BORDERLANDS
SOURCEBOOK

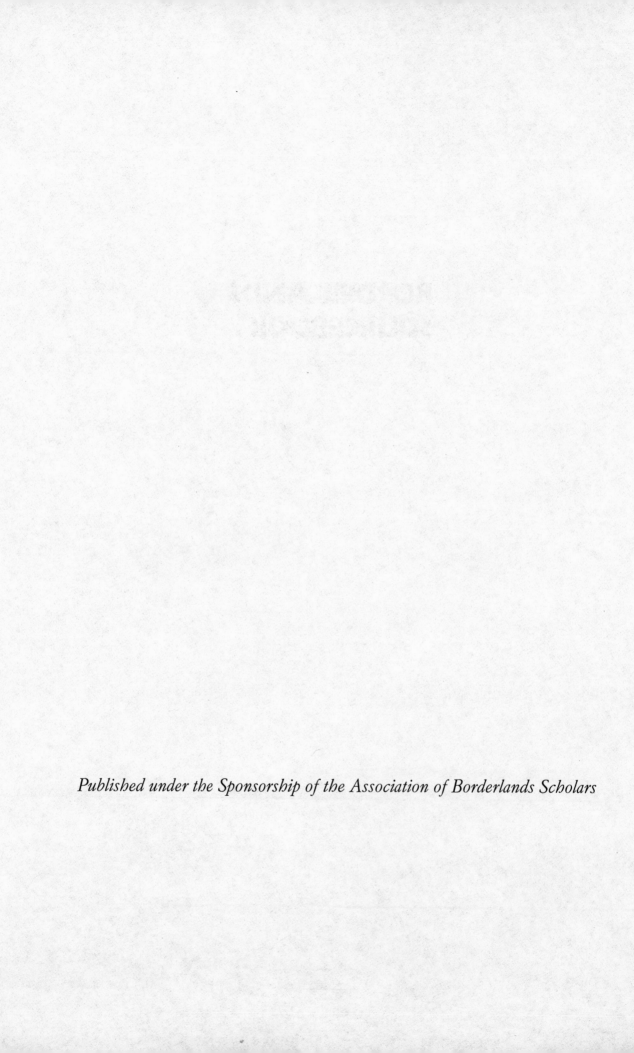

Published under the Sponsorship of the Association of Borderlands Scholars

BORDERLANDS SOURCEBOOK

A GUIDE TO THE LITERATURE ON NORTHERN MEXICO AND THE AMERICAN SOUTHWEST

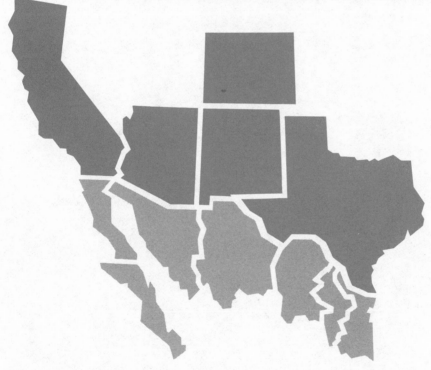

EDITED BY ELLWYN R. STODDARD, RICHARD L. NOSTRAND, AND JONATHAN P. WEST

UNIVERSITY OF OKLAHOMA PRESS : NORMAN

Library of Congress Cataloging in Publication Data

Main entry under title:

Borderlands sourcebook.

Bibliography: p.
Includes index.
1. United States—Boundaries—Mexico—Bibliography. 2. Mexico—Boundaries—United States—Bibliography. 3. Southwest, New—Bibliography. 4. Mexico—Bibliography. 5. United States—Boundaries—Mexico—Historiography. 6. Mexico—Boundaries—United States—Historiography. 7. Southwest, New—Historiography—Addresses, essays, lectures. 8. Mexico—Historiography—Addresses, essays, lectures. I. Stoddard, Ellwyn R. II. Nostrand, Richard L. (Richard Lee), 1939- . III. West, Jonathan P. (Jonathan Page), 1941- . IV. Association of Borderlands Scholars.
Z1251.S8B67 1982 [F786] 016.979   82-40331

Contents

Contents

Illustrations

Tables

This *Borderlands Sourcebook* began as a dream—to have in one volume a handy reference to most of the reputable source materials on border-area topics written and evaluated by leading Borderlands scholars. The project was conceived in the spring of 1976, and by late in that year many potential authors had been invited to write bibliographic essays on a host of topics. No funding was promised; authors were told only that they would receive a copy of the final product. Prior commitments and the distances between the editors and the many contributors kept pushing the completion date forward, and it was difficult to incorporate the most recent literature in successive revisions. But inasmuch as this collection is the only basic, comprehensive work on the United States-Mexico Borderlands available in any form, we anticipate that it will be of value to research scholars and others.

In the nineteenth and early twentieth centuries, research on specific aspects of the Borderlands was done by anthropologists, historians, and others who worked alone and were usually careful to stay within the boundaries of their own disciplines. Visitors added to the store of Borderlands knowledge with their journalistic accounts of the region and its quaint and novel people.

Only in the mid-1950s was this pattern altered when Charles P. Loomis, with grants from the Carnegie Corporation and other sources, assembled at Michigan State University an assortment of historians, archivists, demographers, anthropologists, and sociologists to undertake research on the Borderlands. This multidisciplinary group carefully described the demographic characteristics of people living on both sides of the U.S.-Mexico border (Beegle et al., 1960), and it compiled many of the existing source materials dealing with the border region and its history (Cumberland, 1960*a*). Added to this descriptive profile and bibliography were research projects dealing with comparative political structures, health and health delivery systems, comparative studies of education and values, and disaster perception and relief systems. Studies of paired cities, such as Nogales, Arizona, and Nogales, Sonora, continued this tradition, as geographers, economists, sociologists, and demographers cooperated to capture the complex interrelationships of border communities. But by the mid-1960s this flurry of multidisciplinary social-science activity had languished.

Intercultural exchanges between Mexican and American universities had meanwhile become common after World War II. These exchanges sometimes included reciprocal academic summer-school and specialized programs. Binational university consortia also formalized coordinated efforts, but these seldom involved joint research or scholarly activity as a major focus.

Preface

By the end of the 1960s informal liaisons of interested border researchers in various disciplines gradually coalesced around Ellwyn R. Stoddard, a former participant in the Michigan State University border project and now a faculty member at the University of Texas, El Paso (UTEP). Stoddard's initial contacts with anthropologist John A. Price (formerly of San Diego State University, now of York University), geographers Charles R. Gildersleeve (University of Nebraska, Omaha) and Ronald C. Sheck (New Mexico State University), historian Ralph H. Vigil (formerly of UTEP, now of the University of Nebraska, Lincoln), sociologist Jorge Bustamante (Colegio de México), and others resulted in a multidisciplinary group of interested colleagues. This roster was enlarged and published to promote Borderlands studies (Stoddard, 1974).

What followed was a more formal assessment of Borderlands studies: selected scholars in history, political science, geography, sociology and anthropology, and economics wrote status reports for their disciplines (Stoddard, 1975*a*). Then in April, 1976, a permanent professional organization called the Association of Borderlands Scholars (ABS) was organized in Tempe, Arizona. ABS membership soon grew to include more than two hundred leading experts from three countries and twenty states of the United States; today its membership constitutes the largest reservoir of interdisciplinary expertise available to border policy makers anywhere. Recently Jamail (1980) has prepared a guide to the institutions, organizations, and scholars concerned with and interested in the Borderlands.

In responding to the need for an up-to-date review of Borderlands literature, the three editors, working largely within the ABS membership, commissioned about sixty bibliographic essays. Some essays were completed with dispatch, while others were longer in the writing. Some had to be reassigned, and a few were never completed. Among the latter were six requested of Mexican scholars; fortunately, some of the Mexican sources that might have been cited have been compiled by Bustamante (1980). Most topics that were deemed worthy of coverage were addressed, however, and, indeed, most authors complied with our request to review the literature and write bibliographic essays about the Borderlands, which we defined as including only northern Mexico and the American Southwest.

For Borderlands scholars, researchers, agency personnel, policy makers, planners, and students this volume should serve as a highly useful tool for gaining an overview of most border-area phenomena and the literature pertaining thereto. It should help to prevent many hours of fruitless bibliographic research that accompany inquiry into any Borderlands topic.

The sourcebook comprises three parts and a composite bibliography. Part One introduces the problem of delineating the U.S.-Mexico Borderlands, discusses borders and frontiers, and compares the Mexican and Canadian borders. Part Two contains various sections within which separate chapters deal with specific border phenomena. Because some of the chapters do not address the entire Borderlands through all of time, maps and time scales are given to assist readers in rapidly conceptualizing the spatial and temporal content of each chapter. Part Three discusses certain Borderlands information resources. The composite bibliography contains the references for all three parts.

ELLWYN R. STODDARD

RICHARD L. NOSTRAND

JONATHAN P. WEST

Acknowledgments

The formation of the Association of Borderlands Scholars in 1976 made possible the coordination of the voluntary efforts that were necessary to publish this encyclopedic volume. The contributions of Alvar W. Carlson and Ralph H. Vigil deserve special mention. Manuscript editing by Noel Parsons, Sarah Morrison, and Kathleen McGary and bibliography checking by Robbie Jane Holderman added to the quality of the volume. Others too numerous to mention by name contributed ideas, helped to elicit manuscripts from colleagues, and generally provided professional encouragement to the project. The families of the editors deserve highest praise for their patience during this long ordeal.

Token contributions from the Southwest Border Region Commission and the University of Texas at El Paso provided funds for assembling and editing the volume, and funds from the Association of Borderlands Scholars furnished some of the typing support. Publication of this volume would not have been possible without financial assistance from the University of Oklahoma Foundation.

PART ONE. FRONTIERS, BOUNDARIES, AND BORDERLANDS

In the twentieth century the number of international borders has proliferated, and there has been a new awareness of the complex problems in dealing with border areas. The border realignments associated with the rapidly changing geographical landscape of Europe following World War II and the plethora of emergent African nations have created massive problems for policy makers, diplomats, and scholars. In just the two decades after 1945 the number of contiguous national borders rose from 166 to 412 (Starr and Most, 1976: 582). As treaty obligations have linked noncontinguous nations for purposes of trade, mutual defense, and social or political exchanges, the problems of international and binational borders have become even more complex than before. Both the seasoned researcher and the beginning student investigating a border area sense the overwhelming complexities of such multinational, multicultural regions and the need for broadly based, multidisciplinary training to comprehend what is going on in a given region (Stoddard and McConville, 1978). Moreover, each border region of the world is somewhat like other border areas and yet has a uniqueness

1

Overview

ELLWYN R. STODDARD
Department of Sociology and Anthropology
University of Texas, El Paso

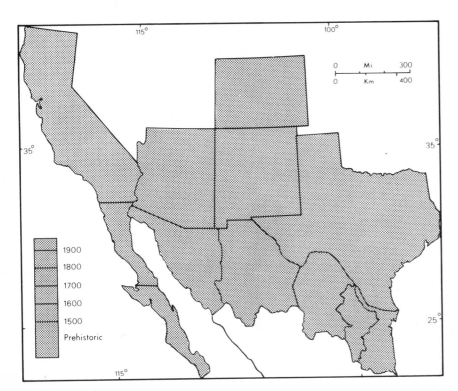

of its own that only becomes apparent with familiarity and time.

The United States-Mexico border region has become better known in the last two decades because of the focus of mass media on problems such as drug trafficking, illegal aliens, and other unlawful enterprises, but there is, of course, much more to the region than those tangential issues. Although the recent discovery of vast petroleum reserves in Mexico has made most Americans superficially aware of our need for Mexico as a future ally, this awareness has failed to alter our society's traditional perception of Mexicans as inferiors. It is in America's interest to eschew the traditional unilateral declarations of Mexican-U.S. policy that were so prevalent in earlier decades and assume a much more equalitarian stance on the policy issues common to our countries. The U.S.-Mexico Borderlands continues to be the milieu in which American and Mexican cultures adapt over the years and where the successful articulation of the two systems must be developed. In order to be knowledgeable about the Borderlands region, it is critical to know its unique history, institutions, and people.

The U.S.-Mexico border region is not a single borderland but rather a composite of many. What constitutes the entity varies among different academic disciplines, among the different ethnic groups occupying the territory, and according to the perceptions and the eras of the people defining it. First and foremost, the 2,000 mile-long political demarcation between the U.S. and Mexico has a schizoid character in terms of climate and topography. The "river borderlands," which extends from the Gulf of Mexico to El Paso-Ciudad Juárez, are quite distinct from the "desert borderlands," which extends from those twin cities westward at imprecise angles across a wasteland devoid of natural-terrain survey points. Within each of those segments are a dozen subareas with soil, climate, and natural resources quite unlike those of the other subareas (E.D.A., 1958). Border poverty is more highly concentrated in the lower Rio Grande Valley of Texas and less so as one moves toward the western end of the boundary. Yet, with all of this diversity, residents all along the U.S.-Mexico border have in their backyards that federal installation called a national border, over which they have little control and which capriciously divides cities, institutions, families, and countries.

For most vacationing Americans the U.S.-Mexico Borderlands is a vague southwestern region—a quaint culture area with a slowed-down life-style, or a sparsely settled open area demanding marathon automobile drives to cross it during a short vacation jaunt. The Borderlands lies somewhere between the moist climates and greenery of New Orleans and San Francisco, but most Americans are not sure just where. For border residents, however, daily life includes the task of living with the artificiality of the international boundary, and there is no question that they live in the Borderlands.

For serious scholars the problem of what should be included in Borderlands studies is a real dilemma, accentuated by the restrictions and scope of their academic disciplines. In one professional article or book the border area may be characterized by exciting possibilities, while in another the outlook appears dismal. Noggle (1959), while discussing the emergence of the "Southwest Borderlands" concept, illustrated extremes that ranged from the glowing and emotional accounts of Lummis (1925) to Blackmar's (1891) fears of Hispanic defilement of a pure Teutonic heritage. One scholar, intent on giving some delimitations to "the Southwest," opined, "We cannot name our area, we can only try to define it" (Parry, 1972: 299-300). Caughey (1952) went so far as to suggest that the area's regionalism rested in the "unconscious of its inhabitants' mental-sets." As a result, with tongue in cheek, Dobie (1952: 13-14) defined it as follows: "The principal areas of the Southwest are . . . Arizona, New Mexico, most of Texas, some of Oklahoma, and anything else north, south, east, or west that anybody wants to bring in. The boundaries of culture and rainfall never follow survey lines." We find a similar lack of consensus when attempting to define what constitutes "the Borderlands."

Historically, Nasatir (1965) traced the shifting Borderlands boundary as Spain's northern land claim, which sprawled from Florida to the "Spanish Lake" of Balboa (the Pacific Ocean) and northward to British Columbia. Later this line was drawn from the Yellowstone in Wyoming across the Rockies to the Pacific. With the loss of Florida and the constant threat of encroachment by the French in Louisiana, the boundary was again redrawn from the Gulf of Mexico through the Great Basin to the West Coast. As a purely Mexican domain the Borderlands was diminished even further, becoming crystalized in the mid-1800s by wars and treaties. The pioneer work of the historian Bolton (Caughey, 1953: 110) described the Spanish Borderlands as the "northern fringe of the Spanish empire in America, from Florida and Georgia on the Atlantic to the Californias on the Pacific," and thus legitimized it as a region for concentrated scholarly investigation; but except for its historical importance in academia Bolton's circumscription is too broad for most contemporary studies of our southern border.

In some disciplines it is common to name regions for the peoples or cultures inhabiting them. For example, *La Gran Chichimeca,* an arid zone encompassing most of the arid southwestern United States as well as the Chihuahua-Sonoran desert, was named for the roving Chichimecs, who inhabited this general area at the time of the arrival of the Spanish explorers. This designation excluded most of east Texas and the Texas lower Rio Grande Valley, as well as the coastal areas in both the Californias. Likewise, Jimenez Moreno (1958: 35-36), in his usage "arid America," selectively excludes the watershed segments of the present U.S.-Mexico border. If one excludes the Californias, either Beals's (1943) "Greater Southwest" or León-Portilla's (1972: 83) "Mexican American Southwest" would be useful to designate the Borderlands region.

The American Borderlands have been carefully delimited by Nostrand (1970) as a demographic region where Spanish-surnamed peoples are relatively significant, whereas Galarza (1972) referred emotionally to a "Border Belt" of Spanish-American poverty devoid of territorial or areal outlimits. Analytical scholars sometimes view the Borderlands as a cluster of isolated urban centers, each radiating its influence into the rural countryside surrounding it but lacking an outlying periphery to distinguish it as a specific region. For archaeologists, early historians, and Chicano historiographers the border does not exist. Thus some arbitrariness must be allowed to designate one concept of "Borderlands" as a point of departure for all of these different but justifiable definitions.

For most of the social scientists and those concerned with contemporary policies, the Borderlands might be defined as an areal domain consisting of a parallel tier of political-legal administrative units (U.S. and Mexican states) lying in juxtaposition along a previously determined arbitrary binational boundary that extends from the Gulf of Mexico to the Pacific Ocean. Even with this the consistent use throughout this volume of the concept *Borderlands* (in the plural) is a reminder that multidisciplinary approaches contain slightly varied designations of what constitutes the region or its people. By avoiding the monistic terms "*a* border" and "*the* borderland" (singular) except when a single discipline or framework is being employed, the term "Borderlands" reflects a collection of unique overlays—with some similarities and some differences being manifest in each.

In still another dimension, the qualities of the border itself are perceived as functionally different. Some regard the border as a barrier that separates the United States from Mexico. In support of this position are the agencies of government that deal with immigration and naturalization, customs, and political-legal rights to curtail uncontrolled border leaks which might adversely affect the territorial integrity of our nation. Such a position denies the necessary symbiotic relationships that permeate any political-legal boundary. A second group perceives the border as a "permeable membrane," a potential obstacle through which the flow of goods, services, and people must be accelerated to achieve local and national interests. When complicated governmental regulations obstruct those flows, legislative and administrative mechanisms are developed to promote a more open border. A third view is that the border is an arbitrary line through a binational, functional "buffer zone" that is penetrated by cultural forms and common problems. In this view such phenomena as rabies epidemics, pollution, water allocations, mosquito control, and transportation routes tie one side to the other; such phenomena have a major impact on the border zone in the neighboring country, so that the entire binational zone should be treated as a common entity (Stoddard, 1978*a*; Whiteford, 1979). Only when the symbiotic linkages between the border zones in both countries are recognized can effective border policies and programs be devised that are not detrimental to one side or the other, or both.

As presently enforced, federal mandates to Mexican or U.S. border communities, *municipios*, or counties often create overwhelming problems capable of reducing border life to eventual extinction. As a result Borderland communities traditionally survive by ignoring federal procedures, circumventing them, or translating them into border customs that are culturally, historically, and functionally acceptable for daily border intercourse. This aspect of borderlands expertise creates enormous disparities between the reality of how border jurisdictions work and the official reports and statistics that are brought in from federal or state officials to define a local border problem. For this reason border policies created in nonborder regions do not work effectively when directly applied to border concerns. On a daily basis local border officials carry on foreign policy with their sister cities and counterparts through a network of informal linkages in the public and private sectors (Stoddard, 1980, 1982).

To make available a maximum of resource materials concerning the U.S.-Mexico Borderlands, this *Sourcebook* contains short, concentrated statements on available resources and areas in need of future research. The first four items (of which this introduction is one) are substantively oriented for the purpose of giving a broad, general background within which to study other specific areas of investigation and issues of concern. Professor Nostrand (chapter 2) provides a well-documented sequence of the changing images of the Borderlands as perceived by Spaniards, Mexicans, and Americans. Professor Kutsche (chapter 3) discusses how natural culture areas, when arbitrarily replaced with cartographic referents (national boundaries), created the genesis of contemporary border strains. The comparison of the U.S.-Canada border with its counterpart between the U.S. and Mexico by Professor Price (chapter 4) allows us more easily to separate out the characteristics common to our two national boundaries from the characteristics unique to one border or the other. The remainder of the volume contains bibliographical essays on various subjects and issues designed to guide the reader to the most reliable resources on any given subject.

Gratefully acknowledged is the permission of the *Social Science Journal* editors to utilize, in modified form, some of my previously published materials found in vol. 12 (October, 1975) and vol. 13 (January, 1976), pp. 5-7.

2

A Changing
Culture
Region

RICHARD L. NOSTRAND
Department of Geography
University of Oklahoma

Narrowly defined, a "borderland" is the area adjacent to a political border. The area that straddles the United States-Mexico border has long been a borderland of special importance. Historically, it was a Spanish-Mexican colonizing frontier, a part of which "North Americans" (as citizens of the United States are known in Mexico) infiltrated and wrested from Mexico. More recently it has been the zone where the sharply contrasting Anglo and Latin cultures have converged to produce significant subcultures.

This particular borderland has come to be known as the Borderlands because of the influence of Herbert Eugene Bolton and his many historian students who wrote under a "Spanish Borderlands" label.[1] Bolton was impressed with the area's subregional variations, and in his seminal *The Spanish Borderlands* (1921), the work in which this now celebrated "Borderlands" label apparently first appeared in print, Florida, New Mexico, Pimería Alta (present-day southern Arizona), Texas, Louisiana, and California were each treated separately. Bolton clearly emphasized the border fringe of the southern United States, yet northern Mexico

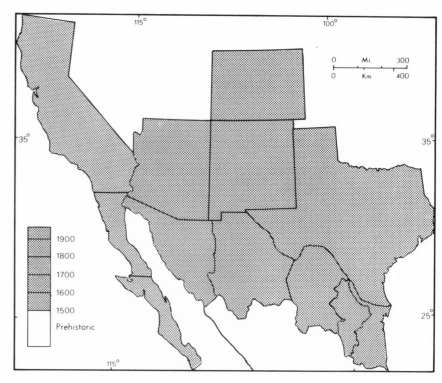

was discussed by way of background; it was the sum of the border-straddling parts that he called the "Borderlands."[2]

Bolton's view of a "Spanish Borderlands"—by which he meant the Spanish and Mexican northern frontiers—is only one way in which the Borderlands have been conceptualized historically. My purpose in this chapter is to identify several post-Columbian images of this region, whether real or imagined, and to suggest their consequences, whether realized or potential. My treatment is admittedly superficial. Perhaps others will identify additional images or will sort out just when given perceptions were held and by whom, but the identification of the following images is nevertheless of value as a beginning point for putting the Borderlands into historical and spatial perspective.

A Northern Frontier

Perhaps the earliest European-held Borderlands image was that of New Spain's northern frontier (Fig. 2-1). In 1521, Spaniards conquered the Aztecs and quickly brought under their control the Tarascans and other culturally advanced peoples. They were soon lured to the north in their search for mineral wealth, and rich strikes at Zacatecas (1546), Durango (1563), and San Luis Potosí (1573-74) attest to their success. Farther north in the present-day United States, however, Coronado failed to find gold and silver in the early 1540s. Missionaries bent on taking Roman Catholicism to the aborigines also ventured into this northern frontier, although the "Chichimecs" whom they encountered were gen-

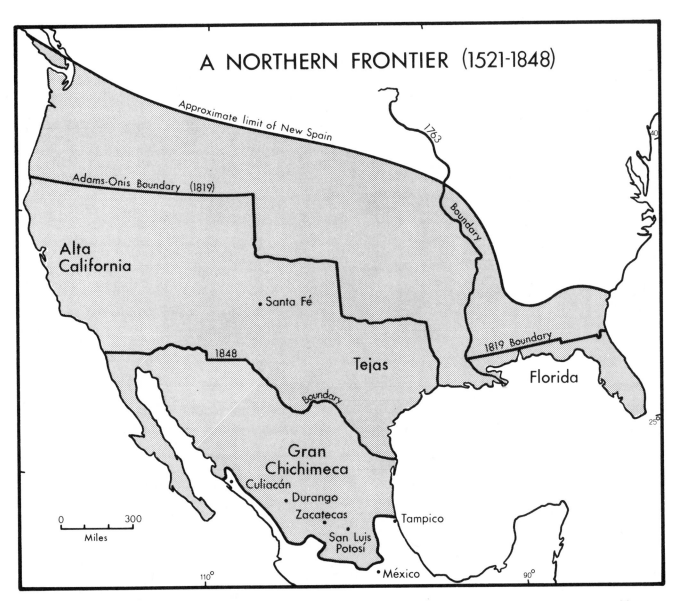

Fig. 2-1. *The Spanish-Mexican northern frontier, 1521-1848. The northern boundary of high culture (Culiacán to Tampico) is after Sauer (1941b: 355).*

7

erally hostile, nomadic, and less culturally advanced than the Indians farther south.[3] In an effort to strengthen its claim to the frontier, the Spanish crown also encouraged colonists to enter this northern area, and garrisons of soldiers were sent to protect the colonists and missionaries (Bolton, 1930).

During the late 1500s the southern boundary of the northern frontier advanced beyond the silver-rich communities such as Zacatecas. What remained a frontier, however, was immense. This frontier was also remote, dangerous (because of its Indians), and uninviting (because of its apparent lack of minerals), and it was generally perceived as such. During the long colonial era there were undoubtedly many specific images of this vast area, and one that was commonly held of a part of the frontier was that of the Gran Chichimeca—the domain of the formidable, barbaric Chichimec (Fig. 2-1). The area north of the silver-rich communities never did become an integral part of New Spain or of Mexico. Indeed, as a relatively uninviting frontier, this area was analogous to southern Chile and Argentina at the opposite end of Spain's New World empire (Gibson, 1966: 201; Zavala, 1957).

In consequence of its remoteness, its paucity of tractable Indians, and its apparent lack of mineral wealth, the northern frontier was only sparsely settled. This lack of effective occupation, and the fact that this frontier lay on the periphery of New Spain's political control, made it difficult for Spain—and then Mexico—to maintain jurisdiction over the area. In consequence, the frontier was whittled away, in part in 1819 when Florida was transferred from Spain to the United States and the western boundary of the Louisiana Purchase was established, and again in 1848 when Mexico was forced to cede its northern lands (Fig. 2-1). Interestingly, these shifts in political borders gave rise to the *Spanish Borderlands* label which is used in the twentieth century by North American students of the area—a term, it should be noted, which is technically anachronistic for much of the Spanish Colonial period.

A Part of Manifest Destiny

During the first half of the nineteenth century, North Americans became aware of the Spanish-Mexican northern frontier through the firsthand accounts of travelers such as Zebulon M. Pike, James Ohio Pattie, Richard Henry Dana, and Josiah Gregg. The image gained from these descriptions was one of an exotic, mineral-rich land inhabited by provincial, Spanish-speaking folk and ubiquitous, hostile Indians. Another image which pertained in part to the northern frontier, and which generated much excitement, was the expansionist notion of "manifest destiny" (Fig. 2-2).

Many North Americans subscribed to the imperialistic idea that it was their destiny—as sanctioned by Providential design—to extend their institutions and control to the Pacific (Weinberg, 1935). Indeed, by allowing North Americans to infiltrate its northern frontier, Mexico facilitated the fulfillment of this design. By 1836, North Americans outnumbered Mexicans by perhaps seven to one in Texas, and

they and their Mexican allies were successful in their revolt for independence.[4] Texas was annexed as a state in 1845, but North Americans wanted still more of Mexico. War was declared, and during its course in 1847, President James Polk gave his commissioner a draft treaty which specified that North America's territorial acquisition should not extend beyond the Rio Grande, the Gila, and Baja California (Prescott, 1965: 77–78, fig. 2B). Except for the last, that is what the United States acquired—to the chagrin of Senator Sam Houston, who during the debate on the treaty's ratification introduced a resolution in Congress which declared that the United States should annex all of Mexico south to a line drawn west from Tampico (Paullin, 1932: 65, plate 94A).

Mexico's northern frontier was clearly coveted by many North Americans, and the idea of manifest destiny justified its infiltration and acquisition. In consequence of infiltration, two frontiers came to overlap, and two people came into contact—and conflict. Mexicans regarded North Americans as haughty, greedy, and crude, and North Americans thought Mexicans were bigoted, indolent, and degenerate. The North American was a *yanqui* or *patón* (*gringo,* meaning "foreigner," was used, but not with reproach until after the Mexican War), and the Mexican was a "greaser" (Paredes, 1961). General antagonism and estrangement reached its highest level in Texas, but feelings of hatred were widespread. The unfortunate (and still-present) attitude that Mexicans were the subordinates in the eyes of many Anglos (as members of the dominant southwestern society are known) thus stems from this unstable zone of cultural convergence during the Mexican era (Lowrie, 1932; McLemore, 1973).

A Mexican Irredentism

The North Americans' manifest destiny was in good part fulfilled as a result of the Mexican War. Mexico was forced to cede Alta California and New Mexico and to recognize the Rio Grande as her international boundary. (She had refused to recognize the independence of Texas in 1836 or to concede that Texas was annexed by the United States in 1845.) As a result of the Mexican Cession in 1848 and the sale of land south of the Gila River in 1853, Mexico lost more than half her territory (Brand, 1966: 73, 136). Yet most Mexicans considered this politically realigned frontier to have been immorally acquired and to be an irredentism (Fig. 2-3).

To this day some in Mexico view the American Southwest as unredeemed territory. Evidence lies in the fact that as recently as World War II, maps were being used in Mexican schools which had the words "territory temporarily in the hands of the United States" written across the Southwest (McWilliams, 1949a: 103). Flags having 44 of the then 48 stars—the omitted ones representing California, Arizona, New Mexico, and Texas—were also being displayed (Peyton, 1946: 146).

The Southwest thus is disputed territory for many Mexicans, and stemming from the irredentist view of the extremists has been at least one plot to reacquire the area. This was the so-called Plan de San Diego, an ambitious proposal osten-

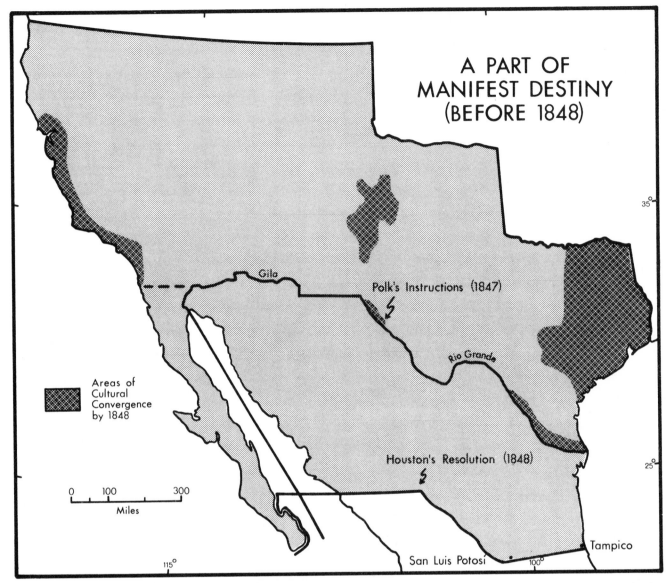

Fig. 2-2. *A part of North America's manifest destiny before 1848. Polk's maximum acquisition line is after Prescott (1965: 77-78, fig. 2B), and Houston's proposed boundary is after Paullin (1932: 65, plate 94A).*

sibly written in the South Texas community of San Diego yet apparently drafted by Mexicans in Monterrey (Cumberland, 1953-54: 290).[5] It called for an uprising on the part of Mexicans who, with the aid of Mexican Americans, were to seize California, Arizona, New Mexico, Colorado, and Texas; declare them an "independent republic"; and, if "expedient," request their annexation to Mexico (Gerlach, 1968: 205-207; Gómez-Quiñones, 1970a: 128-31). The plan was uncovered by authorities in the lower Rio Grande Valley a month before its February, 1915, implementation date, and although it was not taken seriously at the time, it seems to have been one reason for an outbreak of murders and depredations which ravaged the lower Rio Grande Valley in the

summer and early fall of 1915 (Cumberland, 1953-54: 290-91, 308, 311).

A Mexican American Homeland

When the Southwest changed hands, the resident Mexicans became Mexican Americans. In 1850 there were more than eighty thousand Mexican Americans, yet even at that early date this number represented only 20 percent of the enumerated southwestern population (Nostrand, 1975: 383, 390). During the latter half of the nineteenth century this proportion decreased, a situation which prompted some to assert that

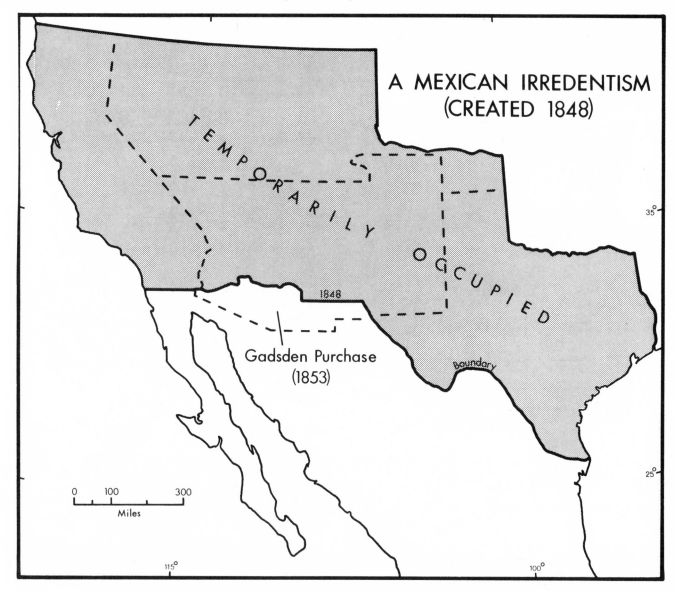

Fig. 2-3. *Mexico's unredeemed frontier, created as a result of the Mexican Cession in 1848.*

"Mexicans" were a "disappearing subculture" (McWilliams, 1968: 8). That prominent authors of the time romanticized the Spaniard of an earlier era while ignoring the seemingly more prosaic Mexican American is a telling commentary on the period.[6] In the twentieth century, however, the viability of this people was no longer in doubt, because immigrants from Mexico began to pour into the United States, where they contributed significantly to raise the southwestern minority total to nearly five million (13 percent) by 1970.[7]

Some of these twentieth-century immigrants (and some southwestern minority members) went to destinations outside the Southwest, and Mexican Americans thus became a national minority. The majority of the immigrants settled in the Southwest among the old stock, however, and today the preponderance of this minority inhabits the five states shown in Fig. 2-4. Within the Southwest, Mexican Americans are concentrated near the U.S.-Mexican border in a zone which some perceive to be a Mexican American region or homeland. The perceived existence of this entity lies in the attempts of several to regionalize it. For example, in the 1920s Bushee (1923: 150) likened this zone of Spanish colonization and Mexican American concentration to a fan whose handle was in Mexico and whose tip was at Santa Fe and which, when fully unfolded, arched from California to New Orleans. McWilliams (1949a: 48, 54) apparently borrowed this simile when writing 25 years later about a "fan of Spanish-Mexican influence" whose opened edge he traced between Santa Barbara and Corpus Christi. More recently I (Nostrand, 1970: 655-59) have added to these attempts to regionalize this Mexican American homeland (Fig. 2-4).

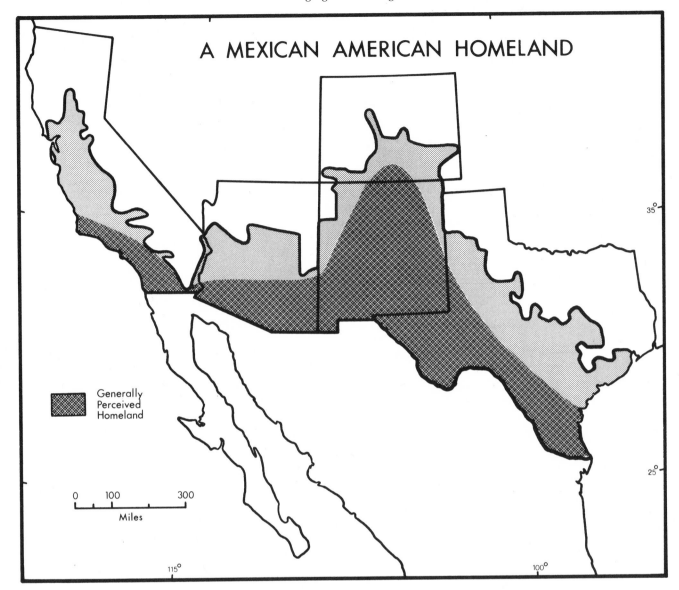

A MEXICAN AMERICAN HOMELAND

Generally
Perceived
Homeland

0   100   300
Miles

35°

25°

115°

100°

Fig. 2-4. *The Mexican American region. The boundary delimitation (outliers and inliers omitted) is based on 1960 census data and is after Nostrand (1970: 655-59).*

However areally defined, the homeland is where Mexican Americans are concentrated, but it is more than a demographic region. When first created in the mid-nineteenth century, it was a spatial discontinuity: Northern Mexico was then part of the United States, yet the area's Mexican inhabitants were only nominally "Americans." In time, however, this discordant quality blurred as these Mexicans, and those who joined them, acculturated. Acculturation produced a new and distinctive subculture, and the homeland is where this subculture is most intense. The homeland is also where the Mexican Americans' roots are deepest and the Spanish-Mexican legacy is richest. And it is where Anglos have to a certain extent been "Hispanicized," as revealed by their fondness for tacos, enchiladas, and burritos; their use of Spanish

Colonial architecture; and their choice of Spanish names for new communities and the curvilinear streets therein. In consequence, the Mexican American homeland today is one of America's genuine culture regions.

Aztlán

During much of their experience, Mexican Americans made conscious efforts to assimilate with Anglo-Americans.[8] Then in the mid-1960s many, especially younger and more militant minority members, began to reject this strategy. Pointing out that Mexican Americans had failed in their attempts to be accepted by Anglos, these persons demanded separate but equal status. For the first time they self-consciously asserted their subcultural differences; they organized politically to achieve social and economic ends;[9] they argued successfully for self-study programs in institutions of higher education (Bongartz, 1969); they articulated a new pride in their heritage; and they seized upon "Chicano"—an old, in-group term—as a self-referent with which to identify (Nostrand, 1973: 398-99).

Aztlán is an areal manifestation of the Chicano movement. As used by some Chicanos, Aztlán means the ancient southwestern Aztec cradle from which Aztecs migrated south (Steiner, 1970: 131).[10] Because these Chicanos argue that they are descended from Aztecs, and because they state that Aztlán was wrested from their ancestors by North Americans, they claim this areally nebulous fatherland (which is too vague to be mapped) by right of original possession. This notion gained support in 1969 at the first national Chicano Youth Liberation Conference held in Denver; there, Chicanos adopted "El Plan Espiritual de Aztlán," which proclaimed Aztlán to be an independent "mestizo nation."[11]

The Chicanos' concept of Aztlán has been called a myth and Chicano propaganda (Womack, 1972: 14, 17). It would be, nevertheless, a potentially explosive idea were militant Chicanos to use it to justify secessionist efforts (Hilton, 1972: 337, 338, 344). Indeed, the Aztlán mentality has already seen expression: in 1966, to call attention to their goal of legally restoring Spanish-Mexican land grants to Hispanos,

members of the Reies Tijerina-led Alianza took possession of the Carson National Forest campground in northern New Mexico under the proclaimed legal existence of the "Corporation of San Joaquin del Rio de Chama." Although secession was not the purpose, their attempt was to forcibly reacquire a portion of an 1806 Spanish grant (Swadesh, 1968: 170). In 1968, Gutiérrez found that economic, political, and social conditions in South Texas were ripe for a Chicano revolution; according to Guerra (1972), one of the less radical objectives of the incipient revolutionaries was for the Chicano-majority South Texas counties to secede as a fifty-first Chicano state. That these revolutionary notions were generated where minority proportions are highest in the Southwest is perhaps more than coincidental.

El Norte

The number of Mexican Americans in the Southwest far exceeds that of "American Mexicans" (Mexicans of American descent or citizenship) in northern Mexico. Some Mexican Americans have repatriated, and other Americans, including Mormons, have moved to northern Mexico, yet in 1960 only sixty thousand persons born in the United States lived in Mexico's six border states.[12] On the other hand, Mexicans in northern Mexico have been more "Anglicized" than southwestern Anglos have been "Hispanicized." *Norteño* Anglici-

Fig. 2-5. *Mexico's* Norte. *The region's southern boundary is after Cline (1953: 107).*

zation and its corollary North American influence are important reasons why Mexico's Norte is distinctive.

The *norteño* is seen by non-*norteños* as one who lives almost in the jaws of the giant: he caters in English to a heavy tourist trade;[13] he commutes to a local American manufacturing plant or to some job across the border (Dillman, 1970*a*, 1970*b*, 1970*c*); he spends his Yankee dollars for American consumer goods;[14] and he builds his new home in the middle of a grass-covered, suburban lot (Nelson, 1963: 83). So powerful is the giant's perceived influence that non-*norteños* often refer to *norteños* as *pochos,* or persons who have been "bleached" through their exposure to North Americans and their culture (Brand, 1966: 56).[15] This influence and the degree of perceived Anglicization diminish with increasing distance from the boundary; Cline's (1953: 107) southern border of the Norte may demarcate the approximate extent of *pochismo,* although North America's influence reaches still deeper into Mexico (Fig. 2-5).

One consequence of North America's influence is that the Norte has been Mexico's "dynamic front," at least in political life.[16] It has produced a disproportionate share of leaders, including Francisco I. Madero and Francisco ("Pancho") Villa, who authored and executed revolutionary "plans." Perhaps these plans germinated in the Norte because the area was on the periphery of dictatorial control (Dumke, 1948: 289). Sheer propinquity to the United States would also seem to be a factor, however. Gamio (1930: 161-62) noted that revolutionary ideas, including the right of labor to unionize and the need for agrarian land redistribution, were probably obtained by Mexicans in the United States. Cosío (1968-69: 35-36) pointed out that "the American tract of land close to the Mexican border" has been used as "a nest for subversive or revolutionary movements organized by Mexicans against the authorities of their own country." And Peyton (1946: 264) affirmed that San Antonio, Texas, has been a staging ground for dozens of insurrections, including the Revolution of 1910.

A Cultural Province

Some see the Norte and the Southwest as one large province of Anglo-Latin ("Latin" meaning Spanish and Indian here) cultural transition (Fig. 2-6).[17] They see Anglicization and Hispanicization as overlapping processes which operate with decreasing effectiveness in opposite directions.[18] Throughout the province Anglos and Latins have come into contact, have blended, and have even fused.[19] This mixing is most intense in a boundary-straddling corridor, and some see the counterpart communities in that corridor as hearth areas of an incipient hybrid or "third" culture (Price, 1968-69: 10; McConville, 1965: 241-43). For them the international boundary is a sharp divide politically but not in other respects (Busey, 1958-59).

Others view the Norte and the Southwest as one province because *norteños* and Mexican Americans are essentially "one people" (McWilliams, 1949*a*: 290). They point out that the entire province has Spain's indelible stamp. The

area's Spanish-Mexican inhabitants also have had to grapple with similar problems stemming from aridity. And the international boundary—which they contend has never been more than an "imaginary line" (Rippy, 1931: 382; Samora, 1971: 13)—has been crossed and recrossed by Mexicans and Mexican Americans wishing to sustain family contacts and by migrants who have pushed north to reinforce the Mexican American element.

This latter image belittles the significant differences between *norteños* and Mexican Americans, and it wrongly implies that southwestern immigrants have been derived only from the Norte. Nevertheless, the notion of a cultural province—whether conceived of as a zone of cultural transition or as the habitat of one people—does have potential consequences. For example, international cooperation is needed for the equitable division of that regionally scarce resource—water—and for the control of illegal border crossings and contraband traffic. This province could be the problem-solving unit (Busey, 1953-54). It could also be a hemispheric "bridge" used by Mexico and the United States as a training ground for diplomats or as a testing zone for new hemispheric policy. In this context the counterpart communities which now punctuate the length of the boundary could serve as conference sites for discussing public policy and for generating innovative solutions to problems.

In Perspective

The foregoing images help to put the Borderlands into temporal-spatial perspective. For example, they point up the Borderlands' changing significance as (1) a remote, dangerous, and uninviting northern frontier, (2) a part of a coveted western frontier, (3) disputed territory, (4) a zone of Mexican American concentration, (5) territory claimed by Chicanos, (6) an area of North American influence, and (7) a zone of cultural transition. The last image—the Borderlands as a cultural province—also underscores the region's fundamental significance as the Western Hemisphere's major zone of Anglo-Latin cultural convergence.

The convergence of Anglos and Latins has produced a distinctive Borderlands culture, and while this culture is becoming increasingly complex, its subcultures are still identifiable as Mexican Americans, Hispanicized southwesterners, "American Mexicans," Anglicized *norteños,* and the hybrid, borderline people. In perspective, the Mexican American subculture would appear to be the Borderlands' product of singular importance. In time, for example, this subculture has seen the greatest degree of Anglo-Latin cultural fusion, and in this respect it can be compared only with the hybrid, borderline subculture which is much more recent in origin. In space, moreover, the Mexican American's presence north of the international boundary contrasts sharply with the relative absence of American Mexicans (the Mexican American's counterpart) south of that line, and this imbalance means that, in a demographic sense, Latin America shades off north of the international boundary, whereas Anglo-America essentially ends at that boundary.

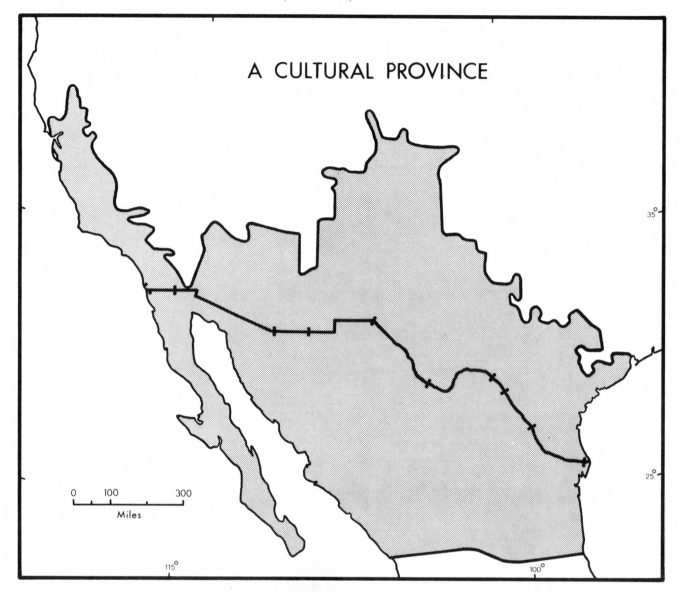

Fig. 2-6. *The zone of cultural transition and/or one people's habitat. Province boundaries are from Figs. 2-4 and 2-5.*

The editors thank Gary S. Elbow, editor of *International Aspects of Development in Latin America: Geographical Perspectives,* proceedings of the Conference of Latin Americanist Geographers, vol. 6 (Muncie, Ind.; Department of Geography-Geology, Ball State University, 1977), for permission to reprint this paper, which appeared on pages 9-28.

1. Caughey (1953a: 110) credited Bolton with the "effective discovery" of the "Spanish borderlands" as a field for historical research and also with the origin of the label itself. Bannon (1970: 239) noted that one of Bolton's editors for his *Spanish Borderlands* may have originated the term.

2. Bolton's usage is followed in the contemporary literature. For example, Stoddard (1974) conceived of the region as including present-day northern Mexico and the adjacent United States.

3. Sauer (1941b: 355) delimited the boundary between the "ruder" northern cultures and the "high" southern cultures.

4. In 1836 Henry M. Morfit estimated that thirty thousand Anglos and five thousand Negroes inhabited Texas, compared with 3,470 Mexicans (Bell, 1935: 37). The number of Mexicans was probably underestimated; two years earlier Almonte (1924-25: 186, 209) gave the figure 3,900.

5. Gomez Quiñones (1970b: 127) speculated that Mexican Americans may have authored the plan; if further research substantiates that idea, the plan may still be considered as a Mexican attempt to reclaim the Southwest, because allegiance to Mexico among South Texas Mexican Americans seems to have been strong. It is unclear just who the plan's backers were. Gerlach (1968) argued that the plan was part of Victoriano Huerta's German-supported re-

volutionary plot to regain the Mexican presidency.

6. Robinson (1966: 8-9) gave Gertrude Atherton's *The Splendid Idle Forites* as an example.

7. Persons of Spanish surname in the five southwestern states numbered 4,667,975 (12.9 percent). U.S. Bureau of the Census (1973: Table I, p.vii).

8. Assimilation was an important implied goal of the influential League of United Latin American Citizens founded in South Texas in 1929 (Garza, 1951: 19-21; page numbers are from the R and E Research Associates' 1972 reprint of this thesis).

9. The success of La Raza Unida in gaining control of Crystal City's school board and city council during 1970-71 is an example (Rivera, 1972).

10. Hilton (1972) noted that the Chicanos' concept of Aztlán (as given in Steiner) is "inaccurate" (p. 338); he asserted that "Aztecs" were the last Chichimec tribe to conquer the Valley of Mexico (p. 339) and that *Aztlán* was a seventeenth-century term for the idealized pre-Spanish Aztec capital of Tenochtitlán in the Valley of Mexico (p. 343).

11. Forbes (1973: 174-77) reproduced this plan. See also Vigil (1973*a*, especially p. 191).

12. Only first-generation data are available. Almost two-thirds of the one hundred thousand persons born in the United States who live in Mexico live in Mexico's six border states (Brand, 1966: 31).

13. Tourism is Mexico's principal earner of foreign exchange, and in 1967 the border area accounted for nearly three-fourths of this trade (Dillman, 1970*b*: 501).

14. United States border merchants estimate that more than half of their trade is with Mexicans (Dillman, 1970*b*: 495).

15. León-Portilla (1972) noted the North Americans' influence (pp. 109 and 113) but developed more fully other aspects of the *norteños'* ethos.

16. Sauer (1941*a*: 22-23) described Mexico's "northern border" as being its "dynamic front," although he did not specify that exposure to North Americans was a reason for this dynamism.

17. The border area's transitional nature is an implied theme in Cumberland (1960*a*: especially 1-2, 193). Busey (1953-54) was more explicit about this transitional nature.

18. There may be subconscious opposition to Anglicization and Hispanicization. For example, Harvard anthropologist Vogt (1970) observed that Mexican food becomes more *picante* the closer one gets to the international boundary, and that it has its greatest *chile* content in the Southwest.

19. John G. Bourke, a West Pointer who resided in the Southwest in the 1870s, "was one of the first to show a realization that cultural fusion was taking place" in the New Mexico- and Arizona-centered Borderlands (Noggle, 1959: 125).

3

Borders and
Frontiers

PAUL KUTSCHE
Department of Anthropology
Colorado College

The term *borderland* is ambiguous enough to encompass both boundaries and frontiers. This lack of precision is convenient, since borderland scholars are sometimes concerned with one and sometimes with the other. *Boundary* denotes a new concept that dates only from the rise of nation states in modern Europe (Spicer, 1976). It pertains to political and administrative sovereignties juxtaposed along an arbitrary but formally demarked line. *Frontier* denotes a phenomenon as old as differences in societies and cultures. A frontier is seen by most scholars not as a line of authority but as a zone of influence. At any given time boundaries are precise, while the width of frontiers is indefinite. Most of the essays in this sourcebook are concerned with the Mexican-U.S. boundary and its consequences; this essay summarizes certain lines of thinking about frontiers.

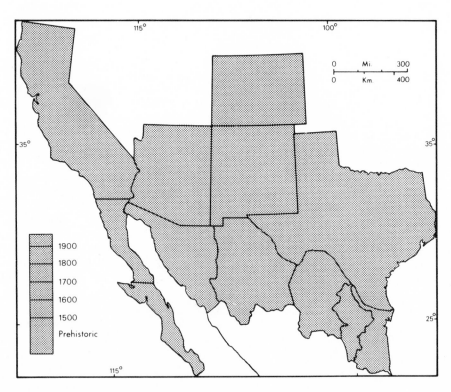

Theories of Frontiers

One must start with Frederick Jackson Turner's 1893 "Significance of the Frontier in American History" (Turner, 1938: 185-229). Turner first raised the question whether frontiers have special properties, and his resounding yes has withstood sharp and vigorous critical attack. Frontiers, said Turner, produce people who act independently of their cultural and governmental centers, tend toward equality, and reduce the cultural baggage of material and ideological characteristics to those items that are useful in the frontier environment.

Most frontier theories have in common a geographical point from which culture spreads. This point is variously termed *focus* (Kroeber, 1953), *central place* (Berry and Harris, 1968; Christaller, 1966), *metropolis* (W. P. Webb, 1952; Cockcroft, Frank, and Johnson, 1972), or *center of gravity* (Lattimore, 1962). Such a point is implied by Wallerstein's *world-system* (1974). The idea was probably born of the attempts of nineteenth-century European museums to bring order out of the chaos of artifacts which travelers dumped upon them; the German-Austrian diffusionists labeled the resulting theory *Kulturkreis,* or "culture circle" (Graebner, 1903).

A. L. Kroeber illuminates both focus and frontier in his introduction to North American culture areas:

Where the influences from two culture climaxes or foci meet in equal strength is where a line must be drawn, if boundaries are to be indicated at all. Yet it is just there that differences often are slight. Two peoples classed as in separate areas yet adjoining each other along the inter-area boundary almost inevitably have much in common. It is probable that they normally have more traits in common with each other than with the peoples at the focal points of their respective areas. This is almost certain to be so where the distance from the foci is great and the boundary is not accentuated by any strong physical barrier or abrupt natural change. . . . What boundaries really show is not so much clefts occurring in nature, as relative extent and strength of influences emanating from foci. [Kroeber, 1953: 5-6.]

Central places form patterns which "fit into a global system of areal organization: tributary areas are seen as organized around these points, which are connected both with one another and with the tributary areas by lines of human movement" (Berry and Harris, 1968: 366). They may be ranked in hierarchies "in a 'nesting' pattern of dominance, subdominance, and competition" (Berry and Harris, 1968: 368).

Metropolis-frontier theory uses a global stage, where central-place theory is regional. For Walter P. Webb (1952) the metropolis is Western Europe from 1500 to 1900, and the frontiers are the Americas, South Africa, Australia, and New Zealand. He concentrates on the impact of frontier upon metropolis—in a word, the creation of an economic boom. Before 1500, Europe had too many people and too little food and other resources. After frontier exploitation Europe became people-poor and resource-rich. The boom ended when population caught up with land and resources. As a cultural, rather than political, historian Webb ignores the boundaries of nation states and colonies and concentrates on technological processes and institutions. Metropolis-satellite theory (for example, Cockcroft, Frank, and Johnson, 1972) conceives metropoles as points rather than regions. At the one extreme are centers of economic and political power, such as Seville, London, and Tokyo; at the other are peasant villages in "underdeveloped nations" (a term which, for these theorists, is laced with irony). In between are the regional capitals, which mediate between metropolis and satellite, and whose elite are brokers in the exchange. Any given chain may have many nodes of power brokerage between the extremes.

Of the frontier theories Owen Lattimore's is perhaps the most comprehensive. In his study of northern China he speaks of frontier zones marginal to "centers of gravity." These zones tend to be more like their neighbors—which are marginal to other centers of gravity—than they are like their own centers. Illegal activities (for example, smuggling) are frequent. The range of power from the center varies according to the activity —greatest for the sharp thrust of a military raid and least for economic integration. Economic range and technology (especially transportation) are closely interdependent; rail and water transport greatly increase economic range, while airplanes ignore natural barriers completely (Lattimore, 1962: 480). Because of the tenuous ties between frontier peoples and centers of gravity, their loyalties are uncertain and their fortunes rise or fall in rhythms different from those of the centers.[1]

A quite different question sometimes asked by theorists is the effect of frontiers upon values at the cultural centers. Turner implies the question, and Webb follows with his economic boom argument. Jorge Mañach (1975: 6) looks at frontiers as areas where civilizations confront each other in "contiguity and opposition." Mañach attributes to the frontier of classical Greece that culture's "intense spiritual activity, the determined application of intelligence to speculation and to practical inquiries, and the heroic sense of life" (1975: 12). Likewise the national cultures of Reconquest Castile and the nineteenth-century United States were also formed by their frontier activities (Mañach, 1975: 14; cf. Hallowell's [1975a and 1975b] American Indian influence on U.S. society as a "backwash").

Cultural geographers and some historians and ethnologists focus their attention on changes in colonizing cultures which are imposed by frontier environments. Carl Sauer emphasizes the meticulous work that must be done on the environment of each frontier area and also on the culture history of both colonized and colonizer (Sauer, 1930b; cf. Thompson, 1973: 8-9), while Bowman (1931) sees environmental factors as setting limits beyond which new frontier cultures cannot develop (cf. Meggers, 1954). For these historians and ethnologists both the reduction of parent cultural inventory and the invention of new traits on frontiers are seen as ecological adaptation. Walter P. Webb's Great Plains studies (1930, 1931) are the classics in historical writing, with his famous examples of the six-shooter, the barbed-wire fence, the windmill, and the McCormick reaper. Ethnologists often focus on the correlation between ecological niche and social organization; for example, market agriculture pushes toward intra-community competition, while subsistence agriculture pushes toward cooperation (Casagrande, Thompson, and Young, 1964; Thompson, 1973; Doolittle, 1973).

Last and least among theoretical approaches to frontiers is an attempt, presaged by Turner and pursued by the U.S. Census Bureau and some geographers, to locate frontier areas by changes, over time, in population densities (see Wishart, Warren, and Stoddard, 1969, for a review of the history of this idea).

The Gran Chichimeca, A Constant Frontier to Changing Centers

The frontier which concerns this sourcebook extends north from the Tropic of Cancer to the divide between the drainages of the Rio Grande and the Mississippi (or, according to some, farther north to include the Arkansas drainage). Ethnologists are beginning to adopt the Aztec label for this area, *Gran Chichimeca*. The term is preferable to *Southwest United States* or *Northwest Mexico* because it is more geographically accurate and avoids modern "cultural imperial" implications (Di Peso, 1966). The continuity of this frontier, from the rise of Mesoamerican civilization to the present, is striking, as described in Mary Helms's succinct summary of "heartlands and frontiers" (1975, chaps. 7 and 13). The centers to which the Chichimeca is frontier, on the other hand, have moved from the Valley of Mexico to Spain to such contemporary metropoles as London, Tokyo, and New York, with equally transient intermediate nodes such as Chihuahua, El Paso, Dallas, and Santa Fe.

Charles Di Peso's (1974) large-scale study of Casas Grandes, the prehistoric northern Chihuahua site, offers a model similar in some respects to the one Lattimore creates for Mongolia. Military and administrative domination by the Valley of Mexico never traveled much higher than the Tropic of Cancer, but Mesoamerican cultural influence was heavy in the Chichimeca through the institution of the *puchteca*—trading families who established durable transmission of both material goods and such intangibles as religious systems over a long period of time. Di Peso believes that these traders also directed the construction of the most monumental buildings at Casas Grandes. Mesoamerican influence probably extended at least as far north as Chaco Canyon in northwestern New Mexico. So we may infer from architectural technology, the presence of the god Quetzalcoatl, and numerous smaller items of material culture (cf. Hedrick, Kelley, and Riley, 1974). Pailes and Whitecotton (1979) find Chichimecan-Mesoamerican relations a good fit to Wallerstein's world-system concept.

Edward Spicer's comprehensive *Cycles of Conquest* (1962) focuses on contact between Chichimecans and the three European civilizations—Spanish, Mexican, and U.S. He describes the failure of Spanish *reducción* policy either to bring nomads into centers or to assimilate nomadic and sedentary Indians. By and large tribes retained their "sacred man-land relationships" (Spicer, 1962: 577). Warfare against Indians actually promoted the Indians' group identity—among the Pueblos as well as among tribes with a greater reputation for military lust. The *encomienda* system was not reinstituted in the Chichimeca after the Pueblo Revolt of 1680; tribute was seldom expected and even more seldom extracted. Although the Mexican government assimilated Indians somewhat more vigorously than did the United States (which set up administratively separate reservations), none of the European powers managed to incorporate Chichimecan tribes into their own civilizations.

George Foster clarified numerous processes common to the frontiers between European and Mesoamerican civilizations in *Culture and Conquest* (1960). Like F. J. Turner and W. P. Webb, Foster notes:

Conquest culture . . . represents but a small part of the totality of traits and complexes that comprise the donor culture. Then, through a second screening process in the geographical region of recipient peoples, conquest culture is still further reduced. . . . Spanish forms were welcomed when they were recognized by the Indians as useful, and when there were no [or only rudimentary] indigenous counterparts. . . . Conversely, where there were satisfactory native counterparts, Spanish influence was much less marked. [1960: 227-28.][2]

Foster adds a concept that I have not seen elsewhere, "cultural crystallization." Iberian and native elements went through a fluid period of a few decades, he says, after which they integrated and became as resistant to further change as either parent culture was before contact (1960, chap. 17).

Among scholars of the Hispanic conquest of the Americas, Silvio Zavala (1957) has an unusually broad scope. He notes in passing that the Mesoamerican and Andean heartlands were densely settled at contact, and he concentrates on the peripheries—the Chichimeca, the pampas of Argentina, and the Auracanian portion of southern Chile. He finds numerous parallels in these frontiers, including freedom from imperial domination in the pre-Columbian period, considerable independence from the Spanish empire, the predominance of mining in Spain's exploitation of all three areas, and the role of the Spanish horseman (especially as *vaquero*). He speculates that perhaps frontiersmen, particularly in the Chichimeca, were more liberal, more jealous of liberty, than others: ". . . The northern frontier was seen [by Mexicans] not merely as a different society more favorable for growth of democratic life but also a hope for the regeneration of all Mexico" (Zavala, 1957: 50). This statement is much like Mañach's that a nation without a frontier must "nourish itself on its own inner substance, and its culture . . . [loses] dimensions of variety and universality" (Mañach, 1975: 15). But, says Zavala, even the frontier "did not signify an absolute guarantee of liberty since it could become the refuge of bossism . . . and local abuses." (Zavala, 1957: 50).

Influence of Boundaries on Frontiers

Firmly established boundary lines, protected by armies and staffed by immigration and customs agents, make a surer and more abrupt impact upon frontier zones than the influence of physical environment and cultural tradition. The term *border region* is an appropriate label for this phenomenon. The influence of Mexico and the United States, for instance, interpenetrates a considerable distance. Stoddard (1978*a*) suggests establishing a legal "buffer zone" in each country to handle common problems. By comparison, shifting boundaries in Europe have a great influence on frontier economics, and the emerging European customs union will affect those areas more than the hinterlands (Hansen, 1977). Endless other examples could be cited.

Future Research

Social scientists studying frontiers agree on several points, although they do not yet have common definitions (Hudson, 1977). They see centers from which frontiers extend, reduction of cultural traits on a continuum from center to frontier, the frontier as a zone and not a boundary, the influence of geographical environments and historical traditions to produce idiosyncratic results, and a freedom to innovate correlated with weak center control.

They differ in assumptions about the object of study, although these assumptions are seldom stated. First, most of them examine the frontiers of a single civilization, usually European and expanding. They analyze the impact of frontier environment on pioneers, producing frontier culture, and the impact of frontier culture on metropolitan culture. Turner, Webb, Sauer, Bowman, Mañach, Thompson, and Zavala are examples. Wells's attempt to conceptualize "frontier systems" (1973) assumes that all frontiers are of this type. A parallel in anthropology is countless ethnographic studies of culture change among nonliterate and peasant peoples, showing massive changes to their cultures, minor changes to the colonizing cultures. (Such studies often use imperialism theories, but seldom use frontier theory.) Second, very few theorists study frontiers between civilizations. Those who do, investigate the special properties of frontier societies, their similarities across boundaries, and their differences from metropolitan societies. Kroeber and Lattimore are prime examples. Foster's research is relevant to both schools of frontier study.

What no theorist has yet constructed is a model of the logical possibilities of contact along frontiers. In the hope of providing a single framework within which all frontier research might fit, I offer the outline of such a model, on a power continuum:

1. *Human societies confronting only a nonhuman environment.* Examples in the Americas: both poles, mountain zones.

2. *Gross inequality of power.* Examples: the pampas and Tierra del Fuego in South America, northwestern European contact with native Americans on the eastern seaboard and in the temperate woodland areas of the United States.

3. *Creation of strong frontier peoples by frontier conditions.* Examples are all the by-products of the adaptation of horses as weapons of battle among the Mongols of Siberia and among the Apaches, Comanches, and other Chichimecans, who were unconquered until the invention of the repeating rifle and similar industrial artifacts (Zavala, 1957: 46).

4. *Imposition of superior power upon a complex stable society, producing patron-client relations with heavy reciprocal exchanges of cultural inventory.* Examples: Old World Bronze and Iron Age conquests, Mesoamerica from the Olmec period (c. 1500 B.C.), the Spanish empire in nuclear America; in the Chichimeca such a relationship characterizes Spanish-Indian relations badly, but Anglo-Hispano relations reasonably well.

5. *The meeting of equals, whether power is equal in the foci or only in the frontier settlements.* Examples are rare in frontier literature, but staples of European history: Alsace-Lorraine, the Scottish borderlands, Poland and Bohemia, the Pyrenees, Hispanic-Indian relations in the Chichimeca from about 1700 A.D. (Swadesh, 1974: 194-97; Simmons, 1971; Stoller, 1976; Kutsche [ed.], 1979).

Frontier data organized according to this model should demonstrate clusters of similar cultural patterns, with significant differences between clusters, and enhance our ability to make theory out of historically unique sequences of events.

---

1. This point fits the Chichimeca during the Spanish and Mexican periods particularly well. Spanish armies at rare intervals put on brilliant military shows as far north as the Grand Canyon and the Arkansas River, but at other times left the northern provinces to fend for themselves. Smuggling and other illegal activities (for example, growing tobacco in violation of the state monopoly) were common. Community relations on both sides of the frontier were egalitarian. Loyalty to centers was so weak that Texas easily broke away to become independent, New Mexico shifted allegiance to the United States with minimal trauma, and the Chihuahua and Sonora provinces were marked by hatred for the European-oriented regime of Porfirio Díaz and became seedbeds of the 1910 revolution which followed.

2. The reduction of traits transmitted from donor to recipient culture has been independently discovered by several scholars in addition to Turner, Webb, and Foster—for example, Wolf (1959: 160), Malinowski (1974: 17), and Linton (1940: 496-97).

4

Mexican and Canadian Border Comparisons

JOHN A. PRICE
Department of Anthropology
York University

Why were international borders located where they are? What kinds of unique cultural processes develop along international borders? Does the condition of different legal jurisdictions foster certain kinds of economic arrangements in border areas? How does a border context affect the development of border cities? These are the kinds of theoretical questions that I, as an anthropologist, find significant in the field of border studies, and, of course, they overlap with other social science interests.

One of the frontiers of anthropological research is the study of large, fast-changing, and broadly integrated cultural systems such as cities and a wide variety of urban subcultures. There is a potential for development of border studies, probably drawing mostly from urban anthropologists. For example, anthropologists will want to compare many different kinds of borders—those between the territories of primate social groups, between ethnic groups, between a metropolis and its hinterland, between provinces and states, and so forth, as well as international borders. This essay contains three potential research areas for comparing

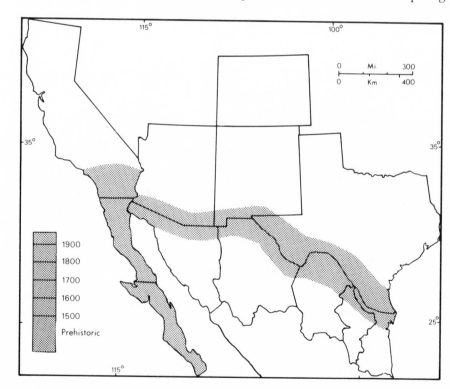

U.S. borders with Mexico and Canada: (1) location of borders, (2) native Indians and borders, and (3) border cities. Table 4-1 contains a more detailed and succinct comparison of the U.S.-Mexican and U.S.-Canadian borders.

Location of the Borders

The location of the Mexican border developed out of the historic Anglo-American-Mexican struggle, a conflict between two quite different cultures. It took place fairly rapidly, with the settlement of Anglos in Texas, the U.S.-Mexican War, and the 1848 Treaty of Guadalupe Hidalgo. The borderlines were established by river and marine features, because the borderland had not been surveyed: the Rio Grande, the junction of the Gila and Colorado rivers, and then a line to one marine league south of the port of San Diego. This simplistic solution to a border location was unfortunate and yielded numerous problems for later generations because of such characteristics as meanderings of the Rio Grande and the lack of a reasonable route for a road between the Mexican mainland and Baja California. Even more disastrous to Mexico was the 1853 Gadsden Purchase by the Americans, because it covered the only reasonable east-west crossing north of the Sierra Madre Occidental. The final border was 2,013 miles long.

The location of the Canadian border developed out of a much longer struggle among Anglo-Americans with the American Revolution, the Jay Treaty of 1794, the War of 1812, the 1814 Treaty of Ghent, the establishment of the 49th parallel as the western boundary in 1846, and, finally, the formation of the Alaskan border in 1903. A precise delineation of the whole international boundary was ratified in Washington, D.C., in 1909.

The boundaries of the Great Lakes and the 49th parallel have worked out fairly well. The cleanup and prevention of water pollution are severe problems on the Great Lakes; many difficulties, such as dams, water use, and water pollution, also concern the rivers winding back and forth between the two countries. A greater problem, however, is that the borderline across New Hampshire and Maine should have continued along the 45th parallel instead of making the huge jog northward (to include northern Maine). This jog is a by-product of an early British move to deflect French-Canadian trade and influence away from New England. It serves to isolate the Maritime Provinces from the rest of Canada. Another serious problem is that the United States took the northern half of the British Columbian coast while determining Alaskan territory. The final land border was 5,525 miles long, over twice the length of the U.S.-Mexican border. It is often called "the longest undefended border in the world."

Native Indians and Borders

The cultural environments of the United States and British Canada have been basically similar for native American Indians and contrast with the Mexican and French Canadian

Table 4-1. *Canada-United States-Mexico Comparisons*

	Canada	United States	Mexico
Population (millions)	23	220	60
Population density (per km²)	2	23	28
Population growth rate	1.8 percent	1.1 percent	3.2 percent
Population location	Border region	Scattered	Scattered
Legal tradition	British	British	Roman
Official languages	French-English	English	Spanish
Common borders	5,525 miles	2,013 miles	
Greater frequency of border crossings	Canadians	Mexicans	
Border city development	Low	Moderate	High
Border screening —out	Survey data	Low	None
Border screening —in	Moderate	High	Low
Health, people	Low	Low	Low
animals	Moderate	High	Low
plants	Low	Moderate	None
Migration	Moderate	High	Moderate
Customs	Moderate	High	Low
Smuggling, general	Low	Moderate	Moderate
Smuggling, drugs	Moderate	High	Very low
Illegal immigration	Moderate	Very high	Very low
Border military defense	Very low	Very low	Very low
Border research cooperation by government agencies	Low	Moderate	Very low

cultural environments. The Yaquis who moved into Arizona from their Mexican ancestral home have become like other U.S. Indians, while those Yaquis who stayed in Mexico are still much like other northern Mexican Indians; the contextual Mexican or U.S. cultures made a difference in their development. A similar thing happened for a band of Kickapoos who went in the other direction, from Illinois to Oklahoma and then to Mexico. Those who went to Mexico tended to remain culturally traditional.

The U.S. and British Canadian cultures, on the other hand, have been very similar environments for the Indians. The Iroquois allied with the British during the Revolutionary War were harassed by the Americans at the end of the war and went to Canada, where in 1784 they were given seventy thousand acres of land. The Canadian Iroquois are still very similar to Iroquois in the United States through parallel developments and actual continuing migrations. In fact, the Iroquois are somewhat unique in North America and are comparable to the Basques of southern France and northern Spain, since they are culturally unified and nationalistic and live in a broad area on both sides of an international border.

A matter of continuing importance to the Iroquois is their freedom to cross the international border. Jay's Treaty of Amity, Commerce and Navigation in 1794 between the United States and Britain included provisions for the Indians living in the eastern border area to freely cross without customs duties for their personal goods.

After Santee Sioux attacks in Minnesota there were American counterattacks, and in 1862 some Sioux came to Canada as refugees. The Sioux who escaped harassment in the United States after the Battle of Little Big Horn also came to Canada under the leadership of Sitting Bull and Medicine Bear in 1876 and 1877. The descendants of those people are still very similar to U.S. Sioux.

From the Micmacs of the Maritimes to the Salish of the Vancouver-Seattle area, native societies were totally disregarded while the border was established and were divided by U.S.-Canadian border decisions. It has not made much difference. For example, among the major Indian population in Boston today (about three thousand) are Micmacs from the Canadian Maritimes. The Indians have simply followed the Maritimers working in New England. Looking west to British Columbia, we know that the Salish visit each other and intermarry across the international line. There is a network of spirit dancing groups, "smokehouse" churches, and Salish winter ceremonials that span the international border.

Indian territories in the U.S.-Mexican border were also disregarded in the drawing up of boundaries, but their location has made more of a difference to the Indians there than is the case in the U.S.-Canadian area. There are some international ties between Indians along the U.S.-Mexican border, but much fewer. Thus, Indians in Baja California who are very close linguistically and culturally to the Diegueño Indians in California occasionally attend the Diegueño festivals. Most of the Indians of Baja California, though, died out in historic times; the few who are left speak Spanish and are quite assimilated into the Mexican population. Also, the Diegueño festivals attract far more U.S. Indians than Mexican Indians. Many of these U.S. Indians, such as Luiseños, Cahuillas, and Yumans, are not Diegueños.

French Canada has stood out as a significantly different and, in modern times, a generally better environment for Indians than has British North America. Compared with other Indians, those in the French environment have higher average incomes, more intermarriage with whites, lower suicide rates, lower arrest rates, and more prohibition of alcoholic beverages, as a decision of Indian leaders. Their greater assimilation and acceptance of white society has meant they have less of an organized reaction against white society.

Compared to the Indians in British Canada, French Canadian Indians have a lower level of Indian political activity, fewer voluntary associations, and fewer ethnic newsletters and other signs of modern ethnic organizations. The French assumption that Indians will naturally assimilate into their culture has been so great that there has been very little development of a separate Indian policy. The French, like the Spanish in Mexico, did not make land cession treaties with Indians and did not create Indian reservations, although mission settlements did become Indian.

Border Cities

El Paso, Texas, and Ciudad Juárez, Chihuahua, form a dual city on the U.S.-Mexican border. It is a challenge to holistic ethnological analysis to understand how an international dual city works, particularly how the two separate parts solve local problems when they are in separate nations. It is difficult to isolate problems that arise simply out of conflict between local and national cultural systems. We must ask such questions as, In what ways is this problem characteristic of (1) international borders, (2) the more encompassing phenomenon of intercultural relationships, or (3) some special analytical slice such as language or economic relationships?

The contrast between the U.S.-Canadian and U.S.-Mexican borders illustrates the markedly different characters of the international borders for a single nation and suggests the difficulty the United States faces in creating a single set of border-related laws to solve screening problems without creating international inequities. There is also much to learn by comparing border-city relationships along and between the two borders.

Sault Sainte Marie, Ontario, and Sault Sainte Marie, Michigan, are international dual cities with similar cultures. They would make a good case study, since their local-national conflict could easily be more isolated and analyzed than in most dual cities. There is much more cultural difference between the dual cities of *southern* Ontario and *southern* Michigan because the U.S. cities there are more industrial and more populous and include the American black culture, which is absent on the Canadian side. Thus, dual cities such as Sarnia-Fort Huron, Windsor-Detroit, Fort Erie-Buffalo, and Niagara Falls in Ontario and New York all have quite strong cultural contrasts.

Border communities along the rest of the U.S.-Canadian border are not usually large enough to be called cities, but they are culturally quite similar. In fact, in most of the U.S.-Canadian border zone, regionality is stronger than nationality, certainly as a predictor and perhaps as a determinant of behavior. Therefore, southern British Columbia is culturally similar to Washington, Alberta to Montana, and so on. This international regionality is weak in the Onatrio area for reasons stated earlier and particularly weak across from French Canada. However, it is somewhat true even in the French-speaking parts of the Canadian border (Quebec) because so many French Canadians have bought farms and summer homes in adjacent New York. Along the northern parts of the New Brunswick-Maine line there are French-speaking towns on both sides of the international line. Canadian Maritime cultures are quite similar to those of New England, forming a kind of North Atlantic region or cultural area that contrasts with the regional panorama across the continent to the west. If French Canada ever separates, as a nation, from the rest of Canada, there will be a similar kind of separatist movement in Atlantic Canada, perhaps favoring alliance with the United States.

None of these U.S.-Canadian differences, even at the extremes of Niagara Falls, New York-Niagara Falls, Ontario, or along the Quebec-New York border, are of the same order as those along the U.S.-Mexican border. The latter is a zone where the "first world," the industrial capitalist world, is in contiguous and extensive contact with the "third world"—poorer countries struggling to industrialize. When the economic differences are so great at the border, they tend to be the major factor setting the pattern for other relationships. When the economic differences are minor, factors such as language, ethnic identity, and national affiliation predominate.

The Canadian population has settled in the southernmost parts of that country, close to but not in border cities. Most Canadians live within one hundred miles of the American border, both because of the economic integration with the United States, which seems to be the primary cause behind Mexico's border cities, and because of historical and ecological factors that are unrelated to or even opposed to economic integration with the United States—for example, the fact that commercial agriculture is only possible in the southern part of Canada for climatic reasons, requiring farmers to live in the south.

Cities such as Quebec and Montreal were located on the Saint Lawrence River because that was the historic transportation route. Toronto and Ottawa, however, were purposely located a considerable distance away from the U.S. border for military defense, and even so, Toronto (Fort York at the time) was captured by Americans in 1813. The national capital (Ottawa) was also purposely located on the French and British Canadian border, on the Ottawa River, because river and canal transportation was important and went into the Canadian interior at that time.

Canada has very little border-city development that depends upon economic integration with the United States. If the United States did not exist, Niagara Falls, Ontario, would still be a tourism center, although as a smaller city; Windsor, Ontario, would probably be just a small farming town instead of an industrial city integrated with Detroit, Michigan; and Sault Sainte Marie would be a smaller fishing and transportation center. The last probably would not have its steel mill and paper mill without the American market. There is nothing in Canada comparable, however, to the economic dependency on the United States of Mexican border cities such as Tijuana, Mexicali, Nogales, Juárez, Nuevo Laredo, and Matamoros. Canada has a much greater economic integration with the United States than Mexico does, but this integration is not achieved through border cities.

There are five major dual cities along the U.S.-Canadian border, and they all involve Ontario, where there are strategic transportation links, since all have bridges across the straits of the Great Lakes. These five are Sault Sainte Marie in Ontario and Michigan; Sarnia-Fort Huron; Windsor-Detroit; Fort Erie-Buffalo; and Niagara Falls in Ontario and New York. U.S. cities tend to be more deteriorated and to have higher crime rates. Canadian images of the United States are negatively influenced by the fact that the only parts of the United States that millions of Canadians have ever seen are such cities as Detroit and Buffalo. Comparably, often the only Mexican cities that millions of Americans see are the border cities, which tend to be deteriorated because of their excessive growth rates and poor capacity to provide facilities and services.

PART TWO. MAJOR TOPICAL CONCERNS

Section I. History and Archaeology

History, most simply defined, is our knowledge of the past. It includes biography, the study of man in his social aspects, political-institutional history, and study of the ways in which people have made a living in particular times and places. But because history tries to tell a story that has meaning, it is more than a collection of facts. Causality is emphasized by historians, and cultural events are described, analyzed, and judged. History thus includes the study of organized human behavior and has close ties with philosophy, literature, sociology, anthropology, geography, political science, economics, and other modern specializations. As such, history is both art and science and has immense variety. Historians are a heterogeneous lot and write in various genres. History itself ranges from dry-as-dust technical publications never meant to be read by the general public to dramatic interpretations of the past based on a morphology of human society.

In their study of the Borderlands, historians have not clearly fixed the geographic or cultural limits of the region, but Herbert Eugene Bolton, *the* Borderlands historian, considered the area to be the northern outposts of New Spain

5

Historical Overview

RALPH H. VIGIL
Department of History
University of Nebraska, Lincoln

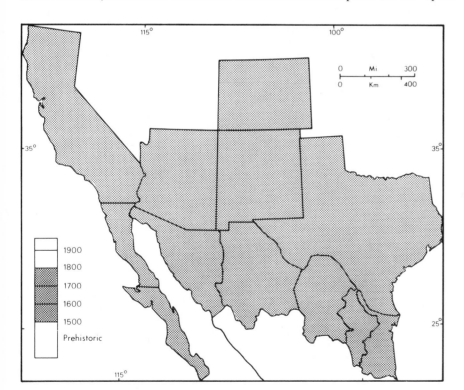

from Florida to the Californias (Bolton, 1921: vii-x, 188-206). Following Bolton's lead, later historians have defined the Borderlands as including northern Mexico and the southern tier of the present-day United States, yet the emphasis has usually been placed on the former Spanish provinces from Texas to California. In this restrictive sense the Borderlands embrace the states of California, Arizona, Texas, and New Mexico and portions of Colorado. Southern Colorado is included within the Hispanic Southwest because, although it was settled by New Mexico pioneers in the nineteenth century, its land titles often derive from original Mexican grants, and the rivers, valleys, and mountains of the region have Hispanic toponyms. In addition, Spanish-American settlements in southern Colorado "formed the northward thrust of a cultural tradition," and *plaza* settlements dominated the countryside throughout the nineteenth century (Onís, 1976; Taylor and West, 1973). The Hispanic Southwest is where settlements were firmly established, where the attempt was made to force the native inhabitants into patterns determined for them in Madrid or Mexico City, and where institutions such as the *presidio,* the mission, and the Spanish-Mexican civil settlement created temporal and spiritual control of the surrounding land and its inhabitants.

Borderlands history properly begins with the spectacular movement commonly referred to as the expansion of Europe, which includes the sixteenth-century meeting of ethnically different Spaniards and heterogeneous Indian societies in what would become the northern fringe of the Viceroyalty of New Spain. Borderlands history thus includes not only the history of the Southwest, where two frontiers collided and a fusion "which is still in progress" began (Bannon, 1970: 3), but also the ethnologically complex Iberian and Indian pasts in an area that in the nineteenth century would become part of Mexico and the United States.

Historians interested in the colonial Borderlands have concentrated on the Spanish conquest of the various Indian civilizations; the advance of Spanish civilization as reflected in the careers of Spanish explorers, conquerors, missionaries, government officials, and institutional development; and on international rivalry. However, excursions into the region's pre-Columbian past have also been made by historians, an example of whom is Hubert Howe Bancroft, who has been called the "West's most versatile and significant early historian" (Caughey, 1969: xv). Bancroft attempted to describe Indians "as they were first seen by Europeans along the several paths of discovery before the withering hand of civilization was laid upon them." The result was five volumes on the "Native Races" (1875-76) utilizing "what was essentially the culture area device" (Caughey, 1946: 126). Bancroft's account of Indian cultures suffers when compared with recent anthropological studies, but his synthetic work was based on numerous sources and had great utility in the late nineteenth century. Moreover, Bancroft "put his finger on the weakness of arbitrary technological criteria of cultural progress" and correctly observed that the terms "Savage and Civilized, as applied to races of men, are relative and not absolute terms" (Keen, 1971*b*: 391).

In addition to his pioneer work in anthropology, Bancroft

was "the first determined collector" of books and manuscripts pertaining to western America. He was also the first to undertake to chronicle its history comprehensively and exhaustively, and his thirty-nine volumes make him "the largest and the basic contributor to the history of Spanish North America" (Caughey, 1969: 126, 130).

In the same period that Bancroft was producing his volumes on Mexico and the Spanish Southwest, Frederick Jackson Turner called attention to the significance of the frontier in American history. Important as an historical declaration of independence, Turner's "frontier hypothesis" stressed the role of the distinctive environment of the wilderness in Americanizing settlers and their institutions. Unfortunately, Turner's "West" was, "in large measure, what has come to be termed the Trans-Allegheny," and the work of "Turner and his school tended to limit the historians' vision unduly" (Bannon, 1964: 4).

Although Bancroft and Turner brought the American West into focus, the importance of the Spanish Borderlands as "another frontier" and the dream of "Parkmanizing" the history of the Hispanic Southwest was first attempted and realized by Herbert Eugene Bolton. Bolton, a student of Frederick Jackson Turner, first became interested in the Spanish Borderlands when he taught at the University of Texas. As teacher and productive scholar there and at Stanford University and the University of California, Bolton made the Spanish Borderlands "an accepted and enduring division of the American story." Moreover, the Bolton "approach" to American history encompassed all the Americas. As early as 1920, Bolton and T. M. Marshall shocked an editorial critic by devoting nearly one-third of their textbook entitled *The Colonization of North America, 1492-1783* "to the period before 1606, that is to say, before there were any permanent English settlements in America" (Bannon, 1968: 11). That the Bolton approach proved popular is demonstrated by the success of the 1920 book, for it had its tenth printing by the MacMillan Company in 1956. Bolton's many students have continued his work, and the result has been a greater understanding of the history of the Americas and the Borderlands. A knowledge of this "other frontier" has led to the realization that "the Anglo-American experience, magnificent and thrilling though it was, actually was not quite as unique as it is sometimes pictured and chauvinistically thought to be. The Anglo-American frontier can be better understood and more properly evaluated by process of comparison" (Bannon, 1970: 3).

In the tradition of their master, Boltonians and neo-Boltonians have diligently mined archives in Spain, Mexico, and the United States, and "it is probable that no other part of colonial Spanish America has stimulated so extensive a program of research" (Gibson, 1966: 189). Lyle Saunder's *Guide* (1944) testifies to the enormous quantity of published and unpublished materials bearing only on cultural relations in just the New Mexico Borderlands. Though not a complete bibliography, it lists over five thousand items. Many outstanding studies of the Borderlands have appeared in article form in historical journals, and the interested reader should consult periodicals such as *New Mexico Historical Review, El*

Palacio, Pacific Historical Quarterly, Arizona and the West, Southwestern Historical Quarterly, The American West, Journal of the West, California Historical Society Quarterly, The Americas, and *Hispanic American Historical Review.*

In spite of the volume of published and unpublished materials concerning the Borderlands, regional synthetic histories are few. Bolton's 1921 study remained the standard work until the appearance in 1970 of John Francis Bannon's new synthesis. Bannon's scholarly but colorful work compresses "the results of hundreds of investigators who have studied aspects of the Borderlands story in the half-century since Bolton's volume appeared" (Ray Allen Billington in Bannon, 1970: vii). Also worthy of note are works by Richardson and Rister (1934), Peyton (1948), Perrigo (1960), Hollon (1961), and Faulk (1968).

Students have observed that as the nineteenth century dawned, Borderlands subcultures had already come to exist. These regional variations, which stemmed from differences in times of colonization and the nature of the localities settled, became more pronounced after Mexican independence in 1821. Provincial economies largely account for different patterns of life in the Mexican borderlands. For example, it was only in the nineteenth century that the livestock industry in New Mexico became more important than farming. The rise of the sheep industry created a class of *ricos* and the *patrón* system, but it also destroyed the egalitarianism that had characterized the early farming villages of this part of the Borderlands. In California, on the other hand, the secularization of the missions by the Mexican government created a new social order dominated by cattle ranchers. These land-based aristocrats soon became the leading political figures of the province and supervised Indian labor on their small principalities.

In addition, Mexico's decision to open the Borderlands to American trade and Anglo-American settlers allowed hide and tallow traders, Santa Fe traders, and Texas pioneers to begin their assault on the Mexican Borderlands. In Texas, colonists of the 1820s achieved a bilingual-bicultural arrangement which the wave of Anglo immigrants of the 1830s destroyed at San Jacinto. Ray A. Billington's *The Far Western Frontier, 1830-1860* (1956) and his *Westward Expansion* (1949) incorporate and appraise many books and articles concerning the Mexican Borderlands, the annexation of Texas, the conquest of California, and the war with Mexico. Billington's scholarship is based on an extensive study of the ample literature available on the Trans-Mississippi frontier, and his viewpoints are singularly free of bias.

Between 1850 and 1900, native Californios, Tejanos, and Hispanos declined in socio-political-economic importance as Anglo-Americans assumed political and economic control of the Southwest. The result was some cultural fusion and much cultural conflict. Central to the origins of cultural conflict was the land-grant problem. The transfer of land in the Southwest from natives to recently arrived Anglo-Americans happened in the area from Texas to California and was characterized by a combination of force and legal chicanery. The prototype of the entrepreneur had not yet developed among Mexican Americans, and they were relatively helpless before

the influx of merchants, businessmen, land speculators, venal politicians, cattle barons, squatters, lawyers, and others who soon controlled the economy and government of the Southwest. An excellent but limited study interpreting this period is Howard Roberts Lamar's (1966) survey of the territorial history of New Mexico, Colorado, Utah, and Arizona. Another fine study of the confrontation between different ethnic groups and cultures is Leonard Pitt's (1966) extensively documented monograph on the decline of the Californios. Pitt's study is a contribution not only to state and local history, but also to the ethnic history of the United States. His work proves that the predicament of Mexican Americans solidified prior to 1900 "and not after the turn of the century, as some suppose" (Pitt, 1966: 296).

The status of the Spanish-speaking people of the Borderlands as a victimized out-group was an apparent fact by 1900 and is largely explained by the influx of new peoples and an economic order that replaced the older agrarian economy. Well before this date, the Spanish-speaking society had come to be known as a "greaser" population by Anglo-Americans. Mexican Americans, in turn, called the new arrivals *gringos*, "foreigners." But in spite of the hostility and opposition toward minority groups that came about after the United States assumed control of the Southwest, the more than eighty thousand Mexicans (Nostrand, 1975) who became subjects of the nation in its triumphant march to the Pacific would have been assimilated, and by now may have become "regular Americans," had it not been for a continual Mexican immigration that began as early as 1848 when gold was discovered in California.

In his study of the Spanish-speaking Californians, Leonard Pitt notes that ethnic groups in the United States are destined "to be thrown together with people of 'their own kind' whom they neither know nor particularly like—perhaps even despise" (Pitt, 1966: 53). At the turn of the century, approximately 100,000 Mexican-born immigrants were located in Texas, Arizona, California, and New Mexico. By 1930 there was an amalgamation of perhaps 1,200,000 persons of Mexican descent in the Southwest, and today the number has grown to approximately 7,200,000.

Wherever Mexican immigrants have located in large numbers, as in Texas and California, all of the Spanish-speaking have been lumped together by the "Anglo" population, who often view them collectively as "interlopers," "foreigners," and "greasers." The reason for this, of course, is that Mexican immigration, whether permanent or temporary, legal or illegal, has created below-minimum-wage labor pools, legal peonage, social ostracism, and a negative stereotype. Organized labor in the Southwest has resented the Mexican immigrants, claiming that their presence has depressed wages. Consequently, the Mexican American today is underrepresented in professional, technical, and managerial skills and competencies.

It should be understood, of course, that Mexican immigrants are not to blame for their condition. Lacking opportunity in Mexico, they came to the United States in response to the encouragement of large-scale fruit and vegetable growers, railroad companies, ranchers, contractors, and others who desired cheap labor. Moreover, in the case of the *bracero* program, which ended in 1964, Mexico and the United States entered into a bilateral agreement whereby the U.S. government would subsidize American growers by allowing the importation of low-wage workers for temporary jobs in agriculture (Galarza, 1964).

Mexican immigration since 1900 has created a society in the Southwest that is stratified along class lines with overtones of a caste system. Perhaps the best definition of the Spanish-speaking people of the Borderlands is that of an ethnic minority that legally exists in free association with the majority but is still not accepted as socially equal and is subjected to both overt and covert discrimination. Because of discrimination and the attendant difficulty of succeeding in American society, many Mexican Americans have suffered and continue to endure anxiety and disaffection. This situation began to change during and after World War II when members of *la raza* became politically oriented in significant numbers. By the 1960s the Chicano movement, and manifestations of conflict and resistance as well as the progress Mexican Americans had made in freeing themselves from subordinate status, had created widespread interest in Mexican Americans. No longer were the Spanish-speaking "invisible" outside the Southwest or "forgotten Americans" within the Borderlands (Sánchez, 1940; Samora, 1966). Mexican Americans or ethnic history had come of age and were "a viable topic of research and exposition" (Almaráz, 1976: 16).

With the inclusion of Mexican American studies as an academic discipline, Borderlands historians are aware of the need to reassess the older historiography. Further studies of ethnic and national individuals and groups who have settled in the Borderlands are needed, as is a new synthesis that might emphasize the older research in light of contemporary views concerning the past and the present.

In conclusion, Borderlands history is the history of a frontier and a region in which various cultures have met, clashed, and blended. Borderlands history is part of European, Mexican, and U.S. history; it cannot be understood except in the context of the epic of greater America. Not only does it include local, state, regional, national, and international history, but it is also one example of "phases common to most portions of the entire Western Hemisphere" (Bannon, 1968: 303). It embraces the pre-Columbian civilizations of the region, European discovery, exploitation and colonization, race mixture and cultural fusion, international rivalry, the rise of independent nations following the American revolutions, the planting of Anglo-American political institutions and culture in the Spanish-Mexican Borderlands, internal colonization, and the efforts of Mexican Americans and Indians to find their place in the sun of a region that is, "from the point of view of the Hemisphere, the most truly American of all regions" (Howard W. Odum as quoted in Lamar, 1966: xiv).

Two traditions concerning Spanish New World conquest and colonization still flourish. One, the Black Legend, maintains that Spaniards in America were uniquely cruel in their treatment of Indians and that the Spanish colonial record is one of tyranny and corruption. The other, the White Legend, addresses Spanish altruism and tolerance and "that portion of Spanish history for which one can find moral or other defensive arguments" (Gibson, 1971). The origins of the Black and White legends, if their meanings are restricted to Spain's colonial record in America, are found in sixteenth-century Spanish writings, largely reflecting "the divergent and conflicting interests of the social groups which appeared in America after the Conquest" (Friede, 1971). That the controversy surrounding Spain's New World actions still continues is demonstrated by the lively debate between Benjamin Keen (1969, 1971a) and Lewis Hanke (1971).

Benjamin Keen and Charles Gibson (1964) have amassed an impressive body of evidence that the Black Legend's substantive content, "stripped of its rhetoric and emotional coloration, and with due regard for its failure to notice less

6

Exploration and Conquest

RALPH H. VIGIL
Department of History
University of Nebraska, Lincoln

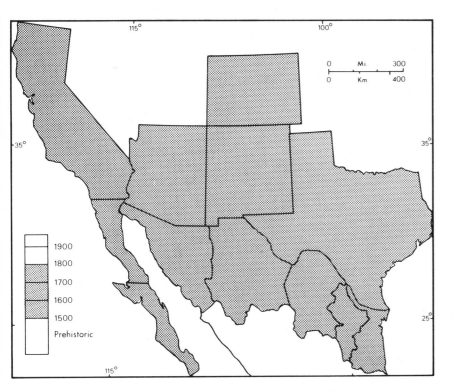

dramatic forms of Spanish exploitation of the Indians (land usurpation, peonage, and the like) is no legend at all" (Keen, 1969: 703-19). Middle American military conquest was accompanied, or shortly followed, by Spanish settlement, appropriation of Indian lands, and cruel Indian exploitation by labor systems and practices that contributed to the disastrous Indian population decline. In addition, Indians under Spanish rule became a deculturated minority victimized by prejudice and discrimination, and Spanish laws written for their protection were all too often neglected.

On the other hand, while one can agree that all conquests are evil, the Spanish conquest of America not excepted, it may also be conjectured that future research and comparative analysis may confirm that the Spanish imperial enterprise had positive features lacking in other conquests. Although more research is needed for concrete generalizations, a significant number of students of the Spanish Conquest have generally agreed that "no other nation made so continuous or so passionate an attempt to discover what was the just treatment for the native peoples under its jurisdiction than Spaniards" (Hanke, 1965: 1; 1970: 107).

Not all Spaniards exploited Indians, and a goodly number were passionate champions of Indian rights. Greatest among the pro-Indian reformers was, of course, Bartolomé de Las Casas (Wagner and Parish, 1967). Another was Judge Alonso de Zorita (1963). Las Casas, Zorita, Viceroy Luis de Velasco, and other Crown officials and friars who opposed Conquest evils were themselves Spaniards, representatives "of an important aspect of Spanish character, an aspect that is Christian, compassionate, egalitarian, and unimpeachable. In this view, a Spain that could produce a figure such as Las Casas cannot be condemned out of hand as morally irresponsible" (Gibson, 1971). By contrast, the English imperial enterprise is marked by values which "less enlightened" ages denounced as social vices; this enterprise lacked spokesmen such as Las Casas. Most Englishmen did not even consider Indians to be lost sheep and potential Christians like themselves (Toynbee, 1934-61, vol. I: xvii, 211-49; Pearce, 1953; Nash, 1974). Unlike Spaniards, English frontiersmen did not view Indians as a necessary part of society, and "counterparts to the friars and the padre rarely figured prominently in the story of the Anglo-American westward movement" (Bannon, 1970: 5; Cook, 1970: 23-42).

Spanish exploration and conquest in the New World may be considered the dramatic prologue to the more prosaic work of settlement and possession. Borderlands exploration and conquest is intimately related, since medieval times, to the expansion of the Spanish frontier, and the Iberian background is pertinent in understanding Spanish America and the Borderlands. New World Spanish explorers and *conquistadores* of the "Renaissance" were cultural heirs of the Iberian *reconquista*. Centuries of reconquest and raids marked by countless battles between Christians and Moslems formed the world view of Castilian nobility and peasantry alike, and the Spanish conquest of the New World has been called "a projection of the Spanish Middle Ages in space and time" (Sánchez-Albornoz, 1970). Military and spiritual ideals were joined in the quest of the New World utopia; glory, adventure, wealth, honor, and fame were found in the pursuit of gold, subjects, and souls (Wolf, 1959: 152-75; Picón-Salas, 1968: 27-41).

Imperial Spain's origins and rise to power under the Hapsburgs may be found in a number of excellent, readily available works. A standard is Roger Bigelow Merriman's *The Rise of the Spanish Empire in the Old World and in the New* (1918-34). Merriman's volumes stress military, political, and diplomatic history and may be supplemented by Jean Hippolyte Mariejol's (1961) history of life and manners in the Spain of the Catholic kings. Benjamin Keen's (1961) translated edition of Mariejol's entertaining and scholarly work, first published in 1892, corrects minor dating errors and revises some statements not accepted by present-day scholars of Isabelline Spain, but Keen remains faithful to the French original's meaning. In addition, Keen's translation contains a scholarly comment on bibliographies and guides, sources for the reign of the Catholic sovereigns and the era's institutions, works on social and intellectual life, and a glossary of terms and persons.

Spanish occupation of the Greater Antilles was directed by the Catholic kings; the ways in which Spanish culture was transmitted were repeated on the mainland. The larger West Indian islands also gave the Spaniards a foothold in the New World, establishing that region's future role as a supply base for exploration, discovery, conquest, and settlement of lands now included within Mexico and the United States.

After transforming the Española Arawaks into tribute payers and cheap labor, sugar planting and stock raising began in the area. Restless colonials, however, almost immediately commenced slave-hunting raids and searched for new islands and regions to exploit. These ventures extended geographical knowledge, soon leading to the discovery of the Mexican mainland and the exploration of North America.

The most durable work emphasizing the early period of discovery, exploration, and conquest is Edward Gaylord Bourne's *Spain in America, 1450-1580* (1904). This concise and admirable survey was reprinted by Benjamin Keen (1962) with a new introduction and selective bibliography. Bourne wrote his brilliant synthesis when the United States became a colonial empire, and Keen correctly observes that Bourne's views on Spain's Indian policies were influenced by "the new imperialist climate of opinion" in the United States.

Bourne's lucid discussion of Spanish colonial policy and activities in the Caribbean from 1492 to 1519 may be supplemented by more recent works. C. H. Haring's *The Spanish Empire in America* (1952) is a scholarly, factual, and objective account of the beginnings of New World royal government and its colonial evolution. It remains the best single-volume institutional history of Spanish New World colonies. Carl O. Sauer's *The Early Spanish Main* (1969) is an outstanding study of the circum-Caribbean area from discovery to 1519. The newly discovered islands and lands were soon being worked by the natives. Excessive and cruel forced labor destroyed these Indians: "By 1519 the Spanish Main was a sorry shell," and most Spaniards now desired to "seek their fortunes in parts as yet untried and unknown" (Sauer, 1969: 294).

According to Charles Gibson, the invasion and subjugation of the Caribbean lands and peoples prior to 1519 were conquests "only in a limited or preliminary sense," and the true "age of conquest" commenced in 1519, when Hernán Cortés and his fellow adventurers "proceeded to march against and subdue the huge populations of the mainland" (Gibson, 1966: 25). Today the narrative epic of conquest and the heroic stance of the men who brought it about no longer receive most historians' attention, but it remains a topic of interest in textbooks. Edited and translated accounts of exploration and conquest are common.

William H. Prescott's *History of the Conquest of Mexico,* first published in 1843, is the classic account of the Aztec Confederacy's defeat by Spaniards who brought Christianity and dispelled "those dark forms of horror which had so long brooded over the fair regions of Anahuac" (Prescott, 1898, vol. I: 80). This narrative epic is short on analysis, but it remains a valuable work essential to an understanding of the most dramatic event in Mexican history. However, Prescott was a product of his time, and his romantic attitudes concerning progress and providence, and his basic anti-Indian prejudice, date the work.

Studying the Spanish conquest of Aztec civilization, historians have strongly relied on three traditional sources: (1) Hernán Cortés's five major letters of relation to Charles V (1519-26); (2) the account given by Francisco López de Gómara, Cortés's chaplain in later years, in his *Historia de la conquista de México,* which forms the second part of the *Historia general de las Indias;* and (3) Bernal Díaz del Castillo's *Historia verdadera de la conquista de la Nueva España.* A. R. Pagden's 1971 translation of Cortés's letters is the best English version to date, containing ample notes, a glossary, and maps. Gómara's disciplined and classical history of Cortés and the Mexican enterprise has been edited and translated by Lesley Byrd Simpson (1964). Bernal Diaz's "true history" of the conquest of Mexico remains the most popular, and new editions of the work "averaged more than one a year in the decade of the 1960s" (Gibson, 1975). Unfortunately, none of these editions "makes a significant scholarly contribution."

Of all sixteenth-century Mexican sources, Cortés's letters have usually been accorded first rank because they were written so soon after the described events. A recent study by Vigil (1974*b*) of the Second Letter of Relation and other documentary data relating to April-June, 1520, events in Mexico proves that Cortés's relation is a source of the first importance.

From their island bases in the Caribbean and from Mexico City, bands of *conquistadores*-explorers soon advanced northward, beginning the history of New Spain's northern frontier, or the Spanish Borderlands. They were led to the resolution of the "northern mystery" by the desire to find another Mexico, by tall tales of the Fountain of Eternal Youth and the Seven Cities of Gold, and by the need to find the transcontinental Strait of Anián, the fabulous land of Quivira, and other El Dorados rich in precious minerals and gems, Amazons, giants, and pygmys. In their search for rich and exotic civilizations, Spaniards questioned Indians and were obligingly told that these kingdoms were just a short distance

beyond. In that fabulous country "there were fishes as big as horses" in great rivers and "everyone had their [*sic*] ordinary dishes made of wrought plate, and the jugs and bowls were of gold" (Pedro de Castañeda in Hodge and Lewis, 1907: 314).

Spanish exploration of the southeastern United States is adequately covered by Bourne (1962). In the same period, John Gilmary Shea wrote an informed and critical account of "Ancient Florida" in Justin Winsor's *Narrative and Critical History of America* (1886, vol. II: 231-98). Another convenient summary is Herbert Eugene Bolton's *The Spanish Borderlands: A Chronicle of Old Florida and the Southwest* (1921). This little volume, as Father John Francis Bannon observes, "set the name for the area" (Bannon, 1970: 257). Bannon himself has an interesting chapter on Spanish conquest in North America in his *History of the Americas* (1952, vol. I: 75-92). These accounts may be supplemented by Woodbury Lowery's two volumes on the Floridas (1901, 1905), Anthony Kerrigan's translation of Andrés G. Barcia's *Chronological History of the Continent of Florida* (1951), and Darío Fernández-Flórez's *The Spanish Heritage in the United States* (1965).

Southwestern exploration and the history of European-Indian relations begin with the 1528 Florida expedition of Pánfilo de Narváez. When colonists reached the Florida coast, a series of disasters depleted the expedition; the survivors constructed makeshift boats and set out westward across the Gulf of Mexico in search of Pánuco, Mexico. Most men were lost at sea, but part of the flotilla did reach the Texas coast. The castaways finally dwindled to four survivors, who finally arrived near the Sinaloa River on a spring day in 1536. There, on the frontier of New Galicia, Alvar Núñez Cabeza de Vaca and his three companions came upon a Spanish slave-hunting party.

After the wanderers reached Mexico City, a report of the remarkable overland journey was made to the Audiencia of Santo Domingo. This relation was used by Gonzalo Fernández de Oviedo in his celebrated *Historia general y natural de las Indias.* The more famous narrative of Cabeza de Vaca was first printed in 1542 at Zamora; a translation of this epic journey is in *Spanish Explorers in the Southern United States, 1528-1543* (1907), edited by Frederick W. Hodge and Theodore H. Lewis. This narrative has great charm and interest and was written by an honest and humane soldier who advised the Crown: "to bring all these people [the Indians] to be Christians and to the obedience of the Imperial Majesty, they must be won by kindness, which is a way certain, and no other is" (Cabeza de Vaca in Hodge and Lewis, 1907: 110).

While traveling overland, Cabeza de Vaca and his companions heard of populous towns with very large houses whose inhabitants grew cotton. This modest report, and the fact that the rainbow seekers had seen "clear traces of gold and lead, iron, copper, and other metals" and precious stones ("emeralds" and turquoise), impressed the viceroy of New Spain and led to the idea that perhaps there was another rich Mexican empire in the north ready for the taking.

Viceroy Antonio de Mendoza originally suggested to Cabeza de Vaca and another survivor of the Narváez expedition that they return north to chase down the rumor of "another Mexico." When this offer was declined and Cabeza de Vaca returned to Spain, Mendoza arranged to have the Franciscan friar Marcos de Niza explore the region beyond Culiacán. Esteban, the black slave who had been a member of the Narváez expedition and the property of one of the Spanish survivors, would guide Fray Marcos. It was also thought that, because he had knowledge of the northern Indians, he would ensure their friendship. In early 1539 the expedition left Culiacán, and because Esteban was sent ahead of the main party, he reached the Zuñi settlements before Fray Marcos. He asked the Cibola Indians for turquoises and women, but since the Indians thought it unreasonable for him "to say that the people were white in the country from which he came and that he was sent by them, he being black," he was killed along with most of the Sonora Indians who were with him (Pedro de Castañeda in Hodge and Lewis, 1907: 289). When Fray Marcos heard of Esteban's death, he returned to Mexico and claimed to have seen Cíbola, a pueblo of fine appearance, with stone houses, terraces, and flat roofs, and larger than the city of Mexico. Fray Marcos's report has been the subject of several studies: some writers consider him to have been a liar; others state that his glowing report of the New Kingdom of San Francisco was based on a view of Hawikuh from a nearby hill and of what he thought the Indians accompanying him had told him (Baldwin, 1926; Bandelier, 1890; Bloom, 1940).

Fray Marcos's report to Viceroy Mendoza precipitated Francisco Vásquez de Coronado's expedition. This left Compostela, Mexico, in 1540 and returned two years later after a fruitless search for the Quivira riches. The most important account of the expedition is that of Pedro de Castañeda, a private soldier under Coronado who went in search of "that better land." A translation of Castañeda's 1565 narrative may be found in Hodge and Lewis (1907). The best modern accounts of the expedition are by Herbert E. Bolton (1949) and A. G. Day (1940). Both works have excellent bibliographies. Bolton recognized that the 1540–42 Coronado expedition "was a necessary antecedent to the colonization" of the Borderlands (Bolton, 1949: 395). Hodge observes that Coronado's quest in North America "combined with the journey of De Soto in giving to the world an insight into the hitherto unknown vast interior of the northern continent and formed the basis of the cartography of that region. It was the means also of making known the sedentary Pueblo tribes of our Southwest and the hunting tribes of the Great Plains, the Grand Cañon of the Colorado and the lower reaches of that stream, and the teeming herds of bison and the absolute dependence on them by the hunting Indians for every want" (Hodge and Lewis, 1907: 280). More recently Jack D. Forbes (1960) has described Coronado's men as "wealth-hungry" bandits who alienated both sedentary and nomadic American Indians by their immorality and injustice.

Despite Coronado's failure, the idea that vast wealth was to be found in the north continued. Coronado was "criticized for withdrawing to Mexico, and within five years of his return there was official talk of sending a new expedition to colonize Quivira" (Bolton, 1949: 400). In the 1550s the utopian dream

of the spiritual conquest of northern New Spain, including lands visited by Coronado, was proposed by Alonso de Zorita and the Mexican Franciscan friars. Moreover, northern Mexico's expansion and settlement south of the Rio Grande were accelerated by the discovery of rich silver mines at Zacatecas; prospecting was undertaken even further north. Durango was founded in 1563; by the 1580s, southern Chihuahua had Spanish outposts. The account of the northward advance and the Spanish-Indian struggle in the land of the Chichimecas is in Philip W. Powell's definitive work (1952). J. Lloyd Mecham's study (1927) of Francisco de Ibarra also describes problems of the northward advance. As Powell notes, Spanish domination of the Gran Chichimeca was finally achieved only after the military approach failed. After 1585, Spanish domination was won by a combination of diplomacy, purchase, religious conversion, gifts of food and clothing, and the promise of good land, seed, and agricultural implements to prospective Indian farmers. "Out of the experience of this pacification grew the mission system that was to serve Spain so well in later expansion on the American continent" (Powell, 1952: 204).

It was from Santa Barbara, Chihuahua, in 1581 that Fray Agustín Rodríguez, accompanied by two other Franciscans, set out for New Mexico. When the ten soldiers who accompanied the friars returned south without them, a relief expedition headed by Antonio de Espejo was sent north to rescue the missionaries. After learning the friars all had met their deaths at the hands of Indians, Espejo and his men explored the region for mineral wealth. Some evidence of mines was discovered (one explanation for the area's settlement). Two other factors were the desire to Christianize the reputedly advanced sedentary Pueblo Indians and the need for a base to defend the Pacific Ocean from the English when it was rumored that Francis Drake had discovered a transcontinental strait north of Mexico.

At the same time that Coronado was exploring the buffalo plains and Hernando de Soto was searching for riches in the southeastern United States, the Pacific Coast exploration of New Spain by Juan Rodríguez Cabrillo was conducted. By 1543 the coastline from the Straits of Magellan to Oregon had been traced, and California had been named by a Spaniard familiar with Garci Rodríguez de Montalvo's novel of chivalry entitled *Las Sergas de Esplandián.* However, California sea colonization proved impossible in the sixteenth century: voyages north were hindered by contrary winds, an ocean current, and fierce storms. Additionally, Spaniards failed to find gold or silver in California, and the land was inhabited by nonagricultural Indians unable to provide a regular food supply to the parasitic Spaniards. California settlement finally happened in the eighteenth century because of Jesuit and Franciscan missionary efforts and the foreign threat posed by Russians and English.

The first steps on the long road to settling California are skillfully synthesized by John Francis Bannon (1970: 49–71). Another excellent summary of the discovery and eventual settlement of this Spanish province is John Walton Caughey's *California* (1953a). Caughey's study also contains an extended appraisal of published materials on California history. Readers will also find Herbert Eugene Bolton's *Spanish Exploration in the Southwest, 1542-1706* (1908) a valuable source. This work contains critical introductions and translations of the Cabrillo and Vizcaíno expeditions as well as accounts of exploration and settlement in New Mexico, Texas, and Arizona. Also important are Hubert Howe Bancroft's valuable volumes on the *History of California* (1884-90) and shorter works by Chapman (1916) and Richman (1911).

With the exception of New Mexico, New Spain's northern frontier beyond the Rio Grande remained unsettled until the late seventeenth and eighteenth centuries. Permanent occupation of Texas, for example, was a Spanish response to French occupation of Louisiana. The final settlement of Texas, however, was not a sudden event. As early as 1519, Alonso de Pineda mapped the coast from Florida to Pánuco, Mexico. In the seventeenth century, New Mexican settlers visited the Jumano Indians of the upper Colorado River; Texas was also explored from the south. Approaches to Texas before the

settling of this defensive Borderlands province may be found in Bolton (1912) and Steck (1932). Carlos E. Castañeda's extensive study (1936-50) also has much information on early Texas. For Spanish-Indian relations in this Borderlands region, see W. W. Newcomb (1961) and John (1975).

European presence in the United States thus begins in the Spanish Borderlands. Exploration of the Atlantic and Pacific coasts, and the vast interior of the continent, extended geographical knowledge and was a dramatic and necessary prologue to settling the Southwest and Florida. American frontier history antedates the founding of Jamestown and Plymouth and formally begins with the *conquistadores*-explorers. These precursors of colonization "did not find the riches of which they had been told, but they found a place in which to search for them and the beginning of a good country to settle in, so as to go on farther from there" (Pedro de Castañeda in Hodge and Lewis, 1907: 284).

7

Colonial Institutions

RALPH H. VIGIL
Department of History
University of Nebraska, Lincoln

The institutional history of the Spanish colonies from discovery to independence has been admirably synthesized by C. H. Haring (1952). His study is "concerned with the transfer of Spanish modes of government and society from the Old World to the New, and with their evolution in a remote and very different American environment." Topics include race and environment, territorial organization, royal government in the Indies, the municipal corporation or *cabildo,* the church in America, school and society, literature, scholarship and the fine arts, agriculture and industry, the royal exchequer, and the Spanish commercial system. Although not a definitive study, this comprehensive volume continues to be recognized as a useful reference and "the fundamental modern treatment of Spanish colonialism" (Gibson, 1958).

Political administration in the Borderlands north of the Rio Grande begins with the settlement of New Mexico. The form and character of government in seventeenth-century New Mexico has been adequately described by France V. Scholes (1935). Juan de Oñate was governor, captain general, and *adelantado*

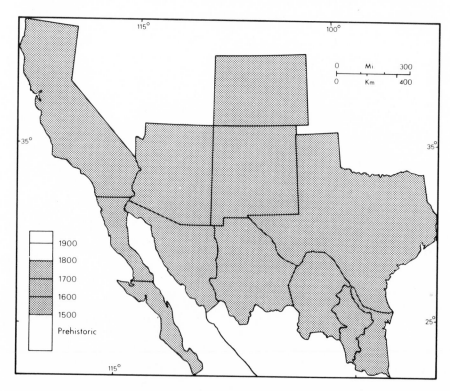

(lord proprietor) of the colony until he resigned his offices and titles in 1607. In 1609 the first royal governor of New Mexico, Don Pedro de Peralta, arrived and assumed control. Peralta and his successors acted as agents of the Crown, and their appointments were made in Mexico City. As Scholes (1935: 75) observes, the provincial governor's "powers were wide enough to permit an honest and energetic man to maintain discipline and secure justice, or to make it possible for a self-seeking official to become a local tyrant."

From about 1660 the province of New Mexico was divided into two major administrative districts. "These were known as the Río Arriba and the Río Abajo, i.e., the upper and lower districts of the Rio Grande Valley and the neighboring districts" (Scholes, 1935: 91). The Río Arriba district was commanded by the governor. The Río Abajo was under the jurisdiction of the lieutenant governor.

Between six and eight rural subdivisions, called jurisdictions, were administered by *alcaldes mayores.* These lesser officials, appointed by the governor, administered petty justice. Because they held office at the governor's pleasure, they were often "nothing more than tools of the governors" (Scholes, 1935: 92). In fact, "confiscation of Indian supplies for the benefit of the *alcaldes,* forced labor, mistreatment of Pueblo women and the appropriation of Indian land were major subjects of most 18th century Franciscan accounts" (Jenkins, 1971: 97; Morfi, 1977: 30-34).

Borderlands government was rudimentary until the eighteenth century. With the occupation of southern Arizona, Texas, and California and the acquisition of Louisiana, however, politics became more complex. Boundary expansion and frontier defense against the Indians of the north and the threat posed by France, Great Britain, and Russia led to government reorganization and military reform in northern New Spain.

Inspection of the Borderlands and recommendations concerning the region resulted in the 1776 creation of the Commandancy General of the Interior Provinces. The Commandancia General, or frontier military district, underwent several reorganizations, but in 1792 it included the provinces of Sonora, Nueva Vizcaya, New Mexico, Coahuila, and Texas (Navarro García, 1964: 486). California, initially part of the Interior Provinces, militarily and politically was subordinated to the viceroy early in 1793 (Bancroft, 1890: 503).

As is apparent from his title, the commandant general's primary duties were military. The highest royal official in the Interior Provinces, he sent information to the viceroy in Mexico City but communicated directly with the Crown from his Chihuahua City headquarters. The commandant general was aided by commandant inspectors and the governors of the several provinces, who acted as military commanders in their respective governments.

The story of the Interior Provinces is skillfully related by Bannon (1970: 167-89). For the role of José de Gálvez in reorganizing the northwestern frontier of New Spain, see Herbert I. Priestley's *José de Gálvez, Visitor-General of New Spain, 1765-1771* (1916). The best study to date of the Interior Provinces is Luis Navarro García's *José de Gálvez y la Commandancia General de las Provincias Internas* (1964). It is based on an intensive study of documentary sources and

discusses the institutional changes of the commandancy, the creation of bishoprics and the intendancy system, economic and missionary problems, and the transformation of the Borderlands' defensive system. A detailed account by Simmons (1968) of Spanish government in New Mexico during its last fifty years as a Spanish province describes New Mexico's relationship within the commandancy system.

In spite of eighteenth-century concerns for improving political administration, the government of the Interior Provinces was fragmented, and local abuses were common. In Texas, for example, San Antonio's provincial governor was under the supervision of the commandant general politically and militarily, but in fiscal affairs he was responsible to the intendant of San Luis Potosí. Justice was administered by magistrates generally ignorant of the laws, and appeals of their decisions could be made only to the Audiencia of New Galicia in Guadalajara. Ecclesiastical matters were supervised by the bishop of Nuevo León. "The consequences of this arrangement are self-evident. So great were the distances of the places where appeals could be made that recourse to these could be had but by few persons; and as the magistrates—generally military men—had no legal adviser, justice could not be properly administered even under the best disposed governor, while the system afforded every opportunity for the exercise of tyranny" (Bancroft, 1889: 4).

Because the Borderlands were essentially "defensive salients" extending beyond the more developed parts of New Spain's viceroyalty, the region may be viewed as a far northern frontier in which Spain used two typical frontier institutions, the *presidio* and the mission.

The *presidio,* or military post, was designed to "protect occupied territory rather than to overrun additional lands" (Moorhead, 1975: 5). Temporary and permanent garrisons eventually extended from Saint Augustine, Florida, to San Francisco, California. Presidial garrisons in northern Mexico were initially very small, and the strength of a typical company in the late sixteenth century "was usually only fourteen troops or less" (Moorhead, 1975: 11). In the seventeenth century most forts had between 25 and 30 troops, but after the Pueblo Revolt of 1680 the *presidio* of El Paso del Norte was assigned a company of 50 men. With the 1693 reoccupation of New Mexico, the presidial company of Santa Fe was assigned 100 men.

Odie B. Faulk, in his overview of the presidial system, emphasizes the weakness and failures of the institution. He notes that soldiers received poor training, received little money, had low morale, and were equipped with inferior weapons and that the *presidio* "all too often was a farce" as an offensive weapon (Faulk, 1974: 70-77). Paige W. Christiansen has made a case study of the Janos *presidio* in Nueva Vizcaya and concludes that in spite of barely serviceable riding equipment, lack of basic military necessities, and inadequate clothing, the soldiers of Janos exerted "a powerful stabilizing influence on the frontier, and it was because of them, because of men like those in the company at Janos, that the frontier was held at all" (Christiansen, 1974*a*: 78-86). In his study of the *soldado de cuera,* Max L. Moorhead reinforces Christiansen's conclusion and observes that in spite of great physical and budgetary strains, the leather-armored soldier of the northern frontier managed to hold his Indian adversary at bay and enabled "the Spanish frontier to survive that continuous effort to roll it back" (Moorhead, 1974a: 87-102).

In his comprehensive work on the *presidio* as a bastion of the Spanish Borderlands, Max L. Moorhead (1975) first discusses the historical evolution of this frontier institution and then gives a descriptive analysis of the fort, the presidial company, the payroll, the civilian settlement, and the Indian reservation. Because this work is confined to the *presidios* of the Provincias Internas, California and Florida are not considered. He does, though, call attention to studies by L. G. Campbell (1972), Chatelain (1941), and others analyzing such coastal fortresses.

Over the years the *presidio* was transformed from a defensive bastion that protected isolated communities "into the nucleus of a civilian town" (Moorhead, 1975: 4). As Moorhead observes, the *presidio,* in addition to guaranteeing "the very survival of Spanish civilization," attracted civilian settlers. "The lure of the presidial payroll, the promise of military protection, and, eventually, the offer of government subsidy and special privileges were all potent enticements. Thus, scores of towns developed in the shelter of these far-flung bastions" (Moorhead, 1975: 270). Also, the *presidio* "in the role of an agency for an Indian reservation . . . made one of the most substantial contributions to the pacification and Europeanization of the hostile tribes" (Moorhead, 1975: 243). Indian prisoners of war, volunteer auxiliaries, peace-seeking bands, detribalized Indians, and mixed-bloods became part of presidial society. Although Moorhead does not specifically discuss presidial society, it is obvious that the congregation of Spanish colonials, mestizos, and Indians contributed to miscegenation and the undermining of the Society of Castes. As Magnus Mörner pointed out, eighteenth-century authorities trusted the declarations of interested parties, and expressions "such as 'taken for Spaniard' or 'reputed to be Spanish' abound in contemporary documentation" (Mörner, 1967: 69).

Although the military post on the Spanish frontier "was not wholly distinctive as an institution on the path of expansionist advance," the mission "was *par excellence* a frontier institution" (Bannon, 1970: 5; 1968: 49). Alongside the presidial soldier went the missionary, and the royal treasury charged expenses for both garrisons and missions to the same account. Moreover, because royal control of the American Church was legalized and granted by papal concessions in the early sixteenth century, permission to found missions and appropriations for upkeep were "usually given in councils of war and finance" (Bannon, 1964: 187-211).

The Church in Spanish America has been intensively studied. The interested reader may find an excellent selected reading list in Oakah L. Jones's significant reprint anthology entitled *The Spanish Borderlands: A First Reader* (1974: 244). John Francis Bannon's *The Spanish Borderlands Frontier* (1970) lists numerous important mission studies in his bibliographical notes. Two outstanding bibliographical sources are H. R. Wagner's *The Spanish Southwest* (1937) and Francis Borgia Steck's guide (1943). Both list important older mission works. An outstanding study of the sixteenth-century

mendicant friars in New Spain is Robert Ricard's renowned *The Spiritual Conquest of Mexico* (1966). The most famous study of the mission as a frontier institution is Herbert E. Bolton's article published in 1917 and reprinted in Bannon (1968).

The Spanish Crown, from the outset of the New World Conquest, wished to convert, civilize, and exploit native inhabitants. The Crown had jurisdiction over everything concerning the Church in the Indies, but cross and scepter generally supported each other. This is most apparent in the mission, the chief institution responsible for Hispanic culture's extension on the Spanish frontier. As Bolton observes, "whoever undertakes to interpret the forces by which Spain extended her rule, her language, her law, and her traditions, over the frontiers of her vast American possessions, must give close attention to the missions, for in that work they constituted a primary agency" (Bannon, 1968: 189).

New Spain's missionaries on the northern frontier were essentially agents of both church and state. While they spread the faith, they also were political, economic, and social agents who helped to control and civilize the frontier. The first task of a missionary was to persuade Indians to concentrate into a compact village, centered around a church, which would serve as the focus of community activity. When the missionaries met Indians already living in permanent settlements (as was the case with the New Mexican Pueblos) a church and quarters for the missionary and his soldier escorts were built to one side of the village. Once the Indians were "reduced" or gathered together, preaching and the baptism of Indian children took place. Then the families of the baptized children were persuaded to build a structure that might serve as a provisional church. In time, the missionary colony came to contain a permanent "well-built mission arranged around a great court or patio, protected on all sides by the buildings, whose walls were sometimes eight feet thick" (Bannon, 1968: 199). One wing might contain the church, and the rest of the quadrilateral building might contain dormitories for the monks, overseers, and travelers; additionally, there would be workshops, schoolrooms, storehouses, a hospital, and a monastery for young Indian girls. In New Mexico those missions, usually established next to the Indian pueblos, "often formed part of a walled compound that also contained the priests' quarters, workshops, storerooms, and stables. When the imposing ruins of these buildings are viewed today, at Pecos or Gran Quivira national monuments, it is at once obvious that the tight Spanish cluster dominated the original Indian town. That was the effect, of course, that the friars were trying to achieve" (Simmons, 1977a: 57-58).

The missionary was helped in his duties by Indians who acted as appointed assistants. Initially these were a catechist and an administrator of church affairs. Eventually every successful mission community had one or more catechists, one or more administrators, and a choir of singers "selected, trained, and officially appointed by the missionaries" (Spicer, 1972: 290).

At the same time that the missionary priests built a church organization, they structured the Indian community along

Spanish lines. In the Indian villages the principal native officials were appointed to, or confirmed in, their offices by the missionary or a Spanish official. Indian community governors and native *alcaldes* exercised restricted judicial and administrative authority and aided the missionary in transforming the southwestern Indian societies.

Organizing the Indian community along Spanish lines required an agency for social change and control. This agency came about through mass education. In New Mexico the Franciscans taught reading, writing, singing, and the making of musical instruments and how to play them as well as carpentry, stock herding, irrigation, and other crafts and arts. In Texas the Franciscans emphasized vocational subjects and practical trades, including "pottery, carpentry, masonry, the making of shoes, hats, clothes, soap and candles, the tanning of hides, spinning, blacksmithing, and the planting of crops" (Barth, 1945: 150). Christian doctrine, as well as industrial and agricultural skills, was taught in the California missions, but only those boys who had a desire and aptitude to learn were taught to read and write. The absence of formal reading and writing schools in California was an exception to the general Franciscan policy in Spanish North America and is explained by "lack of personnel, especially of lay brothers, difficulty of procuring instructional materials from Mexico, failure of the government to support such educational projects, and, especially, lack of native ability and the need for manual laborers in a frontier setting" (Barth, 1945: 157).

In addition to functioning as preachers, teachers, farmers, cattlemen, manufacturers, traders, bankers, and innkeepers, the missionaries acted as diplomatic agents by counteracting foreign influence among their charges. They also explored new frontiers, acted as peace emissaries to hostile tribes, and recorded their experiences in historical chronicles.

The long-term effects of the missions brought about mass changes in Indian theological concepts and social institutions. Indians were Christianized and Hispanicized; by the end of the eighteenth century non-Indian colonials had intermixed with the original Indian mission population. After Mexican independence and mission secularization, many Indian communities became mestizo towns. Even before secularization, cumulative non-Indian influences and the friars' rigid control had changed Indian life.

Students of the New World mission system have evaluated the friars' work in different ways. Blackmar, for example, stated that the Paraguay Jesuits created an "ideal state, equal to any dreamed of by St. Simon, Fourier, or Bellamy. It was successful enough; and the natives were very happy until they came in contact with the natural selfishness and avarice of the European" (Blackmar, 1891: 118; see also Mörner, 1965: 69-78, 79-87; Forrest, 1929: 19; Hodge, Hammond, and Rey, 1945: 99-103). Blackmar (1891: 151) also claimed that "no other system came so near accomplishing the reduction of the barbarous races to a state of civilization as that of the padres of California." Depending upon the personality and the energy of the particular missionary, there is probably some truth in this romantic version of Borderlands history (Bannon, 1968: 212-25). Another view of the missions stresses coercion and violent change, the missions' high mortality

rate, and the idea that the Indians had cultures of their own and should have been left alone (Haring, 1952: 201-202; Mörner, 1965: 63-68). This version also has some truth. Indians were flogged, psychic upset was present among mission Indians, and neophytes frequently escaped (Richman, 1911: 174-84, 219-22; Borah, 1970: 11-13). What one should not forget, though, is that the methods and intentions of the Jesuits and Franciscans were honorable, done in good faith. In addition, one cannot blame the friars "for not knowing the germ theory before anyone in the world knew about germs" (Borah, 1970: 21). The friars did protect the Indians and considered them to be "a necessary part of society" (Borah, 1970: 13). In contrast, Anglo-Americans were almost completely indifferent to Indian religious welfare, and in the Anglo-American economic system native Americans were given no place, or "at best were relegated to abject serfdom" (Cook, 1970: 23-42).

Another important northern frontier institution was Spanish civil settlements. These differed in size and nomenclature, but the most important civil settlement was the urban community with the title of *ciudad* or *villa*. Cities and towns had municipal corporations called *cabildos,* and municipal authority was vested in its officers. An excellent discussion of the town council's origins and powers in Spanish America is in Haring (1952: 158-78). The municipality in northern Mexico is generally discussed by Leonard Cardenas, Jr. (1963).

Gibson (1966: 191) has noted that the "most important towns from the ordinary secular Spanish viewpoint were the mining towns, particularly those in the central corridor north from Mexico." In addition to producing wealth, mining towns functioned as "administrative and social centers, as well as markets and depots for supplies other than silver" (Gibson, 1966: 191). In the seventeenth century, the most important town north of Mexico City was Zacatecas. In 1608 its population consisted of over 1,500 Spaniards, mostly creoles, and about 3,000 Indians and Negroes, some of whom were mestizos and mulattoes (Bakewell, 1971: 268). In contrast, Durango, "though an important trading and mining center, had, in 1605, little more than fifty Spanish families, a hundred or so Negroes and mulattoes, and a few hundred Indians" (Israel, 1975: 3). Spanish mining towns like Zacatecas and Durango "were few in number, but where they did develop they became the visible models of Spanish culture for the Indians" (Spicer, 1972: 301). However, because such towns were few and widely scattered, this type of civil settlement "exerted by no means as uniform an influence on the Indians as did the mission community" (Spicer, 1972: 298).

New World mining is covered in general fashion by Carlos Prieto (1973). His informative, provocative, and frequently insightful book has an excellent bibliography of interest to both the general reader and the researcher. Unfortunately, Prieto neglects to analyze the labor system used in colonial mining. The importance of seventeenth-century Zacatecas as a mining center is the subject of P. J. Bakewell's important monograph (1971). Although Bakewell concentrates on Zacatecas's mines and miners, his observations and conclusions concerning the city and district (with certain noted exceptions) probably represented institutions imposed on, and developed by, miners in other parts of northern Mexico. The importance of Guanajuato and the significance of miners and merchants in Bourbon Mexico are ably covered by D. A. Brading (1971).

Few towns of any size existed north of the Rio Grande in the colonial period. Marc Simmons observes that available evidence confirms only the existence of Santa Fe, New Mexico's single *cabildo* throughout most of the colonial period, although there were three other *villas* (Santa Cruz, Albuquerque, and El Paso) and many smaller communities called *plazas* or *ranchos* (Simmons, 1968: 166; 1969: 12). There were three Spanish civil settlements in California during the eighteenth century: San José, Los Angeles, and present-day Santa Cruz. Spanish Texas had only three civil settlements of any importance. These were San Antonio de Béxar, La Bahía del Espíritu Santo, and Nacogdoches.

The population outside Borderlands towns might be found in *haciendas,* Indian and creole villages, mining camps, ranches, and hamlets. Northern Mexican settlement patterns reflected both New World and Old World influences. American Spaniards searched for mineral wealth; mining was important, but for the average New World immigrant the principal sources of wealth were almost immediately farming and stock raising. In addition, when mining experienced a recession in seventeenth-century Mexico, miners and merchants invested in land, accelerating the formation of large rural estates.

As recently as 1964, Charles Gibson observed that a systematic investigation of the Mexican *hacienda* and the historical problems that it raises is needed (Gibson, 1964: 406-407). Although our knowledge of the history of *haciendas* in all areas of Mexico is limited, Gibson and François Chevalier (1963) have both observed that the advance of the *hacienda* was one of cumulative usurpation of Indian lands. The tempo and periodization of land concentration, however, varied from region to region. For example, William B. Taylor's study of land tenure in colonial Oaxaca observes that *caciques* and *pueblos* in this region retained "about two-thirds of the Valley's agricultural land during the last hundred years of Spanish rule (1972: 201). In contrast, considerably more than half of the Valley of Mexico's agricultural and pastoral lands were acquired by Spaniards "during the first century after the conquest" (Gibson, 1964: 277).

The great *hacienda,* or "manorial estate," eventually became the typical and predominant form of landholding in northern Mexico. The great proprietors of the north lacked adequate labor services and frequently recruited free Indians in southern Mexico to work on their rural estates. Northern *hacendados* also settled captive nomadic Indians and pacified natives on their holdings. "For want of anyone better, cattle barons had recourse to the motley crews of adventurers and vagrants whom travelers would meet in fear and trembling on the northern highways" (Chevalier, 1963: 169).

In the new environment of the *hacienda,* the Indian became another *peón* serving his "hacendado-patriarch-judge-and-jailer" (Stein and Stein, 1970: 38). Because he "mingled with people belonging to other ethnic groups," the Indian settled on the great estate "necessarily adopted the Spanish language. Woodrow Borah therefore states that 'Debt peon-

age, ironically, helped to forge the Mexican nation'" (Mörner, 1967: 97).

Colonial New Mexican settlement and village patterns have been studied by Simmons (1974: 54-69). He notes that in the seventeenth century the majority of the population was "dispersed throughout the rural areas in isolated farms, ranches, and hamlets." In the eighteenth century, "the character of settlement underwent a significant change":

Loose agglomerations of small farmsteads termed ranchos *became the typical unit of colonization in marked contrast to the seventeenth century during which the* hacienda *had predominated. In considerable measure, this shift from large landholdings to farms of more modest size may be attributed to the decrease in Pueblo Indian population, which greatly reduced the labor supply, and to the increase in the numbers of Spanish colonists, whose arrival created a heavy demand for farmlands in the old core area of the Rio Grande Valley.*

Although New Mexico had four *villas,* these municipalities, including the capital of Santa Fe, consisted of many small *ranchos. Ranchos* "were generally referred to as *poblaciones,* or if the population consolidated for mutual defense, as *plazas"* (Simmons, 1974: 61). New Mexico in the early nineteenth century had 102 *plaza* settlements. *Plazas* took their name from the shape of their construction. Built of adobe and arranged "to give an advantage both in attacking and defending behind the walls," they measured two hundred by five hundred *varas* in diameter and had embrasures and bastions (Carroll and Haggard, 1942: 27).

Borderlands population and society were essentially rural during the colonial period. Colonial differences were largely determined by the economic life that developed in the various provinces and the nature of aboriginal population.

New Mexico, the oldest and most populous colony north of the Rio Grande, was dedicated "not to mining, industry, or exploitative agriculture, but to subsistence farming, herding, and evangelization of the Indian people" (Simmons, 1977a: 8). Although New Mexico's sheep industry gradually led to the rise of a *patrón* group, subsistence agriculture prevailed until the nineteenth century. In this isolated world, families "were closely interrelated, needs were few, cooperation was the order of the times" (Sánchez, 1940: 6). As late as 1812, all the settlements enjoyed "sufficient land to enable their residents to make a living by agriculture," and there were no vagrants or beggars (Carroll and Haggard, 1942: 27). If a *patrón* system developed in New Mexico, it probably was not a major element until the nineteenth century and even then had little in common with the *patrón-peón* system found on northern Mexico's great rural estates. New Mexican *haciendas* were small farms usually worked by an extended family; even in the last years of Mexican rule virtually all New Mexicans had the same economic standards because there was "a tract of land for everyone," and New Mexicans placed a limited premium on economic wealth.

In contrast, all California economic activity was centralized, first in the missions and later in the ranch establishments. Cattle were raised by both Franciscans and presidial soldiers turned ranchers after 1784 (Cleland, 1941: 8-9), but California's pastoral era properly began after mission secularization. During the Mexican period, and until the 1860s, the ranch with its "cattle on a thousand hills" became the principal economic unit "and [before 1848] the entire economy depended on the production of cattle for the hide and tallow trade." California village life was overshadowed by ranch life, and the social order was based upon ranchers' authority. An Indian laboring class worked the land and acted as servants or cowboys (Pitt, 1966: 11).

As in the rest of New Spain, ethnic mixture was prevalent in the Borderlands. By the eighteenth century, miscegenation had so greatly weakened the caste system that there were few individuals of "pure" race in New Spain, except for recent immigrants and isolated Indians (Mörner, 1967: 1; 1970*a:* 22-23; Stein and Stein, 1970: 115-16). Mexican society, from an early date, separated into three broad categories: Spaniards (Europeans and creoles), mixed-bloods (mestizos, mulattoes, *zambos,* and so on), and Indians. However, individuals were enrolled into the caste system by their sociocultural status; most Spaniards were genetically mestizos (Brading, 1971: 20). "Spaniard" was synonymous with *blanco, gente de razón,* and *vecino,* but never implied absolute purity of blood. One who was one-eighth Indian was white, as was an individual who was one-sixteenth Negro. As Angel Rosenblat notes, this caste system was removed from an exaggerated racist conception; the term *white* was very flexible (Rosenblat, 1954, vol. II: 133-45; Vigil, 1973*b:* 32-39). Miscegenation in Mexico became a social leveler, especially on the frontier.

By the late-eighteenth-century society, California was divided into the Hispanic community, the *gente de razón,* and the Indians (Chapman, 1921: 384-85). In 1812, Don Pedro Pino declared that there were only two types of people in New Mexico: Spaniards and Indians. There were no castes of African origin, and Pueblo Indians hardly differed from Spaniards (Carroll and Haggard, 1942: 9).

An idea of the culture and character of the Borderlands Hispanic population is gained from various sources. Fray Angelico Chávez states that New Mexicans had fortitude, piety, constant courage, and a marked sense of idealism and nobility (Chávez, 1954: xv). Simmons writes that New Mexicans were "respected and respectable frontiersmen" and cites various sources attesting to their bravery, hospitality, and kindness (Simmons, 1977*a:* 10). Josiah Gregg was ambivalent concerning the New Mexicans but declared that the yeomanry of the country was inured to fatigue and danger, and he had personally seen "persons of the lower class" do things which indicated superlative courage (Gregg, 1954: 155-56).

California also has a rich Hispanic tradition. Richard Henry Dana, another ambivalent Anglo-American, was struck by the Californians' pride, manner, and voice (Dana, 1963: 58-61). Leonard Pitt states the gentry regarded themselves as grandees without a court—as aristocrats in a republic—and declares that "the rancheros, who had behaved like aristocrats even while poor, eased into affluence naturally, as if living up to a pre-established level of life—say, that of Spain in the eighteenth century" (Pitt, 1970: 12-13).

8

New Mexico–
Colorado History

MARC SIMMONS
Cerrillos, New Mexico

Any consideration of New Mexico's history must take into account the shifting nature of the area's boundaries over the centuries. Throughout colonial years, the limits of New Mexico remained imprecisely defined but, in vague terms, were considered to include modern Arizona north of the Gila River; much of present-day Colorado and a slice of Utah; and a band of High Plains country, shading into western Kansas, Oklahoma, and Texas. Pedro Bautista Pino, near the end of the Spanish period, noted that on its outer limits New Mexico bordered upon "Louisiana and other territories that have not yet been named" (Carroll and Haggard, 1942: 20).

New Mexico's southern boundary with Nueva Vizcaya became a subject of dispute as early as 1682 when refugee officials and settlers, driven south by the Pueblo Revolt, raised the issue with the viceroy. They claimed that El Paso del Norte, where they had resettled, was within New Mexico's jurisdiction, which extended south to the Río Sacramento (twenty miles north of today's Chihuahua City). It was at that stream that Don Juan de Oñate allegedly had taken possession

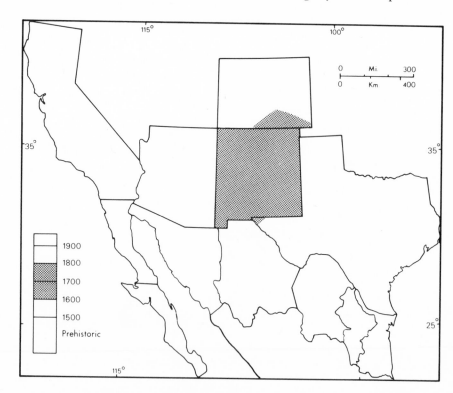

of the kingdom in 1598. The viceroy confirmed the Sacramento as the boundary, but during the following century the line was often moved northward, closer to El Paso (Twitchell, 1925: 14).

The imprecision of colonial boundaries was gradually rectified after New Mexico became part of the United States. The 1850 establishment of a formal territorial government was accompanied by an adjustment of the Texas border. The 1853 Gadsden Purchase completed the boundary with Mexico. Creation of Colorado Territory in 1861 and Arizona Territory in 1863 resulted in considerable loss of ground to New Mexico, rounding out the state's present limits.

The colonial history of New Mexico encompasses a vast stretch of the Borderlands. Furthermore, the initial settlement of southern Colorado, commencing during the decade of the 1850s, was carried out largely by Hispanos when the area was still part of New Mexico. Thus, much of New Mexico's early story must include events transpiring outside modern state boundaries.

Several general histories of the area, produced in the latter half of the nineteenth century, emphasized the high points of Spanish conquest and colonization. The works of Davis (1869), Bancroft (1889), and Bandelier (1890) sketched what little was then known concerning Vásquez de Coronado's quest, Oñate's colonization project, beginnings of the mission program, and the Pueblo Revolt. Twitchell (1911-12) and Read (1912) added small pieces to these stories and, through use of New Mexico's Spanish Archives, began to fill in the large gaps for the eighteenth and nineteenth centuries.

After 1920 a small army of Borderlands scholars, following the lead of Herbert E. Bolton, invaded the principal archives of Mexico and Spain. They discovered a wealth of primary documents on New Mexico and other northern provinces of New Spain. Among this new generation of researchers was France V. Scholes, who almost singlehandedly carved out Spanish New Mexico's history prior to the Pueblo Revolt. His writings (1930, 1935, 1937, 1942) for the first time, illuminated the workings of the mission supply service, the details of the bitter Church-state conflict, and the character of seventeenth-century provincial government and society.

George P. Hammond (1927), after an exhaustive search of archives in Spain, brought out a full narrative account of Oñate's founding of New Mexico. Working with Agapito Rey, he subsequently translated all the Oñate documents and published them in two volumes as part of the Coronado Cuarto Centennial Publications (Hammond and Rey, 1953). Hammond and Rey (1966) later translated the chronicles of lesser expeditions to New Mexico from 1580 to 1594.

Building upon the Coronado documents originally collected and published by George Parker Winship (1896), Professor Bolton accumulated new material and wrote his definitive and highly readable, *Coronado, Knight of Pueblos and Plains* (1949). Bolton's only other significant item of New Mexicana was his translation and narrative summary of the 1776 Domínguez-Escalante expedition from Santa Fe to the Great Basin (1950).

Charles Wilson Hackett, as early as 1911, settled upon the Pueblo Revolt as his area. Over the next several years he issued a series of monographs on the subject (Hackett, 1912, 1917), and ultimately edited a voluminous collection of translated documents (1942). At the same time, J. Manuel Espinosa (1942), drawing upon hitherto unused sources, compiled the story of Don Diego de Vargas and the reconquest of New Mexico. Hackett made a further contribution, editing three volumes of colonial documents on New Mexico and Nueva Vizcaya originally collected by Adolph F. Bandelier (1923-37) from Mexican archives.

Despite the abundance of published documentation, monographic studies, and detailed narratives of single episodes, synthesis works for the first half of the colonial period are few. Forbes's *Apache, Navajo and Spaniard* (1960) stands as the soundest of these, even though its strong anti-Hispanic bias perpetuates the Black Legend. Although focusing on Pecos Pueblo, Kessell's *Kira, Cross, and Crown* (1979) casts much new light on the colonial period generally.

For the early period, two standard volumes by colonial writers must be noted. One is Gaspar Pérez de Villagrá's firsthand account of the initial phase of the Oñate venture (Espinosa, 1933). The other is the *Memorial* of Fray Alonso de Benavides, giving a clear and comprehensive picture of 1630 mission activity (Hodge and Lummis, 1916).

The most valuable presentation of eighteenth-century events in New Mexico is found in the studies of Alfred B. Thomas (1932, 1935, 1940). Much of his material on Indian warfare is summarized in the early chapters of Kenner's *A History of New Mexican-Plains Indian Relations* (1969). Scholars should also refer to Jones's (1966) work on Pueblo Indian auxiliaries. French intrusion into New Mexico before 1763, as well as the trailblazing activities of Pierre (Pedro) Vial on behalf of the Spaniards, are treated in detail by Loomis and Nasatir (1967).

The Church's deteriorating position following the reconquest can be inferred from a close reading of Bishop Tamarón's report of his 1760 visit to New Mexico (Adams, 1954), Father Domínguez's description of the missions in 1776 (Adams and Chávez, 1956), and Father Morfi's general indictment of 1778 provincial affairs (Simmons, 1977b). Simmons (1968) surveys complexities of political institutions during the last half century before independence. A remarkable work of social history, offering summary accounts of each family in colonial New Mexico, is provided by Chávez (1954).

All writers from Bancroft to the present have heavily depended upon Pedro Bautista Pino's peerless *Exposición,* first published in 1812, for information on New Mexico in the last years of the colonial era (Carroll and Haggard, 1942). The writings of Lieutenant Zebulon M. Pike also give insights into Spanish New Mexico during the early nineteenth century available nowhere else (Jackson, 1966).

Unfortunately, the Spanish regime's waning years have not received anything comparable to the attention scholars focused upon the earlier conquest, colonization, and revolt periods. A general review of New Mexican history from 1700 to 1821 still awaits a writer.

The same holds true for the period 1821-46. New Mexico, like other Borderlands areas, has suffered considerable neglect in this historical phase. David J. Weber (1976: 279) sums up the situation: "Historians have produced a substantial number of studies of this vast region during the Mexican era, but that historiography has been notably unbalanced, ethnocentric, and incomplete." Weber himself (1982) attempts to remedy this situation with an admirable synthesis covering the history of the entire Mexican Borderlands.

The only specific overview of New Mexico under Mexican administration is an outdated monograph by Lansing B. Bloom (1913-15) which appeared serially in the journal *Old Santa Fe.* Most remaining studies treat the province from the perspective of American expansionism, concentrating on single themes, such as the Santa Fe Trail, the fur trade, the Texan Santa Fe expedition, or military conquest at the time of the Mexican War.

Essential to a study of these years is Rittenhouse's *The Santa Fe Trail: A Historical Bibliography* (1971), a compilation of 718 annotated entries. Of the numerous general trail histories, the most recent is Connor and Skaggs (1977). Moorhead (1958) uses extensive documentation from Mexican sources to hypothesize that the Santa Fe Trail should properly be viewed as an extension of the Chihuahua Trail (the Camino Real of colonial days). The old Spanish Trail, from Santa Fe to Los Angeles, is the subject of a volume by Hafen and Hafen (1954).

Activities of the mountain men and development of the southwestern fur trade, which centered upon Taos, are described by Cleland (1950) and Weber (1971). Lavender (1954) tells the story of Bent's Fort in southern Colorado, documenting its connection with northern New Mexico's history. The standard biography of Kit Carson remains an old work by Sabin (1914), but it should be used in conjunction with H. L. Carter (1968), a study which dispels many myths about the famous scout and trapper.

Among the numerous contemporary chronicles by Americans or Englishmen visiting New Mexico during the Mexican period, researchers should especially note James's (1962) eyewitness account of 1821-24 affairs and two reports by participants in the Texan Santa Fe expedition (Kendall, 1935; Falconer, 1930). Almost in a category by itself is Gregg's *Commerce of the Prairies* (1954), a storehouse of information on daily life and custom. Most later descriptions of the Santa Fe trade rest on this book, first published in 1844.

For the first year of the Mexican War, 1846, literature is voluminous. For high drama and historical detail, three narratives by youngsters head the list. Seventeen-year-old Lewis H. Garrard came over the trail from Bent's Fort to Taos in time to witness the trial and execution of the rebels who had slain Governor Charles Bent and other Americans. Moreover, his book (1955), which first appeared in 1850, is a prime source for mountain men's customs and speech. Another young man, the Britisher George Frederick Ruxton, also traveled through New Mexico in this turbulent period and composed a valuable memoir (Hafen, 1950). Susan Shelby Magoffin, teenage bride of trader James Magoffin, left a fine diary giving an insider's view of General Kearny's taking of Santa Fe (Drumm, 1926).

Military operations in New Mexico and the Southwest during 1846-47 can be followed in contemporary accounts by Cutts (1847), Cooke (1878), Edwards (1847), Connelley (1907), Emory (1848), and Gibson (1935). A standard source on the Mormon Battalion's march to Santa Fe is Tyler (1881). Historian Ralph Emerson Twitchell (1909) summed up U.S. conquest, but, since he wrote, several new journals have come to light which enlarge understanding of this significant event.

There exist several trustworthy accounts of New Mexico's territorial period. Chief among them is Lamar's *The Far Southwest, 1846-1912* (1966), which also contains significant material on the territories of Colorado, Arizona, and Utah. Keleher (1952) fully narrates events for the period up through the 1868 incarceration of the Navahos at Bosque Redondo. Territorial events can be traced through Larson's definitive study of the long statehood movement (1968). The same author has also given us an excellent history of New Mexico populism (Larson, 1974).

Short biographies of individual territorial governors, from James S. Calhoun in 1851 to the close of Lew Wallace's term in 1881, are in Horn (1963). Especially rich on Indian affairs material is Calhoun's official correspondence, edited by Abel (1915). Several prominent figures of the period have been dealt with in separate studies, including New Mexico Secretary and Special Indian Agent William F. M. Arny (Murphy, 1972), Chief Justice Kirby Benedict (Hunt, 1961), controversial land grant lawyer and later U.S. Senator Thomas Benton Catron (Westphall, 1973), and U.S. District Attorney Colonel Albert Jennings Fountain (Gibson, 1965).

Sources for the Civil War in New Mexico are plentiful. A starting point for anyone entering the field is Rittenhouse's (1961) bibliography on the subject, listing 32 items. Comprehensive military campaign surveys are provided by Hall (1960) and Kerby (1958). The Colorado Volunteers' role in holding New Mexico for the Union is told by Whitford (1906).

Indian troubles following the Civil War receive attention in Hunt's biography of General Carlton (1958). Thrapp (1974) tells of the last days of Victorio and the Mimbres Apaches, while McNitt (1972) treats in full the Navaho wars. Kenner (1969) summarizes the last military engagements against New Mexico's Plains Indians. Much on the history of the territory's military posts can be found in Frazer (1968), Emmett (1965), and Brooks and Reeve (1948).

Economic development in the second half of the nineteenth century centers around ranching, mining, stagecoach lines, and railroads. Towne and Wentworth (1946) cover the history of sheep raising, including sidelights on cattle ranching for the entire Southwest, emphasizing New Mexico and Colorado. French's (1965) narrative of southwestern New Mexico ranch life during 1883-99 is from the viewpoint of a British participant, while Fabiola Cabeza de Vaca (1954) offers recollections of the last traditional Hispanic days of ranching on the High Plains. A brief but readable summary of New Mexico mining history is given by Christiansen (1974a). Morris F. Taylor (1971) traces major stagecoach lines in the northern part of the territory, and Conkling (1947) gives a complete account of the Butterfield line in the south. A handy guide to territorial New Mexico's many small railroads has been published by Myrick (1970). Of the several studies on building the Santa Fe Railroad, Marshall's (1945) is recommended. Finally, the rise of two of the territory's leading mercantile companies has been examined by Parish (1961) and Kelly and Chauvenet (1972).

Social problems growing from the land-grant controversy, activities of the notorious Santa Fe Ring, and the Colfax County and Lincoln County wars constitute a distinct chapter in territorial history. The interconnection of these events is demonstrated in Otero (1935), Keleher (1975), Cleaveland (1971), and Westphall (1973). Printed matter on Lincoln County troubles is extensive (consult Dykes's lengthy 1952 bibliography).

Hispanic Colorado has generally been neglected by that state's scholars. Two recent anthologies (Echevarría and Otero, 1976; Onís, 1976) attempt to remedy the deficiency but fail, largely due to most of the essays' ephemeral nature. One exceptional book considering area land-grant problems is Blackmore (1949). A full history of the New Mexican settlement of southern Colorado still awaits a competent researcher.

There are a number of standard reference tools that should be familiar to all students. Especially praiseworthy is Twitchell's (1914) two-volume annotated listing of documents in New Mexico's Spanish Archives, now housed at the State Records Center and Archives, Santa Fe. A similar calendar for the Archdiocese of Santa Fe Archives, 1678-1900, has been published by Chávez (1957). Many printed sources on colonial New Mexico are noted in Wagner's Spanish Southwest bibliography (1937).

Saunders's (1944) guide to New Mexico cultural relations points to a wealth of material, much from obscure sources, on the state's history, anthropology, sociology, and folklore. A comprehensive listing, together with the archival location of early New Mexico newspapers, is provided by Grove, Barnett, and Hansen (1975). Pearce's (1965) geographical dictionary of New Mexico place names deserves a place at the elbow of all researchers. Dickey (1949) and Boyd (1974) illuminate Hispanic folk arts.

To date, no thorough New Mexico history has appeared to make utmost use of the bountiful research from the past fifty years. New information, particularly on Spanish-Indian relations, folk culture, economic practices, and territorial politics, has caused revision of many long-held ideas and has increased the need for a thoughtful and up-to-date synthesis.

9

Texas History

FÉLIX D. ALMARÁZ, JR.
Division of Social Sciences
University of Texas, San Antonio

Texas historiography roughly parallels the state's political evolution, with disproportionate (yet understandable) emphasis given to the landmark events of the Texas Revolution, the Mexican War, and the Confederacy. It would appear, therefore, to begin with the seige of the Alamo, an event creating, by consistent repetition, a stereotyped awareness in the American consciousness. An important outcome has been that, to the average American, modern Texas emerged from the ashes of the Alamo and San Jacinto completely devoid of Spanish and Mexican antecedents. On the threshold of the '80s, as residents of the Lone Star State prepare to celebrate their sesquicentennial, it is commendable to observe that Texas historiography has progressed from outright chauvinism to open-minded objectivity.

In nineteenth-century Texas, following the battles of independence from Mexico, two writers dominated the historiographical field—Henderson R. Yoakum (1855) and John Henry Brown (1892, 1896). Although Yoakum acknowledged Spanish contributions to Texas history, he devoted considerable attention to

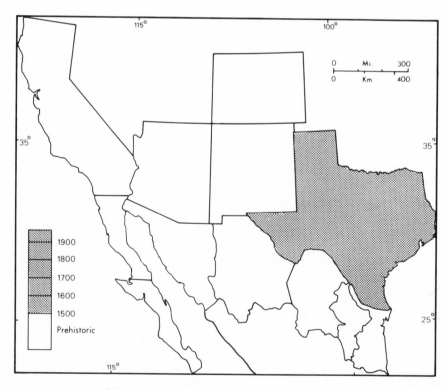

the achievements of Anglo-American immigrants. Retracing much of Yoakum's earlier work, Brown continued the survey through the Civil War into the post-Reconstruction decades. Unchallenged in the nineteenth century, both authors were the standard references. Thematically, Sowell (1900) and Wilbarger (1889), who studied intercultural contact and conflict with Indians, were close to Brown. Until the mid-twentieth century, most writers viewed Texas Indians as a monolithic entity blocking the path of material advancement. In an environment of ethnic tolerance, revisionist scholars have reinterpreted the history of Texas natives in light of recent archival, archaeological, and anthropological research. Notable among these writers are Newcomb (1961), Place (1978), and Rothe (1963). Berlandier (1969) is in a separate category inasmuch as the translation of his insightful nineteenth-century travel journal was only recently published.

For the Spanish period in Texas history, Herbert Eugene Bolton initiated the revisionist school in the first decade of the twentieth century. Slightly earlier, Hubert Howe Bancroft (1889), peerless bibliophile of San Francisco, published a two-volume work on the northern Mexican states and Texas, but it was Bolton who pioneered the new Borderlands school of historiography. Although reprinted in several editions, Bolton's seminal work, *Texas in the Middle Eighteenth Century,* is still a classic reference. Before following Bolton to California campuses, William E. Dunn (1917) contributed a monograph on intercolonial rivalry between Spain and France in the Gulf of Mexico, also comparing Florida and Texas.

In Mexico, the outstanding scholar who interpreted Texas history was Alessio Robles (1938). Using the eclectic system, Alessio frequently consulted the best materials from both sides of the Rio Grande for his accounts.

Steeped in the Boltonian tradition, Carlos Eduardo Castañeda, Mexican born and American educated, devoted nearly 25 years of his professional life to researching meticulously and writing the seven volumes of *Our Catholic Heritage in Texas.* Perhaps misnamed by the leadership council of the Knights of Columbus (the organization underwriting the publication), each volume bears a descriptive subtitle, with delimiting dates for the watershed phases of Texas colonial history from 1519 to 1836. Twenty years after the last volume was published, Castañeda was considered as *the* bedrock source for Spanish-Mexican Texas, with only tangential coverage (volume seven) given to the contemporary Catholic Church.

Within Bolton's conceptual framework (refined by Castañeda), other scholars have concentrated on specific subthemes, such as the missionary frontier. Among the Franciscan religious community, Habig and Leutenegger are the most prolific writers of the mission process in San Antonio de Béxar. For missions located on the periphery of Spanish Texas, contributions by Starnes (1969) and Weddle (1964, 1968a) are reliable pieces of scholarship. Recent specialized studies include Sonnichsen (1968) on El Paso del Norte; Ashford (1971) on the origins and application of Spanish jurisprudence; John (1975) on Hispanic-French competition for the allegiance of native groups in Texas and the Southwest; Myres (1969) on the evolution of ranching; and Weddle (1973) on the Spaniards' search for La Salle's colony.

The final years of Spanish Texas, especially the revolutionary movement for Mexican independence, attracted several scholars. In the order their contributions appeared in print, the group includes Garrett (1939), Vigness (1963), Faulk (1964a), and Almaráz (1971).

Anglo-American immigration into Texas during Mexican rule is amply documented. Eugene Campbell Barker, dean of the Texas historians, led the phalanx with a probing inquiry—*Mexico and Texas, 1821-1836* (1928)—followed by his classical biography of Stephen Fuller Austin (Barker, 1949). Plausibly due to the complexity of the issues, the Texas Revolution interested only two gifted writers, Castañeda (1928) and Binkley (1952). In his first serious excursion into the realm of historical scholarship, Castañeda translated and interpreted an anthology of journals, diaries, and reports, all written by the principal Mexican participants in the battles resulting in a non-Anglo Texas perspective of the conflict. Binkley, a quarter-century later, produced a small volume which succinctly analyzed the causes and effects of the Texas revolt against Mexican authority.

Not surprisingly, the siege of the Alamo, replete with high drama and powerful emotion, drew its complement of investigative writers. The most representative are Walter Lord (1961), John Myers (1948), and Lon Tinkle (1958). From the Mexican vantage point, a recently controversial first-hand account is Carmen Perry's (1975) translation of José Enrique de la Peña's diary, *With Santa Anna in Texas,* an important document that Castañeda did not incorporate into his *Mexican Side of the Texas Revolution.* Interestingly, the dominant personality in the conflict, Santa Anna, whose policies and decisions ruptured Texas's union with Mexico, engaged the scholarship of only Callcott (1964) and O. L. Jones, Jr. (1968) for solid, full-length biographies. Not one to be excluded from published memoirs, Santa Anna wrote an autobiography that Crawford (1967) edited for an American readership.

The successful outcome of the revolution, which created the independent Republic of Texas, undoubtedly contributed to the plethora of books on the subject. In the field of Texas diplomacy, the premier scholar was Joseph W. Schmitz (1941). Contemporary writers studying different aspects of this subject were Hill (1937) and Siegel (1956). Of later vintage, with a continental scope, is Pletcher's (1973) survey.

The disastrous Texas Santa Fe expedition which complicated negotiations at the conference table is examined by Kendall (1929) and N. Loomis (1958). Closely related was the multifaceted question of armed confrontation and its consequences which Connor (1965), Nance (1962, 1965), and Webb (1935) painstakingly researched.

Social history, a challenging topic fraught with problems and promises, appealed to four mature scholars—Broussard (1967), Hogan (1969), Schmitz (1960), and Wheeler (1968)—who surveyed the question from various points of view, ranging from a straightforward description of cultural development to urban growth analysis. Reflecting the broad spectrum of social history were the biographies of the Texas Republic presidents by Herbert Gambrell (1934, 1948) and Llerena B. Friend (1954). Often overlooked is the land issue which Thomas Lloyd Miller critically analyzed in two separate volumes (1967, 1971). Peripherally integrated with social history is the monograph by Richardson (1933) on settlement patterns in the South Plains of Texas.

Between the Mexican War and Reconstruction, writers were motivated toward various topics and charted an uneven record of accomplishment. Stephenson (1921) and Singletary (1960) are notable for their studies of the American War with Mexico. Jordan (1966) concentrated on German immigration; Lea (1957) on the genesis of the ranching empire founded by steamboat Captain Richard King; and McComb (1969) on the growth and expansion of the bayou city of Houston. Not unexpectedly, the Civil War and Reconstruction generated the most interest among Texas writers. Illustrative of the earlier generation of scholars are Ramsdell (1910) and Evans (n.d.). During the centennial observance of the Civil War and its aftermath, Ashcraft (1962) and M. J. Wright (1965) produced reliable accounts. Finally, indicative of the new generation of scholarship are Alwyn Barr (1971) and Ronnie C. Tyler (1974).

Interlaced with political conservatism and reform, the economic expansion of the last quarter of the nineteenth century, extending into the succeeding period, denoted the emergence of unfamiliar forces that rapidly thrust Texas into the era of maturity and modernity. Historiography lagged far behind. Revisionist historians devoted attention to the earlier epochs, particularly events and achievements associated with the centennial of independence (1836-1936). In the reflective mood of the post–World War II era, writers began to study the transitional years of Texas history when the late-nineteenth-century social-economic-political forces collided with the traditional image of rugged individualism. Chris Emmet (1953) and J. Evetts Haley (1949, 1953) artfully composed biographies of colorful cattle barons who were being displaced by faceless corporate structures. Robert C. Cotner (1959), taking a different approach, researched the political career of James Stephen Hogg, Texas's only reform public servant of the nineteenth century (attorney general and governor).

Further illuminating the changes in Texas politics and business on the eve of modernity are the studies by Ben

H. Procter (1962) and William C. Holden (1970, 1976). Continuing the political-economic theme into the twentieth century, Spratt (1970) reviewed the changes that culminated at Spindletop, the fabulous Lucas gusher that spurted near Beaumont on January 10, 1901, symbolically propelling Texas into the forefront of material progress. Seth McKay and Odie Faulk (1965) combined talents for a survey of Texas after that oil discovery.

In the present generation, five authors have written general histories of Texas. Rupert N. Richardson (1958), elder statesman of the quintet, produced the model that remained the orthodox reference for nearly a decade. Next, T. R. Fehrenbach (1968) came out with a popular version, flamboyantly entitled *Lone Star*, frequently cited with mixed appraisals. D. W. Meinig (1969) offered refreshing insights on cultural geography in his provocative *Imperial Texas*. Then Seymour V. Connor (1971) entered the ranks of contemporary revisionists with his volume bearing the unfoliated title of *Texas: A History*. Finally, in the euphony of the Bicentennial, Joe B. Frantz (1976) wrote a compact interpretation of Texas history across the centuries that has the ingredients of a minor classic.

Unlike other states of the Union, Texas history is complex owing to the various phases of human experience and the multitude of writers who, sometimes indiscriminately, chose topics of great promise and meager outcome. The commentary would be exceedingly lengthy if the vast periodical literature were incorporated. This brief survey is not intended to be a comprehensive checklist of all the writings on Texas but rather a commentary on the principal books from which the author gleaned a salient idea or theme. In any essay on Texas historiography, omissions will probably arouse as much criticism as inclusions. Be that as it may, the authors and titles selected for this essay represent a balanced cross-section encompassing a range of viewpoints from biased chauvinism to scholarly objectivity. The next generation of historians will be responsible for evaluating the quality of scholarship in the second half of the twentieth century.

California has long been of special interest to historians who have produced an abundance of state histories dating back to Josiah Royce's philosophic *California* (1886) and Theodore Hittell's four-volume *History of California* (1885-97). Even more extensive than Hittell was Hubert H. Bancroft's production-line seven-volume state history (1884-90). In more recent years a number of excellent one-volume works have been written, including Robert G. Cleland's *From Wilderness to Empire* (1944), Andrew F. Rolle's *California: A History* (1963), and Walton Bean's *California: An Interpretive History* (1968). The last (and most recent) of the three has a brief bibliographic essay at the end of each chapter. There is also John W. Caughey's older but very readable and enduring *California: A Remarkable State's Life History* (1970), which has recently been revised extensively and updated in its third edition and includes an excellent forty-page bibliographic essay. Another readable general account of the diverse factors in the state's development is Ralph J. Roske, *Everyman's Eden: A History of California* (1968). Mention must also be made of Kevin Starr's *Americans*

10

California History

MATT S. MEIER
Department of History
University of Santa Clara

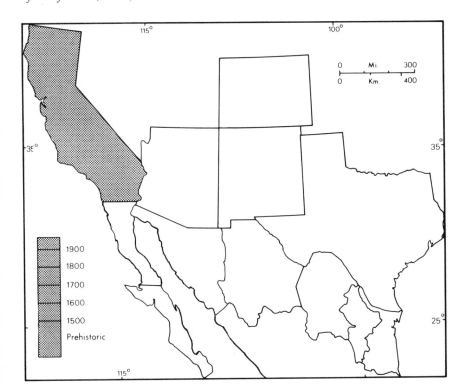

and the California Dream (1973), a cultural and literary history that stresses northern California's leadership, and of *California: Five Centuries of Cultural Contrasts* (1976) by Julian Nava and Bob Barger, which includes treatment of minorities.

The history of man in California is relatively recent. Except for some inconclusive evidence (supported by the late Louis S. B. Leakey) of man's presence near Calico in the Mohave Desert some fifty thousand years ago, the generally accepted antiquity of man in California is set at about thirty thousand years. Direct evidence of human remains dates only to about ten thousand years ago, and an abundance of shell mounds indicates a fair-sized population as early as 6000 B.C. When Europeans arrived, California probably had a higher population density than any area north of Mexico. The approximate numbers are a matter of disagreement; C. Hart Merriam (1905) estimated one-quarter million, a figure twice that given by A. L. Kroeber (1925), although Kroeber later raised his estimate. More recently the late Sherburne Cook's (1976*b*) estimate of approximately 300,000 has been generally accepted. In addition to those scholars' works, the following are of great value in understanding California's Indians: Merriam's *Studies of the California Indian* (1955), Robert Heizer and M. A. Whipple's collection of articles and primary accounts in *California Indians: A Source Book* (1951), Robert Heizer and Albert B. Elsasser's *Natural World of the California Indians* (1980), and Theodora Kroeber's personal account of the last Indian of the Yahi tribe in *Ishi in Two Worlds* (1961).

Summary accounts of the European discovery, exploration, and settlement of early California may be found in early chapters of John Caughey's *California* (1970) and in chapters 4 and 9 of John Francis Bannon's concise *The Spanish Borderlands Frontier, 1513-1821* (1970). The area's history began with exploration of Baja California under the direction of Hernán Cortés in the 1530s. Although the peninsula proved less than hospitable to Europeans who first explored and tried to settle it, investigation was made farther north by Juan Rodríguez Cabrillo, who on September 28, 1542, "discovered" San Diego Bay and then sailed north perhaps as far as Oregon (Wagner, 1929). Francis Drake's brief visit nearly four decades later alerted the Spaniards to the threat of British encroachment and actually prompted their settlement of New Mexico, but not California. At the end of the sixteenth century there was some further coastal exploration by Manila galleons. In 1602, Sebastián Vizcaíno gave names to many of California's prominent coastal features and described Monterey Bay as Alta California's most commodious natural harbor. Still, Spaniards did not find California sufficiently attractive economically to establish settlements.

Toward the end of the seventeenth century Father Eusebio Kino began exploring, mapping, and establishing missions on the Mexican mainland in Pimería Alta (Bolton, 1936) and thus rearoused interest in Baja California and prepared "Arizona" as a base on the road to California. Partly because of Kino's efforts, Father Juan María Salvatierra then laid the foundations of the California missions in Baja California. The establishment of missions in that area by Jesuits, beginning in 1697, was a long and difficult process that eventually led to the founding of eighteen before all Jesuits were expelled from the barren and forbidding peninsula in 1767. Two years later, after the Crown ordered the settlement of Alta California, the Baja California missions provided its initial economic base.

Spanish colonization of this northern region was only somewhat less difficult than in Baja California. Food was scarce locally, the Indians had no surplus, and the supply routes from Mexico, whether by land or sea, were arduous in the extreme (Bolton, 1931). Nevertheless, led by stalwarts like the Franciscan Junípero Serra and military leaders Gaspar de Portolá, Juan Bautista de Anza, Pedro Fages, and Felipe de Neve, two pueblos, one villa, four presidios, and twenty-one missions were eventually established. Almost at the same time, a number of visitors began to arrive in Upper California. Some, like Jean François La Pérouse, Alessandro Malaspina, and George Vancouver, were distinguished; others were sea otter poachers and beaver trappers. The best single-volume history of this early period is still Charles E. Chapman's *A History of California: The Spanish Period* (1921), despite his views on the Indians and his acceptance of the Chinese "discovery" of California. A second valuable account is Irving B. Richman's *California under Spain and Mexico, 1535-1847* (1911).

California's missions have attracted considerable popular interest and have led to a good deal of scholarly controversy about the positive and negative effects that missionaries had on Indians. The most comprehensive treatment of the missions is Zephyrin Engelhardt's *The Missions and Missionaries of California* (4 vols., 1908-15); unfortunately it is flawed by a defensive tone and lapses in historical impartiality. Maynard Geiger's two volumes (1959) present a more balanced, if less comprehensive, picture of the missions. For detail, especially about daily routine, Edith Webb's *Indian Life at the Old Missions* (1952) is excellent. Sherburne Cook puts forward the anthropologist's somewhat different viewpoint in *The Conflict Between the California Indian and White Civilization* (1976*a*); he points out that "the Indians were forced to make a rapid and very difficult adaptation which cost them dear in lives and suffering" (pp. 156-57).

The first Anglo-Americans to come to California were Boston traders who arrived by ship. They were soon followed in the mid-1820s by fur trappers and traders who blazed trails over the towering Sierra Nevada. The story of the first group is vividly related by eyewitness Richard Henry Dana in his *Two Years Before the Mast* (1964), and the saga of the fur trade is given excellent coverage by Robert G. Cleland in *This Reckless Breed of Men* (1950) as well as by Dale Morgan (1953) in his outstanding biography of Jedediah Smith.

Before 1840, fewer than one hundred Anglo-Americans resided in Mexican California, but by the end of 1846 this element had increased to nearly seven hundred as immigrants' wagon trains rolled in (George R. Stewart, 1936, 1962). Settling mostly in the north because Spanish-Mexican cattle ranchers dominated the secularized mission lands, these newcomers began exploiting the agricultural potential of the region under the concerned eyes of Mexican officials. This

Anglo penetration facilitated American acquisition of California, and in 1846 the Bear Flag revolt proclaimed California a republic. Before a new government could be organized, the U.S.-Mexican War occurred, and California was quickly occupied by American military forces. By the time the Treaty of Guadalupe Hidalgo had been ratified, gold was discovered, further upsetting orderly development of California. Unfortunately there is no monograph covering the topic of the American conquest and acquisition of California. The topic of military rule in this period is given good coverage in Theodore Grivas's *Military Government in California, 1846-1850* (1963).

Rodman Paul (1947) and John Caughey (1948) have written basic works on the many fascinating aspects of the California gold rush. From all over the world thousands of miners flocked to the diggings, rapidly populating the state and quickly reducing the Californio population to a powerless minority, as detailed by Leonard Pitt in his *Decline of the Californios* (1966). Two books of popular history, Joseph H. Jackson's *Bad Company* (1949) and Stanton Coblentz's *Villians and Vigilantes* (1936), and the more recent *Furia y Muerte: Chicano Social Banditry* (1973), edited by Pedro Castillo and Alberto Camarillo, vividly portray some of the problems engendered by a weak civil government which led to the constitutional convention of 1849 and California statehood the following year (Ellison, 1950). On the economic side, the gold rush led to a rapid development of transportation, communication, agriculture, and business, the causative factors of which are ably interpreted by Forest Hill in "The Shaping of California's Industrial Pattern" (1955). The first climax of this movement was the juncture of the Union Pacific and Central Pacific railroads in 1869, and within another decade the railroad had also united southern and northern California (Lewis, 1938).

The nationwide depression of the 1870s heralded the coming of a long period of economic, social, and political unrest that sharply modified the trend of California's history by the end of the century. Whereas the first quarter-century of California's history as a state centered largely in the north, the second quarter saw a considerable shift to the southland. The 1887 entrance of the Santa Fe Railroad into Los Angeles ended the Southern Pacific Railroad's transportation monopoly and helped lead to a rapid influx of settlers from the Midwest and East—and an equally rapid decline of the southern Californios. Robert G. Cleland's *The Cattle on a Thousand Hills* (1941) gives an excellent account of the southland's transition from Mexican California to the United States.

Glenn S. Dumke's *The Boom of the Eighties in Southern California* (1944) and Osgood Hardy's "Agricultural Changes in California, 1860-1890" (1929) describe how the former "cow counties" of the south were soon being subdivided into family farms and towns and how the citrus industry sparked a diversified agricultural boom that soon included such crops as wheat, olives, sugar beets, cotton, grapes, avocados, and a wide variety of fruits (Paul, 1974). The discovery of oil fields in Los Angeles, Fresno (Coalinga), Orange, and Kern counties and elsewhere in the southland led to an oil boom in the 1890s (Cleland and Hardy, 1929). This economic trans-

formation was fueled by a constant stream of immigration, which has been one of the enduring patterns in California history.

California's first immigrants came from Asia, presumably by way of the Bering Strait, to be followed much later by Hispanicized Mexicans from the south at the end of the eighteenth century. The gold rush of the mid-1800s brought new floods from Mexico, Chile, Peru, the east coast of the United States, France, England, and as far away as Hawaii, Australia, and China. The latter decades of the century saw the addition of Japanese, Hindustanis, and Filipinos to this immigrant blend, and at the turn of the nineteenth century there began what was soon to be a flood tide of Mexican immigrants, legal and illegal (Rischin, 1974). This growth and change in California's population is broadly delineated by Warren Thompson (1955), and the accompanying problem of nativism is covered by Roger Daniels and Harry Kitano in *American Racism* (1970). In recent years the problems of Mexicans (Pitt, 1966), Chinese (Barth, 1964), and Japanese (Daniels, 1962) have been given particular attention by historians.

Paralleling economic development were equally important political changes. Democratic control of state government disappeared after the Civil War and was replaced by Republican dominance. The unrest of the 1870s led to the 1879 constitution, a detailed and conservative document, and to a rising tempo in Southern Pacific's domination of state politics. Fed by the depression of the early 1890s, California's populist reform movement was characterized by the San Francisco graft prosecutions in the north (Bean, 1952) and the Good Government movement in Los Angeles. The climax of this trend came with the election of Hiram Johnson, the Lincoln-Roosevelt League candidate, as governor and California's delayed embracing of the national Progressive reform movement (see George Mowry, *The California Progressives,* 1951). Hiram Johnson's administration quickly brought to California the entire roster of Progressive reform legislation, but this tide of Progressivism in California was dealt crushing blows by the McNamara brothers' 1911 confession and the Mooney and Billings Preparedness Day, 1916, bombing (Bean, 1968). What these two events had initiated, the emotional antiradical hysteria of World War I brought to a climax in the passage of state antisyndicalism legislation (Cross, 1935).

Following the end of World War I, California entered a boom that quickly outstripped the fondest dreams of earlier California boosterism (Nash, 1964; Cleland and Hardy, 1929). More than two million people migrated to the state—mostly to the southern part, where the phenomenal development of the film industry and tourism soon made that section stereotypical of the whole state in the eyes of the world. Fulton (1960) and Wagenknecht (1962) describe the growth and tremendous social impact of Hollywood movies. In agriculture, new crops like cotton and lettuce modified the earlier pattern (McWilliams, 1939), and in the Los Angeles and San Francisco areas industry got a firm foothold; the expansion of the oil industry, shipping, and construction supplied additional jobs and state revenues.

This phenomenal economic growth was rudely interrupted

at the end of the 1920s by the Great Depression. During the preceding two decades California had received thousands of workers from Mexico; now many Mexicans were repatriated while their places in migratory agriculture were taken by an influx of economic refugees from Oklahoma and Arkansas (Stein, 1973). Noticeably, the southern half of the state furnished a majority of the schemes for alleviating the woes of the depression. Such schemes as Howard Scott's Technology, Upton Sinclair's End Poverty in California, Dr. Francis Townsend's Old Age Revolving Pensions Plan, and the infamous Thirty Dollars Every Thursday are ably described by Carey McWilliams in *Southern California Country* (1946). In *Olson's New Deal for California* (1952), Robert Burke presents an admirable study of the late impact of the New Deal on the state after Culbert Olson's 1938 election. World War II alleviated the many problems of the depression.

Carey McWilliams's *California the Great Exception* (1949a) is a broad survey of the tremendous impact World War II had on the state. A pioneer area in airplane manufacturing during the war, California greatly expanded that industry in the southland and also became a center for naval construction, with the Bay Area accounting for 60 percent of all U.S. shipbuilding during the war. In addition, iron and steel manufacturing was increased remarkably, as was oil production; agricultural production, with the aid of *braceros* from Mexico, (Galarza, 1964) expanded from $626 million in 1939 to $1,744 million in 1944.

World War II marked a watershed for California, and in the postwar years a new economy and society emerged in the state, as ably described by Remi Nadeau in *California, the New Society* (1963). A large pool of skilled workers attracted to California during the war years, existence of excellent educational centers, and postwar federal spending policies led to the development of electronics and aerospace industries, which soon became virtually synonymous with California. Sparked by housing demand, the construction industry expanded rapidly, and in a society based heavily on the automobile, Los Angeles soon became second only to Detroit in automobile assembly. By 1950 the state's population had passed the ten million mark, making California number two among the fifty states in population. But with all of these diversifying economic changes, agriculture still remained the state's most important single industry, and California led the nation in producing wines, fruits, and vegetables and in their processing—bottling, canning, freezing, and drying. Twenty percent of the state's jobs are agriculture-related (Nadeau, 1963).

This rapid growth has been accompanied by numerous problems that have risen to plague the state in the last quarter of the twentieth century. The most important single problem is perhaps water (Nadeau, 1950, 1963). Approximately two-thirds of California's farmland is irrigated, and agricultural requirements account for 90 percent of the state's water use. While the Oroville Dam and the Central Valley Project have been important steps in conservation, the statewide drought of 1976 and 1977 has brought home the seriousness of the water problem. Water and air pollution, especially in the greater urban centers, has had an adverse effect on human health, has caused considerable damage to flora, and has generally deteriorated the quality of life in California. The problem of low-paid agricultural labor (McWilliams, 1968), especially migratory harvest labor, has recently (1975) been alleviated, if not solved, by passage of a state Agriculture Labor Relations Act. There are additional problems of pressing importance connected with an increasingly technological society, such as rapid population expansion due largely to immigration, the destruction of prime agricultural lands by urban expansion, the need for mass transportation systems, and the rising rate of drug use and of crime (see Raymond F. Dasmann, *The Destruction of California,* 1965).

California has undergone great changes, both quantitatively and qualitatively, as its economic base changed from rural to industrial to technological. The image conjured up by the "green and golden" state has changed from orange groves and mission chapels to aircraft factories, silicon chips, and space technology. The only sure thing that can be said of the future is that change in California will probably be even more rapid than it has been in the past.

Settlement of the middle and lower Rio Grande region began with native Americans who established temporary and permanent villages before the arrival of the Spaniards. European penetration of the Texas-Tamaulipas frontier came in 1519, but it was not until 1749 that a permanent colony (Nuevo Santander) was established. Between 1749 and 1755, Spaniards settled the towns of Camargo, Reynosa, Revilla, Mier, and Laredo. To the west, missionaries founded the El Paso del Norte mission (present-day Ciudad Juárez) in 1659, and two decades later the Franciscans established Ysleta, Senecu, and Socorro, when New Mexican settlers fled southward during the Pueblo Revolt of 1680. In the Sonora-Arizona frontier, the famous Father Eusebio Francisco Kino founded San Xavier del Bac (south of Tucson) in 1700. In California, the San Diego mission dates from 1769.

In the nineteenth century, the Borderlands area underwent profound change. With Mexican independence in 1821, Spain no longer had jurisdiction over these remote settlements. Mexico, however, lost the towns lying north of the

11

Border Cities

OSCAR J. MARTÍNEZ
Department of History
University of Texas, El Paso

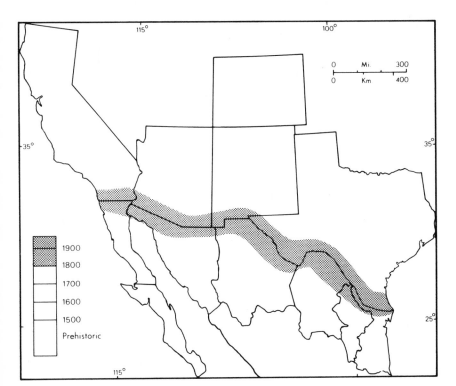

Rio Grande as a result of the U.S.-Mexican War of 1846-48. Following this conflict, new settlements emerged on both sides of the boundary. Texas communities like Brownsville, Rio Grande City, Roma, Edinburg, and El Paso evolved from old Spanish/Mexican *ranchos* or former U.S. military forts established during the war. On the south bank of the Rio Grande, Mexican refugees from the United States founded such towns as Nuevo Laredo and Guadalupe (near El Paso del Norte).

As frontier conditions waned in the late nineteenth century, the border regions experienced considerable growth. In the lower Rio Grande Valley of Texas, Europeans and American Southerners arrived to conduct mercantile operations and to settle on cheap land. In West Texas, the arrival of the railroads in the 1880s transformed El Paso into a prominent transportation and trading center. In San Diego, a gold strike in 1870, the arrival of the railroads, and several land booms caused the population to swell to forty thousand by the 1880s. On the Mexican side, the establishment of the Free Zone from 1885 to 1905 brought commercial prosperity, yet the Mexican towns remained smaller than their American counterparts.

Since 1900 the border region has endured periods of boom and bust because of the area's delicate dependence on external forces. The Mexican Revolution brought recurring disruptions to international trade between 1910 and 1920. Prohibition stimulated tourism in the '20s, but during the '30s the Great Depression triggered unemployment, poverty, and slow population growth. With World War II, however, the border cities entered a period of unprecedented progress. Expansion of Borderlands agriculture, industry, trade, tourism, and government spending contributed to increased urbanization. By 1950 about 800,000 people lived in the Mexican frontier, and by 1970 that figure had soared to 2.3 million, resulting in an annual growth rate of 5 percent during the 1960s (compared to the national rate of 3.2 percent). On the U.S. side, the population of the border counties increased from 1.5 million in 1950 to 2.6 million by 1970.

The Literature

Information concerning the general evolution of the border region can be obtained from materials which treat the Mexican border states and those works which direct attention to the U.S. Borderlands. Cumberland (1960*a*), in his monumental bibliographical work, has compiled an exhaustive list of published works dealing with both sides of the demarcation line. A perusal of that bibliography indicates that although the literature is uneven and many works lack quality, there are few topics that have not commanded at least some attention. Books and articles dealing with areal description, geography, travel, land resources, and myriad aspects of life and culture in the binational Borderlands are plentiful. Historiographically, scholars early had an interest in Spanish institutional patterns that evolved in the area, but the greatest emphasis in the literature has been on diplomatic relations between Mexico and the United States. Since conflict

has characterized many events which have occurred at or near the international boundary, it is not surprising to find much written about such topics as the Texas Revolution, the War of 1846-48, treaties between the two nations, boundary delimitation and resulting controversies, filibustering, outlaw and Indian depredations, the Mexican revolution, transborder forays, border traffic (particularly illegal immigration into the United States), and the distribution of the waters in the rivers that flow through the region.

Publications regarding the broader aspects of the evolution of the Mexican and U.S. Borderlands furnish the student interested in the frontier settlements with necessary perspective, but they frequently lack information that has specific applicability to the binational twin-city complexes. State histories provide some aid, but the focus of such works is understandably not on the fringe areas. Sketches of local communities are also helpful, but since a great many of these sketches are written by nonacademic historians, the pattern is customarily one of poor documentation, poor organization, and lack of perception. Further, an analytical framework is seldom provided, and the emphasis is usually on colorful, romantic, sensational, or provincial concerns. However, often one finds data that suggest further investigation.

Such tendencies are evident in the literature of Ciudad Juárez-El Paso, the largest binational complex along the boundary. Among studies of the state of Chihuahua, the works of Almada (1955, 1964) contain useful data about the border, but the emphasis is on political events emanating from Chihuahua City. For Ciudad Juárez, Chávez M. (1959, 1970) offers greater assistance than can normally be expected from the writings of local authors who are not academics. Additionally, Irigoyen's (1935) collection of primary materials relating to the Free Zone provides abundant social and economic data for Ciudad Juárez and other border communities. Complementing these studies are a few brief and superficial articles and the following more substantial unpublished works: R. White (1968), Valencia (1969), and Langston (1974). More recently, Martínez (1978) has traced aspects of the social and economic evolution of Ciudad Juárez to illustrate border-wide patterns of dependency and interdependency vis-a-vis the United States.

As one would expect, the materials on Ciudad Juárez are far surpassed in volume by the publications available on the history of El Paso. Texas and New Mexico state histories, as well as regional surveys such as that by Meinig (1971), can be counted upon to provide some information on local events as well as to offer perspective. On the city itself, "popular" surveys include the works of O. White (1923, 1925), Sonnichsen (1968), and Bryson (1973). In addition, a large number of shorter monographs, articles, theses, and dissertations treat a vast and varied number of El Paso topics. One of the greatest shortcomings in the historical literature on El Paso (as well as U.S. border cities) is the lack of data regarding Chicanos. When information is provided on this group, it is superficial and oftentimes downright racist. Prior to Garcia's work (1975*a*, 1975*b*), little had been done to document the experience of this ethnic group locally.

Of all the border zones, the lower Rio Grande Valley has

received the most attention from regionally oriented scholars. Two outstanding unpublished works are those by Graf (1942) and Dillman (1968). Significant studies in the published literature include those by Pierce (1917), Scott (1937), Foscue (1939), Da Camara (1949), and Stambaugh and Stambaugh (1954). Two anthropological studies which should be used with caution because of their biased and stereotyped perspectives are by Madsen (1964) and Rubel (1966).

A perusal of the cited works quickly reveals that professional historians have contributed relatively little to the understanding of the border cities. However, members of other disciplines from both sides of the Rio Grande have been busy during the last decade and one-half expanding knowledge of the area. The recent literature reflects Mexico's contemporary concern with the lack of integration of the frontier with the rest of the republic and with the increasing apprehension in the United States concerning the socioeconomic problems prevailing north of the boundary, many of which have their roots on the Mexican side.

Studies of the Mexican border cities are generally concerned with population explosion in the area and the development programs established by Mexico City. Among the important works emphasizing these themes written by American scholars are Dillman (1970b), Baerresen (1971), Ladman and Poulsen (1971), Vetterli (1972), R. Fernández (1973b), Ugalde (1974), Van der Spek (1975), North American Congress on Latin America (1975), and Martínez (1978). The effect of border migration and related phenomena on the U.S. Borderlands is treated in Briggs (1974) and Martínez (1977a, 1978). From south of the boundary, Antonio J. Bermudez (1968), the principal architect and first director of the Programa Nacional Fronterizo (PRONAF), outlined the Mexican strategy for integrating the frontier cities into the national economy. Enrique Sodi Alvarez (1970), another director of PRONAF, placed the northern frontier in a broad historical, geographic, and philosophical context. Since 1961, the Mexican government has issued a number of reports which describe and analyze socioeconomic conditions at the border and outline solutions to important problems. Official publications include those of the Programa Nacional Fronterizo (1961, 1963a), and the Secretaría de Industria y Comercio (1972, 1974a, 1974b, 1974c, 1974d).

Despite the increasingly available literature, which helps to place the border cities in a broader context, superficial and stereotypical notions about the nature of the region still abound. In his sensational book, Demaris (1970) has not only accentuated old images of frontier lawlessness and "wickedness," but has also maligned the entire Mexican Republic by offering a startling answer to an often asked question: Is the border like the rest of Mexico? (with implicit reference to unsavory features). "The answer," declares Demaris, "as far as I was able to determine is a resounding Yes!" (p. 155). Fortunately, recent scholarship is yielding a more objective and larger picture of border life. Anthropologist John A. Price's work (1973a) is a major contribution to the literature. Although his chapters suffer from unevenness and repetition, and the historical treatment is sketchy, Price adds dimension and perspective to the Tijuana scene. He reveals a keen understanding of the varied roles played by the border, including that of cultural adaptation and international symbiosis. Although primarily concerned with Ciudad Juárez, Martínez (1978) may be consulted for historical trends applicable to other border areas as well.

The dynamics of interaction between the various sets of twin cities along the frontier have received attention from various scholars. Stone et al. (1963) investigate many social and cultural aspects of both Nogaleses; D'Antonio and Form (1965) provide insights into elite behavior in El Paso-Ciudad Juárez which are updated by a recent study of informal networks, information sources, and attitudes of community influentials of El Paso and Ciudad Juárez in the public and private sectors (Stoddard et al., 1979). McConville (1965) outlines interdependence and cooperation between these two cities, and Dillman discusses the symbiotic relationship between Brownsville and Matamoros. The impact of Mexico's most recent peso devaluation on American border cities from San Diego to Brownsville was summarized by Stoddard and West (1977).

This brief review of the literature on the growth and development of the border cities reveals that the field is now in a state of transition. The general past neglect on the part of scholars is slowly being rectified. The recent emphasis has been on economic events since 1960, which is understandable since Mexico's frontier has experienced remarkably rapid growth, and attendant social problems have caught the attention of the public, policy makers, and academicians. The studies of the past several years have been helpful in broadening our understanding of the region. From the historian's point of view, however, these works suffer seriously from the lack of time perspective. Historical investigation remains a basic ingredient in laying the foundation for more thorough research on border topics.

Portions of this essay previously appeared in Oscar J. Martínez, *Border Boom Town: Ciudad Juárez since 1848* (Austin: University of Texas Press, 1978) and are reprinted by permission of the publisher.

12

Traditional Historiography

JAMES T. STENSVAAG
Air Force Nuclear Test Personnel
Review
Brooks Air Force Base,
San Antonio, Texas

What constitutes a traditional view of Borderlands history? What, for that matter, constitutes a traditional view of the composition of the Borderlands? A geographical definition is perhaps the most generally accepted answer to the second question, at least for twentieth-century history. Most traditional historians (if that phrase is taken in it most superficial sense to mean older scholars) have thought of the area as the Southwest, for which geographic definitions are about as nebulous as the Borderlands is easily defined.

For this essay we shall assume that Borderlands and the Southwest are roughly synonymous. This will not include all of what everyone has defined as the Southwest; Walter Prescott Webb, for example, seems in *Divided We Stand* (1944) to include every part of the United States that is not the Northwest. Webb's great friend, J. Frank Dobie, on the other hand, might not have included much beyond the outermost limits of Texas cattle drives. We will consider works treating border states, even if their coverage extends north or east, or both.

The first of the two questions posed above—What constitutes traditional Bor-

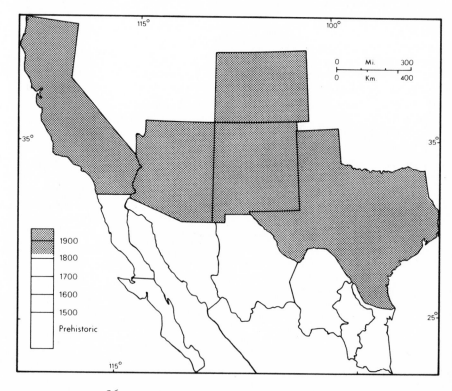

derlands history?—also defies easy answers. Since this essay appears together with a bibliographical study of Chicano history, readers might assume that the perspective of traditional historiography is not particularly racially or culturally diverse. In some measure, at least, that assumption is correct. As increasing numbers of Chicanos and Indians have assumed the white man's historical idiom to express their cultural viewpoints, the older, less culturally oriented history has become "traditional." The existence of new angles on Borderlands history, though, has also affected the traditionalist perspective. Hence, the distinction between traditional history and newer forms is also a measure of the growth of historical professionalism in general and Borderlands studies in particular. Even formerly traditional historians, especially the younger, are now writing nontraditional history within this definition. Where the shift begins, where traditional history ends and newer forms begin, is beyond the confines of this essay, since such a definition would also largely depend upon readers' conceptions. Works included here, if taken as a body, will distinguish traditional views of the twentieth-century Borderlands; most originated before 1970.

Avoiding controversial judgments is one reason for bypassing newer works; another is that perspectives have changed dramatically, even in the last decade. A renowned southwestern student wrote, in 1968, that "the Southwest has a good record of race relations. The Indians are widely accepted as an asset to the region. . . . The largest minority bloc in the Southwest is the Latin-American community, where again [as with the Indians] there is little discrimination. . . . While Southwesterners can point with pride to the strides that have been made, much remains to be done, particularly for the Indian" (Faulk, 1968: 320-21). Contemporary scholars, including that author, would be a bit more cautious, perhaps with even more emphasis upon bridges currently under construction or yet to be built.

Care must be taken to avoid making the word *traditional* either euphemistic or pejorative. Traditional histories may not include all of the cultural leavening that contemporary scholarship finds vital, but their paramountly economic, political, or social viewpoints are necessary for a full regional understanding. Traditional histories deal with the dominant culture, seldom with subcultures except as they disrupt the dominant order. Such traditional analyses are valuable in the overall picture, however short of balance they may be, since historical accuracy includes many linked perspectives.

No historiographical appraisal of the West is complete unless it faces Frederick Jackson Turner. Although Turner wrote little history of the twentieth century, his focus was on the new era. Turner's main concern was the impact of the frontier (the physical frontier, at least) passing from American life—and with it, all of its positive values. He focused upon the twentieth century through his musings about the nineteenth, at the same time emphasizing regional studies' importance to an understanding of each part of American history (Turner, 1920).

The first historian to effectively apply these principles to the twentieth-century Southwest and the Borderlands was Walter Prescott Webb. As a recent biography of Webb shows, although his theories grew independently from Turner's, they stemmed from the same concerns and were similar enough to meld satisfactorily (Furman, 1976).

Webb's postulations, when spun out into the twentieth century, show the Southwest to be culturally defined by the environment. Aridity swept away previous experiences for any conquerors. For the Anglo culture to succeed in developing the Borderlands, the environment first had to be mastered (Webb, W. P., 1931). For Webb, as for Turner, the greatest misfortune was the disappearance of the frontier. In *Divided We Stand* (1944) and again in *The Great Frontier* (1952), Webb theorized that areas such as the Southwest, which has been colonialized, solely for resources, first by Spain, then Mexico, and last the United States, could no longer be considered as mere colonies fit only for plunder. The frontier aura was gone, and with it the temporary aberration of western society's great wealth, all regions needed to work as partners to help ease the crisis of ending the frontier era.

Even though their seminal ideas helped direct attention toward the Southwest as an area worthy of consideration, neither Turner nor Webb has dominated the twentieth-century Borderlands studies. Few historians dispute that environment played a major role in southwestern history; few would acknowledge, however, the preeminence of the frontier ideal. Scholars in several disciplines have now begun to say more about the growth of the American Southwest and the interaction of culture and environment that geographer Carl Sauer (1925: 53) called cultural landscape.

Most authors avoided tackling themes on as grand a scale as Webb's and have instead contented their readers with description. Much literature in the early part of the century, such as Charles Lummis's *Mesa, Canyon, and Pueblo* (1925a), described the region in awestruck tones. The profession matured, however, and more concrete studies, such as Rupert N. Richardson and Carl Coke Rister's *The Greater Southwest,* began to consider economic, social, and cultural factors as well as regional grandeur. Rister also collaborated with LeRoy Hafen in 1941 to produce *Western America,* which exemplifies both the durability and flexibility necessary in a work on the West. It went into its third edition in 1970, Hafen and Eugene Hollon having carried on the work after Rister's death in 1955, and these two authors have acknowledged their debt in the subsequent edition. The newest edition put greater emphasis on "conservation and utilization of natural resources, the rise and growth of Western cities," and the "expansion of industrial and military establishments." Indians, including natives of Alaska and Hawaii, were also given "fuller and more sympathetic treatment" (Hafen, Hollon, and Rister, 1970: vii). Even then the more literary treatment given the Southwest by Haniel Long in *Pinon County* dealt with a wide range, including politics, race relations, labor troubles, and more. Eugene Hollon went on to produce *The Great American Desert* (1966), a quite personal honing of Webb's environmental arguments.

The appearance of books on the Southwest did not stop speculation about whether the region was actually unified in any way. In the early 1950s, the *Arizona Quarterly* carried two such speculative articles proclaiming regionalism's limitations and the qualified existence of the Southwest (Winther, 1952; Shirer, 1953), and even in the early 1960s an analyst could go no farther than calling the Southwest a "collection of familiarities" rather than a deep-set region in any scientific sense (Moore, 1964). Such doubts evidently did not plague Ray Allen Billington, who saw in the West the general persistence of frontier traits such as faith in political democracy, social mobility, casual wastefulness, belief in hard work, and genteel respect for women (Billington, 1966). For Billington, the existence of the West, or any subregion, was more a matter of mind than geography.

Perhaps the definitive statement about the existence of the Southwest came from John Walton Caughey, whose essay "The Spanish Southwest: An Example of Subconscious Regionalism" tied the twentieth-century Borderlands to a more economic and cultural unity. The region made its mark after 1900, Caughey explained, by furnishing perishables, serving as a kind of national sanatorium, becoming a tourist attraction, and developing its oil industry (Caughey, 1969: 29-38). Caughey's analysis, while more precise, was not entirely new; Morris Garnsey had argued for the politico-economic definition of the mountain West in 1950.

Two surveys show the transition from traditional Southwestern historiography to newer models. The first, Lynn Perrigo's *The American Southwest* (1971), deals with the political and economic twentieth century, but Perrigo also begins to contend with cultural abrasion. Gerald D. Nash puts the twentieth-century American West in perspective in his concise *The American West in the Twentieth Century: A Short History of an Urban Oasis* (1973).

Economic development became one of the main themes as historians looked at the Southwest and Borderlands more closely, especially in studies of the twentieth century. Walter Webb's main complaint in *Divided We Stand* (1944) was the Northeast's domination of the Southwest. The same theme motivated A. G. Mezerik's 1946 analysis *The Revolt of the South and the West.* Garnsey's appraisal of the mountain states, together with two articles, "Economic Diversification in the Southwest" by A. S. Lang and "Recent Economic Development of the Southwest" by Stephen L. McDonald, give positive analyses of increasing regional industrial and general economic potential. Part of that growth pattern came from resource exploitation, two facets of which are covered in Carl C. Rister's *Oil! Titan of the Southwest* (1949) and Robert C. Cleland's *A History of Phelps-Dodge, 1834-1950* (1952). Cleland's accounts of labor relations are balanced in Vernon Jensen's history of the Western Federation of Miners, *Heritage of Conflict* (1950).

Besides minerals and oil, two other resources became eminently more valuable in the twentieth-century Southwest, particularly in the Borderlands—the land itself and water. The first of these two was initially scrutinized in 1942 by Roy Robbins, resulting in *Our Landed Heritage: The Public Domain, 1776-1936.* Robbins was mainly concerned with integrating the land's history with already written economic and political history; in the twentieth century, his focus came naturally to the Southwest. Also important is E. Louise Peffer's *The Closing of the Public Domain: Disposal and Reser-*

vation Policies, 1900-1950 (1951), which traces changes in the philosophy of land policy from one of land held in escrow for future use to that of land held in perpetuity for public interest—from the time of the Reclamation Act of 1902, a vital piece of legislation for the Borderlands. Water, the reclamation agent, was also the subject of international controversy throughout the twentieth century as both Mexico and the United States claimed riparian rights on the Rio Grande. Norris Hundley, Jr., first discussed the problem in *Dividing the Waters* (1966); his first study was followed in 1975 by Jerry Mueller's *Restless River,* which discusses water and land as foci for controversy over the meandering Rio Grande.

Political history is one of the foci for traditional historiography, and consequently the history of political relations between Mexico and the United States has generated a long list of studies by traditionally oriented scholars on both sides of the border. Perhaps the most widely read general text, north of the border at least, has been J. Fred Rippy's *The United States and Mexico* (1926). Rippy characterized Mexico's political history as generally chaotic, with governments frequently bankrupt, unrepresentative, and subject to foreign intervention. U.S. interests, on the other hand, pursued active, enterprising, aggressive policies which sometimes appeared exploitive to Mexican governments beset with internal problems. American dynamism and Mexican sensitivity led to "exaggeration of intent" on both sides, Rippy wrote, and intensified problems between the nations in the process. Similarly, James M. Callahan noted in *American Foreign Policy in Mexican Relations* (1932) that American attitudes toward Mexico grew not only out of self-interest, feelings of superiority, and impatience with Latin temperament, but also from more laudable hemispheric concerns and antagonism toward European intervention. According to Callahan, American actions were sometimes misguided out of ignorance, but nonetheless were "always accompanied by an attitude of good will and frequently by unusual patience."

More recent scholarship in the traditional mode has not strayed far from the themes struck by Rippy and Callahan. Luís Zorilla's *Historia de las relaciones entre México y los Estados Unidos de America, 1800-1958* (1965) is the most complete of any of the diplomatic surveys and is drawn, Zorilla states in the preface, primarily from U.S. sources, such as Clarence C. Clendenen's *The United States and Pancho Villa* (1961a), a defense of President Woodrow Wilson's border policies. Clendenen later produced *Blood on the Border: The United States Army and the Mexican Irregulars* (1969), a view of hostilities from the dirt soldier's vantage point with an underpinning of righteous-cause philosophy. Like Clendenen's work, much of the traditionalist literature dealing with binational relations focuses on the obviously troubled times of the late 1840s and the second decade of the twentieth century. Other examples include Berta Ulloa's *La revolución intervenida: Relaciones diplomáticas entre México y los Estados Unidos, 1910-1914* (1971), with its emphasis upon the "rupture of the status quo" between the two countries during those years, and P. Edward Haley's *Revolution and Intervention: The Diplomacy of Taft and Wilson with Mexico, 1910-1917*

(1970), which charts the conventional views of Taft as dollar diplomat and Wilson as moralist and champion of democracy. Daniel Cosío Villegas provided a counterpoint to the emphasis on the years of military strife with his *Historia moderna de México: El Porfirato* (1960), volumes five and six of which provide analysis of *La vida política exterior* during the Díaz years. As this smattering of sources indicates, a capsulized version of the traditionalists' vision of Mexican-U.S. relations, much simplified, has the United States as a politically matured neighbor watching with concern the continuing turmoil in Mexico, and intervening with well-intentioned (if sometimes ill-conceived) motives. More recent literature in this genre is more sophisticated than the writings of the 1920s and '30s, but it starts with the same general premise.

U.S. domestic policies, at least the traditional view of Borderlands political activity, can be deciphered from three books. The first is *Politics in the American West* (Jonas, 1969), a collection of essays of varying quality. The second is *Urban Politics in the Southwest* (Goodall, 1967), a collection with heavy politico-economic emphasis put together by the Institute of Public Administration at Arizona State University. The third is *Ethnic Minorities in Politics* (Tobias and Woodhouse, 1969), which contains essays by Frances Swadesh on the Alianza movement and Suzanne Simmons on Pueblo Indians.

The most important resource of the area, of course, is its people. In the Tobias and Woodhouse (1969) collection, Swadesh and Simmons address two peoples of the Southwest. Other essays in that collection address the interplay of other cultures in the Borderlands. No single work tells the story of the Hispanic-Indian and Anglo-Indian cultural interaction better than Edward Spicer's *Cycles of Conquest* (1962). Supplementing Spicer's work are Wilcomb E. Washburn's *Red Man's Land/White Man's Law* (1971) and Stan Steiner's *The New Indians* (1968). Concerning the Hispanic population,

few authors have been as sensitive as Carey McWilliams in his treatment of migrant labor in *Ill Fares the Land* (1944) and his more general *North from Mexico: The Spanish-Speaking People of the United States* (1949a).

No essay of this length can pretend to name all of the most important works in such a broadly worked area. As that disclaimer is written, though, it must also be noted that the work is far from done, even in the "traditional" fields. The most needed task is the melding of perspectives, a first-rate survey of Borderlands history giving just attention to all cultures. In economics, work needs to be done on labor relations after the Gallup strike and before the drive to organize farm and migrant labor. Much more can be done on resource management, especially the evolution and entanglements of land laws. More needs to be done to study the ethnic diversity within larger cultural groups and the impact of such diversity on local intercultural relations. For example, were French or German settlers different from true Anglo-Americans in their relationships with preexisting cultures? Certainly the impact of industrialization and economic exploitation (or resource utilization) is not yet known, partly because the full story has not yet been spun out, but also because historians can do more work. The list goes on.

One essay collection points the way for all Borderlands students. *Views Across the Border: The United States and Mexico* (Ross, 1978) includes the proceedings of a 1975 binational conference during which most general topics of importance, including culture, politics, economics, migrants, health, ecology, and so on, were touched upon. Scholars can draw an important lesson from that collection, namely, the necessity for untraditional approaches to traditional concerns. Borderlands history, like the region itself, must be both traditional and venturesome to fulfill its function—seeking to help us understand our relationship to our environment and our responsibilities to each other.

13

New Chicano Historiography

CARLOS E. CORTÉS
Department of History
University of California,
Riverside

The Chicano movement of the 1960s and '70s has had a major quantitative and qualitative impact on the course of Borderlands historiography. In a general sense, it has increased interest in and led to expanded research and writing about Borderlands history, particularly the period since the 1846 U.S. conquest of northern Mexico. More specifically, it has generated challenges to traditional interpretations of the Chicano experience and has altered the spectrum of current Borderlands historiography by expanding the relative emphasis on Chicanos (Mexican Americans) as well as by shifting much of the focus away from elites and institutions to the experiences of people in the broader sense.

The new Chicano historiography is that body of scholarship about the Mexican American past that has developed since the mid-1960s greatly as a result of the impetus created by the Chicano movement. Although the new Chicano historiography is obviously not the exclusive province of Mexican American scholars, the past decade has witnessed a dramatic increase in the number of Chicanos involved in the analysis and presentation of their own heritage. Nor is the new Chicano

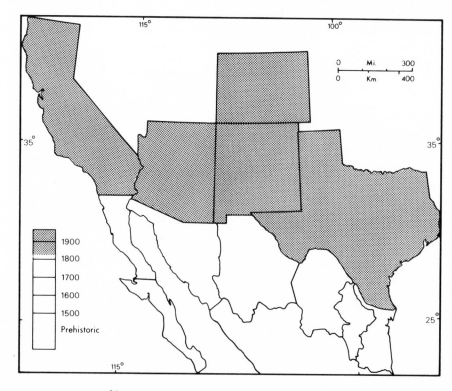

historiography the private preserve of professional historians, as scholars from other disciplines as well as journalists and other writers have contributed to the re-creation and reinterpretation of the Chicano experience. Moreover, while there is no lock-step philosophical unity and while conceptual and analytical disagreements inevitably abound among contemporary scholars, the new Chicano historiography has been preponderantly revisionist and has introduced a variety of new perspectives and paradigms for the study of Borderlands history.

Prior to the 1960s, most scholarship on Mexican Americans could be characterized as "assimilationist" in orientation and consisted heavily of contemporary sociological and anthropological investigations. Examples are such community studies as Ruth Tuck's *Not with the Fist: Mexican Americans in a Southwest City* (1946) and Margaret Clark's *Health in the Mexican-American Culture: A Community Study* (1959). There were a few notable exceptions to this assimilationist assumption, such as George I. Sánchez's classic *Forgotten People: A Study of New Mexicans* (1940), Américo Paredes's remarkable *"With His Pistol in His Hand": A Border Ballad and Its Hero* (1958), economist Paul S. Taylor's (1930-34, 1934) jolting analyses of Mexican workers in the United States, and Mexican anthropologist Manuel Gamio's (1930, 1931) revealing studies of Mexican immigrants. However, implicitly, and sometimes explicitly, most pre-1960 books on Mexican Americans addressed the same underlying questions: How "successful" has the United States been in assimilating Chicanos or how "successful" have Chicanos been in assimilating into mainstream America? How "well" have Chicanos shed their cultural characteristics and immersed themselves into the U.S. melting pot?

While many current scholars still operate under this assimilationist assumption, the new Chicano historiography has created a vigorous challenge. "Success" has been redefined in such terms as community survival, development of a dynamic, syncretic culture, resistance to the homogenizing forces of total assimilation, and political-economic progress without cultural surrender. Reflective of this new scholarly vibrancy have been the publication of numerous insightful theoretical articles and the development of a stimulating debate over interpreting the Chicano past. Foremost among theoreticians of the new Chicano historiography is the perceptive, contemplative Juan Gómez-Quiñones (1971; Gómez-Quiñones and Arroyo, 1976). Representative of the historiographical debate is the provocative exchange in the *Pacific Historical Review* between assimilationist Arthur F. Corwin (1973) and revisionist Rodolfo Acuña (1974).

Not surprisingly, in view of the wealth of recent and revisionist scholarship in this area, there is as yet no fully adequate general introductory history of Mexican Americans. Still valuable is Carey McWilliams's passionate, trailblazing *North from Mexico: The Spanish-Speaking People of the United States* (1949a), which vigorously exposes discrimination and exploitation encountered by Chicanos. Yet despite this promising start, not until 1972 did another full-length general history appear—*The Chicanos: A History of Mexican Americans*, by Matt S. Meier and Feliciano Rivera (1972).

Following in McWilliams's philosophical footsteps, Meier and Rivera extended the historical account through the 1960s, with greater scope and factual accuracy, but with less power and artistry. While useful introductory reading for the facts of Mexican American history, the Meier-Rivera book is weak in analysis and fuzzy in interpretation. However, after nearly a decade, in their book has yet to be surpassed as a general history, except for David Weber's incisive synthesis of nineteenth-century Chicano history in the lengthy section introductions of his documentary collection, *Foreigners in Their Native Land: Historical Roots of the Mexican American* (1973). Other general surveys, such as Manuel A. Machado's mediocre *Listen Chicano! An Informal History of the Mexican American*, fall far short of the level achieved by Meier and Rivera.

In addition to these general works there are a number of more conceptual historical interpretations. Most significant is historian Rodolfo Acuña's vibrant *Occupied America: A History of Chicanos* (1981), a landmark study of Anglo-American oppression and Chicano resistance which is broader in scope than the 1972 version. Another example is political scientist Mario Barrera's *Race and Class in the Southwest: A Theory of Racial Inequality* (1979), a political-economic history of Chicanos emphasizing a class-analysis frame of reference.

Scholars of other disciplines have included historical reinterpretations in their general works. Economist Raúl A. Fernández applied a rigidly economic deterministic framework to Chicano history in his *The United States-Mexico Border: A Politico-Economic Profile* (1977). Geographer Richard L. Nostrand provided unique historical demographic insights in his *Los chicanos: Geografía histórica regional* (1976). Sociologist Joan W. Moore's *Mexican Americans* (with Pachón, 1976), still the best short introduction to Chicanos currently available, has a historical orientation. Finally, the massive, 777-page *The Mexican American People: The Nation's Second Largest Minority* by Leo Grebler, Joan W. Moore, and Ralph C. Guzman (1970), the most complete reference work on Chicanos, devotes considerable attention to history as viewed through an assimilationist prism.

As building blocks for general historical surveys, the new Chicano historiography needs comprehensive state-level histories of the Chicano experience. Among pre-1960 efforts to create such surveys were George Sánchez's aforementioned *Forgotten People* (1940) and Carlos E. Castañeda's seven-volume *Our Catholic Heritage in Texas, 1519-1936* (1936-58), whose last volume focuses on Texas since the formation of the Lone Star Republic. While limited to the nineteenth century, Leonard Pitt's *The Decline of the Californios: A Social History of Spanish-Speaking Californians, 1848-1890* (1966) and Robert Rosenbaum's doctoral dissertation *"Mexicano versus Americano: A Study of Hispanic-American Resistance to Anglo-American Control in New Mexico Territory, 1870-1900"* (1972) hint at the possibilities for full-scale Chicano state histories. Two anthropological studies—Nancie L. Gonzales's *The Spanish-Americans of New Mexico: A Heritage of Pride* (1969) and Frances Leon Swadesh's *Los Primeros Pobladores: Hispanic Americans of the Ute Frontier*

(1974)—moved in that direction, although they are restricted by their emphasis on the northern part of the state. A few small-scale studies have been published, such as Vicente V. Mayer's *Utah: A Hispanic History* (1975). However, the new Chicano historiography still awaits major state historical surveys.

To date, the most significant contributions of the new Chicano historiography have been in the exploration of more limited themes rather than in the creation of general surveys. Because of the unique dual conquest-immigration origins of Mexican Americans, these two themes rank among the most important topics for historical study. Yet while strides have been made in the past decade, much work is yet to be done.

The themes of U.S. westward expansion into northern Mexico, the Texas Revolution and Lone Star Republic, and the U.S.-Mexican War have generated a massive literature and sharply conflicting interpretations. Exemplary is the often vitriolic historiography of the U.S.-Mexican War, in which historians have erected clear battle lines. One scholarly contingent consists of those who emphasize U.S. expansionism, racism, guilt, and wartime atrocities. This school traces its roots to mid-nineteenth-century analyses like Abiel Abbot Livermore's *The War With Mexico Reviewed* (1850). More recent examples are Glenn W. Price's *Origins of the War with Mexico: The Polk-Stockton Intrigue* (1967) and Gene M. Brack's *Mexico Views Manifest Destiny, 1821-1846: An Essay on the Origins of the Mexican War* (1975).

In contrast are the pro–United States apologias, symbolized by Justin Smith's *The War with Mexico* (1919), the anti-Mexican interpretations of which have unfortunately become nearly standard fare in most U.S. elementary- and secondary-school history textbooks. Among recent heirs to the tradition of "Smithism" is *North America Divided: The Mexican War* by Seymour V. Connor and Odie B. Faulk. A new, balanced, comprehensive study of the Mexican War reflecting the considerable recent research is badly needed.

Like the Mexican War, Mexican immigration, the other component of the duality of Chicano origins, is wide open for historical research and reinterpretation. For the most part, scholarship on Mexican immigration has been contemporary in nature. The initial major wave of Mexican immigration during the first three decades of this century led to several major studies. These included the previously mentioned books by economist Paul Taylor (1930-34, 1934) and anthropologist Manuel Gamio (1930, 1931) as well as sociologist Emory S. Bogardus's *The Mexican in the United States* (1934). However, not until historian John R. Martínez's 1957 doctoral dissertation, "Mexican Emigration to the United States, 1910-1930" did that phenomenon receive a thorough historical retrospective.

The termination of that era of immigration through the ensuing repatriation program is analyzed by Abraham Hoffman in his *Unwanted Mexican Americans in the Great Depression: Repatriation Pressures, 1929-1933* (1974). While generally solid in its analysis of the role of governmental and private institutions, the book is limited by its focus on southern California and its neglect of the perspectives and experiences of the repatriated people themselves. Overviews of both the first immigration and the repatriation periods are provided by Mark Reisler's *By the Sweat of Their Brow: Mexican Immigrant Labor in the United States, 1900-1940* (1976), and Lawrence A. Cardoso's *Mexican Emigration to the United States, 1897-1931: Socio-Economic Patterns* (1980).

The 1960s and 1970s have brought a new boom in studies about Mexican immigration, with scholars of various disciplinary backgrounds as well as journalists participating. Special recent emphasis has been on two themes—the *bracero* program and the undocumented worker. Examples are Ernesto Galarza's stunning *Merchants of Labor: The Mexican Bracero Story* (1964), Richard B. Craig's *The Bracero Program: Interest Groups and Foreign Policy* (1971), Julian Samora's *Los Mojados: The Wetback Story* (1971), Grace Halsell's *The Illegals* (1978), Dick J. Reavis's *Without Documents* (1978), Juan Ramón García's *Operation Wetback: The Mass Deportation of Mexican Undocumented Workers in 1954* (1980), and María Herrera-Sobek's *The Bracero Experience: Elitelore Versus Folklore* (1979).

While such "hot" topics as *braceros* and undocumented workers have received most of the attention, some strides have been made toward general reinterpretations of the history of Mexican immigration, including the post-World War II period. An early effort was Leo Grebler's brief *Mexican Immigration to the United States: The Record and Its Implications* (1966). A variety of interpretations by both U.S. and Mexican scholars can be found in historian Arthur F. Corwin's *Immigrants—and Immigrants: Perspectives on Mexican Labor Migration to the United States* (1978a).

Conceptual frameworks, philosophies, methodologies, and themes have varied, including such topics as politics, economics, religion, linkages with Mexico, resistance against societal oppression, and biographies of major Chicano figures. Unfortunately, biographical efforts to date have been overly concentrated on contemporary leaders such as César Chávez and Reies López Tijerina. This essay will illustrate the new trends through a discussion of four areas: urban history, labor history, Chicana history, and cultural history.

Some of the most exciting and revealing work has been done in the areas of urban history and labor history, with the dividing lines between urban, labor, and immigration history often blurred and inappropriate. In urban history, in particular, innovative oral history techniques and statistical methodologies have been applied with excellent results by such scholars as Albert Camarillo, Pedro Castillo, Erasmo Gamboa, Mario García, Gilbert González, Richard Griswold del Castillo, Louise Año Nuevo Kerr, Judith Fincher Laird, Oscar Martínez, Ricardo Romo, F. Arturo Rosales, Ciro Sepulveda, and Joyce Carter Vickery. While the results are still mainly in the form of doctoral dissertations, an increasing number of articles and even some books are now resulting from this new scholarly explosion.

Several interesting trends can be noted. In his excellent *Border Boom Town: Ciudad Juárez since 1848* (1978) and the rest of his border city research, historian Oscar J. Martínez has demonstrated the critical importance of studying the U.S.-Mexican twin-city phenomenon as an integral part of the Chicano experience. In his *Chicanos in a Changing*

Society: From Mexican Pueblos to American Barrios in Santa Barbara and Southern California, 1848-1930 (1979), Albert Camarillo has made superb use of a comparative approach to the history of Mexican Americans in four California cities—Santa Barbara, Los Angeles, San Diego, and San Bernardino. Other noteworthy recently published urban histories of Chicanos include Mario T. García's *Desert Immigrants: The Mexicans of El Paso, 1880-1920* (1981) and Richard Griswold del Castillo's *The Los Angeles Barrio, 1850-1890: A Social History* (1979). Such historians as Louise Año Nuevo Kerr in her "The Chicano Experience in Chicago: 1920-1970" (1976) and Judith Fincher Laird in her "Argentine, Kansas: The Evolution of a Mexican-American Community, 1905-1940" (1975) have helped to destroy the myth of Chicanos as a regional minority and to dramatize the importance of studying the history of Chicanos throughout the United States.

Rivaling urban history in the attention it has received during the past decade has been labor history. In addition to the works discussed under the category of immigration, probably the best known are the journalistic books on César Chávez and Ernesto Galarza's incisive studies of farm labor organizing, *Spiders in the House and Workers in the Field* (1970) and *Farm Workers and Agri-Business in California, 1947-1960* (1977). As in the case of urban history, however, most of the written work to date has been in the form of dissertations and articles reflecting the research of such scholars as Luis Leobardo Arroyo, Alvar Ward Carlson, Victor Nelson Cisneros, Camille Guerin, George Kiser, David Maciel, Joseph Park, Herbert Peterson, Roberto Villarreal, Devra Anne Weber, Charles Winn, Charles Wollenberg, and Emilio Zamora. *La clase obrera en la historia de México: Al norte del Río Bravo,* by David Maciel and Juan Gómez-Quiñones (scheduled for publication in 1981), should be a major addition to the literature on Chicano labor history.

Chicana history—the experiences of Mexican American women—is finally beginning to receive long overdue attention. Before the 1960s, much of the published discussion of Chicanas took the form of romanticized essays on Mexican American culture or stereotypical depictions of Chicanas in "traditional roles." Within pre-1960 historiography, one of the most valuable works is Fabiola Cabeza de Baca's *We Fed Them Cactus* (1954), a sensitive recollection of life in New Mexico.

In recent years young scholars, such as Laura E. Arroyo, Adelaida del Castillo, Richard García, Carlos Larralde, Francine Medeiros, Ana Nieto-Gómez, Adaljiza Sosa Riddell, Gloria Rodríguez, Richard Rodríguez, Vicki Ruiz, Adela de la Torre, Patricia Zavella, and Maxine Baca Zinn, have begun to write about the Chicana past. To date there has been no full-scale history of Chicanas. Useful introductions, however, are provided in Marta Cotera's *Profile of the Mexican-American Woman* (1977) and in *La Chicana: The Mexican-American Woman,* by Alfredo Mirandé and Evangelina Enríquez (1979), the best book on the Chicana yet published.

Finally, in the past decade, numerous scholars have worked toward creating comprehensive historical surveys of various aspects of Chicano cultural expression. Among these are Raymond Paredes and Philip Ortego (literature); Jorge Huerta (theatre); and Jacinto Quirarte (art), whose *Mexican American Artists* (1973) helps to establish the rich pre-1960 Chicano artistic heritage in the United States. Mention should also be made of Cecil Robinson's *Mexico and the Hispanic Southwest in American Literature* (1977), which devotes considerably more attention to Chicano literature than did his earlier edition, the classic *With the Ears of Strangers: The Mexican in American Literature* (1963).

Additional evidence of the vitality of the new Chicano historiography can be found in the success of Chicano scholarly journals, the richness of reprint series of Chicano historical materials, and the numerous general and topical Chicano bibliographies. The most important journal for Chicano social science research has been *Atzlán, International Journal of Chicano Studies Research* (1970-   ), while the *Journal of Mexican-American History* has dedicated itself more exclusively to historical concerns. Foremost among the reprint series are the two edited for Arno Press by Carlos E. Cortés—the 21-volume *The Mexican American* (1974) and the 55-volume *The Chicano Heritage* (1976). These two collections contain numerous little-known works on the Chicano past, including rare government, religious, pamphlet, and ephemeral press publications.

Because of the rapid recent increase in Chicano historiography, the many bibliographies, while useful, are inevitably out of date by the time they are published. Possibly the most comprehensive bibliographical aid to date for studying Chicanos is *The Mexican American: A Critical Guide to Research Aids* by Barbara J. Robinson and J. Cordell Robinson (1980). This thoroughly annotated bibliography of bibliographies also provides an excellent overview of other types of sources, such as genealogical and biographical guides.

Borderlands history has benefited from the challenge and dynamism of the Chicano movement. Yet the new Chicano historiography is not dependent on this social movement for its current motive force, as it now possesses the self-contained momentum for long-term development and, even more important, enjoys a growing cadre of fine young scholars. The future is indeed bright for the reinterpretation and clarification of the Chicano, Borderlands, and U.S. past.

I would like to thank the Academic Senate of the University of California, Riverside, for an Intramural Research Grant which supported this research.

14

Prehistory Overview and California–Baja California Archaeology

THOMAS R. HESTER
*Center for Archaeological
Research
University of Texas at
San Antonio*

In this section, the authors have concentrated on the prehistoric human occupations of the Borderlands. These native American cultures span a period from the earliest documented presence at prior to 9000 B.C. to contemporary native American peoples. Most Borderlands literature focuses on modern issues or problems of relatively recent history; the temporal parameters for Borderlands archaeologists go back some 11,000 years or more.

At present, there are at least two major factors of concern which involve the prehistoric sites. One is restoration (especially in New Mexico and Arizona; see Lekson, Chapter 15 of this *Sourcebook*), which serves to both preserve sites and to make them available as tourist attractions. A second major concern is with site preservation. With all of the activity and growth in the Southwest and other parts of the Borderlands, visitors, tourists, engineers, agency workers, planners, and developers must be made aware of how easily the evidence of prehistoric cultures can be destroyed through thoughtless acts and neglect.

The early hunting and gathering peoples were mobile. They lived by roaming

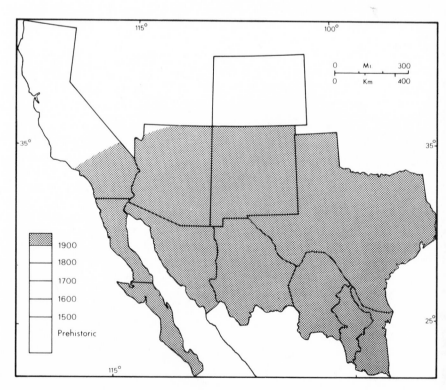

over the land, obtaining their food resources from the environment. However, this was not a haphazard way of life. Archaeological research has indicated that their utilization of resources was done in a scheduled and organized fashion. Unlike the residues of the sedentary agricultural peoples of later times (whose dwellings, tools, and utensils are found in permanent villages), the sites of the nomadic hunter-gatherers are sometimes difficult to recognize. These early sites often consist of scattered flint flakes, projectile points, and burned rocks (representing cooking and food processing). Such sites are in a sense "fragile" in that even casual artifact-collecting from the surface can render the remaining information almost useless to the professional archaeologist.

The archaeological remains of both the agricultural communities and of the nomadic peoples are vitally important in the study of the cultural heritage of the Borderlands. The data that result provide us with a fuller understanding of man's successful adaptation to the region's environment. However, the archaeological sites of the Borderlands are rapidly being lost. These often faint traces of the ancient past have been vandalized and looted by an unconcerned public. Relic collectors and rock hounds often unknowingly ruin archaeological sites in the pursuit of their hobbies. There is even systematic looting of village sites (as in the Mimbres Valley of New Mexico) in order to obtain pottery vessels for the antiquities market (see Michel, 1981).

Many sites in the Borderlands are in the public domain and need better protection from Federal supervisory agencies. Other sites are on private property and can be protected only if the landowner is aware of the scientific value of these remains. The best hope for site preservation lies in the training of skilled avocational archaeologists, who with proper scientific orientation, can help to conserve the dwindling archaeological record (Hester, 1980).

Equally devastating to the archaeological resources of the Borderlands has been site destruction caused by expanding populations, urbanization, and land development. Construction projects, such as roads, highways, canals, dams, and housing subdivisions, have had a tremendous, and very adverse, impact on archaeological remains. Projects that are federally-funded or require licensing must, by law, have archaeological surveys done prior to any land modification. Furthermore, it is the responsibility of the agency, whether private, local, state, or federal, to use the data from the archaeological surveys to help avoid the disturbance of these ancient cultural remains. Although there are a variety of state and governmental agencies in Texas, New Mexico, Arizona, and California responsible for antiquities preservation, they cannot possibly deter every private developer from destroying, through ignorance or apathy, this irreplaceable information.

In the chapters that follow are bibliographical essays on the prehistoric and certain early historic populations of the Borderlands area. The emphasis is on the native American cultures, as other cultures or ethnic groups are treated elsewhere in the volume.

The California-Baja California region is covered in this section only insofar as some key references are provided. For the California region, rather complete bibliographical collections are available. Heizer and Elsasser (1977) have published the prime reference on the archaeology, ethnography, and Indian history of the state. Heizer (1978) has edited the California volume in the *Handbook of North American Indians* series produced by the Smithsonian Institution. More than 70 chapters are devoted to syntheses of data on specific California Indian groups, as well as summaries of California archaeology, native languages, demography, social organization, and treaties. Another important reference is by Bean and Vane (1977). Additionally, several summaries exist on the archaeology of the southern California desert Borderlands (Heizer, 1964; Hester, 1973; P. J. Wilke, 1976; Aiken, 1978; Davis, 1980).

South of the current binational border in Baja California, the key archaeological and ethnohistorical summaries are by Massey (1966) and an updated collection by Price and Smith (1971). Willey (1966) also briefly reviews Baja California archaeology. For those interested in historic and prehistoric culture and ecological settings in southern California and Baja California, see Aschmann (1959a, 1959b, 1966).

15

Southwestern Archaeology

STEPHEN H. LEKSON
Chaco Center
National Park Service

Early archaeological studies in the Borderlands between the lower Colorado River and the El Paso district were dominated by half a dozen anthropological research foundations. Two of these, the Gila Pueblo (in Globe, Arizona) and the Amerind Foundation (in Dragoon, Arizona) have each produced a series of monographs which are basic archaeological references (the Gila Pueblo's *Medallion Papers,* 1928-50, and the Amerind Foundation's *Publications,* beginning in 1940). The Arizona State Museum, often in cooperation with the Department of Anthropology at the University of Arizona, has sponsored numerous archaeological projects in southern Arizona and northern Sonora. Two series of University of Arizona publications, the *Social Science Bulletins* and the *Anthropological Papers,* contain numerous papers pertinent to Borderlands archaeology. *The Kiva,* the journal of the Archaeological and Historical Society (an affiliate of the Arizona State Museum), includes many relevant articles and reports (Gell and Robinson, 1966; Kaemlein and Reinhart, 1975). The Peabody Museum of Harvard University conducted seminal investigations in southwestern New Mex-

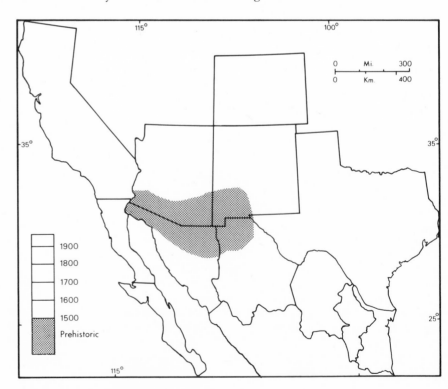

ico in the 1920s and '30s, inspiring other large institutions to undertake field projects in this area (Kidder in Cosgrove and Cosgrove, 1932). The School of American Research in Santa Fe followed in the Cosgroves' footsteps with its Hidalgo Project (McCluney, 1962: vii), a series of archaeological operations in the extreme southwestern corner of New Mexico.

In addition to the University of Arizona, mentioned above, several other universities have conducted archaeological research in the Borderlands. The University of New Mexico and the University of Colorado fielded several expeditions, principally in the Sierra Madre Occidental of northern Chihuahua and Sonora (Lister, 1960). Arizona State University has conducted projects in southern Arizona, several of which are reported in the *Arizona State University Anthropological Research Papers.* Case Western Reserve University supported much of the work of the Upper Gila Project (Fitting, 1972*b*), reported in the *Southwestern New Mexico Research Reports.* The Columbia University Hidalgo Archaeological Project (Findlow and de Ately, 1976) conducted research in extreme southwest New Mexico. The University of Oklahoma has fielded a series of projects in the Río Sonora Valley of Mexico (Pailes in Braniff and Felger, 1976).

The most important Mexican institution operating in the Borderlands is the northwest regional office of the Instituto Nacional de Antropología e Historia located in Hermosillo, Sonora. In a cooperative project the Joint Casas Grandes Expedition, consisting of the Amerind Foundation and the Instituto Nacional de Antropología e Historia, conducted an extensive study of the important Casas Grandes archaeological zone in northern Chihuahua (Di Peso, 1974).

Field notes, site survey reports, and unpublished manuscripts form a large body of data that must be considered in any appraisal of the archaeology of the Borderlands. All the institutions named above maintain libraries and archives that house this kind of material. However, the Gila Pueblo ceased operation in 1951 and transferred its collection to the Arizona State Museum in Tucson. The site-survey files of the Arizona State Museum and the Museum of New Mexico's Laboratory of Anthropology have important inventories of known archaeological resources in the Borderlands.

Various Federal agencies are becoming increasingly important sources of both archaeological reports and regional syntheses. In particular, these would include the USDA Forest Service (particularly in reference to Coronado National Forest), with central bibliographic control at its Southwest Regional Office in Albuquerque; the National Park Service, with its Western Archaeological Center in Tucson, and the Organ Pipe National Monument and other smaller units in southern Arizona; and the Bureau of Land Management, through its state offices in Arizona and New Mexico and its local district offices. Several of these agencies have prepared or are preparing Cultural Resource Overviews for their local units (e.g., LeBlanc and Whalen, 1979). The overviews summarize past archaeological work and archaeological remains in the unit and address specific topics for future research.

The prehistory of the New Mexico-Chihuahua and Arizona-Sonora Borderlands can be divided into three generalized stages: the earliest Paleo-Indian stage, followed by the Archaic, and then the Ceramic. The Paleo-Indian stage constitutes the most ancient human occupation of the area, from at least fifteen thousand to perhaps eight thousand years ago. Traces of man from this stage are often found with the remains of extinct animals. The Archaic stage, from about eight thousand years ago to the time of Christ, had an essentially modern environment with more familiar fauna. Archaeological evidence suggests that the human adaptation during this period was preagricultural, with foodstuffs procured through hunting and gathering. The final prehistoric stage is that of fully agricultural peoples living in permanent villages and producing ceramics (the definitive artifact of this stage). The Ceramic stage lasted from shortly before the time of Christ to about A.D. 1500, when Spanish influences became paramount in the history of the Borderlands. Of these three stages—the Paleo-Indian at least seven thousand years in length; the Archaic perhaps six thousand years long; and the Ceramic only fifteen hundred years in duration—we know least about the longest and most about the shortest and most recent. Little is known about the archaeology of the Paleo-Indian and Archaic stages because sites from only two or three areas are available to describe them. By contrast, the relative abundance of reports about the Ceramic stage will require geographic subdivision of the Borderlands.

The most abundant records for the Paleo-Indian and Archaic stages occur in southeastern Arizona. Important Paleo-Indian sites include Naco (Haury, 1953), Lehner (Haury, Sayles, and Wasley, 1959) and Escapule (Hemmings and Haynes, 1969), where the remains of extinct mammoths were found in association with dart points of Paleo-Indian hunters. Dart points have also been reported in southwestern New Mexico (Fitting and Price, 1968) and northwestern Chihuahua (Di Peso, 1965), and they probably occur in northern Sonora (Di Peso, 1974: 64). One of the most important sites is Ventana Cave in the Arizona Papagueria (Haury, 1950). At Ventana Cave, materials from Paleo-Indian, Archaic, and Ceramic stages were found in good stratigraphic progression, establishing a firm archaeological sequence for the Borderlands.

The major Archaic tradition in the Borderlands is termed the Cochise Culture; it was discovered in the San Pedro Valley of southeastern Arizona (Sayles and Antevs, 1941). Cochise Culture sites have been well documented in southeastern Arizona (Whalen, 1975; Windmiller, 1973) and are known from southwestern New Mexico (Fitting, 1972*a*), Sonora (Fay, 1956*a*, 1959), and northern Chihuahua (Di Peso, 1974: 73).

Shortly before the time of Christ, ceramics and agriculture were introduced to the Borderlands. Archaeological cultures of the Ceramic stage are much better known than those of the preceding Paleo-Indian and Archaic stages. Because of the relative abundance of published material about the Ceramic stage, this review will be limited to an area about one hundred kilometers on either side of the international boundary.

The archaeology of the Ceramic stage of southern Arizona and southwestern New Mexico can best be understood with some knowledge of more extensively studied cultures to the north and south. Basic references and recent summaries of cultures north of the international boundary include Martin and Plog (1973) and Ortiz (1979). In Arizona, the important Hohokam Culture (Haury, 1976) centered on the middle Gila River area. The Salado complex, often associated with later Hohokam material, is known from several Borderlands areas in southeastern Arizona and southwestern New Mexico (Doyel and Haury, 1976). In southwestern New Mexico the Mogollon Culture (Wheat, 1955; LeBlanc and Whalen, 1979; and Everitt, 1973) is best known in the mountains and valleys north of the border, but also extends to the south. Readers interested in the archaeology of Chihuahua and Sonora should consult Di Peso (1966), A. E. Johnson (1966), T. Bowen (1976), Braniff and Felger (1976), and Bell (1974).

With increasing detail in archaeological knowledge, it becomes necessary to delimit archaeological areas. Such areas are the most convenient way to handle the published literature, reflecting the historical vagaries of archaeological fieldwork. At best, archaeological areas only approximate geographic divisions that might have been approved by prehistoric inhabitants. There is an interesting correspondence between the cultural areas defined by archaeologists and the national and state boundaries within which archaeologists operate. Rightly or wrongly, the international boundary is frequently projected onto archaeological data. Many archaeologists working in the southwestern United States see the archaeology immediately south of the border as an extension of the Southwest, while many archaeologists working in Mexico consider the Southwest a peripheral region of Mesoamerica. This point seems more important to Southwesternists than to Mesoamericanists (Riley and Hendrick, 1978).

The Chihuahua area, which is not synonymous with the state of Chihuahua, lies between the alkali flats below El Paso and the continental divide along the crest of the Sierra Madre Occidental. The area extends north into the extreme southwest corner of New Mexico. This area is best known for its large adobe towns of the Casas Grandes Culture. One of the largest of these, the trading center of Paquime at Casas Grandes, Chihuahua, was the focus of a large archaeological project during the late 1950s and early 1960s. The report of this project (Di Peso, 1974), in eight volumes, offers the definitive treatment of the archaeology of northern Chihuahua from A.D. 700 to colonial times. Earlier works (Sayles, 1936; Brand, 1935, 1943) are effectively superseded by Di Peso's report.

North of Chihuahua are the Animas and Playas valleys of southwestern New Mexico. The early work of the Peabody Museum (Cosgrove and Cosgrove, 1932; Kidder, Cosgrove, and Cosgrove, 1949), followed by several expeditions of the School of American Research (McCluney, 1962; Lambert and Ambler, 1961), defined the Animas phase. The term *Animas phase* has been used with several meanings in the archaeological literature, but the original definition refers to large, adobe, pueblolike towns associated with later Casas Grandes material and lasting up to colonial times. For more recent work in this area see Findlow and de Ately (1976).

The Sierra Madre Occidental, in part included in the Chihuahua area, is best known through the work of Robert H. Lister (1958, 1960). Cave sites, including masonry dwellings

in caves, were excavated by crews under Lister's direction. These sites show similarities with those of the Mogollon Culture of southwestern New Mexico. Large, open, pueblolike sites are known in the Río Bavispe Valley and in other valleys in the Sierra Madre Occidental, but none of these sites have been scientifically excavated and reported.

The area west of the Sierra Madre Occidental in northeast Sonora is the location of the Sonora Culture, best known through the reports of Pailes (in Braniff and Felger, 1976, and Riley and Hendrick, 1978). Architecture includes blocks of rooms, isolated rectangular structures and pithouses.

North-central Sonora, and particularly the upper tributaries of the Río Magdalena, are known archaeologically as the center of the Trincheras complex. *Trinchera,* meaning "fortification," refers to the most visible remains of this area, the concentrically walled and terraced *cerros de trincheras.* Prehistoric terracing of hills, which is quite extensive in some areas of north-central Sonora and extends into southern Arizona (Hoover, 1941) and southwestern New Mexico (Osborne and Hayes, 1938), may have been used for agriculture but more likely served a defensive function. Excellent early descriptions of Trincheras sites were given in Sauer and Brand (1931) and later in Hinton (1955) and A. E. Johnson (1963, 1966). Extensive systems of prehistoric agricultural check dams, also called *trincheras,* in the drainages of the Sierra Madre Occidental are described by Herold (1970).

The western end of the Arizona-Sonora Borderlands from the Colorado River to the Río Sonoita and Gila Bend, Arizona, and from the Gulf of California to the Gila River is not well known archaeologically. Paul H. Ezell, working in part for the National Park Service, reported on surveys of this area (Ezell, 1954, 1955) and outlined the distribution of ceramic types and associated cultures. Prehistoric architecture consists mainly of small rubble circles presumed to represent wickiuplike structures.

South central Arizona, called the Papaguería after the native Papagos, is better known than the western Arizona-Sonora area. Ventana Cave, mentioned above, is located there. Two village sites, Valshni (Withers, 1944, 1973) and Jackrabbit (Scantling, 1939), give some indication of the sequence and types of sites present, and several surveys (Gladwin and Gladwin, 1929; Stacy, 1975) indicate their distributions. An excellent summary of archaeological work in this area can be found in Masse (1980).

Southeastern Arizona is the most intensively studied of all archaeological areas along the border. Much of the work of the Gila Pueblo, the Amerind Foundation, and the Arizona State Museum has centered on this area, and the inventory of archaeological publications about it is extensive. In this review, only major reports and recent publications with complete bibliographies are noted.

Southeastern Arizona is a series of basins and ranges including the Santa Cruz, San Pedro, Sulphur Springs, and San Simon valleys. The early survey work of Sauer and Brand (1930) and Gladwin and Gladwin (1935) indicated that several cultural frontiers (including the Hohokam, Mimbres, and Salado cultures) were present, and subsequent work has demonstrated that this situation tends to give each valley a distinctive archaeological sequence (a situation which probably prevails over much of the Borderlands). Some outstanding reports of research in the Santa Cruz Valley include Di Peso (1956), Hayden (1957), Zahniser (1966), Greenleaf (1975), Grebinger (1976), and Doyel (1977). On the San Pedro River, Tuthill (1947) established a chronological framework that was later investigated by Di Peso (1951, 1958) and Franklin and Masse (1976). The Sulphur Springs Valley has had less intensive archaeological work, but major excavations of late Ceramic stage sites have been reported by Mills and Mills (1966) and Johnson and Thompson (1963). In the San Simon Valley, the major chronological divisions in the Ceramic stage were defined by Sayles (1945) and have not been altered in any major way by subsequent work. Because of the multitude of archaeological cultures and cultural frontiers in this area, no easy synthesis is possible and apparently none has been published. Sayles (1945), Sauer and Brand (1930), and Doyel and Haury (1976) probably offer the best overall picture of the area.

Archaeological work continues in the Borderlands. The reader interested in ongoing archaeological research in Arizona-Sonora and New Mexico-Chihuahua should contact the directors and staffs of two institutions which often function as clearinghouses for this sort of information: the Arizona State Museum and the Museum of New Mexico's Laboratory of Anthropology.

Beyond the intrinsic value of prehistoric archaeological sites, they must be considered as cultural resources to be conserved. Site destruction for commercial or other nonscientific purposes is noted in the earliest literature of the region and has continued unabated. Those most affected have contained Casas Grandes, Mimbres, and Salado artifacts, yet sites of any culture, at any stage, are subject to looting. Intact sites of the Mimbres Culture of southwest New Mexico are virtually nonexistent, and Casas Grandes sites on both sides of the border are rapidly meeting the same fate. The archaeological community is surprisingly fatalistic about this destruction, but some archaeologists (for example, LeBlanc, 1975) are attempting to slow the rate of archaeological pillaging through community education and legislation. However, the problem is largely economic, and its solution is beyond the control of professional archaeologists.

16

**Middle-Lower
Rio Grande
Archaeology**

THOMAS R. HESTER
*Center for Archaeological
Research
University of Texas at
San Antonio*

JACK D. EATON
*Center for Archaeological
Research
University of Texas at
San Antonio*

For purposes of this brief review, we define the lower and middle Rio Grande Borderlands as a zone roughly one hundred miles wide extending from the vicinity of the Big Bend National Park southward to the mouth of the Rio Grande. Diverse prehistoric and historic archaeological remains are found within this region. We first examine the long-lived hunting and gathering lifeways which dominated the region in prehistoric times. A discussion of the historic archaeology (written by Eaton) follows.

Prehistoric Archaeology

Although the chronological framework of the regional prehistory is not, for the most part, particularly well known, we can divide the archaeological evidence into three major temporal units: Paleo-Indian, Archaic, and Late Prehistoric. The Paleo-Indian period (cf. Hester, 1977) dates between 9200 B.C. and 6000 B.C.

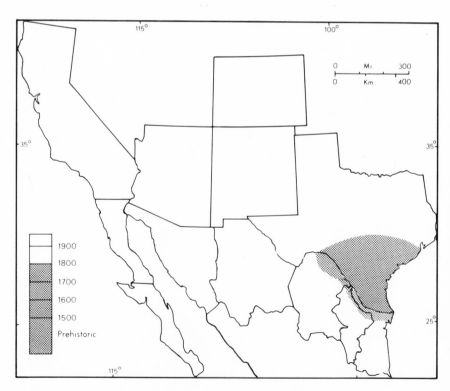

Within the early part of this era, hunting and gathering groups operated in a late Pleistocene environment. The most important Paleo-Indian site of this early phase, dating to ca. 8500 B.C., is Bonfire Shelter, located on a tributary canyon of the Rio Grande near Langtry, Texas (Dibble and Lorrain, 1968). The site was a kill locality used by peoples of the Folsom and Plainview complexes; groups of bison (*Bison antiquus* or *B. occidentalis*) were driven over the steep canyon wall and butchered in a sheltered area below. Several other sites are keys to our understanding of this period, particularly the later part. They reflect the shift from Pleistocene to early Holocene (essentially modern) environments. These sites include Devil's Mouth (Johnson, 1964; Sorrow, 1968) and Baker Cave (Word and Douglas, 1970; Hester, 1978*a*). At the latter locality there are well-preserved plant and animal remains associated with cultural materials of the Golondrina complex, radiocarbon dated at 7000 B.C.

The Archaic period represents a continuing hunting and gathering lifeway found along the entire middle and lower Rio Grande of Texas. An extensive array of chipped stone projectile points and tools, milling stones for the processing of plant food, and rock paintings in shelters and overhangs are all characteristic of this period, which lasted from 6000 B.C. to A.D. 1000. In the upper part of this region, in the area of the Big Bend and the lower Pecos River, rock shelters contain deposits with well-preserved Archaic cultural residues. Along the lower Rio Grande, open occupation sites are found on the terraces overlooking the river and its tributaries. The environment during the period was essentially a modern one, with moist and dry cycles but with a persisting trend toward aridity over time. This seven-thousand-year epoch has left a rich archaeological record throughout the region.

In the Late Prehistoric period (A.D. 1000 to historic contact) the hunting and gathering pattern continued throughout the region, but with the addition of new technological traits. Paramount among these was the introduction of the bow and arrow along with some new forms of chipped stone tools and, in some areas, the manufacture of plainware ceramics. In the Big Bend area, evidence of an agriculturally based population is found at La Junta de los Ríos (the confluence of the Rio Grande and the Río Conchos), influenced by cultural patterns of the American Southwest (see J. C. Kelley, various dates).

With the advent of European peoples, the hunting and gathering societies of the region were disrupted, with many groups being absorbed into the Spanish mission systems. At roughly the same time, in the late seventeenth and early eighteenth centuries, Apache and Comanche groups began to move into the area, further disturbing the cultural traditions which had developed over an eleven-thousand-year period.

Major Research in the Region

The lower and middle reaches of the Rio Grande in Texas and northern Mexico still have not been adequately investigated by archaeologists. There are exceptions, such as the Lake Amistad vicinity near the confluence of the Pecos and Devil's rivers with the Rio Grande. We review here some of the major research efforts—and resulting publications—within the region. The region is divided into four units: the Big Bend, the lower Pecos, the area from Eagle Pass to Falcon Reservoir, and the area of the mouth of the Rio Grande.

The Big Bend. This rugged area, part of the Chihuahuan Desert, has been investigated on a sporadic basis for more than fifty years. Early studies were reported in brief fashion (for example, Setzler, 1935; Coffin, 1932; V. J. Smith, 1931). The first comprehensive research program to encompass parts of the Big Bend was by Kelley, Campbell, and Lehmer (1940). In the 1960s, T. N. Campbell conducted two seasons of archaeological reconnaissance in the Park area (Campbell, 1967, 1970). More recently, the archaeology of the area has been summarized in a report prepared at Southern Methodist University (Bousman and Rohrt, 1974). Curtis Tunnell and his associates have also carried out a series of site studies within the deep canyons of the Rio Grande extending from Brewster to Terrell counties (Mallouf and Tunnell, 1977).

Typical archaeological sites in the Big Bend area include rock shelter occupations, open occupation sites, quarries, sites with numerous hearths, mortar hole areas (plant processing locales?), occasional burned rock middens, boulder enclosures, and rock art sites (both petroglyphs and pictographs).

An agriculturally based cultural pattern, with architecture and ceramics, is found at La Junta de los Ríos. These archaeological remains have been described as the Bravo Valley Aspect but have not been fully published (J. C. Kelley, 1949; Suhm, Krieger, and Jelks, 1954).

Lower Pecos Area. Prior to the period 1950-60, research in this area was also sporadic, although some major excavations like the work of Pearce and Jackson (1933) were undertaken. The area is typified by deeply entrenched canyons along the Rio Grande and the Pecos and Devil's rivers and the many canyon systems that are tributary to these rivers. Rock shelters are the dominant type of site, and because of the aridity and shelter afforded by such sites, they often contain well-preserved cultural remains. This phenomenon has made the rock shelters an important source of information for professional archaeologists, but it has also lured destructive relic collectors and looters who have destroyed literally hundreds of these irreplaceable sites.

When planning began on the construction of Diablo (later Amistad) Reservoir in the 1950s, a large-scale program of archaeological salvage was initiated (Graham and Davis, 1958). During the 1960s, surveys and excavations produced a wealth of scientific information on the sites of the area. While work did focus on the rock shelter sites, other types, including buried terrace, open occupation, and rock art sites, were also studied. Major reports include those for Eagle Cave (Ross, 1965), Parida Cave (Alexander, 1970), Centipede and Damp caves (Epstein, 1963), Devil's Mouth (L. Johnson, 1964; Sorrow, 1968), and others reported through testing and survey (Collins, 1969; Dibble and Prewitt, 1967).

The filling of Lake Amistad meant that hundreds of sites

in the canyons of the Rio Grande and the lower reaches of the Pecos and Devil's rivers were inundated and lost. Unfortunately, the presence of the lake also created easier access to some sites just above the waterline and on ranches which had, before the lake filled, been of difficult access. Thus, "motorboat pothunting" has led to even further destruction of surviving sites adjacent to the lake.

Avocational archaeologists have also carried out work in the area. The most notable project is the work of Word (1970) at Baker Cave on the fringe of the Amistad Lake area. Professional research has continued in the area in recent years, including excavations at Hinds Cave (Shafer and Bryant, 1977) and again at Baker Cave (Hester, 1978*a*).

As noted above, rock shelters are the major type of site in the area. Dry, dusty deposits within these sites will often be stratified, yielding a record of hunting and gathering cultures stretching back to Paleo-Indian times (cf. Word, 1970; Hester, 1978*a*). Along with chipped and ground artifacts, a wealth of other cultural materials is found, including such normally perishable artifacts as basketry, woven matting, sandals, nets, carved wood artifacts, plant remains, human coprolites, and other residues of daily life.

The shelters in which rock art (pictographs) occur are famous for panels of polychrome paintings probably related to hunting cults (Kirkland and Newcomb, 1967). One major site, Panther Cave, is accessible by boat but has been protected from vandals by the installation of a high chain-link fence across the mouth of the shelter.

Eagle Pass to Falcon Lake. This area, sometimes referred to as the "Middle Rio Grande" by Texas archaeologists, is rather poorly known. Terraces of the Rio Grande and its major tributary creeks contain both buried and exposed archaeological sites. Most of these are campsites which contain thousands of chipped stone artifacts and debris. The eroded surface sites have suffered a great deal from intensive arrowhead collecting by local relic hunters, deer hunters, oil-field workers, ranch personnel, and Border Patrol officers. Still, many of the sites on both sides of the Rio Grande offer substantial archaeological potential. Work by J. P. Nunley (part of the Gateway Project of The University of Texas at San Antonio) resulted in the documentation of more than 150 sites on both sides of the river from just above Eagle Pass, Texas, downstream to the vicinity of Guerrero, Coahuila. Nunley also conducted excavations at the Stockley site, a buried terrace site upstream from Eagle Pass (see Nunley, 1975, 1976).

In this same zone, work has been rather extensive in Texas some forty to fifty miles to the east. Sites of all cultural periods have been documented through research at Chaparrosa Ranch (T. R. Hester, 1975*a*, 1978*b*; Montgomery, 1978) and in nearby areas (cf. Hester and Hill, 1975; Hill and Hester, 1971).

To the south, in the Laredo area, site depredations by relic collectors have been devastating. However, Nunley (1971*b*), Shiner (1969), and Fox and Uecker (1978) have provided scientific data at a few sites. Downstream from Laredo, salvage archaeology in the early 1950s, preceding the construc-

tion of Falcon Dam, led to the recovery of data from both open and buried sites along the Rio Grande and its tributaries on both sides of the river (Cason, 1952; Aveleyra Arroyo de Anda, 1951). However, most of this research still remains unpublished.

Research in Mexico in the Eagle Pass-Falcon Reservoir zone has been minimal, aside from the work related to the construction of Falcon Dam noted above. The only significant published work is that by Mullerreid (1934), who described artifacts found during a survey of surface sites along the Río Sabinas in Coahuila.

Area of the Mouth of the Rio Grande. Aerial coverage includes the zone from just south of Falcon Reservoir to the mouth of the Rio Grande. In the upper part of this area, much archaeological work has been done in Starr County, Texas, particularly along the Arroyo los Olmos, a major tributary of the Rio Grande. Weir (1956) documented La Perdida, a major Paleo-Indian locality situated along the stream. More recent work by the University of Texas at San Antonio (UTSA) Center for Archaeological Research has led to the documentation of more than three hundred sites in the county (Nunley and Hester, 1976; notes on file at UTSA).

In the lower area, in Hidalgo, Willacy, and Cameron counties, some important work has been done by amateur archaeologists, including the pioneer research by A. E. Anderson (1932) and more recent field work by A. Vela (Mallouf, Baskin, and Killen, 1977). Much of this region is a flat alluvial delta which has been heavily modified by agriculture; this cultivation has, unfortunately, destroyed many sites in the area.

R. S. MacNeish (1958) conducted an extensive survey in the region on both sides of the river. He defined the Brownsville and Barril complexes, contemporary Late Prehistoric cultural patterns which are characterized by an important shell-working industry and apparent trade contacts with the Huastecan area of Mexico (see also Prewitt, 1974). Agricultural and municipal development in the area has revealed other archaeological remains, including large cemeteries related to the Brownsville complex (Hester, Collins, and Weir, 1969; Hester and Rodgers, 1971). In the past few years, additional survey work has been done as part of the planning process for various governmental projects for land modification. An outstanding example of such research is the monograph prepared by Mallouf, Baskin, and Killen (1977).

Syntheses. Recent syntheses of the archaeology of this region have been prepared by T. R. Hester (1978*c*, 1980) and may be consulted for additional details. Several papers or monographs have been published which synthesize the archaeology of the four subareas just reviewed. For the Big Bend, see Bousman and Rohrt (1974) and Lehmer (1960); for the lower Pecos area, see Shafer and Bryant (1977); for the Eagle Pass-Falcon Reservoir area, see Hester (1975*a*, 1975*b*, 1976); and for the lower Rio Grande, see MacNeish (1958), Nunley and Hester (1975), Mallouf, Baskin, and Killen (1977), and Hester (1978*c*). Some earlier syntheses of these regions are now largely outdated because of recent research; however, useful information is to be found in Sayles (1935); Suhm, Krieger, and Jelks (1954); and Kelley (1959).

Aboriginal Culture in the Early Historic Period

The native historic groups of this region were hunters and gatherers, apparently the descendants of millenia of local cultural groups. In the extant literature they are often referred to as "Coahuiltecans," a name, first applied in the nineteenth century, based on the misconception that these hundreds of hunting and gathering groups spoke the same language. Recent research by I. Goddard (1979) indicates the presence of at least six major linguistic groups in the South Texas area alone; it is probable that we will never know anything about many more such linguistic entities that were present throughout the region.

Additionally, the scattered and sketchy historic accounts about these groups left by the Spanish have been molded into an ethnographic mythology which attempts to characterize the "Coahuiltecan" lifeway (Ruecking, 1955b; Newcomb, 1961). These studies should be viewed with extreme scepticism, as more recent archival work done by T. N. Campbell indicates that we actually have very little cultural information which relates to specific hunting and gathering groups in the region in the early Historic period (cf. Campbell, 1975, 1977). Certainly the archaeology of the region serves to support the concept of considerable diversity among these ancient populations (cf. Hester, 1975c).

Historic Archaeology

The Historic period of the lower and middle Rio Grande of Texas is traditionally defined as that time when Europeans first entered the area during the mid-sixteenth century and is usually recognized by the presence of European cultural materials at archaeological sites.

In the Big Bend and lower Pecos areas of the Rio Grande the Historic period began with the *entrada* of Cabeza de Vaca in 1535. This *entrada* was followed by expeditions such as those of Rodriguez in 1581, Espejo in 1582, Gaspar de Sosa in 1590, and Juan Dominguez de Mendoza in 1684 (Bannon, 1964; Bolton, 1916; Hallenbeck, 1940; Hammond, 1927). In the early eighteenth century, missions and *presidios* were established in the middle Rio Grande region, and eventually ranches, mining camps, and small towns developed (Pierce, 1917). Our concern here will be only the archaeology done at sites of the Historic period along the middle and lower Rio Grande of Texas and the reports which have been published about these sites.

Although there have been a number of archaeological projects concerned with prehistoric sites in the Big Bend and lower Pecos, and nearly all of these are on the American side of the Rio Grande, a relatively small amount of work on historic sites has been done in this region. From the 1930s into the 1950s, J. C. Kelley conducted archaeological surveys and excavations in the Big Bend area, some of which dealt with prehistoric- and historic-period Indian pueblos at sites near Junta de los Ríos. In addition to descriptions of archaeological investigations of pit houses, Kelley's reports contain the locations and history of the area's aboriginal pueblos and also historical villages, missions, and settlements (Kelley, 1939, 1949, 1952, 1953). Some historical background dealing with the Rio Grande's Mexican side of this area is provided by Griffin (1969).

Other archaeological surveys conducted in the Big Bend area have located a variety of historical sites, but other than sampling by surface collections, few actual excavations were undertaken. A survey of the Presidio-Ojinaga area recorded historic Indian pit houses as well as Spanish and Anglo campsites (Holliday and Ivey, 1974). A reconnaissance in the lower canyons of the Rio Grande in the Big Bend-Pecos region located and described several historic sites which included ranch camps and candelilla wax camps (Mallouf and Tunnell, 1977). Archaeological investigations at Fort Leaton Historic Site have included excavations of several rooms providing artifacts dating the occupation of the fort from 1850 to 1920 (Jelks, 1969; Ing and Kegley, 1971). In the lower Pecos River area an archaeological survey was conducted of late-nineteenth-century Chinese labor camps on the Southern Pacific Railroad (Briggs, 1974).

In 1655 a military force led by Fernandez de Azcue on a punitive expedition against the Cacaxtles crossed the Rio Grande somewhere downstream from the present Eagle Pass (Bannon, 1964). This expedition appears to have been the first Spanish *entrada* into the area of the middle Rio Grande. During the later part of the seventeenth century several small missionary expeditions crossed the Rio Grande in the same area with the purpose of establishing contact with certain Indian groups living north of the river. These early crossings were probably made at Paso Pacuache and Paso de Francia located just a few miles from the present town of Vicente Guerrero in Coahuila, Mexico, where important Spanish colonial missions were later established at the beginning of the eighteenth century (Weddle, 1968a).

An architectural survey conducted in 1972-76 by the University of Texas at Austin School of Architecture recorded historical buildings in Eagle Pass, Texas, and Villa de Guerrero, Coahuila, Mexico (Osborne et al., 1976). In Eagle Pass the survey documented several structures dating from the middle to late nineteenth century, including the courthouse, residential houses, and structures at Fort Duncan. The architectural survey in Guerrero included the documentation of remaining buildings of Presidio del Rio Grande, the San Juan Bautista parish church, San Bernardo Mission church, and other structures in Guerrero of eighteenth- and nineteenth-century construction.

During 1975-76, the University of Texas at San Antonio conducted archaeological excavations at the sites of missions San Juan Bautista and San Bernardo, founded in 1700 and 1702, respectively. The missions, which were formally secularized in 1792, were finally abandoned shortly after the 1810 revolution (Adams et al., 1975, 1976, 1977). At the San Bernardo Mission site, where there still stands the mission church, UTSA excavations located the buried remains of the original mission church, monastery, and Indian housing. The San Juan Baustista mission excavations located the buried remains of several mission buildings, including the church, monastery, granary, workshops, and Indian housing. Also uncovered were the remains of a large circular bastion attached to the Indian apartments.

At Fort McIntosh in Laredo, Texas, extensive testing in several areas of the Old Fort McIntosh Historical District sampled cultural materials dating from both the early (1853) and later (1897) periods of fort use. Fort McIntosh was originally founded in 1849 and served as an important frontier post until it was officially closed as a U.S. Army establishment in 1949 (Ivey, Medlin, and Eaton, 1977; Fox, 1978).

Downstream from Laredo, in the Falcon Lake area, extensive salvage archaeology at prehistoric sites was undertaken; however, historic site work was limited to locating 21 historic sites during surveys (Krieger and Hughes, 1950), excavating four historic houses at two of the sites, and documenting historical architecture dating from 1760 and 1850 in the Falcon Reservoir area between Rincon and Falcon, Texas (George, 1975).

Very little historic archaeology has been done in the lower and delta regions of the Rio Grande. A survey in Hidalgo County where flood control construction was planned located two historic Anglo occupation sites (Brown, 1972). Downstream, in the Brownsville area, some archaeological work was done at the Palo Alto battleground located 12 miles north of Brownsville. The first battle of the Mexican War took place here in 1846 (Baxter and Killen, 1976). At the nearby Mexican War battlefield of Resaca de la Palma, M. B. Collins, T. R. Hester, and T. S. Ellzey, in 1967, conducted emergency excavations of a mass burial of Mexican soldiers killed in the battle. The burials had been exposed by subdivision development (Hester, 1978c).

Just above the mouth of the Rio Grande, in the delta region along the Brownsville Ship Channel, and on Brazos Island, three historic sites were recorded and tested (Hall and Grombacher, 1974). The sites included an early historic-period Indian campsite and a military encampment site near the ship channel. The Brazos Santiago Depot—a port facility, military encampment, and supply depot on Brazos Island—was also studied. This site was intermittently occupied by various peoples and facilities from 1523 until it was abandoned in the 1880s.

Section II. Geography and the Environment

Aridity in varying degrees dominates the physical environment of the Border-lands. From the mouth of the Rio Grande to Baja California, dryness is re-vealed in the vegetation and landforms. The breadth of the Borderlands is char-acterized from east to west by the progression from semiarid steppe to the ultimate in aridity, the desert. The major interruptions in this pattern are the forests found in the high elevations of the southern Rocky Mountains and their two southerly prongs in Mexico, the Sierra Madre Occidental and the Sierra Madre Oriental. Even at high elevations, one senses the dryness in the air; views the clear, spacious sky above and in the distance the haze caused by dust, sand, and heat; and enjoys the cooler temperatures largely by imagining the heat in the settlements below. Aridity is a fact in the Borderlands, and man's perception of how to cope with it has largely determined his settlement locations and land use patterns.

17

Environmental Overview

ALVAR W. CARLSON
Department of Geography
Bowling Green State University

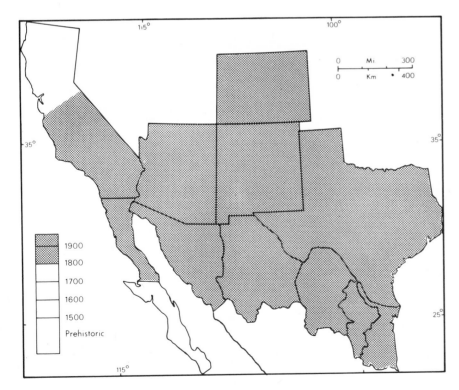

Climate

It is fortunate for those who use the land that the region receives most of its annual precipitation in the summer months when it can be beneficial to crops and pastures. An exception to this pattern is found in southern California, where most of the annual precipitation occurs in winter. For much of the Borderlands, the major source of summer precipitation is the Gulf of Mexico. Moist tropical air, associated with a high-pressure cell, is swept by winds or storms from the Gulf inland as far west as the Sierra Madre Occidental and eastern Arizona. The storms and showers that begin in early July are referred to collectively as the "monsoon" season (Hales, 1974*b*). Aside from the highest mountainous areas and coastal California, the coastal lowlands of Texas and Tamaulipas receive the greatest amounts of annual precipitation in the Borderlands—approximately 30-35 inches. On occasion, hurricanes generate some of this precipitation. Similar amounts of precipitation occur in the Sierra Madre Occidental, with slightly lesser amounts in other high elevations such as the Sangre de Cristo and San Juan mountains of the upper Rio Grande Valley in south central Colorado and northern New Mexico, the Sacramento and Guadalupe mountains of southeastern New Mexico, the Mogollon Rim of central Arizona, and the San Gabriel and San Bernardino mountains of southern California. These areas of comparatively high precipitation constitute only small parts of the Borderlands.

The rest of the area influenced by the Gulf of Mexico receives between ten and twenty inches of precipitation annually, except for the Rio Grande trough, the Jornado del Muerto (located between Albuquerque and El Paso), and that part of the Mesa del Norte found in eastern Chihuahua between the Sierra Madre Oriental and the Sierra Madre Occidental. The latter area, referred to in Mexico as the Chihuahuan Desert, receives five to ten inches of precipitation annually.

It is to the west of the Sierra Madre Occidental that the driest conditions prevail and that desert, particularly the Sonoran Desert and its various components, dominates the landscapes (Ives, 1949; Vivó and Gomez, 1946). The entire area receives less than ten inches of precipitation annually, with certain locales, such as central Baja California and the Colorado River delta, receiving less than five inches. Although the Pacific Ocean is the primary source of precipitation in the western Borderlands, the upwelling of colder water in summer, particularly along the California coast, and the offshore southward-flowing cool water of the California Current produce only modest amounts of atmospheric moisture. Furthermore, the Sonoran Desert is in the rain shadow of air masses moving over the Sierra Madre Occidental in summer and the peninsular mountains of Baja California in winter. The Sonoran Low, which is centered over the desert in summer, also works against producing precipitation. Occasionally there is considerable precipitation in late summer and early fall that results from the tail ends of tropical cyclones or hurricanes *(chubascos)* that originate off the west coast of Mexico in the Pacific Ocean (Aschmann, 1959*a*;

Henderson, 1966; Jaeger and Smith, 1966). Southern California receives most of its precipitation in winter as the high-pressure cell located in the northern Pacific Ocean in summer moves southward, weakens, and becomes centered off Baja California. Storms with considerable precipitation occur in December in the Los Angeles area, for example, and they even extend inland as far as northern Arizona.

Throughout the Borderlands, precipitation is basically seasonal; there are comparatively wet and pronounced dry seasons. Most of the precipitation originates with the flow of air masses, but there is also some precipitation, largely local, produced by thunderstorms caused by convective activity due to high temperatures. The summer storms are intense but quite localized, and they may cause floods (Leopold, 1942, 1945). Generally, the amount of summer precipitation tends to be less variable from year to year than does the amount of winter precipitation. Severe and extensive summer droughts do occur in this arid region. They have been diagnosed as occurring in cycles in which the added deficiency greatly affects the surface and underground sources of water (Thomas et al., 1963*a*-1963*e*). It is believed that there are climatic changes taking place in the Borderlands which could further affect the availability of water resources (Von Eschen, 1958).

Winds are important in bringing precipitation to the different parts of the Borderlands, yet they also contribute to aridity. Coupled with the intense sunshine and heat resulting from cloudless days, especially in summer, and the subtropical location in latitude, winds help to evaporate moisture from the ground and air and produce conditions of low relative humidity. It is the excessive evaporation—up to one hundred inches annually—that makes deserts of certain areas. Numerous localized dust devils, sand spouts, or whirlwinds *(tornillos)* occur in late spring and summer as the high temperatures intensify. Sandstorms and *haboobs,* convectional dome-shaped dust clouds that can rise to ten thousand feet and extend to one hundred miles in breadth and become thunderstorms, characterize these deserts (Idso, 1974). Destructive tornadoes also develop in the Borderlands; annually there are approximately five in Arizona and several dozen in Texas.

Although temperatures are quite predictable throughout the year, extremes are experienced in both winter and summer. Below-zero Fahrenheit temperatures and considerable snow can make winters severe in northern New Mexico and Arizona (Tuan, Everard, and Widdison, 1969). Most of the Borderlands has a mild, dry winter with much sunshine, however. Occasionally, cold northers or *nortes* move into the Borderlands as far south as coastal Tamaulipas, bringing with them killing frosts. Except for the higher elevations in northern New Mexico and Arizona, the first killing frost in the fall normally occurs after September 30. Thus, much of the Borderlands has over 160 frost-free days. In the Rio Grande Valley of Texas, the desert areas of southwestern Arizona and southern California, the coastal area of southern California, and the border states of Mexico, the first killing frost comes after November 30. These areas have growing seasons of over 240 frost-free days (Espenshade and Morrison, 1978; Foscue, 1932*b*; Sellers and Hill, 1974).

Natural Vegetation

The consequences of aridity are vividly revealed in the amounts, types, and distributions of natural vegetation in the Borderlands. Generally, the area influenced by Gulf air masses has more perennial steppe grasses and forests than do the desert areas west of the Sierra Madre Occidental. Coastal Tamaulipas, the lower Rio Grande Valley, and central Texas are characterized by patches of short mesquite grass and mesquite. Halophytes are found in the salt marshes of the Rio Grande delta. In Texas, the mesquite vegetation fades into the grassy oak-hickory forests to the northeast and into the gramas and buffalo grasses of the High Plains in western Texas and eastern New Mexico. The large *meseta,* including the Chihuahua Desert, between the Sierra Madre Oriental and the Sierra Madre Occidental features mostly clumps of broadleaf deciduous shrubs. These are xerophytes, principally mesquite and sotol interspersed by short bunch grass. The taproot of a mesquite may penetrate forty to fifty feet in search of water. Mesquite forests can be very useful for firewood (Olson, 1940).

Needleleaf evergreen trees are found in the high elevations of the Sierra Madre Occidental and in the mountainous areas of the American Borderlands. They are largely pines or a combination of pines and junipers. Growing in the high Sangre de Cristo Mountains in northern New Mexico are spruce and fir trees and the deciduous aspen. Alpine tundra can be found above the timberline, which is over eleven thousand feet in the case of the San Francisco Mountains of northern Arizona. Piñon pines and scrub oaks often grow at lower elevations in the foothills. Between these mountainous areas are expanses of semiarid short gramas interspersed with sagebrush.

Patches of true desert shrubs cover most of the desert west of the Sierra Madre Occidental except in coastal southern California and northern Baja California. Creosote bush and other broadleaf evergreen shrubs constitute much of the desert vegetation, and where there is alkalinity, saltbush is found. Woody plants without leaves are also characteristic of the desert. These include ocotillo, palo verde, yuccas, and various types of cacti, the notable desert succulents. The vegetation of coastal southern California and northern Baja California is characterized by sagebrush, manzanita, and chamise, all broadleaf evergreen shrubs. Chaparral is, however, the distinctive vegetation there.

It is difficult to generalize about natural vegetation in a region that surpasses all others in the United States in its number of different major classifications of plants (Espenshade and Morrison, 1978; Hastings, Turner, and Warren, 1972). Local conditions such as exposure, terrain, elevation, alkalinity, and amount of precipitation create microbiotic niches for some exotic plants. Examples include the giant daggers *(Yucca carnerosana)* of northern Coahuila, the saguaro of south central Arizona, and the Joshua tree of the Mojave Desert.

Physiography

There is no doubt that the Borderlands are topographically varied, but they can be described as a region of parallel, discontinuous southerly extensions of the major mountain systems of the western United States that flank either intermontane plateaus or linear basins, valleys, and troughs. This description does not, however, apply to most of Texas, especially the High Plains and the Gulf Coastal Plain extending into Tamaulipas. One major extension of the Rocky Mountains is the high Sangre de Cristo Range of south central Colorado and north central New Mexico which leads discontinuously to the Sacramento and Guadalupe ranges of southern New Mexico and western Texas and eventually to the Sierra Madre Oriental in Coahuila and Nuevo León. Another major extension of the Rocky Mountains is the San Juan Range of southwestern Colorado and northwestern New Mexico. This extension reappears in several low ranges west of the Rio Grande and in southeastern Arizona and then becomes the Sierra Madre Occidental in Chihuahua and eastern Sonora. It forms the continental divide which separates the two major watersheds of the Borderlands: the Rio Grande, which drains to the Gulf of Mexico, and the Colorado River, which drains to the Gulf of California (Sykes, 1937).

All these mountain ranges serve as barriers to moisture-laden air which comes mostly from the Gulf of Mexico, and thus they produce both orographic precipitation at higher elevations and rain shadows. Much of the orographically produced runoff eventually reaches the Rio Grande system, but a considerable portion enters interior drainage basins. Long and narrow structural basins, known as *bolsones,* frequently have no external drainage and are the sites of playas (Hovey, 1905). Much of the *meseta* between the Sierra Madre Oriental and the Sierra Madre Occidental is drained to the interior, as in the case of the Bolsón de Mapimi of Coahuila and eastern Chihuahua. Other extensive areas of interior drainage are found along the border in northern Chihuahua, southeastern Arizona, southwestern New Mexico, and western Texas.

The coastal mountains of southern California extend into Baja California and in essence separate the Pacific Ocean from the Gulf of California. Fault lines lie parallel to these mountains. The Sierra Nevada reaches into southern California where the San Gabriel and San Bernardino mountains enclose the heavily populated Los Angeles Basin. The desert and Colorado Plateau found between these mountains and the continental divide are drained by the Colorado River system. Elevations in this vast area range from below sea level in Death Valley and the Salton Sea to the high source of the Colorado River in the Rocky Mountains west of Denver. The Colorado River drains a huge watershed that not only provides much valuable water for the driest sections of the Borderlands but also deposits detrital material in the form of an extensive delta in the Gulf of California. California's Mojave Desert and Death Valley are not in this drainage system.

Instead, they belong with most of Nevada in a vast area of interior drainage.

Continuous weathering and erosion have had their impact upon the arid and sparsely covered landforms of the Borderlands and in many cases have resulted in spectacular sites for tourists. There are the unique arches, spoollike pinnacles, and colorful strata of Arizona's Painted Desert and especially the awesome Grand Canyon and the Canyon de Chelly. Desert *pedregales* or glazed stone pavements form fascinating mosaics. Because of the incessant winds and lack of dense vegetal cover, fairly large sand dunes *(médanos)* and small knob dunes are fairly widespread; the most spectacular of them are the Great Sand Dunes in the San Luis Valley of south central Colorado. The color and feeling of the Borderlands' landforms have been captured by artists like Georgia O'Keeffe and in pictorial magazines, particularly *Arizona Highways.*

Perceptions of the Physical Environment

Anglo-American perceptions of this physical environment have changed. In the 1800s the eastern part of the region was included in what was labeled as the Great American Desert. The notion that the Borderlands were a region of barren, brown wastelands, badlands or *malpais,* and stifling hot deserts was commonly held by many eastern Anglos. Some undoubtedly still perceive the area this way. For years the American Southwest was shunned by settlers, some parts such as the Big Bend country of west Texas longer than others (Madison, 1968).

Interestingly enough, in the late 1800s the Borderlands came to be known for their reputedly therapeutic values which enhanced one's longevity. The cool nights, dry air, sunshine, low relative humidity, lack of fog, high elevations, well-drained soils, and coastal salt breezes all reportedly contributed to a mild, comfortable climate that was excellent for recovery from pulmonary diseases (Carrington, 1907; B. M. Jones, 1967; Splitter, 1969; Tuan and Everard, 1964). Consequently, different areas of the Southwest became known for their natural sanatoriums. The popularity of the region grew, and, for example, from the 1890s onward Tucson was sought out for heliotropic reasons of health and pleasure (Parker, 1948). Earlier, the Spaniards were to consider some of the same health-related environmental factors in selecting settlement sites (Stanislawski, 1947).

Not all Anglo-Americans thought that the Borderlands were a healthful place to live. There was considerable controversy over the practice of irrigation in California's Central Valley. Opponents of irrigation contended that large-scale irrigation caused insalubrious or miasmatic conditions which gave rise to diseases such as ague (malaria) (Thompson, 1969a, 1969b). It was also suggested that the frequent sandstorms on the High Plains of western Texas and eastern New Mexico were detrimental to health (Sidwell, 1938). They were linked to the comparatively high incidence of ear, throat, and sinus problems and pneumonia.

Man-made Changes

In the past century, people have rather dramatically changed the Borderlands' physical environment and landscapes. For example, they have diverted surface water and have mined underground aquifers. Both activities have by and large anchored man in this arid region. Although the Indians and Spaniards practiced irrigation, Anglos are responsible for the large irrigation projects found today in many valleys and on the High Plains. Agriculture has historically been the region's largest consumer of water, but there have been growing demands by industrial, urban, and recreational interests.

These demands have led to the construction of numerous canals and reservoirs and several transmountain projects which take water from high-yield watersheds to the rainshadow sides of given basins. Water reclamation, desalination, and weather modification efforts such as cloud seeding to artificially induce precipitation have been attempted to increase the supply of water. The overall scarcity of water has led to the development of water management, irrigation districts, and controversies which have intrastate, interstate, and international implications. This is not to mention the questions that arise over the doctrines of rights applied to both surface and underground water. The problem of salinity caused by irrigation has led to abandonment of cropland and considerable controversy between Mexico and the United States in the lower Colorado Valley. Probably the most visible man-made changes to the physical environment related to water have been in the draining of Owens Lake and the creation of the Salton Sea and the many large reservoirs.

Early accounts of parts of the Borderlands mention luxuriant natural vegetation, especially the "stirrup-high" grasses. Vegetational changes—namely, the disappearance of lush grasslands and the continuous invasion of less desirable plant types—have prompted considerable explanatory research (Bahre and Bradbury, 1978; Buffington and Herbal, 1965; Cooper, 1960; Harris, 1966; Humphrey and Mehrhoff, 1958; Leopold, 1951; Shreve and Hinckley, 1937; York and Dick-Peddie, 1969). First, the lush grasses described in the early accounts may have been very localized, and it may be a fallacy to apply such descriptions to most of the region. It is generally conceded, however, that grasslands have been invaded rather rapidly by a number of woody species, commonly mesquite. Why has there been a general diminution of grass cover which has allowed this invasion to occur? Most of the research points to overgrazing by livestock as the major cause. Other explanations include periodic droughts, the lack of range fires which would have prevented the seeds from propagating, the dissemination of seeds by livestock, and the lowering of water tables which precluded the growth of the indigenous plants but was conducive to the new, undesirable plants. Tampering with stream flow has also led to the replacement of indigenous plants by exotic plants as, for instance, in the Grand Canyon (Dolan, Howard, and Gallenson, 1974).

Vegetational changes in the Borderlands are surely related to an increased number of arroyos. Arroyos are gullies or stream entrenchments with rather steep walls and flat floors. There are basically two theories to explain the accelerated erosion of the past century. One is that overgrazing by livestock reduced and changed the vegetal cover, leading to more surface runoff, and the other is that there have been climatic changes or at least fluctuations which, in general, have produced greater aridity (Bryan, 1925, 1928, 1940; I. A. Campbell, 1970; Cooke and Reeves, 1976; Denevan, 1967; Deppa, 1948; Fleming, 1933; Hastings, 1959; Hastings and Turner, 1965a; Judson, 1952; Leighly, 1936; Thornthwaite, Sharpe, and Dosch, 1941, 1942; Tuan, 1966). These fluctuations have also been characterized by an increase in high-intensity showers. The latter argument is advocated by those who note that there is evidence of prehistoric gullies in alluvium before man introduced livestock to the region. Even among these researchers there is a consensus that livestock grazing has had some impact on accelerating the erosion process. Arroyos have caused loss of irrigable land and have increased downstream sedimentation or siltation, a problem for a number of reservoirs.

Although there have been mining activities in the region for centuries, few operations have so changed the physical landscape or aroused people as those currently underway in the Four Corners area and at Black Mesa in northern Arizona (Durrenberger, 1972). The large-scale strip mining of coal there since 1971 has raised questions concerning revegetation and the impact upon the quality of both surface and ground water.

Without doubt, man's behavior has changed the air quality of the Borderlands. Spatially, some areas have worse air quality than others, but in nearly all cases the problem areas are associated with urbanization. Based upon several aerial contaminants, a number of the region's cities—El Paso, Denver, Phoenix, Albuquerque, and Los Angeles—rank near the top nationally in air pollution. Air pollution is attributable to many factors, including vehicular emissions, power generation, waste elimination, and industrial activity. Particular physiographic features may entrap the foul air, as in the case of Los Angeles, and accentuate the persistence and severity of the problem (Applegate and Bath, 1974; Bland, 1974a, 1974b, 1976; Haagen-Smit, 1964; Mason, 1974; Reith, 1951; Telloz, 1972; Utton, 1973).

Basic Source Materials

Regional studies that contain information on the physical environment of most of the American Borderlands include those by John W. Morris, *The Southwestern United States;* Clifford M. Zierer, *California and the Southwest;* and Elna Bakker and Richard G. Lillard, *The Great Southwest: The Story of a Land and Its People,* a colorful photographic account. There are many more state studies that can be recommended. For California there are Robert W. Durrenberger, *Elements of California Geography;* David N. Hartman, *California and Man;* David W. Lantis et al., *California: Land of Contrast;* and the more specialized works of Edmund C.

Jaeger and Arthur C. Smith, *Introduction to the Natural History of Southern California;* Harry P. Bailey, *The Climate of Southern California;* and Ernest L. Felton, *California's Many Climates.* For Arizona there are *Arizona: Its People and Resources* (the first edition was edited by Jack L. Cross et al.); Charles H. Lowe, *Arizona's Natural Environment, Landscapes and Habitats;* U.S. Congress, Committee on Interior and Insular Affairs, *Mineral and Water Resources of Arizona;* and the more specialized publications by William D. Sellers and Richard H. Hill, editors, *Arizona Climate, 1931-1972* (the first edition was edited by Christine R. Green and William D. Sellers); H. V. Smith, *The Climate of Arizona;* and Frank W. Gould, *Grasses of Southwestern United States.* For New Mexico there are Paige W. Christiansen and Frank E. Kottlowski, editors, *Mosaic of New Mexico's Scenery, Rocks, and History,* and Yi-Fu Tuan et al., *The Climate of New Mexico.* And for Texas there are Robert B. Orton, *The Climate of Texas and the Adjacent Gulf Waters,* and Richard J. Russell, "Climates of Texas," *Annals, Association of American Geographers.*

It is interesting that studies which tend to disregard political boundaries concern deserts. Notable among these are Roger Dunbier, *The Sonoran Desert, Its Geography, Economy, and People;* Ronald L. Ives, "Climate of the Sonoran Desert Region," *Annals, Association of American Geographers;* Edmund C. Jaeger, *The North American Deserts;* M. P. Petrov, *Deserts of the World;* and John C. Van Dyke, *The Desert.* There are also those studies of deserts which are limited to one side of the international border: Ruth Kirk, *Desert: The American Southwest;* Philip Welles, *Meet the Southwest Deserts;* Edmund C. Jaeger, *The California Deserts;* and Homer Aschmann, *The Central Desert of Baja California: Demography and Ecology.* Other studies which overlap the border are Howard G. Applegate and C. Richard Bath, *Air Pollution along the United States-Mexico Border;* C. Wayne Burnham, *Metallogenic Provinces of the Southwestern United States and Northern Mexico;* Fred B. Kniffen, *The Natural Landscape of the Colorado Delta;* and Godfrey Sykes, *The Colorado Delta.*

Although there is no study pertaining only to the physical environment of the Mexican Borderlands, there are a good number of general works which contain much information on the area. One should consult the following: Claude Bataillon, *Las regiones geográficas en Mexico;* Donald D. Brand, *Mexico, Land of Sunshine and Shadow;* Jesus Galindo y Villa, *Geografía de la República Mexicana;* Hans G. Gierloff-Emden, *Mexico: Eine Landeskunde;* David A. Henderson, "Land, Man, and Time" in *Six Faces of Mexico* (edited by Russell C. Ewing); Jorge L. Tamayo, *Geografía general de México* (Vols. I and II); Jorge A. Vivó, *Geografía de Mexico;* Thomas E. Weil et al., *Area Handbook for Mexico;* and Robert C. West and John P. Augelli, *Middle America: Its Lands and Peoples.* More specialized publications include those by M. Walter Pesman, *Meet Flora Mexicana;* Ben Tinker, *Mexican Wilderness and Wildlife;* Jorge A. Vivó and José C. Gomez, *Climatologia de Mexico;* and Stuart D. Scott, *Dendrochronology in Mexico,* mostly concerning northwestern Chihuahua. Other excellent studies on Chihuahua are by Donald D. Brand, *The Natural Landscape of Northwestern Chihuahua;* and Robert H. Schmidt, Jr., *A Geographical Survey of Chihuahua.*

The following useful bibliographies might also be consulted: Ellen C. Barrett, *Baja California II, 1535-1964;* Alvar W. Carlson, "A Bibliography of the Geographers' Contributions to Understanding the American Southwest (Arizona and New Mexico) 1920-1971," *Arizona Quarterly;* Charles C. Cumberland, "The United States-Mexican Border: A Selective Guide to the Literature of the Region," *Rural Sociology;* Robert W. Durrenberger, "A Selected California Bibliography," *California Geographer;* Lyle Saunders, *A Guide to Materials Bearing on Cultural Relations in New Mexico;* Frances Leon Swadesh, *20,000 Years of History: A New Mexico Bibliography;* and Richard Yates and Mary Marshall, *The Lower Colorado River: A Bibliography.* An excellent source of references is the *Research Catalog of the American Geographical Society,* Vol. 5, *United States-South Central and West,* and Vol. 6, *Mexico and Latin America,* and the subsequent monthly additions of *Current Geographical Publications.*

Geology is concerned with the age, composition, structure, and distribution of rock units. Each rock is assigned to one of four geological eras: Precambrian rocks are older than 600 million years, Paleozoic rocks are 225 million to 600 million years old, Mesozoic rocks date back 65 million to 225 million years, and rocks younger than 65 million years are assigned to the Cenozoic Era (Table 18-1). Because rocks of the older eras tend to be buried by younger deposits, their surface expression in the Borderlands is restricted to areas in which unstable portions of the earth's crust have been uplifted. The further division of the Mesozoic and Cenozoic eras into periods is especially helpful in discussing the geology of the Borderlands because practically all Borderlands rock structures and the landscapes developed on them are no older than Mesozoic.

Most Borderlands rocks are sedimentary in origin, having accumulated on the floors and coasts of ancient seas, along river courses, in desert basins, and even on lake bottoms. The older of the sedimentary units are well compacted and

18

Geology and Landforms

JERRY E. MUELLER
Department of Earth Sciences
New Mexico State University

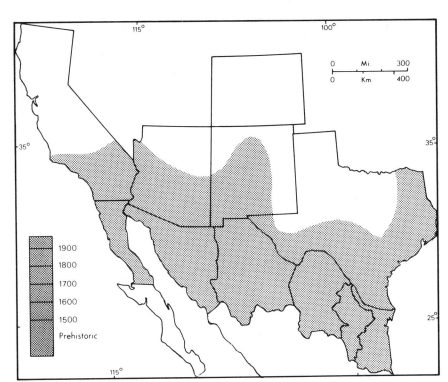

Table 18-1. *Geologic Time Scale*

Era	Period	Age (millions of years before present)
Cenozoic	Quaternary Tertiary	
		65
Mesozoic	Cretaceous Jurassic Triassic	
		225
Paleozoic	Undifferentiated here	
		600
Precambrian	None recognized	
		4500

consolidated, whereas many of the Tertiary and Quaternary deposits are only poorly consolidated. Some rocks of the Borderlands are classed as igneous, having solidified from molten magma that either invaded older rocks or made its way to the earth's surface in the form of lava flows. A few rocks are classed as metamorphic—those sedimentary and igneous units which have been altered by heat and/or pressure in areas of mountain building and volcanic activity. Particularly useful geologic maps that show the distribution of these rock types within the Borderlands include those of Dane and Bachman (1965); Jennings (1977); King and Beikman (1974); López Ramos (1976); Renfro, Feray, and King (1973); and Wilson, Moore, and Cooper (1969).

Geomorphology is concerned with the origin and description of landforms. Most landforms in their broadest outline reveal a strong geologic influence, especially that of rock structure (whether the rock is folded, faulted, domed, or so on), whereas many of the intricate features of the landscape are attributable to erosional agents such as running water and the wind. Broad geologic structures and the landforms developed on them have been regionalized into physiographic units by a number of geographers and geologists. In the discussion which follows, the physiographic regions of the Borderlands have been adapted from Fenneman (1931, 1938), Ordoñez (1936, 1941), Atwood (1940), Lobeck (1948), Raisz (1964), Thornbury (1965), and Hunt (1974).

Gulf Coastal Plain

The Coastal Plain extends uninterrupted along the West Gulf Coast region of Texas and Tamaulipas (Fig. 18-1). Its western boundary is the abrupt escarpment of the Edwards Plateau in south central Texas and the eastern base of the Sierra Madre Oriental in Mexico. In general, the Coastal Plain is wider in the United States than in Mexico, reaching a maximum width of 250 miles in the zone between the Rio Grande and the Nueces River in South Texas. The structure underlying the Coastal Plain is one of poorly consolidated sedimentary marine units which dip gently toward the Gulf of Mexico. Upper Cretaceous limestones, chalks, and clays in the west are overlapped seaward by progressively younger Tertiary and Quaternary clays, sands, and river alluvium, offering evidence of a retreating shoreline since Cretaceous times.

Elevations on the Coastal Plain range from sea level at the coast to one thousand feet near Del Rio, Texas. Relief across this plain is very low, averaging less than a few hundred feet toward the interior and less than fifty feet along the immediate coast (Hammond, 1963). Most prominent among the Coastal Plain features are cuestas: long, narrow belts of hills that run parallel to the coast and are developed on the outcrop of the more resistant limestones and sandstones. Cuestas typically are steeper on the west than on the east and usually attain heights of no more than a few hundred feet above the surrounding plain. The Bordas-Oakville Cuesta of South Texas and its Mexican equivalent, the Reynosa Cuesta, form a continuous belt that extends for hundreds of miles on both sides of the border and is breached only by the Rio Grande near Camargo (Murray, 1961: 536-37).

The immediate coastline is best described as a prograding or depositional one. There, rivers have built large deltas into the Gulf, while wave action and longshore currents have remolded some of the sand into huge offshore bars that fringe the coast. Padre Island, which parallels the Texas coast for more than one hundred miles between Brownsville and Corpus Christi, averages one to two miles in width and is surmounted by sand dunes that occasionally reach seventy-five feet in height. Equally large offshore bars dominate the coast of Tamaulipas between the mouths of the Rio Grande and the Río Soto la Marina. Between the bars and the coast are numerous lagoons and irregular embayments. The bays, called estuaries, represent the mouths of coastal rivers that have been drowned by the postglacial rise in sea level of approximately 250 feet.

Crustal movements along the western margin of the Coastal Plain have exposed a few igneous rocks. Near Uvalde, Texas, the Cenozoic Balcones Fault system has exposed portions of a Cretaceous intrusion that invaded a still older sedimentary cover. Early Tertiary intrusions into Cretaceous rocks have been described in several domed and folded uplifts that occur along a line between Tampico and Ciudad Acuña, most notably in the Sierra San Carlos and the Sierra de Tamaulipas (Eardley, 1962: 661). A real anomaly with respect to Coastal Plain geology is the extensive late Tertiary volcanic field of the Sierra del Aldama some fifty miles north of Tampico. In general the Coastal Plain is narrower, is more deformed structurally, has greater relief, and has more volcanic activity in the vicinity of Tampico than in the areas to the north.

Edwards Plateau

West of the Coastal Plain in south central Texas is an uplifted structural plain known as the Edwards Plateau. The southern and eastern margins of the plateau are rather sharply

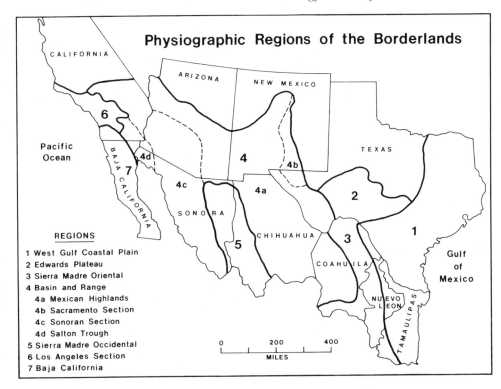

Physiographic Regions of the Borderlands

REGIONS
1 West Gulf Coastal Plain
2 Edwards Plateau
3 Sierra Madre Oriental
4 Basin and Range
  4a Mexican Highlands
  4b Sacramento Section
  4c Sonoran Section
  4d Salton Trough
5 Sierra Madre Occidental
6 Los Angeles Section
7 Baja California

Fig. 18-1.
*Physiographic
regions of the
Borderlands.*

defined by the outward-facing escarpment of the Balcones Fault. The western extension of the plateau into Trans-Pecos Texas, known as the Stockton Plateau, terminates at the eastern boundary of the Basin and Range Physiographic Province. To the north, the Edwards Plateau merges almost imperceptibly into the High Plains of West Texas.

The surface elevations of the plateau decrease from west to east, with maximum elevations of about four thousand feet on the Stockton Plateau and an average of only fifteen hundred feet at the Balcones Escarpment. Underlying this surface is a sequence of Lower Cretaceous sedimentary marine units that dip gently eastward. Several of these units are collectively known as the Fredericksburg Group, of which the Edwards Limestone is the dominant caprock on the plateau. The Edwards Limestone is a relatively pure, massive, resistant carbonate rock that reaches thicknesses of six hundred to seven hundred feet along the southeast margins of the plateau (Sellards, Adkins, and Plummer, 1932: 322-59).

Relief on the Edwards Plateau varies considerably. Most of the streams which originate on the plateau drain eastward and cross the Balcones Escarpment in a series of steep canyons and valleys. These rivers and their tributaries have dissected the escarpment into a series of high rolling hills. Farther west, the Stockton Plateau has been severed from the main Edwards Plateau by the one-thousand-foot-deep canyon of the Pecos River, the only drainage line to cross the entire plateau. According to Hammond (1963), most of the central portion of the Edwards Plateau classifies as a tableland, or relatively flat upland of moderate relief (three hundred to five hundred feet). There, most of the relief is provided by numerous dry valleys whose floors absorb much of the rainfall runoff. Some of this water later emerges at the surface in the form of springs, especially along the Balcones scarp. In some areas a deep soil mantles the surface, whereas in other areas shallow solution depressions in the limestone and a rock-littered surface dominate the landscape.

Sierra Madre Oriental

South of the Rio Grande and west of the Mexican Gulf Coastal Plain is the Sierra Madre Oriental. This upland comprises numerous mountain ranges aligned northwest-southeast and separated by intermontane valleys and basins. Both Lobeck (1948) and Raisz (1964) draw the northern limit of the eastern sierra at the Rio Grande, whereas Ordoñez (1936: 1287) considers the Big Bend region of Brewster and Presidio counties, Texas, as the northern extension of the sierra. Atwood (1940: 329-31), on the other hand, treats the eastern sierra as an extension of the Rocky Mountains, probably due in large part to its similarities in orientation and geologic structure. On the west, the Sierra Madre Oriental merges gradually with the Mexican Highlands section of the Basin and Range Physiographic Province.

From the Rio Grande to Monterrey, the eastern sierra is characterized by narrow, widely spaced, even-crested ranges whose elevations average perhaps five thousand feet. These rugged ranges are cored by thick, massive Cretaceous limestones that have been upfolded into a series of parallel anticlinal ridges. Between the mountain ranges are structural

valleys and basins (downfolded synclines or downfaulted gra-
bens) which have been filled to a great thickness by alluvium
removed from the uplands during Tertiary and Quaternary
erosional cycles. There is a major late Tertiary volcanic field
superposed on the central portion of the Sierra del Carmen
in northern Coahuila, and scattered exposures of early Cenozoic intrusive igneous rocks occur throughout the region
where erosion has stripped the Cretaceous sedimentary cover
(López Ramos, 1976).

The section of the Sierra Madre Oriental south of Monterrey is much more rugged, highly elevated, and closely
folded than the area to the north. An imposing fault scarp
representing several thousand feet of displacement forms an
abrupt eastern boundary. In this section, elevation of the
ranges is double that of the area to the north, and increasing
proximity to maritime air from the Gulf of Mexico promotes
greater rainfall, runoff, and river development. The western
flank of the eastern sierra here, as elsewhere, is arid to semiarid, perennial streams are few, and large alluvial fans at the
mouths of deeply incised canyons are common (Ordoñez,
1936: 1287-89).

To the south of a line running between Saltillo and Torreón
is a western extension or peninsula of the eastern sierra in
which the predominantly folded ranges are oriented east-west.
Middle and late Tertiary faulting superposed on the folded
structures is more prevalent here than in the area to the
north, but like the northern sections, ranges are widely separated by broad structural basins veneered with Quaternary
alluvium. These western ranges, however, plus those to the
south of Monterrey, have a greater exposure of Triassic and
Jurassic rocks in their cores than do the less deformed ranges
of the north (Kellum, Imlay, and Kane, 1936).

Basin and Range

Well over half of the Borderlands region lies within the
Basin and Range Physiographic Province. This province extends from Big Bend National Park in the east to the Imperial Valley of the Californias in the west. To the north,
the province is restricted by the southern margin of the
Colorado Plateau that runs along a line from Prescott, Arizona, to Socorro, New Mexico. To the south, it occupies
all the area between the western and eastern sierras north
of Torreón, as well as the coastal strip of the Sonoran Desert
adjacent to the Gulf of California.

Vast seaways which covered most of this province during
the Paleozoic and Mesozoic eras accumulated great thicknesses of sedimentary rock. Most of the original horizontal
structure of these rocks was deformed into a series of folds
in late Cretaceous times during a period of mountain building known as the Laramide Orogeny. By the middle of the
Tertiary, the folds were truncated by numerous faults which
ultimately gave rise to the modern landscape of upthrust
ranges and downthrown basins. The block-fault origin of the
mountains was first recognized by Gilbert (1928) some one
hundred years ago and has been confirmed by numerous
workers since. Evidence that many of the ranges continue to

rise along their boundary faults comes from the numerous
earthquakes reported in the province each year and from
fairly fresh offsets in rocks and alluvial fans along the mountain fronts.

Other than the drainage systems of the Rio Grande and the
Colorado River, this vast area of the Borderlands has few
outlets to the sea. Instead, most of the runoff from the highlands is trapped in a series of bolsons, or basins of interior
drainage, underlain to a great depth by alluvium eroded from
the ranges during the middle and late Cenozoic. As a result,
much surface water is diverted underground by seepage into
the desert sands and gravels, although on occasion surface
water reaches the low points of the bolsons, where it ponds
and forms temporary lakes. According to Ordoñez, American
geologists and geographers misapply the term *playa* to these
lakes, when in fact these ephemeral features are best termed
barrials (Ordoñez, 1936: 1290).

Mexican Highlands. This section is dominated by high desert
basins which range in elevation from one thousand feet in
the west to four thousand feet in the El Paso-Juárez area.
Long, narrow, *en echelon* fault-block mountains typically rise
another two thousand to five thousand feet above the desert
floor. Most ranges are oriented from north-northwest to
south-southeast, although those along the Arizona-Sonora
border are lineated almost due north-south. In general, Cretaceous sedimentary rocks cap the ranges, and associated
middle Tertiary volcanics are common. Several ranges are
dominated by Paleozoic rocks, and a few, such as Mount
Graham in Arizona and the Organ-San Andres Mountains
of New Mexico, have broad exposures of Precambrian granites
(Wilson, Moore, and Cooper, 1969; Dane and Bachman,
1965). In addition, there are several major Quaternary volcanic fields nested against the international boundary. These
include the West Potrillo of southern New Mexico; the Palo-
mas of northern Chihuahua; and the San Bernardino of southeastern Arizona and northeastern Sonora (López Ramos,
1976).

Along the axis of the Rio Grande Valley, from south central Colorado to the Presidio area of West Texas, is a thirty-
to one-hundred-mile-wide strip in which faulting has been especially active during the last 25 million years. This zone,
known as the Rio Grande Rift, is characterized in the Borderlands by uplifted and tilted horst ranges, downfaulted
basins with deep alluvial fills, and recent volcanism. Vertical
offsets along boundary faults are exceedingly great, with a
minimum of 25,000 feet recorded for the Franklin Mountains
at El Paso. Between the ranges are relatively flat-floored
valleys developed on basin fills 2,000-8,000 feet thick. Major
structural valleys include the Tularosa, Jornada del Muerto,
Mesilla, and Mimbres basins of southern New Mexico, the
Hueco Basin in West Texas, and the Los Muertos Basin of
northern Chihuahua. Evidence presented by Chapin and Seager (1975) suggests the rift zone is geologically more active
than most other areas of the Mexican Highlands.

External drainage to the sea from the Mexican Highlands
is limited to the Rio Grande, to its major tributary from
Mexico, the Río Conchos, and to a few tributaries of the

Colorado River in Arizona. Most of the drainage is internal and provides significant recharge to local groundwater aquifers. Three major drainage lines extend off the northeast flank of the western sierra and terminate in a series of large desert lakes in northern Chihuahua. These rivers and their respective lakes are the Río de Casas Grandes and the Laguna de Guzmán; the Río Santa María and the Laguna Santa María; and the Río del Carmen and the Laguna de Patos (Schmidt, 1973: 21-23). During the great ice age, when a climate decidedly cooler and wetter than today's existed, numerous large freshwater lakes occupied the desert basins. Evidence of these lakes comes from locally thick and fine-grained lake sediment, old beach lines that follow the contour of the basin borders, and remnant saline lakes on the basin floors.

Sacramento Section. This section lies between the Rio Grande Rift and the Pecos River Valley. It is less well deformed structurally and lacks the recent volcanic activity and deep basin fills of the rift. Most of the mountains are fault blocks dipping gently eastward and capped by late Paleozoic sedimentary rocks. The Precambrian granite of the Pedernal Hills and the Tertiary igneous rocks of the Sierra Blanca area are exceptions (Dane and Bachman, 1965). In the north, the Sandia-Manzano Mountains to the west are separated by the Estancia Valley from Glorietta Mesa and the Pedernal Hills to the east. In the south, the Diablo Plateau on the west is separated from the Guadalupe-Delaware Mountains to the east by the Salt Basin. The Estancia and Salt Basin lowlands are structural valleys characterized by internal drainage, salt lakes, sand dunes, and remnant shorelines of ice-age lakes. Near the center of this section are the Sacramento Mountains and the Sierra Blanca, the latter reaching twelve thousand feet in elevation (Hunt, 1974: 504-505).

Salton Trough. This depression is the landward extension of the Gulf of California that was severed from the sea by the building of the Colorado River delta. It lies in an area of very active faults, including the San Andreas, San Jacinto, and Elsinore faults, and it has associated hot springs and geothermal development in the Imperial Valley. Much of the trough lies below sea level, including the Salton Sea with a surface elevation of −235 feet. This sea occupies the site of freshwater Lake Cahuilla, which existed for at least one thousand years immediately before the time of Columbus. The lake basin was inundated during the period 1904-1907 by floodwaters originating in irrigation canals of the Colorado River. Evaporation since 1907 has lowered the Salton Sea to its current level. To the east of the Imperial Valley and the old Lake Cahuilla shorelines is a vast area covered by the Algodone Dune field (Thornbury, 1965: 494-98).

Sonoran Desert Section. This section includes the Mojave Desert of southeastern California, the Gila Bend-Yuma Desert region of southwestern Arizona, and the Sonoran Desert proper between the Sierra Madre Occidental and the Gulf of California in western Sonora. The section is geologically and topographically less spectacular than the rest of the Mexican Highlands. Broad, open basins between the ranges typically lie at elevations of one thousand to two thousand feet, and the fault-block ranges rise another one thousand to three thousand feet above the basin floors. A very few ranges along the Arizona-Sonora border have peak elevations of six thousand to eight thousand feet.

The major boundary faults along which the mountains have risen date back to the middle Tertiary, and apparently little movement or structural deformation has occurred in the last ten million years (Eberly and Stanley, 1978). As a result, the ranges have been lowered through prolonged erosion to the point where they are mere vestiges of once lofty uplands. On their flanks the ranges are encroached by broad, sloping, low-angle rock platforms called pediments. These surfaces serve to transport water and sediment from the highlands to the basins and indicate prolonged backwearing of the mountain front under stable conditions (Fenneman, 1931: 367-75). Because erosion has consumed so much of the original uplands, the rocks exposed in mountain cores are decidedly older than those elsewhere in the Mexican Highlands. A major exception is the constructional Pinacate volcanic field in northwestern Sonora, which dates from the Quaternary.

Most of the exterior drainage for this section is provided by the Colorado River, its major tributaries, the Gila and Williams rivers, and several shorter streams in western Sonora which drain directly from the western sierra to the Gulf of California. The Mojave Desert, by contrast, is one of closed basins and numerous saline lakes, including Soda, Bristol, and Danby lakes. These lakes were much larger, interconnected freshwater bodies during the ice age and may at one time have had a direct outlet to the Colorado River.

Sierra Madre Occidental

The western sierra extends from Guadalajara in the south to the southern boundary of Arizona in the north and from the Sonoran Desert in the west to the Mexican Highlands in the east. It is both shorter (eight hundred miles) and broader (one hundred to two hundred miles) than the eastern sierra and is capped by several thousand feet of Tertiary volcanic material. The Sierra Madre Occidental is best described as a highly elevated, seven-thousand- to ten-thousand-foot volcanic plateau that trends north-northwest to south-southeast and is generally higher in the east than in the west. Its accordant or level summits are occasionally interrupted by deep canyons, or *barrancas*, that run both parallel to and transverse to the dominant structure. Faulting has produced bold scarps and steep slopes along the eastern and western margins of the plateau (Hawley, 1969).

The geologic history of the Sierra Madre Occidental is only poorly known. Evidence from outcrops along faults and canyon walls suggests an underlying basement of Paleozoic sedimentary and metamorphic rocks that were folded and faulted prior to the periods of volcanic outpouring. Intrusive and extrusive igneous rocks which date from 100 million to 45 million years ago form the lower volcanic complex. From 45 million to 32 million years ago volcanic activity virtually ceased, tilting and faulting of the volcanics occurred, and erosional agents cut a topographic surface of great relief. This surface was subsequently buried by a younger volcanism that culminated some 32 million to 23 million years ago. Radiometric dates of volcanic rocks in the western sierra as well as throughout the Borderlands suggest the eruptive phases are associated with periods of pronounced faulting and shifts along crustal plate boundaries (McDowell and Keizer, 1977).

Most of the drainage from the Sierra Madre Occidental originates in the higher elevations of the eastern and central sections of the plateau and is carried to the adjacent desert lowlands through a series of deep canyons. This pattern is especially true in the west, where almost all coastal streams between the Río Sonora and the Río Grande de Santiago originate in the sierra. Major rivers from north to south include the Río Yaqui, Río Mayo, Río Fuerte, and Río Culiacán. Of these, the Río Fuerte has the largest watershed and greatest discharge of all west-slope streams (Schmidt, 1976*a*: 32-35). Drainage to the east of the plateau is largely confined to enclosed basins and desert lakes. The only through-flowing system is the Río Conchos and its tributaries. Near Boquilla, the Conchos has been dammed to form Lago Toronto, a reservoir of approximately two million acre-feet storage capacity (Mueller, 1975: 90).

Los Angeles Ranges

This province is characterized by a series of east-west ranges whose orientation is transverse to the general north-south structural trend of the West Coast. Thrust faulting, especially in the eastern section, has juxtaposed very old rocks across from, and over, younger rocks. The San Bernardino and the San Gabriel mountains, separated from each other by the San Andreas Fault, reach elevations greater than ten thousand feet and are cored in part by Precambrian granites and gneisses that are more than one billion years old (Jennings, 1977). Most rocks in the western section are Tertiary in age

and represent a mixture of marine and terrestrial sediment. Structural lowlands near the coast, such as the Los Angeles and Ventura basins, are filled to a great depth by Tertiary and Quaternary deposits, and their submerged westward extensions form coastal channels, including the Santa Barbara. Multiple marine terraces along the immediate coast, some more than one thousand feet above modern sea level, offer evidence of general regional uplift during the past few million years (Norris and Webb, 1976: 190-244).

Baja California

This province extends south of the Los Angeles Ranges and includes all of Baja del Norte. It is underlain by a huge magmatic intrusion of Cretaceous granite, known as the Southern California Batholith, which forms the backbone of this westward-tilted, plateaulike structure. Paleozoic and Mesozoic metamorphic rocks are associated with the intrusion, and some Mesozoic sedimentaries outcrop on the western slopes. Tertiary marine rocks, locally thick in upraised coastal ranges, are absent over most of the province. Unconsolidated Quaternary deposits, prominent elsewhere in western North America, are restricted to a few valley fills and coastal sediments, including the Vizcaíno Desert at the border with Baja del Sur (Oakeshott, 1971: 335-43; López Ramos, 1976).

Great uplift along eastern boundary faults has produced asymmetrical ranges with bold eastward-facing escarpments. The major ranges in California are the Santa Rosa and Santa Ana mountains, with San Jacinto Peak reaching an elevation of 10,805 feet. Just south of the international boundary are two rugged ranges whose eastern escarpments overlook the Imperial Valley, the Sierra de Juárez to the north and the cresty Sierra San Pedro Mártir to the south—the latter reaching 10,126 feet. There is some evidence that the Elsinore Fault, a major structure in the Los Angeles Ranges and the Imperial Valley, may form the eastern escarpment of the Sierra de Juárez (Norris and Webb, 1976: 169-89).

Water, or perhaps more accurately the lack of it, is one of the most pressing concerns for much of the U.S.-Mexican Borderlands. Since the region is largely either arid or semiarid, it is also chronically short of water. Fortuitously, several major streams flow through it, bringing water from more humid regions. Extensive aquifers also supply groundwater, though this resource is often used beyond its capacity to be naturally recharged. Most surface-water resources are used to the maximum. There have been further attempts to rearrange regional water resources through interbasin water diversion, but these plans are often accomplished only after great expense and considerable political and social turmoil. Certainly no other natural resource imposes stricter limits on both borders' growth and productivity.

It is especially difficult to discuss Borderlands water resources as an integrated whole because the hydrology and water resources are anything but integrated, either by man or by nature. Hydrologically, the region is an artificial one, and the political boundaries do not conform in any way to the watershed

19

Water

OTIS W. TEMPLER
Department of Geography
Texas Tech University

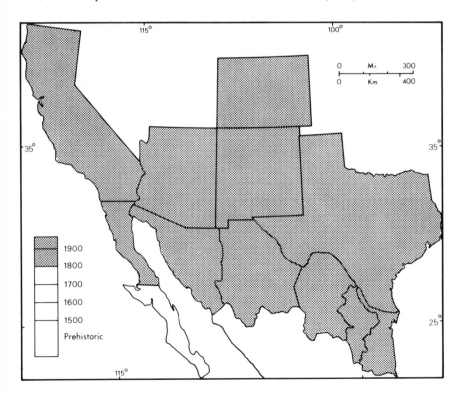

boundaries of surface hydrologic units or to the limits of groundwater aquifers (Fig. 19-1). First, the region is split by the Continental Divide, which directs drainage westward toward the Pacific Ocean or Gulf of California and eastward toward the Atlantic Ocean through the Gulf of Mexico. Large central interior drainage basins further complicate the hydrography. Second, the Borderlands are separated along a general east-west line by the international border, with all its controversial implications for water resource development and management. State boundaries in the United States further disrupt the resource. Finally, the two major watersheds of the region, the Colorado River and the Rio Grande, encompass parts of both countries.

The Rio Grande, known in Mexico as the Río Bravo del Norte, rises in southern Colorado and flows across New Mexico to Texas, where, for 1,244 miles—from El Paso to the Gulf—it forms the international boundary. The total watershed contains 182,000 square miles, of which 89,000 are in the United States and 93,000 are in Mexico. From its headwaters to Fort Quitman, Texas (below El Paso), almost all stream flow is consumed; downstream the major flow contributions are from several Mexican tributaries, notably the Ríos Conchos, Salado, Alamo, and San Juan.

The Colorado River differs markedly in that only 2,000 square miles of its 242,000-square-mile basin lie in Mexico. It rises on the Rocky Mountains' western slopes in central and southern Colorado. The Gila River, after it turns south, is its only important tributary along Arizona's border. Except for the rivers of northern California and eastern Texas, most streams flow through either arid or semiarid regions and thus are often intermittent or highly seasonal.

Because of the variable and widely dispersed nature of the surface-water supply, groundwater is a highly significant part of the region's resources. On the U.S. side, most aquifers are small and generally found within basin fill or the alluvium of stream valleys. Two major exceptions are the Ogallala aquifer of the High Plains, which extends from West Texas and eastern New Mexico northward into eastern Colorado and beyond, and the huge aquifer that occupies most of California's Central Valley. In Mexico, the major aquifers are located in interior drainage basins, on the coastal plains, and in narrow bands along major streams.

There are no comprehensive hydrologic studies of Borderlands water resources. The interested researcher must extract information from a wide range of general sources or combine several more specific ones. An admirable comparative study is Dunbier's *The Sonoran Desert* (1968: chaps. 5 and 9), which surveys resources of Arizona and Sonora. For the United States, excellent general sources are *The Nation's Water Resources* (U.S. Water Resources Council, 1968) and *Water Atlas of the United States* (Geraghty et al., 1973). In addition, there are literally hundreds, if not thousands, of very specific, and some more broadly regional, investigations of surface water and groundwater by the U.S. Geological Survey, the U.S. Bureau of Reclamation, state water agencies, and academicians. Though not specifically cited, a number of these studies' helpful examples are included in the composite bibliography.

Rivers of the West (editors of Sunset Books, 1974) and *Ten Rivers in America's Future* (U.S. President's Water Resource Policy Commission, 1950) cover useful material on southwestern rivers. There are numerous general studies of the Colorado River (Khalaf, 1951; Waters, 1946; Watkins, 1969a, 1969b), the Rio Grande (Arbingast, 1955; Fergusson, 1955; Gilpin, 1949; Horgan, 1954a; Stambaugh and Stambaugh, 1954), and some smaller streams like the Gila (Corle, 1951). Among these are historical and regional studies which use a river basin as the organizing concept and emphasize water's importance as an integrative settlement factor.

There are fewer studies of water resources for the Mexican Borderlands. Tamayo and West (1964), noting that there are almost no modern scientific hydrologic studies for Mexico, provide a general survey of surface resources from which Borderlands information can be extracted. Useful maps of various aspects of hydrology and of the use and development of water resources are in several atlases (Arbingast et al., 1975; García de Miranda and Falcon de Gyves, 1972; Tamayo, 1962b). Other recommended materials are by Arenal (1969), Blasquez-López (1959), and García-Quintero (1951, 1955). According to Arenal, a first-priority item in Mexican water resource policy is basic research on both surface water and groundwater resources. Studies of groundwater supply in several small areas are published by the Instituto Geológico de México and, more recently, by the Secretaría de Recursos Hidráulicos.

Water Resource Use and Development

Water has been a critical Borderlands resource since pre-Columbian times. In central Arizona, an advanced hydraulic society, the Hohokam, practiced sophisticated flood irrigation along the Salt and Gila rivers. That civilization reached its peak about 1200 A.D. and disappeared shortly thereafter, perhaps because of a rising water table associated with waterlogged and saline soils. Elsewhere, Pueblo Indians also practiced irrigation along the New Mexico Rio Grande. Woodbury (1963) summarizes early southwestern Indians' water use and control practices. Even the nomadic hunting and gathering peoples were attracted, on occasion, to lakes and streams for water and food resources; Tamayo and West (1964) discuss the use of surface water by Amerindians in the Mexican Borderlands.

Borderlands Spanish and Mexican settlers brought their Mediterranean irrigation techniques and institutions and often practiced successful irrigation agriculture in favored locales. Many of their techniques and institutions, such as water law, remain today as a part of the region's cultural heritage (Dobkins, 1959; Glick, 1972; Hutchins, 1928; Ressler, 1968; Templer, 1978c).

After 1850, innumerable small private or cooperative irrigation schemes were developed in the American West (Connor et al., 1973; Thomas, 1948). In 1870 the first major Great Plains irrigation project, the Greeley Union Colony, was established in northern Colorado. After 1902 and the passage of the Reclamation Act (P. S. Taylor, 1970), many

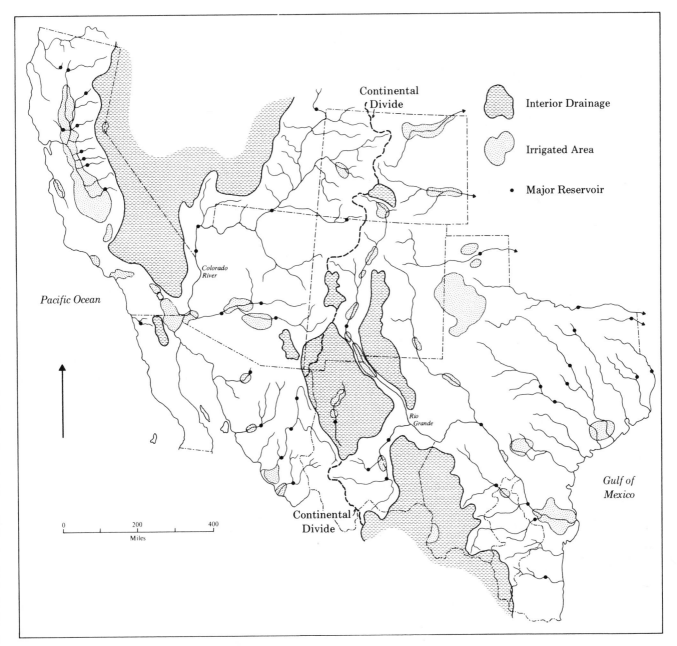

Fig. 19-1. *Surface-water features and drainage. Sources: Adapted from Cantor (1970), García de Miranda and Falcon de Gyves (1972), Geraghty et al. (1973), Tamayo and West (1964), and U.S. Department of the Interior, Geological Survey (1970).*

large federal irrigation projects were developed, especially in California, Arizona, Colorado, and New Mexico. Despite the importance of these projects, most of the irrigated area of the American Borderlands was privately developed.

The Salt River Project (McMullin, 1967; C. L. Smith, 1972), the first reclamation project in the Southwest, resulted from the 1911 completion of Roosevelt Dam. Six major dams have been built on the Colorado River: first Hoover Dam (U.S. Department of the Interior, 1971; Sut-

ton, 1968), then Davis, Parker, and Imperial dams downstream, and more recently Glen Canyon and Flaming Gorge dams upstream. Lake Mead and Lake Powell, formed by Hoover and Glen Canyon dams, respectively, are the largest man-made reservoirs in the United States. Fig. 19-1 indicates these and other major Borderlands reservoirs. Almost all major streams in the American Borderlands have been developed for multiple-purpose use and are controlled by reservoirs, so disastrous flooding and extremely erratic flow have been largely eliminated. A highly recommended survey of many of these projects is *Water Resource Planning and Development in the Southwestern United States* (Humlum, 1969). There are also water development studies for most of the states, especially California (Cooper, 1968; Harding, 1969; Seckler, 1971) and Arizona (Kelso et al., 1973).

In the Mexican Borderlands the era of water resource development also started soon after 1900, but in contrast with the American side, most development was federal and proceeded at a much slower pace. Dunbier (1968: 201) observes that in Mexico more centralized government planning, communal land ownership, and other social factors combined with less sophisticated technology to produce the significant differences in Mexican development of water resources. Of the twenty largest Mexican reservoirs, most completed after World War II, ten are located in the Borderlands; some of the most successful Mexican irrigation projects are also located in the arid north (Centro de Investigaciones Agraria, 1957; Cummings, 1972; Dozier, 1963; Henderson, 1965). Inaccurate or incomplete hydrologic and topographic data have hampered several projects' operation; for example less than three-fourths of the projected acreage in the Laguna district of Durango and southwestern Coahuila proved irrigable. On the Sonora River, the Rodriguez Dam reservoir has never filled to designed capacity and consequently provides much less irrigation water than originally anticipated (Dunbier, 1968: 202-203).

Falcon and Amistad reservoirs, the two major international storage facilities on the Rio Grande, were authorized by the 1944 Mexican Water Treaty and are operated by the International Boundary and Water Commission. Most major reservoirs in both countries serve multiple purposes, though they were designed primarily for irrigation and flood control. Irrigation consumes by far the most water. The major irrigated areas of the Borderlands, many of which are downstream from large reservoirs, are shown in Fig. 19-1. For a discussion of the various irrigation projects, see Cantor (1970).

Some irrigation districts in the American Borderlands are largely dependent on groundwater. This is especially true on the High Plains of Texas and New Mexico (Green, 1973), where practically all irrigation water comes from wells. Bowden (1965) provides an excellent diffusion study of the technology of groundwater irrigation on Colorado's eastern plains. Recently, center-pivot irrigation using well water (Splinter, 1976) has become a distinctive landscape feature in the southwestern United States. Groundwater is responsible for the development, in northwestern Mexico, of Sonora's Costa de Hermosillo, which has transformed an estimated 236,000 acres of desert into a productive agricultural area.

Because of the limited supply of water, there is continual interest in increasing or redistributing water resources through such innovations as interbasin diversion, weather modification, and desalination. At present, interbasin diversion is the most feasible technique. Quinn (1968) examines major water transfer problems in the western United States. Most existing transfers are located in the American Borderlands; almost all are intrastate instead of interstate because of state control and rivalry over water resources. Water diversion has generated useful summaries (Bagley and Smiley, 1969), bibliographies (Whetstone, 1970-71), and economic analyses (Hartman and Seastone, 1970; Howe and Easter, 1971).

The Imperial and Coachella valleys in the Salton Trough (Glendinning, 1949; Hosmer, 1966; Taylor, 1973) were served by an early Colorado River diversion project. Today, water is diverted at Imperial Dam, where it passes through a desilting works and is then channeled through the All-American Canal to the valleys. Another landmark diversion is the Colorado-Big Thompson Project (Loeffler, 1970; U.S. Department of the Interior, 1962; N. A. Evans, 1972), where water is taken from the headwaters of the Colorado River and transferred, through the Continental Divide, to irrigate the eastern slopes of the Rocky Mountains. This Bureau of Reclamation project, capable of supplementing only seasonal water shortages, has been criticized for its excessive costs. In California, the Central Valley Project, initiated in 1937 and completed in 1951 by the Bureau of Reclamation, supplies water for the single most productive Borderlands agricultural area (Taylor, 1968). It involves the transfer of surplus water from northern California to the dry San Joaquin Valley. The Central Arizona Project (R. Johnson, 1977), a recently authorized reclamation venture, will convey the state's share of Colorado River water to help mitigate the critical groundwater overdraft in the Phoenix and Tucson areas, supplying approximately 1.2 million acre-feet (maf) per year.

The search for water by Los Angeles is well documented (Hall, 1963; Nadeau, 1950; Ostrom, 1953). The metropolis is almost solely dependent on imported water, having turned early in this century to the Owens Valley, then the Colorado River, and finally to northern California, which represents, in the world's most extensive water transfer, the California Water Project (Bain et al., 1966; California Department of Water Resources, 1957; Cantor, 1969; J. F. Davis, 1971; Golze, 1967; Langman, 1971; Wilcock et al., 1976). The project, begun in 1960 and completed in 1971, is designed to deliver 4.2 maf of water annually from northern California to central and southern parts of the state. Original construction and escalating operation costs seem to assure that the cost/benefit ratio will never be favorable.

The Texas Water Plan (Fickessen, 1970; Texas Water Development Board, 1968), a project of similar magnitude, has not been implemented. It contemplates the transfer of water from the more humid eastern region and from sources outside the state to South and West Texas, especially the High Plains. In contrast to the situation in California, where the majority of the people live in the water-deficient area, the people of Texas are concentrated where the water supply is greatest, and their continued opposition to water transfer (Clay, 1970, 1971) imposes a formidable barrier.

Many other water diversion plans have been devised, some involving sources far beyond state or regional boundaries (Arguello and Kazmann, 1973; Laycock, 1970), but none has yet been implemented. The most grandiose of all transfer schemes, the North American Water and Power Alliance, or NAWAPA (Barr, 1975; Sewell, 1967; 1974), envisions transferring surplus water from Canada and Alaska to the drier western United States and northwestern Mexico, but this plan has not been viewed favorably in Canada. Though apparently it is technologically feasible, its economic, ecological, social, and political implications make it unlikely that the plan will ever be fully developed.

There is also much interest in Mexican interbasin diversion, but there are no existing projects of the magnitude described above. The much-discussed Northwest Project (PHLINO) would transfer water from nine watersheds in Sinaloa and southern Sonora northward, terminating in the Costa de Hermosillo district. The Mexican government decided to go ahead with this project despite questionable economic feasibility (Cummings, 1974). Another plan under consideration would channel water from the Panuco River northward across the Tamaulipas coastal plain toward the Rio Grande (Arenal, 1969).

Neither weather modification nor desalination has proven technologically fully practical. Several nontechnical desalination summaries are available (Popkin, 1968; U.S. Department of the Interior, 1968; Woodbury, 1967), as are economic analyses of the process (Clawson et al., 1969; Clawson and Landsberg, 1972). Hodges (1969) reports on a desert seacoast desalination project in Sonora. Weather modification is even less developed, and there is little agreement over its ultimate hydrologic impact (Kane, 1973; Seely and DeCoursey, 1975). A historical weather modification account is provided by Townsend (1975). Its current application mainly involves increasing the snowpack in mountainous areas (Hurley, 1967; Weisbecker, 1974).

Water Problems

The major water problem of most of the Borderlands is dividing a limited supply among a growing number of people. Recently, a noted water scientist observed: "Much of the southwestern United States is living on borrowed water and on borrowed time. A whole lifestyle will have to be changed in this area, but very few people are worried about or are doing anything about it" ("The Mighty Colorado . . . ," 1978: 52). The Colorado River is the most noteworthy example. Some predict that within a decade this overused stream will be incapable of supplying those dependent on it. Both the Colorado River and the Rio Grande have been the subjects of continuing controversies which have both internal and international implications.

The internal controversies over the Colorado River have produced monumental historical and political studies (Hundley, 1976; Terrell, 1965-66). Its water use is regulated by a series of documents, collectively known as the "Law of the River," which includes the Colorado River Compact, the Boulder Canyon Project Act, the Mexican Water Treaty of 1944, the Supreme Court decision and decree in *Arizona* v. *California* (1964), the Colorado River Basin Project Act, and numerous lesser compacts and agreements. The Supreme Court decree provides that if 7.5 maf of water are available annually for consumption by the lower basin, Arizona is entitled to 2.8 maf, California to 4.4 maf, and Nevada to 0.3 maf. *Water and Choice in the Colorado River Basin* (National Research Council, 1968) gives an excellent overview of various alternatives for water management of the embattled Colorado River. Even more current are the papers of the Lake Powell Research Project (Mann, 1976). Notable studies of man's impact on the Colorado River are by Dolan et al. (1974) and Luten (1967).

The Rio Grande and its tributaries have been the subject of protracted battles among Colorado, New Mexico, and Texas. An ongoing dispute continues over water deliveries under the Rio Grande Compact, which apportions stream flow between states (Reynolds and Mutz, 1974). Presently, Texas and New Mexico are engaged in a federal court dispute over water deliveries under the Pecos River Compact. Studies of man's impact on the river have been done by Duisberg (1957) and Hay (1963).

At the international level, the United States and Mexico have long argued over both the Colorado River and the Rio Grande. Shortly after 1900, upstream Rio Grande diversions threatened the water supply of the El Paso-Juárez area. A 1906 treaty with Mexico guaranteed the annual delivery of sixty thousand acre-feet of water to the Juárez Valley after completion of Elephant Butte Dam in the Rio Grande Valley Reclamation Project. In 1944, a more comprehensive treaty was completed between the two countries, regulating use for both the Rio Grande and the Colorado River. The landmark treaty study is Hundley's *Dividing the Water* (1966; also see Hundley, 1964).

Because of Mexico's important contribution to the Rio Grande flow below El Paso, equitable water division there was not so difficult as it was for the Colorado River, where practically all flow originates on the American side. The final agreement stipulates that the Unites States is to receive all the flow of the principal American tributaries, one-third of the flow from the major Mexican tributaries (except the Río San Juan and the Río Alamo), and one-half of any flow not otherwise allotted. In turn, the United States was to provide the principal means for building Falcon and Amistad dams. In the case of the Colorado River, Mexico is guaranteed the annual delivery of 1.5 maf of water. Managing the Rio Grande and the Colorado River is the task of the International Boundary and Water Commission (Herrera-Jordan and Friedkin, 1967). Several studies detail the problems of international management of the Rio Grande (Day, 1970, 1972, 1975; Mueller, 1975). J. E. Hill (1965, 1968) has investigated the Chamizal dispute over the Rio Grande and the Colorado River international boundary problems.

The full development of surface-water resources has also led to indiscriminate mining of limited groundwater supplies. This overuse has produced rapidly falling water tables in central and southern Arizona, southern California, and western Texas and in some areas has led to increased or prohibitive pumping costs and decreasing water yields (Lacewell et al., 1976; Osborne, 1973; Pifer, 1969; Williford et al., 1976). The problems of economic and social adjustment to this dwindling resource are not fully understood. A Bureau of Reclamation study of the problems of water resource depletion of the High Plains Ogallala Formation, currently underway and scheduled to be completed in the early 1980s, may provide some answers. Only recently have international boundary groundwater problems come under study (Bradley and DeCook, 1978; Day, 1978; Hernandez, 1978).

Salinity is a problem plaguing many Borderlands irrigation districts. Nowhere is the problem worse than on the lower Colorado River (Findley and O'Rear, 1973; Moore et al., 1974; Oyarzabal-Tamargo and Young, 1978). The *Natural Resources Journal* recently featured a symposium ("International Symposium on the Salinity of the Colorado River," 1975) on the problem. Until recently, Colorado River water supplied to Mexico was often so salty from frequent reuse upstream that it was unsafe for irrigation. Extensive acreage in the Mexicali area was permanently ruined. In 1973 the United States agreed to improve the quality of water delivered to Mexico. The Bureau of Reclamation built a drain near Yuma for the highly saline return flow, and soon a desalination plant will go into operation. Salinity control is also a problem in California's Sacramento–San Joaquin Delta (MacDiarmid, 1975).

Other severe water problems are siltation in reservoirs, cessation of freshwater inflow to estuaries, and phreatophyte control. Rapid reservoir siltation is becoming increasingly serious, and removal of silt is prohibitively costly. Decreasing freshwater inflow to estuaries resulting from the development of inland water is a problem on the Texas Gulf Coast (Chapman, 1971; Nelson et al., 1973). The brackish water of the estuaries is critically important to many species of marine life. Phreatophytes, deep-rooted water-wasting plants which thrive in riparian situations, are responsible for great water losses (Fletcher and Elmendorf, 1955; Harris, 1966; Hughes, 1968), and their control has proven difficult and expensive. Municipal and industrial water pollution is largely confined to major urban concentrations, especially the Texas Gulf Coast.

Water Resource Institutions

Another major problem affecting Borderlands water resource use and management relates to the institutional complex controlling the allocation of water—primarily questions of water rights and law. Some investigators believe this institutional complex is the most significant obstacle to improved water management (Martin and Young, 1969). An inherent problem is that the law has traditionally divided water moving through the hydrologic cycle into separate legal classes, applying different laws to the ownership and use of each class (Templer, 1973a). This unnatural division makes integrated water resource management difficult, if not impossible (Radosevich and Sutton, 1972; Templer, 1976).

Two major doctrines of water rights, the riparian system and the system of prior appropriation, pertain to water in American streams (Hamming, 1958). The riparian system is unregulated, based chiefly on custom or common law, and is tied to riparian landownership. The appropriation system is

administered by a state agency and requires a water use permit. As settlement moved westward, most states adopted the riparian system then in existence in the East. It soon became apparent that this system was ill-suited to conditions in the more arid West, and either it was replaced by the system of prior appropriation or the two doctrines were recognized together. It is difficult to correlate dissimilar water rights where the two systems exist concurrently (Cook, 1968; Hutchins, 1954; Hutchins and Steele, 1957; Templer, 1973a, 1973b, 1978c; Trelease, 1954). Unfortunately, the riparian system prevailed for some time in many western jurisdictions, now making legal revisions even more difficult (Mann, 1963b: 399-402). Because interbasin diversion normally involves surface water, there have been several investigations of attendant legal problems (Johnson and Knippa, 1965; Jensen and Trock, 1973; Weinberg, 1969). *International Water Law Along the Mexican-American Border* (Knowlton, 1968a) discusses water rights pertaining to international streams.

In general, the differences between riparian and appropriation systems also apply to groundwater. The appropriation system may pertain, as it does in New Mexico and Colorado. Three common-law variations have been developed for groundwater. Under the strict common-law rule, which applies in Texas, groundwater is considered part of the land, and the landowner can pump and use it without regard for the effect on adjoining landowners (Templer, 1978b). Two less stringent variations have evolved—the doctrines of reasonable use (in Arizona) and of correlative rights (in California). A comparative survey of groundwater law in the Borderlands states is found in *Southwestern Groundwater Law* (Chalmers, 1974).

Texas's common-law rule has been criticized as encouraging a race for available water and promoting rapid and sometimes wasteful use (Bagley, 1961; Jones and Schneider, 1972; Snyder, 1973; Templer, 1978b; Thomas, 1955, 1972). Clawson (1963: 438) has observed that such a legal system ". . . almost forces each landowner to use whatever water he can get and all he can get before someone else uses it," making rational aquifer management increasingly difficult (Williams, 1972). At present, the trend is toward applying the appropriation system or the more equitable rules of reasonable use or correlative rights (Hutchins, 1955). The controversy continues over the visible impact of contrasting systems of groundwater law along the Texas–New Mexico border ("Apollo 9 Eyes Water Management," 1970; McMillion and Olsson, 1972; C. C. Reeves, 1974). Though there is little precedent for international or interstate groundwater management (Fischer, 1974), recent studies have given attention to the U.S.-Mexican border's legal problems (Burman and Cornish, 1975; Clark, 1978; Dworsky, 1978; Hayton, 1978).

Mexican water institutions are much more centralized than those of the United States (Anaya, 1967; Hernandez-Tiran, 1967; Teclaff, 1972; United Nations, 1974). Mexican water law is derived chiefly from Spain, with an infusion of customary Indian practice. The Mexican Constitution of 1917 decreed that most flowing water was national property, thus subject to federal control. Notwithstanding the government's centralized control over surface water, groundwater is generally considered the property of the landowner, similar to the Texas situation. A permit is required for groundwater exploitation in only a few prohibited zones or regulated areas.

Despite the diverse legal systems of Mexico and the United States, there is a somewhat common heritage, and it is possible to trace the diffusion of these legal systems and the cultural and environmental changes they have undergone. The Hispanic element is particularly important in Texas water law (Dobkins, 1959; Glick, 1972; McKnight, 1966) and can affect contemporary water management (Templer, 1978c).

Other legal classes of water less immediately significant are diffused surface water, runoff before it reaches a stream, and atmospheric moisture. Surface runoff can generally be intercepted by a landowner in stock tanks or farm ponds, often with little regulation. A recent study (Texas Society of Professional Engineers, 1974) concluded that the interception of diffused surface water by such small private reservoirs results in major water losses and has a significant impact on established downstream surface water rights. Water rights involving atmospheric moisture are more poorly defined, but all Borderlands states have legislation regulating weather modification, and it remains a highly controversial issue (Carter, 1973; Lansford, 1972; Scoggins et al., 1975; Templer, 1976), with possible interstate and international ramifications. Issues concerning Indian water rights (Nelson and Booke, 1977) and reserved water rights on federal lands are not yet clearly defined and will continue as problems in the years ahead.

Summary and Conclusions

This exploratory essay has surveyed the nature of the water resources, their use and development, and the more important Borderlands water problems. As previously indicated, the hydrologic entities of the Borderlands do not conform to the region's delimiting and subdividing political boundaries. The chief hydrologic integrative factors are the Colorado River and Rio Grande watersheds, shared by both countries and their Borderlands states. The cited references were chosen from a much more comprehensive list of materials.[1]

Obstacles to an all-inclusive survey are the greatly varying amounts of data, available literature, and degree of water resource development between the respective countries. Only recently has Mexico begun making notable strides in gathering the basic data for comprehensive water resource planning and comparative analysis with the United States. Water control fragmentation in the United States between the various states, regions, and the federal government also makes generalizations and comprehensive planning difficult, despite the much greater volume of material.

1. Many of the cited references were selected from *The Geography of Arid Lands: A Basic Bibliography* (Templer, 1978a). This bibliography, containing over thirteen hundred sources, provides useful material to Borderlands scholars.

20

Climate

ROBERT H. SCHMIDT, JR.
Department of Geological
Sciences
University of Texas, El Paso

Studies of climate are normally confined to continents, nations, or particular types, and there is no single study that pertains specifically to the weather and climate of the United States-Mexico border region. Although many detailed climatic studies exist for the conterminous United States, there are relatively few such studies for Mexico. Although much of the synoptic (macroscale) information and data pertaining to the U.S. Southwest can be applied to northern Mexico, this information's utility is often limited because it is subject to unknown and unobserved atmospheric vagaries occurring further southward.

General Sources

In the United States, basic climatic data are readily available from the Environmental Data Service, various state climatologists, other government agencies, and private groups. Two sources that should be consulted are the *World Survey*

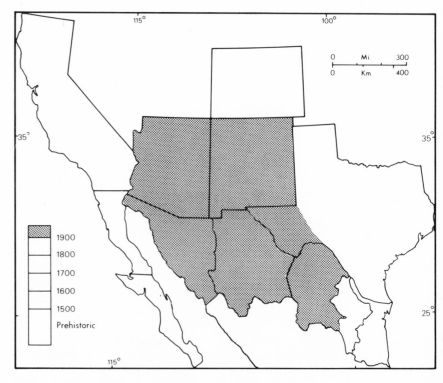

of Climatology, Vol. 11, *Climate of North America,* edited by Bryson and Hare (1974), and the *Climatic Atlas of the United States,* published by the Environmental Data Service (1968). The U.S. Geological Survey's *National Atlas of the United States* (1970) is another general source available at most libraries.

Within the past 15 to 20 years, Mexico has greatly aided climatologists by improving its network of stations and publishing data in several significant and much-needed sources. These include the *Carta de climas de la República* by the Instituto de Geografía (1970), the series *Precipitación y probabilidad de lluvia en los Estados de . . . ,* the *Normales climatologicas: periodo 1941-1970* (1976) published by the Servicio Meteorológico Nacional, Alvarez's *Boletin Meteorológico, Estado de Chihuahua 1957-1971,* and Hastings's *Climatological Data* for Baja California (1964) and Sonora (1969). Certain additional information, especially concerning rainfall extremes and related stream flow data, is available regionally in various issues of *Boletin Hidrológico* published by the Secretaría de Recursos Hidráulicos (the SRH, now the Secretaría de Agricultura y Recursos Hidráulicos—SARH).

In addition to the above-mentioned sources, imagery from U.S. weather satellites and special investigations such as the unique satellite temperature monitoring system developed by the Health Applications Group of the National Aeronautics and Space Administration, Lyndon B. Johnson Space Center (NASA, JSC), in cooperation with the National Commission of Outer Space of Mexico and the U.S. Department of Agriculture screwworm eradication program (Barnes et al., 1977), are examples of relatively sophisticated tools for advancing knowledge of border weather and climate.

Macroclimatic Controls

The U.S.-Mexican border is located in the subtropical latitudes where dry subsiding air, clear skies, and high pressure dominate. There are no sharp seasonal contrasts. Hot summers and mild winters generally predominate, with short intervening spring and fall transitional periods. Altitude is the most important factor affecting temperature differences in the Borderlands: the lower the altitude, the higher the temperature, and vice versa. Interior locations are subjected to continental influences and to being fanned by the tail ends of northern cold fronts during the winter. Inland areas thus have greater temperature variations than coastal locations, which are tempered by stored offshore heat. The moderating effect of the oceans is particularly noticeable on the Pacific Coast, where the relatively cool California Current imparts its influence on the prevailing westerly winds moving over the water surface. Not only does this relatively cool air account for mild year-round coastal temperatures; it also contains relatively little moisture.

Most of the border region's precipitation falls as rain, during summer, in brief thunderstorms. West of the Colorado River (Rio Colorado), a winter maximum precipitation prevails (McDonald, 1965; Hastings and Turner, 1965). The

Sonoran Desert of central Arizona, located between winter and summer maximum regimes, experiences two precipitation maxima (Bryson, 1957). This phenomenon produces moisture over a greater portion of the year and accounts for the relatively dense and "lush" vegetation in this arid zone.

Weather and Climate

The most obvious climatic characteristic of the 3,131-kilometer (1,947 mile) international boundary is its general domination by arid and semiarid climates. The characterization of border towns as hot and dusty possesses a great deal of truth. Some climatic maps, such as Meigs's (1953) "World Distribution of Arid and Semi-Arid Homoclimates" and Thornwaite's (1931) "Climates of North America" show the borderline itself entirely dominated by arid and semiarid climates. The well-known Köppen climate classification (and subsequent modifications) excludes only a very small portion of the boundary from the B (dry) climates (Fig. 20-1; also see Vivó E., 1964). The Köppen classification used for mapping the Mexico portion of Fig. 20-1 was modified by García (1964); this scheme was used by the Instituto de Geografía (Universidad Nacional Autonoma de México) in mapping Mexico's climates at a scale of 1:500,000 for the Comisión de Estudios del Territorio Nacional (Instituto de Geografía, 1970). The latter map series, which includes isotherms and isohyets, fulfills an important basic need, as it is one of the most detailed climatic map series ever produced by a large country. The Köppen classification, as modified by García, incorporates precipitation subdivisions indicating the driest, intermediate, and wettest areas within a major climatic type.

Fig. 20-1 represents a composite of the foregoing maps which were joined, with some liberty, to a climatic map of the United States. The latter was constructed from a composite of my own work (Schmidt, 1975, 1979), a modification by Hastings, Turner, and Warren (1972) of Shreve's 1964 Sonoran Desert map, and the Köppen-Russell (1931) map of the arid West. Fig. 20-2 shows all of the international boundary area to be arid and semiarid, with two exceptions: a small area of temperate-subtropical climates adjacent to the mouth of the Rio Grande and a very small portion of the Laguna Mountains-Sierra de Juárez highlands extending across the border just inland from the Pacific Coast. Lines on this map represent transition zones between different climatic types and should not be interpreted as areas of abrupt change in weather and climate or vegetation. Climatic boundaries are derived, of course, from averages of atmospheric conditions constantly subject to change.

The Köppen system (and most subsequent modifications) do not show the Borderlands Pacific coastal lowlands as a West Coast fog desert (Bn; n = *nebel*). Instead, this area is generally classified as a cool, semiarid climate (BSk). Russell (1931) pointed out that "The Köppen-Geiger (world) map recognizes foggy deserts . . . along the coasts of western South America and Africa, but, strangely, fails to do so for the Baja California coast." Russell and Van Royen (1927)

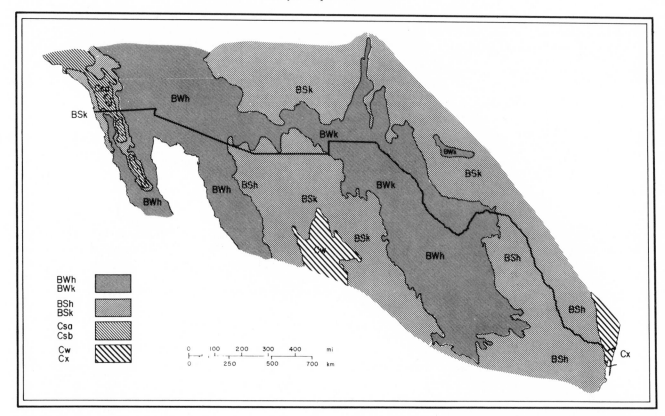

Fig. 20-1. *Climates of the Borderlands. Source: Based on Köppen-García system (Instituto de Geografía, 1970) and a composite of other sources (see text).*

have presented formidable arguments for changing the criterion of a mean annual isotherm of 18° C (64° F) for the differentiation of warm (Bh; h = *heiss*) and cool (Bk; k = *kalt*) dry climatic types, as this value has little to no significance in North America.

Although potential evaporation rates exceed precipitation totals in nearly the entire boundary zone, climatic variations are encountered. Altitude differences and proximity of the ocean are the most important. Along the Pacific littoral, the climate is a West Coast fog desert (Bn). This climatic type, which extends from the Baja region to north of San Diego, is classified as semiarid with a winter maximum of rainfall. The cool offshore waters result in aridity, frequent fogs, and smaller annual and diurnal temperature ranges than would be expected for most dry climates. A mountainous ridge separates the coastal plain from the extremely arid lowlands of the Colorado and Yuman deserts. There, rainfall totals—among the lowest on the continent—are less than 100 mm (4 in.; Fig. 20-2). Mean annual temperatures exceed 22° C (72° F). Further inland in the arid Arizona and Sonora Uplands Desert, a slight summer maximum of precipitation predominates, but significant moisture quantities are received during the winter months which result, as noted previously,

in a relatively luxuriant desert vegetation. On many small-scale maps, the Colorado, Yuman, and Arizona and Sonora Uplands deserts are lumped together as the Sonoran Desert. Generally, precipitation totals in this area range from 200 to 300 mm (8 to 12 in.), and mean annual temperatures are between 18° and 22° C (64° and 72° F).

The highlands of the central interior of the continent, which receives from 300 to 500 mm (12 to 20 in.) of moisture each year, is classified as semiarid. The higher altitude results in cooler mean annual temperatures, with a range of about 14° to 18° C (57° to 64° F). On the eastern slope of the Continental Divide, the border traverses the Chihuahuan Desert, which extends to about 101° west (the Del Rio-Ciudad Acuña area). This arid zone has a distinct summer precipitation maximum, with moisture totals averaging from 200 to 300 mm (8 to 12 in.) and mean annual temperatures from about 16° C (61° F) on the west margins to approximately 21° C (70° F) on the east. Eastward from the interior desert, the coastal lowlands are dominated by a semiarid climate receiving 300 mm (12 in.) to more than 600 mm (24 in.) of rainfall, most of which falls during the summer. Mean annual temperatures vary from 21° C (70° F) on the west to about 24° C (75° F) on the east.

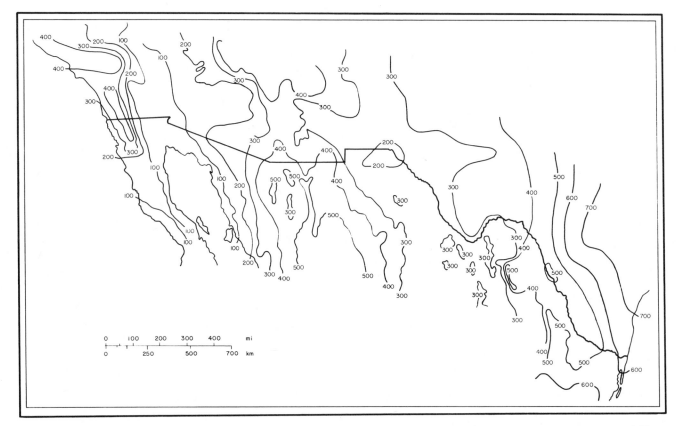

Fig. 20-2. *Mean annual precipitation (mm) in the Borderlands. Source: Instituto de Geografía (1970) and Bryson and Hare (1974).*

The climatic maps used by Vivó (1964) and the Instituto de Geografía (1970), based upon the Köppen system, classify the area adjacent to the mouth of the Rio Grande as a temperate subtropical climate [(Cx'w') and (A)C(x'), respectively]; that area receives relatively small quantities of rain in all months, with a precipitation maximum occurring in the fall.

For most of the border region, the greatest amount of precipitation is recorded in August. In the Colorado and Yuman deserts, precipitation is very erratic, not concentrated into one particular month or season. January is the dominant precipitation month from the Pacific coastline to near Mexicali. Almost the entire border area receives less than 150 mm (6 in.) of snow annually, and snow cover seldom remains on the ground more than a day or two.

The border region is truly in the Sunbelt. Possible mean annual sunshine ranges from 60 percent along the coastal lowlands of Texas to more than 90 percent in the lower Colorado River area; solar energy reaching the earth's surface varies from 380 langleys at La Jolla (San Diego County) to 536 langleys in El Paso (Environmental Data Service, 1968; Handy and Durrenberger, 1976).

The most significant unusual weather activity in the border area results from tropical storms which sometimes reach hurricane intensity. These storms, which occur in both the eastern-north Pacific Ocean and the Gulf of Mexico, seldom result in damage to border communities, but adjacent coastal areas have been devastated with loss of life and property. These storms do have a positive value, in that they bring considerable moisture to dry interior areas. Unusually wet years experienced by border communities are almost exclusively the result of these large tropical storms penetrating into the interior of the continent. Other unusual phenomena include whirlwinds, the warm, dry, föhn-type Santa Ana winds of coastal southern California, and periods of high humidity coupled with high summer temperatures that occasionally affect the area immediately north of the Gulf of California.

Within the border region there are a number of place names attesting to the climate's dryness and the consequences thereof. Representative examples include Yermo, Bagdad, Mecca, Thermal, Ocotillo, Yucca Valley, Desert Center, Desert Shores, Desert Springs, Winterhaven, Arroyo Seco, Sunnyside, Joshua Tree, Organ Pipe Cactus, White Sands, Playas, Rancho El Oasis, Bolsón de los Muertos, Jornada del Muerto, Canyon del Diablo, and Contrabando Mountain and Canyon.

21

Vegetation and Soils

ROBERT ARTHUR BYE, JR.
*Department of Environmental,
Population, and Organismic
Biology
University of Colorado, Boulder*

Plants and their rooting matrix are critical to human existence. An understanding of the variations in, and the exploitation and alteration of, these components is fundamental to man's survival and development. Vegetation is determined by the interactions of various plant-community species with climate and soils and their geological sources, topography and biota (including man). Soils, in turn, are products of the alteration of parent bedrock modified by plants, animals, and climate. The development of vegetation and soils is complexly interrelated (Eyre, 1968).

Vegetation

Descriptions and classifications of vegetation by scholars of different schools of plant ecology have led to considerable confusion and disagreement. Two widely recognized vegetation units include (1) the formation: a group of com-

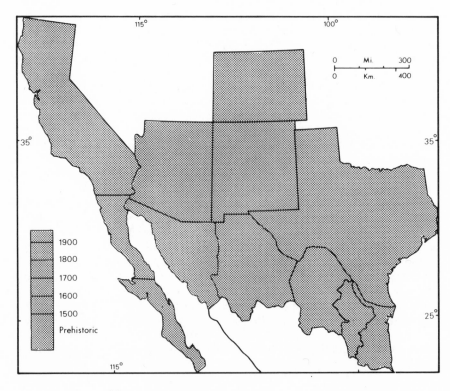

munities in a single continent of similar physiognomy and related climatic and environmental conditions, and (2) the association: a unit defined by floristic composition, character, and differential species and constancy. A summary of various concepts applied to vegetation classification can be found in Chapman (1976) and Schimwell (1971). The physiognomic concept has been clarified (Fosberg, 1967) to consist of (1) physiognomic characteristics (external appearances of vegetation such as leaf size and color), (2) functional characteristics (life form, phenology, periodicity, and dispersal mechanisms), and (3) structural characteristics (biomass distribution in vertical and horizontal spaces and abundance of each species). An important point to keep in mind is that plant communities are formed of assemblages of individual species which occur together along independent gradients of time, space, and environment (Whittaker, 1967). The vegetation study of the Santa Catalina Mountains of southeastern Arizona (Whittaker and Niering, 1965) is an important regional contribution to the development of this basic ecological concept.

Caution must be exercised when describing modern vegetation. Human activities such as agriculture, introduction of alien plants, and grazing have altered the natural vegetation. Often we must attempt to base vegetation maps on potential natural vegetation. Although the assumption may be unfounded, we assume that a disturbed area will return to natural climax vegetation after abandonment. However, continued or periodic land use activities by man and the theory of polyclimax (rather than monoclimax) can alter our perception of the vegetation. Also, descriptions are often based upon dominant vascular plants while less noticeable plants (for example, mosses) are usually not considered.

The cataloging and identification of vascular plants of an area are important in determining the composition and variety of the vegetation. The flora—that is, the assemblage of species in a defined area—includes such information as plant distribution and characteristics. Floras are usually written for a given ecological region or political unit. Some of the basic floras and related vegetation references for the Borderlands region are listed in Table 21-1. Unfortunately, there has not been a uniform floristic treatment for the Southwest, much less for northern Mexico. In addition to references cited in Table 21-1, information on certain Mexican vascular plants can be found in the following sources: trees and shrubs in Standley (1920-26), flowering plants in Langman (1964), and ferns in Jones (1966).

Borderlands vegetation has been examined, for the most part, on a political-geographical basis by individual scholars and by government agencies such as the Soil Conservation Service, the Forest Service, and the U.S. Geological Survey and by the Mexican Dirección de Agrología. Some useful sources for additional information on potential natural vegetation are listed in Table 21-2. Other references to regional vegetation maps can be found in Küchler and McCormick's (1965) bibliography. Mapping vegetation can present special problems which should be considered (Küchler, 1967).

For the purposes of this chapter, I will base my discussion of the major vegetation types upon the recent ecoregion

Table 21-1. *Floras and Vegetation Studies in the Borderlands.*

Texas	Correll and Johnston, 1970. *Manual of the Vascular Plants of Texas.*
	Gould, 1969. *Texas Plants: A Checklist and Ecological Summary.*
New Mexico	Castetter, 1956. The Vegetation of New Mexico.
	Dittmer, Castetter, and Clark, 1954. *The Ferns and Fern Allies of New Mexico.*
	Martin and Hutchins, 1980. *A Flora of New Mexico.*
	Wooton and Standley, 1915. Flora of New Mexico.
Arizona	Kearney and Peebles, 1960. *Arizona Flora.*
Arizona-New Mexico	Tidestrom and Kittell, 1941. *Flora of Arizona and New Mexico.*
Colorado	Harrington, 1964. *Manual of Plants of Colorado.*
	W. A. Weber, 1976. *Rocky Mountain Flora.*
California	Barbour and Major, 1977. *Terrestrial Vegetation of California.*
	Munz, 1974. *A Flora of Southern California.*
	Munz and Keck, 1973. *A California Flora with Supplement.*
Nuevo León	Muller, 1939. Relations of the Vegetation and Climatic Types in Nuevo León, Mexico.
Coahuila	Muller, 1947. Vegetation and Climate of Coahuila, Mexico.
Chihuahua	Knobloch and Correll, 1962. *Ferns and Fern Allies of Chihuahua, Mexico.*
	LeSueur, 1945. *The Ecology of the Vegetation of Chihuahua, Mexico, North of Parallel Twenty-eight.*
Sonora	White, 1948. The Vegetation and Flora of the Region of the Rio Bavispe in Northeastern Sonora, Mexico.
Sonora-Chihuahua	Gentry, 1942. *Rio Mayo Plants: A Study of the Flora and Vegetation of the Valley of the Rio Mayo, Sonora.*
Baja California	Wiggins, 1979. *Flora of Baja California.*
Intermountain United States	Cronquist, Holmgren, Holmgren, and Reveal, 1972. *Intermountain Flora.*
Chihuahuan Desert	Henrickson, 1977. Saline Habits and Halophytic Vegetation of the Chihuahuan Desert Region.
	Johnston, 1977. Brief Resume of Botanical, Including Vegetational, Features of the Chihuahuan Desert Region with Special References on Their Uniqueness.
	Johnston, in prep. *Chihuahuan Desert Flora.*
Sonoran Desert	Hastings, Turner, and Warren, 1972. *An Atlas of Some Plant Distributions in the Sonoran Desert.*
	Shreve and Wiggins, 1964. *Vegetation and Flora of the Sonoran Desert.*

Table 21-2. *Vegetation Maps and Descriptions of Vegetation in the Borderlands.*

United States	Bailey, 1978. Gerlach, 1970. Potential Natural Vegetation. Küchler, 1964.
New Mexico	Castetter, 1956. Soil Conservation Service, 1974.
Arizona	Nichol, 1952. University of Arizona, 1965.
Colorado	R. E. Gregg, 1963. Natural Vegetation of Colorado, modified from Colorado Agricultural Experiment Station map, 1935.
Mexico	Flores Mata et al., 1971. Miranda y Hernandez X., 1963. Rzedowski, 1978.
Southwestern United States and adjacent Mexico	Brown and Lowe, 1980.

concept of the United States (Bailey, 1978), with modifications based upon Küchler (1964), Flores Mata et al. (1971), and my interpretations of associations and formations. For specific details of the vegetation, one might consult the references in Küchler and McCormick (1965) and Tables 21-1 and 21-2.

The ecoregions are arranged in a descending hierarchy from domains to divisions, provinces, and sections. Each unit is characterized by vegetation as well as by fauna, soils, land-surface forms, and climate. The units covering the Borderlands are summarized in Table 21-3 and Fig. 21-1.

Three domains cover the Borderlands: the Humid Temperate Domain in eastern Texas and western California, the Dry Domain stretching from central Texas to eastern California, and the Dry Subtropical Domain scarcely reaching the southern parts of the Mexican states considered.

The Humid Temperate Domain includes two divisions in Texas. The Subtropical Division covers eastern Texas with the Outer Coastal Plain Forest Province of beech, sweetgum, magnolia, pine, and oak forests in the south and the Southeastern Mixed Forest Province with oak, hickory, and pine in the north. The Prairie Division is found in central Texas. The Prairie Parkland Province contains open oak stands mixed with bluestem grasslands. The Prairie Brushland Province is composed of three sections: the Mesquite-Buffalograss Section to the north, the Juniper-Oak-Mesquite Savanna with buffalograss and bluestem in the center, and the Mesquite-Acacia Savanna with bluestem and bristlegrass in the south into Mexico.

The Dry Domain dominates the greater part of the Borderlands. The Steppe Division covers much of the domain in the United States and extends down along the cordilleras into Mexico. The Great Plains-Shortgrass Prairie Province, with grama, buffalograss, and sunflowers, ranges from east-

ern Colorado through eastern New Mexico and northwestern Texas. Islands of grama and shortgrass prairie flank the eastern and western margins of the Chihuahua Desert into Mexico. The Rocky Mountain Forest Province covers the mountain chain with nearly pure stands of a few species of pines, spruce, Douglas fir, and aspen. In contrast, the Sierra Madrean Forest Province clothes the eastern and western

Table 21-3. *Vegetation of the Ecoregions of the Borderlands*

Fig. 21-1 Map Code	Domain/Division/Province/Section
1000	Humid Temperate Domain
1100	Subtropical Division
1110	Outer Coastal Plain Forest Province
	Beech-Sweetgum-Magnolia-Pine-Oak Forest Section
1120	Southeastern Mixed Forest Province
1200	Prairie Division
1210	Prairie Parkland Province
	Oak-Bluestem Parkland Section
1210	Prairie Brushland Province
1211	Mesquite-Buffalograss Section
1212	Juniper-Oak-Mesquite Savanna Section
1213	Mesquite-Acacia Savanna Section
1300	Mediterranean Division
1310	California Grassland Province
1320	Sierran Forest Province
1330	California Chaparral Province
1400	Marine Division
1410	Pacific Forest Province
1411	Redwood Forest Section
1412	California Mixed Evergreen Forest Section
2000	Dry Domain
2100	Steppe Division
2110	Great Plains-Shortgrass Prairie Province
	Grama-Buffalograss Section
2120	Rocky Mountain Forest Province
2130	Sierra Madrean Forest Province
2140	Upper Gila Mountains Forest Province
2150	Colorado Plateau Province
2151	Juniper-Piñon Woodland with Sagebrush-Saltbrush Mosaic Section
2152	Grama-Galleta Steppe with Juniper-Piñon Woodland Mosaic Section
2160	Mexican Highland Shrub Steppe Province
2200	Desert Division
2210	Chihuahuan Desert Province
2211	Grama-Tobosa Section
2212	Tarbush-Creosote Bush Section
2220	American Desert Province
2221	Creosote Bush Section (Mojave Desert)
2222	Creosote Bush-Bur Sage Section (Sonoran Desert)
2223	Cactus Forest Section (Sonoran Desert)
3000	Dry Subtropical Domain
3110	Subtropical Deciduous Forest Province

Source: Based on Bailey (1978).

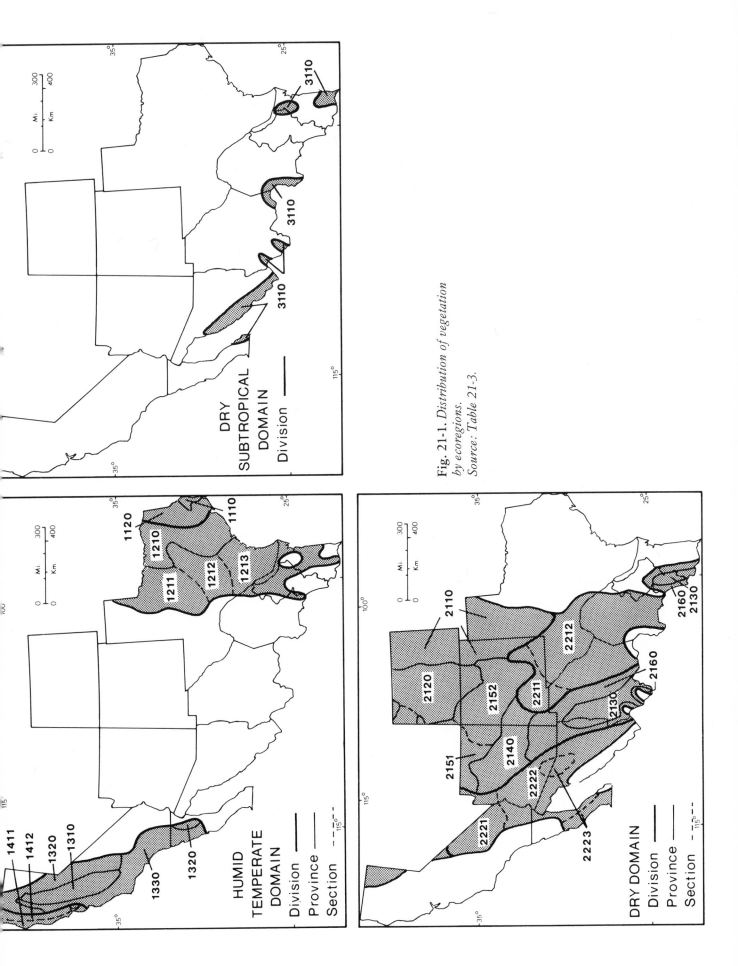

DRY SUBTROPICAL DOMAIN
Division ———

3110

3110

3110

HUMID TEMPERATE DOMAIN
Division ———
Province ———
Section – – –

1411
1412
1320
1310

1330
1320

1120
1210
1110
1211
1212
1213

DRY DOMAIN
Division ———
Province ———
Section – – –

2110
2120
2151
2152
2140
2211
2212
2222
2221
2223
2130
2160
2160
2130

Fig. 21-1. Distribution of vegetation by ecoregions.
Source: Table 21-3.

Mexican mountain chains with mixed forests of many species of pines, oaks, madroños, and aspen. Douglas fir and spruce form isolated pockets. The Upper Gila Mountains Forest Province of central Arizona and northern New Mexico consists of oak, juniper, and piñon woodlands at lower elevations, and ponderosa pine, Douglas fir, spruce, and aspen at higher elevations.

The Colorado Plateau Province of western Colorado, northern Arizona, and northwestern New Mexico includes two sections: (1) in the northwest, the Juniper-Piñon Woodland with Sagebrush-Saltbrush Mosaic, and (2) in the southeast, the Grama-Galleta Steppe with Juniper-Piñon Woodland Mosaic. The Mexican Highland Shrub Steppe Province, composed of shrubs, small trees, cacti, and grasses in open oak-juniper woodlands, flanks the Sierra Madrean Forest Province on the eastern and western slopes of the Mexican mountain chains and extends into southeastern Arizona and adjacent New Mexico.

The Desert Division is characterized by sparse vegetation and is located in north central Mexico and adjacent Texas and New Mexico and in northwestern Mexico and adjacent Arizona and California. In the east, the Chihuahuan Desert Province is divided into the Grama-Tobosa Section with scattered small trees, shrubs, and grassland and the Tarbush-Creosote Bush Section, with its characteristic creosote bush. Isolated islands of grasslands and pine, juniper, and oak woodlands are scattered throughout the province. In the west, the American Desert Province consists of the Mojave Desert (Creosote Bush Section) with creosote bush and chamiso, and with the prominent Joshua tree, juniper, and piñon at higher elevations. The Sonoran Desert contains two sections. The Creosote Bush-Bur Sage Section is dominated by low shrubs, while the Cactus Forest Section consists of columnar cacti such as the saguaro, organ pipe, and cardon as well as shorter chollas.

The Dry Subtropical Domain is found along the eastern and western coastal plains and extends up the canyons of the Sierra Madre and also in central Mexican highlands. The Subtropical Deciduous Forest Province is characterized by many small trees and shrubs of the legume and other tropical families which drop their leaves in the dry season as well as by xeric plants such as cacti and agaves.

The Humid Temperate Domain of western California and adjacent Baja California is represented by two divisions. The Mediterranean Division includes the California Grassland, Sierran Forest, and California Chaparral provinces. Today the California grassland of California's Central Valley is dominated by agricultural fields and grasslands composed of European annual grasses such as oats, brome, barley, and fescue. The Central Valley is flanked on the north and east by the Sierran Forest Province with junipers, piñons, oaks, buckbrushes, and manzanitas in the foothills and various pines, firs, and oaks at the higher elevations. A similar range is isolated in northern Baja California. Bordering the western and southern sides of the Central Valley is the California Chaparral Province of woody plants with thick evergreen leaves. The forest communities (sclerophyll forest) of oaks and junipers are intertwined with the shrub communities (chaparral) of manzanitas, chamiso, oaks, and mountain mahogany. The Pacific Forest Province of the Marine Division is limited to a narrow band along the northwestern coast of California. Along the coast proper is the Redwood Forest Section characterized by giant redwood trees. Inland from the coast is found the California Mixed Evergreen Forest Section with oaks, hemlock, and madroño.

Climax vegetation changes over geological time as a result of evolutionary pressures and climatic, pedeological, and geological alterations. The movement and development of elements and communities of vegetation over the past 140 million years in the Borderlands are only partially understood (Axelrod, 1958; Daubenmire, 1978). More recent changes in the vegetation of the southwestern United States can be documented by pollen records (Martin, 1963; Martin and Mehringer, 1965) and phytogeography (Weber, 1965). Since the late Quaternary period, the vegetation of the northern area of the present-day Chihuahuan Desert has shifted from mesic, subalpine forests of spruce and pine to xeric woodlands of piñon, juniper, and oak to the present desert vegetation (Bryant, 1977; Van Devender and Worthington, 1977; Van Devender et al., 1977; Wells, 1977). In contrast to this relatively slow process, the impact of man on natural vegetation can be rapid.

The employment of fire in the forests and grasslands by the American Indians probably represented the earliest major human force to alter the vegetation in western North America (Lewis, 1973, 1981; Mitchell, 1978; Stewart, 1951, 1954, 1955a, 1955b, 1956). Exploitation of native plants by American Indians in the greater Southwest has been an important component of man's interaction with the natural vegetation. Castetter (1935) has summarized the uncultivated food plants for the area. Elements of the Borderlands' vegetation sold, traded, and employed to improve human health can be found in *Las Yerbas de la Gente* (Ford, 1975). Other useful native plants have been recorded for California (C. B. Clarke, 1977), New Mexico (Standley, 1911), and Texas (Johnston, in prep.). Certain cultural groups have had their economically important plants recorded: Apaches (Castetter and Opler, 1936), Cahuillas (Barrows, 1900; Bean and Saubel, 1972), Hopis (Whiting, 1939), Navahos (Vestal, 1952), Mexican Pimas (Pennington, 1980), Papagos (Castetter and Underhill, 1935), Seris (Felger and Moser, 1974b, 1976), Southern Paiutes (Bye, 1972), Tarahumaras (Pennington, 1963b), Tepehuans (Pennington, 1969), and Zunis (Stevenson, 1915; Camazine and Bye, 1980). The exploitations of distinctive Borderlands plants such as *Prosopis,* mesquite and screwbean (Bell and Castetter, 1937; Felger and Moser, 1971), *Agave,* century plant (Bye, Burgess, and Mares Trias, 1975; Castetter, Bell, and Grove, 1938; Felger and Moser, 1970) and various cacti (Castetter and Bell, 1937; Felger and Moser, 1974a) have been examined. Agricultural practices of the Hopis (Whiting, 1936, 1937), Yumas (Castetter and Bell, 1951), and Pimas and Papagos (Castetter and Bell, 1942) have been documented. Other references to native American employment of natural vegetation have been summarized by Whiting (1966).

The introduction of cattle, sheep, goats, and other grazing and browsing animals by Hispanic and Anglo cultures rapidly diminished the dry grasslands of the Southwest, which yielded many edible wild grains for natives (Bohrer, 1975). Grazing, erosion, and fire control have been credited with the change of the desert grasslands to scrubland of mesquite and cacti *(Opuntia)* (Humphrey, 1958) in the last hundred years in northeastern Mexico and adjacent Texas (Johnston, 1963), southern New Mexico (York and Dick-Peddie, 1969), and southern Arizona (Glendening, 1952). Changes in the vegetation over a seventy-year period have been visually documented in what has been called the "Changing Mile" (Hastings and Turner, 1965). Current studies at the Research Ranch in southeastern Arizona are focusing on the response of once heavily grazed grassland to release from grazing (Bahre, 1977).

Other human activities also affect natural vegetation. Lumbering for fuel, construction material, and tannin has altered the oak and subtropical woodlands and coniferous forests. Rapid expansion of agriculture and associated irrigation have transformed southern and central California, Arizona, and other areas of the Borderlands (Austin, 1972; Gerlach, 1970; *World Atlas of Agriculture*). Attempts to increase and improve grazing lands by chaining, dozing, and firing the piñon-juniper forests have led to the clearing of many areas (Aro, 1971). Recreation vehicles, power and pipeline construction, and road building have modified portions of the Mojave Desert vegetation (Davidson and Fox, 1974; Johnson, Vasek, and Yonkers, 1975; Vasek, Johnson, and Brum, 1975; Vasek, Johnson, and Eslinger, 1975). As population and exploitation of natural resources for food and fiber increase, the arid region of the Borderlands will undergo changes that will further affect natural vegetation (McGinnies, Goldman, and Paylore, 1971). Also the changes in the patterns of land use in the American Southwest caused by the shift from Native American cultures to Euro-American cultures has led to the local extinction of a number of useful plants (Bohrer, 1978).

Introduced plants have taken over many Borderlands areas. The European tamarix *(Tamarix pentandra)* has spread along waterways at a rapid rate and threatens water supplies (Harris, 1966). Introduced grasses such as wild oats *(Avena fatua* and *A. barbata)* and brome grass *(Bromus tectorum)* dominate many parts of the natural grasslands. Alien plants in California have received much attention with respect to their importance in the state flora (Smith and Noldeke, 1960), in agricultural conditions (Robbins, Bellue, and Ball, 1951), and along roadsides (Frenkel, 1970). Eurasian tumbleweeds *(Salsola iberica* and *Kochia iranica)* move across the high plains and grasslands. Filaree *(Erodium cicutarium),* native of Europe, provides a common herbage for cattle in our southwestern states.

Soil

Soils are complex products of geological alteration of bedrock by climatic and biotic interactions. A new system of soil classification (Soil Survey Staff, 1975) has replaced the old system, which was based on presumed pathways of soil genesis. The new system is based primarily on soil properties instead of climatology, geology, and assumed genesis processes. The classification is arranged in a descending hierarchy from orders to suborders, great groups, subgroups, families, series, and types. Caution must be exercised when consulting the state, regional, and local maps and descriptions from the Soil Conservation Service. The type of classification employed, the sampling techniques used, and the purpose of the survey must be evaluated before using the large- and small-scale soil reports and maps available from local and regional Soil Conservation offices (Bartelli et al., 1966).

Six soil orders are located in the Borderlands (Fig. 21-2) (Buckman and Brady, 1969; Fuller, 1975; Gerlach, 1970; Soil Survey Staff, 1975; Secretaría de Recursos Hidráulicos, 1972). The dominant regional order, Aridisol, is composed of arid, mineral soils which are dry in all horizons more than six months of the year and have pedogenic horizons, low natural leaching, and low organic matter. With irrigation, these soils are very productive agriculturally. Entisol also includes mineral soils which are scattered throughout the region but exhibit no natural distinctive horizons. These vary between highly productive soils and infertile barren sands.

Mollisol contains many important agricultural soils which developed under grasslands and forests. They are defined by black, organic-rich surface horizons with high base supply. Alfisol also includes good productive agricultural soils which developed under grass and forest communities. They are characterized by gray to brown surface horizons with medium to high base supply and subsurface horizons with clay accumulation. Although generally moist, these soils are often dry during the warm season.

Ultisol soils are not naturally fertile but respond well to good agricultural management. These acidic soils developed in moist, warm, forested areas and are located in the northeastern and northwestern margins of the Borderlands. Vertisol, the most restricted soil order, is located in eastern Texas and adjacent northeastern Mexico. This order has limited agricultural productivity due to the drying and cracking of the soils. The mineral soil is high in swelling clay which develops wide cracks during the dry season and causes inversions of the soil by allowing the upper profile to drop into the deep cracks.

The Future

There are many problems facing Borderlands researchers. As one can gather from the above text, there are no standardized or uniform vegetation and soil treatments of the whole Borderlands. Even the fragmentary studies are inadequate. Many floristic, ecological, and taxonomic studies by American scientists end at the border, implying that the plants respect recent political boundaries. The only study on the biota of this entire stretch was conducted by the U.S. government under the direction of Emory (1857) after the formation of the boundary following the Mexican-American War. Perhaps an international effort by present-day scholars would be appropriate on a large scale; a start that focuses

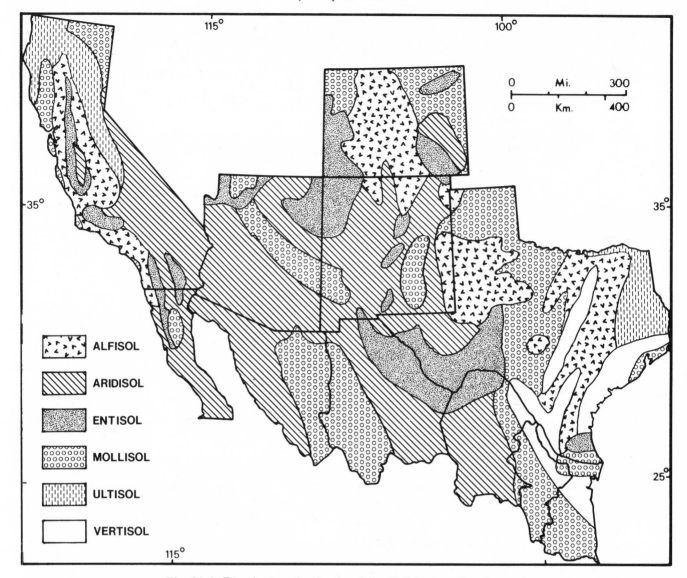

Fig. 21-2. *Distribution of soil orders (New Soil Survey Classification).*

on the Chihuahuan Desert has recently begun (Wauer and Riskind, 1977). Also, a recent international conference discussed the vegetation, soil, and plant resources of the arid lands including the Borderlands region (Goodin and Northington, 1979).

Very basic research still presents a challenge to the life scientists. Many areas have only recently been studied by botanists. In some areas the populations of species new to science are being destroyed before the plants can be described (for example, *Tauschia allioides;* Bye and Constance, 1979). Very fundamental questions related to the evolution, development, and movement of the desert and mountain flora remain unanswered. In the light of increased field work, the development of ecological theories, and the acceleration of human alterations of the Borderlands environment, the definitions, processes, and classifications of plant communities up to biotic provinces are seriously in need of urgent re-evaluation.

The exploitation of and interaction with the ambient vegetal environment by native peoples are vast research areas open to life and social scientists; to date we know relatively little about the biological diversity and bases of man's employment of these resources which represent thousands of years of experimentation and codevelopment. Natural and man-made changes in the plants and vegetation from archaeological and micro and macro fossil investigations are poorly documented. In-depth inquiry into these and other areas can provide thousands of years of insight into the relationships of human populations with vegetation and soils of the past. This information, along with increased knowledge of our present dependent relationship with the Borderlands environment, can help us plan an improved interaction.

Borderlands settlement and patterns of land use existed before the arrival of the Spaniards. The small seed-gathering and hunting populations who inhabited desert areas left practically no permanent imprints upon the landscapes. However, the sedentary peoples who lived near available water or on elevated, defensible sites did leave their mark. Even though their settlements were widely separated, resulting in an overall appearance of a sparsely populated region, some of the most densely populated communities in pre-European North America were found in the Borderlands.

Pre-Spanish Imprints

These settlements were compact agglomerations of residences which, in many cases, displayed some kind of alignment pattern. The Puebloans, in particular, had small plazalike layouts that often consisted of multiple plazas centered upon

22

Rural Settlements and Land Use

ALVAR W. CARLSON
Department of Geography
Bowling Green State University

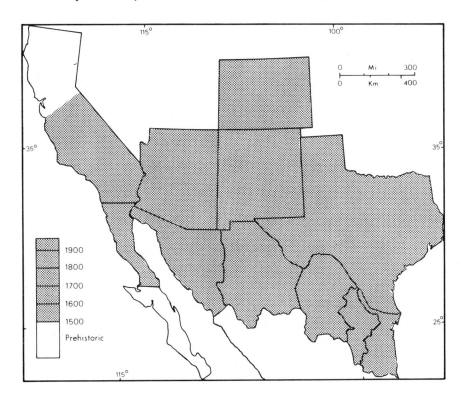

kivas which were enclosed by buildings, mostly multistoried structures (Fliedner, 1975; Scully and Current, 1971). Pit houses surrounding plazas and streets were evident in some of the settlements found on mesetas between the Sierra Madre Oriental and the Sierra Madre Occidental. Other peoples, such as the Mogollons and the Hohokams, apparently made little effort to align or orient their settlements in any repetitive fashion (Reed, 1956). The cliff dwellings were yet another type of village. Notable examples are found in Bandelier National Park and Puye Cliffs in northern New Mexico and in western Chihuahua (Haas, 1926; J. Kelley, 1956; Mindeleff, 1898). Among these cliff dwellings there were often multiroom buildings of masonry, tabular stone, adobe, or a combination of these. These building materials were used by most sedentary peoples.

Irrigation agriculture sustained the densest sedentary settlements in the Borderlands, especially on the floodplains in the upper Rio Grande and Gila River valleys. In the latter case, the Hohokams constructed an elaborate irrigation system with canals. Floodwater farming on the level lands became fairly extensive, but it was eventually hindered by the increasing number of arroyos (Bryan, 1929, 1941). Sanddune farming was also practiced, as among the Anasazis in northern Arizona. Peoples may have moved from piedmont locations to river valleys as they learned the techniques of irrigation (Dickson, 1975). Most settlements were below 7,500 feet in elevation to allow the crops, chiefly corn, to mature in a longer growing season. Several site qualities were therefore considered in establishing an agricultural settlement. The farmland was probably cultivated in common, as there is little evidence of private landownership.

No topic concerning the imprints left by pre-Spanish peoples has been examined more carefully than that of the *cerros de trincheras* (Herold, 1965; Hoover, 1941; Howard and Griffiths, 1968; Sauer and Brand, 1931). These are hills with small rock terraces or entrenchments built as residential sites or as defense walls. Examples can be found in Sonora, Arizona, and New Mexico. The term, especially the word *trincheras,* is also applied to the stone-wall dikes arranged in tiers in canyons and gulches of the high Sierra Madre Occidental to catch alluvium and reduce runoff. Most of this building activity dates from 1100 to 1450 A.D., with evidence that some of it continued until the early 1800s.

Hispanic Imprints

In colonizing the Borderlands, Spaniards used several landholding systems. First, many *encomiendas* were awarded which involved large tracts and the right of the *encomendero* to extract labor from the local inhabitants (L. Simpson, 1950). *Encomenderos* also practiced animal husbandry, which led to the beginnings of the extensive use of land for agriculture. This land system existed in the upper Rio Grande Valley until the Pueblo Revolt of 1680. It was replaced by a system of land grants given either to individuals or to groups of petitioners in order to establish a colony. The individual land grants were again usually huge tracts used for livestock grazing.

In settling colony grants, considerable attention was given to the site, because irrigation agriculture was to complement livestock grazing. Consequently, these grants embraced floodplain areas that were eventually carved into a rather dense settlement pattern, particularly in New Mexico's Rio Arriba. In an egalitarian manner, the limited irrigable land was partitioned into small plots which extended across the floodplain perpendicular to the river in order to assure each landowner equal cropland, accessibility to the community *acequia,* and proper drainage toward the river. This riverine long-lot system of partitioning land was accentuated in time by the custom of subdividing land parcels lengthwise upon inheritance, resulting in an even narrower series of ribbonlike fields (Carlson, 1975a; Harper, Cordova and Oberg, 1943; Leonard, 1970). The Rio Arriba still has a high density of farms under ten acres in size. Because the inhabitants preferred to live near their fields, their houses were located on the upslope edges of the irrigated land, resulting in linear villages. This long-lot system of settlement was also used by Spanish Americans as they acquired land in many of the Pueblo Indian grants, especially after Spanish and Mexican rule (Carlson, 1975b). The Spanish Americans also had the communal use of their grants' remaining uplands for their livestock. In addition, commons were established occasionally near the villages for the local grazing of livestock; an existing example can be found near San Luis in south central Colorado (Carlson, 1967). The long-lot system was also used along several rivers in southern Texas, where the land parcels were much larger than those in the Rio Arriba.

After Spanish rule, the Mexican government continued to make both individual and colony grants in the American Borderlands (Bowden, 1971). It also used the *empresario* system whereby a colonizer or a promoter received a large tract of land if he settled it with a certain number of families and within a specified time.

Spaniards used metes and bounds to describe large grants bestowed in more rugged terrain such as the upper Rio Grande Valley of New Mexico and Colorado. If a unit of measurement was used in this area, it was the league, which amounted to slightly over two and one-half miles. One square league, a *sitio,* was equal to approximately 4,400 acres. The league and the *sitio* were used in the rest of the Borderlands, especially in California, southern Arizona, southern Texas, and northern Mexico (Allen, 1935; Arneson, 1925; Daniell, 1948; Houston, 1961; Mattison, 1946). In the colony grants, the small landholdings were measured in *varas* (one *vara* was equal to 33 inches), which were recorded by the width of the parcel. A number of other units of measurement were used, such as the *caballeria* (approximately 106 acres), but there is also evidence that small parcels of varying sizes were given to people according to the amount of land needed to plant several *fanegas* of seed. In southern Texas, a land unit usually one mile along a river by up to fifteen miles deep was known as a *porción* (Foscue, 1939; Jordan, 1974). These different cadastral methods have had a lasting impact upon rural landscapes, especially in road patterns and political boundaries (Hornbeck, 1976).

Other Hispanic legacies evident in the rural landscapes are the styles of architecture and the use of certain building materials. Adobe brick was used extensively to construct the thick walls of houses, and *terrones*—sod bricks cut from the ground—were used to a lesser degree. Wood was also commonly used, especially in the case of poles for the ubiquitous flat-roofed dwellings. Although the flat roof typified rural houses in both the Mexican and American Borderlands, it is claimed that the Spaniards were responsible for its northward diffusion from aboriginal origins in Mexico (West, 1974). There was normally a greater use of wood in settlements established in close proximity to woodlands found in the higher elevations. There, many buildings were of log or pole construction and were chinked and plastered with adobe (Bunting and Conron, 1966; Gritzner, 1971; Winberry, 1974). An example was a version of the *jacal*, a small one- or two-room, flat-roofed dwelling associated with poorer people. Gable-roofed farmhouses of log frames were built in the mountainous settlements of the upper Rio Grande Valley. They were probably prototypes from Spain (Conway, 1951*b*). In the same area, water-driven gristmills were also built of logs (Gritzner, 1974). Many of the individually owned grants in the Borderlands were characterized by hacienda-type buildings—large masonry houses often with masonry corrals which altogether gave the appearance of small fortresses (Conway, 1951*a*). Common among many of the houses on ranches, and to a lesser extent on the properties of the small landholders, was the *placita,* or private plaza formed by extensions built onto the house to enclose a small area like a courtyard. Because of the yearlong grazing in much of the Borderlands, corrals were in greater use than barns, although barns were built in some of the higher elevations.

A quasi-Spanish rural colonial settlement was the mission. Some missions were large agricultural operations based upon extensive landholdings. Consequently, physical conditions such as soil, water supply for irrigation, and topography were factors in the selection of their sites. Other factors included distance between missions and the number of aborigines in an area who were potential converts to Christianity. Missionaries introduced cattle and numerous crops and horticultural plants to California and Texas (Gentilcore, 1961; Gordon, 1961).

Even the establishment of the early Spanish *pueblos* or civil settlements was based partially upon adjacent agricultural lands. In Los Angeles, settlers received both town lots and equal amounts of irrigable planting fields *(suertes),* which were located between the main irrigation ditch and the river (Baugh, 1942). They also received equal amounts of nonirrigable land, presumably for grazing purposes. Townsites were to be carefully selected, and, again, there tended to be an egalitarian approach to granting land in a semiarid area. Although strategic reasons were paramount in the site selection of forts or *presidios,* there was also some consideration given to the nearby agricultural potentialities of the surrounding land.

Anglo-American Imprints

Beginning in the mid-1800s, many people from other sections of the United States migrated to the American Borderlands to acquire land and pursue farming or ranching. The American system of disposing of land was introduced by the U.S. General Land Office. Initially, the land beyond the recognized Spanish land grants was surveyed in townships and ranges based on the Land Ordinance of 1785. Consequently, a rectangular order was placed upon the land by which prospective settlers could acquire 160-acre homesteads or parcels of up to 640 acres under subsequent legislative acts. These larger parcels were mainly to support the establishment of grazing operations in areas of low carrying capacity. Sometimes many sections were put together to form large livestock ranches. Homesteaders and those who received similar-sized bounty grants, especially in Texas, generally raised crops either by dry farming or, if more fortunate, by irrigation (Miller, 1962). Usually there was a scarcity of land which could be irrigated, for water was not readily available. General farming on many homesteads was deemed unprofitable, and these parcels were frequently combined to form larger operations, primarily ranches. In the settlement of the West, several Borderlands states were important sources of sheep and cattle (Carlson, 1969; Haskett, 1936). The rugged Edwards Plateau of southwestern Texas has long been known for its sheep and goats (Chambers, 1932).

Although much land today is used for livestock grazing, there are areas within the agricultural matrix which are important for their commercial crop specializations. Much intensive crop farming is based on irrigation, which has relied on the development of large projects using surface water or pumps to obtain groundwater. In attempts to find the optimum crop or crops for a given time and place, patterns of land use have changed through time. For example, sugar cane and rice were raised in the lower Rio Grande Valley in the early 1900s before the area was turned into a "winter garden" known for its vegetables and citrus fruits (Dillman, 1970*d*; Foscue, 1932*a*). These and other crops ranging from pinto beans to date palms are raised in southern Arizona, southern California, and elsewhere (Birle, 1976). Cotton has emerged as a leading crop. Some of the large farms producing and processing these different crops have been characterized as farm factories and plantations (Gregor, 1962). Mechanization has allowed for the farming of larger individual land units as well as fragmented units.

On the whole, only a small percentage of each state's land is irrigated. Irrigated land is both the most valuable and the most productive in the Borderlands. Continuous urban sprawl has resulted in the loss of considerable amounts of this valuable land and in cases has altered the nature of the surrounding agricultural production (Griffen and Chatham, 1958; Preston, 1965). Overall, the total number of farms has declined just as dramatically here as in the rest of the country, and less than 2 percent of the people in the Borderlands states live on farms today. The number of farms declined by 48 percent from 548,000 in 1950 to 284,000 in 1974. The farm population constituted nearly 11 percent of the total population in 1950. Between 1950 and 1974, there were significant declines in the number of acres in farms, acres of cropland harvested, and acres of total cropland. The acres of irrigated land, however, increased by nearly 40 percent in the same period. Although each of the five states had sizable increments, the acres of irrigated land doubled in Texas.

Changes have also characterized the livestock industry. Large feedlots have been established, notably on the High Plains and in the Imperial Valley of California. Even the location of dairy cattle has changed, as more and more are found today in drylots in close proximity to the markets of metropolitan areas. In general, Anglo-Americans transformed the rural economy of the American Borderlands from one based largely upon pastoral and subsistence activities to one which has become highly commercialized and diversified.

The diversity in rural landscapes can be attributed in part to differences in the settlers. Ethnic groups such as the Italian Swiss became dairymen in San Luis Obispo County, California; Germans started vineyards near Anaheim, California, and introduced *fachwerk* architecture to the Texas Hill Country north of San Antonio; Japanese specialized in market gardening in southern California and in the San Luis Valley of south central Colorado; and Dutch and Portuguese became dairymen in Los Angeles and Orange counties, California (Fielding, 1962; Iwata, 1962; Jordan, 1966; Raup, 1932*a*, 1935, 1936). The cultural baggage of the midwesterner was manifested by large frame house styles. Southerners, especially the mountaineers, left their imprints in the eastern half of Texas, as they preferred to settle in the hilly terrain (Jordan, 1970*b*). Their initial perception of the environment led them to avoid the prairies, a decision which was also made by some other people.

Mormons also left a notably distinctive imprint on the rural landscapes of both the United States and Mexico. In the latter half of the 1800s they settled many colonies, including Mesa, Saint Johns, and Snowflake in Arizona; Ramah and Fruitland in western New Mexico; San Bernardino in southern California; and Manassa in south central Colorado (Carlson, 1967; Landgraf, 1954; McClintock, 1921; Meinig, 1965). A half-dozen also came to exist in northwestern Chihuahua and northern Sonora beginning in 1885 (Romney, 1938). The Mexican colonies were for the most part depopulated during the Mexican Revolution (Mills, 1954). These agricultural communities were based largely on stock raising and crop irrigation; consequently, they were located near streams, even in the case of the mountain colonies of Mexico. A spacious grid pattern was used in laying out towns, and in the large village blocks, large house lots contained residences, barns, and sheds. Each colonist farmed a rectangular plot of land in the surrounding countryside. Other elements of the Mormon landscape included the town's wide streets lined with tall shade trees, usually cottonwoods; the ward church; substantial brick or stone houses; and hay derricks in the fields (Francaviglia, 1970, 1978; Nelson, 1952).

Although rural landscapes inevitably change, some do so faster than others. For example, the numerous ghost towns,

many associated with early mining operations, tell another part of the Borderlands' economic history (Sherman and Sherman, 1969, 1975). Attempts to colonize for unusual reasons also failed, as in the case of the Boer and Land of Shalam ventures, both near Las Cruces, New Mexico, about 1900 (Keleher, 1944; Maluy, 1977). Generally, an understanding of man's imprint on the present-day rural landscape, when combined with a knowledge of local settlement and economic history, provides insights into many of his struggles to exploit the region.

Mexican Rural Settlements

As in the American Borderlands, settlements in northern Mexico are widely scattered largely because of diverse terrain and limited water resources. Most of the Mexican Borderlands, despite its low carrying capacity, is used for grazing. Large livestock ranches, *ganaderías,* are located throughout the Mexican Borderlands, some having been established in the late 1500s (Brand, 1961). Cattle drives were made from northern Mexico to Mexico City as late as the 1830s. A number of cattle barons owned huge estates (Chevalier, 1963).

Other private landholdings include the *hacienda,* a large tract owned by a single family wherein general farming and ranching are emphasized (McBride, 1971). As land sizes get smaller, crops are increasingly emphasized. Farms of a fairly large size, *particulares,* are found in the irrigated valleys where cotton and wheat are grown commercially (Dozier, 1963). Mexican law has restricted the maximum amount of irrigated land that a private person can own to one hundred hectares. A small privately owned parcel of land may be referred to as a *colono,* and often as a *rancho.* One remaining type of private landholding is the plantation, exemplified by those which produce henequen in Tamaulipas (Fox, 1965).

In the early 1900s very few heads of families owned land. Land reform measures were instituted, and a considerable number of the large holdings, latifundia, including irrigable land were expropriated by the government and redistributed to landless families, *agraristas.* Much of this land was incorporated into *ejidos,* which comprised numerous small parcels usually of ten hectares or smaller (E. Simpson, 1937). The government leased the parcels to the *ejidatarios* rent free and in perpetuity. By 1940 there were approximately 2,300 *ejidos* in the six Borderlands states, constituting approximately one-sixth of those in Mexico (Whetten, 1948). Agrarian reform policies to reduce the number of landless families have continued to be an integral part of the country's land tenure systems, especially with the expansion of irrigated farming since 1940 (Henderson, 1965).

Under governmental guidance, a new land tenure system, the village corporation (Empresa Agropecuaria Ejidal), has been introduced into northwestern Mexico within the past decade. The land is divided into sections of one hundred to three hundred hectares and assigned to section chiefs who have laborers, and all are under a professional manager (Haissman, 1971).

Aside from the private and governmental landholdings, several ethnic and religious groups other than the Mormons acquired land in the Mexican Borderlands. Mennonites settled largely in Chihuahua along the eastern flank of the Sierra Madre Occidental, but not until the 1920s. Their homogeneous, compact settlements, based upon diversified farming, manifested elements of the *Strassendorf* or line-village settlement pattern found in Germany (Sawatzky, 1971; Schmiedehaus, 1954). Approximately fifteen to thirty families lived in each of the one-street villages in house lots that contained both residences and barnyards. They farmed adjacent fields that were laid out in strips *(koerls)* in order to equalize the type of land and soil for each family. Farm sizes were fairly large, ranging from thirty to over one hundred hectares. In 1905, a Russian colony of one hundred families located near Ensenada in Baja California Norte. Their *Strassendorf* village and adjacent lands were allocated, the latter in small, noncontiguous parcels in order to assure that each family received equal amounts of good and bad land (Schmieder, 1928). Using the *mir* land tenure system, all of the land belonged to the parish, with no colonist receiving an individual title. After the harvests, the fields became common pastures.

Indian Rural Settlements

Although many Indians of the American Borderlands have moved to cities, a large percentage still live in rural areas, especially on reservations. The Spanish government was the first to set aside lands for the Indians, giving grants to the different Pueblo Indians in New Mexico. The reservation system was formally introduced by the American government largely to subdue the Indians and to open up lands for non-Indian settlement. Reservations occupy much of the land in both Arizona and New Mexico. There are a number of small mission Indian reservations in southern California.

Navahos came to live on the Borderlands' largest reservation, which is located mostly in northern Arizona and northwestern New Mexico. They established a pastoral economy based upon seminomadism, and their large numbers of livestock, mostly sheep, eventually led to overgrazing, accelerated erosion, and more recently a stock reduction program (Fonaroff, 1963; Hoover, 1931, 1937). In cases, this program led from a dependence upon grazing to an agricultural economy such as the use of irrigated land at Fruitland, New Mexico (Sasaki, 1960). Most Navahos live dispersed in isolated hogans, hexagonal or octagonal dome-shaped structures, scattered here and there upon the reservation. In the past, many families moved to nearby valleys in the summer to cultivate small plots where they had temporary tents or *ramadas* (Page, 1937). A reliance upon a pastoral economy was adopted by several other tribes who possessed fairly large reservations, namely the San Carlos Apache, Acoma, Laguna, and Ute Indians. Overgrazing has been a problem on these last reservations.

Various tribes continued to farm much as they had done for years without depending greatly upon livestock. The Hopis, whose reservation is in the midst of the Navaho Reservation, continued to follow their cultural preference for agriculture (Bradfield, 1971; Forde, 1931; Hack, 1942; Hoover, 1930). Living in tabular stone and adobe houses enclosing courts within nucleated villages upon the high Black Mesa, they farmed fields some distance away. The field sites depended largely upon the availability of water. Some Hopi farmers practiced floodwater farming at the mouths of arroyos. Their irregularly shaped plots were known as *akchin* fields, but the increasing incision of arroyos greatly limited this type of farming. Some selected field sites on sand dunes, which possessed adequate groundwater supplies and inhibited arroyos, and others cultivated fields in cliff terraces where springs provided water. Most of the farmers were, and still are, horticulturists who tilled several isolated patches, as they believed that farming a number of sites would reduce the risk of total crop failure. Some of the families were resettled in an irrigation project along the Colorado River beginning in the mid-1940s (McIntire, 1969*a*). Not far away, the Havasupai Indians also continued intensive irrigated farming upon communally owned land. Similarly, the Pueblo Indians in the upper Rio Grande Valley of New Mexico continued to practice basically subsistence irrigated agriculture. Their irregularly shaped fields surrounded the pueblo, which focused on a plaza enclosed by adobe houses. The kiva was a focal point of the plaza.

In the Mexican Borderlands, Indian tribes that remain are less distinguishable than those in the American Borderlands. Most of them continue to live on their aboriginal lands where they were found by the early Spaniards. Their lands today are assigned to them, and in certain cases *ejidos* have been established. The major tribes include the Mexican Kickapoos (who originated in the United States) in northern Coahuila, the Northern Tepehuans in southern Chihuahua, and the Tarahumaras in the Sierra Madre Occidental of northwestern Mexico (Gajdusek, 1953; Latorre and Latorre, 1976; Pennington, 1969). The Tarahumaras live in isolated conditions, and some are seminomadic herdsmen while others farm small plots. The Northern Tepehuans are also engaged largely in horticultural practices. Mexican Kickapoos depend greatly upon native plants and subsistence farming (Latorre and Latorre, 1977). Each tribe has used different types of housing according to environmental conditions and their economy. The Kickapoos and Tarahumaras have seasonal habitations for winter and summer. Most interestingly, the Tarahumaras use caves in barranca walls for their winter lodgings. The Kickapoos live in wigwams in the winter and open-sided houses in summer. Log dwellings are used by the Tepehuans. Aside from the Pimas and the Papagos, who reside mostly on reservations in southern Arizona, there are only a few remnants of the desert tribes on either side of the border. Their native habitations varied from the circular wattle *kee* used by the Pimas to the roofless windbreaks of the Seris on the very arid Tiburon Island in the Gulf of California (Waterman, 1924). Most of these peoples, including the Yaquis in Sonora, are engaged primarily in subsistence irrigated agriculture (Spicer, 1940, 1954).

Preserving Natural Areas

In the American Borderlands much of the public domain has now been set aside for natural areas and forests. Besides those lands surrounding the spectacular features such as the Grand Canyon which are designated as national parks and monuments, large areas were placed in preserves, namely the federal and state forests. Many areas were established upon the concept of wilderness. In fact, the nation's first wilderness area, the Gila Wilderness, was set aside in 1924. New Mexico and California rank among the states with the most wilderness land today. Nearly 45 percent of the land in California and Arizona is federally owned, while over one-third of the land in New Mexico and Colorado is federally owned. By contrast, less than 2 percent of Texas is in federal ownership. More recently, attempts are being made to preserve other types of lands—for example, the coastline of California and parts of the Mojave Desert. Metropolitan peoples want to be assured that there is "open space" surrounding them. All of these lands have recreational values for both the Borderlands' resident and transient populations. Urbanization has caused the loss of arable land, but on the other hand the demands of urbanites have also placed a premium on preserving the countryside.

Mexico has approximately fifty national parks, of which seven are located in the Borderlands. Its largest national park (Cumbres de Monterrey) covers over 600,000 acres near Monterrey, Nuevo León. Of the Mexican Borderlands states, only Sonora has no national park (Taplin, 1962).

Three historical traditions coexist uneasily in New Mexico—those of the American Indian, the Spanish American, and the Anglo-American. The recent rise of a small group of native American historians, as well as the spread of interest in Indian history among sympathetic Anglo historians, is bringing about a reinterpretation of the Indian historical tradition. The few Spanish American historians who have emerged have until very recently worked within Anglo-American historical conventions and have written in English for a predominantly Anglo audience. Unfortunately, Anglo historians have largely ignored the Spanish American and the American Indian. Weber's comment about southwestern historiography during the Mexican period applies to much Anglo-American historical writing about New Mexico: "unbalanced, ethnocentric, and incomplete" (Weber, 1973).

Sociologists and anthropologists have sporadically been involved in scholarly research among Spanish Americans. From time to time, especially in the 1930s, sociologists have been employed by federal agencies to conduct studies among the rural Spanish American village population. Few of these studies were ever pub-

23

Land Grants

CLARK S. KNOWLTON
Department of Sociology
University of Utah

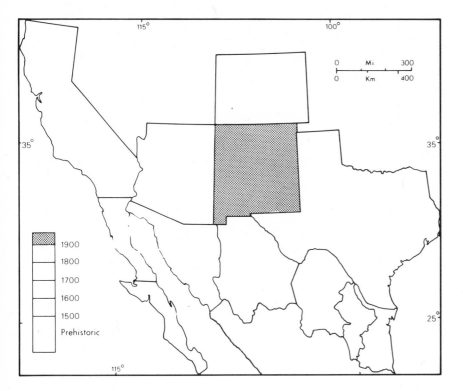

lished. Anthropologists also sporadically studied specific villages. Unfortunately, most of these studies are currently out-of-date and do not cover many geographical regions of Spanish American settlement. However, for the areas studied, they do provide an important socioeconomic base line against which subsequent socioeconomic change can be measured.

No social issue in the history of the Spanish American people has caused as much unrest, violence, and conflict among Spanish Americans and Anglo-Americans as have the questions of Spanish and Mexican land grants. Large numbers of Spanish Americans are convinced, rightly or wrongly, that they were deprived of these land grants by Anglo-Americans through unacceptable legal, political, and violent means. Anglo-Americans often do not realize that in New Mexico the land-grant problem is currently a smoldering issue.

Most of this conflict is caused by value differences between Anglo-Americans and Spanish Americans over ownership and use of land. From the perspective of Anglo-American law, land is to be bought and sold like any other commodity. Private ownership is preferred over communal ownership, and private owners have freedom to use their land as they see fit, with little consideration of community welfare. On the other hand, from the Spanish American viewpoint, land is not a commodity to be bought and sold. It is the very basis of family and community life. Communal ownership is as important as private ownership, and landownership is subordinated to the public good. Even today many rural Spanish Americans believe that it is wrong for individuals or the government to monopolize large sections of land when family heads need access to land to support their families (Knowlton, 1967*a*: 3-4; Nabakov, 1969: D1, D2).

The Spanish and Mexican Land Tenure Systems

Only rarely have scholars questioned the original basis for the Spanish Crown's (that is, Queen Isabella's and her immediate family's) claim to America by the simple declaration of Columbus on the beach of Hispaniola. But the reassertion of property rights of God's Earth to his representative (papal authority) by the pronunciamento preceding each major Spanish conquest is overlooked in current land-grant research (Stoddard, 1973*d*). Once the premise is accepted that the Spanish Crown did indeed have legitimate right to own and dispose of lands in the western hemisphere, the problem of Spanish and Mexican land grants becomes a major historical issue of legal and moral caprice.

The Spanish land tenure system in New Mexico vested ownership of all lands in the Crown of Spain. The existing sovereign could, through his governors in New Mexico, concede land to individuals or groups of applicants who, fulfilling certain legal obligations, received a grant of land called a *gracia* or *merced.* The sovereign retained ultimate title to all land granted. Those who received land were given a right of occupation and use. If they failed to meet the legal require-ments, the land reverted back to the Crown. All ungranted land, known as *tierras realengas y baldías* ("royal and vacant land"), remained in the possession of the crown (Simmons, 1969: 8). According to Simmons, three types of land grants were given: (1) land granted to an individual or to a group of individuals or families who wished to found towns and communities, (2) land granted to private owners for the establishment of farms or stock ranches or for other proper and legal purposes, and (3) titles giving Indian pueblos full and complete possession to the lands they occupied (Simmons, 1974: 56). Perrigo would separate Simmons's first type into two distinctive categories—the town proprietary grant awarded to an individual for the purpose of founding one or more towns, and the community land grant given to heads of ten or more families who desired to establish an agricultural village (Perrigo, 1960: 79-80).

Spanish laws required that each settler of towns and rural communities receive a house lot and enough farmland to sustain himself and his family. As additional settlers came in, they also received farmland as long as it was available. All pastures, watering sites, and lands unsuitable for farming in community land grants became the *ejido,* or common lands of the communities. The *ejidos* belonged to the land-grant communities, not individual settlers on the grant. The commons were very important in village economic systems, as all residents of the village, poor and rich alike, had the right to graze livestock and use the other natural resources. Settlers were usually required to reside on the grant for a specific period of time. Grants were allocated so they would not infringe upon Indian rights, or those of other parties, but a limited knowledge of New World vastness did cause many problems for subsequent territorial claims. The Crown usually reserved the right to all mineral lands. Other requirements might be imposed, depending upon local conditions and the government's desire to attract settlers (Simmons, 1974: 56; Perrigo, 1960: 79-80). The Spanish land tenure system was adopted by the Mexican government, and some subsequent grants overlapped "existing Royal grants," causing legal problems later.

When Anglo-Americans arrived, the majority of the numerous Spanish American communities that still dot New Mexico were nestled on community land grants. The United States, through the Treaty of Guadalupe Hidalgo that ended the Mexican American War in 1848, committed itself to protect the property and civil rights of the population of conquered and annexed territories. It promised to protect Spanish American community land-grant rights, but the Office of Surveyor General established in 1854 failed to work effectively because of differences in land law and unscrupulous legal chicanery. As a result of the growing clamor in New Mexico over unsettled land titles, Congress established a specialized Court of Private Land Claims to adjudicate land-grant titles in Arizona, Colorado, and New Mexico. The system was so cumbersome, so complicated, and so expensive that the Spanish Americans were never able to effectively protect or defend their land rights.

Historians and Social Scientists

The first important group of historians to write about New Mexico was Anderson (1907), Bancroft (1889), Blackmar (1891), Haines (1891), Prince (1883), Read (1912), Ritch (1885), Twitchell (1912), and the unknown author of *An Illustrated History of New Mexico* (1891). Anderson and Haines were local New Mexican historians with little knowledge of Spanish Americans. Bancroft and his associates wrote a comprehensive and well-balanced history of Arizona and New Mexico, free from ethnic or racial prejudice, as part of their multivolume history of the American West. Prince, Read, Ritch, and Twitchell, all lawyers, played influential roles in the political, economic, and legal history of New Mexico. These last four were involved in land-grant litigation and were believed to have been members of the "Santa Fe Ring." Their impressionistic works represent the point of view of the Republican oligarchy that controlled New Mexican political and economic affairs, with Read being the only Spanish American. All of these early historians lived at a time when Anglo-Americans were still a small though powerful minority and were forced to interact intimately with all levels of Spanish American society. Thus, they were more familiar with the Spanish language, Spanish American culture, values, and social classes than were most later historians, and they were more sympathetic to the points of view of the Spanish American merchants and political leaders. This sympathy comes out very clearly in the writings of Bancroft (1889: 430-31), Read (1912: 445), and Prince (1883: 313) as they discuss the Ortiz and Archuleta plot and the Taos Revolt.

Blackmar (1891) discussed Spanish institutions in the Southwest, and though he expressed sympathy for the Spanish-speaking land claimants, he maintained a somewhat segregationist attitude toward the non-Anglo peoples of the Southwest. In Anderson's (1907) work, the long-existing Anglo-American negative attitudes toward the Spanish Americans found a voice.

Little of the concern of land grants and land loss by political and business leaders of New Mexico during the 1880s and 1890s penetrated the pages of these historians. It was not until the 1930s that a generation of scholars interested in the Spanish American people came into existence. The majority of these were employed by New Deal agencies to conduct studies and surveys of socioeconomic conditions in the rural Spanish American village populations.

For example, Harper, Cordova, and Oberg (1943) published a significant comprehensive regional survey of the middle Rio Grande Valley. They analyzed ecological, social, and economic conditions of the middle Rio Grande Valley from the Colorado border on the north and Elephant Butte Reservoir on the south, focusing primarily on the American Indian and Spanish American inhabitants. Johansen (1941), working in the stretch of territory along the Rio Grande from the southern edge of Elephant Butte Reservoir to the Texas line, described the poverty and land loss of Spanish American inhabitants of that region. Walter (1939) found almost

the same general socioeconomic conditions in northern New Mexican villages. Leonard and Loomis (1941), acute observers of the Spanish American village, published a community study of El Cerrito, and a study by Leonard (1948) discussed the natural environment and dependency of the village populations upon the region's natural resources. In the late 1950s, Loomis (1942, 1958) revisited El Cerrito to study village migration and how a massive exodus brought about fundamental changes in social structures and cultural values among those who left and those who remained.

Sánchez (1940), a noted ethnic historian, wrote one of the most revealing books of the 1930s and early 1940s on rural Spanish Americans. Harvey and Erna Fergusson (1955), children of a prominent New Mexican political leader, both produced highly perceptive cultural and social histories of New Mexico reflecting a deeply rooted sympathy for both the American Indian and Spanish American peoples. The scholarly lawyer Keleher (1964) has written a series of well-researched volumes on New Mexican history which includes much on the land-grant controversies.

World War II brought an end to government programs for the study of Spanish American problems, and the social scientists involved in these field studies departed. They were never replaced. During the 1940s little interest existed in the plight of the rural Spanish American village population. The several writers who did comment on Spanish Americans following the war devoted little attention to the land-grant issue: Laughlin (1947) and Calvin (1948) wrote about Spanish Americans and the mystical influence of the natural environment on them.

A volume by Herbert O. Brayer (1949), the state archivist of Colorado, contains a detailed and revealing analysis of the often unethical methods used to exploit both the original Spanish American owners and the purchasers of land grants. His book is highly critical of the methods used by the federal government to resolve land-grant titles.

During the 1950s, field research among the rural Spanish American population turned from legal concerns to interpretive comparisons and "value orientations" (Kluckhohn and Strodtbeck, 1961; Edmonson, 1952; Mead, 1955; Vogt and Alvert, 1969). Horgan (1954b) described the achievements of southwestern minorities, and Burma (1954) described a minority within a minority—the Penitentes.

With the agitated years of the 1960s and their War Against Poverty programs, new concepts of social and economic change were introduced into many rural villages of New Mexico. The Alianza Federal de Mercedes, under the leadership of Reies Tijerina, its charismatic founder, became the most formidable protest movement for almost a century. It demanded the return of the Spanish and Mexican land grants to Spanish Americans. It prompted an outpouring of books about Spanish Americans and their land grants by historians, social scientists, and journalistic observers. However, some authors lacked knowledge about or sympathy for the Spanish American peoples, and they often had a contemptuous attitude toward this minority (Armstrong, 1969; Beck, 1962).

Other authors of the '60s amplified the functions of Spanish Colonial government, especially in terms of the right to land (Simmons, 1968), and the mechanisms through which the Spanish Crown and Mexican Republic granted land (Perrigo, 1960). Espinosa (1962) covered the history of Spanish and Mexican grants, including land-grant obligations under the Treaty of Guadalupe Hidalgo and the function of the Surveyor General. Gates's massive study of the evolution of public land law in the United States compared land-grant owners in Missouri, Louisiana, and Florida with New Mexico owners and claimants and found that the former were treated far more liberally than were those of New Mexico (Gates, 1968: 75-119). Other authors outlined the historical evolution of sociocultural political and/or economic systems of New Mexico (Gonzalez, 1969; Holmes, 1967; Parish, 1961; Lamar, 1962, 1966) and the geology and geography of the region (Reeve, 1961). Stratton's (1969) history of the New Mexico Spanish press of the 1880-1920 period illuminates many of the land-grant controversies and possible public information channels.

During the 1970s there was a sharp increase in books and articles devoted to the study of land grants or materials written about them. This increase may have been a product of the Alianza agitation of the 1960s and a general increase in awareness of the land loss. In the '70s the literature focusing on Spanish and Mexican land-grant problems, particularly in New Mexico, has grown very rapidly. One of the broadest and best-documented sources of current land-grant scholarship is a symposium totally devoted to this subject, especially featuring legal and illegal land loss in New Mexico (Knowlton, 1976). Another symposium edited by Knowlton (1964b) contains several articles on the relationship of land losses in desert and arid zones to the New Mexico experience. Finally, a report from a contracted study on Spanish and Mexican land grants (White, Kelly, and McCarthy, 1972) covers the obligations of the Treaty of Guadalupe Hidalgo, New Mexico statutes relating to land ownership, and a lengthy description of currently existing land titles.

Many articles and books on specific land grants and problems associated with land claims have become available. Jenkins (1961, 1972), the state archivist of New Mexico, has published articles on the Pueblo Indian land grants and the difficulties the Pueblo Indians had in protecting their land grants from Spanish American and Anglo-American encroachments. M. F. Taylor (1965, 1968, 1972, 1976) has written several articles on land grants in Colorado. His work in New Mexico has focused on the land grants in northeastern New Mexico, such as the Maxwell Land Grant, the Una de Gato Grant, and the two grants received by Gervacio Nolan, one in Colorado and the other in New Mexico. The Maxwell Land Grant also attracted the scholarly interest of Dunham (1955), who used it as an example of the litigious problems involved in the adjudication of land-grant titles by the U.S. Government and courts of law. Murphy (1967) has also written an article on the early history of the Maxwell Land Grant, which he believes should be called the Beaubien and Miranda Land Grant. Archibald (1976) discussed the problems of early settlement in the Cañon de Carnue Grant close to Albuquerque. W. T. Jackson turns his attention to

Scottish investment in the Chavez Land Grant purchased by the Scots from a Spanish American land speculator (W. T. Jackson, 1952). Metzgar has done the same with the Atrisco Land Grant, delineating its history from 1692 to 1777 (Metzgar, 1977). And Bowden (1971) has written a brief historical sketch of each Spanish and Mexican land grant in the areas in western Texas and southern New Mexico that once belonged to the Mexican state of Chihuahua.

The process of land claims and resolution of conflicts over landownership has been the subject of various writers. Dick (1970), Duncan (1970), and Westphall (1965) have studied the distribution procedures involving the public domain; Dick and Duncan for the nation as a whole, and Westphall in New Mexico. Bradfute (1975) has described and analyzed the activities of the Court of Private Land Claims, enabling the reader to understand the complex process of landownership resolution. And Westphall (1974) has severely attacked the frauds perpetrated by Anglo-American and Spanish American land speculators as they wrested control of land-grant territories from their original Spanish American owners or heirs.

The social movements arising from organized protest over land loss by Spanish Americans have been studied by various authors (Larson, 1974; Rosenbaum, 1973). Knowlton (1964b, 1967a, 1969) has written extensively on this subject, relating the question of land loss to the poverty and dependency of rural Spanish Americans. McCarty (1969), a reporter for the *Albuquerque Journal,* wrote a series of articles on land grants during the period of agitation in New Mexico. Morrill (1973) also published a very different reaction to the problem in her charming book of personal impressions of Taos (see her chapter entitled "The Land Grant, the Curse of New Mexico").

Certain authors have discussed the background material necessary if the land-grant question is to be resolved. W. B. Taylor (1975) wrote on the evolution of land and water rights in the Viceroyalty of New Spain. Greenleaf (1967, 1972) described the changing policy of the Spanish government toward land and water rights and eighteenth-century land conflicts in the Atrisco Valley located near present-day Albuquerque. Patrick (1976) described the policy of the Spanish Colonial Governor Pedro Fermín de Mendinueta in making land grants, while Simmons (1969) analyzed settlement patterns designed to concentrate New Mexico's population into defensible communities under the Spanish government. García and Hain (1976) have arranged a fine set of readings on the structure and functions of the New Mexico state government within which the legal validity of land grants must be established.

Other background materials include a small general sketch of New Mexico history with a surprising amount of social data (Jenkins and Schroeder, 1974) and studies of diverse aspects of indigenous and Spanish American society and history (Sunserai, 1975; Swadesh, 1974; Zeleny, 1944; Waters, 1973). Meinig (1971), a social geographer, has produced an excellent study of the Spanish American and Anglo-Texas settlement patterns in the nineteenth century and the role of the railroad as the aggressive Texan solidified his hold on West Texas and eastern New Mexico. Spicer and Thompson

(1972) have compiled overall descriptions of minority groups of the region, including various Indian tribes, Mormons, Mexican Americans, and northern Mexicans; these demonstrate the heterogeneity of the region and the complexity of land usage.

The story of Spanish and Mexican land grants is still something of a mystery that is being further obscured by many writers who represent some special interest and who lack a knowledge of archival records and facility in Spanish. Often, popular writers unfamiliar with native Spanish American rural inhabitants interpret current conditions within a distorted historical framework. Those spokesmen for land-grant heirs who, without questioning the original Spanish claims to the New World, seek only to legitimize Royal decrees to give away land they may not own are also of concern. In the distorted historiography of the Southwest in general and New Mexico in particular, land-grant conflicts can hardly be viewed objectively. Although the Alianza Movement has subsided in New Mexico, it seems inevitable that, new protest movements demanding the return of the lost land grants will develop among the Spanish Americans as they have since the 1870s. Unrest among the rural Spanish American over the issue seems endemic. Scholarly research on the socio-economic history of the land grants is badly needed to fill in major gaps in New Mexican history and to determine whether the land grants were lost through force, fraud, or violence or through the natural workings of the market place.

24

Cultural Landscapes

CHARLES F. GRITZNER
Department of Geography
South Dakota State University

The cultural landscape may be defined as the totality of mankind's tangible imprint upon the earth's surface. Each human society, operating within the existing parameters of its respective cultural system, functions as an active ecological agent. Each culture uses and modifies the elements of its natural habitat in its own characteristic way while in quest of food, shelter, protection, mobility, resources, and a host of other essentials to economic survival, material well-being, and physical comfort. While it does so, there emerge distinct patterns of cultural imprint which, for the society in question, have both spatial and temporal associations. Among the more obvious visible elements of the cultural landscape are patterns of land use and division, settlements, resource use, architecture, plant and animal husbandry, and the material manifestations of aesthetic values, religious practices, social and economic conditions, and traditions.

In this essay emphasis is focused upon the cultural landscape which has evolved during nearly four centuries of settlement in the hearth of Hispanic culture of the upper Rio Grande Valley and highlands of northern New Mexico. It is there,

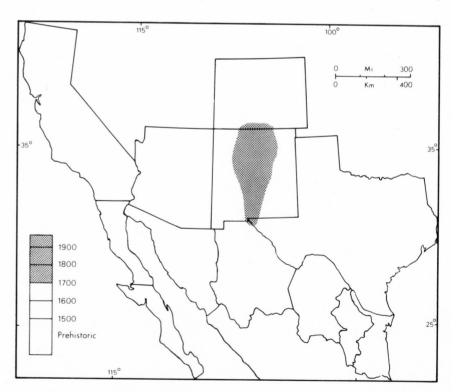

particularly in the small farming villages, that the imprint of traditional Hispanic cultural practices has best been retained within the Hispanic American Borderlands. Folkways have been preserved within this portion of the realm for several reasons, including relative geographic and social isolation, strict adherence to traditional ways of life until recent decades, the relatively high percentage of Spanish-speaking peoples inhabiting the area (Nostrand, 1975, 1980), and the absence of any appreciable Anglo-American intrusion or cultural impact until the present century in the more remote areas of Hispano settlement. The region remains today as one of the last and most pronounced cultural enclaves in the United States, thereby making it an ideal living laboratory for the study of folk-culture practices and resultant features of the cultural landscape. Elsewhere within the Hispano-American Borderlands (Nostrand, 1970), traditional life-styles have given way to acculturation of the Hispano population, in varying degrees, into the mainstream of the American cultural "melting pot."

Few authors have attempted to contribute to the further understanding of Hispano cultural landscapes in New Mexico, or elsewhere within this country, by providing detailed comprehensive information on the region as a whole. Such studies as do exist generally have been written for the layman and often provide little more than a cursory descriptive overview without attention to explanation, analysis, or synthesis of the landscape and its constituent elements.

Scholarly works have focused overwhelmingly on the individual components of the Hispano cultural landscape—for example, agricultural practices, field patterns and land division, practices of land use, architecture, villages, social and environmental planning, economic conditions, and demographic change. Each element within a landscape constitutes a part of the culturally, and often functionally, integrated whole. Information on individual landscape features, while illuminating in its own regard, fails to provide the reader with a holistic impression and understanding of a distinct landscape. Such studies, it may be argued, are necessary if a comprehensive overview ever is to be achieved.

The importance of an integrated approach to landscape research can be illustrated by those aspects of landscape which result from the Hispano's preference for bread made from wheat flour: *hornos*, the outdoor "beehive"-shaped ovens which are still associated with many homesteads; small gristmills with horizontal waterwheels which were common to most settlements prior to the 1930s when commercially milled flour became available to mountain villagers; *acequias*, the small ditches used to divert water from streams to mill sites for power and to agricultural fields for irrigation; *trojas* or *dispensas*, small buildings adjacent to many houses which serve as a storage facility for foodstuffs, including flour, and other household items; the myriad of barn types, identified by a number of names, which are used for housing draft animals and for the storage and protection of fodder; agricultural tools and implements used in planting, harvesting, and threshing wheat, and the structures in which they are housed; tillage practices; the location of farmlands relative to village sites and other land uses; patterns of land division and fencing; and the preferred location of wheat fields themselves.

Very few written works are devoted exclusively to the Hispano cultural landscape. In addition to those references cited in this chapter, the reader is referred to other entries in this volume which are devoted to topics having landscape manifestations—for example, agriculture and ranching, art and architecture, land grants and landownership, spatial overview, land use and settlement patterns, and colonial institutions. In essence, any source of information which contributes to a further understanding of the visible imprints of Hispano cultural activity, from the earliest period of settlement to the present, could be included within a comprehensive bibliographic listing. Any such enumeration would include specific reference to written and photographic documents from archival depositories in New Mexico and elsewhere in the Southwest. Such sources are of paramount importance to the scholar attempting to reconstruct earlier landscape patterns or to determine the rate and nature of landscape change. Place names, too, frequently suggest some aspect of past or present landscape conditions. T. M. Pearce's *New Mexico Place Names: A Geographical Dictionary* (1965) provides a storehouse of information for research based on toponymy.

Cultural Heritage

The Hispano cultural landscape of New Mexico reflects a heritage nurtured in Spain and, to a lesser degree, Mexico. Very few of those cultural practices existing in New Mexico today, or in the past, resulted from invention, innovation, or discovery by peoples living on the remote frontier of Spanish New World settlement. As often is true of societies existing in relative isolation from their cultural hearth (in this case, Iberia), an apparent devolution of culture traits occurs. Viewed in a historical context, perceived cultural degeneration of such traits as language, architecture, religious practices, and technology may be a relative occurrence; that is, the isolated society remains somewhat static, whereas the mother culture continues to evolve. In other instances, actual devolution does take place. This is particularly true for those aspects of cultural activity which are dependent upon economic factors, the application of technology, and sustained support from, or adherence to, such formal institutions as government, religion, and education.

The individual components and composite patterns of a cultural landscape can be understood only in light of those cultural conditions which governed the collective actions of the society which created them. Cultural behavior can be classified into several broad categories: sociological institutions, including those means by which a society controls the interaction among its members and regulates behavior; ideological institutions, which include the totality of knowledge and beliefs shared by a culture and the means by which these traits are communicated; technological institutions, including all tools, techniques, and skills; and established attitudes, sentiments, customs, and perceptions which combine to influence individual and group behavior. Most, if not all, of these behavioral characteristics exercise some impact, be it direct or indirect in nature, upon the evolution of cultural landscapes.

Several keystone studies exist which delineate Hispanic cultural linkages. George M. Foster's *Culture and Conquest* (1960) provides brilliant analysis and synthesis of Spanish culture. Though emphasis is placed on Old World cultural patterns, this work serves as a reliable foundation for the development of an understanding of those culture traits which were transferred to New Spain. Each of Foster's descriptive chapters (4 through 6, 8, and 10 being of particular significance to the study of cultural landscapes) is introduced with a brief synthesis of Spanish American cultural patterns, as background for Iberian data, and concludes with comparisons and comments which attempt to further link the two areas together. Fray Angelico Chávez's *My Penitente Land: Reflections of Spanish New Mexico* (1974) serves as a no less scholarly companion study of the Spanish cultural imprint on New Mexico, with emphasis placed on institutions and practices in the latter setting, where, he observed, "it is the landscape which nurtures and preserves [the] basic culture" (Chávez, 1974: 271). Cultural links between Mexico and New Mexico have been detailed in Carey McWilliams's classic work *North from Mexico* (1949a). Additional studies which invoke cultural diffusion or tradition in explanation of Hispanic cultural practices include Whitaker's (1929) analysis of Spanish contributions to American agriculture, Mosk's (1942) study of the influence of tradition on New Mexican agriculture, Reynolds's (1976) assessment of the influence of traditional Hispanic attitudes about land use on the acceptance of innovation in economic decision making, and Eastman et al. (1971) on contrasting Anglo and Hispano attitudes toward land and its use in New Mexico.

Nineteenth-Century Anglo Perceptions

A folk culture seldom leaves written record of its achievements, activities, or landscape. Perhaps those features are deemed to be unworthy of mention; in the context of landscape, it is the exotic or unusual elements which attract attention, and such perceptions are most apt to be held by individuals who are alien to the culture in question. As a result, narrative accounts of landscape perceptions are conditioned by the observer-writer's own experience and cultural background. The great majority of early Anglo accounts of conditions in New Mexico were both subjective and disparaging in nature. Early descriptions of New Mexican adobe villages serve as a case in point; they were described by various writers as resembling "a brick yard" and a "prairie-dog town" and as being "dirty little mud villages," "dirty mud towns," and "of miserable mud-built hovels."

Nineteenth-century Anglo perceptions of Hispanic cultural landscapes have been studied by J. P. Bloom (1959) and D. Hornbeck (1975). The latter author concluded that the literature offers little information of practical use and notes that "except for a few individuals who were keenly aware . . . , almost all recorders revealed a lack of understanding of New Mexico's culture. [Most statements] may be attributed to the absence of sound geographical knowledge [and the] persistence of multiple popular images." Collectively, the descriptive literature contributed by nineteenth-century travelers suffers from a plethora of meaningless subjective impressions, a glaring lack of attention to detail, little concern for anything but the most exotic elements of the landscape (for example, adobe architecture, poverty, and "backward" technology), and distributional limitation to observations made along the well-traveled Santa Fe Trail, Rio Grande Valley, and roads to Taos.

The keenest and most reliable observations of conditions in New Mexico during the mid-nineteenth century are those of J. Gregg (1952). It is unfortunate that an observer as astute as Gregg failed to venture into those areas of settlement which were remote from the larger population centers and major corridors of travel. Additional narratives, from which random descriptions of cultural landscape features can be gleaned, include those of Zebulon M. Pike, which were written during the first decade of the nineteenth century (Coues, 1965); "Dr. Willard's Journal," an account of travels made during the 1820s (Flint, 1829); and mid-century writings contributed by J. W. Abert (1848), F. A. Wislizenus (1969), G. Ruxton (Porter, Porter, and Hafen, 1950), L. H. Garrard (1939), and W. W. H. Davis (1938).

Elements of Cultural Landscape

Surprisingly few sources exist which provide the reader with a comprehensive overview of the cultural landscape and its integral features. Considerable detail can be found piecemeal in the American Guide Series volume *New Mexico: A Guide to the Colorful State* (Federal Writers' Program, WPA, 1940) and in the several hundred background reports which were prepared under the auspices of this WPA-funded program. The background research manuscripts are housed in the New Mexico State Archives in Santa Fe; their use is facilitated by a detailed topical index.

Perhaps the best general description and analysis of New Mexico's Hispano landscape is that found in a series of three travel guides which were written by the founder and long-time editor of *Landscape* magazine, J. B. Jackson (1962, 1963a, 1963b). Jackson is internationally known and respected for his pioneering contributions to landscape research. His attention to details of the Hispanic cultural imprint of selected areas within a day's drive of Santa Fe is exceptional, even though it was prepared for laymen's use. Works which provide some sense of feeling for landscape patterns within defined geographical areas include A. W. Carlson's (1971a) geographic appraisal of the Spanish-American homeland in the upper Rio Grande Valley; Harper, Cordova, and Oberg's (1943) analysis of economic resources and environmental degradation in the middle Rio Grande Valley; a detailed report prepared by the Interagency Council for Area Development Planning (n.d.), New Mexico State Planning Office, on the Embudo watershed; and J. G. Widdison's (1959) study of the historical geography of the middle Rio Puerco Valley.

The impact of direct or indirect human activity is often imprinted upon the earth's surface in ways which may escape the attention of the casual viewer. The use of any natural resource will, of necessity, cause some change. A discussion of resource selection and use appears in M. M. Taylor's (1960) study of patterns in rural north central New Mexico. Environmental change is particularly evident in the form of vegetation change, soil erosion, and gully formation in this semiarid region. Man-caused fires, overgrazing of livestock, the cutting of forests, and tilling of cropland are major agents of culture-induced alteration of natural landscapes. The grazing of sheep, in particular, has been damaging to vegetation, soil, and drainage patterns (Carlson, 1969; Denevan, 1967; Leopold, 1951). Deforestation has been extensive in many areas; wood has long been a vital resource for fuel, the construction of buildings and fences, and material for a variety of native crafts (Jones, 1932).

Throughout much of rural New Mexico, agricultural landscapes are the most evident imprint of human activity. The literature pertaining to farmscapes is scant, though several references merit mention. The southwestern colonial farm was described in detail by Conway (1951*a*). Carlson (1975*a*) has made an excellent contribution to the understanding of land division practices and long-lot field patterns in the Rio Arriba region. In the arid to semiarid climate of the state's northern region, many crops require irrigation. "Mexican" irrigation systems of the mid-nineteenth century were discussed in detail by W. W. H. Davis (1938: 195-200). In many locations, contemporary practices differ little from those of the distant past. Hutchins (1928) and Simmons (1972) have made notable contributions to the store of knowledge on Hispanic irrigation practices, including the picturesque *acequias,* or community ditches. Most articles devoted to specific agricultural crops are horticultural in their emphasis, with little if any detail on landscape expression. Notable exceptions include the works by Campa (1934) and Calkins (1937*b*) on New Mexico's famed chili.

Small farming villages, located in close proximity to a reliable source of water and suitable agricultural land, dominate the pattern of settlement. Indeed, these communities may constitute the most valid stereotype impression of the Hispano cultural landscape. Numerous studies delineate the social and cultural factors which underlie a preference for community living, a trait which has roots in distant Iberian antiquity. A general description of village life and conditions from the sociological viewpoint is presented in Walter's (1939) assessment of the Spanish-speaking community in New Mexico. Conditions and activities related to village life in the 1930s have been compiled and edited from Federal Writers' Project field notes published by Brown, Briggs, and Weigle (1978). Village types, settlement patterns, and village plans are discussed in detail by Conway (1952) and Simmons (1969). Visual impressions from the late 1920s can be acquired from Morgan's (1929) photographic essay on six His-

pano villages. Perhaps the most definitive single source of detailed information is that presented in the 1935 Tewa Basin study recently edited and reissued by Weigle (1975).

Studies of individual communities include Borhegyi's (1954) analysis of landscape evolution in Chimayó and Leonard and Loomis's (1941) classic work on the culture of El Cerrito, with a companion photo essay on the same community by Rusinow (1942). Other works devoted to specific villages include Carlson (1979), on El Rancho and Vadito; Hillerman (1967) on Las Trampas; Hurt (1934) on Chimayó; and Woods (1943) on Córdova.

New Mexico's Hispano architecture has been the subject of a considerable body of literature. Interest has focused primarily on building materials, architectural techniques, and structure forms. The contributions of Bainbridge Bunting on these features are without peer. His recent volume, *Early Architecture in New Mexico* (Bunting, 1976), presents a lucidly written and vividly illustrated summary of research findings gleaned from some two decades of active study devoted to the further understanding of Hispano architecture in the Southwest. Additional works by him include a study of architectural patterns in the Embudo watershed (Bunting, 1962), a detailed analysis of architecture in northern New Mexico (Bunting and Conron, 1966), and an architectural guide to the region (Bunting, 1970). An overview of New Mexico architecture appears in Hasselden (1943).

Sources of information on specific building characteristics, types, or functions can be found in Conway's (1951*b*) description of a northern New Mexico house type, Jackson's (1952) catalog of New Mexico farm-building terms, Jackson's (1959-60) study of Hispano perceptions and functional uses of house space and design, and Gritzner's (1974*b*) study of Hispano gristmills. West's (1974) seminal study of the flat-roofed folk dwelling in rural Mexico provides background information on its New Mexico counterpart. Housing conditions in rural New Mexico during the 1930s have been detailed in several works (Hollinger and Strong, 1936; Bureau of Home Economics, 1939).

A plethora of studies has been published on adobe. Two, in particular, merit citation: Bainbridge Bunting's *Taos Adobes* (1964), which was the first historical account of the domestic architecture of nineteenth-century New Mexico, and *Adobe: Past and Present* (New Mexico, Museum of New Mexico, n.d.), in which several authors have contributed to the better understanding of this distinct trait of the Hispanic cultural landscape.

Hispanic New Mexicans developed a flourishing tradition of log architecture, both in vertical-post *(jacal)* and horizontal-notched-log construction. Contrary to notions expressed by several students of New Mexican architecture (for example, Ahlborn, 1967), the Hispanic log tradition seems to have evolved from cultural influences in Mexico rather than having been borrowed from Anglos on the southwestern frontier. Log housing was widespread in the highlands of Mexico (Winberry, 1974), and the techniques appear to have diffused northward from there into the forested highlands of northern New Mexico (Gritzner, 1971, 1979-80). Gritzner (1974*a*) has contributed an assessment of those perceptions and considerations which influenced the selection and use of various construction materials in New Mexico's Hispanic folk housing tradition.

Religious architecture in New Mexico has been studied in great detail. George Kulber's publications in this field (1962*a*, 1973) remain classics in both scholarship and detail. Penitente *moradas* and other landscape features resulting from Penitente rites have been described by Ahlborn (1968), Henderson (1937), and Weigle (1970). Newhall (1962) has written on El Santuario de Chimayó. References to other landscape features include Bloom (1925) on early bridges, Benrimo et al. (1966) on *camposantos,* and Chávez's (1977) study of *hornos.* Various folk arts and crafts, some of which have landscape expression, have been detailed by Boyd (1974), Dickey (1949), and Tryk (1977).

Landscape Change and Preservation

Since the 1930s, traditional Hispano landscapes have undergone rapid change and deterioration. Changes in occupation (Leonard and Cleland, 1976), agricultural technology (Marr, 1967), and both social and demographic patterns (Knowlton, 1969*a*) have been cited as paramount factors in landscape transformation. Increased government attention to the need for social and environmental planning also has been instrumental in giving rise to changes in traditional patterns of settlement and land use (Van Dresser, 1960, 1972; Atencio, 1964; Oberg, 1940). Hispano rural communities have undergone marked population decline, yet one author (Riley, 1969) foresees their revitalization in future decades, a trend that has been confirmed in a recent study by Nostrand (1981).

Traditions fade slowly within a folk culture. Nonetheless, signs of erosion in traditional life-styles are evident throughout Hispanic New Mexico. Conflicts between the older and younger generations and between Hispano and Anglo values (Van Ness, 1976; Apodaca, 1952) become increasingly apparent with time.

Vestiges of the Hispano landscape and way of life will remain for some time, and through planning and preservation (Kimbro, 1974; New Mexico, Cultural Properties Review Committee, 1971, 1973), selected remnants will remain for future generations to reflect upon—in memory of a culture which persisted on a remote frontier and the landscape which it nurtured.

Section III. The Economy

When we look at a map of the U.S.-Mexican border, it becomes readily evident that the two countries are joined together by ten major (plus various minor) pairs of neighboring communities. Although politically separated, such border cities customarily provide a cohesive network of services and institutional and personal relationships for the economic operation and growth of the local region and the linkage of economic activities between the two countries. These paired communities present the most apparent points of impact and comparison of the national economies of Mexico and the United States, with their notable differences in wage levels, rates of inflation, methods of financing, labor laws and unions, pricing and other regulatory policies, unemployment rates, patterns of distribution, and growth of population and income. The massive devaluation of the Mexican peso in 1965 further emphasized these differences, which induce economic activity and determine its level and composition (Stoddard and West, 1977). The paired communities form funnels through which passes much of the visible portion of this activity and upon which these communities are largely dependent for their livelihoods.

25

Economic Overview

DONALD W. BAERRESEN
Division of Business
Laredo State University

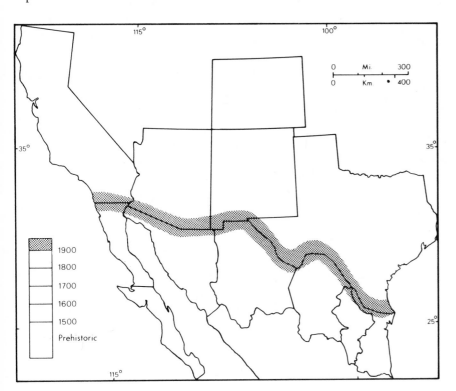

Most border cities lie on traditional north-south trade routes so that the economies of the neighboring communities first became intertwined because of their original purpose of providing gateways for the official transit of merchandise and travelers between the two countries. Over time, and in self-interest for the furtherance of this traffic, there developed within each pair of border communities personal ties between Mexican and U.S. customs brokers, freight forwarders, transportation managers, warehouse operators, bankers, insurance brokers, and the like.

Specialization in merchandising, which caused the economies of the neighboring border communities to become further interrelated, also developed. As personal incomes rose, transportation improved, and leisure time increased, ever larger numbers of people from the interiors of both countries visited the border cities to take advantage of opportunities on the other side of the frontier, so specialization was strengthened and catering to the tourist became a major industry.

Most of the border communities are removed from urban centers in the interiors of their respective countries, and, as a consequence of this relative isolation, there has been a solidifying of local social structures which span the border within many of the pairs of communities. This cross-boundary social contact has led to many intermarriages and business relationships.

The economic linkage between the two members of each pair of border communities has been further reinforced by development of Mexico's Assembly Program. When begun in 1965, this endeavor was called the Border Industrialization Program and was designed to encourage U.S. manufacturers to invest in assembly operations in order that work might be provided to some of the many unemployed people in Mexico's northern border cities. Under the program, which has since been expanded to include almost all of the country, non-Mexicans and Mexicans may own and operate factories in Mexico and import materials, components, and equipment into Mexico free of duty if the resulting products are exported from the country.

The advantages for a U.S. manufacturer are: (1) easy access to the large available supply of low-cost (that is, by U.S. standards), dexterous, and normally docile Mexican labor, and (2) the proximity (compared to foreign alternatives) to his headquarters, principal sources of supply, and markets.

Complementing Mexico's Assembly Program are two U.S. tariff provisions that permit duty-free return to the United States of components of U.S. origin which are assembled abroad and United States-made metal products which are processed abroad. Substantial import tax savings can be realized with use of these tariff provisions. As a consequence of these tax savings and the labor situation, Mexico's Assembly Program has been growing and contributing importantly to economic development in communities on both sides of the border. In 1977 there were operating under the program 447 assembly plants, employing 76,000 people, with 404 of these plants, employing 69,000 people, located in the Mexican border communities. (Banco Nacional de México, 1977: 362).

Not only have the U.S. border communities received increased international trade and spending in their stores due to the assembly operations in Mexico, but they have also benefited from related new investment in local factories and warehouses on their side of the frontier. This development is generally called the "twin plant concept."

According to this idea, a manufacturing operation can sometimes be most profitably conducted when there are two plants within a pair of border communities. The Mexican plant provides the labor-intensive portions of production which comply with the special tariff provisions mentioned, while the U.S. plant provides the portions of production which are capital-intensive and subject to U.S. import taxation. One manager and one staff can direct and supply the support functions for both plants.

An inducement for establishing twin plants (rather than only one in Mexico) has been the relatively low wages (by U.S. standards). Some of these border communities, especially in Texas, have the highest rates of unemployment in the United States because, in addition to local residents in the labor force, thousands of Mexican citizens living across the border have permits to commute to and work in the United States. Often the federal minimum wage (or less) is the going wage, and union activity has generally been weak. These wage levels and certain tax dispensations have attracted additional industrial enterprises to the U.S. side of the border not in relation to the Assembly Program. This latest phase of industrialization is beginning to provide these communities with an important source of income which, unlike the traditional principal income sources of international trade, retailing and tourism, is not directly dependent upon governmental policies and economic relationships between the United States and Mexico.

The United States is Mexico's dominant trading partner, purchasing 55 percent of Mexico's total exports and supplying 63 percent of her imports, according to official figures. Most of this trade (except for crude petroleum) moves by land over the border. Much economic activity in the border area is associated with this trade, which is far more extensive than is officially reported. Informed sources indicate that narcotics smuggled into the United States may, in recent years, have been the largest single source of export earnings for Mexico, while weapons and many other items routinely enter Mexico illegally on a large scale from the United States. The networks of business, financial, and family relationships of the border area are instrumental in servicing, developing, and sometimes controlling the legal and illegal trade as it moves between the two countries.

A recent innovation in the border area is creation of international distribution centers through use of privately owned warehouses and yards that are bonded and administered in compliance with the regulations of the U.S. Customs Service. Foreign merchandise may be held exempt from U.S. import duties in such a warehouse or yard until that merchandise enters into the commerce of the United States. For example, Mexican products may be stored duty-free in the United States under these conditions. As orders are filled, some of the merchandise may be sent on to Canada, Japan, and Europe, all free of U.S. duty, while other merchandise may be entered into the U.S. market, and only then will duty be assessed on this last type of transaction. Similarly, products destined for Mexico from Canada and other countries outside of the United States may be held in properly bonded U.S. facilities duty-free. In many instances such storage is less expensive than would be the direct importation into Mexico and storage there of the same merchandise until it is used or sold. There exist certain transportation cost advantages, plus ease of communication between the two countries, which often make conducting international distribution most economical from the border area.

International trade across the U.S.-Mexican border has received an important impetus from use of the "land-water bridge" concept. Accordingly, in many instances it is cheaper and faster to move merchandise between the interior of Mexico and Europe or Japan through the United States rather than by way of Mexican seaports. For example, many products from Mexico City are transported by railroad and/or trucks through Laredo, Texas, to New York or Houston, where they are loaded aboard ships for delivery in Europe. The high costs, union difficulties, lack of adequate facilities, and infrequent sailings associated with various Mexican seaports provide the economic justification for the routing of much Mexican international trade with other countries through the border area and the United States.

Many Mexican products have received a strong export stimulus to the United States from the Generalized System of Preferences (GSP), which the United States introduced in January, 1976. Under the GSP, some 2,500 specified products may be imported duty-free into the United States from certain developing countries, including Mexico. Therefore, Mexican products that conform to the GSP regulations have become cheaper, by the amount of the import duty that would otherwise be levied, for U.S. purchasers. As a consequence of the GSP, northbound trade across the border has increased considerably. Moreover, some of this merchandise that was formerly sold in Mexican border cities to tourists and wholesalers from the United States has been moved in large volume to the northern side of the border, where it is now sold at retail and wholesale levels and distributed throughout the United States and to other countries. This change has occurred because, before the availability of the GSP, it was cheaper to store the Mexican products in Mexico and to have the tourists use their import duty tax exemptions for bringing these products into the United States.

Most border communities of both countries depend upon tourism as a major source of income for their economies. Tourism for the border is of two kinds. Transient tourism stems from people who pass through the border area while en route to or from their more distant tourist destinations. For many other people the border is their tourist destination, and the primary attraction for them is what lies just on the other side.

Shopping is a principal objective of most tourists stopping at the border. Many people from the interior of Mexico confine their purchasing to the Mexican border cities, where imported items (from the United States and other countries) are more accessible and taxed much less than in the cities of the interior. This condition results from preferential policies granted by the Mexican government for encouraging shoppers to patronize Mexican merchants who must compete with their U.S. counterparts directly across the border. It is estimated that 30-35 percent of all merchandise sold in most Mexican border cities of the north is of foreign origin, while for Tijuana it is between 80 and 90 percent (Banco Nacional de México, 1978: 78). For Mexicans wishing to shop in the United States, only those persons who possess the appropriate documents are authorized to do so. By contrast, the Mexican government presents no restrictions on entry into the Mexican border cities for tourists from the United States.

Sales in stores on the United States side of the border are basically to three kinds of Mexican customers: (1) those who live in neighboring Mexican cities and shop regularly (that is, several times a week) on the other side of the border for their personal consumption; (2) people from the interior of Mexico who normally visit the border area once or twice a year for purchases (sometimes several thousand dollars' worth) of merchandise for the personal consumption of themselves, their family, and their friends; and (3) runners or brokers, colloquially called *"chiveros,"* who resell in the interior of Mexico without formally importing the merchandise into Mexico on a commercial basis. *Chiveros* normally specialize in certain items (for example, perfume, electronic equipment, children's clothing) and often have well-established credit relations with their Mexican customers and the U.S. stores which serve as their sources of supply.

Many of the stores on the U.S. side of the frontier deal almost exclusively with *chiveros,* who buy in large volumes at low unit prices. It is not unusual for a store catering to this type of trade to sell between two and four million dollars' worth of merchandise a year from a plain-looking sales area of only six hundred square feet, or less. This *chivero* activity explains, at least partially, why some of the highest-volume (and highest-priced) retail selling space in all of the United States is found in those communities that border Mexico.

No one knows the exact extent of retail sales from U.S. border stores to citizens of Mexico. A reasonable estimate would be around one billion dollars annually, which is an amount equal to 15 percent of the total value of Mexico's commercial imports.

The northern border cities of Mexico are experiencing some of the highest rates of population expansion in that nation as their citizens are attracted from the interior to possible employment in assembly plants or other expanding border enterprises. Their border location also enhances their chances for entry into the United States. The continued rapid growth of these Mexican border communities represents increased potential markets for American border retail stores which cater to Mexican consumers.

Mexico's capacity for increased border trade of all kinds depends largely upon the successful commercialization of her massive deposits of oil and natural gas. These deposits represent Mexico's single great hope for significantly increasing her national per-capita income, which would likely increase the buying power of Mexicans and increase sales and tourism in the United States, with the border area being a primary beneficiary. In addition, with the decline of the U.S. dollar in overseas markets, products from and tourist services to Mexico should become more attractive for U.S. citizens, who formerly preferred Europe and Asia for tourism. A continued high rate of inflation in Mexico could nullify many of these advantages, but in spite of possible dislocations in the Mexican economy, the long-run effects seem to be for greatly expanded economic activity in the U.S.-Mexican border area.

Bibliographical essays in this section deal with some internal Mexican economic considerations such as taxation and fiscal policies as well as the development of petroleum and energy resources. The areas of international trade, tourism, and labor markets (with added emphasis of migrant labor) which bind both countries into a single economic system are examined in greater detail. Also singled out for examination are the border resources of mining and agriculture, which contribute heavily to the border economy.

A salient fact stands out in the romantic and always exciting history of the Borderlands: mineral resources and mining, at every level and in every period, are central to the theme and story. It is a persistent theme, transcending Indian, Spanish, and Anglo influences, and seems to grow in strength and vitality with the passage of time. It shows up in legend and folklore across the Borderlands; it gave the region's Indians a unique trading position with other tribes and laid the foundation for the exploration and conquest of a significant portion of the Borderlands. Mineral wealth was the basis for a continuing dream of opulence in the minds of the Spanish and has been a constant and vital theme during the one and one-half centuries of American influence.

The Indian miner did his job like so many to follow. He supplied materials for his contemporaries to build their cities; he searched out minerals for craftsmen to make tools; he prospected and mined the clays for the potters; and to the far-flung trade routes he supplied the native copper and turquoise. Like the Spanish and American miners who followed, he left his glory holes, dumps,

26

Mining

PAIGE W. CHRISTIANSEN
Department of Humanities
New Mexico Institute of
Mining and Technology

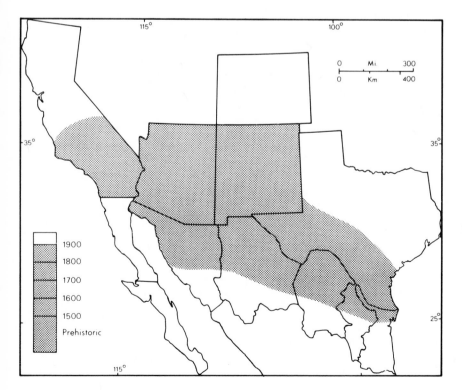

and debris, but to our knowledge he had no roaring camps and left no mining ghost towns. None of the Indian ruins that dot the landscape of the Borderlands today can be traced to mining activity. History left us no record of the Indian prospector or miner, who must have played a significant role in his society, yet the Borderlands' remote canyons once resounded with the blows of his stone hammer.

Mining during the Spanish period was no less important, but it was not as general or as rich as frequently reported. The most significant mining regions were in what are now the northern Mexican states (contiguous with the U.S. border). The Spanish frontier provinces of Texas and New Mexico had few mining centers. Arizona (always a part of Sonora during the Spanish period) had important silver along its extreme southern border.

Important mining centers during the Spanish period include silver in Coahuila, relatively rich silver production in Chihuahua, silver in Sonora (including Arizona), and copper at Santa Rita (New Mexico). These areas were truly commercial mining operations and showed the full impact of available technology in mining, milling, and smelting. Some individual mines were quite rich at times and were large-scale operations for frontier provinces. Over the remainder of the Borderlands, where some mining was apparent (Texas, New Mexico, and California), it was largely subsistence mining in nature and only locally significant.

During the Mexican period there were no major changes in the Borderlands' pattern of mining activity. Problems plaguing the newly founded Mexican nation allowed little opportunity for the development of the northern frontier. Those areas important in the late Spanish colonial period remained mining centers, but few new areas emerged.

America's great westward push in the nineteenth century brought renewed vigor to the search for mineral resources, not only in those areas which became part of the United States after 1848, but also in northern Mexico. The theme came alive, with more of all things needed to make the search exciting—even dramatic—if not always successful: technology, capital, increasing population, transportation, means to settle the problem of hostile Indians (mostly Apaches), and a culture that came to dominate and tame the environment.

The early years of Anglo-American control emphasized the search for precious metals, as had been done for several centuries. Following 1865, however, a slow transition began which gradually changed the nature of mining in the Borderlands. The increasing pressure of an industrial America shifted the emphasis from gold and silver to a variety of other minerals, such as copper, coal, iron, and zinc. Later, potash, molybdenum, uranium, and low-grade copper ores were added until gold and silver assumed secondary importance. This stage ended the romantic, reckless years in the Borderlands' mining camps—the age of individual miners pitting their simple skills and technology against nature, of reckless speculation, of small companies, and of small boom camps. But the death of the stark, yet romantic, mining camps must not overshadow the great gains made by industrial mining. Productivity, not romance, is the measure of success in modern mining, and productivity in the most recent century leaped ahead at a frantic rate.

Thus, the scientist replaced the prospector and the mining company the individual miner, and every Borderlands outcrop was evaluated by its mineral value. Massive mining operations, such as the copper mines at Cananea in Sonora or across southern Arizona or at Santa Rita and Tyron in New Mexico, became the pattern. The *arastras* and adobe furnaces were replaced with great automated mills and smelters such as the mills at Bisbee, Tyron, and across northern Mexico. And, of course, the great smoke-belching smelters across the Borderlands in the nineteenth century changed to the modern style—relatively clean, computerized, and automated.

While prospectors, glory holes, boom camps, mining districts, and industrial mining areas make up the most direct part of mining in the Borderlands, they are not the whole story. The story includes the evolution of mining law, so central to the miner's claim, placer, or lode; his water rights; and the society he tried to develop out of the raw mining camp. His methodology and technology in both mining and ore reduction (mills and smelters) had interesting facets. Where the miner got his capital—and how—was another aspect. Transportation was always the key to success for the miner, and then there were central economic ingredients such as wages, taxes, and profits. Woven into the story of searching prospectors and sweating miners, these elements combined to make a whole fabric.

In general no attempt has been made to review and evaluate the historic importance of mining in the Borderlands. A number of works have touched on special areas or have dealt with special aspects, but none have attempted an overall interpretation. The following bibliographical materials represent only a select listing of books, manuscripts, periodicals, and printed documents relating to mining history in the Borderlands.

The first and most obvious sources are those which have been published. Printed materials for the Spanish and Mexican periods include such items as chronicles, reports, documents of a varying nature, and travel literature. For example, George Hammond and Agapito Rey (1940), George Hammond (1953), J. Lloyd Mecham (1927), and other general historical sources regarding the Spanish thrust into northern Mexico and the American Southwest all have many references to mineral resources and mining. However, they are general, only dealing with mining in a small or incidental way.

There are some general sources which specifically discuss mining. They vary in quality but contain much valuable information about some areas and special aspects of mining history such as social life, law, technology, and so on. The writings of Trinidad García (1895), Robert West (1949), P. J. Bakewell (1883), Charles Dahlgren (1883), and Carlos Prieto (1973) all contain useful reviews of mining activity in northern Mexico. Several works giving special interpretations include Clement Motten (1950), Alexander Von Humboldt (1966), and David Brading (1971).

Northern Mexican sources dealing with specific periods or areas are also available, although they are not completely reliable and are largely undocumented. They are, however, useful and interesting. Thomas Rickard (1907) describes a number of mines in northern Mexico, as does A. Wisleyenus (1828). George Lyon (1828) describes mines and mining conditions. Lyon was an agent representing British capital. For later periods (after 1900), Marvin Bernstein's (1964) book is useful, as is the work of J. R. Southworth (1905). The latter has detailed descriptions and excellent photographs of many major mines in the Mexican part of the Borderlands.

For localized materials, one must turn to regional or state studies. For example, Charles Chapman (1916) provides considerable information on the mines of Sonora and Arizona, these as prelude to the founding of California. A highly specialized item on Sonora is F. J. H. Merrill (1908: 360-61). For specific mines and mining districts of consequence in northern Mexico, an excellent source is the variety of publications of the U.S. Geological Survey (USGS), *Bulletins, Professional Papers and Memoirs.* The USGS sent experts to study many Mexican mining areas of interest to the United States. These publications are well done and contain much historical data.

Finally, Spanish American mining methodology, technology, and general mining history can be found in Otis Young (1970) and in Alan Probert (1969: 90-124).

With the coming of American influence after 1848, the intensity of Borderlands mining gradually increased, particularly in the American Southwest. With this new intensity the volume of historical material relating to mining also increased. Added to this development was the emergence of the academically trained mining or geology specialist who added significant literature relating to mining lore. While these items were mostly technical, they have much historical data and are perhaps some of the finest source material available.

Some of the general material on the American influence should include Otis Young's works (1976, 1979), which give considerable information regarding mining methods and technology. They offer little about individual mines. Frank A. Crampton (1956) and Clark C. Spence (1970) deal with human elements of mining, some applied to the Borderlands. Such general histories as H. H. Bancroft's studies (1886, 1888, 1889a, 1889b), R. E. Twitchell's (1911), and those of Frank Reeve (1961) all have considerable mining history mixed in with other material.

An interesting series which contains much detailed information about a variety of mining areas is the *International Industrial Record,* published in El Paso at the turn of the century. It is devoted to general mining interests in the Southwest and northern Mexican states; it is undocumented, and its accuracy might be challenged; it has some good photographs. John R. Bartlett's personal narrative (1965) contains material on mining activity in New Mexico, Chihuahua, Sonora, and Arizona, much of it eyewitness accounts. Thomas A. Rickard (1932), mining engineer and prolific writer on all phases of mining, has some material on the Borderlands.

Since legend and folklore play such a vital role in Borderlands mining history, several works dealing with this material should be mentioned. Frank Dobie's writings (1930, 1939) are delightful, showing the importance of legend and myth as they relate to mining. Muriel V. S. Wolle (1953) gives some information on mining camps and ghost towns in the Southwest, some of which is useful as local color.

For more specific or local items on mining in the American Southwest, one must turn to state histories or special studies. For New Mexico, Paige Christiansen (1974a) describes, in popular form, the main mining centers through the nineteenth century. Stuart Northrup, a geologist, deals with much mining history in his earlier work (1959), and more specifically in his later publication (1975). William Long (1964), in his University of New Mexico master's thesis, has considerable details on certain aspects of Spanish mining. Fayette Jones (1904), mining engineer and twice president of the New Mexico School of Mines, prepared his work on New Mexico mines and minerals as a promotional giveaway for the Territory of New Mexico at the World Exposition in Saint Louis in 1905. It has considerable information on specific mines and mining districts in New Mexico. It must be used with care, but has some materials not available elsewhere. The numerous references of H. H. Bancroft (1889) are previously mentioned.

Of primary interest for New Mexico mining history are the publications of the New Mexico Bureau of Mines and Mineral Resources. While this series is concerned with technical mining or geologic material, scattered in each volume are valuable historical data. They have been prepared by qualified experts and are reliable.

Materials on Texas are not as numerous, for mining did not play the major role there that it did in other Borderlands areas. H. H. Bancroft (1889a) has some data, as does Vito Alessio Robles (1930, 1934). H. E. Bolton (1915) has considerable detail on Texas for a short span of time, although mining is only incidental. More modern publications of the U.S. Geological Survey and the U.S. Bureau of Mines have more current material.

Arizona, like New Mexico, has had a colorful and productive mining history; a number of items are available. Charles Dunning's (1959) account of American mining was based on Arizona material, although he tries to deal with the whole of American mining. It is useful for Arizona mining history. Richard Hinton (1878) is an early source giving insight into individual mines of historical and legendary importance. William P. Blake's (1902) book on Tombstone's mines is typical of material dealing with a specific camp. Rex Arrowsmith (1963) deals mainly with Arizona material, and largely older mines which have long since disappeared. The Arizona Bureau of Mines publishes technical materials relating to mines and mineral resources and is a significant source of material. Of particular interest is the bureau's *Gold Placers and Gold Placering in Arizona* (1961). Finally, the various federal government publications (U.S. Geological Survey, U.S. Bureau of Mines) contain numerous items of Arizona mines and minerals.

California is represented by many publications on the gold-rush period. Rodman Paul (1947) and John W. Caughey (1948) deal adequately with the California gold-rush story. More specific information about individual mines or placers is available in Charles Haley (1923/1965). The federal government publications, particularly U.S. Treasury Department *Reports on Western Mining,* beginning in 1854, are valuable. State of California publications are also useful.

Mining law, so essential to the proper development of activity, is even of greater interest in the Borderlands where two systems of law have evolved, both influencing modern legal concepts regarding mineral wealth. Several sources are available that give some insight into this aspect of mining. Eduardo Martínez Baca (1901) shows one side of the process, while Charles Shinn (1949) covers the American side. Herbert C. Hoover and L. H. Hoover (1912: 823-25) give a brief but useful discussion of mining law.

While technical materials have been mentioned previously, it is important to point out that numerous technical series (periodical or government agency publications) are among our best sources of mining history. For example, the publications of the U.S. Geological Survey cover a vast area of western and northern Mexico. They are primarily geologic, but most contain valuable historical information collected by highly trained specialists. The same can be said for the publications of the U.S. Bureau of Mines *(Bulletins, Circulars, Reports of Investigations,* and *Mineral Resources Yearbooks).* The Mexican government also published mineral resource development materials, but they are less valuable than U.S. publications. Publications of state agencies are equally as good, where such agencies exist, as in Arizona and New Mexico. Technical journals are full of historical data, perhaps the most valuable of all published sources. The *Mining and Scientific Press* and the *Engineering and Mining Journal,* both issued weekly or bimonthly for long periods of time, contain news material and chronology as well as good reviews of technological developments.

The real excitement in chasing after mining history lies in the search for unpublished manuscripts. Much of the story and the frenzy of the times will be buried in thousands of letters, reports, essay records, and travel accounts and a multitude of other documents.

There are, then, many manuscripts scattered across the Borderlands, and the historian becomes the prospector and miner. If the historian has the time and the grubstake, the historical wealth will be revealed and the time for work begins. In the final analysis, though, the historian, like the prospector, will discover that the search itself, not the finding, is the adventure.

As the decade of the 1980s dawns, global and regional events combine to focus increased attention on energy in Mexican-U.S. relations and, more specifically, on the border states as both producers and consumers of the two nations' energy resources. On the global scene, the 1973 Arab oil embargo and the subsequent continuing rise in oil prices prompted a flurry of activity in Mexico and the United States. In Mexico, decision makers initiated a crash program to develop petroleum resources, building upon the 1972 hydrocarbon discoveries in the nation's south. The mid-1970s witnessed dramatic increases in these endeavors. As new reserves were announced, Petróleos Mexicanos (PEMEX, the state petroleum monopoly) pushed hell-bent to exploit the nation's new-found wealth and to build an increasingly sophisticated petrochemical industry from exploration through final production. Less intensely, Mexico also pushed the development of its coal, geothermal, and nuclear resources.

In the United States, the embargo resulted in a series of demands for establishing a comprehensive national energy policy which would promote the

27

Energy Resources

EDWARD J. WILLIAMS
Department of Political Science
University of Arizona

HANNA J. CORTNER
School of Renewable
Natural Resources
University of Arizona

STEPHEN P. MUMME
Department of Political Science
University of Arizona

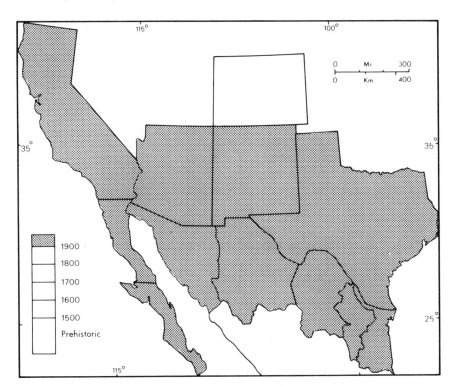

development of alternative energy sources as well as preach a new ethic of energy conservation. While decision makers struggled to agree upon the contents of such a national policy, various research and development efforts, especially for coal and nuclear power, moved forward. Energy conservation also began to receive some attention, but at a level of commitment far less than some had hoped. Finally, a series of bureaucratic reorganizations, culminating in the establishment of the Department of Energy in 1977, attempted to mitigate the management problems created by a fragmented administrative structure for energy policy making.

In the context of Mexican-U.S. relations, the 1973 energy crisis and subsequent reactions on both sides of the border triggered the evolution of ever-closer bilateral energy relations. These relations not only reflected a new-found mutual interest in energy development, but also intensified some traditional policy disputes between the two nations. Thus, concomitant with increased opportunities for cooperation and reciprocity, U.S.-Mexican energy relations grew pockmarked by mutual suspicion and occasional examples of recrimination.

Energy in the Border Region

On the Mexican side of the border, significant energy reserves are extant or potential. Most of Mexico's hydrocarbons are located in the nation's southeastern quadrant, but two important gas fields have already been verified in the border states. The larger of the two fields is in the northeast and stretches roughly from Nuevo Laredo, Tamaulipas, through Nuevo León to Monclova, Coahuila, a distance of some one hundred miles. In his first policy statement upon assuming office in late 1976, Jorge Díaz Serrano, the director general of PEMEX, declared his optimism about the region's possibilities (Petróleos Mexicanos, 1976: 3; Salinas Ríos, 1977: 1). He noted that only one-third of that area had been explored and predicted a reserve of more than one trillion cubic feet. In addition to being optimistic about gas production in the area, PEMEX officials have also become increasingly confident that the potential for oil production may exist.

Baja California is the location of the second promising gas field, although some of the original optimism seems to have been tempered since the first enthusiastic promotion of the area in 1974. At that time, flamboyant statements attested to the area's manifest potential. While one PEMEX official talked hopefully about the region's "propitious conditions," another topped his assessment by declaring that "Baja California alone has a deposit which could change the face of the nation" (Goodsell, 1975). In mid-1976, PEMEX brought in Baja's first gas well, located about halfway down the peninsula, and announced that the area offered "attractive possibilities for immediate production." Although that may be so, exploratory drilling has progressed rather slowly. An intensive exploratory drilling program, for example, was put off because PEMEX's equipment and budget were stretched thin. Many geologists, though, agree with the Mexican company's original estimation of the region's potential. Large portions

of Baja California are probably structurally similar to the rich Santa Barbara gas fields of California. If future conditions warrant, PEMEX will no doubt make a renewed effort to explore these possibilities.

In addition to these two gas discoveries, announcements have also appeared concerning the possibilities of oil in the border state of Chihuahua. In late 1978, an even more positive statement declared the existence of oil reserves in the border state of Sonora.

With hydrocarbons supplying about 90 percent of Mexico's energy needs, other sources pale in their significance. Nevertheless, some other sources have measurable potential, others exhibit special innovative characteristics, and still others exemplify the role of the border region in the nation's overall energy mix. Coal, for example, is not now supplying much of Mexico's energy needs, but total reserves are estimated at over two billion tons. The border region is significant in the nation's overall coal reserve and production picture. While almost all domestic output now comes from the border state of Coahuila, more abundant reserves of bituminous coal exist in another border state, Chihuahua. Anthracite deposits have also been located in the border states of Sonora and Tamaulipas. In general, however, Mexico has been slow to develop its coal reserves; not much more than 10 percent of the nation has been surveyed. If Mexico pushes its program to locate additional coal deposits, however, the northern border states may well become increasingly important as major coal suppliers (Banco Nacional de Comercio Exterior, 1977a: 60; Martin, 1977: 253).

As new uranium reserves were located in the late 1970s, the border region assumed increasing salience in Mexico's nuclear picture. Although the nation's first nuclear energy plant is located in the Gulf state of Veracruz, uranium reserves are found primarily in the border states of Chihuahua, Coahuila, Nuevo León, and Tamaulipas (in addition to the southern state of Oaxaca). Mexico has continued to push further exploration and development in the field; in late 1978 it created a new governmental agency, the Comisión Nacional de Energía Atómica (CNEA), to oversee and coordinate the nation's nuclear activities. Optimistic predictions are that Mexico may well become the world's third largest uranium producer in the foreseeable future, with the border states assuming a leading role (*Latin American Economic Report,* 1978: 336; *Mexico Update,* 1978: 4; Martin, 1977: 253).

Mexico's initiatives in geothermal energy have long attracted the attention of experts in the United States and elsewhere, and, again, the border region is particularly significant. Although studies are underway in the states of Chiapas and Michoacán, the nation's only functioning geothermal units are located at Cerro Prieto, in the northern part of Baja California del Norte. By the mid-1970s, two units were operating and a third was near completion.

Finally, in the area of solar and tidal energy, some initial work was underway by the late 1970s, but it had not progressed very far. In both instances, the border states exhibited some development possibilities, with particularly promising potentials in solar energy. The states of Baja California del Norte, Chihuahua, and Sonora count the nation's highest annual average daily radiation yield.

The United States' part of the border-region equation is much better known, of course, so consequently it does not warrant extensive documentation here. Nevertheless, enumeration of several of the important characteristics of the border states of Arizona, California, New Mexico, and Texas is in order. Texas, for example, has long been important as a major supplier of the nation's hydrocarbon energy resources, and California has also been significant in supplying its own gas from the Santa Barbara fields. By far the most consequential aspect of the contemporary energy situation, though, derives from the border states' possible future contributions for development of alternative sources.

By the turn of the century, New Mexico may well be the most important of the border states as a source of alternative energy. By the mid-1970s, production of the state's enormous coal reserves had already made New Mexico one of the nation's leading suppliers of coal. The state also ranked sixth in oil production, fourth in natural gas production, and first in uranium production and reserves. New Mexico has also committed large sums—large for a relatively small and poor American state—to develop other possibilities. Funding for research and development, for example, averaged $2 million to $2.5 million a year during the mid-1970s, and, by late 1978, legislation proposing increases to $4 million was in the offing (Cortner, 1977; Morton, 1978). Notable work was underway on innovative technology in geothermal energy, and New Mexico's importance in solar energy was also beginning to attract increased attention. Arizona's solar energy initiatives also progressed. These initiatives included development of solar production facilities as well as implementation of an attractive tax-credit structure for solar energy applications, insulation, and energy-saving devices (Arizona, ACCES, 1978). Some attention to geothermal development evolved, new explorations for hydrocarbon reserves began in the eastern part of the state, and construction of the state's first nuclear plant also was begun.

California expended much effort in negotiating for energy importation from Arizona, New Mexico, the state of Utah, and Mexico's Baja California. Concurrently, several wide-ranging research and development initiatives centered on alternative energy sources. A long-time interest in geothermal development, particularly in the southern part of the state, was rejuvenated, and newer beginnings in solar sources moved forward. Some efforts also surfaced in more esoteric fields such as tidal and biomass energy.

Aided by the availability of federal financial assistance, all of the U.S. border states initiated work in energy conservation. States, for example, began to prepare comprehensive energy conservation plans and to organize energy extension services. The 1978 National Energy Act also included several important incentives which promised to move states toward more innovative activity in energy conservation.

In sum, on both sides of the border a plethora of activities characterized the policies and programs of the two nations.

In many instances the border states in both Mexico and the United States continued to play a key role, and in others they promised an even larger potential.

Context and Problems

In both Mexico and the United States, special features define the context and peculiar problems impinging on national and border energy development. Parts of the context are common to both nations, but others imply problems more germane to one side of the border than the other. In Mexico, increasing domestic demand couples with export ambitions and limited investment capital to create impediments to the fulfillment of projected plans.

The domestic debates that emerged in the train of Mexico's oil discoveries present several implications for the overall energy picture. In the first case, both scholars and polemicists have spilt much ink in ongoing controversy concerning projections of Mexico's domestic energy consumption. The predictions and calculations vary to some degree, but substantial consensus exists on projecting a yearly increase in domestic consumption of about 7-9 percent (Instituto Mexicano del Petrol, 1975: 61 ff.; Franssen, 1975: 79; Mejías, 1976: 1). Mexico's border region is among the most rapidly growing sections of the nation, of course, and energy demands there are running significantly ahead of the national average.

Additionally, Mexico's ability to muster investment is also limited. The international bankers have been generous (to a fault?) with PEMEX, but official statements are studded with allusions to the problem of raising sufficient monies to push ahead on the nation's ambitious program of energy development. In both hydroelectric and uranium power, for example, contemporary information and technology promise a much larger potential than is now being exploited, but in both fields insufficient monies have deterred further progress. Beyond financial resources, technological sophistication is also scarce in most areas. Mexico's human resources are up to snuff in hydrocarbon production, but in other fields there exists a chronic lack of specialists for exploration and exploitation. Even when efforts are put forth, moreover, development of energy resources is a time-consuming business, and that long-range aspect of the nation's energy development program must also be construed as a problem for the time being. In some areas, to be sure, Mexican nationalism has played a role. All of the major energy sources are nationally owned, and Mexican decision makers insist on national development and exploitation of the riches. In that sense, political nationalism combines with economic scarcity to retard more expeditious exploitation of the nation's energy wealth.

Finally, reflecting a more serious problem endemic to Mexico's national development, the border region is not well connected with the national distribution system. Thus, despite some excess capacity in other parts of the country, the border states must often import energy from the United States.

Mexico's gas and oil pipeline system, for example, extends only as far as Hermosillo and Chihuahua in the north, thereby leaving the booming border cities dependent on surface transportation from the interior or from north of the border. Baja California is the only border state boasting self-sufficiency in energy. The problem of energy scarcity is particularly serious in Ciudad Juárez, the border's fastest-growing city. Lack of energy has been a noteworthy problem there, impeding industrial expansion and, in turn, weakening the municipality's response to debilitating unemployment (Urquidi and Méndez Villarreal, 1978: 156).

As is true with the catalog of energy resources, energy problems on the U.S. side of the border are generally better known than those on the Mexican side. Some of these problems are not totally dissimilar from those in Mexico, but all have their special characteristics, and some mirror the more developed milieu in the United States.

Like Mexico, the U.S. border region encompasses some of the most rapidly growing states in the nation. The border states are part of the southern and southwestern "sunbelt" states which are witnessing high rates of in-migration from the cooler, northern "snowbelt" states. Immigrants to the region are placing new and increasing demands on the area's available energy supplies. In some sections, natural gas is no longer available for new facilities, or the waiting period for hook-up tends to be extraordinarily long.

Transportation problems, reflecting the long distances between population centers, also affect the energy picture in the border region. Heavily dependent on the automobile to cover these vast areas, the region is particularly susceptible to gasoline shortages or cutbacks.

Water scarcity has special meaning for energy development in the border states. Because of the aridity of the area, water has always been a scarce and valued commodity. Increased energy development is placing an additional burden on the region's limited water supply, and experts predict that if future energy development proceeds as planned, demands for surface water will soon exceed the available supply (Weatherford and Jacoby, 1975). The waters of the Colorado River are a focal point in this scenario. There is some concern, for example, that the border states may seek to satisfy future water demands by circumventing their treaty and legal obligations to supply Mexico with its share of usable (nonsaline) Colorado River water. Future water demands for energy production in the border region are thus intrinsically linked to the long-standing dispute between the United States and Mexico over the Colorado River.

Environmental considerations also play a special role in border-region energy development, perhaps reflecting the heightened concern of the more developed nation for questions of environmental quality. While development of the region's energy resources promises to raise the states' per capita incomes and permit a significant regional contribution toward resolution of the nation's energy supply problems, it also has serious implications for the states' environmental and life-style amenities—clean air, open space, fragile arid ecosystems, and numerous recreation areas. Debates over energy-environment trade-offs have thus been the core of most controversial energy policy issues in the border region. In several cases, environmental considerations have won out, and proposed energy developments have been either cancelled or significantly modified. Such actions, whatever their ultimate vices or virtues, have nonetheless served to further complicate border-region energy development.

The region's Indian tribes present another unique twist to the energy scenario in the border states of Arizona and New Mexico. Many of the region's energy resources are located on Indian lands in those two states, and because of the semisovereign status of the Indian reservations, the tribes exercise considerable control over the extraction and production of these resources. However, tribal development of energy riches located on Indian lands is complicated, since tribes exist as economically impoverished enclaves in the midst of a developed society. In this respect, the tribes face many of the same problems of energy and economic development that the Mexican border states face (Cortner, 1974; Schaller, 1978).

Finally, interstate rivalry impinges on cooperative energy efforts in the border region. Such rivalry often leads to heated controversy, ranging from vituperative charges of exploitation to drawn-out legal proceedings. California is a major factor in this equation. Because it is relatively energy poor, it must import energy from the other border states and its Mexican neighbor, Baja California. In every instance, these importations have been fraught with extensive negotiations and have been pockmarked by controversy. New Mexico, as previously mentioned, sits on the opposite end of the energy spectrum; it is an energy-rich state. Nevertheless, it fears exploitation of its energy resources and is markedly chary of pressures from other states and the federal government. Concerned that energy production benefits could flow out of the state, leaving significant economic and environmental costs for the state's residents to assume, state officials and influential groups keep constant vigil against outsiders' energy claims.

The context and problems on the U.S. side of the border therefore exhibit some differences from the Mexican side, but they are equally contentious. Perhaps most cogent for border scholars, however, is that there has been little cooperation in energy development beyond mutual exploration. The California-Baja California relationship implies the beginning of some mutual accord and cooperation, and some progress is possible on elements of the water issue, but those initiatives are much beyond their infancy stage. Fruitful areas for cooperative efforts between Mexico and the United States exist in solar, geothermal, and hydrocarbons development. In each case the sources of those energy potentialities cross the line of the political border. Fugitive and ad hoc initiatives are occasionally broached in those areas, but nothing substantial has developed. National self-interests defined in American and Mexican terms continue to dominate the scenario. A germ of interdependence has evolved, however, and the discontinuous efforts at bilateral cooperation may bear some fruit in the future, but optimism is not warranted.

Research Sources

Research on energy-related subjects in the Borderlands has been greatly facilitated by the proliferation of technical studies, publications, conferences, and both official and unofficial interests in energy matters generally since the 1973 energy crisis. There are, however, two caveats which should guide the scholar interested in border-region energy subjects—namely, that few materials exist which focus exclusively on the energy activities of the U.S.-Mexican Borderlands, and that the preponderance of energy-related materials available to a scholarly quest originate within the United States. The search for energy-related information concerning the Borderlands must then incorporate a diverse range of general and technical literature which, fortunately, is likely to be accessible to the English-speaking scholar.

Reference and Statistical Works. Abetting the locating of energy materials is a range of reference works from official and unofficial agencies in the energy field. Since the early 1970s, the U.S. government, through its several principal energy agencies, has sponsored various abstracting services covering a range of energy-related publications and periodicals. Under the auspices of the U.S. Department of Energy (DOE) and the Energy Research and Development Administration (ERDA), it has published the *Energy Abstracts for Policy Analysis* (monthly) and the *ERDA-Energy Research Abstracts* (biweekly). Both of these publications abstract by corporate source, author, and subject of work. The U.S. Department of Commerce's National Technical Information Service (NTIS) publishes a weekly abstracting service, *Weekly Government Abstracts: Energy.* Another abstracting service of particular interest to the student of the Borderlands is *The Energy Index,* published by the Environment Information Center's Energy Reference Department in New York. The last work provides a useful geographical index to a range of newspapers and periodicals, some foreign, and is published annually.

Supplementing the abstract services are a number of directories of energy sources and agencies which, though tending to emphasize U.S. sources of energy information, provide ready access to a range of useful tools for scholarly research. The monthly *Directory of Federal Energy Data Sources,* published by the Federal Energy Administration (FEA), in addition to providing major reference abstracts also monthly focuses on special topics. Patricia Baade's *Directory of International Energy Statistics* (1976, with 1977 supplement) and the *Energy Guide: A Directory of Information Resources* (1977) by Virginia Bemis are likewise potentially valuable points of departure. For the scholar interested in U.S. newspaper sources in the Borderlands, frequently new developments and late-breaking energy news may be found in *Newsbank: Business and Economic Development Index,* which provides a full and up-to-date index of energy-relevant news published in over 160 U.S. newspapers, including all the major newspapers in the U.S. Borderlands.

While the reference materials tend to be heavily weighted toward U.S. energy information sources, the Borderlands scholar fares somewhat better with respect to Mexican statistical sources of information. Government publications on both sides of the border are especially fruitful data sources on energy matters. Worthy of mention on the U.S. side are two similarly titled publications, *Energy Facts II* (1975) and *1976 Energy Facts.* In Mexico the *Annuario estadístico,* published by the Secretariat of Industry and Commerce, as well as *México en cifras,* by the quasi-official Nacional Financiera, are important sources of industrial and energy data. International agencies are likewise important sources of statistical information for the scholar interested in national energy trends, though they infrequently provide regional breakdowns of data. The United Nations' *Statistical Yearbook* is perennially useful, as is its regionally oriented *Economic Bulletin for Latin America* studies. The Organization of American States' (OAS) *America en cifras, situación económica: Industria,* among other publications of the OAS, also provides a comparative source of energy-relevant data.

Government Agencies. In addition to the publications summarized above, government agencies at various levels are fruitful sources of information and referral regarding energy matters. Especially in the United States, regional and state agencies frequently publish and serve as clearinghouses for energy information. Such services in the U.S. Borderlands are highly useful, though similar services on the Mexican side are lacking.

At the federal level in the United States, the principal energy-related agencies include, in addition to the DOE, the Federal Energy Regulatory Commission, the Nuclear Regulatory Commission, and the Geological Survey. Each of these agencies publishes extensively and provides various referral services on request; for example, the National Energy Information Center of the DOE's Energy Information Administration may be contacted for answers to a wide variety of general energy questions. Also at the federal level, congressional hearings and reports contain a wealth of technical and policy information for the energy scholar. *Congressional Quarterly,* which provides a weekly report on important congressional activities, is a good information source for current policy issues.

At the regional level, several bodies are of special interest to the border energy scholar, including the Western Governors' Policy Office, the Western Interstate Energy Board, and the Rocky Mountain Mineral Law Foundation. The Four Corners Regional Commission serves as a clearinghouse and publications agency for state energy matters; its *Publications Catalog* should be consulted for a range of salient, energy-related documents. New Mexico's Energy and Minerals Department serves as a clearinghouse in conjunction with the New Mexico Energy Extension Service Information Center. At the University of New Mexico, two pertinent organizations are the Technical Information Center, a part of the Applied Research Service, and the Technology Application Center. In Texas, the Office of Energy Resources, the Energy Advisory Council of Texas, and the Oil and Gas Division of the Texas State Railroad Commission all serve in various ways as sources of information on energy.

Arizona has established a State Energy Information Center with a toll-free "hotline" service. The interested scholar might contact the Energy Programs Division in the Office of Economic Planning and Development, the Arizona Solar Energy Research Commission, the Oil and Gas Conservation Commission, the Arizona Power Authority, and the Arizona Atomic Energy Commission. Additionally, M. E. Hale's *Arizona Energy* (1976), published by the University of Arizona, provides a useful introduction to that state's energy resources and problems. Finally, *Acces-Energy,* a publication of the Council for Environmental Studies at the University of Arizona, provides a useful bimonthly summary of recent publications, major information services and events, and significant Arizona energy activities.

In Mexico, the principal governmental or quasi-governmental agencies in energy matters are at the federal level. In particular, Petróleos Mexicanos (PEMEX) is a vital source of information for both oil and other energy-related matters in Mexico. The most valuable of the petroleum monopoly's annual publications is the *Memoria de labores,* but the company also issues *El Petróleo, Petróleos Mexicanos Construye,* and oddments covering things like the present state of the company's merchant fleet, pipeline systems, and the like. In addition to those regular publications, PEMEX also issues a steady stream of speeches, press releases, and special reports, all invaluable to the scholar interested in Mexican energy. The Instituto Mexicano del Petróleo, PEMEX's research and development arm, also issues occasional studies. Beginning in the mid-1970s, it began to publish a series of comprehensive studies on Mexican domestic energy demands under the general title of *Energéticos.*

The Comisión Federal de Electricidad and its subordinate agency, the Comisión de Energéticos, are especially useful sources on the hydroelectric industry. The Comisión de Energéticos' *Inventario de approvechamento hydroeléctricos, reporte final* (1975) should be consulted. Other sources of energy information include the semiofficial Banco Nacional de Comercio Exterior, which publishes several periodicals, including the survey *Mexico* (1976) and *Comercio Exterior,* and the Comisión Nacional de Energía Nuclear, the Mexican clearinghouse for atomic energy information.

Journals and Other Periodicals. Nowhere is the proliferation of energy information in the '70s more evident than in the periodical literature which either exclusively or occasionally focuses on energy related subjects. It would be impossible to provide a complete coverage or mention of the range of this literature on either side of the border, but a brief listing of the most important publications on border energy should be a useful point of departure.

The periodical literature on both sides of the border can generally be differentiated into two categories: trade publications and professional journals, and general scientific or economic publications. Among the former, the student should consult the *Oil and Gas Journal, American Association of Petroleum Geologists Bulletin, Geothermal World Directory,*

Energy User News, Petroleum Economist, Petroleum Engineer, Petroleum International, Petroleum Today, Petroleum Times, Petroleum Geology, Hydrocarbon Processing and Petroleum Engineering, Bituminous Coal Facts, Coal Facts, Coal Age, Coal Mining and Processing, Bulletin of the Atomic Scientist, and *Atomic Energy Review,* among others.

Of a more general scientific and economic bent are *Energy Systems and Policy, Annual Review of Energy, Energy Policy, Energy Review, American Economic Review,* and *Natural Resources Journal.* The last periodical deserves special mention for its coverage of environmental and energy-related subjects in the Borderlands, with special emphasis on legal and sociopolitical ramifications of energy and natural resources developments. Also of enhanced interest to the Borderlands scholar is *The Journal of Energy and Development,* which focuses on developing nations. Among the many more general periodicals of interest, such publications as *Scientific American, Science and Public Affairs,* and *Science* should not be overlooked as potential information sources.

While the number of energy-related materials in Mexico is considerably less among trade and professional journals, the student should see the *Instituto Mexicano de ingenieros químicos (Revista), El economista mexicano, El trimestre económico, Industria mexicana, Foro internacional,* and *Boletín bibliográfico de oceanografía y geofísica americanas.* Important sources of energy information appear regularly in Mexico's more general economic and public-interest news periodicals. Among the most useful of the latter are the Banco Nacional de Comercio Exterior's *Comercio Exterior,* Banamex's *Review of the Economic Situation in Mexico,* and *Mex-Am Review,* all of which appear in English-language editions. Spanish-language general-interest publications include such newsweeklies as *Proceso, Visión,* and *Tiempo,* substantially focusing on business and economic development. *El mercado de valores* (Nacional Financiera) focuses on financial and economic matters.

Trade Associations, Corporations, Foundations, Public-Interest Research, and so on. While the foregoing publications are generally the most regularly reliable energy information sources, they by no means exhaust the wide range available on this ubiquitous topic. Among important sources are the various proceedings of the professional associations and related compilations of conference papers. Among recent proceedings of interest to Borderlands energy research are the *1977 Annual Meeting of the Geological Society of America, South Central Section; Proceedings of the Council of Economics' 105th Annual Meeting of Mining, Metallurgical and Petroleum Engineers* (1976); *Proceedings of the Geothermal Resource Development Institute Conference* (1977); and *Proceedings of the American Institute of Chemical Engineers, Eleventh Inter-society Energy Conversion Engineering Conference.*

In addition to the proceedings of learned societies and scientific associations, publications of major private corporations involved in energy-related activities should be familiar to the scholar. Virtually all of the major oil companies, for example, publish pamphlets, reviews, and occasional papers on energy. Of worthwhile mention are Exxon Corporation's Background Series (see *World Energy Outlook,* 1977) and the various publications of the petroleum industry's major trade association, the National Petroleum Council.

A host of foundations, private research institutions, workshops, and associations are occasionally alternative information sources. The activities, for example, of the American Association for the Advancement of Science produced numerous energy publications. Among foundations actively involved in energy research are the Ford Foundation, Resources for the Future, the Conservation Foundation, the Environmental Law Institute, the Center for the Study of Democratic Institutions, and the Battele Institute. Considerable energy information is also made available by civic groups such as the League of Women Voters and by a variety of national and local environmental groups concerned about the environmental impacts of energy production. The prestigious Committee for Economic Development also issues a series of energy-related publications of national and international interest, as does the Workshop on Alternative Energy Sources (under the auspices of the Massachusetts Institute of Technology). Along the same line, the research activities of various universities and scholarly centers, especially those located in the border region, are fertile ground for energy-related studies in the Borderlands.

28

Agriculture and Ranching

ROBERT B. KENT
Department of Geography
Syracuse University

The nature of political, economic, and cultural differences along a border modifies the agricultural landscapes that will evolve, while environmental conditions may be exactly the same. This rule does not mean that border agricultural landscapes must be inherently different; they may be hardly distinguishable. In a study of the German-Dutch border in the 1950s, Platt (1958) found almost no significant difference in agricultural economies and landscapes of the two nations along nearly three hundred miles. Recent research along the U.S.-Canadian border in the western part of the continent (Reitsma, 1972), however, revealed striking contrasts between the two nations' agricultural landscapes. Even within nation states, dramatic agricultural differences may develop on provincial or state boundaries. Rose (1955) showed the development of distinct agricultural economies along a portion of the Queensland-New South Wales (Australia) frontier as the result of differing land development policies by state officials. Intensive orcharding developed in Queensland after active government encouragement, while ranching remained the staple economy in New South

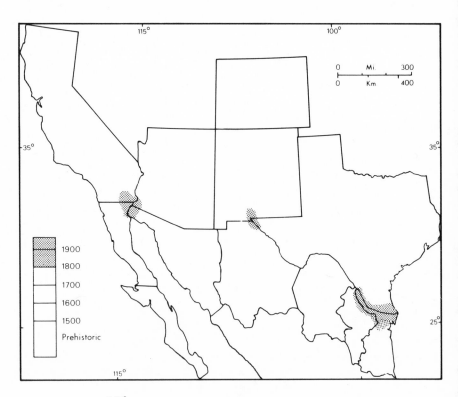

Wales. The political, economic, and cultural differences that exist between the United States and Mexico are evident, in some degree, to even the most casual observer. These differences produce distinctive agricultural landscapes in the border region, although there are some strong similarities among them as well.

Agriculture on the U.S.-Mexican border is distinguished by the recency of its development and by the importance and uniqueness it plays in each nation's agricultural economy. Commercial agricultural activity serving regional, national, and international markets is primarily a post-1900 development. In both Mexico and the United States, the agricultural development of the border was a product of massive irrigation projects, planned and financed by private capital in some cases and by the respective national governments in others. The agricultural production of this region is of major significance to both agricultural economies. This temperate to subtropical region, however, often provides products of a different nature to each economy. This variability is due to the climate of the region relative to that in the agricultural heartland of each country, creating a comparative advantage for the growing of particular crops on each side of the border. It permits and encourages the cultivation of valuable subtropical crops on the northern side and the cultivation of temperate crops on the southern side. In the United States, the Borderlands are major producers of fresh vegetables, citrus fruits, dates, and cotton (Collier, 1970: 337; Jumper, 1969: 316; Hullihen, 1966: 34; Hill, 1963: 50; Lutz, 1964; Smith, 1967: 8). In Mexico, about 29 percent of the alfalfa, 25 percent of the cotton, 20 percent of the sorghum, and 10 percent of the wheat harvested are grown in the border region, as is a significant portion of the country's grape harvest (Brown, 1967: 1; Urquidi and Villarreal, 1978: 145-46; Wellhausen, 1976: 136; West and Augelli, 1976: 373).

This chapter examines the agricultural landscapes of the border in their historical context, focusing primarily on irrigated crop cultivation. It reviews the characteristics of border agriculture and its principal and secondary production regions. The border region reviewed here is restricted to the territory along or immediately adjacent to the present international border. Specifically, these are counties or *municipios* that border on the frontier, although in one or two cases agricultural activity which is very close to the frontier is also mentioned.

Characteristics

Agriculture on the border exhibits similarities discernible in both countries. Primary among these are the use of irrigation water, the cultivation of high-value crops, and the economic structure of the farm units. First, agriculture is dependent upon irrigation water supplied either through irrigation projects financed by national governments, through local irrigation districts, or simply through the private pumping of groundwater. This need for irrigation water has created problems between the two nations which are centered on the quantity and quality of water delivered by the Colorado River

and Rio Grande (Sepúlveda, 1974*b*: 60; Smith, 1961: 115). The question of water quality was resolved in the International Water Treaty of 1944, which dictated the quantities of water deliverable to each nation from the Tijuana and Colorado rivers and the Rio Grande. Water quality, measured by the amount of dissolved salt solids carried in the water, later proved to be a serious problem for Mexican farmers using Colorado River water. Fortunately, these problems were resolved through agreements between the two countries in 1973 (Sepúlveda, 1974*b*: 64). The depletion of groundwater reserves has also created conflict, leading in one case to an accord that limits groundwater pumping along the Arizona-Sonora border to 160,000 acre-feet annually for each nation (Sepúlveda, 1974*b*: 65).

The dependence of border agriculture on irrigation water leads to a generalization about cropping patterns. Irrigation farming is expensive; hence, there is a tendency among agriculturalists to grow high-value crops (Birle, 1976: 22; Venezian and Gamble, 1969: 43). The cropping mixture varies from place to place and often reflects the source of irrigation water. Farmers using water provided by nationally financed irrigation projects may grow crops of lower value because their water costs are low, whereas farmers who are dependent on water supplied from local irrigation districts, or who pump their water from wells, must grow higher-value crops because their costs are high (Birle, 1976: 70). Normally, in areas of low water costs, forage and grain crops predominate, while with higher water costs, citrus, vegetables, and cotton become the principal crops (Pifer, 1969: 547). Farmers in areas of low-cost water often continue to grow low-value crops, ignoring the possibilities of a greater return because of an unwillingness to change, the marketing risks inherent in high-value crops like vegetables, or the higher development costs of a tree crop such as citrus. Growers may also choose to diversify with both high- and low-value crops in order to reduce their risks (Durfee, 1969: 10).

Finally, agriculture on both sides of the border is characterized by large-scale commercial farming operations (Gregor, 1970*a*, 1970*b*, 1976: 55; Urquidi and Villarreal, 1978: 145-46; Venezian and Gamble, 1969: 43). Farm units in the Mexican portion of the region are unusual in their national context. The landholdings are large and well capitalized, and they experience considerable technical inputs, in contrast with the small, poorly capitalized farms in the central and southern parts of the country. This type of contrast does not occur with farm units on the American side, which are large, privately owned, and capital-intensive like many throughout the American West and Southwest.

There are pronounced differences in both agricultural economies in cropping mixture, land tenure, and aspects of agricultural labor supply. National policies and market demands often determine crop plantings; therefore, areas of similar environment which fall in different national territories may exhibit distinct agricultural patterns (Prescott, 1965: 91; Reitsma, 1972: 6). Cotton, for example, is cultivated in the Imperial Valley, the Yuma area, and the Valle de Mexicali, but historically the acreage on the Mexican side of the border in the Valle de Mexicali has been several times greater than that on the American side (Dunbier, 1968: 249). Wheat cultivation has also been more intensive on the Mexican side, while lettuce, melons, and sugar beets are almost absent from it but are valuable commodities in the north (Dunbier, 1968: 252, 259). Import duties and trade restrictions in the United States eliminate the possibility of the competing cultivation of vegetables or fruits by the Mexicans. Cotton acreage, however, has decreased dramatically on the Mexican side in the last few years because of changes in government agricultural policy in Mexico and cotton prices on the international market. Mexican entrepreneurs have moved away from cotton to the production of food crops with government encouragement (Johnson, 1976: 2). Along the lower Rio Grande similar patterns are evident. Citrus cultivation is absent from the Mexican side, but occupies 75,000 acres in Texas (Hill, 1963: 121; Mexico, 1975a: 226-27; U.S., 1977d).

Land tenure constitutes another contrasting element of border agriculture. In the United States, all agricultural land is privately owned, except in the rare cases where land is rented from the state or federal government or is part of an Indian reservation. The passage of the Reclamation Act of 1902 (R. A. Fernández, 1977: 97) and the construction of several irrigation projects under the auspices of the federal government brought tens of thousands of acres under cultivation and under nominal government control. Under the terms of this act, each farmer was restricted to using government water to irrigate a maximum of 160 acres (320 acres for a married couple). Farmers in the Southwest, and especially in California, avoided these regulations through a number of subterfuges and the tacit approval of some U.S. government agencies. The issue has recently raised controversy in the West, including the border region, but it has still not been entirely resolved.

In Mexico, land tenure is somewhat different. The *ejido*, a form of land tenure in which the individual has usufruct rights to the land, is very common. Two of the major irrigated zones, Río Colorado and Ciudad Juárez, have about half of the irrigated land in *ejidos*, while along the lower Rio Grande and San Juan River, this figure decreases to one-fourth of the irrigated land, the balance being held privately (Mexico, 1968: 295-97). These *ejidos* are classified as either individual or collective. On the individual *ejido* the family head is assigned a personal plot, while on the collective *ejido* the *ejiditario* works for a wage or a share of the entire farm's return. Individual *ejido* units far outnumber the collective ones in both acreage and number. In the north and the border region, however, the collective *ejido* is the dominant type, in contrast with the southern and central parts of Mexico, where the individual *ejido* prevails. The concentration of the collective form in the north and the border region was undoubtedly encouraged by the excellent opportunities for mechanization and crop specialization present on the large, flat tracts of land.

Privately held land in Mexico is subject to some of the same kinds of regulations that exist on the American side. Owners of private farms, small property owners and *colonos*, are legally restricted from ownership of more than one hun-

dred hectares of irrigated land. These regulations stem from the Mexican land reform after the 1910 Revolution. Farmers in Mexico, however, have been as adroit as their counterparts in the United States in avoiding these regulations, and frequently private holdings exceed the hundred-hectare limit.

Agricultural labor exhibits contrasts and similarities on both sides of the border. Mechanization is very important today throughout the border region, and while it has served to reduce the need for seasonal laborers, large numbers are still required on both sides of the border. Agriculture in the West and Southwest of the United States has long required large numbers of seasonal laborers. In California, Chinese, Japanese, and Filipino laborers supplied this need until about the 1920s. Then Mexican nationals became increasingly common in the fields, as they did in other border areas. This increase in Mexicans was related to labor shortages in agriculture during World War I (Marshall, 1978: 68) and to their greater suitability as a seasonal labor force (R. A. Fernández, 1977: 116). The Mexicans could, and often would, return to Mexico during the off season, returning dependably for work the following year. Asian farm workers were unable to return seasonally to their homelands and eventually began farming themselves or seeking stable occupations in the cities, forcing farmers to search for other labor sources.

Dependence upon Mexican nationals in agriculture increased and led in 1941 to requests by American growers for the establishment of a contract labor program. This program was institutionalized in the following year in the form of the *bracero* program (Briggs, 1978: 206). This program continued, with a lapse of only four years between 1947 and 1951, until 1964, when it was terminated by the U.S. government (Briggs, 1978: 207). Since 1964, the U.S. government has refused to reinstate the program despite requests from U.S. growers and the Mexican government. Illegal aliens and workers with green cards now constitute the principal sources of agricultural labor for American fields in the Borderlands.

The large population concentration in Mexican border cities is seen by some as a large reserve supply of cheap labor for the needs of U.S. agriculture (R. A. Fernández, 1977: 116). Farming on the Mexican side of the frontier, however, also requires the services of a large seasonal labor force. For example, nearly thirty thousand seasonal workers were required each fall to assist with the cotton harvest in the Mexicali area during the late 1960s (Bataillon, 1969, as cited in Bassols, 1972: 282). Thus, labor flows not only from Mexico to the United States, but also from the interior of Mexico to its northern agricultural areas. Many of these workers are employed in agricultural occupations on both sides of the border during one season.

Principal Regions

There are three major regions of irrigated agriculture on the U.S.-Mexican frontier (Fig. 28-1). The largest of these is on the alluvial soils of the lower Rio Grande and Río San Juan valleys in the states of Texas and Tamaulipas. Browns-

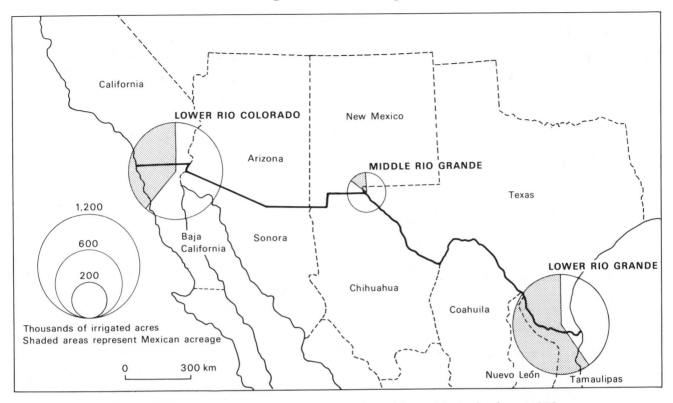

Fig. 28-1. *Principal agricultural regions of the United States-Mexico border ca. 1975.*

ville and Matamoros are the principal urban centers. Another agricultural region lies along the lower Colorado and lower Gila rivers and includes portions of the states of California, Arizona, Baja California, and Sonora. The Imperial Valley, the Valle de Mexicali, and the benchlands around Yuma are the areas of concentrated agriculture. El Centro, Mexicali, and Yuma are the principal urban service centers. The last area of significant and concentrated irrigation agriculture focuses on the twin cities of El Paso and Ciudad Juárez in the states of Texas, New Mexico, and Chihuahua. Agriculture there extends northwest on the Rio Grande into the Mesilla and Rincon valleys and southeast along the Rio Grande in the Valle de Juárez. Irrigated agriculture on a smaller scale and livestock raising are practiced in several other less concentrated locations on the frontier. The remaining discussion focuses on the historical antecedents and contemporary agricultural landscapes of the three major regions and then briefly on several of the less significant areas of agriculture and livestock raising.

Lower Rio Grande. The earliest agricultural settlement of this region was attempted near the confluence of the Rio Grande and the Río San Juan in the mid-eighteenth century (Foscue, 1934: 126). Crop raising was not successful, but within a few years livestock raising rapidly became the principal economic activity (Foscue, 1934: 128). The land was held in common by the Hispano pueblos for about twenty

years until the awarding of individual land grants destroyed the communal structure of landholding (Foscue, 1934: 128-29). The vagaries of changing political control little affected the agricultural economy of this region. Although limited, subsistence-oriented irrigation agriculture was undoubtedly practiced, and some experiments were attempted with commercial cultivation of sugarcane and other crops towards the end of the nineteenth century, livestock raising remained the main agricultural activity until after the beginning of the twentieth century (Day, 1970: 164).

The first large-scale efforts at commercial crop cultivation occurred in the early 1900s on the American side of the river. The railroad arrived in 1904, and immediately private land developers began the process of promoting land sales and irrigation development. The lure of citrus cultivation played prominently in these promotional appeals to midwesterners (Hill, 1963: 13). Cameron and Hidalgo counties, which contain nearly all of the irrigated land north of the river, reported over 50,000 irrigated acres by 1909 (U.S., 1913-14: 710-11). The further development of the valley was impeded by the Mexican Revolution of 1910 and by World War I. Sugarcane, one of the earliest commercial crops, had all but disappeared after the war (Foscue, 1932: 4) and was replaced with the cultivation of citrus, winter truck crops, and cotton. In the early 1930s, the concentration of these crops into separate districts had been recognized (Dillman, 1970d: 9). Citrus dominated in the west, while winter truck crops and cotton occupied the southeast and the north. Irrigated acreage then stood at 220,000 acres (U.S., 1936: 782, 789). Acreage expanded during the forties, reaching nearly 600,000 acres at the end of the decade (U.S., 1956a: 84-93). Acreage has gradually decreased since then. At the last agricultural census, approximately 450,000 acres were irrigated (U.S., 1977d).

Irrigated agriculture on the southern side of the Rio Grande developed at a large scale during the 1940s and 1950s. Before World War II, about fifty thousand acres were farmed. Half of this acreage was used by employing the floodwaters of the Rio Grande, while the other half was dry-farmed, depending only on rainfall for water (Bustamente, 1951: 272). Cotton constituted a near monoculture at that time (Dillman, 1970d: 9). The international agreements embodied in the treaty of 1944, including the construction of the Falcon Dam across the Rio Grande, paved the way for the development of massive irrigation works by the Mexican government (Rodríguez, 1950: 145; Dillman, 1970d: 9). Irrigated acreage soared to levels comparable to those in Texas by the mid-1950s and early 1960s (Day, 1970: 167). The tendency in Mexico, as it was in Texas, was initially to irrigate more land than could continue to be adequately supplied in years of little water (Day, 1970: 166). Acreage since the late fifties has grown steadily from around five hundred thousand acres to nearly seven hundred thousand acres in the mid-seventies (Mexico, 1960, 1976: 607).

Presently, on the U.S. side of the border there are 450,000 acres of irrigated cropland (U.S., 1977d), much of which is planted with sorghum. During 1974, about 650,000 acres of sorghum were harvested, representing extensive double cropping (Texas, 1975: 60). In fact, this area's latitudinal position allows double cropping of most annual crops. Cotton and vegetables each occupy about 100,000 acres annually (Texas, 1976: 9). They are frequently interplanted in young citrus orchards or planted as an alternative crop by citrus growers after their orchards have suffered severe frost damage (Schoffelmayer, 1960: 216).

Citrus, especially pink grapefruit, has been important to the valley's economy since the 1930s (Webber, 1929: 269). Curiously, the seedless pink-fleshed grapefruit, which has been grown widely in the region and which now dominates citrus production, developed as a mutation from a variety of pink grapefruit (with seeds) after a severe freeze in the valley in 1929 (Hill, 1963: 60). Oranges are also important, and the Valencia is a favorite variety because it is a late-season orange that finds a ready market in the north during the winter months (Hill, 1963: 63). Citrus occupied about 90,000 acres in 1961 and about 75,000 acres in 1974 (Hill, 1963: 50; U.S., 1977d). Generally, citrus plantings favor the well-drained, sandy terraces in the west in Hidalgo County, while truck crops and cotton occupy the heavy clay soils to the east in Cameron County (Day, 1970: 98; Hill, 1963: 22).

On the southern side of the river, in Mexico, the agricultural sector is both similar to and different from that in the north. There are 700,000 acres of irrigated land there, much of it also double-cropped (Mexico, 1976: 607). Sorghum, too, is the principal crop in total acreage, accounting for 650,000 acres annually. Corn follows with 200,000 acres, and lesser amounts of land are devoted to beans and cotton, totaling approximately 50,000 and 20,000 acres, respectively. The small cotton acreage today stands in stark contrast to a cotton monoculture described by Dillman (1970: 3) in the early 1960s. Also notable is the near absence of citrus cultivation on the Mexican side. Only six acres were reported in 1974 (Mexico, 1975a: 228). A thriving poultry industry exists, however, boasting nearly a million chickens (Mexico, 1975a: 47).

Lower Colorado. Commercial agricultural exploitation of the lower Colorado River region has occurred within the last ninety years. Yet the irrigation of the lands in the Salton Depression was discussed seriously as early as 1849. Ten years later, O. M. Wozencraft had obtained a concession from the California state legislature for the state rights to sixteen hundred square miles of desert in exchange for their reclamation. He planned to divert Colorado River water into one of its old channels, the Alamo channel in Mexican territory, and have the water flow by gravity into the below-sea-level Salton Depression (Freeman, 1923: 387). Wozencraft never received the necessary federal approval for his endeavor, and the desert did not bloom first in the Salton Depression but instead in the vicinity of Yuma along the lower Gila River at its confluence with the Colorado. Over 500 acres were under irrigation in that area in 1889, increasing to nearly 4,500 acres by 1899 (U.S., 1902: 824-25). Later, agricultural development in the Yuma area was aided tremendously by the federal government. Soon after the U.S. Reclamation Service was formed in 1902, it initiated the Yuma Project and the construction of the Laguna Diversion Dam across the Colorado, bringing nearly 54,000 acres under irrigation in the area by 1922 (Freeman, 1923: 376).

Plans for the reclamation of the Salton Depression were finalized in April, 1900, and by May, 1901, water was delivered through the Imperial Canal, which crossed about fifty miles of Mexican territory. This impressive effort, undertaken with private capital organized under the California Development Company, produced dramatic results. With tens of thousands of acres under cultivation, a flood of the Colorado River in 1905 destroyed the company's levees, and the flow of the river was diverted to the northwest and into the Salton Depression, creating the Salton Sea (Boyle, Graves, and Watkins, 1971: 146). Had this flow not been stopped by the concerted efforts of the Southern Pacific Railroad, water would have continued to fill the depression until its level would have topped the elevation of the accumulated sediments at the mouth of the Colorado and would have created a body of water several times larger than the present-day Salton Sea, eliminating entirely the possibility of farming on the American side of the border. Luckily, only 488 square miles of land were flooded in the two years before the Southern Pacific returned the river to its original course (Beck and Hasse, 1974).

In spite of these problems, the development of the valley continued generally unabated, and by 1909 there were 190,000 irrigated acres of farmland (U.S., 1913-14: 178). This growth continued after 1910, but at a more moderate rate. Irrigated acreage was reported at 235,000 and 450,000 acres in 1934 and 1949, respectively (U.S., 1936: 953; 1956: 55). The Imperial Valley remained a private development until 1940, when the completion of the Imperial Dam on the Colorado River and the All-American Canal by the U.S. Reclamation Service brought valley farmers, who used government water, under acreage limitations (160 acres per individual and 320 acres per married couple). These regulations have been only laxly enforced, to the benefit of farmers with large acreages under irrigation. Irrigated acreage in the valley has remained in the vicinity of 450,000 acres since 1949.

The development of the Imperial Valley in the United States allowed the subsequent colonization of its southern counterpart, the Valle de Mexicali. American capitalists financed the construction of the Imperial Canal across fifty miles of Mexican soil and in so doing opened the way for the agricultural exploitation of the Mexican side of the border. It was also American capitalists who enjoyed most of the benefits of this reclamation for the next thirty to forty years. Cotton, most of which was marketed in the United States, was almost immediately the only major crop, and by 1920, nearly 100,000 acres were harvested annually (Compañía Mexicana del Terrenos del Río Colorado, S.A., 1958: 282). This represented about half of all irrigated acreage at that time (Freeman, 1923: 408). The full impact of the agrarian reform legislation passed immediately after the 1910 Revolution did not affect the Valle de Mexicali until the mid-1930s. American companies were still firmly entrenched in 1931, when they controlled nearly 1,000,000 acres, although it is estimated that only 20 percent of that acreage was under irrigation. One firm, the Colorado River Land Company, successor to the California Land Development Company that developed the Imperial Valley, controlled 800,000 acres. By comparison, Mexican nationals and the Mexican government apparently controlled only 35,000 acres, on which were established modest agricultural colonies (Tout, n.d., as cited in Compañía Mexicana del Terrenos del Río Colorado, S.A., 1958: 135).

In a series of moves initiated in 1929, the Mexican government began to progressively reduce the holdings of American companies by forcing them to subdivide and sell to Mexican nationals and the government (Compañía Mexicana del Torrenos del Río Colorado, S.A., 1958: 139, 164-65). This process culminated in 1945-46 when the Mexican government purchased the remaining holdings of the Colorado River Land Company, including nearly 150,000 irrigated acres. The purchase allowed the establishment by the Mexican government in 1946 of the Compañía Mexicana de Terrenos del Río Colorado, S.A., which was charged with the Mexicanization and colonization of lands regained from the Americans and an expansion of irrigated acreage in the Valle de Mexicali (Compañía Mexicana del Terrenos del Río Colorado, S.A., 1958: 166). Since 1958, irrigated acreage in the valley has hovered around 400,000 acres (Mexico, 1960; 1970: 291; 1976: 607).

The Imperial Valley presently comprises about 450,000 acres of irrigated land (U.S., 1977b). Forage crops, espe-cially alfalfa, occupy the largest acreages, with grain crops, notably sorghums and barley, ranking second (Birle, 1976: 22; Lantis, Steiner, and Karinen, 1973: 75). While occupying less land, cotton and vegetables such as lettuce, melons, and tomatoes represent a much higher financial return per acre. Feed crops and pasture make up nearly seven times the acreage of vegetables, but income from vegetable production is 50 percent greater (Lantis, Steiner, and Karinen, 1973: 75). Cotton was a major crop in the 1920s, when it ranked first in total acreage among all crops, but its fortunes depend in large measure on government agricultural policy and foreign competition, and over the years both have worked to reduce the importance of cotton in the valley (Darnell, 1959: 96; Mandell and Tweeten, 1971: 335). It is not a major crop today. Sugar beets, too, are a part of the agricultural landscape, and by-products of its processing are used to feed some of the hundreds of thousands of cattle held in feed lots in the valley. In fact, large quantities of alfalfa and grain which are grown in the valley never leave, because they are sold to local feed lots. Cattle feeding is a major component of the agricultural sector, and in the late 1960s the Imperial Valley was one of the top cattle-feeding counties in the United States (Boswell, 1967: 135).

East of the Imperial Valley and across the Colorado River in Arizona, 230,000 acres of irrigated cropland occupy the environs of Yuma (U.S., 1977a). Agriculture and related industries are the mainstay of the area's economy as they are in the Imperial Valley (Leaming and de Gennaro, 1970: 11). Alfalfa, sorghums, barley, lettuce, melons, and cotton are the leading crops. Citrus, grapes, and dates distinguish this region from the Imperial Valley, where they are absent. Citrus acreage has been expanded recently, with Valencia oranges and lemons as the most common plantings, but lesser quantities of grapefruit and navel oranges have also been planted (Dunbier, 1968: 300; Hillman, 1972: 261-62; Hullihen, 1966: 34). Plantings of table grapes were made on a large scale in the late 1960s (Hillman, 1972: 262). The date industry, however, has suffered a slow decline in the recent past (Smith, 1967: 92).

South of the border, the Valle de Mexicali contains a distinct agricultural economy, with about 420,000 acres of irrigated cropland which are also fed by the Colorado River (Mexico, 1975a: 6). In contrast to the northern side of the border, cotton occupies nearly half of all irrigated land, followed by wheat and safflower, each covering about one-fifth of the irrigated acreage. Barley, alfalfa, and rye grass are secondary crops. Both cattle and poultry are raised—some 125,000 and 225,000 head, respectively (Mexico, 1975b: 5).

Middle Rio Grande. The middle Rio Grande region has an agricultural history of long duration. The earliest agricultural activity dates to Pueblo peoples in prehistoric times. Early Spanish explorers found these agriculturalists irrigating the Rio Grande in the vicinity of El Paso and for nearly two hundred miles to the north along the river (Meinig, 1971: 6). Hispanic agricultural efforts first focused on the El Paso-Ciudad Juárez area, where a mission was established in the mid-seventeenth century. A hundred years later it had attained a population of approximately four thousand. The indigenous crops of corn and beans, as well as the introduced grape, were the foremost agricultural commodities (Martínez, 1978: 9). To the north in the Mesilla Valley, settlement was limited almost exclusively to Pueblo Indians until the middle of the nineteenth century. The Mexican government tried to encourage settlement in the early 1800s by making large land grants, but effective settlement did not take place until the 1840s (Foscue, 1931: 7; Baldwin, 1938: 316). Grains, including corn, forage crops, fruit, cattle, and sheep were all elements in the valley's early agricultural economy (Baldwin, 1938: 316).

During the last hundred years agriculture has grown on both sides of the river despite occasional setbacks. The Mesilla and Rincon valleys, just to the north of El Paso and Ciudad Juárez, have long dominated in the total number of irrigated acres. In 1889, over 11,000 irrigated acres were reported for Doña Ana County, where the Mesilla and Rincon valleys constitute essentially all irrigated acreage (U.S., 1894: 196). To the south, in the environs of El Paso and Ciudad Juárez, it is assumed that the total irrigated acreage at this time was less, because even ten years later, only 4,826 irrigated acres were reported for El Paso County. At that time, Doña Ana County reported over 17,000 acres of irrigated land (U.S., 1902: 852).

Water availability became an increasing problem as agricultural acreage expanded locally and upstream in northern New Mexico and Colorado. On the American side of the river, farmers were better equipped to supplement surface-water supplies by pumping groundwater, while Mexican farmers apparently lacked capital for these kinds of improvements (Martínez, 1978: 33). Besides these problems, agriculture on the Mexican side of the river suffered an almost complete collapse during the 1890s because of extremely unfavorable trade regulations initiated by the Mexican government (Martínez, 1978: 28). Soon, however, the construction of Elephant Butte Dam in New Mexico, which would supply water to both the Mexican and American sides of the river, significantly improved the prospects for agriculture on the Mexican side. The dam, the product of the Treaty of 1906 and constructed under the auspices of the U.S. Bureau of Reclamation, was completed in 1915 and brought increased agricultural prosperity (Beck, 1962: 12; Martínez, 1978: 33). Surface-water supplies have been inadequate to meet irrigation needs since the early 1940s, and the pumping of groundwater has been necessary since then (Martínez, 1978: 108; Wright et al., 1976: 4). Thus, the expansion of crop acreage has been constrained several times by water availability.

Irrigated acreage has expanded even these constraints. By the early 1930s, acreage had reached nearly 65,000 acres in Doña Ana County and also about the same amount in Texas along the river where El Paso and Hudspeth counties are the statistical reporting units (U.S., 1936: 779, 782, 869). On the Mexican side of the river, acreage stood near 30,000 acres at this time (Martínez, 1978: 61). Cotton and alfalfa were the most important crops throughout the entire region. Acreage has grown steadily, reaching nearly 100,000 acres

by the early 1970s (Lansford and Sorensen, 1973: 16). In the El Paso area, irrigated acreage has experienced considerable fluctuations but now stands around 85,000 acres (U.S., 1977d). The situation on the Mexican side of the river is analogous. Irrigated acreage, especially cotton plantings, fluctuated wildly during World War II and the postwar period (Martínez, 1978: 108) but stabilized in the late fifties and has remained between 30,000 and 40,000 acres since then (Mexico, 1961: 233; 1970: 291; 1976: 608).

The Mesilla and Rincon valleys in New Mexico account for slightly less than half of all irrigated land in this border region. Between 85,000 and 105,000 acres are harvested each year in these valleys, making them the most important agricultural area in the state of New Mexico (Anonymous, 1969: 4; Lansford and Creel, 1970: 21). Cotton and alfalfa are the dominant crops, accounting respectively for approximately 50 percent and 15 percent of the total annual acreage (Lansford and Creel, 1970: 21; Williams and Gray, 1968: 3). Spring lettuce, fall lettuce, chiles, onions, tomatoes, and other vegetables occupy some 10-20 percent of all cropland (Birle, 1976: 174; Burke, 1966: 2, 8, 9; New Mexico, 1975: 29-30). Pecans are a high-value tree crop found on about 7 percent of the total irrigated land, with young orchards often interplanted with cotton, alfalfa, or onions (Birle, 1976: 174; Gilpin, 1949: 152; Lansford and Creel, 1970: 21). Chickens and eggs are both produced here and are distributed to a large tributary area in both New Mexico and Texas (Anonymous, 1969: 4; New Mexico, 1975: 45).

In the El Paso area, agricultural activity varies from that in the Mesilla and Rincon valleys. While cotton and alfalfa are also the principal crops, they are the only crops grown on a large scale in the El Paso area. They have traditionally accounted for over 90 percent of eighty thousand to ninety thousand acres which are irrigated each year (Birle, 1976: 174; Bonnen, 1960: 34; Hughes and Motheral, 1950: 23; U.S., 1977d). Although the area is well suited to both vegetable and pecan production, these activities total less than 2 percent of all irrigated cropland (Birle, 1976: 174; Bryant and Lyerly, 1954: 3). It has been suggested that the more diverse crop pattern found in the Mesilla and Rincon valleys is attributable to the presence of Japanese farmers and the proximity of the New Mexico State University in Las Cruces (Birle, 1976: 176).

The Valle de Juárez is one of the four major areas of irrigated agriculture in the state of Chihuahua (Schmidt, 1973: 47). It exhibits an agricultural sector very similar to that of El Paso. There are 35,000 acres of irrigated crops, two-thirds of which are planted with cotton (Mexico, 1975a: 37-38; Lister and Lister, 1966: 282). Alfalfa, the other important crop, occupies about one-fifth of the cropland. Lesser areas are devoted to sorghums, wheat, and oat hay (Mexico, 1975a: 37-38).

Secondary Regions

A number of lesser agricultural areas are found in the border region. Citrus, avocados, vegetables, and grapes are all grown in San Diego County, where just less than sixty thousand acres are cropped (Blick, 1976: 129; Harmon, 1964; Lutz, 1964: 130). Dairying is also important here, but even with over twenty thousand head, this number is insufficient to meet the milk needs of the area's large population (Blick, 1976: 131). Across the border in the chaparral country between Tecate and Ensenada and south along the Pacific Coast lies one of the few grape-growing districts in Mexico (Brown, 1967: 1). Olive orchards give the landscape a Mediterranean cast. Some truck crops are cultivated just to the south of Ensenada and at San Quintín further south.

Livestock raising has been practiced since the early days of Spanish and Mexican colonization in Arizona and Sonora. It did not, however, assume the proportions of a business enterprise in the United States until the 1880s (Wagner, 1949: 230) and probably not until the last thirty or forty years in Mexico. Grazing practices have contrasted on each side of the border. A recent study of vegetation change in southeastern Arizona and northeastern Sonora has shown that differing grazing practices and histories have left grass taller and ground cover greater on the American side (Bahre and Bradbury, 1978: 145). In this vicinity, small acreages of pecans and alfalfa are grown along the Santa Cruz River valley from Nogales north to Tucson.

Irrigated crop agriculture becomes widespread to the east in Cochise County, Arizona, and Luna County, New Mexico. In both, heavy dependence is given to groundwater pumping. Each county has nearly doubled irrigated acreage during the last twenty years (U.S., 1956b: 46, 196; 1977a; 1977c). Wheat, sorghums, barley, cotton, and peaches are the main crops on the one hundred thousand irrigated acres in Cochise County (Arizona, 1976: 7, 13, 15, 19, 44; U.S., 1977a). Range cattle are also grazed in this county (Snow, 1969: 60). In Luna County, a cotton and grain economy similar to that of Cochise County covers fifty thousand acres (Birle, 1976: 177-79; U.S., 1977c).

Numerous small irrigation districts are found along both sides of the Rio Grande between El Paso–Ciudad Juárez and the mouth of the river (Fuentes, 1970: 81, 89; James, 1969: 89). The most important of these comprises ten thousand acres at the confluence of the Río Conchos with the Rio Grande in Chihuahua, twelve thousand acres near Ciudad Acuña in Coahuila, and twenty thousand acres in Texas's Maverick County (Mexico, 1976: 609; Busch, 1978: 349; U.S., 1977d). A major vegetable-growing district known as the Texas Winter Garden is located just to the east of Maverick County in the counties of Zavala and Dimmit (Tiller, 1971: 6). To the northwest, the Edwards Plateau which fronts on the Rio Grande is one of the chief areas of sheep and Angora goat raising in the United States (Bonnen, 1960: 21; Gilpin, 1949: 201).

Summary

Industrial farming characterizes the agricultural landscapes of the U.S.-Mexican border. Agriculture is dependent on irrigation water provided by surface water or groundwater. Large, well-capitalized farm units, growing relatively high-value crops and dependent on a large seasonal labor force, are found on both sides of the border. Specific cropping patterns, however, are modified by the climatic advantage each side of the border has within its own agricultural economy, differing agricultural policies by each government, and restrictive trade duties on the import of certain agricultural commodities from Mexico to the United States. The principal regions of irrigation agriculture are found on the lands adjacent to the lower Colorado River, along the middle Rio Grande northwest and southeast of El Paso and Ciudad Juárez, and at the mouth of the Rio Grande. Several other areas of lesser agricultural significance dot the border region, with livestock raising practiced in most areas except the deserts.

The author wishes to acknowledge the financial assistance of the Dellplain Latin American Geography Program at Syracuse Univerisity and the support of its director, Professor David J. Robinson.

29

Border
Industrialization

C. DANIEL DILLMAN
Department of Geography
Northern Illinois University

As set forth in the IX Censo Industrial, 1971, the 1970s began with industrial activity along Mexico's northern border strip confined almost entirely to eleven *municipios:* Ensenada, Tijuana, Tecate, and Mexicali, Baja California; Nogales, Sonora; Ciudad Juárez, Chihuahua; Piedras Negras, Coahuila; and Nuevo Laredo, Reynosa, Río Bravo, and Matamoros, Tamaulipas (Secretaría de Industria y Comercio, 1974*a*). Two clusters of four *municipios* each, located in the western and eastern portions of the border zone in Baja California (45 percent) and in Tamaulipas (30 percent), accounted for three-fourths of all industrial establishments and employees and for four-fifths of the gross aggregate value of production in 1970 (Table 29-1). On the basis of these criteria, five centers represented the greatest concentration of industrial activity: Tijuana, Mexicali, Ciudad Juárez, Nuevo Laredo, and Matamoros. The peripheral position of the border *municipios* and their tenuous connections to Mexico's core region were reflected by a very small contribution (3 percent) to total national output and by similarly low proportions of total establishments and of employees in manufacturing (Table

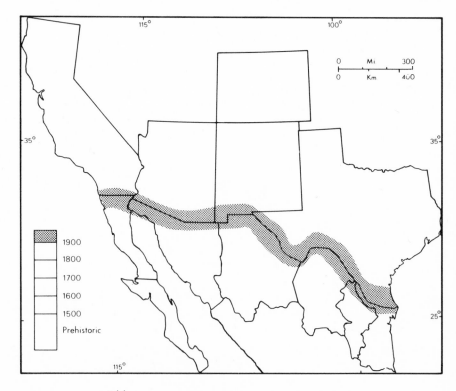

144

29-1). Although food processing was the first- or second-ranking industry type in nine of the eleven *municipios,* electrical/electronic industries had taken over first rank in three centers (Tijuana, Nogales, and Nuevo Laredo), second in three others (Tecate, Piedras Negras, and Matamoros), and third in Ciudad Juárez and Mexicali, largely in response to the Border Industrialization Program (BIP) (Table 29-2). The absence of the electrical/electronic industries from the border zone would have reduced the number of employees in manufacturing by 25 percent, the value of production by just under 20 percent, but the number of establishments by only 3 percent.

The Globally Integrated Production System

The success of countries in the Far East in attracting factories that specialized in labor-intensive assembly and processing of United States-manufactured items for the U.S. market encouraged Mexico to launch the BIP in September, 1965 (Hunt, 1970; Giblin, 1969). In this fashion, foreign capital was drawn to the border communities without altering Mexico's policy of reserving its internal market for domestic industry. Regulations attending the capitalization of foreign companies were modified specifically for participants in the BIP (Dillman, 1976b; Secretaría de Industria y Comercio, 1973). Once limited to the northern border strip, assembly-in-bond plants *(maquiladoras)* now can be located in virtually all of Mexico as a result of changes effected in the legal

bases of the program during the 1970s. If all production from the plants is reexported, complete tax exemptions may be obtained by firms for the importation of raw materials, semifinished products, machinery, and tooling deemed necessary for assembly or processing activities. Conflict between use of the BIP's import privileges and Mexican tariff regulations is avoided by requiring firms to guarantee payment of import levies by means of bonding arrangements—pledge of assets, an authorized bond, cash deposit, or deposit in a bonded warehouse.

Beginning in the early 1960s, manufacturing structures of the larger U.S. corporations became ever more international in scope with the appearance of the "globally integrated production system" (Moxon, 1974). Fundamental to the successful functioning of the system was an international division of labor. Generally, workers in the United States were responsible for more capital-intensive, highly skilled tasks, while workers in less developed countries (LDCs) were used for labor-intensive, unskilled jobs. In addition, the global context of production demanded an innovative approach to foreign investment, the offshore installation, which eventually assumed two forms, the export platform and the satellite plant.

Export platforms spearheaded efforts by U.S. corporations to regain supremacy in their domestic market, lost to the inroads of foreign competition, by lowering production costs (Barnet and Müller, 1974). Corporate strategies focused upon relocation of production facilities in such low-wage areas of the LDCs as the Mexican border zone, which could

Table 29-1. *Distribution of Manufacturing in Northern Border-Zone Municipalities of Mexico, 1970.*

State, Municipality	No. of Establishments	Percentage of Border Zone	No. of Employees	Percentage of Border Zone	Gross Aggregate Value†	Percentage of Border Zone
Baja California, N.	1,660		31,443		1,502,137	
Ensenada	249	7	4,588	8	198,370	9
Tijuana	856	23	12,198	20	497,395	21
Tecate	35	1	1,330	2	228,179	10
Mexicali	520	14	13,327	22	578,193	25
Sonora	1,703		27,223		1,325,984	
Nogales	106	3	3,468	6	95,204	4
Chihuahua	2,145		40,059		2,210,855	
Ciudad Juárez	680	19	9,612	16	278,762	12
Coahuila	2,175		52,397		3,252,913	
Piedras Negras	108	3	2,352	4	113,402	5
Tamaulipas	2,725		26,899		869,944	
Nuevo Laredo	362	10	5,175	9	137,238	6
Reynosa	289	8	1,760	3	35,395	2
Río Bravo	104	3	1,066	2	36,180	2
Matamoros	347	9	4,936	8	128,448	6
Border Zone	3,656	3*	59,812	4*	2,326,766	3*
Mexico	119,963		1,581,247		82,382,641	

Source: *IX Censo Industrial, 1971, Datos 1970,* "Industrias Extractiva y de Transformación (Excepto Extracción y Refinación de Petróleo e Industria Petroquímica Básica)," México, D.F., 1974.

*Percentage of total for Mexico.

†Millions of pesos.

Table 29-2. *Distribution of Manufacturing in the Northern Border Zone of Mexico According to Industry Class, 1970.*

Municipality, Industry Class	No. of Establishments	Percentage of Municipality	No. of Employees	Percentage of Municipality	Gross Aggregate Value†	Percentage of Municipality
Ensenada						
Food processing	117	47	3,076	67	97,779	49
Metal products	15	6	322	7	32,595	16
Mineral products	14	6	346	8	32,163	16
	146	59	3,744	82	162,537	81
Tijuana						
Electrical/electronic	38	4	4,695	38	114,107	23
Food processing	234	27	1,904	16	87,003	17
Footwear/apparel	150	18	1,059	9	24,639	5
	422	49	7,658	63	225,749	45
Tecate						
Beverages	4	11	350	26	199,702	86
Electrical/electronic	3	9	526	40	11,330	5
	7	20	876	66	211,032	91
Mexicali						
Food processing	187	36	2,638	20	141,057	24
Transportation	5	1	842	6	106,742	18
Electrical/electronic	17	3	1,895	14	61,218	11
	209	40	5,375	40	309,017	53
Nogales						
Electrical/electronic	16	15	2,241	65	51,638	54
Food processing	32	30	162	5	11,069	12
	48	45	2,403	70	62,707	66
Ciudad Juárez						
Beverages	11	2	2,122	22	70,848	25
Food processing	288	42	1,780	19	67,842	24
Electrical/electronic	11	2	1,142	12	39,228	14
	310	46	5,044	53	177,918	63
Piedras Negras						
Basic metals	4	3	812	35	76,252	67
Electrical/electronic	6	6	717	30	16,107	14
Wood/cork products	3	3	189	8	8,483	7
	13	12	1;718	73	100,842	88
Nuevo Laredo						
Electrical/electronic	5	1	2,313	45	50,875	37
Food processing	116	32	763	15	25,469	19
	121	36	3,076	60	76,344	56
Reynosa						
Food processing	88	30	522	30	13,064	37
Mineral products	39	13	279	16	3,824	11
	127	43	801	46	16,888	48
Río Bravo						
Paper products	3	3	194	18	16,527	46
Food processing	45	43	667	63	13,255	37
	48	46	861	81	29,782	83
Matamoros						
Food processing	158	46	1,850	37	40,161	31
Electrical/electronic	16	5	1,521	31	31,267	24
	174	51	3,371	68	71,428	55

Source: *IX Censo Industrial, 1971, Datos 1970,* "Industrias Extractiva y de Transformación (Excepto Extracción y Refinación de Petróleo e Industria Petroquímica Básica)," (Mexico City).
†Millions of pesos.

supply goods to the United States at competitive prices. By 1970 Mexico was the world's foremost assembler of components made in the United States for reexport across the border. The predominant share of the output from *maquiladoras* has been absorbed by the United States, but an emerging trend in the 1970s has been the use of the facilities as satellite plants to decrease costs of exports to third countries, thereby applying the springboard effect of low-cost labor to improve penetration into global markets. About one-quarter of production in the early 1970s was destined for these areas (Rivas Sosa, 1973). Satellite plants no longer were mere appendages of a firm's domestic operations. *Maquiladoras* and their counterparts elsewhere in the LDCs represented, for multinational corporations (MNCs), the next stage in the sequence of resource exploitation and manufacturing for import substitution (Helleiner, 1973). Both export platforms and satellite plants embodied changes in the financing and organization of production that led to process, not product, innovation. The labor-intensive industries that Mexico promoted in order to expand sorely needed job opportunities in and to diversify the economic bases of the rapidly growing border communities (which, as a group, rely heavily upon the United States for tourist expenditures, goods and services, and employment) thus are best understood in the context of globally integrated production systems.

The Border Industrialization Program

By January, 1970, less than four years after inception of the industries plan, the Mexican government had approved about 160 American-owned enterprises, and approximately twenty thousand jobs had been created (A. Ericson, 1970). The Baja California centers of Tijuana and Mexicali had experienced the greatest degree of industrial development, with twice as many operating plants as in the other major centers of activity: Ciudad Juárez, Nuevo Laredo, and Matamoros (Dillman, 1970c). Subsequent movement into Mexican border communities by U.S. firms was stimulated by the decision of the U.S. Tariff Commission in September, 1970, to sustain value-added duty provisions, contrary to vociferous opposition by organized labor to the proliferation of "runaway" industries along the border strip. Moreover, in 1971, Mexico introduced the trusteeship system to circumvent the constitutional ban on foreign ownership of land within one hundred kilometers of the border or fifty kilometers of the coast (Dillman, 1976b).

The BIP has offered attractive potentials to firms, in a variety of industries and across a range of sizes, concerned with improving their competitive postures or with investigating avenues of survival. Generally, industries that have been best suited for the program manufacture high-labor-cost/low-duty-rate goods. Firms realizing the greatest advantage from location in the border zone usually have been those for whom labor costs amounted to 50 percent or more of finished product cost, and those for whom U.S. tariff rates on finished or semifinished products assembled in Mexico were not above 25 percent of the value of returning items.

Relatively low wages in Mexico have allowed U.S. firms to obtain economies of production by performing the most labor-intensive phase in the sequence of production, combining phases in the sequence, or establishing parallel production runs of dissimilar items.

Proximity of burgeoning Mexican border communities with high rates of unemployment and low government-regulated minimum wages helped to maximize the flexibility provided by substitution of labor for other costs. Such substitutions have been associated with (1) change in cost structure, (2) use of old equipment, (3) reduction of seasonal variation in production, (4) efforts to improve quality control, (5) economies in product distribution costs, and (6) savings in time and cost of transportation (Dillman, 1976b). Furthermore, the opportunity for firms to establish foreign operations close at hand, in a stable political atmosphere, has blended with the ability to expedite maintenance and repair services from the United States. Locating assembly activities in border centers also has permitted families of U.S. managerial personnel to reside in the U.S. twin communities. To an important degree, greatly accelerated growth of assembly-in-bond operations during the first half of the 1970s can be traced to the development of discrete manufacturing enclaves in or near the Mexican border communities. With the advent of industrial parks, firms could begin production almost immediately through a subcontractor, while potential costs and problems of quality control were analyzed without investment risk; upon subsequent decision to transfer operations to the border, firms received a trained labor force without a hiatus in production.

Mexican facilities, like U.S. assembly plants in other foreign countries, enjoy access to the special tariff schedules, Items 807.00 and 806.30, enacted for return of goods previously fabricated partly in the United States and therefore eligible for duties levied primarily on the value added by foreign labor (U.S. Tariff Commission, 1970). Between 1966 and 1976 products entering the United States from *maquiladoras* jumped in value from $7 million to more than $1 billion (Baerresen, 1971; U.S. Department of Commerce, 1976). Item 807.00 applies to any product whose parts originate in the United States and are sent abroad for assembly; no further processing is necessary upon reentry into the United States. Firms using Item 807.00 produce textiles and apparel, engines, sewing machines, office equipment, television and radio parts, and electronics articles. Item 806.30, on the other hand, refers to any metal product whose form is altered abroad and returned to the United States for additional processing. The most common articles listed in Item 806.30 trade include aircraft parts, semiconductors, and electronics parts of various descriptions. Mexico was the chief recipient of United States-made goods in trade monitored by 807.00 and 806.30 in 1975 (44 percent), furnished 12 percent of the value added in all foreign countries, and accounted for 30 percent of the dutiable value among LDCs in 1977 (U.S. Congress, House of Representatives, Committee on Ways and Means, 1976; Banco Nacional de México, 1979).

The advantages for offshore operations in Mexico, as well as in companion LDCs, by U.S. firms have been particularly important for producers of apparel and electronics goods, industries well suited to labor-intensive assembly functions. No single industry better illustrates the nature of the globally integrated production system than electronics, called the "industry on the wing" (North American Congress on Latin America, 1977). The sophisticated technology of the electronics industry, along with its strong dependence upon hand labor, made easy and profitable the geographical separation of highly technical phases of production from those associated with labor-intensive inputs involving repetitious and tedious assembly tasks quickly mastered by unskilled workers. There was no migration of U.S. electronics firms to foreign areas before 1960; instead it was in the mid-1960s that most of the relocation process occurred. Electronics plants immediately began to appear in the Mexican border zone with the inauguration of the BIP in 1965, and by 1973 the region possessed 175 facilities (Dillman, 1974; Secretaría de Industria y Comercio, 1973). Mexican installations, numerically superior to those in Taiwan and Hong Kong and slightly more numerous than those in Puerto Rico, were the principal concentration of U.S. electronics assembly operations at the time (North American Congress on Latin America, 1977).

Thirty-eight percent of the *maquiladoras* in 1977 produced electrical and electronics goods and employed 63 percent of the labor force in the BIP (Banco Nacional de Comercio Exterior, 1978). Well-known multinational corporations involved in the BIP included General Electric, GTE-Sylvania, Fairchild, Litton Industries, Zenith, RCA, and Texas Instruments. Smaller companies have opened *maquiladoras* in the border cities, but the growing dominance of the largest firms has hastened their disappearance in line with the overall trend in the electronics industry. Often acting as subcontractors or producing specialized devices, the smaller firms have been forced to economize on production costs to a greater extent than the large manufacturers. The Mexican experience during the seventies clearly demonstrated the inherently transitory character of semiconductor assembly operations which seek areas of lowest labor costs. A more important source of semiconductors early in the decade, Mexico by 1977 supplied only 6 percent of 806.30 and 807.00 imports (Banco Nacional de México, 1979).

Some apparel manufacturers in the United States have set up offshore facilities to carry out all aspects of production, but the more common procedure has been to transfer only those stages that would benefit from U.S. Tariff Item 807.00, which led to rapid proliferation of linkages with foreign contractors. In 1977 approximately 130 *maquiladoras,* 29 percent of the plants, were assembling articles of apparel with about one-fifth of the labor force in the BIP (Banco Nacional de Comercio Exterior, 1978). Although some of the factories were directly affiliated with large U.S. clothing manufacturers such as Levi-Strauss, Puritan, Kennington, and Kayser-Roth, the greater portion were much smaller, temporary shops handling subcontracts for U.S. firms. The apparel operations were typically far smaller than the electronics assembly plants, seldom employing more than fifty workers, and they possessed a larger proportion of Mexican capital investment (North American Congress on Latin America, 1975). Locational ad-

vantage explained the 75 percent share of apparel imports from Mexico and Caribbean countries using Item 807.00 in 1975 (Garlow, 1978). The nearness of the Mexican border zone, in particular, permitted swift turnaround time and shorter return hauls to parent firms in the United States.

Impact of the BIP

The industries' scheme has had marked economic impact upon Mexican and U.S. twin communities and has intensified preexisting symbiotic relationships and patterns of interaction between them. Much of the income generated by *maquiladoras* has been channeled into expanded retail sales on the U.S. side of the border, where employees in the BIP have spent up to 75 percent of their income on goods and services (Loehr and Bulson, 1974). Further, many U.S. firms have discovered that economies of production and management could be achieved by shuttling products between Mexican facilities and twin plants *(plantas gemelas)* in U.S. border cities. Using the twin-plant concept, one manager and his staff could direct activities and provide support functions for both installations. The U.S. plant generally was much smaller and employed many fewer workers, some of whom were Mexican residents crossing the border daily. The U.S. facilities could either transship parts from parent plants or regulate two-way parts shipments while performing capital-intensive operations with skilled labor. For every three jobs in its Mexican unit, one job usually was created in the U.S. plant (J. S. Evans, 1972; Alisky, 1973).

To date, the success of the BIP as a regional development instrument can be tied less directly to the localized distribution of relatively modest capital investment than to the expansion of job opportunities (and consequent diffusion of income within the border centers) by the labor-intensive nature of *maquiladoras.* Employment in the assembly plants had grown to roughly 10 percent of the region's total labor force during the first half of the 1970s, and in Tamaulipas and Coahuila, BIP facilities accounted for one of every two industrial employees (Dillman, 1976a). In contrast to the multitude of migrant farm workers thrust into unemployment by cancellation of the *bracero* program in the mid-'60s, members of the predominantly female labor force in the BIP have become permanent and economically viable residents contributing to fundamental social and economic changes in the border zone. A total of over 83,000 in the *maquiladoras* at peak 1974 employment were said to have supported 600,000 dependents, in addition to supplying increased tax revenue at local and national levels (Butler, 1975). Thousands of Mexican women, many of whom were the sole wage earners in their families, had gained unprecedented freedom of action and economic independence. That a larger segment of the labor force had acquired a more reliable income and stable employment was exemplified by the emergence, to some degree, of consumer credit to finance expensive local purchases. Participation in the social security program also made workers and their families eligible to receive benefits and services otherwise unavailable to them.

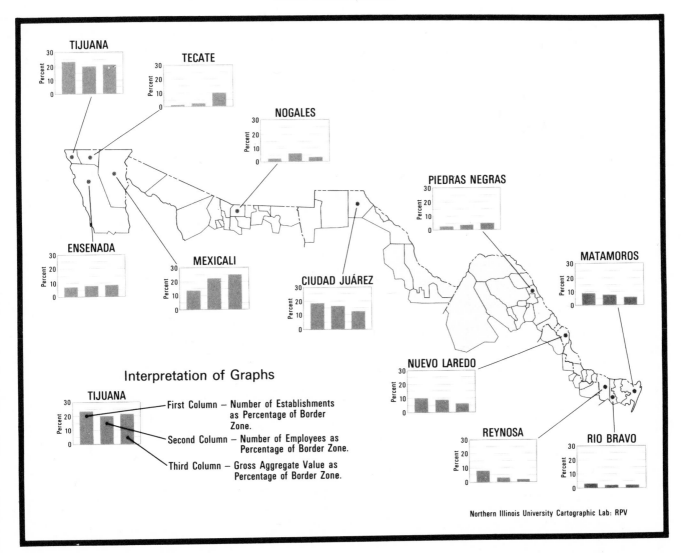

Fig. 29-1. *Selected characteristics of manufacturing in the northern border zone, 1970. Source:* IX Censo Industrial, 1971 *(México, D.F., 1974).*

The BIP's role in effecting change in social and economic patterns should not disguise the program's continuing inability to absorb greater numbers of the male labor force. During the 1960s, unemployment in the border zone rose approximately 90 percent, in large measure the result of steadily mounting pressure from migrants arriving from the interior added to the multitude dislocated by the termination of the *bracero* program. In 1970, newcomers comprised almost 30 percent of the population, but fewer than 3 percent had found employment in *maquiladoras* (Secretaría de Industria y Comercio, 1974c). Conservative estimates in 1974 placed unemployment at over 210,000, despite an increase of 10,000 jobs from the previous year. Men usually were hired only for night shifts or when technical skills or physical strength gave them the competitive edge for jobs. For the border zone as a whole, eight of ten workers were mainly young women.

To the extent that the BIP has acted to swell the ranks of migrants from the interior, it is likely that male newcomers have been largely excluded from employment by the use of resident and migrant young women and have been diverted instead toward limited opportunities in the service sector.

Crisis in the Mid-'70s

Affiliates of major U.S. electronics MNCs were registering the largest increases of new *maquiladoras* and employment at mid-decade. Also, the likelihood of an abbreviated period of operation in the border zone was considerably greater for Mexican-owned or joint ventures than for entirely U.S.-owned firms, because the former were handicapped by lack of size and dependence upon contract arrangements with

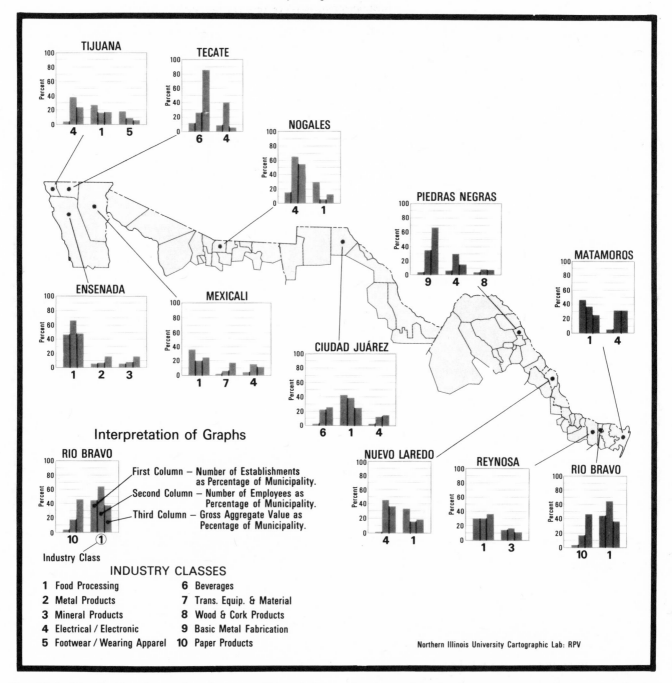

Fig. 29-2. *Distribution of manufacturing according to industry class in northern border zone municipalities, 1970. Source:* IX Censo Industrial, 1971 *(México, D.F., 1974).*

other companies. Border communities with available space in industrial parks and the greatest degree of labor tranquility appeared to be the most attractive sites for *maquiladoras.* By spring, 1975, however, recession in the United States, coupled with increased minimum wage levels and labor unrest in the Mexican border communities, had disrupted the 1970s upsurge in assembly activities (Duncan, 1976). Recession

greatly narrowed the market for products from border plants; most affected by the downturn in demand were smaller companies lacking the flexibility of productive structure possessed by multinational firms. Employment in *maquiladoras* dropped by approximately 35,000, accompanied by an estimated annual wage loss of Mex.\$300 million (U.S. \$24 million) (Butler, 1975). For many firms, heightened aggressiveness by Mexican labor unions and increasing labor costs were central to their decision to cease operation. Although wage increases had barely kept pace with inflation in Mexico, the cumulative effect in time of U.S. recession initiated reevaluation of alternative sites in the interior of Mexico, Central America, the Caribbean, and Asia. A larger wage differential existed, relative to the United States, than two years earlier, but the substantial gap in wage levels was partially offset by other costs (Dillman, 1977*b*). In competition with labor markets in other LDCs, however, most of the advantages for labor-cost substitution by U.S. manufacturers in Mexico were disappearing.

As 1977 began, the in-bond industries had recovered from the brief, though serious, mid-decade slump. U.S. firms, aided by the American Chamber of Commerce in Mexico, had successfully used the threat of a large-scale exodus from the border communities to secure concessions from the Mexican government that weakened regulatory measures covering the BIP labor force (Duncan, 1976; North American Congress on Latin America [NACLA], 1975). Many plants were using more of their excess capacity and were hiring additional labor on a permanent, instead of temporary, basis for specific jobs, as had frequently happened the year before (Banco Nacional de México, 1976). Reduction of labor conflict, Mexico's approval of new administrative procedures, employment practices, and fiscal incentives for the BIP, and, most importantly, peso devaluation led to resurgent production from existing *maquiladoras* and to construction of new facilities. *Maquiladoras* were concentrated heavily (90 percent of them) in the northern border corridor, where more than half of the plants were found—mainly in Tijuana, Ciudad Juárez, and Mexicali. In December, 1976, 552 firms employed almost 81,000 workers, or roughly 2,000 below the peak figure in 1974. Ciudad Juárez, with one-third of the total production from assembly plants, held undisputed first place among other Mexican border communities (Banco Nacional de Comercio Exterior, 1977).

Where increasing minimum-wage levels seemingly diminished prospects for future growth and development of assembly industries, devaluation of the peso generated huge savings, sufficient to restore much of the competitive advantage relinquished to other offshore sites in the hemisphere and Asia. U.S. firms, which converted dollars into pesos to meet Mexican payrolls, were able to purchase more labor for fewer dollars, as wages effectively were lowered 40-50 percent (Stoddard and West, 1977). Many firms tempted to relocate in Central America, Haiti, Taiwan, or South Korea elected to remain in Mexico. Devaluation greatly stimulated interaction across the border involving assembly operations, yet the cheaper peso had the opposite effect for Mexican workers who regularly patronized merchants in U.S. twin communities. Thousands employed in *maquiladoras* no longer could afford to do much of their shopping in the United States, when the cost of goods and services was more than doubled by the lower purchasing power of the peso (Stoddard and West, 1977). Had devaluation not occurred, expanded employment in the Mexican centers normally would have been tied to increased retail sales in those sectors of U.S. border cities most dependent upon Mexican clientele.

Multinational Corporations: Development Polemics

Criticism of the BIP, and similar programs elsewhere in the LDCs, finds basis in dependency theory, which censures MNCs for their exploitative rather than developmental strategies (R. A. Fernández, 1973*b*). Viewed in this context, the host country is highly vulnerable to decisions and interests of multinational enterprises whose policies must ultimately undermine sovereignty and weaken local initiative in planning for development consistent with national requirements (Weinert, 1977). To ideological critics, the BIP's open invitation to foreign firms is yet another step away from the ideals of the Mexican Revolution. Other critics reject the premise that assembly industries can lessen unemployment in the border zone, for any absolute increase in jobs draws more migrants from the interior (Fouts, 1973). Some authorities further assert that dependence upon imported inputs by *maquiladoras* retards linkage effects and discourages the emergence of domestic ancillary industries (Evans and James, 1976). To the contrary, findings from investigation of offshore operations in Asia deny the inevitability of such circumstances; supportive industries can arise, given adequate incentives from government sources. Organized labor in the United States, angered at the loss of jobs attributed to foreign assembly plants, has demanded corrective legislation (Tyler, 1973). In 1971-74, for example, the AFL-CIO pressed hard for passage of the unsuccessful Burke-Hartke Foreign Trade and Investment Act, Part III of which some observers thought would have eliminated access to the BIP by U.S. firms. That unemployment in the U.S. could be traced directly to "runaway industries" was not the viewpoint of those who studied the phenomenon with greater objectivity (Krause and Mathiesen, 1971). Components assembled in Mexico largely were manufactured in the United States and thus provided employment and tax revenue in contrast to offshore operations in Asia and Europe which brought no direct benefits to the American economy (U.S. Congress, Subcommittee on Inter-American Economic Relationships, 1977). Protests from U.S. unions later in the seventies were aimed more toward assembly plants in regions where wages did not revert to the United States as they did in part in U.S. twin communities along the border.

Mexico, as opposed to some competing nations in Europe and Asia, produces few of the components assembled in its offshore facilities, probably as a response not only to Mexico's nearness to the United States but also to Mexico's failure to reach the self-reinforcing stage of industrial development via assembly technologies. The continuing trend of a much higher percentage of U.S.-made components in the Item 807.00 imports from Mexico, as against the diminishingly smaller portion in Taiwan's shipments, signals the latter's growing capacity to manufacture components for local assembly (Baerresen, 1975).

In addition to its goal of creating 175,000 jobs (66,000 in the border zone and 109,000 in the interior), the six-year plan of the López Portillo administration for expansion of assembly industries attempts to promote, through joint ventures involving Mexican and foreign enterprises, the manufacture of goods now acquired abroad (Mitchell, 1977). However, replacement of foreign with Mexican inputs, even in modest amounts, probably will be determined by the (1) reliability, quality, and price of local supplies; (2) effect of reduced eligibility for duty-free treatment under offshore assembly provisions of the U.S. tariff schedules; and (3) the degree to which *maquiladoras* function as satellite plants.

Perspective

If the BIP is fully to realize its potential to absorb surplus labor, direct and immediate action must be taken to employ far greater numbers of men in the border zone's *maquiladoras.* Moreover, viable job opportunities also must be created in those interior districts identified as principal sources of migration toward the border. The extension to such areas of an expanded program of assembly industries could presumably assist in relieving the ever-mounting pressure of the border-community population and combat the spreading interior social unrest stemming from unemployment. The designation of statewide free zones in the interior, such as Durango, San Luis Potosí, Jalisco, and Yucatán, where wages are so much lower than along the northern border, could effectively change the production strategies of firms seeking additional sites for in-bond operations.

Assembly industries, unlike capital-intensive, labor-saving, import-substitution manufacturing, offer more immediate prospects for a substantial decrease in the ranks of the unemployed. As the motive force in the globally integrated production system, MNCs thus assume the pivotal role in maximizing job opportunities in Mexico and in other LDCs (Van Dam, 1971). International firms loom as the prime source of innovative modes, permitting conversion to labor-intensive manufacturing through reverse engineering because they are the central repositories of technical expertise and risk capital and, additionally, have access to world markets (Barnet and Müller, 1974). The potential of the BIP (in present or altered form and distribution) as a medium for transfer of technology will be negated should technological inputs tend toward obsolescence (R. A. Fernández, 1973*b*). Given the magnitude of Mexico's employment problem, emphasis on the domestic production of labor-intensive machinery and equipment (thereby multiplying job opportunities and swelling the number of trained technicians) might provide a feasible option in long-range development planning. Such an alternative future for Mexico naturally presupposes cooperation among governments, manufacturers, and workers in the metropolis, plus a more sedentary presence by multinational firms in the periphery.

Problems for Further Study

Future investigation in the border zone might be concerned with the analysis of (1) attempts to attract industry to U.S. border communities under the twin-plant concept; (2) the frequency of relocation within the border zone by BIP firms —that is, the incidence of intraregional mobility; (3) the extent to which the economies of the border communities have become oriented to tertiary activities by in-migrants encouraged by the presence of *maquiladoras;* (4) the legal or illegal penetration of Mexico's domestic market by products from *maquiladoras;* and (5) the diffusion into northern Mexico of technical, managerial, and marketing innovations from foreign- to domestic-controlled firms.

The United States dominates Mexico's international merchandise trade both as a supplier of goods and as a customer. In 1978 the U.S. market absorbed 65.3 percent of Mexican exports of merchandise, and even this high proportion excludes goods shipped to the United States from Mexico's *maquiladora* plants operating along the border. Of Mexico's total merchandise imports, 60.2 percent were purchased from the United States (Table 30-1). Although having a much more modest impact on the merchandise trade of the United States, Mexico nonetheless is important to the larger nation's commerce. She ranks fifth as a purchaser of U.S. goods and sixth as a source of imports (Table 30-2).

Since 1971, most categories of goods traded between the United States and Mexico have shown only minor changes in terms of their total import or export percentage. As Table 30-3 indicates, however, both U.S. exports and imports of foods, feeds, and beverages and Mexico's purchases of industrial supplies and materials showed marked proportional changes.

30

Trade and Merchandising

DILMUS D. JAMES
Department of Economics and Finance
University of Texas, El Paso

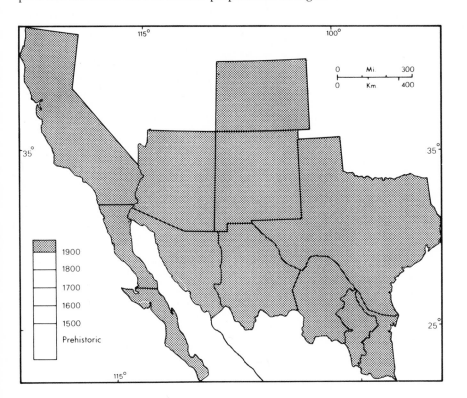

Table 30-1. *Merchandise Trade of Mexico, 1978, by Economic Bloc and Geographic Area.*

Country or Region	Exports (millions of dollars)	Percentage of Exports	Imports (millions of dollars)	Percentage of Imports
United States	$3,548,476	65.3	$4,549,310	60.2
Canada	46,985	0.9	125,456	1.7
Central American Common Market	127,081	2.3	8,919	0.1
Latin American Free Trade Association	406,043	7.5	304,299	4.0
Caribbean Common Market	10,340	0.2	6,240	0.1
Other American countries	87,775	1.6	67,188	0.9
European Economic Community	291,455	5.4	1,397,701	18.5
European Free Trade Area	53,745	1.0	219,937	2.9
Soviet Bloc countries*	15,901	0.3	29,384	0.4
Other countries	401,922	7.4	852,378	11.3
Adjustment for currency changes	448,184	8.2		
Total	$5,437,907	100.1	$7,560,742	100.1

Source: Banco Nacional de Comercio Exterior, *Comercio exterior* 29 (February, 1979): 257-58. Preliminary figures. Operations of border *maquiladora* plants are excluded.

Cuba is included in "Other American countries."

The officially reported data on merchandise trade drastically understate the actual magnitude of commerce. Trade in services or "invisibles" is not included, since, with the exception of expenditures on tourism, its data are not conveniently obtainable on a geographic area basis. Also, there is a substantial volume of economic transactions involving illegally traded goods. Both tourism and smuggling constitute lively issues nationally as well as in the border region, but in view of their coverage elsewhere in this volume, nothing further need be said here about them. Another topical issue entails the future trade in petroleum and natural gas. The issue of Mexico as a potential source of these hydrocarbons for the United States is perhaps most dramatically demonstrated by the controversial Presidential Review Memorandum No. 41 (PRM-41), a draft study by the U.S. National Security Council, which recommends considering trade concessions on immigration, winter farm products, and other products coming from Mexico. The quid pro quo, of course, would be large imports of hydrocarbons from Mexico. The report, which was "leaked" to the *Washington Post* in mid-December, 1978, was widely interpreted in Mexico as a belated rediscovery by the United States of her southern neighbor, a rediscovery prompted solely by narrow pragmatic needs. Negotiations on the sale of Mexican natural gas to the United States broke down over disagreements concerning price (Grayson, 1978). As of April, 1981, Mexico was exporting about 300 million cubic feet per day to the United States through Reynosa. Another pipeline is being constructed to Ciudad Juárez, and natural gas sales to the United States are expected to flow through this point also.

In January, 1979, Mexico's official proven reserves of petroleum, now standing at 40.1 billion barrels, were disputed by outside sources, but even a far more conservative estimate of 28.9 billion barrels by Morgan Guaranty Trust Company placed Mexico well ahead of Venezuela (18 billion barrels) and the North Sea (21.9 billion barrels) and about on a par with the United States (28.5 billion barrels) (Banco Nacional de México, *Review of the Economic Situation of Mexico,* March, 1978: 176). The same source (p. 175) estimated that by 1985, total oil and gas exports by Mexico will range from $11 billion to $19 billion, depending on post-1982 petroleum production policies. Already petroleum exports to the United States, shown in Table 30-4, have increased rapidly in recent years.

Table 30-2. *U.S. Trade with the World and Major Trading Partners, 1977.*

Country	Exports (millions of dollars)	Imports (millions of dollars)
Australia	$ 2,356	$ 1,184
Belgium-Luxembourg	3,138	1,453
Brazil	2,490	2,240
Canada	25,788	29,599
Federal Republic of Germany	5,989	7,238
France	3,503	3,032
Iran	2,731	2,802
Italy	2,790	3,037
Japan	10,529	18,550
Mexico	4,822	4,694
Netherlands	4,812	1,488
Saudi Arabia	3,575	6,347
United Kingdom	5,951	5,141
Venezuela	3,172	4,084
Other countries	39,592	56,781
Total	$121,242	$147,670

Source: U.S. Department of Commerce, *United States Trade with Major Trading Partners 1971-1977,* Overseas Business Reports OBR 78-49, December, 1978, p. 3.

Table 30-3. *U.S. Trade with Mexico by End-Use Categories, 1971 and 1977.*

End-Use Category	1971 (millions of dollars)	1971 (percentage of total)	1977 (millions of of dollars)	1977 (percentage of total)
U.S. EXPORTS				
Foods, feeds, and beverages	$ 90.4	5.6	$ 580.2	12.1
Industrial supplies and materials	483.8	29.9	1,420.2	29.5
Capital goods, including trucks and buses	608.4	37.6	1,679.0	34.9
Consumer goods, nonfood, including automobiles and parts	337.2	20.8	867.5	18.0
Special-category and other exports	100.2	6.2	259.1	5.4
Total	$1,620.0	100.1	$4,806.1	99.9
U.S. IMPORTS				
Foods, feeds, and beverages	$ 564.8	44.8	$1,237.4	26.4
Industrial supplies and materials	275.0	21.8	1,645.2	35.1
Capital goods, including trucks and buses	151.3	12.0	749.4	16.0
Consumer goods, nonfood, including automobiles and parts	189.9	15.1	833.0	17.8
Special-category and other exports	80.6	6.4	219.8	4.7
Total	$1,261.6	100.1	$4,684.8	100.0

Source: U.S. Department of Commerce, *United States Trade with Major Trading Partners, 1971-1977,* Overseas Business Reports OBR 78-49, December, 1978, p. 35.

Trade in energy resources is, of course, not the only issue concerning international economic intercourse in the Borderlands. There are important concerns revolving around smuggling activities, *maquiladora* plant operations, and tourism, but these topics are treated at length elsewhere in this volume. Similarly, the importation of Mexican winter vegetables, opposed by U.S. producing interests, receives some attention elsewhere herein. Further background information and a complete bibliography are found in C. Richard Bath's (1979) political-economic analysis of the controversy. Finally, there is a more theoretical contention that economic exchange between developing and developed countries can be detrimental to the poorer nations. For this "dependency school" position regarding Mexican trade with the United States, see the work of Olga Pellicer de Brody (1974).

In concluding this section, we might note several recent changes in Mexican trade policy that are of interest to any prospective researcher on economic relations between the two countries. Although it seemed certain that Mexico would join the General Agreement on Tariffs and Trade (Álvarez Gurza, 1979), Mexico, in a surprise move early in 1980, declined to become a member. The entire February, 1980, issue of *Commercio Exterior* (Spanish edition), a monthly publication of Banco Nacional de Comercio Exterior, is devoted to this controversy. Partly as an antiinflationary measure, Mexico has begun to replace import controls by requiring import permits with import tariffs. The tariffs, although restrictive, are generally thought to be less so than the permits. Also, Mexico is currently in the process of adjusting both import and export tariffs downward in order to stimulate trade. In early 1977, Mexico, in a reorganization of cabinet duties, divided the responsibilities of the old Secretariat of Industry and Commerce, with international trade being handled by the Secretariat of Commerce and industrial development by the Secretariat of National Resources and Industrial Growth (*BOLSA Review,* February, 1977: 93).

Table 30-4. *U.S. Imports of Crude Petroleum (millions of barrels).*

Country or Region	1972	1973	1974	1975	1976	1977	1978
Canada	322.58	399.70	311.14	234.08	156.84	110.43	92.37
Mexico	7.52	7.19	2.37	27.84	32.73	62.60	112.15
Western Europe	.41	3.08	.96	6.10	26.60	53.31	100.30
OPEC	664.27	1,011.41	1,161.65	1,420.11	1,933.54	2,357.34	2,154.34
Other	43.18	68.63	78.48	83.32	112.35	150.73	149.63
Total	1,037.96	1,490.01	1,554.60	1,771.45	2,262.06	2,734.41	2,608.79
Average unit value per barrel	$2.57	$3.33	$11.00	$11.45	$12.11	$13.29	$13.29

Source: Bach (1979: 43).

U.S.-Mexican Border Trade

Fortunately for the scholar exploring border economic conditions, both the United States and Mexico report data on border spending and receipts (see Tables 30-5 [and 31-1]). While the data are not identical, presumably because of differences in definition and methods of estimation, they tend to exhibit similar trends. For one thing, the United States treats purchases of U.S. goods and cash taken to Mexico by Mexican residents who make frequent border crossings to work in the United States as payments to services instead of "travel expenditures." For a complete rundown on how the U.S. data are estimated, see Miller and Font (1974: 28). In 1974, more frequent and comprehensive surveys and consultations with Banco de México resulted in an upward revision of U.S. payments and receipts as calculated by the U.S. Department of Commerce's Bureau of Economic Analysis. The new estimates were applied retroactively to include 1971 data.

Perhaps one of the surest routes to appreciating the importance of trade across the border is to examine the results of sharp disruptions in the flow of goods and services. One such occurrence was Operation Intercept, a unilateral tightening of customs inspections by the United States designed to combat the inflow of drugs from Mexico. Lasting for about a month in 1969, the operation caused sales on both sides of the border to drop dramatically (Martínez, 1978: 126). A far more important and lasting disruption attended the series of peso devaluations and floats during late 1976. The immediate effect on U.S. border merchants' sales to Mexican commuter shoppers was catastrophic, especially in the portions of U.S. border cities closest to Mexico. These effects are well described by Stoddard and West (1977) in their valuable study of the peso devaluation's impact on the U.S. side of the border. Corroborative evidence is supplied by Baylor (1977) in a preliminary paper analyzing data on

retailing in the El Paso-Ciudad Juárez region before and after the devaluation.

Scholars researching the border marketing situation will be disappointed at the lack of data on incomes, income distribution, spending patterns, and prices; fortunately, we are not yet entirely in the dark. Stoddard, in his *Patterns of Poverty along the U.S.-Mexico Border* (1978) provides a thorough analysis of income distribution by geographic region. As a rough generality, incomes are abnormally low on the U.S. side of the border, compared to those of the United States as a whole, and abnormally high for the Mexican border, compared to the Mexican national situation. Furthermore, there is a tendency for U.S. incomes to fall and Mexican incomes to rise as one moves from east to west along the border.

Some sources of information regarding international spending patterns along the border are found in the chapter on tourism in this volume. Other sources which report on spending by region and product categories are the devaluation studies of Stoddard and West and of Baylor cited above; occasional articles in *El mercado de valores,* such as "Aspectos económicos de la franja fronteriza norte" (1976); several studies by the now reorganized Mexican Secretariat of Industry and Commerce, perhaps the most valuable of which is *Estudio del desarrollo comercial de la frontera norte,* produced in 1976; an insightful analysis by Urquidi and Villarreal (1975); and Oscar Martínez's economic history of Ciudad Juárez, which emphasizes the economic interaction of the El Paso-Ciudad Juárez complex (1978). Perhaps deserving of special mention is "The Impact of El Paso Television in Cd. Juárez, Chihuahua," by a private research firm, Thomas F. Lee and Associates (1979), since it is one of the few investigations of the impact of the media along the border and contains some information on postdevaluation spending habits by Juárez residents in Mexico.

Several research efforts that are in progress should also enrich our knowledge of trade and merchandising patterns in the border region. The Department of Geography of the University of Utrecht, Netherlands, has three field studies, being conducted by graduate students, underway in the border region. The home university, which has the students attached to Mexican or U.S. universities during performance of the field research, hopes to have a total of sixteen economic-geography or social-geography investigations completed over the next several years.

One of the three studies, conducted by S. J. Smith, includes information on spending patterns by lower-class workers who have recently migrated to the border from the interior of Mexico. Further information can be obtained from the supervising professor, Dr. Otto Verkoren, University of Utrecht, Netherlands.

Professor Glenn Palmore (1974), Department of Business, University of Texas at El Paso, who captained a research study on the socioeconomic conditions of Ciudad Juárez, has updated the earlier work. At present there is no intention of publishing the work, but interested researchers can contact Dr. Palmore. A more ambitious and comprehensive survey of the socioeconomic status of Ciudad Juárez was sponsored

Table 30-5. *Border Transactions in the U.S.-Mexican Border Area, Mexican Data*

	Foreign Spending in Mexico's Border Area (millions of dollars)	Mexican Spending in the U.S. Border Area (millions of dollars)
1967	$ 599.6	$ 359.1
1968	713.5	450.4
1969	761.2	501.5
1970	878.9	585.0
1971	966.9	612.5
1972	1,057.0	649.3
1973	1,207.7	695.0
1974	1,372.9	819.2
1975	1,541.6	957.7
1976	1,609.7	1,056.7
1977	1,506.3	786.4
1978	1,654.4	784.1

Sources: 1967-76, Nacional Financiera, *Statistics on the Mexican Economy* (México, D.F.: Nafin, 1977): 380-81; 1977-78, Banco de México, *Informe Anual, 1978:* 141.

by the Mexican government and conducted by the Universidad Autónoma de Ciudad Juárez, Chihuahua. The project involved an extensive questionnaire administered to a sample of five thousand households. For the status of the full survey, contact the Universidad Autónoma de Ciudad Juárez. For computerized information based on an adjusted sample of 1,250 of the original 5,000 interviews, contact the Center for Inter-American Studies, University of Texas at El Paso.

Published information on price levels along the border is also available to students of the border area. Consumer price indices are reported for Mexicali and Ciudad Juárez in Banco de México's *Informe anual.*

Some price information is available on the United States side of the border. The State National Bank of El Paso releases a monthly El Paso consumer price-index figure to the press. Other large banks or bureaus of business and economic research along the border would be potential sources of information.

Undoubtedly one of the most original institutional arrangements for affecting border trade is Mexico's *artículos ganchos* program, in operation since 1971, which was begun in recognition of massive smuggling of consumer goods into the Mexican border area as well as the potential for capturing a larger share of the U.S. border market. Essentially the program allows the duty-free purchase of specified foreign consumer goods for resale in the Mexican market. A detailed description of the program is provided by Martínez (1978: 129-31).

A severe transportation bottleneck throughout Mexico affects the volume of border commerce. The railway system operates largely single track routes, uses old locomotives, and relies heavily on telegraphic communication. The system is short of diesel-electric locomotives and rail cars. Limited port facilities, docking room, material landing equipment, and covered storage have further stretched the inadequate railway operations. Inevitably, these shortcomings have also overloaded highway transportation. For a discussion of Mexico's railroads see "Railroads: A Much-Needed Boost" (Comercio Exterior, 1981: 261-278).

Additional Sources and Suggestions for Further Research

Merchandise trade by Mexico, broken down by country, geographic region, or economic bloc, can be found in the monthly *Indicadores económicos* (Banco Nacional de México), the monthly *Comercio exterior* (Banco Nacional de Comercio Exterior), and the annual *La economía mexicana en cifras* (Nacional Financiera). The most convenient source of U.S. trade by country is found in the *United States Trade with Major Trading Partners,* published by the U.S. Department of Commerce in its Overseas Business Reports Series; in this source, merchandise trade by country is broken down in detail by products, dollar value, and physical quantity. This same series also periodically produces a "Marketing in Mexico" issue (for example, Tower, 1977).

Border trade figures are reported annually by the United States in the monthly *Survey of Current Business* (the article usually appears around mid-year). Mexican data on frontier trade are available in the statistical appendix of *Informe anual* or *La economía mexicana en cifras.* Excellent trade data also appear in the International Monetary Fund's monthly *Directions of Trade,* which gives monthly exports and imports by country, and the IMF's monthly *International Financial Statistics,* which emphasizes financial data such as reserve levels, balance of payments, exchange rates, and so on. An excellent, but expensive, source of information on Mexican markets is the privately produced annual *Guide to Mexican Markets* (see bibliography). Exports by state (for example, Industry and Trade Administration, 1978) are covered by the U.S. Department of Commerce.

Often research connected with proposals for free-trade zones are useful sources (see J. K. Ross, 1978; Utah, Salt Lake City Corporation, 1978). The Ross study (p. 82), for instance, contains information compiled from U.S. customs data which indicate that the cumulative difference between actual and predicted exports going to Mexico through El Paso was $255.6 million for the five quarters immediately after the peso devaluation. A highly promising source which I have not personally seen is *Anuario estadístico del comercio exterior de los Estados Unidos Mexicanos,* published by Mexico's Secretaría de Programación y Presupuesto. Researchers delving into *los artículos ganchos* will find helpful the *Informe mensual del ejército de los artículos de consumo* and the *Informe mensual de cuotas de consumo fronterizo "Gancho,"* both published by the Secretaría de Comercio.

Several references are extremely useful in doing historical or current research on day-to-day changes in trade policy or trends between Mexico and the United States. The monthly periodical *BOLSA Review* (Bank of London and South America) covers Mexican economic events in each issue, with subsections dealing with international commerce; the monthly *Review of the Economic Situation of Mexico* (Banco Nacional de México), very frequently will have a section on international trade; and the monthly *Comercio exterior* (Banco Nacional de Comercio Exterior) contains a valuable subsection, "Recuento nacional," which records changes in Mexican trade policy. In addition, *Comercio exterior* is a superb publication on the broader aspects of world trade. The researcher will find much material pertaining to border economic affairs in two sources of journalistic publications. *Information Service on Latin America* contains excerpts of news pertaining to Latin America appearing in one foreign and several major U.S. newspapers. The reference is arranged chronologically by country. The other source entails indices for most large city newspapers along the U.S. border. Usually these indices are available at the public libraries, university libraries, or newspaper offices.

I can confidently predict that future researchers will be struck by the glaring deficiencies in our knowledge of trade, marketing, and merchandising along the border. Four of the most troubling gaps will be briefly discussed by way of conclusion. First, very little is known about the extent of and effects of "culture-bound" marketing methodologies applied to each side of the border. The Thomas F. Lee and Associates study (1979) dealing with television's impact on Ciudad

Juárez citizens was prompted by the fact that one large U.S. media research firm makes no allowance for Mexican shoppers when conducting media impact surveys in the Borderlands. Very likely, Mexican merchants could also improve their merchandising policies. Perhaps some further light can be shed on the matter in a book in progress by Dr. Carlos C. Restrepo of Bermudez y Asociados Consultores, S.C., in Ciudad Juárez. While his *Investment Opportunities and Marketing in Mexico* will not deal entirely with the border, several components of the book will treat the border region specifically.

Second, there remains plenty of room for studies shedding additional light on shopping patterns in the border area. Little is known about the details of U.S. border residents' spending in Mexico either by product categories or proportion of income. Also, conventional wisdom along the border holds that Mexican spending on U.S. medical and financial services is underreported. At the very least, some limited studies are warranted to determine the potential value of more comprehensive investigations.

Third, despite the enormous outpouring of literature on technology transfer, I know of only one solid study dealing with the border zone. Joseph Nalven (1979) challenges the orthodox view that advanced technology provides a poor "fit" to conditions in developing countries by contending that the conditions along the U.S.-Mexican border are amenable to fruitful transfer of computer technology to northern Mexico. Regardless of whether we accept his conclusion, his work is exemplary of the type of research work that is sorely needed.

Finally, I might cite the cavalier way in which income multipliers are plucked out of the air and used in regional studies pertaining to the border. An income multiplier of two seems popular, but I have seldom seen sufficient justification beyond intuition, nor does one often encounter evidence that the expanded international-trade multiplier, which can take into account trade repercussions on a trading partner's income, has been applied to the border region. The expanded international trade multiplier is laid out by Kindleberger and Lindert (1978: 304-308) or most other standard works on international economics. For one bright spot in filling the void, see Jerry R. Ladman's (1979) article in which he attempts to combine elements of a regional economic multiplier with foreign-trade multiplier models. His theoretical analysis is aimed at contiguous border or "twin" cities. Despite Ladman's excellent beginning, much more effort is needed to pin down reasonably accurate empirical estimates of induced income changes in border cities as a reaction to alterations in the level or pattern of spending.

This chapter serves as a guide to the major issues surrounding U.S.-Mexican tourism, especially in the border region; provides leads on the availability of data; and generally reduces the "start-up" costs for research into border tourism. It focuses on U.S. tourism in Mexico and Mexican tourism in the United States, with special attention in the latter section to the economic impact of Mexican tourism in southern California and Arizona. The chapter concludes with a review of relevant sources of data and significant research gaps.

As Table 31-1 amply demonstrates, tourism between the United States and Mexico is big business by any absolute measurement. In relative importance to the two countries, however, there is a pronounced asymmetry. While Mexican tourism and border spending in the United States accounted for less than 1 percent of total U.S. goods and services in 1977, the corresponding percentage for Mexico exceeded 28 percent. Mexican tourism and border spending represented 23 percent of all travel payments of foreigners in the United States in 1977, but travel expenditures by U.S. citizens were approximately 85 percent

31

Border Tourism

JONATHAN P. WEST
Department of Politics and
Public Affairs
University of Miami

DILMUS D. JAMES
Department of Economics
and Finance
University of Texas, El Paso

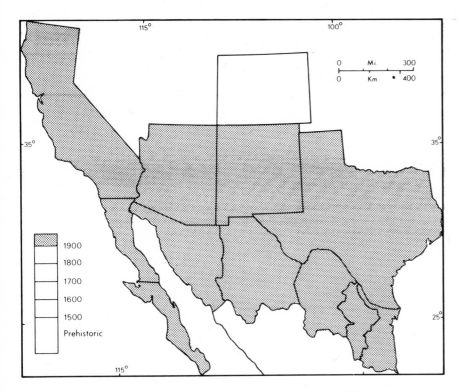

Table 31-1. *United States Travel Payments to Mexico and Travel Receipts from Mexico.*

	Travel Payments of U.S. Visitors to Mexico (millions of dollars)		Travel Receipts from Mexican Visitors to the United States (millions of U.S. dollars)	
	Mexico	Mexican Border Only	Mexico	U.S. Border Only
1967	602	372	457	n.a.
1968	638	390	493	n.a.
1969	692	405	530	n.a.
1970	778	463	583	520
1971	959	589	681	516
1972	1,135	626	720	525
1973	1,264	715	830	598
1974	1,475	904	1,142	858
1975	1,637	1,047	1,311	972
1976	1,723	1,007	1,364	1,023
1977	1,918	1,165	1,316	967
1978	2,121	1,128	1,459	954

Source: *Survey of Current Business,* various issues.

of Mexico's total travel receipts. Thus, the U.S.-Mexican tourism industry is proportionately much more important, indeed crucial, to the economic well-being of Mexico.

U.S. Tourism in Mexico

In contrast with the situation in the United States, where tourism is left primarily to the private sector, in Mexico, government agencies are heavily and directly involved. At the end of 1974, the Secretaría de Turismo replaced the Departamento de Turismo; as the chief agency in the tourist sector, it formulates and coordinates national tourism policies. The Consejo Nacional de Turismo (CNT) is responsible for publicity and information dissemination aimed chiefly at attracting conventions to Mexico.

Fondo Nacional de Fomento al Turismo (FONATUR), which also was established in 1974, is the Mexican financial organization promoting tourist activities. During 1977, FONATUR, which resulted from a merger of Fondo de Promoción de Infraestructura Turista and Fondo de Garantía y Fomento al Turismo, lent Mex.$ 1,309.4 million for new hotel and condominium construction, hotel expansion, hotel remodeling, and infrastructure needed for tourist sites (Banco Nacional de Comercio Exterior, 1978: 930-31).

In the biennium 1978-79, FONATUR was expecting to invest Mex.$ 2,660 million that would be coupled with Mex.$ 2,700 million of private funds for a total of Mex.$ 5,360 million. It appears, however, that the larger portions of the funds were to be spent away from the northern border. Eighteen hundred rooms were slated for Puerto Vallarta, at a cost of Mex.$ 480 million; a Holiday Inn expansion in Guadalajara was to cost Mex.$ 60 million; a Marriott Hotel in Cancun carried a price tag of Mex.$ 270 million; and a

whopping Mex.$ 2,500 million was earmarked for an installation at Las Hadas, Manzanillo (Banco Nacional de Comercio Exterior, 1978: 930-31).

Along the border, the predominant concern over tourism is the regional economic impact, especially the direct and indirect effects on local spending. Studies are ordinarily couched in tourist numbers, spending, and regional spending multipliers. Occasionally an attempt is made to relate changes in income volume, generated by tourism, to fluctuations in employment levels. Generally, local border impact studies are not concerned with price and income elasticities of demand—that is, the percentage change in the demand for tourism associated with a percentage change in either tourist income or the prices tourists pay. There are, however, economic models available in the literature incorporating such effects, and presumably these models could be easily modified to fit border researchers' requirements. *International Travel-International Trade* (Gray, 1970), for example, gives a formula for deriving the income elasticity of U.S. demands for travel-related "imports" from Mexico.[1] Joseph and Jud (1973) show demand elasticities for tourists to Latin America in a model that incorporates purchaser income, prices of commodities in the tourism "exporting" countries relative to those in closely competing countries, and the cost of international travel. Krause and Jud (1973) arrive at an income elasticity figure of 1.38 for U.S. foreign travel exports to Mexico between 1948 and 1970. An excellent general methodology for measuring tourism is in chapter 5 of John M. Bryden's (1973) work dealing with the Commonwealth Caribbean. Bryden considers tourist income multipliers, economies of scale, external economies and diseconomies of scale, uncertainty and risk, and tourism's social impact.

Nationally, the balance of payments and employment level attract more attention. At one point, Mexico voiced a concern that the rapid growth of international travel by Mexicans would cause Mexico's net foreign exchange earnings from tourism to evaporate (Banco Nacional de Comercio Exterior, 1976). It appears, however, that the 1976 devaluation has averted any immediate danger of a narrowing tourism gap. With respect to employment, Mexican sources estimate that 0.75 persons are directly employed and 2.5 persons indirectly employed per hotel room (Banco Nacional de Comercio Exterior, 1978: 930). Traditionally, tourism has been considered a labor-intensive industry that required a very low level of imported inputs. Inter-American Development Bank and World Bank studies, however, lead one to believe that there are stronger balance-of-payments "leakages" and more modest job creation effects than had been believed previously (Hansen, 1974; World Bank, 1972). Presumably such leakages along the border would be considerably higher than for tourists in the interior.

Although not a discernible issue along the northern Mexican border, there are increasing complaints, regarding Mexico as a whole, that tourism can cause socioeconomic and cultural damage by increasing the incidence of crime (Jud, 1975), loosening the fabric of cultural values, raising income expectations, and increasing Mexico's dependency on external forces (L. A. Pérez, 1975; Bugnicourt, 1978). Perhaps the leading writer, consultant, and exponent for rendering tourism more socially and culturally compatible is Herbert Hiller.[2] An interesting addition to the dependency argument is the Jewish tourist boycott of Mexico, a reaction to a Mexican vote in the United Nations General Assembly during late 1975 which Jewish groups felt associated Zionism with racism. Tourism, as well as other Mexican exports, fell sharply from the trend line of previous years. Indeed, at least one economist attributes the inevitability of the 1976 peso devaluation to the Jewish boycott of Mexico (LaBarge, 1978).[3]

Mexican Tourism in the United States

A variety of factors affect the flow of more than two million visitors from Mexico to the United States annually. The first factor resulted from the alteration in the currency exchange rate with the floating of the Mexican peso during the latter half of 1976. This development became an obvious deterrent to travel in the United States in the closing months of 1976, as evidenced by a nearly 20 percent decline of Mexican travel to the United States in September and a nearly 11 percent decline for the year (U.S. Travel Service, 1976, 1977b). A second factor which has had some impact on Mexican travel to the United States is the imposition of restrictive regulations on travel (for example, higher charges by the Mexican government for issuing and renewing passports). The effects of such prices, coupled with the peso devaluation, have impeded the flow of outbound tourism (U.S. Travel Data Center, 1976). A third factor affecting the number of Mexican visitors coming to the United States has been the attraction of competitive travel destinations. The major competitors with the United States for Mexican travelers are domestic destinations within Mexico and destinations in Europe. In recent years Mexicans have been more inclined to look toward their own country as a travel destination, partly because of a government campaign urging travel within the country rather than abroad. Despite these adverse impacts, recent forecasts by the U.S. Travel Service (USTS) anticipate increases in the volume of Mexican arrivals and spending.

The USTS collected survey data in 1970, 1974, and 1976 which identified characteristics of Mexican visitors in the United States.[4] These three USTS surveys briefly summarize the sex, age, marital status, education, occupation, income residence, foreign language capability, and family composition of Mexican visitors. In general, these surveys indicated that Mexican travelers to the United States were consistently more affluent, better educated, and more cosmopolitan than those who stayed within Mexico, or the population as a whole (see Table 31-2). The surveys also identify the characteristics of Mexican visitors' trips, including the size of the traveling party, reasons for travel, mode of transportation, destinations, length of stay, accommodations, expenditures, and seasonal patterns (see Table 31-3).

The 1976 USTS study segmented data for nine separate regions of the United States and its possessions. Highlights were published for only four regions, however, since the sample sizes for other regions were too small to allow statistically reliable analysis. One of the regions for which data could be studied was the Frontier West, which encompasses six states: Arizona, New Mexico, Texas, Oklahoma, Kansas, and Missouri. Of the 952 Mexican travelers to the United States interviewed by USTS, 36 percent mentioned the Frontier West as a destination. This USTS report (1977a) provides both the Mexican traveler and trip characteristics for those included in the sample.

Little detailed information is available on the impact of Mexican foreign visitors on Texas. While county by county travel data are available from the U.S. Travel Data Center in their annual "Impact of Travel on Texas Counties," Mexican tourists are not reported separately. The Texas State Department of Highways and Public Transportation, Travel and Information Division produces a yearly "Report on the Texas Visitor Industry," in which Mexican data are ordinarily not separated out. The 1979 report does indicate that Mexican tourists in Texas spent an average of $1,163.91 per party per trip, compared to $1,010.35 in 1978. Total expenditures were approximately $3.6 billion in 1979, up from $3.3 billion in 1978. Average group size for Mexican tourists was 2.75 persons in both years. As might be expected, Mexican tourists topped the list of foreign tourists coming to Texas, with 34.4 percent of the total in 1979. One other point of interest is that, of all non-Mexican tourists coming to Texas in 1979, 27.1 percent of those who stayed in Texas for less than 30 days also visited Mexico; for longer-term visitors, the proportion jumps to 69.1 percent.

In Southern California tourism has long been an important component of San Diego County's economy. According to an Economic Development Administration (EDA) study (1977), tourism provided employment for approximately 55,000 persons in late 1976 and accounted for more than one billion dollars in tourist spending, goods and services produced for them, and wages from businesses catering to their needs. Tourism's fortunes hinge, to a significant degree, on developments south of the border. For example, San Diego depends in part on attractions of Baja California, in general, and Tijuana, in particular, to lure tourists to San Diego. Tijuana, in turn, benefits and depends on attractions in San Diego to bring American tourists to it. San Diego benefits again in that much of the money which Americans and Mexican tourists spend in Tijuana and Ensenada returns, since residents and merchants cross the border to buy in San Diego County. With this symbiotic relationship it is surprising that the city's detailed 1974 study by Arthur D. Little, Inc., on the impact of tourism on San Diego did not mention Mexico once. Nevertheless, Baja California and San Diego tourist officials are attempting to tie together the tourist fortunes of the two areas.

The section on tourism and conventions in the EDA study reported that "Mexican nationals coming northward showed a 120 percent increase between 1960 and 1975, with crossings exceeding 23 million a year now (the bulk of these are shoppers, merchants, and Mexicans who work in the United States, such as the 10,000 Green Card holders)" (EDA, 1977: 8).[5] Al Anderson, president of the San Diego Convention

Table 31-2. *Characteristics of Mexican Travelers, 1976.*

Traveler Characteristic	Travelers to the U.S. (percent unless otherwise stated)	Non-U.S. Travelers Inter-continental (percent unless otherwise stated)	Non-U.S. Travelers Intra-continental (percent unless otherwise stated)	Total International Travelers (percent unless otherwise stated)	Domestic Travelers (percent unless otherwise stated)
(Base)	(952 persons)	(788 persons)	(180 persons)	(1,920 persons)	(574 persons)
Sex*					
Male	51	39	46	50	51
Female	49	61	54	50	49
Age*					
Median number years	27.5 years	30.4 years	28.0 years	28.2 years	23.8 years
Marital status†					
Married	53	46	39	52	53
Unattached	47	54	61	48	47
Education‡					
Elementary/primary	2	2	3	2	4
High school/secondary or higher	78	72	77	77	72
Technical/vocational	20	26	20	21	25
Occupation‡					
Professional/executive/management	54	50	54	53	45
Clerical	8	10	9	8	10
Student	15	15	18	15	17
Sales/merchant	7	7	5	7	8
Other	16	18	13	16	20
Annual household income†					
Under $14,400	31	23	27	30	49
$14,400 to $24,000	35	35	41	35	35
Over $24,000	35	42	33	35	16
Median	$19,700	$21,655	$19,780	$19,940	$14,650
Size of household†					
1 person	4	6	3	4	2
2 persons	14	13	11	14	10
3 persons	15	15	19	15	19
4-6 persons	50	49	47	50	49
7 or more persons	17	17	19	17	20
Median number persons	5.0 persons	5.0 persons	5.0 persons	5.0 persons	5.2 persons
Average number persons	4.7 persons	4.7 persons	4.8 persons	4.7 persons	5.0 persons
Children (under 18) in household†					
No children	35	44	41	37	28
1 child	18	19	21	18	23
2 children	21	20	13	20	22
3 or more children	26	19	25	25	28
Language capability†					
Speak or read English	84	79	77	83	65

Source: U.S. Travel Service, Department of Commerce (1977b: 11).
Note: Percentages may not add to 100 percent due to rounding.
  *Computed for members of the entire traveling party.
  †Reflects data concerning the respondent.
  ‡Reflects data concerning the primary decision maker for the trip.

and Visitors Bureau, estimated that Mexican tourists accounted for only 2 to 4 percent of San Diego's out-of-state tourist traffic. Unmeasured, according to this report, are the number of Mexican nationals who, as shoppers or workers, also visit tourist attractions. Similarly, no hard data are available on the level and distribution of expenditures by Mexican travelers in San Diego County. For example, the portion of the EDA preliminary report on retail employment reads:

Disagreement exists as to the amount spent annually in San Diego by Mexican nationals. In 1969, according to an Economic Research Bureau report, the San Diego Convention and Visitors Bureau estimated that Mexican Nationals spent almost $95 million in San Diego County during 1968. In its January, 1977, Bulletin, the Research Bureau estimated the figure to be $80 million; Cecil Scaglione, financial writer for the San Diego Union, recently estimated the figure to be

Table 31-3. *Characteristics of the Trip, Mexican Travelers, 1976**

Trip Characteristic	Trips to the U.S. (percent)	Non-US Trips Inter-continental (percent)	Non-US Trips Intra-continental (percent)	Total International Trips (percent)	Domestic Trips (percent)
(Base)	(952 persons)	(788 persons)	(180 persons)	(1,920 persons)	(574 persons)
Purpose of trip†					
Vacation	77	87	82	78	83
Visit relatives	18	22	17	19	21
Visit friends	10	11	9	10	10
Business	15	10	11	14	8
Attend convention	4	6	2	4	4
Study/formal schooling	6	11	7	6	1
Other	13	8	9	12	7
Inclusive-tour travel					
Yes	13	27	28	15	9
No	87	73	72	85	91
Size of traveling party					
1 person	26	29	31	27	15
2 persons	31	39	38	32	25
3 persons	25	12	6	14	18
4 or more persons	29	20	25	27	42
Relationship of party members to respondent†					
Spouse	32	30	26	30	42
Parent	15	13	15	13	19
Son/daughter	43	20	28	38	69
Brother/sister	16	15	9	15	26
Other relative	19	14	7	17	23
Business colleague	5	2	12	5	4
Friend	42	48	45	40	51
Traveled alone	26	29	31	27	15

Source: U.S. Travel Service, Department of Commerce (1977*b*: 16).

*Percentages may not add to 100 percent due to rounding.

†Multiple responses; percentages may add to more than 100 percent.

$200 million. A study done for the Organization of U.S. Border Cities on impact of peso devaluation, and released in March 1977, would place the figure at more than $176 million a year. [EDA, 1977: 7.]

Data on the economic impact of Mexican visitors in Arizona were recently collected and analyzed by the Division of Economic and Business Research at the University of Arizona under a grant from the Arizona Office of Tourism (de Gennaro and Ritchey, 1978*a*, 1978*b*).[6] This study sought to identify demographic-economic characteristics of Mexican visitors to Arizona; points of origin, mode of transportation, length of stay and points visited, expenditure levels by types of goods or services purchased, state and local taxes derived from visitor expenditures, and the extent to which public facilities are used or affected by these visitors. The study sample consists of 2,348 interviews obtained randomly at six border points (Douglas, Lukeville, Naco, Nogales, Sásabe, and San Luis) between Arizona and Mexico and at two Arizona international airports (Tucson and Phoenix).

The authors found that in the one-year study period (April, 1977–March, 1978), Mexican visitors spent in excess of

$315 million for goods and services. The greatest impact was in Arizona border towns, with Nogales receiving the largest proportion of total direct expenditures (44 percent), followed by Yuma (30 percent), Tucson (12 percent), and Douglas (8 percent).

Mexican visitor parties were generally headed by an adult male, typically with another adult. The occupation of the head of the household for the party was most likely from the unskilled worker group; however, there were almost as many from the professional/technical/managerial classification. Both types usually spent less than one day in Arizona. Their main reason for visiting was shopping, business, and personal matters assuming lesser importance.

While Mexican visitors come from many states in northwestern Mexico, the overwhelming majority (96 percent) come from Sonora, Arizona's adjacent state to the south. The nearby states of Jalisco, Sinaloa, and Baja California accounted for the rest. Almost half the Sonoran parties came from Nogales, with San Luis Colorado, Agua Prieta, and Hermosillos also contributing substantially.

The typical Mexican visitor party (two or fewer persons) spent approximately $50 per visit; persons traveling by air spent considerably more ($315) than those traveling by motor vehicle ($30) and pedestrians ($23). Residents of Mexican border towns spent less per trip than visitors whose trips originated in Mexican interior cities, but the numerous visits by border-town residents contributed much more to the total impact. Not surprisingly, traveling parties headed by persons in the professional/technical/managerial occupational group spent considerably more per visit than those headed by unskilled persons.

A categorical analysis of expenditures revealed that $137 million (44 percent of total direct dollar impact) was spent in department stores, with business expenditures (25 percent), food (7 percent), transportation (4 percent), lodging (3 percent), and medical expenses (2 percent) also contributing to a portion of the state total. Mexican visitors paid $8.7 million in taxes, of which $5.7 million went to state government and $3.0 million went to local governments.

The public facility used most frequently was the post office, and the "attractions" most visited were shopping centers, department stores, small city parks, restaurants, and night clubs. Sightseeing and picnics were the most frequent recreation activities.

Sources of Data

Regarding data sources, the U.S. Department of Commerce's Bureau of Economic Analysis publishes the monthly *Survey of Current Business,* which contains an annual article, usually appearing around mid-year, analyzing U.S. receipts and expenditures from international travel (for example, Bolyard, 1978: 64-67). Data breakdowns are presented by world geographic area, expenditures, number of tourists, duration of stay, and mode of transportation. Separate figures on U.S.-Mexican tourism are available, as well as expenditures within the border region.[7] Since 1974, the estimate of Mexican spending in the U.S. border area has been based on more comprehensive surveying methods as well as revised data furnished by Banco de México (Miller and Font, 1974: 24-28). Retroactive recalculation for 1971-74 resulted in substantially higher estimates of Mexican spending in the U.S. border area.

A variety of other publications are prepared by the U.S. Department of Commerce. For example, the U.S. Travel Service published "Foreign Visitor Arrivals by Selected Ports" (for example, 1978*a*) for each calendar year. This publication analyzes foreign travelers by their residence and arrival city in the United States. A separate breakdown on Mexico is included. The same agency also produces "Profiles of Travel to the United States from Selected Major Tourism Generating Countries" (U.S. Travel Service, 1978*b*), which contains sections on arrivals, expenditures, current developments affecting the travel market (including the Mexican market), trip profiles, and competitive considerations (such as the tourists' image of the United States).

A convenient Mexican source, showing the aggregate tourist activity, with a breakdown on United States spending in the border zone,[8] is *Indicadores económicos,* published monthly

by Banco de México. A more refined data breakdown is found in *Indicadores turísticos,* published quarterly by FONATUR. Those interested in obtaining the latter publication should write Gerencia General de Planeación Urbano-Económica, Isabel la Católica No. 24, 4 Piso, México 1, D.F. Of particular interest to border scholars, some data are available by states, showing border spending on a monthly basis. In addition, there is *Boletin mensual FONATUR,* which will contain articles (for example, FONATUR, 1978) helpful to tourism researchers.

A similar monthly publication, *Sectur,* is produced by the Secretaría de Turismo and contains such articles as "Termometro turístico: Estadísticas de afluencia y gastos obtenidos durante el primer trimestre de 1978" (1978). Also, Nacional Financiera's bimonthly *El mercado de valores* frequently reports on the investment and financial aspects of tourism (for example, 1978), and Banco Nacional de México's monthly *Review of the Economic Situation in Mexico* will sporadically survey the economic performance of the tourist sector (for example, 1978*b*).

Beyond these national sources, researchers should check what is available from U.S. state highway departments. As an example, for the past three decades the Texas Department of Highways and Public Transportation has reported on the tourism industry through its "Report on the Texas Visitor Industry." A vast variety of data is provided, including average length of stay, how tourists spend their money, visitors' demographic characteristics, and the like. There is a special section on visitors from Mexico. State tourist offices have an equally rich variety of information. For a list of state tourist office addresses, see the periodical *Hotel and Motel Management* (1977).

City Travel Bureaus on the U.S. side of the border should not be neglected. Not only will they often have locally generated figures on hotel occupancy ratios, local impact of tourist expenditures, and so on, but also often much relevant state, national, and sometimes Mexican literature in their offices. Moreover, they will usually be aware of federal funding proposals, city planning studies, doctoral dissertations in progress, commercial market research studies, and similar activities that may relate to tourism. Finally, many travel bureaus will belong to the private tourism association, the U.S. Travel Data Center, which compiles and distributes studies and data to members.

On the Mexican side, valuable information can be found at the local branch offices of the Departamento de Turismo. Branches are located in all major cities of the border region. Typically, they will have their own information, serve as a repository of other Mexican literature, and provide referrals to individuals, agencies, or organizations. FONATUR presently has no local offices, but there are tentative plans to establish them in the future.

Universities in the border region are important sources; bureaus of business and economic research are good places to start. Illustratively, the Bureau of Business and Economic Research of the University of Texas at El Paso has recently conducted a feasibility study for expanding the Sun Bowl football stadium, home of the annually staged Sun Bowl game (George et al., 1979); at the request of the Arizona Office of Tourism, the previously mentioned study by the Division of Economic and Business Research of the University of Arizona investigated the contribution of Mexican visitors to Arizona's economy.

Research Gaps

We will conclude this chapter by mentioning several areas deserving more research. First, while some attention has been given to price elasticity of tourism expenditures, an extremely relevant issue in a world of flexible exchange rates is cross-elasticities of demand with respect to tourism costs for major competing areas. More specifically, with most European and Japanese currencies appreciating relative to the dollar and the dollar-tied Mexican peso, if one can make the seemingly tenable assumption that U.S.-Mexican tourism is a close substitute for trips from either American country to Europe or Japan, some expansion of intra-North American travel can be expected. An estimate of the expected magnitude and timing of such a cross-elasticity effect would be useful.

Second, turning to a potential damping effect, what are the likely effects of future energy shortages, whether short-term crises or long-run scarcities, on border tourism? Given potential contraction of tourism in the region, are there alterations in travel accommodations and promotional techniques that can ameliorate the damage?

Third, although it is at the very heart of most regional economic models, the regional expenditure multiplier is almost universally selected arbitrarily. More elaboration on this point is found in "Trade and Merchandising" (chapter 30).

Fourth, local or regional promotional efforts resemble an industry characterized as "monopolistic competition"—that is, the presence of many "sellers" who heavily differentiate their product. Promotional expenditures raise each entity's costs, but much of the potential gain is offset by rivals' competitive claims. Efficiency could be enhanced by the identification of instances for which endeavors for cooperative promotion are justified by the expansion of the total market of participating cities or regions.

Fifth, studies such as the one recently completed in Arizona, measuring the current economic impact of travel by Mexican visitors, could be undertaken profitably in New Mexico, Texas, and California. Such baseline data then can be used in monitoring future changes for this portion of the tourist industry.

Finally, there is plenty of room at both applied and theoretical levels for investigations and experiments leading to a more desirable socioeconomic and cultural effect on tourist-receiving regions. This is especially true of Mexico, where, as we have seen, the tourism is proportionately much more important than is the case for the United States.

1. Tourist expenditure in the host country is considered an "export" by the host country and an "import" by the home country of the tourist.

2. Hiller's recommendations are discussed in Goulet (1977: 108-109). Also see Hiller (1976).

3. At the time of the presentation of his paper, Professor La Barge did receive comments from discussants who pointed out that increasing expectations of a devaluation and growing fears of political instability coincided with the sharp downturn in Mexican exports, including tourism.

4. In the first of these three USTS surveys (1970), the universe of the study included adults (21 or older), excluding the lowest socioeconomic class, residing in cities of ten thousand inhabitants or more in the northern and central regions of Mexico. The 1974 and 1976 surveys differ from the 1970 study in two important respects: the southern area of the country is included in the two most recent studies, as are Mexicans between the ages of 18 and 20. These differences should be kept in mind when 1970 results are compared with those from later surveys. The term *Mexican visitor* as it is used here refers to individuals who reported having taken a trip lasting 48 hours or more outside of Mexico during the two years prior to the reported survey and who either traveled to or through the United States on that trip.

5. Green cards may be issued to Mexican citizens upon request to the U.S. Immigration and Naturalization Service if the Mexican citizens are employed in the United States or have regular business requiring frequent commuting trips across the border.

6. In this study a "Mexican visitor" is a permanent resident of Mexico who enters Arizona, maintains his Mexican permanent address, and returns home. The crossing into Arizona may be made at the international boundary between the United States and Mexico or by commercial or private aircraft at several ports of entry in Arizona. While virtually all of these visitors are Mexican citizens, they could include citizens of other nations who permanently reside in Mexico. The length of time the visitor spends in Arizona could range from a few minutes to several months.

7. Much of what is included in border transactions is routine shopping rather than tourism *per se.* For this reason further elaboration is included in Chapter 30, "Trade and Merchandising," of this volume.

8. Mexican data are not identical to those reported in the United States. Orders of magnitude and general trends, however, tend to be compatible.

32

Transportation

RONALD C. SHECK
Department of Earth Sciences
New Mexico State University

Transportation, the movement of goods and people, is an activity that takes place on many levels and involves distinct patterns and dimensions within the Borderlands. Though transportation has many characteristics, the key element is movement. Some movements are occasional and random, while others are repetitious and frequent. Some are highly local, and some involve great distances. The organized, common movements blend together to produce flows and provide an organizational structure to movement, connecting places of settlement and regions of production and consumption.

Because most movements are purposeful and reflect the spatial distribution of settlements and economic activity, they congregate on particular routes or paths. It is along these paths and routes that the physical structures of transportation are found: roads, railroads, natural or improved waterways, and, more recently, legally defined air routes. Associated with these routes are the various modes of transportation: automobiles, trucks, buses, trains, boats and ships, and aircraft. Walking or the use of animal-drawn wagons and carts, pack animals, bicycles,

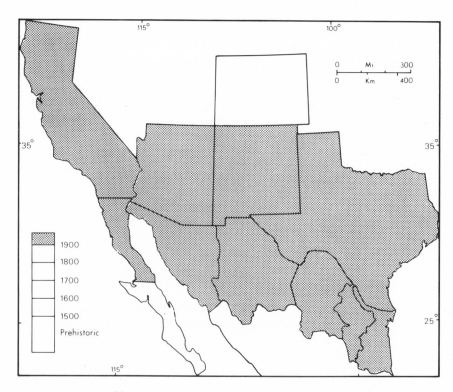

and so on, cannot be overlooked as means of transportation. While routes and rights-of-way refer to fixed structures, the modes are the vehicles or means of transportation.

Literature covering the totality of transportation in the Borderlands simply does not exist. Published material covers only pieces and fragments of the Borderlands transportation picture. Regional histories (for example, Horgan, 1954a) and geographies (Meinig, 1971) often document the growth process of transportation development. Monographs on railroad companies (for example, Kerr, 1968) or urban transportation operators (for example, Dodge, 1960) enrich the detail of transportation history of the region. Local and regional monographs (McGee, 1958; Pennington, 1963; Schmidt, 1973) help to fill in gaps with additional detail. Graphic portrayal of transportation networks is available largely on a macro scale through national atlases (Bonine et al., 1970; García de Miranda and Falcón de Gyves, 1972; U.S. Geological Survey, 1970) and regional atlases (Durrenberger, 1965; Beck and Haase, 1969). More detailed information at larger scale is provided through city maps and special-purpose atlases (Dunscombe and Rose, 1949; Pool, 1975). A wealth of information exists in various government studies and reports on airline, railroad, and highway traffic and in urban planning documents for the local scene. Federal, state, and local agencies in both the United States and Mexico are repositories of quantities of transportation information that have yet to be analyzed and presented in a scholarly format. Materials referenced in this essay should be considered as examples of particular types of source material rather than an exhaustive bibliography.

Movement in the Borderlands

The Borderlands are a region that produces unique patterns of movement. Location on the periphery of the United States and Mexico has an intensity and direction of movement different from that in the core area of either nation. Movement between these two nations takes place here in this zone of contact, and on the U.S. side, the Borderlands are also a zone of transit for movements between the eastern core region of the United States and the high population growth area of the Pacific Coast.

Sparsely inhabited until the twentieth century, the region nonetheless was the site of early cross-border movements. In fact, the border's delineation in the mid-nineteenth century superimposed a political boundary on already existing routes of trade and traffic: the mission trail into California and Arizona, the Camino Real into the middle Rio Grande Valley, and areas of Mexican frontier settlement in South Texas. The crossings established on this now permanent boundary remain the major land contact points between the two nations (Sonnichsen, 1968). Movement is channeled through these few crossings where towns and cities have sprung up on either side of the border. Although a number of other border crossings developed in the late nineteenth and early twentieth centuries, they generally remain subsidiary to the initially established crossings of Tijuana, Nogales, Paso del Norte, Laredo,

and Brownsville. The importance of contact at these points has led to rapid growth of towns and cities, and today the U.S.-Mexican frontier has become the world's most urbanized border. The greatest number of cross-border movements takes place between these binational cities and is a highly localized phenomenon.

Land journeys between the two nations are all funneled through the border twin cities; secondary to local traffic of the urban dwellers are commercial and tourist trips between the hinterlands that lie behind the frontier of either nation. The movement of goods also flows through these land ports of entry, predominantly by truck and train. In general, this movement is a northward flow of produce, other agricultural commodities, and mineral raw materials. Manufactured goods, machinery, and other finished products make up the bulk of goods flowing south into Mexico, though the movement of grain has become increasingly important since 1978. While goods originating in Mexico that cross northward into the United States originate primarily in the border hinterland or in northern Mexico, the flow in the opposite direction has its origins largely outside the Borderlands area in the midwestern manufacturing belt; however, goods produced in southern California are found in growing quantity.

A changing pattern can be noticed in additional traffic in local goods in the border cities as complementary industries of the plants of the border twins grow in number and in productivity. The importation into the United States of beef cattle is more diffused than that of other products, often taking place at scattered, small crossings away from urban centers. A new pattern of movement is that of natural gas entering the United States in the lower Rio Grande Valley by pipeline from the Mexican Gulf Coast.

Though there is a strong international flow of tourist traffic from major U.S. metropolitan areas that lie outside the border region to tourist destinations deep in Mexico, most of these trips are made by air, and planes simply overfly the Borderlands. An exception to this traffic is, of course, that generated in metropolitan centers of California and Texas.

Movements from the Borderlands areas of the United States and Mexico to their respective national core areas are extremely important. The transportation infrastructure greatly facilitates these movements in Mexico, as visual inspection of a highway and railway map shows quite well. The pattern of infrastructure is of equal importance in the United States but is less visibly definable because transportation routes have greater interregional linkages. The Borderlands of both nations are recent recipients of large-scale migration, and a great deal of movement reflects the ties of the new immigrants into these regions with the areas from whence they came. Growing industrial development as well as the expansion of mining activities and increased agricultural production has created additional movements of goods between the national Borderlands and the core areas. In Mexico these movements are reflected in the flow of grain and irrigated crops from the northwest and the Rio Grande Valley area to the central highlands and in movements of mineral ores to supply the growing industrial base of the central plateau and the Monterrey-Saltillo industrial center. Out of the U.S. Borderlands moves a large share of the country's fresh produce and agricultural specialty crops (citrus fruits and avocados) as well as mineral commodities. The development and growth of irrigated agricultural lands in southern California, Arizona, New Mexico, West Texas, and the lower Rio Grande Valley was in part a consequence of rail transportation, which after 1900 had the technical capability to move perishable goods (Meinig, 1971; Ullman, 1957). Imports from core areas include agricultural machinery, manufactured goods, foodstuffs, and consumer goods. Greater trade of semimanufactured goods is taking place in both directions as border-area industrialization increases.

Internal movements within the region on each side of the border include both local and regional traffic. Urbanization has brought about patterns of commuting and the need to supply growing cities with perishable foodstuffs, meat, and milk products produced locally. Another locally important movement is that of building materials. Regional traffic includes movement of mineral supplies, copper to smelters and refineries, and the like.

An important Borderlands movement appearing on the U.S. side, which is lacking in Mexico, is the region's role as a transit route for east-west traffic. The border region from El Paso west across southern New Mexico, Arizona, and California lies astride an important transcontinental route from the midwest to the Pacific Coast. The low gradients and warmer climate of this route were a major reason for territorial acquisition by the United States in the mid-nineteenth century. The pattern remains today, with much of the movement of California produce and other products shipped eastward in exchange for manufactured goods and grain. Winter tourism follows this route to Arizona and southern California, and a growing east-west traffic in both goods and people parallels the border from the Texas Gulf Coast to Los Angeles and San Diego.

Transportation Networks

Following the initial period of Spanish exploration, the first established land route through the area we have come to call the Borderlands was the route from Mexico to the colonies along the northern Rio Grande (Horgan, 1954a). Trails connecting mission settlements and ranches with the south provided a north-south alignment; in the nineteenth century the pattern was superseded by east-west patterns of trails, stagecoach roads (Loomis, 1968), and then railroads (Moorhead, 1958), confirming the policies of manifest destiny of the United States in newly acquired territory.

Today, well-developed highway systems exist on both the U.S. and Mexican sides of the border. Predominant in Mexico are north-south major routes that converge from various points in the border region on Mexico City—a reflection of the highly centralist organization of the Mexican Republic and the urban primacy of the capital city. In the U.S. Borderlands, major highways follow the east-west trend, although north-south connectors link up the major routes. It is yet impossible to traverse Mexico's northern tier of states from the Gulf to the Pacific by highway. The regional and local highway infrastructure is well developed north of the border, while local roads remain nonexistent or at least unpaved beyond the immediate environs of the Mexican border cities. The highways of the two nations are linked together at seventeen border crossings, but the most heavily used routes are those that breach the boundary at Tijuana, Calexico-Mexicali, the twin cities Nogales, El Paso–Juárez, Laredo-Nuevo Laredo, and Brownsville-Matamoros.

Railroad construction in the Borderlands initially involved the east-west transcontinental lines, the first being the Santa Fe-Southern Pacific route linked at Deming, New Mexico, in 1881 (McNeely, 1964; Myrick; 1968). Subsequent construction pushed eastward across Texas from El Paso (Wilson and Taylor, 1952). The north-south trend in Mexico followed the routes of original trails, again focusing on Mexico City. Two thrusts developed during the Porfirian era of railroad building: one by companies pushing up from the south, and another by U.S. companies (Clark, 1958) extending towards Mexico. The latter came from Texas into Chihuahua (Kerr, 1968) towards the Gulf of California and from Arizona along Mexico's Pacific Coast. Lesser lines crossed the border from the north to tap mineral and forest resources in the Sierra Madre Occidental (Dunscomb and Rose, 1949). The Mexican side of the Borderlands has seen active railroad construction in the mid-twentieth century with the completion of the Sonora-Baja California Railway in 1948 and the Chihuahua Pacific Railway in 1962. The former provided an all-Mexican rail route to the lower Colorado River area around Mexicali, and the latter marked the first major transportation link (Secretaría de Comunicaciónes y Obras Públicas, 1954, 1961) between the Chihuahuan Plateau and the Pacific Coast. The rail lines of the two nations are connected at nine points (Rand McNally, 1973), but the major links are at Mexicali-Calexico, Nogales, El Paso–Juárez, and Laredo-Nuevo Laredo. El Paso–Juárez is the most important node in the Borderlands rail system; three U.S. and two Mexican railways meet here. The limited capacities of rail yards in the Mexican border cities produced serious traffic bottlenecks in the late 1970s as transborder traffic grew to unprecedented levels. The Mexican government has developed a multiyear investment program to upgrade the national system, which will relieve congestion (*Railway Gazette International*, 1980: 671-82).

Commercial aviation in the Borderlands developed in the 1930s largely on a regional basis on both sides of the border. The first airports were constructed in the larger cities and at intermediate small communities where it was necessary to refuel the small aircraft with limited range. Although international flights between the two countries were initiated before World War II from Texas and California cities and from Mexico City, the short flight segments and frequent intermediate stops initially included landings at border points for customs inspections. Four-engine aircraft after 1946 and jet aircraft in the 1960s resulted in a general overflying of the Borderlands by most international flights. Exceptions are the major terminals of Los Angeles and San Diego, which are gateway points for flights to and from Mexico. Border-city airfields handle mainly national traffic. Most of the international air services maintained by the two Mexican and six U.S. airlines crossing the frontier originate and terminate beyond the confines of the Borderlands. Routes and services are tightly regulated by binational treaties.

No regularly scheduled coastal shipping services remain in the Borderlands today, although in the nineteenth and early twentieth centuries services were operated on both the Pacific and Gulf coastal routes, and a riverboat serviced the lower Colorado.

The most recent element in the across-border transportation network is the emergence of pipelines as Mexico is in the process of becoming an exporter of natural gas to the United States. Previously, pipelines in the Borderlands have been oriented toward moving oil and natural gas toward national sources of consumption.

Transportation Modes

Motor vehicles—autos, trucks, and buses—are the most ubiquitous carriers of goods and people in the Borderlands area. The oxcart, wagon, horse, and mule, historical carriers, may remain locally important in isolated areas of Sonora, Chihuahua, and Coahuila, but with each year, they continue to lose ground; even rudimentary dirt roads increasingly bring motor vehicles and more rapid connection with the outside world. The high rate of automobile ownership in the United States is exemplified in the Borderlands area by the number of multicar families. In Mexico, outside of the Federal District, the border states have the highest automobile ownership— a reflection of the increasing income gradient towards the northern frontier. However, the rate of automobile ownership is still about five times as great on the U.S. side of the boundary. Public transportation is virtually nonexistent except along the major highways of the U.S. Borderlands; on the Mexican side, buses reach into almost every village with a motorable road. In the United States, intercity bus service, although limited in scope, remains in the hands of private operators, while urban passenger transportation has become publicly owned. Both urban and intercity services in Mexico are largely privately operated. Trucks are almost the exclusive local and regional movers of goods on both sides of the border and take care of much of the international movements as well. For example, most of the produce moving into the United States from Mexico is brought by refrigerated truck.

Railway traffic in the Borderlands tends to be a main-line movement. Examination of railway maps reveals a paucity of branch lines. They exist only where a mine or mill generates a large volume of traffic. Urban industrial areas, mines, and farming zones are the real traffic generators, but the amount of agricultural commodities moving by rail across the border is rather low, although some increase in rail piggyback operations is taking place. Again, the east-west flow components of U.S. railroads contrast with the north-south ones of Mexico. Passenger train traffic in the region has declined drastically on the U.S. side since the late 1950s. Only one east-west train is operated three times a week by Amtrak connecting Los Angeles to New Orleans through Phoenix, Tucson, El Paso, San Antonio, and Houston. Since October, 1981, this train has carried through coaches and sleeping cars to and from Chicago via a connecting service north of San Antonio. The only other border city served by U.S. passenger trains is San Diego, where seven trains a day link that city with Los Angeles. Mexican passenger train service continues to be maintained over the four routes emanating from Mexico City to Mexicali, Nogales, Ciudad Juárez, and Laredo. Additional local train service operates out of these Mexican border cities. No through international train service exists, although such service was maintained between San Antonio and Mexico City via Laredo and Monterrey until 1965. Although railways in the Borderlands were constructed almost exclusively by private capital and remain in corporate holdings in the United States, those in Mexico have been gradually nationalized (Villafuerte, 1959; McNeely, 1964).

Internal airline flights in Mexico connect all of the Borderlands cities to the national capital and also provide the only east-west links across Mexico's northern tier of states. The frequence of flights is somewhat less than on the U.S. side of the border, but all routes operate daily, and some, two or three times a day. The U.S. Borderlands air flights are heavily geared to major metropolitan areas, connecting these areas to one another. The greatest volume of flow is to and from areas outside of the Borderlands (*Official Airline Guide,* 1981). Multiple flight frequencies are operated on all routes, and route density is much greater than in Mexico. For international air traffic, most of the carriers' flights do not originate in the Borderlands, with the exception of the California, Arizona, or Texas interior cities which have direct flights not only to Mexico City but also to West Coast resort cities and now even to Yucatán. Protectionist policies of the Mexican government severely restricted direct flights from U.S. border cities into Mexico until 1978, when flights between El Paso and the interior of Mexico were inaugurated. The growing importance of tourism has resulted in a relaxation of earlier policies.

Another increasingly important mode of tourism in the Borderlands area is the cruise ships operating into Mexican ports from southern California. A similar development is beginning to emerge from Texas ports to the Mexican Gulf Coast and Yucatán. These services are seasonal.

The importation of energy resources (natural gas and petroleum) from Mexico will probably accelerate the construction of pipelines across the border.

Border Urban Transportation

A sizable number of rapidly growing urban centers straddle the international border between the United States and Mexico. Although separate "twin" cities exist on each side of the boundary, they function in many ways (Sheck, 1974) as single urban centers. Most of the 75 million annual crossings of the border take place in these towns and cities. Urban residents make most of these trips, occasioned by a wide range of reasons—employment, shopping, recreation, acquisition of medical and health services, and visits to friends and relatives. The recent escalating population growth rate of both the U.S. Sunbelt and the northern tier of Mexican states has had a heavy impact upon the growth of border cities. Population of these cities has tripled since 1950, reaching an estimated 5 million by 1978. The twin cities range in combined size from Nogales-Nogales, containing 45,000 inhabitants, to El Paso–Juárez, with over 1 million.

Because the number of border crossings is limited to one or two points in each binational urban area, following a pattern set in the nineteenth century, the resulting heavy movement of people is channeled into extremely high-volume corridors, with problems of automobile and pedestrian traffic congestion, air and noise pollution, and so on (El Paso Mass Transit Technical Study, 1977; Stoddard, 1980: 10-13). The low incidence of automobile ownership in Mexico and a lower-than-average pattern in the U.S. border cities indicate the need for alternative solutions. Public transportation is poorly developed or nonexistent across these urban borders. El Paso and Juárez were linked by a streetcar system until 1974, when the franchise was canceled in Mexico. After a two-year lack of mass transit, a Juárez bus operator has been permitted to serve the international traffic (Price and Price, 1981). The sheer magnitude of movement encourages public transportation as a means of alleviating many of the problems.

The last decade has seen beginnings of a reversal in the deterioration of urban transit in the United States, and a number of American border cities (Brownsville, Laredo, El Paso, San Diego) have become active participants in transit programs and projects. However, these have focused only on serving the U.S. portion of the binational urban areas. Federal law in fact prohibits the use of government funds for projects that would operate outside of U.S. territory. Though interest has surfaced recently in revitalizing public transit across urban international boundaries between the United States and Mexico, limited or complete lack of knowledge and experience in urban transportation in the border context is a major barrier to development and implementation of transit programs. For example, a new light rail line opened in July, 1981, between San Diego and the Mexican border at Tijuana (*Rail Travel News,* 1978: 7; *Passenger Transport,* 1981: 1). The primary users will be travelers between the two cities, but the trip will require a mode change at the border. Ironically, this new service replicates an electric interurban railway abandoned in 1916 (Hilton and Due, 1960).

Research Needs

In Borderlands research there has been a noticeable lack of concern with transportation as movement of goods and people. The focus has been primarily modal and often on a single portion of one mode: a railway company, highway flows along a particular route, airline traffic potential between two points, or streetcar operations in a single city. The intrinsic value of these studies is well recognized, and the studies provide useful information upon which to build a slowly emerging overall picture of transportation within this broadly defined region.

An important need for transportation research is to determine the effect of the international boundary on movement, particularly at the local scale where most of it occurs. Understanding the pattern and processes of movement across the border is basic to the identification of contemporary transportation problems. The resolution of these problems in a sound manner can only occur after basic research is carried out. While the past is well documented through a broad array of historical research, a new focus on contemporary transportation issues is needed.

Since the end of World War II the phenomenal growth of Mexico's border communities has been accompanied by a growth in intervention by the central government. This intervention has sought to promote the growth of these communities while simultaneously assuring their conformity with the government's political and economic objectives. These objectives have included raising living standards, generation of foreign exchange, creation of employment, soothing interest groups, and strengthening the government's political control over the area.

Two important fiscal incentives for border development date from the 1930s: the free-zone status on the western portion of the border area and the allocation of small fixed percentages of customs revenues to municipalities *(municipios)* serving as ports of entry.

Since the 1930s the free-zone portion of the border area has consisted of Baja California Norte, Baja California Sur, the northwestern edge of Sonora, and the northern Sonoran communities of Nogales and Agua Prieta. While the status of

33

Taxation and Fiscal Policy

JOHN S. EVANS
Department of Economics
University of Alabama

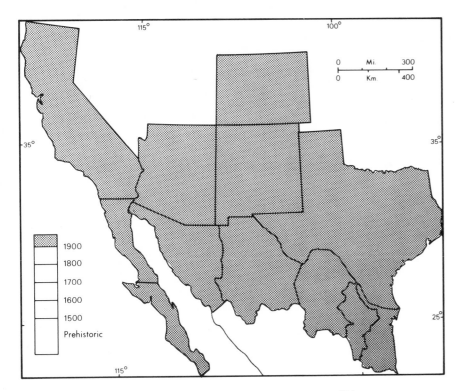

this zone is reviewed periodically under the threat of termination or severe modification, and while some restrictions have been imposed upon the zone's imports, the government has always bowed to the pressures which have favored the retention of the zone's special status.

For many years 3 percent of the general duty on imports and 2 percent of the general duty on exports collected in the customs stations of the border communities and other ports of entry were turned over to local federal material-betterment boards (*juntas federales de mejoras materiales,* or JFMM). During the López Portillo administration (1976–82) the JFMM were abolished; however, the same percentages of import and export duties are now given directly to the *municipios* in which they are collected. In addition, special treatment is now accorded to exports of petroleum, natural gas, and their derivatives. The communities from which such exports take place are allocated 1 percent of the duties collected on them, subject to the restriction that by 1983, 90 percent of this 1 percent must be used to form a municipal development fund *(fondo de fomento municipal).* Since exports of petroleum and related commodities have become extremely important in Mexico's foreign trade, and since the duties levied on exports of crude petroleum and natural gas have recently been set at about 58 percent of value, it is anticipated that the revenues resulting from such exports will be of great benefit to the communities through which they are funneled.

Historically, the attitude of the central government toward border development has been ambiguous. On the one hand it is difficult for the government to ignore the opportunities for economic gain resulting from Mexico's proximity to the United States. On the other hand the migration of people to the remote border strip complicates political management and reduces the demand for domestically manufactured goods, since border residents look to the United States for most of their consumer goods.

By 1960, however, the rapid population growth of the border communities and their obvious potential as a source of dollars tipped the scales in favor of the active promotion of border development. The first major response by the government in recognition of the growing importance of border development was the launching in 1961 of the National Border Program (Programa Nacional Fronterizo, or Pronaf), whose stated objectives were the substitution of domestically produced goods for imports, the promotion of visits by foreigners, and the improvement of the social environment of the border communities (Nacional Financiera, 1970: 177). Although, beginning in 1971, the Echeverría administration (1969–76) phased Pronaf out, the program's objectives have continued to be emphasized.

The National Border Program was entrusted to an agency of the same name, whose primary activity consisted of the planning and execution of public works financed by disbursements of Mexican treasury revenues funneled through Nacional Financiera, the giant government development bank. Nacional Financiera thereby assumed something of a supervisory role in the affairs of Pronaf. Subsequently several other autonomous agencies of the government involved in

steering funds into border development were placed under the general supervision of Nacional Financiera.

Pronaf was also given the responsibility for recommending two types of fiscal subsidies subject to the approval of the Ministry of Finance. These consisted of rebates of freight charges and exemptions from the then 1.8 percent federal portion of the 3.0 percent general tax on commercial receipts, in cases where domestically manufactured goods were sold to buyers residing in border communities.

The use of fiscal incentives related to indirect taxes was expanded in 1971 with the introduction of the tax rebates known as *certificados de devolución de impuestos,* or *cedis.* These amounted to a complete refund of the estimated indirect taxes imposed at all stages of production on domestically manufactured goods that subsequently were either exported or sold to buyers resident in the border area. While the *cedis* were granted for indirect taxes paid, they had a substantial income-tax effect. This occurred because the rebates received were excluded from taxable income even though firms were allowed to deduct the tax payments for which the *cedis* were granted. In general the tax benefit conferred by *cedis* amounted to approximately 20 percent of the sales value of the goods shipped to the border area after taking into account their income-tax effect.

Following the downward float of the peso against the dollar that began on August 31, 1976, the *cedis* and various other tax incentives designed to stimulate exports and border area sales were suspended. The use of *cedis* to promote exports was restored in 1977; however, they were not restored on border-area sales. The government argued that the depreciation of the peso had corrected the overvaluation that had justified their use on sales to border residents.

Nevertheless, the border area has continued to be given preferential treatment in the field of indirect taxation. Beginning in 1971, when the commercial-receipts tax rate was raised substantially on certain goods and services classified as "luxuries," sales within the border area continued to be taxed at the lower general rate (which was raised in 1973 from 3 to 4 percent). When the commercial-receipts tax was replaced in 1980 by the value-added tax (VAT), it was provided that, while the general rate of the VAT was to be 10 percent, the rate applied on sales to individuals or firms resident in the border area would be 6 percent.

Of the various fiscal incentives that have contributed to border development, the best known has been the elimination of import duties for goods used in the assembly of products for export. Since its introduction in 1965 as the cornerstone of the Border Industrialization Program, the policy of promoting assembly operations *(maquiladoras)* has stimulated the opening of hundreds of plants along the border. Whereas the conferral of fiscal incentives to private firms requires a majority of domestic ownership in virtually all other cases, the *maquiladoras* operate without such a restriction.

Even in the late 1960s it was possible for a firm in the interior to receive *maquiladora* status, and over time the government has sought to increase the percentage of assembly operations that are carried out in the interior. The promotion of such interior operations, however, has not been accompanied by measures of discrimination against the *maquiladoras* of the border. Indeed, it should be noted that there has been a tendency for the *maquiladoras* to locate in industrial parks, many of which are located in border communities, and that the government began to promote the establishment of such parks through fiscal incentives and other measures as early as 1970. In effect, the policy of the government has been to give foreign firms the option of locating in the interior when lower labor costs and other favorable factors there outweigh the locational advantage of being on the border.

Beginning in 1971, the government adopted a policy of liberalizing the importation of consumer goods into those sections of the border fringe not included in the free zone. Since it was clear that the residents of the border communities were crossing into the United States for most of their purchases of household goods (popularly known as *gancho,* or "clothes-hanger," articles), it was reasoned that the liberalization of import policy along the border would ensure that Mexican retailers would capture some of the profits from imports without stimulating a significant increase in import volume.

As a logical follow-up to the liberalization of imports of consumer goods, the government introduced in 1972 a program of fiscal and credit incentives for the construction of shopping centers in border communities. The fiscal incentives have consisted primarily of the elimination of import duties and the use of accelerated depreciation. At least 50 percent of the merchandise stocked must be of Mexican origin. In addition, these centers are permitted to operate "in-bond" storage facilities for firms engaged in *maquiladora* operations (Touche Ross, 1979: 24).

Beginning in 1972, various other fiscal measures have been introduced which have been designed, at least in part, to promote border development. Under Echeverría these measures included fiscal incentives for border-area industrial firms (especially small ones) producing for local markets, the construction of tourist facilities, and the promotion of area agricultural production and food processing. Under López Portillo these measures, consisting mostly of the liberalization of imports, were essentially maintained. More significant for border development than their retention, however, was the decision of López Portillo to restructure drastically the fiscal and other incentives designed to promote industrial decentralization.

The drive for industrial decentralization began officially with a presidential decree in July, 1972, which divided the country into three types of zones on the basis of eligibility for a wide variety of fiscal and credit incentives. This decree did not single out the border area for special treatment, but the entire area was included in the zone that qualified for the most favorable incentives to be conferred under the provisions of the decree. Although the benefits allowable under this decree were generous in scope, various factors prevented it from serving as a major stimulant for investment in the border area. In particular, investments in numerous communities lying short distances from the major industrial centers of Mexico City, Monterrey, and Guadalajara were eligible for the decree's benefits. Not surprisingly, most of the benefits granted went to firms for investments made in or near such

communities (Banco Nacional de Comercio Exterior, 1977*b*: 920). Also, because fiscal and credit incentives having nothing to do with industrial decentralization were available under other decrees, the incentive was reduced for firms to avail themselves of the provisions of the decree of July, 1972 (Evans, 1982).

Under López Portillo there was a reclassification of the country geographically for the purpose of applying incentives for decentralization, and there has been a strong effort made to harmonize the overall system of taxes, credit, and other incentives for economic development with the objective of decentralization. According to a decree of February, 1979, there were to be three basic types of geographic zones for the purpose of executing the program of industrial decentralization. The highest degree of eligibility for tax and other concessions was accorded to communities designated by the federal government as priority areas for port and urban development. A second basic type of zone was that of the state priority areas, which were to be determined subsequently by joint action of state and federal authorities. The state priority areas were to be somewhat less eligible for benefits than the designated priority areas. A third basic type of zone delineated by the decree was appropriately classified as areas of low priority; it consisted of communities that were to have a very limited eligibility for tax and other benefits. The low-priority areas consisted of the Federal District and nearby communities in the states of México, Hidalgo, Tlaxcala, Puebla, and Morelos (López Portillo, 1979).

Almost all of the larger cities of the border area, including Tijuana, Mexicali, Ensenada, Nogales, Juárez, Nuevo Laredo, Reynosa, and Matamoros, have been included among the designated priority areas. Other border area communities assigned this classification include Tecate, Agua Prieta, Acuña, and Piedras Negras (López Portillo, 1979). Some other border communities, most notably San Luis Río Colorado and Miguel Alemán, have been included among the state priority areas determined after the publication of the decree of February, 1979 (Nacional Financiera, 1980: 227). While many communities elsewhere in Mexico have been classified either as designated priority areas or as state priority areas, the uniformity with which the border communities have been assigned these classifications indicates that the program of industrial decentralization has assigned a high priority to the development of the border area.

During the second half of the López Portillo administration there has been a pronounced expansion in the use of such incentives as tax concessions, credit allocations, and favorable prices for public utilities, petroleum, and natural gas. The evidence available so far indicates that in practice the government is using these incentives to promote the objective of decentralization of industry and that the border area is receiving a very significant proportion of the assistance granted. Thus in the first half of 1981 the Guarantee and Development Fund for Small and Medium Industry (Fogain) conferred credits of 7.6 billion pesos, of which 1.6 billion pesos went to firms located in border states, excluding Nuevo León (Nacional Financiera, 1981*a*: 971).

The proliferation of programs and agencies involved with

border development induced the Echeverría administration to form in 1971 the Interministerial Commission for the Economic Development of the Northern Border Fringe and the Free Zones and Perimeters, which assumed the primary responsibility for the implementation of most programs affecting the economic development of the border area. Local committees of economic promotion were formed under the supervision of the Interministerial Commission, with responsibilities in such matters as the selection of public-works projects and the allocation of quotas for *gancho* articles to individual firms.

In June, 1977, President López Portillo issued a decree replacing the Interministerial Commission with the Coordinative Commission of the National Program for the Development of the Border Fringes and Free Zones. The Coordinative Commission was made responsible for gathering the necessary information for the execution of an overall border development program, in which the strategy of border development would be indicated and the roles of the different public agencies involved would be assigned. It took over from its predecessor the responsibility for constituting committees of economic promotion, which were to function as auxiliary and consultative agencies (Banco Nacional de Comercio Exterior, 1977*a*: 779).

The Coordinative Commission includes representatives from most of the cabinet-level ministries of the federal government. Its chairman is appointed by the minister for programming and budgeting. The commission has an input into the process of conferring fiscal and other concessions for border development, but the power to grant such concessions lies with specific ministries. Tax incentives are primarily the responsibility of the ministries of commerce, patrimony and industrial development, and finance, while the power to allocate credit lies basically with the ministries and agencies that control particular credit or trust funds.

During the López Portillo administration there has been an expansion in the number and scope of the agencies that are involved in the allocation of credit for economically desirable purposes. The agencies include the following: the Guarantee and Development Fund for Small and Medium Industry (Fogain), the National Fund for Industrial Development (Fomin), the Funds for the Development of Agriculture and Livestock (Fira), the National Fund for the Development of Tourism (Fonatur), the Fund for Industrial Equipment (Fonei), the Fund for the Development of Exports of Manufactured Products (Fomex), the Trust Fund for Industrial Complexes and Parks and Commercial Centers (Fidein), and the National Fund for Studies and Projects (Fsp). While these agencies provide funds to government agencies, they are also involved in lending to private borrowers and guaranteeing the obligations of financial institutions that provide credit to the private sector.

In November, 1981, López Portillo released a long decree announcing the approval of the national program for the development of the border fringes and free zones, which was formulated by the Coordinative Commission. The decree indicates that while there has been a slowing down in the extraordinary population growth of the border area, it has great potential for growth, provided that its economic infrastructure is improved and the proper incentives for private investment are made available. While the decree recognizes that the economic integration of the area into the national economy will be severely limited for a long time to come, it stresses that much can be gained by the continued expansion of the *maquiladora* and other exports of manufactured goods, the promotion of tourism and personal services, and the production and processing of agricultural products. In addition, the decree indicates that the area has a potential for the production of manufactured goods for shipment into the interior, especially in cases when there is not a direct displacement of goods already being manufactured there (Nacional Financiera, 1981*b*: 1229-30 and 1981*c*: 1253-56). It is too early to tell what the impact of the new border development program will be, but there can be little doubt that the decree of November, 1981, represents a major commitment on the part of the government to give a renewed impulse to border development.

Any person who is serious about doing research on the federal government's present involvement in the promotion of border economic development can scarcely avoid a trip to Mexico City for the purpose of visiting the agencies that have major responsibilities in this field. The people who make border development policy are there, as well as most of the people who have major responsibilities in the implementation of it. In Mexico City one can obtain annual reports and statistical information not readily available elsewhere. Table 33-1 gives gives English translations of the names of selected Mexican government agencies.

One of the first steps that should be taken by an individual doing research on border economic development is to visit the U.S. Embassy, whose staff economists and commercial specialists can be helpful in providing information about Mexican government policies and in establishing contacts with Mexican officials who are in a position to provide useful information. The library and other facilities of the embassy can also be useful sources of information.

In the past it has been difficult to obtain good statistical information on the use of tax and credit incentives, but the López Portillo administration has moved in the direction of making such information more readily available. Some information of a statistical nature is now published in an appendix to the annual report to the nation presented on September 1 of each year. By visiting the ministries of patrimony and industrial development, programming and budgeting, commerce, and finance, it should now be possible to obtain a great deal of information of a statistical nature as well as various documents giving the laws and decrees applying to border development and explaining, from the government's point of view, how they operate. The headquarters of Nacional Financiera and the Bank of Mexico are potential sources of statistical information and information about the operation of the various funds involved in the conferral of credit related to border development.

It is, of course, desirable that field trips be made to border cities, especially since this provides an opportunity to compare the reality of what is happening with the official version presented by government officials and publications.

Several sources of information should be consulted that represent or cater to the interests of U.S. firms. In Mexico City the offices of major accounting firms, such as Price Waterhouse, Arthur Andersen, and Touche Ross, provide a good deal of information to their clients about the legal and administrative aspects of tax and credit incentives. The same type of service is provided by several law firms that specialize in assisting foreign firms operating in Mexico. Along the border local chambers of commerce in the United States may prove to be useful sources of information about the functioning of the Mexican government's programs related to border development.

Finally, one would do well to maintain subscriptions to the free government publications *Comercio Exterior* and *El Mercado de Valores.* The former publishes a great deal of information about economic developments and frequently has interpretive articles about government policy that are very worthwhile. The latter publishes virtually all important public documents dealing with economic matters. Also available without charge is the *Review of the Economic Situation of Mexico,* a monthly publication of the Banco Nacional de México. The *Review* is one of the best sources of information on the Mexican economy.

Table 33-1. *The Names of Selected Mexican Government Agencies Translated into English*

Government Agency	English Translation
Comisión Coordinadora del Programa Nacional de Desarollo de las Franjas Fronterizas y Zonas Libres	Coordinative Commission of the National Program for Development of the Border Fringes and Free Zones (Codef)
Comisión Intersecretarial para el Fomento Económico de la Franja Fronteriza Norte en las Zonas y Perimetros Libres	Interministerial Commission for the Economic Development of the Northern Border Fringe and the Free Zones and Perimeters
Comité de Promoción Económica	Committee of Economic Promotion (local government agency)
Fideicomisos de Fomento a la Actividades Agropecuarias	Trust Funds for the Development of Agriculture and Stock-raising (Fira)
Fondo de Equipamiento Industrial	Fund for Industrial Equipment (Fonei)
Fondo de Fomento Municipal	Municipal Development Fund (established by local governments)
Fondo de Garantía y Fomento a la Industria Mediana y Pequeña	Guarantee and Development Fund for Small and Medium Industry (Fogain)
Fondo Nacional de Estudios y Proyectos (formerly Fondo Nacional de Estudios de Preinversión)	National Fund for Studies and Projects (Fsp), formerly National Fund of Preinvestment Studies (Fonep)
Fondo para el Fomento de las Exportaciones de Productos Manufacturados	Fund for the Development of Exports of Manufactured Goods (Fomex)
Programa Nacional Fronterizo	National Border Program (Pronaf)
Secretaría de Agricultura y Recursos Hidraulicos	Ministry of Agriculture
Secretaría de Asentamientos Humanos y Obras Públicas	Ministry of Housing and Public Works
Secretaría de Comercio	Ministry of Commerce
Secretaría de Hacienda y Crédito Público	Ministry of Finance
Secretaría de Patrimonio y Fomento Industrial	Ministry of Patrimony and Industrial Development
Secretaría de Programación y Presupuesto	Ministry for Programing and Budgeting
Secretaría de Turismo	Ministry of Tourism

34

Labor and
Labor Markets

REFUGIO I. ROCHÍN
*Department of Agricultural
Economics
University of California, Davis*

NICOLE BALLENGER
*Department of Agricultural
Economics
University of California, Davis*

A free-enterprise labor market is an intangible economic system wherein labor is allocated and its price, or wage, is largely determined by the market forces of supply and demand. It exists whenever and wherever prospective employers and employees meet to negotiate the purchase and sale of human services. The characteristics and conditions found in any such "marketplace" are wrought from the local geography, history, culture, and accompanying human institutions, such as employer and worker organizations and labor laws. These are factors which determine the nature and extent of employment opportunities, the qualifications and size of the work force, and the dynamics of the exchange between workers and employers. The characteristics of the labor market situated along the U.S.-Mexican border are unique in many respects and are largely the product of historical and economic relations between the two countries. This chapter attempts to offer a brief summary of the literature describing employment and labor market conditions along the border, framed within an overview of the region. Data on the size, distribution, and composition of the labor force are included to assess

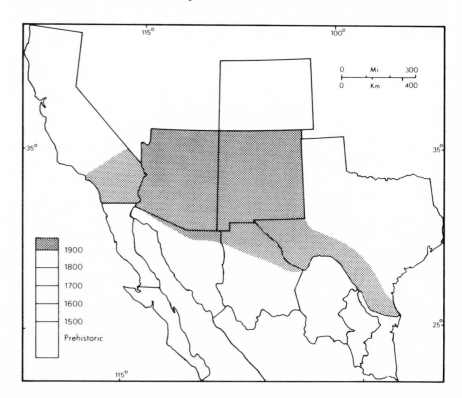

176

the current status of labor-market participants.

Until the mid-1960s the description of Borderlands employment patterns was limited to state and local reports and an occasional discussion in a text which dealt with social problems of unorganized labor and immigrants. Such pre-1960 references (mostly products of the 1930s) include the works of Paul S. Taylor, Carey McWilliams, John Steinbeck, Emery S. Bogardus, Varden Fuller, and Manuel Gamio. Their publications dealt generally with characteristics of poor Mexicans, whites, and farm workers of the Southwest.

Carey McWilliams, for instance, in a classic 1939 portrayal of the migrant farm worker, *Factories in the Field*, writes:

In all America it would be difficult to find a parallel for this strange army in tatters. It numbers 200,000 workers and a more motley crew was never assembled in this country by a great industry. Sources of cheap labor in China, Japan, the Philippine Islands, Puerto Rico, Mexico, the Deep South, and Europe have been generously tapped to recruit its ever expanding ranks. . . . It is an army that marches from crop to crop. Its equipment is negligible, a few pots and pans, and its quarters unenviable. It is supported by a vast horde of camp followers, mostly pregnant women, diseased children and fleabitten dogs. Its transport consists of a fleet of ancient and battered Model T Fords and similar equipage. No one has ever been able to fathom the mystery of how this army supports itself or how it has continued to survive. . . . Today the army has many new faces as recruits have swarmed in from the dust bowl area eager to enlist for the duration of the crops at starvation wages. But, in substance, it is the same army that has followed the crops since 1870. [Pp. 7-8]

Bogardus wrote in the early '30s of the many types of Mexicans in the United States, each with distinctive backgrounds and "interesting" characteristics. He reported also:

The occupations which the Mexican immigrants have entered are, first of all, agricultural. Raising and picking cotton, the beet industry, the cultivation of lettuce, walnuts, oranges and lemons, grapes, cantaloupes, and a large number of similar activities are representative. . . .

If migratory agricultural workers constitute one class of Mexican immigrants, then a second classification includes the Mexicans who have "settled down" on ranches or in small camps. Even these, however, are sometimes subject to migration. They are also the victims of changing economic conditions.

. . . In the third place are the railroad workers. Many of these live in box cars and are continually on the move.

. . . A large fourth group are the unskilled Mexican laborers in the cities. . . . They congregate at certain centers, sometimes on given street corners, to which employers come whenever they want "a hand" or any number of unskilled laborers.

. . . There may also be noted, fifth, the Mexican skilled laborer, living in cities. A number of Mexicans is found in the skilled trades, such as carpentry, painting, plumbing, and masonry. The opportunities are not numerous. Another difficulty is the attitudes of those "Americans" who believe that "once a Mexican, always a Mexican," which means that the Mexican has few chances of advancement.

. . . A sixth occupational type is the Mexican in business. Mexican businessmen operate small stores in Mexican communities. . . . They cater chiefly to the elemental wants of their own people; hence, the stimuli to develop are not exciting.

. . . The professional group, a seventh classification, is not to be ignored. Small in numbers, they are able to eke out only a fair living at best. . . . [Bogardus, 1934, 1970: 37-38]

Thus, the stage is set within which many of the pre-1960s authors relate labor-market conditions, especially for Mexicans, along the border. Since 1960, writings by Acuña, Briggs, Jr., Bustamente, Gilbert Cardenas, Gilberto Cardenas, Corwin, Fogel, Hawley, Hoffman, Jones, North, Rochín, Samora, Stoddard, and Barrera focus more on the problems of poverty, Mexican immigration, and employment with particular attention to Chicanos of the Southwest and the importance of labor-market institutions in molding current conditions. Very few studies have dealt exclusively with Borderlands labor-market conditions per se, wherein the focus would encompass the way a border affects the supply and demand of labor and vice versa.

Historical and geographical factors are certainly important to the contemporary understanding of labor and employment conditions along the border. Before the 1900s the labor market changed relatively little from the period of the Spanish Conquistadores in the 1500s, through the time of Mexican occupation, and during the U.S. military campaigns of the 1860s-1890s. Settlements were sparse and far between. Employment was relegated to farming and cattle ranching and, to a limited extent, to mining and private occupations in small towns. At the turn of the century, employment patterns diversified as border towns grew. San Diego rose in importance as a major seaport and as a primary border location for nonfarm jobs. Other border communities prospered from economic foundations of farming, cattle, and mining. Several communities, such as Calexico-Mexicali, Nogales-Nogales, and El Paso-Juárez, developed as "twin cities," that is, cities that nestle side-by-side along the border, with shared economies and a thin dividing line between the U.S. and Mexican labor markets. What gave rise to a distinct set of jobs and a concomitant laboring class, largely unskilled and low-paid, were the resources found and exploited at the turn of the century. Mario Barrera's book (1979) is one well-documented account of how the economic development of the Southwest's mineral and land resources shaped employment patterns and labor conditions along the border, an account we turn to in some of the descriptions below.

Resources and Factors of Employment

Minerals and Mining. Minerals and mining have long been an important source of jobs and income in areas of the Southwest. The first great California gold rush brought Anglo immigrants and a new prosperity from the East to the West, and California gold mining continued to be an important industry for some time. In Arizona, silver mining was developed in the 1850s, and copper became an important resource in the 1870s. Gold, silver, copper, and lead also assumed importance in New Mexico. Early mining operations were worked on a very small scale, but well before the turn of the century, mines in California and Arizona were heavily capitalized. With the adoption of new mining technologies, large-scale mining operations with wage workers replaced the individual self-employed miners.

In the twentieth century, copper production continued to expand in New Mexico and Arizona. Petroleum production became a major economic enterprise in Texas and California. Industrial development, such as ore processing plants and the manufacturing of extraction machinery, was a by-product of these activities. The discovery of oil stimulated the development of the Texas chemical industry and led to the expansion of important transportation systems.

Today, the border regions of Arizona, New Mexico, and Texas supply a significant share of the United States' copper and oil requirements, in addition to lead, zinc, molybdenum, silver, gold, sand, gravel, and limestone. Arizona leads the nation in copper production, with some of the major mines located in Pima County, along the border. In Texas, the eastern border counties, including Maverick, Webb, Zapata, Starr, Hidalgo, Cameron, and part of Kinney, are endowed with a number of gas and oil fields, and production of both fuels has been increasing, although compared with other areas in Texas the output is relatively small (Title V Regional Action Planning Commission, 1976, pp. 4 and A.8). In Mexico, minerals and mining are valuable sources of jobs in the border states of Baja California and Sonora. Mining for copper in Sonora, especially in the vicinity of Cananea, is particularly important.

Agriculture and Ranching. The California gold rush and the resulting surge in population growth brought on a cattle boom during the 1850s. Although cattle later decreased in importance to Californians, ranching became and remained an important part of the economy of the Southwest border and, in particular, that of Texas. By the 1880s, large companies supplied with eastern and foreign capital had fenced and taken control of the rangelands, and the railroads had replaced the cattle trails. Cattle and sheep ranching also spilled over into New Mexico, Arizona, and Colorado.

But agriculture came to be far more valuable than ranching to the southwestern states of California and Texas. Wheat and other grains, fruits and vegetables, and cotton were cultivated extensively during the latter half of the nineteenth century. From 1900 to 1930 the production of cotton led to the inception of textile mills, and food processing industries grew up in conjunction with the raising of fruits and vege-

tables. Meat packing also became an important business in the Southwest.

The expansion of southwestern agriculture was closely related to the development of irrigation systems (particularly in areas such as the Imperial Valley in California, the Salt River Valley in Arizona, and the Rio Grande Valley and Winter Garden areas of Texas) made possible by the Reclamation Act of 1902. During that period the trend in agriculture was toward more specialized and more commercial crop production. Although grain farming quickly became highly mechanized, the growing of fruits, vegetables, and cotton required, until more recent times, very large quantities of seasonal hand labor.

It was mainly through agriculture that a characteristic pattern of labor conditions emerged, especially in the rapidly transforming state of California. Several factors converged, bringing about the change from mainly extensive wheat and beef cattle production to the cornucopia of commodities produced today. Dry farming in California and other parts of the Southwest was a risky venture, but as irrigation developed, value was added to the land which then in turn required the production of higher-valued crops. The railroad and refrigerated cars opened up eastern markets for Southwest-grown perishables. Successful experiments with new crops and new processing techniques further encouraged the development of fruit, grape, nut, and vegetable crops. On the eve of such labor-intensive crop production, three alternatives were open to landowners: to grow land-intensive crops of the past like wheat or cotton, to sell land and divide large holdings into family-sized units, or to hire a large pool of low-cost labor. It was soon evident that the third alternative was the most profitable.

Between 1860 and 1870 some ten thousand Chinese laborers were available for farm work in California, having completed work on the transcontinental railroad. Some fifty thousand other Chinese were in California working in mines and in light manufacturing in the cities (Meister and Loftis, 1977). After the gold rush, competition from white workers drove many Chinese from the mines and cities to join the former railroad workers in farm work. Both on the railroad and in the mines the Chinese had been accustomed to working in gangs under contract, a system which was readily adopted by growers. By the 1880s, more than half of California's farm labor force was Chinese.

Most of the Chinese had been tenant farmers in their home country and were highly skilled. They taught their employers the intricacies of fruit and vegetable growing, and did much of the work of building levees, reclaiming marshlands and developing irrigation systems that opened large new areas of the state to farming. . . . Growers were so pleased with their labor that they imported thousands more workers directly from China, with the help of merchants and others who also profited from the immigration. [Meister and Loftis, 1977: pp. 6-7]

In spite of fruit and vegetable growers' high satisfaction with the performance of Chinese workers, political agitation from small growers, white unionists, and small manufacturers about "cheap" Chinese labor resulted in 1882 in the Exclusion Act, which prohibited further immigration of Chinese labor. Another law passed in 1894 during an economic depression was intended to force the deportation of many Chinese, but it was largely ignored by the growers. During this period, bands of unemployed white workers actually invaded farm labor camps, forcing Chinese to flee to the cities, where many took jobs unwanted by white workers and established their own separate communities. From 1900 on there was a rapid decline in the importance of Chinese in California agriculture as their numbers dwindled to a relatively insignificant portion of the farm labor force.

Growers, concerned about their labor supply, talked of importing Portuguese, Italians, Mexicans, or blacks from the South or of introducing more capital-intensive, labor-saving farming methods. In 1885, emigration was legalized by the Japanese government, and in time it was the Japanese who filled the labor vacuum left by the Chinese.

At first, during the difficult economic times of the 1890s the Japanese resorted to wage cutting in order to get established in farm work. They were well accepted by growers because they, like the Chinese, organized themselves into hard-working gangs, provided their own food and housing, and lived apart in their own communities (Fuller, 1939). After 1900, the employment of Japanese increased rapidly until they represented a majority of the work force in labor-intensive crops.

The story of the Japanese in California agriculture, however, did not end there, for once established in agricultural employment, many industrious and ambitious workers began taking advantage of the labor contract system to move up and out of the seasonal farm-worker class. The beginnings of farm-worker trade unionism can be traced to their collective bargaining tactics such as "quickie" strikes when fruit was ripe; the refusal to scab against fellow nationals; the provision of fewer men than needed, to drive wages up; and the boycotting of certain growers. Growers soon found that leasing land to Japanese on a share-crop system was more advantageous to both parties than labor contracts which could not be counted on when most urgently needed. By 1910, one-fifth of the Japanese in California were farming their own land as owners, lessees, or sharecroppers (Meister and Loftis, 1977). By 1920, the Japanese owned 74,769 acres of farmland and leased another 383,287 acres. They controlled 91 percent of the berry acreage, 81.2 percent of the onions, 65.4 percent of the asparagus, 58.8 percent of the green vegetables, 53.3 percent of the celery, and substantial portions of the acreage in several other commodities (Nagai, 1977).

Japanese farm workers worked intensively for Japanese growers. Ethnic cooperation paid off handsomely until they were subjected to even stronger discrimination than that endured by the Chinese. The buildup of anti-Japanese pressure resulted in the state Alien Land Law of 1913, which prevented immigrant Japanese from owning or leasing land more than three years—a law which was strengthened in 1920. In 1924, further Japanese immigration was cut off by national legislation. By 1930, the Japanese had lost their position of dominance in the California hired farm labor force, although they continued as tenants on farms vested in the names of others.

Under the pressure of real or threatened labor scarcity, other foreign farm labor groups were welcomed by California growers. The Hindustanis (Pakistanis or Indians), and smaller numbers of Greeks, Armenians, Portuguese, Italians, and other Europeans were hired for farm work. Hindustanis were subjected to much of the same discrimination that was applied to Orientals in general. The Europeans were not long in becoming farmers themselves or in migrating to the cities. The Portuguese made important contributions in dairying; the Italians, in viticulture; the Armenians, in marketing. Between 1920 and 1930 the number of Filipinos in California increased tenfold from 2,700 to 30,500. These immigrants were predominantly young males experienced in agriculture; they, like the Chinese and Japanese, worked in gangs, each under a contracting boss (Fuller, 1939).

Before 1900, relatively few Mexicans came to work in the United States, but their numbers increased substantially from 1900 up until the Great Depression of the 1930s. A revolution in Mexico had created economic depression and unemployment there, World War I cut off immigration from Europe, and representatives of growers' associations and industrial companies actively recruited in Mexico for workers (Hoffman, 1974). For these and other reasons, in the 1920s the Mexican population in California tripled from 121,000 in 1920 to 368,000 in 1930 (Fuller, 1939).

The Great Depression and the drought conditions in Oklahoma and Arkansas brought an influx of poor whites to California, reducing employment opportunities for Mexicans in California and discouraging further immigration. Unemployed Mexicans in the United States meant an additional burden on already strained social agencies, and pressure was brought upon the Mexicans to return to their home country. By the end of the 1930s, more than four hundred thousand Mexican aliens had been repatriated to Mexico, leaving the farmlands to be worked largely by white "refugees" (Hoffman, 1974).

At the beginning of World War II when the national employment rates rose, absorbing most domestic unemployed, urgent demands were voiced by growers for the importation of Mexican farm workers. Among the first petitioners were sugar beet growers who sought approval from the U.S. Department of Agriculture to recruit contract workers in Mexico. After Mexico declared war on the Axis powers in June, 1942, the provision of contract Mexican agricultural labor was considered part of the war effort. Soon the workers came to be known as *braceros*, which means "laborers"—particularly those who do hand labor. Although at the conclusion of the war there was some talk of ending the *bracero* program, both agriculturalists and workers liked the arrangement and wanted it continued. Thus, in 1950, Public Law 78 was passed giving the secretary of labor the authority to recruit Mexican workers for employment—including those in the United States illegally provided they had been here five years.

In time, the costs of the *bracero* program began to be resented, particularly in view of the fact that only a relatively few large growers—those who could provide labor camps, transportation, and other facilities—were benefited. Furthermore, once again the claim was made that the presence of foreign workers was detrimental to domestic ones, depressing wages and taking away jobs. Under pressure from organized labor, Public Law 78 was officially ended on December 31, 1964, but the *bracero* program continued and tapered off gradually until August, 1968, under emergency provision of the Immigration and Nationality Act, Public Law 414. In its 26 years of existence, from 1942 to 1968, nearly five million *braceros* were contracted.

It has frequently been stated that the termination of the *bracero* program would have spelled disaster for the California tomato processing industry had it not been for the fortuitous development of the tomato harvester and a variety of tomato capable of being mechanically harvested. The fact is, however, that masses of former *braceros* returned to California, legally or illegally, and continue returning there to this day.

Despite the tradition of agricultural employment, many illegals are now employed in nonagricultural jobs such as the garment industry, but, nevertheless, a very large labor pool is still available to southwestern agriculture today, as in the past.

Since the Southwest's and California's agricultural work force has been composed of such diverse groups differing from each other and from society at large in nationality, language, and culture, a labor system evolved for coping with the situation which kept the workers from cooperating to better their lot. The inability of most workers to speak English secured their dependence on a bilingual labor contractor who dealt with the grower, sometimes at considerable personal profit to himself. Farmer-laborer relations remain impersonal, even to the point of the workers' being anonymous, identified only by their social security card numbers. Employers did have racial-group preferences, however, and differing wage rates were once paid to different nationalities. Thus, those in one ethnic group would regard those in another as competitors, and mutual suspicion was aroused. Sometimes mixed crews were used to destroy the solidarity that inevitably grew up in homogeneous groups. The system meant that effective worker bargaining power was a long time coming.

It was not until the mid-1960s that unionization came about under the leadership of César Chávez. A series of labor laws gave the workers a greater voice in employer-employee relationships. The Agricultural Labor Relations Act provided a forum for settling disputes and a mechanism for redress. Other protective legislation was enacted on behalf of the laborers, and civil rights policies and social welfare programs also contributed toward the improvement of farm labor working and living conditions.

The present situation in California and the Southwest border region reflects the social history just recounted. The great bulk (from 50 to 70 percent) of the hired farm labor force is Mexican or of Mexican descent. In certain crops, in particular asparagus and lettuce, Filipinos are prominent. Anglos, Chinese, and Basque shepherds are also found.

Agricultural production continues to provide income and employment, particularly in San Diego County, in the fertile alluvial fields of the Imperial Valley, and in areas of Texas. The best quality pastureland along the border is located in central Texas counties, including Val Verde County and parts of Terrell and Kinney counties.

Along the Mexican side of the border the amount of arable land is small. Of 32.4 million acres in the Mexican states of Baja California Norte, Sonora, Chihuahua, Coahuila, Nuevo León and Tamaulipas, only 7.6 percent, or 2.5 million acres, is arable land. In the border states, however, 0.65 percent of the Mexican territory is suitable for pasturage and the raising of livestock. Unfortunately, historical accounts of labor and labor market conditions are hard to find. Certainly a historical analysis, done in the manner of the early writers of the Southwest, would be very welcome today.

Manufacturing. Manufacturing and the retail and service sectors presently account for most of the income and employment along the border. Some of these jobs are, as mentioned above, related to the mining and agricultural bases in this region. Other manufacturing businesses (electronic components, computers, aircraft and parts, and the garment industry) seeking an abundant and inexpensive labor supply have located in the Southwest. In 1965, the Border Industrialization Program (BIP) was initiated in Mexico to encourage the establishment in the border cities of plants for assembling, processing, and exporting American products. U.S tariff regulations are also designed to encourage the location of these plants in Mexico (Briggs et al., 1977). The purpose of the BIP was to establish industrial parks to provide jobs for a swelling border population and to stay emigration to the U.S. side. The number of these plants increased from only 20 in 1966 to 120 in 1970 and 476 in 1974 (Urquidi and Méndez Villarreal, 1978: 148). Employment in the *maquiladora* plants reached 53,680 in 1974, repesenting over 30 percent of the employment in border manufacturing. More recently, the number of border plants has risen to 521, and employment is nearly 110,000, compared with 89,600 at the end of 1978 (*Wall Street Journal,* July 15, 1980). The most important BIP city is Juárez, Mexico, where U.S. companies such as RCA, General Motors, and General Electric have assembly plants. Companies from Belgium and Japan are also located in Juárez, and more foreign investment is expected to be attracted to the city by the presence of Mexico's natural gas pipeline.

In providing jobs and relatively higher wages than elsewhere in Mexico, border industrialization actually induced large migrations of people from the interior of Mexico to the border region. As a consequence, border trade and marketing have increased at a rapid rate, providing for numerous jobs in small business. However, socioeconomic problems along the border have mounted as the capacity of the *maquiladoras* to provide jobs has been exhausted. As unemployment and crime rates have risen, border communities have found themselves unequipped to provide proper municipal services to the multitude of immigrants. In his historical account of the industrialization program in Juárez, Oscar Martínez (1975) notes:

Male unemployment has been only minimally reduced, primarily due to the practice of staffing factories largely with women. BIP has encouraged more migrants from Mexico's interior to head toward the border, thus contributing to overpopulation. With industrial expansion have come attendant social ills, such as inadequate housing, alarming shortage of public services, increased crime, and family disintegration. Worse yet, an air of uncertainty continues to hang over the future of the maquiladora *program, although in the short run it seems probable that the border will experience continued expansion of twin-plant activity. . . . Mexicans fear that "the view of [American] organized labor might prevail in the U.S. government, and that action might be taken to revoke the [tariff provisions] . . . which have been so helpful in the establishment of the border industry program. [Pp. 151-52]*

Government. The government—the military, in particular—is a major employer in parts of the Southwest where vast areas of desert provide the required empty spaces and clear skies. In some areas—for example, in the vicinity of Laredo, Texas—the dependence on military installations for jobs is very high, and military cutbacks or closures have led to severe disruptions of the local economy (Title V Regional Action Planning Commission, 1976: D.24).

Despite the importance of agriculture and mining to the economy of the Southwest, the chief constraint facing the growing labor market is the limitations of the physical economic resources in the border region. The Title V Regional Action Planning Commission (1976) reports that "Deserts, mountains, and above all, aridity are the dominant elements of the landscape. Exploitable minerals, with the exception of copper in Arizona and New Mexico and oil and gas in Texas, have not been found in any quantity (in recent decades). Although half of the area is defined as farmland, much of it is poor pasture used for extensive grazing, and only in a few valleys can the land be cropped extensively with the help of irrigation" (p. 1). The commission does point out, however, that unexploited potential exists in the use of the region's land resources for recreation and tourism.

Labor-Force Characteristics: The 1970s

Within the four U.S. states which border Mexico there are 26 "border" counties: 2 very large counties in California, 4 in each of Arizona and New Mexico, and 16 small counties in Texas.[1] In 1970, the total population in these counties was over 2.8 million, but the population of San Diego County alone was nearly half that figure. The populations of the rest of the border counties ranged, in 1970, from 359,291 and 351,667 in El Paso, Texas, and Pima, Arizona, respectively, to less than 2,000 in Jeff Davis County, Texas. Ten counties in Texas and New Mexico had fewer than 10,000 people (see Table 34-1). Table 34-1 also indicates that in the period 1970-75, all but 3 of the border counties showed impressive population increases. In 1975 the U.S. border population totaled 3,420,187, a 20 percent increase over 1970. The burgeoning numbers of people have put stress on all the border labor markets, but the diversity found from one county to another makes it difficult to generalize the magnitudes and dimensions of labor-market problems.

Urban residents, defined broadly by the U.S. census as persons living in places with 2,500 or more inhabitants, made up approximately 75 percent of the border population in 1970 (see Table 34-1). The farm population constituted 1 percent of border inhabitants; the remaining persons were designated nonfarm rural. It is likely that during the decade of the 1970s the percentage of urban residents increased, as the number of farms and agricultural employment opportunities declined over that period (see Table 34-2).

The civilian labor force within the U.S. border counties totaled 943,842 in 1969. San Diego County had a civilian labor force of 459,679 in 1969, followed by Pima County with 122,311 and El Paso County with 112,825. In most of the other border counties, the labor force was less than 10,000 (see Table 34-3). Approximately 65 percent of the labor force was male in 1969. Labor-market participation rates, measured as a percentage of the population over 18 years of age and in the labor force ranged from about 40 percent to 60 percent. By 1975, the civilian labor force in San Diego County increased some 36 percent as the labor force grew to 621,000. The civilian labor force also grew in all other border counties combined, but to a lesser extent (Title V Regional Action Planning Commission, 1967).

A large proportion of the supply of labor in the border regions comes from the rapidly growing Chicano population. Spanish-speaking people and people with Spanish surnames are the largest minority in the Southwest. In New Mexico the Spanish-language, Spanish-surname population is 40 percent of the total, and this census figure and figures for other states are thought, by Briggs and his coauthors to be significantly understated (Briggs et al., 1977: 5). Most of these people have their origin in Mexico; others trace their heritage in this country to a time when Santa Fe was a provincial capital for Spain. Still others have their roots in countries of all parts of Central and South America. Mexico is the primary source today, though, of a stream of peoples who continue to enter the United States both legally and illegally, seeking employment opportunities and higher wages on this side of the border. Consequently, in 20 of the 26 border counties, over 20 percent of the population is Mexican-born or of Mexican parentage. In 14 counties, mostly in Texas, over 30 percent of the population is of recent Mexican origin or descent. Additionally, thousands of undocumented Mexican aliens and border commuters enter the United States each

Table 34-1. *Population along the Border*

State and County	Total Population 1970	Total Population 1975	1970-75 Percentage Change in Total Pop.	Net Migration 1960-70 (percent)	Net Migration 1970-75 (percent)	1970 Urban Population (percent)	1970 Foreign Stock (percent)	1970 Leading Country of Origin (as percentage of foreign population)*	1970 Median Grade Level Completed
Arizona	1,770,900	2,225,077	25.6	17.4	18.7	79.5	16.7	M 38.4	12.3
Cochise	61,910	73,950	19.4	− 6.5	11.6	64.4	28.5	M 67.0	12.2
Pima	351,667	443,958	26.2	17.7	19.9	85.3	21.0	M 40.6	12.4
Santa Cruz	13,966	17,543	25.6	6.2	15.5	63.9	63.6	M 87.7	10.5
Yuma	60,827	66,020	8.5	11.7	7.6	62.4	18.0	M 62.3	12.0
California	19,957,715	21,202,559	6.2	13.4	1.9	90.9	25.0	M 22.3	12.4
Imperial	74,492	84,276	13.1	−15.1	6.2	67.8	37.7	M 80.8	10.8
San Diego	1,357,782	1,584,583	16.7	16.4	12.4	93.5	20.8	M 23.2	12.4
New Mexico	1,016,000	1,143,827	12.6	−13.6	5.8	70.0	8.7	M 42.6	12.2
Doña Ana	69,773	79,593	14.1	− 8.2	6.0	66.4	24.5	M 79.2	12.2
Grant	22,030	24,377	10.6	1.3	4.3	48.2	16.7	M 78.8	11.7
Hidalgo	4,822	5,820	20.7	−23.7	11.7	75.2	25.4	M 83.6	10.5
Luna	11,706	14,421	23.2	− 2.6	17.7	69.8	24.4	M 75.0	10.6
Texas	11,195,431	12,244,678	9.4	1.5	3.7	79.8	10.7	M 59.3	11.6
Brewster	7,780	7,867	1.1	5.1	− 5.2	78.8	14.5	M 76.5	11.9
Cameron	140,368	176,931	26.0	−32.1	8.7	77.6	42.3	M 91.1	8.5
Culberson	3,429	3,485	1.6	− 7.4	− 3.1	—	29.3	M 89.6	10.6
Dimmit	9,039	10,881	20.4	−30.0	8.8	59.8	37.5	M 94.9	6.2
El Paso	359,291	424,479	18.1	−10.6	5.1	96.3	40.1	M 80.9	12.0
Hidalgo	181,535	227,853	25.5	−25.4	8.4	74.1	44.3	M 93.3	7.4
Hudspeth	2,372	2,968	25.1	−45.6	11.2	—	43.3	M 90.6	9.9
Jeff Davis	1,483	1,456	− 2.0	−21.1	− 8.4	—	18.1	M 85.5	9.5
Kinney	2,025	2,253	11.2	−32.6	9.4	—	24.7	M 82.4	7.2
Maverick	18,093	22,164	22.5	−15.9	6.9	86.2	66.8	M 97.3	6.6
Presidio	4,842	4,810	− 1.0	−28.3	−11.6	56.8	36.5	M 96.1	7.1
Starr	17,707	20,885	17.9	−23.9	4.8	32.1	34.2	M 95.7	5.9
Terrell	2,006	1,834	− 9.0	−33.3	− 8.7	—	16.3	M 89.9	10.6
Val Verde	27,471	31,943	16.2	−17.4	2.6	90.4	35.0	M 91.9	10.6
Webb	72,859	81,009	11.2	−17.8	− 4.9	96.2	48.7	M 93.0	7.6
Zapata	4,352	4,828	10.9	−22.9	6.2	—	40.1	M 97.2	6.2
Total	2,850,000	3,420,187							

Source: *City and County Fact Book, U.S. Census of Populations,* 1972 and 1977.
Definitions: *Urban Population:* All persons living in places of 2,500 or more. *Foreign Stock:* The foreign-born population and the native population of foreign or mixed parentage. *Net Migration:* The difference between the number of persons moving into a particular area and the number of persons moving away from that area. Estimated by substracting "natural increase" (births−deaths) from the net population change. *Leading Country of Origin:* The country which was the leading source of the foreign stock and its percentage share of the total foreign stock residing in the area.
  *M = Mexico

day seeking residence and/or employment.[2] Briggs, Fogel, and Schmidt's book (1977) is the most comprehensive description of "the Chicano."

Although Chicanos are a significant part of the labor force in every sector of the border economy, labor-force participation rates are generally lower for Chicanos than for people of Anglo descent. This disparity is especially marked between Anglo and Chicano women (Rochín, 1973; Briggs, 1977: 31). In addition, people with Spanish surnames (and other minorities) are far more heavily employed in operative and service jobs, and as laborers, than are Anglos. In 1970, by contrast,

18.7 percent of Anglo males held professional jobs in the Southwest, but only 6.4 percent of Chicanos were professionals (see Table 34-4). Not surprisingly, Chicanos have, in general, lower levels of skills and education than do their Anglo neighbors; thus, the Chicano's search for work takes place primarily in the "secondary" job sector. Since the labor supply for these jobs is abundant, wages tend to be depressed, conditions tend to be poor, and prospects for worker organization are not encouraging.

Labor-force participation is influenced by the unemployment rate. As job seekers get discouraged, they often aban-

Table 34-2. *Farm Population and Farmlands: U.S.-Mexican Border Areas.*

State and County	Farm Population				Farms				Land in Farms			
	Total 1970	Percentage Change 1960-70	Median Family Income 1969	Persons below Low Income Level (percent) 1969	Total 1969	Total 1974	Percentage Change 1964-69	Percentage Change 1969-74	Total Acreage	Total Acreage 1974	Percentage Change 1964-69	Percentage Change 1969-74
Arizona	23,273	−52.9	6,624	32.3	5,890	5,803	− 9.1	− 1.5	38,203	37,944	− 5.8	− .7
Cochise	1,349	−48.0	7,681	18.5	713	721	− 9.9	1.1	2,105	2,112	−13.8	.3
Pima	1,384	−50.5	7,764	24.4	343	328	−13.8	− 4.4	3,727	3,877	−13.6	4.0
Santa Cruz	312	−55.4	—	24.4	126	113	5.9	−10.3	284	286	−14.9	.8
Yuma	1,145	−66.3	10,789	11.8	658	699	15.8	6.2	507	491	− 3.4	− 3.1
California	184,875	−44.7	9,683	11.6	77,875	67,674	− 3.7	−13.1	35,722	33,386	− 3.5	− 5.5
Imperial	1,693	−69.3	9,607	18.9	896	771	− 5.0	−14.0	609	513	2.6	−15.6
San Diego	5,242	−44.4	10,404	11.6	4,081	3,829	− 3.1	− 6.2	616	687	−11.5	11.6
New Mexico	37,487	−35.7	6,450	28.7	11,641	11,282	−18.1	− 3.1	46,792	47,046	− 1.8	.5
Doña Ana	3,688	−38.0	5,894	17.5	768	767	−11.6	− .1	645	482	− 2.5	−25.2
Grant	543	−17.4	9,833	13.1	245	199	2.5	−18.8	1,348	1,188	16.0	−11.9
Hidalgo	375	−54.4	7,278	26.4	151	145	−12.7	− 4.0	1,392	1,363	3.6	− 2.1
Luna	806	−28.4	6,850	39.5	239	241	− 8.1	.8	801	826	−16.4	3.1
Texas	386,174	−44.4	6,483	20.2	213,550	174,068	4.1	−18.5	142,567	134,185	.6	− 5.9
Brewster	107	−74.6	—	34.6	115	94	8.5	−18.3	2,586	2,536	11.3	− 2.0
Cameron	4,215	−60.1	6,287	36.2	1,750	1,324	− .2	−24.3	452	404	6.1	−10.7
Culberson	97	−76.5	—	46.4	80	73	8.1	− 8.7	1,844	1,624	8.9	−11.9
Dimmit	237	−72.0	—	34.6	212	210	24.7	− .9	885	833	13.9	− 5.9
El Paso	506	−84.9	10,176	26.5	452	317	12.2	−29.9	387	446	−24.8	15.3
Hidalgo	5,962	−58.4	6,552	27.2	4.124	2,827	43.8	−31.5	773	849	4.9	9.8
Hudspeth	403	−62.5	4,400	32.0	131	144	− 5.8	9.9	1,737	2,168	− 8.3	24.8
Jeff Davis	186	−35.9	—	11.8	68	63	− 9.3	− 7.4	1,363	1,455	−20.2	6.8
Kinney	142	−74.7	—	16.9	126	93	65.8	−26.2	719	714	− 9.3	− .7
Maverick	284	−53.1	—	9.5	160	134	− 4.2	−16.2	825	893	70.8	8.2
Presidio	170	−70.1	—	85.9	177	134	19.6	−24.3	1,995	1,930	− 8.8	− 3.2
Starr	1,205	−51.3	4,194	35.0	777	784	49.4	.9	591	486	19.5	−17.7
Terrell	108	−70.5	—	19.4	80	72	− 5.9	−10.0	1,448	1,277	9.6	−11.8
Val Verde	237	−68.1	—	27.8	195	195	7.7	—	2,029	2,000	− 4.5	− 1.4
Webb	325	−49.5	—	15.7	305	342	67.7	12.1	1,954	1.943	44.0	− .5
Zapata	123	−44.3	—	56.9	278	294	41.1	5.8	551	520	20.8	− 5.7
Total	34,000											
Average	1,172											

Source: *City and County Fact Book, U.S. Census of Population,* 1972 and 1977.
Definitions: *Median Family Income:* Sum of income received by all family members 14 years old and over. The median divides the distribution into two equal groups. *Poverty Income Level 1969:* Ranged from $1,487 for a female unrelated individual 65 years old living on a farm to $6,116 for a nonfarm family with a male head and seven or more persons. Average for a nonfarm family of four headed by a male was $3,745. Income refers to money income and does not include government support.

don the search. Vernon Briggs, Jr. (1977), indicates how "Census reports show that, in the search for jobs, Chicanos fare less favorably than do Anglos. In 1970, their rate of unemployment in the five [southwestern] states ranged from 25 to over 100 percent larger than that of Anglos . . ." (p. 34). But even overall, the employment situation along the border can best be described as dismal. In 1969, the rate of unemployment was around 5.5 percent of the civilian labor force. By 1975, the rate of unemployment had nearly doubled to around 9.5 percent, with some of the highest rates of unemployment found in the larger counties, including San Diego County (11.6 percent, up from 6.3 percent in 1969), Pima County (7.6 percent, up from 4.0 percent in 1969), and El Paso County (8.7 percent, up from 5.2 percent in 1969).

Labor-Market Conditions

The U.S.-Mexican border region is a rich blend of Indian, Spanish, Mexican, Chicano, and Anglo tradition. And yet it is a troubled region in terms of persistent under- and unemployment in the labor market.

Table 34-3. *Labor-Force Participation and Employment in U.S. Border Counties of the Southwest.*

State and County	Civilian Labor Force 1970	Percentage of Population over 18 Years Old in Civilian Labor Force	1970 Labor Force Males	1970 Labor Force Females	1970 Total Employed	Unemployment 1970	Unemployment 1975
Arizona	641,000	57	401,109	239,891	614,055	4.2	9.7
Cochise	18,559	48	12,005	6,554	17,621	5.1	9.2
Pima	122,311	53	76,616	45,695	117,405	4.0	7.6
Santa Cruz	4,588	57	2,921	1,667	4,416	3.7	13.9
Yuma	20,739	54	13,225	7,514	19.746	4.8	8.1
California	7,992,168	60	4.945,195	3,046,973	7,484,690	6.3	9.9
Imperial	25,257	58	16,619	8,638	23,479	7.0	15.5
San Diego	459,679	49	281,759	177,920	430,495	6.3	11.6
New Mexico	342,482	56	218,825	123,657	322,837	5.7	7.2
Doña Ana	23,024	56	14,739	8,285	21,552	6.4	7.8
Grant	7,358	54	5,231	2,127	6,993	5.0	7.3
Hidalgo	1,561	57	1,084	477	1,505	3.6	4.4
Luna	4,004	57	2,547	1,457	3,676	8.2	8.4
Texas	4,297,786	60	2,692,016	1,605,770	4,141,529	3.6	5.4
Brewster	2,939	55	1,863	1,076	2,822	4.0	2.1
Cameron	43,014	54	26,572	16,442	40,178	6.6	9.4
Culberson	1,292	69	898	394	1,252	3.1	4.5
Dimmit	2,606	52	1,741	865	2,391	8.3	9.5
El Paso	112,825	53	68,299	44,526	106,919	5.2	8.7
Hidalgo	55,321	55	35,146	20,175	52,073	5.9	9.8
Hudspeth	834	63	587	247	805	3.5	4.1
Jeff Davis	602	62	397	205	593	1.5	4.0
Kinney	705	57	479	229	666	5.5	5.3
Maverick	5,068	53	3,213	1,855	4,573	9.8	20.1
Presidio	1,555	52	1,076	479	1,471	5.4	5.6
Starr	4,280	44	2,816	1,464	4,016	6.2	36.6
Terrell	646	54	465	181	637	1.4	3.3
Val Verde	7,290	45	4,595	2,695	6,852	6.1	16.0
Webb	20,360	49	12,886	7,474	18,974	6.8	16.2
Zapata	1,029	38	706	323	983	4.5	11.2
Total	947,446				892,093		

Source: *City and County Fact Book, U.S. Census of Population,* 1972. Unemployment figures from Title V Regional Action Planning Commission Report.
The employed were defined as civilians who were either at work or with a job but not at work. Excluded were housewives, charitable workers, and volunteers.

According to most socioeconomic indicators, the border region on the U.S. side, while it has a far healthier economy than that of Mexico's border states, is significantly underdeveloped and lags substantially behind the rest of the nation in providing stable and growing employment and sufficient incomes. For example, in 12 of Texas's border counties, more than 25 percent of all families had median family incomes below the low-income level.[3] In New Mexico, 18.6 percent of all families fall into this poverty category (see Table 34-5). Although some businesses of relatively healthy economic activity exist, especially in the areas of advanced technology, they have a limited impact in creating jobs.

The proximity of Mexico continues to pose a special set of problems which impede socioeconomic development in the Southwest. The large influx of undocumented workers, especially, may be an important depressant to the wages and income levels of many border residents, although the research of Smith and Newman (1977) tends to downplay the extent to which wages are depressed. Briggs, Jr. (1977, p. 85), notes that although the *bracero* program was officially terminated in 1964, "The detrimental effects of the combined numbers of illegal entrants and commuters upon the economic opportunities for Chicanos cannot be overstated" (see also Table 34-6). The favorable, that is, low, wage levels have attracted manufacturing concerns to the border towns, but a great deal of investment still tends to be too capital intensive to be of much value in contributing to solutions for massive under- and unemployment. The increasing demographic tensions,

Table 34-4. *Occupational Distribution of Men in the Southwest.*

	Men with Spanish Surnames				Anglos	Negroes
Occupation	1930	1950	1960	1970	1970	1970
Professionals	.9%	2.2%	4.1%	6.4%	18.7%	6.9%
Managers	2.8	4.4	4.6	5.2	14.0	3.5
Salesmen	2.4 ⎰	6.5	⎱ 3.6	3.9	9.1	2.5
Clerical workers	1.0 ⎱		⎰ 4.8	6.6	7.2	8.7
Craftsmen	6.8	13.1	16.7	20.8	21.1	15.7
Operative workers	9.1	19.0	24.1	25.4	14.4	26.2
Servicemen	4.0	6.3	7.5	10.5	7.1	17.6
Laborers	28.2	18.7	15.2	12.1	4.7	15.9
Farmers	9.8	5.1	2.4	.9	2.1	0.4
Farm laborers	35.1	24.7	16.8	8.1	1.4	2.4
Total	100.0	100.0	99.8	99.9	99.8	99.8

Sources: 1970: U.S. Bureau of the Census, "Persons of Spanish Surname," 1970 Census, Subject Reports, PC(2)-ID, Table 10, pp. 60–77; Detailed Characteristics, PC(1)-Di, U.S. Summary, Table 224, pp. 746–48; 1930–60: Walter Fogel, "Job Gains of Mexican-American Men," *Monthly Labor Review* 91, no. 10 (October, 1968): 23.

coupled with the limited creation of jobs, result in a depressed labor-market situation.

The growth in job opportunities in the Southwest cannot keep up with the burgeoning population. Unfortunately, many low-skilled jobs, particularly in agriculture and food processing but also in mining, have also disappeared as mechanization has replaced hand labor. The problem is especially acute because most workers in agriculture (primarily Chicanos) are not equipped to engage in much other than unskilled labor activities. Of course the problem is exacerbated by the insufficiency of off-farm jobs and the lack of government attention to training programs and facilities to provide displaced farm workers with new sets of skills. Table 34-4 indicates, for example, that although only 8.1 percent of Mexican American males were employed in farm labor in the Southwest in 1970, as compared with 16.8 percent in 1960, the occupational distribution for these men did not shift significantly toward jobs requiring higher levels of skill or education.

Where a large underemployed, low-skilled labor pool exists, working conditions for those who hold jobs are often poor. It is also such a situation that makes prospects for unionization very dim. Briggs speaks of these difficulties in the context of the garment industry in Texas and New Mexico and of the efforts to unionize farm workers under César Chávez (Briggs, 1977: 42, 87). Quite a number of authors, such as Rochín (1973), Salandini (1964), Weber (1973), and Wollenberg (1969), have told parts of the history of strikes and organizing efforts that have long been a part of the lives of agricultural laborers. In general, "Attempts to organize farmworkers in California have a long history, depicted for the most part as either unstable, volatile, or both. . . . Several reasons can be cited for the failure of these unions. For one, the general problems inherent in low levels of income, uncertain seasonal employment, discrimination, lack of organizing skills, and ineffective communication thwarted labor's attempts to organize effectively against employer wealth and intimidation" (Rochín, 1973).

Table 34-5. *Income and Poverty in U.S. Border Counties of the Southwest.*

State and County	Per Capita Income 1974	Average Annual Change 1969–74	1969 Median Family Income	Percentage of Families below Poverty Level 1969*
Arizona	4,530	8.7	9,185	11.5
Cochise	3,871	8.2	8,333	13.4
Pima	4,643	8.9	8,942	10.8
Santa Cruz	3,638	9.0	7,948	20.0
Yuma	3,935	8.4	8,188	13.6
California	5,114	6.9	10,729	8.4
Imperial	3,479	6.9	8,469	16.2
San Diego	4,837	7.2	10,129	8.6
New Mexico	3,601	7.8	7,845	18.6
Doña Ana	3,162	6.9	7,392	20.7
Grant	3,574	8.5	7,907	11.8
Hidalgo	3,119	9.7	6,564	22.1
Luna	3,055	7.7	6,470	20.5
Texas	4,188	8.1	8,486	14.7
Brewster	2,931	7.7	5,640	27.1
Cameron	2,389	8.3	5,070	38.6
Culberson	2,818	6.1	7,216	18.6
Dimmit	2,015	9.5	4,059	51.0
El Paso	3,423	7.6	7,790	17.4
Hidalgo	2,220	8.1	4,761	42.2
Hudspeth	2,638	9.4	5,314	28.2
Jeff Davis	2,961	8.9	5,590	26.5
Kinney	2,559	10.5	3,899	45.7
Maverick	1,991	8.8	4,508	44.1
Presidio	2,484	8.7	4,184	40.9
Starr	1,680	8.1	3,593	52.3
Terrell	3,355	8.7	6,564	23.6
Val Verde	2,966	8.2	6,472	24.5
Webb	2,329	8.2	4,970	38.5
Zapata	2,012	9.1	3,788	50.6
Average	4,358		6,145	

Source: *City and County Fact Book, U.S. Census of Population*, 1972 and 1977.

*$3,745; see definitions, Table 34-2.

Table 34-6. *Studies of Employment Distribution of Apprehended Mexican Illegal Aliens by Economic Sector.*

Economic Sector*	Study			
	Southwest Border Regional Study† (percent)	Cornelius Study‡ (percent)	North and Houstoun§ (percent)	INS (1976) Data# (percent)
Agriculture	50.6	45.0	26.2	32.8
Manufacturing	10.1	20.8	28.2	33.0
Commerce	22.5	14.0	13.9	—
Construction	3.3	10.6	20.8	8.2
Services	13.3	8.6	10.4	26.0
Other	0.2	1.0	0.4	—
Total	100.0	100.0	99.9	100.0

Source: *Illegal Aliens: Estimating Their Impact on the United States,* Report to the Congress of the United States by the Comptroller General, 1980.
  *Agricultural occupations include farmers and farm workers such as farmhands and laborers, and employment in forestry and fisheries. Manufacturing occupations include operatives, such as sewers and stitchers, laborers, craft workers, and managers and administrators. Commerce includes occupations in transportation, such as truck drivers and retail sales clerks. Construction occupations include craftsmen, operatives, and laborers. Service occupations include private household, food service, health service, and protective service workers.
  †Southwest Border Regional Commission, table 14. Sample size = 691.
  ‡Cornelius, 1978: 54. Sample size = 994.
  §North and Houstoun, p. 113. Sample size = 481.
  #Immigration and Naturalization Service, *Estimated Total Number of Illegal Aliens and Employed Illegal Aliens by INS District,* November 22, 1976. Sample size = 3,817,350.

Since the Agricultural Labor Relations Act now provides a forum for settling disputes and a mechanism for redress for farm workers in California, other protective legislation enacted on behalf of the laborers and civil rights policies and social welfare programs have also contributed toward the improvement of working and living conditions along the border. Collective bargaining, minimum wage requirements, better health and safety standards, and further social legislation are ways of making the Southwest a healthier economic environment for those who have jobs. Many authors agree, though, that a consistent and stringent border policy that would curtail the employment of Mexicans in the United States is the only way to increase employment opportunities and raise the standard of living for legal residents. The dynamics of the border region's labor market are indeed something of a vicious circle: Mexico's closeness and the labor pool it offers attract businesses to the border area; these businesses then provide incentive for further emigration from Mexico—and socioeconomic problems may only compound. A closed border could result in higher wages, but possibly in fewer jobs, too. And a closed border will not provide real growth in economic activity for the Southwest.

1. Another two counties of New Mexico, Eddy and Otero, lie very near the border.
2. Commuters are Mexicans who are permitted to work in the United States with entry permits indicating their desire to become residents of the United States. There are approximately forty thousand commuters who live in Mexico and cross the border to work on the U.S. side. For an informative discussion, see Sosnick (1978: 408-30).
3. Average poverty income level for a nonfarm family of four headed by a male was $3,745 in 1969.

The scope of this overview is limited, briefly covering a complex, comprehensive, and sometimes emotionalized topic which has many ramifications and implications for Borderlands scholars. It primarily introduces the reader to the many issues inherent in American migrant labor and serves as a guide to significant literature and documents which are readily available to prospective researchers and others interested in this field.

Over the last century, migrant labor in America has consisted of many diverse populations: Anglos, blacks, Mexican nationals *(braceros),* Chinese, Japanese, Filipinos, Hindustanis, other immigrant groups, and Mexican and native Americans. These migrants have shared similar fates, as chronicled over the years by historians, sociologists, anthropologists, economists, novelists, journalists, government officials, and countless others. The search for cheap seasonal labor by farmers and agribusiness, combined with the economic needs of displaced American farmers, newly arrived immigrants, and the accessible Mexican labor pool, produced what is known today as migrant agricultural labor. The plight of these

35

Migrant Labor

ROBERTO S. GUERRA
Economic Opportunity Division
Texas Department of Community
Affairs, Austin

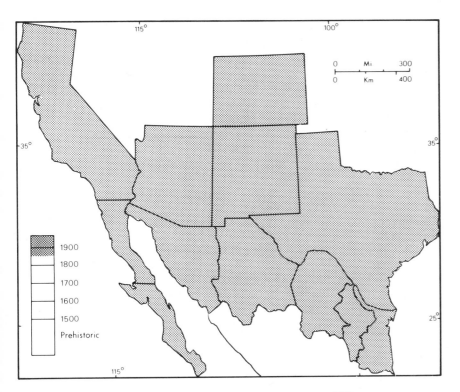

"invisible," "forgotten," and "neglected" peoples has, for the most part, been one of hardship, poverty, and exploitation by public and governmental institutions and employers.

From about 1875 until the 1882 Exclusion Act, agricultural labor was Chinese. The Chinese were then supplanted by Japanese, and later Filipinos, at the turn of the century. Additionally, during the Depression years, Dust Bowl Anglo refugees from Oklahoma, Texas, and other states, displaced from their small farms during the 1930s, resettled and left the migrant stream. This pattern is not so evident among today's minority migrant labor populations.

Mexican people have made an important contribution to the agricultural development of this country, but their history has taken curious twists. Recruited as farm workers in the 1920s, Mexican nationals and many American citizens were repatriated during the Depression years (possibly as "scapegoats" for the country's economic ills). The early 1940s saw the creation of the *bracero* program, a formalized arrangement between the United States and Mexico both to employ Mexican nationals as farm workers, thus relieving manpower shortages created by World War II, and to provide a formalized safety valve for large numbers of unemployed Mexican nationals. This program continued, with brief interruptions, until December, 1964, when the United States terminated the program. Thus, for over twenty years, growers had an unlimited Mexican labor supply. Under these circumstances, it was difficult to improve living and working conditions for migrant agricultural workers.

After 1965, however, foreign workers could be imported only if a real and proven shortage of workers existed. Despite farmers' predictions, shortages of labor did not result as the character and nature of migrant labor changed. The migrant stream then became mostly American citizens, blacks, Chicanos, and poor whites. This era also saw the creation of President Johnson's War on Poverty and other social legislation to alleviate working and living conditions of American poor, including agricultural workers.

Migration Patterns and Ethnicity

Rural America, Inc., estimates that there are nearly five million migrant and seasonal farm workers and dependents in the country today (Spellman, 1977). Although estimates vary, the farm-worker population has historically been composed of ethnic and minority groups. Farm workers who migrate beyond their own state generally follow three main travel patterns or "streams": eastern, midwestern, and western.

The largest and most diverse stream is the midwestern, originating in lower Texas in early spring as Mexican American families arrive to harvest fruits and vegetables in most midwestern and western states. The eastern stream originates in Florida, spreading to the New England states. It is composed predominantly of black workers, although there are also whites, Puerto Ricans, West Indians, and some Mexican Americans; this group consists primarily of individuals instead of traveling families. The western stream, made up

primarily of Mexican Americans, is concentrated in southern California and the Pacific Coast states.

There are, of course, many variations of these patterns; in some instances migrant workers resettle in places other than their original home states. In the 1930s, the "Okies" settled in California. Some Mexican Americans have settled in such states as Washington, Michigan, Minnesota, Ohio, and Illinois.

Literature and Legislative Review

The publication of the novel *The Grapes of Wrath* dramatized the desperate situation of Dust Bowl refugees during the Great Depression and triggered some governmental investigation of agricultural workers' conditions and treatment. This activity marked the beginning of a long and continuous battle to establish minimal protective legislation for migrants.

Perhaps the best documentation of the situation in the 1930s is provided by Carey McWilliams (1942). McWilliams presents a comprehensive analysis of the changes befalling American agriculture and their social consequences. The displaced farm workers, habitual migratory workers, and findings of the La Follette commission are chronicled in detail. Another McWilliams (1935) book focuses on the impact that Dust Bowl refugees from Oklahoma and Texas had on the California migrant labor movement between 1933 and 1937. Both books provide excellent insights into that era's labor problems and contain useful, detailed bibliographies. A more recent publication by Stein (1973) also covers this subject.

A Mexican anthropologist (Gamio, 1930, 1931), through detailed life histories of Mexican immigrants, describes and evaluates the 1918-30 era of immigration from Mexico, touching peripherally on migrant labor. Taylor's (1932) studies of Mexican labor in the United States contain individual accounts of Mexican immigrants settling in California, Texas, Colorado, Pennsylvania, Illinois, and other midwestern agricultural and industrial centers. These studies by Taylor are significant, representing one of the earliest attempts to document the "settling-out" process of Mexican migrant laborers in different parts of the United States.[1]

Although the American migrant labor supply consisted of a diverse group, Mexicans in the early 1940s were treated in a very special way. A formalized agreement in 1942 between Mexico and the United States resulted in the *bracero* program, which continued, with minor interruptions, until 1964. Galarza's (1964) landmark study of the Mexican *bracero* provides a description of this arrangement. Initiated under U.S. Public Law 45, the Mexican Labor Program assured American farmers a steady supply of farm workers through a recruitment and transportation program (Jones, 1945; Swartz, 1945). The *bracero* program, under Public Law 45, was terminated in 1945 but continued informally until 1951, when the Korean conflict created farm-worker shortages. Revived in 1951 under Public Law 78, the program extended until December, 1964, when the *bracero* program was unilaterally terminated by the United States.

Some of the last chapters of Sosnick's (1978) recent volume contain an excellent overview of the various types of Mexican workers in the migrant stream. Samora's (1971) book on the "wetback" contains some migration patterns during this century of Mexican undocumented workers, persons often confused with Mexican American migrant workers.

Unionization and Migrant Labor

Sustained unionization of farm workers has been a relatively recent phenomenon, although sporadic efforts were initiated in the 1920s and 1930s (Jamieson, 1945; Moore, 1965, chap. 11). Agricultural unions have been minimal because of farm workers' mobility, the reluctance of major unions to organize groups with narrow bases of support, and the early discriminatory practices of many labor unions (Grebler, Moore, and Guzman, 1970). The one exception is César Chávez in California, who has struggled since the early 1960s to obtain collective bargaining rights and other protective legislation for farm workers.

The story of César Chávez's unionization efforts is well documented by Mathiessen (1970), Day (1971), Dunne (1967), Nelson (1968), and Sosnick (1978: 297-384). Additionally, the reader is referred to Fodell's (1974) annotated bibliographical essay of books and pamphlets, annual reports and proceedings, unpublished materials, and articles which refer to Chávez, the United Farm Workers, the grape strike and boycotts, and activities of the Migrant Ministry. Chávez's struggle has attained national prominence, but most of his victories have been in California.

When the *bracero* program was phased out, the migrant stream changed to primarily a labor pool of American citizens. Mexican nationals and other foreign farm workers could only be imported through the U.S. Department of Labor's Certification Program, which mandated that no foreign labor could be imported until domestic labor was unavailable for specific harvests. Moreover, the lapse of the *bracero* program coincided with a sharp and continuing rise in Mexican illegal immigration, but this influx was also directed to nonagricultural employment in large urban areas across the country. Schmidt (1964), Briggs (1973*b*, 1974, 1975*b*, 1975*c*), Samora (1971), North (1971), and others provide excellent insights and analyses of changes in the labor market during and after this period.

Issues of the 1980s

A continuing issue for the farm labor population is the increasing mechanization of agribusiness and its concurrent social and economic impact on farm workers. As technology and mechanization become more intensified, the need for migrant labor decreases, although some writers contend that hand labor will still be an integral part of agribusiness for many years (Moore, 1965). More recently, the University of California (1978), Division of Agricultural Sciences, published a collection of papers addressing technological change, farm mechanization, and agricultural employment. Hall's (1968) bibliography focuses on agricultural mechanization and labor, providing excellent background materials. An Arizona case study by Padfield and Martin (1965) dealt with mechanization in specific terms.

The mechanization of agricultural labor is peripheral to a number of other migrant-labor concerns: alternative employment opportunities; the relocation and "settling-out" processes which have occurred, and will increasingly occur; and the whole range of government policy toward farm workers and their families.

Few studies document the relocation and settling-out processes of migrant workers. Choldin and Trout (1969) looked at Michigan urban residents, former migrant workers who dropped out of the migrant stream and relocated outside their home-base state. Under a federally funded project, Favors (1975) investigated the settling-out processes of various migrant subgroups and developed an agricultural continuum more adequately describing them. The President's Commission on Mental Health, in its *Task Panel Report on Migrant and Seasonal Farm Workers* (1978), felt that settling out and relocation among migrants were accelerating in certain parts of the country. This whole issue needs additional study, since changing migration patterns have significant implications for government policies toward farm workers and border agriculture.

Private and Public Assistance to Migrant Workers

Over the years, efforts to assist the farm workers have been made by various sources. Church groups, such as the American Friends Service Committee, the Migrant Ministry of the National Councils of Churches of Christ, the National Advisory Committee on Farm Labor, the Catholic Rural Life Conference, and the Campaign for Human Development, among others, have actively and consistently addressed the concerns of farm workers. Many states have created migrant committees or commissions, but most of these efforts have been ineffective.

National organizations and committees, though, have generally been more supportive of the agricultural worker. The NAACP, LULAC, the GI Forum, and other such traditional special-interest groups continually advocate for migrant farm workers. In recent times, however, assisting and establishing policy for agricultural labor has been shifted to the federal government.

The migrant laborer has been the subject of many governmental hearings and reports initiated as a result of the popular interest caused by exposés such as Steinbeck's *The Grapes of Wrath* (1939), the CBS documentary *Harvest of Shame* (1960), and *A Day Without Sunshine* (1976). These reports exposed the hardships encountered by migrant families, triggering governmental action and assistance, although little has been done toward a national solution for such long-range needs as migrant poverty and illiteracy.

In the late 1930s, agricultural laborers first received national attention. Two presidential commissions were formed during the 1950s: the President's Commission on Migratory Labor (1951) of President Truman and the President's Committee on Migratory Labor (1954) of President Eisenhower. These two landmark commissions laid the groundwork for some of the legislation enacted in the early 1960s to improve the living and working conditions of American agricultural laborers. The 1964 Economic Opportunity Act mandated federal intervention to assist farm workers in education, housing, training, and other areas.

Various congressional committees today address the issue of migrant and seasonal farm workers. Most prominent of these are the Senate Committee on Labor and Public Welfare, Subcommittee on Migratory Labor, and the House Committee on Education and Labor, Subcommittee on Agricultural Labor. These subcommittees' reports provide a detailed documentation of agricultural labor issues, concerns, programs, legislation, socioeconomic and health conditions, and other related topics. They also periodically keep national interest focused on the plight of the agricultural worker.

Two other recent reports of a presidential commission touch on migrant labor in the United States. The President's National Advisory Commission on Rural Poverty produced *The People Left Behind* (1967), which includes the commission's recommendations, and *Rural Poverty in the United States* (1968), which presents a number of background papers. The President's Commission on Mental Health of 1978, despite its focus, provides an excellent background on the migrant and seasonal farm worker in America. It also analyzes federal programs that have an impact on the farm worker and submits a variety of well-documented recommendations to improve the overall structure and delivery of social, health, employment, and educational services to agricultural workers.

In spite of governmental awareness of migrant conditions, however, farm workers and their dependents still remain economically disadvantaged; poorly educated, nourished, and housed; politically powerless; at times culturally and geographically isolated; and extremely vulnerable to social and economic changes beyond their control. Increased mechanization and technology have created a sense of uncertainty about their future livelihood. Adding to the farm workers' dilemma is their exclusion from many federal and state laws concerning fair labor practices, minimum-wage laws, collective bargaining, and minimum health and housing standards. In some cases, administrative directives deprive them of much-needed assistance. Existing laws to protect the farm worker are, at times, not enforced, and most attempts at unionization have met with little success.

General Readings on Migrant Farm Workers

The living and working conditions of the agricultural worker have been well chronicled in the last two decades. In addition to the aforementioned studies and government reports, many books describe the American farm worker's plight. Although

not inclusive, the following list is representative of this period (1960-78):

Hard Traveling: Migrant Farm Workers in America (Dunbar and Kravitz, 1976)
Wandering Workers: The Story of American Migrant Farm Workers and Their Problems (Heaps, 1968)
No Harvest for the Reaper: The Story of the Migratory Agricultural Workers in the United States (Hill, 1960)
The Slaves We Rent (Moore, 1965)
The Harvesters: Story of the Migrant People (Shotwell, 1961)
They Harvest Despair: The Migrant Farm Worker (Wright, 1965)
Hired Hands: Seasonal Farm Workers in the United States (Sosnick, 1978)

Robert Coles has produced two best-selling books which have aroused the American social conscience: *The Migrant Farmer: A Psychiatric Study* (1965) and *Uprooted Children: The Early Life of Migrant Workers* (1970). Dr. Coles has also testified before several congressional committees, shocking people with his findings on the living conditions of many eastern-seaboard farm workers.

Summary

Although selective and limited, this survey indicates a great reservoir of information concerning the plight of migrant workers in America. However, one should not assume that, because data are available defining and documenting their

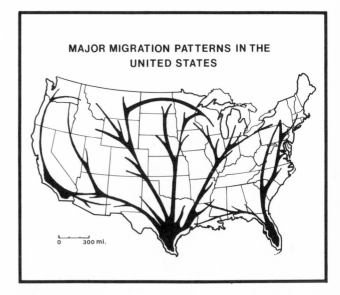

Fig. 35-1. *Major migration patterns in the United States. Source: National Migrant Referral Project, Inc. (Austin, Texas, 1978).*

problems, their substandard conditions have subsided appreciably. Just as the report of the President's Commission on Mental Health on migrant and seasonal farm workers (1978) concludes: "Despite the billions of dollars spent by the federal government over the past fifteen years, American farmworkers still live and work under conditions which are cruel and harsh by any standards . . ." (p. 1196).

Studies on rural poverty in the South (Rungeling et al., 1977) and along the U.S. border (Stoddard, 1978c) show the desperation of families from these two areas to merely survive by remaining in the migrant farm-worker stream (see map of migration patterns and origins, Fig. 35-1). As long as agribusiness needs for farm labor exist (and they will in the foreseeable future), migrant workers will be tied to a cycle of poverty. Migrant American farm workers will continue to be confused with the stream of illegal Mexican aliens drawn to the U.S. agricultural sector, and this factor alone will reduce legislative and judicial support for public programs to better their quality of life.

Included in the many issues concerning migrant labor which need to be researched are the differential treatment and legal guarantees covering farm workers on a state-to-state comparative basis (see Craddock, 1976) and the general impact of mechanization on farm labor.

Alternate occupations and life-styles for displaced workers need to be explored, as do relocation and "settling out" of migrant labor, the increasing and ever-present role of government and legislation, inflation's impact on migrants and the U.S.-Mexican immigration dilemma. On the other hand, promising new developments in agricultural demand and the energy field can open opportunities for this segment of society. The whole issue of agricultural migrant labor is not yet a static one. The future promises to be dynamic and challenging.

---

1. "Settling out" refers to the process whereby migrant families ultimately establish permanent residency in areas to which they had previously migrated on a yearly basis.

Section IV. Politics, the Law, and Demography

Political/ Demographic Overview

C. RICHARD BATH
*Department of Political Science
University of Texas, El Paso*

36

Any assessment of Borderlands political and legal problems must recognize initially the existence of two separate and historically different political structures. In the literature, observers seem to stress the interrelationships and interdependency between them, which in many respects offer a key to understanding particular phenomena within the social and economic spheres. Nevertheless, it should be reiterated that these political systems are distinct and autonomous, merely happening to lie in juxtaposition to each other. And Borderlands observers and scholars who wish to understand the mechanisms by which these political systems are articulated must possess more than just a nodding acquaintance with the system on each side of the international boundary.

Some major differences in the political and legal systems of Mexico and the United States are readily apparent. Although both are ostensibly federal, Mexico's operates as a strongly centralized and personalized structure in which state and municipal roles are subordinated to the needs and dictates of the governmental leadership in Mexico City. The federal system within the United States is a

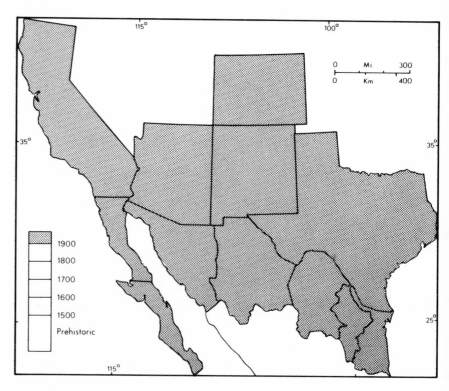

"marble-cake" situation in which selected issues are dominated by states while others are the province of national policy. On this side, power tends to be more diffuse and fragmented than in Mexico, seemingly lacking in cohesion and therefore much more difficult to diagnose, analyze, and predict in specific sensitive areas. In many important areas of public concern, power may be either unused or insufficient to crystalize public sentiment so that a particular policy might be implemented with public support and lasting impact.

At first glance, the Mexican system appears to have a far more visible and centralized mechanism for establishing consensus on a given issue, but even on this subject the scholar is left to inferential conclusions because of a paucity of information on how decisions which result in the adoption of public policies are reached. Unless a researcher has access to key policy informants or participants in Mexico, the nature of the decision-making process will more than likely remain a secret. On the other hand, the sheer quantity of public information available on a given issue in the United States creates problems of selection and discrimination from the plethora of sources, documentary evidence, public commentary, and opinions of key decision makers. Thus, comparable data from these two neighboring countries might be substantively similar and yet vastly different in impact of policy.

Dissimilarities in the legal systems of Mexico and the United States also complicate legal comparisons and analysis. Whereas the Mexican legal system is based on the codified European law, the U.S. system derives its base from the adversary common-law practices. To illustrate, the current debate over universal human rights for U.S. citizens focuses on their distrust of the Mexican judicial and penal system and the reported mistreatment of U.S. citizens in Mexican jails. On the other hand, one of the major concerns of the Mexican government is to protect the undocumented workers in the United States and to ensure their human rights through public denouncements of illegal or unhuman treatment while they reside in this country. Such issues clearly show that the resolution of political and legal controversies across the binational border must include the political structure and nature of each legal system as well as existing relationships between governments or leaders of the two adjoining nation states.

In this section an attempt has been made to cover some of the most crucial political, legal, and demographic subjects in which border observers or Borderlands scholars have focused their interest and research. While the authors have made every effort to be as inclusive as possible in the space available, many aspects were, by necessity, excluded. The coverage given many times reflects the concerns with recent developments or limited perspectives. Little attention is given to land-use policy or law, although recent agreements between the two border nations include guidelines for solving the effects of decertification along their common border. This topic is so new it has received little attention from political scientists or legal scholars. Likewise, recent events appear to link the political systems on both sides of the border to organized crime, although far more evidence will have to be uncovered before such relationships can be accurately demonstrated.

Readers will note that on certain subjects, such as political activity and voting patterns, information for Mexico is not included for the simple reason that such information is not readily available. And although West's article on border linkages demonstrates the type of relationships necessary to carry on the functional aspects of border jurisdictions, a great void exists in listing and categorizing the many interest groups which have influence over border activity and policy as well as their veto power over activities by border entities. Some interest groups may have visible and potent political power in local issues and have little or no impact beyond the city limits of a border city. Others may be far removed from the physical border but have almost exclusive control over segments of border life. For example, the position taken by Zero Population Growth (ZPG) from Washington, D.C., against illegal Mexican aliens reflects that organization's attempts to influence policy in an area in which it has no clientele. Many political agreements are made in far-off Washington, D.C., or México, D.F., which determine landownership, immigration quotas and standards, import-export duties, and even the monetary policies and exchange rates between the countries. Although many talk about border interdependency, because of the number of exchanges of goods, services, and people between the two countries, in the final analysis it must be recognized that border statutes and restrictions will be made at the federal level of the respective nations.

Because of the close association of border policy with demographic characteristics of Mexican border regions, chapters dealing with the problems of urbanization, migration, and some quasi-legal aspects of cross-border movements of Mexican citizens are included elsewhere. Among the demographic characteristics and trends that have substantial socioeconomic effects on a region are the size, growth rate, density, and geographic distribution of the population; the ratio of the dependent population to the labor force and the ratio of males to females; and the distribution of the population by age, income, education, ethnicity, and race. These variables affect economic development, the physical environment, social interaction, and the demand for and techniques required to provide governmental services such as education, roads, public transportation, subsidized housing, welfare, law enforcement, fire protection, water, public health programs, and pollution control. Perhaps no other region in the world contains such a sharp demographic contrast between two of its parts as the U.S.-Mexican Borderlands. The Mexican area has the high fertility, high growth rate, and very rapid urbanization commonly found in developing countries.

The U.S. area, by comparison, has low fertility, low growth, and an already predominantly urban population. When one realizes that fertility, mortality, and migration are the components of population growth rates, it becomes immediately apparent that demographic characteristics are closely aligned with border congestion and increased migration—whether legal or illegal—across adjoining borders. Thus, the demographic processes are inextricably linked with political and legal efforts to resolve emergent socioeconomic issues. It is quite clear that if even the lowest projections of population growth for Mexico are attained, the resolution of current political problems associated with the U.S.-Mexican border are very insignificant in comparison to those which must be faced by federal, state, and local border jurisdictions before the end of the twentieth century.

Public administration comprises all activities that carry out the policies of elected officials and some activities associated with the development of those policies (Starling, 1977: 1). Such a definition stresses administrative involvement in both formulation and implementation of public policy. A recent survey assessing Borderlands research in political science observed that "the subdiscipline of public administration has not been visibly responsive to problems in the Borderlands region" (Bath, 1975: 64). While the study of Borderlands policy formulation and implementation has received limited attention, public administrators interested in the border might identify profitable research areas by reviewing selected studies from other disciplines which touch on some traditional and contemporary concerns of public administration at the local level. This review will give special attention to studies published in English which deal with local administration and coordination of organized activity along the border.[1] Following a brief discussion of the border administration's political environment, this chapter reviews selected studies of Mexican border cities, twin cities on the Texas-Mexican and Arizona-Mexican borders, and Chicanos and politics.

37

Public Administration and Local Coordination

JONATHAN P. WEST
Department of Politics and Public Affairs
University of Miami

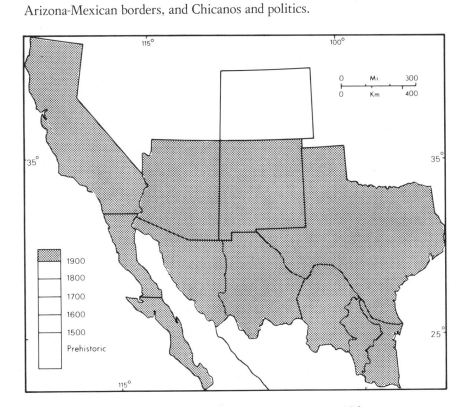

The Environment of Border Administration

Since organizations do not operate in a vacuum, public administrators need knowledge of governmental institutions, power, processes, and relationships. These cannot be understood without an awareness of the basic differences between Mexican and U.S. political systems. Scholars studying modern Mexico generally agree about the structure and operating characteristics of Mexico's political system. Mexican political machinery is described by Brandenburg (1964), Cline (1963), Casanova (1967), Fernandez (1969), Padgett (1966), Scott (1964), Vernon (1963), and others. A useful summary of many studies on the Mexican political system is offered by Needleman and Needleman (1969). Harmon (1977) has compiled an annotated guide to government and politics in Mexico.

While local and comparative and community studies will be the primary focus of this chapter, a few studies of the national bureaucracy in Mexico deserve attention. For example, Ebenstein's (1945) early work on public administration in Mexico briefly examines administrative control, planning, and the civil service; Scott (1955, 1971) describes the operation of Mexico's budget system; and Grimes and Simmons's (1969) study of bureaucracy and political control in Mexico points to the changing character of the bureaucracy in the direction of the expert or technician instead of the politically oriented members of the Partido Revolucionario Institucional (PRI). Grindle (1977) emphasizes that public administrators trained in technical and managerial skills who also possess political skills are increasingly important in policy making. Purcell (1975) uses the framework of political-system analysis and decision-making process in her excellent case study of how and why a particular public policy (the constitutional provision for profit sharing) was made and implemented in Mexico in the 1960s. Insights can also be gleaned from Smith's (1969) doctoral dissertation on Mexico's administrative process, Poitras's (1973) research on the Social Security Institute, Gruber's (1971) exploration of career patterns of Mexico's political elite, Tuohy's (1973) discussion of the impacts of centralism within the Mexican system, Anderson and Cockcroft's (1966) analysis of control and cooperation in Mexican politics, Drake's (1970) examination of Mexican regionalism, Craig's (1971) assessment of the *bracero* program, Greenburg's (1970) analysis of the Ministry of Water Resources, and Grindle's (1977) study of the National Popular Subsistence Corporation. The works of Kantor (1969: 11-54), Fagen and Tuohy (1972: 18-41), Craig (1980: 691-701), Monson (1973: 594-614), Camp (1971: 188-214; 1979: 417-41), Tuohy (1974: 289-307), and Ugalde (1970: 85-133) also have sections touching on administrative concerns. The remainder of this review will examine studies and governmental characteristics at the subnational level.

The structural and operating characteristics of Mexico's political system and the way they differ from those in the United States are important in considering local decision making and administration along the border. For example, Professors Mecham (1940) and Spain (1956: 620-32) point out that Mexican federalism is not U.S. federalism, and Cardenas (1963, 1965) indicates how Mexican *municipios* differ from U.S. municipal jurisdictions. Unlike the United States, the bulk of major decisions affecting the local community in Mexico are made by "outside holders of political and economic power" (Ugalde, 1970: xviii; Klapp and Padgett, 1960: 402; Price, 1973b: 44).

In Mexico, centralization means that each subordinate level in the federal-state-local government chain is weaker, controls fewer resources, and performs fewer functions than the level above. Dillman (1970b) best describes this condition:

Local officials can be removed from their positions by the governor. This does not mean that state governments are strong political entities; on the contrary, they are of slight importance both constitutionally and politically. Important decisions commonly are made at the national level and implemented by federal agencies. If states administer programs, they do so as agents of federal authority. [P. 505]

This system of outside control constrains border municipalities in solving their problems. Such barriers are evident in the collection and use of public monies, where local officials lack sufficient revenues, since local taxes often accrue to higher authorities and "the municipalities, as a rule, cannot directly control their budgets, which . . . must be approved in the state capital" (Dillman, 1970b: 505). While financial resources and decisional latitude at subnational levels are severely circumscribed because of centralization in Mexico, Alisky's studies of state and local government stress that such units can provide vital daily services and serve as a link between the citizenry and the national capital. Alisky (1963a, 1963b, 1971a, 1971b) has provided descriptive guides to the border-state governments of Sonora, Nuevo León, and Baja California. He also discusses the role of Mexico's special districts—the municipal civic betterment boards and federal betterment boards—as the financial right arms of municipalities (Alisky, 1965, 1970). Other studies suggest that once in office, local officials have a certain amount of independence as long as they act in conformity with or fail to antagonize their superiors in state or federal governments (Graham, 1968: 52; Scott, 1964: 47; Furlong, 1972: 62).

A number of local comparative and community studies have been conducted in the border area which indirectly provide insights on administrative matters. I will select and briefly summarize six key studies of Mexican border cities and then examine several more dealing with twin cities which straddle both sides of the international border.

Studies of Mexican Border Cities

Of the six studies to be reviewed dealing directly or indirectly with Mexican border cities, two were conducted by political scientists (Purcell and Purcell, 1974; Furlong, 1972), who analyze the "organizational capacities" and "political processes" of Mexican local governments; two others are the work of sociologists (Ugalde, 1970; Klapp and Padgett, 1960), who focus on "group conflict" and "power structure";

one is by an anthropologist (Price, 1973a, 1973b), who discusses the "symbiosis" of political units along the international boundary; and one is by a historian (Martínez, 1978), who uses a long-term "evolutionary" framework in analyzing the growth of a major border city. The excellent work of Cardenas (1963, 1965), while not reviewed here, is essential background for understanding local government in Mexico.

Susan and John Purcell (1974) in a survey of information gathered in 45 Mexican community studies (including a few in the border region), attempted to explain the distribution of resources in the Mexican political system from the viewpoint of the local community by focusing on the relationship between local organizational capacities and levels of benefits to the community. This study emphasizes the importance in resource acquisition of a local system's capacity to create a community-wide political organization which cultivates linkages between itself and higher authorities in the state and federal governments.

Furlong (1972) investigated 10 cities in the northern Mexican state of Sonora and compared them to 25 cities throughout Peru. He examined the formal government structure; the attitudes of public officials; the municipalities' capabilities to perform extractive, distributive, and regulatory functions; and patterns of political socialization, recruitment, participation, and conflict. His study emphasized two major barriers to local political solutions of problems: the previously mentioned restrictions on municipal activities because of lack of money, and creation of functional agencies at the national level designed to resolve problems without participation of local officials.

Unlike the two comparative studies by the Purcells and Furlong, the four remaining studies deal with single communities located on or near the border. Antonio Ugalde's (1970) excellent book on Ensenada examined group conflict and the conflict-solving processes used in this city. He identifies the plurality of mechanisms whereby labor-management relations have been routinized; the crucial role of the PRI, which contributes to societal integration and reduces social tensions; and the proliferation of poorly coordinated federal agencies, each of which operates on a personalistic basis. Differing with Vernon (1963), who characterizes Mexico's dilemma as government's struggle between rising citizen demands and the economic system's inability to generate resources to satisfy these demands, Ugalde thinks that the economy can produce the necessary resources to meet urgent demands. However, he attributes the scarcity of public resources to the inefficiencies of uncoordinated bureaucratic machinery and the diversion of public funds to the private use of bureaucratic functionaries (Ugalde, 1970: 182). His sections on bureaucratic behavior and the functioning of local, state, and federal governments are of particular interest to students of public administration.

A reputational study of the power structure and decision-making process in Tijuana was conducted by Klapp and Padgett (1960) in the late fifties. They found that no single group within the city ran things and that major power sources were either outside the community (in Mexicali, the state capital, or Mexico City) or outside the structure of government institutions. The Tijuana power structure was found to be composed primarily of businessmen who operated through informal liaisons and personal connections. While Tijuana was substantially influenced by southern California, Klapp and Padgett point out the weakness of formal political integration between San Diego and Tijuana. However, subsequent work by Price (1973a: 78) suggests that this integration has increased since they wrote nearly two decades ago.

John Price's more recent community studies of Tijuana (1973a) and the neighboring community of Tecate (1973b) are significant contributions to the Borderlands literature. The former summarizes urbanization trends in northern Mexico, describes the history of and contemporary life in Tijuana, explores special problems (smuggling and prison life) of that city, and compares tourist-oriented Tijuana with industry-oriented Tecate. The concluding chapters in Price's book (1973a) are more theoretical and useful in that they provide keen insights into the various roles played by the border, including that of cultural adaptation and international symbiosis. His more limited study of Tecate (1973b) shows a city whose development pattern is the antithesis of that of Tijuana. Tecate was deliberately kept small to avoid pollution, and it developed manufacturing industries to avoid dependence on outside tourism. Price found that Tecate's border location had no direct impact on city politics, although indirect influences from the United States in the form of social and economic ties were important. Tecate was able to avoid the pattern of many Mexican border towns because of its relatively isolated location and history of self-determination.

The most recent of these studies of Mexican border cities is Oscar Martínez's (1978) perceptive analysis of Ciudad Juárez. He traces the city's 130-year growth from a small Mexican settlement into a "boom town" of over seven hundred thousand people, illustrating in the process how the city's economy has a strong external orientation and how vulnerable Mexican border communities are to external conditions. One of the most interesting sections of this work is an examination of the Programa Nacional Fronteriza, the Border Industrialization Program, and the *articulos gancho* project, but Martínez concludes that the results of these policies have been mixed and that further efforts are required to successfully integrate the Mexican frontier into the national economy. While primary attention is centered on Juárez, the book provides brief but useful comparisons with other Mexican frontier cities to illustrate border-wide patterns. In this sense, its value transcends that of a single case study, and some insights are provided concerning the general workings of international boundaries.

These six works, together with those of Cárdenas (1963, 1965), would provide useful background as a starting point for public administrators who might wish to apply the theory and methodology of their field in the Mexican border setting.

Numerous scholars from a variety of disciplines have conducted studies in the "paired" or "twin" cities dotting the nineteen-hundred-mile binational border. Our brief analysis of selected studies with administrative implications will be limited to those conducted on both the Texas-Mexican and Arizona-Mexican borders.

Studies of Texas-Mexican Border Cities

Two of the most valuable contributions to border research are the sociological studies by D'Antonio et al. (1961) and D'Antonio and Form (1965), which show how the institutional structures representing the power elite in El Paso differ substantially from those in neighboring Ciudad Juárez. The power elite in Juárez is described as more concentrated and less diverse, with those at the apex of the power pyramid serving primarily in formal government positions; on the other hand, El Paso's power structure is seen as pluralistic, with leaders of economic and social organizations sharing power with those filling official government positions. On the U.S. side, significant social changes undertaken on behalf of the community were often instigated, approved, and implemented using private resources and without the approval or assistance of government office holders. In Juárez, formal governmental authorities are expected to make and execute all significant community decisions. D'Antonio and Form (1965) describe the personal characteristics and methods of operation of influential citizens in both communities. They point out that influential people in Juárez have a better understanding of political/social institutions and cultural values in the United States than El Paso leaders had of institutions and values in Mexico. However, when "successful" bicultural relations occurred between Juárez and El Paso, the authors note, there was a pronounced tendency for Mexican representatives to defer to the values and requests of American leaders. Although substantive portions of D'Antonio and Form's study may now be out of date, their generalizations about relations among elite groups and power structures of the two cities are still valid, as substantiated by a recent study of influential citizens of El Paso and Ciudad Juárez (Stoddard et al., 1979). A team of scholars representing both Mexico and the United States, and the disciplines of sociology, anthropology, history, and public administration, obtained the leaders' reactions to the "Tortilla Curtain" episode which occurred in the fall of 1978. An intensive analysis of how local informal networks across the border circumvent the restrictive federal policies invoked by each country was further extended into the information sources and contact frequencies of public- and private-sector elites. These types of comparative studies continue to be illuminating in showing the informal circumvention of official command and communication channels.

Other studies have examined the interactions between the twin cities along the Texas-Mexican border strip. McConville (1965) discusses interdependence and cooperation in El Paso-Juárez. The symbiotic ties between a pair of cities in the lower Rio Grande Valley are discussed by Dillman (1969a). These two studies are helpful in understanding cultural dynamics in a border setting.

Natural disasters affecting residents on both sides of the border offer unique opportunities to compare the reactions of twin cities as they mobilize disaster relief operations. Disaster studies in the border region have been conducted by Clifford (1955, 1956) and Stoddard (1961). Clifford analyzes the differing responses to the devastating Rio Grande flood of 1954 in the twin border cities of Eagle Pass, Texas, and Piedras

Negras, Coahuila. In Piedras Negras, Clifford finds that the citizenry relied more heavily on kinship ties than upon relief organizations for assistance. Further, the cultural values of Mexican officials made them reluctant to accept help from relief sources, since accepting such aid was seen as questioning their ability to provide the necessary assistance to needy victims in Piedras Negras. In Eagle Pass, neighborhood cooperation and community-wide relief structures were quickly organized and readily used by those in need. Stoddard (1961) reports a similar negative reaction to Anglo-dominated relief organizations among the Mexican American population affected by the 1958 Rio Grande flood. In a subsequent analysis Stoddard observes: "The conclusions made from this investigation. . . were that the manner in which the aid was extended and the social relationships extant between the giver and receiver were the critical criteria for seeking relief help, and not the quality or quantity of goods or services offered . . ." (1969: 484).

Richard Bath, a political scientist, draws on the concepts of interdependency prevalent in the field of international relations and applies them to the El Paso-Juárez microcosm. He concludes that while the microcosm does possess most of the attributes of interdependency attributed to global politics, the resolution of major issues "will more likely be within the framework of North-South conflict than by common perceptions of interdependency" (Bath, 1978a: 25). Another attempt to apply interdependency theory was undertaken by Bath, Carter, and Price (1977), who prepared three case studies from the El Paso-Juárez region dealing with law enforcement, regulation of air pollution, and transportation. In three separate studies, Thomas Price (1977) explores the possibility of an international role for local governments by focusing on an incident involving the international transportation system between El Paso and Juárez, Marshall Carter (1978) studies the transnational dimension of local law enforcement in El Paso-Juárez, and Richard Bath (1974b) examines the problem of air pollution in the El Paso-Juárez region from an ecosystemic perspective. The problems of air pollution are more comprehensively treated in Applegate and Bath (1974), which contains a collection of papers presented at the First Binational Symposium on Air Pollution along the U.S.-Mexico Border.

A few studies have examined political activities and attitudes at the subcommunity level of the neighborhood or barrio. Ugalde (1974) analyzed the urbanization process in Juárez, focusing on one small barrio. He found that residents were not marginal to the political system; instead, they made demands for services, voted in elections, participated in political groups, and had some knowledge of the functioning of the political system. On the other side of the border, Stoddard (1973b) explored the adjustment patterns of Mexican American families experiencing residential relocation in the Chamizal area of El Paso. These residents were less concerned about both the distance from their dwellings to community agencies and the physical characteristics of their new living unit than they were about the preservation of social relationships developed in the mini-neighborhoods of the barrio.

An important comparative study on the border resulted from a two-year cooperative effort by the Institute for Urban Studies of the University of Houston and the Instituto Tecnológico y de Estudios Superiores de Monterrey. This project, funded by the Tinker Foundation of New York, contained a component on intergovernmental and international relations. The objective of this component was to examine the process and patterns of contact and cooperation among border public officials and administrators in five separate twin-city complexes on the Texas-Mexican border. Within each of the twin-city complexes the study sought to identify any formal or informal agreements between contiguous border-city governments; the extent, type, subject, and source of initiation of contacts between officials and agencies in both cities; the role of professional, social, business and personal associations as an arena for meeting people working in the twin cities; the role of "community influentials" in public policy decisions; the compatibility of goals pursued by government officials on both sides of the border; and the extent that public officials are knowledgeable concerning government activities in the twin cities. Special emphasis was placed on determining how and in what policy areas border officials interact with one another and delineating those factors which promote bicommunity cooperation in meeting the common problems of these border cities (West and Sloan, 1976*a*, 1976*b*).

Preliminary findings from this exploratory research are reported by Sloan and West (1976*b*), who examine cooperation among border officials in Laredo and Nuevo Laredo. Building on this case study, the authors collected additional data on informal policy making among twin-city officials in four other twin-city complexes in the lower Rio Grande Valley (Sloan and West, 1977), and West (1979) subsequently replicated this study along the Arizona-Mexican border in both Nogaleses and Douglas-Agua Prieta. In these studies the authors describe the interactions, attitudes, and policy behavior of border officials. They stress the feelings of vulnerability among border officials to outside decision makers, describe the patterns of contact among official counterparts in twin cities, point out the use of informal as opposed to formal agreements to achieve policy cooperation, and identify factors which affect policy cooperation among border-city officials. Table 37-1 summarizes the major problems identified by officials in these seven twin-city areas, and Table 37-2 reports the comparative strength of factors deemed important in facilitating cooperation in each paired city.

Among the factors found to be helpful in explaining variations in border relations among twin cities were characteristics of officials (language, ethnic background, kinship patterns, and turnover rates), the officials' interaction network (visiting and friendship patterns, work-related contact, and shared membership in social and professional organizations), and attitudes of officials (perceived interdependence, feelings of vulnerability, and shared policy priorities). As a consequence of these and other factors, officials in the twin cities have learned to cooperate with each other in such fields as law enforcement, fire control, public health, education, trans-

portation, and public works. The cooperation across the formal boundary line is built upon informal liaisons among border officials seeking to mutually resolve their common problems. Yet there is more cooperation among some border cities than others. For example, in Laredo-Nuevo Laredo and Eagle Pass-Piedras Negras there is a relatively high level of cooperation, while relatively low levels of cooperation were found in McAllen-Reynosa and Del Rio-Ciudad Acuña. Moderate levels of cooperation were discovered in Brownsville-Matamoros on the Texas-Mexican border and in both Nogaleses and Douglas-Agua Prieta on the Arizona-Mexican border.

Informal policy cooperation is the most useful means of handling daily routine problems of a border community; however, local officials often lack sufficient resources or adequate authority to implement permanent solutions to more complex border-related problems (for example, smuggling of aliens, drugs, and contraband). As these more complicated problems are shifted from local to state or federal levels for solution, an incredibly intricate web of government structures is likely to become involved. External decision makers are often insensitive to needs of the border cities and may make decisions which have disastrous effects on twin communities if they restrict the flow of commerce over the border (for example, Operation Intercept). It is not suprising, then, that officials in the border setting feel vulnerable to the effects of decisions by outside (state and federal) policy makers. However, concern about the lack of "border awareness" among state and federal policy makers is more widespread (or more openly acknowledged) among border officials on the U.S. side than it is by their Mexican counterparts (Sloan and West, 1977; West, 1979). Given these attitudes, one can understand why border officials strive whenever possible to fashion local solutions to their problems through informal understandings that do not require the participation of higher levels of government.

As twin cities grow larger, it is predictable that there will be more irritants and a greater need for more complex cooperation. The study by Sloan and West (1977) has not yet been replicated in the growing El Paso-Juárez area, and the patterns there might be quite different. Indeed, Bath (1978*a*: 11) has noted that "observation does not confirm the amount of interaction (in El Paso-Juárez) found in the two Laredos." More comparative studies are needed which use a common methodology to collect and analyze extensive data drawn from several twin cities if we are to better understand attitudes and behavior of policy makers and administrators along the border.

Studies of Arizona-Mexican Border Cities

The paired cities of the Nogaleses and Douglas-Agua Prieta, situated on the Arizona-Mexican border, have provided a research laboratory for economists, geographers, political scientists, historians, sociologists, and anthropologists who have conducted comprehensive studies of land use (Gildersleeve, 1974; McCleneghan and Gildersleeve, 1964, 1965*b*; and

Table 37-1. *Twin-City Officials' Perceptions of Major Problems Facing Their Communities.*

Problem Area	Texas-Mexican Border Cities																Arizona-Mexican Border Cities							
	Brownsville (N=81)		Matamoros (N=77)		Eagle Pass (N=74)		Piedras Negras (N=86)		Del Rio (N=74)		Ciudad Acuña (N=72)		McAllen (N=69)		Reynosa (N=62)		Nogales, Arizona (N=60)		Nogales, Sonora (N=38)		Douglas (N=62)		Agua Prieta (N=58)	
	%	Rank	%	Rank	%	Rank	%	Rank	%	Rank	%	Rank	%	Rank	%	Rank	%	Rank	%	Rank	%	Rank	%	Rank
Smuggling, control (drugs, contraband)	77	1	40	7	73	1	46	5	78	1	40	6	78	1	57	2	93	1	90	1	82	1	66	1
Improved public schools, higher education	63	2	66	1.5	72	2.5	79	1	53	3	61	1	57	2	63	2	68	2	40	5	39	6	62	2
Increased police protection	49	3	32	8	34	6.5	38	7	57	4	36	7	46	5	40	5	31	7.5	32	7	45	4	24	11.5
Low-cost housing	44	4	53	3	35	5	35	8	30	7	50	4	40	6	38	6	31	7.5	29	8.5	48	3	38	7.5
Health care for people who cannot afford to pay for it	43	5	18	11	50	4	22	10	39	5	21	9.5	49	4	37	7	43	5	29	8.5	34	7	40	6
Attracting industry	38	6.5	41	6	72	2.5	58	2	60	2	57	3	54	3	73	1	62	3	34	6	55	2	60	3
Uses of water	38	6.5	49	4	3	13	34	9	3	12.5	21	9.5	29	8	32	8.5	50	4	84	2	21	10	36	9
Improvement of roads, highways, bridges	31	8	66	1.5	34	6.5	43	6	37	6	47	5	32	7	43	4	7	13	45	3	24	9	45	4
Public transportation	25	9	27	9	12	11.5	17	12	27	8.5	6	12.5	18	10	32	8.5	14	10.5	16	11.5	18	11.5	41	5
Control of pollution	19	10	26	10	15	10	21	11	12	11	15	11	16	11.5	17	11	20	9	16	11.5	15	13	19	13
Improved air service	12	11.5	4	13	31	8	55	3	27	8.5	31	8	16	11.5	–	13	10	12	24	10	42	3	24	11.5
Better parks and recreation	12	11.5	47	5	19	9	50	4	22	10	60	2	12	13	28	10	40	6	42	4	26	8	38	7.5
Improved fire prevention	8	13	10	12	12	11.5	12	13	3	12.5	6	12.5	21	9	12	12	14	10.5	3	13	18	11.5	28	10

Source: Adapted from West and Sloan, 1976a, and West, 1979.

Note: Comparable data were not collected in Laredo-Nuevo Laredo. Column percentages refer to the proportion of officials selecting this item as one of the five most important problems facing their particular city.

Table 37-2. *Factors Which Increase Policy Cooperation among U.S.-Mexican Twin-City Officials.*

	Texas-Mexico					Arizona-Mexico	
	Laredo-Nuevo Laredo	Eagle Pass-Piedras Negras	Brownsville-Matamoros	McAllen-Reynosa	Del Rio-Ciudad Acuña	Nogales-Nogales	Douglas-Agua Prieta
Characteristics of officials							
Bilingualism	N.A.	+	+	−	−	+	+
Kinship ties	N.A.	+	−	−	−	+	−
U.S. officials with Spanish surname	+	+	+	−	−	−	−
Longevity in office	N.A.	+	−	−	−	−	−
Elite interaction network							
Visits to sister city	N.A.	+	+	−	−	+	+
Work-related contact	+	−	+	−	−	+	−
Friendship patterns	+	+	−	−	−	+	−
Social organizations	+	+	−	−	−	−	−
Professional organizations	+	+	−	−	−	−	−
Attitudes of officials							
Perceived interdependence	+	+	+	+	−	+	+
Shared feelings of vulnerability to outside decision makers	+	+	+	+	+	+	+
Shared attitudes on policy priorities	+	+	+	−	−	+	+
Informal agreements							
Law enforcement	+	+	+	N.A.	−	+	+
Fire protection	+	+	+	+	−	+	+
Public health	+	+	+	+	−	+	+
Education	+	−	+	−	−	−	+
Transportation planning	+	−	+	−	−	+	+
Other							
Historical tradition	+	+	+	−	−	+	+
Geographic proximity	+	+	+	−	−	+	+
Geographic isolation	+	−	−	−	−	−	+
Natural disaster	+	+	−	−	−	−	−
Economic interdependence	+	−	+	−	−	+	−

Source: Sloan and West, 1977, and West, 1979.
N.A. = data not available

McCleneghan, 1964), socioeconomic profiles (Rivera, 1963; Leaming, 1963), industrial development potential (Tansik and Tapia, 1970; Ladman and Poulson, 1972), historical origins (Dumke, 1948), and cultural dynamics (Stone et al., 1963). Studies in these twin border complexes have also examined such problem areas of concern to public administrators as health care, crime and delinquency, education, and housing (Weaver and Downing, 1975; García and Lytle, 1975; and West, 1979). One of the most innovative studies of a border town was that of Weaver and Downing (1975). They analyze such problems as health, education, and housing and crime in Douglas, especially as these problems affect Mexican American residents. Four characteristics are identified which the authors use in explaining why the city is the way it is. These characteristics include its one-company-town status, its proximity to the border, its small size, and its multiethnic composition. More comprehensive community studies of this type are needed.

García and Lytle (1975) examine a single problem—that of Mexican juveniles and crime in Arizona's Santa Cruz and Cochise counties. Their policy recommendations for deterring Mexican juveniles from entering the country include better border fencing and surveillance, increased joint U.S.-Mexican cooperation among law enforcement officials, and use of modern detection equipment. The study is useful from an administrative perspective in that it points out weaknesses in the American system regarding the rehabilitation and handling of Mexican juveniles. It also reinforces the point made earlier that effective impetus for solutions to many border problems must come from the federal government.

Chicanos in the Borderlands

A special thematic issue of *Aztlan* (vol. 5 [Spring and Fall, 1974]), entitled "Politics and the Chicano," contains some material of interest to public administrators. The authors point out that there is little basic research and critical analysis of empirical data that can aid our understanding of the Chicano political experience (Muñoz, 1974: 2). According to Muñoz, the very limited research available addresses questions concerning co-optation of Chicano leadership by Anglo elites, the relationship between Anglo racism and Chicano oppression, challenges to the assumption that Chicanos are politically apathetic regarding participation in community organizations, explanations for the lack of Chicano political power based on historical conflicts between Anglo and Mexican cultures, typologies of Chicano political development over time, examination of Chicano politics either from the viewpoint of altered political relations between Chicanos and Anglos or from the perspective of increasing self-assertiveness resulting from considerable Chicano activity in the Southwest (Muñoz, 1974: 2).

None of the articles in the special edition of *Aztlan* is devoted exclusively or in major part to Chicano representation in public administration. Nevertheless, those scholars interested in public administration in the Borderlands will likely find useful Muñoz's (1974: 1-8) overall assessment of the literature on Chicanos and politics; Barrera's (1974: 9-26) explanation for the low level of Chicano representation in political office; Padilla and Ramirez's (1974: 189-234) study of Chicano representation in the state legislatures of California, Colorado, and New Mexico; Padilla's (1974: 261-94) examination of socialization of Chicano judges and attorneys; Gutierrez and Hirsch's (1974: 295-312) exploration of the Chicano's perception of his own powerlessness; and Lemus's (1974: 313-409) compilation of a national roster of Spanish-surnamed elected officials. Rocco (1977) provides a more recent review of the literature on the relationships between Chicanos and the institutions of politics in the United States.

Another useful source in interpreting the Chicano political experience is a recent book by García and de la Garza (1977), especially the sections dealing with the Chicanos' political potential, the politics of coalitions, and the problems of leadership. In addition, Banfield (1965) and Strauss (1968) give sketchy and dated descriptions of the Mexican American in El Paso politics; de la Garza (1974: 235-60) provides a more up-to-date analysis of Chicano voting behavior in El Paso. A. G. Gutierrez (1978) has examined electoral politics along the Texas-Mexican border and the emergence of the Chicano movement as well as La Raza Unida. Shockley (1974) and Miller and Preston (1973) have written an interesting account of the Chicano revolt in Crystal City, Texas. Students of public administration will be especially interested in Shockley's account of the first year of rule of La Raza Unida.

Concern about the "representativeness" of government agencies has become increasingly pronounced in recent years. The issue of equal employment opportunities for minorities in municipal government was addressed by Hall and Saltzstein (1977) in their study of 26 Texas cities (some of them border cities) above fifty thousand population. They found that factors affecting employment differ in the case of blacks and

Spanish-surnamed individuals. Specifically, they discovered that Mexican American employment is more strongly related to characteristics of that minority population (size and education of the Spanish-surnamed work force and percentage of professionals) than is the case for blacks. Their data suggest that government strategies to improve the employment status of minorities should take into account the specific group (blacks or Mexican Americans) requiring assistance. Achieving affirmative action or equal employment in bureaucracy is complicated by struggles among the major minority groups for the same positions. Interminority group competition has been studied in federal agencies (Rosenbloom, 1973; Rosenbloom and Grabosky, 1977). Díaz de Krofcheck and Jackson (1974) discuss "nativism" as a concept existing in public institutions which excludes Chicanos in modern society, and Herbert (1974) discusses the problems and dilemmas of the minority administrator in the public sector. Davis and West (1978) examined the attitudes of Mexican American supervisors and administrative personnel in a southwestern community (Tucson, Arizona) toward affirmative action issues using demographic and job-related controls. Not surprisingly, they discovered that Mexican Americans were considerably more supportive of affirmative action than Anglos; however, there was considerable variation in commitment to affirmative action among subgroups within the sample of Chicano supervisors.

With the advent of affirmative action programs and the gradual influx of Mexican Americans into administrative positions, an increasingly important question concerns the relationship between the kinds of job incentives offered by local government and those preferred by differing subgroups of public employees. A number of researchers have suggested that nonwhite employees attach less importance to intrinsic dimensions of work, such as the amount of responsibility, the challenge of job assignment, and organizational advancement, than do their Anglo colleagues, but they express a correspondingly greater interest in extrinsic factors, such as pay, working conditions, and interpersonal relations with coworkers (Bloom and Barry, 1967; Champagne and King, 1967; O'Reilly and Roberts, 1973). This tendency found partial confirmation in a recent study by Davis and West (1980) which compared the attitudes of Anglo and Mexican American supervisors in Pima County (Tucson), Arizona, while controlling for sex, age, education, job tenure, and occupational level. They discovered that Mexican American public supervisors were significantly less likely than Anglos to prefer such intrinsic job rewards as the "challenge of work itself," and they were slightly more inclined to prefer such job inducements as pay or opportunity for advancement. The relationship between ethnicity and the intrinsic job reward was unaffected by controls.

Several books are available on the state governments in California, Arizona, New Mexico, and Texas. Some of these works contain brief sections which are useful in understanding government decision making in a border setting. For example, McClesky (1972) and Nimmo and Oden (1971) point out the dominant influence of political machines and the Democratic party on political and administrative decision making in many South Texas cities and counties. Other authors have focused more broadly on the border region. Stoddard (1978c) has examined poverty along the border, and Cehelsky (1976) has assessed the feasibility of using multistate regional approaches to ameliorate problems in the border region and to improve the economic and social well-being of the U.S. states adjacent to Mexico. On the other side of the border, in addition to Alisky's brief descriptions of state governments in northern Mexico (1963a; 1963b; 1971a; 1971b), Coleman (1978) discusses diffuse support for political institutions and the problem of voter abstention, and Johnson (1971) examines electoral and administrative politics in the northern states of Nuevo León, Sonora, and Baja California. Ugalde (1978) has examined the U.S.-Mexican border and its influence upon the culture, economy, and politics of the Mexican states bordering the United States. He concludes that there is a significant amount of influence crossing the border from the United States which affects the culture and economy of the Mexican side of the border; however, he finds little evidence of American influence on Mexican politics.

In sum, academic literature on the Borderlands by public administrators is minimal. That which exists is limited in theoretical scope and weak in critical analysis of empirical data. Within the major subject areas in the field of public administration—general management; personnel administration; budgeting and finance; policy, planning, and programming; organization theory; administrative law; and others —there have been few historical, behavioral, or normative studies addressing problems of the Borderlands region. This chapter has reviewed some of the Borderlands studies by writers from other disciplines which might be useful to those in the field of public administration. I agree with Bath (1976) that future research by public administrators in the Borderlands is needed in the general area of public policy, with specific attention to the effects of policy in the border area. Related areas deserving further study include comparative studies of selected border problems (for example, law enforcement, environmental pollution, and public health), of administrative structures and processes, and of international organizations; studies of the effects of border urbanization and industrialization; studies of community decision making; examination of horizontal and vertical intergovernmental relations; analysis and evaluation of binational programs of cooperation (for example, drug control and international health); exploration of the attitudes and behavior of minority administrators; and analysis of the consequences of diverse proposals dealing with immigration, unemployment, and economic assistance.

1. Scholarly interest in public administration in Mexico has increased in recent years (*Revista de Administración Pública* is now published, a Society of Public Administration operates, and university courses in public administration are offered); however, this review is limited to works available in English.

38

Mexican Migration and Illegal Immigration

ELLWYN R. STODDARD
*Department of Sociology and
Anthropology
University of Texas, El Paso*

Though the categories of legal and illegal immigration appear to be clearly separate, they represent a legal distinction not easily made in the real world. Indeed, between these polar extremes there is found an incomprehensible morass of contradictory immigration statutes, historical traditions and practices, and "approved" exceptions that produce a broad range of "degrees of legality." It is not unusual for one family member to gain legal residency status through quasi-illegal means and then apply for "family unification" for the remaining family. Thus, many of today's illegal residents are tomorrow's citizens (Portes, 1974a; 1978b). In addition to this legal-illegal continuum, euphonic labels for more diplomatic usage between countries—such as the term *undocumented worker*—have been coined which technically do not describe the phenomena. A great number of illegal Mexican aliens (hereafter referred to as IMAs) in this country are here with fraudulent documents or illegal legitimate documentation (Office of Planning and Evaluation, 1976). On the other hand, although illegal Mexican migration is conceived in "legalese," the phenomenon and ac-

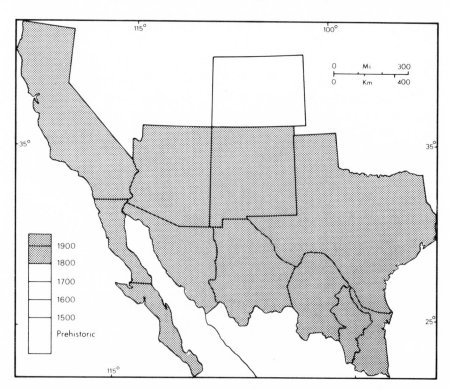

tions to ameliorate its consequences are not within the patch-work of current immigration law (Fragomen, 1973; Keely, 1975*b*; Piore, 1976; Stoddard, 1976*b*).

Field researchers from Taylor (1932) to the present have always averred that there are no available means to accurately count illegal aliens in the United States at any time. But because policy makers and agencies responsible for their control must act on any available data, official "guesstimates" have become more and more acceptable as reliable for public policy and media accounts. Recently, the Immigration and Naturalization Service (INS) began plans for more accurate IMA estimates in this country by contracting with Lesko Associates (1975) for a more sophisticated system of prediction. Their number of 5,222,000 (based upon long-term trends of legal immigration to this country from Europe) has been severely criticized by researchers who maintain that Mexican migration, both legal and illegal, in no way parallels the European experience (Houstoun and North, 1975; Keely, 1977). An INS project to estimate U.S. IMAs was heavily criticized during its $750,000 contract when "door-to-door canvassing" was used as a major technique to verify IMAs present in a given community.

Equally suspect is a Los Angeles "working paper" that locates demographic concentrations of Spanish-speaking Mexican Americans throughout the city and then apportions the illegal Mexican population among them (Los Angeles Department of City Planning, 1976). The traditional manipulation of IMA figures by the INS and the U.S. Customs Service for budgetary justifications and in proceedings (Aberson, 1975) has created a lack of credibility of official statistics and estimates. Politically inspired declarations, such as that of former INS Commissioner Chapman, of a "silent invasion" and the willing collusion of a sensationalist press (Bustamante, 1976*a*; Jacoby, 1977; Gutierrez, 1978) have created a public reaction of fear mixed with disbelief. Most scholars knowledgeable in the field feel the estimate of 10-20 million to be extremely high; most would support estimates of 2.5 million to 5 or 6 million, depending upon the season of the year and what "kinds" of illegals are included within the category. A more realistic approach is reflected in a recent sophisticated demographic analysis which yields an annual illegal flow of from 82,000 to 230,000 per year (Heer, 1979). Yet even this estimate is modified by labor certification problems for limited numbers of "legal Mexican laborers" (Cazorla, 1975); the status of border "commuters," legal and illegal (USSC, 1968; Ericson, 1970; North, 1970); and legal-status changes of permanent alien residence criteria (Fragomen, 1975).

An understanding of present IMA activity requires some historical background and knowledge of traditional as well as present binational migration patterns. For a readable overview of Mexican migration, see Corwin's (1973*a*, 1973*c*) bibliographical essays. Grebler's (1966) or Corwin's (1973*a*) summary of contemporary trend is useful, as is the volume of conference papers by Bryce-Laporte (1979), concerning the "new immigration." For the most up-to-date overview on Mexican immigration and immigration literature, see the annotated bibliography from the INS (North and Grodsky,

1979), the scholarly discussion of migration in Mexico with theoretical implications (Weaver and Downing, 1976), and the recent Battelle Center working paper which critically assesses much of the available data on illegal migration and its various effects (Cross and Sandos, 1979) as well as listing some of the salient investigators/scholars on the subjects with addresses and telephone numbers.

Illegal migration from Mexico begins chronologically with our preoccupation with Chinese immigrants into El Paso, which prompted our first immigration law in 1882 (Farrar, 1970). During the decades which followed, our concern about the "yellow peril" culminated in the Gentlemen's Agreement in 1907; our seasonal need for agricultural workers coupled with the Mexican refugees fleeing the 1910 Mexican Revolution brought many Mexican families into the Southwest. Those who did not return after the revolution or during the trying years of the Great Depression account for about one-third of all Mexican American citizens in the United States today.

One of the earliest volumes dealing with Mexican migration and its problems is the pioneer work of Gamio (1930). Later, over a two-decade period, McWilliams (1933, 1939, 1942, 1949*a*) became the spokesman for humane treatment and consideration for migrant workers of Mexican descent, both citizens and noncitizens. However, some of his data concerning forced repatriation of Mexicans during the Great Depression have been seriously questioned in a recent analysis by Hoffman (1972). In addition to the well-known historical works of that period are recent scholarly contributions by Cardoso (1974, 1976) and Reisler (1976) as well as many of the selections included in the excellent edited volume of Latin American anthropologists by Camara and Kemper (1979). Descriptions of forced repatriation and its agonies are examined by American scholars (Hoffman, 1974) and Mexican researchers (Carreras de Velasco, 1974). A comparison of repatriation patterns in California with the plight of Mexicans in Texas, which unlike California did not have universal welfare assistance, illustrates the extreme variations of policies and living conditions endured by Mexicans during the Depression years (Shapiro, 1952).

A unilateral *bracero* program was initiated by the United States during World War I, although the beginning of the 1942 *bracero* program during World War II is the one most people think of when they hear the word *bracero*. It served as a "pump-priming" mechanism for illegal migration following its 1964 demise (Hadley, 1956; Scruggs, 1961; Galarza, 1964; Grebler, 1966; Greene, 1969*a*; McCain, 1970; Copp, 1971; H. L. Campbell, 1972; Kiser and Kiser, 1969: 67-123; García, 1980). Moreover, its termination affected the labor conditions, housing, and patterns of American migrant labor as well (McElroy and Garret, 1965). Most of these sources which deal with *braceros* also cover the 1953-54 "Operation Wetback," the methodical rounding up of all U.S. residents of Mexican ancestry without legitimate papers or proof of citizenship which sent up to one million persons per year back to Mexico. Many authors focus on the inconsistency of U.S. immigration policies and the unspoken "federal policy" of allowing Mexican labor to enter the United

States without documentation when an unskilled labor supply is needed and then tightening controls and pursuing "clean-up" operations when such labor is no longer needed.

There are a few comprehensive volumes detailing many of the problems of the contemporary IMA migration such as the annotated bibliography by North and Grodsky (1979), the preliminary report of the Domestic Council's Committee on Illegal Aliens (1976), the earlier pioneer volume by Samora (1971), and some important edited volumes such as those by Corwin (1978a), Ross (1978), and Kiser and Kiser (1979). Although most writers inadvertently indicate some positive and negative contributions made by the IMA migrations, the spokesmen for domestic labor and its organizations are the most consistently negative in their criticisms (Briggs, 1975b, 1976; Marshall, 1978; North and LeBel, 1978). Sources presenting a more positive view of IMA contributions to American society usually consider the functional contributions of the aliens (Stoddard, 1976a; Salandini, 1977; Smith and Newman, 1977; Villalpando et al., 1977; Cardenas, 1978a, 1978b). Moreover, since the U.S. Borderlands is the most chronic poverty region in the entire United States (Galarza, 1972; Stoddard, 1978c; Miller and Maril, 1979), the illegal alien phenomenon is used as a "scapegoat" to blame for this endemic condition even though there are only tangential relationships between the two. In fact, the patterns of illegal alien labor along the border are far more integrated with societal structures and institutions than elsewhere in the United States (Stoddard, 1976a, 1978d, 1979b).

Within the decade of the 1970s, a large number of empirical studies have been completed, although unfortunately many do not reach the public, resting instead in the musty tomes of professional journals. Some have been accurate accounts through participant observation: the classical work by Bustamante (Samora, 1971: 108-27), who entered the United States as a "wetback" and, while working, seeking work, or in the containment center, contacted 493 other IMAs and described their feelings and experiences; the work of journalist Davidson (1979), who began with a group of Mexican laborers entering the United States illegally but who could not continue with them because of reasons of health and stamina; the personal experience of an IMA by Nelson (1975); Portman's (1979) experiences working on a Texas ranch with legal and illegal aliens; and other scattered "personal experience of an IMA" in professional and popular literature. Also available are the small studies of 20 IMAs in urban California (Dagodag et al., 1975) and 102 families living in the United States and working in border agriculture (Stoddard, 1976a), and Johnson's (1979; Johnson and Ogle, 1978) experiences with IMAs in rural areas of Arizona, Missouri, and Illinois. Some scholarly studies have dealt with unapprehended illegal aliens, as did the analysis by Moore et al. (1975) of 1,258 persons who used the One Stop Immigration Service of Los Angeles to become legal alien residents. To support the findings of the comprehensive investigation by Villalpando et al. (1977) of IMAs in San Diego County and their use of services, a local religious leader and scholar mingled freely with the IMAs and verified many of the official findings (Salandini, 1977).

An even more recent and thorough study of undocumented workers in San Diego County (C.R.A., 1980), though somewhat critical of the earlier Villalpando estimates and procedures for determining IMAs within the county, was generally supportive of the earlier conclusions—and reaffirmed the positive as well as negative impact of undocumented workers on the economic well being of San Diego County.

A few field studies have compared samples of apprehended and nonapprehended respondents for their motivations for coming to the United States, their demographic and personal characteristics, and so on (López, 1977; Kelly, 1979; Polinard and Wrinkle, 1979) to see if studies of apprehended aliens tell us about those who are not caught. The most widely known studies on illegal aliens are studies of aliens in custody: the North and Houstoun (1976a) study of 793 illegal aliens (of which 481 were Mexican) scattered throughout many states in nineteen detainment centers; Bustamante's (1976b) interviews with 919 Mexicans recently deported from the United States and awaiting processing in eight Mexican border receiving centers; and others.

A comprehensive study by Centro de Información y Estadísticas del Trabajo, Secretaría del Trabajo y Revisión Social (1978), of sixty thousand households should yield important data on Mexican migration flows, while their 1978 interviews of 25,138 deported Mexicans interviewed by Mexican government researchers have been used to question or substantiate many studies published in the United States (see comparisons in Cross and Sandos, 1979).

Using secondary source materials from 3,204 apprehended IMAs in California, Dagodag (1975) has described their characteristics in some detail. Toney (1973, 1977) has related the arrest records of 850,000 illegals along a section of the Texas border with the activity reflected in U.S. Customs and INS reports. From these same source materials representing official arrest and deportation information, Frisbie (1975) has projected such trends over a twenty-year time frame, giving a time dimension to a problem which seems to have had a rather recent origin.

A unique contribution to literature on the illegal or undocumented Mexican worker and his decision to come north, arrest experiences, rate of pay, and recidivist tendencies is a number of scientific studies done in Mexico, usually in "sending communities" from which large numbers of aliens have been known to originate. The works of Cornelius and Díez-Canedo (1976), Dinerman (1978), Stuart and Kearney (1978), and Reichert and Massey (1979) follow the flows to the United States, the earnings and push-pull factors, and the social milieu in which northward migration is conceived and carried out. In addition, Cornelius (1977a, 1978) has reissued increasingly complete compilations of existing studies and research, often comparing their results with those gained from his own research in Mexico.

Inasmuch as scholars as well as policy makers have tended to think of "the alien problem" in categorical terms instead of breaking down the various kinds of migration which are subsumed under the legalistic "illegal alien" umbrella, policies designed to ameliorate one IMA effect have exacerbated others. Some scholars have attempted to show the diversity of IMA activity (Ríos, 1970; Stoddard, 1976b, 1978d; Marshall, 1978: 21-22; Johnson, 1979) which would in turn require a flexible policy to deal with IMAs other than the single young males seasonally employed in agriculture.

Recent federal court rulings have mandated schooling for children of IMAs, but not all of the side issues (including the disproportionate economic strain on border school districts) have been settled at this time. Unresolved also are the problems of how to dispense selective medical and social services to IMAs who currently pay for them through withholding taxes, hospital insurance, Social Security payments, and so on, while avoiding public censure for "putting all illegal aliens on the dole."

The impact of Mexican migration to the northern border communities has been a serious problem for Mexican community leaders as well as for U.S. interests. The two-decade growth of border communities in Baja California (255 percent per decade) or those adjacent to the Texas border (155 percent) from 1940 to 1960 creates municipal problems and strains on medical and social services on both sides of the binational border (Stoddard, 1978b). The stereotype of IMAs being on welfare, public doles, and the like has been scientifically rejected in many studies cited in Cornelius (1978b). However, the impact of legal aliens as well as some illegals on school districts whose boundaries lie alongside the border has been verified by a study of border Texas districts (Hensley, 1976) and more recently by a study of border districts of all four border states (Hartman and Chávez, 1979) which advocates legislative assistance for those areas in the form of congressional impacted area funds. The direct and indirect effect of aliens on employment and wages in border areas has been studied by Smith and Newman (1977) using an economic model. G. Cardenas (1978b) found little or no impact on the labor market in San Antonio caused by the large numbers of illegal Mexican aliens in that city. The U.S. Department of Labor is currently initiating biographical searches for data evaluating the labor effect of IMAs; these searches might well be followed by extensive research into this very sensitive area.

A sizable body of literature has been dedicated to a "structural approach" to the IMA phenomenon. This approach focuses on disjunctive aspects of U.S.-Mexican economic power and dependency, the role of multinational corporations, and the role of capitalism in creating the exploitive IMA situation (R. A. Fernández, 1977; Bach, 1978; Jenkins, 1978; Portes, 1978c); these features are, in turn, questioned by scholars who find dependency theory oversimplistic (Bath and James, 1976). In addition to those focusing on macrosystems, many researchers find IMA activity inextricably connected with existing social and economic institutions (Galarza, 1970; Bustamante, 1972b, 1978a, 1978b; Stoddard, 1976b; Piore, 1979), although they do not totally agree with the operating "exploitation" motif.

Traditionally, U.S. immigration policy has been controlled by Congress's northeastern political bloc, with European constituencies of European ancestry. Thus, national immigration statutes are scarcely adaptable to unique Caribbean and Mexican migration problems (Piore, 1975; Bustamante, 1978b;

Keely et al., 1977). Scholars also deal with models more applicable to European urban migration than to that of the U.S.-Mexican Borderlands (Goldlust and Richmond, 1974). Immigrant profiles (Keely, 1975a) reflect *official* immigration rather than the very numerous "family uniting" exceptions performed almost daily at the Mexican-U.S. border. Quite naturally, therefore, policy changes are geared to northeastern legislators (Rodino, 1971, 1972) instead of border jurisdictions (White, 1975). The popularity of holding IMAs responsible for unfavorable economic conditions has been seen in the 1905 Alien Law in London (Gainer, 1972) and provides an interesting scenario for current U.S. reactions to Mexican border crossers, both legal and illegal.

For legislative aspects of proposed changes to the immigration law, see Hohl and Wenk (1971), Hohl (1974, 1975), and Waddle (1977). Criticisms of the Carter "amnesty proposals" and related issues are available in well-researched, readable form (Cornelius, 1977b; Fragomen, 1977; Schey, 1977; Storer et al., 1977; Waddle, 1977); policy alternatives and criticisms are in Piore (1974, 1976), Houstoun and North (1975), NCEP (1976), and Stoddard (1978a). Openly debated are proposals and justifications for keeping the Mexican-U.S. border open (Gordon, 1975) or those suggesting it be closed to protect native minorities (Briggs, 1975a). A suggestion to use the "guest worker" concept currently operating in Europe is seen as one way to legitimize current migrating Mexican labor practices, legal and illegal (Hansen, 1978), although this plan would be anathema to supporters of domestic labor who see Mexican labor as a threat to the U.S. labor market.

A moral dimension arises as a result of paradoxically restricting legal immigration while attempting to protect illegal aliens' civil rights. The "reasonable suspicion" practices of border control agencies are constantly tested (Rose, 1976; Terry, 1976); the raid on and confiscation of records from an IMA counseling center in the celebrated *Manzos* case (Cowan, 1977; Furlong, 1977) show the incompatibility of alien surveillance and human rights. Centers similar to the Arizona Manzos unit, the One Stop Immigration Center in Los Angeles (Moore et al., 1975; García, 1977), the Illinois Migrant Council (Johnson, 1979), or the Catholic Conference's Migration and Refugee Service in El Paso (López, 1977) have bridged this delicate balance of furnishing information and counsel within a system while their presence is legally incompatible. Many authors plead for human rights for aliens—especially for the civil rights of Mexican Americans—since this minority is often suspected of being and treated as illegals until proven innocent (Bustamante, 1972a; Corona, 1972; Cortés, 1978; Corwin, 1978a: 305-46; Portes, 1978a), while others attempt to legally protect them (G. Cardenas, 1975; Carliner, 1977; Schey, 1977).

Since taking office, INS Commissioner Leonel Castillo has made alien human rights a top-priority issue among his agency's supervisory and line personnel. Supreme Court decisions on alien rights are summarized by Fragomen (1974a; 1974b) and Rosberg (1977), while aliens' rights to public-service employment (Limón, 1975), the teaching profession (Babby, 1975), and other occupations are evidence of judicial concern for aliens as potential victims or lawbreakers.

The IMAs' illegal status is perhaps one reason why they seek to avoid criminal activities which might lead to their deportation (Fragomen, 1973; Portes, 1974a; Stoddard, 1976b). With a rising new generation of Chicano researchers and authors (see Cortés, "New Chicano Historiography," chapter 13 in this volume), legal histories which have traditionally created the Texas Rangers' impeccable morality and courage may be rewritten, exposing many illegal practices and procedures. Though some of these writings may suffer from minority ethnocentrism, they do offer some historical alternatives to southwestern society's presently biased narratives. Other border control agencies might expect similar treatment.

Future research needs surrounding the problems that accompany massive Mexican migration and illegal border crossers are many. Perhaps three are timely and critical: (1) the coordination of immigration and border control agencies; (2) present and future implications of contradictory and overlapping immigration policies; and (3) legal and political aspects of citizen children of IMA parents. The political and economic questions of realigning border control agencies from their traditional (and inefficient) executive departments and legislative committees are currently shunted because of political sensitivity. The pressure to maintain more ports of entry from New York City north to Quebec rather than along the Mexican border is one of organizational maldistribution. As far as immigration policies are concerned, the continued justification for family reunification; lack of "favored-nation" status for Mexican and Canadian neighbors; and treatment of white Mexican Mennonites currently in the United States illegally, compared to treatment of brown-skinned IMA families who have been here for many years, need to be explored. The possibilities of creating "guest-worker" programs, shifting immigration violations from criminal to civil, and providing additional IMA counseling centers protected from legal search and seizure might be looked into. An overall change of our immigration policies from a single European-based model to one responding to distinct migration pressures of Caribbean and Mexican border areas is a paramount need in future policy research.

Compared with the many reports of IMAs currently detained by U.S. agencies, relatively few authors have had intimate contact with IMA families permanently living in the United States, and few perceive that those families may have motivations quite different from those attributed to them by arresting officers, Chicano leaders, middle-class Anglo writers, and others with limited personal contact. Were IMA expectations and experiences better known and understood, public resentment toward them as "welfare cases" and "criminals" (which they are not) might be reduced; the problems of educating their children (especially U.S.-born citizen children) and providing limited social or health services might be seen as economically and morally less expensive than the possible indemnification payments due them after two decades of neglect. Economic studies of their positive contributions to this country, the few worthwhile positions they hold in the labor market, and similar subjects can only be made by intimate contact with the IMAs themselves.

Drug abuse problems in the United States have received considerable attention in recent years. By the mid-1970s, approximately one-half million Americans were addicted to heroin, while at least fifteen million were regular or casual users of marijuana. None of this heroin originates domestically, and only a small percentage of the marijuana is home-grown. Consequently, the questions of source and shipment have become cardinal to most analyses of drug use and abuse in the United States.

Mexico has long been the primary source of high-potency marijuana. Despite the recent influx from Colombia and Jamaica, Mexico still supplies an estimated 30-40 percent of the annual American consumption, or some three million pounds. More importantly, Mexico is now the source of 60 percent of the heroin on the U.S. market, an alarming ten thousand to fifteen thousand pounds annually. Furthermore, Mexico is both a primary transshipment route for cocaine, an increasingly popular drug originating in South America, and the source of vast quantities of psychotropic substances.

39

Illegal Drug Traffic

RICHARD B. CRAIG
Department of Political Science
Kent State University

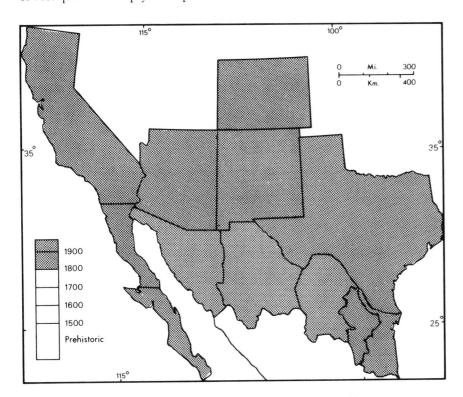

The overwhelming majority of these drugs, whether they originate in Mexico or elsewhere, enter the United States clandestinely along the border. As a result, narcotics traffic has become a crucial aspect of the border ambience. Despite its admitted social, economic, and political import, though, very little has been written on the production and shipment of narcotic drugs in Mexico and across the frontier. This paucity of research is particularly glaring within the scholarly communities of both countries.

In Mexico

If one assumes, as do most U.S. politicians and journalists, that America's drug problem must be attacked primarily at its foreign source, he must face the reality of Mexico's capacity to cultivate, process, ship, and transship enormous quantities of opium, heroin, marijuana, psychotropics, and cocaine. Historically, Mexican narcotics production has been geared almost exclusively to the realities of poverty, profit, and American demand. Marijuana can be, and is, grown in virtually every Mexican state. As is the case with opium and heroin, the cultivation, use, and sale of marijuana are prohibited by both the federal Código Penal and the Código Sanitario. Yet in the Sierra Madre Occidental alone, literally hundreds of tons are grown and processed annually. In the case of heroin, Mexico quickly filled the gap in the American market during the early 1970s with the curtailment of illicit production in Turkey and the demise of the infamous French Connection. According to Pera (Senate Hearings, August, 1976), there are some 375,000 square miles of Mexican territory capable of growing the opium poppy; Craig (1976) documented the existence of some thirty thousand plots in six states alone during 1975-76. The full extent of Mexican heroin production is unknown, but reliable sources estimate it between seven and ten tons annually. In other words, Mexico is currently the source of more than enough heroin to supply the annual demand of American addicts. The twin realities of poverty and profit combine to explain why Mexico has become the source of such vast quantities of illicit narcotic drugs.

Despite impressive economic advances in recent years, in many respects Mexico is still a very poor country. This is particularly true of the rural sector, which, despite rhetoric to the contrary, has largely been neglected by Mexico City. It is no accident that such key marijuana- and opium-producing states as Sonora, Guerrero, and Sinaloa are also centers of grinding rural poverty. These and other drug centers have long been the scenes of guerrilla movements, land seizures, and rural unrest. They lie outside the mainstream of Mexican life and are populated by contemporary *olvidados,* the great majority of whom are economically desperate. Desperate men seek desperate solutions to their problems. They turn to alcohol; leave their villages and families; become "wetbacks"; migrate to the teeming slums of Mexico City, Guadalajara, and Monterrey; seize haciendas or *ejidos;* become guerrillas; or become drug cultivators or traffickers,

or both. Such is the plight of these *campesinos* that, according to Craig (1976), "they literally have nothing to lose and much to gain by cultivating or trafficking in illicit drugs." As long as he lacks land, water, fertilizer, and credit—all of which add up to human dignity—the *campesino* in drug-producing areas will continue to view federal police and soldiers as enemies.

Yet, while the Mexican *campesino* may earn $3,000-$5,000 annually by cultivating marijuana or opium poppies, his profits are infinitesimal compared to the enormous sums earned by those who finance Mexico's illicit drug industry. The *campesino,* for example, receives approximately $10 per pound for his marijuana, the Mexican wholesaler in the interior $30, the U.S. border-state importer $70, the border-state wholesaler $150, a midwestern wholesaler $250, and a midwestern retailer $400. By the time it reaches the American consumer, the original $10 pound of marijuana is purchased for $800-$1,000. While enormous, such profits pale compared to those reaped from heroin. A Mexican trafficker purchases ten kilograms of raw opium for approximately $16,000. The raw opium is then converted in clandestine laboratories to one kilogram of morphine base, which, in turn, yields a minimum of one kilogram of 60-90 percent pure heroin. Reduced in purity to 6 percent, one kilogram of heroin brings some $925,000 on the streets of America's cities, finding its way to twenty thousand addicts. Mexican heroin sales alone constitute at least a $5 billion annual business in the United States. Marijuana sales are far greater.

La Campaña (The Campaign)

Faced with the realities of accelerating production and trafficking, increased U.S. pressure, and a burgeoning domestic drug problem, the Mexican government has responded with an impressive effort designed, first, to halt the cultivation of opium poppies, marijuana, and psychotropics and the production of drugs from them, and, second, to prevent internal and external traffic in these and other drugs. Barona Lobato (1976) asserts that, since 1948, Mexico has conducted an eradication campaign against marijuana and opium. Until quite recently, when it embarked on a massive year-round herbicide program, the government's approach primarily consisted of seasonal search-and-destroy missions by soldiers into such key producing states as Sinaloa, Sonora, Durango, and Guerrero. In 1975, however, the complexion of the eradication program changed dramatically when the government launched a "permanent" airborne offensive, using helicopters to spray defoliants over thousands of poppy and marijuana plots. The results, when compared to earlier army stick-beating expeditions, have been very impressive. During calendar year 1976, for example, Mexican federal agents and soldiers destroyed 32,284 plots of opium on 7,601 hectares of land, dismantled 13 heroin processing laboratories, and destroyed 14,705 marijuana fields encompassing 3,185 hectares of land. Interdiction-phase results of the *campaña* were equally impressive, with 4,031 individuals arrested on drug-related charges, 247 kilograms of heroin and 403,929 kilograms of marijuana seized, and 211 kilograms of South American cocain confiscated.

Despite the statistical success of the antidrug campaign and the loss of lives from the armed resistance of growers and *traficantes,* however, Mexico's productive capacity has been curtailed, but it has not been eliminated. Marijuana and heroin still flow north in response to American demand. This flow poses a serious problem for Mexican officials and a continuing basis for criticism from U.S. politicians and journalists who expect more positive results from the $38 million in technical aid provided Mexico from 1970 through 1976 for its antidrug campaign.

Craig (1976) writes that Americans have criticized the Mexican *campaña* on one or more of the following grounds during the 1970s: failure to commit adequate resources, lack of administrative and political control over particular drug-producing areas, lack of control over certain states and local governments and their officials, failure to adequately share drug-related information, involvement by police and judicial officials in drug trafficking, lack of adequate coordination and cooperation between the Mexican attorney general's office and particular army officers, refusal, until 1975, to employ herbicides, inability to arrest major traffickers and disrupt their networks, refusal to extradite known drug dealers to the United States, and the maltreatment of Americans arrested on narcotics charges.

Mexican officials have categorically denied such charges or termed them gross exaggerations of minor problems. They invariably remind such critics that Mexico is making an all-out effort at great expense and the loss of many lives to aid in solving a neighboring country's problem. "If it were not for the American demand," they contend, "there would be no reason for Mexicans to illegally cultivate, manufacture, and transport narcotic drugs" (Craig, 1976; Barona Lobato, 1976).

Knowledgeable Mexicans realize, however, that although curtailed, drug production and shipment continue despite their best efforts, and they privately acknowledge the validity of particular American charges. Furthermore, they now more than ever realize the dangers to Mexican citizens posed by such illicit activities, for the government has openly admitted the existence of a burgeoning domestic drug problem (Fernández, 1973; García Ramirez, 1974; Rodríguez, 1974; and Craig, 1977*b*). Finally, Mexican and American officials acknowledge that if drug abuse in either country is to be solved primarily by a law-enforcement approach, success must come at the cultivation and manufacturing stage, since once the narcotic enters the trafficking stream, odds in favor of it reaching an addict in either country are approximately ten to one.

At the Border

Mexican federal police and army patrols have been no more successful in interdicting drugs in transport than have their American counterparts. Untold quantities of narcotics are transported north from interior growing and processing centers by motor vehicles, airplanes, and boats. Roadblocks, customs searches, and helicopter surveillance have confiscated only a fraction of the total en route to the border. At that point, the chances of it being intercepted are quite minimal.

International borders are, by their very nature, hubs of smuggling activities. However, no frontier more clearly evidences a contraband *ambiente* than the approximately two-thousand-mile artificial barrier between Mexico and the United States. Despite elaborate statutes in both countries, thousands of items and people illegally traverse the border daily. In the words of a Laredo customs agent: "Anything that doesn't cross this border illegally in one direction or the other at one time or another just hasn't been invented." Unfortunately for America's drug abuse problem, narcotic drugs are not a recent invention.

Border drug smuggling has been described by politicians and journalists as "enormous," "unbelievable," "overwhelming," "incredible," "massive," "unprecedented," "out of control," and "unstoppable." Despite the media attention it receives and its admitted social, economic, political, and human effects in both nations, though, the phenomenon of drug traffic across the U.S.-Mexican border has remained virtually unexplored by either country's scholars. With two exceptions (Price, 1971, 1973*a*; Craig, 1977*a*), academicians have written nothing on the topic. More to the point, no U.S. or Mexican government publication has addressed the specific situation. Even popular writers (Demaris, 1970; Finlator, 1973) and drug traffickers themselves (Kamstra, 1974; Tichborne, 1970) have paid only cursory attention to the border conduit.

Although no one knows the exact figures, approximately six to eight tons of Mexican heroin, millions of pounds of marijuana, huge quantities of South American cocaine, and untold amounts of psychotropic drugs are smuggled across the border annually by every conceivable means. No possible carrier is neglected, including individuals, automobiles, trains, buses, boats, and lately most important, airplanes.

Air transport has radically transformed border narcotics smuggling. Thousands of drug-laden planes traverse the frontier annually. Reliable estimates number more than twenty each night. At least one thousand pilots run the border corridors, generally flying at treetop levels to escape radar detection. Although they are known to carry a variety of drugs, such pilots generally specialize in transporting marijuana (because of its bulk). Narcotics officials generally believe most heroin and cocaine is smuggled by individuals, automobiles, and boats. Detection becomes a needle-in-the-haystack proposition.

In 1975, for example, 46,428,629 vehicles legally entered the United States from Mexico at border checkpoints. During the same year, 26 million individuals crossed the border from Ciudad Juárez into El Paso alone. Given such figures, it would, in the words of an Illinois Legislative Investigating Commission (1976: 14), "require a total failure of the imagination not to be able to conceive of 50 ways to smuggle a package across that border, and most likely all of them have been tried." If pedestrian and automotive traffic did not present enough of a problem for customs officials, consider the smuggling potential of trains and commercial trucks daily crossing the border. Then add to these legal crossings the reality of hundreds of miles of virtually unpatrolled desolate border areas and the large number of ocean craft plying East and West Coast waters, and one can understand why drug smuggling constitutes a monumental problem for border officials.

Efforts to Contain the Flood

The dedication and ingenuity of U.S. customs and narcotics officials stemming the flow of drugs has been equaled, and apparently surpassed, only by the cunning and bravado of smugglers themselves. Congressional testimony from Customs Service and Drug Enforcement Administration (DEA) officials discloses a vast array of devices and technology currently employed to intercept narcotics at the border: primary and secondary searches of persons and vehicles, motorized patrols, informants, dogs to sniff out drugs, boat tracking and locating devices, passive electronic mechanisms, interdiction vehicles, unattended ground sensors, airborne and hand-held radar, X-ray and vapor detection devices, ultrasonic and neutron radiographic techniques, high-performance aircraft equipped with radar and infrared detection devices to permit nighttime surveillance, night vision devices, convoy techniques for trailing smugglers, and a computerized interlocking intelligence system (EPIC) headquartered in El Paso. Despite such technology and the efforts of hundreds of law-enforcement officials on both sides of the border, however, the problem, in the words of Congressman Lester Wolff, "looks almost unsurmountable." According to the knowledgeable New York representative, "We really have a Maginot Line. It is outflanked, overflown, and infiltrated." Such pessimism notwithstanding, there are those who feel the "line" could be considerably strengthened through improved cooperation and through effective prosecution of major drug smugglers, and, if need be, it could be made virtually impenetrable if American officials were willing to pay the price.

There is widespread agreement about the need for more effective coordination and information sharing between Mexican and American officials and, more pointedly, between U.S. law-enforcement agencies at the border. While the sharing of drug-related intelligence between Washington and Mexico City has markedly improved in recent years (Craig, 1976), this improvement does not hold true for American border officials and their Mexican counterparts. U.S. customs and DEA officers, for example, are convinced that Mexican customs personnel are only halfheartedly committed to checking northbound drug traffic. While rejecting the charge, Mexican *aduaneros* reluctantly admit they could perhaps accelerate their efforts if American counterparts would reciprocate more enthusiastically in other areas. Of primary concern is general contraband merchandise smuggling (which, accord-

ing to Mexican officials, totals some $12 million monthly) and particularly the smuggling of guns into Mexico. The Mexican government is seriously concerned about the apparently large flow across the border of weapons, many of which wind up with revolutionary groups (U.S. Senate Committee on Government Operations, 1977).

A second and more urgent problem is the need for more effective coordination among American border agencies involved with drug traffic. In addition to state and local police agents, there exists a plethora of federal committees, intelligence networks, and agencies directly or indirectly involved in halting the border narcotics flow. Of particular concern to antidrug critics is the longstanding feud, or lack of cooperation, between the U.S. Customs Service and the DEA.

In July, 1973, a reorganization plan creating the DEA was implemented to settle the squabbling between the Customs Service and the Bureau of Narcotics and Dangerous Drugs, thereby improving the overall program against international drug traffic. The plan involved a merger of several drug-related agencies and the transfer to DEA of some six hundred customs agents and two hundred support personnel. More importantly, it stripped Customs of the responsibility for narcotics intelligence gathering, making DEA solely responsible for drug trafficking investigative and law-enforcement functions. For narcotics, Customs was only left with the responsibility of border interdiction.

Unfortunately, consolidating narcotics enforcement within a lead organization did not end interagency friction. In fact, so much tension resulted between Customs and the DEA that a memorandum of understanding was issued in December, 1975, which attempted to outline more explicitly each agency's operating guidelines. Jointly signed by the heads of the DEA and Customs, the document also warned both organizations' personnel to "refrain from offering or lending support to any derogatory remarks regarding the other agency." While relations between the two key agencies have improved since signing the "peace treaty," resentments still linger, especially in Customs. According to its chagrined commissioner, Vernon D. Acree, the reorganization has been counterproductive, and responsibility for gathering drug-related intelligence should be restored to Customs (Craig, 1977*b*). Ultimately, problems associated with border drug traffic may create a new "super" agency to oversee and coordinate overlapping and often competitive operations of antismuggling organizations.

Further reorganization would undoubtedly have its supporters and detractors among border law-enforcement personnel. All would agree, however, on the need for a more immediate curtailment of the Mexican narcotics flow: prosecution and long-term sentencing of major drug traffickers. In the words of DEA head Peter Bensinger, judicial handling of major drug cases "makes a mockery of the serious concern of the public about hard drug abuse." One-third of the four thousand persons convicted on federal narcotics charges in 1975 were given probation. Of those sentenced on heroin or cocaine charges, one-third received terms of three years or less. The so-called crisis in our court and bail systems has had an especially demoralizing effect on border law-enforcement officials, who strongly support Bensinger's legislative proposals to (1) require mandatory minimum prison sentences for selling heroin, (2) enable judges to deny bail, (3) raise the administrative forfeiture limit to $10,000, and (4) extend forfeiture provisions to include cash and personal property (U.S. Senate Committee on Government Operations, 1976).

In the long run, however, greater cooperation between Mexican and American border officials, improved interagency coordination, and more stringent sentences for traffickers of hard drugs can only marginally improve law-enforcement agencies' ability to interdict frontier narcotics. Given the realities of Mexican production and American demand, some sources advocate more stringent actions, which amount to unacceptable diplomatic and economic pressure against Mexico. Such naive proposals would virtually seal the border to coerce Mexico into "solving" the U.S. drug problem. In effect, these proposals call for renewal, on a long-term basis, of the ill-fated and short-lived "Operation Intercept" launched in September, 1969. Described by government sources as "the largest peacetime search and seizure operation in American history," Operation Intercept was an economic catastrophe for both countries and a diplomatic disaster for the United States. Any effort to reinstitute such a program would, according to Craig (1977a), make it "highly doubtful that American authorities would ever secure the level of cooperation so sorely needed to impair the cultivation and trafficking of drugs in Mexico and across the border."

40

Law Enforcement

MARSHALL CARTER
Officer, Foreign Service
Department of State

The development of resources in the study of border law enforcement has suffered under a double handicap. Border studies in general have been underfunded and underrated. Research in law enforcement remains something of a pariah, particularly within the discipline of political science. Despite its preoccupation with the role of the military in politics, the mainstream of the discipline has awarded the cognate role of police agencies to criminal justice.

Spurred perhaps by the flurry of attention to law enforcement-related issues in the mass media, however, the scholarly community is beginning to examine this area of political life. Much of the resulting work is found in unpublished conference papers that are not widely available. The discussion that follows will also be concerned with both absent and present resources, noting areas where basic research—and publication—is needed to support the existing studies.[1]

The border is a rich laboratory for testing interdisciplinary and comparative methodologies and hypotheses (Stoddard, 1969a; Bath, Carter, and Price, 1977). The border context may present a particular advantage in examining the main-

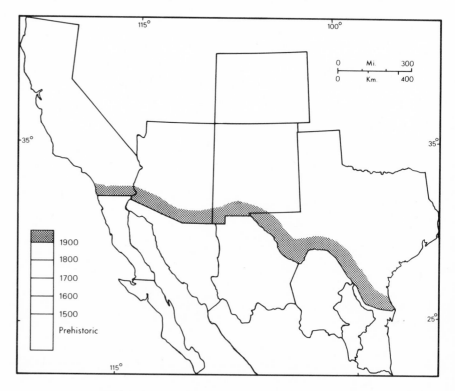

tenance of order by the political system, for it is on the peripheries that the limits of authority are at once vague and clear-cut and the invisible presence of the state is inescapable (Stoddard, 1979).

Structure and Context

Perhaps the most basic approach or perspective is simply the description and analysis of the complex systems of law enforcement, including courts, police, prosecutors, and prisons, found on both sides of the border. There are several important theoretical underpinnings for such emphases. First, there is the federal dimension. Law enforcement on both sides of the border is "federalized"; that is, its operations are dispersed throughout the various levels of the two federal systems that touch at the border. Relationships within the law-enforcement system affect, and are affected by, the distribution of power within the overall political system— intergovernmental relationships (Carter, 1979c; Winkle, 1975). These relations are likely to be most challenging and complex in the border context, where an extensive array of national agencies with police powers is present in force along with numerous state and local agencies (Carter, 1978a; Northcott, 1978). Second, the problems of public order and criminal activity are transnational, and there must accordingly be constant contact, antagonistic or cooperative, between U.S. and Mexican agencies at all levels (Carter, 1978a; T. J. Price, 1977). This contact further heightens the complexity and the intrinsic interest of law-enforcement work in the Borderlands (Carter, 1980, 1981).

Some historical and contemporary descriptive material is available, although much remains for future scholarship to provide.[2] Governmental and university organizations in the border area are compiling basic statistical profiles of the Borderlands and sectors therein, including data on criminal justice agencies (New Mexico State University Center for Business Services, 1977). The Organization of U.S. Border Cities and Counties and particularly the Southwest Border Regional Commission will serve as repositories for basic information. Several useful accounts, by historians and social scientists, have appeared which deal either with the border as a whole or with specific communities. A great amount of information on law enforcement reflecting the importance of the control of disorder in the frontier zones in both the past and present is imbedded in these studies (F. A. Broaddus, 1963; Fernández, 1977; Martínez, 1978; J. A. Price, 1973a). Stanley Ross (1978) has edited a comprehensive collection summarizing many aspects of the border.

On the U.S. side, some specific studies of important police agencies on the border have been done, in part reflecting the substantial support given to police studies by the federal government since the mid '60s. These include an excellent history of police in the western states (Prassel, 1972) and studies of some individual agencies (Samora, Bernal, and Pena, 1978; Perkins, 1978; Webb, 1935), with some case studies of particular cities (M. Carter, 1978c, 1979a).

Unfortunately, the same cannot be said for the Mexican side of the border. Studies of Mexican politics, in the main, have given only a passing nod to the law-enforcement structure, and comparative police studies do little better; states such as Japan, India, and Nigeria have been far more extensively studied in this regard. Basic statistics are available in a recent survey (Dorey and Swidler, 1976). Prassel (1972) makes some interesting comparisons with both Mexico and Canada in his history of police work in the American West. Selected Mexican communities are included in some of the statistical profiles, such as the Center for Business Services compilation (1977) cited above. Beyond that, description and analysis of Mexican police and judicial work (except of highly publicized operations such as Operation Condor) remain virtually untouched. The systemic constraints on police and courts are discussed by Schwarz (1973) and F. N. Baldwin (1976), and these constraints are an essential aspect for understanding the differences from and similarities to the U.S. system.

The conduct of law enforcement at the border itself occurs within the framework of a specialized set of laws relating to it. On this subject the law reviews must be the major resource (again, we refer primarily to U.S. law). Milchen (1969) provides a general overview, supplemented by the more narrowly focused studies of matters such as border stops or searches (Rose, 1976; Terry, 1976; Waples, 1974). The controversial exchange of prisoners between the United States and Mexico was treated by both academic and popular-press articles (Hoffman, 1977; Meyer, 1977; *Harvard Law Review* "Notes," 1977). It would be very useful to have comparative material on the Mexican legal context and perspective.

The question of international transactions directs attention to another important aspect of border law enforcement. Although the bulk of law-enforcement work on both sides of the border may be said to be more or less indistinguishable from that of the "interior," there will be some effect from conditions in the contiguous extranational territory. Criminal activities respect political borders no more than they do other social limits. The two thousand miles of border are bridged by various informal and institutionalized contacts among the law-enforcement agencies of the two nations. These contacts are shaped by the concerns and perceptions of both national and local communities and policy makers. At the national level in the United States, one major law-enforcement concern is the issue of illegal immigration. Extensive citations on that subject are given elsewhere in this sourcebook and will not be repeated here; those that consider the connection between general law enforcement and immigration policy are of particular relevance (Johnson and Ogle, 1978). The antidrug campaign on both sides of the border has similar ramifications, which are nicely elucidated in Richard Craig's work (1979b, 1980). More attention to national Mexican interest in law-enforcement problems of the northern border would be useful. There is more balance in studies of the local elites; a number of empirical investigations of opinion on both sides have been carried out, notably by Sloan and West (1976a, 1977) and by West (1978, 1979). Some related material is found in García and Lytle (1975) and Carter (1978*b*). Journalistic accounts give vivid, if impressionistic, overviews (Hurt, 1977).

Policy Specifics

Certain problem areas for law enforcement on one or both sides can be readily identified: drugs, smuggling, illegal immigration, and associated crime (Craig, 1977, 1980; Gooberman, 1974; Northcott, 1977; Stuller, 1978; García and Lytle, 1975; Jud, 1976; J. A. Price, 1971; Johnson and Ogle, 1978). Of many of these it might be said that we know enough to know how little we know. The work of gathering and analyzing data on border crime is very much in its infancy. On the U.S. side, government agencies such as the El Paso Intelligence Center are compiling mountains of data, but much of this is not for public dissemination. Other data are scattered throughout the annual reports of federal agencies such as the Immigration and Naturalization Service or buried in the records of state and local forces, as yet uncollated and unpublished. The potential for case studies as well as for a border-wide reporting system, perhaps sponsored by the Organization of U.S. Border Cities and Counties or the Southwest Border Regional Commission, is substantial, but the researcher will have to turn to primary sources in the interval—to government documents or to the raw files of police agencies.

The Political Impact: Human Rights

In the more recent works on the border and the U.S. Southwest there is increasing evidence of interest in the human-rights aspects of border policies. Not surprisingly, law enforcement receives much of the attention and the criticism. This emphasis is in part a result of the national focus on human rights that was inaugurated with and by the Carter administration. Within that emphasis, certain questions have been raised that require "rethinking" of border policy. The general principles of U.S. immigration policy, and the mechanisms of its enforcement, have been queried, with particular reference to political versus nonpolitical distinctions and exceptions for groups such as Haitians, Vietnamese, and Cubans. Second, the increasing domestic power of the Hispanic minority, and its assertion of concern on matters affecting Mexican (and other Spanish-speaking) immigrants—legal or illegal—has placed issues of Borderlands human rights on the national agenda. This shift of priorities has been buttressed by the great increase in attention given to Mexico in U.S. foreign policy. Mexico itself has also shown signs of interest in the treatment of Chicanos and Mexicans in the United States. Studies primarily concerned with immigration policy have touched on these matters to some extent, and we are now seeing the beginning of specific studies of border and immigration problems from the human-rights point of view (Baer, 1978; Corwin, 1978*d*; Johnson, 1978; Chapman, 1977; Midgley, 1978; Mollan, 1979; Rosberg, 1977).

Not entirely coincidentally, an assessment of human rights and law enforcement within Mexico is also underway. Craig (1980*a*) has considered the rights implication of the antinarcotics program. The official response to public protest is examined by Stevens (1978) and to emigration problems by Mumme (1978). Johnson and Ogle (1978) note a number of border-related issues. These specific studies illuminate the more general points raised by Schwarz (1973) and Baldwin (1976), which in turn supplement the systemic critiques (Johnson, 1971; Reyna and Weinert, 1978; Goldman and Jacoby, 1978). At a still further remove, the policy and practice of both Mexico and the United States should be seen in the context of human rights in the Americas (Buergenthal, 1975; LeBlanc, 1977; Mower, 1972; Ronning, 1979; Tardu, 1976; Wiarda, 1978).

Looking Ahead

Studies of border law enforcement, to sum up, run the gamut from the technical to the philosophical, local to hemispheric, and descriptive to theoretical. In all of the areas considered, there are still more gaps than connections. The available literature provides a useful, if restricted, array of data: case studies, journalistic accounts, econometric models of crime, historical description, policy critiques, and advocacy. There is a great deal more to be done, and a great deal more data are buried in agencies and archives of all kinds. Many of the gaps in the data base could be filled nicely by doctoral theses or by short articles and monographs. Many of the assumptions of comparative and international politics, as well as those of American or Mexican studies, could be tested in the context of border law enforcement. This is an area that will richly repay some scholarly effort.

The opinions expressed in this chapter are those of the author and do not represent those of the United States Department of State.

1. Considerations of time and space limit this assessment to English-language sources. A number of these studies (for example, Craig, 1977*b*; Johnson and Ogle, 1978) give Spanish-language references.

2. It should be noted that both locally and nationally oriented newspapers (the *Los Angeles Times, New York Times,* and *Washington Post*) have provided extensive coverage of border issues both through current-events reporting and through news analysis. Such resources are not to be overlooked in examining border crime, although nonborder writers may distort situations from ignorance about the workings of the binational boundary.

An abnormally high population growth rate of 3 percent or more is expected to continue in those areas of Mexico contiguous to the U.S.-Mexican border. Not only is this rate much higher than the average for the Republic, but it is also one of the highest anywhere in the world. The city of Tijuana has doubled or tripled its population every decade since 1930, when it was 11,271. Estimates call for Tijuana's population to reach more than 1.5 million by 1990 and for Ciudad Juárez nearly to double its present 800,000 population. From 1940 to 1960 these Mexican border cities increased from 155 to 250 percent in each of the two decades. Although the cities on the U.S. side of the binational border have had a much less dramatic growth—from 25 to 40 percent per decade during the 1940-60 period (Stoddard, 1978b)—the larger communities of the arid Southwest, such as Tucson, Yuma, and El Paso, continue to grow, as do smaller communities throughout the Sun Belt. Finding enough potable water, maintaining clean air and surface water, and dealing with pollution are a real challenge for the future when one considers future projections of rapidly rising popula-

41

International Resource Law

ALBERT E. UTTON
School of Law
University of New Mexico

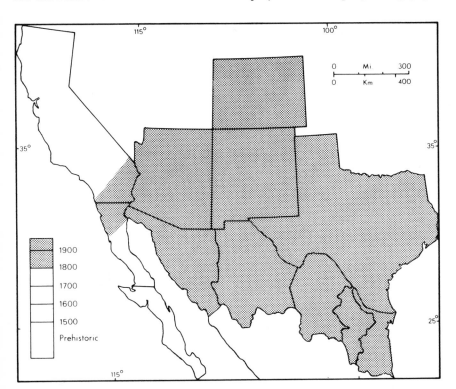

tion. Quite appropriately, then, considerations of population growth are central to understanding the border area's resource problems.

Literature dealing with the Borderlands' natural resources is varied. The best single work about Mexico's population is by Francisco Alba (1977*a*). Also helpful in understanding Mexico's problems are several articles in volume 17 of the *Natural Resources Journal* (1977), some of which deal with political-economic conditions affecting Mexico's northern frontier (Alba, 1977*b*), the potential for growth in counties bordering Mexico (Carpenter and Blackwood, 1977), and an economic perspective on water and air problems in U.S. border communities caused by industrial growth (Ayer and Hoyt, 1977). Stoddard (1978*b*) provides essential insight into the impact of population growth along the border.

Air Quality and Resources

The demands on the border-region air shed are greatest near urban areas; industry-induced pollution is most likely to occur in the two metropolitan areas of San Diego-Tijuana and El Paso-Ciudad Juárez. In addition, several smelters are located between El Paso and Ajo, Arizona, making the pollution level very high in spots between El Paso and San Diego. In the El Paso-Ciudad Juárez area, particulates are very high, and benzine-soluble compounds are extremely high in the commercial area of Juárez. Since the development of the central-valley water project near Phoenix, Arizona, the air once prized as the cleanest in the world has deteriorated severely with the mixing of the moisture from irrigated agriculture with the pollutants from recently constructed industrial sites. Similar air quality problems are developing at specific locations along the Texas-Mexican border as well.

Literature providing an understanding of border air quality problems includes two essential books: *Pollution and International Boundaries* and *Air Pollution along the United States-Mexican Border,* edited respectively by Utton (1973) and Applegate and Bath (1974). The latter is the more comprehensive, containing essays by experts from both countries addressing air problems from automotive emissions to agricultural insecticides and from electrical generation to open trash burning. In addition, Applegate and Bath (1978) update some of these conditions in chapter 42 of this sourcebook, "Pollution and Toxicity." Bath (1978*b*) gives a provocative analysis of the political and institutional aspects of cooperatively solving border air quality problems, while Becker et al. (1976) definitively narrate positive and negative attempts to cooperate across the San Diego-Tijuana border.

Groundwater

Water availability is a critical element in the future growth and development along the border, especially in the arid segment stretching from El Paso to San Diego. In the largest population concentration on the border, El Paso-Ciudad Juárez, a combined population of more than one million

persons must depend heavily upon groundwater sources for municipal needs as well as new wells for agricultural irrigation. Hydrologic studies indicate that pumping of groundwater significantly exceeds the recharge rate. To avoid future shortages and binational conflict, international agreement becomes increasingly important (Utton, 1979).

Between Arizona and Sonora, several drainage basins flow through transfrontier physiographic regions: the Yuma-San Luis; Papago-Río Sonoito; Nogales-Santa Cruz River; Cananea-San Pedro River; and Douglas-Río Yaqui. Groundwater is used heavily in the Yuma-San Luis region for irrigated agriculture, and it is used in the other regions for small-scale domestic, industrial, and municipal purposes. The exploiting of common reservoirs frequently occurs where legal and institutional arrangements for conservation and restricted usage do not exist.

In spite of the fact that the largest U.S. groundwater users are those states which border Mexico, surprisingly little information can be found in legal literature. Of great value are articles by Bradley and DeCook (1978) on groundwater problems encountered along the border and Day's (1978) discussion of the El Paso-Juárez Hueco Bolson.

Regarding the international legal questions, a trio of articles supplies important information. Professor Robert Emmet Clark, the leading American authority on groundwater law, has written on institutional alternatives for managing these resources (1978); a paper by Hayton (1976) provides an excellent world overview of international law and its specific application to the U.S.-Mexican border. Utton (1978) discusses institutional alternatives for managing transboundary aquifers such as those existing along our southern border. Analogically of interest is the problem of shared oil deposits along the binational boundary (Onorato, 1968). Contributions by Hernandez (1978), Burman and Cornish (1975), and Stoddard (1979*a*) provide pertinent insights into the U.S.-Mexican water situation and its precedents. For an excellent treatment of intrastate problems, see Fischer's (1974) article detailing the inadequate legal response to the U.S. transboundary groundwater problems. Economists seem to be far ahead of the legal profession in understanding groundwater management, as seen in the contributions of Veeman (1978) and Kelso et al. (1973).

Surface Water

Continued economic growth in the Colorado River Basin, particularly in developing large energy resources, is placing additional demands upon the resources of that river basin. Present water policies already have degraded Colorado River quality, with increasing salinity a particular concern to both the United States and Mexico. Under Minute 242 to the 1944 Colorado River Treaty, the United States is committed to improve the quality of water delivered to Mexico, including building a reverse-osmosis desalting plant at Yuma. This facility will deliver quality water to the Colorado which, when mixed with existing supplies, will improve the overall quality at the Mexican supply point, the Morelos Dam. However, the increasing agricultural development of the region, combined with increased industry and energy facilities in the Colorado River Basin, furnishes an increased level of saline water that affects surface water on both sides of the border. Recent joint U.S.-Mexican research on the Colorado River salinity developed an estimate of direct economic damages to Mexican users which also serves as a point of departure in determining future economic impacts in Mexico from water quality changes caused by water management policies of the United States.

Surface-water literature is extensive. The best overall view is provided by Hundley (1966) in his discussions of the Rio Grande and Colorado River treaties. Meyers (1967) focuses on the negotiations and ambiguities of the Colorado treaty. The *Natural Resources Journal,* volume 15 (1975), contains an excellent set of articles dealing with salinity problems of the Colorado River. Weatherford and Jacoby (1975) detail the complex legal regimes of the Colorado River and the crucial question of water availability. Brownell (1975), the principal U.S. negotiator of Minute 242—the definitive solution of the Colorado salinity problem—discusses this aspect. Both Bishop (1977) and Brown (1977) provide excellent discussion on the limited water supplies of the Colorado Basin and the demands that energy development will force on the existing resources. Two recent narratives (Hill, 1979; Kennedy, 1979) conclude that Mexican users of surface water are more responsive to their problems of shared resources and potential pollution than are their U.S. counterparts.

Change Factors and Institutional Responses

The physical forces that are inducing change in the boundary region include urbanization and economic development. The changing scene with respect to energy is an added, major force. Resource scarcity, agricultural land, water, energy, clean air, and other environmental amenities, including view, open space, and natural scenic resources, are at the forefront of the forces for change. The concern about the increased vulnerability of society to both resource scarcity and the use of highly sophisticated technology that requires very careful control must be given serious consideration.

The question that confronts the U.S.-Mexican border area is not whether there are forces for change in the physical world and in the world of ideas, but whether we can propose practical ways to allow existing institutions to adjust to these forces while maintaining the strengths they have provided in the past.

The governments of Mexico and the United States have been successful in constructing an institution capable of facilitating and implementing boundary water policies. The International Boundary and Water Commission (IBWC) has specific responsibilities for allocating and distributing the waters of the Rio Grande and the Colorado River between the two countries. The responsibilities include supervising and carrying out allocation formulas by measurement or other monitoring procedures. Flood control and the maintenance of the rivers as boundary waters also are tasks assigned under these treaties. Additionally, under the 1944 treaty, sanitation and quality of rivers are matters in which the IBWC is involved.

The commission has some responsibility for groundwater in relation to the Colorado River salinity agreement. Under that, the IBWC will "study and explore" the advisability of a treaty covering groundwater. Currently, the commission is exchanging groundwater data on basins where there are problems. The salinity agreement also opens the door to information concerning economic development in parts of the boundary region. The IBWC has a start in the joint publication of information, since it makes available consolidated reports on stream flow, water in storage, and similar data for both countries and their citizens. These are substantial tasks done well, but broader questions of transboundary resources call for a reevaluation of the institutional alternatives and opportunities to meet new and potentially serious problems.

Some of the more general questions of international resource law and possible institutional arrangements to carry out those laws effectively are included in an edited volume by Hargrove (1972) and articles by Utton (1967, 1978). For the more specific question of U.S.-Mexican resources law, Sepulveda (1974a, 1978) suggests some excellent institutional alternatives, and Bath (1978b) discusses air quality institutions on the border. Stoddard (1978a) considers functional Borderlands models which would facilitate federal-local coordination of Borderlands resource problems and needs. Substantive discussions on pollution and international boundaries are contained in the edited volume by Utton (1973), which includes the Mexican arguments on the Colorado salinity question (Sepulveda, 1973; Sobarzo, 1973).

It is quite clear that resource management and policies will have to deal more directly with a variety of border resource problems. The patterns of population growth and economic development will determine those areas in greatest need of resource management. Only an enlightened, multidisciplinary approach which considers these human and physical limitations can establish and articulate effective resources policies for the U.S.-Mexican Borderlands region.

42

Pollution and
Toxicity

HOWARD G. APPLEGATE
Department of Civil Engineering
University of Texas, El Paso

The increased urbanization and industrialization of recent decades have contributed heavily to the environmental problems within the Borderlands region. This region though, is only a jurisdictional one. Pollution and toxicity data have to be gathered from border counties or municipalities one by one and summarized by special investigations to conform to the Borderlands region. In addition, the various aspects of pollution and handling of toxic materials are so distinct that they require a separate discussion of each.

Municipal Solid Waste

Legislation controlling the handling of solid wastes has not changed in border states for more than twenty years, while the problem of handling it has increased markedly. It is estimated that the amount of solid waste generated per capita daily will increase from 2.3 kilograms in 1970 to 3.1 kilograms in 1980, 3.9 kilograms

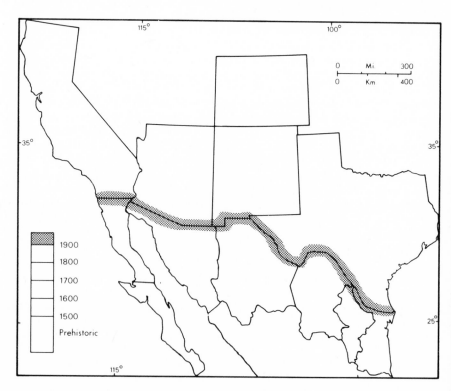

220

in 1990, and 4.4 kilograms in the year 2000. Thus, not only is the increased population creating strains on present solid-waste disposal units, but the per-capita amount is on the increase as well, further complicating the problem.

No county along the border has a problem of finding open areas for a sanitary landfill. The low cost of rangeland and the abundance of arroyos makes such a disposal method extremely attractive from an economic point of view. Such landfills may be regarded as "resource banks" of the future if it becomes economically feasible to convert such concentrated dumps to energy conversion units. For most of the Borderlands (other than the lower Rio Grande Valley of Texas), the low humidity and small rainfall lead to extraordinary preservation of buried solid waste. In the El Paso area, newspapers buried in landfills are still readable after twenty years. Obviously, these sites could be mined as recycling ventures when the technology and economics make it feasible.

A discussion of recycling usually generates more waste heat than fruitful action. Along the border, the sole question at present is, Can recycling be done either to show a profit or at least not to cost more than a sanitary landfill? The answer is no, except for San Diego County. Too great a distance to market and too few materials to be recycled, coupled with unfavorable freight rates, make total recycling along the border economically unsound. Arguments may be advanced that criteria other than economics should be considered in cleaning up the border environment. Although idealism is desirable, any added strain to the present poverty conditions of the U.S.-Mexican border region must be realistically considered in a larger perspective of economic priorities. For the foreseeable future, the "resource bank" of maintaining sanitary landfills for mining seems to be the most economically feasible plan currently available.

Unknown to record keepers and statisticians of municipal solid waste, a great amount of unofficial recycling takes place now along the border. Many Mexican nationals and commuters collect discards such as lumber, worn-out appliances, tires, cardboard, newspapers, and the like for resale or use in homes or small manufacturing firms across the border, but the magnitude of this recycling has not been estimated to date.

Water Pollution

The basic engineering reference for industrial water pollution from the processing of materials and the side effects of these processes is found in Azad (1976). This is a general work which does not have any specific application to border conditions and problems, however.

Water pollution is a problem along the entire border where water resources are shared by border communities. Most Mexican municipalities discharge untreated sewage directly onto the land or into the rivers, and, as yet, no binational controls for such practices are available. No river or lake along the entire border will meet the 1983 Environmental Protection Agency (EPA) goals for fishing, swimming, and irrigation. Only California, of all the border states, has a definite plan for recycling sewage as an alternative to the lack of water and the need to meet EPA standards (Koyasado, 1976). This problem is political, not technical, inasmuch as the technology exists but the political mechanisms to encourage and enforce standards are lacking.

The best source materials for data on water pollution in the Borderlands are the *Water Quality Data Base Report* (no date) of the Lower Rio Grande Valley Development Council for the area from the Gulf of Mexico to Falcon Lake and the *Water Quality Management Plan for the Upper Rio Grande Basin* (1977) of the Texas Department of Water Resources for the area from Falcon Lake to Elephant Butte Reservoir in New Mexico; for groundwater problems in these two areas, see Carter et al. (1965). The lower Colorado River Basin is discussed in various water bulletins from New Mexico, the latest being *New Mexico Water Resources* (1976). Unpublished materials are also available from the Water Research Institute at New Mexico State University. Water pollution in Arizona is covered in yearly bulletins issued by the Arizona Water Commission, while the specific problems of Tucson are discussed by Marum and Marum (1973). California divides the Borderlands portion of its state into two hydrologic areas: south coastal and Colorado Desert. Monthly, semiannual, and annual bulletins on both areas are issued by the California Department of Water Resources, making California water problems much simpler to examine than those other border states.

Air Pollution

The only volume dealing exclusively with air pollution along the U.S.-Mexican border (Applegate and Bath, 1974) discusses the problem of future threats to both countries of a continued absence of binational standards. That work discusses the political barriers to proposed legislation as well as some current pollution along the two-thousand-mile borderline.

Emission surveys for selected counties can be obtained from respective state agencies, but they are mostly estimates instead of actual measurements. When the amount of industrial raw materials used or the quantity of a given product produced is known, then estimates of air pollution can be made from the EPA's book *Compilation of Air Pollution Emission Factors.*

A little-known fact is that vehicular pollution is the primary air pollution problem along the U.S.-Mexican border. One reason for this type of pollution is the free movement of Mexican-registered vehicles, which are not subject to such rigorous inspections and emission standards across the border. This source also complicates the estimates of air pollution from the EPA's *Compilation of Air Pollution Emission Factors,* which uses raw data on vehicle numbers and surface miles (kilometers) traveled on various surfaces for standard U.S. automobiles. Another unique source of vehicular pollution is from the long lines of cars and trucks waiting to pass through the customs at ports of entry. The number of crossings can be obtained from the U.S. Bureau of Customs. Calculated vehicular emissions can be estimated by the length of time spent waiting for entry. Many unlicensed home factories in poor border towns add to pollution. Federal regulations controlling EPA equipment do not allow the agency to measure pollution levels in Mexican border cities, although sometimes this measurement is done "informally," contrary to existing statutes, until it is strictly prohibited by written mandate. The problems of weather inversions in such industrial centers as El Paso also increase the pollution level above what would normally exist if pollutants were not prohibited from moving away from the population centers unimpeded.

Agriculture and Toxicity

More than three dozen specific reports on various rates of pesticide contamination of border areas are summarized in Applegate et al. (1971) and Applegate (1979). These are the most up-to-date and precise of any other available sources. The U.S. Department of Agriculture publishes a yearly summary of agricultural statistics for each state, and each state also publishes a detailed statistical crop report (that is, fruit and pecan statistics, vegetable statistics, and so on) which may be obtained from the state departments of agriculture. The state statistics are not, however, dealt with solely as Borderlands phenomena even though they are more up-to-date than the federal statistics.

Agriculture has been a major industry along the border in various "pockets" as the long growing season has encouraged the shift from earlier family-sized farm units to large corporate agriculture. (The long growing season has encouraged outside capital to buy up family farms for their investment potential.) Such change has produced greater use of chemical fertilizers, insecticides, herbicides, and so on, together with more and better machinery to spread these materials. These developments have increased environmental degradation from agricultural practices.

Wastes generated in processing crops vary greatly from year to year and from crop to crop. Air pollution is increased from residue either in the field (as occurs with cotton after the harvest) or at the processing plant. In Arizona, New Mexico, and Texas, field burning is uncontrolled for all practical purposes, and only in proximity to larger cities are the discharges of processing plants regulated. On the other hand, California has strict and enforced controls on agricultural burning.

Pesticides (insecticides, herbicides, larvicides, and the like) are an essential part of Borderlands agriculture. The kinds, amounts, and types used vary greatly from year to year. Current information can be obtained from the various state departments of agriculture. The *Pesticides Monitoring Journal* (Government Printing Office) is the best single source for information on these compounds' effects. Various state agricultural experiment stations have a plethora of bulletins, pamphlets, and so on, of more specialized data. Caution must be used in extrapolating field data from the more mesic, colder parts of the United States to the arid, warmer Borderlands. Applegate et al. (1971) has shown that pesticides applied in the Borderlands have different half-lives, degradation products, and effects on nontarget organisms than they do farther north. The dangers to humans from pesticides and residues along the Rio Grande Texas-Mexican border are found in some relatively unknown professional papers and publications (Lahser and Applegate, 1966; Queveda and Applegate, 1978) as well as other fugitive materials unavailable at this time.

The U.S.-Mexican border is important both for crossing cattle from Mexico and for feedlots. Data on cattle crossing can be obtained directly from the port of entry or from the U.S. Customs Bureau. The number and capacity of feedlots can be obtained from the U.S. Department of Agriculture Livestock Reporting Service or the state departments of agriculture. Both air and water pollution from feedlots are discussed in Graber (1974); if the number of cattle is known, their waste products can be calculated with this publication.

Summary and Future Prospects

Environmental degradation is increasing within the Borderlands. The large population can be maintained by importing outside water, which is becoming more difficult to obtain. Sewage recycling is repugnant to many and potentially hazardous. Nevertheless, municipal sewage is both the greatest single source of water pollution in the Borderlands and the greatest remaining untapped water source.

The usually superb climate of the Borderlands can cause air stagnation, in which situation anything put into the air during these periods tends to stay. Obviously, this condition leads to air pollution. Vehicles are the greatest sources of air pollution along the border. The sprawling cities, often long distances from each other, make vehicles a necessity rather than a luxury. Inadequate mass transit systems, or the total lack of them, contribute to the problem. Mexican vehicle inspection is not even a token effort.

Unfavorable freight rates plus long distances to industrial centers make recycling of solid waste unlikely. Fortunately, the arid climate preserves such material when it is properly disposed of in landfills, which can be mined in the future.

Mexico contributes an unknown but obviously large amount of air and water pollutants to the Borderlands. Depressed economic conditions make local authorities unwilling to offend even the more blatantly polluting industries. The need to clear all actions with federal authorities in Mexico City also impedes progress toward pollution control in Mexican border areas as well as toward binational pollution standards and control procedures.

There is little indication that worsening of the environment along the border has been halted or even slowed; there is no evidence whatsoever that it is improving. For many years, the Borderlands have been the stepchild of distant capitals, both state and federal. Unless these capitals recognize that the Borderlands are indeed a special place, environmental degradation will continue.

National Sources of Information

For environmental-health purposes the Borderlands has been defined by the United States-Mexico Border Health Association as counties and *municipios* abutting the border. The United States-Mexico Border Health Initiative includes a much larger area that is heavily influenced by traffic across the border. The association maintains a limited file of health statistics and a small reference library. In 1981 the Initiative was awaiting approval by the Secretary of Health, Education, and Welfare. Both programs have provisions for environmental-health studies. Information on the programs can be obtained from the Pan-American Health Organization, 509 U.S. Court House, El Paso, Texas 79901.

The Subsecretaria de Mejoramiento del Ambiente (SMA), Secretaria de Salubridad y Asistencia is the leading agency in Mexico for environmental-health information. Unfortunately, it is virtually impossible to obtain data from them. Moreover, most of their efforts are confined to Mexico City, Monterrey, and Guadalajara.

The Environmental Protection Agency (EPA) and the President's Council on Environmental Quality are the two leading agencies for such information in this country. The Government Printing Office indexes and sells their publications. Virtually all their data are reported by federal region (Region 6 comprises Arkansas, Louisiana, New Mexico, Oklahoma, and Texas; Region 9 comprises Arizona, California, Hawaii, Nevada, Guam, and American Samoa). It is difficult at times to separate out data for the border region.

State Sources of Information

Each Mexican border state has a Jefe de los Servicios Coordinados de Salud Publica and a Promotor Estatal, SMA. Data are most difficult to obtain from either office.

State and city departments of health are rich sources of information in the United States. Their health data can be correlated with environmental data obtained from state environmental agencies. Regional Planning Commissions often gather environmental health data: Permian Basin Regional Planning Commission, Middle Rio Grande Valley Development Council, Pima Association of Governments, Lower Rio Grande Valley Development Council, Southern New Mexico Council of Governments, West Texas Council of Governments, and so on. Occasionally these bodies generate their own data, but usually their publications are just compilations of city and county data. The local addresses of regional bodies can be obtained from county judges.

Specific Publications

Only three publications dealing exclusively with border environmental problems have been found: *Pollution and International Boundaries* (Utton, ed., 1973); *Air Pollution Along the United States-Mexico Border* (Applegate and Bath, eds., 1974); *Environmental Problems of the Borderlands* (Applegate, 1979). The data from the two earlier volumes are old, but both contain excellent presentations of the political difficulties attendant to resolving border environmental problems. The latest book is essentially a collection of data on air, water, solid-waste, and vehicular pollution. No attention is given in it to political or economic problems. None of the three books covers health effects of pollution.

Various agencies of Borderlands universities issue occasional publications that sometimes deal with border environmental problems, for example, Border State University Consortium for Latin America, Occasional Paper no. 7, "Environmental Problems Along the Border"; University of Arizona Office of Arid Land Studies, Arid Land Resource Information Paper no. 14, "International Water Use Relations Along the Sonoran Desert Borderlands"; Univeristy of Texas at El Paso Center for Inter-American Studies, Occasional Paper no. 5, "Air Quality Issues in the El Paso/Cd. Juárez Border Region."

The *Natural Resources Journal* (published by the University of New Mexico, School of Law) specializes in border-related environmental problems. As might be expected from the affiliation, the coverage is usually from a legal or political viewpoint.

Other Sources

Data on pesticide poisoning can be obtained from the Pesticide Incident Monitoring System (PIMS). Each state in the United States has a local office; the national office is in the Department of Epidemiology and Public Health, University of Miami (Florida). Reporting is strictly voluntary; the data are thus often incomplete. Reporting is by county, however, so that borderland counties can be identified. In 1981 the program was not to be included in the next federal budget.

Mexico does not have anything analogous to PIMS. The only laboratory capable of analyzing samples from humans for pesticides is Delegado de Mejoramiento del Ambiente, Gomez Placio, Durango. They do not share data readily.

Hospitals and the Cruz Roja (Red Cross) clinics are willing to make data available in Mexico. The chief difficulty is the filing system: records are filed chronologically by department. To determine the incidence of a particular environmental health problem, such as lead poisoning, it is necessary to go through the entire filing system. This requires both a working knowledge of Spanish and ample time.

It is virtually impossible to obtain similar data in the United States. Hospitals require signed release forms from both the patient and the doctor before records can be searched.

Most university libraries have the capability to search computer data banks via telephone. The data banks range from the huge, multidisciplinary Lockheed Data Bank to highly specialized ones, such as Index Medicus. A trained librarian can put the world's data on a given subject at your fingertips. Arid Land Abstracts may be the most useful for Borderlands specialists to consult.

43

Political Activity
and Voting

ROBERTO E. VILLARREAL
Department of Political Science
University of Texas, El Paso

The electoral process stands as the cornerstone of democratic theory and practice in many parts of the world. It is through electoral participation that citizens have the formal opportunity to exercise political influence. According to Campbell, "the study of voting . . . is concerned with a fundamental process of political decision . . ." (see Campbell et al., 1960; Key, 1966; Flanigan, 1972). In fact, much of the debate on the quality of political life centers around the extent of voting participation (Verba and Nie, 1972). However, to discuss the quality of voting participation, we must consider numerous variables defining several levels of participation. For example, in the United States, high voter turnout is closely associated with high educational levels, professional and other white-collar occupations, metropolitan residence, and membership in voluntary associations. On the other hand, nonvoting is associated with low educational and economic levels, unskilled occupations, rural living, nonmembership in organizations, and the deprived conditions of racial and ethnic groups (Greenstein, 1963). In Milbrath's (1965) classical study of political participation, he con-

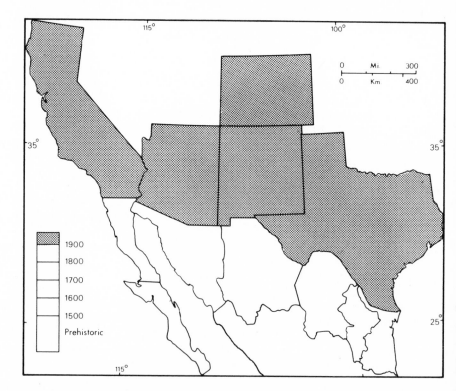

cludes that no matter how class is measured, studies consistently show that higher-class persons are more likely to participate in politics than are lower-class persons.

While it is logical that these same general correlations apply on the border, the heavy ethnic concentration, a generally depressed economic environment, a constant migration flow, and a history of more extreme class distinctions combine to distinguish its patterns of political behavior from those of other U.S. regions.

A review of the current literature of political participation and voting behavior in the Southwest region reveals a disarray of scholarly activities that lack border orientation, comprehensiveness, data bases, comparability, rigor, and definition.[1] In fact, studies of voting behavior strongly reflect the status in the discipline of political science on Borderlands studies (Bath, 1975).

First, there is lack of definable parameters to separate border from nonborder regions (Stoddard, 1975a, 1978c; Frantz, 1978). Second, the bulk of studies deals with distinct communities (de la Garza, 1977; Freeman, 1974; Shockley, 1974; A. G. Gutierrez, 1978), political subdivisions (Merrill, 1976; García, 1974; Vigil, 1977), and the ethnic factor.[2] What has been done attempts to mobilize Chicano political strength (Southwest Voter Registration Education Project, or SVREP). Those studies that offer comprehensive analysis of voting behavior limit their interpretation to intraethnic voting behavior (Grebler, Moore, and Guzman, 1970; García and de la Garza, 1977).

Third, on the Mexican side of the border the limitations to study voting behavior far exceed those of the United States, since the "Mexican government is reluctant to make accessible 'electoral data'" (Ugalde, 1978: 103-104). Finally, the diversification of socioeconomic, political, geographic, and ethnic concerns in the border region does not facilitate a comparative and comprehensive analysis of political participation.

The Border Phenomenon

A study of voting behavior reveals that the border region is uniquely characterized by a highly stratified economic structure, "with a small elite dominating virtually every aspect of life" (A. G. Gutierrez, 1978). Economically, the border is one of the nation's poorest areas, with the highest level of unemployment. The distribution of wealth is relatively uneven; incomes are higher along the California border and gradually decrease as one approaches the Texas Gulf (Stoddard, 1978c). Within this economically deprived region lives a heavy concentration of ethnic groups, each exhibiting distinct cultural and socioeconomic patterns. Further differences are found in their separate levels of political participation and control. There are also rural-urban cleavages (with the highest concentrations of people in several southwestern metropolitan areas). Somewhat parallel with the ethnic factor is the social stratification of dominant and subordinate groups.

Since the border region demonstrates a comparatively lower level of formal education, which is generally an important determinant in voter participation (Milbrath, 1965; Bennett and Klecka, 1970), one would expect voter participation also to be lower than in other regions of the United States—as is, in fact, the case. Recent trends, though, indicate that the level of formal education among border residents, especially among minorities (Carter, 1970), is increasing rather rapidly; so too should voter participation.

In the border region perhaps no variable for voting behavior creates more consternation and controversy than ethnicity. Ethnicity denotes diversity of interests, and diversity is the nucleus for potential, if not real, conflict.

Part of the uniqueness of the border phenomenon is the presence of the Chicano population since time immemorial (Sanchez, 1966). Together, the native American Indians, who have recently taken a more active political role (García and Winkle, 1971), and the Mexican Americans form the "only territorial minority" (de la Garza, Kruszweski, and Arciniega, 1973) in the United States. Obviously, because of this historical presence and the proximity to Mexico, the heaviest concentrations of Mexican American communities are found along the U.S.-Mexican border. In the lower Rio Grande Valley of Texas, for example, Mexican Americans are the most numerous ethnic group by a four-to-one ratio over other ethnic groups (Miller and Maril, 1979). In another survey A. G. Gutierrez (1978) found that "only two [border] counties in Texas (Brewster and Terrell) have less than a majority of Chicanos within their boundaries" (p. 119).

With the exception of a small acculturated minority, the Chicano population has lived in extreme poverty. A significant part of this population has become increasingly restive under such conditions. In spite of economic expansion along the border, Mexican American and other minority groups have been excluded from economic and political participation. Stoddard notes that, proportionate to their percentage of the total Borderlands population, Amerindians, Mexican Americans, and black Americans carry "two to three times more poverty families" than the Anglo population (Stoddard, 1978c). Furthermore, the proportion of urban-area minority groups remains high, despite Anglo numbers, partly as a function of inmigration and partly because of a high birth rate among families long established in the border region (Crow, 1971). Although economic poverty levels among different groups are highly diversified, as a region the U.S.-Mexican Borderlands is poverty-prone (Stoddard, 1978c). In their recent study of "Poverty in the Lower Rio Grande Valley of Texas," Miller and Maril categorize the border subregion at *the bottom of U.S. urbanized areas in terms of income* (1979: 6). Ethnically, over 90 percent of the poor are Mexican Americans.

Border Participation and Behavior

Border-region social conditions suggest a lower political participation level, especially among minority groups struggling with a political environment relatively unsuitable for political participation. A review of the literature on Chicano voting behavior reveals the recurring theme of voter apathy and nonparticipation in major population centers in the border region.

The first major effort to systematically evaluate Chicano participation was the UCLA Project. In their study of the Southwest, Grebler, Moore, and Guzman reinforced the notion that Mexican Americans, as a group, have appeared to be less disposed to participate in the electoral process than have other minorities. Moreover, Mexican Americans have had limited impact in the political system; their political efficacy seems low (1970).

The notion of lower Chicano participation gains additional support from a study by McCleskey and Nimmo on registration and turnout which concluded that, under the poll-tax system, Mexican Americans registered less frequently than Anglos and blacks. Although the removal of the poll tax in the late 1960s improved matters, the registration rate still fell comparatively short. The study did indicate, though, that once Chicanos qualified to vote, their turnout was almost as high as that of the two other groups (McCleskey and Nimmo, 1968; Nimmo and McCleskey, 1969). In another Texas study by McCleskey and Merrill (1973) of fifteen Texas counties where heavy concentrations were found, Mexican Americans registered at about the same level as, and at times higher than, the rest of Texas. In terms of voting turnout, however, this group participated from 5 percent to 15 percent lower than the entire state (McCleskey and Merrill, 1973b). To A. G. Gutiérrez (1978), "getting people registered to vote has little to do with getting them to the polls on election day" (p. 135). Shinn (1971) reflected similar conclusions. In his study of border Chicanos he found a positive correlation between turnout and Spanish surnames. Freeman's (1974) study of South Tucson concludes that although Chicanos constitute better than 60 percent of the population and dominate local politics, Mexican Americans simply do not participate in the political process.

In *The Ethnic Factor* (1972), Levy and Kramer claimed that the Spanish American vote declined steadily at a time when black voters in the South were making considerable gains. In fact, the downward trend in Chicago voting participation continued to 1972. According to the authors, by 1972 the figures showed a remarkable gap between Mexican American voter participation and Anglo population. During the same period, the U.S. Bureau of the Census reported that the percentage of the Spanish-origin population of voting age that actually voted was 37.5 percent, compared with 64.5 percent for whites and 52.1 percent for blacks (SVREP). Mexican-American registration rates may be lowest in Arizona. Kimball (1972) maintains that in some Pima County (Tucson) districts, Chicanos average a 13 percent lower registration rate than do Anglos.

Despite the low voting levels among Mexican Americans and other minorities in the border region, the sheer potential of these groups still remains. The historical and social conditions of the border region, however, underscore the great difficulty involved in mobilizing the nonvoter who continues to view the electoral process as distant thunder. Gomez (1978) clearly points out this dilemma when he states that the "greatest unresolved task confronting Chicanos desirous of using political and governmental means to improve their condition is mobilizing the Mexican American population living along the . . . border into an election-influencing voting bloc" (p. 388). Nevertheless, the population growth, increased level of education, and economic conditions of Chicanos are variables that indicate potential change. For example, in a 1973 study of population data and the 1972 congressional election districts, the Mexican American voting-age population is larger than the 1972 victory margin in 26 congressional districts in the states of Arizona, California, Colorado, New Mexico, and Texas. "In twelve of these districts the Spanish-speaking voting-age population was at least twice that of the 1972 victory margin" (Southwest Voter Registration Education Project: 6). Moreover, the pattern of low-level Chicano voter participation does not remain constant for the entire region. The New Mexican experience is an exception to voting participation levels and political impotence. In his study of New Mexico, Vigil (1977) concludes that, at least in the 1974 primary elections, Mexican Americans had a higher voting turnout than Anglos, and he found them ". . . contributing significantly to victories by Hispanics in six of eight statewide races" (pp. 347-48). Holmes, in *Politics in New Mexico* (1967), claims that the Hispanic voting record reflects communities "whose voters long ago developed highly organized, stable, competitive two-party politics at village as well as precinct and county levels" (p. 67).

The low level of Chicano political participation has led to a historical pattern of political impotence. For example, in an empirical study by Padilla and Ramirez (1974), it was noted that "only nine Chicanos have served in the California Legislative Senate since it was first organized" (p. 190). Slightly better representation is found in other parts of the border region.

Besides socioeconomic and educational considerations, there are diverse explanations for the low level of voting participation. Vigil (1977) argues that there are two different explanations for Chicano nonparticipation—the racial and cultural one and the legal or structural one. The former suggests that Chicano nonparticipation in the electoral process is due to the Mexican culture, wherein "the common citizen is prone to expect and rely on elites to govern" (p. 307). The legal explanation suggests that the dominant social group has a definite control of legal-political structures and has "imposed legal or procedural barriers that have served to exclude Chicanos" (p. 308).

The bulk of recent literature on voter participation stresses legal and structural factors as participation barriers. De la Garza's (1977) study of El Paso concluded that low voting participation is more a result of "systematic variables" which operate to inhibit participation. Grebler et al. (1970) contend that the history of contacts between the Mexican American people and the U.S. government is replete with incidents of prejudice against the Chicano people. Similar claims are documented by McWilliams in his classical study, *North from Mexico* (1968). Garcia's *Political Socialization of Chicano Children* (1972) arrives at a similar explanation for low voting participation, including discriminatory practices by the larger society and the recent migration of Chicanos from rural areas to the vibrant cities. Neighbor's (1976) studies of El Paso voting representation contend that, through at-large representation, the Chicano vote has been diluted and that "nonpartisanship" inflates the vote of those who culturally dominate and dilute ". . . the vote of the culturally discriminated, because of the lesser need of the former and the greater need of the latter to identify political interest with party label" (Neighbor, 1977). Other gerrymandering has been documented by Taebel; in "Minority Representation on City Councils" (1978) he concludes that minority representation is more "a function of the number of city council seats than the type of election plan." Additional reasons for nonparticipation are "deliberate obstacles" such as intimidation, residency laws, and the threat of loss of employment.[3]

The Democratic party in the border region has been labeled a "highly efficient operation." For many decades that party's predominance has been so phenomenal that Republican and third-party attempts to win control have been minimal. To what extent has the Democratic party served as a catalyst for political activity and voter participation? To some researchers the role of the Democratic party has been detrimental to voter participation, since its "sole concern is to mobilize [voters] to vote a straight ticket" (A. G. Gutiérrez, 1978: 132). To others, groups like the Mexican Americans have aligned with Democrats (Liberals) because a "substantial part of the liberal creed is concerned with the rights and opportunities of minority groups . . ." (McCleskey et al., 1978: 116). Although historically Mexican Americans and other groups have been committed to the Democratic party, it "has not rewarded Mexican Americans in proportion to the support received from them" (de la Garza, 1977: 65). To Corona, the history of the Democratic party in California is a "history of political repression and exploitation" (Juárez, 1974: 304).

The arrogant mood of the Democratic leadership, the general upheaval in American politics in the mid-1960s, the emergence of Chicano leaders in more assertive political roles, and some shifts in party electorate support were important factors in creating La Raza Unida (LRU), an alternative to a two-party system unable or unwilling to represent the Chicano community (see Merrill, 1976). As a product of the border region La Raza Unida enjoyed some degree of conventional and unconventional success, especially at the local level. The most compelling experiences have been those in Crystal City and Zavalla County in Texas. La Raza Unida leaders have controlled city and county politics since the early 1970s. Third parties are, however, limited by their lack of uniformity, political strength, and acceptance, especially in state and national elections. Moreover, the success of LRU depended on several characteristics not necessarily common throughout the border region (Shockley, 1974).

The decline of La Raza Unida party brought a considerable number of supporters back to the Democratic party. The return to the traditional party brought a significant change for Chicano leaders: the creation of a permanent organiza-tion within the Democratic party. Both the Hispanic American Democrats (HAD) and Mexican American Democrats (MAD) made their debut in 1978.[4] The shift back to the Democratic party was not complete. A comparison of the Southwestern Mexican vote in the 1976 and 1980 presidential elections indicated a shift of this group's support from the Democratic presidential candidate to the Republican and Independent candidates.[5]

Political participation and representation present many critical issues for the Hispanic leaders in the 1980s. One of the most critical issues relating voter participation on the border is the considerable number of people who still do not vote; they comprise "at least half and possibly as much as three-fourths of the potentially eligible electorate along the border" (A. G. Gutierrez, 1978: 135). Mobilizing this potential electorate amid extreme poverty, political alienation, illiteracy, unemployment, discrimination, migration, a one-party system, and ethnic traditions that exclude voter participation presents one of the most intriguing, yet stubborn, challenges to democratic theory in the border region. Another critical issue is gerrymandering. Mexican Americans are "the most gerrymandered and malapportioned people in the United States."[6] Without adequate redistricting at the county, city, state, and federal levels voter-registration drives are considered to be futile. It has been predicted that Hispanics will become the largest minority group in the United States by the end of the 1980s. Partial solutions to these critical issues will definitely give this group a considerable leverage in community affairs.

The study of border-region voting behavior has suffered from scholarly neglect, although recent attention has brought an interest that will probably have far-reaching effects. The success of such study will depend upon rigorous definitions of what constitutes the border region, emphasis on comprehensive and comparative studies that cover border diversity, the impact of migration and population growth on voting behavior, and the potential mobilization of the nonpartici-pant.

1. Mainly, the area examined includes the states that border with Mexico.

2. The greater part of the literature on political participation emphasizes the ethnic variable.

3. The number of obstacles that limit voter participation is considerable. See F. Chris García and Rudolph de la Garza (1977: chap. 7).

4. For a discussion of these organizations see Howard Kim, "Our *Voz* Within the Democratic Party," *Nuestro,* August 25, 1980, p. 25.

5. According to a study by the Southwest Voter Registration Education Project, "the Republican support among Latinos increased by 53 percent, compared to the 16 percent for the Democrats." See Choco Gonzales Meza, *The Latino Vote in the 1980 Presidential Elections* (San Antonio: Southwest Voter Registration Project, 1981).

6. See Gloria Rubio, "Hispanic Impact on the Political Process," *Agenda,* January-February, 1980, pp. 8-10.

44

Mexican
Demographic
Trends

LAWRENCE A. CARDOSO
Department of History
University of Wyoming

Gross population trends partially explain migration of Mexicans within the twentieth-century Borderlands. National culture, history, psychology, economic trends, and the desire for self-betterment have also affected Mexico's internal and external migration. Strong "push" factors, particularly in rural Mexico, continue to complement even stronger "pull" forces in the United States, and the number of Mexicans in the U.S. Borderlands is growing rapidly (see Dillman, "Border Urbanization," chapter 46 in this sourcebook).

Mexico's Population Growth

The 1910 Mexican Revolution and the aftermath of intense nationalism gave rise to an official pro-natalist policy. Revolutionary politicians and intellectuals, as they interpreted their nation's history, felt that Mexico's small population caused many past disasters. According to them, Mexico had lost one-half of her

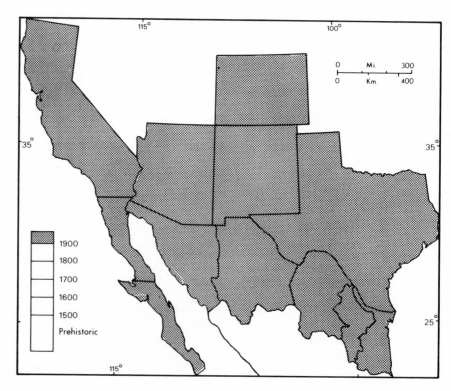

territory in 1848 to the United States because of her inability to field sufficiently large armies to fight off the Yankee invaders and was unable to repel two additional U.S. invasions in the twentieth century. With only relatively small population clusters in her northern desert region, what losses might ensue in another conflict? This perceived relationship between national defense and population was best expressed by the head of the Federal Department of Health in 1927: "The destiny of a people is fundamentally tied to its demographic potency" (González Navarro, 1974, vol. I: 121). Moreover, it was generally believed in Mexico that a rapid rise in the standard of living had not occurred since the 1821 independence, partially because of the small national population. More people would pressure the government, at all levels, for better services and facilities. The standard of living, in short, would rise as more and more people demanded, by their very presence, that it do so. This attitude was deeply embedded within Mexican culture, as symbolized by the Spanish maxim from colonial days: *gobernar es poblar* ("to govern is to populate"). With these beliefs and hopes, demographic spokesmen of the revolution such as Gilberto Loyo planned a national program to increase the total population (Loyo, 1935; Stycos et al., 1971: 63; Corwin, 1963).

However, little incentive to limit the number of children has existed outside the numerically small middle class until very recent efforts in populous urban centers. Indeed, given the low wages available to most working people and the nearly total lack of social security programs for insurance and old-age benefits, children are a positive economic addition to the typical family. They are kept out of school to supplement their parents' earnings. Meanwhile, the Catholic Church, traditionally an opponent of birth control, has kept silent (Urquidi, 1967; Navarrete, 1967: 136; McCoy, 1974*b*: 377-93).

Medical advances since the 1940s, including penicillin and other wonder drugs, caused the death rate to plummet, especially for the very young. Government-supported medical facilities began to deliver quality medical programs for the first time. Intensive campaigns were launched to improve food preparation, provide safe drinking water, and deliver prenatal care. The mortality rate dropped sharply, the birth rate stayed high, and the young had a good chance of survival (Cook and Borah, 1971, vol. II: 409-35; Benítez Zenteno, 1967; Gutierrez de MacGregor, 1968: 10-11).

Statistics of overall Mexican population growth, shown in Table 44-1, tell the story eloquently. The revolutionaries'

Table 44-1. *Mexican Population Growth, 1940-2000.*

1940	19,815,000
1950	26,640,000
1960	34,040,000
1970	50,718,000
1980	68,000,000*
2000 (est.)	135,000,000†

Source: Mexican census data.
*Mexican census data.
†Sánchez-Albornoz (1974: 258).

pro-natalist policy was so successful that demographic growth far exceeded most projections (United Nations, 1954: 16; Sánchez-Albornoz, 1974: 5-6).

Other components of this plan for national greatness, however, did not proceed with such linear development. The status of rural working people is basic to understanding emigration pressures. Increases in rural population have brought disaster for the majority of families. The adult working force now numbers almost nine million men and women. Mexican economist Edmundo Flores estimates that more and more of the working force is becoming landless; underemployment and unemployment, for which no reliable statistics are available, are chronically at about 66 percent of the work force (Flores, 1976: 75-79). Less food is produced as the years go by because of soil depletion, and the average annual wage for rural toilers is less than U.S. $120. Because of this "atavistic cruelty," in the words of sociologist Carlos A. Echanove (1969: 44), we see a steadily increasing emigration (Flores, 1976: 113-14; Ronfeldt, 1973: 171-215; R. Wilkie, 1971: 131-42).

Displaced rural people see Mexico's cities as attractive alternatives, but urban areas usually fail to live up to the migrants' expectations. Higher wages; the chance to earn money by washing cars, shining shoes, and performing other marginal services; and the availability of subsidized housing, medical services, and other benefits of the modern Mexican welfare state induce thousands to flee the countryside every week. Mexico City is the primary destination for the displaced, although Monterrey and other cities have witnessed an influx of rural poor in search of jobs and personal security (Loyo, 1970: 33; Pontones, 1976: 162; Gollás and García, 1976: 436-39; Balán et al., 1973: 61, 64).

So great has been the influx of the rural poor, however, that whatever advantages might have awaited them in the cities have vanished. The Mexican economic "miracle" since 1940 has indeed brought about quick and impressive growth in the gross national product, but when measured on a per-capita basis, a steady decline in personal income has also occurred. More and more people in the country are receiving a smaller and smaller share of the pie. Underemployment and unemployment in the cities have afflicted one-third of the adult working force. And with eight hundred thousand young people yearly entering the job market for the first time, prospects for the future are not good. The "miracle" has not been miraculous enough (Reynolds, 1970: 36-43; Flores, 1976: 114-16; Wilkie, 1970).

After Mexico's industrialized centers, northern Mexico's border area is the second most popular internal destination of the displaced rural migrants. The magnetism of the international zone has been strengthened through the Border Industrialization Program's building of hundreds of factories. Ironically, this program's "employment net," established in large part to slow down emigration to the United States, has succeeded in drawing far more people than there are jobs available. This situation, in turn, has led to the creation of large pools of unemployed, restless workers just on the other side of the border. Tourism and commuter work have also drawn hundreds of thousands from the central part of the country. Ciudad Juárez's population, for example, has grown from 424,000 in 1970 to an estimated 700,000 in 1975; Tijuana and other border towns show a similar population growth. Julian Samora estimates that by 1980 the northern frontier region of Mexico may have 14,000,000 people (Samora, 1971: 132-34; Martínez, 1978: 148; Price, 1973*a*: 1-21; Urquidi, Méndez and Villarreal, 1978: 141-62; Corwin and McCain, 1978: 68-69).

Only recently have Mexico's leaders attempted to deal with the problems of population growth. In 1973, President Luis Echeverría made available voluntary family planning services to the general population through the Secretariat of Health. The General Population Law (1973) calls for *paternidad responsable* ("responsible parenthood") with the aims of strengthening family life, raising the standard of living, and pursuing more qualitative national development. The Roman Catholic Church, through its silence, has given its tacit support to the new program. Even Gilberto Loyo, the major spokesman for increased population growth, has expressed his concern over the slowing down of economic growth because of the population explosion. While it is too early to judge the overall importance of this program, it may in the long run help to ameliorate some current problems and thus lessen migration pressures (Loyo, 1974: 186, 193-94; McCoy, 1974*a*: 394-98; Sanders, 1974).

Emigration to the United States

Whatever future developments in Mexico may occur, the United States has been and will remain for many decades one of the principal outlets for Mexicans who wish to improve their lot. The sheer weight of precedent argues for this view. Since the turn of the century, Mexican muscle has provided an indispensable element for economic growth in the Borderlands and far beyond. U.S. federal authorities, working in close cooperation with southwestern employers and espousing the ideals of Pan American goodwill, have allowed large-scale immigration to meet the needs of regional development and to improve often shaky relations with our sister republic south of the Rio Grande. This policy has been the *sine qua non* of economic development in the Borderlands, given the relatively low population density of the area. Only in times of recession or depression has this policy been reversed (Cardoso, 1977; Hoffman, 1974; Bustamante, 1976*c*; Corwin, 1978*b*: 136-75; García, 1980).

Since World War II, moreover, the rising expectations of Americans and their lowering birth rate have meant that fewer and fewer people in the United States are willing to do unpleasant, semiskilled, low-paid work. Somebody has to pick the crops and perform other arduous tasks. More often than not in the Borderlands the Mexican immigrant has been the only one willing to do these things. He is eagerly accepted by employers, and dramatic changes in this situation seem improbable (Spengler, 1975: 15, 28; Corwin and McCain, 1978: 67-107).

For these very practical reasons there has been little effective exclusion from this country, despite our generally very restrictive immigration laws. Indeed, at times, in the words of Paul S. Taylor, we see "a long, dismal history of immigration laws that have never been fully enforced [along the Mexican border]" (Taylor, 1978: 351). The Immigration Law of 1924, which placed an effective block to "new" immigrants from southern and eastern Europe, excluded the Mexican from its restrictions so that economic interests in the Borderlands could have their cheap labor. The Immigration Act of 1965 did place a maximum quota of forty thousand on entrants from any one Latin American nation, but it is quite clear that this paper barrier is not operable for Mexico. This recent law excluded those coming here to join relatives. The extensive kinship network in Mexican culture thus allows almost double the number of Mexicans to enter the United States, in sharp distinction to the limits placed on other countries of the Western Hemisphere (Briggs, 1978: 210).

And then there is the matter of illegal migration. The United States Immigration and Naturalization Service now estimates that the number of illegal migrants may be as large as three million (R. A. Fernández, 1977: 116). Although migration statistics are "largely a game of conjectures and calculated guesses," it is clear that the Mexican addition to our permanent-resident population since the year 1900 exceeds five million people (Corwin, 1978*c*: 108-35; Ehrlich et al., 1979).

Some Effects of Mexican Migration

The open-door policy of the U.S. government benefits more people than it harms. The labor exodus creates a safety valve for Mexico's excess population and thus reduces the possibility of political unrest in our neighboring republic. Demands for labor are met in the booming Sun Belt states. And, all inflammatory rhetoric of many restrictionists aside, most of the newcomers are young, "on the make," and very hard-working (Dagodag, 1975: 499-511; González Navarro, 1974, vol. II: 202-203). The money they earn here may be taken back to Mexico, where it is used to improve the migrants' standard of living. The newcomer may also decide to stay in one of the numerous and growing Chicano barrios and usually becomes a good citizen (Norquest, 1972; García Tellez, 1955: 27-28; Nelson, 1975).

Many of those who remain in the United States do not settle permanently in one place. Instead, they join internal migratory streams in this country. Often, the recent migrant may move on because of depressed wages caused by the continuing arrival of immigrants from his native country. Chicanos, suffering from low wages caused in part by the influx of Mexicans, are at times also forced to join the migratory stream. San Antonio and the lower Rio Grande Valley are the two primary sites of this "bumping" northward of workers (Kemper, 1969; Peón, 1966).

Continuing immigration has also slowed down the assimilation process for Chicanos and Mexican Americans in ways which are not yet totally clear. Within the context of American history, immigrant groups and their descendants begin rapid assimilation only *after* the drastic reduction of the number of newer arrivals to the group. We see this most remarkably in the cases of southern and eastern Europeans after 1924 (Higham, 1975). Continuing Mexican immigration provides constant cultural replenishment to local established communities, however, and traditional community patterns of life are reinforced: a premium is often not set on assimilation but on striving toward closer identification with the original immigrant group. This insulation, particularly strong near the border but not confined to that region, will doubtless provide for the continued and vigorous existence of the most important ethnic group in the Borderlands (Breton, 1964: 141-46; Browning and McLemore, 1964).

Research Needs

I have sketched only the outlines of the demographic picture as it affects migration. We need more case studies, similar to those by Ronfeldt (1973), Raymond Wilkie (1971), and Perez Lizaur (1975), of Mexican *ejidos* and private property holdings. For far too long the rhetoric of Mexican revolutionaries has blinded us to the gnawing persistence of rural misery which has remained largely untouched by the social programs of national reconstruction. The internal and external migratory processes are not completely understood. In my *Mexican Emigration to the United States, 1897 to 1931* (1980), I offer a partial explanation of the push and pull factors during the first wave of massive emigration in this century. Many recent published works rightly downplay the importance of government statistics and policy statements, concentrating, instead, on the human element of the process. Samora (1971), a valuable exception, will hopefully stimulate other studies in search of answers to new questions. Martínez's recent monograph (1978) of the role played by immigrants in the development of the Ciudad Juárez-El Paso area is outstanding for its perceptions, close analysis, and thorough research. Its incisive model provides a goal for other much-needed local studies of urban areas in the Borderlands. Other important recent works include García (1981) and Herrera-Sobek (1979). We still need to know more about the effects of the immigrants' presence on established Chicano communities. Scholars of the Borderlands from all disciplines should analyze closely these processes—as they have affected and will continue to affect the evolution of the Chicano group. This will enable us to go far toward understanding the complex nature of the region's development.

45

Fertility and Mortality

JOHN J. HEDDERSON
Department of Sociology and
Anthropology
University of Texas, El Paso

Fertility and mortality in the U.S.-Mexican Borderlands from 1930 to 1975 are discussed in this chapter. Demographics on both sides of the border are analyzed separately, and these findings are then integrated.

Reviewing the literature on Borderlands fertility and mortality is difficult. Studies are almost nonexistent. The data for the U.S. Borderlands are poor, while those for the Mexican Borderlands are even worse. An ideal demographic analysis of fertility and mortality requires not only accurate information on births and deaths but also accurate data on the size and age-sex structure of the population being studied. The available Borderlands data are not complete and allow only rough estimates of Borderlands fertility and mortality.

U.S. Borderlands Demographic Data

The Bureau of the Census estimates that in 1970 a little more than 2 percent of the total population was not counted (Siegel, 1974). The undercount was

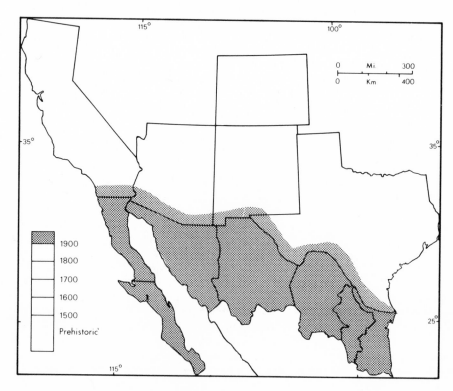

232

much higher for low-income groups, young adults, and minorities. Passel (1976) estimates that the American Indians were undercounted by about 7 percent in the 1970 census. The Bureau of the Census calculates that in 1970, 8 percent of all blacks and 20 percent of black males aged 25-29 were missed (U.S. Bureau of the Census, 1973). The Bureau could not estimate precisely the undercount of people of Spanish origin in 1970 because the question concerning Spanish heritage had not been asked of all households. One Bureau analysis concluded, however, that the undercount of persons of Spanish origin was somewhere between the white and black undercounts (Siegel and Passel, 1979). In the U.S. counties bordering Mexico there are unusually large proportions of young adults, illegal aliens, and non-English speakers as well as a generally low socioeconomic level; the undercount in 1970 of the U.S. Borderlands population therefore may have been quite high. This undercount would bias upward both fertility and mortality measures, because their calculation involves dividing births or deaths by either the total population or specific age-sex groups. The infant mortality rate is an exception, since the denominator is the annual number of births, but it, too, may be biased in border counties because of underregistration of infant deaths.

In the United States, records of births and deaths are compiled at the county level through continuous registration of these events as they occur. The U.S. border counties generally were among the last to have registration complete enough to be included in the annual publication of the National Center for Health Statistics, *Vital Statistics of the United States.* Border-county records still are below national standards, because high poverty levels and border crossings make record keeping difficult. High poverty levels mean that more births and deaths occur outside hospitals, and a vital event occurring outside a hospital is less likely to be registered. Proximity to the border contributes to the inaccuracies because (1) the residence of a person dying or of a woman giving birth may be misreported, and (2) births to and deaths of foreign nationals may not be reported to their government. The stereotypic example is of Mexican resident women having children born in the United States and giving a false U.S. address. But the large amount of traveling and temporary residence of U.S. nationals in Mexico undoubtedly leads to U.S. nationals giving birth, having abortions, or dying in Mexico. The number of these events is not known, but it is highly probable that the net effect is to inflate birth enumeration and deflate death enumeration in the U.S. border counties.

Information on births in U.S. border counties can be obtained from the National Center for Health Statistics, and information on population can be obtained from the Bureau of the Census (see the sources of Table 45-1). Both birth and population data are necessary for the calculations of most fertility measures such as the crude birth rate (number of births per thousand population). The crude birth rate is termed "crude" because it only standardizes for population size, although age and sex structure also affect the number of births for a population. The Bureau of the Census does not estimate age-sex structure at the county level except for cen-

Table 45-1. *Birth Rate, Death Rate, Growth Rate, Infant-Mortality Rate, and Population of U.S. Borderlands Counties, 1980.*

	Crude Birth Rate	Crude Death Rate	Natural Growth Rate (percent)	Infant Mortality Rate	Population
California					
San Diego	17	7	1.0	11	1,861,800
Imperial	25	7	1.8	5	92,100
Arizona					
Yuma	20	8	1.2	9	90,600
Pima	17	8	0.9	8	531,300
Santa Cruz	24	6	1.8	6	20,500
Cochise	18	7	1.1	10	87,700
New Mexico					
Hidalgo	23	9	1.4	14	6,000
Grant	21	6	1.5	9	26,200
Luna	19	12	0.7	7	15,600
Doña Ana	19	5	1.4	10	96,300
Texas					
El Paso	21	5	1.6	10	479,900
Hudspeth	22	8	1.4	0	2,700
Culberson	29	6	2.3	10	3,300
Jeff Davis	21	6	1.5	0	1,600
Presidio	11	8	0.3	0	5,200
Brewster	19	8	1.1	14	7,600
Terrell	15	9	0.6	0	1,600
Val Verde	24	7	1.7	8	35,900
Kinney	18	14	0.4	0	2,300
Maverick	39	7	3.2	4	21,400
Webb	27	6	2.1	12	99,300
Zapata	23	9	1.4	20	6,600
Starr	28	6	2.2	17	27,300
Hidalgo	27	6	2.1	10	283,200
Cameron	26	7	1.9	9	209,700
United States	16	9	0.7	13	225,500,000

Sources: California Department of Health Services, Arizona Bureau of Vital Records and Information Services, New Mexico Health and Environment Department, Texas Department of Health.

Definitions: Crude birth rate = births per thousand population, crude death rate = deaths per thousand population, and natural growth rate = annual percentage of growth.

sus years, so between census years the crude birth rate is the only measure of fertility that can be calculated.

In addition to the statistical sources listed above, one can obtain data by writing directly to state and federal agencies. They can often provide relevant data that are not yet published—and in some cases will not be published. For example, the Texas Bureau of Vital Statistics tabulates Spanish-surname births and deaths by county; it does not publish these data but will provide them on request.

U.S. Borderlands Fertility

Table 45-1 presents the crude birth rates for U.S. border counties. Ranging from a low of 11 per thousand in Jeff Davis County to a high of 31 per thousand in Starr County, in general they are well above the U.S. crude birth rate of 15 per thousand. Even allowing for upward biases because of an underenumeration of population and because of births to Mexican residents who report themselves as U.S. residents, the U.S. Borderlands counties, with few exceptions, clearly have higher than average fertility for the nation. This high fertility is as expected because the border counties have an untypically large proportion of their population below the national medians in income and education and an untypically large proportion of Mexican Americans. Low socioeconomic groups and Mexican Americans have higher than average fertility. In part, the higher than average fertility of Mexican Americans is because that group has a disproportionately large percentage of people below median socioeconomic levels.

The unusually low crude birth rate of Jeff Davis County likely results from an unusually low proportion of its population being in the childbearing years because of the outmigration of its young adults. This explanation seems likely when one notes that the crude death rate for Jeff Davis is high for a border county, suggesting that it has a disproportionately old population. Starr County, which has the highest crude birth rate, also has the highest percentage of families (52 percent) living in poverty according to the 1970 census and the highest percentage (98 percent) of Spanish-surname families (Stoddard, 1978c: 33).

U.S. Borderlands Mortality

Many readers may be surprised to note in Table 45-1 that the crude death rates and infant mortality rates of U.S. border counties are generally below the national averages. How can there be low mortality in a poverty belt? For the crude death rate (number of deaths per thousand population) the reason is age structure. The higher the fertility of a population, the younger will be its age structure, and a young population has a lower crude death rate. The border counties have high fertility, which contributes to their generally having low crude death rates.

The infant mortality rate (number of deaths of children under one year old per thousand births) is not affected by age structure, but it is affected by border crossings. There are children born in the United States to Mexican residents giving a U.S. address. When these infants return to Mexico, some of them die, and their deaths are not recorded in the U.S. counties in which they were born. These unrecorded infant deaths bias downward the infant mortality rates for U.S. border counties. The severity of the border-crossing bias, however, may be overestimated by some authors who calculate the underregistration of Spanish-surname infant mortality as high as 20 percent (Palloni, 1978). Other work suggests that the border crossing bias is not substantial and

that the Spanish-surname population does, in fact, have very low infant mortality for a population with a high proportion of poor families (Hedderson and Dandistel, forthcoming). In examining infant mortality rates, one must also realize that counties with small populations have so few births that the infant mortality rate may be erratically low or high; as in Zapata County, where just three infant deaths resulted in an extremely high infant mortality rate by U.S. standards.

The U.S. Borderlands is an area with glaring differences in mortality between the two most numerous ethnic groups: Hispanics and Anglos. The 1970 census categorized Spanish-surname and Spanish-language households together, while previous censuses had used only a Spanish-surname category. "Anglo" is not a Bureau of the Census classification, but is a useful, albeit vague, category for non-Hispanic whites. (Note that Spanish-surname and Hispanic Americans are included in the "white" census category.) Hispanic Americans are mostly Mexican Americans in the Borderlands, but also include those with Spanish, Puerto Rican, Cuban, and other Hispanic origins. There have been no adequate national-level studies of the mortality of Hispanic Americans.

Regional studies indicate, however, that the Spanish-surname population, especially the Mexican Americans within it, have higher than average mortality for the United States (Bradshaw and Fonner, 1978). Life expectancy for the Spanish-surname population in San Antonio was around 63 years in 1950 as compared to 72 years for the Anglo population (Ellis, 1962). In Texas life expectancy in 1970 was 70 for the Spanish-surname population and 72 for Anglos (Siegel and Passel, 1979). How much of the difference in mortality is due to the Mexican American population being generally poorer has not been studied, but one would hypothesize that this is the major cause. Inferior public education and health services because of language barriers and other discriminating forces are also likely to be causing higher mortality among Mexican Americans.

Mexican Borderlands Demographic Data

Resources of the Mexican government available for registration of vital events and the conducting of censuses are fewer than those available in the United States. At the same time, having a less literate, poorer population makes accurate data gathering much more difficult. In Mexico a larger proportion of vital events occurs outside of hospitals and a larger proportion of the population is transient or living in temporary shelters. Since 1950, the Mexican Borderlands have been one of the fastest growing regions of the nation; consequently, record keeping is even more difficult there. Local records on births, deaths, population size, and age-sex structure are further skewed by the migration of Mexican and American nationals back and forth across the border. At this time one can only extrapolate from national trends to make judgments about likely fertility and mortality in the Mexican Borderlands. In the future sample surveys and sample registration programs would probably be the best possibilities for obtaining adequate data from these areas. Most of the national fertility and mortality figures presented below are adjusted estimates by United Nations demographers based on the incomplete registration of births and deaths and the decennial census. These estimates are fairly accurate, but it is unlikely that they are exactly on the mark.

Mexican Borderlands Fertility

Mexico had one of the highest crude birth rates in the world, and Table 45-2 shows it did not decline until the 1970s, when it dropped sharply. Mexico's crude birth rate in 1980 was estimated to be 33 per thousand, compared to the world crude birth rate of 29 per thousand and the U.S. crude birth rate of 16 per thousand. The persistently high fertility, despite substantial socioeconomic development, had led some demographers to contend that the theory of demographic transition could not explain current fertility in Mexico (Seiver, 1975, 1976). (Transition theory posits that societies change from high fertility and high mortality to low fertility and low mortality because of socioeconomic development.) Other scholars believed that they detected the beginnings of development-linked fertility declines in Mexico (Hicks, 1974), and the 1970s decline confirmed their position.

There is evidence from the National Fertility Survey of 1976 that the Mexican family program begun in 1972-73 may have lowered the crude birth rate from 45 per thousand in 1970 to 41 per thousand by mid-1976 (Nagel, 1978: 28). Victor Urquidi, president of El Colegio de México, a leading center for economic and demographic research, estimated the mid-1978 annual population growth at 2.9 percent (Intercom, 1978). This rate would correspond to a crude birth rate of 37 per thousand and bodes well for achieving President Lopez Portillo's goal of lowering natural growth to 2.5 percent by 1982 and 1 percent by 2000. There is a tendency for officials interested in lowering fertility to overestimate

declines, but, if there was in fact a decline in the crude birth rate from 45 to 33 per thousand between 1970 and 1980, it represents a salient turning point in Mexico's demographic history.

The Mexican Borderlands may have a crude birth rate above the national average because the migration of young adults into the region increases the proportion of the population in the childbearing years. This effect would be dampened to the extent that the sex ratio of the in-migrants is not balanced, creating a surplus of males or females in the region. Although the exact levels are unknown, it is safe to conclude that the Mexican Borderlands are one of the regions of highest fertility in the world. Demographic transition theory predicts that this fertility will begin to decline if it has not already, but the possibility exists that Mexico and her Borderlands will continue to be an exception to this theory.

Mexican Borderlands Mortality

The best available indicators of Mexican Borderlands mortality are national mortality rates calculated by demographers from incomplete records (Benitez-Zenteno and Cabrera-Acevedo, 1967; Alba, 1977a). These rates show that Mexico's mortality has been declining steadily and is low by world standards even though it is much higher than that of affluent nations. Mexico does, of course, have one of the lowest crude death rates in the world, but this is substantially due to Mexico's young age structure. Mortality measures that control for age structure provide a better comprehension of mortality levels in Mexico.

The infant mortality rate is a good indicator of mortality levels because it is not affected by age structure and is easier to compile than life expectancy. The Population Reference Bureau (1981) estimated that infant mortality in Mexico was 70 per thousand births. The Borderlands of Mexico have higher socioeconomic levels than the national average, so one would expect that the infant mortality there is a little lower, perhaps about 65 per thousand. Both figures compare favorably to the total world infant mortality rate of 99 per thousand but are much higher than Sweden's 1978 infant mortality rate of 8 per thousand, the lowest recorded by any nation. The steady decline in the infant mortality rate of Mexico suggests that there have been improvements in both medical care and living standards in the past 45 years. The recent slight increase may be due to more complete registration of infant deaths and not an increase in the actual rate.

Life expectancy at birth is a measure of mortality levels which is not biased by age-structure effects. Life expectancies for Mexico calculated for the past five decades show that life expectancy has been increasing and is currently five years greater than the world standard of sixty years (Table 45-3). In Mexico, as almost everywhere, life expectancy is greater for women than for men. This sex gap in life expectancy tends to increase as life expectancy increases. How much of this gap is due to the genetically superior resistance of

Table 45-2. *Crude Birth Rate, Crude Death Rate, and Natural Growth Rate for Mexico and the United States, 1930-80.*

	Mexico			United States		
Year	Crude Birth Rate	Crude Death Rate	Natural Growth Rate (percent)	Crude Birth Rate	Crude Death Rate	Natural Growth Rate (percent)
1930	45	26	1.9	21	11	1.0
1940	—	—	—	19	11	0.8
1950	46	16	3.0	24	10	1.4
1960	44	11	3.3	24	10	1.4
1970	45	10	3.2	18	9	0.9
1980	33	8	2.5	16	9	0.7

Sources: Mexico, 1930-50—United Nations, *Statistical Yearbook, 1955,* Tables 2 and 3; 1960—United Nations, *Demographic Yearbook, 1961,* Table 14; 1970-75—Nagel (1978); 1980—*1981 World Population Data Sheet* (Washington, D.C.: Population Reference Bureau). United States, 1930-75—U.S. Bureau of the Census, *Statistical Abstract of the United States, 1977; 1980—1981 World Population Data Sheet* (Washington, D.C.: Population Reference Bureau).

Table 45-3. *Infant Mortality and Life Expectancy by Sex for Mexico and the United States, 1930-80.*

	Mexico				United States			
	Infant Mortality*	Life Expectancy			Infant Mortality*	Life Expectancy		
Year	tality*	Total	Male	Female	tality*	Total	Male	Female
1930	147	37	36	37	65	60	58	62
1940	125	41	40	42	47	63	61	65
1950	101	50	48	51	29	68	66	71
1960	74	59	58	60	26	70	67	73
1970	68	61	59	63	20	71	67	75
1980	70	65	—	—	13	74	70	78

Sources: Mexico, 1930-60—Raul Benitez and Gustavo Cabreera Acevedo, *Tablas Abreviadas de Mortalidad de la Población de Mexico, 1967* (Mexico City: El Colegio de México), pp. 25, 63; 1970—United Nations, *Demographic Yearbook, 1974, 1975,* Tables 22 and 33; 1980—*1981 World Population Data Sheet* (Washington, D.C.: Population Reference Bureau). United States, 1930-70—U.S. Bureau of the Census, *Statistical Abstract of the United States, 1979,* Table 100; 1980—*Statistical Bulletin* 61 (no. 4): 13.

*Per thousand over one year.

the female to degenerative diseases and how much is due to differences in life-styles is undetermined, but both factors seem to be involved.

Currently in the Mexico Borderlands, life expectancies are probably above national levels because the average income for the region is above the national average. The averages, however, obscure the existence of severe poverty in the Mexico Borderlands, especially among the new in-migrants to the border cities. Some of the new arrivals are forced to live in caves dug into hillsides or in cardboard and scrap-lumber shacks while trying to improve their lot. The mortality of this impoverished group most likely is high by world standards.

Conclusions

When considered as a totality, the U.S.-Mexican Borderlands are from a demographic perspective quite heterogeneous. In the U.S. Borderlands, fertility and mortality rates are both low by world standards, although they are higher than rates for the entire United States. In the Mexican Borderlands, fertility is high by world standards and much higher than on the U.S. side, and mortality is low by world standards but considerably higher than on the U.S. side of the Borderlands. Fertility and mortality are probably lower in the Mexican Borderlands than for all of Mexico. This combination— the U.S. Borderlands having high fertility and mortality for the United States and the Mexican Borderlands having low fertility and mortality for Mexico—reduces the national difference in vital rates in the Borderlands. Even with this reduction in differences, however, the U.S.-Mexican Borderlands are one of the most demographically diverse regions in the world and will remain so for at least the next few decades.

The Mexico-United States boundary is the world's longest land border separating high- and low-income countries. Along this unique demarcation line, paired or twin urban clusters from Tijuana-San Diego (San Ysidro) in the west to Matamoros-Brownsville in the east reflect this economic disparity (Pederson, 1978). Most countries stringently control traffic across their borders, yet the sharp economic contrasts across the Mexican-U.S. boundary have led to a relatively open border, or, in many respects, even a porous barrier. Interaction between the paired communities in retail trade, commuter workers, and tourism has fostered a high degree of mutual symbiosis, the absence of which would severely impair the economic health of each side. The urban twins are not individual entities; they are in reality divided cities.[1]

Mexican municipalities during the 1970s continued to face the complex problems of burgeoning population growth, urban sprawl, high unemployment, and squalor experienced in the '50s and '60s (Cárdenas, 1970). The economies of the Mexican border centers have been dominated increasingly by U.S. assembly

46

Border
Urbanization

C. DANIEL DILLMAN
Department of Geography
Northern Illinois University

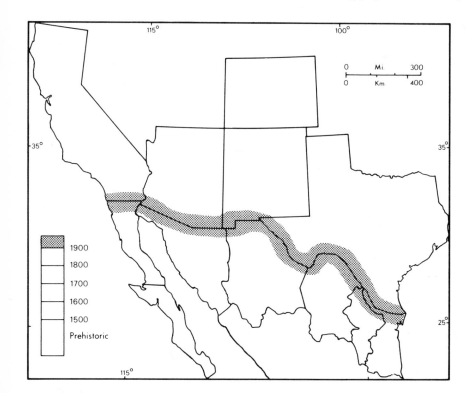

plants (Dillman, 1977*b*; Bosse, 1973), vegetable shipments northward to the United States (Gildersleeve, 1974), the southward influx of U.S. tourists to Mexico (Secretaría de Industria y Comercio, 1974), the movement of contraband in both directions, the passage of illegal drugs into the United States (R. Fernández, 1977), and the thriving trade in commercial sex (Demaris, 1970). In terms of goods and services, Mexico's northern border has had more important foreign than domestic connections (Dillman, 1970*b*). The narrow functional base of Mexican municipalities has provided insufficient employment opportunities for a population rapidly expanding in response to (1) migration northward for higher wages and better living conditions, (2) change from rural to urban residence, (3) high rates of natural increase, and (4) decentralization of industry associated with the Border Industrialization Program (BIP).

The "Border Paradox"

The juxtaposition of a highly developed nation next to a developing one contributes to the "border paradox" (Stoddard, 1978*c*). Incomes in Mexico rise with proximity to the border zone; in the United States the reverse holds true. The U.S. side of the border is an area of general poverty, particularly in the lower Rio Grande area of Texas, where Brownsville, McAllen, and Laredo were the lowest-ranking U.S. cities in per capita income in 1970. Isolation, lack of resources, and restrictions imposed by the international boundary have hindered population growth and economic expansion in U.S. border centers. This side has lagged far behind most other U.S. areas in industrial development (Nathan, 1968). Economic systems of American border towns would be weakened seriously without access to cheap Mexican labor, consumer purchases by Mexican nationals, and tourist revenues. Nevertheless, to people in Mexico, the other side of the border looms as a region of wealth and opportunity (O. J. Martínez, 1976).

Population Distribution and Change

Population in *municipios* and counties adjacent to the international boundary stood at just under six million in 1970, with slightly over one-half that number south of the border. The *municipios* of Ciudad Juárez, Mexicali, and Tijuana held 40 percent of the Mexican border population; Matamoros, Nuevo Laredo, Reynosa, and Ensenada accounted for two-fifths of the residents (Schmidt, 1976*b*). In the United States, San Diego, El Paso, and Pima counties were the most populous, with a concentration of more than 70 percent of the U.S. border population. Approximately one of every three persons on the border lived either in San Diego County or in the *municipio* of Tijuana. Excluding San Diego, but including San Ysidro, Mexican border cities were several times larger than their U.S. counterparts (Tables 46-1 and 46-2).

The northern Mexico border strip was more urbanized

in 1970 and had become so more swiftly than the rest of the republic (Dillman, 1970*b*). While national urban population climbed from 51 to 60 percent between 1960 and 1970, urban dwellers in northern border states increased from 64 to 85 percent. The border zone, moreover, has experienced the highest population growth rate of any major Mexican region since 1940 (Price, 1973*a*). Since 1950, an average annual increment of roughly 5 percent also has made the northernmost municipalities one of the world's fastest growing areas. Population in border municipalities swelled from 841,000 in 1950 to 2,335,000 in 1970, a mean annual rate of 5.2 percent compared to 3.2 percent for the entire republic and 3.6 percent for the six northern states (Subsecretaría de la Presidencia, 1974).

On the other hand, an almost 200 percent population increase in the largest border municipalities from 1950 to 1970 disguised a greatly reduced growth rate during the 1960s (Table 46-2). Generally, population rose at decreasing rates throughout the decade except in Matamoros, which grew even more rapidly, and Piedras Negras, which lost population. Estimates for the seven largest Mexican cities in 1990 project the highest increments for the western half of the border zone and show Tijuana and Nuevo Laredo changing their ranks from third to second and sixth to fourth, respectively (Banco Nacional de Comercio Exterior, 1978).

Borderward Migration

Relatively higher living levels and proximity to the United States have provided strong stimuli for in-migration from other parts of Mexico. As a result, a far larger share of the border population (29 percent) than in the rest of the republic (15 percent) or the northern border states (20 percent) did not reside in the states of their birth, according to the 1970 census. Tijuana received the largest absolute influx of migrants during the 1960s, followed by Mexicali and Ciudad Juárez, with less than one-half as many newcomers (Table 46-3). With one of every two residents born elsewhere, Tijuana vividly illustrated the magnetism of real or imagined opportunities offered by border communities.

Seen in the context of borderward migration, Mexican border municipalities have served as gateways, stopover points, and favored destinations (O. J. Martínez, 1977*b*). In the first instance, Mexican centers have been "springboards" into the United States for two transborder working groups: daily commuters and seasonal laborers. Mexican cities also have provided temporary respite for countless *repatriados* and *deportados* whose arrival has closely coincided with periods of economic distress in the United States. Further, the border stopover function has enabled migrants ultimately bound for distant U.S. locations to prepare themselves for culture shock *al otro lado*. The attraction of certain cities for in-migrants was greatly enhanced in the first half of the 1970s by accelerated growth of the BIP, although expanded operations by *maquiladoras* did little to ease massive unemployment among males (Dillman, 1978).

Table 46-1. *Population Growth in Nine U.S. Border Cities.*

City	Population			Percentage Increase		
	1950	1960	1970	1950-60	1960-70	1950-70
San Diego	334,387	573,224	696,769	71	22	108
Calexico	6,433	7,992	10,625	24	33	65
Nogales	6,153	7,286	8,946	18	23	45
Douglas	9,442	11,925	12,462	26	5	32
El Paso	130,485	276,687	322,261	112	17	147
Eagle Pass	7,276	12,094	15,364	66	27	111
Laredo	51,910	60,678	69,024	17	14	33
McAllen	20,067	32,728	37,636	63	15	88
Brownsville	36,066	48,040	52,522	33	9	46
Total	602,219	1,030,654	1,225,609	X̄ 48	X̄ 18	X̄ 75

Source: *U.S. Census of Population,* 1970. The most reliable estimates of the populations of the nine cities prior to the 1980 census were San Diego, 842,000; Calexico, 15,000; Nogales, 12,000; Douglas, 15,000; El Paso (County), 600,000; Eagle Pass, 25,000; Laredo, 100,000; McAllen (Hidalgo), 75,000; Brownsville, 90,000 (Milton H. Jamail, *The United States-Mexico Border: A Guide to Institutions, Organizations, and Scholars* [Tucson: University of Arizona Latin American Area Center, 1980]).

Table 46-2. *Population Growth in Ten Mexican Border Municipalities.*

Municipio	Population			Percentage Increase		
	1950	1960	1970	1950-60	1960-70	1950-70
Ensenada	31,077	64,934	115,423	109	78	271
Tijuana	65,364	165,690	340,583	153	106	421
Mexicali	124,362	281,333	396,324	126	41	219
San Luis Río Colorado	13,593	42,134	63,604	210	51	368
Nogales	26,016	39,812	53,494	53	34	106
Ciudad Juárez	131,308	276,995	424,135	111	53	223
Piedras Negras	31,665	48,408	46,698	53	-4	47
Nuevo Laredo	59,496	96,043	151,253	61	57	154
Reynosa	69,428	134,869	150,786	94	12	117
Matamoros	128,347	143,043	186,146	11	30	45
Total	680,656	1,293,261	1,928,446	X̄ 98	X̄ 48	X̄197

Source: Secretaría de Industria y Comercio, Dirección General de Estadística, *VIII and IX Censos de Población, 1960 and 1970* (México, D.F.). The most reliable estimates of the populations of the nine cities before release of official population totals for 1980 were Tijuana, 1,000,000; Ciudad Juárez, 1,000,000; Mexicali, 800,000; Matamoros, 350,000; Nuevo Laredo, 300,000; Reynosa, 300,000; San Luis Río Colorado, 150,000; Nogales, 120,000; Piedras Negras, 120,000 (Milton H. Jamail, *The United States-Mexico Border: A Guide to Institutions, Organizations, and Scholars* [Tucson: University of Arizona Latin American Area Center, 1980]).

Hybrid Urban Centers

The current interweaving of economic, social, and cultural interests in a binational, bicultural, and bilingual regional setting graphically exemplifies symbiotic relationships long prevailing in the twin communities (McWilliams, 1976; Stone et al., 1963). Adjacent to the international boundary is a transitional corridor of culture overlap and blending. A third culture, neither completely Latin nor Anglo-Saxon, has appeared as a syncretization of the two. Cultural fusion has affected the development of distinctive city forms and organizations instead of mere facsimiles of either Mexican or U.S. urban centers. Innovations in language, diet, dress, and customs attest to dynamic cultural change as one travels toward the border. Government institutions have adapted to unique border milieus, facilitating the flow of ideas, goods, and people across the international line (O. J. Martínez, 1976). Paired communities rely heavily upon informal functional relationships (which circumvent federal jurisdictional constraints and regulatory policies) to coordinate activities resulting from proximity and interdependence (Sloan and West, 1977).

Tijuana, the world's fastest-growing city (Ridgely, 1977), a focus of internal migration and a center of Mexican economic development efforts, clearly manifests the hybridization of urban culture. Ever-present cultural and economic interaction is reshaping values, attitudes, and preferences as traditions from Mexico's heartland mingle and fuse with southern California's urban culture. Probably no other part of Mexico is as vulnerable as Tijuana to cultural stress; as a result, its urban landscape is eclectic in the extreme (Griffin and Ford, 1976).

The impact of different cultures upon each other in closely linked urban centers has been treated by Sheck (1974) for

Table 46-3. *In-migration, Mexican Border Municipalities.*

Municipio	Total Pop. 1970	Percentage Born Elsewhere*	Number of Arrivals 1960-70†	Percentage of Total Pop.	Percentage Distribution Length of Residence (yrs.)			
					<1	1-2	3-5	1965-70
Ensenada	115,423	36	23,448	20	18	23	29	70
Tijuana	340,583	50	106,908	31	17	21	27	65
Tecate	18,091	38	4,298	24	19	21	28	68
Mexicali	396,324	35	57,239	14	13	17	26	56
San Luis Río Colorado	63,604	37	13,143	21	16	18	28	62
Nogales	53,494	18	4,751	9	16	21	26	63
Ciudad Juárez	424,135	25	50,527	12	14	17	24	55
Piedras Negras	46,698	14	3,047	6	17	18	29	64
Nuevo Laredo	151,253	36	27,211	18	17	20	27	64
Reynosa	150,786	33	22,005	15	14	19	27	60
Matamoros	186,146	24	14,904	8	19	20	23	62
Total	1,946,537	X̄ 31	327,481	X̄ 16	X̄ 16	X̄ 19	X̄ 27	X̄ 63

Source: Secretaría de Industria y Comercio, Dirección General de Estadística, *IX Censo General de Población 1970.* México, D.F., 1972.

*Includes foreign-born: Ensenada, 0.9 percent; Tijuana, 2.1 percent; Tecate, 1.2 percent; Mexicali, 1.3 percent; San Luis, 1.5 percent; Nogales, 1.3 percent; Ciudad Juárez, 2.8 percent; Piedras Negras, 2.3 percent; Nuevo Laredo, 3.3 percent; Reynosa, 2.1 percent; Matamoros, 2.6 percent; Total, *municipios,* 2.1 percent.

†Specifically, during the intercensal period ending 1968.

Ciudad Juárez and El Paso. Each city was examined initially for landscape elements that could be explained by the other urban entity and culture, after which spatial arrangements of both cities were studied to identify the visible imprint of one upon its neighbor. Two highly noticeable effects of Anglo culture in the residential morphology of Juárez were (1) the widespread occurrence of "house-on-lot" arrangements ("flush-with-the-street" housing apparently still was preferred by low-income migrants with rural or small-town origins), and (2) the degree of separation and exclusiveness of residential land use. The greatest Anglo impact on the spatial structure of Juárez, however, has been the appearance of two urban nodes, that is, the Programa Nacional Fronterizo center and the older downtown area. In El Paso the survival of small- and medium-sized retail outlets on the southern margin of the central business district (CBD) and the variety in form, distribution, and intensity of Mexican culture in residential and commercial landscapes, clearly signaled the nearby existence of Juárez. Retail links with Mexico and the channeling of border-oriented traffic through the city center have been instrumental in preventing deterioration of downtown El Paso.

In Gildersleeve's (1974) comparison of two twin cities, Ambos Nogales and Douglas-Agua Prieta, distribution patterns of land use indicate the meeting of two cultures. Cities in Mexico possessed an ecological character much akin to Latin counterparts, but tourism and industrialization (based on foreign capital) were adding the veneer of a western, or industrial, city. The U.S. twins exhibited the internal structure of an Anglo city with a strong export base, and CBDs in the U.S. cities served clientele from both sides of the border. Whereas business zones in the Mexican twins catered chiefly to U.S. tourists, scattered neighborhood establish-

ments provided for the daily needs of residents. Industrial activities were found in similar locations on each side of the border, although Mexican centers were geared to participation in the BIP with its assembly and processing plants.

Spatial Interaction: Economic Symbiosis

Transborder Trade. The common boundary shared by Mexico and the United States has always accounted for border business interchanges. Disparity in development of local commercial establishments in Mexican municipalities has fostered strong economic symbiosis with their Anglo neighbors (for example, Price, 1978; Dillman, 1968). A stout volume of trade based on individual expenditures by both Mexicans and Americans on trips to the other side has been a continuing and intrinsic feature of border spatial interaction. Each paired community has benefited from these exchanges, although the United States has enjoyed the much greater advantage (Dillman, 1970b).

Improved socioeconomic conditions and rising per capita income in Mexico, following expansion in irrigated agriculture and in manufacturing, usually have been associated with increased U.S. business activity. In addition to purchases by commuter workers, many other Mexican residents have depended heavily upon goods and services supplied by U.S. twin cities. Transborder shopping excursions in this regard have been made by preference and necessity (Dillman, 1970a, 1970c). A recent survey of the buying habits of U.S. and Mexican shoppers revealed that most purchases by the latter in U.S. border centers were for foodstuffs, clothing, appliances, and other items of subsistence; expenditures by U.S. shoppers in Mexico were mainly restricted to tourist categories—arts and crafts articles, food, beverages, and entertainment. Foremost among the border crossing points for intercity trade are (1) Tijuana–San Ysidro–San Diego, (2) Mexicali–Calexico, (3) Ciudad Juárez–El Paso, (4) Ambos Nogales, (5) Laredo–Nuevo Laredo, and (6) Matamoros-Brownsville (Stoddard and West, 1977).

Mexican expenditures in U.S. cities are not confined to those by residents of the border strip. U.S. wholesale and retail establishments serve market areas deep in northern Mexico. Affluent Mexicans from Monterrey and beyond, for example, typically journey to Laredo for specialized purchases, mostly in clothing stores, thus giving the Texas city a higher volume in apparel sales than in automobiles (R. A. Fernández, 1977). Nogales attracts a retail and wholesale clientele from as far south as Ciudad Obregón, Mazatlán, and Guadalajara. Brownsville, in particular, exemplifies the close economic ties of U.S. border cities with northern Mexico, but to a greater degree and probably with more far-reaching effects than elsewhere (Dillman, 1969a). Brownsville merchants long have maintained distant links of retail purchases southwest and south to San Luis Potosí, Torreón, and Tampico. As Mexico's second leading port after Veracruz at the beginning of the 1970s, Brownsville was serving a vast export hinterland encompassing northern Mexico east of the Sierra Madre Occidental south to Zacatecas and San Luis Potosí (Dillman, 1969b, 1969c).

Commuter Workers. In the 1960s the largest percentage of wage income in six of nine major Mexican border municipalities went to individuals daily crossing the border to work legally or illegally (Dillman, 1970a). Only in Mexicali, Nogales, and Ensenada were wages received abroad not the leading salaried sector of their respective economies. In all of the municipalities except Ensenada, roughly one-fifth to more than one-third of the wage income originated in the United States. The most dependent cities were, in order, Ciudad Juárez, Tijuana, Nuevo Laredo, and Matamoros.

Daily journeys across the border by large numbers of "green card" holders and a smaller group of U.S. citizens residing in Mexico has become a common feature of interaction between twin communities (North, 1970; North and Houstoun, 1976; Dillman, 1970a, 1977a; Stoddard, 1978d; A. Ericson, 1970). The Alien Registration Receipt, or green card, permits persons designated as legal resident aliens to live and work in the United States for an indefinite period of time, not contingent upon application for U.S. citizenship. Green card holders may choose, however, to commute to their U.S. jobs. In September, 1976, the U.S. Immigration and Naturalization Service (INS) identified some 46,000 such persons crossing the border each day, returning to Mexico at night. Moreover, the figure excluded uncounted tens of thousands of illegal workers in U.S. border counties who were either EWIs (those who "enter without inspection") or VAs (visa abusers, those with 72-hour entry permits for the purpose of recreation, shopping, and visitation; Stoddard, 1976a).

Most commuting aliens cross the border to work in a variety of low-paying, blue-collar jobs in an urban setting; more than half of the commuters are employed in or near San Diego and El Paso. Additionally, green card workers are more likely to be men than women, although large numbers of women hold domestic and clothing manufacturing jobs. Many Mexico-based workers still had agricultural jobs at mid-decade, but according to North and Houstoun (1976), they represent a decreasing proportion of total commuting employees, as farm laborers opt for other occupations. The intrusion of Mexican farm and urban workers into the U.S. labor market, where wages are low and unemployment is high, has had an adverse effect on lower-income U.S. residents, especially in communities east of San Diego, and more so in the mid-1970s than in the late 1960s. In 1975, the number of unemployed residents of U.S. border counties exceeded the commuting labor force by some 65,000 persons (16,000, excluding San Diego County). The only areas where commuters were more numerous than unemployed residents were the agricultural counties of Imperial County, California; Yuma County, Arizona; and Maverick County, Texas. In the face of opposition by organized labor and U.S. farmworkers to Mexican commuting workers, the Supreme Court (in 1974) affirmed that residence in the United States by green card holders was not a prerequisite for employment (North, 1975).

Tourism. The economies of Mexican border municipalities are generally structured to serve foreign tourists (Dillman, 1970c). Were they to be denied the infusion of tourist spending and earnings by commuting workers, Mexican border centers would face severe economic hardship. Tourism not only is a major revenue source for virtually all large border cities except Mexicali (Schmidt, 1976b) but is the most readily discernable economic element. The existence of night clubs, restaurants, liquor stores, *bordellos,* perfume and jewelry shops, handicraft emporiums, and modern port-of-entry facilities (often associated with shopping centers, or *centros*) at major crossing points betoken the importance of border-focused tourist traffic. U.S. border cities lying at the principal entries to Mexico similarly benefit from a robust volume of Mexico-bound tourists as well as visits by affluent Mexican travelers. U.S. communities house, feed, and clothe tourists and supply a variety of goods and services. El Paso, for example, cites tourism as its third-ranking source of revenue and thus is highly sensitive to fluctuations in border tourist traffic (Stoddard and West, 1977).

Tourism earned $836 million for Mexico in 1976. Until receipts from the tourist trade were surpassed by the revenues from crude-oil exports late in the '70s, tourism was traditionally the country's chief source of the foreign exchange needed to balance the outflow of pesos (Banco de México, 1977). The Mexican government therefore has aggressively promoted tourism in the border zone, where nearly two-thirds of tourist transactions occur. Over 50 percent of 1974 foreign visitors crossed into Ciudad Juárez (33 percent) and Tijuana (21 percent); smaller, though locally important, numbers of tourists entering Nuevo Laredo (8 percent), Matamoros (6 percent), and Mexicali (5 percent) accounted for an additional 20 percent, as the five cities received almost three-quarters of the foreign visitations (Schmidt, 1976b).

Occupational Structure in Mexico

The economically active population (EAP) of border municipalities at the beginning of the 1970s was engaged mainly in commerce and services (46 percent) and secondarily in primary activities (22 percent) and industry (25 percent). In the same year, the national average in each category stood at 32, 40, and 23 percent, respectively. The service sectors in Nogales, Ciudad Juárez, Nuevo Laredo, and Tijuana absorbed over 50 percent and in Tijuana 52 percent, of the EAP. Such percentages mirrored the unbalanced productive system in the Mexican border corridor, for many activities were characterized by low productivity and by low levels of remuneration, representing disguised unemployment.

In view of the service sector's continuing dominance of the economically active population (Table 46-4), it is tempting to hypothesize not only that *maquiladoras* have attracted large numbers of migrants who usually have been absorbed —at least in part—by the tertiary sector, or who have joined the unemployed and marginal segments of the potential work force, but also that the BIP has led—at least indirectly—to increasing dominance of tertiary employment (Bustamante, 1976). Establishing *maquiladoras* along the frontier presumably became a causative factor in the borderward migration of the 1970s, acting in concert with local and external stimuli already present. However, during the first five years of the BIP (roughly 1965-70), *maquiladoras* were heavily concentrated in the western centers of Tijuana and Mexicali and in Ciudad Juárez (Dillman, 1970c). As a result, the full impact of assembly industries upon border employment since 1965

was unrevealed by the 1970 census, which predated the BIP's accelerated growth in the early 1970s.

The supposed trend during the 1960s toward greater relative emphasis on tertiary occupations can be measured by expressing the service sector as a percentage of secondary and tertiary occupations in 1960 and 1970 (Table 46-4) to obtain an index showing the relative importance of service activities. In this context, border-zone municipalities became slightly less oriented to tertiary occupations (0.655 versus 0.648), although the region's EAP still exhibited greater involvement with supply of services than was the case of the republic as a whole. Whereas the number and concentration of BIP plants before 1970 seem not to have supported increased relative tertiary dominance, the new industries failed to diminish rising unemployment or thin the marginally employed. The percentage of unemployed and underemployed in the cities with the five largest EAPs ranged from 20 percent in Tijuana, Mexicali, and Ciudad Juárez to 23 percent in Nuevo Laredo and 25 percent in Matamoros (Torres, 1976).

Mexico's Border Development Programs

The Mexican government historically has viewed the borderward population flow with little enthusiasm. The northern frontier always has been poorly connected to the national economic system and remote from the republic's centrally positioned heartland. The inception in 1961 of the National Border Program (Programa Nacional Fronterizo—PRONAF) signaled a special federal effort to integrate the northern border zone into the mainstream of the Mexican economy, to present a more attractive image of border communities to tourists, to raise the level of living, and to effect urban changes consistent with the requirements of modern city

Table 46-4. *Economically Active Population (EAP), Border-Zone Municipios, 1960 and 1970.*

Municipio	Total No.	EAP 1960 Percentage I	S	A	Service Index*	Total No.	EAP 1970 Percentage I	S	A	Service Index*	Index Change 1960-70
Tijuana	32,832	25	47	20	.653	89,013	30	52	9	.634	−.019
Ensenada	21,999	22	38	34	.633	30,163	23	47	25	.671	+.038
Mexicali	90,378	15	29	53	.659	98,738	21	39	33	.650	−.009
San Luis Río Colorado	13,030	12	29	60	.707	16,422	13	38	41	.745	+.038
Nogales	13,265	25	57	18	.695	14,229	27	59	7	.686	−.009
Ciudad Juárez	85,989	29	50	19	.633	108,078	27	56	9	.675	+.042
Piedras Negras	13,381	25	34	32	.576	12,130	31	45	16	.592	+.016
Nuevo Laredo	30,576	22	54	23	.711	39,463	27	54	11	.667	−.044
Reynosa	44,925	19	30	51	.612	38,032	34	43	16	.558	−.054
Matamoros	45,882	16	35	49	.686	49,467	21	46	27	.687	+.001
Border zone†	480,638	20	38	39	.655	586,951	25	46	22	.648	−.007
Mexico	11,332,016	19	26	54	.578	12,994,392	23	32	40	.582	+.004

Source: Secretaría de Industria y Comercio, Dirección General de Estadística. I = Industry, S = Service, A = Agriculture. Percentages for *municipios*, border zone, and Mexico exclude activities insufficiently specified.

*Service as percentage of industry + service.

†All *municipios*.

planning (Dillman, 1970*b*, 1970*c*). In its formative years, PRONAF provided some infrastructural improvements to facilitate the development of import-substitution manufacturing and made cosmetic alterations to enhance often unseemly border towns (Dillman, 1970*c*). All major ports of entry and many minor crossing points were destined to receive ultramodern, commercial-cultural, gateway complexes (Dirección de General Relaciones Culturales, 1962; PRONAF, 1963). Termination of the *bracero* program, and the ever-present arrival of migrants from the interior, spurred unemployment and soon erased potentially beneficial effects of PRONAF on the jobless sector. Given the scale of federal funding, PRONAF was incapable of responding to consequent socioeconomic problems.

Within this context, the BIP was created in 1965 to bring foreign-owned (primarily U.S.), labor-intensive, assembly industries to the border zone without revising Mexico's policy of reserving the internal market for domestic manufacturers (Baerresen, 1971; Dillman, 1976*b*). The industries experienced remarkable growth in number of plants, especially during the first half of the 1970s, and by 1976 had earned $520 million in foreign exchange (Banco de México, 1977). Viewed from more than a decade of existence, the BIP has strengthened Mexico's dependence upon border transactions while complementing strategies of regional development and industrial decentralization (Secretaría de Industria y Comercio, 1973). Success in lowering male unemployment has been minimal at best, yet the program's impact probably could not have been otherwise in the absence of a concerted attack on root causes of unemployment and underemployment in the interior.

In 1971 the federal government reacted to growing economic dependence on the United States—largely due to the BIP's success—by inaugurating a new containment policy for the border-zone economy. Announced program goals were to raise employment, keep the Mexican consumer within the domestic market, replace the increasing flow of imported goods with national products, and increase the balance of border trade in favor of Mexico. Responsibility for design and implementation of economic and social policies in the renewed assault on border-zone problems was given to the Inter-Ministerial Commission for the Economic Development of the Northern Border Zone and Free Zones (founded by President Luis Echeverría in May, 1972). Moreover, the new frontier program included construction and operation of shopping centers, offering Mexican consumers a variety of goods and facilities competitive with those in neighboring U.S. cities.

To reduce spending by Mexican nationals in U.S. twin communities, a series of tax incentives (or selective tax concessions) has been introduced since the early 1960s to increase sales of domestically manufactured goods within the border zone and to enable local merchants to recapture retail business from U.S. merchants. Beginning in 1961, annual subsidies of freight rate reductions and refunds of commercial tax receipts on sales of Mexican-made items were granted to manufacturers serving the border-zone (Dillman, 1970*c*). Two decrees by the federal executive in March, 1971, consid-erably broadened earlier inducement policies (Evans, 1975; Nacional Financiera, 1971). Qualifying firms were authorized to receive refunds of total import duties on materials in products sold in the border zone and refunds on local transactions equivalent to 11 percent of product value. Since December, 1971, the entire border strip has enjoyed a modified *zona libre,* or free zone, because of the *artículos gancho* program allowing duty-free entry of "enticement" or "hook" articles (popular consumption goods) previously obtained in U.S. stores. Purchases of Mexican goods presumably would be similarly stimulated, those goods being displayed along with the "hook" articles. A subsequent August, 1972, decree permitted accelerated depreciation and refunds of import levies for shopping centers along the border (Nacional Financiera, 1972). A decree published eighteen months later was aimed at stimulating commodity production for domestic consumption by subsidizing Mexican-owned small and medium industrial enterprises. Exemptions from import duties on machinery and equipment (up to 100 percent) and raw materials (60 percent) could be sought if Mexican inputs comprised one-fifth of production costs (Subsecretaría de la Presidencia, 1974).

Despite an uninterrupted rise in Mexican expenditures for imported goods prior to devaluation of the 1976 peso, tax incentive schemes met with immediate and substantial success. Amounts of tax concessions, approved on sales of domestic products, increased sharply from 1971 to 1973 (Mex.$ 187 million to Mex.$ 1,485 million); the share of consumption purchases for domestically produced items grew from 28 to 50 percent (Banco Nacional de Comercio Exterior, 1974). Furthermore, transborder trade in Mexico's favor improved by almost 80 percent during the first half of the 1970s. On the other hand, the Inter-Ministerial Commission's development policies had no visible impact upon massive unemployment and underemployment and, in the view of some critics, augured intensified dependence on U.S. economy (R. A. Fernández, 1977).

Common Problems

The U.S. border zone traditionally has been a region of economic hardship and deprivation. Although poverty in Mexico increases away from the border, in the United States the reverse obtains. Border-zone counties currently exhibit the largest concentration of poverty families of any region of the United States in addition to having the highest rates of unemployment and the lowest family income (Stoddard and West, 1977). Regional planning and relief programs modified for use in the U.S. border zone should recognize that real poverty (as opposed to regulated and to relative poverty) is greatest in the lower Rio Grande Valley of Texas, decreasing westward toward the Pacific Coast. Over 50 percent of all families in poverty are found in Texas; therefore, poverty in U.S. border counties is determined mainly and measured by conditions in Texas (Stoddard, 1978*c*). Because the economies of Mexican-U.S. twin cities are more closely linked to each other than to their respective national systems, poverty in U.S. communities can be attributed, in part, to circumstances in and exchanges with Mexico, but also reflects the social, economic, and political milieu in the U.S. Borderlands. The great abundance of cheap Mexican labor, chiefly the result of springboard, receptacle, and Hong Kong-Taiwan functions, has exacerbated preexisting socioeconomic problems of U.S. Chicanos. A previous *campesino* background, the relative scarcity of good-paying blue-collar jobs, and pervasive racial discrimination in the United States make outmigration a viable alternative to local poverty for many Chicano residents.

Urban centers in the U.S. border zone, except for San Diego, generally suffer from a higher than average taxation rate for governmental, social, educational, and health services imposed on a lower than average wage and income base, thus creating a negative development component. Further, the relatively sparse population in the U.S. border region, in competition with large metropolitan centers in the interior Southwest, commands scant attention from state and federal policy makers. Residents of U.S. border cities must subsidize the national boundary, a responsibility that reduces funds for essential public services. To prevent this exploitation, the international boundary could be designated a federal installation, the servicing of which would qualify local communities for border-area equity supplements or impacted area reimbursements (Stoddard, 1978*a*).

The ability of the Mexican municipalities to initiate corrective policies has been hamstrung by their lowly position in the Mexican government's administrative hierarchy. Most major local taxes, including land assessments, have accrued to state governments; consequently, local officials have been forced to cope with deficient revenue. The municipalities, as a rule, have lacked direct control over their budgets, which usually must be approved in the state capital. Local officials also can be removed from their positions by the governor. This does not mean that state governments are strong political entities; on the contrary, they are of slight constitutional and political importance. Important decisions commonly are made at the national level and carried out by federal agencies. If states administer programs, they do so as agents of centralized authority (Goodman and MacDonald, 1966).

U.S. unemployment, falling retail sales, a rising level of business transactions, and Mexican inflation during the last half of 1976 reemphasized the border zone's vulnerability to external influences, especially policies formulated by distant national governments. Widespread negative social and economic effects stemming from recent peso devaluation signaled the latest phase in a cyclic pattern inseparable from international economic processes (O. J. Martínez, 1977*a*). Although past wage and price adjustments have prompted a relative return to previous transborder trade levels, economic conditions in the second half of the 1970s were clearly unlike those in earlier periods. Mexican attempts to recapture the border consumer market and attract more U.S. shoppers appeared to have had positive results (*Christian Science Monitor,* 1978). Such circumstances bode ill for U.S. merchants whose trade depended heavily upon economic symbiosis with Mexican municipalities. The prospect of improved connections between the border corridor and the Mexican interior underscores the compelling need for expanded binational cooperation to rationalize the border zone's economic system, thus realizing socioeconomic potentials on both sides of the boundary.

1. The most recent and comprehensive treatment of the historical background of Mexican-U.S. border twin cities appears in Gildersleeve (1978). Other useful sources are Martínez (1978); Dillman (1971, 1970*b*, 1968), and Stoddard (1978*b*).

Section V. Society and Culture

For slightly more than four centuries, Spanish- and English-speaking peoples have been exploring and settling the region that now makes up the Borderlands of the United States and Mexico. Documentary evidences of this Western European expansion into a once sparsely populated and largely arid region consisted of diaries, official records, and correspondence during the early years. These documents eventually came to include more elaborate and specialized writings of a descriptive and purposive nature, culminating in rather formal disciplinary products of the sort which now make up the basic writings of the social sciences and humanities.

The chronicles of the Spanish explorers and the research reports of the contemporary sociologist have one salient feature in common: both are essentially imported perspectives based on readily identifiable cultural traditions that are reflected in the very language through which journals, reports, and other accounts are assembled. The study of man by man inevitably imposes language values, whether these are norms or are highly personal. In either case the filtering of

47

Border Culture Overview

J. LAWRENCE McCONVILLE
San Francisco, California

245

the phenomena observed and described is both pervasive and inevitable.

The more complex procedures of the contemporary social scientist may achieve some sort of standard of rigor within a profession, but this rigor in no way sets such methods apart, qualitatively, from modes of description and analysis belonging to other disciplines or eras. This does not imply, however, that a native social science among precolonial peoples would have been preferable—even if the first Borderlands inhabitants had developed a written language and made it a possibility. External perspectives of chroniclers, commentators, officials, historians, and researchers have yielded highly varied documentaries of social science during the Anglo-Iberian penetration of the region. Social science is a peculiarly distinctive endeavor within Western Civilization and relies heavily on documentary accounts in a few Indo-European tongues. Substantive knowledge available for survey and inspection therefore bears the heavy impress of writers' ends and purposes. Likewise, gaps in Borderlands knowledge have not all arisen out of carelessness and neglect but have partially sprung from culturally defined activities which initially produced those documents.

These observations may not seem especially remarkable in a worldwide context, since Western Civilization's extension throughout the planet has brought about many analogous situations in other continents. In the U.S.-Mexican Borderlands, however, there are considerations which make the study of "doing social science" especially intriguing.

Perhaps the most important reason to survey the Borderlands sociocultural situation stems from its emergence as a zone where the establishment of highly artificial and arbitrary boundaries has actually served to attract large numbers of people to a region that, on ecological grounds alone, would appear to have rather limited prospects for extensive human occupation. This development was not due to any rational plan for relating U.S. and Mexican societies, but sprang from human needs that transcend and circumvent officially promulgated social realities appearing on maps and in compendia of laws and regulations. The interpenetration of the two countries and their cultures has been so pervasive that practically every aspect of social order has been affected.

The assembling of Anglo-Iberian institutions and customs in the remote, sparsely settled, and ecologically inauspicious habitats of the arid Borderlands has sometimes been poignant, pathetic, bizarre, and audacious, but above all it has been accompanied by a sense of marginality. Habitat conditions have left it a lightly populated fringe area on the margins of larger sociocultural influences. This marginality, and the effects of time and distance, have diluted both meanings and forms of the cultural baggage wanderers have brought. Even modern technology and the imposing institutions of contemporary nation-states often take on a forlorn and withered appearance, somewhat like tropical plants brought into the desert and neglected. The Anglo-Iberian enclaves of the Borderlands have a peculiar transparency, as if the sunshine's clarity renders social framework susceptible to examination. Perhaps a practical awareness of this has made the inhabitants cling all the more to their fragile cultural forms and symbols

and nurture them so intensely. These communities possess something akin to the mood of an earthling colony on the far side of the moon—an awareness that their habitat is almost entirely sustained through calculated environmental manipulations terribly dependent upon linguistic meanings.

To a considerable extent the persons drawn to this region have been, in one sense or another, marginal members of the societies from which they came. The Borderlands have not drawn so much from the "core," or central elements of the societies which supposedly control the region, but instead from the ragged edges of the social fabric, from the human surpluses, and from the "ravines" and "gullies" of the social order into which some have inevitably stumbled.

Perhaps the oddest thing about the Borderlands is the contrast between the newcomers' ambitions and the pervasive austerity of the natural habitat. Wave after wave of Anglo-Iberian immigrants have been pushed into this vast "Empty Quarter" of North America through population pressures in the core regions, where competition, increase in numbers, and diminishing quantities of productive land have brought occupation of zones considered relatively unattractive. The Borderlands' meteoric population rise to forty million people in recent years reflects the massive technological intervention necessary to maintain these imported life-styles in a region obviously resistant to large-scale human occupation.

There are ominous indications that this massive occupation may be short-lived, given the gloomy forecasts concerning the region's water resources. Ironically, the Borderlands' expansionist spirit has actually revived a man-over-nature aggressiveness fast becoming obsolete in old power centers in parent countries. As marginal elements from both Mexico and the United States continue to move to the Borderlands, what was once a desolate zone along two nations' boundaries is fast becoming a powerful magnet where the very differences between contributing societies sustain the region's economy. Indeed, one of the most fascinating aspects of Borderlands urbanization is that it has depended so little upon the region's natural resources. The economic foundation of this expansion has been and continues to be the cultural configuration of the groups in contact.

The intermingling of English- and Spanish-speaking immigrants in fast-growing cities flung far out along the edges of the parent countries is having consequences neither foreseen nor intended. The gathering together of marginal men in ecologically marginal habitats along the margins of two societies is, in short, marginality "raised to the third power," and a mutual dependency developing far from the national monitors can only lead to unknown cultural change. Comprehensive social science studies in the Borderlands are necessary to understand the dynamics transforming national life and the world order as presently conceived.

The historically sparse settlement of the region, recent large-scale occupation, and a relatively manageable body of research materials (stemming partially from significantly neglected areas) assess the social science enterprise in this part of the world as a real possibility. There are, however, some obstacles, not the least of which is that data gathering has been confined to political research jurisdictions. Since the political partitioning of the Borderlands has disregarded ecological and cultural units, severe discontinuities in data production have plagued the region for the last 130 years. National, state, and local jurisdictions have typically only gathered data required by applicable laws, ordinances, and regulations. Since these laws vary, a rationale for dealing with long-term and geographically dispersed phenomena has often been unavailable.

There is also a disparity between the two countries in research since the Mexican economy has not sustained social science research efforts as much as has the economy of the United States. This inequity has made the international boundary something of a border between zones of research intensity—although this is less true in anthropology and history, for which internationalism in the scholarly community has somewhat prevailed.

Both countries have shown considerable indifference to studies of Borderlands human interaction. The two nations' research has focused on geological and topographic surveys, flora and fauna, climate, mineral and water resources, agricultural productivity, and historical concerns dull or remote enough that they run little risk of disturbing the tranquility of the assumed social order. This neglect is hardly surprising, however, for the national cultures' attempts to sustain a faith in all regions' conformity to a generalized, nationwide pattern are often the least effective in marginal areas that are also zones of culture contact. Any world traveler of even modest perspicacity soon detects the rather limited and superficial way such Borderlands conformity is actually obtained.

The region's cultural ecology has fostered a largely undocumented and unmonitored "intimacy in isolation," which, in turn, has brought forth an array of distinctive cultural niches. These cultural niches not only have facilitated a certain amount of cultural alloyage between and among the contributing peoples, but also have helped to preserve communities of older traditions, folkways, and mores persisting despite nearby technological interventions and population changes. Time and again one finds evidences of continuity within regional change—or, as several observers have remarked, "old wine in new bottles."

From the point of view of monitors of national integrity, the Borderlands are an administrative nuisance, a region drifting into cultural divergence, an array of curiously nondescript enclaves barely held together by isolational inertia and a thin veneer of forms and symbols supposedly showing some affiliation with the larger units fancifully drawn on maps. It is hardly surprising, therefore, that many sensitive aspects of Borderlands culture have been so carefully sidestepped, so systematically avoided, and so thoroughly unsubsidized. The lack of Borderlands materials may well have originated in a neglectful attitude toward national margins, but continued neglect of a region containing forty million people requires an alternative explanation—one which recognizes that the Borderlands growth has motivated a drift toward virtually uncontrolled cultural amalgamation of unforeseeable characteristics.

The respective countries' institutions plod on, resurrecting time-honored images, symbols, and shibboleths of the two national cultures, skittishly avoiding anything discrepant with ossified notions. Attempts to sustain traditional ideas about institutional order range from comical to bizarre. The result is not unlike the tunnel vision employed by two middle-aged matrons who prefer to judge their appearance with a hand mirror, inspecting themselves from the neck up only, conveniently ignoring the transformations in other body parts that might not fit the image they wish to convey.

Despite their scientific pretensions, the social sciences are far from immune to the constraints operating in the milieu. Research undertakings bear the heavy impress of cultural residues channeling research modes and topics along well-traveled paths. A survey of Anglo-Iberian writers' research products unmistakeably points to this. If shallowness, conventionality, and an almost touching dose of "sociological innocence" in adhering to canons of disciplinary procedure have been the usual fare in the region's research, the Borderlands have also nurtured a most extraordinary intellectual environment—one in which the very absence of heavy institutional interference and the transparency of man's norm-based conduct combine, enabling some to transcend the ethnocentrisms of both tribe and scholar, to penetrate the interactional haze, and to achieve clarity, cogency, and perspicacity in unveiling the human condition.

48

Health and Health Care

ELLWYN R. STODDARD
*Department of Sociology and
Anthropology
University of Texas, El Paso*

GUSTAVO M. QUESADA
*Department of Extension
Federal University of Santa Maria
(Brazil)*

Major differences on each side of the U.S.-Mexican border are more explicitly manifested in health conditions and practices than in any other border institution. The literature on this subject is overly abundant and scattered among various technical journals, professional outlets, and popular publications; unfortunately, relatively little of it is more than generalized impressionistic views based upon a paucity of accurate data. The gathering of empirical data along the border area is indeed a special problem. Not only is the National Center of Health Statistics failing to facilitate general Southwest data gathering (according to some leading researchers), but also some border states—especially Texas—are uncooperative in making available health data on those with Spanish surnames (Teller and Clyburn, 1974*a*). Reliability of data, such as the U.S. child mortality rates, also suffers. The births to Mexican parents of children born in the United States (or reported so by midwives wishing to give the newborn "American" citizenship) who subsequently die in Mexican border towns add to the positive side of infant health; unreported deaths do not balance the scale. Thus, although health con-

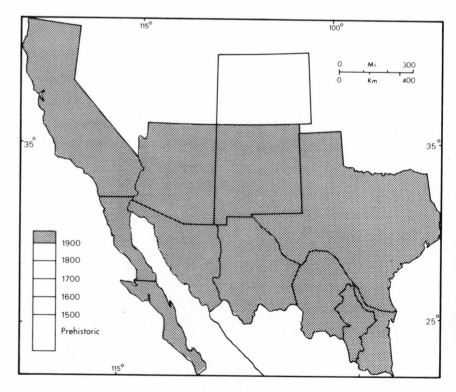

248

ditions are relatively poor in the U.S. border area, some border cities report that region to be the safest place in the country to have a baby (compare Steglich and Deardorff, 1968, with Teller and Clyburn, 1974b: 245ff.). Also, Mexico's border-city populations are largely illiterate and/or poorly educated; census data and vital statistics are questionable, when available (Roberts and Askew, 1972).

For an overview of health conditions in the Mexican border area, Loewe Reiss (1978) is one of the best current sources. Information on the public health system and an evaluation of border health centers in Mexico is provided by Candelas (1971) and A. C. García (1970). The full range of state comprehensive health plans is also available (Castellanos, 1973; Farias, 1973; Felix, 1973; Flores, 1973; Gutiérrez, 1973). There are a few studies of health organizations in operation (Fernández and Vides, 1970; Guel, 1972; Gonzalez and Intriago, 1972); occasionally there is an overview of the border region's sociocultural *ambiente* ("milieu") (Martínez, 1970). Reports of specific programs, such as a vaccination program in Ciudad Juárez (Ortiz, 1971) or the status of the border rabies problem (Cárdenas, 1971), are sometimes available. Comparative binational surveys or studies, such as that of Walker (1972), along various points of the U.S.-Mexican binational border or the more intensive work comparing life stress conditions in Ciudad Juárez and El Paso reported in Durham and Hough (1979) provide an increased accuracy but are focused on specific communities in a given time frame. The intensive study of Douglas, Arizona, with implications for the Mexican sister city (Weaver and Hubbard, 1975), provides tangential Mexican health data. Generally, though, ongoing statistical data for Mexican border areas are unavailable or unknown at this time.

On the U.S. side of the border, health studies of the dominant ethnic minority—Mexican Americans—become synonymous with Borderlands health information. Such overall summaries as that of Moustafa and Weiss (1968) and the critical literature review of Weaver (1973b) are basic for anyone beginning a study of border health conditions and practices. Also available are some excellent edited volumes. Riedesel (1971) edited nine articles concerned with health and health care in the arid Southwest, covering topics from physical diseases peculiar to such climates and border minority problems. A very recent volume of twenty medical anthropology papers (Velimirovic, 1978a) expresses research interests, information, and professional perspectives on minority health care in the general border region. Many government documents, such as the Office of Economic Opportunity (OEO) report on deficiencies in nutrition and Texas's rejection of governmental nutrition programs (U.S. Commission on Civil Rights, 1970), have accumulated data relevant to border health, but such information is often found "stored" in mimeograph form instead of being published for popular consumption by border agencies whose budgets depend upon state political moods.

One of the most fruitful sources of current border information is the Pan American Health Organization (PAHO) field office, located at 509 U.S. Court House, El Paso, Texas 79901. Its history goes back to 1942, when the International

Sanitary Bureau was formed, later coming under the auspices of the World Health Organization and its regional outlet, the Pan American Health Organization (PAHO). This field office not only has served to carry on the responsibilities of the parent organization, but also has acted as a continuous data source for border health information and needs. The PAHO-sponsored U.S.-Mexican Border Health Organization (C. L. Williams, 1972) has been a forum for Mexican and American physicians, nurses, health workers, and research scholars to exchange views and solutions. Commentary from attendees at these meetings indicates that, because Mexican physicians are somewhat less secure and dogmatic than their American counterparts, there is less chance of initiating programs involving paraprofessionals or those with less than professional training in health care. In the United States there seems to be a broad interest in expanding the paraprofessional role, not only to alleviate the critical shortage of licensed health personnel, but also in treating minority clientele. An annotated discussion of previous paraprofessional experiments among Mexican American clientele is the comprehensive literature review of McLaughlin (1980). Perhaps this thrust will subvert the common stereotypes of Mexican American rejection of Western medical theories and focus on the health-care delivery personnel instead.

Epidemiographic patterns vary considerably between Mexican and U.S. Borderlands. Throughout Latin America, in Mexico generally, and in the rapidly growing northern border cities (Stoddard, 1978c), migration's impact adds to the high incidence of communicable (but avoidable) diseases (Velimorovic, 1979), whereas degenerative diseases and malignant neoplasms are more common in the United States and along the U.S. border, despite the region's poverty (Stoddard, 1978b). Loewe Reiss (1978) reports that influenza and various forms of dysentery are the principal causes of death in Mexico, especially in the six northern border states. In contrast, Teller (1978) reports these same diseases ranking 14th to 21st in Texas, particularly in the impoverished lower Rio Grande Valley, whereas heart disease, malignant neoplasms, and cerebrovascular diseases, which rank quite low in Mexico, are the top three in the United States. Quite obviously, Mexican health problems are directly linked to disease prevention and control and to nutrition and the availability of health care, whereas U.S. health problems are related to the stresses and life-style of an urban industrialized nation and the use or availability of highly sophisticated health treatment.

From the 1930s, the availability of "cultural laboratories" has attracted ethnologists and researchers interested in cultural patterns, including patterns of health. One of the outcomes of the last 25 years of studying indigenous cultures is a latent consequence of stereotyping certain ethnic groups, especially Mexican Americans (Stoddard, 1973b: 38-51; Weaver, 1973b: 86-100; Farge, 1977). Two major themes begun in the Southwest have crystalized into current "health myths": the "value-orientation" model and the "folk-culture" influence. Relying somewhat on Florence Kluckhohn's value-orientation approach developed at Radcliffe College and applied in her doctoral field studies in New Mexico, "Los Atarquenos" (Kluckhohn, 1961), there emerged a Mexican American and Anglo American set of values which were supposedly of ethnic origin. These, in fact, represent more clearly social-class values of lower- and middle-class America, irrespective of ethnic origins, but they became the framework within which external and ethnic observers identified Mexican American culture or cultural deviants. The second theme was imagining Mexican Americans as nothing more than transplanted "folk-culture" residents from isolated areas of Mexico. Using field techniques developed for isolated, homogeneous indigenous peoples (Leeds, 1968), observers mistakenly assumed that their "folk-culture" respondents (who were actually from Mexican peasant society; see Foster, 1953*b*: 170, for folk/peasant differences) who relied on "folk healers" did so because of their folk-culture beliefs, thus rejecting more conventional health practices because of cultural determinism. One of the first studies of Southwestern health care was the classic by Saunders (1954), who combined many realistic health problems with these conceptual frameworks. Subsequent studies reinforcing these cultural differences, in response to cultural determinants, were Clark's (1959) on San Jose, Rubel's (1960, 1966) and Madsen's (1961, 1973) in the lower Rio Grande Valley, and Edmundson's (1957) in New Mexico. Heller (1964, 1966) legitimized these cultural determinants without regard to variations in social class. Probably the most stereotyped analysis, however, comes from the medical profession itself in the work of Kiev (1968), who worked in San Antonio public clinics and talked with four *curanderos,* representing such folk healers as the mainstream of Mexican American health practice.

With the rise of the Chicano movement, emotional reactions against such ethnic stereotyping (which by now had become accepted as *the* ethnic model for Mexican Americans) were seen in articles by Romano V. (1968, 1969), Vaca (1970*a*, 1970*b*), Montiel (1970), and others. An edited volume of ethnic representatives protesting Mexican American mental health treatment based upon "Anglo" values shows that even in such discussions, the value-orientation model has no place for "middle-class Mexican Americans" and "lower-class Anglo Americans" (Boucher, 1970).

Some alternative explanations for Mexican American poverty and lack of occupational mobility or access to social services began to emphasize structural restraints or institutional programming of minority failure. Reminiscent of Jaco's (1959, 1960) work a decade earlier, which found that in Texas, first-time admittance of Mexican American clients to mental health centers resulted in a three-to-one ratio of institutionalization, Karno and Edgerton (1969) found that low facility use ratios by Mexican Americans were not a result of negative beliefs toward such clinics but of the absence of any available clinics in their communities or neighborhoods. An ad hoc committee of medical sociologists took up this argument of minority exclusion and, with an American Sociological Association grant coupled with support from the Carnegie Foundation, compiled a large volume of articles and position papers dealing with barriers against Mexican American clientele seeking health services (Quesada et al., 1974). A summary of these papers is available (Quesada and

Heller, 1977), but the larger volume is not in published form.

Many empirical investigations into Mexican American behavior toward health needs began to challenge the simplistic cultural determinism explanations of value-orientation and folk-culture models. Although folk healers and practices are prevalent among rural or barrio Mexican American families, these practitioners often serve to cure "folk diseases" which cannot be diagnosed by Western medicine. Moreover, their reluctance to use available health clinics and programs more often than not stems from factors other than cultural beliefs (Farge, 1977). McLemore's (1963) study of Mexican American beliefs about hospital care showed much change as educational levels increased; Weaver (1973*a*) found this trend only among Anglo-American clients in a biethnic clinic. In Balch and Miller's (1974) results, the less fortunate Mexican Americans had to use public health mental facilities where psychiatric personnel with ethnic preconceptions provided inadequate treatment.

Bloombaum et al. (1968) found health personnel were tolerant of ethnic and racial minorities but held firm stereotypes of their clients' motivations. Weaver (1969) compared lower-class Anglos and Chicanos, finding similar views and preferences among clients of health clinics about practices and procedures, but found that low use by Anglos of Chicano paraprofessionals limited them to Mexican clients, labeling the clinic as a "Mexican health center."

Martínez and Martin (1966) found that Mexican American clients were anxious to use available, relatively inexpensive public health facilities which were locally situated and staffed with "friendly" personnel. Wolkon et al. (1974) concluded that differential responses to health care were equated with social class instead of ethnicity. Nall and Spielberg (1969) found folk healers and medical physicians working within the same community, often serving the same clientele (but the use of folk healers had no impact on the desire for medical attention for tuberculosis). Karno and Edgerton (1969) found that Mexican Americans wanted health services but used them differentially on the basis of language factors, formality in patient contact, and location of or lack of available facilities.

Little impact was felt from value orientations or folk beliefs toward disease and modern medicine. Weclew (1975) found that folk healers were largely used because they listened to a person's problems, made house calls, and offered personalized services. Public clinics' long lines, combined with the distance from the client's home, resulted in low Mexican American use in the lower Rio Grande Valley (Chavira and Trotter, 1957). Lindstrom (1975) found that previously unsatisfactory contacts with health services blunted the efforts of Mexican Americans to seek medical attention. Individuals from Michigan or even from Mexico were able to adjust to a children's clinic better than Texas migrant families. While these situational and social-class factors have rarely been communicated to practicing medical personnel (Paynich, 1964; Cadena, 1970), the steady outpouring of "commonsense" rules for handling a socially and culturally homogeneous Mexican American culture have filled the literature and popular media (see Leninger, 1970; White, 1977, etc.). Many practicing medical professionals who have limited experience with poverty or the barrio have diagnosed all Mexican American families and reactions as similar to those of the people with whom they have had intimate contact.

During the wave of social-action government programs to raise the quality of life among southwestern minorities, there have been sincere but abbreviated efforts to cope with indigenous and minority cultural diversity. Such programs as the Area Health Education Centers (American Medical Association, 1973), areawide Comprehensive Health Planning Agencies, Migrant Health Programs, Community Services Administration grants to local clinics, National Institute of Mental Health (NIMH) grants to Indian health programs, and the recently reinstituted Regional Medical Program have tried to reduce the distance between health facilities and potential users. These programs have also included cost subsidies, cross-cultural training, and the growing use of paraprofessionals (McLaughlin, 1980). Some programs have been aimed exclusively at dental health (Pettibone and Soliz, 1973; García and Juárez, 1978), while others deal with socioeconomic and cultural dimensions in defining and dealing with life stress situations (Durham and Hough, 1979). Specific surveys and studies of alcohol use, compared to popular stereotypes about Mexican Americans (Maril and Zavaleta, 1978), as well as methods of working with alcoholism among this minority, are available (Trotter, 1979a, 1979b).

Although not as prominent the homogeneous stereotype of "the Indian" has recently become popular, as if sedentary reservations Pueblos would react the same way as urbanized Plains Indian militants. Much is available about Indian reservation health services and government hospitals for selected Indian tribes (though relatively little appears in professional journals and other unbiased formats), for example, health services on a Pima and Papago reservation (Kahn et al., 1975; Rabeau and Rund, 1971), Papago problems off the reservation (Waddell, 1970), Indian intoxication in general and Navaho and Uintah-Ouray case studies in particular (Dozier, 1966b; Ferguson, 1968; Slater and Albrecht, 1972; Kunitz and Levy, 1974), and Navaho suicide patterns (Levy, 1965). Additional references on health care among native Americans can be found in chapter 56 in this sourcebook.

Medical personnel untrained in cultural differences do not realize that certain practices and patterns successful among members of one tribe are not applicable to clients of other tribes; instead, these problems are considered to be the fault of the clients, since stereotypes depict "the Indian" as having a single homogeneous set of beliefs and cultural practices. Quite obviously, more accurate information might break this single category of "Indian" into different cultural areas, each with its practices and taboos. The more successful Indian health programs have adopted this procedure by combining cultural anthropologists with medical personnel who are willing to adjust somewhat to local beliefs and customs through personnel training programs (Justice, 1978).

Another aspect of border health is the potential for minority-sensitive health-career training to provide effective health delivery systems to minority or ethnic clientele. Even as medical school curricula reflect an increase in physician speciality training (Bean, 1976), the need for increased effectiveness in health delivery systems by general practitioners located in multiracial or multiethnic areas is becoming well known. Not only has a shortage of professionally trained nurses and medical helpers increased the necessity for hiring paraprofessionals, but there is also an increasing realization among professional medical personnel that the "bridging function" of minority paraprofessionals is an intricate part of the health delivery system itself. Perhaps the most complete review of the use of ethnic paraprofessionals is by McLaughlin (1980). Although D'Antonio and Samora (1962) found little room at the top for minority members, an increasing number of scholarships and special medical programs to bring ethnic professional and client ratios into balance have become available during the last decade. Possibly this drive for a greater number of Spanish-surnamed personnel has found foreign-trained doctors willing to fill the positions, thus drying up the sparse number of physicians in Latin American countries (Kidd, 1967; Portes, 1969, 1976).

Perhaps the most authoritative view of future health needs (many of which apply to both sides of the U.S.-Mexican Borderlands) is outlined by Davis (1976) in his recommendations to the Association of American Medical Colleges:

1. Encourage more efficient and responsive health-care delivery, preferably at community centers.
2. Attract more health professionals to underserved areas (rural regions and poverty areas, such as the U.S. border region) by a point-merit system.
3. Leave many patients at home among familiar surroundings and supportive kin and friends.
4. Encourage the use of nonphysician health professionals without lowering quality health-care standards.

Because of the different needs for the Mexican border region, a wholly different set of priorities would need to be formulated.

In summary, in the poverty belt of the U.S. Borderlands, where costs of health care are sometimes equal to outlays for food and shelter, public health programs are extremely critical. The current trend to replace existing ethnic-racial stereotypes regarding attitudes and motivation toward health-care services and procedures will allow medical personnel to be more effective. At the same time, this movement should promote an increased tolerance toward the folk practitioner and his clientele. Social-class variations in understanding of, and receptivity to, medical services need to be understood outside of ethnic or cultural determinism. Such training and increased sensitivity to minorities, especially those heavily concentrated in poverty categories, should help to remove structural barriers around public health services which cannot be penetrated by minority clients without the overt efforts and cooperation of medical personnel.

49

Education

CELESTINO FERNÁNDEZ
Department of Sociology
University of Arizona

Although general information about Borderlands educational experiences concerns those who encounter the greatest difficulties in education—that is, the native American, black, and Hispanic minorities—the greatest thrust of this chapter will concern the largest numerical minority, Hispanic Americans. Approximately three million Hispanic students are enrolled in elementary and secondary schools throughout the United States, and 70 percent of them are located in the four border states (California, Arizona, New Mexico, and Texas) and Colorado. Of those students more than 95 percent are of Mexican descent (Brown, Rosen, Hill, and Olivas, 1980; U.S. Commission on Civil Rights, 1971: 15-20). Thus border Hispanic problems are Mexican American problems.

Table 49-1 shows that over eight million students attend elementary and secondary schools in the Southwest. Of those eight million students 17 percent are Mexican American. Among Catholic students a slightly higher proportion are Mexican American (20 percent). The bulk of the border Mexican American students (80 percent) are enrolled in schools in California and Texas. Almost

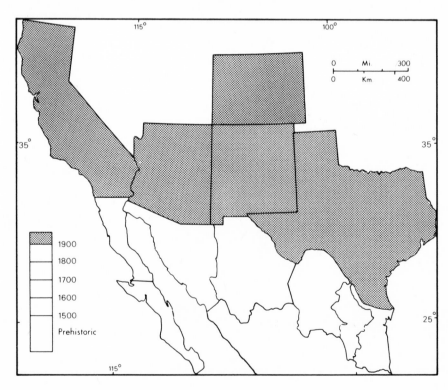

Table 49-1. *Ethnic Breakdown of Enrollment in the Southwest.*

State	Anglo Number	Anglo Percentage of Total Enrollment	Mexican American Number	Mexican American Percentage of Total Enrollment	Black Number	Black Percentage of Total Enrollment	Other Number	Other Percentage of Total Enrollment	Total Number	Total Percentage
California	3,323,478	74.2	646,282	14.4	387,978	8.7	119,642	2.7	4,477,381	100.0
Texas	1,617,840	64.4	505,214	20.1	379,813	15.1	7,492	0.3	2,510,358	100.0
New Mexico	142,092	52.4	102,994	38.0	5,658	2.1	20,295	7.5	271,040	100.0
Arizona	262,526	71.6	71,748	19.6	15,783	4.3	16,402	4.4	366,459	100.0
Colorado	425,749	82.0	71,348	13.7	17,797	3.4	4,198	0.8	519,092	100.0
Southwest	5,771,684	70.9	1,397,586	17.2	807,030	9.9	168,030	2.0	8,144,330	100.0

Source: U.S. Commission on Civil Rights (1971: 17).

Table 49-2. *Enrollment in the Southwest by School Level and Ethnicity.*

Ethnic Group	Elementary Number of Pupils	Elementary Percentage of Total Pupils	Intermediate Number of Pupils	Intermediate Percentage of Total Pupils	Secondary Number of Pupils	Secondary Percentage of Total Pupils	All School Levels Number of Pupils	All School Levels Percentage of Total Pupils
Anglos	3,209,813	68.8	1,043,391	71.6	1,518,480	75.3	5,771,684	70.9
Mexican Americans	866,774	18.6	233,106	16.0	297,707	14.8	1,397,586	17.2
Blacks	490,264	10.5	154,261	10.5	162,505	8.1	807,030	9.9
Others	101,809	2.1	27,060	1.9	39,162	1.9	168,030	2.0
Total	4,668,660	100.0	1,457,818	100.0	2,017,854	100.0	8,144,330	100.0

Source: U.S. Commission on Civil Rights (1971: 17).

50 percent are found in California alone.

Figure 49-1 illustrates concentrations of Chicano students in southwestern states. In Arizona and Texas these concentrations are mostly along the binational border. In Arizona, 55 percent of Chicano students are in the southern part of the state, whereas in other border states major Mexican American concentrations are found in urban centers (that is, Los Angeles, San Jose, Denver, and Albuquerque).

In all five southwestern states the proportion of Chicano students decreases at every level from elementary schools through colleges and universities. Table 49-2 shows the proportion of Mexican American enrollment decreasing from 18.6 percent attending elementary schools to 16 percent in junior high and 14.8 percent at the senior high level. Although the table does not present data on blacks residing in the Borderlands, their patterns show the same trend, as do the trends of native Americans, particularly those residing on reservations. On the other hand, Anglo enrollment increases at every level—from 68.8 percent at the elementary level to 71.6 percent in junior highs and 75.3 percent in high school. There are three major causes for the higher proportion of Chicano students in the lower grades and the larger proportion of Anglo students in the upper grades: (1) higher birthrates among Mexican Americans than among Anglos, yielding more young Chicanos in the primary grades; (2) a higher rate of grade repetition for Mexican Americans than for Anglo students, particularly in the early years of elementary school; and (3) a higher attrition and dropout rate for Chicanos than for Anglos, especially at the intermediate and secondary levels. Of these three factors the most significant is the last. It is in the junior and senior high schools that the educational system takes its greatest toll of minority students (Chicanos, native Americans, and blacks) in the Borderlands.

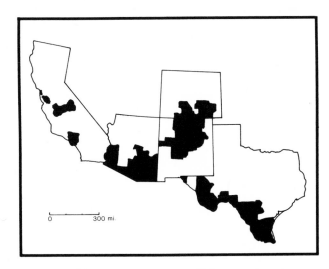

Fig. 49-1. *Major concentrations of Mexican American students in the Southwest. Source: U.S. Commission on Civil Rights, 1971, p. 19.*

The current situation outlined above presents a bleak picture of education in the Southwest. Although it is a well-known and accepted fact that the Chicano (and native American) experience in schools is problematic in terms of language, culture, socioeconomic status, and other aspects, relatively little research has been devoted to such matters. While the Chicano experience in education has not been totally ignored, there still exists considerable room for improvement.

Review of Available Resources

A basic resource describing educational statistics for the Borderlands region is chapter 7 of Grebler et al. (1970), and, although the data are now dated, some of the interregional, interethnic, and interracial comparisons made there are extremely valuable in noting the overall trends. For a wealth of unpublished materials and research reports having to do with educational problems in the Southwest, including those of the border minorities, the Educational Resources Information Center-Clearinghouse on Rural Education and Small Schools, or ERIC-CRESS (which has its regional outlet at New Mexico State University, Las Cruces, New Mexico 88003) contains many professional papers, survey reports, and other fugitive materials that cannot be obtained in other resource locations. Various other substantive summaries and reviews of educational topics relevant to the Borderlands include work by Demos (1962), C. Fernández (1977), N. G. Hernández (1973), and Weinberg (1977: chapter 4).

In studies of border educational problems there are two overall theoretical orientations into which research and analysis fall. The first might be called the "motivational school" and represents the bulk of current educators and administrators. When students fail, this orientation claims, it is from lack of effort and stamina, from low aspiration, and from the limitations "inherent" in racial, ethnic, and religious values. In opposition to this orientation, which blames the individual student for all of his failures, is the "structural" approach, which claims that the institutional structure itself shares some, or most, of the blame for educational failure among vast numbers of its students. This latter orientation is the theme of Chicano researchers and educators and the recent thrust of the social scientists in Borderlands studies.

The major resources emphasizing the institutional barriers that have a negative effect upon minority students in border schools are the six reports of the U.S. Commission on Civil Rights (1971-74), Carter and Segura's (1979) book on majority neglect in the education of Mexican Americans, an edited volume by Johnson and Hernández (1970) on the same theme, and a more recent report by Brown et al. (1980). Their works strongly underline the criticism of existing educational processes, procedures, and measurement instruments.

The six reports of the Commission on Civil Rights are based upon a thorough and lengthy investigation of schools, curricula, facilities, classroom management, placement practices, and school financing in the Southwest over a five-year period. The first of these reports discusses the extent to which Mexican American students experience segregation in schools and the low representation of Mexican Americans as teachers, school administrators, and school board members. The second report talks of measurements and interpretations of placement tools as well as of the failure of schools to educate Mexican American and other minority students, as evidenced by reading achievement levels, dropout rates, grade repetition, "over-ageness," and participation in extracurricular activities. The third report identifies and diagnoses overt and covert exclusionary practices. The study concludes that schools use various "exclusionary practices" which deny Mexican American students use of the Spanish language, pride in their ethnic heritage, and the direct support of their community. The remaining three reports cover different funding for majority and minority schools, processes of classroom interaction detrimental to the minority student, and final recommendations for action. One summary of the second report concludes:

. . . Minority students in the Southwest—Mexican Americans, Blacks, American Indians—do not obtain the benefits of public education at a rate equal to that of their Anglo classmates. This is true regardless of the measure of school achievement . . . used. [*U.S. Commission on Civil Rights, 1971, Vol. II:41*]

These six reports constitute the most comprehensive and extensive documentation of problems facing the Spanish-speaking student in the Southwest. Subsequent research data, such as those of Espinosa and García (1976) for California and Maldonado and Byrne (1978) for Utah, further substantiate the commission's findings by showing the limited number of Spanish-surnamed individuals in supervisory or educational policy-making positions.

Carter, a sociologist, and Segura, an educator, discuss a wide range of topics and cover them thoroughly in their book (1979). They review research produced in the following areas in the past decade: the academic achievement of Mexican Americans versus other groups, the effects of bilingualism on educational performance, self-concept, poverty, segregation, cultural exclusion, failure of the schools as opposed to failure of the culture, intellectual capacity, cognitive style, teacher perceptions and behavior, and other factors within the framework of institutional failure. The onus is left with the larger society to provide opportunities and channels of educational mobility and success for its minority students. Their conclusion, however, is not very encouraging:

It is axiomatic that predicting the future requires understanding the present and its antecedents. Although it is impossible to predict with certainty, it is possible to suggest future educational directions. Barring catastrophic events, there is every reason to believe schools will change little in the next ten years; they have changed little in the . . . past. [*Carter and Segura, 1979:381*]

The report by Brown et al. (1980) presents a comprehensive set of tables, figures, and graphs on the current educational experience of Mexican American and other Hispanic students compared to the educational status of whites. While the report offers little in the way of theoretical or explanatory discussion of the findings, a substantial amount of data is presented on numerous measures of Hispanic participation in elementary and secondary schools and institutions of higher education. In addition, the report contains a section on outcomes of schooling (e.g., employment, income, and so on). Upon review of the empirical evidence presented in this document, one must agree with Carter and Segura's conclusion: the gap in educational achievement between Anglos and Mexican Americans is still great, and there is no reason to expect it to diminish in the next ten years.

In any case, these materials offer the most comprehensive assessment of the nature and extent of opportunities available to Mexican American students in the public schools of the Borderlands.

Educational Achievement

There is total consensus on the outcomes of present educational systems and practices in terms of the number of formal years of education students achieve. Under constant scrutiny are the reasons for the discrepancies between Anglo students and minority pupils. As a group Chicanos score lower on both verbal and math achievement tests, have higher dropout rates, are less likely to graduate from high school, and attend college in fewer numbers. Also fewer graduate from college or attend graduate and professional schools (see Brown et al., 1980; Carter and Segura, 1979; Coleman et al., 1966; Crossland, 1971; Espinosa et al., 1975, 1979; Fernández et al., 1975; Gordon et al., 1968; Grebler, 1967; Jensen, 1961; Manuel, 1965; Sánchez, 1932; and U.S. Commission on Civil Rights, 1971-74, vol. 2). These findings are also true for native Americans and blacks.

The explanations advanced to account for these differences have tended to focus on the family or the culture, which are viewed as the "damaging causes" that bring about the lower performance of Chicano students. Such explanations have also been employed to explain differences in school outcomes between blacks or native Americans and Anglos in the Southwest.

Such claims show an ignorance of the role of ethnicity versus the importance of large concentrations of minority peoples in lower-class strata (Casavantes, 1969). Away from ethnic concentrations lower-class Anglo youth have much the same problems with the middle-class educational institution at which their middle-class Anglo classmates shine. Yet for many decades the literature of education and social science developed stereotypes of a homogeneous Mexican American culture and a foreign-born genetic legacy of incompetence (Vaca, 1970a, 1970b; Weinberg, 1977). Only recently have social scientists and other writers questioned these earlier family and culture models of deprivation (see Armstrong, 1972; Barton and Clasen, 1971; California State Department of Education, 1969; Castañeda et al., 1974; Davis and Personke, 1968; Fernández and Marenco, 1980; Fernández

et al., 1975; Galván, 1978; Hernández, 1970; Kuvlesky and Juárez, 1975; Mercer, 1971; Moreno, 1970; Ortega, 1971; Ramírez and Castañeda, 1974; Romano, 1968; Vásquez, 1972, and Vogler, 1968).

The results show that one's language ability, social origins, and cultural patterns may not be legitimately measured on presently existing IQ and achievement tests. Although testing per se may entail no biases, interpretation of performance as an accurate measure of "inherent ability" is erroneous. It is at present unknown whether test results for lower-class Mexican American barrio students legitimize discriminatory treatment by prejudiced individuals or whether middle-class bias is so strong among educational personnel (including many Spanish-surnamed individuals with middle-class origins) that they cannot distinguish "ability" when measuring instruments are inadequate. What is known is that discrimination, whether intentional or unintentional, affects the chances for success of Chicano students in the Southwest, in some areas more than others.

Among Mexican American pupils wide discrepancies exist between students from rural and urban areas because the rural areas offer fewer possibilities for schooling. One exception to this situation is in the state of Colorado, where two decades of programs exclusively directed at the rural and migrant Mexican American children of school age have greatly reduced the rural-urban schooling gap. Also years of formal schooling for Mexican Americans are fewer in Texas than in California. The Mexican American population in the lower Rio Grande Valley, or Mexican American families from that area who have dropped out of the migrant stream, have less formal education than other Mexican Americans. In Lubbock, Texas, migrant dropouts from the lower Rio Grande Valley who have settled in the area have eight to nine years less schooling than their Anglo counterparts (Grebler, 1967: table 6). Matthiesson (1968) and Lindstrom (1975) found that the reactions to education and the health of Mexican Americans in Wisconsin and Michigan cities were best among native-born individuals, next best among those born in Mexico, and least positive among those who came from Texas. Inasmuch as most of the Borderlands poverty is also concentrated in Texas (Stoddard, 1978c), it is quite obvious that certain structural determinants are responsible for these wide variations in educational experiences. To be sure, the current situation presents a bleak picture of education for minorities in the Southwest.

Self-Concept and Aspirations

Self-concept is a variable commonly associated with the low academic status of Chicano and native American students. It is argued that Chicano and native American pupils have lower self-esteem than do Anglo students because of discrimination, cultural conflict, and subordinate status in the larger society. A search of the literature, however, reveals mixed findings. As C. Fernández (1977) and Hernández (1973) have noted, the question whether Mexican American students have lower self-concepts than Anglo students remains largely unanswered.

Numerous studies report a significant difference in the academic self-evaluations of Chicanos and Anglos, with Chicano students holding lower views of their academic abilities (for example, Coleman et al., 1966; Firma, 1970; Gustafson and Owens, 1971; Hishiki, 1969; Mabry, 1968; Palomares, 1968). Other studies report no significant differences in self-concept between the two groups (for example, Carter, 1968; DeBlassie and Healy, 1970; Dornbusch et al., 1974; Larkin, 1972; Linton, 1972; Valenzuela, 1971).

No doubt some of the variation in the findings is a result of the different designs of the studies and the numerous instruments used for measuring self-concept. Yet it is conceivable that both sets of findings are accurate. One can even envision studies that find that Chicano students have higher self-concepts than Anglos, as Soares and Soares (1969) claim. There is a need to study in greater detail the conditions under which self-concepts differ for minority groups vis-à-vis the dominant group.

Research for more than a decade by Kuvlesky et al. (1971) separates from the feelings of self-worth of Mexican American, black, and Anglo youth in South Texas the element of "goal deflection" caused by the realities of the world about them. Since a minority person is seldom able to break away from poverty or menial occupational work, younger minority members are "deflected" from their goals because of invisible barriers within the structure which they do not understand but the effects of which they are able to scrutinize closely as highly motivated members of their minority fail to achieve.

Aspirations are another variable that has often been linked to academic achievement. It is argued that high educational and occupational aspirations among students, peers, and parents result in higher motivation on the part of the individual student and that this motivation in turn brings about higher achievement. This proposition has been generally supported by research.

In the case of Chicano students in the Borderlands the findings are fairly consistent. The earlier literature took for granted the "fatalistic" and "present-day" orientation of the Mexican American stereotype and thus assumed that Chicanos had low aspirations. Research findings strongly challenge this belief. Although a few studies (Demos, 1962; Mabry, 1968) report lower aspirations among Chicano students and parents than among Anglos, most recent research finds no significant differences in the level of aspirations of these two ethnic groups (Anderson and Johnson, 1971; Heller, 1964; Johnson, 1970; Juárez and Kuvlesky, 1969).

These findings are encouraging. Chicano students care about their schooling, and their parents support them in their view of the importance of school. Undue emphasis on this factor is unwarranted, however, for it is unrealistic to believe that Mexican American students will reach their high educational and occupational aspirations. Given the institutionalized deterrents to minority achievement within the educational institutions of the Borderlands, the level of student motivation among Mexican Americans cannot be a major determinant of success unless the student launches forth from a middle-class milieu.

Bilingual and Bicultural Education

Bilingual and bicultural education as a curricular model for minority-language children has a very short history. In 1968 the Bilingual Education Act initiated the official involvement of the federal government in the education of children whose home language was other than English. This act was designed simply to supply seed money to school districts to meet the special needs of children of limited English-speaking ability who lived in areas with a high concentration of families with incomes below $3,000 a year. In 1970 the Department of Health, Education, and Welfare required school districts with federally funded programs to "rectify the language deficiency in order to open the instruction to students with language deficiencies."

It was not until 1974, when the U.S. Supreme Court handed down a unanimous decision in the *Lau* v. *Nichols* class-action case, that schools were obligated by law to give special assistance to children with limited ability to speak English by providing them with bilingual and bicultural programs. During their short history bilingual and bicultural programs have been under attack from conservative politicians, school officials, and the general population. Most recently, President Reagan has expressed his lack of support for such programs. The need for special language programs for minority language children in the Borderlands remains, however.

According to the U.S. Commission on Civil Rights an estimated 50 percent of the Chicano first-grade students in the Southwest do not speak English as well as the average Anglo first-grader does. Bilingual and bicultural education is the one recent method most widely employed by the schools in an attempt to reach and, more importantly, to raise the educational achievement of Chicanos. Bilingual and bicultural education has been defined as "instruction in two languages used concurrently within the classroom with emphasis on the history and culture associated with both languages" (Aguirre and Fernández, 1976-77: 19). Although, in broad outline, this approach appears to be relevant to the education of Chicano students in the Southwest, the specific programs that have emerged, such as Foreign Language for English Speakers (FLES) and English as a Second Language (ESL), are not without their drawbacks (Anderson, 1969).

Social-science purists quietly suggest that only when the programs become multilingual, multicultural, and multiclass-oriented will they be more successful than such programs have been in the past. To assume that middle-class English materials directly translated into middle-class Spanish will be applicable to the vocabulary, interests, or experience of the barrio child is to promote failure. Among families where the father is completely absent, gone for extended periods of time, or arrives home very late from work, the children see no familiar experiences in pictures showing a father carrying a briefcase and dressed in a suit as he returns with his car and greets a mother, complete with white apron, who has a picture-book kitchen and table setting. On the other hand, the success of television shows like "Sesame Street" derives from the presence of familiar street scenes, including a garbage can and a neighborhood store, with a furry monster who likes cookies; such a scene relates to English and Spanish-speaking children from most social levels. Only when the various functions of language (that is, communication, identity, and a cultural reservoir of items and experience) are considered separately and programs aim to emphasize them one at a time can a greater return on "bilingual and bicultural" education be felt (Stoddard, 1973a: 107-22).

Another dimension to bilingual and bicultural education is the goal to which a given program is directed. Fishman (1977: 27-30) has identified three categories of bilingual and bicultural education: compensatory, enrichment, and group maintenance. Programs of the compensatory type are geared to overcoming "diseases of the poor." The primary goal is to increase overall achievement by using the mother tongue (Spanish) for instruction until the child develops sufficient skill in the dominant language (English) that English alone can be used as the medium of instruction. Enrichment programs, geared most often to the middle and upper social classes, seek to "enrich" the education and lives of these children by exposing them to different languages and cultures. Group-maintenance programs are intended to preserve and enhance minority groups as such, whether poor or rich. Because in the Borderlands governmental support focuses principally upon the patronizing compensatory programs instead of maintaining and promoting cultural diversity, the last two types of programs are not enthusiastically received and appear to be failing. Moreover, compensatory programs that are merely transitional or remedial are unlikely to raise the achievement levels of Chicano students, while they do promote stereotypes of "cultural disadvantage." Such programs serve only to sooth the feelings of the people responsible for educational policies in the Southwest by illustrating that something is being done. Not until programs of the compensatory type are shifted so that their primary goals are cultural maintenance and enrichment will such programs be vigorously supported by the Chicano community.

Bilingual education is also an important issue on the Mexican side of the U.S.-Mexico border. Mexicans, however, have been more willing to embrace the English language as part of their educational programs than Americans the Spanish language. Mexicans strongly encourage their children to learn English. Often children of the middle and upper classes are sent to the U.S. sometime during their schooling years to learn English. Many universities in the Southwest offer language programs during the summer months that cater to Mexican high school and college students.

Other Border Issues

One of the most important issues to surface in the Borderlands in recent years has been the education of children of undocumented (illegal) Mexican immigrants. The question is whether these children have a right to a tuition-free public education or whether the schools have the right to require

these students to pay tuition. Although the issue has been raised in all four border states, it came to a head in the form of a court case in Texas. In July, 1980, Judge Woodrow Seals decided in favor of the students, stating that children of undocumented immigrants should not be penalized by excluding them from a free public education. Moreover, these children should be given equal educational opportunity in order that they may move up the social and economic ladder. Exclusion from a free public education, he argued, would further contribute to their second-class resident status and lead to unemployment, crime, and reliance on social welfare programs.

Judge Seals made his decision on the basis of research which indicates that few Mexican immigrants—less than 10 percent—remain permanently in the United States. Moreover, the typical undocumented immigrant is male, single, and between twenty and thirty years of age. Thus the number of children of undocumented workers who are attending the schools is very small. In addition, the research has consistently found that undocumented immigrants pay taxes in many ways, for example, when purchasing gasoline, food, and clothing (Cornelius, 1978; Zazueta, 1980). Furthermore, settled immigrants file income taxes, and the overwhelming majority of undocumented immigrants rent homes, thus indirectly contributing to the ad valorem taxes that finance public schools.

The Texas ruling, however, has been contested, and the U.S. Supreme Court has decided to hear the case. Although, as of this writing, the Supreme Court has not heard the case, we can be sure of two things: (1) this case is highly political, and (2) the decision will have an impact on both U.S.-Mexico relations and Anglo-Mexican American relations, particularly in the Borderlands.

Another Borderlands educational issue, which is not as political or as well studied as the one discussed above, is the attendance of Mexican students in schools on the U.S. side of the border. There seems to be a substantial number of Mexican students residing in border cities on the Mexican side of the border who attend public schools on the U.S. side. Often the student provides the school system with an address in the U.S., usually that of a relative or friend, in order to be eligible for a free public-school education. This phenomenon seems to be peculiar to border towns and cities, for example, Juárez-El Paso, Nogales, Arizona-Nogales, Sonora, Mexicali-Calexico, and so on.

From my own work it appears that such students are usually from the middle and upper classes and that their incentive for crossing the border daily to attend school is their parents' perception that U.S. schools are providing a better all-around education. Equally important is the fact that these students are able to become fluent bilinguals; that is, they use the U.S. schools to learn and perfect their English.

Although, as noted above, a great deal of research needs to be done on the subject, it appears that these border crossings to attend school may have deleterious effects on the Mexican educational system. The parents with the most power to improve the quality of the educational system along the Mexican border are the ones who take their children out of the Mexican schools and place them in American schools. Thus the border crossings to attend school indirectly affect the educational system on the Mexican side of the border as well as on the American side.

Summary

Because the traditional approach to education is so well documented in the existing literature, this essay has attempted to emphasize the other orientations that are currently being developed and supported by Borderlands minorities. These orientations have not had wide distribution among school functionaries, teachers, and educational researchers, and at present they are in need of further research and polishing to increase their potential effectiveness. It is no longer enough to collect data showing that Mexican Americans and other border minorities do not find the present educational experience as satisfying or rewarding as do members of the dominant society. It is critically important that the salient factors that contribute to this pattern be isolated and that policies be developed that deal with the causes of the problem instead of its symptoms. It is equally critical that school officials no longer expect or accept a lower level of achievement for Chicano students and that they begin to respond to their strengths instead of perceived weaknesses.

Chicano researchers are looking for more humane theoretical models that will better explain the Chicano experience in education and differentiate that experience from those of other minorities and the larger society. Meanwhile, other social scientists are attempting to separate the experiences that arise out of poverty and social class patterns from experiences that are solely ethnic and cultural in nature. But, even if divergent viewpoints were articulated and conflicts resolved, there is little evidence that the educational system in the Borderlands would respond rapidly to the special needs of its minorities.

The family holds a highly significant position in the U.S.-Mexican Borderlands. As in most Latin American societies, Mexicans and Mexican Americans consider the family infinitely more important than the individual. The family is the primary and basic social unit; for example, individual duties are generally performed first to the family and second to one's employer. Strict social sanctions exist to see that behavior conforms to this pattern, although modernization is modifying those sanctions to some degree.

Until the last two decades, research on the Borderlands family was almost nonexistent. In the 1940s prominent sociologist Kingsley Davis (1942: 100) stated that Latin America was "the dark continent, sociologically speaking" and that more was known about Africa than about cultures south of the Rio Grande. Two decades later, after completing a book on world marriage systems, researchers David and Vera Mace remarked (cited in Bridges, 1961: 6): "As yet, we know practically nothing of Latin America. It is about the only area of the world which has not been included in our studies." Until the late 1960s this

50

Family Life

JULIAN C. BRIDGES
Department of Sociology and Social Work
Hardin-Simmons University

same paucity of empirical research existed concerning Chicano marriage and family systems.

For family life before the mid-1960s the principal bibliographical sources in English (although they contain Spanish references) are Aldous and Hill's *International Bibliography of Research in Marriage and the Family* (1967); the *Journal of Marriage and the Family* (formerly *Marriage and Family Living, 1954-*); and *Handbook of Latin American Studies, 1950-* (sections on sociology and anthropology).

The most comprehensive bibliographies in studies of marriage and the family conducted since 1964 (in addition to the sources mentioned above) are Aldous and Dahl's *International Bibliography of Research in Marriage and the Family, 1965-1972* (1974) and Olson and Dahl's *Inventory of Marriage and Family Literature, 1973-1974* (1975) and *1975-1976* (1977).

Other bibliographical sources very helpful in reviewing literature on family life, particularly in Mexico and Latin American countries, are *Bibliography of the Center for Latin American Research in the Social Sciences, 1960-; Dissertation Abstracts, 1960-;* and *List of Books Accessioned and Periodical Articles Indexed at the Pan American Union Columbus Memorial Library, 1965-.*

Significant Mexican family studies published in English during the early period (before 1965) are Burnight et al. (1956) on rural-urban fertility; Cancian (1964) on village family interaction patterns; Corwin (1963) on attitudes toward population size; Díaz Guerrero (1955) on neurosis and family structure; Fernández et al. (1958) on a comparison of Mexican and Puerto Rican family values; and Whetten (1948) on rural family life.

Probably the most comprehensive early treatments of Mexican family life are by Hayner (1942, 1954) and Humphrey (1952). Moore (1952) offers insight into working-class attitudes toward fertility control, while Ramírez (1957) provides the perspective of a Mexican psychoanalyst toward Mexican family organization.

By far the most outstanding anthropological contributions about the Mexican village family in early years are the works of Redfield (1936, 1941) in the Yucatán region and Lewis (1949, 1951, 1953a, 1953b, 1956, and 1959b) in Tepoztlán, Morelos (near Mexico City). Lewis also studied urban families and became the most prolific writer on family life to date (1959a, 1959b, 1961, 1964a, 1964b, and 1969a). His book *Five Families: Mexican Case Studies in the Culture of Poverty* (1959a) is the most extensive treatment of Mexican family life in print, while his *The Children of Sánchez: Autobiography of a Mexican Family* (1961) is the most intensive analysis of a single family. Lewis's highly significant insight into sociological patterns among the growing number of families in Mexican urban slums makes a stellar contribution to social science which will be pertinent for decades to come.

Finally, four very early studies, while not of an empirical nature, offer historical comparison on the basis of the writers' observations. Gann (1918) makes rather extensive comments about Maya marriage and children. Shontz (1927) cites changes in family relationships as compared to even earlier periods of Mexican history. Toor (1932) talks extensively, but generally, of courtship and marriage patterns, and Miller (1938) writes of women in Mexico's isthmus region.

The single most definitive work in Spanish before 1965 is that of María Bermúdez (1955). Although her book contains many comments not supported by empirical research, later investigations have tended to corroborate and confirm many of Bermúdez's assumptions. Other significant early, general studies of the Spanish family are Iturriaga (1951), Lewis (1959b), Martínez (1949), and Villaseñor Martínez (1964), the last being the best treatment, although it is unpublished. For an English summary of this work, see McGinn (1966).

Some specific Spanish early studies worthy of note are Davis (1964) on the age of marriage; Gómez (1959) on the economic conditions of the middle-class family; González Pineda (1961) on sociopsychological aspects of family members; Ramírez and Parres (1957b) on marriage in a rural village; Ramírez (1959) on the psychological motivations of family members; and Stavenhagen (1959) on co-parenthood in a Zapotec village.

The best current, somewhat general, studies published in English of the family in Mexico are McGinn (1966) on the middle-class family and Peñalosa (1968) on Mexican family roles. Studies in Spanish include Altmann Smythe (1967) on the social reality of the family; Elu (1965) on a sociology of the family; López Mercado (1965) on various aspects of the Mexican family; and Díaz Guerrero (1975) on psychological and sociocultural family structure.

Bridges (1980) has written a comprehensive article on the Mexican family. Some of the findings which follow should be viewed primarily as hypotheses to be tested, since there has been little empirical research on the Mexican family.

Before any adequate discussion of Mexican family life, several precautionary statements should be made. First, it must be constantly remembered that much more research has been conducted among families of lower socioeconomic class than among the middle or upper classes. While the former aggregate constitutes by far the largest single segment of Mexico's population, the American reader must continually guard against the ethnocentric tendency to compare the familial norms of those who are less economically fortunate with the customs of U.S. middle-class families.

A second precaution lies in the fact that there are considerable variations of family behavior within the same social classes. For example, there is a wide divergence of family patterns between rural and urban residents, those members who visit cities regularly and those who do not, those who live in villages directly affected by modernization or industrialization and those hardly touched by these developments (cf. Reck, 1978), those that are headed by females and those in which both parents are present, those whose members may migrate at least temporarily to and from the United States and those who never migrate (Cornelius, 1977a), and those in which the wife works outside the home and those of the more traditional pattern.

The family must be studied as a dynamic instead of static institution, as variegated instead of uniform in the tones and colors it reflects within one social class or another. Numerous variables interact and influence the behavior patterns from each household.

The third major observation of a precautionary nature is that empirical research on the Mexican family is still in its swaddling clothes. It is a truism, but hard data are difficult to accumulate. Much of what has been written on the Mexican family (though by some of Mexico's most respected writers) has been more from the philosophical (Ramos, 1961; Paz, 1962) or psychoanalytical (González Pineda, 1961; Ramírez, 1959) perspective than scientific sampling. Montiel (1970, 1973), while discussing the background of the Chicano family, analyzes the weaknesses of approaches based on the Mexican "national character."

I have proposed the ideal type (Bridges, 1979a) as a valuable theoretical construct for studying the Mexican, Mexican American, or Chicano family. Such types, while they do not necessarily exist in reality, are useful models with which to compare empirical studies of actual families. Using such an approach, polar opposites like the traditional extended family (TEF) and the modern nuclear family (MNF) are paradigms to measure the investigations of all families with respect to how completely they correspond to the models.

Thirty-three aspects of each of two polar types have been outlined; for example, in geographical location, the TEF model is extremely rural, while the MNF model is extremely urban. According to the 1970 census of population, only 35.3 percent of Mexico's inhabitants lived in localities of 20,000 or more persons, and only 11.5 percent resided in cities of 500,000 or more (Bridges, 1973: 89-94). On the other hand, only 41.3 percent of the population still lives in localities of fewer than 2,500 persons. If this category can be defined as extremely rural, and cities above 500,000 are defined as extremely urban, almost half of Mexico's population now lives in neither category. They live in medium-sized localities.

Another example of the 33 aspects is in child discipline. The TEF tends toward corporal punishment, while the MNF uses withdrawal of approval. Studies seem to show that a distinction is definitely made in disciplining sons and daughters. During the first year of life, both sexes are given a great deal of affection and freedom. This freedom continues considerably for sons, but not for daughters, after the first year. Sons, however, receive more corporal punishment than do their sisters. This punishment is usually administered by the father, who maintains more distance from sons than does the mother. The mother-son relationship is usually quite close, but not as close as that of the mother-daughter (Peñalosa, 1968; McGinn, 1966).

Space permits only a cursory treatment of other aspects of the two ideal types. The chief occupation of the TEF male head is generally agriculture, with that of the MNF head being manufacturing, transportation, or government. Outside of strictly rural locales, however, many Mexican family members today hold jobs in construction, commerce, and services. In 1970 almost one-fifth of the population was occupied in this latter group, while approximately one-half was dedicated to farming and one-fourth to manufacturing, transportation, or government (Bridges, 1973: 188).

In the father's affection toward his children, the TEF model of withholding affection from the sons is approximated more closely in most studies, although increased urbanization seems to be altering this pattern, particularly in the middle class. Affection on the part of the MNF mother, though, toward both male and female offspring is diminished compared to that of the TEF mother; most Mexican mothers incline very strongly toward the TEF model. However, when children arrive in rapid succession, time does not permit the attention and affection each desires (González Pineda, 1963: 252; Peñalosa, 1968: 686).

Concerning sexes, the TEF emphasizes male superiority, whereas the MNF is more equalitarian. Although studies stress the former in describing the Mexican model, my eight years of observation in Mexico City, and extensive travel throughout all regions of the country, lead me to believe that this is an area in considerable flux, especially among the middle and upper classes. Role segregation is still strong, but there is great respect for the power and influence of the wife-mother. While the authority pattern tends to be publicly patriarchal, it is often equalitarian or even matriarchal in family interaction.

Until recent years a strict double standard existed for premarital sexual relations. Thus, there was a very close TEF model approximation instead of MNF equalitarian opportunities. With the arrival of contraceptives in Mexico and a national family planning program sponsored by the government, university coeds in Mexico City today engage in premarital intercourse without worrying about the loss of reputation as they did in the past. Although the percentage following this practice is probably very small, and will remain so for some years, the younger Mexican generation's attitudes are becoming considerably more liberal.

Marriage preparation frequently follows a semi-TEF pattern among nuclear families with both parents present. The traditional pattern called for courtship chaperoned strictly by adults. Today children are the most frequently used chaperones, if chaperones are used at all. Much furtive and surreptitious courting occurs today in large urban areas. Maids from rural districts who obtain urban employment have no family member to supervise their relationships.

Authority for mate selection is no longer parental arrangement (TEF), yet it has not arrived at a level of absolute individual decision (MNF). Today it tends to be by mutual consent on the part of both families and *novios* concerned. The source of one's spouse tends still to be primarily endogamous, in terms of social class, although exogamy is more frequent when, for example, prospective partners have achieved the same level of educational preparation.

In the TEF, the legal marriage constitution tends to be sanctioned more by the clan or extended family, while among the MNF, the government defines legal matrimony. Mexican families today are definitely moving toward the latter practice. In 1970, 42 percent of the population of marriageable age were legally married; only 13 percent were married only by the church (not legal in Mexico) or living in consensual union. In 1930, these figures were 28 and 30 percent, respectively. Age of first marriage tends to be low in the TEF model and higher in the MNF paradigm (Whetten, 1948: 388). Today, Mexican young people are definitely marrying later, largely because of extensive migration of young people from rural to urban areas, where they tend to marry at later ages (Bridges, 1973: 147-51).

Today, marriage in Mexico takes the form of neither polygyny (TEF) nor strict monogamy (MNF); instead, the pattern of the male having one legal wife but mistresses (monogyny) still persists tenaciously. However, as women obtain higher levels of education and become companions to their husbands as well as bearers of the children, monogamy tends to predominate. Machismo is diminishing in modern Mexico, particularly since the federal government has launched an active campaign against it in conjunction with its family planning program.

Female retaliation against husbands' extramarital sex relations is becoming more frequent in Mexico, although extramarital sex is still tolerated by the vast majority of women (Bridges, 1961: 98-102). Dissolution of marriage among the poor occurs primarily by male desertion. Divorce still carries considerable stigma, and the rate is very low compared to that in the United States. However, the proportion of divorced Mexicans has increased 57 percent for females and 100 percent for males from 1940 to 1970 (Bridges, 1973: 160).

Mexican descent and inheritance is patrilineal, although each person has two last names (the bisexual surname pattern). Residence after marriage tends to be neolocal, but proximity is often great to at least one set of parents. Kinship ties are strongly bilateral. Both husband and wife look for frequent opportunities to visit their parents by birth and marriage. Increased geographical mobility has created the modified extended family pattern, in which communication is frequent even though children and offspring are widely separated.

A great deal of deference is still given to age among Mexican families, but the elderly authority—particularly in urban areas—diminishes with advancing age. The individual is still subservient to the family, but the eldest son or daughter is often backed through family financial sacrifices so he or she may obtain an education. Children usually feel great responsibility for the welfare of their parents, and often for younger brothers and sisters, even after they are married.

Finally, as fertility and infant mortality decline in Mexico, it is expected that the individual will become a more important part of the family unit. The pattern, however, of warm hospitality extended to relatives who may need to move into one's area is deeply ingrained in Mexican society. For example, in Mexico City, where many students come from all over the nation, there exists the lowest ratio of heads of households per nonnuclear family relatives living in the home. Conversely, rural districts have the smallest proportion of extended-type families, challenging the assumption that extended families still predominate rurally (Bridges, 1980).

By far the best treatment of the literature of Chicano family studies is in a recent article by Mirandé (1977). The writer, a Chicano himself, discusses "the social science myth" of the Mexican American family, sympathetic views toward the Chicano family, and his own synthesis of the two. Another discussion of both the traditional assumptions and the more recent Chicano perspective is Stoddard (1973a: 99-106). Grebler et al. (1970) present valuable research findings based upon their sample surveys drawn in San Antonio, Albuquerque, and Los Angeles. Moore and Panchon (1976: 101-21) offer some additional research material while discussing patterns of change in the modern Chicano family.

Primarily sympathetic with the Chicano perspective are Montiel (1970: 56-63; 1973: 22-31), Romano (1968: 43-56), and Murillo (1971: 97-108). Empirical research supporting the Chicano perspective is that of Alvírez and Bean (1976) and Goodman and Beman (1971). Mexican American intermarriage is dealt with on a comprehensive level by Murguía and Frisbie (1977). Finally, Bean, Curtis, and Marcum (1977) confirm doubts concerning the influence of social class instead of ethnicity in explaining behavior differences between Mexican American marital partners. Obviously, much more research is needed to test these numerous hypotheses.

From prehistoric times human beings have lived and traveled in the shared border regions of what are now Mexico and the United States. The native peoples of this region and the Spaniard, Mexican, Chicano, and Anglo who came later have all contributed to this area's art development. This chapter is an overview of the type of art prevalent in this region over time, focusing on painting and, to a lesser extent, on sculpture and architecture. It is important to remember that much of this art is not wholly unique to the border region. It must, to some extent, be understood as part of the art of a larger society in which this region was or is a part—for example, of the Spanish colonial empire or the United States of America.

Native American Prehistoric Period

This period covers the years from before the birth of Christ until approximately the sixteenth century and the arrival of the Spanish. With the exception of

51

Art and Architecture

LOUIS M. HOLSCHER
Department of Sociology
University of Arizona

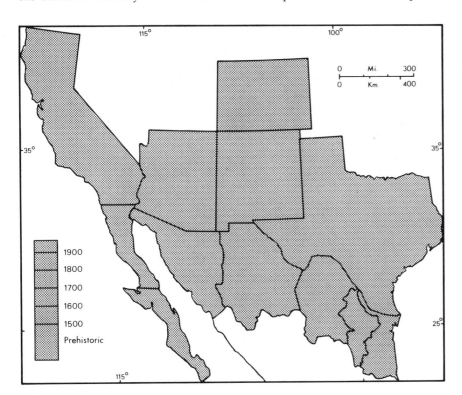

decorated dart shafts in Gypsum Cave (Nevada), the earliest border art is from the Hohokam Estrella phase, dated 100 B.C. to A.D. 100, and the early Mogollón Culture of about the same period (Tanner, 1973: 16), both having left painted pottery. Three civilization groups are apparent, mainly in what is now part of the United States: Anasazi, Hohokam, and Mogollón-Mimbres (Lehmann, 1962: 107).

The Anasazi, often called Pueblos, inhabited the vast plateau region. Their basketry appeared first, but they used decorated ceramics as early as A.D. 500-700. Such ceramics were almost always painted in black on a white ground (Lehmann, 1962: 107). The forms and the decoration became more varied over time so that by Pueblo III (1050-1300) the pottery was very skillfully executed (Lehmann, 1962: 108). During Pueblo IV (1300-1700) excellent pottery continued to be produced. Lehmann (1962: 108) states that birds and insects appeared, along with animals, masked persons, and flowers, and that colors were more varied. Brilliant kiva mural decorations were executed in the Hopi and Rio Grande areas during Pueblo IV (Dutton, 1975: 254). Tanner (1976: 9) believes that much of this art reflected high religious attainment plus the costumes and customs of the people.

Dutton's (1963:22) excellent work on the murals of Kuaua (an ancient pueblo near Bernalillo, New Mexico) indicates that the earliest cultural remains date to the early fourteenth century. Dutton learned much about the Kuaua paintings by showing them to contemporary Pueblo men knowledgeable about traditional religious practices, indicating a continuity from the past (Dutton, 1963: 25).

The Hohokam civilization inhabited the southern Arizona desert area. Today's Pimas and Pápagos are their probable descendants. There appears to be a strong Mexican influence in even the very early years of this culture. Tanner (1976: 11) believes that Mexican-featured figurines associated with the Hohokam peoples definitely came from the south. They appeared as early as A.D. 300-500 (Lehmann, 1962: 108).

Colonial-period pottery (A.D. 500–900) featured motifs of birds, turtles, and quadrupeds (Lehmann, 1962: 108). Overall, the red and cream colors and a free-style painting not found elsewhere in the Southwest characterize Hohokam wares (Tanner, 1976: 12). The Mogollón-Mimbres peoples inhabited the mountains of eastern Arizona and southwestern New Mexico. They appeared about 300 B.C. and disappeared about A.D. 1300. Their first pottery was plain, but later it was decorated with red paint; still later they developed red-on-white ware (Tanner, 1976: 13).

The Mimbres, in southwestern New Mexico, represent one of the border's major ceramic developers. Their black-on-white decorated wares, often said to be influenced by the Anasazi, reached a high point between 1050 and 1200 (Lehmann, 1962: 110). The motifs include human figures, birds, insects, and so on, usually appearing on the inside bottom of cups and pots. Two books entirely about Mimbres wares, both with excellent pictures, are Snodgrass (1975), and Giammettei and Reichert (1975); also, see Brody (1977).

The foremost authority on these civilizations' art is Clara Lee Tanner, long associated with the University of Arizona.

Her book *Prehistoric Southwestern Craft Arts* (1976) relates art to the people's culture; her discussion of materials, techniques, and forms is the basis for a discussion on design styles and artistic development. Smithsides's comprehensive work of native southwestern art has nearly three hundred illustrations of geometric ornamentation, patterns, borders, and so on, from prehistoric to contemporary times.

A number of books have been published on southwestern architecture. Sanford's work *The Architecture of the Southwest* (1971) includes sections on native American (both prehistoric and modern), Spanish colonial, and American architecture. *Early Architecture in New Mexico* (1976), by Bunting, covers the prehistoric and Spanish colonial periods up to the coming of Anglos and the railroad (1880-1912). Current and Scully's book *Pueblo Architecture of the Southwest: A Photographic Essay* (1966) includes pictures of Chaco Canyon, Canyon de Chelly, and Navajo National Monument, giving the reader a good visual idea.

Most works on prehistoric Mexican art do not discuss what is now that country's northern frontier. Kubler (1962), in nearly four hundred pages on Mexican, Mayan, and Andean ancient art, has only two pages on the Huastecan civilization, which ranged from the Mexican Highlands north into eastern Texas, lasting from about 1100 B.C. until the coming of the Spanish. These people painted densely patterned murals about 1100 A.D. (for example, at Tamuin) and carved monumental sculptures during the Toltec periods (Kubler, 1962b: 80).

One cannot fully discuss prehistoric art and culture without including the works and ideas of Charles Di Peso on Casas Grandes and the Gran Chichimeca. This area extends as far north and east as San Francisco and Wichita, and south as far as the Tropic of Cancer. He believes that the peoples from the Mexican central valleys directly and indirectly influenced the economy, culture, and art of people far to the north.

Cave and rock painting was another prehistoric artistic endeavor of the border area; there are numerous books available on this subject. Crosby (1975) has an excellent book on central Baja California cave paintings. These paintings, many of them much larger than life-sized, were probably from A.D. 500-1500. Most prehistoric North American people engaged in some sort of rock art, creating a vast reservoir of carvings, paintings, and engravings. Kirkland and Newcomb (1967) provide a good overview of Texas rock art. The definitive source on New Mexico rock art is Schaafsma (1972). Like the book on Texas, it covers both prehistoric and historic periods. Heizer and Clewlow's *Prehistoric Rock Art of California* (1973) is a general survey of that state.

Native American Art, Historic to Contemporary

This section will mainly emphasize native art from the southwestern United States. It is very difficult to locate materials from Mexico's northern frontier.

Native American art, over the past few hundred years, has been greatly affected by the arrival of the Spanish and the

Anglo-Americans. Painting in the Southwest, at the outset of the historic period, included ceramics, textiles, blankets, skins, the decorating of kiva walls, and cliff wall paintings. Tanner (1973: 9) believes that the Spanish had only a slight influence on ceramic decoration and that Mexican painting influences seem to be nonexistent. One important Spanish effect, though, was the introduction of sheep to the Navahos and the subsequent use of wool in their weaving.

During this period, pottery was for utilitarian and ceremonial purposes only. Bowls and jars dominated, as they had during the two thousand years of Southwest ceramics (Tanner, 1968: 85). As in prehistoric times, only a small percentage of ceramics were painted. Pottery, though, was the greatest of all prehistoric arts and continued to be some of the most successful decorative native art in the Southwest during the sixteenth to nineteenth centuries (Dockstader, 1973: 17). A good introduction to Pueblo pottery during 1600-1800 is the book by Frank and Harlow (1974). With the U.S. conquest of northern Mexico in the 1840s, many rapid changes came to affect native American culture. The railroad and traders introduced many metal pots to the native Americans and influenced pot design (Tanner, 1968: 85). By the early part of the twentieth century, pottery had begun to wane and in some instances had virtually died out among certain Rio Grande Pueblos (Dutton, 1975: 245).

There are many books and articles available on contemporary Pueblo pottery and its important artists; see, for example, LeFree (1975), and Maxwell Museum of Anthropology (1974). Bunzel's work, first published in 1929, covers the pottery of the Zuñi, Acoma, Hopi, and San Ildefonso peoples and is mostly concerned with design principles. A good reference guide for New Mexico's Pueblo pottery is Toulouse (1977).

Sand painting, a well-known Navaho art form, was probably adopted from the Pueblo people, who had used it since prehistoric times (Dockstader, 1973: 17). Outside of ritual, much sand painting is now made for the tourist. A good source on the symbolism of Navaho sand painting is Newcomb and Reichard (1975). Dry painting is still used by the Pueblos during certain ceremonies. The Jicarilla Apaches and Pimas also use dry painting (Dutton, 1975: 255).

Native Texas peoples did not paint as extensively as did their neighbors to the west. Berlandier (1969), in his chapter on artifacts, does mention that Comanches painted their shields. Of course there was rock art in that area. Painting on canvas, that is, easel painting, is a fairly recent phenomenon in native American art forms. Brody (1971) begins her discussion on painting about 1885. Both Berlandier (1969) and Brody (1971) are the best introductions to native American painting in the Southwest. Brody provides the reader with a chronological framework detailing the relationship between the native artists and their white patrons, white instructors, and a number of institutions.

Tanner's book (1973) is a merging of history, culture, and art. She stresses that new art is emerging, one with traditional subject matter in the contemporary idiom. Other works of interest on native American painting of the Southwest include *Art and Indian Individualists* by Guy and Doris Monthan

(1975). That book stresses the evolution of native American art as a natural course of events influenced by modern technological society. Southwestern sculpture is limited because of the scarcity of suitable basic materials. The most common carvings are small painted and decorated *kachina* dolls made by the Hopis and Zuñis (Dockstader, 1961: 17). *Kachinas,* not really dolls, are important in Pueblo social organization (Dutton, 1975: 259).

There have been many books published on contemporary southwestern arts and crafts over the past few years. Probably the best is Tanner's *Southwest Indian Craft Arts* (1968), which includes chapters on textiles, baskets, silver and jewelry, *kachinas* and carvings, and minor crafts. For a comprehensive work on California native peoples, see Kroeber (1976). Possibly these peoples' greatest art contribution has been in basketry (Dockstader, 1961: 16). The best may be Pomo, with its decorations of bird feathers, shells, and other ornaments.

Spanish Colonial Art

This section summarizes the art of the Spanish-speaking people of Mexico's northern frontier from approximately the early part of the seventeenth century until Mexico's independence from Spain in the 1820s. The focus will be on New Mexico, because it was there that Spanish traditions were the strongest (Ahlborn, 1975: 41). Generally speaking, in New Mexico, Texas, Arizona, and California, Hispanic artistic differences derived from varying supply sources and local political chronology as well as church and social history (Ahlborn, 1975: 41).

The 1680 Pueblo revolt drove most Spanish from northern New Mexico. Subsequently, most material objects from the seventeenth century were destroyed. Little remains from this period except the Palace of the Governors in Santa Fe and a few early missions in what is now New Mexico (Boyd, 1959: 6). For art, the eighteenth and nineteenth centuries are important.

Hundreds of religious paintings were made on hides in New Mexico during the eighteenth century. There was much religious art at that time. Panels and altar screens were extensively painted by 1800; the artists were Franciscans and lay image makers, including many native Americans.

The *santero,* the maker of images, came into his own during the nineteenth century. *Santeros* created thousands of *bultos* (statues) and *retablos* (paintings), common in every Catholic home, both Spanish and Pueblo (Boyd, 1959: 31-33). Most early New Mexican art was influenced by prints, easily carried from Spain and Flanders (Boyd, 1974: 80).

Much of the work by the *santeros* is anonymous, but both Steele (1974) and Boyd (1974) provide extensive information on what is known about the men who painted the *retablos* and sculptured the *bultos*. For the best overview on this region's art before 1848, see Boyd's *Popular Arts of Spanish New Mexico* (1974). That book has a lengthy bibliography. There are a number of excellent books on border architecture during Spanish colonial times. Sanford (1971) and Bunting (1976) have already been mentioned. Kubler's *Religious Architecture of New Mexico* (1962) relates architecture to the changing society and the limited construction materials in New Mexico. Boyd (1974) also has an extensive section on both domestic and religious architecture. The Hispanic tradition in early Colorado art and architecture is presented by Adams (1974).

Most books on Latin American art history or Spanish art in the Americas are not concerned with the northern frontier region of Mexico or with what is now the southwestern United States. A good example of this selectivity is the work of Castedo (1969). Although he does mention that the Baroque splendor of Central Mexico is largely missing in the North, Chihuahua City's cathedral is an exception. Toussaint's massive work *Colonial Art in Mexico* (1967) has some information on the North and contains an extensive bibliography in Spanish.

Mexican Period, 1820 to the Present

The 1821 independence from Spain brought a cultural break, especially in art. The Baroque style that dominated the Hispanic world since the early 1600s was displaced by a neoclassic French-influenced style lasting throughout much of the nineteenth century. Late in the 1800s French impressionism also made inroads into Mexican art. In the outlying provinces, including the North, there were antiacademic and popular tendencies being nourished. Castedo (1969: 217) states that most of these "popular" painters' names are unknown. One tremendously popular artist was José Guadalupe Posada.

The major event in Mexico in the twentieth century was the Revolution of 1910. Its effect on art has been tremendous, especially in theme, color, and design. Additionally, Central Mexican presence in the northern states and the U.S. Southwest has increased as a result of the tremendous upheavals in Mexico that began in 1910 (Quirarte, 1973: chap. 3).

The most important twentieth-century development in Mexican painting has been the mural movement. It has often been very political, carrying forth the belief that art should belong to all people and should be revolutionary. Today, murals can be found in most Mexican cities, including the North and many parts of the United States. The three most prominent muralists were David Alfaro Siqueiros, José Clemente Orozco, and Diego Rivera (Cardoza y Aragón, 1966; Edwards and Bravo, 1966). Many important twentieth-century Mexican artists have either been born in the North or have lived (and exhibited) in the United States (see V. Stewart, 1951).

Folk art is found everywhere in Mexico; its forms of expressions are manifold. Because of the mass movement northward in the twentieth century and the American tourist trade, much folk art of Oaxaca, the Huicholes in Nayarit, Taxco, and so on, has either influenced the border folk art or found its way north fairly intact. A good short introduction is Dorner (1962). A much more extensive work, and one that is beautifully done, is Fondo Editorial de la Plastica Mexicana, *The Ephemeral and the Eternal of Mexican Folk Art* (1971).

Chicano Period

The Chicano period of border art includes works by persons of Mexican heritage after 1848 who live permanently in the United States. Works of the later *santeros* in northern New Mexico should technically be included here, but historically and culturally they fit better into the Spanish colonial period and are discussed in that section.

The first major book about this area is by Quirarte (1973). It contains a concise overview of border history during the Spanish colonial period; a brief essay on art and architecture in the seventeenth, eighteenth, and nineteenth centuries; and a short piece on Mexican muralists in the United States. The major body of Quirarte's book is the second section, which gives detailed information on and illustrations of the work of many important twentieth-century Chicano artists. The major points in his discussion are that Chicano artists have been definitely influenced by their Mexican cultural heritage and their experiences as a minority in the United States. It is also clear that Chicano artists have been affected by the same events that have affected and revolutionized twentieth-century art in general. A more recent work by Barrio (1975) discusses Mexican art's influence on the Chicano artist and how the Chicano's cultural heritage has affected his art. Quirarte's book has one shortcoming: it does not adequately discuss the emergence of mural painting by young Chicano artists in the late 1960s and early 1970s. These paintings have appeared throughout the Southwest and in many northern cities. For an analysis of their uses and themes, see Holscher (1976) and Kahn (1975).

Anglo Art

Much of the emphasis in this chapter is on those artists who painted the evolving Southwest panorama as it changed from Mexican and Indian control to that of the United States. Many paintings depict the cowboy and the native American. Cawelti (1976), in his essay on the frontier and the native American, discusses four cultural images of the American West:

1. The West as a dangerous and empty wilderness to be conquered and civilized. Here the native American is basically an obstacle to be removed.
2. The West as an empty wilderness to be transformed into a model of Christian civilization (for example, the image of the Mormons).
3. The West as a place of escape from artificial and corrupting social boundaries. George Catlin's paintings are a good example, symbolizing the native American as an heroic natural man doomed to extinction by the onrush of civilization (Ewers, 1973).

4. The West as a place of sudden wealth and power (for example, the El Dorado legends and many stories of lost mines).

The two most famous western artists are Charles M. Russell and Frederic Remington. Both have been written about extensively, and both painted throughout the West, although Remington especially painted in the Southwest. Remington was a pictorial historian: in his works are explorers, pioneers, soldiers, Apaches, cowboys, *vaqueros,* miners, ranchmen, and a depiction of the change from buffalo to cattle (Hassrick, 1973; McCracken, 1966). Russell painted mostly in Montana, but his works include paintings of Plains Indians, frontiersmen, and animals that relate to the Southwest (Renner, 1968; McCracken, 1966).

A good introduction to nineteenth-century Texas artists is Pinckney (1967). Besides Remington and Russell, there are numerous other western artists of importance. Among them are Edward Borein (Davidson, 1974), George Phippen (Phippen, 1969), Buck Schiwetz (Lindsey, 1972; Schiwetz, 1960), Theodore Gentilz (Kendall, 1974), Louis Akin (Babbitt, 1973), and Peter Hurd (Horgan, 1965).

Two books including works by many of the above-mentioned artists, and a good many others including Albert Bierstadt, are by Ewers (1973) and Howard (1976). The first book stresses the role of the frontier artist as explorer and historian as well as painter. The latter is a history of the Cowboy Artists of America, an organization of western artists.

In contrast to these artists and paintings is the establishment of art colonies in Taos and Santa Fe in the late 1800s. Coke (1963) describes the major figures and their paintings in the years 1882 to 1942, stressing that New Mexico was the most flourishing arts center in the "far West."

For Taos and Santa Fe artists, native American culture determined much of their work, although Spanish American and Anglo life was not neglected. A recent book on Santa Fe artists is by Robertson and Nestor (1976). Garman (1976) provides a good introduction to the art of Raymond Jonson, whose works have gained much recognition in New Mexico over the past forty years.

Summary

This chapter on border art has attempted to give an overview of this region's art types and some idea of the relationship between art and the peoples inhabiting the area. Sources are, for the most part, readily available and in English. Many of the books on the Spanish colonial and Mexican periods have excellent bibliographies, which include books and articles only available in Spanish. By purposely avoiding sources in Spanish, I have neglected the art of the native peoples of northern Mexico, especially the Yaquis, Seris, and Tarahumaras. One must remember that there was no such thing as a border until 1848. Because of subsequent political influences, border economic and cultural changes take on meaning after that time. In the middle part of the nineteenth century, massive Anglo intrusion into the Southwest began to affect both Spanish colonial and native American art. Given the cultural differences between the United States and Mexico, it is safe to assume that the border will continue to play a major role in defining a boundary for art and for artists.

52

Languages and Dialects

J. HALVOR CLEGG
Department of Spanish and Portuguese
Brigham Young University

The Spanish spoken along the U.S.-Mexican border is a subdialect of Castilian Spanish. A genealogy of this subdialect would show that the original source, Castilian, was carried into southern Spain during the reconquest of the peninsula from the Moors, later becoming known as Andaluz. In turn, Andaluz was carried into America, since early colonists were largely represented by southern Spaniards who spoke the southern Castilian subdialect. Those colonists provided a framework for the Spanish spoken in America and specifically in Mexico.

The early history of northern Mexico and the border region is one of limited occupation. Colonial expansion into the area was initiated by priests establishing missions to convert the Indians. Relatively few areas were conducive to permanent settlements of civilian colonists. Presidios were established throughout the region to protect settlements against nomadic attacks.

At the time of the 1848 Treaty of Guadalupe Hidalgo, the total number of Spanish speakers in the United States probably did not exceed fifty thousand. The only area where speakers of pre-1848 Spanish have remained in any number

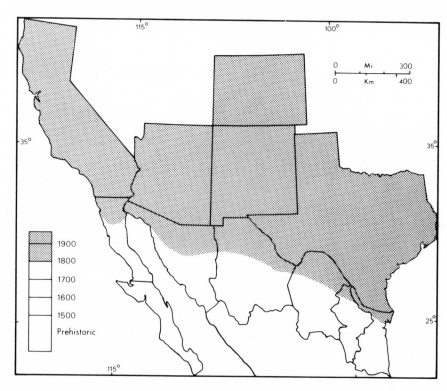

is northern New Mexico and southern Colorado. These people call themselves "Hispanos." The Hispano dialect reflects the area's early isolation from the evolution of mainstream Mexican Spanish in its archaisms and phonetic distinctions as well as some vocabulary differences.

In reality there is only one other major dialect along the border—one that might be called the "new wave" dialect. The "new wave" is defined as those settlers who came to the United States during the twentieth century or the children of those settlers. Statistics show that the large majority of these people came between 1910 and 1930. McWilliams (1949*a*) pointed out that 10 percent of the Mexican nation migrated to the United States by 1930, with the number of migrants exceeding 700,000. Considering how few Tejanos and Californios were already present, it is not surprising that the new wave immediately overwhelmed the earlier Hispanos in all areas except northern New Mexico and southern Colorado.

There are many writers who make subtle divisions within the new wave dialect; however, these distinctions can readily be disputed on several different bases. Some recognize dialects within the respective states. This division is obviously too facile, but some subtle differences do exist: people from South Texas can recognize the subtle differences between themselves and people from the El Paso, Texas, area and the differences between them and Californians. However, these differences are largely lexical. Additionally, there is a dialectical mix in northern Mexico because of the migration from different areas in southern Mexico, and again a mix within the United States as well. There is also much mobility among Mexican Americans within the United States itself. The result is the creation of the new wave dialect.

The speakers of the new wave dialect are generally uneducated in Spanish or marginally educated in English, in contrast to Hispanos, who are educated largely in English with some Spanish. The new wave has a long tradition of no education, since they generally descend from the *peones.* Although their ancestors were freed from peonage in the Mexican War of Independence, they still were uneducated; those in Mexico received a limited education. Mexican education was not successful until after World War II. Consequently, the Spanish of the new wave is a spoken language like that of Spanish American and Spain; many of the forms which are considered typically "Chicano Spanish" are simply forms spoken in Madrid, Buenos Aires, and Mexico City. The distinction between spoken and written Spanish is an important sociolinguistic distinction.

A third important dialect area is on the Mexican side of the border. A national study of Mexican dialects is being carried out by Juan Manuel Lope Blanch and a team of co-workers. This study surveyed about three hundred Mexican cities; the results are being compiled. Professor Lope Blanch indicates there are some sixteen dialect regions in Mexico. His divisions have not been published; when they are, they will be of acute interest to students of the border Spanish language. It is anticipated that there will be at least three northern divisions, but the distinctions will be quite subtle.

Study of Linguistics

The study of the Spanish language of the border should be considered relative to the history of linguistics. There have been several bibliographies printed, especially recently, concerning border Spanish. For practical purposes the two most efficient bibliographies are *The Spanish and English of U.S. Hispanos: A Critical, Annotated, Linguistic Bibliography* by Teschner, Bills, and Craddock (1975) and a supplement to that bibliography, by the same authors, which appeared in *Hispania* (May, 1977: 347-58).

Linguistics study along the border can be divided into five approaches: the traditional, the structural, the generative, the educational, and the sociolinguistic.

Traditional Studies. These types of studies are characterized by phonologies, dictionaries, lexicons, and so forth, appearing from the late-nineteenth through twentieth centuries. Traditional studies are still being done. The work by Espinosa (1946) on New Mexico is probably the best example of phonology done in the entire area. An example of California phonology is a descriptive analysis of Los Angeles Spanish by Phillips (1967). In Arizona, Anita Post (1934) did her work on the Arizona Spanish. In Texas there have been works by Lozano (1961), Clegg (1969), and Poulter (1973).

Several lexical items were done in New Mexico. The first and most famous was done by Kercheville and McSpadden (1934), but others have been added, such as that of Aranda (1975). A recent and extremely useful dictionary is *El diccionario del español Chicano* by Galván and Teschner (1975). In that dictionary they have summarized the works of several other writers from each region as well as the *Barrio Language Dictionary* by López and Fuentes (1975) and the *Dictionary of Pachuco Terms* by Rodolfo Serrano (1976).

The best lexicon on California Spanish is Blanco, *La lengua española en la historia de California* (1971), or Phillips's dissertation (1967). Two works on Texas Spanish are the *Diccionario del español de Tejas* by Galván and Teschner (1975) and the earlier work by Cerda et al. (1943*a*, 1943*b*, 1957). The best work on Arizona is by Trejo (1951).

Structural Studies. This category is quite limited, largely due to the focus of structural linguists. By choice they prefer not to deal in lexically limited semantics. An example of a structural work is that of Bowen (1952) on the Spanish of San Antonito, New Mexico. Other examples are morphological works like that of Sawyer (1964) in San Antonio. More recent morphological studies are typified by that of Bowen and Ornstein (1976) in "Studies in Southwest Spanish" on the structural analysis of the Spanish New Mexican verb system.

Generative Studies. Works of this type will predictably be few because of the highly theoretical nature of generative theory. Some studies have been done, though, such as work by Hensey (1976) and by Harris (1974). These studies are of marginal use for the Borderlands scholar. A dissertation by Rosaura Sanchez (1972) is probably the most valuable work on the generative plane. The structural works were done through the 1950s, '60s, and '70s; the generative works, of course, in the 1960s.

Education Studies. The most fruitful area of language study has been explored by people in education. Their studies can be divided into six basic categories: (1) standard versus nonstandard Spanish, (2) bilingualism, (3) the relationship of Spanish to English, (4) code switching, (5) tests and testing, and (6) materials developed.

Standard versus Nonstandard Spanish. The concern with standard versus nonstandard Spanish goes back to the question of written Castilian or written Mexican Spanish from the grammars versus spoken Hispano Spanish and the new wave speech. This particular bias, when viewed from a general perspective—that of written versus spoken language generally—relegates many studies to a secondary position, since spoken Spanish is very similar throughout the Spanish world. Nevertheless, some examples of differentiation between standard and nonstandard Spanish can be found in textbooks such as that by Pauline Baker (1966), probably the first to seriously attempt to write a book for border Spanish speakers—*Español para los Hispanos.* By its title, one can see that it is from New Mexico. In her textbook, Baker indicates Hispano Spanish errors and the proper form from the written tradition. Her disciple and follower Marie Esman Barker wrote *Español para el bilingüe* somewhat later (1970). Though her work was a little broader, she based it on Baker's, including some structuralist orientation that has drills with Baker's same basic forbidden forms. Even at this date there are several works on standard versus nonstandard Spanish in the lexical area: that is, a dissertation by Webb (1974), a programmed book by de León (1976), and a short article by González-Mena de LoCoco (1974).

Bilingualism. This very fruitful category of study was brought about, particularly in the last two decades, by the U.S. government's push for bilingual education. For theoretical reflections on bilingualism, see D. N. Cárdenas (1975) or Cohen (1974). A second thrust has been King's (1976) concern with bilingualism, language, and academic achievement. Another particular concern of bilingual education has been language acquisition, the subject of a study by Padilla (1976). These studies have become more and more complex, as evidenced by the dissertations of Collado-Herrell (1977) and Hocker (1973). Still another concern is that of language dominance, reflected by Zirkel (1977). A more scholarly work is that of Yolanda Solé (1977).

The Relationship of Spanish to English. This linguistic category focuses on the relationship of border Spanish to English dialects. Its studies also can be divided into several subcategories. First are the works which are done on a purely linguistic basis, such as those of Ramírez (1974) and Riegelhaupt-Barkin (1976). A second subcategory of concern has been the evaluative reactions of different speakers to varying dialects. Examples of these are Carranza (1975) and Fretz (1974). A related focus is a study done by MacIntosh and Ornstein (1974). English itself is in the process of being studied, as illustrated by Dubois's (1975) study.

Code Switching. A fourth category generated by bilingual eduation is code switching. There are several definitions of code. One of the more important is social code, the code meaning the language used by each individual's group—i.e. with father, with child, with mother, with gang, etc. A second definition of code is language per se, meaning Spanish, English, or any other. In our writings, code has been defined as language, meaning language switches. Articles have been written on code switching by Sánchez (1976) and by Valdés-Fallis (1973).

Tests and Testing. This important educational category is a subject of interest because of the many difficulties suffered by young Chicanos on poorly designed tests. Examples of works that have been done are tests by Burt et al. (1976) and James (1977) and a dissertation by Randle (1975).

Bilingual Materials. The sixth important bilingual subcategory is the development of materials. A brief history shows that the first materials were in literary Spanish and impossible for the children to use, since they had difficulty with the lexicon. The second materials were from areas like Puerto Rico and were, for Chicanos, again a source of lexical problems. The third set of materials was developed from Mexican literary materials, but it created another gap because of its variation from the spoken Spanish. Finally, materials had to be developed in the spoken Spanish of the border. As a result, resource centers were set up in Texas, first in Austin and then in San Antonio; in Las Cruces, New Mexico; and in San Diego, California. Since that time, many other smaller centers have begun to develop bilingual information.

Sociolinguistic Studies. The last and probably most important area to Borderlands scholars is sociolinguistics. Early works are almost nonexistent. An exception is the interesting work on *pachucos* by Barker (1947), and another is by Coltharp (1965). Later works are characterized by a highly fragmented approach; various authors have given different definitions of just what the study of sociolinguistics is. There have been few studies by highly trained sociolinguists. In the studies that have been done on border Spanish, we have some theoretical treatises suggesting what might be done. Untrained people have used the term; we have people who have used theories based on the work of great sociolinguists such as Fishman and LaBov. The Fishman trend seems to be more predominant in border studies. As for theoretical treatises, Jacob Ornstein is one of the more important writers. He published articles from 1971 to 1976 on different theoretical aspects of sociolinguistics, and a book, *Recent Developments in U.S. Sociolinguistics* (1975). In addition to Ornstein, Hensey wrote articles in 1974 and 1975. Other important sociolinguistic writers have been the Solés (Carlos and Yolanda) in 1975 and 1976.

The majority of writers have been in the Fishman, or macrolinguistic (broad), mold. Some early examples are one of Ornstein's early works, done together with colleagues, called the "Sociolinguistic Background Questionnaire Measurement Instrument for the Study of Bilingualism" from the University of Texas, El Paso, Cross-Cultural Southwest Ethnic Study Center (1975). Other examples of the Fishman type of approach are found in an article by one of the important people in early sociolinguistic considerations, Chester Christian—"Sociolinguistics Criteria for Choice of Spanish Lexicon in Training Teachers of Mexican-Americans in Texas" (1976). Another is a dissertation by Olivares, "Ways of Speaking in a Chicano Community: A Sociolinguistic Approach" (1977). Also available are Lawton on "Chicano Spanish: Some Sociolinguistic Considerations" (1975) and several articles done by Ornstein, such as "A Sociolinguistic Study of Mexican-American and Anglo Students in a Border University" (1975).

There are many areas of study in which people could use the LaBovian, or microlinguistic (narrow), approach, meaning the analysis of the many social variables that affect language. These variables are so numerous that no complete list has yet been created. It would be easy to list at least a dozen major social factors in speech, including such things as sex, age, origin, social level, and education. An early sociolinguistic example is William P. Kuvlesky's work based on interviews with teenagers, "The Use of Spanish and Aspirations for Social Mobility Among Chicanos: A Synthesis and Evaluation of Texas and Colorado Findings" (1973), presented to the Rocky Mountain Social Sciences Association in Laramie, Wyoming. Other examples include the works of McDowell and Luhman (1977) and Yolanda Solé (1977). Another narrow sociolinguistic study is the work by Ortiz (1975). Also, an important example is the study by Patella and Kuvlesky (1975); another related study is that of Sierra Cantú (1975).

Some work has been done on language learning among Spanish-speaking children. An example is a dissertation by McKay and Rodriguez Brown (1975). There is also an article by Yolanda Lastra de Suárez (1977), and another very interesting article by Gustavo González (1977).

This brief overview reflects general trends of research on border language. For in-depth materials, the bibliographies may be consulted.

53

Religion and Church

ELLWYN R. STODDARD
*Department of Sociology and
Anthropology
University of Texas, El Paso*

JULIAN C. BRIDGES
*Department of Sociology and
Social Work
Hardin-Simmons University*

If religion is that "unified system of beliefs and practices relative to sacred things," as Durkheim holds it to be, it ranks as a major social force in every region of the world, including the Borderlands (Durkheim, 1915: 47; Smith and Zopf, 1970: 346). Although a large proportion of the population of a given region may not formally identify with a given church or denomination, an understanding of existing religious systems may yield understanding of the values and culture under investigation, inasmuch as ingrained religious traditions, even those not expressed by church rituals, have great impact on human behavior.

Steck (1943) has compiled a bibliography of older works dealing with church and religion in the Borderlands. Cumberland's volume (1960a), usually a strong resource for border-related topics, gives the subject of religion a mere one-half page. A reader by Jones provides not only topical information but also a reading list for church topics. A very recent archival resource to the Catholic Church repositories in Mexico (Mounce, 1979) is indeed a scholar's friend and might be supplemented by perusing archival and documented or periodical resources

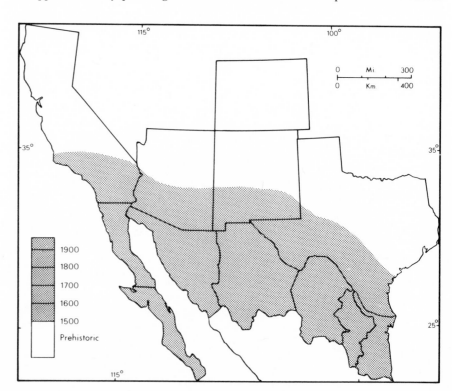

272

covered by Cardoso's "Mexican Resources," chapter 59 of this sourcebook.

On the U.S. side, Grebler's (1970) two chapters of current Mexican American practices in Los Angeles and San Antonio, with some history and a survey of the literature, are perhaps the most readily available general resources, but care must be taken not to generalize their findings toward nonurban Mexican Americans or other Catholic ethnic groups in the Southwest. Hough's (1972) survey of unpublished literature covers Catholicism among Hispanos and Mexican Americans, Protestantism, religious work among various Indian groups, and Mormonism; it is an unpolished jewel for interested scholars trying to pull together available literature extant a decade ago and earlier, as is the short synthesis by Stoddard (1973*a*: chap. 4).

A background in the New World's conquest by Spain and other European countries which brought their social institutions and religious and racial dogmas is needed for a scholar to interpret contemporary Borderlands religious conditions. Among the better historical volumes focusing heavily upon the role of the church are those of Bannon (1970), Gibson (1966), and Cumberland (1968), which emphasize the institutional impact of conquest and colonialism. Older volumes, such as that of Haring (1952), are somewhat more romanticized. Prescott's (1936) volume, considered by many as a classical reference, is a highly speculative extrapolation of early Spanish diaries reflecting a conquest ideology rather than a well-documented reference for scholarly research.

More accurately, the New World conquerors' transference of European institutions and motives can be found in the enlightening discussion of premodern Spanish institutions (Glick, 1975) and the "Society of Castes" transferred and maintained in America (Mörner, 1967). The comparison of the "White Legend" cultural and religious enlightenment brought by the Europeans to New World native inhabitants with the "Black Legend" view of arrogant, insensitive opportunists creating mayhem, raping, and pillaging must be raised, although few scholars can resolve this polar disparity as purely one or the other (Las Casas, 1542; Ives, 1939; Collier, 1947; Wagner and Parish, 1967; Keen, 1969; Hanke, 1971; Vigil, 1976). In this, as in other historical dilemmas dealing with New World exploitation, the meticulous record-keeping tradition of early Church padres in the Americas must be balanced with the ideological declarations of European church ecclesia. Such pronouncements as papal bulls, laws made by the Council of the Indies and other similar contemplating bodies, and writings of elites from the peninsula should not be equated with actual behavior toward native American peoples working in the fields and mines in the Western Hemisphere, so far from surveillance and control.

The initial exploration and subsequent development of the continent were greatly affected by individual friars, including Fray Marcos de Niza, whose account of the "Seven Cities of Cibola" (Arteaga y S., 1932) legitimized the Spanish expenditures for colonization of the interior provinces to the north. Also, the ventures of Rodríguez, López, and Espejo (Mecham, 1926*a*, 1926*b*) and Father Escalante's exploration of the Great Basin (Auerbach, 1943) accelerated the development of the

southwestern United States. The cultural impact of individual priests is also noteworthy: the work of Father Kino among the Pimas and Pápagos in Arizona and Baja California (Bolton, 1932, 1936; Burrus, 1962; Faulk, 1968), Father Neumann, the Jesuit priest, among the Tarahumaras (Christelow, 1939; Neumann, 1969), the perspective of Fray Junípero Serra in California (Tibesar, 1955; Geiger, 1963), Fray Sedelmeyr among the Arizona Maricopas and Yumas (Ives, 1939), and the legendary Mother Marie de Agreda—"the beautiful Woman in Blue"—who worked among the Jumanos and East Texas Jémezes (Bolton, 1912) all reflect the stereotype of "padres on horseback" which was, in reality, quite different from the role of the Church generally in the years of conquest and colonization in America.

Bolton (1917), Auerback (1934), and others give a succinct overview of early religious institutions in the New World. The political implications of the Catholic *Patronato Real* tie to New World claims and legitimization, the 1571 Mexican Inquisition, the role of the Church in native rebellions (Poole, 1965), and the secular struggle to counter the growing influence of the Jesuits and to expel them from the Americas in 1767 (Mörner, 1965) are but a few of the highlights of the Catholic Church's role in the development of the American hemisphere—north and south.

The Church's struggle to maintain and expand its influence in the New World can only be understood in combination with Spain's priority in seeking mineral wealth and her military capability of protecting this wealth and claims to wealth-producing areas. Providing protection for gold and silver from mine to distant disembarcation points to the Spanish Peninsula (Powell, 1952) reduced the number of soldiers available for established presidios. Spanish missions, established jointly with the presidios, usually had two to four priests who were financed from the War Fund. The continuity of a mission related directly to being able to show some labor or potential returns equivalent to those of a similar expenditure on the military force. Presidios normally had from twenty to sixty ill-equipped, poorly trained soldiers who were ill-suited for acquiring additional territory or fighting major campaigns (Moorhead, 1975) but whose presence "discouraged" Christianized Indians at the mission from departing and also legitimized the Spanish claim to the nearby territory. A paired church-presidio perimeter extended from Florida to California: San Augustín, Appalache, and Pensacola in Florida; Los Adaes in Louisiana; San Antonio, La Bahía, and San Juan Bautista in East Texas; San Elizario and others in the upper and lower Rio Grande Valley in West Texas and New Mexico; Janos, Fronteras, Tubac, and Altar across the arid lands to the Pacific; and the coastal pairs in San Diego, Santa Barbara, Monterrey, and San Francisco (Bolton, 1917: 53). Specific problems of the frontier missions, such as supplying them in far-flung areas as northern New Mexico (Scholes, 1930) or the combination of indigenous beliefs and shamans with Catholicism and padres (Vought, 1967), are only a few of those addressed by scholars.

Initially, missions were designed as a temporary institution to convert an indigenous group of people to a manageable community within a ten-year period. This process—known as *reducción*—was rather successful among the more sedentary tribes of Central Mexico but was more of a failure among the nomadic peoples of the northern interior provinces of Texas, southern New Mexico, and Arizona. Still, Bolton (1917) and others correctly argue that it was the most suitable institution available to Spain for the colonization and control of the wild frontier region. Many accounts describe the establishment and life within missions located in various Borderlands regions: in California (Englehardt, 1908-15; Bolton, 1919; Webb, 1952; Tibesar, 1955; Simpson, 1962; Geiger, 1965, 1971; Hutchinson, 1965; Starnes, 1969; Borah, 1970; Garr, 1972); in Sonora-Arizona (Englehardt, 1899; Geiger, 1939; Bannon, 1955; Pontones Chi., 1958; Hastings, 1961; Polzer, 1972); and in Texas (Francisco López, 1785; Persons, 1953; Habig, 1968a, 1968b; Weddle, 1964, 1968a, 1968b; Boren, 1968; Leutenegger and Habig, 1974).

The regions where the various religious orders were dominant varies according to time and events. Generally, Dominicans were with the early Spanish strongholds in the Antilles and later in Lower California. The Jesuits, who learned the native language and customs instead of demanding indigenous peoples to acculturate, were found in Florida; in the Southwest among the Yaquis or Sonoras; among the Seris, Tarahumaras (Dunne, 1948) and other cultures in Mexico's states of Sonora, Sinaloa, and Chihuahua; and also in Baja California (Decorme, 1941). They also founded missions in southern Arizona among the Pimas and Pápagos (Donahue, 1960) and were as far north and east as New Mexico before their expulsion in 1767 (Dunne, 1944). The Franciscans, in Central Mexico initially, extended further northward into New Mexico, East Texas, Louisiana, West Texas, and Arizona (Kelly, 1941; Kessell, 1964; Polzer, 1972). Known for their work among the Pueblos and Zuñis, they are more remembered in popular literature for their string of southern California missions beginning with San Diego—the building of which they began when the expelled Jesuits had relinquished their control of that general region. Other smaller orders, such as the Oblate Fathers from France, who came to Texas in 1847, the Spanish Claretin Fathers from Spain, representatives from the Immaculate Heart Mission, the Vicentian Fathers, the Piarists, and others made less noticeable impacts on southwestern history, but they did make many local contributions in establishing missions, schools, and similar services (Grebler et al., 1970: 451).

Except for a few rare instances, the Church was aligned with elite or conservative institutions in the homeland as well as in the New World. Occasionally an awkward situation emerged, as when a liberal Spanish Crown moved to liberalize a conservative colonial regime or when a recently liberated Republic of Mexico moved rapidly to secularize missions in southern California which had been loyal to the Spanish Crown. The separation of church and state begun by President Benito Juárez, as reflected in the 1856 Lerdo Laws, transferred vast church-held lands to governmental control, thus isolating the Catholic Church in Mexico from its formal power base (Mecham, 1929; Schmidt, 1954). Revolts of the clergy against the government sanctions and restrictions that suppressed the continuous and unlimited immigration of "foreign priests" during the first quarter of the twentieth century further dismantled the organized influence of the Church throughout Mexico. Mexicans who were to emigrate to the United States would retain their dedication to "religiosity," but most would retain only a nominal identity with the Catholic Church. This erosion of influence and insensitivity to the changing needs of the populace alienated the Church from its followers (Lamar, 1966; Vallier, 1970; Grebler et al., 1970: 667-68). As Cumberland (1968: 179) so graphically expressed it: "The Church had made the average Mexican merely a surface practitioner of a religious rote, deeply imbued with a form of religiosity but not necessarily loyal to the Church."

Against this background can be seen the religious legacy carried to the United States by the waves of Mexican immigrants during the first quarter of the twentieth century. This legacy is in direct contradiction with the many stereotypes heaped constantly upon the Mexican American minority by writers in professional and popular literature during the post-World War II era. Protests against such facile stereotyping are summarized by Stoddard (1973a: 84-96).

Contemporary Catholicism in the Southwest

Catholics, like all other religious groups, vary in dedication, identification, integration, and socialization. A typology by Spitzer (1960) clarifies four basic Catholic patterns. First are the dedicated formal Catholics, monastic replacements who support parochial schools and church budgets. Second are the nominal Catholics who carry the tradition and name but who are not heavily influenced by ceremonial contact (Clark, 1959; Foy, 1962; Ulibarrí, 1966; Wagner, 1966). Women and children who attend church without older males perhaps represent more than 80 percent of Church members, with home and neighborhood being more important socializing agents than the Church or Church schools (Fishman, 1961). Third are cultural or social Catholics whose allegiance is to church social activities or membership acceptance rather than credos or deeply held religious dogmas. Fourth are folk Catholics, remnants of whom are reported by Madsen (1964) and Loomis and Samora (1965) in rural or traditional areas like Texas's Lower Valley.

Southwestern Catholicism has always suffered from the lack of financial support characteristic of the poverty endemic to that region—few clergy, serious economic problems, and visible needs. Since their beginning in 1847, parochial schools in the Rio Grande Valley have been manned by foreign religious orders; Borderlands' clergy-member ratios have always been high compared to those of eastern locations (Moore, 1970a: 86-87; Grebler et al., 1970: 473-77) and are becoming, as is all American Catholicism, less and less distinct from American Protestantism (McCready and Greeley, 1972).

Available research materials point out wide discrepancies among orthodox Catholic expectations and beliefs (that is, concerning church attendance, use of clerics for marriage and baptisms, attitudes and behavior toward birth control, and so on; Grebler et al., 1970) and similar discrepancies among ordained priests (Greeley and Schoenherr, 1971; Greeley, 1972*a*) characterized by Moore (1972) as a breakup of a theological system over the issue of birth control. During recent decades, liberalizing of the lower clerical echelon, as well as the departure of large numbers from monastic orders to pursue secular social action or their isolation within the Church for their activist stance (McNamara, 1968, 1969) as they demanded more and more from the Catholic Church to support the goals of the Chicano movement (Barragán, 1969), has been viewed with alarm. According to some observers, the militant Chicano movement was a substitute for the estranged ecclesiastical structure and the rigid posture of the Church. However, just as there are activist or liberalized lower echelons of priests and padres, so there were sympathetic leaders like Bishop Donohoe of Fresno, who provided "priests at large" for Delano grape strikers (as did Archbishop Lucey of San Antonio, whose priests spearheaded early social action demonstrations). In 1969, a group called Priests Associated for Religion, Education, and Social Rights (PADRE) organized and made themselves felt in subsequent Church conventions (Barragán, 1969: 50, 54-57). Higher-level Mexican American church officials were conspicuously absent before 1970, when a few were named to these more visible posts. Also, the University of Notre Dame has become an institutionalized refuge for various types of Chicano studies and Church-related research on border conditions.

Although discrimination against Mexican Americans within today's Catholic Church is denied, it was present in the recent past (Grebler et al., 1970: 475-76). A study from Pomona, California, however, indicates that only two of every ten churchgoing Mexican American adults worship in predominantly Anglo congregations (Peñalosa, 1963: 147), with much lower expectation for Texas, where segregated housing and linguistic problems are more pronounced.

The relationship of Protestantism to former Catholic Mexican Americans, where factors other than ideational creeds are credited with religious "conversions," is discussed by various authors (Grebler et al., 1970: chap. 20; Stoddard, 1973*a*: 96-99). Some studies report that conversions to Protestant views result in upward mobility (Bronson, 1966); others maintain that such upward mobility is nil or explained by such factors as educational differences (Lazerwitz, 1961; Featherman, 1971; Greeley and Rossi, 1966; Glenn and Hyland, 1967). Remy (1969) shows that in areas of strong Catholic traditions (such as the lower Rio Grande Valley of Texas), Protestants are still predominantly Anglo. In other areas, such as the Rio Grande from El Paso to Big Bend Park, an active "river ministry" to the border hamlets has been sponsored by the Southern Baptist Convention since 1967. McCarty (1980) provides an interesting linkage between Protestantism in Texas and legal restraints against alcohol usage from the mid-1850s to the Depression years of the mid-1930s. Other Protestant influences are found inextricably combined with immigrants from the State-Church countries of Western Europe and are included under discussions of Ethnic Minorities.

Church and Religion in Contemporary Mexico

Unlike the United States, which does not request census information on religious behavior, Mexico does gather such information, as do 69 areas of the world (United Nations, 1964: 330-37). General information on denominations and some information on affiliation is available from the Mexican census (Dirección General Estadística, 1972, vol. XIX: 55-56); an intensive analysis of Catholic and Protestant (or Evangelical as they prefer to be called in Mexico) denominations and Judaism has been completed by Bridges (1973*a*: 116-38).

In Mexico, 96.2 percent declared themselves to be Catholic in 1970, whereas Evangelicals constituted only 1.8 percent of the population. Jews represented 0.1 percent; those of other religious groups, 0.3 percent; and 1.6 percent of the nation's inhabitants indicated that they had no religion at all. Roman Catholicism is strongest generally in the central and north-central regions of Mexico (Báez-Carmargo and Grubb, 1935: 109-17; Mecham, 1966: 393-94, 404-405). Evangelicals have their highest proportions (8.3 percent) in the southeastern state of Tabasco and border *municipios*. These urban concentrations give the Evangelicals a 2.4 percent average throughout the six border states next to the United States (Bridges, 1969). Jews and other non-Catholics historically have concentrated in major cities, and in 1960, 42 percent of the Evangelical adherents were living in only 2 percent of the country's *municipios* (Sorokin and Zimmerman, 1929: 108-109, 142; Bridges, 1973*b*: 40-44).

From 1900 to 1970 the absolute number of Roman Catholics increased almost 350 percent. During the same period the small Evangelical population increased 4.6 times as fast. Assuming the continuation of present trends and continuation of the high percentage of participation by the Evangelical churches' membership, the latter could become more influential (though probably not more numerous) than Catholics in selected *municipios* of southeastern Mexico and the U.S. border by the year 2000 (Bridges, 1973*b*: 45-63).

For information on population trends for various Evangelical denominations, see McGavaran et al. (1963: 22-55) and Read et al. (1969*a*: 165-74); for clergy-member ratio patterns, refer to Ramos et al. (1963: 61, 77) and Bridges (1972: 248-51). Growth projections for all of Latin America in 1980 show a total of 27 million Protestants (Read, 1969*b*: 6).

Numbers are not the only measure of religious influence. The statement by a high Catholic Church official (Excelsior, 1972) that less than 20 percent of Mexican Catholics in Mexico City are practicing members indicates a very high proportion of nominal Catholics. This low level of interest seems to be common throughout most Latin American countries and in Mexican border states as well (Rycroft, 1958: 34-35; Willems, 1967: 34-35; Bridges, 1969: 53-54). It should not, though, indicate that the Catholic Church in Mexico is currently an outdated bastion of monolithic conservatism, inasmuch as a haven for Latin American leftist authors and writers who advocate socialism and its more radical varieties as a desirable substitute for capitalism (Gheerbrant, 1970: 258-80). Thus, the outspoken Bishop of Cuernavaca felt relatively secure criticizing the Church for not supporting political and economic reform (Mendez Arceo, 1968: 239-47). His opening of his diocese as a refuge to such iconoclastic clerics as Ivan Illich shows today's diversity among Mexican Catholic leaders. Additionally, a small minority of more liberal denominations, constituting Mexico City's theological community, have been more vocal in recent years concerning the need for national and Third World social and economic change.

Although Evangelicals number slightly less than 2 percent of Mexico's population, their higher proportion of loyal adherents reflects a much greater influence than their small numbers indicate (Rycroft, 1959: 34; Solís Garza, 1971: 85). At the present time, however, Protestants in Mexico, though widely divergent in their political views, largely remain theologically conservative and politically apathetic, undoubtedly partially because of their position as a minority group.

Mormons

The Church of Jesus Christ of Latter-day Saints, often called Mormons, besides being one of the fastest-growing churches in Latin America and Mexico because of their overt proselyting, are historically integrated into the history of the Southwest and Borderlands. General summaries of their eastern U.S. origins, and their westward movement under Brigham Young in the mid-1800s, are available (Arrington and Bitton, 1979; O'Dea, 1975) as is discussion of their presence in the Great Basin as a barrier to indigenous and Spanish northward expansion (Meinig, 1965, 1970). Along with this region's native American cultures, Mormons were included by Harvard scholars to be studied in their monumental comparative research project on cultural values (O'Dea and Vogt, 1970; Hough, 1972: 60-67) and a later case study of pluralism existing in current Southwest society (Spicer and Thompson, 1972).

Various secular issues and events about Mormon colonization in the West include the attempt to establish their own State of Deseret (Anonymous, 1940; Clark, 1958; Hansen, 1963), which would have included Utah, Nevada, southern California, northern Arizona, and parts of other intermountain jurisdictions and the fight for continued congressional representation when the Church practiced polygyny (erroneously referred to as polygamy) before 1890 (Arrington and Bitton, 1979: chap. 10). Their village-centered pattern of land settlement has been studied in depth (Nelson, 1952). Of interest to borderlands historians is the march of the all-volunteer Mormon Battalion and its trail from Iowa through El Paso to San Diego during the 1846 War with Mexico (Gracy and Gugeley, 1965; Yurtinas, 1975; see Simmons, "New Mexico-Colorado History," chapter 8 of this sourcebook, also). The Mormon colonizing efforts in Chihuahua (Romney, 1938; Hardy, 1963, 1965, 1969; Frost, 1976) and in Sonora (Burns and Naylor, 1973) as well as their exodus

from Mexico in 1913 (Mills, 1954) are a vital link for early Anglo-Mexican relations. The Mormon opening of parts of Arizona to colonization (McClintock, 1921; Arrington, 1966; Peterson, 1973) and their unsuccessful attempts in Nevada (Bowen, 1976) show the early impact of their colonization efforts. The Mormon Trail is a contemporary western transportation route. Only recently has scholarly work appeared analyzing the earliest Mormon economic systems that led to survival in the barren Utah desert (Arrington, 1958) and the Mormons' unique "self-help" philosophy of today (Fisher, 1978).

The history of Mormon-native American contacts is somewhat different from the proselyting of other religious bodies among Indian tribal groups (Hamilton, 1948; Berkhofer, 1965). The Mormon theology declared Indian people to be a "remnant of Israel" whose history is contained within the Book of Mormon and whose future is a glorious one. Mormons actively sought to raise Indian peoples to their scriptural destiny through education and evangelization (Coates, 1969) while inadvertently leading to their economic destruction by diverting rivers and streams to irrigated farms and agriculture. Brigham Young's maxim, "It's cheaper to feed them than to fight them" (Morgan, 1948; James, 1967), was practiced in frontier days, but aid and technical assistance programs to Mormon and non-Mormon Indian groups throughout North America reflect current Church policy as a temporary Mormon responsibility to increase native Americans' self-reliance and self-sufficiency (James, 1968).

Mennonites

Located in northern Chihuahua not far from the Mormon colonies (and sometimes confused with them) are the Mennonite peoples, whose history of colonization in Mexico is available (Schmiedehaus, 1954; Sawatzky, 1971). Relatively isolated and not involved in most border problems of the past, some of them currently have emerged as a major test of racism with regard to immigration policies. A small Mennonite contingent emigrated to central Texas, thinking to relocate their colony, but through legal technicalities were refused permanent visas. Characterized as an industrious and frugal people, whose dedication to a sedentary life devoid of modern society's technological advancements and moral codes is indeed noteworthy, their fight against deportation back to Mexico has been taken up by such political powers as Senator Lloyd Bentsen of Texas, although for Mexicans seeking access to the north, this selectivity smacks of racism. Mennonites have Western European origins, while illegal Mexicans, stereotyped as social and economic liabilities to the United States, are refused entry regularly. This polemic will undoubtably fan the flame of "favoritism for white immigrants" in the eyes of Mexicans patiently awaiting legal entry to the United States.

Mennonites do not attempt to affect the larger society and are therefore less visible than some other religious minorities of the region. They are often studied by scholars who are concerned with ascetic microcosms which persist within a shrinking world of integrated cultures.

Exotic Religious Groups

Most Borderlands native American cultures are covered in chapters 54, 55, and 56 of this sourcebook, and ethnologies describing their religious practices are cited there. The two entities with more popular appeal are the Penitente cult of northern New Mexico and the southwestern peyote cults, and these deserve brief mention.

Some romanticized or superficial accounts of the Penitentes are far from accurate and should be used with extreme care (Lummis, 1925; Horka-Pollick, 1969; etc.). The Penitentes, a third order of Franciscans, believed to have been a flagelation sect, were brought to the New World during the Spanish Conquest and carried to northern New Mexico near the beginning of the seventeenth century. The sect's rituals are highly emotional and realistic, including the alleged crucifixion of one of their own number in annual Easter ceremonies (Henderson, 1937; Woodward, 1940; Burma, 1954: 188-98; 1963*b*; Chávez, 1954). Work by Weigle (1970; 1976), especially her more recent volume, provides far more documentation, background explanatory material, and accuracy than even some of the other original scholars quoted so often in the literature.

There are some rather scholarly and yet readable references on peyote cults (Aberle, 1966; Collins, 1967; LaBarre, 1969) which describe the use of the small peyote cactus crown or "button," extracted from plants indigenous to northern Mexico, in religious ceremonials and rituals in which hallucinations or dreams occur. When the use of peyote spread northward to the Plains Indians, cultures such as the Kiowas initially felt threatened inasmuch as their own dream-producing substance did not produce the fantasies in color. In recent decades, the fight has continued between these groups and various federal drug control agencies on grounds of First Amendment freedom of religious practices. The ethical and moral issues for the courts seem to be made more complex by the "loophole" which such religious use would allow for persons who use peyote and other hallucinogens for recreational purposes only. Meanwhile, the Native American Church and its traditional peyote ritual continues on.

54

Indian Cultures of Northern Mexico

N. ROSS CRUMRINE
Department of Anthropology
University of Victoria

Several indigenous cultural groups still exist in the far north of Mexico, south of the U.S.-Mexican border. Since these groups pattern in differing natural and cultural areas, regional materials are summarized. Jorge Vivó (1943) divides the area into five natural parts: Gulf Coast plain, high Central Plateau, western Sierra Madre, Gulf of Cortes and Sonoran coastal plain, and Baja California. Each of these parts represents an extension of North American natural areas: Gulf Coast lowlands, High Plains, Rocky Mountains, Colorado Plateau, and Sierra Nevada. Generally the climate is dry and hot, a steppe in the east and desert in the west, with scattered summer rainfall and slight winter rains. Northwestern Baja California, characterized by winter rains, proves an exception. Parts of Baja California, the western Sierra Madre, and a few scattered mountain areas of the high Central Plateau are more humid and support pine forests (see Map 5 in Kroeber, 1939). Other areas are characterized by scrub growth, especially mesquite, yucca, agave, and a range of differing cacti (see also West, 1964). For modern culture areas, Howard Cline (1972: 167) divides northern

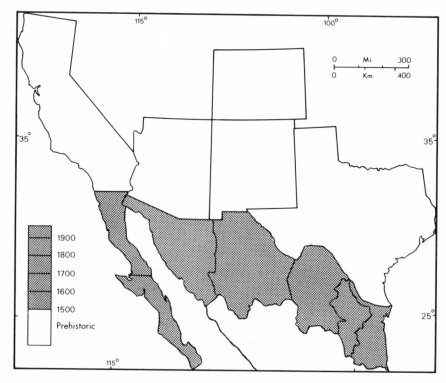

278

Mexico into northeastern, north central, and northwestern regions and Baja California, although it seems best to retain a division between the western Sierra Madre area and the Sonoran coastal plain. Moving from east to west, except for the Gulf Coast lowlands, indigenous groups may be listed: in the high Central Plateau, immigrant Kikapús (Kickapoos); in the western Sierra Madre, Guarijíos and Tarahumaras; in the Sonoran coastal plain, Cucapás (Cocopas), Pápagos, Pimas, Opatas, Seris, Yaquis, and Mayos; and in Baja California, Cumiais, Paipais, Cochimís, and Kiliwas (see map in Instituto Nacional Indigenista, 1977, no. 1).

Culturally, Kroeber (1939: Map 6) delineates areas similar to the natural ones mentioned above: Tamaulipas and the North Mexican Interior Plateau are included with the supra-area of Mexico and the northern Sierra Madre (Tarahumaras), central Sonora (Pimas, Pápagos, Opatas), Sonora coast (Seris), and lower Colorado River. Baja California he includes as part of the southwestern supra-area. Following Beals's study *The Comparative Ethnology of Northern Mexico before 1750* (1932a) and Mendizábal's "Influencia de la sal en la distribución geográfica de los grupos indígenas de México" (1930), Kroeber argues that the groups of Tamaulipas (Tamaulipecs, Olives, and Coahuiltecs) and the interior plateau (Zacatecs, Guachichils, Laguneros, Conchos, Pames, and Janambres) were chiefly hunters and collectors and have since disappeared, whereas the groups in the Sierra Madres and to the west (with the exception of the Seris) were farmers, still existing today although changed considerably. These intact western groups represent enclaved societies surrounded by modern Mexican technology and economics. Some group members still speak indigenous languages. They all belong to the Uto-Aztecan group, with the exception of the eastern Pames, Janambres, Olives, Tamaulipecs, and Coahuiltecs (most of which are probably extinct) and the western Seris, Cocopas, and Baja California groups from the Hokan language family (see Kroeber, 1934 and 1939: 124-25; Sauer, 1933; and Flores, 1967). Kroeber (1939: Table 18) lists the area's aboriginal population as slightly over two hundred thousand, with one hundred thousand in Tamaulipas and the Interior Plateau and slightly over one hundred thousand in northwestern Mexico, although Kroeber always tended to be low in his Mexican population estimates. Sauer's estimate (1935: 32-33) of "an aboriginal population between Gila and Río Grande de Santiago in excess of half a million" is considerably more than Kroeber's figure. Sauer does not include north central and northeastern Mexico but does encompass groups living north of the U.S.-Mexican border and south of the Mayos of southern Sonora and northern Sinaloa. Drawing from the 1950 census, Flores (1967) lists the numbers of Indian-language speakers: Baja California, 428 (9 monolinguals); Sonora, 25,058 (1,892 monolinguals); Sinaloa, 8,940 (954 monolinguals); Chihuahua, 22,448 (9,707 monolinguals); Coahuila, 500 (141 monolinguals); Nuevo León, 198 (6 monolinguals); and Tamaulipas, 696 (1 monolingual)—nearly 1,400 for the eastern groups and 57,000 for the western.

Concluding the general introduction, we shall note several important general sources on modern northern Mexican in-

digenous groups. For general bibliographical lists, Parra and Moreno (1954) *Bibliografía indigenista de México y Centroamerica (1850-1950)* and Bernal (1962) *Bibliografía de arqueología y etnografía, Mesoamérica y Norte de México, 1514-1960* are excellent and include indexes listing materials by state, tribe, and subject (although they are somewhat dated and not complete). The *Boletín bibliográfico de antropología americana* is also excellent and more up-to-date, but somewhat more time-consuming. The Braniff and Felger (1976) *Sonora: antropología del desierto,* with a long bibliography, is very inclusive, quite up-to-date, and of high quality but tends to be restricted to Sonora; also, articles in that volume summarizing the research and knowledge of the area should prove extremely useful for scholars and students. The Southwestern Mission Research Center's *Newsletter,* put together by Bernard Fontana and Charles Polzer (among others), also includes long lists of books and articles on southwestern anthropology as well as mission history. More synthesized, the *Handbook of Middle American Indians* (Wauchope, 1964, especially vol. VIII, *Ethnology,* Part 2), includes a number of short sketches on northwestern Mexican Indians, with extensive references. Other volumes of this series also provide useful information. The twenty-volume *Handbook of North American Indians,* edited by William Sturtevant, is being published by the Smithsonian Institution; its volume 10 (1982) includes articles on Indian groups of northwestern Mexico and is the most up-to-date reference on the area.

Most materials presented in the following sections are descriptive reports focusing upon individual groups. The major portion of the anthropological publications aims to describe and explain the existence of modern enclaved Indian groups, usually referring to a single group or, at the most, several groups. The finest exception to this rule is the comprehensive book *Cycles of Conquest,* by Edward Spicer (1962). In the first half of that work Spicer devotes chapters to the history and present conditions of each enclaved group in the Southwest and northwestern Mexico. The second half deals with processes of social and cultural change and the types of contact between the dominant society and the enclaved group which accompany specific processes of change. This book and Spicer's other work are the most imaginative and theoretical approach to northwestern Mexico's indigenous groups. Thus, his works are recommended to anyone interested in a general knowledge of the area's enclaved groups. The Instituto Nacional Indigenista (National Indian Institute) of Mexico has established several coordinating centers in northwestern Mexico at Témoris, Carichi, Guachochi, and Chihuahua, all in Chihuahua for the Tarahumaras; at El Fuerte in Sinaloa and Etchojoa in Sonora for the Mayos; at Vicam in Sonora for the Yaquis; at Bahía Kino in Sonora for the Seris; at Caborca in Sonora for the Pápagos; and at Mexicali in Baja California for the Cucapás-Kiliwas, Paipais, Cochimís, and Comiais (see map in Instituto Nacional Indigenista, 1977, no. 1). As action or applied anthropology organizations, they build schools, health clinics, and homes and bring medical and legal help to indigenous peoples. They publish little bulletins, *Acción Indigenista* and *México Indígena* (1977, no. 1). *Acción Indigenista* briefly reports on individual coordinating centers' activities and proves useful for information on local action programs. Since general materials are extremely limited, we now turn to source data on specific areas and enclaved groups.

East of the Tarahumaras, in western Chihuahua, the map of modern Indian groups in *México Indígena* (Instituto Nacional Indigenista, 1977, no. 1: 4) shows only the Kikapús (Kickapoos) located in northern Coahuila. Saldívar (1943: 49-52) provides a short account of the Tamaulipas Indians. In the northern part of the state he lists two major nomadic hunting and collecting groups, Chichimeca del Norte and La Sierra Madre. Newcomb (1961: 29-57) discusses these hunting-collecting groups, which he calls Coahuiltecans, at greater length since they overlapped onto the Texas southern coastal plain. They hunted deer, javelinas, rabbits, and other small game and collected wild roots, nuts, and berries. They were characterized by patrilineal family bands, with an occasional chief holding informal power over several bands. Bands cooperated in occasional communal hunts and religious ceremonies *(mitotes),* at which time dancing, feasting, and eating of peyote took place. Numerous shamans existed, spoke at *mitotes,* and used their powers. Like the Seri region of western Sonora, the Coahuiltecan area was extremely marginal and a difficult one in which to make a living. By the end of the nineteenth century, because of disease, absorption into the Mexican population, and Apache and Comanche raiding, the Coahuiltecan population had disappeared. Saldívar (1943: 49-52) mentions two additional groups of early Tamaulipas, although neither exists today. A group in the eastern Tamaulipas Mountains, called the Sierra Tamaulipa Oriental, was made up of farmers and was more complex than the Coahuiltecans. A sedentary group, they grew corn, beans, squash, and chile, living in settlements with a circular plaza and producing pottery and stone containers. Their homes of wood and mud, roofed with palm or straw, faced the plaza. The Huaxteco group was located in the south of Tamaulipas. Even more complex, it was characterized by centralized government, a wider crop range, priestly and governing classes, larger villages, and greater craft specialization. In an early article, McGee (1897: 114-19) describes rope making in a Guachichil group of Nahuatlan living in the southern corner of Tamaulipas and Nuevo León. They were farmers and stock raisers, harvesting agave fiber which they exchanged at the *hacienda* store for corn and cloth. I am unaware of additional information on this group.

Moving into the far north of Mexico, the states of Nuevo León, Coahuila, and central and eastern Chihuahua, only one modern group is encountered—the Kickapoos, who are not indigenous to the area but who migrated into Coahuila in the 1850s. Besides Kickapoo materials, numerous scattered references on the area's ethnohistory exist, such as the early article by Kane (1876) on Coahuilan geography and ethnology and the more recent survey articles by Jiménez Moreno (1943, 1960). Beals (1973), Mendizábal (1930), and Newcomb (1961) include materials on this area, although Newcomb concentrates upon the Texas horse nomads and Jumano farmers. This region was an area of hunting and collecting peoples who submitted to the Spanish and later were raided and killed by nomadic Apaches. There are numerous items on the Apaches and raiding Indians in Mexico, such as those by Vizcaya Canales (1968), Valdez Terrazas (1950), and the book by Terrazas Sánchez, *La guerra apache en México* (1974). In a carefully researched article, Forbes (1959) describes the appearance and spread of the horse and the mounted Indian in northern Mexico during the second half of the sixteenth and the seventeenth centuries. Numerous other ethnohistorical sources concerning nomads and Apaches in northern Mexico exist, such as Almada (1950), Cordero y Bustamante (1944), Cessac (1882), Dupoyet (1910), Lambberg (1949), Pérez (1942), and Ramírez (1903). Jiménez Moreno (1943) has constructed an elaborate map of the area's indigenous groups and the mission settlements.

Kirchhoff (1943) describes the culture and society of these nomadic hunting-collecting groups. He suggests numerous parallels to the Baja California collecting groups. Cactus fruits (tunas), agave and palm hearts, and numerous roots were collected and cooked in underground ovens. They gathered honey and made cactus fruit wine and bread from mesquite flour. They also cooked peyote in water as a drink. Rabbits, jack rabbits, and deer were the main game animals, although they also relied upon rats, gophers, and birds and, in certain regions, fish. In the north the bands were small, although marriages were known within or outside the band. There were band chiefs and sacred all-night bonfire dances. Beyond the band groups, which spoke similar dialects, constant warlike relations existed, especially for revenge. Newcomb (1961: 225-45) has written a chapter on the farming Jumanos living along the Conchos River in northeastern Chihuahua and the Rio Grande by El Paso. Galaviz de Capdevielle (1961) discusses Indian rebellions in the north of New Spain during the fifteenth and sixteenth centuries. Huerta Preciado (1966) describes Indian rebellions in colonial northeastern Mexico. Probably the best source on groups of this area is the reconstructed ethnography of these indigenous peoples by Griffen (1969), *Culture Change and Shifting Population in Central Northern Mexico.* Griffen fully describes the history of Spanish-Indian contact up to the extinction of the indigenous peoples and the arrival of the Apaches, also including a long section on material culture, subsistence, social organization, religious and ceremonial life, shamanism, and so on. Turning to immigrant indigenous peoples, Porter has written full articles, "The Seminole in Mexico, 1850-1861" (1951) and "The Seminole-Negro Indian Scouts, 1870-1881" (1952). The major body of data, though, refers to the modern Kickapoos, who represent the only intact indigenous group living in the area today.

In contrast to the scanty information noted above, the Kickapoos have received considerable attention in the popular press as well as in academic publications. In the first half of the nineteenth century, part of the Kickapoos migrated from the United States to northern Mexico. As a reward for aiding in government combat against the Lipan, Apache, and Comanche tribes (who were raiding in northern Mexico), in 1849 the Kickapoos received a land grant in Coahuila. Their present village, El Nacimiento Rancheria, consists of some 85 families, a total of 432 individuals

(Anonymous, 1977a: 50), and is located 25 miles northwest of Múzquiz, Coahuila. Even today they are quite binational and enjoy dual citizenship, traveling to the United States for both college education and wage labor (April until November). Mainly, the Kickapoos hunt deer, bears, pumas, wild boars, squirrels, and other game. In 1923 their area was set aside as a hunting region, with special permission for the Kickapoos to hunt with guns, traps, and so on. Recently their guns have been confiscated. In April, 1977, a group of Kickapoos visited Mexican President José López Portillo to discuss this matter (Anonymous, 1977a: 50-52).

The Kickapoos also do some farming and raise fruit trees, such as *aguacates,* peaches, and oranges. The women own the houses and furnishings, and the men the guns, horses, and farm implements, while automobiles are owned in common. The Kickapoos are endogamous, although one should not marry within the consanguine family. They are additionally characterized by serial monogamy or frequent spouse shifts (Latorre and Latorre, 1968: 268). Matrilocal, they use the Omaha type of kinship system. Kickapoo ceremonialism is crucial and the key in maintaining Indian identity. Of the fourteen surviving clans only four contain ceremonial leaders capable of directing their numerous religious ceremonials. Each clan owns a medicine bundle which plays a major role in the clan's ritual (Latorre and Latorre, 1968: 268-69). Each year, curing groups, or herbal societies, also present their own ceremonials after the conclusion of clan rituals. Naming ceremonies, feasts for the dead, adoption ceremonials, funeral rituals, and so on, are still held. Capitán Papikwano, the tribal chief, is acknowledged by both the Kickapoos and the Mexican government. Dolores and Felipe Latorre have been doing field work for some ten years among the Kickapoos and have published a very complete book, *The Mexican Kickapoo Indians* (1976), on modern Kickapoo life and several excellent papers on Kickapoo religion (1968) and medicine (1969). The book, a descriptive monograph, also explains the role of Kickapoo ceremonialism in preserving their separate identity. A. M. Gibson (1963) has published a Kickapoo history which, in part, deals with the Mexican Kickapoos. Ritzenthaler and Peterson wrote an earlier monograph (1956) and articles on Kickapoo ethnic survival (1955) and on Kickapoo courtship whistling (1954). In 1946, Emilio N. Acosta published an interestingly titled book, *Meníscika* (see Anonymous, 1977a: 51-52), about a Kickapoo man who attended the University of Wisconsin, visited Mahatma Gandhi in India, and acted as a mediator between the Mexican government and the tribe. Also, Carlos Basauri (1940), Alfonso Fabila (1945), and Roberto de la Cerda Silva (1957) have written short descriptive accounts of the Kickapoos, and William Jones has published some Mexican Kickapoo tales (1915). A popular account in *Tiempo* (Anonymous, 1977a) reports the present negotiations between the Mexican government and the Kickapoos, especially concerning hunting rights. Other short articles also exist such as Buntin (1933), Goggin (1951), and Peterson (1956).

One other body of data concerning northern Mexico's indigenous and folk customs should be mentioned. From its mestizo or Indian ancestry the North of Mexico has pro-

duced folk curers, prophets, and a corpus of folklore exhibiting both peasant and indigenous roots. Kelly (1961, 1965) has described folk practices in southern Coahuila, including some information on spiritualism and the famous Mexican curer who spent many years in southern Texas, Don Pedrito Jaramillo. Dodson (1951) has collected a history of and numerous stories of cures by Don Pedrito; Macklin (1967), Macklin and Crumrine (1972, 1973), and N. R. Crumrine and Macklin (1974) have analyzed the sociological, structural, and symbolic elements of Niño Fidencio's curing cult in Nuevo León; Barragan (1966) and Roel (1963) describe Tatita of Nuevo León; Pulido (1965) sketches Cayetano Hernández de Villagrán of Tamaulipas; and Dupoyet (1910) describes curing among the northern Mexican nomadic tribes.

Moving westward into southwestern Chihuahua, Sonora, and Baja California, the western Sierra Madres, the coastal plain of the Gulf of California, and the highlands of Baja California, the major modern indigenous groups are encountered. Three groups live in southwestern Chihuahua and southeastern Sonora: northern Tepehuáns, Guarijíos (Warihios), and Tarahumaras. Some three thousand to four thousand Tepehuáns are scattered over an extremely mountainous area in the tip of southwesternmost Chihuahua. They maintain small subsistence gardens of maize, beans, and squash and occasionally grow wheat, barley, oats, potatoes, and peas. They also raise chickens and a few goats, pigs, cows, and turkeys. They cook and ferment maguey hearts and collect cactus fruits, wild seeds, and roots as foods and medicines. Settlements are scattered and grouped into moiety divisions within six major regions *(gobernancias).* Land inheritance was patrilineal, although modern *ejido* rules have modified this form. Kinship terminology is highly descriptive, with numerous distinctions for grandparents' and parents' siblings. The politicoreligious system is still intact, with each of the six *gobernancias* led by an elected *gobernador* and a set of lesser officials. Religious and curing rituals are also still intact and characterized by a fusion of indigenous and Catholic customs and beliefs. Service (1969) has published a good summary account of the northern Tepehuáns, and Cerda Silva (1943b) and Mason (1912, 1913, 1948, 1952, 1959) have written numerous short articles on both southern and northern Tepehuáns. Pennington (1969) has published a very full and excellent account of modern Tepehuán material culture and an article (1963a) on medicinal plants.

The Guarijíos live northwest of the Tepehuáns along the southwestern border of Chihuahua and Sonora in the higher western foothills of the western Sierra Madres, between the Tarahumaras in the pine-covered high Sierra Madres and the Mayos on the coastal plain of southern Sonora and northern Sinaloa. Like the Tepehuáns, the Guarijíos are quite isolated. In fact, the recent establishment of an Indian center among the Guarijíos was seen by the local newspaper, *El Informador del Mayo,* as a rediscovery of a lost and forgotten tribe (Anonymous, 1977b: 1, 5). Gentry (1963) has published a short but complete description of the Guarijíos which projects a population of about sixteen hundred, although the article in *El Informador del Mayo* reports a population of four hundred (Anonymous, 1977b: 5).

The Guarijíos grow corn, beans, squash, sugarcane, chiles, onions, tobacco, cotton, and amaranth. Like the Tepehuáns, they rely upon chickens and a few cows, goats, sheep, and pigs to supplement their crops. Wild fruits, seeds, and roots are also collected as food and medicine. Additionally, deer and fish, as well as wild birds, pigs, and so on, are hunted and eaten. Gentry's material is quite good; he has also published a volume on Río Mayo plants (Gentry, 1942). The settlement pattern is quite scattered, with no elaboration of Gentry's political roles. There is a chief-curer-ceremonial specialist combined in one role called the *selyeme*. He knows Guarijío songs and conducts the *tuwuri* ceremonial, a two-night ritual. Each household tries to give three such *tuwuris* during late summer and fall as a thanksgiving ritual to "Tata Dios," or God. The *tuwuri* involves praying, singing, ritual dancing by women, *paskola* dancing by men, and ritual foods and feasting. Besides this Gentry publication and a short article by Hilton (1947) on words and phrases in Tarahumara and Guarijío languages, I know of very little additional published material on the Guarijíos.

In contrast, a huge amount of scattered literature exists concerning the high Sierra Madre Tarahumaras in southwestern Chihuahua. Spicer (1962) has written an excellent Tarahumara history, and Fried (1969) has produced a good summary of modern Tarahumara life. Some forty to fifty thousand Tarahumaras still live in the high Sierra Madre Occidental, farming small plots of corn, beans, squash, and potatoes and herding goats and sheep. Wealthier families also own cattle (high-prestige animals), and the more acculturated families keep pigs and chickens. Small scattered household clusters, rancherías, usually of five to six houses (although some include fifteen to twenty units), share a small, flat clearing or patio for working, dancing, or feasting. Households are highly mobile, moving to tend scattered agricultural plots or domesticated animals and to adapt to seasonal changes. The nuclear family is the primary economic unit, although communal work parties *(tesgüinadas)* take place and trade with mestizos for needles, axes, thread, salt, cloth, and the like. Marriage is usually monogamous, but polygamous and polyandrous households also are found. Although kinship terminology is bilateral, patterns are extremely flexible.

Within the ranchería, mutual assistance exists; at the pueblo level (a territorial grouping of rancherías characterized by a religioadministrative center), religious ceremonies, footraces, the adjudication of disputes, and ranchería and pueblo exogamy act as integrating mechanisms, although no tribal leaders or councils exist. The political and religious organization reflects a fusion of indigenous elements and seventeenth-century Christian patterns taught to the Tarahumaras by Jesuit missionaries. An indigenous priest-doctor still is active at the ranchería level, not conflicting with pueblo officials active in Christian-influenced fiestas. The ranchería fiestas (involving dancing, drinking of *tesgüino* corn beer, and food offerings) deal with curing, rain, first-fruit rituals, harvests, and rituals for the dead. On the other hand, pueblo or church fiestas celebrate the Christian calendar and involve prayers, dancing, and drinking.

Beginning with Lumholtz (1902) in the early 1890s, Basauri (1929), Bennett and Zingg (1935), Plancarte (1954), and Pennington (1963) have published full volumes on the Tarahumaras. Each includes additional references. Fried (1953, 1961) and Passin (1942a, 1942b, 1943) have discussed Tarahumara personality and social organization; Zingg (1942), Tarahumara values; and Champion (1955), Tarahumara culture contact and acculturation. Among others we also might mention Basauri (1927), Bennett and Zingg (1946a, 1946b), Brand (1943), Ceballos (1951), Cerda Silva (1943a), Gómez (1948, 1952, and 1953), Neumann (1969), Vega (1943), and Zingg (1932) as well as the highly literary account by Artaud (1963).

Moving west into northern and central Sonora, survivors of several indigenous groups still exist: the Opatas, Pimas, and Pápagos. These peoples were agriculturalists; their modern members still farm small plots in addition to caring for cattle and participating in the modern agricultural wage labor market. In most cases their culture is quite similar to that of the area's poor mestizo farmers and peasants. Hinton (1969, 1976) has published two excellent summaries. He (1969: 881) estimates some four thousand Opatas and Jobas (although they have lost their languages and are difficult to identify), fifteen hundred Pima Bajos, some three hundred Pápagos in Sonora, and an equal number of Sonoran Pápagos living in Arizona. Even though much of traditional Opata culture is now gone, they do retain a unique Easter ceremonial (Owen, 1958). The Pima Bajos and Pápagos attend the large fiestas for San Francisco in Magdalena (Dobyns, 1950) and Maicoba. Kinship and social organization of Opatas and Pima Bajos are highly acculturated; the Pápago family structure still retains a patrilineal bias, and the kinship terminology is Yuman (see Underhill, 1939).

Johnson (1950), Owen (1959), and Hinton (1959) have published modern studies on the Opatas and assimilation among the Opatas, Jobas, and Pima Bajos; Lumholtz (1902) and Brugge (Mason and Brugge, 1958) have written on the Pimas; and Joseph, Spicer, and Chesky (1949); Nolasco (1965, 1969); and Underhill (1939, 1946) have produced works on the Pápagos, including Sonoran materials. As additional references, add Gaillard (1894) on the Pápagos; Hamy (1883) on the Opatas, Pimas, and Tarahumaras; Hewes (1935) and Johnson (1940a, 1940b) on the Piman foot drum and Sonoran dance regalia; and Brugge (1956) on Pima basketry.

The Seris living along the coast just west of Hermosillo are still intact and have struck the imagination of western writers. Thus Moser (1976), in his excellent bibliography on Seri ethnography, lists over 240 items. Today some 415 Seris (Moser, 1976: 365) still live on the Sonoran coast. As were their ancestors, modern Seris are fishermen. In the past they were hunters and collectors, especially hunting for the sea turtle. Today their fishing is more commercial, although they still rely upon wild foods in addition to store-bought items. Traditional social organization exists, and the kinship terminology is Yuman, with monogamous marriage and patrilocal residence. Their religion is non-Christian; shamanism and myth cycles continue. According to Moser, the studies of McGee (1898), Droeber (1931), and Coolidge

(1939) are the most complete. Griffen's study (1959), though, is extensive; Lindig's (1960) is rich and includes an extensive bibliography. Recently, Seris have been carving ironwood in exquisite animal, bird, and fish forms (Johnston, 1968). These art objects are now reaching an international market. Although hundreds of additional items could be mentioned, the following are of specific interest: Fay (1956*b*) on a fertility figure; González Bonilla (1941) and Watkins (1939) on Seri pelican-skin robes; Nolasco (1967) and Moser (1963, 1968) on Seri bands and on two Seri myths; and Instituto Nacional Indigenista (*Acción Indigenista*, 1975, nos. 262 and 265) on their aid and development program among the Seri.

Moving to the far northwest corner of Sonora, one encounters some 240 speakers of Cocopa or Cucapá (Nolasco, 1969: 48). Living in the delta area of the Colorado River, the Cocopas relied upon spring floods to dampen the rich soil for their crops of corn, beans, and pumpkins and upon wild foods such as piñon nuts, acorns, cactus fruit, wild rice, mesquite, and screwbean. However, today many Cocopas are members of agricultural *ejidos,* practice modern irrigation agriculture, and work as agricultural wage labor. They also fished and hunted rabbits, wood rats, quail, and doves. Agricultural ritual and ceremonialism was little developed, although there was a shaman, seer, and curer. Funeral and mourning ceremonies were elaborate and important. The deceased was cremated, and his or her property was burned or distributed to the visitors. The mourning ceremony, which took place after the harvest fiesta, was often held as much as two years after death so that the proper amount of goods could be assembled. Castetter and Bell (1951) have published a recent account of Cocopa agriculture and general culture based upon Kelly's earlier work (1942, 1949), Cocopa social organization and ceremonialism, Gifford's general descriptive study (1933), and the work of Kniffen (1931). The Instituto Nacional Indigenista has established a coordinating center in Mexicali for the Cocopas (Cucapás) and the Baja California groups—Cucapás, Comiais (Diegueños), Cochimís (Tipais), Paipais, and Kiliwas—and has published short notes on the center and its activities (Instituto Nacional Indigenista, *Acción Indigenista,* 1973, nos. 242 and 246; 1975, nos. 263 and 264).

The 26 Comiais live near Tijuana. The Cochimís, the Paipais, and the Kiliwas are located slightly to the south in the northern Baja California central mountain area; they number 137, about 200, and 62, respectively (Instituto Nacional Indigenista, *Acción Indigenista,* 1975, no. 264: 2-3). Today members of these groups work as small-scale farmers and wage laborers on the region's large farms and ranches. They also hunt deer and rabbits and collect wild foods such as acorns, pine nuts, cactus fruit, berries, and seeds. The households are widely scattered; intermarriage within and between the differing groups takes place. Remnants of numerous patrilocal bands still exist, and the kinship terms are basically Yuman in type. The non-Catholic religion focuses upon witchcraft, ghosts, and curing. In the past, curing shamans were important; occasional commemorative fiestas for the dead still occur. Owen (1969) has written a summary

of modern Baja ethnography; Meigs (1939) about the Kiliwas; Drucker (1941) on cultural elements of the Paipais (Akwa'alas) and Tipais; and Gifford and Lowie (1928) on the Akwa'alas. Massey's (1949) aboriginal linguistic distributions, Henderson's (1952*a*, 1952*b*) popular descriptions, Barrett's (1957) bibliography, and Owen's (1962, 1963*a*, 1963*b*, and 1965) account of disease concepts, curing, and the theory of the patrilocal band should be noted. Also, Hinton and Owen (1957), Michelsen and Owen (1967), North (1908), Aschmann (1952), Rodríguez Lorenzo (1938), and Shipek (1968) should be mentioned.

The Yaquis, inhabiting the Sonoran central coast south of the Seris, and the Mayos, living south of the Yaquis along the southern coast of Sonora and the northern coast of Sinaloa, represent the last groups to be discussed in this bibliographical article. Spicer (1969 and 1976), Crumrine (1976*a*), and Griffith (1976) have published summary and bibliographic articles concerning the Mayos and Yaquis, in one of which Spicer (1976) has assembled some three hundred references. Modern Mayo population runs over thirty thousand and Yaqui population over fifteen thousand (Spicer 1969: 830). Many Mayos hold memberships in *ejidos,* whereas Yaquis live on a reservation. Both groups work as small-scale farmers, wage laborers, and fishermen (see L. S. Crumrine and N. R. Crumrine, 1967; N. R. Crumrine and L. S. Crumrine, 1967; N. R. Crumrine, 1977; and McGuire, 1977). They borrow money from the bank, request irrigation water from the government, and plant the recommended commercial crops of corn, sesame, cotton, soybeans, safflower, wheat, and so on. Much of their food (coffee, meat, sugar, bread, and even some tortillas) is purchased in the local mestizo market with cash or credit from their crop sales. Their clothing and much of their material culture are identical to those of rural mestizo peasant farmers.

The Mayo-Yaqui belief and ceremonial system, however, is unique, reflecting the fusion of Christian and indigenous patterns. Among Yaquis, the pueblo organization is highly developed and tightly integrated with ceremonial and mythical organizations. Both groups' saint's-day fiestas are celebrated with feasting, fireworks, and the dancing of specialists, the *paskola,* and deer dancers (see Crumrine, 1977, 1979, and Spicer, 1954*a*, 1964). The Lenten and Holy Week ceremonies include masked Fariseros who crucify Jesus and ultimately are destroyed by God's power (see Crumrine, 1974*c*; and Spicer 1954*a* and 1964). Beals (1943*b*, 1945), Crumrine (1974*c*, 1977), and Erasmus (1961, 1967) have published major monographs on the Mayos, and Fabila (1940), Holden et al. (1936), and Spicer (1954*a*, 1961, 1980) have written on the Yaquis.

Numerous articles have been published on Yaqui-Mayo crafts, dance, folklore, and ceremonialism: Barker (1957, 1958), Cámara Barbachano (1962), Castañeda (1968), Crumrine (1969, 1970, 1973, 1974*a*, 1974*b*, 1976*b*), N. R. Crumrine and L. S. Crumrine (1970), N. R. Crumrine and M. L. Crumrine (1976, 1977), N. R. Crumrine and Macklin (1974), Densmore (1932), Domínguez (1937), Giddings (1959), Griffith (1967, 1972), Krizman (1968), Kurath (1960), Montell (1938), Parsons and Beals (1934), Spicer (1958,

1965), Toor (1937*a*, 1937*b*), Warner (1945), and Wilder (1963). Histories, historical novels, and bibliographies also exist: Acosta (1949), Calderón (1956), Chávez Camacho (1948), Corral (1959), Moisés (1971), Nicoli (1885), Paso y Troncoso (1905), Pesqueira (1966), and Spicer (1961, 1962, 1969).

Fay (1955, 1956*c*, 1958, 1968) has written on area house types, and the following authors have written about curing, new religious movements, and the question of ethnic identity and enclavement: Crumrine (1964, 1966, 1968, 1975, 1977, 1979), Erasmus (1961, 1967), Macklin and Crumrine (1973), Picchioni (1965), and Spicer (1954*b*, 1966, 1970*a*, 1971, 1972, 1980).

The following references should also be mentioned: Beals (1932*a*), Corzo (1954), L. S. Crumrine (1969), L. S. Crumrine and N. R. Crumrine (1967), N. R. Crumrine and L. S. Crumrine (1967, 1969), Delgado Hernández (1951), Erasmus (1955), Ibarra (1944), Spicer (1943, 1945, 1951), and *Acción Indigenista* of the Instituto Nacional Indigenista (1973, nos. 240, 243, 245; 1974, nos. 247, 254; 1975, nos. 259, 261, 263, 265, 267).

In conclusion, most likely the paragraphs on the Kickapoos, Pápagos, Cocopas, Bajo California groups, and Mayos-Yaquis will be of most interest to readers because all these groups either have friends or relatives living on the north side of the border or pass freely back and forth, working or visiting friends in the United States.

Those interested in contemporary native Americans of the Borderlands confront a rapidly growing literature. Much of this material, however, is limited; more of it is simply badly done and not worth the time. Yet given the substantial Indian population of the region as well as the continuities and changes during the era, the subject is a most important one. It is not surprising that some of the best work in Native American studies has been done here.

The term *contemporary,* of course, is open to interpretation. Hodge (1976), for example, defines contemporary as the period since 1875. I define it more narrowly, emphasizing the years since World War II, stressing work completed since 1965.

There are, moreover, arbitrary choices about the focus of such a bibliographical review. I have attempted to include a wide variety of sources, especially many native American works. This essay is organized topically into (1) regional and tribal studies; (2) media sources; (3) economy; (4) population, migration, and urbanization; (5) political and legal affairs; (6) health and health care; (7) edu-

55

Native Americans

PETER IVERSON
Department of History
University of Wyoming

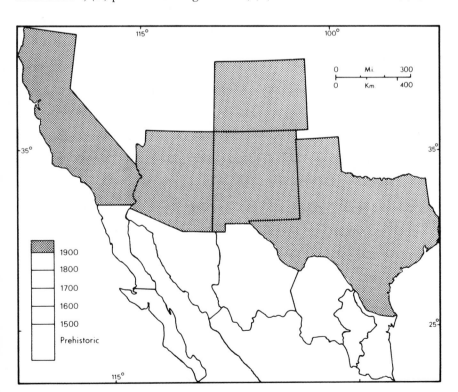

cation; (8) society; and (9) art and literature.

Space limitations make this review hardly comprehensive. Other bibliographical studies should be consulted. Hodge's bibliography on contemporary Indian affairs (1976) includes much that is relevant. The Newberry Library Center for the History of the American Indian is in the process of publishing an extensive bibliographical series, five volumes of which thus far are pertinent (Dobyns, 1976b; Heizer, 1976; Iverson, 1976b; Prucha and Melody, 1977). Heizer, with Nissen and Castillo (1975), earlier compiled a more extensive source guide for California Indian history. Laird has produced an exhaustive Hopi bibliography (1977). Sutton (1975) is enormously helpful for land tenure. Also important are Murdock and O'Leary (1975) and Berry (1969). I readily acknowledge my indebtedness to these and other scholars in compiling sources listed in this essay.

Regional and Tribal Studies

One should begin with Spicer (1962) for a classic overview through 1960. Dozier (1971) is brief but excellent. More limited and more dated are Dale (1949) and Kelly (1953). Spicer and Thompson (1972) include other ethnic groups in addition to native Americans but contain two valuable essays by Spicer as well as articles by Young (1972: 167-238) on the Navahos and Sekaquaptewa (1972: 239-60) on the Hopis. Questions of identity and tribal boundary maintenance are also examined in Helm (1968), Barth (1969), and Bennett (1975). See Fontana (1973: 5-8; 1974: 18-24) for a shorter consideration of modern Borderlands Indian identity.

There are few comprehensive, analytical state studies. For Arizona, Weaver et al. (1974), offers a brief and usually very general survey of contemporary legislation, urbanism, tribal government, living conditions, employment, economic development and assistance programs, and education. The Arizona Commission of Indian Affairs publishes annual reports and a state tribal directory (1966-present, 1967-present). For California, see the work of Forbes (1969, 1971) and various state reports (California, Department of Industrial Relations, 1965; California, State Advisory Commission on Indian Affairs, 1966). The first-rate volume edited by Tewa anthropologist Alfonso Ortiz (1965) has some relevant New Mexico material; other sources for New Mexico include Dozier (1970), Aberle (1948), and Meaders (1963). For oral history, see the Doris Duke tapes at the University of New Mexico (Ellis, 1973: 19-24).

Because of the University of Oklahoma Press's Civilization of the American Indian Series and other of that press's publishing efforts, tribal studies abound. Many of these works, however, place little emphasis on the twentieth century, let alone the contemporary period. Among the general studies, see Crampton (1977), Lange (1959), Underhill (1967), White (1962), James (1974), Tiller (1976), Bean (1972), Brown (1979), Thompson (1950), Nagata (1970), Kluckhohn and Leighton (1974), Leighton and Adair (1966), Hirst (1976), Joseph, Spicer, and Chesky (1949), Sonnichsen (1958),

Whitman (1947), and Bee (1981). The Indian Tribal Series, edited by Dobyns and Euler, provides readable, general introductions to various peoples (for example, see Dobyns and Euler, 1971, 1972; Dobyns, 1971, 1972, 1973). The Zuñis and Navahos collectively have authorized and authored works dealing with their history (Quam, 1972; Roessel, 1973; Roessel and Johnson, 1974; Johnson, 1977a, 1977b; Yazzie, 1971). Generally based on oral history, these perspectives offer an important complementary, and sometimes differing, picture of a people's past; even if they are concerned with an earlier period, the accounts tell much about contemporary viewpoints and values.

Media Sources

Contemporary newspapers, journals, and films are of central importance for a perspective on recent developments. The American Indian Historical Society, based in San Francisco (under the direction of Rupert Costo, a Cahuilla, and Jeannette Henry, a Cherokee) publishes the newspaper *Wassaja;* the journal *The Indian Historian;* and a children's magazine, *The Weewish Tree. Akwesasne Notes,* published sporadically by the New York Mohawk Nation, also covers much Borderlands news. *Wassaja* and *Akwesasne Notes* must be read keeping in mind the editorial perspectives of its staffs. For often very different vantage points, see major metropolitan newspapers such as the *Los Angeles Times, San Francisco Chronicle, Arizona Republic,* or *Albuquerque Journal;* bordertown newspapers such as the *Gallup Independent* devote attention to native American affairs.

A great many other publications feature tribal news, Indian organizations, or Indian concerns. California Indian news is available through *Early American, Five Feather News, Take Ten, The Tribal Spokesman,* and *Whispering Arrow.* Indian newspapers in Arizona and New Mexico include *Canyon Shadows, Fort Apache Scout, Fort McDowell Indian Community News, Views and Events, Hopi Action News, Indian Forerunner, Navajo Times, 19 Pueblo News, Pima Maricopa Echo, Qua'Toqti,* and *Smoke Signals.* Such organizations as the Association on American Indian Affairs *(Indian Affairs)* and the National Congress of American Indians *(The Sentinel Bulletin)* publish their own newsletters. Legal concerns are considered in the *California Indian Legal Services Newsletter* and the University of New Mexico law school's *American Indian Law Newsletter.* Native American students at the University of Arizona publish a journal, *Sun Tracks,* while the Indian education program at Arizona State University sponsors the *Journal of American Indian Education.*

Scholarly journals vary considerably in contemporary attention. Journals such as *Human Organization,* emphasizing applied study, tend to be more helpful. Western law journals often feature articles of central importance. *American Anthropologist, Current Anthropology, Ethnohistory, Journal of Anthropological Research* (formerly *The Journal of Southwestern Anthropology), Plateau, American Indian Quarterly,* and *Western History Quarterly* from time to time have articles of interest. State historical journals, including the *California Historical Quarterly, Arizona and the West, Journal of Arizona History,* and the *New Mexico Historical Review* occasionally publish pertinent articles and, more frequently, useful book reviews. The *American Indian Quarterly* and *Western History Quarterly* both publish recent article listings.

Film is a medium through which increasing amounts of Borderlands Indian information will be transmitted. Adair and Worth (1972) have worked with Navajos, teaching them to be filmmakers *(Seen Through Navajo Eyes—Navajos Film Themselves).* Several filmmakers documented northern California Indian struggles to regain claimed lands *(The Dispossessed, The Earth is Our Mother, Forty-seven Cents),* while another reviewed efforts toward cultural revitalization *(The Way of Our Fathers).* A young Pueblo Indian from New Mexico, Larry Littlebird, helped start Circle Films, a cooperative Indian undertaking resulting in a number of films. In 1977, Laguna Pueblo writer Leslie Marmon Silko proposed what promises to be an important new film series on Laguna life (Laguna Pueblo Film Project). In television, Navaho area residents began receiving the Navajo Nation Report in the mid-1970s. Additionally, educational television stations in Phoenix and Tucson filmed southwestern artists and writers, including Schmitz (1975), Gorman, Laloma, Scholder, Hardin, Houser, Evers (1976), Momaday, Ríos, and Silko.

Economy

Native American economic development affects all residents of the region, although it is vital to Indians and their futures. Native American human and land resources, moreover, are critical to everyone in the Borderlands. Their significance is attested to by a growing literature. A good place to start is a two-volume essay collection published by the U.S. Congress, Joint Economic Committee (1969).

The 1977 dry year underlined water's importance in the Borderlands. Native American water rights, forged through the Winters Doctrine and subsequent court decisions, are being seriously tested for the first time, with the full impact yet to be felt. William Veeder, a Bureau of Indian Affairs specialist in water law, has written widely on the subject (Veeder, 1965, 1969, 1971, 1972). See also Dellwo (1971: 215-40), Nickeson (1974: 174-78), Coffeen (1973: 345-77), MacMeekin (1972), Hilding (1973), S. M. Campbell (1974: 1299-1321), Clark (1971: 48-68), and Ranquist (1971: 34-41).

Indian coal, oil, uranium, and timber resources have been widely used in recent years, with native Americans facing consistent challenges in their attempts to gain a fair return for these resources. Among many relevant works, consult Anderson (1974: 209-26), Chambers and Price (1974: 1061-96), Hackenberg (1976: 303-11), Aberle (1969: 223-76), Berger (1968a: 89-122; 1968b: 675-89), Wolff (1972: 29-41), and Gibbons (1965: 73-105).

Traditional land usage has often included farming and livestock. These practices have recently been affected by increasing population, government regulations, and diversifying tribal economies: see Adams (1971: 77-82), Getty (1961-62, 1963), Martin (1973: 153-62), Downs (1963: 53-67; 1964) and Roessel and Johnson (1974).

A modern wage-work economy has encouraged both off-reservation migration and internal urbanization within Indian reservations. See Dobyns, Stoffle, and Jones (1975: 155-79), R. W. Young (1976), Adams and Krutz (1971: 115-34), Taylor (1970), Waddell (1969), Stoffle (1975: 217-25), Sutton (1964; 1967: 69-89), Padfield and Van Willigen (1969: 208-16), Munsell (1967), and Reno (1970: 8-16). The Indian trader remains important in the most rural areas; W. Y. Adams (1963) and McNitt (1962) present trader portraits, while the Federal Trade Commission (1973) and Southwest Indian Development (1968) criticize the trading post.

Federal and state government regulations, assistance, and policies may generally help or hinder native American economic development: for example, see McFeeley (1972: 71-80), Israel and Smithson (1973: 267-302), Hough (1967), Olson (1972: 81-90), Sorkin (1971; 1973: 115-29), Schaab (1968: 303-30), and Bee (1970: 155-61).

Population, Migration, and Urbanization

Native American population statistics remain impressively unreliable. We do know, or at least suspect, that the Indian population within the United States reached its nadir with the 1920 census and has been rising ever since. The Borderlands are no exception. The Navaho population alone may be 150,000, the largest tribe in the country. Los Angeles has more Indian residents than any other city. The 1980 census will officially reveal California the state with the largest native American population. Arizona and New Mexico, of course, also are among the states with the highest number of Indian people. The cities of San Francisco-Oakland, Phoenix, and Albuquerque, and reservation bordertowns such as Gallup and Farmington, are Indian population centers. The Pápagos and the Navahos have been scrutinized far more frequently for demographic purposes, as the following studies reveal: Dobyns (1976), Alvarado (1970: 9-14), Hackenberg (1961; 1966: 470-93; 1967: 478-92), Hillery and Essene (1963: 297-313), Johnston (1966), D. J. Jones (1962: 1-9), Kelly (1963, 1964), Kunitz (1974a: 7-16; 1974b: 435-51), Niswander et al. (1970: 7-23), Workman and Niswander (1970: 24-49), U.S. Bureau of the Census (1973), Zubrow (1974), Cook (1976), Bodine (1971), California Department of Industrial Relations (1965), and Arizona Commission of Indian Affairs (1967).

Migration to town and city, encouraged by reservation circumstances and the assistance of the Bureau of Indian Affairs (BIA) has increased steadily since World War II; see Cook (1943a: 33-45), W. Hodge (1969), A. Ortiz (n.d.), Uchendu (1966), and Hackenberg and Wilson (1972: 171-86). Town and urban residence is not necessarily permanent, either by choice or situation. For analyses of Indian urbanization in the Borderlands or the urbanization of Borderlands Indians, see Ablon (1963*a*; 1963*b*: 296-304); Goodner (1969); Kunitz, Levy, and Odoroff (1970: 92-106); Luebben (1964); Price (1968: 168-75); Sparks (1968: 706-24); Trillin (1970: 92-104; 1971: 108-14); Uhlmann (1973, 1974); Waddell (1969; 1970: 37-42); Waddell and Watson (1971); and Chaudhuri (1974).

Political and Legal Affairs

Native American tribal governments and political development merit more extensive analysis. Many tribal governments are relatively recent, established during the days of Indian Commissioner John Collier. Some of them are more fully accepted and powerful than others, but given the complex issues these organizations are charged with confronting, all are important. Political movements, such as the one which occupied Alcatraz Island, also need further and continuing attention: Blue Cloud (1972), Pandey (1968: 71-85), Price (1973), Iverson (1975), Shepardson (1963; 1965: 250-53), Young (1961, 1978), M. E. Smith (1968*a*, 1968*b*, 1969, 1971), Williams (1970), Witt (1970: 93-127), Bean (1964: 1-10), Costo (1970: 4-12), Wilson (1964), Navaho Tribe (1969), and Fretz (1966: 581-616).

Legal assistance, from general counsel to tribal governments and attorneys employed to advise individual Indians, has had a profound impact on tribal government development and reaffirmation of native American rights. For a classic framework of Indian law, see Cohen (1971); for readings, documents, and cases, see Price (1973). A recent bibliography is Santini (1973). Dobyns's article on the legal counsel's role (Dobyns, 1970: 268-94) is also important. In addition, see Price (1969: 161-206), Swan (1970: 594-626), and Iverson (1976: 21-34; 1977: 1-15).

Legal issues facing Borderlands Indians are reviewed frequently in various law journals. One central concern has been tribal, state and federal jurisdiction. In addition to Price (1973), Cohen (1971), and Angle (1959), see Aschenbrenner (1971: 485-524); Cree (1974: 1451-1506); Davis (1959: 62-101); Ericson and Snow (1970: 445-90); Kane (1965: 238-55); Keith (1974: 283-92); Nash (1970: 626-34; 1971: 321-34); Olson (1972: 81-90); Ransom and Gilstrap (1971: 196-214); Hacker, Meier, and Pauli (1974: 421-56); Johnson (1974: 1-28); Vollmann (1974: 387-412); Goldberg (1975: 535-94); Baldassin and McDermott (1973: 13-22); and Canby (1973: 206-32). In addition to previously cited articles on economic development, the following studies cover legal matters and government policy: California Indian Legal Services (1968), F. Fernandez (1968: 161-76), K. Johnson (1966), U.S. Bureau of Indian Affairs (1972), Babbitt (1971: 157-58), Busselen (1962), Castile (1974: 219-28), Chambers (1971: 1-20), Cuykendall (1973: 191-212), Davies (1966: 132-51), Schlesinger (1967), Sutton (1970: 1-23), White (1972), de Raismes (1975: 59-106), Ziontz (1975), Shifter and West (1974: 73-106), Bodine (1973: 13-22), Johnson (1973: 973-92), Moriarty (1973: 13-25), Washburn (1973), G. T. Jones (1974: 41-60), Kerr (1969:

311-38), Goodman and Thompson (1975: 397-418), Kickingbird (1975: 243-54), and Strickland (1975: 313-32).

Health and Health Care

Borderlands native Americans are gradually increasing their use of Euro-American health care. Since the demise of the doctor draft the Indian Health Service has been plagued by a shortage of physicians. Still, medical care seems to be improving in quality. More Indians are entering medical fields; many doctors appear to be moving beyond the traditional animosity which has existed between doctor and patient or doctor and native singer or healer. Written work about this transition focuses primarily on the Navahos; see Bahr (1973: 109), Levy (1961), Adair and Deuschle (1970), Mico (1962), Navaho Health Authority (1973), Gorman (1974), and Bergman (1973: 8-15). For additional perspectives on contemporary Indian healing practices and ceremonies, consult Frisbie and McAllester (1978), Bahr (1974), Boyer (1964: 384-419), Devereux (1969), Stewart (1970: 15-24), Smithson (1964), Fox (1960: 291-303), Kaplan and Johnson (1964: 203-29), Leighton and Leighton (1949), Kluckhohn (1967), and Wyman (1970).

The Native American Church, which includes ritual peyote use, is considered by its adherents to be a vital institution for maintenance of health and harmony. It has gained an important membership base in the Borderlands. A valuable work on the Native American Church's growth among one southwestern tribe is Aberle (1966). Other works include those of Collins (1967: 183-91; 1968: 427-49) and Bergman (1971: 695-99).

There remain significant problems in Indian health. For analyses of the contemporary situation, see Adams et al. (1970: 1047-61), Hackenberg and Gallagher (1972: 211-26), Hirschhorn and Spivey (1972: 348-50), Adair et al. (1957: 80-94), Dozier (1966*b*: 72-87), Levy and Kunitz (1969: 11-19; 1974), and Bearn and Wood (1969).

Education

Since World War II there have been a number of important Indian educational developments in the Borderlands: the rise of a public school network on many reservations, the growth of Indian-controlled schools, the great increase in native American college students and graduates, and the enrollment of more Indian children in urban schools. Native Americans in the region have played leading roles in such organizations as the National Indian Education Association; experimental Indian schools here have served as models for Indian communities throughout the nation. Basic difficulties remain, particularly in bicultural schools, but the overall picture is much brighter than it was thirty years ago.

Surprisingly, there are relatively few first-rate general Indian education studies or surveys. In addition to Berry (1968), see Fuchs and Havighurst (1973), Szasz (1974), K. Iverson (1978), Deever (1974), *Journal of American Indian Educa-*

tion, and U.S. Senate, Subcommittee on Indian Education (1969).

The issue of Indian control of Indian schools is considered in the above works, but more particularly in Rosenfelt (1973: 492-550; 1974: 4-8), Henry (1972), Erickson and Schwartz (1969), R. Bergman et al. (1969), Navaho Division of Education (1973*a*, 1973*b*), Warren (1974), Emerson (1970: 94-98), Wax (1970: 62-71), Erickson (1970: 76-93), Muskrat (1970: 72-75), and Platero (1970: 57-58). Sources on a bilingual approach include Spolsky (1970: 19-24), Spolsky and Holm (1971), Holm (1973: 191-202), Murphy (1970: 4-25), and Willink (1973: 177-90). For other perspectives, see Breuing (1975: 51-58); Forbes (1967); National Association for the Advancement of Colored People (1971); Zintz (1957-60); Officer (1956); Parmee (1968); Long, Canyon, and Churchman (1973: 7-14); Padfield, Hemingway, and Greenfield (1966-67: 1-24); Lobo, Bainton, and Weaver (1974: 138-56); and Kelly (1967).

Society

Spicer's analyses of native American cultural change and continuity provide an important perspective (Spicer, 1957: 197-230; 1961; 1962; 1971: 795-800; 1972: 1-76). Also see Warren (1974), Castile (1974: 219-28), Fontana (1973: 18-24; 1974*b*: 18-24), and McNickle (1973). Clearly the degree of continuity and change has varied from one community or tribe to another. For different viewpoints on contemporary Indian societies, consult Lamphere (1977), Ortiz (1965: 389-96; 1969), Basso (1970, 1971), Downs (1972), Negata (1970), Sasaki (1960), White (1962), Simons (1970), Opler (1969), Witherspoon (1970: 55-65; 1975; 1977), Ellis (1953: 385-94; 1959: 325-47), Titiev (1972), Sherer (1966: 1-35), Basehart (1970: 87-106), Melody (1976), Dozier (1964: 79-97; 1966: 172-85; 1970; 1971: 228-56), Aberle (1948), McNeley (1975), Fenton (1974: 297-344), Reno (1963), and Bee (1981). One is struck, in reading through much of the literature, by what Warren calls "continuity within change," the extent to which Indian identities adapt within a changing world. Writing nearly twenty years ago, Vogt noted what he termed the resistant institutional core of the Navahos, "composed of systems of social rela-

tions, ecological adjustments and values forming a coherent and distinctive Navajo pattern" (1961: 278-336). The observation still seems valid, not only for the Navahos, but also for many other Borderlands native American peoples.

Art and Literature

For decades Indian artists and craftsmen from the Borderlands have been recognized for the beauty and the imagination of their work. Native American painting, silverwork, basketry, pottery, weaving, sculpture, and other art forms reached new heights of popularity and critical acclaim during the 1960s and '70s, and with this recognition came an outpouring of description and analysis. A selective sample includes Maxwell Museum (1974), Peterson (1977), Adair (1944), Chapman (1970), Le Free (1975), Brody (1971), Tanner (1968, 1973), Monthan and Monthan (1975), Breeskin and Turk (1972), Dunn (1968; 1972: 150-62), Harlow (1977), Harlow and Young (1965), Marriott (1948), Quoyawayma and Carlson (1964), and Wright and Roat (1970).

It almost goes without saying that the region's native Americans possess a rich traditional literature of stories, legends, and teachings. Indian societies have provided a continuing source for the poet, the essayist, and the novelist. Non-Indian writers such as Frank Waters (1942) long have used the region as the environment for their stories, but increasingly Indian writers are publishing their own work.

Perhaps the best-known contemporary Indian writer is N. Scott Momaday, a Kiowa who teaches English at Arizona. Momaday's parents worked for the Indian Service in Arizona and New Mexico for many years. His novel *House Made of Dawn* (1969) and recent memoir *The Names* (1976) reflect this exposure. Leslie Silko from Laguna Pueblo has emerged as the most prominent of the younger southwestern Indian writers. She was the principal contributor to Rosen (1974) and in 1977 published her first novel, *Ceremony.* Collections such as Rosen (1974, 1975), Milton (1969, 1971), Allen (1974), and Hobson (1977) will introduce the reader to many other writers. Indian student publications such as *Sun Tracks,* from the University of Arizona, are other important sources for new contributors to contemporary native American literature.

56

Negro (Black)
Americans

ELLWYN R. STODDARD
*Department of Sociology and
Anthropology
University of Texas, El Paso*

The contributions of Negro and black peoples in the development of the United States-Mexico Borderlands is for the most part conspicuously absent in texts and popular literature. In this essay the term *Negro,* of historical vintage, is applied to traditional materials, while the term *black* is employed when speaking of more contemporary resources.

More than fifty years before Columbus's voyage to the New World the Portuguese were bringing Negro slaves to Lisbon markets from the Gold Coast and surrounding areas. At Lisbon assessments were incurred, which are recorded as historical evidence of this early slave trade. Black slaves are also mentioned even earlier in archaic references to Spain and her pre-Columbian institutions. The highly stratified caste system operative in medieval Europe, which found people of color settling in the bottom strata, was the model for New World social institutions. To maintain the costly perquisites of the Spanish monarchs, the exploitation of mineral wealth in the New World created a procession of Portuguese, Spanish, French, and British interests supplying African slaves to

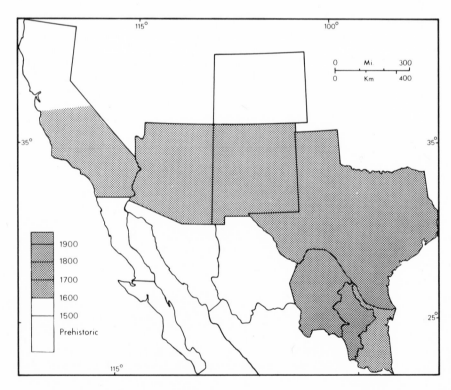

to fill labor voids. The slave trade in and of itself proved to be a highly profitable venture for those wishing to invest in the procurement, transportation, and disposition of Negroes to anxious buyers. For a scholarly approach to the introduction of Negro slavery into the New World, see Mörner (1966, 1967), Bowser (1972), and the short bibliography by King (1944). The classical volume by Freyre (1956) describes Negro slavery, castes, and miscegenation in Brazil. The works of Aguirre Beltrán (1944, 1946), Palmer (1970), Cardoso (1975) and Love (1971) reflect these processes in Mexico and the Borderlands. Texas slavery (Robbins, 1972) and Texas blacks during Reconstruction years (Smallwood, 1974) have also been the subjects of scholarly works. The well-written monograph by Schwartz (1975) describes the legal tensions along the border concerning slavery and the flights of slaves southward to freedom. Carlton's thesis (1977) deals with blacks only in the San Diego region from 1850 to the turn of the century.

Perhaps the most comprehensive source on black history from the pre-Conquest era to modern times is *The Chronological History of the Negro in America* (Bergman and Bergman, 1969), though various authors deal with the evolution of Spanish slavery, slave rebellions, and the difficult roles of slaves and freemen in New World society (King, 1942; Davidson, 1966; Greene, 1972). Besides the European masters, some indigenous American Indian tribes lured slaves into their territories and, as did the Creeks and some Cherokees, engaged in the buying and selling of Africans as early as 1721 (Bailey, 1972; Geist, 1975; Halliburton, 1975; Hudson, 1976). In stark contrast, the Seminoles from Florida's Everglades welcomed Negro slave refugees and allowed the refugees to live among them in a primitive democratic feudalism, many as freemen. Miscegenation occurred, and many of these Seminole Negroes, as they were called, joined their Indian brothers in the First and Second Seminole Wars (1817 and 1835-42), the latter being the most expensive Indian War in which the United States ever participated (Porter, 1951; Katz, 1969, 1971). Some Seminole Negroes fled to Mexico and later were hired as U.S. Army Scouts, helping the border troops to track the marauding Indians who inhabited the Texas-Mexican Borderlands (1873-91), but they were denied Indian rights because they were not included on the official Seminole roll before it was closed in 1866 (Woodhull, 1937; Reeve, 1950; Porter, 1951, 1952).

Negroes in the American South are a popular subject, as evidenced by early journalistic accounts of their servitude (Olmstead, 1904), more detailed social histories (Phillips, 1929; Woofter, 1936), and Marxist explanations of post-Civil War racial exploitation (Mandel, 1978). Religion and racism in the South (H. S. Smith, 1972), personal biographies of Negroes living under the pre- and postwar systems (Brignano, 1974), and the classical, though controversial, treatment of the Negro question in America by Gunnar Myrdal (1944) are the subjects of more analytical studies. Many sources describe the cooperation of Booker T. Washington and the militant rejection of the system by W. E. B. Du Bois, while only recently has the moderate road of challenge through the system been highlighted, as in the career of Gordon Blaine Hancock (Gavins, 1977). Also, as a result of the women's liberation movement, special care is being taken to restore the female Negro heroines, such as Deborah Gannett and Harriet Tubman, whose guerrilla activities in the "underground railroad" led slaves to freedom. The poetic acclaims garnered by Phyllis Wheatly and the suffrage leadership of Sojourner Truth (Isabella Baumfree) and many more black heroes and heroines are now ready to be inserted into our American histories (Drotning, 1968, 1969).

The military contributions made by black troops have been neglected in Hollywood movie portrayals of the Army in the Southwest. Since at least the time of Crispus Attucks, a Negro hero who died at the hands of the British in Boston before the Revolutionary War, Negro soldiers have been a part of American history. They constituted 10 percent of the Union Army until after the Civil War. After disbanding its colored forces in 1864, the army instituted four black volunteer units commanded by white officers. These were the 24th and 25th Infantry regiments and the 9th and 10th Cavalry regiments. One-fifth of all mounted Army troops along the Mexican border from the end of the Civil War to the turn of the century were black. Although they were given inferior rations and supplies, they had only one-fifth the desertion rate of white units, and they distinguished themselves with 28 awards of the Congressional Medal of Honor in one period of only a few years. They were the most effective units against border Indians in army history. Together with the Seminole Negro scouts they became known as "Grierson's Brunettes" or the "Buffalo Soldiers" as they pursued and vanquished marauding Indian groups. Among their scenes of heroism were the victories over Apache chiefs Victorio and Geronimo, the saving of the 7th Regiment from annihilation during the Sioux campaign, the building up and maintaining of most of the forts throughout the Southwest, and the charge on San Juan hill under Colonel Teddy Roosevelt (Flipper, 1963, 1968; Leckie, 1967; Thompson, 1968; Johnson, 1969; Carroll, 1971a, 1971b; David and Crane, 1971; Fowler, 1971; Wakin, 1971; Utley, 1973).

Negroes accompanied Alarcón and Coronado in their explorations of the Southwest. Estevánico, a Negro, guided Fray Marcos de Niza through New Mexico in the search for the Seven Cities of Cibola which started much of the Borderlands colonization. Within our modern era, such frontiersmen as Edward Rose and James Beckwourth are comparatively unknown while their white mountain-men contemporaries Kit Carson and Jim Bridger are well-known folk heroes. Beckwourth scouted for Frémont and discovered the pass through the Rockies near Truckee, California.

Without the black cowboys there might not have been the successful cattle industry in Texas. Such interesting figures as Bose Ikard, James Kelly, Isom Dart, "80 John" Wallace, and the cowboy writer Nat Love *(The Life and Adventures of Nat Love: Better Known in the Cattle Country as "Deadwood Dick"—by Himself)* cannot be separated from the histories of the Santa Fe, Chisolm, and Goodnight-Loving trails. During the thirty-year period 1866-95 one-fourth of the cowhands on the trails were black, mostly working in all-black outfits with white trail bosses (with a few exceptions such as Bose Ikard, who rode the Goodnight-Loving trail). The white saloons and prostitutes of Abilene, Hayes, Newton, Ellsworth, Wichita, Dodge City, and Caldwell were off limits to the black trail hands. As the open range changed to ranching, the critical need for the effective black cowboys diminished, and they became subservient Negro hired hands (Katz, 1969; Cromwell, 1970; Durham and Jones, 1965, 1966).

Black badmen, such as Cherokee Bill and Ben Hodges, the con artist and cattle thief, along with rodeo greats Bill Pickett and Jesse Stahl, have had a major impact on the Southwest and the Borderlands. It should also be remembered among southwestern anthropologists that a black cowboy, George McJunkin, working on the Crow Foot Ranch near Folsom, New Mexico, alerted the experts to the remains of straight-horned Bison and the famed Folsom spearpoints that are some of the earliest signs of mankind in America (Agogino, 1971; Hewett, 1971).

Whereas Negro minstrels are a creation of German-born Gottlieb Graupner (who later organized the Boston Philharmonic) and were popularized by white comedian Thomas D. Rice, Negro spirituals, the blues, and jazz music are black cultural contributions to modern society. Such musicians as W. C. Handy, James Bland, Lionel Hampton, Louis Armstrong, Hubie Blake, and many present-day black entertainers have indirectly affected border life. Negro participation in athletics, restricted by segregation for many decades, is now a dominant part of spectator sports in America, but is not strictly a border phenomenon. However, the successful Texas Ashworths (Muir, 1950) and the spicy account of Lord Beresford and his black Lady Flo (Porter, 1970) represent unusual border situations. The successful fight against the white primary by Dr. Lawrence Nixon of El Paso (Bryson, 1974)—like the careers of early symbols of black politicization, such as Paul Robeson, and modern-day black martyrs, such as Medgar Evers and Martin Luther King—leaves the political history of our country richer for its contribution. Inasmuch as many bibliographies and summaries of contemporary materials relevant to black studies are available, these have not been included in this brief, selective overview of blacks in the Borderlands, but some unpublished dissertations and theses relating to the topic can be found in the bibliography.

Because there is a need to show the scope of contributions to border life from ethnic and racial groups other than Anglo and Mexican Americans, the following short summaries, based on limited materials and expertise, have been included to provide the curious reader or researcher a point of departure for future investigation.

57

Oriental and Other Minorities

Chinese

More than the small number of Chinese immigrants to the United States would imply, the policy decisions made by this country in reaction to their immigration are very important to the overall problems of the contemporary U.S.-Mexican Borderlands. Chinese immigration came in three distinct waves: the first with the 1849 California gold rush and the lure of mining; the second with the recruitment of Chinese to work on the transcontinental railroads, beginning

ELLWYN R. STODDARD
Department of Sociology and Anthropology
University of Texas, El Paso

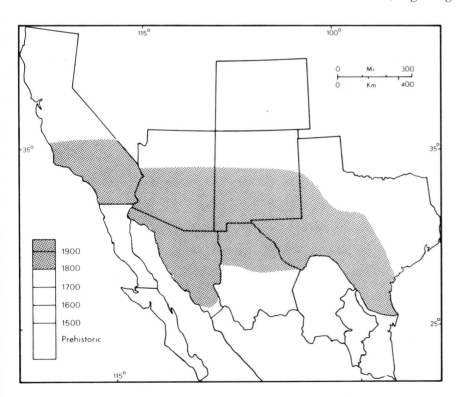

about 1864; and the third following President Roosevelt's lifting of the Chinese exclusion laws in 1943. (The last wave had very little impact on border affairs.)

Canton, in southern China, furnished most of the early 25,000 immigrants who came between 1849 and 1851 to find California's rumored "Mountain of Gold." During the 1850s an estimated 50,000 Chinese were recruited and came to the United States, but many of them returned to China. Of those remaining the unskilled laborer class were referred to as *ku* ("bitter") *li* ("strength"), or "physical workers." They came to be called coolies by Americans, and no other immigrant minority has suffered as much from racial hatred as those Chinese (Lee, 1960; Sung, 1967).

In 1864, as the Central Pacific Railroad owners sought workers to commence the hard road through the Rocky Mountains, they experimented with a few Chinese and found them to be hard and very reliable workers. Before long the bulk of their workers were Chinese, to the chagrin of Mexican and Irish laborers. The histories of the transcontinental railroad and the part played by Chinese workers in completing it range from a conservative account (Dowdell and Dowdell, 1972) to a moderate one (Chu and Chu, 1967) to a highly critical account of deprivation and horror (Saxton, 1966). After the transcontinental line was completed in 1869, many Chinese workers returned to their native country. Those remaining were either hired by other railroads (Union Pacific, Northern Pacific, or, later on, Houston and Texas Central) or driven eastward by persecution and lack of opportunities. The heaviest Chinese concentration in the United States remained in the San Francisco Bay area, and, since 1900, 50 percent or more of the Chinese in the U.S. have always been located in California (Lewis, 1938; Barth, 1964). Following the Emancipation Proclamation, southern owners considered a plan to import Chinese as competition for the newly freed Negroes, but it was never finalized (Peabody, 1967).

The Chinese impact on the Borderlands was chiefly from 1880 until the 1930s depression. By 1881 the Southern Pacific line from California to El Paso had been completed, and 137 Chinese were residents of El Paso's South Side. The population there did not seem to grow, though there was a constant turnover as illegal immigrants (including oriental females "mail-ordered" from China) arrived and others left for other cities. Opium dens, gambling, and a much-feared Tong Society existed along with the hard work of operating thirteen of the fifteen hand laundries in town and three of the twelve restaurants in that border city. Nationwide sentiment against the "Yellow Peril" had brought formal legislation against further Chinese immigration. Those laws included the Chinese Exclusion Act of 1882, the Geary Act of 1892, the extension of 1902, and the 1924 quota immigration law. The last annually allowed 105 persons of Chinese ancestry legally to enter the United States while prohibiting them from citizenship. Locally, the city of El Paso passed three antiopium ordinances between 1882 and 1886, and the state of Texas passed a law forbidding aliens not eligible for citizenship from owning land outside incorporated urban areas (which kept the increasing number of Chinese in East and South Texas from competing in agriculture). At the end of the century there were still only about 700 Chinese in El Paso, but many had entered illegally from Mexico as older residents of the ethnic enclave moved to other cities. Secret maze ways and passages held illegals—some reportedly were brought into the country through a tunnel under the Rio Grande—and constant raids and harassment made life difficult for this small, almost exclusively male population (Chu and Chu, 1967; Farrar, 1970, 1972). The antagonism reflected the national reactions toward nonwhite peoples in that period, as summarized by Oscar Handlin (1957:36): "By the end of the century the pattern of racist practices and ideas seemed fully developed: the orientals were to be totally excluded; the Negroes were to live in segregated enclaves; the Indians were to be confined to reservations as permanent wards of the nation; and all Whites were to assimilate as rapidly as possible to a common standard."

In Mexico the 30,000 Chinese who emigrated there found an even more brutal reception, as they were driven from their homes during the Revolution of 1910 and were massacred in great numbers in 1911 (Cumberland, 1960b). Some of those fleeing for their lives eased through the northern borders to safety. In 1917, General Pershing returned from Mexico with 527 Chinese who had been servicing his troops. By special legislation they were allowed to come to San Antonio (under the supervision of the Department of the Army) and to remain until 1921. Many of them remained and became the core of the most numerous Chinese concentration in Texas (Nims, 1941; Briscoe, 1947, 1959; Rhoads, 1977). In El Paso illegal Chinese immigration had waned. Between 1930 and 1940 its Chinatown died out, as the old bachelors from the earlier era passed away, leaving only a few families and their descendants scattered throughout the community.

In 1943, President Roosevelt signed a decree allowing increased Chinese immigration and citizenship privileges in return for Chinese military support against the Japanese, then our common enemy. Until then there had not been more than 1,000 Texas Chinese at any one time. In 1970, however, there were 435,000 Chinese in the United States, of whom more than half were in California, especially in the San Francisco Bay region, and 7,635 were in Texas, principally in Houston and San Antonio.

Japanese

Members of this minority are classified by generation. Thus an Issei is a Japanese born in Japan who immigrates to the United States, a Nisei is born in the United States of Issei parentage, and a Sansei is born in the United States of native-born parents of Japanese ancestry. A Kibei is a Japanese born in the United States and raised in Japan who has returned to the United States.

Western Japanese immigration was restricted by Japan itself, because it feared that its citizens' desire to leave would lower its prestige among the nations of the world. The earliest Japanese migrations came decades after the first wave of

Chinese, beginning in 1868 with 180 agricultural contract laborers coming to Hawaii. In 1880 only 148 Japanese lived on the U.S. mainland; only 2,000 were here a decade later. By 1900, with Hawaiian Japanese migrating to the continental United States, the total population had reached more than 24,000. In 1910 the Japanese population was 72,157, many of whom came from Japan itself.

Japanese were subjected to the Yellow Peril fears that were directed against all orientals, but they did not establish themselves economically as early as the Chinese and were less of a threat. As a result of the 1907 "Gentlemen's Agreement" no additional Japanese were allowed to enter the United States except for "pictures brides" for those already here. Even that practice terminated in 1924, when quota immigration brought total exclusion of Japanese (Ichihashi, 1969).

Because of the World War II hostilities with Japan, the Japanese population in the United States suffered many indignities, including forced internment, which abrogated many constitutional rights (Kitagawa, 1967; ten Brock et al., 1968; Spicer et al., 1969). Nevertheless, the 442nd Combat Infantry Regiment—the Hawaiian Nisei military unit—was one of the most decorated units in World War II while fighting in Europe (Bosworth, 1967). One researcher has found that, despite the economic losses resulting from the illegal deportation to internment camps, and despite the racism directed toward oriental features and language, the Japanese were able to rise rapidly in socioeconomic standing compared to Mexican Americans, because of late marriage, small families, and concentration on middle-class and English-language skills (Uhlenberg, 1972).

Many Japanese war brides of military personnel now reside in border locations, such as Fort Bliss at El Paso—a fairly recent phenomenon. Other small clusters of Japanese came to border towns upon release from their World War II camps.

Koreans

There are more Koreans in the United States than in any other country except Korea, China, Japan, and the Soviet Union. Korean immigration to the United States began with a few students coming to Hawaii in 1900. By 1905 about 7,200 persons had emigrated there. This immigration was stopped by the Korean government, and subsequent Korean immigration to the United States was categorized as Chinese (H. Kim, 1974). The arrival of Korean war brides following the 1950s American military action in the Far East has been this immigrant group's major impact on the Borderlands. Even later than the formation of the Filipino-American Association in El Paso (1971) came the Korean Association of 1974 (C. Kim, 1974), which is a visible minority heavily identified with the Fort Bliss installation.

Jews

Historically Jewish migration from the Old World to the New World occurred in three general waves. The first wave arrived after the Spanish Inquisition during the last half of the fifteenth century, when they were expelled from Portugal and Spain. The second immigration wave came from Germany and Eastern European countries following the defeat of Napoleon in the middle of the nineteenth century. The third arrived later in the century as a result of the Russian tsar's attempts to crush the impending revolution (Friendman, 1943; Schappes, 1958; Janowsky, 1964). The wave of WW II refugees from the holocaust added numbers, but did not appreciably affect the Jewish pattern of settlement throughout this country.

In the American colonies under English rule (1690), Jews were allowed to hold religious services and to engage in retail trade, activities forbidden them in Europe. They were few in number—less than three thousand at the time of the first U.S. census (1790), and they were heavily concentrated at eastern ports of entry. From 1830 to 1850 their numbers increased from about six thousand to more than fifty thousand as economic and political conditions in Germany and Austria-Hungary drove them elsewhere. Because they had been forbidden to enter trades, many had become expert in the secondhand garment business and in the limited manufacture of new garments. As they came to America, they became peddlers of goods, providing freighting services to expanding western and southwestern areas.

Unlike most other immigration groups Jews came from varied language areas (Spanish, Portuguese, German, Yiddish, Russian, and so on), sharing only the sacred Hebrew language, which was unacceptable as a common vernacular (Learsi, 1954). Thus a few Jews built their businesses around their peddler trades, serving an expanding system of army forts, California gold miners, Arizona miners, and others (Wilson, 1967). A few were found in most of the expanding western communities. For example, in 1850 only 8 Jews were in Los Angeles, and a decade later there were only 100 (Karp, 1976). In 1880 the conditions in Europe and Russia were forcing massive numbers to flee for their lives: 200,000 emigrated from Eastern Europe between 1880 and 1890, and another 200,000 had come by the turn of the century. Only a few came west and settled in the developing areas (mostly those from Western Europe who accompanied German-speaking settlers). As the termination of the Mexican War interrupted commerce with Old Mexico, the void was filled by Jewish peddlers and trade merchants, where no entrenched establishment barred their way, as had been the case in Europe. The careers of businessmen such as the Speigelbergs (Santa Fe bankers), Ernst Kohlberg (El Paso cigar manufacturer and border trader), Herman Ehrenberg and Michael Goldwasser (whose Arizona company eventually became that of the Goldwater brothers in freighting and retail trade), Levi Strauss (who was the pants maker for the California gold miners), and the Schwartz family (successful in dry goods in El Paso) are among the Jewish success stories associated with the Southwest and border areas (Fierman, 1964, 1980; Wilson, 1967; Yaffee, 1968; Levinson, 1968; Kohlbert, 1973). Although they were late arrivals to the area and few in number, the Jews made an enormous impact on the region's economic and political life.

Syrian-Lebanese

In the late 1880s refugees from Lebanon (then a part of Syria) who could not abide the harsh Turkish rule came to America and settled in cities, such as Chicago (Wakin, 1974), and in Texas (Institute of Texas Cultures, 1974). A few came to El Paso and began small trade-goods businesses on pushcarts and wagons (Malooly, 1953). Because of the 1924 immigration quotas some of their relatives waited in Mexico for nearly ten years to enter the United States. Today the third generation of Syrian-Lebanese in El Paso includes some of the most important border importers, trade-goods merchants, and clothing manufacturers found in the border region. Such names as Farah slacks, Azar nuts, Malooly furniture, and Ayoub merchandisers show their business leadership. They have also been leaders in the creation of informal social links with their Mexican counterparts, producing one of the largest and most effective systems of informal cooperation across the entire U.S.-Mexican border. Future models for local cross-national planning and private-sector cooperation would be well based on the Syrian-Lebanese examples.

Western Europeans

Sometimes, by focusing on the more visible ethnic and racial minorities of the Southwest, the kaleidoscope of ethnic, racial, and national minorities usually subsumed in the Anglo-American category is overlooked. The Molokan Russian immigrants of the Los Angeles region (Young, 1932), the French in California and Sonora (Wyllus, 1932; Nasatir, 1945), the German communities of Texas (Jordan, 1966, 1969) and California (Raup, 1932a), the Boer colonization in the Southwest (Maluy, 1977), Czechoslovakian immigrants to the region (Maresh, 1946), the oldest polish settlements in America located in Texas (Baker, 1978), and many more examples illustrate the complex ethnic-racial-cultural-language mosaic in the U.S.-Mexican Borderlands region. Although the non-Spanish surname is lumped into the Anglo classification in the Southwest, this generalization should not cause one to overlook the diverse European historical and ideological identities that are contained in cultural islands within the region.

PART THREE. BORDERLANDS INFORMATION RESOURCES

There is a rich but largely untapped body of resources in Mexico for the study of the American Borderlands. It is the purpose of this study to describe archival and published materials and to suggest some aids which may be of use to scholars in the United States. Many of these resources may be profitably used by historians, economists, anthropologists, political scientists, ethnologists, sociologists, and others.

A few words are in order for those uninitiated in the use of Mexican materials. It is indispensable to establish a good rapport with personnel working in the archives. There is often an incomplete catalog or description of a particular run of materials, and you will have to depend on their often intimate knowledge of their holdings. All researchers should take care to learn and follow the rules and regulations of the archive being used; failure to do so may result in the denial of access to materials. Take nothing in or out of the archive except your own papers, pens, and pencils unless you have secured prior permission to bring in other equipment, such as a typewriter. Photocopying facilities are not always

58

Mexican Resources

LAWRENCE A. CARDOSO
Department of History
University of Wyoming

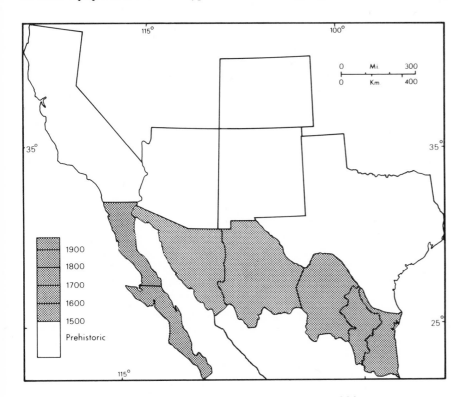

available; when they are, you will find them to be generally expensive and time-consuming. It is helpful to carry a letter of accreditation from your school or research center as well as a U.S. passport for purposes of identification. Archival personnel may want to keep your passport while you are working with their documents. Be extremely careful not to mark or otherwise mutilate materials allowed for your use.

The above advice does not imply that American researchers can expect to do their work in an atmosphere of confrontation. Rather, it is a plea for willingness to understand Mexico and to work within the limits imposed by Mexicans to protect one of their national resources. My experience during the course of several research trips to the archives mentioned below has proven that friendly and eager assistance usually is preferred visiting scholars. Two practical guides which provide more detailed information for the visitor to Mexico are Greenleaf and Meyer (1973) and Blair (1969).

General Guides

There are four general guides to Mexican archives which should be consulted. Herbert E. Bolton's *Guide to Materials for the History of the United States in the Principal Archives of Mexico* (1913) may still be used with profit. Bolton provides detailed calendars of historical manuscripts available in local, state, and national collections. Published in 1913, however, it is not always accurate because of the many documents which have been moved or lost in the past 65 years. The best general guides are the more recent *Archivalia mexicana* by Manuel Carrera Stampa (1952) and Lino Gómez Canedo's *Los archivos de la historia de America* (1961). Both of these works stress materials which pertain to the colonial period (pre-1821) but also contain information on nineteenth-century holdings. As with Bolton, Gómez Canedo and Carrera Stampa deal with local and state archives, both being areas largely ignored by bibliophiles, archivists, and scholars. Beers (1979) is another general guide not to be overlooked for its comprehensive survey of archival materials.

El Archivo Histórico de la Secretaría de Relaciones Exteriores

The Historical Archive of the Secretary of Foreign Relations (AHSRE) is located at Plaza de Tres Culturas in Tlatelolco, in the northern part of Mexico City. Countless millions of documents are the products generated in the United States by a bureaucracy consisting of more than fifty consuls, the office of the Mexican Ambassador, and many special diplomatic and commercial agents. This repository is the richest Mexican source for materials for the study of the Borderlands.

A wide variety of subjects interested the secretary of foreign relations and his employees. Since Mexican law grants citizenship by virtue of the nationality of one's parents as well as place of birth, Mexicans and their American-born children

were viewed as proper causes of concern for the government and its agents. Real and potential difficulties with law enforcement agencies received close scrutiny, with an eye to thwarting encounters with police and court officials. On many occasions diplomatic intervention through the Mexican ambassador in Washington took place when it was believed there had been denial of due process. There are reports regarding investigations and protests during strikes, the draft crises of World War I, the organization of labor unions, and affiliation with radical groups. A report sent by Consul General Teódulo Beltrán in May, 1918, to Secretary of Foreign Relations Cándido Aguilar typifies the kinds of information in AHSRE documents. Beltrán received complaints from field workers in the Spreckles Sugar Company's California sugarbeet fields that working conditions were horrendous, with open-ended hours, irregular pay, poor food, unfit housing, and armed police in the camps to ensure submission to company dictates. The Mexican workers looked to Beltrán for assistance because of the earlier failure of the radical Industrial Workers of the World to organize Spreckles employees. Beltrán filed formal complaints with competent state and federal agencies, and then he began negotiations with the company for better working conditions. Management personnel of Spreckles, faced with a barrage of bad publicity and threatened with the loss of sorely needed Mexican workers because of the wartime labor crisis, signed a new contract on May 25, 1918, and promised to terminate immediately their unfair practices (Beltrán to Aguilar, May 25, 1918, AHSRE, 241 [72:73]/13-14-22).

Other documents from the twentieth century deal with the welfare of expatriates and their families. Consuls frequently sought aid from American public and private charity groups, or from the Mexican government-sponsored Blue Cross and Honorific Commission self-help mutual aid societies. After the onset of the Great Depression in 1929, our sources show that consuls made herculean efforts by seeking money for railroad fares from former employers, trying to arrange employment for those who wished to stay in the United States, and coaxing money from private sources in both nations to aid the destitute. A large number of materials from the nineteenth century, dating back to the 1820s, detail Mexican efforts to control increasing American incursions into the Borderlands.

There are several catalogs and indexes to help locate materials in the seven collections described below. There is a name index to find reports by individual consuls and other government agents as well as the thousands of immigrants and their children who contacted them. A geographic index is invaluable for obtaining materials which relate to a specific city or state. A chronological guide gives the decimal numbers from documents according to the date they were written. Note that items beyond 1940 are generally not open to researchers without special permission. Ulloa (1963) provides a thorough guide to the 259 volumes which make up the set entitled Ramo de la Revolución Mexicana. The Bolton calendar, although largely useless for the specific location of nineteenth-century materials, gives a detailed look for archival holdings from independence to the outbreak of the Revolution of 1910.

Seven major collections out of a total of 32 deal extensively with the Borderlands:

1. Ramo de la Revolución Mexicana. This set contains much information on the history of events along the United States-Mexico border during the first decade of the Revolution. There are reports from consuls and special political agents describing the activities and attitudes of exiles and their allies, the enforcement of U.S. neutrality laws, smuggling, and causes of emigration. The Ulloa (1963) guide makes this collection the easiest one in the archive to use.

2. Ramo Flores Magón. This massive set of documents details the activities of the three Flores Magón brothers in the United States and Mexico from about 1904 to the 1920s. Before the onset of the Revolution they spent much of their time in exile attempting to bring upheavals in Mexico against the dictatorship of Porfirio Díaz. There is much information regarding their campaign to gain funding and political support from other Mexican immigrants and to mount their abortive invasion of 1911.

3. Legajos de Numeración Corrida. Decimal file number 241 in this series is the richest single source of documentation for the area which concerns us here. All consular and other reports relating to emigration, repatriation, labor, strife, and citizen welfare are to be found here. The number of folders is so massive that they can be used effectively only in conjunction with the indexes discussed above. If any matter touched on the Mexican or Chicano population in the United States and came to the attention of the secretary's employees, there is sure to be documentation of the events in file 241.

4. Recortes de Periódicos. This collection has more than five hundred boxes of newspaper clippings, many of them remitted by agents in the Borderlands. This source offers a central and easy-to-use collection of news items from many regions of the United States where matters pertaining to Mexicans and Mexico were discussed in the press.

5. Servicios Culturales de la Secretaría de Relaciones Exteriores. More than one hundred boxes of documents in this collection detail the efforts of the Mexican government to reach out to its expatriated citizens through the use of cultural and patriotic devices. There is information regarding the prospects and problems in establishing libraries and other information centers as well as celebrating national holidays such as the sixteenth of September (Independence Day) and the Fifth of May (the date of the Mexican victory over the invading French army at Puebla in 1862).

6. Comercio Exterior de México. This set of 33 boxes contains information on the Mexican government's efforts to foment export trade to the United States. There is correspondence with members of the foreign business community and reports on the economic vitality of many local markets for Mexican goods.

7. Reclamaciones Generales y Especiales. This is the general title of three groups of claims and counterclaims by the Mexican and U.S. governments for alleged damage to public and private property and the loss of lives of their nationals.

The almost two thousand boxes of materials detail minutely the havoc so common at times along the mutual border of the two countries.

El Archivo General de la Nación (AGN)

This rich repository at Calzada Tacuba 8 in downtown Mexico City has holdings of 170 *ramos.* In addition to Bolton, there are three publications which are of special value for locating its materials: Rubio Mañé (1940), Chávez Orozco (1953), and the ongoing *Boletín del Archivo General de la Nación* (second series, 1929-). The last has detailed indexes to some of the collections. There are also some unpublished guides. Although not always complete, these finding aids yield valuable information on Spanish and Mexican efforts to settle and secure the Borderlands. Two examples are the Californias and Provincias Internas collections, totalling 355 volumes, used so effectively by Bobb (1962). The other 45 *ramos* of the colonial and early national period, with such titles as Misiones, Archivo de Guerra, and Inquisición, have obvious potential for various phases of Borderlands studies.

There are also strong holdings for the twentieth century. By law, the AGN receives all presidential papers and documents from federal agencies. These collections begin with administrations of the latter part of the nineteenth century but are strongest in the post-1910 period. Chief executives often took a keen interest in diplomatic relations with the United States, Mexican expatriates, rebels—real and potential—in the Southwest, border-zone development, and similar matters, and the documentation for presidential initiatives and concerns may be found in their papers. There are also thousands of letters from Mexican emigrants praising or complaining about their conditions in the United States.

The papers of Lázaro Cárdenas, amounting to over nine hundred thick packets, illuminate the types of materials found in the AGN. Cárdenas began a campaign in the late 1930s to repatriate from Texas thousands of workers and their families to new agrarian colonies in the state of Tamaulipas. In order to apprise himself of the magnitude of the project, Cárdenas sent his Under Secretary of Foreign Relations Ramón Beteta and special agent Jesús M. González to Texas on fact-finding missions. The reports submitted (in file number 503.11/3 of Cárdenas's papers) show there were severely limited employment opportunities for those in the expatriate community. More often than not, available jobs were given to white citizens at the expense of Mexicans. Federal and state welfare and employment programs openly discriminated against the immigrants. One major obstacle to repatriation was the accelerating Americanization of youngsters in Texas, Beteta and González reported. Despite all the roadblocks put before them in the United States, many did not look to Mexico as their native land. Familiarity with English and new ways of dressing, living, and eating had convinced many that whatever the future held for them, it would be found in their new homeland. Thus, we see here materials for race relations, employment patterns, governmental policies toward minorities, and trends in assimilation. These few examples could be multiplied many times over in the AGN's other twentieth-century holdings.

Hemeroteca Nacional de México

This is the central repository for newspapers and serials. This valuable archive holds about 200,000 volumes of materials and has complete runs of many periodicals of the nineteenth century and, especially, those of the twentieth century, although there are many holdings from the pre-1821 period. There are many state and provincial publications, particularly from the northern region, which give extensive day-by-day coverage of the border area.

Two major finding aids facilitate research in the Hemeroteca. Located in the National Library, just south of University City, there is a good alphabetical catalog of current holdings. Stanley Ross et al. (1965-67) provide subject citations to newspaper materials for the twentieth century. This latter tool is invaluable, as one no longer has to survey long runs of unindexed newspapers to locate pertinent sources.

Centro de Estudios de la Historia de México

This archive, at Avenida Poniente 140, number 739, Mexico City, is run by Condumex, a subsidiary of the Anaconda Copper Company, and is open to the general public. It is without a doubt the best-organized and -managed collection of those discussed here. It has two collections of note: the Luis G. Cuevas papers, containing documents relating to the U.S.-Mexican War, and the papers of Venustiano Carranza, consisting mostly of incoming correspondence, which supplement those found in the AGN. A brief guide to these and others in the Condumex collection is the company's *Centro de Estudios de la Historia de México* (Condumex, 1969).

State and Local Resources

We lack systematic cataloging and care of local and state archival materials in Mexico. Often money and personnel do not exist to care for these repositories. Acts of God, revolutionary damage, and financial exigencies have resulted in conditions which may only be described as disgraceful. One historian found a large number of colonial manuscripts stored under a bandstand in one state capital; one collection I tried to see in 1972 had been sold to a trash collector and converted into cardboard boxes.

Nevertheless, northern state repositories do have materials relating to the binational, bicultural area. With a great deal of diligence and patience, one will surely root out some information which is of value. The monograph of C. Alan Hutchinson (1969) is an excellent example of what one can do with extant state materials. The best guide to date is that of Bailey and Beezley (1975) for the state of Coahuila. This research aid is quite strong for the twentieth century and describes all

major civil and ecclesiastical archives open to the public in Saltillo. It is hoped that the efforts of Bailey and Beezley will spur others to emulation. In addition to the more general aids discussed above, other guides for some northern areas include Cavazos Garza (1952) on Nuevo León, García Martínez and Lira González (1968) on Querétaro, and de la Mora and González Navarro (1951) on Jalisco, all part of the distinguished series "La historia y sus instrumentos" published in *Historia Mexicana*.

Published Materials

In addition to the manuscript sources there are many publications which touch in part or whole on the Borderlands. It would be futile in the space available here to do more than point out some readily accessible finding aids to printed books and articles. The basic bibliography is the *Handbook of Latin American Studies* (1936-), a yearly, interdisciplinary publication. Scholarly journals which provide a more current inventory include *Inter-American Economic Affairs* (1946-), *Inter-American Review of Bibliography* (1951-), *Journal of Inter-American Studies and World Affairs* (1958-), *Hispanic American Historical Review* (1918-), *Latin American Research Review* (1965-), *Historia Mexicana* (1952-), and *El Trimestre Económico* (1933-). More specialized bibliographies include González y González et al. (1961-68) and Cumberland (1960a). Special note should be made of two major documentary collections which, despite their titles, contain a wealth of information on the Borderlands: Isidro and Josefina Fabela (1964-73) and González Ramírez (1954-56).

Nor should one overlook Mexican governmental publications. The Kerr (1940) guide is useful but dated and not always complete. Ongoing publications which have some materials on the Borderlands include the yearly reports *(Memorias)* of various federal departments, the congressional record *(Diario de los debates),* and state and national *Diarios Oficiales*. The last are comparable to the U.S. *Federal Register,* with its statements of laws, regulations, and public policy.

Conclusion

This article has described only the major collections of manuscript and published materials in Mexico which are of use in the examination of Borderland topics. The guides and bibliographies mentioned will lead the reader to other, more minor, collections. Far from being secondary or tertiary to the study of the Southwest, Mexican materials can—and should—be used with more profit than has been the case hitherto. If we accept the premise that the Borderlands have been and still are a binational, bicultural area, then we may say that students of the area have been seriously remiss in ignoring or underemploying materials from the Mexican component of the equation. The riches of these collections await the interested scholar. Our understanding of the area will be greatly enhanced through their use.

Other important sources of information are atlases and various types of maps. There is no atlas that covers only the Borderlands, or even the American Southwest, but rather a number for the various states. Recommended state atlases are those by Robert W. Durrenberger, *Patterns on the Land: Geographical, Historical and Political Maps of California;* Warren A. Beck and Ynez D. Haase, *Historical Atlas of California;* Henry P. Walker and Don Bufkin, *Historical Atlas of Arizona;* Warren A. Beck and Ynez D. Haase, *Historical Atlas of New Mexico;* Stanley A. Arbingast and Lorrin Kennamer, *Atlas of Texas;* and Bureau of Economic Geology, University of Texas at Austin, *Environmental Geologic Atlas of the Texas Coastal Zone.* Bibliographies and lists of maps that should be consulted are Edward L. Chapin, Jr., *A Selected Bibliography of Southern California Maps;* California State Planning Board, *Surveys and Maps in California;* Jay W. Sharp, "A Collection of Printed Maps of Texas, 1835-1951, in the Eugene C. Barker Texas History Center," *Southwestern Historical Quarterly;* and Jay W. Sharp, "The Maps of the Stephen F. Austin Collection in the Eugene C. Barker Texas

59

Maps, Aerial Photography, and Imagery

ALVAR W. CARLSON
Department of Geography
Bowling Green State University

History Center," *Southwestern Historical Quarterly.* A noteworthy atlas on a special topic is *An Atlas of Some Plant Distributions in the Sonoran Desert* by James Rodney Hastings et al. The U.S. Soil Conservation Service, in cooperation with the different state agricultural experiment stations, has issued many reports with maps. The U.S. Geological Survey has published detailed listings, *Geological and Water-Supply Reports and Maps,* available for each of the states.

The Geological Survey also has published a series of topographic maps at different scales which are available to the public. All of the Borderlands states are covered by maps of 1:250,000 scale. According to the recent indexes (1976 and 1977), each state is mostly covered by the topographic quadrangle maps published in the 7½-minute (1:24,000) or 15-minute (1:62,500) series. Only California is completely covered in this series, while the other states have small areas, usually very sparsely settled, which have not been mapped. Indexes to the various topographic maps and order forms are available from the Branch of Distribution, U.S. Geological Survey, Box 25286 Federal Center, Denver, Colorado 80225. The indexes also list many special maps such as those on the Grand Canyon National Park and the Glen Canyon Recreation Area and the dealers within each state who sell these and the topographic maps.

Two recommended atlases that include considerable information on the Mexican Borderlands are Stanley A. Arbingast et al., *Atlas of Mexico,* and Jorge L. Tamayo, *Atlas geográfico general de México.* Other references with maps that pertain to northern Mexico are provided in the bibliography (Hoy, 1942; Merrill, 1906; Raisz, 1961; and Tamayo, 1949, 1962*b*).

The Mexican government has inaugurated an ambitious project to map the country. By 1978, climatic (1:500,000) and aeronautical maps (1:250,000) were completed for all of northern Mexico. Although topographical maps at a scale of 1:250,000 are not available, about one-half of the Mexican Borderlands are covered by topographic maps at a scale of 1:50,000, particularly large portions of Coahuila, Chihuahua, Sonora, and Baja California Norte. Much of the remaining area is provisionally mapped. In addition, geologic maps are available on nearly all of Baja California Norte, southeastern Chihuahua, and the central portions of Coahuila and Nuevo León. Except for Baja California Norte, these areas are also covered by a series of maps on soils, land use, and potential land use, all at a scale of 1:50,000. Other topics will also be mapped in the future. To obtain an index of available maps, send requests to Dirección General de Estudios del Territorio Nacional, Departamento de Agencias, San Antonio Abad 124, México 8, D.F.

Aerial photography is another important source of information on the physical environment, land use, and settlement patterns of the Borderlands. Recommended publications which include aerial photos of the American Borderlands are *The Look of Our Land: An Airphoto Atlas of the Rural United States* (volumes entitled *The Far West, The Mountains and Deserts,* and *The Plains and Prairies)* by the U.S. Department of Agriculture, Economic Research Service; and *Land Use and Its Patterns in the United States,* by F. J. Marschner.

Current indices and order forms for aerial photography at different scales are available from the U.S. Department of Agriculture, Agricultural Stabilization and Conservation Service, Aerial Photography Field Office, 2222 West, 2300 South, P.O. Box 30010, Salt Lake City, Utah 84125. Local ASCS offices often have photo indices and mosaics for their counties and can offer assistance. The National Archives Cartographic Branch, Washington, D.C., has dated aerial photography, such as the upper Rio Grande project's photography of northern New Mexico in the 1930s. Aerial photography taken in the 1970s, and at varying scales, is also available for all of the Mexican Borderlands. For an index *(avance),* write to the aforementioned Dirección General de Estudios del Territorio Nacional.

In recent years much information has been obtained on the Borderlands from Landsat photography. It has become particularly important in making land-cover inventories. Arizona and Texas have ongoing projects using Landsat images in planning and managing natural resources (Arizona, ARETS, 1971). The satellites, even from 570 miles high, can obtain excellent remote-sensing imagery (color infrared photography) because of the region's relatively little cloud cover. High-altitude imagery has also resulted from the National Aeronautics and Space Administration's use of U-2 and RB-57 aircraft. Recommended publications on high-altitude photography of the American Borderlands are *Applied Remote Sensing of Earth Resources in Arizona;* Leonard W. Bowden, "Remote Sensing of the World's Arid Lands," *Photo-Atlas of the United States* (1973*a*); and Norman J. W. Thrower, "Land Use in the Southwestern United States, from Gemini and Apollo Imagery" (Thrower et al., 1970). Satellite imagery on the American Borderlands from 1972 to the present is available at different scales from the aforementioned U.S. Department of Agriculture, ASCS, Aerial Photography Field Office. Another source is the Geological Survey, EROS Data Center, Mundt Federal Building, Sioux Falls, South Dakota 57198. NASA photographs (1:62,500) of the United States-Mexico boundary line between El Paso, Texas, and the Pacific Ocean, dated July, 1977, are available from the International Boundary and Water Commission, 200 IBWC Building, 4110 Rio Bravo, El Paso, Texas 79902. This agency has also made 1:20,000 photo mosaics of 1972 and 1974 aerial photographs covering the boundary line from El Paso to the Gulf of Mexico. These mosaics are published in three volumes of *International Boundary between the United States and Mexico in the Rio Grande and Colorado River Delineated in Accordance with the Treaty of November 23, 1970,* which are available from NCIC, Western Division, Stop 504, Box 25046, Federal Center, Denver, Colorado 80225.

There is also much Landsat coverage of the Mexican Borderlands. It is available from the aforementioned EROS Data Center, ASCS Aerial Photography Field Office, and Dirección General de Estudios del Territorio Nacional. Another source is the World Bank, Cartography Section, Room N-619, 1818 H Street, N.W., Washington, D.C. 20433. Its index of coverage has been published and titled *Landsat Index Atlas of the Developing Countries of the World.*

BIBLIOGRAPHY

This composite reference bibliography has been organized to give maximum utility with minimum duplication. It comprises three sections: I, Books, Articles, and Cited Dissertations and Theses; II, Unauthored Public Documents and Miscellaneous Resource Materials; and III, A Topical List of Dissertations and Theses.

Abel, Annie Heloise
1915   Editor. *The Official Correspondence of James S. Calhoun, While Agent at Santa Fe and Superintendent of Indian Affairs in New Mexico.* Washington, D.C.: Government Printing Office.

1916   Editor. The Journal of John Greiner. *Old Santa Fe* 3 (no. 11):189-243.

1941   Indian Affairs in New Mexico Under the Administration of William Curr Lane. *New Mexico Historical Review* 16 (nos. 2 and 3):206-32, 328-58.

Aberle, David F.
1966   *The Peyote Religion Among the Navaho.* Viking Fund Publications in Anthropology, no. 42. Chicago: Aldine Publishing Co.

1969   A Plan for Navajo Economic Development. In *Toward Economic Development for Native American Communities: A Compendium of Papers Submitted to the Subcommittee on Economy in Government, Joint Economic Committee, Congress of the United States,* pp. 223-76. 2 vols. Washington, D.C.: Government Printing Office.

Aberle, Sophie D.
1948   The Pueblo Indians of New Mexico: Their Land, Economy, and Civil Organization. *American Anthropologist* 50 (October):1-93.

Aberson, David
1975   Information Gathering Methods in Immigration and Naturalization Service Proceedings. *Chicano Law Review* 2 (Summer):51-65.

Abert, J. W.
1848   Report of J. W. Abert, of his Examination of New Mexico in the Years 1846-1847. H. Exec. Doc. 41, 30 Cong. 1st Sess. Reprinted in Albuquerque: Horn and Wallace, 1962.

Ablon, Joan
1963*a*   Relocated American Indians in the San Francisco Bay Area: Concepts of Acculturation, Success and Identity in the City. Ph.D. dissertation, University of Chicago.

1963*b*   Relocated American Indians in the San Francisco Bay Area: Social Interaction and Indian Identity. *Human Organization* 23 (no. 4):296-304.

Abril, Irene F.
1977   Mexican-American Folk Beliefs: How They Affect Health Care. *American Journal of Maternal Child Nursing* (May-June):168-73.

Section I.

Books, Articles, and Cited Dissertations and Theses

Acosta, Roberto
1949   *Apuntes históricos sonorenses: la conquista temporal y espiritual del Yaqui y del Mayo.* Mexico City: Imprenta Aldina.

Acuña, Rudolph F.
1970   Ignacio Pesqueira: Sonoran Caudillo. *Arizona and the West* 12 (Summer):139-74.
1972   *Occupied America: The Chicano's Struggle for Liberation.* San Francisco: Canfield Press.
1974   To the Editor. *Pacific Historical Review* 43 (February): 147-50.
1981   *Occupied America: A History of Chicanos.* New York: Harper.

Adair, John
1944   *The Navajo and Pueblo Silversmiths.* Norman: University of Oklahoma Press.

———, and Deuschle, Kurt W.
1970   *The People's Health; Medicine and Anthropology in a Navajo Community.* New York: Appleton-Century-Crofts.

———, and Leighton, Dorothea
1966   *People of the Middle Place: A Study of the Zuñi Indians.* New Haven: HRAF Press.

———, and Worth, Sol
1972   *Through Navajo Eyes: An Exploration in Film Communication and Anthropology.* Bloomington: Indiana University Press.

———, et al.
1957   Patterns of Health and Disease Among the Navahos. *Annals, American Academy of Political and Social Science* 311 (May):80-94.

Adams, Eleanor B.
1954   Editor. *Bishop Tamaron's Visitation of New Mexico, 1760.* Albuquerque: Historical Society of New Mexico.
1960   Viva el rey! *New Mexico Historical Review* 35 (October):284-92.
1963   Fray Silvestre and the Obstinate Hopi. *New Mexico Historical Review* 38 (April):97-138.

———, and Chávez, Angélico
1956   *The Missions of New Mexico, 1776, by Fray Francisco Atanasio Domínguez.* Albuquerque: University of New Mexico Press.

Adams, Gyorgy
1972   Some Implications and Concomitants of Worldwide Sourcing. *Acta Oeconómica* 8 (nos. 2 and 3):309-23.
1973   Economic Life: International Corporations in the Early Seventies. *New Hungarian Quarterly* 14 (Spring):207-19.

Adams, Morton S.; Brown, Kenneth S.; Iba, Barbara Y.; and Niswander, Jerry D.
1970   Health of Pápago Indian Children. *Public Health Reports* 85:1047-61.

Adams, R. E. W.
1977   Compiler. *The Archeology and Ethnohistory of the Gateway Area: Middle Rio Grande of Texas. Final Report to National Endowment for the Humanities.* San Antonio: University of Texas at San Antonio.

———, et al.
1975   Archaeology and Ethnohistory of the Gateway Area, Middle Rio Grande of Texas. Report of the Investigations to the National Endowment for the Humanities by the University of Texas at San Antonio.
1976   The Archaeology and Ethnohistory of the Gateway Area, Middle Rio Grande of Texas. Report for the 1976 Investigations to the National Endowment for the Humanities by the University of Texas at San Antonio.

Adams, Robert H.
1974   *The Architecture and Art of Early Hispanic Colorado.* Boulder: Colorado Associated University Press.

Adams, William Y.
1963   *Shonto: A Study of the Role of the Trader in a Modern Navaho Community.* Washington, D.C.: Smithsonian Institution, Bureau of American Ethnology Bulletin no. 188. Government Printing Office.
1971   Navajo Ecology and Economy: A Problem in Cultural Values. In Keith H. Basso and Morris E. Opler, eds. *Apachean Culture and Ethnology,* pp. 77-81. Publications in Anthropology, no. 21. Tucson: University of Arizona Press.

———, and Krutz, Gordon
1971   Wage Labor and the San Carlos Apache. In Keith H. Basso and Morris E. Opler, eds. *Apachean Culture and Ethnology,* pp. 115-34. Publications in Anthropology, no. 21. Tucson: University of Arizona Press.

Agogino, George
1971   The McJunkin Controversy. *New Mexico Magazine* (May-June):41-43.

Aguilar Monteverde, Alfonso
1967   *Teoría y política de desarrollo latinamericano.* Mexico City: Universidad Autónoma de México.

Aguirre, Adalberto, and Fernández, Celestino
1976-77   Mexican Americans and Bicultural Education: A Sociological Analysis. *Atisbos: Journal of Chicano Research* 2 (Winter):15-26.

Aguirre Beltrán, Gonzalo
1944   The Slave Trade in Mexico. *Hispanic American Historical Review* 24 (August):412-31.
1946   *La población negra de México, 1519-1810: estudio etnohistórico.* Mexico City: n.p.

Ahlborn, Richard E.
1967   The Wooden Walls of Territorial New Mexico. *New Mexico Architecture* (September-October):20-23.
1968   *The Penitente Moradas of Abiquiu.* Contributions from the Museum of History and Technology, paper 63. Washington, D.C.: Smithsonian Institution.
1975   Spanish Art in the United States. In *Hispanic Influences in the United States.* New York: Interbook, Spanish Institute.

Ahnert, Frank
1960   The Influence of Pleistocene Climates upon the Morphology of Cuesta Scarps on the Colorado Plateau. *Annals, Association of American Geographers* 50 (June):139-56.

Aiken, C. Melvin
1978   The Far West. In J. D. Jennings, ed. *Ancient Native Americans,* pp. 131-82. San Francisco: W. H. Freeman & Co.

Alba Hernández, Francisco
1977a   *La población de México: evolución y dilemas.* Mexico City: El Colegio de México.
1977b   Condiciones y Políticas Económicas en la Frontera Norte de México. *Natural Resources Journal* 17 (October): 571-84.

Alcalá Quintero, Francisco
1969   Desarrollo regional fronterizo. *Comercio Exterior* 19 (November).

Alcalá Venceslada, A.
1951   *Vocabulario Andaluz.* Madrid: n.p.

Aldous, Joan, and Dahl, Nancy
1974   *International Bibliography of Research in Marriage and the Family, 1965-1972.* Minneapolis: University of Minnesota Press.

———, and Hill, Ruben
1967   *International Bibliography of Research in Marriage and the Family, 1900-1964.* Minneapolis: University of Minnesota Press.

Alessio Robles, Vito
1938   *Coahuila y Texas en la época colonial.* Mexico City: Editorial Cultura.

Alexander, R. K.
1970   *Archeological Excavations at Parida Cave, Val Verde County, Texas.* Austin: Texas Archaeological Salvage

Project, no. 19.

Alfaro, Richard J.
1970   *Diccionario de anglicismos.* Madrid: Gredos.

Alisky, Marvin
1963*a*   *State and Local Government in Sonora, Mexico.* Tempe: Arizona State University.
1963*b*   *Government of Arizona's Other Neighbor, Baja California.* Tempe: Arizona State University.
1965   *Mexico's Special Districts: Municipal Civic Betterment Boards.* Tempe: Arizona State University.
1970   *Mexico's Federal Betterment Boards: Financial Mainstays of Border Municipalities.* Tempe: Arizona State University.
1971*a*   *Government of the Mexican State of Nuevo Leon.* Tempe: Arizona State University.
1971*b*   *Guide to the Government of the Mexican State of Sonora.* Tempe: Arizona State University.
1973   U.S.-Mexican Border Conflicts and Compromises. *Southeastern Latin Americanist* 17 (September):1-5.

Allen, R. H.
1935   The Spanish Land-Grant System as an Influence in the Agricultural Development of California. *Agricultural History* 9 (July):127-42.

Allen, Terry D.
1974   Editor. *Arrows Four: Prose and Poetry by Young American Indians.* New York: Washington Square Press.

Almada, Francisco R.
1950   Los Apaches. *Sociedad Chihuahuense de Estudios Históricos Boletín* 2:5-15.
1955   *Resumen de historia del estado de Chihuahua.* Mexico City: Libros Mexicanos.
1964   *La revolución en el estado de Chihuahua.* 2 vols. Mexico City: Instituto Nacional de Estudios Históricos de la Revolución Mexicana.

Almaráz, Félix D., Jr.
1968   Governor Manuel de Salcedo of Hispanic Texas, 1808-1813: A Reappraisal. *Texana* 6 (Spring):12-31.
1971   *Tragic Cavalier: Governor Manuel Salcedo of Texas, 1808-1813.* Austin: University of Texas Press.
1973   Carlos Eduardo Castañeda, Mexican American Historian: The Formative Years, 1896-1927. *Pacific Historical Review* 42 (August):319-34.
1975-76 The Status of Borderlands Studies: History. *Social Science Journal* 12 (October) and 13 (January): 9-18.

Almond, Gabriel A., and Powell, G. Bingham, Jr.
1966   *Comparative Politics.* Boston: Little, Brown & Co.
1963   *The Civic Culture: Political Attitudes and Democracy in Five Nations.* Princeton: Princeton University Press.

Almonte, Juan N.
1924-25 Statistical Report on Texas [1835] translated by Carlos E. Castañeda. *Southwestern Historical Quarterly* 28 (January):177-222.

Altmann Smythe, Julio
1967   La familia como una realidad social. *Criminalia* 2 (Febrero):80-90.

Alvarado, Anita L.
1970   Cultural Determinants of Population Stability in the Havasupai Indians. *American Journal of Physical Anthropology* 33:9-14.

Álvarez, G. Angel
1973   Boletin Meteorológico, Estado de Chihuahua 1957-1971. Union Ganadera Regional de Chihuahua 10.

Álvarez Gurza, Eric
1979   El ingreso al GATT de paises en desarrollo: elementos jurídicos que deben tomarse en cuenta. *Comercio Exterior* 29 (Febrero):171-78.

Álvarez, Rodolfo
1973   The Psycho-Historical and Socioeconomic Development of the Chicano Community in the United States. *Social Science Quarterly* 53 (August): 920-42.

Alvírez, David
1973   The Effects of Formal Church Affiliation and Religiosity on the Fertility Patterns of Mexican-American Catholics. *Demography* 10 (no. 11):19-36.
———, and Bean, Frank D.
1976   The Mexican American Family. In Charles H. Mindel and Robert W. Habenstein, eds. *Ethnic Families in America,* pp. 271-92. New York: Elsevier.

Amsden, Charles A.
1933   The Navaho Exile at Bosque Redondo. *New Mexico Historical Review* 8 (no.1):31-50.
1949   *Prehistoric Southwesterners: From Basketmaker to Pueblo.* Los Angeles: Southwest Museum.

Anaya, Manuel
1967   Mexico and Its Water Resources Policy. *International Conference on Water for Peace* 8:682-91.

Anderson, A. E.
1932   Artifacts of the Rio Grande Delta Region. *Texas Archeological Society Bulletin* 3:29-31.

Anderson, Arthur J. O.
1958   Frederick Webb Hodge, 1864-1956. *Hispanic American Historical Review* 38 (May):263-67.

Anderson, Bo, and Cockcroft, James D.
1966   Control and Cooptation in Mexican Politics. *International Journal of Comparative Sociology* 7 (March):11-28.

Anderson, David H.
1974   Stripmining on Reservation Lands: Protecting the Environment and the Rights of Indian Allotment Owners. *Montana Law Review* 35 (Summer):209-26.

Anderson, Don L.
1971   The San Andreas Fault. *Scientific American* 225 (November):52-66, 68.

Anderson, George B.
1907   *Complete History of New Mexico: Its Resources and People.* 2 vols. Los Angeles: Pacific States Publishing Co.

Anderson, James G., and Johnson, William H.
1971   Stability and Change Among Three Generations of Mexican Americans: Factors Affecting Achievement. *American Educational Research Journal* 8:285-308.

Anderson, Theodore
1969   Bilingual Schooling: Oasis or Mirage. *Hispania* 52:69-74.

Angle, J.
1959   *Federal, State, and Tribal Jurisdiction on Indian Reservations in Arizona.* Tucson: University of Arizona, Bureau of Ethnic Research.

Apodaca, Anacleto
1952   Corn and Custom: Introduction of Hybrid Corn to Spanish-American Farmers in New Mexico. In Edward H. Spicer, ed. *Human Problems in Technological Change.* New York: Russell Sage Foundation.

Apollo 9 Eyes Water Management
1970   *Cross-Section* 16 (October): 1, 3.

Applegate, Howard G.
n.d.   Carbon Monoxide Concentrations in El Paso for 1977. In Willard P. Gingerich, ed. *Air Quality Issues in the El Paso/Cd. Juárez Border Region.* Occasional Paper, no. 5. El Paso: University of Texas at El Paso, Center for Inter-American Studies.
1979   A Survey of Environmental Problems Along the Border. In James D. Kitchen, ed. *Environmental Problems Along the Border,* pp. 1-37. Occasional papers, no. 7. San Diego: Border-State University Consortium for Latin America.
1979*a*   *Environmental Problems of the Borderlands.* 145 pages. El Paso: Texas Western Press.
———, and Bath, C. Richard
1974   Editors. *Air Pollution Along the United States-Mexican Border.* El Paso: Texas Western Press.

1978   Air Pollution Along the United States-Mexico Border with Emphasis on El Paso-Ciudad Juárez-Las Cruces Air Shed. *Natural Resources Journal* 18 (January):91-100.

——; Hanselka, C. Wayne; and Culley, Dudley D.
1971   Effect of Insecticides on an Ecosystem in the Northern Chihuahua Desert. In William G. McGinnies, Bram J. Goldman, and Patricia Paylore, eds. *Food, Fibers and Arid Lands,* pp. 393-404. Tucson: University of Arizona Press.

Aranda, Charles
1975   *Dichos: Proverbs and Sayings from the Spanish.* Santa Fe: Sunstone Press.

Arbingast, Stanley A.
1955   The Rio Grande. *Texas Business Review* 29 (July):1-4.

——, and Kennamer, Lorrin
1963   *Atlas of Texas.* Austin: University of Texas, Bureau of Business Research.

——, et al.
1975   *Atlas of Mexico.* Austin: University of Texas, Bureau of Business Research.

Archbold, John C.
1966   The Mexicali Valley Water Problem. *California Geographer* 7:47-51.

Archer, Chiston I.
1973   The Deportation of Barbarian Indians from the Internal Provinces of New Spain, 1789-1810. *Americas* 29 (January):376-85.

Archibald, Robert
1976   *Cañon de Carnue:* Settlement of a Grant. *New Mexico Historical Review* 51:313-28.

Arenal, Rodolfo del C.
1969   Water Resources of Mexico. *Water Resources Bulletin* 5 (March):19-38.

Arguello, Ottoniel, and Kazmann, Raphael G.
1973   Mississippi River Water for Texas? *Journal of the Irrigation and Drainage Division, American Society of Civil Engineers* 99 (no. 1R-4):441-48.

Armstrong, Roy A.
1972   Test Bias from the Non-Anglo Viewpoint: A Critical Evaluation of Intelligence Test Items by Members of Three Cultural Minorities. Ph.D. dissertation, University of Arizona.

Armstrong, Ruth
1969   *New Mexico: From Arrowhead to Atom.* South Brunswick, N.J.: A. S. Barnes.

Arneson, Edwin P.
1925   The Early Art of Terrestrial Measurement and Its Practice in Texas. *Southwestern Historical Quarterly* 29 (October):79-97.

Arnold, Brigham A.
1957   *Late Pleistocene and Recent Changes in Land Forms, Climate, and Archeology in Central Baja California.* Publications in Geography, no. 10, pp. 201-317. Berkeley: University of California.

Aro, R. S.
1971   Evaluation of Pinyon-Juniper Conversion to Grassland. *Journal of Range Management* 24:188-97.

Arrington, Leonard J.
1958   *Great Basin Kingdom: Economic History of the Latter-Day Saints, 1830-1900.* Cambridge: Harvard University Press.

1966   Inland to Zion: Mormon Trade on the Colorado River, 1864-1867. *Arizona and the West* 8:239-51.

——, and Bitton, Davis
1979   *The Mormon Experience: A History of the Latter-Day Saints.* New York: Alfred A. Knopf.

Arrowsmith, Rex
1963   Editor. *Mines of the Old Southwest.* Santa Fe: Stagecoach Press.

Artaud, Antonin
1963   *Les Tarahumaras Dècines, Isère: l'Arbalète, Marc Bar-*

bezat. Translated into English as the Peyote Dance. n.p.

Arteaga y S., Armando
1932   Fray Marcos de Niza y el descubrimiento de Nuevo Mexico. *Hispanic American Historical Review* 12 (November):481-89.

Aschenbrenner, P. J.
1971   State Power and the Indian Treaty Right to Fish. *California Law Review* 59 (March):485-524.

Aschmann, Homer
1952   A Primitive Food Preparation Technique in Baja California. *Southwestern Journal of Anthropology* 8:36-39.

1959a   *The Central Desert of Baja California: Its Demography and Ecology.* Ibero-Americana, no. 42. Berkeley: University of California Press.

1959b   The Evolution of a Wild Landscape, and Its Persistence, in Southern California. *Annals, Association of American Geographers* 49 (September-Supplement):34-56.

1960   Retreat of an Agricultural Frontier. *Geographical Review* 50 (July):432.

1966   The Head of the Colorado Delta. In S. R. Jones and G. R. J. Jones, eds. *Geography as Human Ecology,* pp. 231-64. New York: St. Martin's Press.

1974   *Environment and Ecology in the "Northern Tonto" Claim Area.* New York: Garland Publishing, University of California at Riverside.

Ashcraft, Allan C.
1962   *Texas in the Civil War: A Resume History.* Austin: Texas Civil War Centennial Commission.

Ashford, Gerald
1971   *Spanish Texas.* Austin: Pemberton Press.

Atencio, Tomás C.
1964   The Human Dimensions in Land Use and Land Displacement in Northern New Mexico Villages. In Clark S. Knowlton, ed. *Indian and Spanish American Adjustments to Arid and Semiarid Environments,* pp. 44-52. Lubbock: Texas Tech College.

Atwater, Elizabeth V.
1974   *Mode of Life and Tribal Lands of the Jicarilla Apache During the Spanish-American Period, 1601-1849.* New York: Garland Publishing, Stanford Research Institute.

Atwood, W. W.
1927   Utilization of the Rugged San Juans. *Economic Geography* 3 (April):193-209.

1940   *The Physiographic Provinces of North America.* New York: Ginn & Co.

Auerbach, Herbert S.
1943   Father Escalante's Journal with Related Documents and Maps. *Utah Historical Quarterly* 11 (January):1-10.

Austin, M. E.
1972   *Land Resource Regions and Major Land Resource Areas of the United States.* Handbook 296. Washington, D.C.: U.S. Department of Agriculture.

Aveleyra Arroyo de Anda, L.
1951   Reconocimiento arqueológico en la zona de la presa internacional Falcón, Tamaulipas y Texas. *Revista Mexicana de Estudios Antropológicos* 12:31-59.

Avina, Rose H.
1932   *Spanish and Mexican Land Grants in California.* San Francisco: R & E Research Associates.

Axelrod, D. I.
1958   Evolution of the Madro-Tertiary Geoflora. *Botanical Review* 24:433-509.

Ayer, Harry W., and Hoyt, Paul G.
1977   Industrial Growth in the U.S. Border Communities and Associated Water and Air Problems: An Economic Perspective. *Natural Resources Journal* 17 (October):585-614.

Ayer, I. E.
1916   Translator. *Memorial of Fray Alonso de Benavides, 1630.* Chicago: University of Chicago Press.

Azad, Hardan Singh
1976   *Industrial Wastewater Management Handbook.* New York: McGraw-Hill Publishing Company.

Babbitt, Bruce E.
1973   *Color and Light: The Southwest Canvases of Luis Akin.* Flagstaff: Northland Press.

Babbitt, Hattie
1971   State Taxation of Indian Income. *Law and Social Order* 2:355-69.

Babby, Lon S.
1975   Aliens Who Can Teach. *Yale Law Journal* 85 (November):90-112.

Bach, Christopher L.
1979   U.S. International Transactions: Fourth Quarter and Year, 1978. *Survey of Current Business* 59 (March): 38-62.

Bach, Robert L.
1978   Mexican Immigration and the American State. *International Migration Review* 12 (Winter):536-58.

Baer, Joshua
1978   *Illegales:* The New Immigrants. *New Times* (January 23):27-32.

Baerresen, Donald W.
1971   *The Border Industrialization Program of Mexico.* Lexington: D. C. Heath.
1975   Unemployment and Mexico's Border Industrialization Program. *Inter-American Economic Affairs* 29 (no. 2): 79-90.

Báez-Comargo, Gonzalo, and Grubb, K. G.
1935   *Religion in the Republic of Mexico.* London: World Dominion Press.

Bagley, Edgar S.
1961   Water Rights Law and Public Policies Relating to Ground Water "Mining" in the Southwestern States. *Journal of Law and Economics* 1 (October):144-75.

Bagley, Jay M., and Smiley, Terah L.
1969   Editors. Symposium: Water Importation into Arid Lands. In W. G. McGinnies and Bram Goldman, eds. *Arid Lands in Perspective,* pp. 337-421. Tucson: University of Arizona Press.

Bahr, Donald M.
1973   Psychiatry and Indian Curing. *Indian Programs* 2 (no. 4):1-9.
————, Gregorio, Juan; Lopez, David; and Alvarez, Albert
1974   *Piman Shamanism and Staying Sickness.* Tucson: University of Arizona Press.

Bahr, Howard M.; Chadwick, Bruce A.; and Day, Robert C.
1972   Editors. *Native Americans Today: Sociological Perspectives.* New York: Harper & Row.

Bahre, C. J.
1977   Land-Use History of the Research Ranch, Elgine, Arizona. *Journal of the Arizona Academy of Science* 12 (supplement 2):1-32.

Bahre, Conrad J., and Bradbury, David E.
1978   Vegetation Change Along the Arizona-Sonora Boundary. *Annals, Association of American Geographers* 68 (June):145-65.

Bailey, David C., and Beezley, William H.
1975   *A Guide to Historical Sources in Saltillo, Coahuila.* East Lansing: Michigan State University, Latin American Studies Center.

Bailey, David T., and Haulman, Bruce E.
1974   Patterns of Landholding in Santa Fe in 1860 and 1870. Paper presented to the Rocky Mountain Social Science Association, April, at El Paso, Texas.

Bailey, Harry P.
1966   *The Climate of Southern California.* Berkeley: University of California Press.

Bailey, M. Thomas
1972   *Reconstruction in Indian Territory.* Port Washington, N.Y.: Kennikat Press.

Bailey, R. G.
1978   *Description of the Eco-Regions of the United States.* Ogden: U.S. Forest Service, Intermountain Region.

Bailey, Reed W.
1941   Climate and Settlement of the Arid Region. In *U.S.D.A. Yearbook of Agriculture: Climate and Man,* pp. 188-96. Washington, D.C.: Government Printing Office.

Bailey, Wilfred C.
1950   A Typology of Arizona Communities. *Economic Geography* 26 (April): 94-104.
1955   Problems in Relocating the People of Zapata, Texas. *Texas Journal of Science* 7 (March):20-37.

Bain, Joe S., et al.
1966   *Northern California's Water Industry: The Comparative Efficiency of Public Enterprise in Developing a Scarce Natural Resource.* Baltimore: Johns Hopkins University Press.

Baker, George C.
1975   Social Functions of Language in a Mexican American Community. In Richard V. Teschner, ed. *Spanish and English of United States Hispanos: A Critical, Annotated, Linguistic Bibliography.* Arlington: Center for Applied Statistics.

Baker, Oliver E.
1930   Agricultural Regions of North America: Part 8—The Pacific Subtropical Crops Region. *Economic Geography* 6 (April, July):166-90, 278-308.
1931   Agricultural Regions of North America: Part 10—The Grazing and Irrigated Crops Region. *Economic Geography* 7 (October):325-64.
1932   Agricultural Regions of North America: Part 10—The Grazing and Irrigated Crops Region. *Economic Geography* 8 (October):325-77.

Baker, Paulline
1966   *Español para los hispanos.* 2d ed. Skokie, Ill.: National Textbook Co.

Baker, Thomas Lindsay
1978   Silesians in Texas: A History of the Oldest Polish Colonies in America. Ph.D. dissertation, Texas Tech University.

Bakewell, P. J.
1971   *Silver Mining and Society in Colonial Mexico: Zacatecas, 1546-1700.* Latin American Series, no. 15. Cambridge: Cambridge Univerity Press.

Bakker, Elna, and Killard, Richard G.
1972   *The Great Southwest: The Story of a Land and Its People.* Palo Alto: American West Publishing Co.

Balán, Jorge; Jelin, Elisabeth; and Browning, Harley
1972   Editors. *Estudios sobre migración, estructura ocupacional y mobilidad en México.* Mexico City: Instituto de Investigaciones Sociales, UNAM.
————, et al.
1973   *Man in a Developing Society: Geographic and Social Mobility in Monterrey, Mexico.* Austin: University of Texas Press.

Balbas, Manuel
1927   *Recuerdos del Yaqui: principales episodios durante la compaña de 1899 a 1901.* Mexico City: Sociedad de Edición y Librería Franco Americana.

Balch, P., and Miller, K.
1974   Social Class and the Community Mental Health Center: Client and Therapist Perceptions at Presenting Problems and Treatment Expectations. *American Journal of Community Psychology* 2 (no. 3):243-54.

Balchin, W. G. V., and Pye, Norman
1955   Climate and Culture in Southern Arizona. *Weather* 10 (December):399-404.

Baldassin, William E., and McDermott, John T.
1973   Jurisdiction over Non-Indians: An Opinion of the "Opinion." *American Indian Law Review* 1 (December):13-22.

Baldwin, Fletcher N., Jr.
1976   Constitutional Limitations on Government in Mexico, the United States and Uganda. In Richard P. Claude, ed. *Comparative Human Rights.* Baltimore: Johns Hopkins University Press.

Baldwin, Gordon C.
1973   *Indians of the Southwest.* New York: Capricorn Books.

Baldwin, Percy M.
1926   Fray Marcos de Niza and His Discovery of the Seven Cities of Cíbola. *New Mexico Historical Review* 1 (April):193-223.
1938   A Short History of the Mesilla Valley. *New Mexico Historical Review* 13 (July):314-24.

Bale, Jack B., and Minch, John A.
1971   *Coastal and Shore Landforms of Baja California del Norte, Mexico.* Department of Geography and Department of Geology, Technical Report 0-71-2. Riverside: University of California.

Ball, Howard, and Lauth, Thomas P.
1971   Editors. *Changing Perspectives in Contemporary Political Analysis.* Englewood Cliffs, N.J.: Prentice-Hall.

Bancroft, Hubert Howe
1884-90 *History of California, Mexico, Northern Mexican States and Texas, New Mexico and Arizona.* 7 vols. San Francisco: A. L. Bancroft Co.

Bandelier, A. F.
1890-92 *Final Report of Investigations Among the Indians of the Southwestern United States . . . 1880-1885.* American Series Papers, nos. 3 & 4. Cambridge: Archaeological Institute of America.
————, and Hewett, E. L.
1937   *Indians of the Rio Grande Valley.* Albuquerque: University of New Mexico Press.

Banfield, Edward C.
1965   El Paso: Two Cultures. In *Big City Politics,* pp. 66-69. New York: Random House.

Banks, Vera J.
1963   *Migration of Farm People: 1946-1960.* Miscellaneous Publication no. 1963. Washington, D.C.: USDA, Economic Research Service.
1975   *Farm Population Estimates for 1974.* Agricultural Economic Report no. 319. Washington, D.C.: USDA, Economic Research Service.

Bannon, John Francis
1952   *History of the Americas.* 2 vols. New York: McGraw-Hill.
1955   *The Mission Frontier in Sonora, 1620-1687.* New York: U.S. Catholic Historical Society.
1964   *Bolton and the Spanish Borderlands.* Norman: University of Oklahoma Press.
1970   *The Spanish Borderlands Frontier: 1513-1821.* New York: Holt, Rinehart & Winston; also Albuquerque: University of New Mexico Press, 1974.
1971   Herbert Eugene Bolton—Western Historian. *Western Historical Quarterly* 2 (July):261-82.

Barber, Ruth Kerns
1932   *Indian Labor in the Spanish Colonies.* Publication in History no. 15. Albuquerque: Historical Society of New Mexico.

Barbosa-Da Silva, José F.
1968   Participation of Mexican-Americans in Voluntary Associations. *Research Reports in the Social Sciences* 2 (Spring):33-43.

Barbour, M. G., and Major, J.
1977   Editors. *Terrestrial Vegetation of California.* New York: Wiley-Interscience.

Barcia, Andrés G.
1951   *Chronological History of the Continent of Florida.* Translated by Anthony Keggigan. Gainesville: University of Florida Press.

Barker, Eugene C.
1928   *Mexico and Texas, 1821-1835.* Dallas: P. L. Turner Co.
1949   *The Life of Stephen F. Austin: Founder of Texas, 1793-1836: A Chapter in the Westward Movement of the Anglo-American People.* Austin: Texas State Historical Association.

Barker, George C.
1947   Social Functions of Language in a Mexican American Community. *Acta Americana* 5:185-202.
1957   The Yaqui Easter Ceremony at Hermosillo. *Western Folklore* 16 (no. 4):262-65.
1958   Some Functions of Catholic Processions in Pueblo and Yaqui Culture Change. *American Anthropologist* 60: 449-55.

Barker, Marie Esman
1970   *Español para el bilingue.* Skokie, Ill.: National Textbook Co.

Barnes, Charles M.; Spaulding, R. R.; and Giddings, L. E.
1977   *The Screwworm Eradication Data System Archives.* Technical Memorandum X-58197. Houston: NASA, LBJ Space Center.

Barnes, Thomas C.; Naylor, Thomas H.; and Polzer, Charles W.
1981   *Northern New Spain: A Research Guide.* Tucson: University of Arizona Press.

Barnet, Richard J., and Müller, Ronald E.
1974   *Global Reach: The Power of Multinational Corporations.* New York: Simon & Schuster.

Barona Lobato, Juan
1976   *México ante el reto de las drogas.* Mexico City: Impresiones Modernas.

Barovick, Richard L.
1970   Labor Reacts to Multinationals. *Columbia Journal of World Business* 5 (July-August):40-46.

Barr, Alwyn
1971   *Reconstruction to Reform: Texas Politics, 1876-1906.* Austin: University of Texas Press.

Barr, Lorna
1975   NAWAPA: A Continental Development Scheme for North America. *Geography* 60 (no. 2):111-19.

Barragán, Manuel Neira
1966   El tatita. *Hemisferio* (Mayo-Agosto):19 (Monterrey).

Barragán, Miguel F.
1969   Organized Religion and La Raza. In *La Raza Challenges Health and Social Welfare Practices,* pp. 49-59. Tucson: Southwest Council of La Raza, NIMH.

Barrera, Mario
1974   The Study of Politics and the Chicano. *Aztlán* 5 (no. 1 & 2):9-26.
1979   *Race and Class in the Southwest: A Theory of Racial Inequality.* Notre Dame: University of Notre Dame Press.

Barrett, Elinore M.
1974   Colonization of the Santo Domingo Valley. *Annals, Association of American Geographers* 64 (March):34-53.

Barrett, Ellen C.
1957   *Baja California: A Bibliography.* Los Angeles: Bennett & Marshall.
1967   *Baja California II, 1535-1964: A Bibliography of Historical, Geographical and Scientific Literature Relating to the Adjacent Islands in the Gulf of California and the Pacific Ocean.* Los Angeles: Westernlore Press.

Barrio, Raymond
1975   *Mexico's Art and Chicano Artists.* Sunnyvale, Calif.: Ventura Press.

Barrows, D. P.
1900   *The Ethno-botany of the Coahuilla Indians of Southern California.* Chicago: University of Chicago Press.

Bartelli, L. J.; Baird, J. V.; Heddleson, M. R.; and Klingebiel, A. A.
1966   Editors. *Soil Surveys and Land Use Planning.* Madison: American Society of Agronomy and Soil Science Society of America.

Barth, Fredrik
1969   Editor. *Ethnic Groups and Bounderies: The Social Or-ganization of Culture Difference.* Boston: Little, Brown & Co.

Barth, Gunther
1964   *Bitter Strength: A History of the Chinese in the United States, 1850-1870.* Cambridge: Harvard University Press.

Barth, Pios Joseph
1945   *Franciscan Education and the Social Order in Spanish North America, 1502-1821.* Chicago: University of Chicago Press.

Bartlett, John R.
1965   *Personal Narrative of Explorations and Incidents in Texas, New Mexico, California, Sonora, and Chihuahua with the United States and Mexico Boundary Commis-sion, 1850-53.* Chicago: Rio Grande Press.

Bartlett, Katherine
1934   Spanish Contacts with the Hopi, 1540-1823. *Museum Notes of Northern Arizona, Flagstaff* 6 (no. 12):55-60.
1936   The Navajo Wars, 1823-1870. *Museum Notes of Northern Arizona, Flagstaff* 8 (no. 7):33-37.

Barton, Henry W.
1962   Five Texas Frontier Companies During the Mexican War. *Southwestern Historical Quarterly* 64 (July):17-30.

Basauri, Carlos
1927   Creencias y prácticas de los tarahumaras. *Mexican Folk-ways* 3:218-34.
1929   *Monografía de los tarahumaras.* Mexico City: Talleres Gráficos de la Nación.
1940   Los ki-ka-poos. In *La Población Indígena de México,* pp. 643-63. Mexico City: Secretaria de Educación Pública.

Basehart, Harry W.
1971   Mescalero Apache Band Organization and Leadership. *Southwestern Journal of Anthropology* 26:87-106.
1974   *Mescalero Apache Subsistence Patterns and Socio-Political Organization.* New York: Garland Publishing, University of New Mexico.

Basso, Keith H.
1970   *The Cibecue Apache.* New York: Holt, Rinehart & Winston.
1971   To Give up on Words: Silence in Western Apache Culture. *Anthropological Papers of the University of Arizona* 21:151-61.

Bassols Batalla, Angel
1959   *Los aspectos geoeconómicos y humanos de la explotación en el territorio de la Baja California.* Mexico City: Sociedad Mexicana de Geografía y Estadística.
1972   *El noreoeste de México: un estudio geográfico eco-nómico.* Mexico City: *Universidad Autónoma de México.*

Bataillon, Claude
1969   *Las regiones geográficas en México.* Mexico City: Siglo XXI Editores, S.A.

Bath, C. Richard
1974a   An Overview of Environmental Policy Formulation in the United States. In Howard G. Applegate and C. Rich-ard Bath, eds. *Air Pollution Along the United States-Mexico Border,* pp. 58-69. El Paso: Texas Western Press.
1974b   A Personal Perspective of Environmental Decision-mak-ing in Two Cities: El Paso, Texas, and Ciudad Juarez, Mexico. Paper presented to the Southwest Political Science Association, March, at Dallas, Texas.
1974c   Air Pollution Policy Formulation in the U.S. and Mexico: The El Paso-Juárez Region. Paper presented to the Western Political Science Association, April, at Denver, Colorado.
1975-76 The Status of Borderlands Studies: Political Science. *Social Science Journal* 12-13 (October, 1975-January, 1976):55-69.

1978a   The El Paso-Ciudad Juárez Region as a Microcosm of the North-South Conflict: Political Science. Paper pre-sented to the International Studies Association, February, at Washington, D.C.
1978b   Alternative Cooperative Arrangements for Managing Transboundary Air Resources Along the Border. *Natural Resources Journal* 18 (January):181-99.
1979   The Mexican Tomatoe: A Case of Dependency? In John J. Brasch, ed. *Current Latin American Issues and Re-search.* Lincoln: University of Nebraska.
———; Carter, H. M.; and Price, T. J.
1977   Dependence, Interdependence, or Detachment? Three Case Studies of International Relations Between El Paso, Texas, and Ciudad Juárez, Mexico. Paper presented to the Third World Conference, October, in Omaha, Ne-braska.
———, and James, Dilmus D.
1976   Dependency Analysis of Latin America: Some Criticisms, Some Suggestions. *Latin American Research Review* 11 (Fall):3-54.
———, and Peterson, Robert L.
1972   Political Socialization in Northern Mexico: A Prelim-inary Report. Paper presented to the Rocky Mountain Social Science Association, April, at Salt Lake City, Utah.

Baugh, Ruth E.
1937   Land Use Changes in the Bishop Area of Owens Valley, California. *Economic Geography* 13 (January):17-34.
1942   Site of Early Los Angeles. *Economic Geography* 18 (Jan-uary):87-96.

Baxter, E. P., and Killen, K. L.
1976   *A Study of the Palo Alto Battlefield, Cameron County, Texas.* Anthropology Laboratory Report 33. College Sta-tion: Texas A. & M. University.

Bayitch, S. A., and Siqueiros, José Luis
1968   *Conflict of Laws: Mexico and the United States.* Coral Gables: University of Miami Press.

Baylor, Allen O.
1977   The Effects of the 1976 Mexican Peso Devaluation on U.S.-Mexico Border Business: A Case of El Paso, Texas, and Ciudad Juárez, Mexico. Manuscript, University of Texas at El Paso, October.

Beals, Carleton
1932   *Porfirio Díaz, Dictator of Mexico.* Philadelphia: J. B. Lippincott Co.

Beals, Ralph L.
1932a   *The Comparative Ethnology of Northern Mexico Before 1750.* Ibero-Americana, no. 2. Berkeley: University of California Press.
1932b   Aboriginal Survivals in Mayo Culture. *American An-thropologist* 34:28-39.
1943a   Northern Mexico and the Southwest. In *El norte de México y el sur de los Estados Unidos,* pp. 191-99. Mexico City: Sociedad Mexicana de Antropología.
1943b   *The Aboriginal Culture of the Cáhita Indians.* Ibero-America, no. 19. Berkeley: University of California.
1945   *The Contemporary Culture of the Cáhita Indians.* Bureau of American Ethnology Bulletin, no. 142. Washington, D.C.: Smithsonian Institution.
1946   *Cherán: A Sierra Tarascan Village.* Social Anthropology Series, no. 2. Washington, D.C.: Smithsonian Institution.
1973   *The Comparative Ethnology of Northern Mexico Before 1750.* New York: Cooper Square Publishers. Original publication, 1932.

Bean, Frank D.
1973   Components of Income and Expected Family Size Among Mexican-Americans. *Social Science Quarterly* 54 (no. 1):103-16.
———, and Bradshaw, Benjamin S.
1970a   An Exploratory Study of Intermarriage between Mex-ican-Americans and Anglo-Americans: 1850-1960. *Pro-*

ceedings, Southwestern Sociological Association, pp. 120-25.

1970b   Intermarriage Between Persons of Spanish and Non-Spanish Surname Changes from the Mid-nineteenth to the Mid-twentieth Century. *Social Science Quarterly* 51 (September):389-95.

——; Curtis, Russell L., Jr.; and Marcum, John P.

1977   Familism and Marital Satisfaction Among Mexican Americans: The Effects of Family Size, Wife's Labor Force Participation, and Conjugal Power. *Journal of Marriage and the Family* 39 (November):759-67.

Bean, L. J., and Saubel, K. S.

1972   *Temalpakh, Cahuilla Indian Knowledge and Usage of Plants.* Banning, Calif.: Malki Museum Press.

——, and Vane, S. B.

1977   *California Indians: Primary Resources: A Guide to the Manuscripts, Artifacts, Documents, Serials, Music and Illustrations.* Anthropological Papers, no. 7. Ramona, Calif.: Ballena Press.

Bean, W. B.

1976   Medical Practice. Paper presented to American Association of Medical Colleges at San Francisco, California.

Bean, Walton

1952   *Ross Ruef's San Francisco.* Berkeley: University of California Press.

1968   *California: An Interpretive History.* New York: McGraw-Hill.

Beardsley, Theodore S.

1976   Bibliografía preliminar de estudios sobre el español en los Estados Unidos. *Boletín de la Academia Norteamericana de la Lengua Española* 1:49-73.

Beck, Warren A.

1962   *New Mexico: A History of Four Centuries.* Norman: University of Oklahoma Press.

——, and Haase, Ynez D.

1969   *Historical Atlas of New Mexico.* Norman: University of Oklahoma Press.

1974   *Historical Atlas of California.* Norman: University of Oklahoma Press.

——, and Williams, David A.

1971   *California, A History of the Golden State.* Garden City: Doubleday & Co.

Becker, Michael, et al.

1976   San Diego-Tijuana: Plans Across the Border. *Cry California* 2 (Summer):29-35.

Bee, Robert L.

1970   Self-Help at Fort Yuma: A Critique. *Human Organization* 29 (Fall): 155-61.

1981   *Development at Fort Yuma: The Changing Lives of the Quechan Indians.* Tucson: University of Arizona Press.

Beegle, J. Allan; Goldsmith, Harold F.; and Loomis, Charles P.

1960   Demographic Characteristics of the United States-Mexico Border. *Rural Sociology* 25 (March):107-62.

Beers, Henry P.

1979   *Spanish and Mexican Records of the American Southwest: A Bibliographic Guide to Archive and Manuscript Sources.* Tucson: University of Arizona Press.

Beezley, William H.

1970   State Reform During the Provisional Presidency: Chihuahua, 1911. *Hispanic American Historical Review* 50 (August):524-37.

1973   Research Possibilities in the Mexican Revolution: The Governorship. *Americas* 29 (January):309-13.

Beheiry, Salah A.

1967   Sand Forms in the Coachella Valley, Southern California. *Annals, Association of American Geographers* 57 (March):25-48.

Bell, Betty

1974   *The Archaeology of West Mexico.* Ajijic, Jalisco, Mexico: Sociedad de Estudios Avanzados del Occidente Mexico, A.C.

Bell, Mattie

1935   The Growth and Distribution of the Texas Population. Master's thesis, Baylor University.

Bell, Wendell

1971   Comparative Studies: A Commentary. In Fred W. Riggs, ed. *International Studies: Present Status and Future Prospects,* pp. 56-73. Monograph no. 12. Philadelphia: American Academy of Political and Social Science.

Bell, W. H., and Castetter, E. F.

1937   *The Utilization of Mesquite and Screwbean by the Aborigines in the American Southwest.* Biological Series, no. 5 (2). Albuquerque: University of New Mexico Bulletin.

Bender, Averam B.

1974a   *A Study of the Jicarilla Apache Indians, 1846-1887.* New York: Garland Publishing, Harris Teachers College, St. Louis, Missouri.

1974b   *A Study of Mescalero Apache Indians 1846-1880.* New York: Garland Publishing, Harris Teachers College, St. Louis, Missouri.

1974c   *A Study of Western Apache Indians, 1846-1886.* New York: Garland Publishing, Harris Teachers College, St. Louis, Missouri.

Benedict, Ruth

1934   *Patterns of Culture.* Boston: Houghton Mifflin Co.

Benitez, Mario, and Villarreal, Lupita

1979   *The Education of the Mexian American: A Selected Bibliography.* Rosslyn, Va.: National Clearinghouse for Bilingual Education.

Benítez Zenteno, Raúl, and Acevedo, Gustavo Cabrera

1966   *Projecciones de la población de México, 1960-1980.* Mexico City: Banco de México.

1967   *Tablas abreviadas de mortalidad de la población de México.* Mexico City: El Colegio de México.

Bennett, John W.

1975   Editor. *The New Ethnicity: Perspectives from Ethnology.* 1973 Proceedings of the American Ethnological Society. St. Paul: West Publishing Company.

Bennett, Wendell C., and Zingg, Robert M.

1935   *The Tarahumara: An Indian Tribe of Northern Mexico.* Chicago: University of Chicago Press.

1946a   Death Among the Tarahumaras. *Mexican Life* 22 (no. 4):25-27, 54-60.

1946b   Shamans: The Tarahumara Healers. *Mexican Life* 22 (no. 5):27-28, 61-73.

Benrimo, Dorothy; Boyd, E.; and James, Rebecca S.

1966   *Compasantos.* Fort Worth: Amon Carter Museum of Western Art.

Bensinger, Peter B.

1977   DEA Today. *Drug Enforcement* 4 (August):8-11, 35-36.

Benson, Nettie Lee

1960   Texas' Failure to Send a Deputy to the Spanish Courts, 1810-1812. *Southwestern Historical Quarterly* 64 (July):14-35.

1968   A Governor's Report on Texas in 1809. *Southwestern Historical Quarterly* 71 (April):601-15.

Berger, Edward B.

1968a   Indian Land—Minerals—Related Problems. *Rocky Mountain Mineral Law Institute* 14:89-122.

1968b   Indian Mineral Interest: A Potential for Economic Advancement. *Arizona Law Review* 10 (no. 3):675-89.

Bergman, Peter M., and Bergman, Mort N.

1969   *The Chronological History of the Negro in America.* New York: New American Library (Mentor).

Bergman, Robert L.

1971   Navajo Peyote Use: Its Apparent Safety. *American Journal of Psychiatry* 128:695-99.

1973   Navajo Medicine and Psychoanalysis. *Human Behavior* 2:8-15.

Bergman, Robert; Tax, Sol; Witherspoon, Gary; Werner, Oswald; and Muskrat, Joseph
1969   The Rough Rock Demonstration School. In Arthur Harkins and Richard Woods, eds. *Problems of Cross-Cultural Educational Research and Evaluation.* Minneapolis: University of Minnesota Center for Urban and Regional Affairs.

Berkhofer, Robert F., Jr.
1965   Salvation and the Savage: An Analysis of Protestant Missions and American Indian Response, 1787-1862. In Francis Paul Prucha, ed. *The Indian in American History,* pp. 75-84. Hinsdale, Ill.: Dryden Press (1971).

Berlandier, John Louis
1969   *The Indians of Texas in 1830.* Washington, D.C.: Smithsonian Institution.

Bermúdez, Antonio J.
1968   *Recovering our Frontier Markets.* Mexico City: Ediciones Enfesa.

Bermúdez, María Elvira
1955   *La vida familiar del Mexicano.* Mexico City: Antigua Librería Robredo.

Bernal, Ignacio
1962   *Bibliografía de arqueología y etnografía, Mesoamérica y norte de México, 1514-1960.* Memorias VII. Mexico City: Instituto Nacional de Antropología y Historia.

Berni, Giorgio
1973   Border Industry: The Case of Ciudad Juárez, Chihuahua. Paper presented at Conference sponsored by Institute of Latin American Studies, April, at Austin, Texas.

Bernstein, Marvin
1964   *The Mexican Mining Industry, 1890-1905.* Albany: State University of New York at Albany.

Berry, Brewton
1969   *The Education of American Indians: A Survey of the Literature.* Washington, D.C.: Government Printing Office.

Berry, Brian J. L., and Harris, Chauncy D.
1968   Central Place. *Encyclopedia of the Social Sciences.* New York: Macmillan Co. and Free Press.

Berry, Kenneth J., and Martin, Thomas W.
1974   The Synecdochic Fallacy: A Challenge to Recent Research and Theory-Building in Sociology. *Pacific Sociological Review* 17 (April):139-66.

Bertou, Patrick, and Clasen, Robert E.
1971   An Analysis of a Spanish Translation of the Sixteen Personality Factors Test. *Journal of Experimental Education* 39 (Summer):13-21.

Bigart, Robert James
1972   The Social Cost of Space. *Rocky Mountain Social Science Journal* 9 (January):111-15.

Bill, James A., and Hardgrave, Robert L.
1973   *Comparative Politics: The Quest for Theory.* Columbus, Ohio: Charles E. Merrill.

Billington, Ray A.
1949   *Westward Expansion: A History of the American Frontier.* New York: Macmillan Co.
1956   *The Far Western Fronter, 1830-1860.* New York: Harper & Brothers.
1966   *America's Frontier Heritage.* New York: Holt, Rinehart & Winston.

Bimson, Walter R.
1971   *The West and Walter Bimson.* Tucson: University of Arizona Museum of Art.

Binkley, William C.
1952   *The Texas Revolution.* Baton Rouge: Louisiana State University Press.

Birle, Siegfried
1976   *Irrigation Agriculture in the Southwest United States: Regional Variations of Crop Patterns.* Marburger Geographische Schriften, Heft 67. Marburg: Geographischen Institut der Universität.

Bishop, A. Bruce
1977   Impact of Energy Development on Colorado River Water Quality. *Natural Resources Journal* 17 (October):649-71.

Bishop, G. D.
1967   Editor. *Farm Labor in the United States.* New York: Columbia University Press.

Bittinger, M. W.
1959   *Colorado's Ground-Water Problems: Ground-Water in Colorado. Bulletin 504-S.* Fort Collins: Colorado Agricultural Experiment Station.

Blackmar, Frank W.
1891   *Spanish Institutions of the Southwest.* Baltimore: Johns Hopkins University Press.

Blackmore, William
1949   *The Spanish-Mexican Land Grants of New Mexico and Colorado, 1863-1878.* 2 vols. Denver: Bradford-Robinson.

Blair, Calvin, et al.
1969   *Responsibilities of the Foreign Scholar to the Local Scholarly Community.* Washington, D.C.: Latin American Studies Association.

Blaisdell, Lowell L.
1966   Harry Chandler and Mexican Border Intrigue, 1914-1917. *Pacific Historical Review* 35 (November):385-93.

Blake, John Herman
1973   Social Change and Population Trends in Mexico. Ph.D. dissertation, University of California at Berkeley.

Blake, William P.
1902   *Tombstone and Its Mines.* New York: n.p.

Blanco, Antonio S.
1971   *La lengua española en la historia de California.* Madrid: Ediciones Cultura Hispánica.

Bland, Warren R.
1974a   Seasonal Variations in Air Pollution in Los Angeles County. *Professional Geographer* 26 (August):277-82.
1974b   Seasonal and Spatial Patterns of Air Pollution in Los Angeles County. *Yearbook of the Association of Pacific Coast Geographers* 36:25-34.
1976   Smog Control in Los Angeles County: A Critical Analysis of Emission Control Programs. *Professional Geographer* 28 (August):283-89.

Blásquez-López, L.
1959   *Hidrogeología de las regiones desérticas de México.* Instituto de Geología, Anales 15. Mexico City: UNAM.

Bleznick, Donald W.
1977   Editor. *Hispania.* Worcester: American Association of Spanish and Portuguese.

Blick, James D.
1976   Agriculture in San Diego County. In Philip R. Pryde, ed. *San Diego: An Introduction to the Region,* pp. 121-35. Dubuque: Kendall/Hunt Publishing Co.

Bloom, John P.
1959   New Mexico Viewed by Anglo-Americans, 1846-1849. *New Mexico Historical Review* 34 (July):165-98.
1962   Johnny "Gringo" in Northern Mexico, 1846-1847. *Arizona and the West* 4 (Autumn):237-48.

Bloom, Lansing B.
1913-15 New Mexico under Mexican Administration, 1821-46. *Old Santa Fe* 1 (July, October, January, April):3-49, 131-75, 236-87, 348-85.
1925   Early Bridges in New Mexico. *El Palacio* 18:163-82.
1939   The Vargas Encomienda. *New Mexico Historical Review* 14 (October):366-417.
1940   Who Discovered New Mexico? *New Mexican Historical Review* 15 (April):101-32.

Bloom, R., and Barry, J.
1967   Determinants of Work Attitudes Among Negroes. *Journal of Applied Psychology* 55:287-92.

Bloombaum, M.; Yamamoto, J.; and James, Q.
1968   Cultural Sterotyping Among Psychotherapists. *Journal*

of Consulting and Clinical Psychology 32 (no. 1):99.

Blue Cloud, Peter
1972   Editor. *Alcatraz Is Not an Island.* Berkeley: Wingblow Press.

Bobb, Bernard
1962   *The Viceregency of Antonio Maria Bucareli in New Spain.* Austin: University of Texas Press.

Bodine, John J.
1971   Population Structure of Taos Pueblo. *California Anthropologist.* State College of California at Los Angeles.
1973   Blue Lake: A Struggle for Indian Rights. *American Indian Law Review* 1 (Winter):13-22.

Bogardus, Emory S.
1934   *The Mexican in the United States.* Los Angeles: University of Southern California Press.

Boggs, S. Whittemore, and Bowman, Isaiah
1940   *International Boundaries: A Study of Boundary Functions and Problems.* New York: Columbia University Press.

Bohrer, V. L.
1975   The Prehistoric and Historic Role of the Cool-Season Grasses in the Southwest. *Economic Botany* 29:199-207.
1978   Plants that Have Become Locally Extinct in the Southwest. *New Mexico Journal of Science* 18:10-19.

Bolton, Herbert Eugene
1908   Editor. *Spanish Exploration in the Southwest, 1542-1706.* New York: Barnes & Noble. Reprinted in 1952.
1912   The Spanish Occupation of Texas, 1519-1960. *Southwestern Historical Quarterly* 16 (July):1-28.
1913   *Guide to Materials for the History of the United States in the Principal Archives of Mexico.* Washington, D.C.: Carnegie Institution.
1914   *Athanase de Mezières and the Louisiana-Texas Frontier, 1768-1780.* 2 vols. Cleveland: Arthur H. Clark Co.
1915   Texas in the Middle Eighteenth Century. In *Studies in Spanish Colonial History and Administration.* Berkeley: University of California Press.
1916   *Spanish Exploration in the Southwest, 1542-1706; Itinerary of Mendoza.* New York: Scribner's Sons.
1917   The Mission as a Frontier Institution in the Spanish-American Colonies. *American Historical Review* 33 (October):42-61.
1919   The Iturbide Revolution in the Californias: Sobre resistencia de los misioneros de ambas Californias a jurar la independencia. *Hispanic American Historical Review* 2 (May):188-242.
1921   *The Spanish Borderlands: A Chronicle of Old Florida and the Southwest.* New Haven: Yale University Press.
1930   Defensive Spanish Expansion and the Significance of the Borderlands. In James F. Willard and Colin B. Goodykoontz, eds. *The TransMississippi West,* pp. 1-42. Boulder: University of Colorado.
1931   *Outposts of Empire.* New York: Alfred A. Knopf.
1932   *Padre on Horseback: A Sketch of Eusebio Francisco Kino.* San Francisco: Sonora Press.
1936   *Rim of Christendom: A Biography of Eusebio Francisco Kino, Pacific Coast Pioneer.* New York: Macmillan Co.
1949   *Coronado, Knight of Pueblos and Plains.* Albuquerque: University of New Mexico Press.
1950   *Pageant in the Wilderness.* Salt Lake City: Utah State Historical Society.
1962   *Texas in the Middle Eighteenth Century: Studies in Spanish Colonial History and Administration.* New York: Russell & Russell.

Bolyard, Joan E.
1978   International Travel and Passenger Fares, 1977. *Survey of Current Business* 58, part 1 (June):64-67.

Bonaparte, Ronald
1975   The Rodino Till: An Example of Prejudice Toward Mexican Immigration to the U.S. *Chicano Law Review* 2 (Summer):40-50.

Bongartz, Roy
1969   No More Sombreros: The Chicano Rebellion. *Nation* 208 (March 3):271-74.

Bonine, Michael E., et al.
1970   *Atlas of Mexico.* Austin: University of Texas, Bureau of Business Research.

Bonnen, C. A.
1960   *Types of Farming in Texas.* Bulletin no. 964. College Station: Texas Agricultural Experiment Station.

Booth, Alfred W.
1942   The Portales Region: A Pump Irrigation District in the Llano Estacado. *Economic Geography* 18 (January):97-105.

Borah, Woodrow
1951   *New Spain's Century of Depression.* Folcroft, Pa.: Folcroft Press.
1970   The California Mission. In Charles Wollenberg, ed. *Ethnic Conflict in California History,* pp. 1-22. Los Angeles: Tinnon-Brown.

Boren, Carter E.
1968   *Religion on the Texas Frontier.* San Antonio: Naylor Co.

Borhegyi, Stephan F. de
1954   The Evolution of a Landscape. *Landscape* 4 (Summer):24-30.

Bosse, Carle
1973   Nogales, Sonora: Prosperity from Piccolos, Paper Dresses, Printed Circuits. *Industrial Development* 142 (May/June):18-23.

Boster, Ron S.; O'Connell, Paul F.; and Thompson, James C.
1974   Recreation Uses Change Mogollon Rim Economy. *Arizona Review* 23 (August-September):1-7.

Boswell, Thomas D.
1967   Beef Cattle Feeding in the Imperial Valley, California: A Study in Economic Geography. Master's thesis, San Diego State College.

Bosworth, Allan R.
1967   *America's Concentration Camps.* New York: Norton & Co.

Boucher, Stanley W.
1970   Editor. *Mexican-American Mental Health Issues: Present Realities and Future Strategies.* Boulder: Western Interstate Commission for Higher Education.

Boudeville, Jacques R.
1974   European Integration, Urban Regions and Medium-sized Towns. In Margan Sant, ed. *Regional Planning and Policy for Europe.* Lexington: D. C. Heath.

Bourke, John C.
1891   *On the Border with Crook.* New York: Charles Scribner's Sons.

Bourke, John Gregory
1958   *An Apache Campaign in the Sierra Madre: An Account of the Expedition in Pursuit of the Hostile Chiricahua Apaches in the Spring of 1883.* New York: Charles Scribner's Sons.

Bourne, Edward Gaylord
1962   *Spain in America, 1450-1580.* New York: Barnes & Noble.

Bousman, C. B., and Rohrt, M.
1974   *Archeological Assessment of Big Bend National Park.* Dallas: Southern Methodist University, Archaeology Research Program.

Bouvier, Leon F.; Shyrock, Henry S,; and Henderson, Harry W.
1977   International Migration: Yesterday, Today, and Tomorrow. *Population Bulletin* 32 (no. 4).

Bowden, J. J.
1969   *The Ponce de Leon Land Grant.* Southwestern Studies, no. 24. El Paso: Texas Western Press.
1971   *Spanish and Mexican Land Grants in the Chihuahuan Acquisition.* El Paso: Texas Western Press.
1974   *The Ascarate Grant.* New York: Garland Publishing,

University of Texas.

Bowden, Leonard W.
1965   *Diffusion of the Decision to Irrigate: Simulation of the Spread of a New Resource Management Practice in the Colorado Northern High Plains.* Geography Research Paper no. 97. Chicago: University of Chicago.
1973a   *Correlation of Remote Sensing Imagery of the Coast of Southern and Baja California with Terrain Analysis.* Final report 0-73-3. Riverside: University of California, Department of Geography.
1973b   Remote Sensing of the World's Arid Lands. In David H. K. Amiran and Andrew W. Wilson, eds. *Coastal Deserts, Their Natural and Human Environments,* pp. 13-24. Tucson: University of Arizona Press.

Bowen, J. Donald
1952   The Spanish of San Antonito, New Mexico. Ph.D. dissertation, University of New Mexico.
————, and Ornstein, Jacob
1976   *Studies in Southwest Spanish.* Rowley, Mass.: Newbury House.

Bowen, Marshall
1976   Mormon Migration to and from a Northeastern Nevada Agricultural Community. Paper presented to the Western Social Science Association, May, at Tempe, Arizona.

Bowen, Thomas
1976   *Seri Prehistory: The Archeology of the Central Coast of Sonora, Mexico.* Anthropological Papers. Tucson: University of Arizona Press.

Bowman, Isaiah
1931   *The Pioneer Fringe.* New York: American Geographical Society.

Bowman, J. N.
1964   The Birthdays of the California Missions. *Americas* 20 (January):289-308.
1965   The Names of the California Missions. *Americas* 21 (April):263-74.

Bowser, Frederick P.
1972   The Africans in Colonial Spanish America. *Latin American Research Review* 7 (Spring):77-94.

Boyd, Elizabeth
1959   *Popular Arts of Colonial New Mexico.* Santa Fe: Museum of International Folk Art.
1966   With Frances Breese. *New Mexico Santos: How to Name Them.* Santa Fe: Museum of New Mexico Press.
1969   *The New Mexico Santero.* Santa Fe: Museum of New Mexico Press.
1974   *Popular Arts of Spanish New Mexico.* Santa Fe: Museum of New Mexico Press.

Boyd-Bowman, Peter
1973   A Spanish Soldier's Estate in Northern Mexico, 1624. *Hispanic American Historical Review* 53 (February):95-105.

Boyer, Bryce L.
1964   Folk Psychiatry of the Apaches of the Mescalero Indian Reservation. In Ari Kiev, ed. *Magic, Faith and Healing,* pp. 384-419. New York: Free Press.

Boyle, Robert H.; Graves, John; and Watkins, T. H.
1971   *The Water Hustlers.* San Francisco: Sierra Club.

Boysen, Bernadine B.
1970   La Mesa Penetario: An Ethnography of Baja California's State Prison. Master's thesis, San Diego State College.

Brack, Gene
1968   Mexican Opinion and the Texas Revolution. *Southwestern Historical Quarterly* 72 (October):170-82.
1975   *Mexico Views Manifest Destiny, 1821-1846: An Essay on the Origins of the Mexican War.* Albuquerque: University of New Mexico Press.

Bradfield, Maitland
1971   *The Changing Pattern of Hopi Agriculture.* Occasional Paper no. 30. London: Royal Anthropological Institute of Great Britain and Ireland.

Bradfute, Richard W.
1975   *The Court of Private Land Claims.* Albuquerque: University of New Mexico Press.

Brading, David A.
1970   The Mexican Silver-Mining in the Eighteenth Century: The Revival of Zacatecas. *Hispanic American Historical Review* 50 (November):665-81.
1971   *Miners and Merchants in Bourbon Mexico, 1763-1810.* Cambridge: Harvard University Press.
————, and Cross, Harry E.
1972   Colonial Silver Mining: Mexico and Peru. *Hispanic American Historical Review* 52 (November):545-79.

Bradley, Michael D., and De Cook, Kenneth J.
1978   Ground Water Occurrence and Utilization in the Arizona-Sonora Border Region. *Natural Resources Journal* 18 (January):29-48.

Bradley, Raymond S.
1976   *Precipitation History of the Rocky Mountain States.* Boulder, Colo.: Westview Press.

Bradshaw, Benjamin S., and Bean, Frank D.
1973a   Trends in the Fertility of Mexican Americans: 1950-1970. *Social Science Quarterly* 53 (March):688-96.
1973b   Some Aspects of Mexican-American Fertility. In *Report of the Commission on Population Growth and the American Future.* Research papers, vol. 1, pp. 139-64. Washington, D.C.: Government Printing Office.

Bradshaw, Benjamin S., and Fonner, Edwin, Jr.
1978   The Mortality of Spanish-Surnamed Persons in Texas: 1969-1971. In Frank D. Bean and W. Parker Frisbie, eds. *The Demography of Racial and Ethnic Groups.* New York: Academic Press.

Brand, Donald B.
1935   The Distribution of Pottery Types in Northwest Mexico. *American Anthropologist* 37 (no. 2):287-305.
1937   *The Natural Landscape of Northwestern Chihuahua.* Geological Series, vol. 5. Albuquerque: University of New Mexico.
1943   The Chihuahua Culture Area. *New Mexico Anthropologist* 7:115-58.
1961   The Early History of the Range Cattle Industry in Northern Mexico. *Agricultural History* 35 (July):132-39.
1966   *Mexico, Land of Sunshine and Shadow.* Princeton: Van Nostrand.

Branda, Eldons S.
1976   Editor. *The Handbook of Texas.* Vol. 3. Austin: Texas State Historical Association.

Brandenburg, Frank
1964   *The Making of Modern Mexico.* Englewood Cliffs, N.J.: Prentice-Hall.

Brandt, Nancy
1964   Pancho Villa: The Making of a Modern Legend. *Americas* 21 (October):146-62.

Braniff, Beatriz, and Felger, Richard S.
1976   *Sonora: antropología del desierto.* Centro Regional del Noroeste no. 27. Mexico City: Instituto Nacional de Antropología e Historia.

Brawner, Marlyn R.
1973   Migration and Educational Achievement of Mexican Americans. *Social Science Quarterly* 53 (March):727-37.

Brayer, Herbert O.
1949   *William Blackmore: The Spanish-Mexican Land Grants of New Mexico and Colorado, 1863-1878.* Denver: Bradford-Robinson.

Breeskin, Adelyn D., and Turk, Rudy H.
1972   *Scholder/Indians.* Edited by Doris Monthan. Flagstaff: Northland Press.

Breton, Raymond
1964   Institutional Completeness of Ethnic Communities and the Personal Relations of Immigrants. *American Journal*

of Sociology 70 (September):141-46.

Breuing, Robert G.

1975 Schools and the Hopi Self. In John W. Bennett, ed. *The New Ethnicity: Perspectives from Ethnology,* pp. 51-58. 1973 proceedings, American Ethnological Society. St. Paul: West Publishing Co.

Bridges, Julian C.

1961 An Examination of Some Aspects of Family Mortality in Latin America. D.D. dissertation, Southwestern Baptist Theological Seminary.

1969* A Study of the Number, Distribution, and Growth of the Protestant Population in Mexico. Master's thesis, University of Florida, Gainesville.

1972 How Religiously Homogeneous is the Rural Population of Mexico? *Rural Sociology* 37:246-52.

1973a The Population of Mexico: Its Composition and Changes. Ph.D. dissertation, University of Florida, Gainesville.

1973b *Expansión evangélica en México.* El Paso: Mundo Hispánico.

1979 Evangelical Expansion in Mexico: A Study of the Number, Distribution, and Growth of the Protestant Population, 1857-1970. In Lyle C. Brown and William F. Cooper, eds. *Religion in Latin American Life and Literature.* Waco, Texas: Markham Press.

1980 The Mexican Family. In Man Singh Das and Clinton J. Jasser, eds. *The Family in Latin America,* pp. 400-64. New Delhi: Vikas Publishing House.

Briggs, A. K.

1974 The Archeology of 1882 Labor Camps on the Southern Pacific Railroad, Val Verde County, Texas. Master's thesis, University of Texas, Austin.

Briggs, Vernon M., Jr.

1972 Chicanos and Rural Poverty: A Continuing Issue for the 1970s. *Poverty and Human Resources Abstracts* 7 (no. 1):3-24.

1973a The Mexico-United States Border: An Assessment of Policies of the United States upon the Economic Welfare of the Chicano Population. Paper presented to a Conference sponsored by Institute of Latin American Studies, April, at Austin, Texas.

1973b *Chicanos and Rural Poverty.* Baltimore: Johns Hopkins University Press.

1974 *The Mexico-United States Border: Public Policy and Chicano Economic Welfare.* Publication no. 2. Austin: University of Texas, Center for the Study of Human Resources.

1975a Illegal Aliens: The Need for a More Restrictive Border Policy. *Social Science Quarterly* 56 (December):477-84.

1975b Mexican Workers in the United States Labor Market: A Contemporary Dilemma. *International Labour Review* 112 (November):351-68.

1975c *Mexican Migration and the U.S. Labor Market: A Mounting Issue for the Seventies.* Publication no. 3. Austin: University of Texas, Center for the Study of Human Resources.

1976 Illegal Immigration and the American Labor Force. *American Behavioral Scientist* 19 (January-February): 351-63.

1978 Labor Market Aspects of Mexican Migration to the United States in the 1970s. In Stanley R. Ross, ed. *Views Across the Border,* pp. 204-25. Albuquerque: University of New Mexico Press.

———; Fogel, Walter, Jr.; and Schmidt, Fred H.

1977 *The Chicano Worker.* Austin: University of Texas Press.

Brignano, Russell C.

1974 *Black Americans in Autobiography: An Annotated Bibliography of Autobiographies and Autobiographical Books Written Since the Civil War.* Durham: Duke University Press.

Briscoe, Edward Eugene

1947 Pershing's Chinese Refugees: An Odyssey of the South-

west. Master's thesis, St. Mary's University (San Antonio).

1959 Pershing's Chinese Refugees in Texas. *Southwestern Historical Review* 62 (April):467-88.

Broaddus, J. Morgan, Jr.

1963 *The Legal Heritage of El Paso.* El Paso: Texas Western Press.

Brody, J. J.

1971 *Indian Painters and White Patrons.* Albuquerque: University of New Mexico Press.

1977 *Mimbres Painted Pottery.* Santa Fe: School of American Research.

Brody, Olga. See also Pellicer de Brody, Olga

1974 Mexico in the 1970s and Its Relations with the United States. In Julio Cotler and Richard R. Fagen, eds. *Latin America and the United States,* pp. 314-33. Stanford: Stanford University Press.

Bronson, Louise Fisher

1966 Changes in Personality Needs and Values Following Conversation to Protestantism in a Traditionally Roman Catholic Ethnic Group. Ph.D. dissertation, University of Arizona.

Brooks, Bonnie S.; Brooks, Gary D.; Goodman, Paul W.; and Ornstein, Jacob

1975 *Sociolinguistic Background Questionnaire: A Measurement Instrument for the Study of Bilingualism.* El Paso: Cross-Cultural Southwest Ethnic Studies Center.

Brooks, Clinton E., and Reeve, Frank D.

1948 *Forts and Forays, James A. Bennett: A Dragoon in New Mexico, 1850-1856.* Albuquerque: University of New Mexico Press.

Broussard, Ray F.

1967 *San Antonio During the Texas Republic: A City in Transition.* El Paso: Texas Western Press.

Brown, Alan K.

1962 Rivera at San Francisco: A Journal of Exploration, 1754. *California Historical Society Quarterly* 41 (December): 325-41.

Brown, Charles E.

1967 Viticulture in Northwestern Baja California, Mexico. Master's thesis, San Diego State College.

Brown, D. E., and Lowe, C. H.

1980 *Biotic Communities of the Southwest.* General Technical Report RM-78. Fort Collins, Colo.: United States Department of Agriculture, Forest Service.

Brown, D. R.

1972 *An Assessment of the Archeological Resources to be Affected by Construction of Retamal International Diversion Dam, United States Kie and Modified Hackney Floodway and Closure of Mission Floodway, Hidalgo County, Texas.* Research Report 15. Austin: Texas Archeological Survey.

Brown, Dee

1971 *Bury My Heart at Wounded Knee: An Indian History of the American West.* New York: Bantam Books.

Brown, Donald N.

1979 People of the Mountain Place: Picurís Pueblo, New Mexico. Unpublished manuscript.

Brown, F. Lee; Sawyer, James W.; and Khoshakhlagh, Rahman

1977 Some Remarks on Energy Related Water Issues in the Upper Colorado River Basin. *Natural Resources Journal* 17 (October):635-48.

Brown, George H.; Rosen, Nan L.; Hill, Susan T.; and Olivas, Michael A.

1980 *The Condition of Education for Hispanic Americans.* Washington, D.C.: Government Printing Office.

Brown, John Henry

1892 *History of Texas from 1685 to 1892.* 2 vols. St. Louis: L. E. Daniell.

1896 *Indians, Wars and Pioneers of Texas.* Austin: L. E. Daniell.

Brown, Julia S., and Gilmartin, Brian G.
1969   Sociology Today: Lacunae, Emphases, and Surfeits. *American Sociologist* 4 (November):283-91.

Brown, Lorin W.; Briggs, Charles L.; and Weigle, Marta
1978   *Hispano Folklife of New Mexico.* Albuquerque: University of New Mexico Press.

Brown, Ralph H.
1928   Monte Vista: Sixty Years of a Colorado Community. *Geographical Review* 18 (October):567-78.

1936   A Southwestern Oasis: The Roswell Region, New Mexico. *Geographical Review* 26 (October):610-19.

Brown, Robert M.
1927   The Utilization of the Colorado River. *Geographical Review* 17 (July):453-66.

Browne, W. A.
1937   Agriculture in the Llano Estacado. *Economic Geography* 13 (April):155-74.

Brownell, Herbert, and Eaton, Samuel D.
1975   The Colorado River Salinity Problem with Mexico. *American Journal of International Law* 69 (January):255-71.

Browning, Harley L., and Feindt, Waltraut
1968   Diferencias entre la población nativa y la migrante en Monterrey. *Demografía y Economía* 2 (no. 2):183-204.

1969   Selectivity of Migrants to a Metropolis in a Developing Country: A Mexican Case Study. *Demography* 6 (no. 4): 347-57.

1971   The Social and Economic Context of Migration to Monterrey, Mexico. In Francine Rabinovitz and Felicity Trueblood, eds. *Latin American Urban Research,* vol. 1, pp. 45-70. Beverly Hills: Sage Publications.

Browning, Harley L., and McLemore, S. Dale
1964   *A Statistical Profile of the Spanish-Surname Population of Texas.* Austin: University of Texas, Bureau of Business Research.

Brugge, David M.
1956   Pima Bajo Basketry, *Kiva* 22 (no. 1).

Bruggee, David
1964   Vizcarra's Navajo Campaign of 1823. *Arizona and the West* 6 (Autumn):223-44.

Bruun, Kettil; Pan, Lynn; and Rexed, Ingemar
1975   *The Gentlemen's Club: International Control of Drugs and Alcohol.* Chicago: University of Chicago Press.

Bryan, Kirk
1925   Date of Channel Trenching (Arroyo Cutting) in the Arid Southwest. *Science* 62 (October 16):338-44.

1928   Change in Plant Associations by Change in Ground Water Level. *Ecology* 9 (October):474-78.

1929   Flood-Water Farming. *Geographical Review* 19 (July): 444-56.

1940   Erosion in the Valleys of the Southwest. *New Mexico Quarterly* 10.

1941   Pre-Columbian Agriculture in the Southwest, as Conditioned by Periods of Alluviation. *Annals, Association of American Geographers* 31 (December):219-42.

Bryant, Byron D., and Lyerly, Paul J.
1954   *Vegetable Crops for Commercial Production in the El Paso Area.* Publication, no. 115. College Station: Texas Agricultural Experiment Station.

Bryant, V. M.
1977   Late Quaternary Pollen Records from the Eastcentral Periphery of the Chihuahuan Desert. In R. H. Wauer and D. H. Riskind, eds. *Transactions of the Symposium on the Biological Resources of the Chihuahuan Desert Region, United States and Mexico,* no. 3, pp. 3-21. Washington, D.C.: National Park Service.

Bryce-Laporte, Roy S.
1979   *Sourcebook on the New Immigration.* New Brunswick, N.J.: Transaction Books.

Bryden, John M.
1973   *Tourism and Development: The Case of the Commonwealth Caribbean.* Cambridge: Cambridge University Press.

Bryson, Conrey
1973   *The Land Where We Live: El Paso del Norte.* El Paso: Aniversario del Paso.

1974   *Dr. Lawrence A. Nixon and the White Primary.* El Paso: Texas Western Press.

Bryson, Reid A.
1957   The Annual March of Precipitation in Arizona, New Mexico, and Northwestern Mexico. Technical Reports on the Meteorology and Climatology of Arid Regions 6. Tucson: University of Arizona Press.

———, and Hare, F. K.
1974   *World Survey Climatology.* Amsterdam: Elsevier Scientific Publishing Co.

Buckman, H. O., and Brady, N. C.
1969   *The Nature and Properties of Soils.* New York: Macmillan Co.

Buergenthal, Thomas
1975   The Revised OAS Charter and the Protection of Human Rights. *American Journal of International Law* 69 (October):4.

Buffington, Lee C., and Herbel, Carlton H.
1965   Vegetational Changes on a Semidesert Grassland Range from 1858 to 1963. *Ecological Monographs* 35 (Spring): 139-64.

Bugnicourt, Jacques
1978   Un nuevo colonialismo: turismo para los ricos. *Comercio Exterior* 28 (Marzo):301-303.

Buntin, Martha
1933   The Mexican Kickapoo. *Chronicles of Oklahoma* 11: 691-708.

Bunting, Bainbridge
1962   The Architecture of the Embudo Watershed. *New Mexico Architecture* 4 (June):19-26.

1964   *Taos Adobes.* Santa Fe: Museum of New Mexico Press.

1970   Take a Trip with NMA: An Architectural Guide to Northern New Mexico. *New Mexico Architecture* 12 (September-October):13-51.

1976   Early Architecture in New Mexico. Albuquerque: University of New Mexico Press.

———, and Conron, John P.
1966   The Architecture of Northern New Mexico. *New Mexico Architecture* 8 (September-October):14-49.

Bunzel, Ruth L.
1972   *The Pueblo Potter: A Study of Creative Imagination in Primitive Art.* New York: Dover Publications. First published in 1929.

Burdick, Charles B.
1966   A House on Navidad Street: The Celebrated Zimmerman Note on the Texas Border? *Arizona and the West* 8 (Spring): 19-34.

Burgess, Donald Harris
1963   Missionary Efforts Among the Tarahumara Indians. Master's thesis, University of Texas at El Paso.

Burgess, Sherwood D.
1962   Lumbering in Hispanic California. *California Historical Society Quarterly* 44 (September):237-48.

Burke, Gerald M.
1966   *Marketing Chile in the Rio Grande Valley.* Bulletin no. 511. Las Cruces: New Mexico Agricultural Experiment Station.

Burke, Robert E.
1952   *Olson's New Deal for California.* Berkeley: University of California Press.

Burma, John H.
1949   The Present Status of the Spanish-Americans of New Mexico. *Social Forces* 30:133-38.

1954   *Spanish-speaking Groups in the United States.* Durham: Duke University Press.

1962 An Economic, Social and Educational Survey of Río Arriba and Taos Counties. Mimeographed. El Rito: Northern New Mexico State College.

1963 Interethnic Marriage in Los Angeles, 1948-59. *Social Forces* 42 (December):156-65.

1970 Editor. *Mexican Americans in the United States.* Cambridge, Mass.: Schenkman Publishing Co.

Burman, Barbara G., and Cornish, Thomas G.

1975 Needed: A Ground-Water Treaty Between the United States and Mexico. *Natural Resources Journal* 15 (April): 385-404.

Burnham, C. Wayne

1959 *Metallogenic Provinces of the Southwestern United States and Northern Mexico.* State Bureau of Mines and Mineral Resources Bulletin 65. Socorro: New Mexico Institute of Mining and Technology.

Burnight, R. G.; Whetten, N. L.; and Waxman, B. D.

1956 Differential Rural Urban Fertility in Mexico. *American Sociological Review* 21 (January): 3-8.

Burns, Barney T., and Naylor, Thomas H.

1973 Colonia Morelos: A Short History of a Mormon Colony in Sonora, Mexico. *Smoke Signal, Tucson Corral of the Westerners* 27 (Spring):142-79.

Burrus, Ernest J.

1955 An Introduction to Bibliographical Tools in Spanish Archives and Manuscript Collections Relating to Hispanic America. *Hispanic American Historical Review* 35:443-83.

1962 Kino, Historian's Historian. *Arizona and the West* 4 (Summer):145-56.

1970 Rivera y Moncada, Explorer and Military Commander of Both Californias: In the Light of His Diary and Other Contemporary Documents. *Hispanic American Historical Review* 50 (November):682-92.

1972 Two Fictitious Accounts of Ortega's Third Voyage to California. *Hispanic American Historical Review* 52 (May):272-83.

———, and Zubiliaga, Felix

1956-59 Editors. *Historia de la Compañía de Jesús en Nueva España,* by S. J. Alegre and Francisco Javier. Vols. 1-3. New edition. Rome: Institutum Historicum, S.J.

Burt, Marina K.; Dulay, Heidi C.; and Hernández-Chávez, Eduardo

1976 *Bilingual Syntax Measure.* New York: Harcourt, Brace & Jovanovich.

Busch, Arthur W.

1978 Environmental Management: A Basis for Equitable Resource Allocation. In Stanley R. Ross, ed. *Views Across the Border,* pp. 338-59. Albuquerque: University of New Mexico Press.

Busey, James L.

1953-54 The Political Geography of Mexican Migration. *Colorado Quarterly* 2 (Autumn):181-90.

1958-59 The Mexican Border—If Any. *Colorado Quarterly* 7 (Winter):287-98.

Bushee, Alice H.

1923 Spanish Influence in the Southwest. *Hispania* 6 (May): 148-57.

Bushnell, G. H. S.

1965 *Ancient Arts of the Americas.* New York: Praeger Publishers.

Busselen, H. J., Jr.

1962 A Study of the Federal Termination of a California Ranchería and Its Effects upon the Social and Economic Integration of the Indian Population Involved. Master's thesis, California State University, Sacramento.

Bustamante, Jorge A.

1972a The "Wetback" as Deviant: An Application of Labeling Theory. *American Journal of Sociology* 77 (January): 706-18.

1972b The Historical Context of the Undocumented Immigration from Mexico to the United States. *Aztlán* 3 (Fall): 257-82.

1976 *Maquiladoras:* A New Face of International Capitalism in Mexico's Northern Frontier. Paper presented at the Latin American Studies Association, March, at Atlanta, Georgia.

1976a The Silent Invasion Issue. Paper presented to Population Association of America, April, at Montreal, Canada.

1976b Impact of Undocumented Immigration from Mexico on the U.S.-Mexican Economies. Proceedings, San Diego. *Fronteras* 76 (November):28-50.

1976c *Espaldas mojadas: materia previa para la expansión del capital norteamericano.* 2d ed. Mexico City: El Colegio de México.

1978a Commodity Migrants: Structural Analysis of Mexican Immigration to the United States. In Stanley R. Ross, ed. *Views Across the Border,* pp. 183-203. Albuquerque: University of New Mexico Press.

1978b Dimensions of the Migration Phenomenon in Mexico and the Caribbean Basin. Proceedings, Brookings Institution-Colegio de México Symposium, pp. 23-40, June, Washington, D.C.

1979 Toward the Analysis and Prognosis of the Political Implications of Mexican Undocumented Immigration. In Fernando Camara and Robert Van Kemper, eds. *Migration Across Frontiers: Mexico and the United States,* pp. 151-56. Albany: State University of New York at Albany, Institute for Mesoamerican Studies.

1980 *México-Estados Unidos: Bibliografía General Sobre Estudios Fronterizos.* México, D.F.: El Colegio de México.

Bustamante, J. C.

1951 Falcon Dam Stimulates Irrigation in Mexico. *Civil Engineering* 21 (no. 5):42-43.

Butler, M. T.

1975 Inflation in Mexico and Recession in U.S. Threaten Maquiladoras Accomplishments. *Business Review, Federal Reserve Bank of Dallas* (July): 1-7.

Bye, R. A.

1972 Ethnobotany of the Southern Paiute Indians in the 1870s, with a Note on the Early Ethnobotanical Contributions of Dr. Edward Palmer. In D. D. Fowler, ed. *Great Basin Cultural Ecology: A Symposium,* pp. 87-104. Publications in the Social Sciences, no. 8. Reno and Las Vegas: Desert Research Institute.

———; Burgess, D.; and Trias, A. Mares

1975 Ethnobotany of the Western Tarahumara of Chihuahua, Mexico: Notes on the Genus *Agave. Harvard University Botanical Museum Leaflets* 24: 85-112.

———, and Constance, L.

1979 A New Species of *Tauschia* (Umbelliferae) from Chihuahua, Mexico. *Madroño* 26 (1):44-47.

Cabeza de Baca, Fabiola. See also Gilbert, Fabiola Cabesa de Baca

1954 *We Fed them Cactus.* Albuquerque: University of New Mexico Press.

Cable, Dwight R.

1975 Influence of Precipitation on Perennial Grass Production in the Semidesert Southwest. *Ecology* 56 (Summer): 981-86.

Cadena, M.

1970 The Mexican American Family and the Mexican American Nurse. In D. Hymovich and M. Barnard, eds. *Family Health Care.* San Francisco: McGraw-Hill.

Calderón, Estaban B.

1956 *Juicio sobre la guerra yaqui, y génesis de la huelga de Cananea.* Mexico City: Imprenta YMMX.

Calderón, Liborio V.

1973 On the Importance of the "Assembly Industries" to the Mexican Economy. Paper presented at conference sponsored by Institute of Latin American Studies, April, at Austin, Texas.

Cali, Francois

1961 *The Spanish Arts of Latin America.* New York: Viking

Press.

Calkins, Hugh G.
1937a   *Dependency on Migratory Labor in the Upper Rio Grande
         Area.* Soil Conservation Service Bulletin no. 46. Albu-
         querque: U.S. Department of Agriculture.
1937b   *Handling of a Cash Crop (Chili).* Regional Bulletin no.
         46. Albuquerque: U.S. Department of Agriculture.

Callahan, James M.
1932   *American Foreign Policy in Mexican Relations.* New
         York: Macmillan Co.

Callcott, Wilfred Hardy
1964   *Santa Anna: The Story of an Enigma Who Once Was
         Mexico.* Hamden, Conn.: Archon Books.

Callon, Milton W.
1962   *Las Vegas, New Mexico—the Town That Wouldn't
         Gamble.* Las Vegas: Las Vegas Publishing Co.

Calvin, Ross
1948   *Sky Determines.* Albuquerque: University of New Mex-
         ico Press.

Camara Barbachano, Fernando
1962   El Papel de la religión en la integración de la sociedad
         y cultura yaqui. *International Congress of Americanists,
         Proceedings* 2 (35):575-93.
1979   Differential Migration Streams, Economic Growth, and
         Socio-Cultural Changes in Mexican Border Cities. In
         Fernando Camara and Robert Van Kemper, eds. *Migra-
         tion Across Frontiers: Mexico and the United States,*
         pp. 101-26. Albany: State University of New York at
         Albany, Institute for Mesoamerican Studies.

Camara, Fernando, and Van Kemper, Robert
1979   Editors. *Migration Across Frontiers: Mexico and the
         United States.* Albany: State University of New York
         at Albany, Institute for Mesoamerican Studies.

Camarillo, Albert
1979   *From Mexican Pueblos to American Barrios: Historical
         Roots of Chicano Urban Society in Santa Barbara and
         Southern California, 1848-1930.* Cambridge: Harvard
         University Press.

Camazine, S., and Bye, R. A.
1980   A Study of the Medical Ethnobotany of the Zuni Indians
         of New Mexico. *Journal of Ethnopharmacology* 2:365-
         88.

Cameron, Colin, and Edelson, Joanne
1969   *Farm Labor Organizing: An Annotated Bibliography.*
         Madison: University of Wisconsin, Institute for Research
         on Poverty.

Camp, Roderic A.
1971   The Cabinet and the *Técnico* in Mexico and the U.S.
         Journal of Comparative Administration 3 (no. 2):188-
         214.
1979   Women and Political Leadership in Mexico: A Compara-
         tive Study of Female and Male Political Elites. *Journal
         of Politics* 41 (no. 2):417-41.

Campa, Arthur L.
1934   Chili in New Mexico. *New Mexico Business Review* 3:
         61-63.

Campbell, Angus, et al.
1960   *The American Voter.* New York: John Wiley & Sons.

Campbell, Charles E.
1972   Some Environmental Effects of Rural Subdividing in
         an Arid Area: A Case Study in Arizona. *Journal of
         Geography* 71 (March): 147-54.

Campbell, Howard L.
1972   Bracero Migration and the Mexican Economy, 1951-
         1964. Ph.D. dissertation, American University.

Campbell, Ian A.
1970   Climate and Overgrazing on the Shonto Plateau, Ari-
         zona. *Professional Geographer* 22 (May):132-41.

Campbell, Leon G.
1974   The First Californios: Presidential Society in Spanish
         California, 1769-1822. In Oakah L. Jones, Jr., ed. *The*

Spanish Borderlands—A First Reader, pp. 106-18. Los
Angeles: Lorrin L. Morrison.

Campbell, S. M.
1974   A Proposal for the Quantification of Reserved Indian
         Water Rights. *Columbia Law Review* 74 (November):
         1299-1321.

Campbell, T. N.
1967   Archeological Survey of the Big Bend National Park,
         Texas. Part I. Mimeographed report submitted to the
         National Park Service.
1970   Archeological Survey of the Big Bend National Park,
         1966-1967. Mimeographed report submitted to National
         Park Service.
1973   Systematized Ethnohistory and Prehistoric Culture Se-
         quences of Texas. *Texas Archeological Society Bulletin*
         43:1-11.
1975   *The Payaya Indians of Southern Texas.* Special Publi-
         cation no. 1. San Antonio: Southern Texas Archaeo-
         logical Association.
1977   *Ethnic Identities of Extinct Coahuiltecan Indian Pop-
         ulations: Case of the Juanca Indians.* Pearce-Sellards
         Series, no. 26. Austin: Texas Memorial Museum.

Canby, William C., Jr.
1973   Civil Jurisdiction and the Indian Reservation. *Utah Law
         Review* (Summer):206-32.

Cancián, F. M.
1964   Interaction Patterns in Zincanteco Families. *American
         Sociological Review* 29 (August):540-50.

Candelas, J.
1971   El instituto de seguridad y servicios sociales de los traba-
         jadores del estado y la salud pública de la frontera mex-
         icana-estadounidense. *Salud Pública de México* 13:
         195-208.

Cantor, Leonard M.
1969   The California Water Plan. *Journal of Geography* 68
         (September):366-71.
1970   *A World Geography of Irrigation.* New York: Praeger
         Publishers.

Cantú, Ismael Sierra
1975   The Effects of Family Characteristics, Parental Influ-
         ence, Language Spoken, School Experience, and Self-
         Motivation on the Level of Educational Attainment of
         Mexican Americans. Ph.D. dissertation, University of
         Michigan, Ann Arbor.

Cárdenas, Daniel N.
1975   Chicano Language: What? Why? How? *Hispania* 53:
         185-88.

Cardenas, Gilbert
1978a   Toward a Theoretical Approach for the Measurement
         of Discrimination and the Manpower Impact of Illegal
         Aliens. Paper presented to Southern Economic Asso-
         ciation, November, at Washington, D.C.
1978b   The Manpower Impact of Mexican Illegal Aliens in the
         San Antonio Labor Market in the Seventies. Paper, Pan
         American University, Edinburg, Texas.

Cardenas, Gilberto
1975   U.S. Immigration Policy Toward Mexico: An Historical
         Perspective. *Chicano Law Review* 2 (Summer):66-91.
1976   Illegal Aliens in the Southwest: A Case Study. In *Illegal
         Aliens: An Assessment of the Issues,* pp. 66-69. Wash-
         ington, D.C.: National Council on Employment Policy.

Cardenas, L.
1971   Perspectives de control de la rabia en la frontera norte
         de México. *Salud Pública de México* 13:169-74.

Cardenas, Leonard, Jr.
1963   *The Municipality in Northern Mexico.* Southwestern
         Studies, no. 1. El Paso: Texas Western Press.
1965   Contemporary Problems of Local Government in Mex-
         ico. *Western Political Quarterly* 18 (December): 858-
         65.
1970   Trends and Problems of Urbanization in the United

States-Mexico Border Area. In Ellwyn R. Stoddard, ed. *Comparative U.S.-Mexico Border Studies,* pp. 39-54. Occasional Papers, no. 1. El Paso: Border-State University Consortium for Latin America.

Cardoso, Geraldo da Silva
1975   Negro Slavery in the Sugar Plantations of Veracruz and Pernambuco, 1550-1680: A Comparative Study. Ph.D. dissertation, University of Nebraska, Lincoln.

Cardoso, Lawrence A.
1974   Mexican Emigration to the United States, 1900-1930: An Analysis of Socio-Economic Causes. Ph.D. dissertation, University of Connecticut.
1976   Labor Emigration to the Southwest, 1916-1920: Mexican Attitudes and Policy. *Southwestern Historical Quarterly* 74 (April):400-16.
1977   La repatriación de braceros en época de Obregón—1920-1923. *Historia Mexicana* 26 (abril-junio):576-95.
1980   *Mexican Emigration to the United States, 1897-1931: Socio-Economic Patterns.* Tucson: University of Arizona Press.

Cardoza y Aragon, Luis
1966   *Mexican Art Today.* Mexico City: Fondo de Cultura Economica.

Carleton, James Henry
1855   *Diary of an Excursion to the Ruins of ABO, Quarra, and Gran Quivera, in New Mexico Under the Command of James Henry Carleton.* Ninth Annual Report. Washington, D.C.: Smithsonian Institution.
1867   *Condition of the Indian Tribes.* Washington, D.C.: Report of the Joint Special Committee appointed under Joint Resolution of March 3, 1865.

Carliner, David
1977   *The Rights of Aliens.* New York: Avon Books.

Carlson, Alvar W.
1967   Rural Settlement Patterns in the San Luis Valley: A Comparative Study. *Colorado Magazine* 44 (Spring):111-28.
1969   New Mexico's Sheep Industry, 1850-1900: Its Role in the History of the Territory. *New Mexico Historical Review* 44 (January):25-49.
1971a   Mexican Americans and a Bibliography of the Geographical Literature, 1920-1971. *Revista Geográfica* 75 (December):154-61.
1971b   The Rio Arriba: A Geographic Appraisal of the Spanish-American Homeland; Upper Rio Grande Valley, New Mexico. Ph.D. dissertation, University of Minnesota.
1972a   A Bibliography of the Geographers' Contributions to Understanding the American Southwest (Arizona and New Mexico). *Arizona Quarterly* 28 (Summer):101-41.
1972b   A Bibliography of the Geographical Literature on the American Indian, 1920-1971. *Professional Geographer* 24 (August):258-63.
1973a   An Addendum to a Bibliography of the Geographers' Contributions to Understanding the American Southwest (Arizona and New Mexico), 1920-1971. *Arizona Quarterly* 29 (Winter):352-57.
1973b   Seasonal Farm Labor in the San Luis Valley. *Annals, Association of American Geographers* 63 (March):97-108.
1975a   Long-Lots in the Rio Arriba. *Annals, Association of American Geographers* 65 (March):48-57.
1975b   Spanish-American Acquisition of Cropland Within the Northern Pueblo Indian Grants, New Mexico. *Ethnohistory* 22 (Spring):95-110.
1976   Spanish Colonization and the Abiquiu Grant, New Mexico, 1754-1970. *Philippine Geographical Journal* 20 (April, May, June):61-68.
1979   Corrales, New Mexico: Transition in a Spanish-American Community. *Red River Valley Historical Review* 4, (Summer):88-99.
1979   El Rancho and Vadito: Spanish Settlements on Indian

Lands. *El Palacio* 85 (Spring):28-39.

Carlton, Robert Lloyd
1977   Blacks in San Diego County, 1850-1900. Master's thesis, San Diego State University.

Carmen Elu de Leñero, María del. See also Elu, Maria del Carmen
1971   Editor. *Mujeres que hablan: implicaciones psico-sociales en el uso de métodos anticonceptivos.* Mexico City: Instituto Mexicano de Estudios Sociales.

Carpenter, Edwin H., and Blackwood, Larry G.
1977   The Potential for Population Growth in the U.S. Counties that Border Mexico: El Paso to San Diego. *Natural Resources Journal* 17 (October):545-69.

Carranza, Michael A., and Ryan, Ellen B.
1975   Evaluative Reactions of Bilingual Anglo and Mexican American Adolescents Toward Speakers of English and Spanish. *Linguistics* 166:83-104.

Carrera Stampa, Manuel
1952   *Archivalia Mexicana.* Mexico City: UNAM.

Carreras de Velasco, Mercedes
1974   *Los Mexicanos que devolvió: la crisis 1929-1932.* Mexico City: Secretaría de Relaciones Exteriores.

Carrington, Paul M.
1907   The Climate of New Mexico, Nature's Sanatorium for Consumptives. *New York Medical Journal* 86 (July 6):1-10.

Carroll, H. Bailey, and Haggard, J. Villasana
1942   Editors. *Three New Mexico Chronicles: The* Exposición *of Don Pedro Bautista Pino 1812; The* Ojeada *of Lic. Antonio Barreiro 1832; and the Additions by Don José Augustín de Escudero 1894.* Albuquerque: Quivira Society.

Carroll, John M.
1971a   *Buffalo Soldiers West.* Ft. Collins, Colo.: Old Army Press.
1971b   *The Black Military Experience in the American West.* New York: Liveright.

Carter, George F.
1945   *Plant Geography and Culture History in the American Southwest.* New York: Viking Fund.
1959   Man, Time, and Change in the Far Southwest. *Annals, Association of American Geographers* 49 (September-supplement):8-30.

Carter, Harvey L.
1968   *"Dear Old Kit": The Historical Christopher Carson.* Norman: University of Oklahoma Press.

Carter, J. D.; Berger, W. E.; and Dent, O. F.
1965   Reconnaissance Investigation of the Ground-Water Resources of the Upper Rio Grande Basin, Texas. Bulletin 6502. Austin: Texas Water Commission.

Carter, Luther J.
1973   Weather Modification: Colorado Heeds Voters in Valley Dispute. *Science* 180 (June 29):1347-50.

Carter, Marshall
1978a   Cooperation and Conflict: Dilemmas of Transnational Law Enforcement on the U.S.-Mexico Border. Paper presented to Western Social Science Association, April, at Denver, Colorado.
1978b   The Political Economy of Crime in the U.S.-Mexican Borderlands. Paper presented to the North American Economic Studies Association/Southern Economics Association, November, at Washington, D.C.
1978c   Law Enforcement and Federalism: Bordering on Trouble. *Policy Studies Journal* 7 (no. 5):413-18.
1979a   Law Enforcement and Federalism. In Fred A. Meyer and Ralph Baker, eds. *Determinants of Law Enforcement Policies.* Lexington, Mass.: Lexington Books.
1979b   Human Rights and the Border Complex. Paper presented to Rocky Mountain Council on Latin American Studies, May, at El Paso, Texas.
1979c   Federalism and the Judicial Process: A Case Study and Discussion from the U.S.-Mexico Border. Paper presented to the American Political Science Association,

September, at Washington, D.C.

1980   Agency Fragmentation and Its Effects on Impact: A Borderlands Case. *Policy Studies Journal* 8 (no. 6):862-70.

1981   Policy Organization and Impact: Fragmentation in the Borderlands. In John G. Grumm and Stephen L. Wasby, eds. *The Analysis of Policy Impact.* Lexington, Mass.: Lexington Books, D. C. Heath and Co.

Carter, Thomas P.

1968   The Negative Self-Concept of Mexican-American Students. *School and Society* 96:217-19.

——, and Segura, Roberto D.

1979   *Mexican Americans in School: A Decade of Change.* New York: College Entrance Examination Board.

Casagrande, Joseph B.; Thompson, Stephen I.; and Young, Philip D.

1964   Colonization as a Research Frontier: The Ecuadorian Case. In Robert A. Manners, ed. *Process and Pattern in Culture,* pp. 281-325. Chicago: Aldine Publishing Co.

Casanova, Pablo G. See also González-Casanova

1967   *La Democracia en México.* 2d ed. Mexico City: Ediciones ERA.

Casavantes, Edward J.

1969   *A New Look at the Attributes of the Mexican-American.* Albuquerque: Southwestern Cooperative Educational Laboratory.

Cason, J. F.

1952   Report on Archaeological Salvage in Falcon Reservoir, Season of 1952. *Texas Archeological and Paleontological Society Bulletin* 23:218-59.

Castañeda, Alfredo, et al.

1974   Editors. *Mexican Americans and Educational Change.* New York: Arno Press.

Castañeda, Carlos E.

1928   Editor and translator. *The Mexican Side of the Texan Revolution.* Dallas: P. L. Turner Co.

1935   Editor and translator. *History of Texas, 1673-1779,* by Fray Juan Agustín Morfi. 2 vols. Albuquerque: Quivira Society.

1936-58   *Our Catholic Heritage in Texas, 1519-1936.* 7 vols. Austin: Von Boeckmann-Jones Co.

1968   *The Teachings of Don Juan: A Yaqui Way of Knowledge.* Berkeley: University of California Press.

Castedo, Leopoldo

1969   *A History of Latin American Art and Architecture.* London: Pall Mall Press.

Castellanos, M.

1973   *Plan de salud del Estado de Baja California.* Mexico City: 1° Convención Nacional de Salud.

Castetter, E. F.

1935   Uncultivated Native Plants Used as Sources of Food. Biological Series 4 (1). Albuquerque: University of New Mexico Bulletin.

1956   The Vegetation of New Mexico. *New Mexico Quarterly* 26:256-88.

——, and Bell, W. H.

1937   The Aboriginal Utilization of the Tall Cacti in the American Southwest. Biological Series 5 (1). Albuquerque: University of New Mexico Bulletin.

1942   *Pima and Pápago Indian Agriculture.* Albuquerque: University of New Mexico Press.

1951   *Yuman Indian Agriculture: Primitive Subsistence on the Lower Colorado and Gila Rivers.* Albuquerque: University of New Mexico Press.

——; Bell, W. H.; and Grove, A. R.

1938   The Early Utilization and the Distribution of *Agave* in the American Southwest. Biological Series 5 (4). Albuquerque: University of New Mexico Bulletin.

——, and Opler, M. E.

1936   The Ethnobiology of the Chiricahua and Mescalero Apache: The Use of Plants for Foods, Beverages, and Narcotics. Biological Series 4 (5). Albuquerque: University of New Mexico Bulletin.

——, and Underhill, R. M.

1935   The Ethnobiology of the Pápago Indians. Biological Series 4 (3). Albuquerque: University of New Mexico Bulletin.

Castile, George P.

1974   Federal Indian Policy and the Sustained Enclave: An Anthropological Perspective. *Human Organization* 33 (Fall): 219-28.

Castillo, Pedro, and Camarillo, Alberto

1973   Editors. *Furia y muerte: los bandidos Chicanos.* Los Angeles: University of California Press.

Caughey, John Walton

1946   *Hubert Howe Bancroft: Historian of the West.* Berkeley: University of California Press.

1948   *Gold is the Cornerstone.* Berkeley: University of California Press.

1952   The Spanish Southwest: An Example of Subconscious Regionalism. In Merrill Jensen, ed. *Regionalism in America,* pp. 173-89. Madison: University of Wisconsin Press.

1953a   Herbert Eugene Bolton. *Pacific Historical Review* 22 (May):109-12.

1953b   *California.* Englewood Cliffs, N.J.: Prentice-Hall.

1969   *The American West, Frontier and Region: Interpretations.* Edited by Norris Hundley, Jr., and John A. Schutz. Los Angeles: Ward Ritchie Press.

1970   *California: A Remarkable State's Life History.* Englewood Cliffs, N.J.: Prentice-Hall.

Cavazos Garza, Israel

1952   Nuevo León: la historia y sus instrumentos. *Historia Mexicana* 1 (enero-marzo):494-515.

Cawelti, John G.

1976   The Frontier of the Native American. In Joshua C. Taylor, ed. *America as Art.* Washington, D.C.: Smithsonian Institution.

Cazorla, Eugenio

1973   Immigration Law and Practice . . . A Rare Field. *Texas Bar Journal* 36 (February):129-32.

1975   Employers and Aliens: The Labor Certification Process. *Texas Bar Journal* 38 (no. 1):41-47.

Cehelsky, Marta

1976   The U.S.-Mexico Border Area as a Development Region. Paper presented to the Southwestern Social Science Association, April, at Dallas, Texas.

Cerda, Gilberto; Cabaza, Berta; and Farias, Julieta

1970   *Vocabulario español de Texas.* Austin: University of Texas Press.

Cerda Silva, Roberto de la

1943a   Los tarahumaras. *Revista Mexicana de Sociología* 5 (3): 403-36.

1943b   Los tepehuanes. *Revista Mexicana de Sociología* 5 (4): 541-67.

1957   Kikapús. In Francisco Rojas González and René Barragán Avilés, eds. *Etnografía de México,* pp. 671-81. Mexico City: UNAM, Instituto de Investigaciones Sociales.

Cessac, León de

1882   Renseignements ethnographiques sur les Comanches. *Revue d'Ethnographie* 1:94-118.

Chalmers, John R.

1974   *Southwestern Groundwater Law: A Textual and Bibliographic Interpretation.* Office of Arid Lands Studies, no. 4. Tucson: University of Arizona.

Chamberlin, Eugene Keith

1963   Nicholas Trist and Baja California. *Pacific Historical Review* 32 (February):44-63.

Chambers, Reid P.

1971   Discharge of the Federal Trust Responsibility to Enforce Claims of Indian Tribes: Case Studies of Bureaucratic Conflict of Interest. *American Indian Law Newsletter* 4 (September):1-20.

——, and Price, Monroe

1974 Regulating Sovereignty: Secretarial Discretion and the Leasing of Indian Lands. *Stanford Law Review* 26 (May): 1061-96.

Chambers, William T.
1932 Edwards Plateau: A Combination Ranching Region. *Economic Geography* 8 (January):67-80.
1934 Pine Woods Region of Southeastern Texas. *Economic Geography* 10 (July):302-18.
1952 *Texas: Its Lands and Peoples.* Austin: Steck Co.

Champagne, J., and King, D.
1967 Job Satisfaction Factors Among Under Privileged Workers. *Personnel and Guidance Journal* 45:429-34.

Champion, R.
1955 Acculturation Among the Tarahumara of Northwestern Mexico Since 1890. *Transactions of the New York Academy of Science* 17:560-66.

Chapin, Charles E., and Seager, William R.
1975 Evolution of the Rio Grande Rift in the Socorro and Las Cruces Areas. In *Las Cruces Country Guidebook,* pp. 297-321. Socorro: New Mexico Geological Society, Twenty-Sixth Field Conference.

Chapin, Edward L., Jr.
1953 *A Selected Bibliography of Southern California Maps.* Berkeley: University of California Press.

Chapman, Charles E.
1916 *The Founding of Spanish California: The Northwestward Expansion of New Spain, 1687-1783.* New York: Macmillan Co.
1921 *A History of California: The Spanish Period.* New York: Macmillan Co.

Chapman, Charles R.
1971 The Texas Water Plan and Its Effect on Estuaries. In *Symposium on the Biological Significance of Estuaries,* pp. 40-57. Washington, D.C.: Sport Fishing Institute.

Chapman, Kenneth M.
1970 *The Pottery of San Ildefonso.* Albuquerque: University of New Mexico Press.

Chapman, S. B.
1976 Editor. *Methods in Plant Ecology.* New York: John Wiley & Sons.

Chapman, Stephen
1977 Let the Aliens in." *Washington Monthly* 9 (July-August): 5-6.

Chatelain, Verne E.
1941 *The Defense of Spanish Florida, 1565-1762.* Washington, D.C.: Carnegie Institution of Washington.

Chávez, Fray Angélico
1954 *Origins of New Mexico Families.* Santa Fe: Historical Society of New Mexico.
1955 Early Settlements in the Mora Valley. *El Palacio* 62 (November):318-23.
1957 *Archives of the Archdiocese of Santa Fe, 1678-1900.* Washington, D.C.: Academy of American Franciscan History.
1965 The Unique Tomb of Fathers Zárate and De La Llana in Santa Fe. *New Mexico Historical Review* 40 (April): 101-16.
1967 Pohe-Yemo's Representative and the Pueblo Revolt of 1680. *New Mexico Historical Review* 42 (April):85-126.
1974 *My Penitente Land: Reflections on Spanish New Mexico.* Albuquerque: University of New Mexico Press.

Chávez, Tibo
1977 In Search of the Horno. *New Mexico Magazine* 55 (January):28, 46-47.

Chávez Camacho, Armando
1948 *Cajeme, Novela de Indios.* Mexico City: Editorial Jus.

Chávez M., Armando B.
1959 *Sesenta años de gobierno municipal.* Mexico City: Gráfica Cervantina.
1970 *Historia de Ciudad Juárez, Chihuahua.* Mexico City: n.p.

Chávez Orozco, Luis
1953 *Índice de ramo de indios del archivo general de la nación.* 2 vols. Mexico City: n.p.

Chavira, Juan Antonio, and Trotter, Robert T., II
1975 *The Gift of Healing.* Edinburg, Texas: Pan American University.

Chevalier, François
1963 *Land and Society in Colonial Mexico: The Great Hacienda.* Berkeley: University of California Press.
1970 *Land and Society in Colonial Mexico.* Berkeley: University of California Press.

Chilcott, John H.; Campbell, Ernest Q.; Hobson, Carol J.; McPartland, James; Mood, Alexander M.; Weinfeld, Fredric D.; and York, Robert L.
1962 Enculturation in a Mexican Ranchería. *Journal of Educational Sociology* 36:42-47.

Chipman, Donald E.
1963 New Light on the Career of Nuño Beltrán de Guzmán. *Americas* 19 (April):341-48.
1966 The Traffic in Indian Slaves in the Province of Pánuco, New Spain, 1523-1533. *Americas* 23 (October):142-55.
1971 The Status of Biography in the Historiography of New Spain. *Americas* 27 (January):327-39.

Choldin, Harvey M., and Trout, Grafton D.
1969 *Mexican Americans in Transition: Migration and Employment in Michigan Cities.* East Lansing: Michigan State University, Agricultural Experiment Station.

Christaller, Walter
1966 *Central Places in Southern Germany.* Englewood Cliffs, N.J.: Prentice-Hall.

Christelow, Allan
1939 Father Joseph Neumann, Jesuit Missionary to the Tarahumara. *Hispanic American Historical Review* 19 (November):432-42.

Christian, Chester C., Jr.
1961 Some Sociological Implications of Government VD Control. Master's thesis, University of Texas at Austin.
1976 Sociolinguistics Criteria for Choice of Spanish Lexicon in Training Teachers of Mexican-Americans in Texas. *Journal of The Linguistic Association of the Southwest* 2 (August):41-48.

Christiansen, Paige W.
1961 Pascual Orozco, Chihuahua Rebel: Episodes in the Mexican Revolution, 1910-1915. *New Mexico Historical Review* 36 (April):97-120.
1974a *The Story of Mining in New Mexico.* Socorro: New Mexico Bureau of Mines.
1974b The Presidio and the Borderlands: A Case Study. In Oakah L. Jones, Jr., ed. *The Spanish Borderlands—A First Reader,* pp. 78-86. Los Angeles: Lorrin L. Morrison.

———, and Kottlowski, Frank E.
1967 Editors. *Mosaic of New Mexico's Scenery, Rocks, and History.* Socorro: New Mexico Bureau of Mines.

Chu, Daniel, and Chu, Samuel
1967 *Passage to the Golden Gate: A History of the Chinese in America to 1910.* New York: Doubleday & Co.

Church, Phil E.
1947 Snow as an Environmental Factor in the West. *Yearbook, Association of Pacific Coast Geographers* 9:8-14.

Clark, James R.
1958 The Kingdom of God, the Council of Fifty and the State of Deseret. *Utah Historical Quarterly* 24 (April):131-48.

Clark, Joseph Lynn
1939 *A History of Texas: Land of Promise.* New York: D. C. Heath.

Clark, Margaret
1959 *Health in the Mexican-American Culture: A Community Study.* Berkeley: University of California Press.

Clark, Robert E.
1962 New Mexico Water Law Since 1955. *Natural Resources*

Journal 2 (December):484-561.

1967   Editor. *Waters and Water Rights.* 7 vols. Indianapolis: Allen Smith Co.

1971   Water Rights-Problems in the Upper Rio Grande Watershed and Adjoining Areas. *Natural Resources Journal* 11 (January):48-68.

1977   The Role of State Legislation in Ground Water Management. *Creighton Law Review* 10 (March):469-87.

1978   Institutional Alternatives for Managing Groundwater Resources. *Natural Resources Journal* 18 (January):153-61.

Clarke, C. B.
1977   *Edible and Useful Plants of California.* Berkeley: University of California Press.

Clawson, Marion
1952   Land Use Potentialities of Artificially-induced Precipitation in the Western United States. *Land Economics* 28 (February):54-62.

1963   Critical Review of Man's History in Arid Regions. In Carle Hodge and Peter C. Duisberg, eds. *Aridity and Man,* pp. 429-59. AAAS, Publication no. 74. Washington, D.C.

———, et al.
1969   Desalted Sea Water for Agriculture: Is It Economical. *Science* 164 (June 6):1141-48.

———, and Landsberg, Hans H.
1972   Editors. *Desalting Seawater: Achievements and Prospects.* New York: Gordon & Breach.

Clay, Comer
1970   A Review of the Texas Water Plan—Issues and Attitudes. In Corwin W. Johnson and Susan H. Lewis, eds. *Contemporary Developments in Water Law,* pp. 160-72. Symposium no. 4. Austin: University of Texas, Center for Research in Water Resources.

1971   *Issues and Attitudes on the Texas Water Plan.* Austin: University of Texas, Institute of Public Affairs.

Cleaveland, Norman
1971   *The Morleys, Young Upstarts on the Southwest Frontier.* Albuquerque: Calvin Horn Publisher.

Clegg, J. Halvor
1969   Fonética y fonología del español de Texas. Ph.D. dissertation, University of Texas, Austin.

Cleland, Courtney B.
1966   Do We Need a Sociology of Arid Regions. In John W. Bennett, ed. *Social Research in North American Moisture Deficient Regions,* pp. 1-12. AAAS, Publication no. 9. Las Cruces: New Mexico State University.

Cleland, Robert Glass
1944   *From Wilderness to Empire: A History of California, 1542-1900.* New York: Alfred A. Knopf.

1950   *This Reckless Breed of Men: The Trappers and Fur Traders of the Southwest.* New York: Alfred A. Knopf.

1952   *A History of Phelps-Dodge, 1834-1950.* New York: Alfred A. Knopf.

———, and Hardy, Osgood
1929   *March of Industry.* Los Angeles: Powell Publishing Co.
1941   *The Cattle on a Thousand Hills: Southern California, 1850-1870.* San Marino, Calif.: Huntington Library.

Clendenen, Clarence C.
1961a   The Punitive Expedition of 1916: A Re-evaluation. *Arizona and the West* 3 (Winter):311-20.

1961b   *The United States and Pancho Villa: A Study in Unconventional Diplomacy.* Ithaca: Cornell University Press.

1964   Mexican Unionists: A Forgotten Incident of the War Between the States. *New Mexico Historical Review* 39 (January):32-39.

1969   *Blood on the Border: The United States Army and the Mexican Irregulars.* New York: Macmillan.

Clifford, Roy A.
1955   *Informal Group Actions in the Rio Grande Flood: Report to the Committee on Disaster Studies.* Washington, D.C.: National Research Council.

1956   *The Rio Grande Flood: A Comparative Study of Border Communities in Disaster.* National Research Council Publication 458. Washington, D.C.: National Academy of Sciences.

1970   Sociological Study of the Growth and Decline of Mexican Population Centers, 1940-1960. Ph.D. dissertation, University of Florida, Gainesville.

Cline, Howard F.
1953   *The United States and Mexico.* Cambridge: Harvard University Press.

1963   *Mexico: Revolution to Evolution, 1940-1960.* New York: Oxford University Press.

1968   *The United States and Mexico.* rev. ed. New York: Atheneum Publishers.

1972   Ethnohistorical Regions of Middle America. In Robert Wauchope, ed. *Handbook of Middle American Indians,* vol. 12, *Guide to Ethnohistorical Sources,* part 1, pp. 166-82. Austin: University of Texas Press.

Clyma, Wayne, and Lotspeich, F. B.
1966   *Water Resources in the High Plains of Texas and New Mexico.* Agricultural Research Service, pp. 41-114. Washington, D.C.: U.S. Department of Agriculture.

Coalson, George O.
1952   Mexican Contract Labor in American Agriculture. *Southwestern Social Science Quarterly* 33 (December):228-38.

1977   *The Development of the Migratory Farm Labor System in Texas, 1900-1954.* San Francisco: R & E Research Associates.

Coan, Charles C.
1925   *History of New Mexico.* 3 vols. Chicago: Historical Society.

Coates, Lawrence G.
1969   A History of Indian Education by the Mormons, 1830-1900. Ed.D. dissertation, Ball State University.

Coblentz, Stanton A.
1936   *Villains and Vigilantes.* Elmira, N.Y.: Wilson Erickson.

Cockcroft, James D.; Gunder Frank, André; and Johnson, Dale L.
1972   *Dependence and Underdevelopment.* Garden City: Doubleday & Co.

Coffeen, William R.
1973   The Effects of the Central Arizona Project on the Fort McDowell Indian Community. *Ethnohistory* 19 (no. 4):345-77.

Coffin, E. F.
1932   *Archaeological Exploration of a Rock Shelter in Brewster County, Texas.* Indian Notes and Monographs, no. 48. New York: Heye Foundation, Museum of the American Indian.

Cohen, Andrew D.
1974   The Effects of Several Years of Bilingual Schooling on Language Maintenance: What Language is Juanito Using Now? Occasional Papers, no. 1. California Teachers of English to Speakers of Other Languages.

Cohen, Barry M.
1968   The Texas-Mexico Border, 1858-1867: Along the Lower Rio Grande Valley During the Decade of the American Civil War and the French Intervention in Mexico. *Texana* 6 (Summer):153-62.

Cohen, Felix S.
1971   *Handbook of Federal Indian Law.* Albuquerque: University of New Mexico Press. Reprint of 1941 edition.

Cohen, Ronald
1978   Ethnicity: Problem and Focus in Anthropology. *Annual Review in Anthropology* 7:379-403.

Coke, Van Deren
1963   *Taos and Santa Fe: The Artist's Environment, 1882-1942.* Albuquerque: University of New Mexico Press.

Coleman, James S.
1966   *Equality of Educational Opportunity.* Washington, D.C.:

Government Printing Office.

Coleman, Kenneth M.
1976   *Diffuse Support in Mexico.* Beverly Hills, Calif.: Sage Publications.

Coles, Robert
1965   *The Migrant Farm Worker: A Psychiatric Study.* Atlanta: Southern Regional Council.
1970   *Uprooted Children: The Early Life of Migrant Farm Workers.* Pittsburgh: University of Pittsburgh Press.
1971   *Migrants, Sharecroppers, Mountaineers.* Boston: Little, Brown & Co.

Collado-Herrell, Leida Ileana
1976   An Exploration of Affective and Cognitive Components of Bilingualism. Ph.D. dissertation, University of Maryland.

Colley, Charles C.
1970   The Missionization of the Coast Miwok Indians of California. *California Historical Society Quarterly* 49 (July): 143-62.

Collier, James E.
1970   Sources of Fresh Vegetables in United States Markets. *Journal of Geography* 69 (6):335-41.

Collier, John
1947   *Indians of the Americas: The Long Hope.* New York: New American Library (Mentor).

Collins, John James
1967   Peyotism and Religious Membership at Taos Pueblo, New Mexico. *Southwestern Social Science Quarterly* 48:183-91.
1968   A Descriptive Introduction to the Taos Peyote Ceremony. *Ethnology* 7 (October):427-49.

Collins, M. B.
1969   *Test Excavations at Amistad International Reservoir, Fall, 1967.* Austin: Texas Archeological Salvage Project 16.

Coltharp, Lurline H.
1965   *The Tongue of the Tirilones: A Linguistic Study of a Criminal Argot.* University, Ala.: University of Alabama Press.

Colton, Harold S.
1974   *Hopi History and Ethnobotany.* New York: Garland Publishing, Museum of Northern Arizona.

Colyer, Vincent
1872   *Peace with the Apaches of New Mexico and Arizona.* Washington, D.C.: Government Printing Office.

Conkling, Roscoe P., and Conkling, Margaret B.
1947   *The Butterfield Overland Mail, 1857-1869,* 3 vols. Glendale: Arthur H. Clark Co.

Conley, Marita; Soto, Irma; and Stephan, Nelly
1976   *Contemporary Bibliography on Seasonal Agricultural Labor, 1970-1976.* Austin: University of Texas, Center for the Study of Human Relations.

Connelley, William Elsey
1907   *Doniphan's Expedition and the Conquest of New Mexico and California.* Topeka: Privately published.

Connor, Seymour V.
1965   *Adventure in Glory, 1836-1849.* Austin: Steck Co.
1971   *Texas: A History.* Arlington Heights, Ill.: AHM Publishing Corp.
——, and Faulk, Odie B.
1971   *North America Divided: The Mexican War.* New York: Oxford University Press.
——, and Skaggs, Jimmy M.
1977   *Broadcloth and Britches, the Santa Fe Trade.* College Station: Texas A&M University Press.
——, et al.
1973   *Water for the Southwest: Historical Survey and Guide to Historic Sites.* ASCE Historical Publication no. 3. New York: American Society of Civil Engineers.

Conway, A. W.
1951a   Southwestern Colonial Farms. *Landscape* 1 (Spring): 6-9.

1951b   A Northern New Mexico House-Type. *Landscape* (Autumn): 20-21.
1952   Village Types in the Southwest. *Landscape* 2 (Spring): 14-19.

Conway, M. Margaret, and Feigert, Frank B.
1972   *Political Analysis: An Introduction.* Boston: Allyn & Bacon.

Cook, L. D.
1968   *Water Administration in Arizona: A Problem in Coordination.* Tempe: Arizona State University, Institute of Public Administration.

Cook, Ramsey
1971   *The Maple Leaf Forever: Essays in Nationalism and Politics in Canada.* Toronto: Macmillan of Canada.

Cook, Sherburne F.
1943a   *The Conflict Between the California Indian and White Civilization.* Berkeley: University of California Press.
1943b   Migration and Urbanization of the Indians of California. *Human Biology* 15:33-45.
1970   The California Indian and Anglo-American Culture. In Charles Wollenberg, ed. *Ethnic Conflict in California History,* pp. 23-42. Los Angeles: Tinnon-Brown.
1976   *The Population of the California Indians, 1769-1970.* Berkeley: University of California Press.
——, and Borah, Woodrow
1971   *Essays in Population History: Mexico and the Caribbean.* 2 vols. Berkeley: University of California Press.

Cooke, Philip St. George
1878   *The Conquest of New Mexico and California.* New York: G. P. Putnam's Sons.

Cooke, Ronald U., and Reeves, Richard W.
1976   *Arroyos and Environmental Change in the American South-West.* London: Oxford University Press.

Coolidge, Dane, and Coolidge, Mary R.
1939   *The Last of the Seris.* New York: E. P. Dutton.

Cooper, Charles F.
1960   Changes in Vegetation, Structure, and Growth of Southwestern Pine Forests Since White Settlement. *Ecological Monographs* 30 (April):129-64.

Cooper, Erwin
1968   *Aqueduct Empire—a Guide to Water in California: Its Turbulent History, Its Management Today.* Glendale: Arthur H. Clark Co.

Cooper, Kenneth
1959   Leadership Role Expectations in Mexican Rural and Urban Environment. Ph.D. dissertation, Stanford University.

Coplin, William D.
1974   *Introduction to International Politics: A Theoretical Overview.* 2d ed. Chicago: Rand McNally & Co.

Copp, Nelson G.
1963   Wetbacks and Braceros: Mexican Migrant Laborers and American Immigration Policy, 1930-1960. Ph.D. dissertation, Boston University.
1971   *Wetbacks and Braceros: Mexican Migrant Laborers and American Immigration Policy, 1930-1960.* San Francisco: R & E Research Associates.

Cordero, E.
1968   La subestimación de la mortalidad infantil en México. *Demografía y Economía* 2 (no. 1):44-62.

Cordero y Bustamante, Antonio
1944   Los apaches a fines del siglo XVIII. *Sociedad Chihuahuense de Estudios Históricos, Boletín* 5:112-13, 148-60, 194-95.

Corle, Edwin
1951   *The Gila, River of the Southwest.* New York: Rinehart & Co.

Cornbleth, Catherine
1971   Political Socialization and the Social Studies: Beliefs of Mexican American Youth. Mimeographed. University of Texas at Austin.

Cornejo, Gerardo, et al.
1975   *Law and Population in Mexico.* Law and Population Monograph Series, no. 23. Medford: Fletcher School of Law and Diplomacy.

Cornelius, Wayne A.
1977a   *Illegal Mexican Migration to the United States: Recent Research Findings, Policy Implications, and Research Priorities.* Cambridge: Massachusetts Institute of Technology, Center for International Studies.
1977b   Undocumented Immigration: A Critique of the Carter Administration's Policy Proposals. *Migration Today* 5 (October):5-8, 16-20.
1978   *Mexican Migration to the United States: Causes, Consequences, and U.S. Responses.* Cambridge: Massachusetts Institute of Technology, Center for International Studies.

———, and Díez-Canedo, Juan
1976   Mexican Migration to the United States: The View from Rural Sending Communities. Paper presented at Conference on Mexico and the United States: The Next Ten Years, March, at American University, (March) Washington, D.C.

Corona, Bert
1972   *Bert Corona Speaks on La Raza and the "Illegal Alien" Scare.* New York: Path Press.

Corral, Ramón
1959   *Obras Históricas: reseña histórica del estado de Sonora. 1875-1877, biografía de José María Leyva Cajeme, las razas indígenas de Sonora.* Hermosillo: Biblioteca Sonorense de Geografía e Historia no. 1.

Correll, D. S. and Johnston, M. C.
1970   *Manual of the Vascular Plants of Texas.* Renner: Texas Research Foundation.

Cortés, Carlos
1974   Editor. *The Mexican American.* 21 vols. New York: Arno Press.
1976   Editor. *The Chicano Heritage.* 55 vols. New York: Arno Press.

Cortés, Hernan
1971   *Hernan Cortés: Letters from Mexico.* Edited and translated by A. R. Pagden. New York: Grossman Publishers.

Cortés, Michael
1978   Testimony on the Civil Rights Implications of Proposed Federal Policies Concerning Undocumented Workers and Immigrations. Mimeographed. Washington, D.C., National Council of La Raza.

Cortner, Hanna J.
1974   Development, Environment, Indians and the Southwest Power Controversy. *Alternatives* 4 (Autumn):14-20.
1977   Energy Policy Planning, Administration, and Coordination in the Four Corners States. Consultant Report for Four Corners Regional Commission.

Corwin, Arthur F.
1963   *Contemporary Mexican Attitudes Toward Population, Poverty, and Public Opinion.* Gainesville: University of Florida Press.
1972   The New Wetback Infiltration: A Preliminary Report. Manuscript. Report prepared for Senator Stevenson's Subcommittee on Agricultural Labor in the United States.
1973a   Mexican Emigration History, 1900-1970: Literature and Research. *Latin American Research Review* 8 (Summer): 3-24.
1973b   Mexican American History: An Assessment. *Pacific Historical Review* 42 (August):269-308.
1973c   Causes of Mexican Emigration to the United States: A Summary View. *Perspectives in American History* 7: 557-635.
1978a   Editor. *Immigrants—and Immigrants: Perspectives on Mexican Labor Migration to the United States.* Westport, Conn.: Greenwood Press.
1978b   A Story of Ad Hoc Exemptions: American Immigration Policy Toward Mexico. In Arthur F. Corwin, ed. *Immigrants—and Immigrants: Perspectives on Mexican Labor Migration to the United States,* pp. 136-75. Westport, Conn.: Greenwood Press.
1978c   Quien Sabe? Mexican Migration Statistics. In Arthur F. Corwin, ed. *Immigrants—and Immigrants: Perspectives on Mexican Labor Migration to the United States,* pp. 108-35. Westport, Conn.: Greenwood Press.
1978d   A Human Rights Dilemma: Carter and "Undocumented" Mexicans. In Arthur F. Corwin, ed. *Immigrants—and Immigrants: Perspectives on Mexican Labor Migration to the United States,* pp. 320-46. Westport, Conn.: Greenwood Press.

———, and McCain, Johnny M.
1978   Wetbackism since 1964: A Catalogue of Factors. In Arthur F. Corwin, ed. *Immigrants—and Immigrants: Perspectives on Mexican Labor Migration to the United States,* pp. 67-107. Westport, Conn.: Greenwood Press.

Corzo, Francisco
1954   La región de las tribus yaquis, *Boletín de estudios especiales del Banco Nacional de Crédito Ejidal* 1 (no. 11).

Cosgrove, C. B., and Cosgrove, Harriet S.
1932   *The Swartz Ruin, A Typical Mimbres Ruin in Southwestern New Mexico.* Papers of the Peabody Museum of American Ethnology, no. 51. Cambridge: Harvard University Press.

Cosío Villegas, Daniel
1960   *Historia moderna de México.* El Porfirato, vols. 5 and 6: La vida politica exterior. México, D.F.: Editorial Hermes.
1968   Border Trouble in Mexican-United States Relations. *Southwestern Historical Quarterly* 72 (July):34-39.

Costo, Rupert
1970   Alcatraz. *Indian Historian* 3 (Winter):4-12.

Cotera, Marta
1977   *Profile of the Mexican American Woman.* Austin: National Educational Laboratory.

Cotner, Robert C.
1959   *James Stephen Hogg: A Biography.* Austin: University of Texas Press.

Coues, Elliot
1900   Editor. *On the Trail of a Spanish Pioneer: The Diary and Itinerary of Francisco Garcés in His Travels Through Sonora, Arizona and California, 1775-1776.* 2 vols. New York: Francis P. Harper.
1965   *The Expeditions of Zebulon Montgomery Pike.* 3 vols. Minneapolis: Ross & Haines. Reissue of earlier volumes.

Coughlin, Magdalen
1967   Boston Smugglers on the Coast, 1797-1821: An Insight into the American Acquisition of California. *California Historical Society Quarterly* 46 (June):99-120.
1971   Commercial Foundations of Political Interest in the Opening Pacific, 1789-1829. *California Historical Society Quarterly* 50 (March):15-33.

Coulter, John Wesley
1930   Land Utilization in the Santa Lucia Region. *Geographical Review* 20 (July):469-79.

Covarrubias, Miguel
1966   *Indian Art of Mexico and Central America.* New York: Alfred A. Knopf.

Cowan, Margo
1977   Counseling the Undocumented Alien. *Migration Today* 5 (April):27-29.

Cox, Robert W.
1972   Labor and Transnational Relations. In Robert O. Keohane and Joseph S. Nye, Jr., eds. *Transnational Relations and World Politics.* Cambridge: Harvard University Press.

Craddock, Brian
1976   *Guide to Farmworker Protective Laws: An Aide to Texas Based Farmworkers.* Austin: Manpower, Education and Training. Updated 1979.

Craig, Richard B.
1971   *The Bracero Program: Interest Groups and Foreign Policy.* Austin: University of Texas Press.
1976   *La Campaña Permanente:* Mexico's Anti-Drug Campaign. Paper presented to Latin American Studies Association, March, at Atlanta, Georgia.
1977a   Operation Intercept: The International Politics of Pressure. Paper presented to Organization of American Historians, April, at Atlanta, Georgia.
1977b   The Mexico Connection: State and Non-State Actors. Paper presented to the American Political Science Association, September, at Washington, D.C.
1979a   Drug Traffic, the Border, and Mexico-United States Relations. Paper presented to Society for Intercultural Education, Training and Research, March.
1979b   Operation Condor: Mexico's Antidrug Campaign Enters a New Era. Paper presented to Latin American Studies Association, April, at Pittsburgh, Pennsylvania.
1979c   Former paper now published 1980 as Human Rights and Mexico's Antidrug Campaign. *Social Science Quarterly* 60:691-701.
1979d   Contraband and the Mexico-United States Border: The Case of Narcotics. Paper presented to the National Council for Geographic Education, Mexico City (November).
1980a   Human Rights and Mexico's Antidrug Campaign. *Social Science Quarterly* 60 (no. 4):691-701.
1980b   Operation Intercept: The International Politics of Pressure. *The Review of Politics* 42:4.
————, and Turner, Michael A.
1977   International Control of Narcotics: A Synopsis. *Indian Political Science Review* 11 (January):33-47.
Crampton, C. Gregory
1977   *The Zuñis of Cíbola.* Salt Lake City: University of Utah Press.
Crampton, Frank A.
1956   *A Working Stiff in the Western Mine Camps.* Denver: A. Swallow.
Crawford, Ann Fears
1967   Editor. *The Eagle: The Autobiography of Santa Anna.* Austin: Pemberton Press.
Cree, Linda
1974   Extension of County Jurisdiction over Indian Reservations in California: Public Law 280 and the Ninth Circuit. *Hastings Law Journal* 25 (May):1451-1506.
Cromwell, A.
1970   *The Black Frontier.* Lincoln: University of Nebraska Press.
Cronin, J. G.
1964   *A Summary of the Occurrence and Development of Water in the Southern High Plains of Texas.* Water Supply Paper no. 1693. Washington, D.C.: U.S. Geological Survey.
1969   *Ground Water in the Ogallala Formation in the Southern High Plains of Texas and New Mexico.* Hydrologic Investigation Atlas no. 330. Washington, D.C.: U.S. Geological Survey.
Cronquist, A.; Holmgren, A. H.; Holmgren, N. H.; and Reveal, J. L.
1972   *Intermountain Flora, Vascular Plants of the Intermountain West, U.S.A.* Vol. 1, New York: Hafner Publishing Co. Vol. 6, New York: Columbia University Press.
Crook, General George
1946   *General George Crook: His Autobiography.* Edited and annotated by Martin F. Schmitt. Norman: University of Oklahoma Press.
Crosby, Harry
1975   *The Cave Paintings of Baja California.* La Jolla, Calif.: Copley Books.
Cross, Harry E., and Sandos, James A.
1979   *The Impact of Undocumented Mexican Workers on the United States: A Critical Assessment.* Washington, D.C.: Battelle Human Affairs Research Centers.
1980   *Rural Development in Mexico and Recent Migration to the U.S.* Berkeley: University of California Press.
Cross, Ira B.
1935   *History of the Labor Movement in California.* Berkeley: University of California Press.
Cross, Jack L.; Shaw, Elizabeth H.; and Scheifele, Kathleen
1960   Editors. *Arizona: Its People and Resources.* Tucson: University of Arizona Press.
Crossland, Fred E.
1971   *Minority Access to College: A Ford Foundation Report.* New York: Schocken Books.
Crow, John E.
1971   City Politics in Arizona. In Robert D. Winkle, ed. *Politics in the Urban Southwest.* Albuquerque: University of New Mexico Press.
Crumrine, Lynne S.
1969   *Ceremonial Exchange as a Mechanism in Tribal Integration Among the Mayos of Northwest Mexico.* Anthropological Papers, no. 14. Tucson: University of Arizona.
————, and Crumrine, N. Ross
1967   Mundo de la selva vs. tractor: system económico moderno de los indios mayo, en el noroeste de México. *América Indígena* 27 (no. 4):715-33.
1968   Anthropological Antinomy: The Importance of an Empirical Basis for a Concept of Anthropological Fact. *Anthropological Quarterly* 41 (no. 1):34-46.
1969   Capakoba, the Mayo Easter Ceremonial Impersonator: Explanations of Ritual Clowning. *Journal for the Scientific Study of Religion* 8 (no. 1):1-22.
1970   Ritual Drama and Culture Change. *Comparative Studies in Society and History* 12 (no. 4):361-72.
1973   La tierra te devorará: un análises estructural de los mitos de los indígenas mayo. *América Indígena* 33 (no. 4):1119-50.
1974a   God's Daughter-in-Law, the Old Man, and the Olla: An Archaeological Challenge. *Kiva* 39 (nos. 3 and 4):277-81.
1974b   Anomalous Figures and Liminal Roles: A Reconsideration of the Mayo Indian Capakoba, Northwest Mexico. *Anthropos* 69:858-73.
1974c   *El ceremonial de Pascua y la identidad de los mayos de Sonora.* Mexico City: Instituto Nacional Indigenista INI 31.
1975   A New Mayo Indian Religious Movement in Northwest Mexico. *Journal of Latin American Lore* 1 (no. 2):127-45.
1976a   A Survey of Modern Mayo Social Organization and Ceremonial and Ideological Systems, Sonora, Northwestern Mexico. *Katunob* 9 (no. 2):52-61.
1976b   Mediating Roles in Ritual and Symbolism: Northwest Mexico and the Pacific Northwest. *Anthropologica* 18 (no. 2):130-52.
1977   *The Mayo Indians of Sonora, Mexico: A People Who Refuse to Die.* Tucson: University of Arizona Press.
Crumrine, N. Ross
1964   *The House Cross of the Mayo Indians of Sonora, Mexico.* Anthropological Papers, no. 8. Tucson: University of Arizona.
1966   The Problem of Ethnic Identity. *Trans-Action* 3 (no. 6):48-50.
1979   Mayo Indian Myth and Ceremonialism, Northwest Mexico: The Dual Ceremonial Cycle. In N. Ross Crumrine, ed. *Ritual Symbolism and Ceremonialism in the Americas: Studies in Symbolic Anthropology,* 1:89-111. Occasional Publications in Anthropology, Ethnology Series, 33. Greeley, Colo.: Museum of Anthropology, University of Northern Colorado.

————, and Crumrine, Lynne S.
1967   Ancient and Modern Mayo Fishing Practices, *Kiva* 33 (no. 1):25-33.
1969   Where Mayos Meet Mestizos: A Model for the Social Structure of Culture Contact. *Human Organization* 28 (no. 1):50-57.
1970   Ritual Service and Blood Sacrifice as mediating Binary Oppositions: A Structural Analysis of Several Mayo Myths and Rituals. *Journal of American Folklore* 83 (327):69-76.

————, and Crumrine, M. Louise
1976   El Papel integracional del symbolismo ritual de los "folk" santos: la velación de San Cayetano de los indígenas mayo y los mestizos, Sonora, Mexico. *Actas del XLI Congreso Internacional de Americanistas* 3:127-31.
1977   Ritual Symbolism in Folk and Ritual Drama: The Mayo Indian San Cayetano Velación, Sonora, Mexico. *Journal of American Folklore* 90 (355):8-28.

————, and Macklin, Barbara June
1974   Sacred Ritual *v.* the Unconscious: The Efficacy of Symbols and Structure in North Mexican Folk Saints' Cults and General Ceremonialism. In Ino Rossi, ed. *The Unconscious in Culture: The Structuralism of Claude Levi-Strauss in Perspective*, pp. 179-97. New York: E. P. Dutton.

Cruz, Gilbert Ralph
1969   The City Ordinances for the Internal Management and Administration of the Municipal Government of San Antonio of Bejar, 1829. *Texana* 7 (Summer):95-116.

Cukwurah, A. O.
1967   *The Settlement of Boundary Disputes in International Law.* Manchester: University of Manchester Press.

Culbert, James I.
1941a   Cattle Industry of New Mexico. *Economic Geography* 17 (April):155-68.
1941b   Pinto Beans in the Estancia Valley of New Mexico. *Economic Geography* 17 (January):50-60.

Culley, John H.
1940   *Cattle, Horses, and Men.* Los Angeles: Ward Ritchie Press.

Cumberland, Charles C.
1953-54 Border Raids in the Lower Rio Grande Valley—1915. *Southwestern Historical Quarterly* 57 (January):285-311.
1960a   The United States-Mexican Border: A Selective Guide to the Literature of the Region. *Rural Sociology* 25 (June):1-236.
1960b   The Sonora Chinese and the Mexican Revolution. *Hispanic American Historical Review* 40 (May):191-211.
1968   *Mexico: The Struggle for Modernity.* New York: Oxford University Press.

Cummings, Ronald G.
1972   *Water Resource Management in Northern Mexico.* Baltimore: Johns Hopkins University Press.
1974   *Interbasin Water Transfers: A Case Study in Mexico.* Baltimore: Johns Hopkins University Press.

Cutter, Donald C.
1961a   California, Training Ground for Spanish Naval Heroes. *California Historical Society Quarterly* 40 (June):109-22.
1961b   Sources of the Name "California." *Arizona and the West* 3 (Autumn):233-44.
1970   Harbor Entry and Recognition Signals in Early California. *California Historical Society Quarterly* 49 (March):47-53.
1974a   *Jicarilla Apache Tribe: Historical Materials, 1540-1887.* New York: Garland Publishing.
1974b   *Indian Land Rights in the American Southwest in the Jicarilla Apache Area.* New York: Garland Publishing, University of New Mexico.

Cutts, James Madison
1847   *The Conquest of California and New Mexico.* Philadelphia: Carey and Hart.

Cuykendall, Clydia J.
1973   State Taxation of Indians—Federal Preemption of Taxation Against the Backdrop of Indian Sovereignty. *Washington Law Review* 49 (no. 1):191-212.

DaCamara, Kathleen
1949   *Laredo on the Rio Grande.* San Antonio: Naylor Co.

Dagodag, W. Tim
1975   Source Regions and Composition of Illegal Mexican Immigration to California. *International Migration Review* 9 (Winter):499-511.

————; Avila, Jesus H.; and Epstein, Caryn E.
1975   Routes of Illegal Mexican Immigration: Some Empirical Observations. Paper presented to Western Social Science Association, May, at Denver, Colorado.

Dahl, Robert A.
1961   *Who Governs?* New Haven: Yale University Press.

Dahlgren, Charles B.
1883   *Historic Mines of Mexico: A Review of Mines of That Republic for the Last Three Centuries.* New York: n.p.

Dale, Edward Everett
1949   The Indians of the Southwest: A Century of Development Under the United States. Norman: University of Oklahoma Press.

Dana, Richard Henry
1963   *Two Years Before the Mast.* New York: Bantam Books.
1964   *Two Years Before the Mast.* Los Angeles: Ward Ritchie Press.

Dane, Charles H., and Bachman, George O.
1965   *Geologic Map of New Mexico: Scale 1:500,000.* Washington, D.C.: U.S. Geological Survey.

Daniel, James M.
1968   The Spanish Frontier in West Texas and Northern Mexico. *Southwestern Historical Quarterly* 71 (April):481-95.

Daniell, Forrest
1948   Early Land Surveying in Texas. *Surveying and Mapping* 8 (April-May-June):59-63.

Daniels, Roger
1962   *The Politics of Prejudice.* Gloucester, Mass.: Peter Smith.

————, and Kitano, Harry H. L.
1970   *American Racism.* Englewood Cliffs, N.J.: Prentice-Hall.

D'Antonio, William V., and Form, William H.
1965   *Influentials in Two Border Cities.* Notre Dame: University of Notre Dame Press.

D'Antonio, William V., and Press, Irwin
1970   Community Study of Fabens, Texas. Research manuscript, University of Notre Dame.

D'Antonio, William V., and Samora, Julian
1962   Occupational Stratification in Four Southwestern Communities. *Social Forces* 41 (October):17-25.

D'Antonio, William V.; Form, William H.; Loomis, Charles P.; and Erickson, Eugene
1961   Institutional and Occupational Representations in Eleven Community Influence Systems. *American Sociological Review* 26 (June):440-45.

Darnell, William I.
1959   The Imperial Valley: Its Physical and Cultural Geography. Master's thesis, San Diego State College.

Dasmann, Raymond F.
1965   *The Destruction of California.* New York: Macmillan Co.

Daubenmire, R.
1978   *Plant Geography, with Special Reference to North America.* New York: Academic Press.

Davenport, William
n.d.   *Art Treasures of the West.* Menlo Park, Calif.: Lane Magazine & Book Co.

David, Fay, and Crane, Elaine
1971   *The Black Soldier.* New York: William Morrow & Co.
Davidson, Chandler, and Gaety, Charles M.
1973   Ethnic Attitudes as a Basis for Minority Cooperation in Southwestern Metropolis. *Social Science Quarterly* 53 (March):738-49.
Davidson, David M.
1966   Negro Slave Control and Resistance in Colonial Mexico, 1519-1650. *Hispanic American Historical Review* 46 (August):235-53.
Davidson, E., and Fox, M.
1974   Effects of Off-Road Motorcycle Activities on Mojave Desert Vegetation and Soil. *Madroño* 22:381-90.
Davidson, Harold G.
1974   *Edward Borein: Cowboy Artist.* Garden City: Doubleday & Co.
Davidson, James B., and Schlangen, Joseph B.
1970   Cultural and Structural Assimilation Among Catholics in the Southwest. In William T. Liu and Nathaniel J. Pallone, eds. *Catholics in the U.S.A.: Perspectives on Social Change,* pp. 435-56. New York: John Wiley & Sons.
Davidson, John
1979   *The Long Road North.* Garden City: Doubleday & Co.
Davies, Glen E.
1966   State Taxation of Indian Reservations. *Utah Law Review* 17 (July):132-51.
Davis, Charles E., and West, Jonathan P.
1978   Analyzing Perceptions of Affirmative Action Issues: A Study of Mexican American Supervisors in a Metropolitan Bureaucracy. *Midwest Review of Public Administration* 12:246-56.
1980   Job Reward Preferences of Mexican-American and Anglo Public Employees. *Public Productivity Review* 4:199-209.
Davis, E. L.
1980   Evaluation of Early Human Activities and Remains in the California Desert. San Diego: Great Basin Foundation.
Davis, John F.
1971   Some Recent Developments in the Search for Solutions to California's Water Supply Problems. *Tijdschrift Voor Economische en Sociale Geografie* 62 (no. 2):95-103.
Davis, K.
1976   U.S. Health Care. Paper presented to the Association of American Medical Colleges, San Francisco, California.
Davis, Kingsley
1942   Changing Modes of Marriage: Contemporary Family Types. In Howard Becker and Ruben Hill, eds. *Marriage and the Family.* Boston: D. C. Heath.
Davis, Lawrence
1959   Criminal Jurisdiction over Indian Country in Arizona. *Arizona Law Review* 1:62-101.
Davis, O. L., and Personke, Carl R.
1968   Effects of Administering the Metropolitan Readiness Test in English and Spanish to Spanish-speaking School Entrants. *Journal of Educational Measurement* 5:231-34.
Davis, Tom B.
1967   Editor. *Mexico's Recent Economic Growth: The Mexican View.* Austin: University of Texas Press.
Davis, William Robert
1971   The Spanish Borderlands of Texas and Chihuahua. *Texana* 9 (Summer):142-55.
Davis, W. M.
1921   Lower California and Its Natural Resources: A Review. *Geographical Review* 11 (October):551-62.
Davis, William Watts Hart
1869   *The Spanish Conquest of New Mexico.* Doylestown, Pa.: n.p.
1938   *El Gringo: Or New Mexico and Her People.* Chicago: Rio Grande Press. Reprint of 1857 edition.

Dawson, E. Richard, and Prewitt, Kenneth
1969   *Political Socialization.* Boston: Little, Brown & Co.
Day, A. Grove
1940   *Coronado's Quest: The Discovery of the Southwestern States.* Los Angeles: University of California Press.
Day, J. C.
1970   *Managing the Lower Rio Grande: An Experience in International River Development.* Geography Research Paper no. 125. Chicago: University of Chicago.
1972   International Management of the Rio Grande Basin: The United States and Mexico. *Water Resources Bulletin* 8 (October):935-47.
1975   Urban Water Management of an International River: The Case of El Paso-Juarez. *Natural Resources Journal* 15 (July):453-70.
1978   International Aquifer Management: The Hueco Bolson on the Rio Grande River. *Natural Resources Journal* 18 (January):163-80.
Day, Mark
1971   *Forty Acres: César Chávez and the Farmworkers.* New York: Praeger Publishers.
Deasy, George F., and Gerhard, Peter
1944   Settlements in Baja California: 1768-1930. *Geographical Review* 34 (October):574-86.
De Blassie, Richard R., and Healy, Gary W.
1970   *Self-Concept: A Comparison of Spanish-American, Negro and Anglo Adolescents Across Ethnic, Sex and Socioeconomic Variables.* Las Cruces: New Mexico State University, ERIC Clearinghouse on Rural and Small Schools.
Decorme, Gerard
1941   *La obra de los Jesuitas mexicanos durante la epoca colonial, 1672-1767.* 2 vols. Mexico City: Antigua Librería Robredo de J. Porrúa e Hijos.
Deever, R. Merwin, et al.
1974   *American Indian Education.* Tempe: Arizona State University.
de Gennaro, Nat, and Ritchey, Robert J.
1978a   *The Economic Impact of Mexican Visitors to Arizona.* Tucson: University of Arizona, Division of Economic and Business Research.
1978b   Mexican Visitors to Arizona Identified as a Valued Market. *Arizona Review* 27 (August-September):1-9.
De Hoyos, Arturo
1961   Occupational and Educational Levels of Aspiration of Mexican-American Youth. Ph.D. dissertation, Michigan State University.
de la Cerda Silva, Robert. See Cerda Silva, Robert de la
de la Garza, Rudolph O.
1974   Voting Patterns in "Bi-cultural" El Paso. *Aztlán* 5 (nos. 1 and 2):235-360.
1977   Mexican American Voters: A Responsible Electorate. In Frank Baird, ed. *Political Power, Influence or Resource,* pp. 1-108. Lubbock: Texas Tech University, Graduate Studies.
———; Kruszewski, Z. Anthony; and Arciniega, Thomas
1973   Editors. *Chicanos and Native Americans: The Territorial Minorities.* Englewood Cliffs, N.J.: Prentice-Hall.
De la Mora, Miguel, and González Navarro, Moisés
1951   Jalisco: la historia y sus instrumentos. *Historia Mexicana* 1 (Julio-septiembre):154-63.
De la Peña, José Enrique
1975   *With Santa Anna in Texas: A Personal Narrative of the Revolution.* Edited and translated by Carmen Perry. College Station: Texas A&M University Press.
de León, Fidel
1976   *El español del suroeste y el español standard: material programado.* Manchaca, Texas: Sterling Swift Publishing Co.
Delgado Hernández, Filipe
1951   Estudio sobre la rehabilitación económico-agrícola de la

zona correspondiente a las tribus yaqui. *Boletín de la Sociedad Mexicana de Geografía y Estadística* 72 (1-3): 117-44.

Dellwo, R. D.
1971   Indian Water Rights: the Winters Doctrine Updated. *Gonzaga Law Review* 6 (Spring):215-40.

DeLoria, Vine, Jr.
1972   Editor. *Of Utmost Good Faith.* New York: Bantam Books.

Demaris, Ovid
1970   *Poso del Mundo: Inside the Mexican-American Border, from Tijuana to Matamoros.* Boston: Little, Brown & Co.

Demos, George D.
1962   Attitude of Mexican-American and Anglo-American Groups Toward Education. *Journal of Social Psychology* 57:249-56.

Denevan, William M.
1967   Livestock Numbers in Nineteenth-Century New Mexico, and the Problem of Gullying in the Southwest. *Annals, Association of American Geographers* 57 (December): 691-703.

Densmore, Frances
1932   *Yuman and Yaqui Music.* Bureau of American Ethnology Bulletin no. 110. Washington, D.C.: Smithsonian Institution.

DePalo, William A., Jr.
1973   The Establishment of the Nueva Vizcaya Militia During the Administration of Teodoro de Croix, 1776-1783. *New Mexico Historical Review* 48 (July):223-50.

Deppa, James W.
1948   The Formation and Control of Arroyos in the Southwest. *Journal of Forestry* 46 (March):174-79.

de Raismes, Joseph
1975   The Indian Civil Rights Act and the Pursuit of Responsible Tribal Government. *South Dakota Law Review* 20 (Winter):59-106.

Derbyshire, Robert L.
1969   The Adaptation of Adolescent Mexican Americans to United States Society. *American Behavioral Scientist* 13 (September):88-103.

Deutscher, Irwin
1973   *What We Say/What We Do: Sentiments and Acts.* Glenview, Ill.: Scott, Foresman & Co.

Devereux, George
1951   Mohave Chieftainship in Action: A Narrative of the First Contacts of the Mohave Indians with the United States. *Plateau* 23 (no. 3):33-43.
1969   *Mohave Ethnopsychiatry: The Psychic Disturbances of an Indian Tribe.* Washington, D.C.: Smithsonian Institution Press.

DeWeerdt, John L., and Glick, Philip M.
1973   Editors. *A Summary-Digest of the Federal Water Laws and Programs.* Arlington, Va.: National Water Commission.

Dewsnut, Richard L., and Jensen, Dallin W.
1973   Editors. *A Summary-Digest of State Water Laws.* Arlington, Va.: National Water Commission.

Díaz de Krofcheck, Maria D., and Jackson, Carlos
1974   The Chicano Experience with Nativism in Public Administration. *Public Administration Review* 34 (November/December):534-40.

Díaz del Castillo, Bernal
1966   *Historia de la conquista de la Nueva España.* Introduction and notes by Joaquín Ramírez Cabañas. Mexico City: Editorial Porrúa, S.A.

Díaz Guerrero, Rogelio
1955   Neurosis and the Mexican Family Structure. *American Journal of Psychiatry* 112 (December):411-47.
1975   *Psychology of the Mexican: Culture and Personality.* Austin: University of Texas Press.

Dibble, D. S., and Lorrain, D.
1968   *Bonfire Shelter: A Stratified Bison Kill Site, Val Verde County, Texas.* Miscellaneous Papers, no. 1. Austin: Texas Memorial Museum.
———, and Prewitt, E.
1967   *Survey and Test Excavations at Amistad Reservoir,* 1964-1965. Report no. 3. Austin: Texas Archeological Salvage Project.

Dick, Everett
1970   *The Lure of the Land.* Lincoln: University of Nebraska Press.

Dicken, Samuel N.
1932   Dry Farming in the San Joaquin, California. *Economic Geography* 8 (January):94-99.
1935   Galaena: A Mexican Highland Community. *Journal of Geography* 34 (April):140-47.
1936   The Basin Settlements of the Middle Sierra Madre Oriental, Mexico. *Annals, Association of American Geographers* 26 (September):157-78.
1939   Monterrey and Northeastern Mexico. *Annals, Association of American Geographers* 29 (June):127-58.

Dickey, Roland
1949   *New Mexico Village Arts.* Albuquerque: University of New Mexico Press.

Dickson, D. Bruce
1975   Settlement Pattern Stability and Change in the Middle Northern Rio Grande Region, New Mexico: A Test of Some Hypotheses. *American Antiquity* 40 (April):159-71.

Dillman, C. Daniel
1968   The Functions of Brownsville, Texas, and Matamoros, Tamaulipas: Twin Cities of the Lower Rio Grande. Ph.D. dissertation, University of Michigan.
1969a   "Border Town Symbiosis Along the Lower Rio Grande as Exemplified by the Twin Cities, Brownsville (Texas) and Matamoros (Tamaulipas). *Revista Geográfica* 71 (December):93-113.
1969b   Brownsville: Border Port for Mexico and the United States. *Professional Geographer* 21 (May):178-83.
1970a   Commuter Workers and Free Zone Industry Along the U.S.-Mexico Border. *Proceedings, Association of American Geographers* 2:48-51.
1970b   Urban Growth Along Mexico's Northern Border and the Mexican National Border Program. *Journal of Developing Areas* 4 (July):487-507.
1970c   Recent Developments in Mexico's National Border Program. *Professional Geographer* 22 (September):243-47.
1970d   Transformation of the Lower Rio Grande of Texas and Tamaulipas. *Ecumene* 2 (no. 2):3-11.
1971   Occupance Phases of the Lower Rio Grande of Texas and Tamaulipas. *California Geographer* 12:30-37.
1974   Assembly Plants in Mexico's Northern Border Cities and the Border Industrialization Program. Paper presented to Association of American Geographers, April, at Seattle, Washington.
1976a   Mexico's In-Bond Assembly Plants: Impact, Problems and Prospects. Paper presented at Conference of Latin Americanist Geographers, October, at El Paso, Texas.
1976b   *Maquiladoras* in Mexico's Northern Border Communities and the Border Industrialization Program. *Tijdschrift voor Economische e Sociale Geografie* 67 (no. 3):138-50.
1976c   Mexico's Border Industrialization Program (BIP): Current Patterns and Alternative Futures. Paper presented at Latin American Studies Association, March, at Atlanta, Georgia.
1977a   Commuter Workers in the Borderlands—1967. *Frontera* 2 (March):7-8.
1977b   Assembly Industries in Mexico: Contexts for Development. Manuscript, Department of Geography, Northern Illinois University at DeKalb.

1978   Assembly Plants and Multinational Corporations in Mexico. Paper presented to Association of American Geographers, April, at New Orleans, Louisiana.

Dinerman, Ina R.
1978   Patterns of Adaptation Among Households of U.S.-bound Migrants from Michoacán, Mexico. *International Migration Review* 12 (Winter):485-501.

Di Peso, Charles C.
1951   *The Babocamari Village Site on the Babocamari River, Southeastern Arizona.* Publication no. 5. Dragoon, Arizona: Amerind Foundation.
1953   *The Sobaipuri Indians of the Upper San Pedro River Valley.* Publication no. 6. Dragoon, Arizona: Amerind Foundation.
1956   *The Upper Pima of San Cayetano del Tumacacori.* Publication no. 7. Dragoon, Arizona: Amerind Foundation.
1958   *The Reeve Ruin of Southeast Arizona: A Study of Prehistoric Western Pueblo Migration into the Middle San Pedro Valley.* Publication no. 8. Dragoon, Arizona: Amerind Foundation.
1965   The Clovis Fluted Point from the Timmy Site, Northwest Chihuahua, Mexico. *Kiva* 31 (no. 2):83-87.
1966   Archeology and Ethnohistory of the Northern Sierra. In G. F. Ekholm and G. R. Willey, eds. *Archeological Frontiers and External Connections.* Handbook of Middle American Indians, vol. 4. Austin: University of Texas Press.
1968   Casas Grandes and the Gran Chichimeca. *El Palacio* 75 (Winter):45-61.
1974   *Casas Grandes: A Fallen Trading Center of the Gran Chichimeca.* 7 vols. Flagstaff, Arizona: Northland Press.
———, and Matson, Daniel S.
1965   The Seri Indians in 1692 as Described by Adamo Gilg. S.J. *Arizona and the West* 7 (Spring):33-56.

Dismuke, Dewey
1940   Acoma and Laguna Indians Adjust Their Livestock to Their Range. *Soil Conservation* 6 (November):130-31.

Dittmer, H. J.; Castetter, E. F.; and Clark, O. J.
1954   *The Ferns and Fern Allies of New Mexico.* Publication in Biology no. 6. Albuquerque: University of New Mexico Press.

Dixon, Ford
1963   Clayton Erhard's Reminiscences of the Texan Santa Fe Expedition, 1841. *Southwestern Historical Quarterly* 56 (January):424-56.

Dobie, J. Frank
1930   *Coronado's Children: Lost Mines and Buried Treasure of the Southwest.* Dallas: Southern Methodist University Press.
1939   *Apache Gold and Yaqui Silver.* Boston: Little, Brown & Co.
1952   *Guide to Life and Literature of the Southwest.* Dallas: Southern Methodist University Press.

Dobkins, Betty Eakle
1959   *The Spanish Element in Texas Water Law.* Austin: University of Texas Press.

Dobyns, Henry F.
1950   Editor. The Fiesta of St. Francis Xavier: Magdalena, Sonora, Mexico. *Kiva* 16 (nos. 1 and 2):1-32.
1966   Estimating Aboriginal American Population: An Appraisal of Techniques with a New Hemispheric Estimate. *Current Anthropology* 7 (October):395-416.
1971   *The Apache People (Coyotero).* New York: Garland Publishing Co.
1972   *The Pápago People.* New York: Garland Publishing Co.
1973   *The Mescalero Apache People.* New York: Garland Publishing Co.
1974a   *Prehistoric Indian Occupation Within the Eastern Area of the Yuman Complex: A Study in Applied Archaeology.* New York: Garland Publishing Co., Indian Tribal Series (Hualapai Indians).

1974b   Altitude Sorting of Ethnic Groups in the Southwest. *Plateau* 47 (Fall):42-48.
1976a   *Spanish Colonial Tucson: A Demographic History.* Tucson: University of Arizona Press.
1976b   *Native American Historical Demography: A Critical Bibliography.* Bloomington: Indiana University Press.
———, and Euler, Robert C.
1971   *The Havasupai People.* Phoenix: Indian Tribal Series.
1972   *The Navajo People.* Phoenix: Indian Tribal Series.
1974   *Socio-Political Structure and Ethnic Group Concept of the Pai.* New York: Garland Publishing Co., Indian Tribal Series and Ft. Lewis College (Durango).
———; Stoffle, Richard W.; and Jones, Kristine
1975   Native American Urbanization and Socio-economic Integration in the Southwestern United States. *Ethnohistory* 22 (Spring):155-79.

Dockstader, Frederick J.
1973   *Indian Art in America: The Arts and Crafts of the North American Indian.* Greenwich, Conn.: New York Graphic Society.

Dodge, Richard V.
1960   *Rails of the Silver Gate: The Spreckles San Diego Empire.* San Marino: Pacific Railway Journal.

Dodson, Ruth
1951   Don Pedrito Jaramillo, the Curandero of Los Olmos. In Wilson Hudson, ed. *The Healer of Los Olmos and Other Mexican Lore.* Texas Folklore Society publication no. 24. Austin: Southern Methodist University Press.

Dolan, Robert; Howard, Alan; and Gallenson, Arthur
1974   Man's Impact on the Colorado River in the Grand Canyon. *American Scientist* 62 (July-August):392-401.

Domínguez, Francisco
1937   Costumbres yaquis. *Mexican Folkways* 9 (no. 2):6-24.

Donahue, J. Augustine
1960   The Unlucky Jesuit Mission of Bac. *Arizona and the West* 2 (Summer):127-39.

Donnelly, Thomas C.
1940   Editor. *Rocky Mountain Politics.* Albuquerque: University of New Mexico Press.

Doolittle, Graydon H.
1973   Culture and Environment on the Cumberland Frontier. *University of Oklahoma Papers in Anthropology* 14 (no. 1):31-43.

Dorey, M. A., and Swidler, G. J.
1976   *World Police Systems—A Factual Text.* Parts 1 and 2. Boston: Northeastern University Press.

Dornbusch, Sanford M., et al.
1974   *Student Perceptions of the Link Between School and Work.* Palo Alto: Stanford University, Center for Research and Development in Teaching.

Dorner, Gerd
1962   *Folk Art of Mexico.* New York: A. S. Barnes & Co.

Dorroh, J. H., Jr.
1946   *Certain Hydrologic and Climatic Characteristics of the Southwest.* Publications in Engineering, no. 1. Albuquerque: University of New Mexico Press.

Dotson, Floyd
1955   Disminución de la población mexicana en los Estados Unidos de acuerdo con el censo de 1950. *Revista Mexicana de Sociología* 17:151-69.

Douglas, Curt R.
1976   Editor. *Linguistics and Education.* San Diego: San Diego State University, Institute for Cultural Pluralism.

Dowdell, Dorothy, and Dowdell, Joseph
1972   *The Chinese Helped Build America.* New York: Julian Messner.

Downing, Theodore E.
1979   Explaining Migration in Mexico and Elsewhere. In Fernando Camara and Robert Van Kemper, eds. *Migration Across Frontiers: Mexico and the United States,* pp. 159-67. Albany: State University of New York at Al-

bany, Institute for Mesoamerican Studies.

Downs, James F.
1963   The Cowboy and the Lady: Models as a Determinant of the Rate of Acculturation Among the Piñón Navajo. *Kroeber Society Anthropological Papers* 29:53-67.
1964   *Animal Husbandry in Navajo Society and Culture.* Publications in Anthropology, no. 1. Berkeley: University of California Press.
1972   *The Navajo.* New York: Holt, Rinehart & Winston.

Doyel, David E.
1977   *Excavations in the Middle Santa Cruz River Valley, Southeastern Arizona.* Highway Salvage Archeology in Arizona no. 44. Tucson: Arizona State Museum.
———, and Haury, Emil W.
1976   The 1976 Salado Conference. *Kiva* 42 (1).

Dozier, Craig L.
1963   Mexico's Transformed Northwest: The Yaqui, Mayo and Fuerte Examples. *Geographical Review* 53 (October): 548-71.

Dozier, Edward P.
1964   The Pueblo Indians of the Southwest. *Current Anthropology* 5:79-97.
1966a   *Hano: A Tewa Community in Arizona.* New York: Holt, Rinehart & Winston.
1966b   Problem Drinking Among American Indians: The Role of Socio-cultural Deprivation. *Quarterly Journal of Studies of Alcohol* 27 (no. 1):72-87.
1970   *The Pueblo Indians of North America.* New York: Holt, Rinehart & Winston.
1971   The American Southwest. In Eleanor Burke Leacock and Nancy Oestreich Lurie, eds. *North American Indians in Historical Perspective*, pp. 228-56. New York: Random House.

Drake, P. W.
1970   Mexican Regionalism Reconsidered. *Journal of Inter-American Studies and World Affairs* 12 (July):401-15.

Driver, Les
1969   Carrillos Flying Artillery: The Battle of San Pedro. *California Historical Society Quarterly* 48 (December):335-49.

Drotning, Phillip T.
1968   *A Guide to Negro History in America.* Garden City: Doubleday & Co.
1969   *Black Heroes in our Nation's History.* New York: Cowles Book Co.

Drucker, Philip
1941   Culture Element Distributions: XVII Yuman-Pima. *University of California Anthropological Record* 6 (no. 3).

Drumm, Stella M.
1926   Editor. *Down the Santa Fe Trail and into Mexico, the Diary of Susan Shelby Magoffin, 1846-1847.* New Haven: Yale University Press.

Dubois, Betty Lou, and Valdés-Fallis, Guadalupe
1974   *Mexican-American Child Bilingualism: Double Deficit?* Las Cruces: New Mexico State University.

Duisberg, Peter C.
1957   Editor. Problems of the Upper Rio Grande: An Arid Zone River. Special Symposium report, University of New Mexico and New Mexico Institute of Mining and Technology, 1955.

Dumke, Glenn S.
1944   *The Boom of the Eighties in Southern California.* San Marino: Huntington Library.
1948   Douglas, Border Town. *Pacific Historical Review* 17 (August):283-98.

Dunbar, Anthony, and Kravitz, Linda
1976   *Hard Traveling: Migrant Farmworkers in America.* Cambridge, Mass.: Ballinger Publishing Co.

Dunbier, Roger
1968   *The Sonoran Desert, Its Geography, Economy, and People.* Tucson: University of Arizona Press.

Duncan, Cameron
1976   The Runaway Shop and the Mexican Border Industrialization Program. *Southwest Economy and Society* 2 (October-November):4-25.

Dunham, Harold H.
1955   New Mexican Land Grants with Special Reference to the Title Paper of the Maxwell Grant. *New Mexico Historical Review* 30:1-22.
1970   *Government Handout.* New York: Da Capo Press.
1974a   *Spanish and Mexican Land Policies and Grants in the Taos Pueblo Region, New Mexico.* New York: Garland Publishing, University of Denver.
1974b   *A Historical Study of Land Use Eastward of the Taos Indians' Pueblo Land Grant Prior to 1848.* New York: Garland Publishing.

Dunn, Dorothy
1968   *American Indian Painting of the Southwest and Plains Areas.* Albuquerque: University of New Mexico Press.
1972   A Documented Chronology of Modern American Indian Painting of the Southwest. *Plateau* 44:150-62.

Dunn, William Edward
1911   Apache Relations in Texas, 1718-1750. *Quarterly Texas State Historical Association* 14 (no. 3):198-274.
1917   *Spanish and French Rivalry in the Gulf Region of the United States, 1678-1702: The Beginnings of Texas and Pensacola.* Bulletin no. 1705. Austin: University of Texas.

Dunne, John Gregory
1967   *Delano: The Story of the California Grape Strike.* New York: Farrar, Straus, & Giroux. Rev. ed., 1971.

Dunne, Peter Masten
1940   *Pioneer Black Robes on the West Coast.* Berkeley: University of California Press.
1944   *Pioneer Jesuits in Northern Mexico.* Berkeley: University of California Press.
1948   *Early Jesuit Mission in Tarahumara.* Berkeley: University of California Press.
1952   *Black Robes in Lower California.* Berkeley: University of California Press.
1957   *Juan Antonio Balthasar*, Padre Visitador *to the Sonora Frontier 1 44-1 45: Two Original Reports.* Tucson: Arizona Pioneers' Historical Society.

Dunning, Charles H.
1959   *Rock to Riches: The Story of American Mining.* Phoenix: Southwest Publishing.

Dunscomb, Guy, and Rose, Al
1949   *Maps of the Southern Pacific.* Modesto: Rose Lithograph Company.

Dupoyet, Theodore
1910   Quelques observations sur l'art de guérie chez certaines tribus nomades du nord du Méxique. *Congrès International des Américanistes* 17:107-12.

Durfee, Lynn E.
1969   Large Scale Vegetable Farming in Central Arizona. Master's thesis, Arizona State University.

Durham, Mary L., and Hough, Richard L.
1979   Cultural Variations Associated with Physical Illness. Paper presented to the Southwestern Sociological Association, March, at Ft. Worth, Texas.

Durham, Philip, and Jones, Everett L.
1965   *The Negro Cowboys.* New York: Dodd, Mead & Co.
1966   *The Adventures of the Negro Cowboys.* New York: Bantam Books.

Durkheim, Emile
1915   *Elementary Forms of Religious Life.* London: Macmillan Co.

Durrenberger, Robert W.
1964   A Selected California Bibliography: California's Natural Landscape. *California Geographer* 5:75-88.
1965   A Selected California Bibliography: Exploration and Settlement—the Spanish and Mexican Period. *California*

Geographer 6:73-85.

1966 A Selected California Bibliography: Exploration and Settlement—The American Period. *California Geographer* 7:55-81.

1967 Selected California Bibliography: Water Resources, Part I. *California Geographer* 8:47-61.

1968*a* Selected California Bibliography: Water Resources, Part II. *California Geographer* 9:65-77.

1968*b* *Elements of California Geography.* Palo Alto: National Press Books.

1968*c* *Patterns on the Land: Geographical, Historical and Political Maps of California.* Palo Alto: National Press Books.

1972 The Colorado Plateau. *Annals, Association of American Geographers* 62 (June):211-36.

Dutton, Bertha P.

1963 *Sun Father's Way: The Kiva Mural of Kuaua.* Albuquerque: University of New Mexico Press.

1975 *Indians of the American Southwest.* Englewood Cliffs, N.J.: Prentice-Hall.

Duty, Toney E.

1970 The Coronado Expedition (1540-1542). *Texana* 8 (Summer):121-39.

Dworkin, Anthony Gary

1965 Stereotypes and Self-Images Held by Native-born and Foreign-born Mexican Americans. *Sociology and Social Research* 49 (January):214-24.

Dworsky, L. B.

1978 The Management of Water-Land Environmental Resources at International Boundary Regions. *Natural Resources Journal* 18 (January):143-52.

Dykes, Jefferson C.

1952 *Billy the Kid, the Bibliography of a Legend.* Albuquerque: University of New Mexico Press.

Eardley, A. J.

1962 *Structural Geology of North America.* New York: Harper & Row.

Eastman, C.; Carruthers, C.; and Liefer, J. A.

1971 Contrasting Attitudes Toward Land in New Mexico. *New Mexico Business* 24 (March):3-20.

Easton, David

1959 *The Political System.* New York: Alfred A. Knopf.

1965*a* *A Framework for Political Analysis.* Englewood Cliffs, N.J.: Prentice-Hall.

1965*b* *A Systems Analysis of Political Life.* New York: John Wiley & Sons.

Ebenstein, William

1945 Public Administration in Mexico. *Public Administration Review* 5 (Spring):102-12.

Eberly, L. D., and Stanley, T. B.

1978 Cenozoic Stratigraphy and Geologic History of Southwestern Arizona. *Geological Society of America Bulletin* 89:921-40.

Echánove, Carlos A.

1969 *Sociología mexicana.* 3d ed. Mexico City: Editorial Porrúa.

Echevarría, Evelio, and Otero, José

1976 *Hispanic Colorado.* Fort Collins, Colo.: Centennial Publications.

Edmonson, Munro S.

1952 *Los Manitos:* Patterns of Humor in Relation to Cultural Values. Ph.D. dissertation, Harvard University.

1957 Los Manitos: *A Study of Institutional Values.* New Orleans: Tulane University, Middle American Research Institute.

Edwards, Emily, and Alvarez Bravo, Manuel

1966 *Painted Walls of Mexico.* Austin: University of Texas Press.

Edwards, Frank S.

1847 *A Campaign in New Mexico with Colonel Doniphan.* Philadelphia: Carey & Hart.

Ehrlich, Howard J.

1969 Attitudes, Behavior, and the Intervening Variables. *American Sociologist* 4 (February):29-34.

Ehrlich, Paul R., et al.

1979 *The Golden Door: International Migration, Mexico, and the United States.* New York: Ballantine Books.

Ekholm, Gordon F., and Willey, Gordon R.

1966 Editors. *Archeological Frontiers and External Connections: Handbook of Middle American Indians.* Vol. 4. Austin: University of Texas Press.

Elac, John Chala

1961 *The Employment of Mexican Workers in U.S. Agriculture, 1900-1960: A Binational Economic Analysis.* Los Angeles: University of California.

Elías-Olivares, Lucía E.

1976 Ways of Speaking in a Chicano Community: A Sociolinguistic Approach. Ph.D. dissertation, University of Texas, Austin.

Ellis, Florence Hawley

1953 Authoritative Control and the Society System in Jémez Pueblo. *Southwestern Journal of Anthropology* 9 (Winter):385-94.

1959 An Outline of Laguna Pueblo History and Social Organization. *Southwestern Journal of Anthropology* 15 (Winter):325-47.

1974*a* *Anthropological Data Pertaining to the Taos Land Claim.* New York: Garland Publishing, University of New Mexico.

1974*b* *Anthropological Study of the Navajo Indians.* New York: Garland Publishing, University of New Mexico.

1974*c* Anthropology of Laguna Pueblo Land Claims. New York: Garland Publishing, University of New Mexico.

1974*d* Archaeologic and Ethnologic Data: Acoma-Laguna Land Claims. New York: Garland Publishing, University of New Mexico.

1974*e* The Hopi: Their History and Use of Lands. New York: Garland Publishing, University of New Mexico.

Ellis, John M.

1959 Mortality Differentials for a Spanish-Surname Population Group. *Southwestern Social Science Quarterly* 39 (no. 1):314-21.

1962 Spanish-Surname Mortality Differences in San Antonio, Texas. *Journal of Health and Human Behavior* 3 (Summer):125-27.

Ellis, Richard N.

1971 *New Mexico Past and Present.* Albuquerque: University of New Mexico Press.

1973 The Duke Indian Oral History Collection at the University of New Mexico. *New Mexico Historical Review* 48 (July):19-24.

Ellison, William H.

1950 *A Self-governing Dominion: California, 1848-1860.* Berkeley: University of California Press.

Elu, María del Carmen. See also Carmen Elu de Leñero, María del

1965 Consideraciones con respecto a una sociología familiar. *Desarrollo* 1:5-8.

Emerson, Gloria J.

1970 The Laughing Boy Syndrome. *School Review* 78-79 (November):94-98.

Emmett, Chris

1953 *Shanghai Pierce: A Fair Likeness.* Norman: University of Oklahoma Press.

1965 *Fort Union and the Winning of the Southwest.* Norman: University of Oklahoma Press.

Emory, William Hemsley

1848 Notes of a Military Reconnaissance, from Fort Leavenworth, in Missouri, to San Diego, in California, including part of the Arkansas, Del Norte, and Gila Rivers. Washington: Wendell and Van Benthuysen, Printers.

1857 *Report on the United States and Mexican Boundary Sur-*

vey. 2 vols. Sen. Exec. Doc. 108, 34 Cong., 1st sess. Washington, D.C.: Government Printing Office.

Engelhardt, Zephyrin
1899   *The Franciscans in Arizona.* Harbor Springs, Mich.: Holy Childhood Indian School.
1908-15 *The Missions and Missionaries of California.* 4 vols. San Francisco: James H. Barry Co.

Epstein, J. F.
1963   Centipede and Damp Caves: Excavations in Val Verde County, Texas, 1958. *Texas Archeological Society Bulletin* 33:1-129.

Erasmus, Charles J.
1955   Work Patterns in a Mayo Village. *American Anthropologist* 57 (no. 2):322-33.
1961   *Man Takes Control.* Minneapolis: University of Minnesota Press.
1967   Culture Change in Northwest Mexico. In Julian H. Steward, ed. *Contemporary Change in Traditional Societies,* vol. 3, pp. 1-131. Urbana: University of Illinois Press.

Erickson, Donald A.
1970   Custer Did Die for Our Sins! *School Review* 78-79 (November):76-93.
———, and Schwartz, Henrietta
1969   Community School at Rough Rock. A Report submitted to the Office of Economic Opportunity.

Ericson, Anna-Stina
1970   The Impact of Commuters on the Mexican-American Border Area. *Monthly Labor Review* (August):18-27.

Ericson, R., and Snow, D. R.
1970   The Indian Battle for Self-Determination. *California Law Review* 58 (no. 2):445-90.

Espejo, José A.
1951   *Geografía de Chihuahua.* Mexico City: Editorial El Nacional.

Espenshade, Edward B., Jr., and Morrison, Joel L.
1978   Editors. *Goode's World Atlas.* 15th ed. Chicago: Rand McNally & Co.

Espinosa, A. M.
1946   *El español en Nuevo Mexico.* Buenos Aires: Biblioteca de Dialectología Hispanoamericana.

Espinosa, Gilberto
1933   Translator. *History of New Mexico.* Los Angeles: Quivira Society.
1962   New Mexico Land Grants. *State Bar of New Mexico Journal* 2.
1973   *Tomé* v. *Valencia,* 1847: A Dramatic Trial. *New Mexico Historical Review* 48 (January):57-92.
———; Chavez, Tibo J.; and Waid, Carter M.
1970   Editors. El Rio Abajo. Portales, N.M.: Bishop Publishing Company.
———, and Hodge, F. W.
1933   Editors. *History of New Mexico by Gaspar Pérez de Villagrá Alcalá 1610.* Publication vol. 4. Los Angeles: Quivira Society.

Espinosa, José E.
1960   *Saints in the Valleys: Christian Sacred Images in the History, Life, and Folk Art of Spanish New Mexico.* Albuquerque: University of New Mexico Press.

Espinosa, José Manuel
1936   Governor Vargas in Colorado. *New Mexico Historical Review* 11 (no. 2):179-87.
1940   *First Expedition of Vargas into New Mexico.* Coronado Historical Series, vol. 10.
1942   *Crusaders of the Rio Grande.* Chicago: Institute of Jesuit History Publications.

Espinosa, Ruben W.; Fernández, Celestino; and Dornbusch, Sanford M.
1975   Factors Affecting Chicano Effort and Achievement in High School. *Atisbos: Journal of Chicano Research* 1: 9-30.

1977   Chicano Perceptions of High School and Chicano Performance. *Aztlán* 8 (Spring):133-56.
———, and Garcia, Joseph D.
1976   *Credentialed Staff-Pupil Ratios by Ethnicity in the California Public Schools.* Finance Reform Project. San Diego: San Diego State University School.

Etzold, Thomas H.
1978   *Aspects of Sino-American Relations Since 1784.* New York: Franklin Watts.

Evans, Clement A.
n.d.   Editor. *Confederate Military History: Texas and Florida.* Vol. 11. Secaucus, N.J.: Blue & Grey Press.

Evans, John S.
1972   Mexican Border Development and Its Impact upon the United States. *South Eastern Latin Americanist* 16 (June):4-10.
1975   The Use of Incentives for the Development of Mexico's Northern Border Zone. *El Paso Economic Review* 12 (October):1-4.
1982   The Evolution of the Mexican Tax System Since 1970. University of Texas Institute of Latin American Studies Technical Paper, no. 34.
———, and James, Dilmus D.
1976   The Industrialization of the Northern Mexico Border Region: Past, Present and Future. Revision of paper presented to Southwestern Economics Association, March, at Dallas, Texas, in 1974.

Evans, Norman A.
1972   Transmountain Water Diversion for the High Plains. In Donald D. MacPhail, ed. *The High Plains: Problems of Semiarid Environments,* pp. 42-59. CODAZR Publication no. 15. Fort Collins: Colorado State University.

Everitt, Cindi
1973   Black-on-white Mimbres Pottery: A Bibliography. *Artifact* 11 (4).

Ewers, John C.
1973   *Artists of the Old West.* Garden City: Doubleday & Co. Reprinted from 1965.

Eyre, S. R.
1968   *Vegetation and Soils, a World Picture.* London: Edward Arnold.

Ezell, Paul H.
1954   An Archeological Survey of the Northwestern Papagueria. *Kiva* 19 (2-4):1-26.
1955*a* Indians Under the Law: Mexico, 1821-1847. *América Indígena* 15 (no. 3): 199-214.
1955*b* The Archeological Delineation of a Cultural Boundary in Papagueria. *American Antiquity* 20 (no. 4):367-74.
1963   *The Maricopas: An Identification from Documentary Sources.* Anthropological Papers, no. 6. Tucson: University of Arizona.

Fabela, Isidro, and Fabela, Josefina
1964-73 Editors. *Documentos históricos de la revolución mexicana.* 27 vols. Mexico City: various publishers.

Fabila, Alfonso
1940   *Las tribus yaquis de Sonora, su cultura y anhelada autodeterminación.* Mexico City: Departamento de Asuntos Indígenas, Primer Congreso Indigenista Interamericano.
1945   La tribu kíkapoo de Coahuila. Biblioteca Enciclopédica Popular, no. 50. Mexico City: Secretaría de Educación.

Fagen, Richard R., and Tuohy, William S.
1972   *Politics and Privilege in a Mexican City.* Stanford: Stanford University Press.

Falco, Mathea
1977   International Narcotics Control. *Drug Enforcement* 4 (August):12-13.

Falconer, Thomas
1930   Letters and Notes on the Texan Santa Fe Expedition, 1841-1842. New York: Dauber & Pine Bookshops.

Farge, Emile J.
1977   A Review of Findings from "Three Generations" of Chi-

cano Health Care Behavior. *Social Science Quarterly* 58 (December):407-11.

Farías, L. M.
1973   *Plan de salud del Estado de Nuevo León.* Mexico City: I Convención de Salud.

Farrar, Nancy
1970   The History of the Chinese in El Paso, Texas: A Case Study of an Urban Immigrant Group in the American West. Master's thesis, University of Texas at El Paso.
1972   *The Chinese in El Paso.* El Paso: Texas Western Press.

Faulk, Odie B.
1962   The Controversial Boundary Survey and the Gadsden Treaty. *Arizona and the West* 4 (Autumn):201-26.
1964a   Spanish-Comanche Relations and the Treaty of 1785. *Texana* 2 (Summer):44-53.
1964b   *The Last Years of Spanish Texas, 1778-1821.* The Hague: Mouton & Co.
1965   Ranching in Spanish Texas. *Hispanic American Historical Review* 45 (May):257-66.
1967   *Too Far North—Too Far South: The Controversial Boundary Survey and the Gadsden Purchase.* Los Angeles: Westernlore Press.
1968   *Land of Many Frontiers: A History of the American Southwest.* New York: Oxford University Press.
1969   A Colonization Plan for Northern Sonora, 1850. *New Mexico Historical Review* 44 (October):293-314.
1974   The Presidio: Fortress or Farce? In Oakah L. Jones, Jr., ed. *The Spanish Borderlands: A First Reader,* pp. 70-77. Los Angeles: Lorrin L. Morrison.

Favors, Jean
1975   *An Agricultural Continuum: A Descriptive Study of the Farmworker Population and the Settling Out Process.* Washington, D.C.: Department of Health, Education and Welfare.

Fay, George E.
1955a   A Preliminary Report of an Archeological Survey in Sonora, Mexico, 1953. *Kansas Academy of Science, Transactions* 58 (4).
1955b   Indian House Types of Sonora. I: Yaqui. *Masterkey* 29.
1956a   The Peralta Complex, a Sonoran Variant of the Cochise Culture. *Science* 124:1029.
1956b   A Seri Fertility Figurine from Bahía Kino, Sonora. *Kiva* 21 (3-4):11-12.
1956c   Indian House Types of Sonora. II: Mayo. *Masterkey* 30 (1):25-28.
1958   An Indian House Type of Sinaloa. *Masterkey* 32 (4): 126-30.
1959   The Peralta Complex, a Sonoran Variant of the Cochise Culture: New Data. *El Palacio* 66:21-24.
1968   An Indian-Mexican House Type in Sonora, Mexico. University of Northern Colorado Museum of Anthropology Series, no. 5. Greeley, Colo.

Featherman, David L.
1971   The Socioeconomic Achievement of White Religio-ethnic Subgroups: Social and Psychological Explanations. *American Sociological Review* 36 (April):207-22.

Fehrenbach, T. R.
1968   *Lone Star: A History of Texas and the Texans.* New York: Macmillan Co.

Felger, R. S., and Moser, M. B.
1970   Seri Use of the Century Plant, *Agave. Kiva* 36:159-67.
1971   Seri Use of Mesquite *(Prosopis glandulosa* var. *torreyana). Kiva* 37:53-60.
1974a   Columnar Cacti in Seri Indian Culture. *Kiva* 39:257-356.
1974b   Seri Indian Pharmacopoeia. *Economic Botany* 28:414-36.
1976   Seri Indian Food Plants: Desert Subsistence Without Agriculture. *Ecology of Food and Nutrition* 5:13-27.

Félix, S. F.
1973   *Plan de salud del Estado de Sonora.* Mexico City: I Convención Nacional de Salud.

Feller, Abraham H.
1935   *The Mexican Claims Commissions, 1923-1934: A Study in the Law and Procedure of International Tribunals.* New York: Macmillan Co.

Felton, Ernest L.
1965   *California's Many Climates.* Palo Alto: Pacific Books, Publishers.

Fenneman, Nevin M.
1931   *Physiography of Western United States.* New York: McGraw-Hill.
1938   *Physiography of Eastern United States.* New York: McGraw-Hill.

Fenton, William N.
1957   Factionalism at Taos Pueblo, New Mexico. In U.S. Bureau of Ethnology Papers 56, Bulletin 164, pp. 297-344. Washington, D.C.: Government Printing Office.

Ferguson, Frances N.
1968   Navaho Drinking: Some Tentative Hypotheses. *Human Organization* 27 (Summer):159-67.

Fergusson, Erna
1951   *New Mexico: A Pageant of Three Peoples.* New York: Alfred A. Knopf.
1952   *Our Southwest.* New York: Alfred A. Knopf.

Fergusson, Harvey
1955   *Rio Grande.* New York: William Morrow & Co.

Fernández, Adela
1973   *Las drogas: ¿paraíso o infierno?* Mexico City: Colección Duda Semanal.

Fernández, C., and Vides, M. T.
1970   Situación epidemiológica en la frontera norte de México y programa de vigilancia. *Salud Pública de México* 12: 161-82.

Fernández, Celestino
1977   The Chicano Experience in Education: Current State of the Field. *National Directory of Sociology of Education and Educational Sociology* 3.
——— ; Espinosa, Ruben W.; and Dornbusch, Sanford M.
1975   *Factors Perpetuating the Low Academic Status of Chicano High School Students.* Palo Alto: Stanford University, Center for Research and Development in Teaching.
——— , and Marenco, Eduardo
1980   *Group Conflict, Education, and Mexican Americans: A Discussion Paper.* San Francisco: Mexican American Legal Defense and Educational Fund.

Fernández, F.
1968   Except a California Indian: A Study in Legal Discrimination. *Historical Society of Southern California Quarterly* 50:161-76.

Fernandez, Julio
1969   *Political Administration in Mexico.* Boulder, Colorado: University of Colorado, Bureau of Governmental Research and Service.

Fernández, Marina R.; Sierra, E. D.; and Trent, R. D.
1958   Three Basic Themes in Mexican and Puerto Rican Family Values. *Journal of Social Psychology* 48 (November): 167-81.

Fernández, Raul A.
1973a   Economy and Change on the United States-Mexico Border. Paper presented to Association for the Study of North American Integration, December, in New York.
1973b   The Border Industrialization Program on the United States-Mexico Border. *Review of Radical Political Economists* 5:37-52.
1977   *The United States-Mexican Border: A Politico-Economic Profile.* Notre Dame: University of Notre Dame Press.

Fernández-Flórez, Darío
1965   *The Spanish Heritage in the United States.* Madrid: Publicaciones Españolas.

Fernández Kelly, Maria Patricia
1978   Mexican Border Industrialization: Female Labor Force Participation and Migration. Paper presented to American Sociological Association, September, at San Francisco, California.
1979   A Study of the Composition of the Female Labor Force in Mexican-American "Maquiladoras." Ph.D. dissertation, Rutgers University.

Fewkes, Jesse Walter
1903   *Hopi Kachinas, Drawn by Native Artists.* Annual Report no. 21. Washington, D.C.: Bureau of American Ethnology.

Fickessen, Jack W.
1970   Water for Texas Through the Texas Water Plan. *Water Resources Bulletin* 6 (July-August):695-99.

Fielding, Gordon J.
1962   Dairying in Cities Designed to Keep People Out. *Professional Geographer* 14 (January):12-17.

Fierman, Floyd S.
1964   *Merchant Bankers of Early Santa Fe, 1844-1893.* El Paso: Texas Western Press.
1980a   *The Schwartz Family of El Paso: The Story of a Pioneer Jewish Family in the Southwest.* Southwestern Studies, no. 62. El Paso: Texas Western Press.
1980b   *The Spiegelbergs: Pioneer Merchants and Bankers in the Southwest.* El Paso: University of Texas Library, private binding.

Findley, Rowe, and O'Rear, Charles
1973   The Bittersweet Waters of the Lower Colorado. *National Geographic Magazine* 144 (October):540-69.

Findlow, Frank J., and de Atley, Susan P.
1976   Prehistoric land use patterns in the Animas Valley: A first approximation. *Anthropology UCLA* 6:1-57.

Finlator, John
1973   *The Drugged Nation: A "Narc's" Story.* New York: Simon & Schuster.

Fireman, Janet R., and Servín, Manuel P.
1970   Miguel Constansó: California's Forgotten Frontier. *California Historical Society Quarterly* 49 (March):3-19.

Firma, Theresa P.
1970   *Effects of Social Reinforcement on Self-Esteem of Mexican-American Children.* Las Cruces: New Mexico State University, ERIC Clearinghouse on Rural and Small Schools.

Fischer, Ward H.
1974   Management of Interstate Ground Water. *Natural Resources Lawyer* 7 (Summer):521-46.

Fisher, Albert L.
1978   Mormon Welfare Programs: Past and Present. *Social Science Journal* 15 (April):75-99.

Fishman, Joshua A.
1961   Childhood Indoctrination for Minority Group Membership. In Milton L. Barron, ed. *Minorities in a Changing World,* pp. 177-96. New York: Alfred A. Knopf.
1966   *Language Loyalty in the United States: The Maintenance and Perpetuation of Non-English Mother Tongues by American Ethnic and Religious Groups.* The Hague: Mouton & Co.
1977   *Bilingual Education: An International Sociological Perspective.* Rowley, Mass.: Newbury House.

Fitting, James E.
1972a   *Chipped Stone from the 1967 Mimbres Area Survey: Parts I and II.* Southwestern New Mexico Research Reports. Cleveland: Case Western Reserve University.
1972b   Preliminary notes on Cliff Valley settlement patterns. *The Artifact* 10: 15-30.
———, and Price, Theron D.
1968   Two Late Paleo-Indian Sites in Southwestern New Mexico. *Kiva* 34: 1-8.

Flaherty, Peter F.
1977   The Drug Problem on the Scales of Justice. *Drug Enforcement* 4 (August):4-5.

Flanigan, William W.
1972   *Political Behavior of the American Electorate.* 2d ed. Boston: Allyn & Bacon.

Fleming, B. P.
1933   Erosion: A Real Menace in the Southwest. *Science* 78 (November 3):391-95.

Fleming, Randall
1974   Architecture of Earth. *Pacific Discovery* 27 (September-October):16-22.

Fletcher, J. E., and Bender, Gordon L.
1965   Editors. *Ecology of Groundwater in the Southwest United States.* CODAZR Publication no. 5. Tempe: Arizona State University.

Fliedner, Dietrich
1975   Pre-Spanish Pueblos in New Mexico. *Annals, Association of American Geographers* 65 (September):363-77.

Flint, Timothy
1929   Dr. Willard's Journal of Inland Trade with New Mexico. *Western Monthly Review* 2 (April):597-607, (May):649-59.

Flipper, Henry O.
1963   *Negro Frontiersman: Western Memories.* El Paso: Texas Western Press.
1968   *The Colored Cadet.* New York: Homer Lee & Co.

Flores, Anselmo Marino
1967   Indian Population and Its Identification. In Robert Wauchope, ed. *Handbook of Middle American Indians,* vol. 6, pp. 12-25. Austin: University of Texas Press.

Flores, Edmundo
1976   *Vieja revolución, nuevos problemas.* 3d ed. Mexico City: Cuadernos de Joaquín Mortiz.

Flores, Estevan T.
1978   The Limitations of the Push-Pull Demographic Approach: Mexican Immigration and the Circulation of Class Struggle. Paper presented to First Symposium Internacional sobre los Problemas de los Trabajadores Migratorios de México y los Estados Unidos de Norte-américa, July, at Guadalajara, Mexico.

Flores, S. O.
1973   *Plan de Salud del Estado de Chihuahua.* Mexico City: I Convención Nacional de Salud.

Flores Mata, G., et al.
1971   *Mapa y descripción de los tipos de vegetación de la República Mexicana.* Mexico City: Dirección de Agrícola.

Fodell, Beverly
1974   *César Chávez and the United Farm Workers: A Selective Bibliography.* Detroit: Wayne State University Press.

Fogel, Walter
1967   *Mexican Americans in Southwest Labor Markets.* Mexican American Study Project, Advance Report. Los Angeles: University of California.
1975   *Mexican Labor in United States Labor Markets.* Institute of Industrial Relations, Reprint no. 252. Los Angeles: University of California.

Fonaroff, L. Schuyler
1963   Conservation and Stock Reduction on the Navajo Tribal Range. *Geographical Review* 53 (April):200-23.

Fontana, Bernard L.
1973   Savage Anthropologists and Unvanishing Indians of the American Southwest. *Indian Historian* 6 (Winter):5-8.
1974a   The Melting Pot That Wouldn't: Ethnic Groups in the American Southwest Since 1846. *American Indian Culture and Research Journal* 3 (no. 2):18-24.
1974b   *The Pápago Tribe of Arizona.* New York: Garland Publishing, University of Arizona.

Forbes, Jack D.
1959   The Appearance of the Mounted Indian in Northern Mexico and the Southwest, to 1680. *Southwestern Journal of Anthropology* 15 (no. 2):189-212.

1960   *Apache, Navaho, and Spaniard.* Norman: University of Oklahoma Press.

1964   The Development of the Yuma Route Before 1846. *California Historical Society Quarterly* 43 (June):99-118.

1966   Black Pioneers: The Spanish-speaking Afroamericans of the Southwest. *Phylon* 27 (Fall):233-46.

1967   *California Indian Education: Report of the First All-Indian Statewide Conference on California Indian Education.* Modesto, Calif.: Ad Hoc Committee on California Indian Education.

1969   *Native Americans of California and Nevada.* Healdsburg, Calif. Naturegraph Publishers.

1971   The Native American Experience in California History. *California Historical Quarterly* 50:234-42.

1973   Aztecas del norte: *The Chicanos of Aztlán.* Greenwich, Conn.: Fawcett.

Ford, K. C.
1975   Las yerbas de la gente: *A Study of Hispano-American Medicinal Plants.* Anthropological Papers, no. 60. Ann Arbor: University of Michigan.

Ford, Larry, and Griffin, Ernest
1974   Tijuana Landscape Tastes: Form, Character and Image of a Hybrid City. Paper presented to the Association of American Geographers, April, at Seattle, Washington.

Forde, C. Daryll
1931   Hopi Agriculture and Land Ownership. *Journal of the Royal Anthropological Institute of Great Britain and Ireland* 61:357-406.

Foreman, W. James
1950   Changing Land Tenure Patterns in Mexico. *Land Economics* 26 (February):65-77.

Form, William H., and D'Antonio, William V.
1955   The Integration and Cleavage Among Community Influentials in Two Border Cities. *American Sociological Review* 24 (December):804-14.

Form, William H., and Rivera, Julius
1958   The Place of Returning Migrants in a Stratification System. *Rural Sociology* 23 (September):286-97.

1959   Work Contacts and Inter-National Evaluations: The Case of a Mexican Border Village. *Social Forces* 37 (May): 334-39.

Forrest, Earle R.
1929   *Missions and Pueblos of the Old Southwest.* Cleveland: Arthur H. Clark Co.

Fosberg, F. R.
1967   A Classification of Vegetation for General Purposes. In G. F. Peterken, ed. *Guide to the Checklist for I.B.P. Areas.* Handbook no. 4. Oxford, England: Blackwell Scientific Program.

Foscue, Edwin J.
1931   The Mesilla Valley of New Mexico: A Study in Aridity and Irrigation. *Economic Geography* 7 (January):1-27.

1932*a*   Land Utilization in the Lower Rio Grande Valley of Texas. *Economic Geography* 8 (January):1-11.

1932*b*   The Climate of the Lower Rio Grande Valley of Texas. *Monthly Weather Review* 60 (November):207-14.

1934   Agricultural History of the Lower Rio Grande Valley Region. *Agricultural History* 8 (no. 3):124-37.

1938   Influence of Contrasted Soil Types upon Changing Land Values near Grapevine, Texas. *Annals, Association of American Geographers* 28 (June):137-44.

1939   Historical Geography of the Lower Rio Grande Valley of Texas. *Texas Geographic Magazine* 3 (Spring):1-15.

Foster, George M.
1953*a*   What is "Folk Culture"? *American Anthropologist* 55 (no. 2):159-73.

1953*b*   Relationships Between Spanish and Spanish-American Folk Medicine. *Journal of American Folklore* 66:201-17.

1960   *Culture and Conquest.* Chicago: Quadrangle Books.

Foster, John W.
1975   Shell Middens, Paleoecology and Prehistory: The Case from Estero Morua, Sonora, Mexico. *Kiva* 41 (no. 2): 185-93.

Fouts, Susan Carey
1973   Mexican Border Industrialization: An Analogy and a Comment. Paper presented at conference sponsored by Institute of Latin American Studies, April, at University of Texas, Austin, Texas.

Fowler, Arlen L.
1971   *The Black Infantry in the West.* Westport, Conn.: Greenwood Publishing Co.

Fox, D. E.
1978   *Archaeological Testing for Construction of Tennis Courts and Parking Facilities at Fort McIntosh, Laredo Junior College Campus, Laredo, Texas.* Survey Report no. 68. San Antonio: University of Texas at San Antonio, Center for Archaeological Research.

———, and Uecker, H.
1978   *Archaeological Study of the McPherson Road Extension Project, Laredo, Texas.* Survey Report no. 45. San Antonio: University of Texas at San Antonio, Center for Archaeological Research.

Fox, David J.
1965   Henequen in Tamaulipas, Mexico. *Journal of Tropical Geography* 21 (December):1-11.

Fox, Robin
1960   Therapeutic Rituals and Social Structure in Cochíti Pueblo. *Human Relations* 13:291-303.

Foy, Felician A.
1962   Editor. *National Catholic Almanac.* St. Anthony's Guild.

Fragomen, Austin T., Jr.
1973   The Illegal Alien: Criminal or Economic Refugee? Mimeographed. New York: Center for Migration Studies.

1974*a*   U.S. Supreme Court's Decision on Non-Citizenship. *International Migration Review* 8 (Spring):77-78.

1974*b*   Regulating the Illegal Aliens. *International Migration Review* 8 (Winter):567-72.

1975   Permanent Resident Status Redefined. *International Migration Review* 9 (Spring):63-68.

1977   After Amnesty, What? *Migration Today* 5 (April):25-26.

Francaviglia, Richard V.
1970   The Mormon Landscape: Definition of an Image in the American West. *Proceedings, Association of American Geographers* 2:59-61.

1978   *The Mormon Landscape.* New York: AMS Press.

Francisco López, Fray José
1785   The Texas Missions in 1785. *Mid-America* (January, 1940). In Wayne Moquin, ed. *Documentary History of the Mexican Americans*, pp. 106-109. New York: Praeger Publishers.

Frank, Larry, and Harlow, Francis H.
1974   *Historic Pottery of the Pueblo Indians, 1600-1880.* Boston: New York Graphic Society.

Franklin, Hayward H., and Masse, W. Bruce
1976   The San Pedro Salado: A Case of Prehistoric Migration. *Kiva* 42 (no. 1):47-55.

Franssen, Herman T.
1975   *Toward Project Interdependence: Energy in the Coming Decade.* Washington, D.C.: U.S., Cong. Joint Committee on Atomic Energy.

Frantz, Joe B.
1976   *Texas: A Bicentennial History.* New York: W. W. Norton & Co.

1978   The Borderlands: Ideas on a Leafless Landscape. In Stanley R. Ross, ed. *Views Across the Border*, pp. 33-49. Albuquerque: University of New Mexico Press.

Frazer, Robert W.
1968   Editor. *New Mexico in 1850: A Military View.* Norman: University of Oklahoma Press.

Freeman, Donald M.
1974   Party, Vote, and the Mexican American in South Tuc-

son. In F. Chris Garcia, ed. *La causa politica*, pp. 55-66. Notre Dame: University of Notre Dame Press.

Freeman, Lewis R.
1923   *The Colorado River: Yesterday, Today, and Tomorrow.* New York: Dodd, Mead & Co.

Freithaler, William O.
1968   *Mexico's Foreign Trade and Economic Development.* New York: Praeger Publishers.

French, William
1965   *Some Recollections of a Western Ranchman.* 2 vols. New York: *Argosy-Antiquarian.*

Frenkel, R.
1970   Ruderal Vegetation along some California Roadsides. University of California Publications in Geography, no. 20. Berkeley, Calif.

Fretz, Barbara Beers
1974   An Exploratory Study of Foreign Language Acquisition and Evaluative Reactions to Spanish and English Speakers. Ph.D. dissertation, University of Maryland.

Fretz, Burton D.
1966   The Bill of Rights and American Indian Tribal Government. *Natural Resources Journal* 6 (October):581-616.

Freyre, Gilberto
1956   *The Master and the Slaves.* New York: Alfred A. Knopf.

Fried, Jacob
1953   The Relation of Ideal Norms to Actual Behavior in Tarahumara Society. *Southwestern Journal of Anthropology* 9:286-95.

1961   An Interpretation of Tarahumara Interpersonal Relations. *Anthropological Quarterly* 34:110-20.

1969   The Tarahumara. In Robert Wauchope, ed. *Handbook of Middle American Indians,* vol. 8, pp. 846-69. Austin: University of Texas Press.

Friede, Juan
1971   *Las Casas* and Indigenism in the Sixteenth Century. In Juan Friede and Benjamin Keen, eds. *Bartolomé de Las Casas in History: Toward an Understanding of the Man and His Work.* De Kalb: Northern Illinois University Press.

Friedland, William H., and Nelkin, Dorothy
1971   *Migrant Agricultural Workers in America's Northwest.* New York: Holt, Rinehart & Winston.

Friedman, Lee M.
1943   *Jewish Pioneers and Patriots.* Philadelphia: Jewish Publication Society of America.

Friedrichs, Robert W.
1970   *A Sociology of Sociology.* New York: Free Press.

Friend, Llerena B.
1954   *Sam Houston: The Great Designer.* Austin: University of Texas Press.

1965   Sidelights and Supplements on the Perote Prisoners. *Southwestern Historical Quarterly* 48 (January, April): 366-74, 489-96; 49 (July, October):88-95, 516-24.

1966   Sidelights and Supplements on the Perote Prisoners. *Southwestern Historical Quarterly* 49 (January, April): 377-85, 516-24.

Frisbie, Charlotte J., and McAllester, David P.
1978   Editors. *Navajo Blessingway Singer: The Autobiography of Frank Mitchell.* Tucson: University of Arizona Press.

Frisbie, Parker
1975   Illegal Migration from Mexico to the United States: A Longitudinal Analysis. *International Migration Review* 9 (Spring):3-13.

Fromm, Erich, and Maccoby, Michael
1970   *Social Character in a Mexican Village.* Englewood Cliffs: Prentice-Hall.

Frost, Elsa; Meyer, Michael C.; and Vasquez, Josefina Z.
1979   Editors. *Labor and Laborers Through Mexican History.* Tucson: University of Arizona Press.

Frost, Melvin J.
1976   Mormon Colonization, Withdrawal and Resettlement in Northern Mexico. Paper presented to Conference of Latin Americanist Geographers, October, at El Paso, Texas.

Fuchs, Estelle, and Havighurst, Robert
1973   *To Live on This Earth: American Indian Education.* Garden City: Doubleday/Anchor.

Fuentes, Dagoberto, and López, José A.
1974   *Barrio Language Dictionary: First Dictionary of Calo.* Los Angeles: Southland Press.

Fuentes A., Luis
1970   La productividad de los distritos de riego en la República Mexicana. *Informaciones Gegraficos* 20:69-92.

Fuller, Varden
1939   The Supply of Agricultural Labor as a Factor in the Evolution of Farm Organization in California. Ph.D. dissertation, University of California, Berkeley.

Fuller, W. H.
1975   *Soils of the Desert Southwest.* Tucson: University of Arizona Press.

Fullerton, Frank P.
1968   The Implementation of the Chamizal Convention. 2 vols. Master's thesis, University of Texas at El Paso.

Fulton, A. R.
1960   *Motion Pictures: The Development of an Art, from Silent Films to the Age of Television.* Norman: University of Oklahoma Press.

Furlong, Thomas F.
1977   Manzo Case Resolved. *Migration Today* 5 (April):29-30.

Furlong, W. L.
1972   Peruvian and Northern Mexican Municipalities: A Comparative Analysis of Two Political Subsystems. *Comparative Political Studies* 5 (April):59-83.

Furman, Necah S.
1976   *Walter Prescott Webb: His Life and Impact.* Albuquerque: University of New Mexico Press.

Gaillard, D. D.
1894   The Pápago of Arizona and Sonora. *American Anthropologist* 7:293.

Gainer, Bernard
1972   *The Alien Invasion: The Origins of the Aliens Act of 1905.* New York: Crane, Russak & Co.

Gajdusek, D. Carleton
1953   The Sierra Tarahumara. *Geographical Review* 43 (January):15-38.

Galarza, Ernesto
1964   *Merchants of Labor: The Mexican Bracero Story.* Santa Barbara: McNally & Loftin.

1970   *Spiders in the House and Workers in the Field.* Notre Dame: University of Notre Dame Press.

1972   Mexicans in the Southwest: A Culture in Process. In Edward H. Spicer and Raymond H. Thompson, eds. *Plural Society in the Southwest,* pp. 261-97. New York: Interbook.

1977   *Farm Workers and Agri-Business in California, 1947-1960.* Notre Dame: University of Notre Dame Press.

Galaviz de Capdevielle, María Elena
1968   *Rebeliones indígenas en el norte del reino de la Nuevo España.* Vols. 6 and 7. Mexico City: Campesina.

Galindo y Villa, Jesús
1926-27 *Geografía de la Republica Mexicana.* 2 vols. Mexico City: Sociedad de Edición y Librería Franco Americana.

Galloway, Robert W.
1970   The Full-glacial Climate in Southwestern United States. *Annals, Association of American Geographers* 60 (June): 245-56.

Galván, Robert R.
1978   *Bilingualism As It Relates to Intelligence Test Scores and School Achievement Among Culturally-deprived Spanish-American Children.* New York: Arno Press.

Galván, Roberto, and Teschner, Richard
1975   *The Dictionary of the Spanish of Texas.* Silver Spring,

Md.: Institute of Modern Languages.
1977   *El diccionario del español Chicano.* Silver Spring, Md.: Institute of Modern Languages.
Gambrell, Herbert
1934   *Mirabeau Buonaparte Lamar, Troubadour and Crusader.* Dallas: Southern Methodist University Press.
1948   *Anson Jones: The Last President of Texas.* Garden City: Doubleday & Co.
Gamio, Manuel
1930   *Mexican Immigration to the United States.* Chicago: University of Chicago Press.
1931   *The Mexican Immigrant: His Life History.* Chicago: University of Chicago Press.
García, A. C.
1970   Evaluación de los centros de salud de la frontera norte. *Salud Pública de México* 12:140-59.
García, Enriqueta
1964   *Modificaciones al sistema de clasificación climática de Koppen.* Mexico City: Offset Larios, S.A.
———, et al.
1975   *Precipitación y probabilidad de lluvia en los estados de Mexico.* Mexico City: UNAM, Instituto de Geografía, Comisión de Estudios del Territorio Nacional.
García, F. Chris
1972a   Editor. *Chicano Politics: Readings.* New York: MSS Information Corp.
1972b   *Political Socialization of Chicano Children: A Comparative Study with Anglos in California Schools.* New York: Praeger Publishers.
1973   Orientations of Mexican-American and Anglo Children Toward the U.S. Political Community. *Social Science Quarterly* 53 (March):814-30.
1974   Editor. *La Causa Politica: A Chicano Political Reader.* Notre Dame: University of Notre Dame Press.
———, and Garza, Rudolph de la
1977   *The Chicano Political Experience.* North Scituate, Mass.: Duxbury Press.
———, and Hain, Paul L.
1976   Editors. *New Mexico Government.* Albuquerque: University of New Mexico Press.
———, and Winkle, Robert D.
1971   New Mexico: Urban Politics in a State of Varied Political Cultures. In Robert D. Windle, ed. *Politics in the Urban Southwest.* Albuquerque: University of New Mexico Press.
García, Hugo C.
1977   The One Stop Immigration Center: Leading the Way Through the Maze. *Agenda* 7 (September-October): 19-21.
García, John A., and Lytle, Clifford M.
1975   Mexican Juveniles and Crime in U.S. Border Communities. Paper presented to the Southwestern Social Science Association, March, at San Antonio, Texas.
García, John A., and Juárez, Rumaldo Z.
1978   Utilization of Dental Health Services by Chicanos and Anglos. *Journal of Health and Social Behavior* 19 (December):428-36.
García, Juan R.
1980   *Operation Wetback: The Mass Deportation of Undocumented Mexican Laborers in 1954.* Westport Conn.: Greenwood Press.
García, Mario T.
1975a   *Obreros:* The Mexican Workers of El Paso, 1900-1920. Ph.D. dissertation, University of California, San Diego.
1975b   Racial Dualism in the El Paso Labor Market, 1880-1920. *Aztlán* 6 (no. 2):197-217.
1981   *Desert Immigrants: The Mexicans of El Paso, 1880-1920.* New Haven: Yale University Press.
García, Richard A.
1970   Political Ideology: A Comparative Study of Three Chicano Youth Organizations. Master's thesis, University

of Texas at El Paso.
García, Trinidad
1895   *Los mineros Mexicanos.* Mexico City: n.p.
García e Miranda, Enriqueta, and Falcón de Gyves, Zaida
1972   *Nuevo atlas Porrúa de la República Mexicana.* Mexico City: Editorial Porrúa, S.A.
García Martínez, Bernardo, and Lira González, Andrés
1969   Querétaro: la historia y sus instrumentos. *Historia Mexicana* 18 (octubre-diciembre):286-92.
García-Quintero, Andrés
1951   Hydrology of Mexico. *Transactions, American Society of Civil Engineering* 116:1197-1217.
1955   Hidrología de las zonas áridas de México. In *Problemas de las zonas áridas de México,* pp. 43-82. Mexico City: Instituto Mexicana de Recursas Naturales Renobles, Biblioteca Central de la Ciudad Universitaria.
García Ramírez, Sergio
1974   *Delitos en materia de estupefacientes y psicotrópicos.* Mexico City: Ediciones Botas.
García Téllez, Ignacio
1955   *La migración de braceros a los Estados Unidos norteamericanos.* Mexico City: n.p.
Gardner, J. Linton, and Myers, Lloyd E.
1967   Editors. *Water Supplies for Arid Regions.* CODAZR Publication no. 10. Tucson: University of Arizona.
Gardner, Richard
1970   *¡Grito! Reies Tijerina and the New Mexico Land Grant War of 1967.* New York: Bobbs-Merrill Co.
Garlow, David
1978   Offshore Assembly in the Caribbean Basin. *Caribbean Basin Economic Survey* 4:1-11. Atlanta: Federal Reserve Bank.
Garman, Ed
1976   *The Art of Raymond Jonson: Painter.* Albuquerque: University of New Mexico Press.
Garnsey, Morris E.
1950   *America's New Frontier: The Mountain West.* New York: Alfred A. Knopf.
Garr, Daniel
1972   Planning and Plunder: The Missions of Indian Pueblos of Hispanic California. *Southern California Quarterly* 54 (no. 4):291-312.
Garrard, Lewis H.
1938   *Wah-to-yah and the Taos Trail.* Glendale: Arthur H. Clark Co.
1955   *Wah-to-yah and the Taos Trail.* Norman: University of Oklahoma Press.
Garrett, Julia Kathryn
1939   *Green Flag over Texas: The Story of the Last Years of Spain in Texas.* New York and Dallas: Cordoba Press.
Garrigan, Gilbert J.
1946   *A Guide to Historical Method.* Edited by Jean Delanglez. New York: Fordham University Press.
Garza, Edward D.
1951   LULAC: League of United Latin-American Citizens. Master's thesis, Southwest Texas State Teachers College.
Gates, Paul W.
1962   California's Embattled Settlers. *California Historical Society Quarterly* 12 (June):99-130.
1968   *History of Public Land Law Development.* Washington, D.C.: Public Land Law Review Commission.
Gatewood, J. S.; Wilson, Alfonso; Thomas, H. E.; and Kister, L. R.
1964   *General Effects of Drought on Water Resources of the Southwest.* Geological Survey. Washington, D.C.: Government Printing Office.
Gavins, Raymond
1977   *The Perils and Prospects of Southern Black Leadership: Gordon Blaine Hancock, 1884-1970.* Durham: Duke University Press.

Geach, Gwen
1961   *Selected References on Domestic Migratory Agricultural Workers: Their Families, Problems and Programs, 1955-1960.* Bureau of Labor Standards Bulletin no. 225. Washington, D.C.: U.S. Department of Labor.

Geiger, Maynard J.
1939   *The Kingdom of St. Francis in Arizona, 1839-1939.* Santa Barbara: n.p.

1959   *The Life and Times of Fray Junípero Serra, O.F.M.: Or the Man Who Never Turned Back, 1713-1784, a Biography.* Washington, D.C.: Academy of American Franciscan History.

1963   Fray Junípero Serra, Organizer and Administrator of the Upper California Missions, 1769-1784. *California Historical Society Quarterly* 42 (September):195-220.

1965   Biographical Data on the California Missionaries, 1769-1848. *California Historical Society Quarterly* 44 (December):291-310.

1967   New Data on the Building of Mission San Francisco. *California Historical Society Quarterly* 46 (September): 195-205.

1969   Biographical Data on the Missionaries of San Fernando College Serving the California Missions in 1817 and 1820. *California Historical Society Quarterly* 48 (July): 125-51.

1971   Mission San Gabriel in 1814. *Southern California Quarterly* 53 (no. 3):235-50.

Geist, Christopher
1975   Slavery Among the Indians: An Overview. *Negro History Bulletin* 38 (October/November):465-67.

Gell, Elizabeth A. M., and Robinson, William J.
1966   *The Kiva Index: Volumes 1-30, 1935-1965.* Tucson: Arizona Archeological and Historical Society.

Gendarme, René
1970   Les problèmes économiques des régions frontières européennes. *Revue économique* 21 (November).

Gentilcore, R. Louis
1961   Missions and Mission Lands of Alta California. *Annals, Association of American Geographers* 51 (March):46-72.

Gentry, Howard S.
1942   *Rio Mayo Plants: A Study of the Flora and Vegetation of the Valley of the Rio Mayo, Sonora.* Publication 527. Washington, D.C.: Carnegie Institution of Washington.

1943   *The Warihio Indians of Sonora-Chihuahua: An Ethnographic Survey.* Bureau of American Ethnology Bulletin no. 186. Washington, D.C.: Smithsonian Institution.

George, E.
1975   *Historic Architecture of Texas: The Falcon Reservoir.* Austin: Texas Historical Commission, Texas Historical Foundation.

George, Edward Y.; Schauer, David A.; and Neill, Weldon C.
1979   Economic Impact of the Expansion of the Sun Bowl. *El Paso Business Review* 16 (February):2-22.

Geraghty, James J., et al.
1973   *Water Atlas of the United States.* Port Washington, N.Y.: Water Information Center.

Gerald, Rex E.
1974   *Aboriginal Use and Occupation of Certain Lands by Tigua, Manso and Suma Indians.* New York: Garland Publishing, University of Texas at El Paso.

Gerhard, Peter
1972   *A Guide to the Historical Geography of New Spain.* Cambridge, England: Cambridge University Press.

Gerlach, Allen
1968   Conditions along the Border, 1915: The Plan of San Diego. *New Mexico Historical Review* 43 (July):195-212.

1970   Editor. *The National Atlas of the United States of America.* Washington, D.C.: U.S. Geological Survey.

Getty, Harry T.
1961-62 San Carlos Apache Cattle Industry. *Human Organization* 20 (Winter):181-86.

1963   *The San Carlos Indian Cattle Industry.* Anthropological Papers, no. 7. Tucson: University of Arizona.

Gheerbrant, Alain
1970   *La iglesia rebelde de América Latina.* Mexico City: Siglo Veintiuno.

Giammattei, Victor M., and Reichert, Nancy G.
1975   *Art of a Vanished Race: The Mimbres Classic Black-on-White.* Woodland, Calif.: Dillon-Tyler.

Gibbons, Francis M.
1965   Examination of Indian Mineral Titles. *Rocky Mountain Mineral Law Institute* 10:73-105.

Giblin, P. M.
1969   Developments in Mexican Border Industrialization. *Texas International Law-Forum* 5 (Spring):164-75.

Gibson, Arrell M.
1963   *The Kickapoos: Lords of the Middle Border.* Norman: University of Oklahoma Press.

1965   *The Life and Death of Colonel Albert Jennings Fountain.* Norman: University of Oklahoma Press.

Gibson, Charles
1955   The Transformation of the Indian Community in New Spain, 1500-1810. *Journal of World History* 2 (no. 3): 581-605.

1958   *The Colonial Period in Latin American History.* Baltimore: American Historical Association.

1963   Colonial Institutions and Contemporary Latin America: Social and Cultural Life. *Hispanic American Historical Review* 63 (August):279-289.

1964   *The Aztecs Under Spanish Rule: A History of the Indians of the Valley of Mexico, 1519-1810.* Stanford: Stanford University Press.

1966   *Spain in America.* New York: Harper & Row.

1971   Editor. *The Black Legend: Anti-Spanish Attitudes in the Old World and the New.* New York: Alfred A. Knopf.

1975   Writings on Colonial Mexico. *Hispanic American Historical Review* 55 (May):287-323.

Gibson, George Rutledge
1935   *Journal of a Soldier Under Kearny and Doniphan.* Glendale: Arthur H. Clark.

Gibson, Lay J., and Reeves, Richard W.
1970   Functional Bases of Small Towns: A Study of Arizona Settlements. *Arizona Review* 19 (October):19-26.

Giddings, Ruth W.
1959   *Yaqui Myths and Legends.* Anthropological Papers, no. 2. Tucson: University of Arizona.

Gierloff-Emden, Hans G.
1970   *Mexico: Eine Lankeskunde.* Berlin: Walter de Gruyter & Co.

Gifford, Arthur
1972   Joint Ventures: An Approach to the Border Industrialization Program. *El Paso Economic Review* 9 (March).

Gifford, E. W.
1933   The Cocopa. *Publications in American Archaeology and Ethnology, University of California* 31:257-334.

1946   Archeology of the Punta Peñasco Region, Sonora. *American Antiquity* 11 (no. 4):215-21.

———, and Lowie, R. H.
1928   Notes on the Akwa'ala Indians of Lower California. *Publications in American Archaeology and Ethnology, University of California* 23:339-52.

Giffords, Gloria Kay
1974   *Mexican Folk Retablos: Masterpieces on Tin.* Tucson: University of Arizona Press.

Gilbert, Fabiola Cabesa de Baca. See also Cabesa de Baca, Fabiola.
1954   *We Fed Them Cactus.* Albuquerque: University of New Mexico Press.

Gilbert, Grove K.
1928   *Studies of Basin-Range Structure.* U.S. Geological Sur-

vey Paper no. 153. Washington, D.C.: Government Printing Office.

Gildersleeve, Charles Richard

1965   Some Land Use Contrasts in a Border Economy. Paper presented to Nebraska Academy of Science, NCGE Division, April.

1974   Ambos Nogales and Douglas-Agua Prieta: Comparisons of Two Paired Cities on the United States-Mexico Border. Paper presented to the American Association of Geographers, April, at Seattle, Washington.

1975-76   The Status of Borderlands Studies: Geography. *Social Science Journal* 12 (October, 1975):19-28; and 13 (January, 1976):19-28.

1978   The International Border City: Urban Spatial Organization in a Context of Two Cultures Along the United States-Mexico Boundary. Ph.D. dissertation, the University of Nebraska, Lincoln.

Gilmore, N. Ray, and Gilmore, Gladys W.

1963   The Bracero in California. *Pacific Historical Review* 32 (August):265-82.

Gilpin, Laura

1949   *The Rio Grande: River of Destiny.* New York: Duell, Sloan & Pearce.

Gilpin, Robert

1973   *The Multinational Corporation and the National Interest.* Report to the Senate Committee on Labor and Public Welfare. Washington, D.C.: Government Printing Office.

1975   *U.S. Power and the Multinational Corporation.* New York: Basic Books.

Gingerich, Willard P.

n.d.   Editor. Air Quality Issues in the El Paso/Cd. Juárez Border Region. Occasional Paper, no. 5. El Paso: University of Texas at El Paso Center for Inter-American Studies.

Gipson, Rosemary

1967   The Beginning of Theater in Sonora. *Arizona and the West* 9 (Winter):349-64.

Glade, William P., Jr., and Anderson, Charles W.

1963   *The Political Economy of Mexico.* Madison: University of Wisconsin Press.

Gladwin, Winifried, and Gladwin, Harold S.

1929   *The Red-on-Buff Culture of the Papagueria.* Medallion Paper no. 4. Globe, Ariz.: Gila Pueblo.

1935   *The Eastern Range of the Red-on-Buff Culture.* Medallion Paper no. 16. Globe, Ariz.: Gila Pueblo.

Glendening, G. E.

1952   Some Quantitative Data on the Increase of Mesquite and Cactus on a Desert Grassland Range in Southern Arizona. *Ecology* 33:319-28.

Glendinning, Robert M.

1949a   The Coachella Valley, California: Some Aspects of Agriculture in a Desert. *Papers of the Michigan Academy of Science, Arts and Letters* 35:173-95.

1949b   Desert Contrasts Illustrated by the Coachella. *Geographical Review* 39 (April):221-28.

Glenn, Norval D., and Hyland, Ruth

1967   Religious Preferences and Worldly Success: Some Evidence from National Surveys. *American Sociological Review* 32 (February):73-85.

Glick, Thomas F.

1972   *The Old World Background of the Irrigation System of San Antonio, Texas.* Southwestern Studies, no. 35. El Paso: Texas Western Press.

1975   Comparative Ethnic Systems in Premodern Spain. Paper presented to American Sociological Association, August, at San Francisco, California.

Glock, Waldo S., and Agerter, Sharlene R.

1968   Tree Growth and Precipitation near Flagstaff, Arizona. *Yearbook of the Association of Pacific Coast Geographers* 30:79-106.

Goddard, I.

1979   The Languages of South Texas and the Lower Rio Grande. In *The Languages of North America: An Historical and Comparative Assessment.* Austin: University of Texas Press.

Goggin, John M.

1951   The Mexican Kickapoo Indians. *Southwestern Journal of Anthropology* 7:314-27.

Goldberg, Carole E.

1975   The Limits of State Jurisdiction over Reservation Indians. *UCLA Law Review* 22 (February):535-94.

Goldfrank, Esther S.

1967   *The Artist of "Isleta Paintings."* Contributions to Anthropology, vol. 5. Washington, D.C.: Smithsonian Institution.

Goldkind, Victor

1963   Factors in the Differential Acculturation of Mexicans in a Michigan City. Ph.D. dissertation, Michigan State University.

Goldlust, John, and Richmond, Anthony H.

1974   A Multivariate Model of Immigration Adaptation. *International Migration Review* 8 (Summer):193-225.

Goldman, Robert K., and Jacoby, Daniel

1978   *Report of the Commission of Inquiry to Mexico.* New York: International League for Human Rights.

Gollás, Manuel, and García, Adalberto

1976   El desarrollo económico reciente de México. In James W. Wilkie, et al., eds. *Contemporary Mexico: Papers of the Fourth International Congress of Mexican History,* pp. 405-40. Berkeley: University of California Press.

Golze, Alfred R.

1967   Comprehensive Water Development in California. *International Conference on Water for Peace* 8:548-62.

Gómez, R. J.

1959   Condiciones económicas de la classe media mexicana desde la revolución. *Revista Mexicana de Sociología* 21:127-34.

Gomez, Rudolph

1972   Editor. *The Changing Mexican-American.* Boulder, Colo.: Pruett Publishing Co.

1978   The Politics of the Mexican-United States Border. In Stanley R. Ross, ed. *Views Across the Border,* pp. 386-89. Albuquerque: University of New Mexico Press.

———, et al.

1972   Editors. *The Social Reality of Ethnic America.* Lexington, Mass.: D. C. Heath.

Gomez Candeo, Lino

1961   *Los archivos de la historia de América.* 2 vols. Mexico City: Pan American Institute of Geography and History.

Gómez González, Filiberto

1948   *Rarámuri: mi diario tarahumara.* Mexico City: n.p.

1952   *Cuatro mil anos de vida tarahumara.* Mexico City: n.p.

1953   Los tarahumaras, el grupo étnico más numeroso que aún conserva su primitiva cultura. *América Indígena* 13 (no. 2):109-17.

Gómez-Quiñones, Juan

1970a   Research Notes on the Twentieth Century: Notes on Periodization, 1900-1965. *Aztlán* 1 (Spring):115-18.

1970b   Plan de San Diego Reviewed. *Aztlán* 1 (Spring):124-32.

1971   Toward a Perspective on Chicano History. *Aztlán* 2 (Fall): 1-49.

———, and Leobardo Arroyo, Luis

1976   On the State of Chicano History: Observations on Its Development, Interpretations, and Theory, 1970-1974. *Western Historical Quarterly* 7 (April):155-85.

Gonzáles, G. L., and Intriago, M. K.

1972   Estudio sobre los recursos para salud en Matamoros, Tamaulipas. *Salud Pública de México* 14:697-706.

González, Gustavo

1975   The Acquisition of Grammatical Structures by Mexican-American Children. In Eduardo Hernández-Chávez, et al., eds. *El Lenguaje de Los Chicanos*, pp. 220-37. Arlington, Virginia: Center for Applied Linguistics, 1975.

González, Nancie L.
1969   *The Spanish Americans of New Mexico.* Albuquerque: University of New Mexico Press.

González Bonilla, Luis Arturo
1941   Los seris. *Revista Mexicana de Sociología* 3:93-107.

González-Casanova, Pablo. See also Casanova, Pablo G.
1970   *Democracy in Mexico.* New York: Oxford University Press.

González-Mena de LoCoco, Verónica
1974   The Salient Differences Between Chicano Spanish and Standard Spanish: Some Pedagogical Considerations. *Bilingual Review* 1:243-51.

González Navarro, Moisés
1974   Población y sociedad en México, 1900-1970. 2 vols. Mexico City: UNAM.

González Pineda, Francisco
1961   *El mexicano: su dinámica psicosocial.* Mexico City: Pax-México.

González Ramírez, Manuel
1954-56 Editor. *Fuentes para la historia de la revolución mexicana.* 4 vols. Mexico City: Fondo de Cultura Económico.

González y Gonzáles, Luis, et al.
1961-62 *Fuentes de la historia contemporánea de México: libros y folletos.* 3 vols. Mexico City: El Colegio de México.

Gooberman, Lawrence A.
1974   *Operation Intercept: The Multiple Consequences of Public Policy.* New York: Pergamon Press.

Goodall, Leonard E.
1967   Editor. *Urban Politics in the Southwest.* Tempe: Arizona State University.

Goodin, J. R., and Northington, D. K.
1979   *Arid Land Plant Resources.* Lubbock, Texas: International Center for Arid and Semi-Arid Land Studies.

Goodman, James M., and Thompson, Gary L.
1975   The Hopi-Navaho Land Dispute. *American Indian Law Review* 3 (no. 2):397-418.

Goodman, Mary Ellen, and Beman, Alma
1971   Child's Eye-Views of Life in an Urban Barrio. In Nathaniel N. Wagner and Marsha J. Haug, eds. *Chicanos: Social and Psychological Perspectives*, pp. 109-22. St. Louis: C. V. Mosby Co.

Goodman, Mel, and MacDonald, R. J.
1966   The Structure of Mexican Government and Administration. Manuscript, University of Texas at Austin.

Goodner, James
1969   *Indian Americans in Dallas: Migrations, Missions, and Styles of Adaptation.* Minneapolis: University of Minnesota, Training Center for Community Programs.

Goodrich, James W.
1972   Revolt at Mora, 1847. *New Mexico Historical Review* 47 (January):49-60.

Goodsell, James Nelson
1975   Mexico Gets a Second Go—at an Oil Boom. *Christian Science Monitor* 67 (January 14):5.

Gordon, B. L., et al.
1974   *Environment, Settlement and Land Use in the Jicarilla Apache Claim Area.* New York: Garland Publishing, University of New Mexico.

Gordon, C. Wayne; Nasatir, David; Schwartz, Audrey J.; Stanton, Gordon E.; and Wenkert, Robert
1968   *Educational Achievement and Aspirations of Mexican-American Youth in a Metropolitan Context.* Occasional Report no. 36. Los Angeles: University of California, Center for Study and Evaluation.

Gordon, James D.
1961   Texas: Cosmopolitan Cattle Country. *Texas Business Review* 35 (October):7-10.

Gordon, Wendell
1975   A Case for a Less Restrictive Border Policy. *Social Science Quarterly* 56 (December):485-91.

Gorman, Carl
1974   *Navajo Times* Articles on Navajo Healing Sciences. *Navajo Times*, March 7, March 14, March 21, April 18, April 25, and May 2.

Gould, Frank W.
1951   *Grasses of Southwestern United States.* Bulletin 22 (January), Biological Science Bulletin no. 7. Tucson: University of Arizona.
1975   *Texas Plants: A Checklist and Ecological Summary.* MP-585 revised. Texas Agricultural Experiment Station: Texas A&M University.

Goulet, Denis
1977   *The Uncertain Promise: Value Conflicts in Technology Transfer.* New York: IDOC/North America.

Graber, R.
1974   *Agricultural Animals and the Environment.* Stillwater: Oklahoma State University Press.

Gracy, David B., II
1968   *Littlefield Lands, Colonization on the Texas Plains, 1912-1920.* Austin: University of Texas Press.
———, and Rugeley, Helen J. H.
1965   Editors. From the Mississippi to the Pacific: An Englishman in the Mormon Battalion. *Arizona and the West* 7 (Summer):127-60.

Graebner, Fritz
1903   Kulturkreise und Kulturschichten in Ozeanien. *Zeitschrift für Ethnologie* 37:28-53.

Graf, Leroy Phillip
1942   The Economic History of the Lower Rio Grande Valley, 1820-1875. 2 vols. Ph.D. dissertation, Harvard University.

Graham, J. A., and Davis, W. A.
1958   Appraisal of the Archeological Resources of Diablo Reservoir, Val Verde County, Texas. Washington, D.C., Bureau of Interior, National Park Service Report.

Graham, Lawrence
1968   *Politics in a Mexican Community.* Social Science Monographs, no. 35. Gainesville: University of Florida Press.

Graves, Theodore D.
1962*   Time Perspective and the Deferred Gratification Patterns in a Tri-ethnic Community. Ph.D. dissertation, University of Pennsylvania.

Gray, H. Peter
1970   *International Travel-International Trade.* Lexington, Mass.: Heath Lexington Books.

Grayson, George W.
1978   Mexico and the United States: The Natural Gas Controversy. *Inter-American Economic Affairs* 32 (Winter): 3-27.
1980   *The Politics of Mexican Oil.* Pittsburgh: University of Pittsburgh Press.

Grebinger, Paul
1976   *Salado:* Perspectives from the Middle Santa Cruz Valley. *Kiva* 42 (no. 1):39-46.

Grebler, Leo
1966   *Mexican Immigration to the United States: The Record and Its Implications.* Mexican-American Study Project, Advance Report no. 2. Los Angeles: UCLA.
1967   *The Schooling Gap: Signs of Progress.* Mexican-American Study Project, Advance Report no. 7. Los Angeles: UCLA.
———; Moore, Joan W.; and Guzman, Ralph C.
1970   *The Mexican-American People: The Nation's Second Largest Minority.* New York: Free Press.
1973   The Family: Variations in Time and Space. In Livie Isauro Duran and H. Russell Bernard, eds. *Introduction to Chicano Studies*, pp. 309-31. New York: Macmillan Co.

Greeley, Andrew
1972a   *Priests in the United States: Reflections on a Survey.*

New York: Doubleday & Co.
1972*b*   *The Denominational Society.* Glenview, Ill.: Scott, Foresman & Co.

———, and Rossie, Peter H.
1966   *The Education of American Catholics.* Chicago: Aldine Publishing Co.

———, and Schoenherr, Richard
1971   *American Priests.* Chicago: National Opinion Research Center, U.S. Catholic Conference.

Green, Christine R., and Sellers, William D.
1964   Editors. *Arizona Climate.* Tucson: University of Arizona Press.

Green, Donald E.
1973   *Land of the Underground Rain: Irrigation on the Texas High Plains, 1910-1970.* Austin: University of Texas Press.

Greenburg, Edward S.
1970   Editor. *Political Socialization.* New York: Atherton Press.

Greenburg, Martin H.
1970   *Bureaucracy and Development: A Mexican Case Study.* Lexington, Mass.: D. C. Heath.

Greene, Jack P.
1972   Editor. *Neither Slave nor Free: The Freedman of African Descent in the Slave Societies of the New World.* Baltimore: Johns Hopkins University Press.

Greene, Sheldon L.
1969*a*   Operation Sisyphus: Wetbacks, Growers and Poverty. *Nation* 209 (October 20):403-406.
1969*b*   Immigration Law and Rural Poverty: The Problems of the Illegal Entrant. *Duke Law Journal* 19 (no. 3):475-.

Greene, Shirley
1954   *The Education of Migrant Children: A Study of the Educational Opportunities and Experiences of the Children of Agricultural Migrants.* Washington, D.C.: National Council on Agricultural Life and Labor.

Greenleaf, J. Cameron
1975   *Excavations at Punta de Agua in the Santa Cruz River Basin, Southeastern Arizona.* Anthropological Papers, no. 26. Tucson: University of Arizona Press.

Greenleaf, Richard E.
1964   The Founding of Albuquerque, 1706: A Historical-legal Problem. *New Mexico Historical Review* 39 (January): 1-15.
1967   Atrisco and Las Ciruelas, 1722-1796. *New Mexico Historical Review* 42 (January):5-25.
1972   Land and Water in Mexico and New Mexico, 1700-1821. *New Mexico Historical Review* 47 (April):85-112.

———, and Meyer, Michael C.
1973   Editors. *Research in Mexican History.* Lincoln: University of Nebraska Press.

Greenstein, Fred
1963   *The American Party System and the American People.* Englewood Cliffs, N.J.: Prentice-Hall.

Greenwood, N. H.
1963   Feasibility of Transmountain Stream Diversions Across the White Mountains of Arizona. *Journal of Geography* 62 (May):203-209.

Gregg, Josiah
1952   *Commerce of the Prairies.* 2 vols. New York: Lippincott Co. Originally published by Henry G. Langley, New York, 1844.
1954   *Commerce of the Prairies.* Edited by Max L. Moorhead. Norman: University of Oklahoma Press.

Gregg, R. E.
1963   *The Ants of Colorado.* Boulder: University of Colorado Press.

Gregg, Robert D.
1937   *The Influence of Border Troubles on Relations Between the United States and Mexico.* Baltimore: Johns Hopkins University Press.

Gregor, Howard F.
1951   A Sample Study of the California Ranch. *Annals, Association of American Geographers* 41 (December):285-306.
1957   Urban Pressures on California Land. *Land Economics* 33 (November):311-25.
1959*a*   An Evaluation of Oasis Agriculture. *Association of Pacific Coast Geographers Yearbook* 21:39-50.
1959*b*   Push to the Desert: The Pressure of Agriculture on California Arid Land Illustrates the Law of Diminishing Returns. *Science* 129 (May 15):1329-39.
1962   The Plantation in California. *Professional Geographer* 14 (March):1-4.
1963   Urbanization of Southern California Agriculture. *Tijdschrift voor Economische en Social Geografie* 54 (December):273-78.
1964   A Map of Agricultural Adjustment. *Professional Geographer* 16 (January):16-19.
1970*a*   The Large Industrialized American Crop Farm: A Mid-Latitude Plantation Variant. *Geographical Review* 60 (no. 2):151-75.
1970*b*   The Industrial Farm As a Western Institution. *Journal of the West* 9 (no. 1):78-92.
1976   Agricultural Intensity in the Pacific Southwest. *Proceedings of the Association of American Geographers* 8:54-58.

Gregory, Herbert E.
1915   The Oasis of Tuba, Arizona. *Annals, Association of American Geographers* 5:107-19.

Grieb, Kenneth J.
1968   Reginald del Valle: A California Diplomat's Sojourn in Mexico. *California Historical Society Quarterly* 47 (December):316-428.

Griffin, Ernst C., and Ford, Larry R.
1976   Tijuana: Landscape of a Culture Hybrid. *Geographical Review* 66 (October):435-47.

Griffin, Paul F., and Chatham, Ronald L.
1958   Population: A Challenge to California's Changing Citrus Industry. *Economic Geography* 34 (July):272-76.

Griffin, Paul F.; Chatham, Ronald L.; and Young, Robert N.
1968   *Anglo-America: A Systematic and Regional Geography.* 2nd ed. Palo Alto: Fearon Publishers.

Griffin, Paul F., and Young, Robert N.
1957   *California, the Empire State: A Regional Geography.* San Francisco: Fearon Publishers.

Griffin, William B.
1959   *Notes on Seri Indian Culture, Sonora, Mexico.* Latin American Monographs, no. 10. Gainesville: University of Florida Press.
1969   *Culture Change and Shifting Populations in Central Northern Mexico.* Anthropological Papers, no. 13. Tucson: University of Arizona Press.

Griffith, James S.
1967   Mochicahue Judio Masks: A Type of *Fariseo* Mask from Northern Sinaloa, Mexico. *Kiva* 32 (no. 4):143-49.
1972   Cáhitan Pascola Masks. *Kiva* 37 (no. 4):185-98.

Grimes, C. E., and Simmons, C. E. P.
1969   Bureaucracy and Political Control in Mexico: Towards an Assessment. *Public Administration Review* 29 (January/February):72-80.

Grindle, Merilee S.
1977*a*   *Bureaucrats, Politicians, and Peasants in Mexico.* Berkeley: University of California Press.
1977*b*   Power, Expertise, and the "Tecnico": Suggestions From a Mexican Case Study. *Journal of Politics* 39 (no. 2): 399-426.

Griswold del Castillo, Richard
1979   *The Los Angeles Barrio, 1850-1890: A Social History.* Berkeley: University of California Press.

Gritzner, Charles F.
1969   Spanish Log Construction in New Mexico. Ph.D. disser-

tation, Louisiana State University.

1971   Log Housing in New Mexico. *Pioneer America* 3 (July): 54-62.

1974a   Construction Materials in a Folk Housing Tradition: Considerations Governing Their Selection in New Mexico. *Pioneer America* 4 (January):25-39.

1974b   Hispano Gristmills in New Mexico. *Annals, Association of American Geographers* 64 (December):514-24.

1979-80 Hispanic Log Construction. *El Palacio* 85:20-20.

Grivas, Theodore
1961   Alcalde Rule: The Nature of Local Government in Spanish and Mexican California. *California Historical Society Quarterly* 40 (March):11-32.

1963   *Military Government in California, 1846-1850.* Glendale: Arthur H. Clark Co.

Gronet, Richard W.
1969   United States and the Invasion of Texas, 1810-1814. *Americas* 25 (January):281-306.

Grove, Pearce S.; Barnett, Becky J.; and Hansen, Sandra J.
1975   *New Mexico Newspapers: A Comprehensive Guide to Bibliographical Entries and Locations.* Albuquerque: University of New Mexico Press.

Gruber, Wilfried
1971   Career Patterns of Mexico's Political Elite. *Western Political Quarterly* 24 (no. 3):467-82.

Guel, J. R.
1972   Estudio de la organización sanitaria del estado de Coahila. Mimeographed. Mexico City: Escuela de Salud Pública.

Guerra, Carlos
1972   Chicano Movement. Lecture, President of Texas MAYO Chapters, April 11, University of Texas at Austin.

Guerrero, Ricardo
1968   Prostitution in Tijuana. In John A. Price, ed. *Tijuana '68: Ethnographic Notes on a Mexican Border City.* Ethnology Laboratory Publication no. 1. San Diego: San Diego State University.

Guest, Florian F.
1962   The Establishment of the Villa de Franciforte. *California Historical Society Quarterly* 41 (March):29-50.

1966   The Indian Policy Under Fermín Francisco de Lasuén, California's Second Father President. *California Historical Society Quarterly* 45 (September):195-224.

1967   Municipal Government in Spanish California. *California Historical Society Quarterly* 46 (December):307-35.

Gunnerson, Dolores A.
1956   The Southern Athabascans: Their Arrival in the Southwest. *El Palacio* 63:346-65.

Gunnerson, James H.
1969   Apache Archaeology in Northeastern New Mexico. *American Antiquity* 4 (no. 1):32-39.

Günter, Hans
1973   Editor. *Transnational Industrial Relations.* London: Macmillan Co.

Gustafson, Richard A., and Owens, Thomas R.
1971   The Self-Concept of Mexican-American Youngsters and Related Environmental Characteristics. Manuscript. ERIC (ED 053 195). Las Cruces, N.M.: New Mexico State University, ERIC Clearinghouse.

Gutiérrez, Armando G.
1978   The Politics of the Texas Border: An Historical Overview and Some Contemporary Directions. In Stanley R. Ross, ed. *Views Across the Border,* pp. 117-37. Albuquerque: University of New Mexico.

———, and Hirsh, Herbert
1973   The Militant Challenge to the American Ethos: Chicanos and Mexican-Americans. *Social Science Quarterly* 53 (March):830-46.

1974   Political Maturation and Political Awareness: The Case of the Crystal City Chicano. *Aztlán* 5 (1/2):295-312.

Gutiérrez, Felix
1978   Newspaper Coverage of Undocumented Workers: A Pre-

liminary Report. Paper, Office of the INS Commissioner, July, Washington, D.C.

Gutiérrez, José Angel
1968   La Raza and Revolution: The Empirical Conditions of Revolution in Four South Texas Counties. Master's thesis, St. Mary's University.

Gutiérrez, T. E.
1973   *Plan de salud del estado de Coahila.* Mexico City: I Convención Nacional de Salud.

Gutiérrez de MacGregor, María Teresa
1968   *Geodemografía del estado de Jalisco.* Mexico City: UNAM.

———, and Valverde V., Carmen
1975   Evolution of the Urban Population in the Arid Zones of Mexico, 1900-1970. *Geographical Review* 65 (April): 214-28.

Guzman, Ralph C.
1966   Politics and Policies of the Mexican-American Community. In Eugene Dverin and Arthur Misner, eds. *California Politics and Policies,* pp. 350-81. Los Angeles: Addison-Wesley Publishing Co.

1967   *The Socio-economic Position of the Mexican-American Migrant Farm Worker.* Washington, D.C.: National Advisory Commission on Rural Poverty.

1970   The Political Socialization of the Mexican-American People. Ph.D. dissertation, University of California at Los Angeles.

Haagen-Smit, A. J.
1964   The Control of Air Pollution. *Scientific American* 210 (January):24-31.

Haas, William H.
1926   The Cliff-Dweller and His Habitat. *Annals, Association of American Geographers* 16 (December):167-215.

Haase, Edward F.
1970   Environmental Fluctuations on South-facing Slopes in the Santa Catalina Mountains of Arizona. *Ecology* 51 (Autumn):959-74.

Habig, Marion A.
1968a   Mission San Jose y San Miguel de Aguayo, 1720-1824. *Southwestern Historical Quarterly* 71 (April):496-516.

1968b   *San Antonio's Mission San Jose.* San Antonio: Naylor Co.

1968c   *The Alamo Chain of Missions: A History of San Antonio's Five Old Missions.* Chicago: Franciscan Herald Press.

Hack, John T.
1941   Dunes of the Western Navajo Country. *Geographical Review* 31 (April):240-63.

1942   *The Changing Physical Environment of the Hopi Indians of Arizona.* Papers of the Peabody Museum of American Archaeology and Ethnology, no. 35. Cambridge: Harvard University.

Hackenberg, Robert A.
1961   *Pápago Population Study: Research Methods and Preliminary Results.* Tucson: University of Arizona, Bureau of Ethnic Research.

1962   Economic Alternatives in Arid Lands: A Case Study of the Pima and Pápago Indians. *Ethnology* 1 (April):186-96.

1966   An Anthropological Study of Demographic Transition: The Pápago Information System. *Millbank Memorial Fund Quarterly* 44:470-93.

1967   The Parameters of an Ethnic Group: A Method for Studying the Total Tribe. *American Anthropologist* 69: 478-92.

1974   *Pápago Indians: Aboriginal Land Use and Occupancy.* New York: Garland Publishing, University of Colorado.

1976   Colorado River Basin Development and Its Potential Impact on Tribal Life. *Human Organization* 35 (Fall):303-11.

———, and Gallagher, Mary M.
1972   The Costs of Cultural Change: Accidental Injury and

Modernization Among the Pápago Indians. *Human Organization* 31:211-26.

———, and Wilson, Roderick C.

1972 Reluctant Emigrants: The Role of Migration in Pápago Indian Adaptation. *Human Organization* 31:171-86.

Hackenberg, Robert H.

1974 *Aboriginal Land Use and Occupancy of the Pima-Maricopa Indians.* New York: Garland Publishing, University of Colorado.

Hacker, Patrick E.; Meier, Dennis C.; and Pauli, Dan J.

1974 State Jurisdiction over Indian Land Use: An Interpretation of the "Encumbrance" Savings Clause of Public Law 280. *Land and Water Law Review* 9 (no. 2):421-56.

Hackett, Charles W.

1912 The Retreat of the Spaniards from New Mexico in 1689, and the Beginnings of El Paso. *Southwestern Historical Quarterly* 16 (October):137-68.

1913 The Retreat of the Spaniards from New Mexico in 1689, and the Beginnings of El Paso. *Southwestern Historical Quarterly* 16 (January):259-76.

1917 *The Causes for the Failure of Otermin's Attempt to Reconquer New Mexico, 1681-82.* New York: Macmillan.

1923-37 Editor. *Historical Documents Relating to New Mexico, Nueva Vizcaya and Approaches Thereto, to 1773.* 3 vols. Washington, D.C.: Carnegie Institution of Washington.

———, and Shelby, C. C.

1942 *Revolt of the Pueblo Indians of New Mexico and Otermin's Attempted Reconquest, 1680-1682.* Coronado History Series, vols. 3 and 9. Albuquerque: University of New Mexico Press.

Haddox, John

1970 *Los Chicanos: An Awakening People.* Southwestern Studies, no. 28. El Paso: Texas Western Press.

Hadley, Eleanor M.

1956 A Critical Analysis of the Wetback Problem. *Law and Contemporary Problems* 21:334-57.

Hafen, LeRoy R.

1950 Editor. *Ruxton of the Rockies.* Norman: University of Oklahoma Press.

———, and Hafen, Ann W.

1954 *Old Spanish Trail, Santa Fe to Los Angeles.* Glendale: Arthur H. Clark Co.

———; Hollon, W. Eugene; and Rister, Carl Coke

1970 *Western America: The Exploration, Settlement, and Development of the Region beyond the Mississippi,* 3rd ed. Englewood Cliffs, N.J.: Prentice-Hall. Originally published in 1941.

Hager, William M.

1963 The Plan of San Diego: Unrest on the Texas Border in 1915. *Arizona and the West* 5 (Winter):327-36.

Haines, Helen

1891 *History of New Mexico from the Spanish Conquest to the Present Time, 1530-1890.* New York: New Mexico Historical Publishing Co.

Haissman, I.

1971 The Village Corporation: Mexican Experience with a New Land Tenure System. *Land Reform, Land Settlement and Cooperatives* 2:14-20.

Hale, Will

1959 *Twenty-Four Years a Cowboy and Ranchman in Southern Texas and Old Mexico.* Norman: University of Oklahoma Press.

Hale, W. E., et al.

1965 *Characteristics of Water Supply in New Mexico.* Technical Report no. 31. Santa Fe: New Mexico State Engineers.

Hales, John E., Jr.

1974*a* Southwestern United States Summer Monsoon Source —Gulf of Mexico or Pacific Ocean? *Journal of Applied Meteorology* 13 (April):331-42.

1974*b* Southwestern United States Summer Monsoon Source —Gulf of Mexico or Pacific Ocean? *Weatherwise* 27 (August):148-55.

Haley, Charles S.

1923 *Gold Placers of California.* San Francisco: California State Bureau of Mines.

Haley, J. Evetts

1949 *Charles Goodnight: Cowman and Plainsman.* Norman: University of Oklahoma Press.

1953 *The XIT Ranch of Texas and the Early Days of the Llano Estacado.* Norman: University of Oklahoma Press.

Haley, P. Edward

1970 *Revolution and Intervention: The Diplomacy of Taft and Wilson with Mexico, 1910-1917.* Cambridge, Mass.: M.I.T. Press.

Hall, Carl W.

1968 *Bibliography on Mechanization and Labor in Agriculture.* Rural Manpower Center, Special Paper no. 6. East Lansing: Michigan State University.

Hall, Edward T.

1944 Recent Clues to Athabascan Prehistory in the Southwest. *American Anthropologist* 46:98-105.

Hall, G. D., and Grombacher, K. A.

1974 *An Assessment of the Archeological and Historical Resources to Be Affected by the Brazos Island Harbor Waterway Project, Texas.* Research Report no. 30. Austin: Texas Archeological Survey.

Hall, Grace, and Saltzstein, Alan

1977 Equal Employment Opportunity for Minorities in Municipal Government. *Social Science Quarterly* 57 (March): 864-73.

Hall, Martin Hardwick

1960 *Sibley's New Mexico Campaign.* Austin: University of Texas Press.

Hall, Warren E.

1963 Los Angeles: Growing Pains of a Metropolis. In Carle Hodge and Peter C. Duisberg, eds. *Aridity and Man,* pp. 517-28. Publication no. 74. Washington, D.C.: AAAS.

Hallenbeck, C.

1940 *Alvar Núñez Cabeza de Vaca, the Journal of the Route of the First European to Cross the Continent of North America, 1534-1536.* Glendale: Arthur H. Clark Co.

Halliburton, R.

1975 Black Slave Control in the Cherokee Nation. *Journal of Ethnic Studies* 3 (Summer):23-32.

Hallowell, A. Irving

1957*a* The Impact of the American Indian on American Culture. *American Anthropologist* 59:201-17.

1957*b* The Backwash of the Frontier: The Impact of the Indian on American Culture. In Walker D. Wyman and Clifton B. Kroeber, eds. *The Frontier in Perspective,* pp. 229-58. Madison: University of Wisconsin Press.

Halpin, Joseph

1971 Musical Activities and Ceremonies at Mission Santa Clara de Asis. *California Historical Society Quarterly* 50 (March):35-42.

Halsell, Grace

1978 *The Illegals.* New York: Stein & Day Publishers.

Hamby, James E., Jr.

1975 The People of Chihuahua: A Demographic Analysis. Ph.D. dissertation, University of Florida.

Hamilton, H. R., et al.

1966 *Bibliography on Socio-Economic Aspects of Water Resources.* Washington, D.C.: Department of Interior, Office of Water Resources Research.

Hamilton, J. A.

1948 A History of the Presbyterian Work Among the Pima and Papago Indians of Arizona. Master's thesis, University of Arizona.

Hammill, Hugh M., Jr.
1973   Royalist Counterinsurgency in the Mexican War for Independence: The Lessons of 1811. *Hispanic American Historical Review* 53 (August):470-89.

Hamming, Edward
1958   Water Legislation. *Economic Geography* 34 (January): 42-46.

Hammond, Edwin H.
1963   *Classes of Land-Surface Form in the Forty-eight States, U.S.A. Map at scale 1:5,000,000.* Washington, D.C.: Association of American Geographers.

Hammond, George P.
1927   *Don Juan de Oñate and the Founding of New Mexico.* Santa Fe: El Palacio Press.

————, and Rey, Agapito
1927   The Gallegos Relation of the Rodriguez Expedition to New Mexico. *Historical Society of New Mexico, Publications in History* 4:18, 22, 54-55.

1928   *Obregon's History of Sixteenth Century Explorations in Western America, etc., Mexico, 1584.* Los Angeles: n.p.

1929   *The Espejo Expedition into New Mexico Made by Antonio de Espejo, 1582-1583: As Revealed in the Journal of Diego Perea de Luxan.* Vol. 1. Albuquerque: Quivira Society.

1940   *Narrative of the Coronado Expedition.* Albuquerque: University of New Mexico Press.

1953   Editors. *Don Juan de Oñate, Colonizer of New Mexico, 1595-1628.* 2 vols. Albuquerque: University of New Mexico Press.

1966   Editors. *The Rediscovery of New Mexico, 1580-1594.* Albuquerque: University of New Mexico Press.

Hamy, E. T.
1883   Quelques observations sur la distribution géographique des opatas, des tarahumaras et des pimas. *Société d'Anthropologie de Paris, Bulletin* 3 (no. 6):785-91.

Hancock, Richard H.
1959   *The Role of the Bracero in the Economic and Cultural Dynamics of Mexico: A Case Study of Chihuahua.* Stanford: Hispanic American Society.

Handlin, Oscar
1957   *Race and Nationality in American Life.* Garden City, N.Y.: Doubleday Anchor.

————, et al.
1954   *Harvard Guide to American History.* Cambridge: Harvard University Press.

Handy, Robert M., and Durrenberger, R. W.
1976   *Solar Radiation and Sunshine Data for the Southwestern United States, 1966-1974.* Tempe: Arizona State University, Solar Energy Research Commission, Laboratory of Climatology.

Haney, Jane B.
1979   Formal and Informal Labor Recruitment Mechanisms: Stages in Mexican Migration into Mid-Michigan Agriculture. In Fernando Camara and Robert Van Kemper, eds. *Migration Across Frontiers: Mexico and the United States,* pp. 141-49. Albany: State University of New York at Albany, Institute for Mesoamerican Studies.

Hanke, Lewis
1935   *The First Social Experiments in America: A Study of the Development of Spanish Indian Policy in the Sixteenth Century.* Cambridge: Harvard University Press.

1965   *The Spanish Struggle for Justice in the Conquest of America.* Boston: Little, Brown & Co.

1970   *Aristotle and the American Indians: A Study in Race Prejudice in the Modern World.* Bloomington: Indiana University Press.

1971   A Modest Proposal for a Moratorium on Grand Generalizations: Some Thoughts on the Black Legend. *Hispanic American Historical Review* 51 (February):112-27.

Hansen, Kenneth R.
1974   *Latin American Tourism: Prospects, Problems and Alternative Approaches.* Washington, D.C.: Inter-American Development Bank.

Hansen, Klaus J.
1963   The Kingdom of God in Mormon Thought and Practice, 1830-1896. Ph.D. dissertation, Wayne State University.

Hansen, Niles
1973   *Location Preferences, Migration, and Regional Growth.* New York: Praeger Publishers.

1977   The Economic Development of Border Regions. *Growth and Change* 8 (October):2-8.

1978   Alien Migration: Mexican Workers in the United States and European "Guest Workers." *Texas Business Review* 42 (June):107-11.

Hansen, Roger
1971   *The Politics of Mexican Development.* Baltimore: Johns Hopkins University Press.

Harding, S. T.
1960   *Water in California.* Palo Alto: n.p.

Hardy, B. Carmon
1963   The Mormon Colonies of Northern Mexico: A History, 1885-1912. Ph.D. dissertation, Wayne State University.

1965   Cultural "Encystment" as a Cause of the Mormon Exodus from Mexico in 1912. *Pacific Historical Review* 34 (November):439-54.

1969   The Trek South: How the Mormons Went to Mexico. *Southwestern Historical Quarterly* 73 (July):197-210.

Hardy, Osgood
1929   Agricultural Changes in California, 1860-1890. Proceedings of the Pacific Coast Branch, American Historical Association, pp. 216-30.

Hargrove, L.
1972   Editor. *Law, Institutions and the Global Environment.* Dobbs Ferry, N.Y.: Oceana Publications.

Haring, C. H.
1952   *The Spanish Empire in America.* New York: Oxford University Press.

Harlow, Francis H.
1973   *Matte-Paint Pottery of the Tewa, Keres, and Zuñi Pueblos.* Albuquerque: University of New Mexico Press.

1977   *Modern Pueblo Pottery, 1880-1960.* Flagstaff: Northland Press.

————, and Young, John V.
1965   *Contemporary Pueblo Indian Pottery.* Santa Fe: Museum of New Mexico Press.

Harmon, Robert B.
1977   *A Selected and Annotated Guide to the Government and Politics of Mexico.* Council of Planning Librarians Exchange Bibliography no. 1242.

Harmon, Warren W.
1964   The Grape Industry in San Diego County, California. Master's thesis, San Diego State College.

Harper, Allen G.; Cordova, Andrew R.; and Oberg, Kalervo
1943   *Man and Resources in the Middle Rio Grande Valley.* Albuquerque: University of New Mexico Press.

Harrington, H. D.
1964   *Manual of the Plants of Colorado.* Chicago: Swallow Press.

Harris, David R.
1966   Recent Plant Invasions in the Arid and Semi-arid Southwest of the United States. *Annals, Association of American Geographers* 56 (September):408-22.

Harris, James W.
1974*a*   Morphologization of Phonological Rules: An Example from Chicano Spanish. In R. Joe Campbell, et al., eds. *Linguistic Studies in Romance Languages: Proceedings of the Third Linguistic Symposium on Romance Languages.* Washington, D.C.: Georgetown University Press.

1974*b*   Two Morphophonemic Innovations in Chicano Spanish. Paper, Indiana University Linguistics Club, Bloomington, Ind.

Harshbarger, J. W., et al.
1966   *Arizona Water.* Water Supply Paper no. 1648. Washington, D.C.: U.S. Geological Survey.

Hartman, David N.
1968   *California and Man.* Dubuque, Iowa: Wm. C. Brown Co.

Hartman, L. M., and Seastone, Don
1970   *Water Transfers: The Economic Efficiency and Alternative Institutions.* Baltimore: Johns Hopkins University Press.

Hartman, Susan, and Chavez, Leticia
1979   *Impact of Resident Aliens and Migrant School Children on Border Public School Districts.* El Paso: Organization of U.S. Border Cities and Counties, Southwest Border Regional Commission.

Harvey, Byron, III
1970   *Ritual in Pueblo Art: Hopi Life in Hopi Painting.* New York: Museum of the American Indian, Heye Foundation.

Harvey, Gina Cantoni, and Heiser, M. F.
1975   *Southwest Languages and Linguistics in Educational Perspective: Proceedings, Third Annual Southwest Areal Languages and Linguistics Workshop.* San Diego: San Diego State University Institute for Cultural Pluralism.

Haskett, Bert
1936   History of the Sheep Industry in Arizona. *Arizona Historical Review* 7 (July):3-49.

Hasselden, Louis G.
1943   New Mexico Architecture. *New Mexico Quarterly Review* 31 (Autumn):326-32.

Hassrick, Peter H.
1973   *Frederick Remington: Paintings, Drawings and Sculpture in the Amon Carter Museum and Sid W. Richardson Foundation Collection.* New York: Abrams.

Hastings, James Rodney
1959   Vegetation Change and Arroyo Cutting in Southeastern Arizona. *Journal of Arizona Academy of Science* 1:60-67.

1961   People of Reason and Others: The Colonization of Sonora to 1767. *Arizona and the West* 3 (Winter):321-40.

1964   Climatological Data for Baja California. Technical Reports on the Meteorology and Climatology of Arid Regions, no. 14. Tucson: University of Arizona, Institute of Atmospheric Physics.

———, and Humphrey, Robert R.
1969*a*   Editors. *Climatological Data and Statistics for Baja California.* Technical Report no. 18. Tucson: University of Arizona, Institute of Atmospheric Physics.

1969*b*   Editors. *Climatological Data and Statistics for Sonora and Northern Sinaloa.* Technical Report no. 19. Tucson: University of Arizona, Institute of Atmospheric Physics.

———, and Turner, Raymond M.
1965*a*   *The Changing Mile, an Ecological Study of Vegetation Change with Time in the Lower Mile of an Arid and Semiarid Region.* Tucson: University of Arizona Press.

1965*b*   Seasonal Precipitation Regimes in Baja California, Mexico. *Geografiska Annaler* 47 (no. 4):205-23.

———; ———; and Warren, Douglas K.
1972   *An Atlas of Some Plant Distributions in the Sonoran Desert.* Technical Report on Climatology of Arid Regions no. 21. Tucson: University of Arizona Institute of Atmospheric Physics.

Haulman, Bruce, and Bailey, David T.
1973   Ethnic Differences in Two Southwestern Cities, 1860-1870. Paper presented at the Southwestern Sociological Association, March, at Dallas, Texas.

Haury, Emil W.
1950   *The Stratigraphy and Archeology of Ventana Cave.* Tucson: University of Arizona Press. Reprinted in 1975.

1953   Artifacts with Mammoth Remains, Naco, Arizona. *American Antiquity* 19:1-14.

1956   Speculations on Prehistoric Settlement Patterns in the Southwest. In Gordon R. Willey, ed. *Prehistoric Settlement Patterns in the New World,* pp. 3-10. New York: Wenner-Gren Foundation.

1976   *The Hohokam: Desert Farmers and Craftsmen.* Tucson: University of Arizona Press.

———; Sayles, E. B.; and Wasley, William
1959   The Lehner Mammoth Site, Southeast Arizona. *American Antiquity* 25:2-30.

Hawley, Ellis W.
1966   The Politics of the Mexican Labor Issue, 1950-1965. *Agricultural History* 60 (no. 3):157-76.

Hawley, John W.
1969   Notes on the Geomorphology and Late Cenozoic Geology of Northwestern Chihuahua. In *The Border Region Guidebook,* pp. 131-42. New Mexico Geological Society, Twentieth Field Conference.

Hay, John
1963   Upper Rio Grande: Embattled River. In Carle Hodge and Peter C. Duisberg, eds. *Aridity and Man,* pp. 491-98. Publication no. 74. Washington, D.C.: AAAS.

Hayden, Julian D.
1957   *Excavations, 1940, at the University Indian Ruin.* Technical Series, no. 5. Globe, Ariz.: Southwest Monuments Association.

Hayner, Norman S.
1942   Notes on the Changing Mexican Family. *American Sociological Review* 7:489-97.

1954   The Family in Mexico. *Marriage and Family Living* 16 (November):369-73.

1966   *New Patterns in Old Mexico: A Study of Town and Metropolis.* New Haven, Conn.: College and University Press.

Hayton, Robert D.
1976   The Ground Water Legal Regime as Instrument of Policy Objectives and Management Requirements. In *Second International Conference on Water Law and Administration, Annales Juirs Aquarum* 2 (February):272-301.

1978   Institutional Alternatives for Mexico-U.S. Groundwater Management. *Natural Resources Journal* 18 (January):201-12.

Heald, Weldon F.
1963   Arizona's Wilderness Areas. *Arizona Highways* 39 (September):14-27, 40-47.

Healy, Robert G.
1974   Saving California's Coast: The Coastal Zone Initiative and Its Aftermath. *Coastal Zone Management Journal* 1:365-94.

Heaps, Willard A.
1968   *Wandering Workers: The Story of American Migrant Farmworkers and Their Problems.* New York: Crown Publishers.

Hecht, Melvin E.
1963   *Township and Range Index of Arizona.* Tucson: University of Arizona, Bureau of Business and Public Research.

1975   The Decline of the Grass Lawn Tradition in Tucson. *Landscape* 19 (May):3-10.

1978   Climate and Culture, Landscape and Lifestyle in the Sun Belt of Southern Arizona. *Journal of Popular Culture* 11 (Spring):928-47.

Hedderson, John J., and Daudistel, Howard C.
1982   Infant Mortality of the Spanish Surname Population. *Social Science Journal* 19 (October).

Hedrick, Basil C. J.; Kelley, Charles; and Riley, Carroll L.
1971   Editors. *The North Mexican Frontier: Readings in Archaeology, Ethnohistory and Ethnography.* Carbondale: Southern Illinois University Press.

1974   *The Mesoamerican Southwest.* Carbondale: Southern Illinois University Press.

Heer, David M.
1979   What Is the Annual Net Flow of Undocumented Mexican Immigrants to the United States? *Demography* 16 (August):417-23.

Hefferan, Violle Clark
1940   Thomas Benton Catron. Master's thesis, University of New Mexico.

Heizer, Robert F.
1962   The California Indians: Archaeology, Varieties of Culture, Arts of Life. *California Historical Society Quarterly* 41 (March):1-28.

1964   The Western Coast of North America. In J. D. Jennings and E. Norbeck, eds. *Prehistoric Man in the New World,* pp. 117-48. Chicago: University of Chicago Press.

1976   *The Indians of California: A Critical Bibliography.* Bloomington: Indiana University Press.

1978   Editor. *California.* Handbook of North American Indians Series, vol. 8. Washington, D.C.: Smithsonian Institution.

———, and Clewlow, C. W., Jr.
1973   *Prehistoric Rock Art of California.* Ramona, Calif.: Ballena Press.

———, and Elsasser, Albert B.
1977   *A Bibliography of California Indians: Archaeology, Ethnography and Indian History.* New York: Garland Publishing.

1980   *The Natural World of the California Indians.* Berkeley: University of California Press.

———; Nissen, Karen M.; and Castillo, Edward D.
1975   *California Indian History: A Classified and Annotated Guide to Source Materials.* Publications in Archaeology, Ethnology and History, no. 4. Ramona, Calif.: Ballena Press.

———, and Whipple, M. A.
1951   Editors. *California Indians: A Source Book.* Berkeley: University of California Press.

Helleiner, G. K.
1973   Manufactured Exports from Less Developed Countries and Multinational Firms. *Economics Journal* 83 (March): 21-47.

Heller, Celia Stopnika
1964   Ambitions of Mexican-American Youth: Goals and Means of Mobility of High School Seniors. Ph.D. dissertation, Columbia University.

1966   *Mexican American Youth: Forgotten Youth at the Crossroads.* New York: Random House.

Helm, June
1968   *Essays on the Problem of Tribe: Proceedings, 1967 American Ethnological Society.* Seattle: University of Washington Press.

Helms, Mary W.
1975   *Middle America.* Englewood Cliffs, N.J.: Prentice-Hall.

Hely, Allen G.
1969   *Lower Colorado River Water Supply, Its Magnitude and Distribution.* Professional Paper no. 486-D. Washington, D.C.: U.S. Geological Survey.

Hemmings, E. Thomas, and Haynes, C. V., Jr.
1969   The Escapule Mammoth and Associated Projectile Points, San Pedro Valley. *Journal of the Arizona Academy of Science* 5 (no. 3):184-88.

Henderson, Alice C.
1937   *Brothers of Light: The Penitentes of the Southwest.* New York: Harcourt Brace.

Henderson, David A.
1960   Geography of the Sierras Juarez and San Pedro Mártir, Baja California, Mexico. *California Geographer* 1:21-28.

1964   Agriculture and Livestock Raising in the Evolution of the Economy and Culture of the State of Baja California,

Mexico. 2 vols. Ph.D. dissertation, University of California, Los Angeles.

1965   Arid Lands Under Agrarian Reform in Northwest Mexico. *Economic Geography* 41 (October):300-12.

1966   Land, Man, and Time. In Russell C. Ewing, ed. *Six Faces of Mexico: History, People, Geography, Government, Economy, Literature and Art,* pp. 103-60. Tucson: University of Arizona Press.

Henderson, Randall
1952a   Lost Silver Ledge of Santa Catarina. *Desert Magazine* 15 (11).

1952b   Tribesmen of Santa Catarina. *Desert Magazine* 15 (7).

Henrickson, J.
1977   Saline Habits and Halophytic Vegetation of the Chihuahuan Desert Region. In R. H. Wauer and D. H. Riskind, eds. *Transactions of the Symposium on the Biological Resources of the Chihuahuan Desert Region, United States and Mexico,* pp. 289-314. Transactions and Proceedings Series, no. 3. Washington, D.C.: National Park Service.

Henry, Jeanette
1972   *The American Indian Reader: Education.* San Francisco: American Indian Educational Publishers.

Hensey, Fritz G.
1976   Toward a Grammatical Analysis of Southwest Spanish. In J. Donald Bowen and Jacob Ornstein, eds. *Studies in Southwest Spanish,* pp. 29-44. Rowley, Mass.: Newbury House.

Hensley, Jim Bob
1976   *Mexican Immigrant-Alien Student Study, 1975-76.* Edinburg, Texas: Region One Education Service Center, Texas Education Agency.

Herbert, Adam W.
1974   The Minority Administrator: Problems, Prospects, and Challenges. *Public Administration Review* 34 (November-December):534-40.

Hernández, Duluvina
1970   *Mexican American Challenge to a Sacred Cow.* Monograph no. 1. Los Angeles: University of California, Chicano Studies Center.

Hernández, John W.
1973   *Rio Grande Environmental Project.* Las Cruces: New Mexico State University, Water Resources Research Institute.

1978   Interrelationship of Ground and Surface Water Quality in the El Paso-Juarez and Mesilla Valleys. *Natural Resources Journal* 18 (January):1-10.

Hernández, José
1966   A Demographic Profile of the Mexican Immigration to the United States, 1910-1950. *Journal of Inter-American Studies* 8 (July):471-96.

———; Estrada, Leo; and Alvírez, David
1973   Census Data and the Problem of Conceptually Defining the Mexican American Population. *Social Science Quarterly* 53 (March):671-87.

Hernández, Juan
1963   Cactus Whips and Wooden Crosses. *Journal of American Folklore* (July-September):216-24.

Hernández, Norma G.
1973   Variables Affecting Achievement of Middle School Mexican-American Students. *Review of Educational Research* 43:1-39.

Hernández, Timoteo
1943   *Geografía del Estado de Nuevo Leon.* Monterrey, Mexico: n.p.

Hernández-Chávez, Eduardo
1975   Consideraciones sociolinguísticas en materiales para la educación bilingue. In Rudolph C. Troika and Nancy Modiano, eds. *Proceedings of the First Inter-American Conference on Bilingual Education,* pp. 228-38. Arlington, Md.: Center for Applied Linguistics.

———; Cohen, Andrew D.; and Beltrano, Anthony F.
1975   Editors. El lenguaje de los Chicanos. Arlington, Md.: Center for Applied Linguistics.

Hernández-Tiran, José
1967   *Mexico y su política Hidráulica—Mexico and Its Hydraulic Resources.* In Spanish and English. Mexico City: Secretario de Recursos Hidráulicos.

Herold, Laurance E.
1965   *Trincheras and Physical Environment Along the Rio Gavilan, Chihuahua, Mexico.* Publication in Geography, Technical Paper no. 65-1. Denver: University of Denver.

Herrera-Jordan, David, and Friedkin, Joseph F.
1967   The International Boundary and Water Commission, United States and Mexico. *International Conference on Water for Peace* 5:192-206.

Herrera-Sobek, María
1979   *The Bracero Experience: Elitelore versus Folklore.* Los Angeles: UCLA Latin American Center.

Hershberger, Charles E.
1966   The Death of Borunda, Alcalde of Ciudad Juárez: Chihuahuan Politics During the 1930s. *Arizona and the West* 8 (Autumn):207-24.

Herskovits, Melville J.
1948   *Man and His Works: The Science of Cultural Anthropology.* New York: Alfred A. Knopf.

Hester, James J.
1960   Late Pleistocene Extinction and Radio-Carbon Dating. *American Antiquity* 26 (no. 1):58-77.

Hester, Thomas R.
1971   Archaeological Investigations at the La Jita Site, Uvalde County, Texas. *Texas Archaeological Society Bulletin* 42:51-148.

1973   *Chronological Ordering of Great Basin Prehistory Contributions.* Archaeological Research no. 17. Berkeley: University of California.

1974   A Bibliographic Guide to the Archaeology of Southern Texas. *Journal of South Texas* 1 (Corpus Christi).

1975*a*   Chipped Stone Industries on the Rio Grande Plain, Texas: Some Preliminary Observations. *Texas Journal of Science* 26 (nos. 1-2):213-22.

1975*b*   Late Prehistoric Cultural Patterns Along the Lower Rio Grande of Texas. *Texas Archeological Society Bulletin* 46:107-25.

1975*c*   An Overview of Prehistoric Chronology in Southern and South Central Texas. Paper presented to Conference on Prehistory of Northeast Mexico and Texas, in Monterrey, Mexico.

1980   *Digging into South Texas Prehistory.* San Antonio, Texas: Corona Publishing Company.

1976   *Hunters and Gatherers of the Rio Grande Plain and the Lower Coast of Texas.* San Antonio: University of Texas at San Antonio, Center for Archaeological Research.

1977   The Current Status of Paleoindian Studies in Southern Texas and Northeastern Mexico. In E. Johnson, ed. *Paleoindian Lifeways,* pp. 169-87. Museum Journal no. 17. Lubbock, Texas.

1978*a*   *Early Human Occupations in South Central and Southwestern Texas.* San Antonio: University of Texas at San Antonio, Center for Archaeological Research.

1978*b*   *Background to the Archaeology of Chaparrosa Ranch, Southern Texas.* Special Report no. 6. San Antonio: University of Texas at San Antonio, Center for Archaeological Research.

1978*c*   A Cultural Perspective of the Rio Grande Valley: Prehistoric and Historic Archaeology. Paper presented to Conference on Exploration of a Common Legacy, McAllen, Texas.

———; Collins, M. B.; and Weir, F. A.
1969   Two Prehistoric Cemetery Sites in the Lower Rio Grande Valley of Texas. *Texas Archaeological Society Bulletin* 40:119-66.

———, and Hill, T. C., Jr.
1973   Prehistoric Occupation at the Holdsworth and Stewart Sites on the Rio Grande Plain of Texas. *Texas Archaeological Society Bulletin* 43:33-75.

1975   *Some Aspects of Late Prehistoric and Protohistoric Archaeology in Southern Texas.* Special Report no. 1. San Antonio: University of Texas at San Antonio, Center for Archaeological Research.

———, and Rodgers, R. W.
1971   Additional Data on the Burial Practices of the Brownsville Complex, Southern Texas. *Texas Journal of Science* 22 (no. 4):367-71.

Hewes, Leslie
1935   Huepac: An Agricultural Village of Sonora, Mexico. *Economic Geography* 11 (July):284-92.

Hewett, Jaxon
1971   The Bookish Black at Wildhorse Arroyo. *New Mexico Magazine* 49 (January-February):20-24.

Hibben, Frank
1951   Sites of the Paleo-Indian in the Middle Rio Grande Valley. *American Antiquity* 17 (no. 1):41-46.

Hicks, W. Whitney
1974   Economic Development and Fertility Change in Mexico, 1950-1970. *Demography* 11 (no. 3):407-22.

Higham, John
1975   *Send These to Me: Jews and Other Immigrants in Urban America.* New York: Atheneum Publishers.

Hilding, Nancy
1973   American Indian Water Rights on the Rio Grande and Colorado Rivers. Student paper, University of New Mexico, Albuquerque.

Hill, Forest G.
1955   The Shaping of California's Industrial Pattern. Proceedings of the Thirteenth Annual Conference of the Western Economic Association.

Hill, Herbert
1960   *No Harvest for the Reaper: The Story of the Migratory Agricultural Workers in the United States.* New York: NAACP.

Hill, James E., Jr.
1963   Texas Citrus Industry. Ph.D. dissertation, University of Tennessee.

1965   *El Chamizal:* A Century-Old Boundary Dispute. *Geographical Review* 55 (October):510-22.

1967   *El Horcon:* A United States-Mexican Boundary Anomaly. *Rocky Mountain Social Science Journal* 4 (April): 49-61.

1968   The Colorado River International Boundary. *Journal of Geography* 67 (December):545-47.

Hill, Jim Dan
1937   *The Texas Navy in Forgotten Battles and Shirtsleeve Diplomacy.* Chicago: University of Chicago Press.

Hill, Martin
1979   The Big Stink over New River. *California Journal* 9 (February):48-50.

Hill, T. C., Jr., and Hester, T. R.
1971   Isolated Late Prehistoric and Archaic Components at the Honeymoon Site (41 ZV 34), Southern Texas. *Plains Anthropologist* 15 (51):52-59.

Hiller, Herbert
1976   Some Basic Thoughts About the Effects of Changing Values in Receiving Societies. In *Marketing Travel and Tourism,* pp. 199-201. Salt Lake City: University of Utah, Bureau of Economic and Business Research.

Hillerman, Tony
1967   Las Trampas. *New Mexico Quarterly* 37:20-32.

Hillery, George A., Jr., and Essene, Frank J.
1963   Navajo Population: An Analysis of the 1960 Census. *Southwestern Journal of Anthropology* 19:297-313.

Hillman, Jimmye S.
1972   Farming and Ranching. In *Arizona: Its People and Resources*, 2d ed., pp. 257-76. Tucson: University of Arizona Press.

Hilton, George W., and Due, John F.
1960   *The Electric Interurban Railway in America*. Stanford: Stanford University Press.

Hilton, Kenneth S.
1947   Palabras y frases en las lenguas Tarahumara y Guarijío. *Anales del Instituto Nacional de Antropología e Historia* 2:307-13.

Hilton, Ronald
1972   Is Intellectual History Irrelevant? The Case of the Aztecs. *Journal of the History of Ideas* 33 (April-June):337-44.

Hindman, E. James
1975   ¿Confusión o conspiración? Estados Unidos frente a Óbregon. *História Mexicana* 25 (Octubre-Diciembre): 271-301.

Hine, Robert
1968   *Bartlett's West: Drawing the Mexican Boundary*. New Haven: Yale University Press.

Hinton, Richard J.
1878   *The Handbook of Arizona: Its Resources, History, Towns, Mines, Ruins, and Scenery*. San Francisco: n.p.

Hinton, Thomas B.
1955   A Survey of Archeological Sites in the Altar Valley, Sonora. *Kiva* 21 (no. 1-2):1-12.

1959   *A Survey of Indian Assimilation in Eastern Sonora*. Anthropological Papers, no. 4. Tucson: University of Arizona.

1969   Remnant Tribes of Sonora: Opata, Pima, Pápago, and Seri. In Robert Wauchope, ed. *Handbook of Middle American Indians*, vol. 8, pp. 879-88. Austin: University of Texas Press.

———, and Owen, Roger C.
1957   Some Surviving Yuman Groups in Northern Baja California. *América Indígena* 17:87-102.

Hirsch, Herbert
1973   Political Scientist and Other Cameradas: Academic Myth Making and Racial Stereotypes. In de la Garza, et al., eds. *Chicano and Native Americans: The Territorial Minorities*, pp. 10-22. Englewood Cliffs, N.J.: Prentice-Hall.

Hirschhorn, Norbert, and Spivey, Gary H.
1972   Health and the White Mountain Apache. *Journal of Infectious Diseases* 126:348-50.

Hirst, Stephen
1976   *Life in a Narrow Place: The Havasupai of the Grand Canyon*. New York: David McKay Co.

Hishiki, Patricia C.
1969   Self-Concept of Sixth-Grade Girls of Mexican-American Descent. *California Journal of Educational Research* 20: 56-62.

Hittell, Theodore H.
1885-98   *History of California*. 4 vols. Vols. 1 and 2, San Francisco: Pacific Press; Vols. 3 and 4, New Jersey: Stone Co.

Hobson, Gerald
1976   Special Native American issue of *New America: A Review* 2 (summer, fall) published by American Studies Graduate Students, University of New Mexico, Albuquerque.

Hocker, Phillip Norton
1973   Two-Stimulus Transposition as Demonstrated by Spanish/English Speaking Children from Bilingual (Spanish/English) and Monolingual (English) Instruction Classrooms. Ph.D. dissertation, New Mexico State University.

Hodge, Frederick W.
1910   Editor. *Handbook of American Indians North of Mexico* 2 vols. Washington, D.C.: Bureau of American Ethnology. Reprinted in New York, 1959.

1932   Biographical Sketch and Bibliography of Adolphe Francis Alphonse Bandelier. *New Mexico Historical Review* 7 (October):353-70.

———; Hammond, George P.; and Rey, Agapito
1945   *Fray Alonso de Benevides' Revised Memorial of 1634*. Albuquerque: University of New Mexico Press. Also, 1954 edition.

———, and Lewis, T. H.
1907   *Spanish Explorers in the Southern United States, 1528-1543*. New York: Charles Scribner's Sons. Reprinted New York: Barnes & Noble, 1953.

———, and Lummis, Charles Fletcher
1916   Editors. *The Memorial of Fray Alonso de Benevides, 1630*. Chicago: privately printed.

Hodge, William
1969   *The Albuquerque Navahos*. Anthropological Paper no. 11. Tucson: University of Arizona.

1976   *A Bibliography of Contemporary North American Indians*. New York: Interland.

Hodges, Carl N.
1969   A Desert Seacoast Project and Its Future. In W. G. McGinnies and Bram Goldman, eds. *Arid Lands in Perspective*, pp. 119-26. Tucson: University of Arizona Press.

Hoetink, Harry
1967   *The Two Variants in Caribbean Race Relations: A Contribution to the Sociology of Segmented Societies*. New York: Oxford University Press.

Hoffman, Abraham
1972   Mexican Repatriation Statistics: Some Alternatives to Carey McWilliams. *Western Historical Quarterly* 3:391-404.

1974   *Unwanted Mexican Americans in the Great Depression: Repatriation Pressures, 1929-1939*. Tucson: University of Arizona Press.

Hoffman, Peter R.
1978   The Internal Structure of Mexican Border Cities. Paper presented to Association of American Geographers, April, in New Orleans, Louisiana.

Hoffman, P. Browning
1977   Criminal Law—Exchange of Prisoners. *Harvard International Law Journal* 18 (Summer):703-706.

Hogan, William Ransom
1969   *The Texas Republic: A Social and Economic History*. Austin: University of Texas Press.

Hohl, Donald G.
1974   Proposed Revisions of the U.S. Western Hemisphere Immigration Policies. *International Migration Review* 8 (Spring):69-78.

1975   U.S. Immigration Legislation: Prospects in the 94th Congress. *International Migration Review* 9 (Spring):59-62.

———, and Wenk, Michael G.
1971   Current U.S. Immigration Legislation: Analysis and Comment. *International Migration Review* 5:339-56.

Holden, W. C.
1928   West Texas Drouths. *Southwestern Historical Quarterly* 32 (October):103-23.

———; Seltzer, C. C.; Studhalter, R. A.; Wagner, C. J.; and McMillan, W. G.
1936   *Studies of the Yaqui Indians of Sonora, Mexico*. College Bulletin vol. 12. Lubbock: Texas Tech University.

Holden, William C.
1970   *The Espuela Land and Cattle Company: A Study of a Foreign-owned Ranch in Texas*. Austin: Texas State Historical Association.

1976   *A Ranching Saga: The Lives of Electious Halsell and Ewing Halsell*. 2 vols. San Antonio: Trinity University Press.

Holliday, V. T., and Ivey, J. E.
1974   *Presidio-Ojinaga International Flood Control and Channel Relocations Project, Presidio County, Texas: An*

Evaluative Survey of the Archeological and Historical Resources. Research Report no. 48. Austin: Texas Archeological Survey.

Hollinger, E. C., and Strong, Veda A.
1936   *Farm Housing Conditions in New Mexico.* County Reference Material no. 19. Las Cruces: New Mexico Extension Service.

Hollon, W. Eugene
1961   *The Southwest: Old and New.* New York: Alfred A. Knopf.
1966   *The American Desert: Then and Now.* New York: Oxford University Press.

Holm, Wayne
1973   *Bilagaana Bizaad:* ESL in a Navajo Bilingual Setting. In Paul R. Turner, ed. *Bilingualism in the Southwest,* pp. 191-202. Tucson: University of Arizona Press.

Holmes, Beatrice H., et al.
1972   *State Water-Rights Laws and Related Subjects: A Supplemental Bibliography, 1959 to mid-1967.* Miscellaneous Publication no. 1249. Washington, D.C.: U.S. Department of Agriculture.

Holmes, Jack D. L.
1971   Interpretations and Trends in the Study of the Spanish Borderlands: The Old Southwest. *Southwestern Historical Quarterly* 74 (April):461-77.

Holmes, Jack E.
1967   *Politics in New Mexico.* Albuquerque: University of New Mexico Press.

Holmes, Oliver W.
1968   Managing Our Spanish and Mexican Southern Arichival Legacy. *Southwestern Historical Quarterly* 71 (April):517-41.

Holscher, Louis M.
1972   Chicanos in the State of Washington. Paper presented to Southwestern Sociological Association, March, in San Antonio, Texas.
1976   Artists and Murals in East Los Angeles and Boyle Heights: A Sociological Observation. *Humboldt Journal of Social Relations* 3 (Spring-Summer):25-29.

Holtzman, Wayne H.
1968   Cross-cultural Studies in Psychology. *International Journal of Psychology* 3 (no. 3):83-91.

Hoover, Herbert C., and Hoover, L. H.
1912   Notes on the Development of Mining Law. *Engineering and Mining Journal* 94 (November 2):823-25.

Hoover, J. Wenger
1929a   The Indian Country of Southern Arizona. *Geographical Review* 19 (January):38-60.
1929b   Modern Canyon Dwellers of Arizona. *Journal of Geography* 28 (October):269-78.
1930   Tusayan: The Hopi Indian Country of Arizona. *Geographical Review* 20 (July):425-44.
1931   Navajo Nomadism. *Geographical Review* 21 (July):429-45.
1935   House and Village Types of the Southwest As Conditioned by Aridity. *Scientific Monthly* 40 (March):237-49.
1936   Physiographic Provinces of Arizona. *Pan-American Geologist* 65 (June):321-35.
1937   Navajo Land Problems. *Economic Geography* 13 (July):281-300.
1941   Cerros de Trincheras of the Arizona Papagueria. *Geographical Review* 31 (April):228-39.

Hopkins, George E.
1977   How the Dope Traffic Became Airborne. *Washington Monthly* 8 (January):46-53.

Horgan, Paul
1954a   *Great River: The Rio Grande in North American History.* New York: Holt, Rinehart & Winston.
1954b   *The Heroic Triad.* New York: Holt, Rinehart & Winston.

Horgan, Paul
1965   *Peter Hurd: A Portrait Sketch from Life.* Austin: University of Texas Press.

Horka-Pollick, Lorayne
1969   *Los Hermanos Penitentes.* Los Angeles: Westernlore Press.

Horn, Calvin
1963   *New Mexico's Troubled Years.* Albuquerque: Horn and Wallace.

Hornbeck, David
1975   Influence of Early Anglo Images of New Mexico on Landscape Change, 1850-1870. Paper presented to Western Social Science Association, April, at Denver, Colorado.
1976   Mexican-American Land Tenure Conflict in California. *Journal of Geography* 75 (April):209-21.

Hosmer, Helen
1966   Imperial Valley. *American West* 3 (Winter):34-49.

Hough, Henry W.
1967   *Development of Indian Resources.* Denver: World Press.

Hough, Richard L.
1972   Religion and Pluralism in the Southwest: Sociological Perspectives on the Literature. Commissioned manuscript, University of Texas at El Paso, Cross-Cultural Southwest Ethnic Study Center.

Houston, Virginia H. Taylor
1961   Surveying in Texas. *Southwestern Historical Quarterly* 65 (October):204-33.

Houstoun, Marion F., and North, David S.
1975   The "New Immigration" and Presumptions of Social Policy: A Commentary. Manuscript, Linton & Co., Washington, D.C.

Hovey, Edmund Otis
1905   The Western Sierra Madre of the State of Chihuahua, Mexico. *Bulletin of the American Geographical Society* 37:531-43.

Howard, James K.
1976   *Ten Years with the Cowboy Artists of America: A Complete History and Exhibition Record.* Flagstaff: Northland Press.

Howard, William A., and Griffiths, Thomas M.
1968   Algunos aspectos de la distribución de trincheras en la Sierra Madre occidental de México. *Revista Geográfica* 69 (diciembre):107-20.

Howe, Charles W., and Easter, K. William
1971   *Interbasin Transfers of Water: Economic Issues and Impacts.* Baltimore: Johns Hopkins University Press.

Hoy, Harry E.
1942   A New Map on the Surface Configuration of Mexico. *Papers of the Michigan Academy of Science, Arts and Letters* 28:441-43.

Hudson, Charles
1976   *The Southeastern Indians.* Knoxville: University of Tennessee Press.

Hudson, John C.
1977   Theory and Methodology in Comparative Frontier Studies. In D. H. Miller and J. O. Steffen, eds. *The Frontier: Comparative Studies,* pp. 11-31. Norman: University of Oklahoma Press.

Huerta Preciado, María Teresa
1966   *Rebeliones indígenas en el noreste de México en la época colonial.* Series 15. Mexico City: Instituto Nacional de Antropología e Historia.

Hughes, Eugene E.
1968   Phreatophytes: Problems and Perspectives. *Water Resources Bulletin* 4 (August):50-53.

Hughes, William F., and Motheral, Joe R.
1950   *Irrigated Agriculture in Texas.* Miscellaneous Publication no. 59. College Station: Texas Agricultural Experiment Station.

Hull, Dorothy
1916   Castano de Sos's Expedition to New Mexico in 1690. *Old Santa Fe* 3 (no. 12):307-32.
Hullihen, James D.
1966   Arizona Citrus Industry. Master's thesis, Arizona State University.
Humboldt, Alexander Von
1966   *Political Essay on the Kingdom of New Spain.* Facsimile of 1810 edition. 3 vols. New York: AMS Press.
Humlum, Johannes
1969   *Water Development and Water Planning in the Southwestern United States.* New York: Humanities Press.
Humphrey, Norman D.
1948   The Cultural Background of the Mexican Immigrant. *Rural Sociology* 13 (no. 3):239-56.
1952   Family Patterns in a Mexican Middletown. *Social Services Review* 26 (June):195-201.
Humphrey, R. R.
1958   The Desert Grassland, a History of Vegetational Changes and an Analysis of Causes. *Botanical Review* 24:193-252.
———, and Mehrhoff, L. A.
1958   Vegetation Changes on a Southern Arizona Grassland Range. *Ecology* 39 (October):720-26.
Hundley, Norris, Jr.
1963-64 The Colorado Waters Dispute. *Foreign Affairs* 42 (April):495-500.
1966   *Dividing the Waters: A Century of Controversy Between the United States and Mexico.* Berkeley: University of California Press.
1967   The Politics of Water and Geography: California and the Mexican-American Treaty of 1944. *Pacific Historical Review* 36:209-26.
1976   *Water and the West: The Colorado River Compact and the Politics of Water in the American West.* Berkeley: University of California Press.
Hunt, Aurora
1958   *Major James Henry Carleton, 1814-1873, Western Frontier Dragoon.* Glendale: Arthur H. Clark Co.
1961   *Kirby Benedict, Frontier Judge.* Glendale, Calif.: Arthur H. Clark Co.
Hunt, Charles B.
1974   *Natural Regions of the United States and Canada.* San Francisco: W. H. Freeman & Co.
Hunt, L. H., II
1970   Industrial Development on the Mexican Border. *Business Review, Federal Reserve Bank of Dallas* (February):3-12.
Hurley, P. A.
1967   *Augmenting Upper Colorado River Basin Water Supply by Weather Modification.* Denver: U.S. Department of Interior, Bureau of Reclamation, Office of Atmospheric Water Resources.
Hurt, Amy P.
1934   Chimayo: The Village Time Has Blest. *New Mexico Magazine* 12 (November):10-12, 43-44.
Hurt, Harry, III
1977   The Cactus Curtain. *Texas Monthly* 5 (August):8.
Hutchins, Wells A.
1928   The Community Acequia: Its Origin and Development. *Southwestern Historical Quarterly* 31 (January):261-84.
1954   History of the Conflict Between Riparian and Appropriative Rights in the Western States. In *Proceedings of the Water Law Conferences, 1952-54,* pp. 106-37. Austin: University of Texas, School of Law.
1955   Trends in the Statutory Law of Ground Water in the Western United States. *Texas Law Review* 34:157-91.
1971   *Water Rights Laws in the Nineteen Western States.* Vol. 1. Miscellaneous Publications, no. 1206. Washington, D.C.: U.S. Department of Agriculture.
———, and Steele, Harry A.
1957   Basic Water Rights Doctrines and Their Implication for

River Basin Development. *Law and Contemporary Problems* 22 (Spring):276-300.
Hutchinson, C. Alan
1965   The Mexican Government and the Mission Indians of Upper California, 1821-1835. *Americas* 21 (April):335-62.
1969   *Frontier Settlement in Mexican California: The Híjar-Padrés Colony and Its Origins, 1769-1835.* New Haven: Yale University Press.
1973   An Official List of the Members of the Híjar-Padrés Colony for Mexican California, 1834. *Pacific Historical Review* 42 (August):407-18.
Hyman, Herbert T.
1959   *Political Socialization: A Study in the Psychology of Political Behavior.* Glencoe, Ill.: Free Press.
Ibarra, Alfredo Jr.
1944   Entre los Mayos de Sinaloa. *Anuario de la Sociedad Folklórica de México* 4:351-73.
Ichihashi, Yamato
1969   *Japanese in the United States.* New York: Arno Press.
Idso, Sherwood B.
1974   Wild Summer Winds Drive Dust Storms, Called Haboobs, Across the Desert, Endangering Motorists. *Smithsonian* 5 (December):68-73.
Ing, J. D., and Kegley, G.
1971   *Archeological Investigations at Fort Leaton State Historic Site, Presidio County, Texas.* Austin: Texas Parks and Wildlife Department.
International Symposium on the Salinity of the Colorado River
1974   *Natural Resources Journal* 15 (January):1-239.
Interview with Attorney General Pedro Ojeda Paullada
1974   *Drug Enforcement* 1 (Fall):9-13.
Irigoyen, Ulises
1935   *El problema económico de las fronteras mexicanas.* 2 vols. Mexico City: n.p.
1942   El problema económico de las ciudades fronterizas. *Boletín de la Sociedad Chihuahuense de Estudios Históricos* 4:64-68, 89-92.
Isbister, J.
1973   Birth Control, Income Redistribution and the Rate of Saving: The Case of Mexico. *Demography* 3 (no. 1):85-98.
Israel, Daniel, and Smithson, T. L.
1973   Indian Taxation, Tribal Sovereignty and Economic Development. *North Dakota Law Review* 49 (Winter):267-302.
Israel, J. I.
1975   *Race, Class and Politics in Colonial Mexico, 1610-1670.* London: Oxford University Press.
Iturriaga, José E.
1951   *La estructura social y cultural de México.* Mexico City: Fondo de Cultura Económica.
Iverson, Katherine
1978   Civilization and Assimilation in the Schooling of Native Americans. In Philip Altbach and Gail Kelly, eds. *Colonialism and Education,* pp. 149-80. New York: Longman.
Iverson, Peter
1975   The Evolving Navajo Nation: *Dine* Continuity Within Change. Ph.D. dissertation, University of Wisconsin, Madison.
1976a   "Legal Services and Navajo Economic Revitalization." *Journal of Ethnic Studies* 4 (Fall):21-34.
1976b   *The Navajos: A Critical Bibliography.* Bloomington: Indiana University Press.
1977   Legal Counsel and the Navajo Nation Since 1954. *American Indian Quarterly* 3 (Spring):1-15.
Ives, Ronald L.
1936   Desert Floods in the Sonoyta Valley. *American Journal of Science* 232 (November):349-60.
1949   Climate of the Sonoran Desert Region. *Annals, Associa-*

1964   *tion of American Geographers* 39 (September):143-87.

1964   *The Pinacate Region, Sonora, Mexico.* Occasional Paper no. 47. San Francisco: California Academy of Sciences.

1965   Interior Erosion of Desert Mountains. *Journal of Geography* 64 (January):3-14.

1971   A Land Use Map of the Southwest from Satellite Photography. *Geographical Review* 61 (April):299-300.

Ives, Ronald L.

1939   Editor and translator. The Report of the Bishop of Durango on Conditions in Northwestern Mexico in 1745. *Hispanic American Historical Review* 19 (August):314-17.

1960   Navigation Methods of Eusebio Francisco Kino, S.J. *Arizona and the West* 2 (Autumn):213-44.

1966   Retracing the Route of the Fages Expedition. *Arizona and the West* 8 (Spring-Summer):49-70, 157-70.

1973   Father Kino's 1697 Entrado to the Casa Grande Ruin in Arizona: A Reconstruction. *Arizona and the West* 15 (Winter):345-70.

Ivey, J. E.; Medlin, T.; and Eaton, J.

1977   *An Initial Archaeological Assessment of Areas Proposed for Modification at Fort McIntosh, Webb County, Texas.* Report no. 32. San Antonio: University of Texas at San Antonio, Center for Archeological Research.

Iwata, Masakazu

1962   The Japanese Immigrants in California Agriculture. *Agricultural History* 36 (June):25-37.

Jackson, Donald

1966   Editor. *The Journals of Zebulon Montgomery Pike.* 2 vols. Norman: University of Oklahoma Press.

Jackson, Gregg B., and Cosca, Cecilia E.

1974   The Inequality of Educational Opportunity in the Southwest: An Observational Study of Ethnically Mixed Classrooms. *American Educational Research Journal* 11:219-29.

Jackson, J. B.

1952   A Catalog of New Mexico Farm-building Terms. *Landscape* 1 (Winter):31-32.

1953-54   Pueblo Architecture and Our Own. *Landscape* 3 (Winter):20-25.

1959-60   First Comes the House. *Landscape* 9 (Winter):26-32.

1962   *Landscape Autoguide, Tour I: Santa Fe to Taos.* Santa Fe: Landscape Magazine.

1963*a*   *Landscape Autoguide, Tour II: Santa Fe to the Upper Espanola Valley.* Sante Fe: Landscape Magazine.

1963*b*   *Landscape Autoguide, Tour III: Santa Fe to Pecos and Villanueva.* Santa Fe: Landscape Magazine.

Jackson, Joseph Henry

1949   *Bad Company.* New York: Harcourt Brace.

Jackson, Ralph S., Jr.

1968   The Border Industrialization Program of Northern Mexico. Paper presented to Seminar in Latin American Commercial Law, fall, at Austin, Texas.

Jackson, W. T.

1952   The Chávez Land Grant: A Scottish Investment in New Mexico, 1881-1940. *Pacific Historical Review* 26:349-66.

Jaco, E. Gartly

1959   Mental Health of the Spanish-American in Texas. In Marvin K. Opler, ed. *Culture and Mental Health,* pp. 467-88. New York: Macmillan Co.

1960   *The Social Epidemiology of Mental Disorder: A Psychiatric Survey of Texas.* New York: Russell Sage Foundation.

Jacobs, Wilbur R.; Caughey, John W.; and Frantz, Joe B.

1965   *Turner, Bolton, and Webb: Three Historians of the American Frontier.* Seattle: University of Washington Press.

Jacobstein, J. Myron, and Mersky, Roy M.

1966   *Water Law Bibliography, 1847-1965.* Silver Spring, Md.: Jefferson Law Book Co.

1969   *Water Law Bibliography, 1847-1965, Supplement 1, 1966-1967.* Silver Spring, Md.: Jefferson Law Book Co.

1974   *Water Law Bibliography, 1847-1965, Supplement 2, 1968-1973.* Silver Spring, Md.: Jefferson Law Book Co.

Jacoby, Susan

1977   Immigration and the News Media: A Journalistic Failure. *Migration Today* 5 (April):20-22.

Jaeger, Edmund C.

1957   *The North American Deserts.* Stanford: Stanford University Press.

1965   *The California Deserts.* Stanford: Stanford University Press.

———, and Smith, Arthur C.

1966   *Introduction to the Natural History of Southern California.* Berkeley: University of California Press.

Jamail, Milton H.

1980   *The United States-Mexico Border: A Guide to Institutions, Organizations and Scholars.* Tucson: University of Arizona Latin American Area Center.

James, Daniel

1963   *Mexico and the Americas.* New York: Praeger Publishers.

James, Dilmus

1969   An Economic Appraisal of the Mexican Border Industrialization Program. Paper presented to the Western Regional Science Association, February, at Newport Beach, Calif.

1972   The Mexican Border Industrialization Program and the Economic Development of Northern Mexico. Paper presented to Seminar for Visiting Mexican Economists, University of Arizona, at Tucson.

———, and Evans, John S.

1974   The Industrialization of the Northern Mexican Border Region: Past, Present and Future. Paper presented to the Southwestern Economics Association, March, at Dallas, Texas.

James, Harry C.

1974   *Pages from Hopi History.* Tucson: University of Arizona Press.

James, Peter

1977   *James Language Dominance Test: English/Spanish.* Austin: Learning Concepts.

James, Preston E.

1969   *Latin America.* New York: Odyssey Press.

James, Rhett S.

1967   Brigham Young—Chief Washakie Indian Farm Negotiations, 1854-1857. *Annals of Wyoming* (October).

1968   A Nineteenth Century Indian Self-Help Program: Brigham Young and the Shoshones. Manuscript, University of Texas at El Paso.

James, Thomas

1962   *Three Years Among the Indians and Mexicans.* Philadelphia: J. B. Lippincott Co.

Jameson, Donald A.

1969   Rainfall Patterns on Vegetation Zones in Northern Arizona. *Plateau* 41 (Winter):105-11.

Jamieson, Stuart

1945   *Labor Unionism in American Agriculture.* Bulletin no. 836. Washington, D.C.: U.S. Bureau of Labor Statistics.

Jamil, Milton H.; and Ullery, Scott J.

n.d.   Editors. *International Water Use Relations along the Sonoran Desert Borderlands.* 139 pages. Tucson: University of Arizona, Office of Arid Land Studies.

Janeway, William R.

1934   *Bibliography of Immigration in the United States, 1900-1930.* Columbus, Ohio: H. L. Hedrick. Reprinted in 1972 by R & E Research Associates, San Francisco, California.

Janowsky, Oscar I.

1964   Editor. *The American Jew.* Philadelphia: Jewish Publication Society of America.

Jelks, E. B.
1969   *Archeological Excavations at Fort Leaton State Park.* Austin: Texas Parks and Wildlife Department.

Jenkins, J. Craig
1978   The Demand for Immigration Workers: Labor Scarcity or Social Control? *International Migration Review* 12 (Winter):514-35.

Jenkins, Myra E.
1961   The Baltasar Baca Grant: History of an Encroachment. *El Palacio* 68:47-64, 87-105.

1966   Taos Pueblo and Its Neighbors, 1540-1847. *New Mexico Historical Review* 41 (April):85-114.

1971   Land Grant Problems. In Richard N. Ellis, ed. *New Mexico, Past and Present: A Historical Reader,* pp. 96-103. Albuquerque: University of New Mexico Press.

1972   Spanish Land Grants in the Tewa Area. *New Mexico Historical Review* 47 (April):113-34.

1974a   *History of the Laguna Pueblo Land Claims.* New York: Garland Publishing, New Mexico State Records Center and Archives.

1974b   *History and Administration of the Tigua Indians of Ysleta del Sur During the Spanish Colonial Period.* New York: Garland Publishing, New Mexico State Records Center and Archives.

———, and Minge, Ward Alan
1974   *Navajo Activities Affecting the Acoma-Laguna Area, 1846-1910.* New York: Garland Publishing, New Mexico State Records Center and Archives.

Jennings, Charles W.
1977   *Geologic Map of California: Scale 1:750,000.* Sacramento: California Division of Mines and Geology.

Jensen, Arthur R.
1961   Learning Abilities in Mexican-American and Anglo-American Children. *California Journal of Educational Research* 12:147-59.

Jensen, Clarence W., and Trock, Warren L.
1973   *The Texas Water Plan and Its Institutional Problems.* Technical Report no. 37. College Station: Texas A&M University, Texas Water Resources Institute.

Jensen, James M.
1960   Cattle Drives from the Ranchos to the Gold Fields of California. *Arizona and the West* 2 (Winter):341-52.

Jessup, Phillip C.
1973   El Chamizal. *American Journal of International Law* 67 (July):423-45.

Jett, Stephen C.
1964   Pueblo Indian Migrations: An Evaluation of the Possible Physical and Cultural Determinants. *American Antiquity* 29 (January):281-300.

1978   The Origins of Navajo Settlement Patterns. *Annals, Association of American Geographers* 68 (September): 351-62.

Jetton, Elden V.
1966   Stratospheric Behavior Associated with the Southwestern Cut-off Low. *Journal of Applied Meteorology* 5 (December):857-65.

Jiménez Moreno, Wigberto
1943   Tribus e idiomas del norte de México. In *El norte de México y el sur de los Estados Unidos,* pp. 121-33. Mexico City: Sociedad Mexicana de Antropología e Historia.

1958   *Estudios de historia colonial.* Mexico City: Instituto Nacional de Antropología e Historia.

1960   El noreste de México y su cultura. *Academia Mexicana de la Historia, Memorias* 19:176-87.

Johansen, Sigurd A.
1941   Rural Social Organization in a Spanish-American Culture Area. Ph.D. dissertation, University of Wisconsin.

1942   The Social Organization of Spanish-American Villages. *Southwestern Social Science Quarterly* 23:151-59.

1948   *Rural Social Organization in a Spanish-American Culture Area.* Albuquerque: University of New Mexico Press.

John, Elizabeth A. H.
1975   *Storms Brewed in Other Men's Worlds: The Confrontation of Indians, Spanish, and French in the Southwest, 1540-1795.* College Station: Texas A&M University Press.

Johnson, Alfred E.
1963   The Trincheras Culture of Northern Sonora. *American Antiquity* 29:174-86.

1966   Archeology of Sonora, Mexico. In G. F. Ekholm and G. R. Willey, eds. *Archeological Frontiers and External Connections. Handbook of Middle American Indians.* Vol. 4. Austin: University of Texas Press.

———, and Thompson, Raymond H.
1963   The Ringo Site, Southeastern Arizona. *American Antiquity* 29 (no. 4):465-80.

Johnson, Broderick H.
1977a   Editor. *Stories of Traditional Navajo Life and Culture.* Tsaile, Ariz.: Navajo Community College Press.

1977b   Editor. *Navajos and World War II.* Tsaile, Ariz.: Navajo Community College Press.

Johnson, Corwin W., and Knippa, Larry D.
1965   Transbasin Diversion of Water. *Texas Law Review* 43 (October):1035-61.

Johnson, David C.
1974   State Taxation of Indians: Impact of 1973 Supreme Court Decisions. *American Indian Law Review* 2 (no. 1):1-28.

Johnson, H. B.; Vasek, F. C.; and Yonkers, T.
1975   Productivity, Diversity, and Stability Relationships in Mojave Desert Roadside Vegetation. *Torrey Botanical Club Bulletin* 102:106-15.

Johnson, Henry S.
1970   Motivation and the Mexican American. In Henry S. Johnson and William J. Hernandez-M., eds. *Educating the Mexican American,* pp. 108-16. Valley Forge, Pa.: Judson Press.

Johnson, Henry Sioux, and Hernandez-M., William J.
1970   Editors. *Educating the Mexican American.* Valley Forge, Pa.: Judson Press.

Johnson, Jean B.
1940a   The Piman Foot Drum and Fertility Rites. *El México Antiguo* 5:40-41.

1940b   Sonora Dance Regalia. *El México Antiguo* 5:54-56.

1950   *The Opata: An Inland Tribe of Sonora.* Publications in Anthropology, no. 6. Albuquerque: University of New Mexico.

Johnson, Jessie J.
1969   *The Black Soldier: Missing Pages in U.S. History.* Hampton, Va.: J. J. Johnson; paperback edn., Hampton, Va.: Ebony Publishers, 1976.

Johnson, Kenneth
1966   *K-344 or the Indians of California vs. the United States.* Los Angeles: Dawson's Book Shop.

Johnson, Kenneth F.
1971   *Mexican Democracy: A Critical View.* Boston: Allyn & Bacon.

1978   *Amnesty and Human Rights: Dilemmas Affecting Illegal Mexican Aliens in the United States.* Paper presented to Human Rights Internet, International Studies Association, February, at Washington, D.C.

1979   Stranded Mexican Aliens in Missouri and Illinois: The Spectrum of Human Rights Issues. Paper presented to Rocky Mountain Council on Latin American Studies, May, at El Paso, Texas.

———, and Ogle, Nina M.
1978   *Illegal Mexican Aliens in the United States: A Teaching Manual on Impact Dimensions and Alternate Futures.* Washington, D.C.: University Press of America.

Johnson, K. W.
1973   Sovereignty, Citizenship and the Indian. *Arizona Law*

Review 14 (November):973-92.

Johnson, L. Jr.
1964   *The Devil's Mouth Site: A Stratified Campsite at Amistad Reservoir, Val Verde County, Texas.* Archaeology Series, no. 6. Austin: University of Texas.

Johnson, Rich
1977   *The Central Arizona Project, 1918-1968.* Tucson: University of Arizona Press.

Johnson, Robert W.
1976   Mexican Farmers Shift from Cotton to Food Crops. *Foreign Agriculture* 14 (13):2-4.

Johnston, Bernice
1968   Seri Ironwood Carving. *Kiva* 33 (no. 3):155-66.

Johnston, Denis Foster
1966   *An Analysis of Sources of Information on the Population of the Navaho.* Bulletin no. 197. Washington, D.C.: Smithsonian Institution, Bureau of American Ethnology.

Johnston, M. C.
1963   Past and Present Grasslands of Southern Texas and Northeastern Mexico. *Ecology* 33:456-66.

1977   Brief Resume of Botanical, Including Vegetational, Features of the Chihuahuan Desert Region with Special Emphasis on Their Uniqueness. In R. H. Wauer and D. H. Riskind, eds. *Transactions of the Symposium on the Biological Resources of the Chihuahuan Desert Region, United States and Mexico,* pp. 335-59. Washington, D.C.: National Park Service.

In press.   *Edible, Medicinal and Otherwise Useful Plants of Texas.* Austin: University of Texas Press.

————, and Henrickson, J.
In prep.   *Chihuahuan Desert Flora.*

Jonas, Frank H.
1969   Editor. *Politics in the American West.* Salt Lake City: University of Utah Press.

Jones, Billy M.
1967   *Health-Seekers in the Southwest, 1817-1900.* Norman: University of Oklahoma Press.

Jones, Delmos J.
1962   A Description of Settlement Pattern and Population Movement on the Pápago Reservation. *Kiva* 27 (April):1-9.

Jones, Fayette
1904   *New Mexico Mines and Minerals.* Santa Fe: New Mexican Printing Co.

Jones, G. T.
1974   Enforcement Strategies for Indian Landlords. *American Indian Law Review* 2 (Summer):41-60.

Jones, Hester
1932   Uses of Wood by the Spanish Colonists in New Mexico. *New Mexico Historical Review* 7:273-91.

Jones, Lamar B.
1965   Mexican-American Labor Problems in Texas. Ph.D. dissertation, University of Texas, Austin.

Jones, O. R., and Schneider, A. D.
1972   Groundwater Management on the Texas High Plains. *Water Resources Bulletin* 8 (June):516-22.

Jones, Oakah L., Jr.
1962   Pueblo Indian Auxiliaries in New Mexico, 1763-1821. *New Mexico Historical Review* 37 (April):81-111.

1966   *Pueblo Warriors and Spanish Conquest.* Norman: University of Oklahoma Press.

1968   *Santa Anna.* New York: Twayne Publishers.

1974   Editor. *The Spanish Borderlands: A First Reader.* Los Angeles: Lorrin L. Morrison.

Jones, Roberto C.
1945   *Mexican Workers in the United States: The Mexico-United States Manpower Recruiting Program and Its Operation.* Washington, D.C.: Pan American Union, Division of Labor and Social Information.

Jones, William
1915   *Kickapoo Tales.* Publication of the American Ethnological Society, vol. 9. Leyden: E. J. Brill.

Jordan, Terry G.
1966   *German Seed in Texas Soil: Immigrant Farmers in Nineteenth-Century Texas.* Austin: University of Texas Press.

1969   The German Settlement of Texas After 1865. *Southwestern Historical Quarterly* 73 (October):193-212.

1970a   Population Origin Groups in Rural Texas. *Annals, Association of American Geographers* 60 (June):404-405. Map supplement no. 13.

1970b   The Texas Appalachia. *Annals, Association of American Geographers* 60 (September):409-27.

1974   Antecedants of the Long-Lot in Texas. *Annals, Association of American Geographers* 64 (March):70-86.

1978   *Texas Log Buildings, A Folk Architecture.* Austin: University of Texas Press.

Joseph, Alice; Spicer, Rosamond B.; and Chesky, Jane
1949   *The Desert People: A Study of the Pápago Indians of Southern Arizona.* Chicago: University of Chicago Press.

Joseph, Hyman, and Jud, G. Donald
1973   Estimates of Tourism Demand: Latin America. In Walter Krause et al. *International Tourism and Latin American Development,* pp. 25-42. Austin: University of Texas, Bureau of Business Research.

Josephy, Alvin M., Jr.
1968   *The Indian Heritage of America.* New York: Alfred A. Knopf.

1969   *The Indians in the History of America.* New York: Alfred A. Knopf.

1971   Editor. *Red Power: The American Indians Fight for Freedom.* New York: McGraw-Hill.

Juárez, Albert
1972   The Emergence of *El Partido de la Raza Unida:* California's New Chicano Party. *Aztlán* 3 (Fall):177-205.

1974   The Emergence of *El Partido de la Raza Unida:* California's New Chicano Party. In F. Chris Garcia, ed. *La Causa Politica,* pp. 304-21. Notre Dame: University of Notre Dame Press.

Juárez, Rumaldo Z., and Kuvlesky, William P.
1969   Ethnic Group Identity and Orientations Toward Educational Attainment: A Comparison of Mexican-American and Anglo Boys. Paper presented in 1968 to Southwestern Sociological Association, April, at Dallas, Texas.

Jud, G. Donald
1976   Tourism and Crime in Mexico. *Social Science Quarterly* 57 (September):324-30.

Judson, Sheldon
1952   Arroyos. *Scientific American* 187 (December):71-76.

Julian, George W.
1887   Land Stealing in Mexico. *North American Review* (May).

Jumper, Sidney R.
1969   The Fresh Vegetable Industry in the U.S.A.: An Example of Dynamic Interregional Dependency. *Tijdschrift voor Economische en Sociale Geografie* 60 (no. 3):308-18.

Jurado, Miguel David
1970   Mexican American Community Political Organization: The Key to Chicano Political Power. *Aztlán* 1 (Spring):53-79.

Justice, James W.
1978   Training Across Cultural Barriers: The Experience of the Indian Health Service with the Community Health Training Program. In Boris Velimirovic, ed. *Modern Medicine and Medical Anthropology in the United States-Mexico Border Population,* pp. 96-108. Washington, D.C.: Pan American Health Organization.

Kaemlein, Wilma, and Rinehart, Joyce
1975   *The Kiva Index: Volumes 31-40, 1965-1975.* Tucson: Arizona Archeological and Historical Society.

Kahl, Joseph A.
1968   *The Measurement of Modernism: A Study of Values in Brazil and Mexico.* Austin: University of Texas Press.

Kahn, David
1975   Chicano Street Murals: People's Art in the East Los
        Angeles Barrio. *Aztlán* 6 (Spring):117-21.
Kahn, M. W.; Williams, C.; Galvez, E.; Lejero, L.; Conrad, R.;
and Goldstein, G.
1975   The Pápago Psychology Service: A Community Mental
        Health Program on an American Indian Reservation.
        American Journal of Community Psychology 3 (no. 2):
        81-97.
Kalback, Warren E.
1970   *The Impact of Immigration on Canada's Population.* Ot-
        tawa: Dominion Bureau of Statistics.
Kamstra, Jerry
1974   *Weed.* New York: Bantam Books.
Kane, Albert E.
1965   Jurisdiction over Indians and Indian Reservations. *Ari-
        zona Law Review* 6:238-55.
Kane, John
1973   A Case for Scientific Evaluation of Weather Modification
        Activities. *Water for Texas* 3 (June):7-9.
Kane, T. L.
1876   Geography and Ethnology of Coahuila. *American Philo-
        sophical Society Proceedings* 16 (99):561-73.
Kantor, Harry
1969   *Patterns of Politics and Political Systems in Latin Amer-
        ica.* Chicago: Rand McNally.
Kaplan, Bert, and Johnson, Dale
1964   The Social Meaning of Navajo Psychopathology and Psy-
        chotherapy. In Ari Kiev, ed. *Magic, Faith and Healing,*
        pp. 203-29. New York: Free Press.
Karno, Marvin, and Edgerton, Robert B.
1969   Perception of Mental Illness in a Mexican-American
        Community. *Archives of General Psychiatry* 20 (Feb-
        ruary):233-38.
Karp, Abraham J.
1976   *Golden Door to America.* New York: Viking Press.
Katz, William L.
1969   *Eyewitness: The Negro in American History.* New York:
        Pitman Publishing Co.
1971   *The Black West: A Documentary and Pictorial History.*
        Garden City, N.Y.: Doubleday & Co.
Kearney, T. H., and Peebles, R. H.
1960   *Arizona Flora.* 2d ed. with supplement. Berkeley: Uni-
        versity of California Press.
Keely, Charles B.
1975*a* Effects of U.S. Immigration Law on Manpower Charac-
        teristics of Immigrants. *Demography* 12 (May):179-91.
1975*b* Beyond Law Enforcement: Some Implications of and
        Perspectives About Illegal Alien Policy in the U.S. Paper
        presented to Illegal Immigration Briefing, Zero Popula-
        tion Growth Conference, June, in Washington, D.C.
1977   Counting the Uncountable: Estimates of Undocumented
        Aliens in the United States. *Population and Development
        Review* 3 (December):473-82.
1979   *U.S. Immigration: A Policy Analysis.* New York: Popu-
        lation Council.
————; Elwell, Patricia J.; Fragomen, Austin T., Jr.; and Tomasi,
Silvan M.
1977   Profiles of Undocumented Aliens in New York City:
        Haitians and Dominicans. Paper presented to the Latin
        American Studies Association, November, at Houston,
        Texas.
————, and Tomasi, Silvan M.
1976   The Disposable Worker: Historical and Comparative
        Perspectives on Clandestine Migration. Mimeographed.
        Occasional Papers and Documentation. Staten Island,
        New York: Center for Migration Studies.
Keen, Benjamin
1969   The Black Legend Revisited: Assumptions and Realities.
        Hispanic American Historical Review 49 (November):
        703-19.

1971*a* The White Legend Revisited: A Reply to Professor
        Hanke's "Modest Proposal." *Hispanic American His-
        torical Review* 51 (May):336-55.
1971*b* *The Aztec Image in Western Thought.* New Brunswick,
        N.J.: Rutgers University Press.
Keith, Shirley
1974   A Rebuttal to "the Pre-emption Doctrine and Colonias
        de Santa Fe." *Natural Resources Journal* 14 (April):
        283-92.
Keleher, Julia
1944   The Land of Shalam: Utopia in New Mexico. *New Mex-
        ico Historical Review* 19 (April):123-34.
Keleher, William A.
1929   Law of the New Mexico Land Grant. *New Mexico His-
        torical Review* 4:350-71.
1952   *Turmoil in New Mexico, 1846-1868.* Santa Fe: Rydall
        Press.
1962   *The Fabulous Frontier.* Rev. ed. Albuquerque: Univer-
        sity of New Mexico Press.
1964   *Maxwell Land Grant.* Rev. ed. New York: Argosy-Anti-
        quarian.
1975   *Maxwell Land Grant.* Santa Fe: William Gannon.
Kelemen, Pál
1956   *Medieval American Art.* New York: Macmillan Co.
Keller, Gary D.; Teschner, Richard V.; and Viera, Silvia
1976   Bilingualism in the Bicentennial and Beyond. New York:
        Bilingual Press/Editorial Bilingue.
Kelley, J. C.
1939   Archeological Notes on the Excavation of a Pit-House
        near Presidio, Texas. *El Palacio* 44 (10):221-34.
1949   Archaeological Notes on the Excavated House Structures
        in Western Texas. *Texas Archaeological and Paleonto-
        logical Society Bulletin* 20:89-114.
1952-53 The Historic Indian Pueblos of La Junta de los Rios:
        Parts I & II. *New Mexico Historical Review* 27 (no. 4):
        257-95 and 28 (no. 1):21-51.
1959   Archaic Manifestations in the Southwest and Texas.
        American Antiquity 24 (3):276-88.
————; Campbell, T. N.; and Lehmer, D. J.
1940   The Association of Archaeological Material with Geo-
        logical Deposits in the Big Bend Region of Texas. *West
        Texas Historical and Scientific Society* 10:9-173.
Kelley, J. Charles
1956   Settlement Patterns in North-Central Mexico. In Gordon
        R. Willey, ed. *Prehistoric Settlement Patterns in the New
        World,* pp. 128-39. Viking Fund Publications in Anthro-
        pology, no. 23. New York: Wenner-Gren Foundation.
Kelley, Wilfrid D.
1955   Settlement of the Middle Rio Grande Valley. *Journal of
        Geography* 54 (November):387-99.
Kelley, William H.
1974   *The Pápago Indians of Arizona.* New York: Garland
        Publishing, University of Arizona, Bureau of Ethnic Re-
        search.
Kellum, L. B.; Imlay, R. W.; and Kane, W. G.
1936   Evolution of the Coahuila Peninsula, Mexico. *Geological
        Society of America Bulletin* 47:969-1009.
Kelly, Daniel T., and Chavenet, Beatrice
1972   *The Buffalo Head: A Century of Mercantile Pioneering
        in the Southwest.* Santa Fe: Vetgara Publishing Co.
Kelly, Henry W.
1941   *The Franciscan Missions of New Mexico, 1740-1760.*
        Publication in History, vol. 10. Albuquerque: Historical
        Society of New Mexico.
Kelly, Isabel
1961   Mexican Spiritualism. In *Alfred L. Kroeber: A Memo-
        rial,* Kroeber Anthropological Society Papers, vol. 25,
        pp. 191-206.
1965   *Folk Practices in North Mexico: Birth Customs, Folk
        Medicine, and Spiritualism in the Laguna Zone.* Latin

American Monographs, no. 2. Austin: University of Texas Press.

Kelly, Philip
1979   Illegal Mexican Aliens in Southern Colorado: A Sampling of Their Views on Living and Working in the United States and Mexico. Paper presented to Rocky Mountain Council for Latin American Studies, May, at El Paso, Texas.

Kelly, William H.
1942   Cocopa Gentes. *American Anthropologist* 44:675-91.
1949   Cocopa Attitudes and Practices with Respect to Death and Mourning. *Southwestern Journal of Anthropology* 5:151-64.
1953   *Indians of the Southwest: A Survey of Indian Tribes and Indian Administration in Arizona.* Tucson: University of Arizona, Bureau of Ethnic Research.
1963   *The Papago Indians of Arizona: A Population and Economic Study.* Tucson: University of Arizona, Bureau of Ethnic Research.
1964   *Methods and Resources for the Construction and Maintenance of a Navajo Population Register.* Tucson: University of Arizona, Bureau of Ethnic Research.
1967   *A Study of Southern Arizona School-Age Indian Children, 1966-1967.* Tucson: University of Arizona, Bureau of Ethnic Research.

Kelso, M. M.; Martin, W.; and Mack, L.
1973   *Water Supplies and Economic Growth in an Arid Environment: An Arizona Case Study.* Tucson: University of Arizona Press.

Kemper, Conley C.
1969   *Texas Migrant Labor: The 1968 Migration.* Austin: Texas Good Neighbor Commission.

Kendall, Dorothy S.
1974   *Gentilz: Artist of the Old Southwest.* Austin: University of Texas Press.

Kendall, George Wilkins
1929   *Narrative of the Texas Santa Fe Expedition.* Norman: University of Oklahoma Press.
1935   *Narrative of the Texas Santa Fe Expedition.* 2 vols. Austin: Steck Co.

Kennamer, L. G.
1923   A Cattle Ranch in New Mexico. *Journal of Geography* 22 (April):153-160.

Kennedy, Will C.
1979   Ecology and the Border: The Case of the Tijuana Flood Control Channel. In James D. Kitchen, ed. *Environmental Problems Along the Border,* pp. 72-90. Occasional Papers, no. 7. San Diego: Border-State University, Consortium for Latin America.

Kenner, Charles L.
1969   *A History of New Mexican-Plains Indian Relations.* Norman: University of Oklahoma Press.

Kerby, Robert Lee
1958   *The Confederate Invasion of New Mexico and Arizona, 1861-1862.* Los Angeles: Westernlore Press.

Kercheville, F. M.
1934   A Preliminary Glossary of New Mexican Spanish. Albuquerque: University of New Mexico Bulletin.

Kerr, Anita
1940   *Mexican Government Publications.* Washington, D.C.: Government Printing Office.

Kerr, J. R.
1969   Constitutional Rights, Tribal Justice and the American Indian. *Journal of Public Law* 18:311-38.

Kerr, Louise Año Nuevo
1976   The Chicano Experience in Chicago, 1920-1970. Ph.D. dissertation, University of Illinois, Chicago Circle.

Kesseli, John E.
1942   The Climates of California According to the Köppen Classification. *Geographical Review* 32 (July):476-80.

Kessell, John I.
1964   San José de Tumacacori—1773: A Franciscan Reports from Arizona. *Arizona and the West* 4 (Winter):303-12.
1966   The Puzzling Presidio: San Phelipe de Guevavi, Alias Terrenate. *New Mexico Historical Review* 41 (January): 21-46.
1969   Father Ramón and the Big Debt, Tumacacori, 1821-1823. *New Mexico Historical Review* 44 (January):53-72.
1971   Campaigning on the Upper Gila, 1756. *New Mexico Historical Review* 46 (April):133-60.
1973   The Making of a Martyr: The Young Francisco Garcés. *New Mexico Historical Review* 48 (July):181-96.

Kessell, John L.
1979   *Kiva, Cross and Crown: The Pecos Indians and New Mexico, 1540-1840.* Washington, D.C.: National Park Service.

Key, V. O.
1966   *The Responsible Electorate.* Cambridge: Harvard University Press.

Khalaf, Jassim M.
1951   *The Water Resources of the Lower Colorado River Basin.* Publications in Geography, no. 22. Chicago: University of Chicago.

Kickingbird, Kirke
1975   The American Indian Policy Review Commission: A Prospect for Future Change in Federal Indian Policy. *American Law Review* 3 (no. 2):243-54.

Kidd, C. V.
1967   *Migration of Health Personnel, Scientists, and Engineers from Latin America.* Publication no. 142. Washington, D.C.: Pan American Health Organization.

Kidder, Alfred V.
1963   *An Introduction to the Study of Southwestern Archaeology.* New Haven: Yale University Press.
——; Cosgrove, Harriet S.; and Cosgrove, C. B.
1949   *The Pendleton Ruin, Hidalgo County, New Mexico.* Publication no. 585. Washington, D.C.: Carnegie Institute.

Kiev, Ari
1968   Curanderismo: *Mexican-American Folk Psychiatry.* New York: Free Press.

Los Kikapu piden ayuda
1977   *Tiempo* 70 (April 4):50-52.

Kim, Chong-Soon
1974   Assimilation into the Host Society of Four Asiatic Groups, El Paso, Texas. Master's thesis, University of Texas at El Paso.

Kim, Hyong-Chan
1974   Some Aspects of Social Demography of Korean Americans. *International Migration Review* 8 (Spring):23-42.

Kimball, Penn
1972   *The Disconnected.* New York: Columbia University Press.

Kimbro, Harriet
1974   Las Golondrinas. *New Mexico Magazine* 52 (July-August):14-19.

Kindleberger, Charles P., and Lindert, Peter H.
1978   International Economics. 6th ed. Homewood, Ill.: Richard D. Irwin.

King, Francis Xavier
1976   Bilingualism and Academic Achievement: A Comparative Study of Spanish Surnamed Bilingual, Spanish Surnamed Monolingual, and Non-Spanish Surnamed Students. Ph.D. dissertation, United States International University.

King, James F.
1942   Evolution of the Free Slave Trade Principle in Spanish Colonial Administration. *Hispanic American Historical Review* 22 (February):34-56.
1944   The Negro in Continental Spanish America: A Select

Bibliography. *Hispanic American Historical Review* 24 (August):547-59.

1953 The Colored Castes and the American Representation in the Cortes of Cadiz. *Hispanic American Historical Review* 33 (February):33-64.

King, Philip B., and Beikman, Helen M.
1974 *Geologic Map of the United States: Scale 1:2,500,000.* Washington, D.C.: U.S. Geological Survey.

King, William S., and Jones, Delmos J.
1974 *Pápago Population Studies.* New York: Garland Publishing, University of Arizona, Bureau of Ethnic Research.

Kirchhoff, Paul
1943 Los recolectores-cazadores del norte de Mexico. In *El norte de México y el sur de Estados Unidos,* pp. 133-44. Mexico: Sociedad Mexicana de Antropología.

Kirk, Ruth
1973 *Desert: The American Southwest.* Boston: Houghton Mifflin Co.

Kirkland, Forrest, and Newcomb, W. W., Jr.
1967 *The Rock Art of Texas Indians.* Austin: University of Texas Press.

Kirkstein, Peter N.
1977 *Anglo over Bracero: A History of the Mexican Worker in the United States from Roosevelt to Nixon.* San Francisco: R & E Research Associates.

Kiser, George C., and Kiser, Martha Woody
1979 Editors. *Mexican Workers in the United States: Historical and Political Perspectives.* Albuquerque: University of New Mexico Press.

Kitagawa, Daisule
1967 *Issei and Nisei: The Internment Years.* New York: Seabury Press.

Klapp, Orrin E., and Padgett, L. Vincent
1960 Power Structure and Decision-Making in a Mexican Border City. *American Journal of Sociology* 65 (January): 400-406.

Klecka, William
1970 Social Status and Political Participation: A Multivariate Analysis of Predictive Power. *Midwest Journal of Political Science* 14 (August):355-82.

Kluckhohn, Clyde
1967 *Navajo Witchcraft.* Boston: Beacon Press. Reprint of 1944 edition.
——, and Leighton, Dorothea
1974 *The Navaho.* Rev. ed. by Lucy H. Wales and Richard Kluckhohn. Cambridge: Harvard University Press.

Kluckhohn, Florence
1941 *Los Atarqueños:* A Study of Patterns and Configurations in a New Mexico Village. Ph.D. dissertation, Radcliffe College.
1961 The Spanish-American of Atrisco. In Florence R. Kluckhohn and Fred L. Strodtbeck, eds. *Variations in Value Orientations,* pp. 175-257. Evanston: Row, Peterson.
——, and Strodtbeck, Fred
1961 *Variations in Value Orientations.* Evanston: Row, Peterson.

Kneale, A. H.
1950 *Indian Agent.* Caldwell, Idaho: Caxton Printers.

Kniffen, Fred B.
1931 The Primitive Cultural Landscape of the Colorado Delta. *University of California Publications in Geography* 5: 43-66.
1932 The Natural Landscape of the Colorado Delta. *University of California Publications in Geography* 5:149-244.

Knobloch, I. W., and Correll, D. S.
1962 *Ferns and Fern Allies of Chihuahua, Mexico.* Renner, Texas: Texas Research Foundation.

Knowlton, Clark S.
1962 Patron-Peon Patterns Among the Spanish Americans of New Mexico. *Social Forces* 40 (October):12-17.

1963 Causes of Land Loss Among the Spanish Americans in Northern New Mexico. *Rocky Mountain Social Science Journal* 1 (May):201-11.

1964a *Indian and Spanish American Adjustments to Arid and Semiarid Environments.* Lubbock: Texas Technological College.

1964b One Approach to the Economic and Social Problems of Northern New Mexico. *New Mexico Business Review* 17:3, 15-22.

1967a Land Grant Problems Among the State's Spanish-Americans. *New Mexico Business Review* 20:1-13.

1967b Recommendations for the Solution of Land Tenure Problems Among the Spanish-Americans. In *The Mexican-American: A New Focus on Opportunity,* pp. 233-38. Washington, D.C.: Inter-Agency Committee on American Affairs.

1968a Editor. *International Water Law Along the Mexican-American Border.* El Paso: Texas Western Press, AAAS-CODAZR.

1968b The New Mexican Land War: Guerillas of Río Arriba. *Nation* 206:792-96.

1969a Changing Spanish-American Villages of Northern New Mexico. *Sociology and Social Research* 53:459-74.

1969b Tijerina, Hero of the Militants. *Texas Observer* 61:1-4.

1970 Violence in New Mexico: A Sociological Perspective. *California Law Review* 53:1054-84.

1972 Culture Conflict and Natural Resources. In William Burch, Jr., et al., eds. *Social Behavior: Natural Resources and the Environment,* pp. 109-45. New York: Harper & Row.

1975 Neglected Chapter in Mexican-American History. In Gus Tyler, ed. *Mexican-Americans Tomorrow.* Albuquerque: University of New Mexico Press.

1976 Editor. Spanish and Mexican Land Grants in the Southwest: A Symposium. *Social Science Journal* 13 (October):3-63.
——, and Ramirez, Sal
1965 A Comparison of Spanish-American Leadership Systems of Northern New Mexico and El Paso. Paper presented to Texas Academy of Science, December.

Koeninger, Rupert C.
1968 The Law: Rape, Race, Time and Death in Texas. *Proceedings, Southwestern Sociological Association,* April, pp. 192-96.

Kohlberg, Walter L.
1973 Translator. *Letters of Ernst Kohlberg, 1875-1877.* El Paso: Texas Western Press.

Koos, Earl
1957 *They Follow the Sun.* Jacksonville: Florida State Board of Health.

Koyasado, J. S.
1976 Reclamation of Water from Wastes in Southern California. *Water Resources Bulletin,* pp. 80-85.

Kraenzel, Carl F.
1968 The Place of Public Services, Including for Mental Illness, in Sparsely Populated Areas. In *Final Report of Program Development: Conference of 24 Western States on the Development of Mental Health Services in Sparsely Populated Rural Areas,* pp. 1-10. Phoenix: Arizona Department of Health, NIMH.

Kramer, V. Paul
1972 The Spanish Borderlands of Texas and Tamaulipas. *Texana* 10 (Summer):260-72.

Krause, Corrine Azen
1970 The Jews in Mexico: A History with Special Emphasis on the Period from 1857 to 1930. Ph.D. dissertation, University of Pittsburgh.

Krause, Lawrence B., and Mathieson, John
1970 How Much of Current Unemployment Did We Import? In *Brookings Papers on Economic Activity,* no. 2, pp. 417-28. Washington, D.C.: Brookings Institute.

Krause, Walter; Jud, G. Donald; and Hyman, Joseph
1973   Editors. *International Tourism and Latin American Development.* Austin: University of Texas, Bureau of Business Research.

Krause, Walter, and Jud, G. Donald
1973   International Tourism in Latin America: Potential and Requirements. In Walter Krause, G. Donald Jud, and Joseph Hyman, eds. *International Tourism and Latin American Development*, pp. 43-61. Austin: University of Texas, Bureau of Business Research.

Krieger, A., and Hughes, J.
1950   *Archaeological Salvage in the Falcon Reservoir Area.* Progress Report no. 1. Washington, D.C.: Department of Interior, National Park Service.

Kirzman, Richard
1968   Manuel Vaquasewa: A Chair-Maker from Alamos, Sonora, Mexico. *Keystone Folklore Quarterly* 13 (no. 2): 103-20.

Kroeber, Alfred L.
1925   *Handbook of the Indians of California.* Bureau of American Ethnology Publication, no. 78. Washington, D.C.: Government Printing Office.
1939   *Culture and Natural Areas of Native North America.* Publications in American Archaeology and Ethnology, vol. 38. Berkeley: University of California Press.
1953   *Cultural and Natural Areas of Native North America.* Berkeley: University of California Press.
1976   *Handbook of the Indians of California.* New York: Dover Publications. Originally published in 1925.

Kroeber, Theodora
1961   *Ishi in Two Worlds.* Berkeley: University of California Press.

Kubler, George
1962a   *Religious Architecture of New Mexico.* Chicago: Rio Grande Press. Reprint of 1940 ed., Colorado Springs: Taylor Museum of the Fine Arts Center.
1962b   *The Art and Architecture of Ancient America: The Mexican, Maya and Andean Peoples.* Baltimore: Penguin Books.
1973   *The Religious Architecture of New Mexico in the Colonial Period and Since the American Occupation.* Albuquerque: University of New Mexico Press, School of American Research.

———, and Soria, Martin
1959   *Art and Architecture in Spain and Portugal and Their American Dominions, 1500-1800.* Harmondsworth: Penguin Books.

Küchler, A. W.
1964   *Manual to Accompany the Map of Potential Natural Vegetation of the Conterminous United States.* Special Publication no. 36. New York: American Geographical Society.
1967   *Vegetation Mapping.* New York: Ronald Press Co.

———, and McCormick, J.
1965   *Vegetation Maps of North America.* Lawrence: University of Kansas Libraries.

Kuipers, Cornelius
1946   *Zuñi Also Prays.* Christian Reformed Board of Missions.

Kunitz, Stephen
1974a   Factors Influencing Recent Navajo and Hopi Population Changes. *Human Organization* 33:7-16.
1974b   Navajo and Hopi Fertility, 1971-1972. *Human Biology* 46:435-51.

———, and Levy, Jerrold E.
1969   Notes on Some White Mountain Apache Social Pathologies. *Plateau* 42 (Summer):11-19.
1974   *Indian Drinking. Navajo Practices and Anglo-American Theories.* New York: John Wiley & Sons.

Kurath, Gertrude P.
1960   The Sena'asom Rattle of the Yaqui Indian Pascolas. *Ethnomusicology* 4 (no. 2):60-63.

Kutsche, Paul
1979   Editor. *The Survival of Spanish American Villages.* Colorado College Study no. 15. Colorado Springs: Colorado College.

Kuvlesky, William P., and Juárez, Rumaldo Z.
1975   Mexican American Youth and the American Dream. In J. S. Stevens and R. E. Campbell, eds. *Career Behavior of Special Groups*, pp. 241-96. Columbus, Ohio: Charles E. Merrill Publishing Co.

Kuvlesky, William P., and Patella, Victoria M.
1971   Degree of Ethnicity and Aspirations for Upward Social Mobility Among Mexican American Youth. *Journal of Vocational Behavior* 13:231-44.

Kuvlesky, William P.; Wright, D. E.; and Juárez, R. Z.
1971   Status Projections and Ethnicity: A Comparison of Mexican American, Negro and Anglo Youth. *Journal of Vocational Behavior* 1:137-51.

La Barge, Richard A.
1978   The Jewish Devaluation of the Mexican Peso. Paper presented to the North American Economic Studies Association, December, at Mexico City.

La Barre, Weston
1969   *The Peyote Cult.* New York: Schocken Books.

LaBov, William; Cohen, Paul; Robins, Clarence; and Lewis, John
1968   A Study of the Non-standard English of Negro and Puerto Rican Speakers in New York City. 2 vols. Bethesda, Md.: Department of Health, Education, and Welfare, Office of Education.

Lacewell, Ronald D., et al.
1976   *Adjustments Due to a Declining Groundwater Supply: High Plains of Northern Texas and Western Oklahoma.* College Station: Texas A&M University, Texas Water Resources Institute.

Ladman, Jerry R.
1979   The Economic Interdependence of Contiguous Border Cities: The Twin City Multiplier. *Annals of Regional Science,* 13: 23-28.

———, and Poulson, Mark O.
1971   *Economic Impact of the Mexican Border Industrialization Program: Agua Prieta, Sonora.* Center for Latin American Studies, no. 10. Tempe: Arizona State University.

Lahser, C., and Applegate, Howard G.
1966   Pesticides at Presidio III: Soil and Water. *Texas Journal of Science* 18 (no. 4):386-95.

Laird, Judith Ann Fincher
1975   Argentine, Kansas: The Evolution of a Mexican-American Community, 1905-1940. Ph.D. dissertation, University of Kansas, Lawrence.

Laird, W. David
1977   *Hopi Bibliography.* Tucson: University of Arizona Press.

Lamar, Howard R.
1960   Political Patterns in New Mexico and Utah Territories, 1850-1900. *Utah Historical Quarterly* 28:371.
1962   Land Policy in the Spanish Southwest, 1846-1891: A Study in Contrasts. *Journal of Economic History* 22: 498-515.
1966   *The Far Southwest, 1846-1912.* New Haven: Yale University Press.

Lamare, James W.
1971   LULACS and Political Decision-Making in El Paso. Mimeographed, University of Texas at El Paso.
1974   Language Environment and Political Socialization of Mexican American Children. In Richard G. Niemi et al., eds. *The Politics of Future Citizens*, pp. 63-82. San Francisco: Jossey-Bass.

Lambberg, Emilio
1949   Indios salvajes de Chihuahua en el siglo XIX, 1815. *Sociedad Chihuahuense de Estudios Historicos, Boletin* 6:272-81.

Lambert, Marjorie F., and Ambler, J. Richard
1961   *A Survey and Excavation of Caves in Hidalgo County, New Mexico.* Monograph no. 25. Santa Fe: School of American Research.
Lamphere, Louise
1977   *To Run After Them: Cultural and Social Bases of Co-operation in a Navajo Community.* Tucson: University of Arizona Press.
Landgraf, John L.
1950   Land Use in the Ramah Navaho Area, New Mexico. *Transactions of the New York Academy of Science* 13 (December):77-84.
1954   *Land-Use in the Ramah Area of New Mexico: An Anthropological Approach to Areal Study.* Papers of the Peabody Museum of American Archaeology and Ethnology, vol. 42, no. 1. Cambridge: Harvard University.
Landis, Paul H.
1940   *Rural Life in Process.* 1st ed. New York: McGraw-Hill.
Landmann, Robert S.
1980   Editor. *The Problem of the Undocumented Worker.* Albuquerque: University of New Mexico, Latin American Institute.
Lang, A. S.
1940   Economic Diversification in the Southwest. *Southwest Social Science Quarterly* 21 (June):30-41.
Lang, M. F.
1968   New Spain's Mining Depression and the Supply of Quicksilver from Peru. *Hispanic American Historical Review* 48 (November):632-41.
Lange, Charles H.
1959   *Cochití.* Austin: University of Texas Press.
Langman, I. K.
1964   *A Selected Guide to the Literature on the Flowering Plants of Mexico.* Philadelphia: University of Pennsylvania Press.
Langman, R. C.
1971   *California: The Imbalance Between People and Water.* Toronto: McGraw-Hill.
Langston, Edward L.
1974   The Impact of Prohibition on the Mexican-United States Border: The El Paso-Ciudad Juárez Case. Ph.D. dissertation, Texas Tech University.
Langton, Kenneth P.
1969   *Political Socialization.* New York: Oxford University Press.
Lansford, Henry H.
1972   Weather Modification in the High Plains Region: Some Public Policy Issues. In Donald D. MacPhail, ed. *The High Plains: Problems of Semiarid Environments,* pp. 18-26. CODAZR Publication no. 15. Ft. Collins: Colorado State University.
Lansford, R. R., and Creel, B. J.
1970   Irrigated Cropland, Lower Rio Grande River Basin, New Mexico. In *New Mexico Agricultural Experiment Station Research Report no. 168,* pp. 20-21. Las Cruces: New Mexico State University, Agricultural Experiment Station.
Lansford, R. R., and Sorensen, E. F.
1973   Trends in Irrigated Agriculture, 1940-1972. In *New Mexico Agricultural Experiment Station Research Report no. 260.* Las Cruces: New Mexico State University, Agricultural Experiment Station.
Lansing, J. B.; Mueller, Eve; Ladd, W.; and Barth, Nancy
1962   *The Geographic Mobility of Labor.* Ann Arbor, Mich.: Survey Research Center, Institute for Social Research, University of Michigan.
Lantis, David W.; Steiner, Rodney; and Karinen, Arthur E.
1963   *California: Land of Contrast.* Belmont, Calif.: Wadsworth Publishing Co.
1973   *California: Land of Contrast.* 2d ed. Dubuque, Iowa: Kendall-Hunt Publishing Co.

Larkin, Ralph W.
1972   Class, Race, Sex, and Preadolescent Attitudes. *California Journal of Educational Research* 23:213-23.
Larson, Robert W.
1968   *New Mexico's Quest for Statehood, 1846-1912.* Albuquerque: University of New Mexico Press.
1974   *New Mexico Populism.* Boulder: Colorado Associated University Press.
1975   The White Caps of New Mexico: A Study of Ethnic Militancy in the Southwest. *Pacific Historical Review* 44:171-85.
Las Casas, Bertolomé de
1542   La brevíseme relación de la destrucción de las Indias. In John Francis Bannon, ed. *Indian Labor in the Spanish Indies,* pp. 36-39. Boston: D. C. Heath.
Lastra de Súarez, Yolanda
1975   El habla y la educación de los niños de origen mexicano en Los Angeles. In Eduardo Hernández-Chávez, et al., eds. *El Lenguaje de los Chicanos,* pp. 61-69. Arlington: Center for Applied Linguistics.
Latorre, Dolores L., and Latorre, Filipe A.
1968   The Ceremonial Life of the Mexican Kickapoo Indians. In *Proceedings, Eighth International Congress of Anthropological and Ethnological Sciences II,* pp. 268-70. Tokyo: Science Council of Japan.
1969   ¿Hasta que punto los indios Kickapú se han integrado en la medicina popular y moderna de México? *Anuario Indigenista* 29:253-67.
1976   *The Mexican Kickapoo Indians.* Austin: University of Texas Press.
1977   Plants Used by the Mexican Kickapoo Indians. *Economic Botany* 31 (July-September):340-57.
Lattimore, Owen
1962   *Studies in Frontier History: Collected Papers, 1928-1958.* New York: Oxford University Press.
Laughlin, Ruth
1947   *Caballeros.* Caldwell, Idaho: The Caxton Printers, Ltd.
Lavender, David
1954   *Bent's Fort.* Garden City, N.Y.: Doubleday & Co.
Lawton, David
1975   Chicano Spanish: Some Sociolinguistic Considerations. *Bilingual Review* 2:22-33.
Laycock, Arleigh H.
1970   Canadian Water for Texas. *Water Resources Bulletin* 6 (July-August):542-49.
Lazerwitz, Bernard
1961   A Comparison of Major United States Religious Groups. *Journal of the American Statistical Association* 56:568-79.
1964   Religion and Social Structure in the United States. In Louis Schneider, ed. *Religion, Culture and Society.* New York: John Wiley.
Lea, Tom
1957   *The King Ranch.* 2 vols. Boston: Little, Brown & Co.
Leaming, George F.
1963   Recent Trends in Trade Across the Arizona-Sonora Border. *Arizona Review* 12 (November):11-18.
1967   Recreational Tourism: Its Economic Impact on Tucson and Nogales. *Arizona Review* 16 (October):4-8.
———, and de Gennaro, Nat
1970   Arizona's Growing Southwest: The Yuma County Economy. *Arizona Review* 19 (10):9-18.
Learsi, Rufus
1954   *The Jews in America: A History.* Cleveland: World Publishing Co.
LeBlanc, Lawrence J.
1977   Economic, Social and Cultural Rights and the Inter-American System. *Journal of Inter-American Studies and World Affairs* 19 (February):61-82.
LeBlanc, Steven
1975   *Mimbres Archeological Center: Preliminary Report of*

the First Season of Excavation, 1974. Los Angeles: University of California, Institute of Archeology.

———, and Whalen, Michael
1979   *An Archaeological Synthesis of South-Central and South-western New Mexico.* Bureau of Land Management Draft Overview.

Leckie, William H.
1967   *The Buffalo Soldiers: A Narrative of the Negro Cavalry in the West.* Norman: University of Oklahoma Press.

LeCompte, Janet
1973   Manuel Armijo's Family History. *New Mexico Historical Review* 48 (July):251-58.

Lee, David Lopez
1970   Mexican-American Fatalism: An Analysis and Some Speculation. *Journal of Mexican-American Studies* 1 (Fall):44-53.

Lee, Rose Hum
1960   *The Chinese in the United States of America.* Hong Kong: Hong Kong University.

Lee, Thomas F., et al.
1979   The Impact of El Paso Television in Ciudad Juárez, Chihuahua. Research report, University of Texas at El Paso.

Leeds, Anthony
1968   The Anthropology of Cities: Some Methodological Issues. Offprint no. 80. Austin: University of Texas, Institute of Latin American Studies.

LeFree, Betty
1975   *Santa Clara Pottery Today.* Albuquerque: University of New Mexico Press.

Lehmann, Henry
1962   *Pre-Columbian Ceramics.* New York: Viking Press.

Lehmer, D. J.
1960   A Review of Trans-Pecos Archeology. *Texas Archeological Society Bulletin* 29:109-44.

Leighly, John
1936   Meandering Arroyos of the Dry Southwest. *Geographical Review* 26 (April):270-82.

Leighton, Alexander H., and Leighton, Dorothea C.
1949   Gregorio, the Hand-Trembler. *Peabody Museum of American Archaeology and Ethnology Papers* 40 (no. 1): 1-177.

Le Marquand, David G.
1977   *International Rivers: The Politics of Cooperation.* Vancouver: University of British Columbia.

Lemert, Ben F.
1949   Parras Basin, Southern Coahuila, Mexico. *Economic Geography* 25 (April):94-102.

Lemus, Frank C.
1974   National Roster of Spanish-surnamed Elected Officials, 1973. *Aztlán* 5 (nos. 1 and 2):313-409.

Leñero Otero, Luis
1968   The Mexican Urbanization Process and Its Implications. *Demography* 5 (no. 2):866-73.

Leninger, M. M.
1970   *Nursing and Anthropology: Two Worlds to Blend.* New York: John Wiley & Sons.

Leonard, Olen E.
1943   The Role of the Land Grant in the Social Organization and Social Processes of a Spanish-American Village in New Mexico. Ph.D. dissertation, Louisiana State University.

1948   *The Role of the Land Grant in the Social Organization and Social Processes of a Spanish-American Village in New Mexico.* Ann Arbor, Mich.: Edwards Brothers.

1970   *The Role of the Land Grant in the Social Organization and Social Processes of a Spanish-American Village in New Mexico.* Albuquerque: Calvin Horn Publisher.

1972   *Job Mobility and Adjustment: A Test for Relationship Between Mobility Characteristics of Workers Recently Removed from Farms to Towns and Villages of Pinal*

County, Arizona. Tucson: University of Arizona, Department of Sociology, USDA-ERS.

———, and Cleland, Courtney B.
1976   Occupational Changes in North Central New Mexico: A Response to Social and Economic Alterations in a Traditional Agricultural Area. *Social Science Journal* 13 (April):95-101.

———, and Loomis, Charles P.
1941   *Culture of a Contemporary Rural Community: El Cerrito, New Mexico.* Washington, D.C.: U.S. Department of Agriculture.

León-Portilla, Miguel
1960   The Concept of the State Among the Aztecs. *Alpha Kappa Deltan* 30:7-13.

1972   The Norteño Variety of Mexican Culture: An Ethnohistorical Approach. In Edward H. Spicer and Raymond H. Thompson, eds. *Plural Society in the Southwest,* pp. 77-114. New York: Interbook.

Leopold, A. Starker
1950   Vegetation Zones of Mexico. *Ecology* 31 (October):507-18.

Leopold, Luna B.
1942   Areal Extent of Intense Rainfall, New Mexico and Arizona. *American Geophysical Union, Transactions,* part 2:558-63.

1945   Characteristics of Heavy Rainfall in New Mexico and Arizona. *American Society of Civil Engineers, Transactions 1944,* paper 2222:837-66.

1951   Vegetation of Southwestern Water Sheds in the Nineteenth Century. *Geographical Review* 41 (April):295-316.

Lesco Associates
1975   Final Report: Basic Data and Guidance Required to Implement a Major Illegal Alien Study During Fiscal Year 1976. Paper prepared for the Immigration and Naturalization Service, October, Washington, D.C.

LeSueur, H.
1945   *The Ecology of the Vegetation of Chihuahua, Mexico, North of Parallel Twenty-eight.* Publication no. 4521. Austin: University of Texas.

Leutenegger, Benedict
1968   New Documents on Father José Mariano Reyes. *Southwestern Historical Quarterly* 71 (April):583-602.

———, and Habig, Marion A.
1974   Report on the San Antonio Missions in 1792. *Southwestern Historical Quarterly* 77 (April):487-98.

Levinson, Robert Edward
1969   The Jews in the California Gold Rush. Ph.D. dissertation, University of Oregon.

Levy, Jerrold E.
1961   *Navajo Health Concepts and Behavior: The Role of the Anglo Medical Man in the Navajo Healing Process.* Window Rock, Ariz.: U.S. Public Health Service.

1965   Navajo Suicide. *Human Organization* 24:308-18.

———; Kunitz, Stephen J.; and Odoroff, C. L.
1970   A One Year Follow-up of Navajo Migrants to Flagstaff, Arizona. *Plateau* 42 (Winter):92-106.

Levy, Mark R., and Kramer, Michael S.
1972   *The Ethnic Factor.* New York: Simon and Schuster.

Lewis, Henry T.
1973   *Patterns of Indian Burning in California: Ecology and Ethnohistory.* Bellena Press Anthropological Papers, no. 1.

1981   *From Fire to Flood: Historic Human Destruction of Sonoran Desert Riverine Oases.* Bellena Press Anthropological Papers, no. 20.

Lewis, Oscar
1938   *The Big Four: The Story of Huntington, Stanford, Hopkins, and Crocker, and of the Building of the Central Pacific.* New York: Alfred A. Knopf.

Lewis, Oscar
1949   Husbands and Wives in a Mexican Village: A Study of Role Conflict. *American Anthropologist* 51:602-10.
1951   *A Day in the Life of a Mexican Village.* Urbana: University of Illinois Press.
1953a   Tepoztlán Restudied. *Rural Sociology* 18 (June):121-37.
1953b   Husbands and Wives in a Mexican Village: A Study of Role Conflict. In Olen Leonard and Charles Loomis, eds. *Readings in Latin American Social Organizations and Institutions.* East Lansing: Michigan State College Press.
1956   A Day in the Life of a Mexican Peasant Family. *Marriage and Family Living* 18:3-13.
1957   Urbanization but Disorganization: Tepoztecan Families in Mexico City. *América Indígena* 17:231-46.
1959a   *Five Families: Mexican Case Studies in the Culture of Poverty.* New York: Basic Books.
1959b   Family Dynamics in a Mexican Village. *Marriage and Family Living* 21:218-26.
1961   *The Children of Sánchez: Autobiography of a Mexican Family.* New York: Random House.
1964a   *Pedro Martínez, a Mexican Peasant and His Family.* New York: Random House.
1964b   The Extended Family in Mexico. In William Goode, ed. *Readings in Family and Society,* pp. 18-183. Englewood Cliffs: Prentice-Hall.
1969a   *The Children of Sánchez: Autobiography of a Mexican Family.* New York: Random House. Originally published in 1961.
1969b   *A Death in the Sánchez Family.* New York: Random House.

Limón, Gilberto
1975   Discrimination Against Aliens in Federal Public Employment. *Chicano Law Review* 2 (Summer):109-29.

Lindig, Wolfgang
1960   Die Seri: Ein Koka-Wildbeuterstamn in Sonora. *International Ethnography* 41:1-116 (Dresden).

Lindsey, John H.
1972   *The Schiwetz Legacy: An Artist's Tribute to Texas, 1910-1971.* Austin: University of Texas Press.

Lindstrom, C. J.
1975   No Shows: A Problem in Health Care. *Nursing Outlook* 23:755-59.

Linton, Ralph
1940   *Acculturation in Seven American Indian Tribes.* New York: Appleton-Century Co.

Linton, Thomas H.
1972   A Study of the Relationship of Global Self-Concept, Academic Self-Concept, and Academic Achievement Among Anglo and Mexican-American Sixth-Grade Students. Manuscript, ED 063 053. Las Cruces, N.M.: New Mexico State University, ERIC Clearinghouse for Rural and Small Schools.

Lister, Florence, and Lister, Robert
1966   *Chihuahua: Storehouse of Storms.* Albuquerque: University of New Mexico Press.

Lister, Robert H.
1958   *Archeological Excavations in the Northern Sierra Madre Occidentale, Chihuahua and Sonora, Mexico.* Series in Anthropology, no. 7. Boulder: University of Colorado.
1960   History of Archeological Fieldwork in Northwestern Mexico. *El Palacio* 67 (4):118-24.

Little, Arthur D.
1974   Tourism in San Diego: Its Economic, Fiscal and Environmental Impacts. Report to the City of San Diego, California.

Livermore, Abiel Abbot
1850   *The War with Mexico Reviewed.* Boston: American Peace Society.

Lobeck, Armin K.
1948   *Physiographic Diagram of North America: Scale 1:6,000,000.* New York: Columbia University, Geographical Press.

Lobo, Frank; Bainton, Barry; and Weaver, Thomas
1974   Indian Education. In Thomas Weaver, ed. *Indians of Arizona: A Contemporary Perspective,* pp. 138-56. Tucson: University of Arizona Press.

Loeffler, M. John
1970   Australian-American Interbasin Water Transfer. *Annals, Association of American Geographers* 60 (September):493-516.

Loehr, William, and Bulson, Michael E.
1974   The Mexican Border Industrialization Program. *Arizona Business* 21 (October):11-16.

Loesch, August
1954   *The Economics of Location.* New Haven: Yale University Press.

Loewe Reiss, Ricardo
1978   Considerations on the Health Status Along Mexico's Northern Border. In Stanley R. Ross, ed. *Views Across the Border,* pp. 241-55. Albuquerque: University of New Mexico Press.

Logan, R. M.
1974   *Canada, the United States, and the Third Law of the Sea Conference.* Montreal: Canadian-American Committee.

Long, Daniel
1941   *Pinon County.* Edited by Erskine Caldwell. New York: Duell, Sloan & Pearce.

Long, John; Canyon, Lena; and Churchman, David
1973   For Urban Los Angeles: A Tribal American Preschool. *Journal of American Indian Education* 13 (October): 7-14.

Long, William
1964   A History of Mining in New Mexico During the Spanish and Mexican Periods. Master's thesis, University of New Mexico.

Loomis, Charles P.
1942   Wartime Migration from the Rural Spanish Speaking Villages of New Mexico. *Rural Sociology* 7 (December): 384-95.
1958   El Cerrito, New Mexico: A Changing Village. *New Mexico Historical Review* 33 (January):53-75.
1966   A Comparison of Social Distance Attitudes in the United States and Mexico. *Studies in Comparative International Development* 2.
1970   In Defense of Integration: For One Nation and One World. *Centennial Review* 14:125-65.
1974   History and Results of the Michigan State University Carnegie Corporation Border Project. Paper presented to Southwestern Sociological Association, March, at Dallas, Texas.

————, and Leonard, Olen E.
1938   *Standards of Living in an Indian-Mexican Village and on a Reclamation Project.* Report no. 4. Washington, D.C.: Department of Agriculture, Farm Security Administration and Bureau of Agricultural Economics.

————, and Samora, Julian
1965   Prejudice and Religious Activity in Mexico and the United States. *Sociological Analysis* 26 (Winter):212-16.

Loomis, Charles P.; Loomis, Zona K.; and Gullahorn, Jeanne E.
1966   *Linkages of Mexico and the United States.* Bulletin no. 14. East Lansing: Michigan State University, Experiment Station.

Loomis, Noel M.
1958   *The Texan-Santa Fé Pioneers.* Norman: University of Oklahoma Press.
1968   *Wells Fargo.* New York: C. N. Potter.
1969   Commandants-General of the Interior Provinces: A Preliminary List. *Arizona and the West* 11 (Autumn):261-68.

————, and Nasatir, Abraham P.
1967   *Pedro Vial and the Roads to Santa Fe.* Norman: Uni-

versity of Oklahoma Press.

Lope Blanch, Juan M.
1970 *Questionario para le delimitación de las zonas dialectales de México.* Mexico City: El Colegio de México.

Lopez, David T.
1969 Low-Wage Lure South of the Border. *AFL-CIO American Federationist* 76 (June):1-8.

Lopez, Pedro
1977 A Study of Unapprehended and Apprehended Aliens in El Paso: Characteristics and Reported Reasons for Coming to the U.S. Master's thesis, University of Texas at El Paso.

López de Gómara, Francisco
1964 *Cortés, the Life of the Conqueror by His Secretary Francisco López de Gómara.* Translated and edited by Lesley Byrd Simpson. Berkeley: University of California Press.

López Mercado, María
1965 *Algunos aspectos de las bases de la familia.* Mexico City: UNAM.

López Portillo, José
1979 Decreto por el que se establecen zonas geográficas para la ejecución del Programa de Estímulos para la Desconcentración Territorial de las Actividades Industriales. *Diario Oficial,* February 2.

López Ramos, Ernesto
1976 *Carta geológica de la republica mexicana: scale 1:2,000,000.* Mexico City: UNAM, Instituto de Geología.

Lord, Walter
1961 *A Time to Stand.* New York: Harper & Brothers.

Love, Edgar F.
1967 Negro Resistance to Spanish Rule in Colonial Mexico. *Journal of Negro History* 52:89-103.
1971 Marriage Patterns of Persons of African Descent in a Colonial Mexico City Parish. *Hispanic American Historical Review* 51 (February):79-91.

Lowe, Charles H.
1964 *Arizona's Natural Environment, Landscapes and Habitats.* Tucson: University of Arizona Press.

Lowenthal, Abraham F.
1973 United States Policy Toward Latin America: "Liberal," "Radical," and "Bureaucratic" Perspectives. *Latin American Research Review* 8 (no. 3):3-25.

Lowery, Woodbury
1901 *The Spanish Settlements Within the Present Limits of the United States, 1513-1561.* New York: G. P. Putnam's Sons.
1905 *The Spanish Settlements Within the Present Limits of the United States, Florida, 1562-1574.* New York: G. P. Putnam's Sons.

Lowrie, Samuel Harman
1932 *Culture Conflict in Texas, 1821-1835.* Studies in History, Economics and Public Law, no. 1, p. 376. New York: Columbia University.

Loyo, Gilberto
1935 *La política demográfica de México.* Mexico City: S. Turanzas del Valle.
1960 *La población de México: estadísticas actual y tendencias.* Mexico City: Instituto mexicano de recursos naturales renovables.
1966 *La población de México: estado actual y tendencias, 1960-1980.* Mexico City: Ponencia.
1970 *Tres breves estudios.* Mexico City: n.p.
1974 The Demographic Problems of Mexico and Latin America. In T. L. McCoy, ed. *The Dynamics of Population Policy in Latin America,* pp. 183-201. Cambridge, Mass.: Ballinger Publishing Co.

Lozano, Anthony G.
1961 Intercambio de español e inglés en San Antonio, Texas. *Archivum* 11:111-38.

Luebben, Ralph A.
1964 Prejudice and Discrimination Against Navahos in a Min-

ing Community. *Kiva* 30 (October):1-18.

Luhman, Reid A.
1974 The Social Bases of Thinking and Speaking: A Study of Bilingual Chicano Children. Ph.D. dissertation, University of Kansas.

Lumholtz, Carl
1902 *Unknown Mexico.* 2 vols. New York: Charles Scribner's Sons.

Lummis, Charles F.
1925 *Land of Poco Tiempo.* New York: Charles Scribner's Sons. Originally published in 1893.
1925 *Mesa, Canyon, and Pueblo.* New York: Century.

Lumsden, Ian
1970 Editor. *Close the 49th Parallel, Etc.: The Americanization of Canada.* Toronto: University of Toronto Press.

Lupsha, Peter, and Schlegel, Kip
1979 Drug Trafficking in the Borderlands: Its Impact on North-South Relations. Paper presented to Latin American Studies Association, April, at Pittsburgh, Pennsylvania.

Luten, Daniel B.
1967 The Use and Misuse of a River (Colorado River). *American West* 4 (May):47-53.

Lutz, Carl L.
1964 The San Diego Citrus Industry. Master's thesis, San Diego State College.

Lyon, George F.
1828 *A Journal of Residence and Tour in the Republic of Mexico in the Year 1826, with Some Account of the Mines of That Country.* 2 vols. London: n.p.

McBride, George McCutchen
1971 *The Land Systems of Mexico.* Mexico. New York: Octagon Books. First published in 1923.

McCain, Johnny M.
1970 Contract Labor as a Factor in United States-Mexican Relations, 1942-1947. Ph.D. dissertation, University of Texas, Austin.

MacCarry, Timothy J.
1970 Attitudes, Class and Ethnic Relations in Fabens. Manuscript, Sociology Department, University of Notre Dame.

McCarty, Frankie
1969 Land Grant Problems in New Mexico, Reprint of a Series of Articles on New Mexican Land Grants published in the *Albuquerque Journal,* September 28-October 10, 1969. Albuquerque: Albuquerque Journal.

McCarty, Jeanne B.
1980 The Struggle for Sobriety: Protestants and Prohibition in Texas: 1919-1935. Southwestern Studies, no. 62. El Paso: Texas Western Press.

McCleneghan, Thomas J.
1964 Land Use Contrasts in a Border Economy. Paper presented to Regional Science Association, February, at Tempe, Arizona.
1965 Land Ownership in the West. *Arizona Review* 14 (March):13-18.
———, and Gildersleeve, Charles R.
1964 *Land Use Contrasts in a Border Economy.* Tucson: University of Arizona.
1965a A Land Use Comparison of Two "Paired" Cities on the Arizona-Mexico Border. Paper presented to Southwestern and Rocky Mountain Division, AAAS, May, at Flagstaff, Arizona.
1965b Paired Cities on the Arizona-Sonora Border. *Arizona Review* 14 (June):9-13.

McCleskey, Clifton
1972 *The Government and Politics of Texas.* Boston: Little, Brown & Co.
———, et al.
1978 *The Government and Politics of Texas.* 6th ed. Boston: Little, Brown & Co.
———, and Merrill, Bruce

1973   Mexican-American Political Behavior in Texas. *Social Science Quarterly* 53 (March):785-99.

1974   Mexican American Behavior in Texas. In F. Chris Garcia, ed. *La Causa Politica*, pp. 128-42. Notre Dame: University of Notre Dame Press.

———, and Nimmo, Dan
1968   Differences Between Potential Registered and Actual Voters: The Houston Metropolitan Areas in 1964. *Social Science Quarterly* 49 (June):103-14.

McClintock, James H.
1921   *Mormon Settlement in Arizona: A Record of Peaceful Conquest of the Desert.* Phoenix: Manufacturing Stationers.

McCluney, Eugene B.
1962   *Clanton Draw and Box Canyon.* Monograph no. 26. Santa Fe: School of American Research.

McClung, Donald R.
1971   Second Lieutenant Henry O. Flipper: A Negro Officer on the West Texas Frontier. *West Texas Historical Association Yearbook*, pp. 20-31.

McClure, Charles R.
1973   The Texas-Santa Fe Expedition of 1841. *New Mexico Historical Review* 48 (January):45-56.

McComb, David G.
1969   *Houston: The Bayou City.* Austin: University of Texas Press.

McConville, J. Lawrence
1965   El Paso-Ciudad Juárez: A Focus of Inter-American Culture. *New Mexico Historical Review* 40 (July):233-46.

1966   A History of Population in the El Paso-Ciudad Juárez Area. Master's thesis, University of New Mexico.

McCoy, Terry L.
1974*a*   Editor. *The Dynamics of Population Policy in Latin America.* Cambridge, Mass.: Ballinger Publishing Co.

1974*b*   A Paradigmatic Analysis of Mexican Population Policy. In Terry L. McCoy, ed. *The Dynamics of Population Policy in Latin America.* Cambridge, Mass.: Ballinger Publishing Co.

McCracken, Harold
1966   *The Frederic Remington Book: A Pictorial History of the West.* Garden City, N.Y.: Doubleday & Co.

McCready, William C., and Greeley, Andrew M.
1972   The End of American Catholicism? In Patrick H. McNamara, ed. *Religion American Style*, pp. 195-204. New York: Harper & Row.

MacDiarmid, John MacLeod
1975   The State Water Plan and Salinity Control in the Sacramento-San Joaquin Delta of California. *Yearbook of the Association of Pacific Coast Geographers* 37:63-76.

McDonald, James E.
1965   *Variability of Precipitation in an Arid Region: A Survey of Characteristics for Arizona.* Technical Report on the Meteorology and Climatology of Arid Regions no. 1. Tucson: University of Arizona, Institute of Atmospheric Physics.

McDonald, Stephen L.
1965   Recent Economic Development of the Southwest. *Southwestern Social Science Quarterly* 45 (March):329-39.

MacDougal, Daniel Trembly
1906   The Delta of the Rio Colorado. *Bulletin of the American Geographical Society* 38:1-16.

McDowell, Fred W., and Keizer, Richard P.
1977   Timing of Mid-tertiary Volcanism in the Sierra Madre Occidental Between Durango City and Mazatlán, Mexico. *Geological Society of America Bulletin* 88:1479-87.

McDowell, H. G.
1964   Cotton in Mexico. *Journal of Geography* 63 (February):67-72.

McDowell, John H.
1975   The Speech Play and Verbal Art of Chicano Children: An Ethnographic and Sociolinguistic Study. Ph.D. dissertation, University of Texas, Austin.

1977   The Speech Play and Verbal Art of Chicano Children: An Ethnographic and Sociolinguistic Study. In Donald W. Bleznick, ed. *Hispania.* Worcester, Mass.: American Association of Spanish and Portuguese.

McElroy, Robert, and Garret, Earl C.
1965   *Termination of the Bracero Program: Some Effects on Farm Labor and Migrant Housing Needs.* Economic Research Service Report 77. Washington, D.C.: U.S. Department of Agriculture.

McFeeley, Mark B.
1972   Need for a Federal Policy in Indian Economic Development. *New Mexico Law Review* 2 (January):71-80.

McGavaran, Donald; Guegel, John; and Taylor, Jack
1963   *Church Growth in Mexico.* Grand Rapids, Mich.: Wm. B. Eerdmans Publishing Co.

McGee, W. J.
1897   Rope-Making in Mexico. *American Anthropologist* 10:114-19.

1898   *The Seri Indians.* 17th Annual Report. Washington, D.C.: Smithsonian Institution, Bureau of American Ethnology.

McGinn, Noel F.
1966   Marriage and Family in Middle-Class Mexico. *Journal of Marriage and the Family* 28 (August):305-13.

McGinnies, William G.; Goldman, B. J.; and Paylore, P.
1969   *Deserts of the World: An Appraisal of Research into Their Physical and Biological Environments.* Tucson: University of Arizona.

1971   Editors. *Food, Fiber, and the Arid Lands.* Tucson: University of Arizona Press.

McGlynn, Eileen A.
1975   *Middle American Anthropology: Directory, Bibliography and Guide to the UCLA Library Collections.* Los Angeles: University of California, Latin American Center and University Library.

McGregor, John C.
1941   *Southwestern Archaeology.* New York: John Wiley & Sons.

MacGregor, María Teresa G. de, and Valverde, Carmen
1975   Evolution of the Urban Population in the Arid Zones of Mexico, 1900-1970. *Geographic Review* 62 (no. 2):214-28.

McGuire, Thomas R.
1977   Yaqui Farmers, Yaqui Fishermen: Towards a Political Economy of Ethnicity. In *Discovery*, pp. 1-24. Santa Fe: School of American Research.

Machado, Manuel A., Jr.
1978   *Listen Chicano! An Informal History of the Mexican American.* Chicago: Nelson-Hall Publishers.

McIntire, Elliot G.
1969*a*   Hopi Colonization on the Colorado River. *California Geographer* 10:7-14.

1969*b*   The Hopi Villages of Arizona: A Study in Changing Patterns. *Proceedings of the Association of American Geographers* 1:95-99.

1971   Changing Patterns of Hopi Indian Settlement. *Annals, Association of American Geographers* 61 (September):510-21.

MacIntosh, Roderick, and Ornstein, Jacob
1974   A Brief Sampling of West Texas Teacher Attitudes Toward Southwest Spanish and English Language Varieties. *Hispania* 57:920-26.

MacKay, Maryann
1975   Spoken Spanish of Mexican American Children: A Monolingual and Bilingual School Program. Ph.D. dissertation, Stanford University.

McKay, Seth Shepard, and Faulk, Odie B.
1965   *Texas After Spindletop.* Austin: Steck Co.

Mackinnon, J. B.
1975   Investment at the Border: The Maquiladoras. *Mexican-*

American Review 43 (March):61-67.

Macklin, Barbara June
1967   El niño fidencio: un estudio del curanderismo en Nuevo León. In *Anuario Humánitas,* pp. 529-63. Monterrey: Universidad de Nuevo León, Centro de Estudios Humanísticos.

———, and Crumrine, N. Ross.
1972   "Santa" Teresa, El Niño "Santo" Fidencio and "San" Damián: The Structural Development of Three Folk Saints' Movements, Northern Mexico. *XXXIX Congreso Internacional de Americanistas, Memorias* 6:100-109 (Lima).
1973   Three North Mexican Folk Saints' Movements. *Comparative Studies in Society and History* 15 (1):89-105.

McKnight, Joseph W.
1966   The Spanish Watercourses of Texas. In *Essays in Legal History in Honor of Felix Frankfurter,* pp. 373-86. New York: Bobbs-Merrill Co.

McLaughlin, Michael J.
1980   Chicano Paraprofessional Acculturation and Community Mental Health Ideology: Measuring the Bridging Function. Ph.D. dissertation, University of Arizona.

McLean, Malcolm D.
1966   Tenoxtitlán, Dream Capital of Texas. *Southwestern Historical Quarterly* 70 (July):23-43.
1974-77   Editor and compiler. *Papers Concerning Robertson's Colony in Texas.* 5 vols. Fort Worth: Texas Christian University Press.

McLemore, S. Dale
1963   Ethnic Attitudes Toward Hospitalization: An Illustrative Comparison of Anglos and Mexican Americans. *Southwestern Social Science Quarterly* 43 (March):341-46.
1973   The Origins of Mexican-American Subordination in Texas. *Social Science Quarterly* 53 (March):656-70.

MacMeekin, Daniel
1972   The Navajo Tribe's Water Rights in the Colorado River Basin. U.S. Senate Judiciary Committee Report. Washington, D.C.: Government Printing Office.

McNeely, John H.
1964   *The Railways of Mexico: A Study in Nationalization.* El Paso: Texas Western College Press.

MacNeish, R. S.
1958   Preliminary Archaeological Investigations in the Sierra de Tamaulipas, Mexico. *Transactions, American Philosophical Society* 48 (6). *Analysis* 29 (Winter):177-85.
1969   Priests, Protests, and Poverty Intervention. *Social Science Quarterly* 50 (December):695-702.
1971   Prostitution Along the U.S.-Mexican Border: A Survey. In Ellwyn R. Stoddard, ed. *Prostitution and Illicit Drug Traffic on the U.S.-Mexico Border,* pp. 1-21. Occasional Papers, no. 2. El Paso: Border-State University, Consortium for Latin America.

McNeley, James K.
1975   The Navajo Theory of Life and Behavior. Ph.D. dissertation, University of Hawaii.

McNickle, D'Arcy
1973   *Native American Tribalism: Indian Survivals and Renewals.* New York: Oxford University Press.

McNitt, Frank
1962   *The Indian Traders.* Norman: University of Oklahoma Press.
1972   *Navajo Wars.* Albuquerque: University of New Mexico Press.

McSpadden, George E.
1934   Some Semantic and Philological Facts of the Spanish Spoken in Chilili, New Mexico. *University of New Mexico Bulletin/Language Series* 5:71-102.

McWilliams, Carey
1933   Getting Rid of the Mexican. *American Mercury* 28 (March):322-24.
1939   *Factories in the Field: The Study of Migratory Farm Labor in California.* Boston: Little, Brown & Co. Reprinted by Peregrine Press, 1971.
1942   *Ill Fares the Land: Migrants and Migratory Labor in the United States.* Boston: Little, Brown & Co.
1946   *Southern California Country.* New York: Duell, Sloan & Pearce.
1949a   *North from Mexico: The Spanish-Speaking People of the United States.* New York: J. B. Lippincott Co. Reprinted by Greenwood Press, 1968.
1949b   *California, the Great Exception.* New York: Current Books.
1968   *The Mexicans in America: A Students' Guide to Localized History.* New York: Teachers College Press (Columbia University).
1976   The Borderlands: Let Justice Make Us Friends. In K. Skagen, ed. *Proceedings* of San Diego-Tijuana Conference in November, Fronteras Publication no. 3, pp. 1-4.

Maderey, Laura Elena
1974   Relationships Between Stream Load and Physical Elements of the Land in the Basin of Rio Conchos, Mexico. *Geographical Survey* 3 (July):133-50.

Madge, John
1962   *The Origins of Scientific Sociology.* New York: Free Press of Glencoe.

Madison, Virginia
1968   *The Big Bend Country of Texas.* New York: October House.

Madsen, William H.
1961   *Society and Health in the Lower Rio Grande Valley.* Austin: Hogg Foundation for Mental Health.
1964   *The Mexican-Americans of South Texas.* San Francisco: Holt, Rinehart & Winston.
1973   *The Mexican-Americans of South Texas.* 2d ed. New York: Holt, Rinehart & Winston.

Maes, Ernest E.
1941   The World and People of Cundiyo. *Land Policy Review* 4:8-14.

Magoffin, Susan Shelby
1926   *Down the Santa Fe Trail and into Mexico, the Diary of, 1846-1847.* Edited by Stella M. Drumm. New Haven: n.p.

Major, Mabel
1950   *Signature of the Sun: Southwest Verse, 1900-1950.* Albuquerque: University of New Mexico Press.

Maldonado, Lionel A., and Byrne, David R.
1978   *The Social Ecology of Chicanos in Utah.* Iowa City: University of Iowa, Urban Community Research Center.

Maldonado, Oscar
1969   *Los católicos y la paneación familiar: resultados de una encuesta nacional.* Mexico City: Instituto Mexicano de Estudios Sociales.

Malinowski, Bronislaw
1945   *The Dynamics of Culture Change.* New Haven: Yale University Press.

Mallery, T. D.
1936   Rainfall Records for the Sonoran Desert. *Ecology* 17 (January):110-21; 17 (April):212-15.

Maloney, Thomas J.
1964   Recent Demographic and Economic Changes in Northern New Mexico. *New Mexico Business* 17:2, 4-14.

Malooly, Gilbert
1953   Syrian People in El Paso. Undergraduate paper, University of Texas at El Paso Library.

Mallouf, R.; Baskin, B.; and Killen, K.
1977   *A Predictive Assessment of Cultural Resources in Hidalgo and Willacy Counties, Texas.* Survey no. 23. Austin: Texas Historical Commission, Office of the State Archeologist.

———, and Tunnell, C.
1977   *An Archeological Reconnaissance in the Lower Canyons of the Rio Grande.* Survey no. 22. Austin: Texas Histori-

cal Commission, Office of the State Archeologist.

Maluy, Dale C.
1977 Boer Colonization in the Southwest. *New Mexico Historical Review* 52 (April):93-110.

Mañach, Jorge
1975 *Frontiers in the Americas.* Translated by Philip H. Phenix. New York: Teachers College Press (Columbia University).

Mancke, Richard B.
1979 *Mexican Oil and Gas: Political, Strategic, and Economic Implications.* New York: Praeger Publishers.

Mandel, Jay R.
1978 *The Roots of Black Poverty: The Southern Plantation Economy After the Civil War.* Durham: Duke University Press.

Mandell, Paul I., and Tweeten, Luther G.
1971 The Location of Cotton Production in the United States Under Competitive Conditions: A Study of Crop Location and Comparative Advantage. *Geographical Analysis* 3 (no. 4):334-53.

Mangan, Frank
1973 *Bordertown Revisited.* El Paso: Guynes Publishing Co.

Manje, Juan Mateo
1954 Luz de tierra incognita: *Unknown Arizona and Sonora, 1639-1721.* Translated by H. Karns and Associates. Tucson: Arizona Silhouettes.

Mann, Dean E.
1963a *The Politics of Water in Arizona.* Tucson: University of Arizona Press.
1963b Political and Social Institutions in Arid Regions. In Carle Hodge and Peter C. Duisberg, eds. *Aridity and Man,* pp. 397-428. Publication no. 74. Washington, D.C.: AAAS.
1976 *Water Policy and Decision-Making in the Colorado River Basin.* Lake Powell Research Project Bulletin no. 24. Los Angeles: University of California.

Manners, Robert A.
1974a *Havasupai Indians: An Ethnohistorical Report.* New York: Garland Publishing, Brandeis University.
1974b *An Ethnological Report of the Hualapai (Walapai) Indians of Arizona.* New York: Garland Publishing, Brandeis University.

Manuel, Herschel T.
1965 *The Spanish-speaking Children of the Southwest: Their Education and Public Welfare.* Austin: University of Texas Press.

Marcum, John P., and Bean, F. D.
1976 Minority Group Status as a Factor in the Relationship Between Mobility and Fertility: The Mexican-American Case. *Social Forces* 55 (no. 1):135-48.

Maresh, Henry R.
1946 The Czechs in Texas. *Southwestern Historical Quarterly* 50 (October):236-40.

Mariejol, Jean Hippolyte
1961 *The Spain of Ferdinand and Isabella.* Translated and edited by Benjamin Keen. New Brunswick: Rutgers University Press.

Maril, Robert L., and Zavaleta, Anthony N.
1978 Drinking Patterns of Mexican Americans in Brownsville, Texas. Paper presented to Western Social Science Association, April, at Denver, Colorado.

Markham, Charles G.
1972 Baja California's Climate. *Weatherwise* 25 (April):64-76.

Marr, Eldon G.
1967 Agriculture in New Mexico. *New Mexico Business* 20 (October):1-12.

Marriott, Alice
1948 *María, the Potter of San Ildefonso.* Norman: University of Oklahoma Press.

Marschner, F. J.
1959 *Land Use and Its Problems in the United States.* Agriculture Research Service Handbook 153. Washington,

D.C.: U.S. Department of Agriculture.

Marshall, James
1945 *Santa Fe, The Railroad that Built an Empire.* New York: Random House.

Marshall, Ray
1978 Economic Factors Influencing the International Migration of Workers. In Stanley R. Ross., ed. *Views Across the Border,* pp. 163-80. Albuquerque: University of New Mexico Press.
———, et al.
1974 *Human Resource Development in Rural Texas.* Studies in Human Development, no. 1. Austin: University of Texas.

Martin, John F.
1973 The Organization of Land and Labor in a Marginal Economy. *Human Organization* 32 (Summer):153-62.

Martin, P. S.
1963 *The Last 10,000 Years: A Fossil Pollen Record of the American Southwest.* Tucson: University of Arizona Press.
———, and Mehringer, P. J.
1965 Pleistocene Pollen Analysis and Biogeography of the Southwest. In H. E. Wright, Jr., and D. G. Fry, eds. *The Quaternary of the United States,* pp. 433-51. Princeton: Princeton University Press.

Martin, Paul S., and Plog, Fred
1973 *The Archaeology of Arizona: A Study of the Southwest Region.* Garden City: Doubleday/Natural History Press.

Martin, W. C., and Hutchins, C. R.
1980 *A Flora of New Mexico.* Braunschweig: J. Cramer.

Martin, William E., and Young, Robert A.
1969 The Need for Additional Water in the Arid Southwest: An Economist's Dissent. *Annals of Regional Science* 3 (June):21-31.

Martin, William F.
1977 Editor. *Energy Supply to the Year 2000: Global and National Studies.* Cambridge: MIT Press.

Martinez, Cervando, and Martin, Harry W.
1966 Folk Diseases Among Urban Mexican Americans. *Journal of the American Medical Association* 196 (April): 161-64.

Martínez, Gregorio
1949 La familia mexicana. *Revista Mexicana de Sociología* 3:337-53.

Martinez, John
1957 Mexican Emigration to the United States, 1910-1930. Ph.D. dissertation, University of California, Berkeley.

Martínez, Oscar J.
1975 Border Boom Town: Ciudad Juárez since 1880. Ph.D. dissertation, University of California, Los Angeles.
1976 Interaction Along the U.S.-Mexican Border: An Interpretive Essay. Paper presented to the Latin American Studies Association, March, at Atlanta, Georgia.
1977a The Peso Devaluation and the Border: Some Historical Observations. *El Paso Business Review* 15 (Summer): 1-5.
1977b Chicanos and the Border Cities: An Interpretive Essay. *Pacific Historical Review* 46 (February):85-106.
1978 *Border Boom Town: Ciudad Juárez Since 1848.* Austin: University of Texas Press.
1980 *The Chicanos of El Paso: An Assessment of Progress.* El Paso: Texas Western Press.

Martinez, P. D.
1970 Ambiente sociocultural en la faja fronteriza mexicana. *Salud Pública de México* 12:833-39.

Martinez, Vilma S.
1976 Illegal Immigration and the Labor Force: An Historical and Legal View. *American Behavioural Scientist* 19 (no. 3):335-49.

Martínez Baca, Eduardo
1901 *Reseña histórica de las legislación minera en México.*

Mexico City: n.p.

Martínez García, Geronimo
1974   México: una visión demográfica de su composición por regiones. *Pensamiento Político* 17 (October):193-210.

Marum and Marum, Inc.
1973   *A Regional Plan for Water, Sewerage and Solid Waste Project.* Tucson: Pima Association of Governments.

Mason, J. Alden
1912   The Fiesta of the Pinole at Azqueltan. *Mesium Journal* 3:44-50.

1913   The Tepehuán Indians of Azqueltan. *Proceedings of the 18th International Congress of Americanists,* pp. 344-51.

1948   The Tepehuán and Other Aborigines of the Mexican Sierra Madre Occidental. *América Indígena* 8:289-300.

1952   Notes and Observations on the Tepehuán. *América Indígena* 12:33-53.

1959   The Tepehuán of Northern Mexico. *Mitteilungen aus dem Museum für Völkerkunde in Hamburg* 25:91-96.

——, and Brugge, David M.
1958   Notes on the Lower Pima. In *Miscellanea Paul Rivet, Octogenario Dictata,* vol. 1, pp. 277-97. Mexico City: UNAM.

Mason, John Dancer
1969   The Aftermath of the Bracero: A Study of the Economic Impact on the Agricultural Hired Labor Market of Michigan from the Termination of Public Law 78. Ph.D. dissertation, Michigan State University.

Mason, Peter F.
1974   The Distribution of Air Pollution in California: A Study in Spatial Interaction. *Journal of Geography* 73 (December):30-37.

Masse, W. Bruce
1980   Excavations at Gu Achi: a reappraisal of Hohokam settlement and subsistence in the Arizona Papaguería. National Park Service Western Archaeological Center *Publications in Anthropology* 12. Tucson: Western Archaeological Center.

Massey, William C.
1949   Tribes and Languages of Baja California. *Southwestern Journal of Anthropology* 5 (no. 3):272-307.

1966   Archaeology and Ethnohistory of Lower California. In G. F. Ekholm and G. R. Willey, ed. *Handbook of Middle American Indians,* vol. 4, pp. 38-58. Austin: University of Texas Press.

Mathes, W. Michael
1969   A Biographical Note on Isidro de Atondo y Antillón, Admiral of the Californias. *California Historical Society Quarterly* 48 (September):211-18.

Matson, D. S., and Schroeder, A. H.
1958   Cordero's Description of the Apache, 1796. *New Mexico Historical Review* 22:335-56.

Matthiasson, Carolyn W.
1968   Acculturation of Mexican-Americans in a Midwestern City. Ph.D. dissertation, Cornell University.

Matthiessen, Peter
1970   *Sal Si Puedes: César Chávez and the New American Revolution.* New York: Random House.

Mattison, Ray H.
1946   Early Spanish and Mexican Settlements in Arizona. *New Mexico Historical Review* 21 (October):273-327.

Maybry, L.
1968   The Educational and Occupational Aspirations of Anglo, Spanish, and Negro High School Students. Ph.D. dissertation, University of New Mexico.

Mayer, Vicente V., Jr.
1975   *Utah: A Hispanic History.* Salt Lake City: University of Utah Printing.

Mead, Margaret
1955   The Spanish Americans of New Mexico, U.S.A. In Margaret Mead, ed. *Cultural Patterns and Technological Change,* pp. 151-77. New York: UNESCO, Mentor.

Meaders, Margaret
1963   The Indian Situation in New Mexico. *New Mexico Business Reprint* (January, March, July, and August).

Meador, Bruce S.
1951   *Wetback Labor in the Lower Rio Grande Valley.* San Francisco: R & E Research Associates, 1973.

Mecham, J. Lloyd
1926*a*   Supplementary Documents Relating to the Chamuscado Rodriguez Expedition. *Southwestern Historical Quarterly* 29 (January):224-31.

1926*b*   Antonio de Espejo and His Journey to New Mexico. *Southwestern Historical Quarterly* 30 (October):114-38.

1927   *Francisco de Ibarra and Nueva Vizcaya.* Durham: Duke University Press.

1929   The Papacy and Spanish-American Independence. *Hispanic American Historical Review* 9 (May):154-75.

1940   Mexican Federalism: Fact or Fiction. *Annals of the American Academy of Political and Social Science* 208 (March): 23-38.

1966   *Church and State in Latin America.* Rev. ed. Chapel Hill: University of North Carolina Press.

Megee, Mary C.
1958   Monterrey, Mexico: Internal Patterns and External Relations. Research Paper, no. 58. Chicago: University of Chicago, Department of Geography.

Meggers, Betty J.
1954   Environmental Limitation on the Development of Culture. *American Anthropologist* 56:801-24.

Meier, Matt S., and Rivera, Feliciano
1972   *The Chicanos: A History of Mexican Americans.* New York: Hill & Wang.

Meigs, Peveril, III
1935   Historical Geography of Northern Lower California. *Yearbook of the Association of Pacific Coast Geographers* 1:14-17.

1939   *The Kiliwa Indians of Lower California.* Berkeley: Ibero-Americana Publication no. 15.

1953   World Distribution of Arid and Semi-Arid Homoclimates. In *Reviews of Research on Arid Zone Hydrology,* pp. 203-204. Paris: UNESCO.

Meinig, Donald W.
1965   The Mormon Culture Region: Strategies and Patterns in the Geography of the American West, 1847-1964. *Annals, Association of American Geographers* 55 (June): 191-220.

1969   *Imperial Texas: An Interpretive Essay in Cultural Geography.* Austin: University of Texas Press.

1971   *Southwest, Three Peoples in Geographical Change, 1600-1970.* New York: Oxford University Press.

1972   American Wests: Preface to a Geographical Interpretation. *Annals, Association of American Geographers* 62 (June):159-84.

Meister, Dick, and Loftis, Anne
1977   *A Long Time Coming: The Struggle to Unionize America's Farm Workers.* New York: Macmillan Press.

Mejías, José Luis
1976   Petróleo. *El Universal* (2 de Febrero).

Meline, James F.
1867   *Two Thousand Miles on Horseback.* New York: Hurd & Houghton.

Melody, Michael E.
1976   The Sacred Hoop: The Way of the Chiricahua Apache and Teton Lakota. Ph.D. dissertation, University of Notre Dame.

1977   *The Apaches: A Critical Bibliography.* Bloomington: Indiana University Press

Méndez Arceo, Sergio
1968   Desacralización para el desarrollo. In *La Iglesia: el subdesarrollo y la revolución,* pp. 239-47. Mexico City:

Nuestro Tiempo.

Mendizabal, Miguel O. de. See also Othón de Mendizabal, Miguel
1930   Influencia de la sal in la distributión geográfica de los grupos indígenas de México. *Proceedings of the International Congress of Americanists* 23:93-100.

Mendoza Berrueto, Eliseo
1976   The Economic Development of the Mexican Border. Fronteras Publication no. 2, Proceedings of Conference in San Diego, May 7-8.

Menefee, Seldon C.
1941   *Mexican Migratory Workers of South Texas.* Washington, D.C.: Works Progress Administration.

Mercer, Jane
1971   Institutionalized Anglocentrism: Labeling Mental Retardation in Public Schools. *Race, Change and Urban Society* 5:311-38.

Merkx, Gilbert W., and Griego, Richard J.
1971   Crisis in New Mexico. In Norman R. Yetman and C. Hoy Steele, eds. *Majority and Minority: The Dynamics of Racial and Ethnic Relations,* pp. 599-610. Boston: Allyn & Bacon.

Merriam, C. Hart
1905   The Indian Population of California. *American Anthropology* 7:594-606.
1955   *Studies of the California Indians.* Berkeley: University of California Press.

Merriam, Willis B.
1957   Irrigation Progress in the Mexican Northwest. *Journal of Geography* 56 (December):429-33.

Merrill, Bruce D.
1976   Partisanship, Ethnicity, and Electoral Change in Texas. *Public Service* 3, no. 3.

Merrill, F. J. H.
1906   Maps of Mexico. *Bulletin of the American Geographical Society* 38:281-87.
1908   Dry Placers of Northern Sonora. *Mining and Scientific Press* 97 (September 5 and 12):360-61.

Merriman, Roger Bigelow
1918-34 *The Rise of the Spanish Empire in the Old World and in the New.* 4 vols. New York: Macmillan Co.

Metzgar, Joseph V.
1974   Ethnic Sensitivity of Spanish New Mexicans: A Survey and Analysis. *New Mexico Historical Review* 49 (January):49-74.
1977   The Atrisco Land Grant, 1692-1977. *New Mexico Historical Review* 52:269-96.

Metzler, William H., and Largent, Frederic
1960   *Migratory Farmworkers in Mid-Continent Streams.* Research Service Report no. 40. Washington, D.C.: U.S. Department of Agriculture.

———; ———; Loomis, Ralph A.; and Le Ray, Nelson
1967   *The Farm Labor Situation in Selected States, 1965-1966.* Economic Research Service Report no. 110. Washington, D.C.: U.S. Department of Agriculture.

Meyer, Michael C.
1969   Perspectives on Mexican Revolutionary Historiography. *New Mexico Historical Review* 44 (April):167-80.
1971   The Militarization of Mexico, 1913-1914. *Americas* 27 (January):293-306.

Meyer, Neil L., and Bromley, Daniel W.
1974   *Interregional Impacts on Alternative Water Resource Policies for Irrigation in the Western United States.* Madison: University of Wisconsin, Water Resources Center.

Meyer, Peter
1977   Mexican Transfer. *Harpers* 255 (November):26-33.

Meyers, Charles J., and Noble, Richard L.
1967   The Colorado River: The Treaty with Mexico. *Stanford Law Review* 19 (January):367-419.

Mezerick, A. G.
1946   *The Revolt of the South and the West.* New York: Duell, Sloan & Pearce.

Michel, Mark P.
1981   Preserving America's Prehistoric Heritage. *Archaeology* 34:61-62.

Michelsen, R., and Owen, Roger C.
1967   A Keruk Ceremony at Santa Catarina, Baja California, Mexico. *Pacific Coast Archaeological Society Quarterly* 3 (1).

Mico, Paul R.
1962   *Navajo Perception of Anglo Medicine.* Tuba City, Ariz.: Navajo Health Education Project, P. H. S. Indian Hospital.

Midgley, Elizabeth
1978   Immigrants: Whose Huddled Masses? *Atlantic* 241:6-26.

Milbrath, Lester
1965   *Political Participation.* Chicago: Rand McNally & Co.

Milchen, Joseph A.
1969   Criminal Law at the International Border. *San Diego Law Review* 6 (January).

Miller, David E.
1973   Central Pacific Construction Vignettes. In George Kraus, ed. *The Golden Spike,* pp. 45-58. Salt Lake City: University of Utah Press, Utah State Historical Society.

Miller, Etienne, and Font, Rafael I.
1974   International Travel and Passenger Fares in the U.S. Balance of Payments, 1974. *Survey of Current Business* 55 (July):24-28.

Miller, John T., and Brown, Irvin C.
1938   Observations Regarding Soils of Northern and Central Mexico. *Soil Science* 46 (December):427-51.

Miller, Mamie Ruth Tanquist
1941   *Pueblo Indian Culture as Seen by the Early Spanish Explorers.* Social Science Series no. 21. Los Angeles: University of Southern California Press.

Miller, Max
1938   The Women of Tehuantepec. *Mexican Life* (October), pp. 15-16.

Miller, Michael V., and Maril, Robert Lee
1978   *Poverty in the Lower Rio Grande Valley of Texas.* Report prepared for the Texas Agricultural Experiment Station and the South Texas Institute of Latin and Mexican American Research, Texas Southmost College.
1979   *Poverty in the Lower Rio Grande Valley of Texas: Historical and Contemporary Dimensions.* Technical Report 28-2. College Station: Texas A&M University, Agricultural Experiment Station.

Miller, Michael V., and Preston, James D.
1973   Vertical Ties and the Redistribution of Power in Crystal City. *Social Science Quarterly* 53 (August):772-84.

Miller, Thomas L.
1962   Texas Bounty Land Grants, 1835-1888. *Southwestern Historical Quarterly* 66 (October):220-33.
1967   *Bounty and Donation Land Grants of Texas, 1835-1888.* Austin: University of Texas Press.
1971   *The Public Lands of Texas, 1519-1970.* Norman: University of Oklahoma Press.

Mills, Elizabeth H.
1954   The Mormon Colonies in Chihuahua after the 1912 Exodus. *New Mexico Historical Review* 29 (July): 165-82; 29 (October):290-310.

Mills, Jack, and Miles, Vera
1966   *The Kuykendall Site.* Report no. 6. El Paso: El Paso Archaeological Society.

Milton, John R.
1969   Editor. *The American Indian Speaks.* Vermillion, S.Dak.: Dakota Press.
1971   Editor. *American Indian II.* Vermillion, S.Dak.: Dakota Press.

Mindeleff, Cosmos
1898   Origin of the Cliff Dwellings. *Journal of the American Geographical Society* 30:111-23.

Minge, Ward A.
1974   *Historical Treatise in Defense of the Pueblo of Acoma Land Claims.* New York: Garland Publishing.

Miranda, F., and Hernández X., E.
1963   Los tipos de vegetación de México. *Boletín de la Sociedad Botánica de México* 28:29-179.

Mirandé, Alfredo
1977   The Chicano Family: A Reanalysis of Conflicting Views. *Journal of Marriage and the Family* 39 (November): 737-56.

———, and Enríquez, Evangelina
1979   *La Chicana: The Mexican-American Woman.* Chicago: University of Chicago Press.

Mitchell, J. D.
1978   The American Indian: A Fire Ecologist. *American Indian Culture and Research Journal* 2 (no. 2):26-31.

Mitchell, Jacquelyn A.
1977   Preliminary Report on the Impact of Mexico's Twin Plant Industry Along the U.S.-Mexico Border. Tucson: Southwest Border Regional Commission.

Mittelbach, Frank G.; Moore, Joan W.; and McDaniel, Ronald
1966   *Intermarriage of Mexican Americans.* Mexican-American Study Project Advance Report no. 6. Los Angeles: UCLA.

Moisés, Rosalío; Kelly, Jane Holden; and Holden, William Curry
1971   *The Tall Candle: The Personal Chronicle of a Yaqui Indian.* Lincoln: University of Nebraska Press.

Mollan, Robert
1979   Human Rights in South Texas: The Grand Jury Selection Question. Paper presented to Rocky Mountain Council on Latin American Studies, May, at El Paso, Texas.

Momaday, N. Scott
1969   *House Made of Dawn.* New York: Harper & Row.
1976   *The Names.* New York: Harper & Row.

Monson, Robert A.
1973   Political Stability in Mexico: The Changing Role of Traditional Rightists. *Journal of Politics* 35 (no. 3):594-614.

Montell, G.
1938   Yaqui Dances. *Ethnos* 3 (no. 6):145-66.

Montgomery, J.
1978   *The Mariposa Site: A Late Prehistoric Site on the Rio Grande Plain of Texas.* Special Report no. 7. San Antonio: University of Texas at San Antonio, Center for Archaeological Research.

Monthan, Guy, and Monthan, Doris
1975   *Art and Indian Individualists: The Art of Seventeen Contemporary Southwestern Artists and Craftsmen.* Flagstaff, Ariz.: Northland Press.

Motheral, Joe
1944   *Recent Trends in Land Tenure in Texas.* Bulletin no. 641. College Station: Texas Agricultural Experiment Station.

Montiel, Miguel
1970   The Social Science Myth of the Mexican American Family. *El Grito* 3 (Summer):56-63.
1973   The Chicano Family: A Review of Research. *Social Work* 18:22-31.

Moore, C. V., et al.
1974   Effects of Colorado River Water Quality and Supply on Irrigated Agriculture. *Water Resources Research* 10 (April):137-44.

Moore, Joan W.
1970a   *Mexican Americans.* Englewood Cliffs, N.J.: Prentice-Hall.
1970b   Colonialism: The Case of the Mexican Americans. *Social Problems* 17 (Spring):463-72.

———, and Pachón, Henry
1976   *Mexican Americans.* 2d ed. Englewood Cliffs, N.J.: Prentice-Hall.

———; Van Arsdol, Maurice D., Jr.; Carillo, Frank R.; and Galindo, Dennis
1975   The Role of Illegal Immigration in the Southern California Economy. Paper presented to the Population Association of America, April, at Seattle, Washington.

Moore, Mary Lu, and Beene, Delmar L.
1971   The Interior Provinces of New Spain: The Report of Hugo O'Connor, January 30, 1776. *Arizona and the West* 8 (Autumn):265-82.

Moore, Maurice J.
1972   Catholic Priests' Views on Contraception: Breakup of a Theological System. Paper presented at American Sociological Association, August, at New Orleans, Louisiana.

Moore, R. Lawrence
1964   The Continuing Search for a Southwest: A Study in Regional Interpretation. *Arizona and the West* 6 (Winter):275-88.

Moore, Thurman
1965   *The Slaves We Rent.* New York: Random House.

Moore, Wilber E.
1952   Attitudes of Mexican Factory Workers Toward Fertility Control. Paper presented at 1951 Milbank Memorial Fund Conference, New York.

Moorhead, Max L.
1958   *New Mexico's Royal Road: Trade and Travel on the Chihuahua Trail.* Norman: University of Oklahoma Press.
1961a   The Private Contract System of Presidio Supply in Northern New Spain. *Hispanic American Historical Review* 41 (February):31-54.
1961b   The Presidio Supply Problem of New Mexico in the Eighteenth Century. *New Mexico Historical Review* 36 (July):210-29.
1974a   The *Soldado de Cuera:* Stalwart of the Spanish Borderlands. In Oakah L. Jones, Jr., ed. *The Spanish Borderlands: A First Reader.* Los Angeles: Lorrin L. Morrison.
1974b   Rebuilding the Presidio of Santa Fe, 1789-1791. *New Mexico Historical Review* 49 (April):123-42.
1975   *The Presidio: Bastion of the Spanish Borderlands.* Norman: University of Oklahoma Press.

Moquin, Wayne
1971   Editor. *Documentary History of the Mexican Americans.* New York: Praeger Publishers.

Moran, Theodore H.
1974   *Multinational Corporations and the Politics of Dependence: Copper in Chile.* Princeton: Princeton University Press.

Morelos, José B., and Lerner, S.
1970   Proyecciones de la población total y de la población activa de México por regiones, 1960-1985. *Demografía y Economía* 4 (no. 3):349-63.

Moreno, Humberto E.
1974   A Different Kind of Good Neighbor Policy. *Drug Enforcement* 1 (Fall):14-18.

Moreno, Steve
1970   Problems Related to Present Testing Instruments. *El Grito* 3 (Spring):25-29.

Morfi, Juan Agustín
1935   *History of Texas, 1673-1779.* Translated by Carlos E. Casteñada. Albuquerque: Quivira Society.
1977   *Father Juan Agustín de Morfi's Account of Disorders in New Mexico.* Edited and translated by Marc Simmons. Isleta Pueblo, N.Mex.: Historical Society of New Mexico.

Morgan, Dale L.
1948   The Administration of Indian Affairs in Utah, 1851-1858. *Pacific Historical Review* 17 (November):385-92.
1953   *Jedediah Smith and the Opening of the West.* Indianapolis: Bobbs-Merrill Co.

———, and Hammond, George P.
1963   *A Guide to the Manuscript Collections of the Bancroft Library, Vol. 1: Pacific and Western Manuscripts (Except California).* Berkeley: University of California Press.

Morgan, Willard D.
1929   Through Penitente Land with a Leica Camera. *Photo-Era* 62 (February):65-73.

Moriarty, James R.
1973   Federal Indian Reservations in San Diego County. *American Indian Culture Center Journal* 4 (no. 2):13-25.

Mörner, Magnus
1965   Editor. *The Expulsion of the Jesuits from Latin America.* New York: Alfred A. Knopf.

1966   The History of Race Relations in Latin America: Some Comments on the State of Research. *Latin American Research Review* 1 (Spring):17-44.

1967   *Race Mixture in the History of Latin America.* Boston: Little, Brown & Co.

1970a   Editor. *Race and Class in Latin America.* New York: Columbia University Press.

1970b   A Comparative Study of Tenant Labor in Parts of Europe, Africa and Latin America, 1700-1900: A Preliminary Report of a Research Project in Social History. *Latin American Research Review* 5 (Summer):3-15.

Morrill, Claire
1973   *A Taos Mosaic.* Albuquerque: University of New Mexico Press.

Morris, John W.
1970   *The Southwestern United States.* New York: D. Van Nostrand Co.

Morris, Samuel B.
1947   The Colorado River: The Southwest's Greatest Natural Resource. *Journal of the American Water Works Association* 39 (October):945-67.

Moser, Edward
1963   Seri Bands. *Kiva* 28 (no. 3):23-37.
1968   Two Seri Myths. *Tlalocan* 4 (no. 2):157-60.

Mosino Aleman, P. A.
1964   Surface Weather and Upper-Air Flow Patterns in Mexico. *Geofisica Internacional, Technical Conference on Hurricanes and Tropical Meteorology* 4:117-68.

——, and Garcia, Enriqueta
1974   The Climate of Mexico. In R. A. Bryson and F. K. Hare, eds. *Climates of North America,* vol. 11 of *World Survey of Climatology,* pp. 345-404. Amsterdam: Elsevier Scientific Publishing Co.

Mosk, Sanford A.
1942   The Influence of Tradition on Agriculture in New Mexico. *Journal of Economic History* 2 (December, Supplement):34-51.

Motten, Clement J.
1970   *Mexican Silver and the Enlightenment.* Philadelphia: University of Pennsylvania Press.

Mounce, Virginia N.
1979   *An Archivists Guide to the Catholic Church in Mexico.* Palo Alto: R & E Research Associates.

Moustafa, A. Taher, and Weiss, Gertrud
1968   *Health Status and Practices of Mexican Americans.* Mexican-American Study Project Advance Report no. 11. Los Angeles: UCLA.

Mower, A. Glenn, Jr.
1972   The American Convention on Human Rights: Will It Be Effective? *Orbis* 15:1147-72.

Mowry, George
1951   *The California Progressives.* Berkeley: University of California Press.

Moxon, Richard W.
1974   Offshore Production in the Less-developed Countries: A Case study of Multinationals in the Electronics Industry. *New York University, Graduate School of Business Administration, Institute of Finance, Bulletin,* nos. 98-99 (July).

Mueller, Clark Dean
1976   Decision-Making in Mexico: The Politics of Population Policy Formation. Ph.D. dissertation, University of Utah.

Mueller, Jerry E.
1975   *Restless River: International Law and the Behavior of the Rio Grande.* El Paso: Texas Western Press.

Muir, Andrew Forest
1950   The Free Negro in Jefferson and Orange Counties, Texas. *Journal of Negro History* 35 (July):183-206.

Muller, Cornelius H.
1937   Plants as Indicators of Climate in Northeast Mexico. *American Midland Naturalist* 18 (November):986-1000.

1939   Relations of the Vegetation and Climatic Types in Nuevo Leon, Mexico. *American Midland Naturalist* 21 (May):687-729.

1947   Vegetation and Climate of Coahuila, Mexico. *Madroño* 9:33-57.

Müller, Ronald
1973   The Multinational Corporation and the Underdevelopment of the Third World. In Charles K. Wilbur, ed. *The Political Economy of Development and Underdevelopment.* New York: Random House.

Mullerried, F. K. G.
1934   Sobre artefactos de piedra en la porción oriental del estado de Coahuila. *Annales del Museo Nacional de Arqueología, Historia y Etnografía* 2:205-19.

Mumme, Stephen P.
1978   Mexican Politics and the Prospects for Emigration Policy: A Policy Perspective. *Inter-American Economic Affairs* 32 (Summer):67-94.

Munch, Francis J.
1969   Villa's Columbus Raid: Practical Politics of German Design? *New Mexico Historical Review* 44 (July):189-214.

Muñoz, Carlos
1970   Toward a Chicano Perspective of Political Analysis. *Aztlán* 1 (Fall):15-26.

1974   Politics and the Chicano: On the Status of the Literature. *Aztlán* 5 (nos. 1 and 2):1-7.

Muñoz, Humberto; de Oliveira, Orlandina; and Stern, Claudio
1979   Internal Migration to Mexico City and Its Impact upon the City's Labor Market. In Fernando Camara and Robert Van Kemper, eds. *Migration Across Frontiers: Mexico and the United States,* pp. 35-64. Albany: State University of New York at Albany, Institute for Mesoamerican Studies.

Munro, Joan A.
1970   Editor. *The Alaska Boundary Dispute.* Toronto: Copp Clark Publishing.

Munsell, Marvin R.
1967   Land and Labor at Salt River: Household Organization in a Changing Economy. Ph.D. dissertation, University of Oregon.

Munz, P. A.
1974   *A Flora of Southern California.* Berkeley: University of California Press.

——, and Keck, D. D.
1973   *A California Flora with Supplement.* Berkeley: University of California Press.

Murdock, George P., and O'Leary, Timothy
1975   *Ethnographic Bibliography of North America.* 4th ed. New Haven: Human Relations Area Files.

Murguía, Edward, and Frisbie, W. Parker
1977   Trends in Mexican American Intermarriage: Recent Findings in Perspective. *Social Science Quarterly* 58 (December):374-89.

Murguía Rosette, José Antonio
1973   Foreign Investment as a Factor in Development. Paper presented to Institute of Latin American Studies Conference, April, at Austin, Texas.

Murillo, Nathan
1971   The Mexican American Family. In Nathaniel N. Wagner and Marsha J. Haug, eds. *Chicanos: Social and Psychological Perspectives,* pp. 97-108. St. Louis: C. V.

Mosby Co.

Murphy, Lawrence R.
1967   The Beubien and Miranda Land Grant, 1841-1846. *New Mexico Historical Review* 42:27-47.
1972   *Frontier Crusader—William F. M. Arny.* Tucson: University of Arizona Press.

Murphy, Penny
1970   A Brief History of Navajo Literacy. In Bernard Spolsky; Agnes Holm; and Penny Murphy, eds. *Analytical Bibliography of Navajo Reading Materials,* pp. 4-25. Washington, D.C.: U.S. Bureau of Indian Affairs.

Murray, Grover E.
1961   *Geology of the Atlantic and Gulf Coastal Plain Province of North America.* New York: Harper & Row.

Muskrat, Joseph
1970   The Need for Cultural Empathy. *School Review* 78-79 (November):72-75.

Musto, David F.
1973   *The American Disease: Origins of Narcotics Control.* New Haven: Yale University Press.
1974   American Reaction to International Narcotics Traffic. Paper presented to the National Academy of Science, March, at Mexico City.

Myers, John
1948   *The Alamo.* Lincoln: University of Nebraska Press.

Myrdal, Gunnar
1944   *An American Dilemma: The Negro Problem and Modern Democracy.* New York: Harper & Row.

Myres, Sandra L.
1966   The Spanish Cattle Kingdom in the Province of Texas. *Texana* 4 (Fall):233-46.
1969   *The Ranch in Spanish Texas, 1691-1800.* El Paso: Texas Western Press.

Myrick, David F.
1968   A Brief Survey of the Histories of Pioneer Arizona Railroads. Golden, Colo.: Colorado Railroad Museum.
1970   *New Mexico's Railroads.* Golden, Colo.: Colorado Railroad Museum.

Nabakov, Peter
1969   *Tijerina and the Courthouse Raid.* Albuquerque: University of New Mexico Press.

Nabhan, Gary Paul, and Sheridan, Thomas Edward
1977   Living Fencerows of the Rio San Miguel, Sonora, Mexico: Traditional Technology for Floodplain Management. *Human Ecology* 5 (June):97-111.

Nadeau, Remi
1950   *The Water Seekers.* Garden City, N.Y.: Doubleday & Co.
1963   *California, the New Society.* New York: David McKay Co.

Nagata, Shuichi
1970   *Modern Transformations of Moenkopi Pueblo.* Studies in Anthropology, no. 6. Champaign: University of Illinois.

Nagel, John S.
1978   Mexico's Population Policy Turnaround. *Population Bulletin* 33:2-39.

Nall, Frank C., II
1959   Levels of Aspiration of Mexican-Americans in El Paso Schools. Ph.D. dissertation, Michigan State University.
1962   Role Expectations: A Cross-cultural Study. *Rural Sociology* 27 (March):28-41.
——, and Speilberg, Joseph
1967   Social and Cultural Factors in Responses of Mexican-Americans to Medical Treatment. *Journal of Health and Social Behavior* 8 (December):299-308.

Nalven, Joseph
1979   The Transfer of Technology from a Developed to a Less Developed Country: A Look at Computer Utilization Along the U.S.-Mexican Border. Paper presented to Urban and Regional Information Association, August, at San Diego, California.

Nance, Joseph Milton
1962   *After San Jacinto: The Texas-Mexican Frontier, 1836-1841.* Austin: University of Texas Press.
1965   *Attack and Counterattack: The Texas-Mexican Frontier, 1842.* Austin: University of Texas Press.

Nasatir, Abraham P.
1945   *French Activities in California: An Archival Calendar-Guide.* Stanford: Stanford University Press.
1965   The Shifting Borderlands. *Pacific Historical Review* 34 (February):1-20.

Nash, Douglas
1970   Tribal Control of Extradition from Reservations. *Natural Resources Journal* 10 (no. 3):626-34.
1971   Remedy for a Breach of the Government-Indian Trust Duties. *New Mexico Law Review* 1 (January):321-34.

Nash, Gary B.
1974   *Red, White and Black: The Peoples of Early America.* Englewood Cliffs, N.J.: Prentice-Hall.

Nash, Gerald D.
1964   *State Government and Economic Development: A History of Administrative Policies in California, 1849-1933.* Berkeley: University of California Press.
1973   *The American West in the Twentieth Century: A Short History of an Urban Oasis.* Englewood Cliffs, N.J.: Prentice-Hall.

Nathan, Robert R., et al.
1968   See E.D.A., 1968. Unauthored Journal Articles.

Nava, Julian, and Barger, Bob
1976   *California: Five Centuries of Cultural Contrasts.* Beverly Hills: Glencoe Press.

Navarrete, Ifigenia M. de
1967   Income Distribution in Mexico. In Tom B. Davis, ed. *Mexico's Recent Economic Growth: The Mexican View,* pp. 133-71. Austin: University of Texas Press.

Navarro García, Luis
1964   *Don José de Gálvez y la comandancia general de las provincias internas del norte de Nueva España.* Sevilla: Escuela de Estudios Hispanoamericanos.

Needleman, Carolyn, and Needleman, Martin
1969   Who Rules Mexico? *Journal of Politics* 31 (no. 4):1011-34.

Needler, Martin
1971   *Politics and Society in Mexico.* Albuquerque: University of New Mexico Press.

Neighbor, Howard D.
1976   Dilution of the Chicano Vote in El Paso. Paper presented to Western Social Science Association, April, at Tempe, Arizona.
1977   The Case Against Nonpartisanship: A Challenge from the Courts. *National Civic Review* 66 (October):447-52.

Neighbours, Kenneth F.
1974   *Apache Ethnohistory: Government, Land and Indian Policies Relative to Lipan, Mescalero and Tigua Indians.* New York: Garland Publishing.

Nelson, E.
1975   Editor. *Pablo Cruz and the American Dream. The Experiences of an Undocumented Immigrant from Mexico.* Salt Lake City: Peregrine Smith.

Nelson, Eugene
1968   *Huelga: The First Hundred Days of the Great Delano Grape Strike.* Delano, Calif.: Farmworkers Press.

Nelson, Howard J.
1963   Townscapes of Mexico: An Example of the Regional Variation of Townscapes. *Economic Geography* 39 (January):74-83.
1977   The Two Pueblos of Los Angeles: Agricultural Village and Embryo Town. *Southern California Quarterly* 59 (Spring):1-11.

Nelson, Jack C., et al.
1973   The Effects of Water Resources Development on Es-

tuarine Environments (Texas Gulf Coast). *Water Resources Bulletin* 9 (December):1249-57.

Nelson, Jean W.
1974   *Mode of Life and Aboriginal Tribal Lands of the Jicarilla Apache.* New York: Garland Publishing, Stanford Research Institute.

Nelson, Lowry
1952   *The Mormon Village: A Pattern and Technique of Land Settlement.* Salt Lake City: University of Utah Press.

Nelson, Michael C., and Booke, Bradley L.
1977   *The Winters Doctrine: Seventy Years of Application of Reserved Water Rights to Indian Reservations.* Arid Lands Resource Paper no. 9. Tucson: University of Arizona.

Neumann, David L.
1931   Our Architectural Follies. *New Mexico Quarterly* 1:211-17.

Neumann, Joseph
1969   *Révoltes des Indiens Tarahumars, 1626-1724.* Travaux & Mémoires de l'Institut des Hautes Etudes de l'Amérique Latine 24. Paris: Université de Paris.

Newcomb, Franc J., and Reichard, Gladys A.
1975   *Sandpaintings of the Navajo Shooting Chant.* New York: Dover Publishing Co. Originally published in 1937.

Newcomb, Rexford
1973   *The Franciscan Mission Architecture of Alta California.* New York: Dover Publications. Originally published in 1916.

Newcomb, William W.
1961   *The Indians of Texas: From Prehistoric to Modern Times.* Austin: University of Texas Press.

Newhall, Nancy
1962   Sanctuary in Adobe. *American Heritage* 13 (April):68-75.

Newton, Horace E.
1954   *Mexican Illegal Immigration into California, Principally Since 1945.* San Francisco: R & E Research Associates, 1973.

Nichol, A. A.
1952   *The Natural Vegetation of Arizona.* Bulletin no. 127. Tucson: University of Arizona, Agricultural Experiment Station.

Nickeson, Steve
1974   The Political Economics of Arizona Water. *American Indian Law Newsletter,* September 27, pp. 174-78.

Nicoli, José P.
1885   El estado de Sonora—yaquis y mayos—estudio historico. 2d ed. Mexico City: Imprenta de Francisco Díaz de León.

Nimmo, Dan, and McCleskey, Clifton
1969   Impact of the Poll Tax on Voter Participation: The Houston Metropolitan Area in 1966. *Journal of Politics* 31 (August):682-99.

Nimmo, Dan, and Oden, William E.
1971   *The Texas Political System.* Englewood Cliffs, N.J.: Prentice-Hall.

Nims, Amy Elizabeth
1941   Chinese Life in San Antonio. Master's thesis, Southwest Texas State University.

Niswander, Jerry D.; Brown, Kenneth S.; Iba, Barbara Y.; Leyshon, W. C.; and Workman, Peter L.
1970   Population Studies on Southwestern Indian Tribes. I: History, Culture and Genetics of the Pápago. *American Journal of Human Genetics* 22:7-23.

Niswander, Jerry D., and Workman, Peter L.
1970   Population Studies in Southwestern Indian Tribes. II: Local Genetic Differentiation in the Pápago. *American Journal of Human Genetics* 22:24-49.

Noggle, Burl
1959   Anglo Observers of the Southwest Borderland, 1825-1890: The Rise of a Concept. *Arizona and the West* 1 (Summer):105-31.

Nolasco A., Margarita
1965   Los Pápagos, habitantes del desierto. *Anales del Instituto Nacional de Antropología e Historia* 45.
1967   Los Seris, desierto y mar. *Anales del Instituto Nacional de Antropología e Historia* 18:125-94.
1969   *Notas para la antropología social del noroeste de México.* Departamento de Investigaciones Antropológicas Publicaciones 23. Mexico City: Instituto Nacional de Antropología e Historia.

Norquest, Carrol
1972   *Rio Grande Wetbacks: Mexican Migrant Workers.* Albuquerque: University of New Mexico Press.

Norris, Robert M., and Webb, Robert W.
1976   *Geology of California.* New York: John Wiley & Sons.

North, A. W.
1908   The Native Tribes of Lower California. *American Anthropologist* 10:236-50.

North, David S.
1970   *The Border Crossers: People Who Live in Mexico and Work in the United States.* Washington, D.C.: U.S. Department of Labor, Manpower Administration/Trans-Century Corporation.
1971   *Alien Workers: A Study of the Labor Certification Program.* Washington, D.C.: Trans-Century Corporation.
1975   Green Light for Green Cards. *Texas Observer* 47 (January 17):9.
———, and Houstoun, Marion F.
1976a   *Illegal Aliens: Their Characteristics and Role in the U.S. Labor Market: An Exploratory Study.* Washington, D.C.: U.S. Department of Labor/Linton & Company.
1976b   A Summary of Recent Data on and Some of the Policy Implications of Illegal Immigration. In *Illegal Aliens: An Assessment of the Issues,* pp. 36-51. Washington, D.C.: National Council on Employment Policy.
———, and LeBel, Allen
1978   *Manpower and Immigration Policies in the United States.* Special Report no. 20. Washington, D.C.: National Commission for Manpower Policy.

North, Jeannette H., and Grodsky, Susan J.
1979   Compilers. *Immigration Literature: Abstracts of Demographic, Economic, and Policy Studies.* Washington, D.C.: U.S. Department of Justice, Immigration and Naturalization Service.

Northcott, Kaye
1977   All Roads Lead from Roma. *Texas Monthly* 5 (April): 82-87, 100-88.
1978   The Enemy Within. *Texas Monthly* 6 (September):164-68.

Northrup, Stuart
1959   *Minerals of New Mexico.* Albuquerque: University of New Mexico Press.
1975   *Turquoise and Spanish Mines in New Mexico.* Albuquerque: University of New Mexico Press.

Nostrand, Richard L.
1970   The Hispanic-American Borderland: Delimitation of an American Culture Region. *Annals, Association of American Geographers* 60 (December):638-61.
1973   "Mexican American" and "Chicano": Emerging Terms for a People Coming of Age. *Pacific Historical Review* 42 (August):389-406.
1974   Border Communities in a Changing Borderland Context. Paper presented to Association of American Geographers, April, at Seattle, Washington.
1975   Mexican Americans Circa 1850. *Annals, Association of American Geographers* 65 (September):378-90.
1976   *Los Chicanos: Geografía histórica general.* Mexico City: SepSetentas 306.
1977   The Borderlands in Perspective. *Proceedings, Conference of Latin Americanist Geographers* 6:9-28.
1980   The Hispano Homeland in 1900. *Annals, Association of American Geographers* 70:382-96.

1981   El Cerrito Revisited. Paper presented to Association of American Geographers, April, in Los Angeles, California.

Nowell, Charles E.
1962   Arrellano versus Urdaneta. *Pacific Historical Review* 31 (May):111-20.

Nuñez, Theron R.
1963   Cultural Discontinuity and Conflict in a Mexican Village. Ph.D. dissertation, University of California, Berkeley.

Nunley, J. P.
1971*a*   Archaeological Interpretation and the Particularistic Model: The Coahuiltecan Case. *Plains Anthropologist* 16 (no. 54, pt. 1):302-10.

1971*b*   Sociocultural Units of the Southwestern Texas Archaic: An Analytic Approach. Ph.D. dissertation, Southern Methodist University.

1975   Report of Archaeological Survey Activities, 1975. In R. E. W. Adams, assembler. *Archaeology and Ethnohistory of the Gateway Area, Middle Rio Grande of Texas.* Report to the National Endowment for the Humanities. San Antonio: University of Texas at San Antonio.

1976   Report on the Second Season's Survey of Archeological Resources in the Vicinity About Guerrero, Coahuila, Mexico. In R. E. W. Adams, assembler. *The Archaeology and Ethnohistory of the Gateway Area: Middle Rio Grande of Texas.* Report to the National Endowment for the Humanities. San Antonio: University of Texas at San Antonio.

Nunley, J. P., and Hester, T. R.
1975   *An Assessment of Archaeological Resources in Portions of Starr County, Texas.* Report no. 7. San Antonio: University of Texas at San Antonio, Center for Archaeological Research.

Nuttall, Donald A.
1972   The Gobernantes of Spanish Upper California: A Profile. *California Historical Society Quarterly* 51 (Fall):253-80.

Oakeshott, Gordon B.
1971   *California's Changing Landscapes.* New York: McGraw-Hill.

Oberg, Kalervo
1940   Cultural Factors and Land-Use Planning in Cuba Valley, New Mexico. *Rural Sociology* 5 (December):438-48.

Ocampo, Manuel
1950   Historia de la misión de la Tarahumara, 1900-1950. Mexico City: Editorial Buena Prensa.

O'Dea, Thomas F.
1975   *The Mormons.* Chicago: University of Chicago Press.

Officer, James E.
1956   *Indians in School: A Study of the Development of Educational Facilities for Arizona Indians.* Tucson: University of Arizona, Bureau of Ethnic Research.

1964   Sodalities and Systemic Linkage: The Joining Habits of Urban Mexican-Americans. Ph.D. dissertation, University of Arizona.

Ogle, Ralph H.
1940   *Federal Control of the Western Apaches, 1848-86.* Vol. 9. Albuquerque: New Mexico Historical Society.

Ojeda, Mario
1976   *Alcances y límites de la política exterior de México.* Mexico City: El Colegio de México.

Olmstead, Frederick L.
1904   *A Journey in the Seaboard Slave States in the Years 1853-54 with Remarks on Their Economy.* New York: G. P. Putnam's Sons.

Olson, Clarence E.
1940   Forests in the Arizona Desert. *Journal of Forestry* 38 (December):956-59.

Olson, D. H., and Dahl, Nancy
1975   *Inventory of Marriage and Family Literature: 1973-1974.* Vol. 3. St. Paul: Family Social Sciences.

1977   *Inventory of Marriage and Family Literature: 1975-1976.* Vol. 4. St. Paul: Family Social Sciences.

Olson, T. W.
1972   Indian-State Jurisdiction over Real Estate Development on Tribal Lands. *New Mexico Law Review* 2 (no. 1): 81-90.

Onís, José de
1976   Editor. *The Hispanic Contribution to the State of Colorado.* Boulder, Colo.: Westview Press.

Onorato, William T.
1968   Apportionment of an International Common Petroleum Deposit. *International and Comparative Law Quarterly* 17 (Winter):85-102.

Opler, Morris E.
1969   *Apache Odyssey: A Journey Between Two Worlds.* New York: Holt, Rinehart & Winston.

1974   *Lipan and Mescalero Apache in Texas.* New York: Garland Publishing, University of Oklahoma.

Oppenheimer, Alan J.
1974   *An Ethnological Study of Tortugas, New Mexico.* New York: Garland Publishing, University of New Mexico.

Ordoñez, Ezequiel
1936   Principal Physiographic Provinces of Mexico. *Bulletin of the American Association of Petroleum Geologists* 20 (October):1277-1307.

1941   Las provincias fisiográficas de México. *Revista Geográfica, Instituto Panamericano de Geografía e Historia* 1:133-81.

O'Reilly, C., and Roberts, K.
1973   Job Satisfaction Among Whites and Nonwhites: A Cross Cultural Approach. *Journal of Applied Psychology* 57: 295-99.

Ornstein, Jacob
1970   Sociolinguistics and New Perspectives in the Study of Southwest Spanish. In Ralph W. Ewton, Jr., and Jacob Ornstein, eds. *Studies in Language and Linguistics,* pp. 127-84. El Paso: Texas Western Press.

1971   Sociolinguistic Research on Language Diversity in the American Southwest and Its Educational Implications. *Modern Language Journal* 55:223-29.

1973   Toward an Inventory of Interdisciplinary Tasks in Research on U.S. Southwest Bilingualism/Biculturalism. In Paul R. Turner, ed. *Bilingualism in the Southwest,* pp. 321-39. Tucson: University of Arizona Press.

1975   Notes on a Diachronic View of the Development of Sociolinguistic Practice and Theory in the American Southwest. *Journal of the Linguistic Association of the Southwest* 1 (August):5-21.

Ortega, Frank
1971   Special Education Placement and Mexican Americans. *El Grito* 4 (Summer):29-35.

Ortiz, Alfonso
1965   Editor. Dual Organization as an Operational Concept in the Pueblo Southwest. *Ethnology* 4:389-96.

1969   *The Tewa World.* Chicago: University of Chicago Press.

1972   *New Perspectives on the Pueblos.* Albuquerque: University of New Mexico Press.

1979   *Southwest.* Handbook of North American Indians Series, vol. 9. Washington, D.C.: Smithsonian Institution.

Ortiz, C. A.
1971   Evaluación del programa de vacunación con BCG en Ciudad Juárez, Chihuahua, 1970. *Salud Pública en México* 13:693-99.

Ortiz, Leroy I.
1975   A Sociolinguistic Study of Language Maintenance in the Northern New Mexico Community of Arroyo Seco. Ph.D. dissertation, University of New Mexico.

Orton, Robert B.
1964   *The Climate of Texas and the Adjacent Gulf Waters.* Washington, D.C.: U.S. Department of Commerce, Weather Bureau.

Osborne, Douglas, and Hayes, Alden C.
1938   Some Archeological Notes from Southern Hidalgo Coun-

ty, New Mexico. *New Mexico Anthropologist* 3 (2).

Osborne, James E.
1973   Economic Effects of an Exhaustible Irrigation Water Supply: Texas High Plains. *Southern Journal of Agricultural Economics* 5:135-39.

Osborne, L.; Moriarity, T.; Spence, S.; and Almond, K.
1967   *Texas Border Architecture: Eagle Pass, Texas, and Guerrero, Coahuila, Mexico.* Austin: University of Texas, School of Architecture.

Ostrom, Vincent
1953   *Water and Politics: A Study of Water Policies and Administration in the Development of Los Angeles.* Los Angeles: Haynes Foundation.

Otero, Luis Leñero. See Leñero Otero, Luis

Otero, Miguel Antonio
1935   *My Life on the Frontier, 1864-1882.* 2 vols. New York: Press of the Pioneers.

Othón de Mendizabal, Miguel. See also Mendizabal, Miguel O. de
1968   El origin historical de nuestra clases medias. In Ensayos sobre las clases en México, pp. 9-22. Mexico City: Editorial Nuestro Tiempo.

Owen, Roger C.
1958   Easter Ceremonies Among Opata Descendants of Northern Sonora, Mexico. *Kiva,* vol 23, no. 4.

1959   *Marobavi: A Study of an Assimilated Group in Northern Sonora.* Anthropological Papers, no. 3. Tucson: University of Arizona.

1962   The Indians of Santa Catarina, Baja California, Mexico: Concepts of Disease and Curing. Ph.D. dissertation, University of California, Los Angeles.

1963*a*   Indians and Revolution: The 1911 Invasion of Baja California, Mexico. *Ethnohistory* 10:373-95.

1963*b*   The Use of Plants and Non-magical Techniques in Curing Illness Among the Paipai, Santa Catarina, Baja California, Mexico. *América Indígena* 23:319-44.

1965   The Patrilocal Band: A Linguistically and Culturally Hybrid Social Unit. *American Anthropologist* 67:675-90.

Oyarzabal-Tamargo, Francisco, and Young, Robert A.
1978   International External Diseconomies: The Colorado River Salinity Problem in Mexico. *Natural Resources Journal* 18 (January):77-90.

Padfield, Harland; Hemingway, Peter; and Greenfield, Philip
1966-67 The Pima-Pápago Educational Population: A Census and Analysis. *Journal of American Indian Education* 6 (no. 1):1-24.

Padfield, Harland, and Martin, William E.
1965   *Farmers, Workers and Machines: Technological and Social Change in Farm Industries of Arizona.* Tucson: University of Arizona Press.

Padgett, L. Vincent
1966   *The Mexican Political System.* Boston: Houghton Mifflin Co.

Padilla, Amado, and Lindholm, Kathryn
1976   Acquisition of Bilingualism: An Analysis of the Linguistic Structures of Spanish/English Speaking Children. In Gary D. Keller et al., eds. *Bilingualism in the Bicentennial and Beyond.* New York: Bilingual Press/Editorial Bilingue.

Padilla, Fernando
1974   Socialization of Chicano Judges and Attorneys. *Aztlán* 5 (nos. 1 and 2):261-94.

——, and Ramírez, Carlos B.
1974   Patterns of Chicano Representation in California, Colorado and New Mexico. *Aztlán* 5 (nos. 1 and 2):189-233.

Page, Gordon B.
1937   Navajo House Types. *Museum Notes, Museum of Northern Arizona* 9 (March):47-49.

Pailes, R. A., and Whitecotton, Joseph W.
1979   The Greater Southwest and the Mesoamerican "World" System: An Exploratory Model of Frontier Relationships.

In W. W. Savage, Jr., and S. I. Thompson, eds. *The Frontier: Comparative Studies,* pp. 105-21. Norman: University of Oklahoma Press.

Palacios, Fausto E., and Montiel, Guillermo
1967   Industrialization del estado de Baja California. Mexico City: Banco de Comercio.

Palloni, Alberto
1978   Application of an Indirect Technique to Study Group Differentials in Infant Mortality. In Frank D. Bean and W. Parker Frisbee, eds. *The Demography of Racial and Ethnic Groups.* New York: Academic Press.

Palmer, Colin A.
1970   Negro Slavery in Mexico, 1570-1650. Ph.D. dissertation, University of Wisconsin, Madison.

Palmore, Glenn L., et al.
1974   *The Ciudad Juárez Plan for Comprehensive Socio-Economic Development: A Model for Northern Mexico Border Cities.* El Paso: University of Texas at El Paso, Bureau of Business and Economic Research.

Pandey, Triloki Nath
1968   Tribal Council Elections in a Southwestern Pueblo. *Ethnology* 7 (January):71-85.

Paredes, Américo
1958   *"With His Pistol in His Hand." A Border Ballad and Its Hero.* Austin: University of Texas Press.

1961   On *Gringo, Greaser,* and other Neighborly Names. In Mody C. Boatright et al., eds. *Singers and Storytellers,* pp. 285-90. Dallas: Southern Methodist University Press.

Parish, William J.
1961   *The Charles Ilfeld Company: A Study of the Rise and Decline of Mercantile Capitalism in New Mexico.* Cambridge: Harvard University Press.

Park, Joseph F.
1961   The Apaches in Mexico-American Relations, 1848-1861. *Arizona and the West* 3 (Summer):129-48.

1962   Spanish Indian Policy in Northern Mexico, 1765-1810. *Arizona and the West* 4 (Winter):325-44.

Parker, Margaret T.
1948   Tucson: City of Sunshine. *Economic Geography* 24 (April):79-113.

Parmee, Edward A.
1968   *Formal Education and Culture Change: A Modern Apache Indian Community and Government Education Programs.* Tucson: University of Arizona Press.

Parra, Manuel Germán, and Jiménez Moreno, Wigberto
1954   *Bibliografía indigenista de México y Centroamérica, 1850-1950.* Indigenista Memorias, vol. 4. Mexico City: Instituto Nacional.

Parry, John H.
1972   Plural Society in the Southwest: A Historical Comment. In Edward H. Spicer and Raymond H. Thompson, eds. *Plural Society in the Southwest,* pp. 299-320. New York: Interbook.

Parsons, Edmond Morris
1967   The Fredonian Rebellion. *Texana* 5 (Spring):11-52.

Parsons, Elsie Clews
1936   *Mitla: Town of the Souls and Other Zapoteco-speaking Peoples of Oaxaca, Mexico.* Chicago: University of Chicago, Ethnological Series.

1962   Isleta Paintings. In *Bureau of American Ethnology Bulletin no. 181.* Washington, D.C.: Smithsonian Institution.

——, and Beals, Ralph L.
1934   The Sacred Clowns of the Pueblo and Mayo-Yaqui Indians. *American Anthropologist* 36 (no. 4):491-514.

——, and Goldfrank, Esther S.
1970   *Isleta Paintings.* Washington, D.C.: Smithsonian Institution Press.

Parsons, Theodore W.
1965   Ethnic Cleavage in California Schools. Ph.D. disserta-

tion, Stanford University.

Paso y Troncoso, Francisco del
1905   *Las guerras con las tribus yaqui y mayo del estado de Sonora.* Mexico City: Tipografía del Departamento de Estado Mayor.

Passel, J.
1976   Provisional Evaluation of the 1970 Census Count of American Indians. *Demography* 13:397-409.

Passin, Herbert
1942a   Sorcery as a Phase of Tarahumara Economic Relations. *Man* 42:11-15.
1942b   Tarahumara Prevarication: A Problem in Field Method. *American Anthropologist* 44:235-47.
1943   The Place of Kinship in Tarahumara Social Organization. *Acta Americana* 1:361-89, 469-95.

Patella, Victoria M., and Kuvlesky, William P.
1975   *Bilingual Patterns of Nonmetropolitan Mexican American Youth: Variations by Social Context, Language Use, and Historical Change.* Bulletin. College Station: Texas A&M University.

Patrick, Elizabeth N.
1976   Land Grants During the Administration of Spanish Colonial Governor Pedro Fermín de Mendinueta. *New Mexico Historical Review* 51:5-18.

Patten, Roderick B.
1970   Miranda's Inspection of Los Almagres: His Journal, Report, and Petition. *Southwestern Historical Quarterly* 74 (October):223-54.

Paul, Rodman
1947   *California Gold: The Beginning of Mining in the Far West.* Lincoln: University of Nebraska Press.
1974   The Beginning of Agriculture: Innovation Versus Continuity. In George H. Knoles, ed. *Essays and Assays: California History Reappraised.* San Francisco: California Historical Society.

Paullin, Charles O.
1932   *Atlas of the Historical Geography of the United States.* Edited by John K. Wright. Washington, D.C.: Carnegie Institution and American Geographical Society.

Paynich, Mary Louise
1964   Cultural Barriers to Nurse Communication. *American Journal of Nursing* 64 (February):87-90.

Paz, Octavio
1961   *The Labyrinth of Solitude: Life and Thought in Mexico.* New York: Random House. Reprinted in 1962 by Grove Press, New York.
1972   *The Other Mexico: Critique of the Pyramid.* New York: Grove Press.

Peabody, Etta B.
1967   Efforts of the South to Import Chinese Coolies, 1865-1870. Master's thesis, Baylor University.

Pearce, J. E., and Jackson, A. T.
1933   *A Prehistoric Rock Shelter in Val Verde County, Texas.* University of Texas Anthropological Papers, no. 2.

Pearce, Roy Harvey
1953   *The Savages of America: A Study of the Indian and the Idea of Civilization.* Baltimore: Johns Hopkins University Press.

Pearce, T. M.
1965   Editor. *New Mexico Place Names, a Geographical Dictionary.* Albuquerque: University of New Mexico Press.

Pearson, G. A.
1937   Conservation and Use of Forests in the Southwest. *Scientific Monthly* 45 (August):150-57.

Pearson, Jim Berry
1961   *The Maxwell Land Grant.* Norman: University of Oklahoma Press.

Peck, Robert F.
1967   A Comparison of the Value System of Mexican and American Youth. *Revista Interamericana de Psicología* 1 (Marzo):41-50.

———, and Díaz-Guerrero, Rogelio
1967   Two Core-Culture Patterns and the Diffusion of Values Across Their Border. *International Journal of Psychology* 2 (no. 4):275-82.

Pederson, Leland R.
1978   Population Change Along the United States-Mexico Border, 1900-1970. Paper presented to the Association of American Geographers, April, at New Orleans, Louisiana.

Peffer, E. Louise
1951   *The Closing of the Public Domain: Disposal and Reservation Policies, 1900-1950.* Stanford: Stanford University Press.

Pellicer de Brody, Olga. See also Brody, Olga Pellicer de
1974   Mexico in the 1970s and Its Relations with the United States. In Julio Cotler and Richard R. Fagen, eds. *Latin America and the United States: The Changing Political Realities,* pp. 314-33. Stanford, Calif.: Stanford University Press.

Peñalosa, Fernando
1963   Class Consciousness and Social Mobility in a Mexican-American Community. Ph.D. dissertation, University of Southern California.
1967   The Changing Mexican-American in Southern California. *Sociology and Social Research* 51 (July):405-17.
1968   Mexican Family Roles. *Journal of Marriage and the Family* 30 (November):680-88.
1969   Education-Income Discrepancies Between Second and Later-Generation Mexican-Americans in the Southwest. *Sociology and Social Research* 53 (July):448-54.

———, and McDonagh, Edward C.
1966   Social Mobility in a Mexican-American Community. *Social Forces* 44 (June):498-505.

Pennington, Campbell W.
1963a   Medicinal Plants Utilized by the Tepehuán of Southern Chihuahua. *América Indígena* 23 (no. 1):31-47.
1963b   *The Tarahumar of Mexico: Their Environment and Material Culture.* Salt Lake City: University of Utah Press.
1969   *The Tepehuán of Chihuahua: Their Material Culture.* Salt Lake City: University of Utah Press.
1980   *The Pima Bajo (Névome) of Central Sonora, Mexico: Volume I. Material Culture.* Salt Lake City: University of Utah Press.

Peón, Máximo
1966   *Como viven los mexicanos en los Estados Unidos.* Mexico City: B. Costa-Amic.

Pérez, Baudelio
1942   Las tribus aborígenes de la región de Ciudad Juárez. *Sociedad Chihuahuense de Estudios Históricos, Boletín* 4:204-207.

Perez, Louis A., Jr.
1975   *Underdevelopment and Dependency: Tourism in the West Indies.* El Paso: University of Texas at El Paso, Center for Inter-American Studies.

Pérez de Ribas, Andrés
1645   *Historia de los triunfos de nuestra Santa Fe entre gentes las más bárbaras y fieras del nuevo orbe.* Madrid: A. de Parades.

Pérez Lizaur, Marisol
1975   *Población y sociedad: cuatro comunidades del Acolhuacan.* Mexico City: Instituto Nacional de Antropología e Historia.

Perkins, Clifford Alan, and Sonnichsen, C. L.
1978   *Border Patrol.* El Paso: Texas Western Press.

Perrigo, Lynn I.
1960   *Texas and Our Spanish Southwest.* Dallas: Banks Upshaw & Co.
1971   *The American Southwest: Its Peoples and Cultures.* New York: Holt, Rinehart & Winston.

Perry, Robert L.
1971   *Galt, U.S.A.: The "American Presence" in a Canadian*

City. Toronto: Maclean-Hunter.

Persons, Billie
1953   Secular Life in the San Antonio Missions. *The Southwestern Historical Quarterly* 62 (July):45-62.

Pesman, M. Walter
1962   *Meet Flora Mexicana: An Easy Way to Recognize Some of the More Frequently Met Plants of Mexico as Seen from the Main Highways.* Globe, Ariz.: Dale S. King, Publisher.

Pesqueira, Fernando
1962   El desarrollo industrial de Sonora y el problema ocupacional. *Revista Mexicana de Sociología* 24 (no. 2): 437-40.
1966   *Bibliografía antropológica de Sonora.* Hermosillo: Ediciones de la Universidad de Sonora.

Peterson, Charles S.
1973   *Take Up Your Mission: Mormon Colonizing Along the Little Colorado River, 1870-1900.* Tucson: University of Arizona Press.

Peterson, Frederick A.
1956   The Kickapoo Indians of Northern Mexico. *Mexican Life* 30:50-54.

Peterson, Susan
1977   *The Living Tradition of Maria Martinez.* Tokyo: Kodansha International.

Petrov, M. P.
1976   *Deserts of the World.* New York: John Wiley & Sons.

Pettibone, Timothy J., and Solís, Enrique, Jr.
1973   Dental Health Care Models of Southwest Cultures. Mimeographed. Las Cruces: New Mexico State University, Educational Research Center.

Peyton, Green
1946   *San Antonio—City in the Sun.* New York: McGraw-Hill.
1948   *America's Heartland: The Southwest.* Norman: University of Oklahoma Press.

Phillips, Robert N.
1967   Los Angeles Spanish: A Descriptive Analysis. Ph.D. dissertation, University of Wisconsin, Madison.

Phillips, Ulrich B.
1929   *Life and Labor in the Old South.* Boston: Little, Brown & Co.

Phippen, Louise
1969   *The Life of a Cowboy: Told through the Drawings, Paintings, and Bronzes of George Phippen.* Tucson: University of Arizona Press.

Picchioni, Egidio
1965   Curanderos y curaciones entre los mayo del noroeste de México. Suplemento Antropológico de la *Revista del Ateneo Paraguayo* 1 (2), Asunción, Paraguay.

Picón-Salas, Mariano
1968   *A Cultural History of Spanish America from Conquest to Independence.* Berkeley: University of California Press.

Pierce, Frank G.
1917   *A Brief History of the Lower Rio Grande Valley.* Menasha, Wis.: George Banta Publishing Co.

Pifer, Joseph
1969   Water Table Decline and Resultant Agricultural Patterns in the Salt River Valley of Arizona. *Journal of Geography* 68 (December):545-49.

Pinckney, Pauline A.
1967   *Painting in Texas: The Nineteenth Century.* Austin: University of Texas Press.

Piore, Michael
1974   The "New Immigration" and the Presumptions of Social Policy. Paper presented to the Industrial Relations Research Association, December.
1975   The Illegals: Restrictions Aren't the Answer. *New Republic,* February 22, pp. 7-8.
1976   Illegal Immigration in the United States: Some Observations and Policy Suggestions. In *Illegal Aliens: An*

Assessment of the Issues, pp. 25-35. Washington, D.C.: National Council on Employment Policy.
1979   *Birds of Passage: Migrant Labor and Industrial Societies.* New York: Cambridge University Press.

Pi-Sunyer, Oriol
1973   *Zamora: Change and Continuity in a Mexican Town.* New York: Holt, Rinehart & Winston.

Pitt, Leonard
1966   *The Decline of the Californios: A Social History of Spanish-speaking Californians, 1848-1890.* Berkeley: University of California Press. See also 1970 edition.

Place, Marion T.
1970   *Comanches and Other Indians of Texas.* New York: Harcourt, Brace and World.

Plancarte, Francisco M.
1954   *El problema indígena Tarahumara.* Memorias, no. 5. Mexico City: Instituto Nacional Indígena.

Platero, Dillon
1970   Let's Do It Ourselves. *School Review* 78-79 (November): 57-58.

Platt, R. S.
1965   The Changing Landscape of the San Fernando Valley Between 1930 and 1964. *California Geographer* 6:59-72.
1958   Assisted by Paula Bücking-Spitta. *A Geographical Study of the Dutch-German Border.* Westfalen: Münster.

Pletcher, David M.
1973   *The Diplomacy of Annexation: Texas, Oregon, and the Mexican War.* Columbia, Mo.: University of Missouri Press.

Poblano, Ralph
1973   *Ghosts in the Barrio: Issues in Bilingual-Bicultural Education.* San Rafael, Calif.: Leswing Press.

Poitras, Guy E.
1973   Welfare Bureaucracy and Clientele Politics in Mexico. *Administrative Science Quarterly* 18 (no. 1):18-25.

Polinard, Jerry L., and Wrinkle, Robert
1979   Hands Across the Border? The Interaction of Undocumented Workers with Mexican-Americans, Public Agencies and the INS. Paper presented to Western Social Science Association, April, at Lake Tahoe.

Pollitt, D. H., and Levine, S. H.
1960   *Migrant Farmworkers in America.* Senate Committee on Labor and Public Welfare. 86 Cong., 2d sess. Washington, D.C.: Government Printing Office.

Polzer, Charles W.
1972   The Franciscan Entrada into Sonora, 1645-1652. *Arizona and the West* 14 (Autumn):253-78.

Pontones Chi, Eduardo
1976   La migración en Mexico. In James W. Wilkie, M. C. Meyer, and E. Menzonde Wilkie, eds. *Contemporary Mexico,* pp. 135-64. Berkeley: University of California Press.

Pool, William C.
1975   *A Historical Atlas of Texas.* Austin: Encino Press.

Poole, Stafford
1965   War by Fire and Blood: The Church and the Chichimecas, 1585. *Americas* 22 (October):115-37.

Popkin, Roy
1968   *Desalination: Water for the World's Future.* New York: Praeger Publishers.

Porter, Clyde; Porter, Mae R.; and Hafen, LeRoy R.
1950   Editors. *Ruxton of the Rockies.* Norman: University of Oklahoma Press.

Porter, Eugene O.
1970   *Lord Beresford and Lady Flo.* El Paso: Texas Western Press.

Porter, Kenneth W.
1951   The Seminole in Mexico, 1850-1861. *Hispanic American Historical Review* 31 (February):1-36.
1952   The Seminole-Negro Indian Scouts, 1870-1881. *South-*

western Historical Quarterly 55 (January):358-77.

1971   *The Negro on the American Frontier.* New York: Arno Press.

Portes, Alejandro

1969   Dilemmas of a Golden Exile: Integration of Cuban Refugees in Milwaukee. *American Sociological Review* 34 (August):505-18.

1974*a*   Return of the Wetback. *Society* 11 (March-April):40-46.

1974*b*   From Assimilation to Ethnic Consciousness: Changing Trends in the Study of Immigration. In M. Harper et al., eds. *Issues in Mental Health and Social Science Studies of Minority Groups.* Washington, D.C.: National Institute of Mental Health.

1978*a*   Why Illegal Migration? A Human Rights Perspective. In A. Said, ed. *Human Rights and World Order,* pp. 79-89. New Brunswick, N.J.: Transaction Books.

1978*b*   Immigration and the International System: Some Characteristics of Recent Mexican Immigrants to the United States. Paper presented at the Society for the Study of Social Problems, September, at San Francisco, California.

1978*c*   Toward a Structural Analysis of Illegal (Undocumented) Immigration. *International Migration Review* 12 (Winter):469-84.

———, and Ross, Adreain A.

1976   Modernization for Emigration: The Medical Brain Drain from Argentina. *Journal of Inter-American Studies and World Affairs* 18 (November):395-422.

Portman, Robert

1979   A Study of Undocumented Mexican Workers on a Texas Ranch. Undergraduate honors thesis, Dartmouth College.

Post, Anita C.

1933   Some Aspects of Arizona Spanish. *Hispania* 16:35-42.

Poston, Dudley L., and Alvírez, David

1973   On the Cost of Being a Mexican American Worker. *Social Science Quarterly* 53 (August):697-709.

Poulter, Virgil L.

1973   A Phonological Study of the (Spanish) Speech of Mexican-American College Students Native to Fort Worth-Dallas. Ph.D. dissertation, Louisiana State University.

Powell, Philip W.

1952   *Soldiers, Indians and Silver: The Northward Advance of New Spain, 1550-1600.* Berkeley: University of California Press.

Prassel, Frank Richard

1972   *The Western Peace Officer: A Legacy of Law and Order.* Norman: University of Oklahoma Press.

Prescott, J. R. V.

1965   *The Geography of Frontiers and Boundaries.* Chicago: Aldine Publishing Co.

Prescott, William H.

1898   *Mexico and the Life of the Conqueror Fernando Cortes.* 2 vols. New York: Peter Fenelon Collier.

1936   *History of the Conquest of Mexico.* New York: Modern Library.

Presley, James

1963   Mexican Views on Rural Education, 1900-1910. *Americas* 20 (July):64-71.

1968   Santa Anna's Invasion of Texas: A Lesson in Command. *Arizona and the West* 10 (Autumn):241-52.

Preston, Richard E.

1965   The Changing Landscape of the San Fernando Valley Between 1930 and 1964. *California Geographer* 6:59-72.

Prewitt, E. R.

1974   Preliminary Archeological Investigations in the Rio Grande Delta of Texas. *Texas Archeological Society Bulletin* 45:55-66.

Price, Glenn W.

1967   *Origins of the War with Mexico: The Polk-Stockton Intrigue.* Austin: University of Texas Press.

Price, John A.

1968   Tijuana: A Study of Symbiosis. *New Mexico Quarterly* 38 (no. 3):8-18.

1969   The Urbanization of Mexico's Northern Border States. Manuscript. U.S. Mexico Border Studies Project, Notre Dame University, Notre Dame, Ind.

1971   International Border Screens and Smuggling. In Ellwyn R. Stoddard, ed. *Prostitution and Illicit Drug Traffic on the U.S.-Mexico Border,* pp. 22-43. Occasional Papers, no. 2. El Paso: Border-State University, Consortium for Latin America.

1973*a*   *Tijuana: Urbanization in a Border Culture.* Notre Dame: University of Notre Dame Press.

1973*b*   Tecate: An Industrial City on the Mexican Border. *Urban Anthropology* 2:35-47.

———, and Smith, H. C.

1971   A Bibliography on the Anthropology of Baja California. *Pacific Coast Archaeological Society Quarterly* 7:39-69.

Price, Judith M., and Price, Thomas J.

1981   Transportation Policy in an International Setting: The Case of El Paso-Ciudad Juárez. Paper presented at the Annual Meeting of the Western Social Science Association, San Diego, Calif., April 23.

1969   Lawyers on the Reservation: Some Implications for the Legal Profession. *Law and the Social Order* 2:161-206.

1973   *Law and the American Indian: Readings, Notes, and Cases.* Indianapolis: Bobbs-Merrill.

Price, Thomas J.

1977   Noncentral Governments as International Actors: A Case Study and Discussion. Paper delivered to American Political Science Association, September, at Washington, D.C.

Prieto, Carlos

1973   *Mining in the New World.* New York: McGraw-Hill.

Prince, L. Bradford

1883   *Historical Sketches of New Mexico.* Kansas City: Ramsey, Millet & Hudson.

1914   *A Concise History of New Mexico.* Cedar Rapids, Iowa: Torch Press.

Probert, Alan

1961   Bartolomé de Medina: The Patio Process and Sixteenth Century Silver Crisis. *Journal of the West* 8 (January) 90-124.

El problema de las drogas en Mexico

1972   *Revista del Instituto National de Neurología* 6.

Procter, Ben H.

1962   *Not Without Honor: The Life of John N. Reagan.* Austin: University of Texas Press.

Prucha, Francis Paul

1977   *A Bibliographical Guide to the History of Indian-White Relations in the United States.* Chicago: University of Chicago Press.

Pulido, Marco Antonio

1965   Dios en Tamaulipas. *Contenido,* January, pp. 90-96.

Purcell, Susan K.

1975   *The Mexican Profit-sharing Decision: Politics in an Authoritarian Regime.*

———, and Purcell, John F. H.

1974   Community Power and Benefits from the Nation: The Case of Mexico. In F. Rabinovitz and F. Trueblood, eds. *Latin American Urban Research,* pp. 49-76. Beverly Hills, Calif.: Sage Publications.

Quaife, Milo Milton

1925   Editor. *The Southwestern Expedition of Zebulon Pike.* Chicago: n.p.

Quam, Alvina

1972   *The Zuñis: Self-Portrayals.* Albuquerque: University of New Mexico Press.

Quesada, Gustavo M., et al.

1974   Editors. Barriers to Medical Care Among Texas Chicanos. Mimeographed. San Antonio: Southwest Medical Sociology Ad Hoc Committee.

Quesada, Gustavo, M., and Heller, Peter L.
1977   Sociocultural Barriers to Medical Care Among Mexican Americans in Texas. *Medical Care* 14 (May):93-101.

Queveda, H. A., and Applegate, Howard G.
1978   Pesticide Residues in Adipose Tissue in the Middle Rio Grande Valley. Paper presented to United States-Mexico Border Health Association, March, at Reynosa, Mexico.

Quinn, Frank
1968   Water Transfers: Must the American West Be Won Again. *Geographical Review* 58 (January):108-32.

Quirarte, Jacinto
1973   *Mexican American Artists.* Austin: University of Texas Press.

Quoyawayma, Polingaysi (Elizabeth White), and Carlson, Vada
1964   *No Turning Back.* Albuquerque: University of New Mexico Press.

Rabeau, E. S., and Rund, Nadine
1971   Cultural and Social Problems in the Delivery of Health Services for Southwest Indians. In M. L. Riedesel, ed. *Health Related Problems in Arid Lands,* pp. 53-58. Tempe: Arizona State University, CODAZR.

Rader, Jesse L.
1947   *South of Forty, from the Mississippi to the Rio Grande: A Bibliography.* Norman: University of Oklahoma Press.

Radosevich, George F., and Sutton, William M.
1972   Legal Problems and Solutions to Surface-Groundwater Management. In Donald D. MacPhail, ed. *The High Plains: Problems of Semi-Arid Environments,* pp. 32-41. Publication no. 15. Ft. Collins: Colorado State University, CODAZR.

Rahn, Perry H.
1967   Sheetfloods, Streamfloods, and the Formation of Pediments. *Annals, Association of American Geographers* 57 (September):593-604.

Raisz, Erwin
1961   A New Landform Map of Mexico. *International Yearbook of Cartography* 1:113-28.
1964   *Landforms of Mexico: Map at Scale 1:3,000,000.* Cambridge, Mass.: Office of Naval Research.

Ramirez, Arnulfo G.
1974   The Spoken English of Spanish-speaking Pupils in a Bilingual and Monolingual School Setting: An Analysis of Syntactic Development. Ph.D. dissertation, Stanford University.

Ramírez, José Fernando
1903   Notas sobre los comances. *Anales de Museo Nacional de México* 1-7:264-73.

Ramírez, Manuel, and Castañeda, Alfredo
1974   *Cultural Democracy: Bicognitive Development and Education.* New York: Academic Press.

Ramírez, Santiago
1959   Some Dynamic Patterns in the Organization of the Mexican Family. *Inter-national Journal of Social Psychiatry* 3:18-21.

———, and Parres, Ramon
1957   *El matrimonio entre los nativos de Zacoalco.* Guadalajara: Planeación y Promoción.
1959   *El mexicano: psicología de sus motivaciones.* Mexico City: Pax-México.

Ramos, Rutilio; Alonso, Isidoro; and Garre, Domingo
1963   *La iglesia en México.* Fribourg, Switzerland: FERES.

Ramos, Samuel
1962   *Profile of Man and Culture in Mexico.* Austin: University of Texas Press.

Ramsdell, Charles William
1910   *Reconstruction in Texas.* New York: Columbia University Press.

Randle, Janice Ann Whitehead
1975   A Bilingual Oral Language Test for Mexican-American Children. Ph.D. dissertation, University of Texas, Austin.

Rands, Robert L.
1974a   *Acoma Land Utilization.* New York: Garland Publishing, University of Southern Illinois.
1974b   *Laguna Land Utilization: An Ethnohistorical Report.* New York: Garland Publishing, University of Southern Illinois.

Ranney, Austin
1962   Editor. *Essays on the Behavioral Study of Politics.* Urbana: University of Illinois Press.

Ranquist, Harold A.
1971   Effects of Changes in Place and Nature of Use of Indian Rights to Water Reserved Under the Winters Doctrine. *Natural Resources Journal* 5 (no. 1):34-41.

Ransom, R. E., and Gilstrap, W. G.
1971   Indians—Civil Jurisdiction in New Mexico—State, Federal and Tribal Courts. *New Mexico Law Review* 1 (January):196-214.

Rathjen, Fred
1961   The Physiography of the Texas Panhandle. *Southwestern Historical Quarterly* 64 (January):315-32.

Raup, Hallock F.
1932a   The German Colonization of Anaheim, California. *University of California Publications in Geography* 6:123-46.
1932b   Land Use and Water Supply Problems in Southern California: The Case of the Perris Valley. *Geographical Review* 22 (April):270-78.
1935   The Italian-Swiss Dairymen of San Luis Obispo County, California. *Yearbook of the Association of Pacific Coast Geographers* 1:3-8.
1936   Land-Use and Water Supply Problems in Southern California: Market Gardens of the Palos Verdes Hills. *Geographical Review* 26 (April):264-69.
1940a   Piedmont Plain Agriculture in Southern California. *Yearbook of the Association of Pacific Coast Geographers* 6:26-31.
1940b   San Bernardino, California: Settlement and Growth of a Pass-Site City. *University of California Publications in Geography* 8:1-64.
1959   Transformation of Southern California to a Cultivated Land. *Annals, Association of American Geographers* 49 (September, Supplement):58-78.

Ray, Verne F.
1974   *Ethnohistorical Analysis of Documents Relating to the Apache Indians of Texas.* New York: Garland Publishing, University of Washington.

Raymond, Rossiter
1872   *Statistics of Mines and Mining in the States and Territories West of the Rocky Mountains.* Washington, D.C.: Government Printing Office.

Read, Benjamin M.
1912   *Illustrated History of New Mexico.* Santa Fe: New Mexican Printing Co.

Read, William R.; Monterroso, Victor M.; and Johnson, Harmon
1969a   *Latin American Church Growth.* Grand Rapids, Mich.: Wm. B. Eerdmans Publishing Co.
1969b   Growth in Latin America. *Church Growth Bulletin* (September):6.

Reavis, Dick J.
1978   *With Documents.* New York: Condor Publishing Co.

Reck, Gregory G.
1978   *In the Shadow of Tlaloc: Life in a Mexican Village.* New York: Penguin Books.

Redfield, Robert
1930   *Tepoztlán: A Mexican Village.* Chicago: University of Chicago Press.
1936   Marriage in a Maya Village. *Mexican Folkways* 7:154-59.

1941 *The Folk Culture of Yucatan.* Chicago: University of Chicago Press.

——, and Villa, Alfonso R.

1934 *Chan Kom: A Maya Village.* Publication no. 448. Washington, D.C.: Carnegie Institution of Washington.

Reed, Erik K.

1956 Types of Village-Plan Layouts in the Southwest. In Gordon R. Willey, ed. *Prehistoric Settlement Patterns in the New World,* pp. 11-17. New York: Wenner-Gren Foundation for Anthropological Research.

Reeve, Frank D.

1937-38 The Federal Indian Policy in New Mexico. *New Mexico Historical Review* 12:218-69, 13:14-62.

1950 Frederick E. Phelps: A Soldier's Memoirs. *New Mexico Historical Review* 25 (July):187-221.

1956 Early Navaho Geography. *New Mexico Historical Review* 31 (October):290-309.

1960 Navaho-Spanish Diplomacy, 1770-1790. *New Mexico Historical Review* 35 (July):200-35.

1961 *History of New Mexico.* New York: Historical Publishing Co.

Reeve, Frank K.

1974 *Navajo Indians.* New York: Garland Publishing, University of New Mexico.

Reeves, C. C., Jr.

1974 An Apollo Photo and the Texas-New Mexico Line. *Photogrammetric Engineering* 40 (April):461-65.

Reeves, Richard W., and Gibson, Lay James

1974 Town Size and Functional Complexity in a Disrupted Landscape. *Yearbook of the Association of Pacific Coast Geographers* 36:71-84.

Reichert, Josh, and Massey, Douglas S.

1979 Migration from a Rural Mexican Town: Research Report. *Intercom* 7 (June-July):6-7.

Reisler, Mark

1976 *By the Sweat of Their Brow: Mexican Immigrant Labor in the United States, 1900-1940.* Westport, Conn.: Greenwood Press.

Reith, John W.

1951 Los Angeles Smog. *Yearbook of the Association of Pacific Coast Geographers* 13:24-32.

Reitsma, Hendrik J.

1972 Areal Differentiation Along the United States-Canada Border. *Tijschrift voor Economische en Sociale Geografie* 62 (1):2-10.

Remy, Caroline

1969 Protestant Churches and Mexican-Americans in South Texas. Paper presented to Rocky Mountain Social Science Association, May, at Lubbock, Texas.

Renaud, Etienne B.

1928 Evolution of Population and Dwelling in the Indian Southwest. *Social Forces* 7 (December):263-70.

Renfro, H. B.; Feray, Dan E.; and King, Philip B.

1973 *Geological Highway Map of Texas: Scale 1:1,750,000.* Tulsa: American Association of Petroleum Geologists.

Renner, Frederic G.

1968 *Charles M. Russell: The Greatest of All Western Artists.* Washington, D.C.: Potomac Corral, the Westerners.

Reno, Philip

1963 *Taos Pueblo.* Denver: Sage Books.

1970 Manpower Planning for Navajo Employment: Training for Jobs in a Surplus-Labor Area. *New Mexico Business* (December):8-16.

Ressler, John Q.

1968 Water-Control on New Spain's Northwest Frontier. *Journal of the West* 7 (January):10-17.

Restrepo, Carlos E.

1975 The Transfer of Management Technology to a Less Developed Country: A Case Study of a Border Industrialization Program in Mexico. Ph.D. dissertation, University of Nebraska, Lincoln.

Reubens, Edwin P.

1978 Aliens, Jobs and Immigration Policy. *Public Interest* 51: 113-34.

Revueltas, José

1969 *El Apando.* Mexico City: Biblioteca Era Narrativa.

Reyna, José Luis, and Weinert, Richard S.

1978 Editors. *Authoritarianism in Mexico.* Philadelphia: Institute for the Study of Human Issues.

Reynolds, C. Lynn

1976 Economic Decision-Making: The Influence of Traditional Hispanic Land Use Attitudes on Acceptance of Innovation. *Social Science Journal* 13 (October):21-34.

Reynolds, Clark W.

1970 *The Mexican Economy: Twentieth-Century Structure and Growth.* New Haven: Yale University Press.

Reynolds, S. E., and Mutz, Philip B.

1974 Water Deliveries Under the Rio Grande Compact. *Natural Resources Journal* 14 (April):201-206.

Rhoads, Edward J. M.

1977 The Chinese in Texas. *Southwestern Historical Quarterly* 81 (July):1-36.

Ricard, Robert

1966 *The Spiritual Conquest of Mexico: An Essay on the Apostolate and the Evangelizing Methods of the Mendicant Orders in New Spain; 1523-1572.* Berkeley: University of California Press.

Richardson, Robert T.

1975 The Coming of Summer in Southern California. *Yearbook of the Association of Pacific Coast Geographers* 37:63-76.

Richardson, Rupert Norval

1933 *The Comanche Barrier to South Plains Settlement: A Century and a Half of Savage Resistance to the Advancing White Frontier.* Glendale: Arthur H. Clark Co.

1958 *Texas: The Lone Star State.* Englewood Cliffs, N.J.: Prentice-Hall.

——, and Rister, Carl C.

1934 *The Greater Southwest: The Economic, Social and Cultural Development of Kansas, Oklahoma, Texas, Utah, Colorado, Nevada, New Mexico, Arizona, and California from the Spanish Conquest to the Twentieth Century.* Glendale: Arthur H. Clark Co.

Richman, Irving B.

1911 *California Under Spain and Mexico, 1535-1847.* Boston: Houghton Mifflin Co.

Rickard, Thomas A.

1907 *Journeys of Observation.* San Francisco: Dewey Publishing.

1932 *A History of American Mining.* New York: McGraw-Hill.

Ridgley, Roberta

1977 Border Cities Search for Regional Solutions. *Planning* 43 (April-May):28-30.

Riedesel, M. L.

1971 Editor. *Health Related Problems in Arid Lands.* Tempe: Arizona State University, CODAZR.

Riegelhaupt-Barkin, Florence

1976 The Influence of English on the Spanish of Bilingual Mexican-American Migrants in Florida. Ph.D. dissertation, State University of New York, Buffalo.

Riley, Carroll L.

1971 Early Spanish-Indian Communication in the Greater Southwest. *New Mexico Historical Review* 46 (October):285-314.

1973 Las Casas and the Benevides Memorial of 1630. *New Mexico Historical Review* 48 (July):209-222.

1978 *Across the Chichimec Sea: Papers in Honor of J. Charles Kelley.* Carbondale: Southern Illinois University Press.

Riley, Robert B.

1969 New Mexico Villages in a Future Landscape. *Landscape* 18 (Winter):3-12.

Rios, Omar G.
1970   The Chronic Mexican-Alien Immigration Offender. *Federal Probation* 34 (September):57-60.

Rippy, J. Fred
1926   *The United States and Mexico.* New York: Alfred A. Knopf.
1931   *The United States and Mexico.* New York: F. S. Crofts.

Rippy, Merrill
1953   Land Tenure and Land Reform in Modern Mexico. *Agricultural History* 27 (April):55-61.

Rischin, Moses
1974   Immigration, Migration and Minorities in California. In George Knoles, ed. *Essays and Assays: California History Reappraised.* San Francisco: California Historical Society.

Rister, Carl Coke
1940   *Border Captives: The Traffic in Prisoners by Southern Plains Indians, 1835-1875.* Norman: University of Oklahoma Press.
1949   *Oil! Titan of the Southwest.* Norman: University of Oklahoma Press.

Ritch, W. G.
1885   *Aztlán: The History, Resources and Attractions of New Mexico.* Boston: D. Lothrop.

Rittenhouse, Jack D.
1961   *New Mexico Civil War Bibliography.* Houston: Stagecoach Press.
1971   *The Santa Fe Trail, a Historical Bibliography.* Albuquerque: University of New Mexico Press.

Rivas Sosa, E.
1973   Función de las industrias maquiladoras en la promoción de polos de desarrollo industrial. Tesis profesional, UNAM, Escuela Nacional de Economía.

Rivera, Diego, and Wolfe, Bertram D.
1934   *Portrait of America.* New York: Covici Friede Publishers.

Rivera, George, Jr.
1972   Social Change in the Barrio: The Chicano Movement in South Texas. *Aztlán* 3 (Fall):205-14.

Rivera, Julius
1963   Markets to the South: A Look at Some Socio Economic Aspects of Sonora. *Arizona Review* 12 (June):1-12.

Rizenthaler, Robert E., and Peterson, Frederick A.
1954   Courtship Whistling of the Mexican Kickapoo Indians. *American Anthropologist* 54 (6, part 1):1088-89.
1955   The Kickapoos Are Still Kicking. *Natural History* 64 (4):200-206.
1956   *The Mexican Kickapoo Indians.* Publications in Anthropology, no. 2. Milwaukee: Milwaukee Public Museum.

Robbins, Fred
1972   The Origins and Development of the African Slave Trade into Texas, 1816-1860. Master's thesis, University of Houston.

Robbins, Roy
1942   *Our Landed Heritage: The Public Domain, 1776-1936.* Princeton: Princeton University Press.

Robbins, W. W.; Bellue, M. K.; and Ball, W. S.
1951   *Weeds of California.* Sacramento: California Department of Agriculture.

Roberts, Robert E.
1973   Modernization and Infant Mortality in Mexico. *Economic Development and Cultural Change* 21 (no. 4):655-69.
———, and Askew, Cornelius, Jr.
1972   A Consideration of Mortality in Three Subcultures. *Health Services Report* 87:262-70.

Robertson, Edna, and Nestor, Sarah
1976   *Artists of the Canyons and Caminos: Santa Fe, the Early Years.* Salt Lake City: Peregrine Smith.

Robinson, Barbara J., and Robinson, J. Cordell
1980   *The Mexican American: A Critical Guide to Research Aids.* Greenwich, Conn.: JAI Press.

Robinson, Cecil
1963   *With the Ears of Strangers: The Mexican in American Literature.* Tucson: University of Arizona Press.
1966   Spring Water with a Taste of the Land: The Mexican Presence in the American Southwest. *American West* 3 (Summer):6-15, 95.
1977   *Mexico and the Hispanic Southwest in American Literature.* Tucson: University of Arizona Press.

Robinson, W. W.
1948   *Land in California: The Story of Mission Lands, Ranchos, Squatters, Mining Claims, Railroad Grants, Land Scrip, Homesteads.* Berkeley: University of California Press.

Robinson, Warren C., and Robinson, E. H.
1960   Rural-Urban Fertility Differentials in Mexico. *American Sociological Review* 25 (no. 1):77-81.

Robles, Vito Allesio
1934   *Saltillo en la historia y en la leyenda.* Mexico City: n.p.
1938   *Coahuila y Texas en la época colonial.* Mexico City: Editorial Cultura.

Rocco, Raymond A.
1977   A Critical Perspective on the Study of Chicano Politics. *Western Political Quarterly* 30 (no. 4):558-73.

Rochín, Refugio I.
1973   Economic Deprivation of Chicanos: Continuing Neglect in the Seventies. *Aztlán* 4 (no. 1):85-102.

Rock, Michael J.
1974   The Change in Tenure New Mexico Supreme Court Decisions Have Effected upon Common Lands of Community Land Grants in New Mexico. Paper presented to Rocky Mountain Social Science Association, April, at El Paso, Texas.

Rodino, Peter
1971-72   Illegal Aliens. Hearings of the Committee on the Judiciary, U.S. House of Representatives. Washington, D.C.: Government Printing Office.

Rodriguez, Roy C.
1972   Political Activism by Mexican-Americans in Local Voluntary Associations in El Paso, Texas. Paper presented to Cross-Cultural Southwest Ethnic Study Center Workshop, July, at El Paso, Texas.

Rodríguez del Pino, Salvador, et al.
1976   *Proceedings of the National Exploratory Conference on Chicano Sociolinguistics, Las Cruces, New Mexico.* Las Cruces: New Mexico State University, ERIC/CRESS.

Rodríguez L., Antonio
1950   Mexico's Irrigation Possibilities Along the Northeastern Zone Bordering the State of Texas. In *Basic Industries in Texas and Northern Mexico*, pp. 128-47. New York: Greenwood Press, University of Texas Institute of Latin-American Studies.

Rodríguez Lorenzo, Esteban
1938   Expedición a la Nación Guaycura en California. *Anales del Museo Nacional de México* 5 (no. 3):53-69.

Rodríguez Manzanera, Luis
1974   *La drogadición de la juventud en México.* Mexico City: Ediciones Botas.

Roel, Santiago
1963   Nuevo León. In *Apuntes históricos*, pp. 169-70. Monterrey: Undécima Edición.

Roessel, Ruth
1973   *Navajo Stories of the Long Walk Period.* Tsaile, Ariz.: Navajo Community College Press.
———, and Johnson, Broderick H.
1974   *Navajo Livestock Reduction: A National Disgrace.* Tsaile: Navajo Community College Press.

Rohn, Arthur H.
1973   The Southwest and the Intermontane West. In James F. Fitting, ed. *The Development of North American Archaeology*, pp. 185-211. Garden City, N.Y.: Doubleday Anchor.

Rolle, Andrew F.
1963   *California: A History.* New York: Thomas Y. Crowell Co.

Romano V., Octavio
1968   The Anthropology and Sociology of the Mexican-Americans: The Distortion of Mexican-American History. *El Grito* 2 (Fall):13-26.
1969   The Historical and Intellectual Presences of Mexican-Americans. *El Grito* 2 (Fall):32-46.
Romanucci-Ross, Lola
1973   *Conflict, Violence and Morality in a Mexican Village.* Palo Alto, Calif.: National Press Books.
Romney, Thomas Cottam
1938   *The Mormon Colonies in Mexico.* Salt Lake City: Deseret Book Co.
Rompen el aislamiento de los indios Guarifjios
1977*b*   *El Informador,* May 21, pp. 1 and 5.
Ronfelt, David
1973   *Atencingo: The Politics of an Agrarian Struggle in a Mexican Ejido.* Stanford: Stanford University Press.
Ronning, C. Neale
1979   National Priorities and Political Rights in Spanish America. In Adamantia Pollis and Peter Schwab, eds. *Human Rights: Cultural and Ideological Perspectives.* New York: Praeger Publishers.
Rosaldo, Renato; Calvert, Robert A.; and Seligman, Gustav L.
1973   Editors. *Chicano: The Evolution of a People.* Minneapolis: Winston Press.
Rosberg, Gerald M.
1977   The Protection of Aliens from Discriminatory Treatment by the National Government. *Supreme Court Review,* pp. 275-339.
Rose, A. J.
1955   The Border Zone Between Queensland and New South Wales. *Australian Geographer* 6 (no. 4):3-18.
Rose, Mary H.
1976   Illegal Aliens and the Border Patrol: Reasonable Suspicion Not Required When Occupants of Vehicles Stopped for Questioning at Permanent Inland Checkpoints. *United States* v. *Martínez-Fuerte. New York University Journal of International Law and Politics* 9 (Fall).
Rosen, Kenneth
1974   *The Man to Send Rain Clouds: Contemporary Stories by American Indians.* New York: Viking Press.
1975   *Voices from the Rainbow: Contemporary Poetry by American Indians.* New York: Viking Press.
Rosenau, James N.
1969   *Linkage Politics.* New York: Free Press.
Rosenbaum, Robert J.
1973   Las Gorras Blancas of San Miguel County, 1884-1890. In Renato Rosaldo, Robert A. Calvert, and Gustav A. Seligman, eds. *The Evolution of a People,* pp. 128-36. Minneapolis: Winston Press.
1975   *Mexicano* versus *Americano:* A Study of Hispanic-American Resistance to Anglo-American Control in New Mexico Territory, 1870-1900. Ph.D. dissertation, University of Texas at Austin.
Rosenblat, Angel
1954   *La población indígena y el mestizaje en América.* 2 vols. Buenos Aires: Editorial Nova.
Rosenbloom, David H.
1973   A Note on Interminority Group Competition for Federal Positions *Public Personnel Management* 2 (no. 2):47.
———, and Grabosky, Peter N.
1977   Racial and Ethnic Competition for Federal Service Positions. *Midwest Review of Public Administration* 11 (no. 4):281-90.
Rosenfelt, Daniel
1973   Indian Schools and Community Control. *Stanford Law Review* 25 (April):492-550.
1974   Legal Obligations to Provide Education Services for Indians. *Journal of American Indian Education* 13 (January):4-8.

Roske, Ralph J.
1968   *Everyman's Eden: A History of California.* New York: Macmillan Co.
Ross, Irwin
1973   Labor's Big Push for Protectionism. *Fortune,* March, pp. 93-97, 172, 174.
Ross, James K.
1978   *El Paso, Texas Foreign Trade Zone Economic Feasibility Study.* El Paso: Allan L. Lemley & Associates.
Ross, R. E.
1965   The Archeology of Eagle Cave. *Texas Archeological Salvage Project Papers* 7. Austin.
Ross, Stanley R.
1978   Editor. *Views Across the Border.* Albuquerque: University of New Mexico Press.
———, et al.
1965-67   *Fuentes de la historia contemporánea de México; periódicos y revistas.* 2 vols. Mexico City: El Colegio de México.
Roster of State Tourist Offices
1976   *Hotel and Motel Management* (August):27-80.
Rothe, Aline
1963   *Kalita's People: A History of the Alabama-Coushatta Indians of Texas.* Waco.
Rowe, Gene, and Smith, Leslie Whitener
1973   *The Hired Farm Working Force.* Washington, D.C.: U.S. Dept of Agriculture, Economic Research Service. Updated editions in 1974, 1975.
Royce, Josiah
1886   *California.* Cambridge, Mass.: Riverside Press.
Rubel, Arthur J.
1960   Concepts of Disease in Mexican-American Culture. *American Anthropologist* 62 (October):795-814.
1966   *Across the Tracks: Mexican-Americans in a Texas City.* Austin: University of Texas Press.
Rubio Mañé, Ignacio
1940   *El archivo general de la nación.* Mexico City: Editorial Cultura.
Ruecking, Frederick H., Jr.
1953   The Economic System of the Coahuiltecan Indians of Southern Texas and Northeastern Mexico. *Texas Journal of Science* 5 (no. 4):480-97.
1954*a*   *Bands and Band-Clusters of the Coahuiltecan Indians.* Student Papers in Anthropology, vol. 1, no. 2, pp. 1-24. Austin: University of Texas.
1954*b*   Ceremonies of the Coahuiltecan Indians of Southern Texas and Northeastern Mexico. *Texas Journal of Science* 6 (no. 3):330-39.
1955   The Social Organization of the Coahuiltecan Indians of Southern Texas and Northeastern Mexico. *Texas Journal of Science* 7 (no. 4):357-88.
Ruesink, David C., and Watson, T. Brice
1969   *Bibliography Relating to Migrant Labor.* Report no. 69-1 (March). College Station: Texas A&M University.
Ruhe, Robert V.
1964   Landscape Morphology and Alluvial Deposits in Southern New Mexico. *Annals, Association of American Geographers* 54 (March):147-59.
Rungeling, Brian; Smith, Lewis H.; Briggs, Vernon M., Jr.; and Adams, John S.
1977   *Employment, Income and Welfare in the Rural South.* New York: Praeger Publishers.
Rusinow, Irving
1942   *A Camera Report on El Cerrito: A Typical Spanish-American Community in New Mexico.* Publication no. 479. Washington, D.C.: U.S. Department of Agriculture, Bureau of Agricultural Economics.
Russell, Richard J.
1926   Climates of California. *University of California Publications in Geography* 2:73-84.
1931   Dry Climate of the United States. *University of California Publications in Geography* 5 (no. 1).

1945   Climates of Texas. *Annals, Association of American Geographers* 35 (June):37-52.

Rycroft, W. Stanley
1959   *Religion and Faith in Latin America.* Philadelphia: Westminster Press.

Rzedowski, J.
1978   *Vegetación de México.* México City: Editorial Limusa.

Saarinen, Thomas F.
1966   Attitudes Toward Weather Modification: A Study of Great Plains Farmers. In W. Sewell, ed. *Human Dimensions of Weather Modification,* pp. 21-50. Geography Research Paper no. 105. Chicago: University of Chicago.

Sabatini, Joseph D.
1973   *American Indian Law: A Bibliography of Books, Law Review Articles and Indian Periodicals.* Albuquerque: University of New Mexico, Indian Law Center.

Sabin, Edwin L.
1914   *Kit Carson Days, 1809-1868.* Chicago: A. C. McClurg & Co.

Salandini, Victor P.
1964   An Objective Evaluation of the Labor Disputes in the Lettuce Industry in Imperial Valley, California, During January-March, 1961. Master's thesis, St. Louis University.

1977   An Analysis of the Socioeconomic Impact of the Mexican Illegal Alien on San Diego County. Paper presented to Southwest Labor Studies Conference, March, at Tempe, Arizona.

Saldívar, Gabriel
1943   Los indios de Tamaulipas. In *El norte de México y el sur de Estados Unidos,* pp. 49-52. Mexico City: Sociedad Mexicana de Antropología.

Salinas, Estaban; Bagnall, Ruth M.; and Kuvlesky, William P.
1973   *Mexican Americans: A Survey of Research by the Texas Agricultural Experiment Station, 1964-73.* Progress Report 3194. College Station: Texas A&M University, Experiment Station.

Salinas Ríos, Francisco
1977   Enormes yacimientos de petróleo y gas en 3 estados. *Excelsior,* 31 de agosto.

Salmon, Robert Mario
1975   Seventeenth Century Tarahumara: A History of Cultural Resistance. Master's thesis, University of New Mexico.

Samora, Julian
1953   *Minority Leadership in a Bi-racial Cultural Community.* San Francisco: R & E Research Associates (1973).

1961   Conceptions of Health and Disease Among Spanish-Americans. *American Catholic Sociological Review* 22 (Winter):314.

1966   Editor. La Raza: *Forgotten Americans.* Notre Dame: University of Notre Dame Press.

1971   Los Mojados: *The Wetback Story.* Notre Dame: University of Notre Dame Press.

————; Bernal, Joe J.; and Peña, Albert
1978   *Gunpowder Justice: A Reassessment of the Texas Rangers.* Notre Dame: University of Notre Dame Press.

————; Galarza, E.; and Gallegos, H.
1969   *Mexican-Americans in the Southwest.* Chicago: McNally & Loftin.

Sánchez, George I.
1932   Scores of Spanish-speaking Children on Repeated Tests. *Journal of Genetic Psychology* 40 (March):223-31.

1940   *Forgotten People: A Study of New Mexicans.* Albuquerque: University of New Mexico Press. Also 1967 edition, Albuquerque: Calvin Horn Publisher.

Sánchez, Rosaura A.
1972   Nuestra circumstancia lingüística. *El Grito* 6 (Fall):45-74.

1974   A Generative Study of Two Spanish Dialects. Ph.D. dissertation, University of Texas, Austin.

1976   Chicano Code-Switching. In Curt R. Douglas, ed. *Linguistics and Education.* San Diego: San Diego State University, Institute for Cultural Pluralism.

Sánchez-Albornoz, Claudio
1970   The Continuing Tradition of Reconquest. In H. B. Johnson, Jr., ed. *From Reconquest to Empire: The Iberian Background to Latin American History.* New York: Alfred A. Knopf.

Sánchez-Albornoz, Nicolas
1974   *The Population of Latin America: A History.* Translated by W. A. R. Richardson. Berkeley: University of California Press.

Sanderline, Walter S.
1964   A Cattle Drive from Texas to California: The Diary of M. H. Erskine, 1854. *Southwestern Historical Quarterly* 67 (January):397-412.

Sanders, Thomas G.
1974   Mexico 1974: Demographic Patterns and Population Policy. In *American Universities Field Staff Reports, North America Series,* vol. 2, no. 1, pp. 1-28.

1975   Population Factors and Ideology in Mexico's Elementary Textbooks. In *American Universities Field Staff Reports, North America Series,* vol. 3, no. 2, pp. 1-9.

Sandos, James A.
1970   German Involvement in Northern Mexico, 1915-1916: A New Look at the Columbus Raid. *Hispanic American Historical Review* 50 (February):70-79.

1972   The Plan of San Diego: War and Diplomacy on the Texas Border, 1915-1916. *Arizona and the West* 14 (Spring):5-24.

Sandoval, Salvador A.
1971   Political Socialization in Northern Mexico. Master's thesis, University of Texas at El Paso.

Sanford, Trent E.
1950   *Architecture of the Southwest: Indian, Spanish, American.* New York: W. W. Norton & Co.

1971   *The Architecture of the Southwest: Indian, Spanish, American.* Westport, Conn.: Greenwood Press. Originally published in 1950.

Santamaría, Francisco J.
1942   *Diccionario general de americanismos.* Mexico City: Editorial P. Robredo.

1959   *Diccionario de Mejicanismos.* Mexico City: Editorial Porrúa.

Santos, Richard G.
1966   An Annotated Survey of the Spanish Archives of Laredo at St. Mary's University of Texas. *Texana* 4 (Spring): 41-46.

Sasaki, Tom J.
1960   *Fruitland, New Mexico: A Navajo Community in Transition.* Ithaca: Cornell University Press.

Sauer, Carl
1925   *The Morphology of Landscape.* Publications in Geography, vol. 2, no. 2. Berkeley: University of California.

1930*a*   *Basin and Range Forms in the Chiricahua Area.* Publications in Geography, vol. 3, pp. 339-415. Berkeley: University of California.

1930*b*   Historical Geography and the Western Frontier. In J. F. Willard and C. B. Goodykoontz, eds. *The Trans-Mississippi West,* pp. 267-89. Boulder: University of Colorado.

1932*a*   Aztlán: Prehistoric Frontier on the Pacific Coast. *Ibero-Americana,* no. 1.

1932*b*   Road to Cíbola. *Ibero-Americana,* no. 3.

1933   Aboriginal Distribution of Languages and Tribes in Northwest Mexico. *Ibero-Americana,* no. 5.

1935   Aboriginal Population of Northwestern Mexico. *Ibero-Americana,* no. 10.

1941*a*   Foreward to Historical Geography. *Annals, Association of American Geographers* 31 (March):1-24.

1941*b*   The Personality of Mexico. *Geographical Review* 31: 353-64.

————, and Brand, Donald

1930   Pueblo Sites in Southeastern Arizona. *University of California Publications in Geography* 3 (no. 7):415-59.

1931   Prehistoric Settlements of Sonora, with Special Reference to Cerros de Trincheras. *University of California Publications in Geography* 5 (no. 3):67-148.

Sauer, Carl O.

1969   *The Early Spanish Main.* Berkeley: University of California Press.

Sauer, Jonathan

1967   *Geographic Reconnaissance of Seashore Vegetation Along the Mexican Gulf Coast.* Coastal Studies, no. 21. Baton Rouge: Louisiana State University.

Saunders, Lyle

1944   *A Guide to Materials Bearing on Cultural Relations in New Mexico.* Albuquerque: University of New Mexico Press.

1954   *Cultural Differences and Medical Care: The Case of the Spanish-speaking People of the Southwest.* New York: Russell Sage Foundation.

Savenhagen, María Eugenia V.

1959   Compadrazgo en una comunidad Zapoteca. *Ciencias Políticas y Sociales* 5 (septiembre):365-402.

Sawatsky, Harry L.

1971   *They Sought a Country: Mennonite Colonization in Mexico.* Berkeley: University of California Press.

Sawyer, Janet Beck Moseley

1964   Spanish-English Bilingualism in San Antonio, Texas. *Publications of the American Dialect Society* 41 (no. 1): 7-15.

Saxton, Alexander

1966   The Army of Canton in the High Sierra. *Pacific Historical Review* 35 (May):141-52.

1971   *The Indispensable Enemy: Labor and the Anti-Chinese Movement in California.* Los Angeles: University of California Press.

Sayles, Edwin B.

1935   *An Archaeological Survey of Texas.* Globe, Ariz.: Medallion papers, no. 17.

1936   *An Archeological Survey of Chihuahua.* Globe, Ariz.: Medallion Papers, no. 22.

1945   *The San Simon Branch: Excavations at Cave Creek and in the San Simon Valley, I-Material Culture.* Globe, Ariz.: Medallion Papers, no. 34.

————, and Antevs, Ernst

1941   *The Cochise Culture.* Globe, Ariz.: Medallion Papers, no. 29.

Scantling, F. H.

1939   Jackrabbit Ruin. *Kiva* 5 (no. 3):9-12.

Schaab, William C.

1968   Indian Industrial Development and the Courts. *Natural Resources Journal* 8 (April):303-30.

Schaafsma, Polly

1972   *Rock Art in New Mexico.* Albuquerque: University of New Mexico Press.

Schaller, David A.

1978   An Energy Policy for Indian Lands: Problems of Issue and Perception. *Policy Studies Journal* 8 (Autumn): 40-49.

Schappes, Morris U.

1958   *The Jews in the United States.* New York: Citadel Press.

Schey, Peter A.

1977   Carter's Immigration Proposal: A Windfall for Big Business, Anathema for Undocumented Persons. *Agenda* 7 (September-October):4-15.

Schimwell, D. W.

1971   *The Description and the Classification of Vegetation.* Seattle: University of Washington Press.

Schiwetz, E. M.

1960   *Buck Schiwetz' Texas: Drawings and Paintings by E. M. Schiwetz.* Austin: University of Texas Press.

Schlebecker, John T.

1969   *Bibliography of Books and Pamphlets on the History of Agriculture in the United States, 1607-1967.* Santa Barbara: Cleo Press.

Schlesinger, Andrew B.

1971   Las gorras blancas, 1889-1891. *Journal of Mexican-American Studies* 1:87-143.

Schlesinger, R. A.

1967   *The California Indian Lease.* California Practice Book 35. Berkeley: University of California Press.

Schmeckebier, Laurence E.

1939   *Modern Mexican Art.* Minneapolis: University of Minnesota Press.

Schmidt, Fred H.

1964   *After the Braceros: An Inquiry into the Problems of Farm Labor Recruitment.* Los Angeles: University of California, Institute of Industrial Relations.

1970   *Spanish Surnamed Employment in the Southwest.* Washington, D.C.: Government Printing Office.

Schmidt, Robert H., Jr.

1973   *A Geographical Survey of Chihuahua.* Southwestern Studies, no. 37. El Paso: Texas Western Press.

1975   *The Climate of Chihuahua, Mexico.* Technical Report no. 23. Tucson: University of Arizona, Institute of Atmospheric Physics.

1976*a*   *A Geographical Survey of Sinaloa.* Southwestern Studies, no. 50. El Paso: Texas Western Press.

1976*b*   Some Economic Characteristics of the Border Region. *El Paso Economic Review* 13 (October):1-4.

1979   A Climatic Delineation of the "Real" Chihuahuan Desert. *Journal of Arid Environments* 2:243-50.

Schmiedehaus, Walter

1954   A Beleaguered People: The Mennonites of Mexico. *Landscape* 4 (Summer):13-21.

Schmieder, Oscar

1928   The Russian Colony of Guadalupe Valley. *University of California Publications in Geography* 2:409-34.

Schmitt, Karl M.

1954   The Clergy and the Independence of New Spain. *Hispanic American Historical Review* 34 (August):289-312.

Schmitz, Joseph William

1941   *Texas Statecraft, 1836-1845.* San Antonio: Naylor Co.

1960   *Texas Culture, 1836-1846: In the Days of the Republic (Thus they Lived).* San Antonio: Naylor Co.

Schneider, Louis

1969   On Frontiers of Sociology and History: Observations on Evolutionary Development and Unanticipated Consequences. *Social Science Quarterly* 50 (June):6-24.

Schnore, Leo F.

1965   On the Spatial Structure of Cities in the Two Americas. *In* P. Hauser and L. Schnore, eds. *The Study of Urbanization.* New York: Wiley.

Schoffelmayer, Victor H.

1960   *Southwest Trails to New Horizons.* San Antonio: Naylor Co.

Scholes, France V.

1930   The Supply Service of the New Mexico Missions in the 17th Century. *New Mexico Historical Review* 5 (January, April, October):93-155, 186-209, 384-404.

1935   Civil Government and Society in New Mexico in the 17th Century. *New Mexico Historical Review* 10 (April):71-111.

1937   *Church and State in New Mexico.* Albuquerque: University of New Mexico Press.

1940   Documentary Evidence Relating to the Jumano Indians. Carnegie Institution of Washington Publication 523. *Contributions to American Anthropology and History* 4:271-89.

1942   *Troublous Times in New Mexico, 1659-1670.* Albuquerque: University of New Mexico Press.

————, and Mera, H. P.

1940   Some Aspects of the Humano Problem. *Contributions to American Anthropology and History* 6 (no. 34):265-99. Washington, D.C.: Carnegie Institution.

Schoonover, Thomas
1974   Mexican Cotton and the American Civil War. *Americas* 30 (April):429-47.

Schroeder, Albert H.
1965   Unregulated Diffusion from Mexico into the Southwest Prior to A.D. 700. *American Antiquity* 30 (January): 297-309.

1966   Pattern Diffusion from Mexico into the Southwest after A.D. 600. *American Antiquity* 31 (July, part 1):683-704.

1968   Shifting for Survival in the Spanish Southwest. *New Mexico Historical Review* 43 (October):291-310.

1974a   *A Study of the Apache Indians: Part I, Apaches and their Neighbors; Part II, The Jicarilla Apaches; Part III, The Mescalero Apaches.* New York: Garland Publishing, University of New Mexico.

1974b   *A Study of the Apache Indians: "Tonto" and Western Apache.* New York: Garland Publishing, University of New Mexico.

1974c   *A Study of Yavapai History.* New York: Garland Publishing, University of New Mexico.

Schroeder, Richard C.
1975   *The Politics of Drugs: Marijuana to Mainlining.* Washington, D.C.: Congressional Quarterly.

Schulman, Edmund
1956   *Dendroclimatic Changes in Semiarid America.* Tucson: University of Arizona Press.

Schwartz, A. J.
1971   Comparative Study of Values and Achievements: Mexican-American and Anglo Youth. *Sociology of Education* 44 (Fall):438-62.

Schwartz, David C.
1974   Toward a More Relevant and Rigorous Political Science. *Journal of Politics* 36 (February):103-37.

Schwartz, Rosalie
1975   *Across the Rio to Freedom: U.S. Negroes in Mexico.* Southwestern Studies, no. 44. El Paso: Texas Western Press.

Schwarz, Carl E.
1973   Judges Under the Shadow: Judicial Independence in the United States and Mexico. *California Western International Law Journal* 3 (2).

1978   Informal Justice Mechanisms in the United States, Cuba, and Mexico. Paper presented to the Western Political Science Association, March, at Los Angeles, California.

Scoggins, James R., et al.
1975   *An Evaluation of Weather Modification Activities in the Texas High Plains.* Report no. 193. Austin: Texas Water Development Board.

Scott, Florence Johnson
1937   *Historical Heritage of the Lower Rio Grande.* San Antonio: Naylor Co.

Scott, Robert E.
1955   Budget Making in Mexico. *Inter-American Economic Affairs* 9 (Autumn):3-20.

1964   *Mexican Government in Transition.* Urbana: University of Illinois Press.

1965   Mexico: The Established Revolution. In L. W. Pye and S. Verba, eds. *Political Culture and Political Development,* pp. 330-95. Princeton: Princeton University Press.

1971   *Mexican Government in Transition.* Urbana: University of Illinois Press.

Scott, Robin F.
1970   The Sleepy Lagoon Case and the Grand Jury Investigation. In Manuel P. Servín, ed. *The Mexican Americans: An Awakening Minority,* pp. 105-16. Beverly Hills: Glencoe Press.

Scott, Stuart D.
1966   *Dendrochronology in Mexico.* Papers of the Laboratory of Tree-Ring Research, no. 2. Tucson: University of Arizona Press.

Scruggs, Otey M.
1960   The First Mexican Labor Program. *Arizona and the West* 2 (Winter):319-26.

1961   The United States, Mexico and the Wetbacks, 1942-1947. *Pacific Historical Review* 30 (May):149-64.

1963   Texas and the Bracero Program, 1942-1947. *Pacific Historical Review* 32 (August):251-64.

Scully, Vincent, and Current, William
1971   *Pueblo Architecture of the Southwest, a Photographic Essay.* Austin: University of Texas Press.

Scurlock, Dan
1979   *Selected Sources on the Spanish Borderlands, 1492-1850.* Albuquerque: University of New Mexico, Center of Anthropological Studies.

Seckler, David
1971   Editor. *California Water: A Study in Resource Management.* Berkeley: University of California Press.

Seely, Edward H., and DeCoursey, Donn G.
1975   Hydrologic Impact of Weather Modification. *Water Resources Bulletin* 11 (April):365-69.

Segale, Sister Blandina
1949   *At the End of the Santa Fe Trail.* Milwaukee: The Bruce Publishing Company.

Segalman, Ralph
1968   *Army of Despair: The Migrant Worker Stream.* LEASCO.

Seiver, Daniel
1975   Recent Fertility in Mexico: Measurement and Interpretation. *Population Studies* 29:341-54.

1976   Economic Development and Fertility Change in Mexico, 1950-1970 (Comment on W. Whitney Hicks Followed by Reply from Hicks). *Demography* 13 (no. 1):149-52.

Sekaquaptewa, Emory
1972   Preserving the Good Things of Hopi Life. In Edward H. Spicer and Raymond Thompson, eds. *Plural Society in the Southwest,* pp. 239-60. New York: Weatherhead Foundation.

Sellards, E. H.; Adkins, W. S.; and Plummer, F. B.
1932   *The Geology of Texas: Vol. I, Stratigraphy.* Bulletin no. 3232. Austin: University of Texas Press.

Sellers, William D., and Hill, Richard H.
1974   Editors. *Arizona Climate, 1931-1972.* Tucson: University of Arizona Press.

Sepúlveda, Bernardo, and Chumacero, Antonio
1973   *La inversión extranjera en México.* Mexico City: Fondo de Cultura Económica.

Sepúlveda, César
1972   Mexican-American International Water Quality Problems: Prospects and Perspectives. *Natural Resources Journal* 12 (January):215-22.

1974a   Métodos intergubernamentales viables para la cooperación de aire a lo largo de la frontera México-Norteamericana. In Howard G. Applegate and C. Richard Bath, eds. *Air Pollution Along the United States-Mexican Border,* pp. 131-35. El Paso: Texas Western Press.

1974b   Colorado River Management and Internatinal Law. In A. B. Crawford and D. F. Peterson, eds. *Environmental Management in the Colorado River Basin,* pp. 59-66. Logan: Utah State University Press.

1976   *La Frontera Norte de México.* Mexico City: Editorial Porrúa.

1978   Instituciones para la solución de problemas de superficie entre México y los Estados Unidos. *Natural Resources Journal* 18 (January):131-42.

Serrano, Rodolfo G.
1976   *Dictionary of Pachuco Terms.* Bakersfield, Calif.: Sierra Printers.

Service, Elman
1947   Recent Observations on Havasupai Land Tenure. *Southwestern Journal of Anthropology* 3 (Winter):360-66.

1969   The Northern Tepehuan. In Robert Wauchope, ed. *Handbook of Middle American Indians,* vol. 8, pp. 822-29. Austin: University of Texas Press.

Servín, Manuel P.

1961   The Instructions of Viceroy Bucareli to Ensign Juan Pérez.. *California Historical Society Quarterly* 40 (September):237-48.

1964   The Quest for the Governorship of Spanish California. *California Historical Society Quarterly* 43 (March):45-56.

1970   Constansó's 1794 Report on Strengthening New California's Presidios. *California Historical Society Quarterly* 49 (September):221-32.

1972   The Beginnings of California's Anti-Mexican Prejudice. Paper presented to Rocky Mountain Social Science Association, March, at Salt Lake City, Utah.

1973   California's Hispanic Heritage: A View into the Spanish Myth. *Journal of San Diego History* (Winter) 19:1-9.

Setzler, F. M.

1935   A Prehistoric Cave Culture in Southwestern Texas. *American Anthropologist* 31:104-10.

Sewell, W. R. Derrick

1967   NAWAPA: A Continental Water System. *Bulletin of the Atomic Scientists* 23 (September):8-13.

1974   Water Across the American Continent (NAWAPA). *Geographical Magazine* 46 (June):472-79.

Shadow, Robert D.

1979   Differential Out-Migration: A Comparison of Internal and International Migration from Villa Guerrero, Jalisco (Mexico). In Fernando Camara and Robert Van Kemper, eds. *Migration Across Frontiers: Mexico and the United States,* pp. 67-83. Albany: State University of New York at Albany, Institute for Meso-american Studies.

Shafer, H. J., and Bryant, V. M., Jr.

1977   *Archeological and Botanical Studies at Hinds Cave, Val Verde County, Texas.* Annual Report to the National Science Foundation. College Station: Texas A&M Research Foundation.

Shalkop, Robert L.

1969   *The Folk Art of a New Mexico Village.* Colorado Springs: Taylor Museum of the Colorado Springs Fine Arts Center.

Shannon, Lyle W.

1973   *Minority Migants in the Urban Community.* Beverly Hills: Sage Publications.

Shapiro, H. A.

1952   The Pecan Shellers of San Antonio, Texas. *Southwestern Social Science Quarterly* 32 (no. 3):229-44.

Sharp, Jay W.

1960   A Collection of Printed Maps of Texas, 1835-1951, in the Eugene C. Barker Texas History Center. *Southwestern Historical Quarterly* 64 (July):96-123.

1961   The Maps of the Stephen F. Austin Collection in the Eugene C. Barker Texas History Center. *Southwestern Historical Quarterly* 64 (January):388-97.

Shaw, Robert d'A.

1971   Foreign Investment and Global Labor. *Columbia Journal of World Business* 6 (July-August):52-62.

Shea, John Gilmary

1886   Ancient Florida. In Justin Winsor, ed. *Narrative and Critique of America.* Vol. 88. Boston: Houghton Mifflin Co.

Sheck, Ronald C.

1971   Mexican-American Migration to Selected Texas Panhandle Urban Places. Paper presented to Association of American Geographers, August, in San Francisco, California.

1974   El Paso-Juárez: Cultural Impingement in the Urban Setting. Paper presented to Association of American Geographers, April, at Seattle, Washington.

Shepardson, Mary

1963   *Navajo Ways in Government: A Study in Political Process.* Memoir 96. Menasha,Wis.: American Anthropological Association.

1965   Problems of the Navajo Tribal Courts in Transition. *Human Organization* 24:250-53.

Sherer, Lorraine M.

1966   The Clan System of the Ft. Mohave Indians: A Contemporary Survey. *Southern California Quarterly* 48: 1-35.

Sherman, James E., and Sherman, Barbara H.

1969   *Ghost Towns of Arizona.* Norman: University of Oklahoma Press.

1975   *Ghost Towns and Mining Camps of New Mexico.* Norman: University of Oklahoma Press.

Shields, Lora M., and Wells, Philip V.

1962   Effects of Nuclear Testing on Desert Vegetation. *Science* 135 (January 5):38-40.

Shifter, Richard, and West, Richard W., Jr.

1974   Healing v. Jones: Mandate for Another Trail of Tears? *North Dakota Law Review* 51 (Fall):73-106.

Shiner, J. L.

1969   Component Analysis of Archaic Sites. *Texas Archeological Society Bulletin* 40:215-30.

Shinn, Allen M., Jr.

1971   A Note on Voter Registration and Turnout in Texas, 1960-1970. *Journal of Politics* 33 (November):1120-29.

Shinn, Charles H.

1949   *Mining Camps, a Study in American Frontier Government.* New York: Alfred A. Knopf.

Shipek, Florence C.

1968   *The Autobiography of Delfina Guero, a Diegueño Indian.* Baja California Travel Series, no. 12. Los Angeles: Dawson's Book Shop.

Shirer, John

1953   Is There a Southwest? *Arizona Quarterly* 9 (Summer): 101-109.

Shockley, John Staples

1974   *Chicano Revolt in a Texas Town.* Notre Dame: University of Notre Dame Press.

Shontz, O. J.

1927   Land of Poco Tiempo: A Study in Mexican Family Relationships in a Changing Social Environment. *Family* 8:74-79.

Shreve, Forrest

1934   Rainfall, Runoff and Soil Moisture Under Desert Conditions. *Annals, Association of American Geographers* 24 (September):131-56.

1935   The Human Ecology of Baja California. *Yearbook of the Association of Pacific Coast Geographers* 1:9-13.

1936   The Plant Life of the Sonoran Desert. *Scientific Monthly* 42 (March):195-213.

1942   Vegetation of Northern Mexico. *Yearbook of the Association of Pacific Coast Geographers* 8:3-5.

1944   Rainfall of Northern Mexico. *Ecology* 25 (January):105-11.

————, and Hinckley, Arthur L.

1937   Thirty Years of Change in Desert Vegetation. *Ecology* 18 (October):463-78.

————, and Wiggins, I. L.

1964   *Vegetation and Flora of the Sonoran Desert.* 2 vols. Stanford: Stanford University Press.

Shuler, Ellis W.

1940   The Influence of the Shore Line, Rivers and Springs, on the Settlement and Early Development of Texas. *Texas Geographic Magazine* 4 (Autumn):26-31.

Sibley, Marilyn McAdams

1967   Across Texas in 1767: The Travels of Captain Pagés. *Southwestern Historical Quarterly* 70 (April):591-622.

1973   Charles Stillman: A Case Study of Entrepreneurship on the Rio Grande, 1861-1865. *Southwestern Historical Quarterly* 77 (October):227-40.

Sidwell, Raymond
1938   Sand and Dust Storms in Vicinity of Lubbock, Texas. *Economic Geography* 14 (January):98-102.

Siegel, Jacob S.
1974   Estimates of Coverage of the Population by Sex, Race, and Age in the 1970 Census. *Demography* 11:1-23.
———, and Passel, Jeffrey S.
1979   Coverage of the Hispanic Population of the United States in the 1970 Census. U.S. Bureau of the Census, Current Population Reports, no. 23.

Siegel, Stanley
1956   *A Political History of the Texas Republic, 1836-1845.* Austin: University of Texas Press.

Silko, Leslie Marmon
1974   Editor. *The Man to Send Rain Clouds.* New York: Viking Press.
1975   Poems. In Kenneth Rose, ed. *Voices of the Rainbow,* pp. 8-30. New York: Viking Press.
1977   *Ceremony.* New York: Viking Press.

Simmons, Marc
1964   Tlascalans in the Spanish Borderlands. *New Mexico Historical Review* 39 (April):101-10.
1966   New Mexico's Smallpox Epidemic of 1780-1781. *New Mexico Historical Review* 41 (October):319-26.
1968   *Spanish Government in New Mexico.* Albuquerque: University of New Mexico Press.
1969   Settlement Patterns and Village Plans in Colonial New Mexico. *Journal of the West* 8 (January):7-21.
1971   *The Fighting Settlers of Seboyeta.* Cerrillos, N.M.: San Marcos Press.
1972   Spanish Irrigation Practices in New Mexico. *New Mexico Historical Review* 47 (April):135-50.
1977a   *New Mexico. A Bicentennial History.* New York: W. W. Norton & Co.
1977b   *Father Juan Agustín de Morfi's Account of Disorders in New Mexico, 1778.* Santa Fe: Historical Society of New Mexico.

Simmons, Ozzie G.
1952   Anglo-Americans and Mexican-Americans in South Texas: A Study in Dominant-Subordinate Group Relations. Ph.D. dissertation, Harvard University.
1961   The Mutual Images and Expectations of Anglo-Americans and Mexican-Americans. *Daedalus* 92 (Spring): 286-99.

Simons, Suzanne L.
1970   Sandía Pueblo: Persistence and Change in a New Mexican Indian Community. Ph.D. dissertation, University of New Mexico.

Simpson, Eyler N.
1937   *The Ejido, Mexico's Way Out.* Chapel Hill: University of North Carolina Press.

Simpson, Lesley Byrd
1937   Spanish Utopia. *Hispania* 20 (December):353-68.
1950   *The Encomienda in New Spain: The Beginning of Spanish Mexico.* Berkeley: University of California Press.
1962   The Letters of José Señan, O.F.M. Mission San Buenaventura, 1796-1823. In Wayne Moquin, ed. *A Documentary History of the Mexican American,* pp. 111-15. New York: Praeger Publishers.
1964   *Many Mexicos.* Berkeley: University of California Press.

Singer, P.
1973   Population and Economic Development in Latin America. *International Journal of Health Services* 3 (no. 4): 731-36.

Singletary, Otis A.
1960   *The Mexican War.* Chicago: University of Chicago Press.

Skrabanek, R. L., and Upham, W. Kennedy
1974   *The Population of Texas: A Decade of Change.* College Station: Texas A&M University, Agricultural Experiment Station.

Slater, Arthur D., and Albrecht, Stan L.
1972   The Extent and Costs of Excessive Drinking Among the Uintah-Ouray Indians. In Howard M. Bahr, Bruce A. Chadwick, and Robert C. Day, eds. *Native Americans Today: Sociological Perspectives,* pp. 358-67. New York: Harper & Row.

Sloan, John W., and West, Jonathan P.
1976a   Comparative Perceptions of Community Integration and Public Policy Along the U.S.-Mexico Border. Paper presented to the Southwestern Social Science Association, April, at Dallas, Texas.
1976b   Community Integration and Policies Among Elites in Two Border Cities: Los Dos Laredo. *Journal of Inter-American Studies and World Affairs* 18 (November): 451-74.
1977   The Role of Informal Policy-Making in U.S.-Mexico Border Cities. *Social Science Quarterly* 58 (September):270-82.

Smallwood, James M.
1974   Black Texans During Reconstruction, 1865-1874. Ph.D. dissertation, Texas Tech University.

Smiley, Terah L.
1957   Editor. *Climate and Man in the Southwest.* Tucson: University of Arizona Press.

Smith, Barton, and Newman, Robert
1977   Depressed Wages Along the U.S.-Mexico Border: An Empirical Analysis. *Economic Inquiry* 15 (January):51-66.

Smith, Bradley
1968   *Mexico: A History in Art.* New York: Harper & Row.

Smith, Courtland L.
1972   *The Salt River Project: A Case Study in Cultural Adaptation to an Urbanizing Community.* Tucson: University of Arizona Press.

Smith, Dwight
1967   The Date Industry of Arizona. Master's thesis, Arizona State University.

Smith, F. M.
1969   Factors Influencing the Administrative Process in Mexico. Ph.D. dissertation, University of North Carolina.

Smith, G. L., and Noldeke, A. M.
1960   A statistical report on "A California Flora." *Leaflets of Western Botany* 9:117-23.

Smith, H. Shelton
1972   *In His Image, but . . . : Racism in Southern Religion, 1780-1910.* Durham: Duke University Press.

Smith, H. V.
1956   *The Climate of Arizona.* Bulletin no. 279. Tucson: University of Arizona, Agricultural Experiment Station.

Smith, Justin
1919   *The War With Mexico.* 2 vols. New York: Macmillan Co.

Smith, K. M.
1961   Quality and Quantity of Rio Grande Water. *Journal of the Rio Grande Valley Horticultural Society* 15:115-22.

Smith, M. Estelle
1968a   A Comparative Analysis of Tiwa Government and Law. Mimeographed.
1968b   Governing Systems and Cultural Change Among the Southern Tiwa. Paper presented at American Anthropological Association, November, at Seattle, Washington.
1969   Governing at Taos Pueblo. *Eastern New Mexico University Contributions in Anthropology,* vol. 2, no. 1.
1971   Political Entrepreneurship. Paper presented at American Anthropological Association, November, at New York, New York.

Smith, Ralph A.
1962   Apache Plunder Trails Southward, 1831-1840. *New Mexico Historical Review* 37 (January):20-42.
1963   Indians in American-Mexican Relations Before the War

of 1846. *Hispanic American Historical Review* 43 (February):34-64.

1964 The Scalphunter in the Borderlands, 1835-1850. *Arizona and the West* 6 (Spring):5-22.

1965 The Scalp Hunt in Chihuahua, 1849. *New Mexico Historical Review* 49 (April):117-40.

Smith, V. J.
1931 Archeological Notes of the Big Bend Region. *Texas Archeological and Paleontological Society Bulletin* 3:60-69.

Smith, T. Lynn, and Zopf, Paul E., Jr.
1970 *The Principles of Inductive Rural Sociology.* Philadelphia: F. A. Davis Co.

Smithsides, Dorothy
1961 *Decorative Art of the Southwestern Indians.* New York: Dover Publications. Originally published in 1936.

Smithson, Carma Lee
1964 *Havasupai Religion and Mythology.* Salt Lake City: University of Utah Press.

Snodgrass, O. T.
1975 *Realistic Art and Times of the Mimbres Indians.* El Paso: O. T. Snodgrass.

Snow, Ronald W.
1969* The Beef Cattle Industry of Arizona: A Geographical Analysis. Master's thesis, Arizona State University.

Snyder, Stephen E.
1973 Groundwater Management: A Proposal for Texas. *Texas Law Review* 51:289-317.

Soares, Anthony T., and Soares, Louise M.
1969 Self Perceptions of Culturally Disadvantaged Children. *American Educational Research Journal* 6:31-45.

Sobarzo, Alejandro
1973 Salinity in the Colorado: An Interpretation of the Mexican-American Treaty of 1944. *Natural Resources Journal* 12 (October):510-14.

Sodi Álvarez, Enrique
1970 *Frontera.* Mexico City: Programa Nacional Fronterizo.

Solé, Yolanda R.
1975a Sociolinguistic Perspectives on Texas Spanish and the Teaching of the Standard Language. In Gina C. Harvey and M. F. Heiser, ed. *Southwest Languages and Linguistics in Educational Perspective: Proceedings of Third Annual Southwest Areal Languages and Linguistics Workshop.* San Diego: San Diego State University, Institute for Cultural Pluralism.

1975b Language Maintenance and Language Shift Among Mexican American College Students. *Journal of the Linguistic Association of the Southwest* 1 (August):22-48.

1976 Language Attitudes Towards Spanish Among Mexican American College Students. In Curt R. Douglas, ed. *Linguistics and Education,* pp. 327-47. San Diego: San Diego State University, Institute for Cultural Pluralism.

1977 Sociocultural and Sociopsychological Factors in Differential Language Retentiveness by Sex. In Donald W. Bleznick, ed. *Hispania.* Worcester, Mass.: American Association of Spanish and Portuguese, Inc.

1977a Sociolinguistic Perspectives on Texas Spanish and the Teaching of the Standard Language. In Donald W. Bleznick, ed. *Hispania.* Worcester, Mass.: American Association of Spanish and Portuguese, Inc.

1977b Language Maintenance and Language Shift among Mexican American College Students. In Donald W. Bleznick, ed. *Hispania.* Worcester, Mass.: American Association of Spanish and Portuguese, Inc.

1977c Language Attitudes Towards Spanish among Mexican American College Students. In Donald W. Bleznick, ed. *Hispania.* Worcester, Mass.: American Association of Spanish and Portuguese, Inc.

Solís Garza, Hermán
1971 *Los mexicanos del norte.* Mexico City: Nuestro Tiempo.

Solórzano, Rosalía
1979 Attitudes and Migration Patterns: A Comparative Study

of the "Marias" from Ciudad Juarez, Chihuahua, and Tijuana, Baja California, Mexico. Master's thesis, University of Texas at El Paso.

Sonnichsen, Charles L.
1958 *The Mescalero Apaches.* Norman: University of Oklahoma Press.

1968 *Pass of the North: Four Centuries on the Rio Grande.* El Paso: Texas Western Press.

1971 Col. William C. Green and the Strike at Cananea, Sonora, 1906. *Arizona and the West* 13 (Winter):343-68.

———, and McKinney, M. G.
1973 El Paso: From War to Depression. *Southwestern Historical Quarterly* 74 (January):367-71.

Sorkin, Alan L.
1971 *American Indians and Federal Aid.* Washington, D.C.: Brookings Institution.

1973 Business and Industrial Development on American Indian Reservations. *Annals of Regional Science* 7 (no. 2):115-29.

Sorokin, Pitrim A., and Zimmerman, Carle C.
1929 *Principles of Rural-Urban Sociology.* New York: Henry Holt.

Sorrow, W. M.
1968 *The Devil's Mouth Site: The Third Season, 1967.* Austin: Texas Archeological Salvage Project 14.

Sosnick, Stephen H.
1978 *Hired Hands: Seasonal Farm Workers in the United States.* Santa Barbara: McNally & Loftin, West.

Soto Mora, Consuelo, and Jauregui O., Ernesto
1965 *Isotermas extremas e índice de aridez en la república mexicana.* Mexico City: UNAM Instituto de Geografía, Talleres de Edimex.

1968 *Cartografía de elementos bioclimáticos en la república mexicana.* Mexico City: UNAM Instituto de Geografía.

Southwestern Landscapes as Seen from the Air
1951 *Landscape* 1 (Autumn):10-19.

Southworth, J. F.
1905 *The Mines of Mexico.* Mexico City: n.p.

Sowell, A. J.
1900 *Early Settlers and Indian Fighters of Southwest Texas.* Austin: Ben C. Jones.

Spain, August O.
1956 Mexican Federalism Revisited. *Western Political Quarterly* 9 (September):620-32.

Sparks, J. P.
1968 The Indian Stronghold and the Spread of Urban America. *Arizona Law Review* 10 (Winter):706-24.

Spell, Lota M.
1962 The Grant and First Survey of the City of San Antonio. *Southwestern Historical Quarterly* 66 (July):73-89.

Spellman, Karen Edmonds
1977 *Where Have All the Farmworkers Gone? The Statistical Population of Migrant and Seasonal Farmworkers by Federal Agencies.* Washington, D.C.: Rural America.

Spence, Clark C.
1970 *Mining Engineers and the American West: The Lace-Boot Brigade.* New Haven: Yale University Press.

Spengler, Joseph J.
1975 *Population and America's Future.* San Francisco: W. H. Freeman & Co.

Spicer, Edward H.
1940 *Pascua, a Yaqui Village in Arizona.* Chicago: University of Chicago Press.

1943 Linguistic Aspects of Yaqui Acculturation. *American Anthropologist* 45 (no. 3):410-26.

1945 El problema yaqui. *América Indígena* 4 (no. 4):273-86.

1951 The Military Orientation in Yaqui Culture. In Erik Kellerman Reed and Dale S. King, eds. *For the Dean: Essays in Anthropology,* pp. 171-87. Tucson: Santa Fe.

1954a *Potam, a Yaqui Village in Sonora.* Memoir no. 77. Menosha, Wis.: American Anthropological Association.

1954*b*   Spanish-Indian Acculturation in the Southwest. *American Anthropologist* 56:663-78.

1957   Worlds Apart: Cultural Differences in the Modern Southwest. *Arizona Quarterly* 13 (no. 3):197-230.

1958   Social Structure and Social Process in Yaqui Religious Acculturation. *American Anthropologist* 60 (no. 3): 433-41.

1961   Editor. *Perspectives in American Indian Culture Change.* Chicago: University of Chicago Press.

1962   *Cycles of Conquest: The Impact of Spain, Mexico and the U.S. on the Indians of the Southwest, 1533-1960.* Tucson: University of Arizona Press.

1964   Apuntes sobre el tipo de religión de los yuto-aztecas centrales. *International Congress of Americanists, Proceedings for 1964* 2 (35):27-38.

1965   La danza yaqui del venado en la cultura mexicana. *América Indígena* 25 (no. 1):117-39.

1966   Process of Cultural Enclavement in Middle America. *International Congress of Americanists, Proceedings for 1966,* 36 (3):267-79.

1969   The Yaqui and Mayo. In Robert Wauchope, ed. *Handbook of Middle American Indians,* vol. 8, pp. 830-45. Austin: University of Texas Press.

1970*a*   Patrons of the Poor. *Human Organization* 29 (Spring): 12-19.

1970*b*   Contrasting Forms of Nativism Among the Mayos and Yaquis of Sonora, Mexico. In W. Goldschmidt and Harry Hoijer, eds. *The Social Anthropology of Latin America, Essays in Honor of Ralph Leon Beals,* pp. 104-24. Los Angeles: University of California, Latin American Center.

1971   Persistent Cultural Systems: A Comparative Study of Identity Systems That Can Adapt to Contrasting Environments. *Science* 174 (November 19):795-800.

1972   Introduction, and Plural Society in the Southwest. In Edward H. Spicer and Raymond Thompson, eds. *Plural Society in the Southwest,* pp. 1-76. New York: Interbook, Weatherhead Foundation.

1976   The United States-Mexico Border and Cultural Alternatives: The Yaqui Case. Paper presented at Conference on Border Studies, July, at El Paso, Texas.

1980   *The Yaquis: A Cultural History.* Tucson: University of Arizona Press.

———; Hansen, Asael T.; Luomala, Katherine; and Opler, Marvin K.

1969   *Impounded People.* Tucson: University of Arizona Press.

———, and Thompson, Raymond H.

1972   Editors. *Plural Society in the Southwest.* New York: Interbook, Weatherhead Foundation.

Spiess, Lincoln Bunce
1965   Church Music in Seventeenth-Century New Mexico. *New Mexico Historical Review* 40 (January):5-21.

Spitzer, A.
1960   Religious Structure in Mexico. *Alpha Kappa Deltan* 30: 54-58.

Splinter, William E.
1976   Center-Pivot Irrigation. *Scientific American* 243 (June): 90-99.

Splitter, Henry Winfield
1969   Health in Southern California, 1850-1900. *Journal of the West* 8 (October):526-58.

Spolsky, Bernard
1970   Navajo Language Maintenance: Six Year Olds in 1969. *Language Sciences* 13 (December):19-24.

———, and Holm, Wayne
1971   Literacy in the Vernacular: The Case of the Navajo. Mimeographed. Navajo Reading Study Program, Report no. 8. Mimeographed. Albuquerque, University of New Mexico.

Spratt, John S.
1970   *The Road to Spindletop: Economic Change in Texas.* Austin: University of Texas Press.

Springer, Frank
1890   The Private Land Grant in New Mexico. Santa Fe: Minutes of the New Mexico Bar Association.

Stacy, V. K. Pheriba
1975   Archeological Survey in the Arizona Papagueria. *Kiva* 40 (no. 3):181-87.

Stambaugh, J. Lee, and Stambaugh, Lillian
1954   *The Lower Rio Grande Valley of Texas.* San Antonio: Naylor Co.

Standley, P. C.
1911   Some Useful Native Plants of New Mexico. *Annual Report,* pp. 447-62, with 13 plates. Washington, D. C.: Smithsonian Institution.

1920-26   Trees and Shrubs of Mexico. *Contribution from the United States Herbarium* 23:1-1721.

Stanislawski, Dan
1947   Early Spanish Town Planning in the New World. *Geographical Review* 37 (January):94-105.

Starling, Grover
1977   *Managing the Public Sector.* Homewood, Ill.: Dorsey Press.

Starnes, Gary B.
1969   *The San Gabriel Missions, 1746-1756.* Madrid: Ministry of Foreign Affairs.

1972*a*   The Spanish Borderlands of Texas and Coahuila. *Texana* 10:20-29.

1972*b*   Juan de Ugalde and the Coahuila-Texas Frontier. *Texana* 10 (no. 2):116-28.

Starr, Harvey, and Most, Benjamin A.
1976   The Substance and Study of Borders in International Relations Research. *International Studies Quarterly* 20 (December):581-620.

Starr, Kevin
1973   *Americans and the California Dream.* New York: Oxford University Press.

Stavenhagen, Rodolfo
1958   Las condiciones socioeconómicas de la población trabajadora de Tijuana, B.C. *Ciencias Políticas y Sociales* 4 (no. 14):333-89.

1970   Social Aspects of Agrarian Structure in Mexico. In Rudolfo Stavenhagen, ed. *Agrarian Problems and Peasant Movements in Latin America,* pp. 225-70. Garden City: Anchor Books.

Steck, Francis Borgia
1932   Forerunners of Captain De León's Expedition to Texas, 1670-1675. *Southwestern Historical Quarterly* 36 (July): 1-28.

1943   *A Tentative Guide to Historical Materials on the Spanish Borderlands.* Philadelphia: Catholic Historical Society of Philadelphia.

Steglich, W. G.
1974   Language and Ethnic Identification in the American Southwest. Paper presented to International Sociological Association, August, at Toronto, Canada.

———, and Deardorff, Gwen
1968   Some Correlates of Infant Mortality in Lubbock County. *Proceedings of Southwestern Sociological Association,* pp. 93-97.

Stein, Stanley J., and Stein, B. H.
1970   *The Colonial Heritage of Latin America: Essays on Economic Dependence in Perspective.* New York: Oxford University Press.

Stein, Walter J.
1973   *California and the Dust Bowl Migration.* Westport, Conn.: Greenwood Press.

Steiner, Rodney
1960   Two Water Flow Maps of California. *California Geographer* 1:41-44.

1967   Large Landholdings in the Environs of Los Angeles. *California Geographer* 8:115-25.

Steiner, Stan
1968   *The New Indians.* New York: Harper & Brothers.
1970   *La Raza: The Mexican Americans.* New York: Harper & Brothers.
Stelle, Thomas J.
1974   *Santos and Saints: Essays and Handbook.* Albuquerque: Calvin Horn Publisher.
Stephenson, Nathaniel Wright
1921   *Texas and the Mexican War.* New Haven, Conn.: Yale University Press.
Stevens, Evelyn
1965   Mexican Machismo: Politics and Value Orientation. *Western Political Quarterly* 18 (December):848-57.
1978   *Protest and Response in Mexico.* Cambridge: M.I.T. Press.
Stevens, Harry R.
1971   A Company of Hands and Traders: Origins of the Glen-Fowler Expedition of 1821-1822. *New Mexico Historical Review* 46 (July):181-222.
Stevens, Robert C.
1964   The Apache Menace in Sonora, 1831-1849. *Arizona and the West* 6 (Autumn):211-22.
Stevenson, M. C.
1915   Ethnobotany of the Zuñi Indians. *Annual Report, Bureau of American Ethnology* 13:33-102.
Stevenson, Robert J.
1975   *La Zona* in Transition: Bordertown Prostitution in Frontier City, Mexico. Master's thesis, New York University at Stony Brook.
Stewart, George R.
1936   *Ordeal by Hunger: The Story of the Donner Party.* New York: Henry Holt.
1962   *The California Trail.* New York: McGraw-Hill Book Co.
Stewart, Guy R., and Donnelly, Maurice
1943   Soil and Water Economy in the Pueblo Southwest. *Scientific Monthly* 56 (January, February):31-44, 134-44.
Stewart, Kenneth M.
1970   Mohave Indian Shamanism. *Masterkey* 44:15-24.
Stewart, O. C.
1951   Burning and Natural Vegetation in the United States. *Geographical Review* 41:317-20.
1954   The Forgotten Side of Ethnography. In R. F. Spencer, ed. *Method and Perspective in Anthropology,* pp. 221-48, 308-10. Minneapolis: University of Minnesota Press.
1955a   Why Were the Prairies Treeless? *Southwestern Lore* 20:59-64.
1955b   Forest and Grass Burning in the Mountain West. *Southwestern Lore* 21:5-8.
1956   Fire as the First Great Force Employed by Man. In W. L. Thomas, ed. *Man's Role in Changing the Face of the Earth,* pp. 115-33. Chicago: University of Chicago Press.
Stewart, Virginia
1951   *Contemporary Mexican Artists.* Stanford: Stanford University Press.
Stoddard, Ellwyn R.
1961   Catastrophe and Crisis in a Flooded Border Community: An Analytical Approach to Disaster Emergence. Ph.D. dissertation, Michigan State University.
1969a   The U.S.-Mexican Border: A Comparative Research Laboratory. *Journal of Inter-American Studies* 11 (July):477-88.
1969b   Some Latent Consequences of Bureaucratic Efficiency in Disaster Relief. *Human Organization* 28 (Fall):177-89.
1970a   Ethnic Identity of Urban Mexican-American Youth. *Proceedings, Southwestern Sociological Association,* March, pp. 131-35.
1970b   Comparative Structures and Attitudes Along the U.S.-Mexico Border. In Ellwyn R. Stoddard, ed. *Comparative U.S.-Mexico Border Studies,* pp. 1-38. Occasional Papers, no. 1. El Paso: Border-State University, Consortium for Latin America.

1970c   *The Role of Social Factors in the Successful Adjustment of Mexican American Families to Forced Housing Relocation: A Final Report of the Chamizal Relocation Research Project, El Paso, Texas.* El Paso: City of El Paso, Department of Planning Research and Development, Community Renewal Program.
1972   An International Boundary Treaty (the Chamizal) and Its Aftermath. Paper presented to the Rural Sociological Society, August, at Baton Rouge, Louisiana.
1973a   *Mexican Americans.* New York: Random House.
1973b   The Adjustment of Mexican-American Barrio Families to Forced Housing Relocation. *Social Science Quarterly* 53 (March):749-59.
1973c   Mexican-American Identity: A Multi-Cultural Legacy. Paper presented to Southwestern Social Science Association, March, at Dallas, Texas.
1973d   On Buying and Selling America: An Ethnohistorical Approach to Territorial Disputes and Land Grant Claims in the Southwest. Paper presented to Rocky Mountain Social Science Association, April, at Laramie, Wyoming.
1974   U.S.-Mexico Borderlands Studies: An Inventory of Scholars, Appraisal of Funding Resources and Research Projects. El Paso: University of Texas at El Paso, Center for Inter-American Studies.
1975a   Editor. The Status of U.S.-Mexico Borderlands Studies: A Symposium. *Social Science Journal* 12-13 (October, 1975-January, 1976):1-112.
1975b   Real, Regulated and Relative Poverty in the U.S.-Mexico Borderlands. Paper presented to Rural Sociological Society, August, at San Francisco, California.
1975c   Introduction, and The Status of Borderlands Studies: Sociology and Anthropology. In The Status of U.S.-Mexico Borderlands Studies: A Symposium, pp. 3-8, 29-54. *Social Science Journal* 12-13 (October, 1975-January, 1976):1-112.
1976a   Illegal Mexican Labor in the Borderlands: Institutionalized Support of an Unlawful Practice. *Pacific Sociological Review* 19 (April):175-210.
1976b   A Conceptual Analysis of the "Alien Invasion": Institutionalized Support of Illegal Mexican Aliens in the U.S. *International Migration Review* 10 (Summer):175-89.
1978a   Functional Alternatives to Bi-national Border Development Models: The Case of the U.S.-Mexico Region. Paper presented to American Sociological Association, September, at San Francisco, California.
1978b   Selected Impacts of Mexican Migration on the U.S.-Mexico Border. Paper presented to U.S. State Department Panel on U.S.-Mexican Border Issues, October, at Washington, D.C.
1978c   *Patterns of Poverty Along the U.S.-Mexico Border.* El Paso: University of Texas at El Paso, Center for Inter-American Studies and the Organization of U.S. Border Cities and Counties.
1978d   Illegal Mexican Aliens in Borderlands Society. *South Texas Journal of Research and the Humanities* 2 (Fall):197-213.
1979a   A 3-D Perspective of Water Gate Rip-offs Along the Rio Grande: Water Allocations by *Dam, District and Ditchrider.* In James D. Kitchen, ed. *Environmental Problems Along the Border,* pp. 38-71. Occasional Papers, no. 7 (Summer). San Diego: Border-State University, Consortium for Latin America.
1979b   Border and Non-Border Illegal Mexican Aliens: A Commentary. *El Paso Business Review* 16 (May):21-27.
1980   U.S.-Mexico Diplomacy: Its Latent Consequences in the Borderlands. Paper presented at Fifth World Congress of Rural Sociology, August, at Mexico City.
1981   Northern Mexican Migration and the U.S.-Mexico Border Region. Modified version of Stoddard, 1978b. *New Scholar* 9.
———; Martínez, Oscar J.; and Martínez Lasso, Miguel Angel

1979   *El Paso-Ciudad Juárez Relations and the "Tortilla Curtain": A Study of Local Adaptation to Federal Border Policies.* El Paso: El Paso Council on the Arts and Humanities and the University of Texas at El Paso.

————, and McConville, C. Lawrence
1978   The Effectiveness of Sociology in Training and Rewarding Scholars in a Multidisciplinary/Multicultural Field. *Western Sociological Review* 9 (Fall):67-75.

————, and West, Jonathan P.
1977   *The Impact of Mexico's Peso Devaluation on Selected U.S. Border Cities.* Tucson: SW Borderlands Consultants, and Organization of U.S. Border Cities.

Stoffle, Richard W.
1975   Reservation-based Industry: A Case from Zuñi, New Mexico. *Human Organization* 34 (Fall):217-25.

Stoller, Marianne L.
1976   The Early Santeros of New Mexico. Paper presented to American Society for Ethnohistory, Albuquerque.

Stone, Robert C.; Petroni, Frank A.; and McCleneghan, Thomas J.
1963   *Ambos Nogales:* Bi-cultural Urbanism in a Developing Region. *Arizona Review* 12 (January):1-29.

Storer, Desmond; Hawkins, Freda; and Tomasi, Silvan M.
1977   *Amnesty for Undocumented Migrants.* New York: Center for Migration Studies.

Strahler, Arthur N.
1944   Valleys and Parks of the Kaibab and Coconino Plateaus, Arizona. *Journal of Geology* 52 (November):361-87.

1945   Landscape Features of the Kaibab and Coconino Plateaus. *Plateau* 18 (July):1-6.

Strange, S.
1968   *The Mexican American in the Migrant Labor Setting.* East Lansing, Michigan State University.

Stratton, Porter A.
1969   *The Territorial Press of New Mexico, 1834-1912.* Albuquerque: University of New Mexico Press.

Strauss, Melvin Potter
1968   The Mexican-American in El Paso Politics. In Clyde Wingfield, ed. *Urbanization in the Southwest,* pp. 56-61. El Paso: Texas Western Press.

Strickland, Rennard
1975   Friends and Enemies of the American Indian: An Essay Review on Native American Law and Public Policy. *American Indian Law Review* 3 (no. 2):313-32.

Strong, Helen M.
1938   A Land Use Record in the Blackland Prairies of Texas. *Annals, Association of American Geographers* 28 (June):128-36.

Stuart, James, and Kearney, Michael
1978   Migration from the Mixteca of Oaxaca to the Californias: A Case Study. Paper presented to American Anthropological Association, November, at Los Angeles, California.

Stubbs, Stanley A.
1950   *Bird's-Eye View of the Pueblos.* Norman: University of Oklahoma Press.

Stuller, Jay
1978   Hunting the Wild Cargo. *New Times* 10 (June 26).

Sturtevant, William C.
1982   Editor. *Handbook of North American Indians,* vol. 10. Washington, D.C.: Smithsonian Institution, Bureau of American Ethnology.

Stycos, J. Mayone
1965   Opinions of Latin American Intellectuals on Population Problems and Birth Control. *Annals, American Academy of Political and Social Science* 360 (July):11-26.

1973   *Clinics, Contraception and Communication: Evaluation Studies of Family Planning Programs in Four Latin American Countries.* New York: Appleton-Century-Crofts.

————, and Arias, Jorge
1966   Editors. *Population Dilemma in Latin America.* Washington, D.C.: Potomac Books.

————, et al.
1971   *Ideology, Faith, and Family Planning in Latin America: Studies in Public and Private Opinion on Fertility Control.* New York: McGraw-Hill Book Co.

Suhm, D. A.; Krieger, A. D.; and Jelks, E. B.
1954   An Introductory Handbook of Texas Archeology. *Texas Archeological Society Bulletin* 25: entire volume.

Sung, Betty Lee
1967   *Mountain of Gold: The Story of the Chinese in America.* New York: Macmillan Co.

Sunseri, Alvin R.
1975   *New Mexico in the Aftermath of the Anglo-American Conquest, 1846-1861.* Ann Arbor: University Microfilms.

Sutton, Imre
1964   Land Tenure and Changing Occupance on Indian Reservations in Southern California. Ph.D. dissertation, University of California, Los Angeles.

1967   Private Property in Land Among Reservation Indians in Southern California. *Yearbook, Association of Pacific Coast Geographers* 29:69-89.

1968   Geographical Aspects of Construction Planning: Hoover Dam Revisited. *Journal of the West* 7 (no. 3):301-44.

1970   Land Tenure in the West: Continuity and Change. *Journal of the West* 9 (no. 1):1-23.

1975   *Indian Land Tenure. Bibliographical Essays and a Guide to the Literature.* New York: Clearwater Publishing Co.

Swadesh, Frances Leon
1968   The Alianza Movement: Catalyst for Social Change in New Mexico. In June Helm, ed. *Spanish-speaking People in the United States.* Proceedings, American Ethnological Society, pp. 162-77. Seattle: University of Washington Press.

1972   The Social and Philosophical Context of Creativity in Hispanic New Mexico. *Rocky Mountain Social Science Journal* 9 (January):11-18.

1973   *20,000 Years of History: A New Mexico Bibliography.* Santa Fe: Sunstone Press.

1974   *Los primeros pobladores: Hispanic Americans of the Ute Frontier.* Notre Dame: University of Notre Dame Press.

Swank, Irvin C.
1977   North American Heroin. *Drug Enforcement* 4 (January): 2-12.

Swartz, Harry
1945   *Seasonal Farm Labor in the United States.* New York: Columbia University Press.

Sweet, James A.
1974   *Recent Fertility Change Among High Fertility Minorities in the United States.* Working Paper no. 74-11. Madison: University of Wisconsin, Center for Demography and Ecology.

Sykes, Godfrey
1926   The Delta and Estuary of the Colorado River. *Geographical Review* 16 (April):232-55.

1931   Rainfall Investigations in Arizona and Sonora by Means of Long-Period Rain Gauges. *Geographical Review* 21 (April):229-33.

1937   *The Colorado Delta.* Washington, D.C.: Carnegie Institution of Washington, and American Geographical Society of New York.

Szasz, Margaret
1974   *Education and the American Indian: The Road to Self-Determination, 1928-1973.* Albuquerque: University of New Mexico Press.

Taebel, Delbert
1978   Minority Representation on City Councils: The Impact of Structure on Blacks and Hispanos. *Social Science Quarterly* 59 (June):142-53.

Talbert, Robert H.
1955   *Spanish Name People in the Southwest and West.* Fort

Worth: Texas Christian University and L. Potishman Foundation.

Tamayo, Jorge L.
1949 Cartografía. In *Geografía general de México,* pp. 43-96. Mexico City: Instituto Mexicano de Investigaciones Económicas. Vol. 1.
1962a *Atlas geográfico general de México.* Mexico City: Instituto Mexicano de Investigaciones Económicas.
1962b *Geografía general de Mexico.* Mexico City: Instituto Mexicano de Investigaciones Económicas. Vols. 1 and 2 (Geografía Física).
———, and West, Robert C.
1964 The Hydrography of Middle America. In Robert C. West and Robert Wauchope, eds. *Handbook of Middle American Indians,* vol. 1, pp. 84-121. Austin: University of Texas Press.

Tanner, Clara Lee
1968 *Southwest Indian Craft Arts.* Tucson: University of Arizona Press.
1973 *Southwest Indian Painting: A Changing Art.* 2d ed. Tucson: University of Arizona Press.
1976 *Prehistoric Southwestern Craft Arts.* Tucson: University of Arizona Press.

Tanner, John D., Jr.
1969 Campaign for Los Angeles: December 29, 1846, to January 10, 1847. *California Historical Society Quarterly* 48 (September):219-42.

Tansik, David A., and Tapia S., Humberto
1970 Is the Twin Plant Concept in Trouble? *Arizona Review* 19 (December):6-12.

Taplin, Glen W.
1962 The National Parks of Mexico. *National Parks Magazine* 36 (July):8-13.

Tardu, M. E.
1976 The Protocol to the UN Covenant on Civil and Political Rights and the Inter-American System: A Study of Co-existing Political Procedures. *American Journal of International Law* 70 (October):778-80.

Tarter, Donald E.
1970 Attitude: The Mental Myth. *American Sociologist* 5 (August):276-78.

Tax, Sol
1953 *Penny Capitalism: A Guatemalan Indian Economy.* Series no. 16. Washington, D.C.: Smithsonian Institution.

Taylor, Benjamin J.
1968 Indian Manpower Resources: The Experience of Five Southwestern Reservations. *Arizona Law Review* 10 (Winter):579-96.
1970 The Reservation Indian and Mainstream Economic Life. *Arizona Business Bulletin* 17 (December):12-22.
———, and Bond, M. E.
1968 Mexican Border Industrialization. *Michigan State University Business Topics* 16 (Spring):33-45.

Taylor, Jack E.
1962 *God's Messengers to Mexico's Masses: A Study of the Braceros.* Eugene, Ore.: Institute of Church Growth.

Taylor, James R.
1972 *Twin Plants and the Border Industrialization Program.* Vol. 4, *Needs Analysis of the Port of Anapra Development Program.* Las Cruces: New Mexico State University, Center for Business Services.
1973 Industrialization of the Mexican Border Region. *New Mexico Business* 26 (March):3-9.
1975 The Status of Borderlands Studies: Economics. *Social Science Journal* 12-13 (October, 1975-January, 1976): 69-76.

Taylor, James W.
1958 Geographic Bases of the Gadsden Purchase. *Journal of Geography* 57 (November):402-10.

Taylor, Marlowe M.
1960 *Rural People and Their Resources, North-Central New Mexico.* Agricultural Experiment Bulletin 448. Las Cruces: New Mexico State University.

Taylor, Morris F.
1965 Promoters of the Maxwell Grant. *Colorado Magazine* 42:133-50.
1968 A New Look at an Old Case: The Bent Heirs' Claim in the Maxwell Grant. *New Historical Review* 43:213-28.
1971 *First Mail West, Stagecoach Lines on the Santa Fe Trail.* Albuquerque: University of New Mexico Press.
1972 The Two Grants of Gervacio Nolan. *New Mexico Historical Review* 47:151-84.
1974 The Maxwell Cattle Company, 1881-1888. *New Mexico Historical Review* 49:289-24.
1976 The Uña de Gato Grant in Colfax County. *New Mexico Historical Review* 51:121-43.

Taylor, Paul S.
1930 Some Aspects of Mexican Immigration. *Journal of Political Economy* 38 (October):609-15.
1930-34 *Mexican Labor in the United States.* 3 vols. Berkeley: University of California Press.
1931a Mexicans North of the Rio Grande. *Survey Graphic* 66 (May):135-40.
1931b Crime and the Foreign Born: The Problem of the Mexican. *U.S. Commission of Law Observation and Enforcement* 10:199-243.
1934 *An American-Mexican Frontier: Nueces County, Texas.* Chapel Hill: University of North Carolina Press.
1978 The Future of Mexican Immigration. In Arthur F. Corwin, ed. *Immigrants—and Immigrants: Perspectives on Mexican Labor Migration to the United States,* pp. 347-52. Westport, Conn.: Greenwood Press.

Taylor, Paul S.
1968 Water, Land and People in the Great Valley. *American West* 5 (March):24-29.
1970 Reclamation: The Rise and Fall of an American Idea. *American West* 7 (July):27-33.
1973 Water, Land and Environment, Imperial Valley: Law Caught in the Winds of Politics. *Natural Resources Journal* 13 (January):1-35.

Taylor, Walter P., et al.
1946 The Sierra del Carmen in Northern Coahuila: A Preliminary Ecological Survey. *Texas Geographic Magazine* 10 (Spring):11-22.

Taylor, William B.
1972 *Landlord and Peasant in Oaxaca.* Stanford: Stanford University Press.
1975 Land and Water Rights in the Viceroyalty of New Spain. *New Mexico Historical Review* 50:189-212.
———, and West, Elliott
1973 Patrón Leadership at the Crossroads: Southern Colorado in the Late Nineteenth Century. *Pacific Historical Review* 49 (August):335-57.

Taylor, W. W., Jr.
1966 Archaic Cultures Adjacent to the Northeastern Frontiers of Mesoamerica. In Handbook of Middle American Indians, vol. 4, pp. 59-94. Austin: University of Texas Press.
1972 The Hunter-Gatherer Nomads of Northern Mexico: A Comparison of the Archival and Archeological Records. *World Archaeology* 4 (no. 2):167-78.

Teclaff, Ludwick A.
1967 *The Lower Basin in History and Law.* The Hague: Martinus Nijhoff.
1972 *Abstraction and Use of Water: A Comparison of Legal Regimes.* Doc. ST/CH 152. New York: United Nations.

Teller, Charles H.
1973a Nativity, Health Care and Disease: A Study of Diphtheric Mexican American Families in San Antonio. Paper presented to Southwestern Sociological Association, March, at Dallas, Texas.
1973b Annotated Bibliography on the Demography of the Mexi-

can American Population. Paper presented to Conference on Demography of the Mexican American People, May, at Austin, Texas.

1978   Physical Health Status and Health Care Utilization in the Texas Borderlands. In Stanley R. Ross, ed. *Views Across the Border*, pp. 256-79. Albuquerque: University of New Mexico Press.

————, and Clyburn, Steve
1974a   Texas Population in 1970: Trends and Ethnic Differentials in Infant Mortality. *Texas Business Review* 48:240-46.

1974b   *Illness and Access to Medical Care in a Tri-ethnic Texas Community.* Mimeographed. Austin: Department of Research and Transportation.

Telloz, Joaquin
1972   Sources of Atmospheric Pollution at the U.S.-Mexican Border. *Natural Resources Journal* 12 (October):564-66.

Templer, Otis W.
1973a   Water Law and the Hydrologic Cycle: A Texas Example. *Water Resources Bulletin* 9 (April):273-83.

1973b   Institutional Constraints and Water Resources. Water Rights Adjudication in Texas. *Rocky Mountain Social Science Journal* 10 (October):37-45.

1976   *Institutional Constraints and Conjunctive Management of Water Resources in West Texas.* WRC-76-1. Lubbock: Texas Tech University, Water Resources Center.

1978a   The Geography of Arid Lands: A Basic Bibliography. No. 78-1. Lubbock: Texas Tech University, International Center for Arid and Semi-Arid Land Studies.

1978b   Texas Ground Water Law: Inflexible Institutions and Resource Realities. *Ecumene* 10 (April):6-15.

1978c   Texas Surface Water Law: The Legacy of the Past and Its Impact on Water Resource Management. *Historical Geography Newsletter* 8 (Spring):11-20.

ten Brock, Jacobus; Barnhart, Edward H.; and Watson, Floyd K.
1968   *Prejudice, War and the Constitution: Japanese American Evacuations and Resettlement.* Berkeley: University of California Press.

Terjung, Werner
1966   Physiological Climates of California. *Yearbook of the Association of Pacific Coast Geographers* 28:55-73.

Terrazas Sánchez, Filberto
1974   *La guerra apache en México: viento de octubre.* Mexico City: Costa-Amic.

Terrell, John U.
1965-66 *War for the Colorado River.* 2 vols. Glendale: Arthur H. Clark Co.

Terry, James L., Jr.
1976   Reasonable Suspicion for Border Patrol Stops: United States v. Brigoni-Ponce, U.S. Supreme Court, 1975. *Columbia Journal of Transnational Law* 15 (no. 2).

Teschner, Richard V.
1972   Anglicisms in Spanish: A Cross-referenced Guide to Previous Findings, Together with English Lexical Influence on Chicago Mexican Spanish. Ph.D. dissertation, University of Wisconsin, Madison.

————; Bills, Garland D.; and Craddock, Jerry R.
1975   *Spanish and English of U.S. Hispanos: A Critical, Annotated, Linguistic Bibliography.* Arlington: Center for Applied Linguistics.

Thames, John L.
1977   Editor. *Reclamation and Use of Disturbed Land in the Southwest.* Tucson: University of Arizona Press.

Thomas, Alfred Barnaby
1931   Governor Mendinueta's Proposals for the Defense of New Mexico, 1772-1778. *New Mexico Historical Review* 4 (no. 1):21-39.

1932   *Forgotten Frontiers: A Study of the Spanish Indian Policy of Don Juan Bautista de Anza, Governor of New Mexico, 1777-1787.* Norman: University of Oklahoma Press.

1935   *After Coronado: Spanish Exploration Northeast of New Mexico, 1696-1727.* Norman: University of Oklahoma Press.

1940   *The Plains Indians and New Mexico, 1751-1778.* Albuquerque: University of New Mexico Press.

1941   *Teodoro de Croix and the Northern Frontier of New Spain, 1776-1783.* Norman: University of Oklahoma Press.

1974a   *The Mescalero Apache, 1653-1874.* New York: Garland Publishing, University of Alabama.

1974b   *The Jicarilla Apache Indians: A History, 1598-1888.* New York: Garland Publishing, University of Alabama.

Thomas, George
1948   *Early Irrigation in the Western States.* Salt Lake City: University of Utah Press.

Thomas, H. E.
1955   *Water Rights in Areas of Ground-Water Mining.* Circular no. 347. Washington, D.C.: U.S. Geological Survey.

1962   *The Meteorologic Phenomenon of Drought in the Southwest, 1942-56.* Professional Paper 372-A. Washington, D.C.: U.S. Geological Survey.

1963   *General Summary of Effects of the Drought in the Southwest.* Professional Paper 372-H. Washington, D.C.: U.S. Geological Survey.

1972   Water-Management Problems Related to Ground Water Rights in the Southwest. *Water Resources Bulletin* 8 (February):110-17.

————, et al.
1963a   *Effects of Drought Along Pacific Coast in California.* Professional Paper 372-G. Washington, D.C.: U.S. Geological Survey.

1963b   *Effects of Drought in Basins of Interior Drainage.* Professional Paper 372-E. Washington, D.C.: U.S. Geological Survey.

1963c   *Effects of Drought in Central and South Texas.* Professional Paper 372-C. Washington, D.C.: U.S. Geological Survey.

1963d   *Effects of Drought in the Colorado River Basin.* Professional Paper 372-F. Washington, D.C.: U.S. Geological Survey.

1963e   *Effects of Drought in the Rio Grande Basin.* Professional Paper 372-D. Washington, D.C.: U.S. Geological Survey.

Thomas, William L., Jr.
1961   Competition for a Desert Lake: The Salton Sea, California. *California Geographer* 2:31-39.

Thomforde, Duane W.
1969   Political Socialization in South El Paso. Master's thesis, University of Texas at El Paso.

Thompson, Erwin N.
1968   The Negro Soldiers on the Frontier: A Fort Davis Case Study. *Journal of the West* 7 (April):217-35.

Thompson, Jerry Don
1972   Mexican-Americans in the Civil War: The Battle of Valverde. *Texana* 10 (no. 1):1-19.

Thompson, Kenneth
1969a   Insalubrious California: Perception and Reality. *Annals, Association of American Geographers* 59 (March):50-64.

1969b   Irrigation as a Menace to Health in California: A Nineteenth Century View. *Geographical Review* 59 (April):195-214.

Thompson, Laura
1950   *Culture in Crisis: A Study of the Hopi Indians.* New York: Harper & Brothers.

Thompson, Roger M.
1971   Language Loyalty in Austin, Texas: A Study of a Bilingual Neighborhood: Ph.D. dissertation, University of Texas, Austin.

Thompson, R. W., and Robbins, M. C.
1975   Seasonal Variation in Conception in Rural Uganda and

Mexico. *American Anthropologist* 75 (no. 3):676-86.

Thompson, Stephen I.
1973   Pioneer Colonization: A Cross-Cultural View. Module in Anthropology no. 33. Los Angeles: Addison-Wesley Publishing Co.

Thompson, Warren S.
1955   *Growth and Change in California's Population.* Los Angeles: Haynes Foundation.

Thornbury, William D.
1965   *Regional Geomorphology of the United States.* New York: John Wiley & Sons.

Thornthwaite, C. Warren
1931   The Climates of North America According to a New Classification. *Geographical Review* 21 (October):633-55.

———; Sharpe, C. F. Stewart; and Dosch, Earl F.
1941   Climate of the Southwest in Relation to Accelerated Erosion. *Soil Conservation* 6 (May):298-302, 304.

1942   *Climate and Accelerated Erosion in the Arid and Semi-Arid Southwest, with Special Reference to the Polacca Wash Drainage Basin, Arizona.* Technical Bulletin no. 808. Washington, D.C.: U.S. Department of Agriculture.

Thrapp, Dan L.
1974   *Victorio and the Mimbres Apaches.* Norman: University of Oklahoma Press.

Thrower, Norman J. W.
1970   Land Use in the Southwestern United States: From Gemini and Apollo Imagery. *Annals, Association of American Geographers* 60 (March):208-209. Annals Map Supplement no. 12.

———, et al.
1970   *Satellite Photography as a Geographic Tool for Land Use Mapping of the Southwestern United States, 1 July 1968-31 January 1970.* Interagency Report USGS-193, Technical Report 69-3. Washington, D.C.: U.S. Geological Survey.

Tibesar, Antonine
1955   Editor. *Writings of Junípero Serra, 1773,* vol. 1, pp. 295-327. In Wayne Moquin, ed. *A Documentary History of the Mexican Americans,* pp. 98-102. New York: Praeger Publishers, 1971.

Tichborne, Roger
1970   Tales of Mexico and Marijuana. *Scanlans* 1:7-20.

Tidestrom, I., and Kittell, T. A.
1941   *Flora of Arizona and New Mexico.* Washington, D.C.: Catholic University of America Press.

Tiller, James W., Jr.
1971   *The Texas Winter Garden: Commercial Cool Season Vegetable Production.* Austin: University of Texas, Bureau of Business Research.

1973   Truck Farming as a Factor in the Settlement of the Texas Winter Garden. *Ecumene* 5 (May):6-15.

Tiller, Veronica
1976   The History of the Jicarilla Apache Tribe, 1541-1970. Ph.D. dissertation, University of New Mexico.

Timmons, Wilbert H.
1968   Tadeo Ortiz and Texas. *Southwestern Historical Quarterly* 72 (July):21-33.

Tinker, Ben
1978   *Mexican Wilderness and Wildlife.* Austin: University of Texas Press.

Tinkle, Lon
1958   *13 Days to Glory: The Seige of the Alamo.* New York: McGraw-Hill Book Co.

Tipton, William
1943   *Engineering Memorandum on Treaty with Mexico Relating to the Utilization of the Waters of Certain Rivers.* Vol. 2. Six States Committee.

Titiev, Mischa
1972   *The Hopi Indians of Old Oraibi: Change and Continuity.*

Ann Arbor: University of Michigan Press.

Tobias, Henry, and Woodhouse, Charles
1969   Editors. *Ethnic Minorities in Politics.* Albuquerque: University of New Mexico Press.

Toney, W. T., Jr.
1973   *A Descriptive Study of the Control of Illegal Mexican Migration in the Southwestern United States.* Published Master's thesis, Sam Houston State University. San Francisco: R & E Research Associates, 1977.

Toor, Frances
1932   Courtship and Marriage. *Mexican Folkways* (July-September):160.

1937a   Apuntes sobre costumbres yaquis. *Mexican Folkways* (July):52-63.

1937b   Los fiesteros de la fiesta de San Juan en el pueblo de Vicam. *Mexican Folkways* (July):26-31.

Torres, Olga Ester
1976   Algunas observaciones sobre la economía de la frontera norte de México. *Comercio Exterior* 26 (December): 1406-13.

Toulouse, Betty
1977   *Pueblo Pottery of the New Mexico Indians.* Santa Fe: Museum of New Mexico.

Toussaint, Manuel
1967   *Colonial Art in Mexico.* Translated and edited by Elizabeth Wilder Weismann. Austin: University of Texas Press.

Tout, Otis B.
1931   *The First Thirty Years: An Account of the Principal Events of the History of the Imperial Valley.* San Diego: O. B. Tout.

Tower, Frederick J.
1977   Marketing in Mexico. Overseas Business Reports (March). Washington, D.C.: Department of Commerce, Office of International Marketing.

1979   Mexico: Imports to Rise in '79, with Emphasis on Industrial Needs. *World Trade Outlook for Latin America,* March, 7.

Towne, Charles W., and Wentworth, Edward N.
1946   *Shepherd's Empire.* Norman: University of Oklahoma Press.

Townsend, Jeff
1975   *Making Rain in America: A History.* No. 75-3. Lubbock: Texas Tech University, International Center for Arid and Semi-Arid Land Studies.

Toynbee, Arnold J.
1934-61   *A Study of History.* 13 vols. London: Oxford University Press.

Trejo, Arnulfo D.
1951   Vocablos y modismos del español de Arizona. Master's thesis, Universidad de las Américas (Mexico City College).

Trelease, Frank J.
1954   Coordination of Riparian and Appropriative Rights to the Use of Water. *Texas Law Review* 33 (November): 24-69.

Treutlein, Theodore E.
1968   The Portola Expedition of 1769-1770. *California Historical Society Quarterly* 47 (December):291-313.

1972   Fagés as Explorer, 1769-1770. *California Historical Society Quarterly* 51 (Winter):338-56.

Treviño, Julio B.
1969   Border Assembly Operations. *Mexican-American Review* 37 (April):31-33.

Trillin, Calvin
1970   U.S. Journal: Los Angeles. New Group in Town. *New Yorker,* April 18, pp. 92-104.

1971   U.S. Journal: Gallup, New Mexico. *New Yorker,* September 25, pp. 108-14.

Troike, Rudolph C., and Modiano, Nancy
1977   Proceedings of the First Inter-American Conference on

Bilingual Education. In Donald W. Bleznick, ed. *Hispania.* Worcester: American Association of Spanish and Portuguese.

Troncoso, Francisco del Paso y. See under Paso y Troncoso, Francisco del.

Trotter, Robert T., II
1979   Evidence of an Ethnomedical Form of Aversion Therapy on the United States-Mexico Border. *Journal of Ethnopharmacology* 1:279-84.

1982   Ethnic Patterns of Alcohol Use: Anglo and Mexican-American College Students. *Adolescence Journal* 17 (summer):305-25.

Tryk, Sheila
1977   Spanish Colonial Arts and Crafts: Reflections of a Way of Life. *New Mexico Magazine* 55 (January):14-21, 44-45.

Tuan, Yi-Fu
1962   Structure, Climate and Basin Land Forms in Arizona and New Mexico. *Annals, Association of American Geographers* 52 (March):51-68.

1966   New Mexican Gullies: A Critical Review and Some Recent Observations. *Annals, Association of American Geographers* 56 (December):573-97.

———, and Everard, Cyril E.
1964   New Mexico's Climate: The Appreciation of a Resource. *Natural Resources Journal* 4 (October):268-308.

———; Everard, Cyril E.; and Widdison, Jerold G.
1969   *The Climate of New Mexico.* Santa Fe: State Planning Office.

Tuck, Ruth
1946   *Not with the Fist: Mexican Americans in a Southwest City.* New York: Harcourt, Brace.

Tuohy, William S.
1973   Centralism and Political Elite Behavior in Mexico. In Clarence E. Thurber and Lawrence S. Graham, eds. *Development Administration in Latin America,* pp. 260-80. Durham, N.C.: Duke University Press.

1974   Psychology in Political Analysis: The Case of Mexico. *Western Political Quarterly* 27 (no. 2):289-307.

Turnage, William V., and Mallery, T. D.
1941   *An Analysis of Rainfall in the Sonoran Desert and Adjacent Territory.* Publication no. 529. Washington, D.C.: Carnegie Institution of Washington.

Turner, Frederick C.
1974   *Responsible Parenthood: The Politics of Mexico's New Population Policies.* Washington, D.C.: American Enterprise Institute for Public Policy Research.

Turner, Frederick Jackson
1920   *The Frontier in American History.* New York: Henry Holt.

1938   *The Early Writings of Frederick Jackson Turner.* Madison: University of Wisconsin Press.

Turner, Louis
1973   *Multinational Corporations and the Third World.* New York: Hill & Wang.

Turney, Jack R., and Ellis, Harold H.
1962   *State Water-Rights Laws and Related Subjects: A Bibliography.* Miscellaneous Publication no. 921. Washington, D.C.: U.S. Department of Agriculture.

Tuthill, Carr
1947   *The Tres Alamos Site on the San Pedro River, Southeastern Arizona.* Publication no. 4. Dragoon, Ariz.: Amerind Foundation.

Twitchell, Ralph Emerson
1909   *The History of the Military Occupation of the Territory of New Mexico from 1846 to 1851.* Denver: Smith-Brooks Co.

1911-14   *The Leading Facts of New Mexican History.* 2 vols. Cedar Rapids, Ia.: Torch Press.

1914   *The Spanish Archives of New Mexico.* 2 vols. Glendale: Arthur H. Clark Co.

1922   Pueblo Indian Land Tenures in New Mexico and Arizona. *El Palacio* 12 (March 1):31-33, 38-61.

1925   *Old Santa Fe.* Danville, Ill.: Interstate Printers & Publishers.

Tyler, Daniel
1970   Gringo Views of Governor Armijo. *New Mexico Historical Review* 45 (January):23-44.

Tyler, Gus
1973   Labor's Multinational Pains. *Foreign Policy* 12 (Fall): 113-32.

Tyler, Ronnie C.
1966   The Rangers at Zacualtipan. *Texana* 4 (Winter):341-50.

1967   The Callahan Expedition of 1855: Indians or Negroes? *Southwestern Historical Quarterly* 70 (April):574-85.

1969   Santiago Vidaurri and the Confederacy. *Americas* 26 (July):66-76.

1970   Cotton on the Border, 1861-1865. *Southwestern Historical Quarterly* 73 (April):456-77.

1974   *Santiago Vidaurri and the Southern Confederacy.* Austin: Texas State Historical Association.

Tyler, Sergeant Daniel
1881   *A Concise History of the Mormon Battalion in the Mexican War, 1846-1847.* N.p., n.d. Glorieta, N.M.: Rio Grande Press, 1964.

Uchendu, Victor C.
1966   *Navajo Harvest Hands: An Ethnographic Report* (February). Stanford: Stanford University, Food Research Institute.

Ugalde, Antonio
1970   *Power and Conflict in a Mexican Community.* Albuquerque: University of New Mexico Press.

1974   *The Urbanization Process of a Poor Mexican Neighborhood.* Austin: University of Texas, Institute of Latin American Studies.

1978   Regional Political Processes and Mexican Politics on the Border. In Stanley R. Ross, ed. *Views Across the Border,* pp. 97-116. Albuquerque: University of New Mexico Press.

Uhlenberg, Peter
1972   Demographic Correlates of Group Achievement: Contrasting Patterns of Mexican-Americans and Japanese-Americans. *Demography* 9 (February):119-28.

1973   Fertility Patterns Within the Mexican-American Population. *Social Biology* 2 (no. 1):30-39.

Uhlmann, Julie M.
1973   The Impact of Urbanization on the Fertility Behavior of Pápago Indian Women. Ph.D. dissertation, University of Colorado.

1974   Boundary Maintenance in the Urban Environment: The Pápago Case. Paper presented to American Anthropological Association, November, in Mexico City.

Ulibarrí, Horacio
1966   Social and Attitudinal Characteristics of Spanish-speaking Migrant and Ex-Migrant Workers in the Southwest. *Sociology and Social Research* 50:361-70.

Ullman, Edward J.
1957   *American Commodity Flow.* Seattle: University of Washington Press.

Ulloa, Berta.
1963   *Revolución mexicana, 1910-1920.* Mexico City: Secretaría de Relaciones Exteriores.

1965   Las relaciones Mexico-Norteamericanas, 1910-1911. *Historia Mexicana* 15 (July-September):25-46.

1971   La revolución intervenida: Relaciones diplomáticas entre México y los Estados Unidos, 1910-1914. México: El Colegio de México, Centro de Estudios Historicos.

Underhill, Ruth M.
1939   *Social Organization of the Pápago Indians.* Contributions to Anthropology, vol. 30. New York: Columbia University.

1946 *Pápago Indian Religion.* Contributions to Anthropology, vol. 33. New York: Columbia University.

1974 *Acculturation at the Pápago Village of Santa Rosa.* New York: Garland Publishing, Columbia University.

Unikel, Luis

1970 The Process of Urbanization in Mexico: Distribution and Growth of Urban Population. In F. F. Rabinovitz and F. M. Trueblood, eds. *Latin American Urban Research.* Beverly Hills: Sage Publications.

1972 Bibliografía sobre desarrollo urbano y regional en México. *Demografía y Economía* 4 (no. 3):377-408.

Urquidi, Victor

1967 Fundamental Problems of the Mexican Economy. In Tom B. Davis, ed. *Mexico's Recent Economc Growth: The Mexican View,* pp.173-203. Austin: University of Texas Press.

——, and Villarreal, Sofía Méndez

1975 Importa económica de la zona fronteriza del norte de México. *Foro Internacional* 16 (October-December): 149-74.

1978 Economic Importance of Mexico's Northern Border Region. In Stanley R. Ross, ed. *Views Across the Border,* pp. 141-62. Albuquerque: University of New Mexico Press.

Utley, Robert M.

1966 The Range Cattle Industry in the Big Bend of Texas. *Southwestern Historical Quarterly* 69 (April):419-41.

1973 *Frontier Regulars: The United States Army and the Indians, 1866-1890.* New York: Macmillan Co.

Utton, Albert E.

1967 International Streams and Lakes. In Robert E. Clark, ed. *Waters and Water Rights.* vol. 2. Indianapolis: Allen Smith Co.

1972 Pollution and Political Boundaries: U.S.-Mexican Environmental Problems. *Natural Resources Journal* 12 (October):479-614.

1973 Editor. *Pollution and International Boundaries: U.S.-Mexican Environmental Problems.* Albuquerque: University of New Mexico Press.

1974 Editor. *International Environmental Law.* New York: Praeger Publishers.

1978 International Groundwater Management. *Nebraska Law Review* 57 (no. 3):633-64.

Vaca, Nick

1970*a* The Mexican-American in the Social Sciences, 1912-1970. Part 1: 1912-1935. *El Grito* 3 (Summer):3-24.

1970*b* The Mexican-American in the Social Sciences, 1912-1970. Part 2: 1935-1970. *El Grito* 4 (Fall):17-51.

Valdés-Fallis, Guadalupe

1973 Spanish and the Mexican Americans. *Colorado Quarterly* 22:483-93.

Valdez Terrazas, Alberto

1950 El salvajismo apache en Chihuahua. *Boletín de la Sociedad Chihuahuense de Estudios Históricos* 7 (January-February):372-74.

Valencia, Nestor A.

1969 Twentieth Century Urbanization in Latin America and a Case Study of Ciudad Juárez. Master's thesis, University of Texas at El Paso.

Valenzuela, A. M.

1971 The Relationship Between Self-Concept, Intelligence, Socio-economic Status and School Achievement Among Spanish-American Children in Omaha. Field Report. Lincoln: University of Nebraska.

Vallier, I.

1970 *Catholicism, Social Control, and Modernization in Latin America.* Englewood Cliffs, N.J.: Prentice-Hall.

Van Dam, Andre

1971 The World's Work: Who Needs It Most. *Columbia Journal of World Business* 6 (September-October):24-30.

Van der Spak, Peter G.

1975 Mexico's Booming Border Zone: A Magnet for Labor-intensive American Plants. *Inter-American Economic Affairs* 29 (no. 2):33-47.

Van Devender, T. R.; Martin, P. S.; Phillips, A. M.; and Spaulding, W. G.

1977 Late Pleistocene Biotic Communities from the Guadalupe Mountains, Culberson County, Texas. In R. H. Wauer and D. H. Riskind, eds. *Transactions of the Symposium on the Biological Resources of the Chihuahuan Desert Region, United States and Mexico,* pp. 107-13. Transactions and Proceedings Series no. 3. Washington, D.C.: Department of the Interior, National Park Service.

Van Devender, T. R., and Worthington, R. D.

1977 The Herpetofauna of Howell's Ridge Cave and the Paleoecology of the Northwestern Chihuahuan Desert. In R. H. Wauer and D. H. Riskind, eds. *Transactions of the Symposium on the Biological Resources of the Chihuahuan Desert Region, United States and Mexico,* pp. 85-106. Transactions and Proceedings Series no. 3. National Park Service.

Van Dresser, Peter

1960 Rootstock for a New Regionalism. *Landscape* 10 (Fall): 11-14.

1972 *A Landscape for Humans: A Case Study of the Potentials for Ecologically Guided Development in an Uplands Region.* Albuquerque: Biotechnic Press.

Van Dyke, John C.

1918 *The Desert.* New York: Charles Scribner's Sons.

Van Ness, John R.

1974 Spanish-American *v.* Anglo-American Land Tenure and the Study of Economic Change in New Mexico. Paper presented to Rocky Mountain Social Science Association, April, at El Paso, Texas.

1976 Spanish American *v.* Anglo American Land Tenure and the Study of Economic Change in New Mexico. *Social Science Journal* 13 (October):46-52.

Van Royen, W.

1927 The Climatic Regions of North America. *Monthly Weather Review* 55:315-19.

Van Valkenburgh, Richard F.

1974 *Short History of the Navajo People.* New York: Garland Publishing, Bureau of Indian Affairs.

——, and Kluckhohn, Clyde

1974 *Navajo Sacred Places* (83 photographs plus notes). New York: Garland Publishing, Bureau of Indian Affairs and Harvard University.

Vasek, F. C.; Johnson, H. B.; and Brum, G. D.

1975 Effects of Power Transmission Lines on Vegetation of the Mojave Desert. *Madroño* 23:114-30.

Vásquez, James

1972 Measurement of Intelligence and Language Differences. *Aztlán* 3 (Spring):155-63.

Vasquez, Librado Keno, and Vasquez, María Enriqueta

Veeder, William H.

1965 Winters Doctrine Rights: Keystone of National Programs for Western Land and Water Conservation and Utilization. *Montana Law Review* 26:149-72.

1969 Federal Encroachment on Indian Water Rights and the Impairment of Reservation Development. In U.S. Congress, Joint Economic Committee. *Toward Economic Development for Native American Communities,* pp. 460-518. Washington, D.C.: Government Printing Office.

1971 Indian Private and Paramount Rights to Use of Waters. *Rocky Mountain Mineral Law Institute* 16:631-68.

1972 Water Rights: Life or Death for the American Indian. *Indian Historian* 5 (no. 2):4-21.

Veeman, Terrence

1978 Water Policy and Water Institutions in Northern India:

The Case of Ground Water Rights. *Natural Resources Journal* 18 (July):569-88.

Vega, J.
1943   La raza tarahumara y el medio geográfico y social en que vive. *Sociedad Mexicana de Geografía y Estadística Boletín* 58:103-21.

Velasco Valdez, Miguel
1967   Repertorio de voces populares en Mexico. Mexico City: B. Costa-Amic.

Velie, Lester
1970   Poverty at the Border: Mexican Labor Brought in by Greedy U.S. Employers. *Readers Digest* 97:92-97.

Velimirovic, Boris
1978a   Editor. *Modern Medicine and Medical Anthropology in the United States-Mexico Border Population.* Washington, D.C.: Pan American Health Organization.
1978b   Selected Bibliography in Medical Anthropology for Health Professionals in the Americas. Mimeographed. El Paso: Pan American Health Organization, Regional Office.
1979   Forgotten People: Health of the Migrants. *Bulletin of the Pan American Health Organization* 13 (no. 1):66-85.

Venezian, Eduardo L., and Gamble, William K.
1969   *The Agricultural Development of Mexico: Its Structure and Growth Since 1950.* New York: Praeger Publishers.

Verba, Sidney, and Nie, Norman H.
1972   *Participation in America: Political Democracy and Social Equality.* New York: Harper & Row.

Vernon, Raymond
1963   *The Dilemma of Mexico's Development.* Cambridge: Harvard University Press.

Vestal, P. A.
1952   *Ethnobotany of the Ramah Navajo.* Peabody Museum of American Archaeology and Ethnology, vol. 40, no. 4. Cambridge: Harvard University.

Vetterli, Richard R.
1972   The Impact of the Multi-national Corporation on the Power Structure of Mexico and a Mexican Border Community. Ph.D. dissertation, University of California, Riverside.

Vigil, Maurilio
1977   *Chicano Politics.* Washington, D.C.: University Press of America.

Vigil, Ralph H.
1973a   The New Borderlands History: A Critique. *New Mexico Historical Review* 48 (July):189-208.
1973b   The Hispanic Heritage and the Borderlands. *Journal of San Diego History* 19 (July):32-39.
1974a   The Lords of New Spain and Mexico. *Rocky Mountain Social Science Journal* 11 (April):103-12.
1974b   A Reappraisal of the Expedition of Pánfilo de Narváez to Mexico in 1520. *Revista de Historia de America* 77-78 (January-December):101-25.
1976   Alonso de Zorita, Early and Last Years. *Americas* 32 (April):501-13.

Vigness, David M.
1963   *The Revolutionary Decades, 1810-1836.* Austin: Steck Co.
1972   Nuevo Santander in 1795: A Provincial Inspection by Félix Calleja. *Southwestern Historical Quarterly* 75 (April):461-506.

Villafuerte, Carlos
1959   *Ferrocarriles.* Mexico, D.F.: Fondo de Cultura Economica.

Villalobos Calderón, Liborio
1973   On the Importance of the Assembly Industries to the Mexican Economy. Paper presented to Conference at Institute of Latin American Studies, April, in Austin, Texas.

Villalpando, M. Vic, et al.
1977   A Study of the Socioeconomic Impact of Illegal Aliens on the County of San Diego. Report. San Diego: County Human Resources Agency.

Villareal Cárdenas, Rodolfo
1968   The Industrialization of the Northern Mexican Border and the United States Investor. *Arizona Review* 17 (January):6-9.

Villaseñor Martínez, Irene
1964   La Familia Mexicana. Dissertation, ITESCO, Guadalajara, Mexico.

Vines, Robert A.
1960   *Trees, Shrubs, and Woody Vines of the Southwest.* Austin: University of Texas Press.

Viveros, Michael
1972   *Anatomía de una prisión: 1525 días en Lecumberri y Santa Marta.* Mexico City: Editorial Dina.

Vivian, Gordon
1964   *Excavations in a 17th-Century Jumano Pueblo, Gran Quivera, New Mexico.* Archeological Research Series, no. 8. Washington, D.C.: U.S. Department of the Interior, National Park Service.

Vivó Escoto, Jorge A.
1943   Marco geografico del norte de México. In *El norte de Mexico y el sur de Estados Unidos,* pp. 11-16. Mexico City: Sociedad Mexicana de Antropología.
1948   Geografía de Mexico. Mexico City: Fondo de Cultura Económica. Also published in 1953.
1964   Weather and Climate of Mexico and Central America. In Robert C. West, ed. *Handbook of Middle American Indians,* 1:187-215. Austin: University of Texas Press.
1968   El uso del suelo en las ciudades portuarias y fronterizas. *Anuario de Geografía* 8:186-94.

———, and Gómez, José C.
1946   Climatología de México. Mexico City: Instituto Panamericano de Geografía e Historia, no. 19.

Vizcaya Canales, Isidro
1968   La invasión de los indios Bárbaros al nordeste de México en los años de 1840 y 1841. Serie Historia no. 7. Monterrey: Instituto Técnico y de Estudios Superiores.

Vogler, James D.
1968   The Influence of Ethnicity and Socioeconomic Status on the Pictorial Test of Intelligence. Ph.D. dissertation, University of Arizona.

Vogt, Evon Z.
1955   *Modern Homesteaders: The Life of a Twentieth-Century Frontier Community.* Cambridge: Harvard University Press.
1961   Navajo. In Edward H. Spicer, ed. *Perspectives in American Indian Culture Change,* pp. 278-336. Chicago: University of Chicago Press.

———, and Alvert, Ethel M.
1969   *People of Rimrock.* Cambridge: Harvard University Press.

———, and O'Dea, Thomas F.
1953   A Comparative Study of the Role of Values in Social Action in Two Southwestern Communities. *American Sociological Review* 18 (December):645-54.

Vollmann, Tim
1974   Criminal Jurisdiction in Indian Country: Tribal Sovereignty and Defendants' Rights in Conflict. *Kansas Law Review* 22 (Spring):387-412.

Von Eschen, G. F.
1958   Climatic Trends in New Mexico. *Weatherwise* 11 (December):191-95.

Von Humboldt, Alexander. See Humboldt, Alexander Von.

Vought, Martha
1967   Shamans and Padres: The Religion of the Southern California Mission Indian. *Pacific Historical Review* 36 (November):363-73.

Waddell, Jack O.
1969   *Pápago Indians at Work.* Anthropological Papers, no. 12. Tucson: University of Arizona.
1970   Resurgent Patronage and Lagging Bureaucracy in a Pápago

Off-Reservation Community. *Human Organization* 29 (Spring):37-42.

————, and Watson, O. Michael
1971 Editors. *The American Indian in Urban Society.* Boston: Little, Brown & Co.

Waddle, Paula
1977 The Legislative and Judicial Response to the Immigration of Undocumented Workers. *South Texas Journal of Research and the Humanities* 1 (Fall):177-210.

Wagenknecht, Edward
1962 *The Movies in the Age of Innocence.* Norman: University of Oklahoma Press.

Wagner, Henry R.
1929 *Spanish Voyage to the Northwest Coast of America in the Sixteenth Century.* San Francisco: California Historical Society.
1937 *The Spanish Southwest, 1542-1794.* 2 vols. Albuquerque: Quivira Society.

Wagner, Henry Raup, and Parish, Helen Rand
1967 *The Life and Writings of Bartolomé de las Casas.* Albuquerque: University of New Mexico Press.

Wagner, John A.
1966 The Role of the Christian Church. In Julian Samora, ed. *La Raza: Forgotten Americans*, pp. 27-45. Notre Dame: University of Notre Dame Press.

Wagoner, J. J.
1952 *The History of the Cattle Industry in Southern Arizona, 1540-1940.* Tucson: University of Arizona Press.

Wakin, Edward
1971 *Black Fighting Men.* New York: Lorthrop, Lee & Shepard.
1974 *The Lebanese and Syrians in America.* Chicago: Claretian Publications.

Walker, Darthula
1937 Adjustments to the Climate of the Llano Estacado Region of Texas. *Yearbook of the Association of Pacific Coast Geographers* 3:10-15.

Walker, George
1972 Border Health Survey: Final Report on Phase Three of the El Paso-Ciudad Juárez Project. Paper presented to U.S.-Mexico Border Health Association, April, at Chihuahua, Mexico.

Walker, Henry P.
1962 William McLane's Narrative of the Magee-Gutiérrez Expedition, 1812-1813. *Southwestern Historical Quarterly* 66 (October):234-351.
1963 William McLane's Narrative of the Magee-Gutiérrez Expedition, 1812-1813. *Southwestern Historical Quarterly* 66 (January):457-79.

————, and Bufkin, Don
1979 *Historical Atlas of Arizona.* Norman: University of Oklahoma Press.

Walker, Kenneth P.
1965 The "Pecan Shellers" of San Antonio and Mechanization. *Southwestern Historical Quarterly* 69 (July):44-58.

Walker, William O., III
1977 Control Across the Border: The United States, Mexico, and Narcotics Policy, 1936-1940. Paper presented to Organization of American Historians, April, at Atlanta, Ga.

Wallace, Christopher M.
1969 *Water out of the Desert.* Southwestern Studies no. 22. El Paso: Texas Western Press.

Wallace, Ernest, and Anderson, Adrian S.
1965 R. S. MacKenzie and the Kickapoos: The Raid into Mexico in 1873. *Arizona and the West* 7 (Summer):105-26.

Wallace, W. J.
1962 Prehistoric Cultural Development in the Southern California Deserts. *American Antiquity* 28 (October):172-80.

Wallen, C. C.
1955 Some Characteristics of Precipitation in Mexico. *Geo-grafiska Annaler* 37 (Series A):51-85.

Wallerstein, Immanuel
1974 *The Modern World-System.* New York: Academic Press.

Walter, Paul A.
1938 A Study of Isolation and Social Change in Three Spanish-speaking Villages of New Mexico. Ph.D. dissertation, Stanford University.
1939 The Spanish-speaking Community in New Mexico. *Sociology and Social Research* 24 (November-December):150-57.

Waples, Gregory L.
1974 From Bags to Body Cavities: The Law of Border Search. *Columbia Law Review* 74 (January): 53-87.

Ware, G. W.; Estesen, B. J.; and Cahill, W. P.
1968 An Ecological Study of DDT Residues in Arizona Soils and Alfalfa. *Pesticides Monitoring Journal* 2 (December):129-32.

Warner, Louis H.
1931 Conveyance of Property, the Spanish or Mexican Way. *New Mexico Historical Review* 6 (October):334-59.

Warner, Ruth E.
1945 Yaquis of Mexico and the Folk Literature. *Kiva* 8:18-22.

Warner, Ted J.
1966 Frontier Defense. *New Mexico Historical Review* 41 (January):5-20.
1970 Don Felix Martínez and the Santa Fe Presidio, 1693-1730. *New Mexico Historical Review* 45 (October):269-310.

Warren, Dave
1974 Cultural Studies in Indian Education. *BIA Education Research Bulletin,* January.

Warren, Fintan
1961 Jesuit Historians of Sinaloa-Sonora. *Americas* 18 (July):329-39.

Washburn, Wilcomb E.
1971 *Red Man's Land/White Man's Law.* New York: Charles Scribner's Sons.
1973 *The American Indian and the United States.* 4 vols. New York: Random House.

Watanabe, Susumu
1974 Constraints on Labor-intensive Export Industry in Mexico. *International Labour Review* 109 (January):23-45.

Waterman, T. T.
1924 North American Indian Dwellings. *Geographical Review* 14 (January):1-25.

Waters, Frank
1942 *The Man Who Killed the Deer.* Denver: Sage Books.
1946 *The Colorado.* New York: Rinehart & Co.
1973 *To Possess the Land.* Chicago: Swallow Press.

Watkins, Frances E.
1939 Seri Indian Pelican-Skin Robes. *Masterkey* 13 (no. 6):210-13.

Watkins, T. H.
1969a Conquest of the Colorado. *American West* 6 (July):5-9.
1969b *The Grand Colorado: The Story of a River and Its Canyons.* Palo Alto: American West Publishing Co.

Watson, James B., and Samora, Julian
1954 Subordinate Leadership in a Bi-cultural Community. *American Sociological Review* 19 (August):413-17.

Wauchope, Robert
1964 General editor. *Handbook of Middle American Indians.* 16 vols. Austin: University of Texas Press.

Wauer, R. H., and Riskind, D. H.
1977 Editors. *Transactions of the Symposium on the Biological Resources of the Chihuahuan Desert Region, United States and Mexico.* Transactions and Proceedings Series, no. 3. Department of the Interior. National Park Service.

Wax, Murray L.
1970 Gophers or Gadflies: Indian School Boards. *School Review* 78-79 (November):62-71.

Weatherford, Gary D., and Jacoby, Gordon C.

1975   Impact of Energy Development on the Law of the Colorado River. *Natural Resources Journal* 15 (January): 171-213.

Weaver, Jerry L.
1969   *Health Care Service Use in Orange County, California: A Socio-economic Analysis.* Long Beach: California State University, Long Beach Center for Political Research.
1973a   Health Care Costs as a Political Issue: Comparative Responses of Chicanos and Anglos. *Social Science Quarterly* 53 (March):846-54.
1973b   Mexican American Health Care Behavior: A Critical Review of the Literature. *Social Science Quarterly* 54 (June):85-102.

Weaver, Thomas
1974   *Indians of Arizona: A Contemporary Perspective.* Tucson: University of Arizona Press.
———, and Downing, Theodore E.
1976   Editors. *Mexican Migration.* Tucson: University of Arizona, Bureau of Ethnic Research.
———; ———; et al.
1974   Editors. *A Community Study of Douglas, Arizona: A Final Report.* Tucson: University of Arizona, Bureau of Ethnic Research.
1975   *The Douglas Report: The Community Context of Housing and Social Problems.* Tucson: University of Arizona, Bureau of Ethnic Research.
———, and Hubbard, Glee
1975   Health. In Thomas Weaver and Theodore Downing, et al., eds. *The Douglas Report: The Community Context of Housing and Social Problems,* pp. 236-54. Tucson: University of Arizona, Bureau of Ethnic Research.

Webb, Edith B.
1952   *Indian Life at the Old Missions.* Los Angeles: Warren F. Lewis.

Webb, James Josiah
1931   *Adventures in the Santa Fe Trade, 1844-1847.* Southwest Historical Series, no. 1. Glendale, Calif.: Arthur H. Clark.

Webb, Walter Prescott
1930   The Great Plains and the Industrial Revolution. In J. F. Willard and C. B. Goodykoontz, eds. *The Trans-Mississippi West,* pp. 309-39. Boulder: University of Colorado Press.
1931   *The Great Plains.* Boston: Ginn & Co.
1935   *The Texas Rangers: A Century of Frontier Defense.* Boston: Houghton Mifflin. Reissued in 1965, Austin: University of Texas Press.
1936   *The Great Plains.* Boston: Houghton Mifflin Co.
1944   *Divided We Stand: The Crisis of a Frontierless Democracy* (rev. ed.). Austin: Acorn Press.
1952   *The Great Frontier.* Boston: Houghton Mifflin Co.

Webber, H. J.
1929   Citrus Production in the Rio Grande Valley, Texas, and in the Salt River Valley, Arizona. *California Citrograph* 14 (no. 7):269, 292-94.

Weber, David J.
1967   Spanish Fur Trade from New Mexico, 1540-1821. *Americas* 24 (October):122-36.
1971   *The Taos Trappers: The Fur Trade in the Far Southwest, 1540-1846.* Norman: University of Oklahoma Press.
1973   *Foreigners in Their Native Land. Historical Roots of the Mexican American.* Albuquerque: University of New Mexico Press.
1976   Mexico's Far Northern Frontier, 1821-1854: Historiography Askew. *Western Historical Quarterly* 7:279-93.
1982   *Mexico's Far Northern Frontier: The American Southwest Under Mexico, 1821-1846.* Albuquerque: University of New Mexico Press.

Weber, Francis J.
1963   The Pious Fund of the Californias. *Hispanic American Historical Review* 43 (February):78-94.
1967   Jesuit Missions in Baja California. *Americas* 23 (April): 408-22.
1968   The California Missions and Their Visitors. *Americas* 24 (April):319-36.
1970   Irish-born Champion of the Mexican Americans. *California Historical Society Quarterly* 49 (September):233-49.

Weber, W. A.
1965   Plant Geography in the Southern Rocky Mountains. In H. E. Wright, Jr., and D. G. Fry, eds. *The Quaternary of the United States,* pp. 453-68. Princeton: Princeton University Press.
1976   *Rocky Mountain Flora.* Boulder: Colorado Associated University Press.

Webster, Michael G.
1970   Intrigue on the Rio Grande: The Río Bravo Affair, 1875. *Southwestern Historical Quarterly* 74 (October):149-64.

Weclew, Robert V.
1975   The Nature, Prevalence, and Level of Awareness of Curanderismo and Some of Its Implications for Community Mental Health. *Community Mental Health Journal* 11 (no. 2):145-54.

Weddle, Robert S.
1964   *The San Saba Mission: Spanish Pivot in Texas.* Austin: University of Texas Press.
1968a   San Juan Bautista: Mother of Texas Missions. *Southwestern Historical Quarterly* 71 (April):542-63.
1968b   *San Juan Bautista: Gateway to Spanish Texas.* Austin: University of Texas Press.
1973   *Wilderness Manhunt: The Spanish Search for La Salle.* Austin: University of Texas Press.

Weigle, Marta
1970   *The Penitentes of the Southwest.* Santa Fe: Ancient City Press.
1975   *Hispanic Villages of Northern New Mexico.* Reprint of volume 2, 1935, *Tewa Basin Study.* Santa Fe: Lightning Tree.
1976   *Brothers of Light, Brothers of Blood.* Albuquerque: University of New Mexico Press.

Weil, Thomas E., et al.
1974   *Area Handbook for Mexico.* Washington, D.C.: Government Printing Office.

Weinberg, Albert K.
1935   *Manifest Destiny: A Study of Nationalist Expansionism in American History.* Baltimore: Johns Hopkins University Press.

Weinberg, Edward
1969   Intrastate, Interstate, and International Legal and Administrative Problems of Large Scale Water Transfers. In W. G. McGinnies and Bram Goldman, eds. *Arid Lands in Perspective,* pp. 352-58. Tucson: University of Arizona Press.

Weinberg, Meyer
1977   *A Chance to Learn: A History of Race and Education in the United States.* Cambridge: Cambridge University Press.

Weinert, Richard S.
1976   Multinationals in Latin America. *Journal of Inter-American Studies* 18 (May):253-60.

Weintraub, Sidney, and Ross, Stanley R.
1980   *The Illegal Alien from Mexico: Policy Choices for an Intractable Issue.* Austin: University of Texas, Border Studies Program.

Weir, F. A.
1956   Surface Artifacts from La Perdida, Starr County, Texas. *Texas Archeological Society Bulletin* 26:59-78.

Weisbecker, Leo W.
1974   *Snowpack, Cloud-Seeding, and the Colorado River: A Technology Assessment of Weather Modification.* Nor-

man: University of Oklahoma Press.

Welch, Susan; Commer, John; and Steinman, Michael
1973 Political Participation Among Mexican-Americans: An Explanatory Examination. *Social Science Quarterly* 53 (March):785-99.

Welles, Philip
1964 *Meet the Southwest Deserts.* Tucson: Dale S. King, Publisher.

Wellhausen, Edwin J.
1976 The Agriculture of Mexico. *Scientific American* 235 (no. 3):128-53.

Wells, P. V.
1977 Post-glacial Origin of the Present Chihuahua Desert Less Than 11,500 Years Ago. In R. H. Wauer and D. H. Riskind, eds. *Transactions of the Symposium on the Biological Resources of the Chihuahuan Desert Region, United States and Mexico,* pp. 53-66. Transactions and Proceedings, Series no. 3. Washington, D.C.: U.S. Department of the Interior, National Park Service.

Wells, Robin F.
1973 Frontier Systems as a Sociocultural Type. *University of Kentucky Studies in Anthropology* 15:6-15.

Wendorf, Fred
1956 Some Distributions of Settlement Patterns in the Pueblo Southwest. In Gordon R. Willey, ed. *Prehistoric Settlement Patterns in the New World,* pp. 18-25. Viking Fund Publications, no. 23. New York: Wenner-Gren Foundation.

Wertz, Jacques B.
1966 The Flood Cycle of Ephemeral Mountain Streams in the Southwestern United States. *Annals, Association of American Geographers* 56 (December):598-633.

West, Elizabeth Howard
1904 A Brief Compendium of the Events Which Have Occurred in the Province of Texas from Its Conquest or Reduction, to the Present Date by Antonio Bonilla, 1772. *Texas State Historical Association Quarterly* 8 (July): 1-78.

West, Jonathan P.
1978 Informal Policy Making in Ambos Nogales and Douglas-Agua Prieta. Paper presented to the Southwestern Social Science Association, April, at Houston, Texas.
1979 Informal Policy Making Along the Arizona-Mexico International Border. *International Review of Public Administration* 1:435-58.

West, Jonathan P., and Sloan, John W.
1976a Intergovernmental Relations and Public Policy Along the U.S.-Mexico Border. Paper presented to the Western Social Science Association, April, at Tempe, Arizona.
1976b *Comparative Perceptions of Community Integration and Public Policy Along the U.S.-Mexico Border.* Houston: University of Houston, Institute for Urban Studies.

West, Robert C.
1949 *The Mining Communities of Northern New Spain.* Berkeley: University of California Press.
1964 The Natural Regions of Middle America. In Robert Wauchope, ed. *Handbook of Middle American Indians,* vol. 1, pp. 363-83. Austin: University of Texas Press.
1974 The Flat-roofed Folk Dwelling in Rural Mexico. *Geoscience and Man* 5 (June 10):111-32.

West, S. W., and Broadhurst, W. L.
1975 *Summary Appraisals of the Nation's Ground-Water Resources: Rio Grande Region.* Professional Paper no. 813-D. Washington, D.C.: U.S. Geological Survey.

Westphall, Victor
1958 The Public Domain in New Mexico, 1854-1891. *New Mexico Historical Review* 33 (January):24-52.
1965 *The Public Domain in New Mexico, 1854-1891.* Albuquerque: University of New Mexico Press.
1973 *Thomas Benton Catron and His Era.* Tucson: University of Arizona Press.

1974 Fraud and Implications of Fraud in the Land Grants of New Mexico. *New Mexico Historical Review* 59 (July): 189-218.

Whalen, Norman M.
1975 Cochise Site Distribution in the San Pedro Valley. *Kiva* 40 (no. 3):203-11.

Wheat, Joe Ben
1955 *The Mogollon Culture Prior to A.D. 1000.* Memoirs, no. 10. Salt Lake City: Society for American Archeology.

Wheeler, Kenneth W.
1968 *To Wear A City's Crown: The Beginnings of Urban Growth in Texas, 1836-1865.* Cambridge: Harvard University Press.

Whetstone, George A.
1970-71 *Interbasin Diversion of Water: An Annotated Bibliography.* 2 vols. Lubbock: Texas Tech University, Water Resources Center.

Whetten, Nathan L.
1948 *Rural Mexico.* Chicago: University of Chicago Press.
———, and Burnight, Robert G.
1956 Internal Migration in Mexico. *Rural Sociology* 21 (June): 140-51.

Whitaker, Arthur P.
1929 The Spanish Contribution to American Agriculture. *Agricultural History* 3 (January):1-14.

White, C. Langdon; Foscue, Edwin J.; and McKnight, Tom
1974 *Regional Geography of Anglo-America.* 4th ed. Englewood Cliffs, N.J.: Prentice-Hall.

White, Ernestine Huffman
1977 Giving Health Care to Minority Patients. *Nursing Clinics of North America* 12 (March):27-40.

White, Katherine H.
1961 The Pueblo de Socorro Grant. Master's thesis, University of Texas at El Paso.

White, L. C.; Koch, Summer S.; Kelly, William B.; and McCarthy, Jr., John F.
1972 *Land Report,* Santa Fe, N.M.: State Planning Office.

White, Leslie A.
1962 *The Pueblo of Sía, New Mexico.* Bulletin no. 184. Washington, D.C.: Smithsonian Institution, Bureau of American Ethnology.

White, Owen
1923 *Out of the Desert: The Historical Romance of El Paso.* El Paso: McMath Co.
1925 *Them Was the Days: From El Paso to Prohibition.* New York: Minton, Balch & Co.

White, Richard C.
1975 Testimony Offered Before House Judiciary Committee on Immigration, Citizenship and International Law. *Congressional Record,* 94 Cong., 1st sess., vol. 121, no. 55.

White, Russell A.
1968 El Paso del Norte: The Geography of a Pass and Border Area Through 1906. Ph.D. dissertation, Columbia University.

White, S. S.
1948 The Vegetation and Flora of the Region of the Rio de Bavispe in Northeastern Sonora, Mexico. *Lloydia* 11: 229-302.

Whiteford, Linda
1979 The Borderland as an Extended Community. In Fernando Camara and Robert Van Kemper, eds. *Migration Across Frontiers: Mexico and the United States,* pp. 127-37. Albany: State University of New York at Albany, Institute for Mesoamerican Studies.

Whiteford, Scott, and Henao, Luis Emilio
1979 Commercial Agriculture, Irrigation Control, and Selective Labor Migration: The Case of the Tehuacan Valley. In Fernando Camara and Robert Van Kemper, eds. *Migration Across Frontiers: Mexico and the United States,* pp. 25-33. Albany: State University of New York at Albany, Institute for Mesoamerican Studies.

Whitford, William Clarke
1906   *Colorado Volunteers in the Civil War.* Denver: State Historical Society.

Whiting, A. F.
1936   Hopi Indian Agriculture, I. Background. *Museum Notes of Northern Arizona* 8 (no. 10).
1937   Hopi Indian Agriculture, II. Seed Source and Distribution. *Museum Notes of Northern Arizona* 10 (no. 5).
1939   *Ethnobotany of the Hopi.* Northern Arizona Society of Science and Art Bulletin, no. 15.

Whitman, William
1947   The Pueblo Indians of San Ildefonso. *Columbia University Contributions to Anthropology* 34:1-164.

Whittaker, R. H.
1967   Gradient Analysis of Vegetation. *Biological Review* 42: 207-64.

Whittaker, R. H., and Niering, W. A.
1965   Vegetation of the Santa Catalina Mountains, Arizona: A Gradient Analysis of the South Slope. *Ecology* 46: 429-52.

Wiarda, Howard J.
1978   *Democracy and Human Rights in Latin America: Toward a New Conceptualization. Orbis* 22 (Spring):137-60.

Widdison, Jerold Gwayn
1959   Historical Geography of the Middle Rio Puerco Valley, New Mexico. *New Mexico Historical Review* 34 (October):248-84.

Wiest, Raymond E.
1970   Wage-Labor Migration and Household Maintenance in a Central Mexican Town. Ph.D. dissertation, University of Oregon.
1979   Implications for International Labor Migration for Mexican Rural Development. In Fernando Camara and Robert Van Kemper, eds. *Migration Across Frontiers: Mexico and the United States,* pp. 85-97. Albany: State University of New York at Albany, Institute for Mesoamerican Studies.

Wiggins, I. L.
1980   *Flora of Baja California.* Stanford: Stanford University Press.

Wilbarger, J. W.
1889   *Indian Depredations in Texas.* Austin: Hutchings Printing House.

Wilber, G. L.; Jaco, D. E.; Hagan, R. J.; and del Fierro, A. C.
1975   *Spanish-Americans and Indians in the Labor Market.* Vol. 1. Lexington: University of Kentucky, Social Welfare Research Institute.

Wilcock, D. N. et al.
1976   Changing Attitudes to Water Resources Development in California. *Geography* 61 (July):127-36.

Wilder, Carleton S.
1963   The Yaqui Deer Dance: A Study in Cultural Change. Bulletin no. 186, pp. 145-210. Washington, D.C.: Smithsonian Institution, Bureau of American Ethnology.

Wilder, Mitchell
1943   *Santos: The Religious Folk Art of New Mexico.* Colorado Springs: Taylor Museum of Colorado Springs Fine Art Center.

Wilke, P. J.
1976   *Background: The Prehistory of the Yuha Desert Region.* Publications in Anthropology, no. 5. Ramona, Calif.: Ballena Press.

Wilken, Robert L.
1953   *Anselm Weber, O.F.M., Missionary to the Navaho, 1898-1921.* Milwaukee: Bruce Publishing Co.

Wilkie, James W.
1970   *The Mexican Revolution: Federal Expenditures and Social Change Since 1910.* 2d ed. Berkeley: University of California Press.
———, et al.

1976   Editors. *Contemporary Mexico: Papers of the IV International Congress of Mexican History.* Berkeley: University of California Press.

Wilkie, Raymond
1971   *San Miguel: A Mexican Collective Ejido.* Stanford: Stanford University Press.

Willems, Emilio
1967   *Followers of the New Faith: Culture Change and the Rise of Protestants in Brazil and Chile.* Nashville: Vanderbilt University.

Willey, G. R.
1966   Baja California. In *An Introduction to American Archaeology: Vol. 1, North and Middle America,* pp. 356-61. Englewood Cliffs, N.J.: Prentice-Hall.

Williams, Aubrey W.
1970   *Navajo Political Process.* Contributions to Anthropology, no. 9. Washington, D.C.: Smithsonian Institution Press.

Williams, C. L.
1972   Realizaciones de la associación fronteriza mexicana-estadaunidense de la salubridad. *Salud Pública de México* 14.

Williams, Edward J.
1979   *The Rebirth of the Mexican Petroleum Industry.* Lexington, Mass.: D. C. Heath.

Williams, Jean
1972   Ground Water Management Potential. *Water for Texas* 2 (June):4-6.

Williams, Joseph E., and Gray, James R.
1968   *Economic Analysis of Alfalfa Hay Transportation in New Mexico.* Bulletin no. 534. Las Cruces: New Mexico State Agricultural Experiment Station.

Williams, Llewelyn
1967   Occurrence of High Temperatures at Yuma Proving Ground, Arizona. *Annals, Association of American Geographers* 57 (September):579-92.

Williford, George H., et al.
1976   *The Impact of the Declining Groundwater Supply in the Northern High Plains of Texas and Oklahoma on Expenditures for Community Services.* College Station: Texas A&M University, Texas Water Resources Institute.

Willink, Elizabeth W.
1973   Bilingual Education for Navajo Children. In Paul R. Turner, ed. *Bilingualism in the Southwest,* pp. 177-90. Tucson: University of Arizona Press.

Wilson, Andrew W.
1963   Tucson: A Problem in Uses of Water. In Carle Hodge and Peter C. Duisberg, eds. *Aridity and Man,* pp. 483-89. Publication no. 74. Washington, D.C.: AAAS.

Wilson, Don W.
1967   Pioneer Jews in California and Arizona, 1849-1875. *Journal of the West* 6 (April):226-36.

Wilson, Eldred D.
1931   New Mountains in the Yuma Desert, Arizona. *Geographical Review* 21 (April):221-28.
———; Moore, Richard T.; and Cooper, John R.
1969   *Geologic Map of Arizona. Scale 1:500,000.* Washington, D.C.: U.S. Geological Survey.

Wilson, H. Clyde
1964   Changes in the Jicarilla Apache Political and Economic Structures, 1880-1960. *University of California Publications in American Archaeology and Ethnology* 48 (no. 4):297-360.

Wilson, Herbert M.
1897   Topography of Mexico. *Journal of the American Geographical Society* 29:249-60.

Wilson, James A.
1974   *Tejanos, Chicanos and Mexicanos: A Partially Annotated, Historical Bibliography for Texas Public School Teachers.* San Marcos: Southwest Texas State University, Department of Education and Department of History.

Wilson, Neill C., and Taylor, Frank J.
1952 Southern Pacific: The Roaring Story of a Fighting Railroad. New York: McGraw-Hill Book Co.

Winberry, John J.
1974 The Log House in Mexico. *Annals, Association of American Geographers* 64 (March):54-69.

Windmiller, Ric
1973 The Late Cochise Culture in the Sulphur Springs Valley, Southeastern Arizona: Archeology of the Fairchild Site. *Kiva* 39 (no. 2):131-69.

Winkle, John W., III
1975 Intergovernmental Relations in Criminal Justice. In John A. Gardiner, ed. *Crime and Criminal Justice Issues in Public Policy-Making.* Lexington, Mass.: Lexington Books.

Winship, George Parker
1896 *The Coronado Expedition, 1540-1542.* 14th Annual Report, part 1, pp. 329-613. Washington, D.C.: Bureau of American Ethnology.

Winslow, David C.
1949 Classification of Farms in the Southwest. *Southwestern Social Science Quarterly* 30 (December):169-74.

Winther, Sophus K.
1952 The Limits of Regionalism. *Arizona Quarterly* 8 (Spring): 30-36.

Wishart, David J.; Warren, Andrew; and Stoddard, Robert H.
1969 An Attempted Definition of a Frontier Using a Wave Analogy. *Rocky Mountain Social Science Journal* 6 (no. 1):73-81.

Wisleyenus, A.
1848 *Memoir of a Tour to Northern Mexico Connected with Col. Doniphan's Expedition in 1846 and 1847.* Sen. Misc. Doc. no. 26, 30 Cong., 1st sess.

Wislizenus, Frederick A.
1969 *A Tour to Northern Mexico, 1846-1847.* Glorieta: Rio Grande Press. Reprint of 30 Cong., 1st sess., Publication no. 26, 1848.

Wissler, Clark
1940 *Indians of the United States.* Garden City, N.Y.: Doubleday & Co.

Withers, A. M.
1944 Excavations at Valshni Village, a Site on the Pápago Indian Reservation, Arizona. *American Antiquity* 10 (no. 1):33-47.
1973 Excavations at Valshni Village, Arizona. *Arizona Archeologist* 7.

Witherspoon, Gary
1970 A New Look at Navajo Social Organization. *American Anthropologist* 72:55-65.
1975 *Navajo Kinship and Marriage.* Chicago: University of Chicago Press.
1977 *Language and Art in the Navajo Universe.* Ann Arbor: University of Michigan Press.

Witt, Shirley Hill
1970 Nationalistic Trends Among American Indians. In Stuart Levine and Nancy Lurie, eds. *The American Indian Today,* pp. 93-127. Baltimore: Penguin Books.

Wolf, Eric
1959 *Sons of the Shaking Earth.* Chicago: University of Chicago Press.

Wolff, Anthony
1972 Showdown at Four Corners. *Saturday Review* 55 (June 3):29-41.

Wolkon, G. H.; Moriwaki, S.; Mandel, D. M.; Archuleta, J.; Bunje, F.; and Zimmerman, S.
1974 Ethnicity and Social Class in the Delivery of Services: Analysis of a Child Guidance Clinic. *American Journal of Public Health* 64 (no. 7):709-12.

Wolle, Muriel V. S.
1953 *The Bonanza Trail: Ghost Towns and Mining Camps of the Old West.* Bloomington: University of Indiana Press.

Wollenberg, Charles
1969 Huelga, 1928 Style: The Imperial Valley Cantaloupe Workers Strike. *Pacific Historical Review* 38 (February): 45-58.

Wollman, Nathaniel
1962 Editor. *The Value of Water in Alternative Uses, with Special Application to Water Use in the San Juan and Rio Grande Basins of New Mexico.* Albuquerque: University of New Mexico Press.

Womack, John, Jr.
1972 The Chicanos. *New York Times Review of Books* 19 (August 31):12-18.

Woodbury, David O.
1967 *Fresh Water from Salty Seas.* New York: Dodd, Mead & Co.

Woodbury, Richard B.
1963 Indian Adaptations to Arid Environments. In Carle Hodge and Peter C. Duisberg, eds. *Aridity and Man,* pp. 55-85. Publication no. 74. Washington, D.C.: AAAS.

Woodhull, Frost
1937 The Seminole Indian Scouts on the Border. *Frontier Times* 15:118-27.

Woods, Betty
1943 Timeless Town. *New Mexico Magazine* 21 (August): 16-17, 38-39.

Woodward, Dorothy
1940 The Penitentes of New Mexico. Ph.D. dissertation, Yale University.

Woodward, Margaret L.
1968 The Spanish Army and the Loss of America, 1810-1824. *Hispanic American Historical Review* 48 (November):586-607.

Woofter, Thomas J.
1936 *Landlord and Tenant on the Cotton Plantation System.* Washington, D.C.: W.P.A. Division of Social Research.

Wooster, Ralph A.
1964 Texas Military Operations Against Mexico, 1842-1843. *Southwestern Historical Quarterly* 67 (April):465-84.

Wooten, Dudley G.
1899 *History of Texas,* n.p.

Wooton, E. O., and Standley, P. C.
1915 Flora of New Mexico. *Contributions from the United States National Herbarium* 19:1-794.

Worcester, Donald E.
1951 Editor and translator. Instructions for Governing the Interior Provinces of New Spain, 1786. Publication no. 12. Berkeley, Calif.: Quivira Society.

Word, J. H., and Douglas, C. L.
1970 *Excavations at Baker Cave, Val Verde County, Texas.* Bulletin no. 16. Austin: Texas Memorial Museum.

Wright, Barton, and Roat, Evelyn
1970 *This Is a Hopi Kachina.* Flagstaff: Museum of Northern Arizona.

Wright, Dale
1965 *They Harvest Despair: The Migrant Farmworker.* Boston: Beacon Press.

Wright, Marcus Joseph
1965 Compiler. *Texas in the War, 1861-1865.* Hillsboro, Ill.: Hill Junior College Press.

Wright, N. Gene, et al.
1976 *Cost of Producing Crops in the Irrigated Southwest: Part II, New Mexico.* Technical Bulletin no. 222. Tucson: University of Arizona, Agricultural Experiment Station.

Wyllys, Rufus Kay
1932 The French of California and Sonora. *Pacific Historical Review* 1 (September):337-59.
1952 The Historical Geography of Arizona. *Pacific Historical Review* 21 (May):121-27.

Wyman, Leland C.
1970 *Blessingway: With Three Versions of the Myth Recorded*

and Translated from the Navajo by Berard Haile. Tucson: University of Arizona Press.

Xavier, Gwyenth H.
1974 *The Cattle Industry of the Southern Pápago Districts with Some Information on the Reservation Cattle Industry as a Whole.* New York: Garland Publishing.

Yaffee, James
1968 *The American Jews.* New York: Random House.

Yates, Richard, and Marshall, Mary
1974 *The Lower Colorado River: A Bibliography.* Yuma: Arizona Western College Press.

Yazzie, Ethelou
1971 Editor. *Navajo History.* Chinle, Ariz.: Navajo Community College Press, Navajo Curriculum Center, Rough Rock Demonstration School.

Yoakum, Henderson R.
1855 *History of Texas: From Its Settlement in 1685 to the Annexation of the United States in 1846.* 2 vols. New York: J. S. Redfield.

York, John C., and Dick-Peddie, William A.
1969 Vegetation Changes in Southern New Mexico During the Past Hundred Years. In William C. McGinnies and Bram J. Goldman, eds. *Arid Lands in Perspective,* pp. 155-66. Tucson: University of Arizona Press.

Young, Otis E, Jr.
1965 The Spanish Tradition in Gold and Silver Mining. *Arizona and the West* 7 (Winter):299-314.

———, with Lenon, Robert
1970 *Western Mining: An Informal Account of Precious-Metals Prospecting, Placering, Lode Mining, and Milling on the American Frontier from Spanish Times to 1893.* Norman: University of Oklahoma Press.

1976 *Black Powder and Hand Steel: Miners and Machines on the Old Western Frontier.* Norman: University of Oklahoma Press.

Young, Pauline V.
1932 *Pilgrims of Russian-Town.* Chicago: University of Chicago Press.

Young, Robert W.
1961 *The Navajo Yearbook.* BIA Report no. 8. Window Rock, Ariz.: Navajo Agency.

1972 The Rise of the Navajo Tribe. In Edward H. Spicer and Raymond Thompson, eds. *Plural Society in the Southwest,* pp. 167-238. New York: Interbook, Weatherhead Foundation.

1976 Regional Development and Rural Poverty in the Navajo Indian Area. Ph.D. dissertation, University of Wisconsin, Madison.

1978 *A Political History of the Navajo Tribe.* Tsaile, Ariz.: Navajo Community College Press.

Yurtinas, John F. G.
1975 A Ram in the Thicket: The Mormon Battalion in the Mexican War, 2 vols. Ph.D. dissertation, Brigham Young University.

Zahniser, Jack L.
1966 Late Prehistoric Villages Southeast of Tucson, Arizona, and the Archeology of the Tanuqe Verde Phase. *Kiva* 31 (no. 3):103-204.

Zárate, Alván O.
1967 Some Factors Associated with Urban-rural Fertility Differentials in Mexico. *Population Studies* 21 (no. 3):283-93.

1968a Fertility in Urban Areas of Mexico: Implications for the Theory of the Demographic Transition. *Demography* 4 (no. 1):372-73.

1968b Differential Fertility in Monterrey, Mexico: Prelude to Transition? *Milbank Memorial Fund Quarterly* 45 (no. 2):93-108.

Zavala, Silvio
1957 The Frontiers of Hispanic America. In Walker D. Wyman and Clifton B. Kroeber, eds. *The Frontier in Perspective,* pp. 35-58. Madison: University of Wisconsin Press.

Zazueta, Carlos H.
1980 *Mexican Workers in the United States.* México, D.F.: Centro Nacional de Información y Estadísticas del Trabajo.

Zeleny, Carolyn
1944 Relations Between the Spanish-Americans and the Anglo-Americans in New Mexico: A Study of Conflict and Accommodation in a Dual Ethnic Relationship. Ph.D. dissertation, Yale University.

Zelman, Donald L.
1974a Mexican Labor and Settlement in California, 1910-1940. Unpublished paper.

1974b The Deportation of Mexicans from California, 1950s. Unpublished paper.

Zierer, Clifford M.
1934 San Fernando: A Type of Southern California Town. *Annals, Association of American Geographers* 24 (March): 1-28.

1956 Editor. *California and the Southwest.* New York: John Wiley & Sons.

Zingg, Robert M.
1932 Juguetes y juegos de los niños tarahumaras. *Mexican Folkways* 7:107-10.

1942 Genuine and Spurious Values in Tarahumara Culture. *American Anthropologist* 44:78-92.

Zintz, Miles V.
1957-60 *The Indian Research Study: The Adjustment of Indian and Non-Indian Children in the Public Schools of New Mexico.* 2 vols. Albuquerque: University of New Mexico, College of Education.

Ziontz, Alvin J.
1975 In Defense of Tribal Sovereignty: An Analysis of Judicial Error in Construction of the Indian Civil Rights Act. *South Dakota Law Review* 20 (Winter):1-58.

Zirkel, Perry A.
1977 A Method for Determining and Depicting Language Dominance. *TESOL Quarterly* 8:7-16.

Zonn, Leo E.
1978 The Railroads of Sonora and Sinaloa, Mexico: A Historical Geography. *Social Science Journal* 15 (April): 1-15.

Zorilla, Luis G.
1965 *Historia de las relaciones entre México y los Estados Unidos de América, 1800-1958.* Mexico City: Editorial Porrúa.

Zorita, Alonso de
1963 *Life and Labor in Ancient Mexico: The Brief and Summary Relation of the Lords of New Spain.* New Brunswick: Rutgers University Press.

Zubrow, Ezra B. W.
1974 *Population, Contact, and Climate in the New Mexican Pueblos.* Anthropological Papers, no. 24. Tucson: University of Arizona.

Section II.
Unauthored
Public
Documents and
Miscellaneous
Resource
Materials

AFL-CIO
1970   *The Developing Crisis in International Trade.* Washington, D.C.: AFL-CIO, Industrial Union Department.
AMA
1973   *Community Health Delivery Programs: Task Force Report.* Chicago: American Medical Association, Council on Medical Service, Committee on Community Health Care
American Association for the Advancement of Science (AAAS)
1969   *Guidebook of Northern Mexico, Sonoran Desert Region.* Tucson: University of Arizona Press, AAAS Committee on Arid Lands.
American Embassy, Mexico
1978   *Foreign Economic Trends and their Implications for the United States-Mexico.* Prepared by the U.S. Foreign Service, released by U.S. Department of Commerce (June).
American Geographical Society
1960-68 Current Geographical Publications. Additions to the *Research Catalog of the American Geographical Society.* New York.
1962   *Research Catalog of the American Geographical Society.* Vols. 5 and 6. Boston: G. K. Hall & Co.
Arizona, ACCES
1978   *ACCES-Energy III* (October-November). Tucson: University of Arizona, Council for Environmental Studies.
Arizona, ARETS
1971   *Applied Remote Sensing of Earth Resources in Arizona. Proceedings, 2nd Symposium* (November). Tucson: University of Arizona Press.
Arizona Commission of Indian Affairs.
1967-   *Annual Report of the Arizona Commission of Indian Affairs; and Tribal*
present *Directory.*
Arizona Crop Reporting Service
1976   *1975 Arizona Agricultural Statistics.* Phoenix.
Arizona Mining
1961   *Gold Placers and Gold Placering in Arizona.* Tucson: Arizona Bureau of Mines.
Arizona, University of, Faculty Members
1972   *Arizona, Its People and Resources.* Tucson: University of Arizona Press.
Arizona Water
1964   *Arizona Town Hall, 4th, Castle Hot Springs.* Phoenix: Arizona Academy.
1975   *Arizona State Water Plan—Summary: Inventory of Resources and Uses.* Phoenix: Arizona Water Commission.
Banco Nacional de Comercio Exterior, Mexico, *Comercio Exterior* (monthly publication)
1971a   Nuevo reglamento para las industrias maquiladoras de exportación. *Comercio Exterior* 21 (April):290-91.
1971b   Fragmentos del informe de la Comisión de Aranceales de Estados Unidos

sobre las industrias maquiladoras de exportación. *Comercio Exterior* 21 (April):292-308.

1974 VI reunion nacional para el desarollo fronterizo. *Comercio Exterior* 24 (July):686-87.

1977a Alianza para la producción. *Comercio Exterior* 27 (January):45-47.

1977a Diversos aspects de la reforma administrativa. *Comercio Exterior* 27 (July):779-80.

1977b Estímulos y remación de obstáculos. *Comercio Exterior* 27 (April):415-18.

1977b Reorientación de los estímulos fiscales. *Comercio Exterior* 27 (August):918-21.

1977c Recuento nacional: sector financiero. *Comercio Exterior* 27 (July):779

1977d Reorientación de los estímulos fiscales. *Comercio Exterior* 27 (August):918-21.

1977e *Mexico 1976: Facts, Figures, Trends.* Mexico City: Banco Nacional de Comercio Exterior.

1978a La industria maquiladora: evolución reciente y perspectivas. *Comercio Exterior* 28 (April):407-14.

1978b Sector turismo: sus metas, sus logros, sus efectos. *Comercio Exterior* 28 (August):929-33.

1981 Railroads: A Much-Needed Boost. *Comercio Exterior* 31: 261-78.

Banco Nacional de México, S.A., *Review of the Economic Situation of Mexico* (monthly); *Informe Anual* (annually)
1974 Assembly Plants on the Northern Border. *Review of the Economic Situation of Mexico* 50 (no. 579):86.

1976 In-Bond Industry Advancing. *Review of the Economic Situation of Mexico* 52 (no. 607):199-201.

1978a Foreign Trade and Tourism. *Review of the Economic Situation of Mexico* 54 (May):172-77.

1978b Long-Term Prospects for Tourism. *Review of the Economic Situation of Mexico* 54 (June):207-12.

1979 Structure and Prospects of the In-Bond Industry. *Review of the Economic Situation of Mexico* 55:244-52.

Bancroft Library, University of California, Berkeley
1964a *Catalog of Printed Books.* 22 vols. Boston: G. K. Hall & Co.

1964b *Index to Printed Maps.* Boston: G. K. Hall & Co.

1969 First Supplement to *Catalog.* 6 vols.

1974 Second supplement to *Catalog.* 6 vols.

1975 First supplement to *Index.*

Bank of London South American Review (monthly publication)
Boletín Bibliográfico de Antropología Americana
1937- *Bibliographical Bulletin of American Anthropology,* vol.
present 1. Mexico: Instituto Panamericano de Geografía e Historia.

Border-State University Consortium for Latin America
n.d. Environmental Problems along the Border. Occasional Paper, no. 7. 120 pp. San Diego, Calif.: San Diego State University.

Bureau of Economic Geology
1972-78 *Environmental Geological Atlas of the Texas Coastal Zone.* Austin: University of Texas.

Bureau of Home Economics
1939 *The Farm Housing Survey.* Miscellaneous Publication no. 323. Washington, D.C.: U.S. Department of Agriculture.

Cámara Nacional de Comercio (CANACO)
1977 *Articulos Gancho: Su Razon de Ser.* Ciudad Juárez.

California, Department of Education
1969 Spanish-speaking Pupils Classified as Educable Mentally Retarded. *Integrated Education* 5:28-33.

California, Department of Industrial Relations (CDIR)
1965 *American Indians in California.* San Francisco: CDIR, Division of Fair Employment Practices.

California, Department of Water Resources (CDWR)
1957 *The California Water Plan.* Bulletin no. 3. Sacramento: CDWR.

1974 *The California Water Plan: Outlook in 1974.* Bulletin

no. 160-74. Sacramento: CDWR.

California Indian Legal Services (CILS)
1968 *An Explanation of Termination.* Berkeley: CILS.

California, Office of the Lieutenant Governor
1977 *EDA Border Area Development Study: Preliminary Report.* Sacramento.

California, State Advisory Commission on Indian Affairs
1966 *Progress Report to the Governor and the Legislature on Indians in Rural and Reservation Areas.* Sacramento (February).

California, State Planning Board
1940 *Surveys and Maps in California.* Sacramento.

California, University of California
1978 *Technological Change, Farm Mechanization and Agricultural Employment.* Berkeley: University of California, Division of Agricultural Sciences (July).

Centro de Investigaciones Agraria
1957 *Los distritos de riego del noreste: tenencia y aprovechamiento de la tierra.* Mexico City: Instituto Mexicano de Investigaciones Económicas.

Christian Science Monitor
1978 Business Highlights. May 11.

Commission of the Californias
1972 *The Narcotics Laws of Mexico and the United States.* San Diego.

Condumex
1969 *Centro de estudios de historia de Mexico.* Mexico City: Fundacion Cultural de Condumex.

Compañía Mexicana de Terrenos del Río Colorado, S.A.
1958 *Colonizacion del valle de Mexicali B.C.* Mexico City.

Comptroller General of the United States
1974 *Efforts to Stop Narcotics and Dangerous Drugs Coming from and Through Mexico and Central America.* Report to Congress. Washington, D.C.: Government Printing Office.

1975a *Stopping U.S. Assistance to Foreign Policy and Prisons.* Report to Congress. Washington, D.C.: Government Printing Office.

1975b *If the United States is to Develop an Effective International Narcotics Control Program, Much More Must be Done.* Report to Congress. Washington, D.C.: Government Printing Office.

CRA
1980 *Undocumented Immigrants: Their Impact on the County of San Diego.* San Diego: San Diego County and Community Research Associates, Inc.

Dirección General de Estadística
1972 *IX censo general de población, 1970: resumen general abreviado.* Mexico City: Secretaría de Industria y Comercio.

Dirección General de Relaciones Culturales
1962 *Programa nacional fronterizo.* Mexico City.

Domestic Council, Committee on Illegal Aliens
1976 *Preliminary Report.* Washington, D.C.: Department of of Justice (December).

Domestic Council, Drug Abuse Task Force
1975 *White Paper on Drug Abuse.* Washington, D.C.

Economic Development Administration (EDA)
1968 *Industrial and Employment Potential of the United States-Mexico Border.* Washington, D.C.: U.S. Department of Commerce, Economic Development Administration.

Editors of Sunset Books
1974 *Rivers of the West.* Menlo Park, Calif.: Lane Publishing Co.

El Mercado de Valores (Nacional Financiera, S.A.). *La economía Mexicana en cifras*
1970 Actividades del programa nacional fronterizo. 30 (March 30):177-79, 185-88.

1971 Incentivos fiscales a la exportación. 31 (March 22):183-84, 186-87.

1972 Estímulos al establecimiento de centros comerciales en

las zonas fronterizas. 32 (August 21):861.

1976   Aspectos económicos de la franja fronteriza norte. 36 (May 31):408-12.

1977   Ley orgánico de la administratión pública federal. 37 (January 3):1-19.

1978*a*   Comités de promoción económica en ciudades fronterizas. 38 (February 6):92.

1978*b*   Avance de las ciudades industriales. 38 (February 13): 105, 109-11.

1978*c*   Estímulos fiscales a diversas actividades. 38 (March 27): 241-44.

1978*d*   Créditos del FONATUR en 1977. 38 (April 10):269, 275-77.

1978*e*   Plan nacional de desarrollo urbano. 38 (June 19):477, 479-92.

1978*f*   Los fideicomisos de fomento económico. 38 (October 16):858-61.

1978*g*   Estímulos para fomentar la integración económica de la franja fronteriza norte y las zones libres del país. 38 (October 30):893-903.

1980   Zonas de desconcentración territorial de las actividades industriales. 40 (March 10):227-29.

1981*a*   Fogain in el primer semestre de 1981. 41 (September 14):970-71.

1981*b*   Desarrollo de las franjas fronterizas y zonas libres. 41 (November 23):1226-32.

1981*c*   Desarrollo de las franjas fronterizas y zonas libres. 41 (November 30):1253-59.

El Paso Chamber of Commerce
1976   *Directory of Twin Plants, El Paso, Texas-Ciudad Juárez, Chihuahua.*

El Paso Industrial Development Corporation
1974   *El Paso-Juárez Twin Plant Handbook, 1974-75.*

El Paso Mass Transit Technical Study
1977   Houston, Texas: Wilbur Smith and Associates

Energy Facts II
1975   Prepared for the Subcommittee on Energy Research, Development, and Demonstration of the Committee on Science and Technology, U.S. House of Representatives, 94th Cong., 1st session, by the Science Policy Research Division, Congressional Research Service, Library of Congress. Washington, D.C.: Government Printing Office.

Environmental Data Service
1968   *Climatic Atlas of the United States.* Washington, D.C.: Department of Commerce, Environmental Science Services Administration.

Environmental Protection Agency
1973   *Compilation of Air Pollution Emission Factors.* 2d ed. Washington, D.C.: Government Printing Office, AP-42.

Excelsior
1972   Hay seis millones de católicos a su modo en la metrópoli. March 22.

Federal Trade Commission
1973   *Trading Post System on the Navajo Reservation.* Washington, D.C. (June).

Federal Writers' Program, WPA
1940   *New Mexico: A Guide to the Colorful State.* New York: Hastings House. Rev. ed. 1953, 1963.

Fondo Editorial de la Plástica Mexicana
1971   *The Ephemeral and the Eternal of Mexican Folk Art.* 2 vols. Mexico City: Fondo Editorial de la Plástica Mexicana.

Fondo Nacional de Fomento al Turismo (FONATUR) Indicadores Turisticas (quarterly publication)
1978   86,525 empleos en 1978, contribución del turismo al desarrollo de México. *Boletín Mensual FONATUR* 1 (March):2-5.

Government of Canada
1972   *Foreign Direct Investment in Canada.* Ottawa.

Guide to Mexican Markets
    Annual publication, Sinaloa 9, México 7, D.F.: Marynka Olizar.

Harvard Law Review "Notes"
1977   Constitutional Problems in the Execution of Foreign Penal Sentences: The Mexican-American Prisoner Transfer Treaty. *Harvard Law Review* 90 (May):1500-27.

Illinois Legislative Investigating Commission
1976   *Mexican Heroin: A Report to the Illinois General Assembly.* Chicago.

Indiana Advisory Committee to USCCR
1975   *Indiana Migrants: Blighted Hopes, Slighted Rights.* Chicago (March).

Industry and Trade Administration
1978   *Texas Exports.* Washington, D.C.: U.S. Department of Commerce (November).

Institute of Texan Cultures (ITC)
1974   *The Syrian and Lebanese Texans.* San Antonio: Institute of Texan Cultures.

Instituto de Geografía
1970   *Carta de Climas de la República. Scale 1:500,000.* Mexico City: UNAM, Comisión de Estudios del Territorio Nacional.

Instituto Mexicano del Petróleo
1975   *Energéticos: demanda sectorial.* Mexico City.

Instituto Mexicano de Recursos Naturales Renovables
1960   *Mesas redondas sobre los recursos naturales renovables y el crecimiento demográfico de México.* Mexico City.

Instituto Nacional Indigenista (INI), *Acción Indigenista* (boletín mensual)
1977   México Indígena. No. 1 (April).

Inter-America Research Associates (IARA)
1976   *Migrant/Seasonal Farmworker: An Assessment of the Migrant and Seasonal Farmworker Situation in the United States.* Vol. 2: *Findings.* Washington, D.C.: IARA, prepared for Community Services Administration (May).

Intercom
1978   *Mexico Tackles Its Skyrocketing Population Growth.* Washington, D.C.: Population Reference Bureau.

International Labor Office (ILO)
1972   The Relationship Between Multinational Corporations and Social Policy. Paper prepared by ILO, meeting (October-November) in Geneva.

International Monetary Fund, *Directions of Trade* (Monthly); *International Financial Statistics* (Monthly)

International Planned Parenthood Federation
1974   Congress of the United States of Mexico Decrees. *Western Hemisphere Region News Service* 2 (1):3-4.

LAER
1978   Mexican Congress Agrees on Unified Nuclear Industry. *Latin American Economic Report* 6 (November 24) London.

Land Tenure Center
1969   Land Tenure and Agrarian Reform in Mexico: A Bibliography. Madison: University of Wisconsin. Supplements 1 and 2 published in 1971 and 1976.

Los Angeles, County Museum of Art
1964   *Masterworks of Mexican Art* (October 1963 to January 1964).

Los Angeles Department of City Planning (LADCP)
1976   Working Paper: An Estimate of the Illegal Alien Population in Los Angeles. Mimeographed LADCP (July).

Maxwell Museum of Anthropology
1974   *Seven Families in Pueblo Pottery.* Albuquerque: University of New Mexico Press.

Mexican Institute for Foreign Trade
1973   *Regulation of paragraph third, article 327, of the customs code of the United States of Mexico, for assembly plants.* Mexico City.

Mexico Update
1978   *Mexico Update.* Vol. 2 (November). Mexico City: Ameri-

can Chamber of Commerce of Mexico.

Nacional Financiera. See *El Mercado de Valores*

National Advisory Committee on Farm Labor
1967   *Farm Labor Organizing, 1905-1967: A Brief History.* New York.

National Association for the Advancement of Colored People (NAACP)
1971   *An Even Chance.* New York: NAACP, Legal and Defense Fund.

National Council on Employment Policy (NCEP)
1976   *Illegal Aliens: An Assessment of the Issues.* Washington, D.C.

National Migrant Information Clearinghouse (Juarez-Lincoln Center)
1973*a*   *Migrant Programs in California.* Austin.
1973*b*   *Migrant Programs in Florida.* Austin.
1974*a*   *Migrant Programs in Iowa, Kentucky, Minnesota, Missouri and Tennessee.* Austin.
1974*b*   *Migrant Programs in Michigan.* Austin.
1974*c*   *Migrant Programs in the Northeastern States.* Austin.
1974*d*   *Migrant Programs in the Southeastern States and Washington, D.C.* Austin.
1974*e*   *Migrant Programs in the Southwestern States.* Austin.
1974*f*   *Migrant Programs in Wisconsin and Ohio.* Austin.
1974*g*   *Farmworker Programs in Texas.* Austin.
1974*h*   *Farmworker Programs in Florida.* Austin.

National Park Service
1951   *Archeological Excavations at the Falcon Reservoir, Starr County, Texas.* Washington, D.C.: Smithsonian Institution River Basin Surveys, prepared for National Park Service.

National Research Council (NRC)
1968   *Water and Choice in the Colorado Basin: An Example of Alternatives in Water Management.* NRC Committee on Water, Publication no. 1689. Washington, D.C.: National Academy of Sciences.

Navaho Division of Education
1973*a*   *Strengthening Navajo Education.* Window Rock, Ariz.
1973*b*   *Eleven Programs for Strengthening Navajo Education.* Window Rock, Ariz. (December).

Navaho Health Authority
1973   *Health Resources Directory.* Window Rock, Ariz. (September).

Navaho Tribe
1969   *Navajo Tribal Code.* Orford, N.H.: Equity Publishing.

New Mexico, Anonymous
1895   *An Illustrated History of New Mexico.* Chicago: Lewis Publishing Co.
1969   South Central New Mexico: High Country to Space Age Country. *New Mexico Progress* 36 (1). Albuquerque: Albuquerque National Bank.

New Mexico, Crop and Livestock Reporting Service
1975   *New Mexico Agricultural Statistics, 1974.* Las Cruces: New Mexico Department of Agriculture.

New Mexico, Cultural Properties Review Committee
1971   *Historical Preservation: A Plan for New Mexico.* Santa Fe: New Mexico State Planning Office.
1973   *The Historic Preservation Program for New Mexico.* Vol. 2: *The Inventory.* Santa Fe: New Mexico State Planning Office.

New Mexico, Interagency Council for Area Development Planning
n.d.   *Embudo: A Pilot Planning Project for the Embudo Watershed of New Mexico.* Santa Fe: New Mexico State Planning Office.

New Mexico, Maxwell Museum of Anthropology
1974   *Seven Families in Pueblo Pottery.* Albuquerque: University of New Mexico Press.

New Mexico, Museum of New Mexico
n.d.   *Adobe: Past and Present.* Reprinted from *El Palacio* 77 (September, 1971).
1940   *Representative Art and Artists of New Mexico.* Santa Fe: School of American Research. Reissued by Olana

Gallery, Bronx, New York, in 1976.

New Mexico, State Engineer's Office
1967   Compiler. *Water Resources of New Mexico: Occurrence, Development and Use.* Santa Fe: State Planning Office.

New Mexico, State University Center for Business Services
1977   *Inventory of Economic, Sociocultural and Socioeconomic Resources in the Rio Grande Valley from Elephant Butte to Port Quitman, Texas.* Las Cruces.

New York Public Library, Reference Department
1961   *Dictionary Catalog of the History of the Americas.* Boston: G. K. Hall & Co.

North American Congress on Latin America (NACLA)
1975   Hit and Run: U.S. Runaway Shops on the Mexican Border. *Latin America and Empire Report* 9 (July-August): 2-30.
1977   Electronics: The Global Industry. *Latin America and Empire Report* 11 (April):3-25.

Official Airline Guide
1981   *Official Airline Guide.* North America Edition. July 15.

OPE
1976   Fraudulent Entrants Study: Illegal Alien Study. Part 1. Mimeographed. Washington, D.C.: Immigration and Naturalization Service, Office of Planning and Evaluation.

Passenger Transport
1981   Tijuana Trolley Rolls in San Diego. *Passenger Transport* 39 (no. 31):1.

Petróleos Mexicanos
1976   Annual Report, 1975. *Mexican Newsletter* 36 (March 18).

Photo-Geographic
1975   *Photo-Atlas of the United States.* Pasadena: Ward Ritchie Press.

Population Reference Bureau
1964   Mexico: The Problem of People. *Population Bulletin* 20: 173-203.
1980   *World Population Data Sheet.* Washington, D.C.

President's Commission on Mental Health
1978   *Task Panel Report on Migrant and Seasonal Farmworkers,* vol. 3. Washington, D.C.: Government Printing Office.

President's National Advisory Commission on Rural Poverty
1968   *Rural Poverty in the United States.* Washington, D.C.: Government Printing Office (May).

Procuraduría General de la República Mexicana
1974   Código penal para el distrito y territorios federales. Mexico City: Editores Mexicanos Unidos, S.A.
1948-76   *Memoria, 1948-, 1959-, 1975-, 1976.* Mexico City: Talleres Gráfico de la Nación.

Programa Nacional Fronterizo
1961   *Programa nacional fronterizo.* Mexico City.
1962   *Matamoros, Tamaulipas.* Mexico City.
1963*a*   *Programa nacional fronterizo.* Studies of individual border cities. Mexico City.
1963*b*   *Proyecto de un nuevo centro comercial en Matamoros, Tamaulipas: análisis económico.* Mexico City.

Rail Travel News
1978   Urban-Suburban Transit. *Rail Travel News* 8:7.

Railway Gazette International
1980   Focus on Mexico. *Railway Gazette International* 136 (no. 8):671-82.

Rand McNally
1973   *Handy Railroad Atlas of the United States.* Chicago: Rand McNally.
1979   *Road Atlas: United States, Canada, Mexico.* Chicago: Rand McNally.

SCLPW
1969-70   *Migrant and Farmwork Powerlessness.* Washington, D.C.: Hearings of Senate Committee on Labor and Public Welfare, Subcommittee on Migratory Labor.

SCWHI
1969   *The Impact of Commuter Aliens Along the Mexican and*

Canadian Borders. Washington, D.C.: Hearings of Select Commission on Western Hemisphere Immigration.

Secretaría de Comercio, *Informe mensual del ejército de los artículos de consumo; Informe mensual de cuotas de consumo fronterizo "Gancho."*

Secretaría de Industria y Comercio (SIC)
1968   *Programa de industrialización de la frontera norte de México.* Mexico City.
1972   *Estudio del desarrollo comercial de la frontera.* Mexico City.
1973   *Industrial Possibilities, Program for Assembly In-Bond Plants.* Mexico City: Subsecretaría de Industria.
1974a   *IX Censo Industrial 1971, Datos 1970. Industrias Extractiva y de Transformación (excepto Extracción y Refinación de Petróleo e Industria Petroquímica Básica).* México, D.F.
1974b   *Industrial Possibilities: Instruments for Promotion.* Mexico City.
1974c   *Zona fronteriza de Mexico: viabilidad industrial.* Mexico City.
1974d   *Zonas Fronterizas de México: Perfil Socioecónomico.* Mexico City: Dirección General de Estadística.
1974e   *Prontuario legal del programa de fomento económico fronterizo.* Mexico City.
1976a   *Política economica fronteriza, 1971-76.* Mexico City.
1976b   *Estudio del desarrollo comercial de la frontera norte.* Mexico City.

Secretaría de Programación y Presupuesto
  Anuario estadístico del comercio exterior de los Estados Unidos Mexicanos. Mexico City.

Secretaría de Recursos Hidráulicos (Dirección General de Distritos de Riego)
1960   *Estadística agrícola del ciclo 1958-59.* Informe estadístico no. 18.
1961   *Estadística agrícola del ciclo 1959-60.* Informe estadístico no. 20.
1968   *Estadística agrícola del ciclo 1966-67.* Informe estadístico no. 39.
1970   *Estadística agrícola del ciclo 1968-69.* Informe estadístico no. 48.
1972   *Mapa de unidades de suelos de la República Mexicana según el sistema de clasificación FAO/UNESCO. Escala 1:2,000,000.* Mexico City.
1975a   *Estadística agrícola del ciclo 1973-74.* Informe estadístico no. 74.
1975b   *Producción de la ganadería, de las industrias y semillas mejoradas, en los distritos de riego en el ciclo agrícola 1973-74. Informe estadístico no. 78.*
1976   *Estadística agrícola del ciclo 1974-75.* Informe estadístico no. 79.

Secretaría de Salubridad y Asistencia
1973   *Código sanitario de los Estados Unidos Mexicanos.* Mexico City.
  Cámara nacional de la industria de laboratorios químico farmacéuticos. Mexico City.

Secretaría de Turismo
1978   Economia turística: financiamiento a la industria hostelera en México. *Sectur* 1 (June):13-15.

Servicio Meteorológico Nacional
1976   *Normales climatológicas: período 1941-1970.* Mexico City: Dirección General de Geografía y Meteorología, Secretaría de Agricultura y Ganadería.

Sociedad Mexicana de Antropología
1943   *El norte de Mexico y el sur de Estados Unidos.* Tercera Reunión de Mesa Redonda sobre Problemas Antropológicos de México y Centro América. Mexico City: Castillo de Chapultepec (August/September).

Soil Conservation Service
1974   *Vegetation Map of New Mexico.* Albuquerque: Soil Conservation Service.

Soil Survey Staff
1975   *Soil Classification—A Comprehensive System—7th Approximation.* Washington, D.C.: U.S. Department of Agriculture. See also 1960, 1967.

Southwest Border Regional Commission.
1978   Economic Impact of Undocumented Aliens in the California Border Region. California Area Development Study, preliminary draft.

Southwest Indian Development
1968   *Traders on the Navaho Reservation: A Report on the Economic Bondage of the Navaho People.* Window Rock, Ariz.: Southwest Indian Development.

Southwestern Mission Research Center
  Newsletter. Tucson: Arizona State Museum.

Subsecretaría de la Presidencia
1974   Impetus to Small and Medium-sized Industry. *Mexican Newsletter* 38:3-6.

Texas, Amon Carter Museum of Western Art
1964   *Religious Folk Art of New Mexico.* Fort Worth.

Texas, Crop and Livestock Reporting Service
1975   *1974 Texas Field Crop Statistics.* Austin: Texas Department of Agriculture.
1976   *1975 Texas Cotton Statistics.* Austin: Texas Department of Agriculture.

Texas Department of Community Affairs (TDCA)
1975   Juvenile Alien Project. Mimeographed. Austin: State Youth Secretariat Division Report.

Texas Department of Highways and Public Transportation
1976   Texas Visitor Industry Report 1976. Austin.
1977a   Texas Tourism Tops 3.1 Billion During 1976. Austin (September).
1977b   Side Bar Accompanying Texas Tourism 1976. Austin (September).
1978   Report on the Texas Visitor Industry. Austin.
1979   Report on the Texas Visitor Industry. Austin.

Texas Governor's Office on Migrant Affairs
1976   *Migrant and Seasonal Farmworkers in Texas.* Austin.

Texas Lower Rio Grande Valley Development Council
n.d.   *Water Quality Data Base, Technical Plan Report I.* McAllen.

Texas Reynosa-McAllen Joint Industrial Team
1973   *General Information on Mexico's Border Industrialization Program for U.S. Manufacturers at Reynosa, Tamaulipas, Mexico.* McAllen: McAllen Industrial Board.

Texas Society of Professional Engineers
1974   *The Effects of Ponds and Small Reservoirs on the Water Resources of Texas.* Austin.

Texas Water Development Board
1968   *The Texas Water Plan.* 4 parts. Austin.
1975   *Inventories of Irrigation in Texas, 1958, 1964, 1969, and 1974.* Report no. 196. Austin.

Title V Regional Action Planning Commission
1976   *Arizona, California, New Mexico, Texas: Application for Designation.* Washington, D.C.: U.S. Department of Commerce.

Touche Ross International
1979   *Business Study: Mexico.* 2d ed.

United Nations (UN)
1954   *The Population of Central America (Including Mexico), 1950-1980.* New York: UN.
1964   *Demographic Yearbook, 1963.* New York: UN Statistical Office.
1973   *Multinational Corporations in World Development.* New York: UN Department of Economic and Social Affairs.
1974   *National Systems of Water Administration.* New York: UN.

U.S. Bureau of the Census
1894   *Report of Agriculture by Irrigation in the Western Part of the United States at the Eleventh Census, 1890.* Washington, D.C.: Government Printing Office.
1902   *Twelfth Census of the United States, Taken in the Year*

1900. Agriculture: Part 2, Crops and Irrigation, Census Reports 4. Washington, D.C.: Government Printing Office.

1913-14 *Thirteenth Census of the United States Taken in the Year 1910: Agriculture, 1909 and 1910.* Washington, D.C.: Government Printing Office.

1936 *United States Census of Agriculture: 1935. Reports for States with Statistics for Counties and a Summary for the United States.* Second Series, vol. 2. Washington, D.C.: Government Printing Office.

1956a *United States Census of Agriculture: 1954.* Vol. 1: *Counties and State Economic Areas.* Part 26, *Texas.* Washington, D.C.: Government Printing Office.

1956b *United States Census of Agriculture: 1954.* Vol. 1: *Counties and State Economic Areas.* Part 30, *New Mexico and Arizona.* Washington, D.C.: Government Printing Office.

1973 *Census of Population: Subject Reports PC(2)-1D Persons of Spanish Surname; Subject Reports PC(2)-1F American Indians.* Washington, D.C.: Government Printing Office.

1973 *Census of Population and Housing, 1970. Estimates of Coverage by Sex, Race and Age: Demographic Analysis.* Washington, D.C.: Government Printing Office.

1977 *1974 Census of Agriculture.* Vol. 1: Part 5, *California;* Part 3, *Arizona;* Part 31, *New Mexico;* Part 43, *Texas.* Washington, D.C.: Government Printing Office.

U.S. Bureau of Indian Affairs (BIA)
1972 *California Rancheria Task Force Report.* Sacramento: BIA, California Office.

U.S. Commission on Civil Rights (USCCR)
1970 *Food Programs in Texas: Staff Report.* Report no. 365. Washington, D.C.: General Services Administration.

1971 *Political Participation of Mexican-Americans in California: A Report.* Washington, D.C.: USCCR, California State Advisory Committee.

1971-74 Report 1: *Ethnic Isolation of Mexican Americans in the Public Schools of the Southwest.* Mexican American Education Study, USCCR.

Report 2: *The Unfinished Education: Outcome for Minorities in the Five Southwestern States.* Mexican American Education Study, USCCR.

Report 3: *The Excluded Student: Education Practices Affecting Mexican Americans in the Southwest.* Mexican American Education Study, USCCR.

Report 4: *Mexican American Education in Texas: A Function of Wealth.* Mexican American Education Study, USCCR.

Report 5: *Teachers and Students: Classroom Interaction in the Schools of the Southwest.* Mexican American Education Study, USCCR.

Report 6: *Toward Quality Education for Mexican Americans.* Mexican American Education Study, USCCR.

U.S. Comptroller General
1980 *Illegal Aliens: Estimating Their Impact on the United States.* Report to the Congress of the United States.

U.S. Congress
1977 Subcommittee on Inter-American Economic Relationships, Joint Committee. *Hearings, Recent Developments in Mexico and Their Economic Implications for the United States.* 95th Cong., 1 session. January 17 and 24. Washington, D.C.: Government Printing Office.

U.S. Congress, House of Representatives. (Washington, D.C.: Government Printing Office)
  Committee on Armed Services
    1975-76 *Thefts and Losses on Military Weapons, Ammunition and Explosives.* Hearings before Subcommittee, November 18-19, 1975; January 20, 1976.

Committee on Education and Labor, Subcommittee on Agricultural Labor
  1972 *Seminar on Farm Labor Problems.* 92d Cong., 1 sess.
  1972 *Agricultural Child Labor Act of 1971.* 92d Cong., 1 sess.
  1973 *Migrant Manpower Programs.* 92d Cong., 1 sess.
  1974 *Agricultural Labor Management Relations.* 93d Cong., 1 sess.
  1975 *National Office for Migrant and Seasonal Farmworkers.* 93d Cong., 2 session.
  1976 *Federal and State Statutes Relating to Farmworkers.* 94th Cong., 2 sess.
  1976 *Farm Labor Contractor Registration Act Amendment of 1976.* 94th Cong., 2 sess.
  1976 *Oversight Hearing on Migrant Education Programs.* 94th Cong., 1 sess.

Committee on Foreign Affairs
  1973 *The World Narcotics Problem: The Latin American Perspective. Report of Special Study Mission.*

Committee on Government Operations
  1974 *Law Enforcement and the Southwest Border: Hearings Before Subcommittee.* July 10-11, 16, August 14.

Committee on International Relations
  1975-76 *U.S. Citizens Imprisoned in Mexico: Hearings Before Subcommittee.* Part 1: April 29-30, 1975; Part 2: October 25, 1975, January 27, 1976; Part 3: June 29, 1976.
  1976 *The Shifting Pattern of Narcotics Trafficking: Latin America. Report of a Study Mission.*

Committee on Interstate and Foreign Commerce
  1974 *Heroin Traffic and Addiction: Hearing Before Subcommittee.* October 7.

Committee on Ways and Means
  1976 *Background Information and Compilation of Materials on Items 807.00 and 806.30 of the Tariff Schedules of the United States.* Subcommittee on Trade.

Joint Economic Committee
  1969 *Toward Economic Development for Native American Communities.* 2 vols. Subcommittee on Economy in Government.

Select Committee on Narcotics Abuse and Control
  1977a *Decriminalization of Marijuana: Hearings.* March 14-16.
  1977b *Oversight Hearings on Narcotics Abuse and Current Federal and International Narcotics Control Effort: Hearings.* September 21-23, 27-30, 1976.
  1977c *Report of Seven Nation Fact-finding Mission.* November 4-21, 1976.

U.S. Congress, Senate (Washington, D.C.: Government Printing Office)
  Committee on Finance
    1973 *Multinational Corporations: Hearings.* Subcommittee on International Trade.

Committee on Government Operations
  1976a *Federal Narcotics Enforcement, Interim Report.*
  1976b *Federal Drug Enforcement: Hearings before Subcommittee, Part 4: July 27-29; Part 5: August 23-26.*
  1977 *Illicit Traffic in Weapons and Drugs Across the United States-Mexican Border: Hearing Before Subcommittee.* January 12.

Committee on Interior and Insular Affairs
  1969 *Mineral and Water Resources of Arizona.* Washington, D.C.: U.S. Bureau of Reclamation, Arizona Bureau of Mines report.

Committee on Labor and Public Welfare
  1962 *The Migratory Farm Labor Problem in the United*

States. Washington, D.C.: See also reports for 1964, 1965, 1966, 1967, 1968, 1969.

1969   *The Education of American Indians.* 5 vols. *Indian Education: A National Tragedy—A National Challenge.* Washington, D.C.: Subcommittee on Indian Education.

1970   *Migrant and Seasonal Farmworker Powerlessness.* Part 1: *Who are the Migrants?* Part 7A: *Manpower and Economic Problems.* 91st Cong., 1 sess.

1973   *Farmworkers in Rural America, 1971-1972, Part 1.* 92nd Cong., 1 and 2 sess.

1973   *Federal and State Statutes Relating to Farmworkers: A Compilation.* 92d Cong., 2 sess.

Select Commission on Western Hemisphere Immigration (USSC)

1968   *The Impact of Commuter Aliens Along the Mexican and Canadian Borders: Hearings.*

U.S. Department of Agriculture

1970   *The Look of Our Land: The Far West.* Agriculture Handbook 372. Washington, D.C.: Economic Research Service.

1971   *The Look of Our Land: The Plains and Prairies.* Agriculture Handbook 419. Washington, D.C.: Economic Research Service.

1972   *The Look of Our Land: The Mountains and Deserts.* Agriculture Handbook 409. Washington, D.C.: Economic Research Service.

U.S. Department of Commerce

1974   *U.S. Imports for Consumption and General Imports, IA 236-A, TSUSA nos. 806.30 and 807.00.* Washington, D.C.: Social and Economics Statistics Administration, Bureau of the Census, Foreign Trade Division.

1976a   *Arizona, California, New Mexico, Texas: Application for Designation as a Title V Regional Action Planning Commission.* Washington, D.C.: Government Printing Office.

1976b   *U.S. Imports for Consumption and General Imports, IA 236-A, TSUSA numbers 806.30 and 807.00.* Washington, D.C.: Social and Economic Statistics Administration, Bureau of the Census, Foreign Trade Division.

U.S. Department of Health

1965   *Domestic Agricultural Migrants in the United States: Counties in Which an Estimated 100 or More Seasonal Workers migrated into the Area to Work During the Peak Season.* Publication 540. Washington, D.C.: Government Printing Office.

U.S. Department of the Interior

1962   *The Story of the Colorado-Big Thompson Project.* Washington, D.C.

1968   *1968 A-B Seas of Desalting.* Washington, D.C.: Office of Saline Water.

1970   *National Atlas of the United States of America.* Washington, D.C.: Geological Survey.

1971   *The Story of Hoover Dam.* Washington, D.C.

1976   *Geologic and Water-Supply Reports and Maps: Arizona, California, Colorado, New Mexico, Texas.* (Each state separate.) Washington, D.C.: Geological Survey.

U.S. Department of Justice

1976   *Estimated Total Number of Illegal Aliens and Employed Illegal Aliens by INS District.* Special and Irregular Publication of the Immigration and Naturalization Service.

U.S. Department of Labor

1964   *Coverage of Agricultural Workers Under State and Federal Labor Laws.* Bulletin 265. Washington, D.C.: Bureau of Labor Standards.

1974   *Bibliographic Literature on Migrant Seasonal Farmworkers: An Annotated Reference Guide.* Prepared for Manpower Administration by LMC (October).

U.S. News and World Report

1978   The Mighty Colorado: An Ailing Giant? 84 (June 19): 52-55.

U.S. President's Commission on Mental Health

1978   *Task Panel Report on Migrant and Seasonal Farmworkers.* Vol. 3: *Appendix.* Washington, D.C. (February).

U.S. President's Commission on Migratory Labor

1951   *Migratory Labor in American Agriculture.* Washington, D.C.

1954   *Migratory Notes.* Washington, D.C.

1961   *Report to the President's Committee on Domestic Migratory Labor.* Washington, D.C.: U.S. Department of Labor, Bureau of Labor Standards.

U.S. President's National Advisory Commission on Rural Poverty

1967   *The People Left Behind: Report.* Washington, D.C.

1968   *Rural Poverty in the United States.* Washington, D.C. (May).

U.S. President's Water Resource Policy Commission

1950   *Ten Rivers in America's Future.* 2 vols. Washington, D.C.

U.S. Strategy Council on Drug Abuse

1976   *Federal Strategy: Drug Abuse Prevention 1976.*

U.S. Tariff Commission

1970   *Economic Factors Affecting the Use of Items 807.00 806.30 of the Tariff Schedules of the United States.* Washington, D.C.: TC no. 339.

1972   *Competitiveness of U.S. Industries.* Washington, D.C.: TC no. 473.

1973   *Implications of Multinational Firms for World Trade and Investment and for U.S. Trade and Labor: Report to the U.S. Senate Committee on Finance.* Washington, D.C.

U.S. Travel Data Center

1975   *Proceedings: 1976 Travel Outlook Forum.* Washington, D.C. (December). See also for 1976, 1977, 1978.

1978   *Publications Catalog.* Washington, D.C.

1979   *Impact of Travel on Texas Counties.* Washington, D.C.

U.S. Travel Service, Department of Commerce

1971   *A Study of Mexican Travel Habits and Patterns.* Washington, D.C. (March). See also 1975-May; November.

1975   *Summary and Analysis of International Travel to the U.S.* Washington, D.C. See also 1976, 1977.

1977a   *Review of the Market: Mexico.* Washington, D.C.

1977b   *Mexico: A Study of the International Travel Market.* Washington, D.C.

1978a   *Foreign Arrivals by Selected Ports, Calendar Year 1977.* Washington, D.C.

1978b   *Profile of Travel to the United States from Selected Major Tourism Generating Countries.* Washington, D.C. (July).

U.S. Water Resources Council

1968   *The Nation's Water Resources.* 7 parts. Washington, D.C.: Government Printing Office.

University of Arizona

1965   Arizona Natural Vegetation. Tucson: Agricultural Experimental Station and Cooperative Extension Service, Bulletin A-45.

Utah, Salt Lake City Corporation

1978   *Application for Establishment of a Foreign Trade Zone: Salt Lake City, Utah.* Salt Lake City (October 28).

World Atlas of Agriculture

1977   Vol. 3: *Americas.* Novara, Italy: Instituto Geográfico de Agostini S.p.A.

World Bank

1972   *Tourism, Sector Working Paper.* Washington, D.C.

1976   *Landsat Index Atlas of the Developing Countries of the World.* Baltimore: Johns Hopkins University Press.

Section III.

Topical List of Dissertations and Theses

These dissertations and theses were accumulated from various sources, not only the chapters of *Borderlands Sourcebook* but also dissertation abstracts, computer searches, specialty bibliographies relating to the Southwest, and commencement lists of recent years supplied by more than three dozen universities located in, or concerned with, the border region. As in the composite bibliography, Ellwyn R. Stoddard was principally responsible for collecting, collating, and classifying the entries with editing help from various sources. Special mention is due Professor Matt C. Meier and Cindi Everitt for their lists on selected topics.

Economics and Labor

Appleman, Susan Marie
1979   An Analysis of the CETA Participant Selection Process of the Urban Component, Travis County, Texas, of the Capital Area Manpower Consortium. M.A., University of Texas, Austin.

Bergmann, John Francis
1952   Resources and Development of the Pacific and Mountain Divisions of the K.C.M.&O. Railway Route, Mexico. M.A., University of Texas, Austin.

Best, Doris Dunlap
1976   The Responses of Real Estate Lenders and Borrowers to Changing Mortgage Money Market Conditions, San Diego County, 1966-1975. M.A., San Diego State University.

Biderman, Jaime
1974   Enclave Development: The Case of Multinational Assembly Industries on Mexico's Northern Border. M.A., University of California, Berkeley.

Bledsoe, Tod Stewart
1972   Economic Integration in Central America. M.S., San Diego State University.

Boswell, Thomas D.
1967   Beef Cattle Feeding in the Imperial Valley, California: A Study in Economic Geography. M.A., San Diego State University.

Box, Dorothy Mae
1947   A Social and Economic History of the El Paso Area. M.A., North Texas State University.

Brown, Jerald E.
1972   The United Farm Workers Grape Strike and Boycott, 1965-1970. Ph.D., Cornell University.

Bruno, Anthony
1977   The Impact of the 1966 Tax Reform Act upon Taxation of Single-Family Residents in San Diego County, 1966-1976. M.S., San Diego State University.

Burkart, Edward C.
1973   Job Preference Factors at California State University at San Diego. M.S., San Diego State University.

Butts, Robert Andrew
1974   Recreation Travel Behavior. M.A., San Diego State University.

Campbell, Howard L.
1972   Bracero Migration and the Mexican Economy, 1951-1964. Ph.D., American University.

Cardenas, Gilbert
1977   Manpower Impact and Problems of Mexican Illegal Aliens in an Urban Labor Market. Ph.D., University of Illinois, Urbana.

Cauble, Douglas Glenn
1978   A Cost Analysis of Alternative Methods of Harvesting Mesquite for Industrial Use. M.S., Texas Tech University.

Choi, Kwok-on Frankie
1979   A Cross-national Study of the Pattern of Modernization in the Developing Countries, 1965-75. M.S., Texas A&M University.

Clark, Marilyn Noll
1977   Women Aircraft Workers in San Diego During the Second World War. M.A., San Diego State University.

Collier, G. Loyd
1954   The Lower Rio Grande Valley of Texas: Some Problems of an Irrigated Area. M.A., University of Nebraska.

Cook, Edson Carroll
1977   The Travel Agency Industry of the City of San Diego. M.A., San Diego State University.

Couturier, Edith
1965   The Hacienda of Hueyapan: The History of a Mexican Social and Economic Institution. Ph.D., Columbia University.

Daniel, Cletus
1972   Labor Radicalism in Pacific Coast Agriculture. Ph.D., University of Washington.

Dieck-Assad, Clara Marilu
1979   Tourism and Foreign Exchange for Mexico with Emphasis on the Demand and Supply of U.S. Tourism. M.A., University of Texas, Austin.

Dillman, C. Daniel
1968   The Functions of Brownsville, Texas, and Matamoros, Tamaulipas: Twin Cities of the Lower Rio Grande. Ph.D., University of Michigan.

Durfee, Lynn E.
1969   Large Scale Vegetable Farming in Central Arizona. M.A., Arizona State University.

Earley, Sarah Margaret
1974   Consumer Attitudes Towards Production Housing in San Diego County. M.B.A., San Diego State University.

Emish, Barbara Yvonne
1960   The Economic Development of Port Brownsville, Texas. M.A., Southern Methodist University.

Evans, Samuel L.
1960   Texas Agriculture, 1880-1930. Ph.D., University of Texas, Austin.

Fabelo, Antonio
1979   National Identity and Its Relation to the Potential Cultural Effects of Tourism in Developing Nations with Specific Reference to the Cases of Mexico and Peru. M.A., University of Texas, Austin.

Falls, Robert Hoyle
1956   Agricultural Production and Marketing of the Lower Rio Grande Valley. M.A., University of Chicago.

Fardovie, Hadi Oveisi
1979   Entrepreneurial Activities of the Public Sector in the Economic Development Processes: A Comparative Study of Mexico and Iran. Ph.D., University of Texas, Austin.

Fernandez-Cavada, José Luis
1979   International Trade in Fresh Oranges and Tangerines: Analysis of Potential Structural Changes Including EC Expansion. Ph.D., University of California, Davis.

Fernandez Kelly, Maria Patricia
1979   A Study of the Composition of the Female Labor Force in Mexican-American "Maquiladoras." Ph.D., Rutgers University.

Fineberg, Richard A.
1970   Green Card Workers in Farm Labor Disputes: A Study of Post-Bracero Mexican-National Farm Workers in the San Joaquin Valley, 1968. Ph.D., Claremont Graduate College.

Flandi, Stanley Albert
1973   Recruiting, Selecting, and Compensating Classified Employees in San Diego County Community Colleges. M.P.A., San Diego State University.

Fuller, Varden
1939   The Supply of Agricultural Labor as a Factor in the Evolution of Farm Organization in California. Ph.D., University of California, Berkeley.

Garcia, Mario T.
1975   *Obreros:* The Mexican Workers of El Paso, 1900-1920. Ph.D., University of California, San Diego.

Garibay, Lorenzo, Jr.
1977   The Border Industrialization Program of Mexico: A Case Study of the Matamoros, Tamaulipas Experience. M.A., University of Texas, Austin.

Glass, Judith C.
1966   Conditions Which Facilitate Unionization of Agricultural Workers: A Case Study of the Salinas Valley Lettuce Industry. Ph.D., University of California, Los Angeles.

Graf, Leroy P.
1942   The Economic History of the Lower Rio Grande Valley, 1820-1875. 2 vols. Ph.D., Harvard University.

Greer, Scott
1952   The Participation of Ethnic Minorities in the Labor Unions of Los Angeles County. Ph.D., University of California, Los Angeles.

Grossman, Seymour Lester
1971   Bank-Business Firm Relationships: A Survey of San Diego County. M.A., San Diego State University.

Gutierrez, Jesus Leopoldo
1979   The Mexican Banking System and Monetary Policy During the 1970's (1971-1976). M.A., University of Texas, Austin.

Hall, William C.
1942   A Study of 281 Farm Labor Families of South Texas. M.A., Texas A&I University.

Hanson, Stella E.
1926   Mexican Laborers in the Southwest. M.A., Pomona College.

Harmon, Warren W.
1964   The Grape Industry in San Diego County, California. M.A., San Diego State College.

Henderson, David A.
1964   Agriculture and Livestock Raising in the Evolution of the Economy and Culture of the State of Baja California, Mexico. 2 vols. Ph.D., University of California, Los Angeles.

Hershberger, Charles
1962   The El Paso *Labor Advocate* and Its Editors from 1909-1939: A Study of Labor Journalism in the Southwest. M.A., University of Texas, El Paso.

Hill, James E., Jr.
1963   Texas Citrus Industry. Ph.D., University of Tennessee.

Hullihen, James D.
1966   Arizona Citrus Industry. M.A., Arizona State University.

Hulpe, John F.
1963   The Position of California Labor in Regard to the Bracero Program, 1942-1962. M.A., California State University, San Francisco.

Inman, Raymond William
1973   Professionals and Unions: A Case Study of American Federation of Teacher Membership Composed of San Diego State College Faculty. M.S., San Diego State University.

Johns, Bryan T.
1948   Field Workers in California Cotton. M.A., University of California, Berkeley.

Jordan, Mildred
1956   Railroads in the El Paso Area. M.A., University of Texas, El Paso.

Keema, Alexander William
1971   A Study of the Impact of Truth in Lending upon Banks and Finance Companies in San Diego. M.A., San Diego State University.

Killiam, Wilton Hayes
1958   Agriculture in Texas. M.A., University of Texas, Austin.

Kuntz, Edwin C.
1978   An Empirical Analysis of Selected Socially Responsive Behaviors in the Texas Banking Industry. D.B.A., Texas Tech University.

Lee, Mary Antoine
1950   A Historical Survey of the American Smelting and Refining Company in El Paso, 1817-1950. M.A., University of Texas, El Paso.

Lovett, John C.
1973   Analysis of California State University at San Diego School of Business Graduates. M.S., San Diego State University.

Lubach, Robert Gordon
1976   San Diego, California, and United States Business Cycles, 1949-1974: A Comparison. M.S., San Diego State University.

Lutz, Carl L.
1964   The San Diego Citrus Industry. M.A., San Diego State College.

Lytwyn, Richard Dean
1972   Employment Patterns of Community College Data Processing Graduates in San Diego County. M.S., San Diego State University.

McCain, Johnny M.
1970   Contract Labor as a Factor in United States-Mexican Relations, 1942-1947. Ph.D., University of Texas, Austin.

McKann, Michael Hewitt
1975   The Recreation Potential of Chorro Canyon, Presidio County, Texas. M.S., Texas Tech University.

Markey, Lawrence F.
1973   A Study of the Financial Forecasting Systems of Six San Diego County Corporations. M.B.A., San Diego State University.

Mason, John Dancer
1969   The Aftermath of the Bracero: A Study of the Economic Impact on the Agricultural Hired Labor Market of Michigan from the Termination of Public Law 78. Ph.D., Michigan State University.

Miller, Mary Catherine
1974   Attitudes of the San Diego Labor Movement Toward Mexicans. M.A., San Diego State University.

Mitchell, Elizabeth
1955   The Clothing Industry of El Paso from 1919 to July 1955. M.A., University of Texas, El Paso.

Newell-Garcia, Roberto Edwardo
1979   Financial Deepening and Financial Narrowing: The Case of Mexico, 1960-1976. Ph.D., University of Texas, Austin.

Niblo, Stephen Randall
1972   The Political Economy of the Early Porfiriato Politics and Economics in Mexico, 1876 to 1880. Ph.D., Northern Illinois University.

Olliff, Donathon Carnes
1974   Economics of Mexican-United States Relations During the Reforma, 1854-1861. Ph.D., University of Florida.

Orndorff, Helen
1956   History of the Development of Agriculture in the El Paso Valley. M.A., University of Texas, El Paso.

Oyarzabal-Tamargo, Francisco
1976   Economic Impact of Saline Irrigation Water: Mexicali Valley, Mexico. Ph.D., Colorado State University.

Perron, Marius
1928   Employment Agencies on the Mexican Border. M.A., University of Texas, Austin.

Perry, Josef H.
1961   Economic Characteristics of Texas Intrastate Migrants. M.A., University of Texas, Austin.

Peterson, Herbert
1974   Twentieth-Century Search for Cíbola: Post World War I Mexican Labor Exploitation in Arizona. M.A.,* University of Arizona.

Reccow, Louis
1971   The Orange County Citrus Strikes of 1935-1936: The Forgotten People in Revolt. Ph.D., University of Southern California.

Restrepo, Carlos Emilio
1975   The Transfer of Management Technology to a Less Developed Country: A Case Study of a Border Industrialization Program in Mexico. Ph.D., University of Nebraska, Lincoln.

Rivas Sosa, E.
1973   Fundión de las industrias maquiladoras en la promoción de polos de desarrollo industrial. Tesis Profesional, UNAM (Mexico City).

Rochlin, Clifford Barry
1971   California Union Membership: A Relative Decline. M.S., San Diego State University.

Rollins, Audrey Finegold
1975   Mexico's Labor Code and Its Implementation: The Ciudad Juárez Example. Ph.D., Texas Tech University.

Romo, Ricardo
1975   Mexican Workers in the City: Los Angeles, 1915-1930. Ph.D., University of California, Los Angeles.

Rubalcaba, Robert Louis
1973   The Mortgage Money Market in San Diego County, 1960-1972. M.S., San Diego State University.

Rungeling, Brian Scott
1969   Impact of the Mexican Alien Commuter on the Apparel Industry of El Paso, Texas: A Case Study. Ph.D., University of Kentucky.

Salandini, Victor P.
1964   An Objective Evaluation of the Labor Disputes in the Lettuce Industry in Imperial Valley, California, During January-March, 1961. M.A., St. Louis University.
1969   The Short-Run Socio-Economic Effects of the Termination of Public Law 78 on the California Labor Market for 1965-1967. Ph.D., Catholic University of America.

Shane, Robert Allen
1975   A Site Evaluation Model for a Mexican Fast-Food Restaurant. M.B.A., San Diego State University.

Shapiro, Barry Ira
1978   A Shift-Share Analysis of Industrial Composition and Growth in the Lower Rio Grande Valley State Planning Region of Texas. M.S., Texas A&M University.

Shapiro, Harold Arthur
1940   The Workers of San Antonio, Texas, 1900-1940. Ph.D., University of Texas, Austin.

Sheehan, Michael Francis
1979   The Theory of the Limiting Utility Applied to the Development of Natural Resources in Arid Lands. Ph.D., University of California, Riverside.

Smith, Dwight
1967   The Date Industry of Arizona. M.A., Arizona State University.

Snow, Ronald W.
1969   The Beef Cattle Industry of Arizona: A Geographical Analysis. M.A., Arizona State University.

Solis-Flores, Roberto Hiram
1955   Production and Marketing of Cotton in the Matamoros Area of Mexico. M.A., University of Texas, Austin.

Spencer, John H. D.
1955   A Study of the Male, Manual, Manufacturing Labor Force of El Paso, Texas. Ph.D., University of North Carolina, Chapel Hill.

Standefer, Harmon Bishop
1949   Some Economic Aspects and Consequences of Free-Trade Zones in Mexican Border Cities. M.A., University of Texas, Austin.

Starnbaugh, Jacob Lee
1924   The Marketing of Perishable Farm Products Grown in the Lower Rio Grande Valley of Texas. M.A., University of Texas, Austin.

Tawfik, Gilda
1977   An Evaluation of Multinational Corporations. M.B.A., San Diego State University.

Tiller, James Weeks
1969   Some Economic Aspects of Commercial Cool Season Vegetable Production in the Texas Winter Garden. Ph.D., University of Oklahoma.

Toner, David T.
1974   Bias in the Tax Appraisals of Single Family Residences in El Paso, Texas. M.A., University of Texas, El Paso.

Tucker, Leo Robert
1976   A Survey of the Growth of Industrial Arts Plastics Programs in Southern California High Schools, 1969 to 1975. M.A., San Diego State University.

Walton, Roger M. V.
1941   A Study of Migratory Mexican Pea-Pickers in Imperial Valley, August, 1940. M.A., University of Southern California.

Wasserman, Mark
1975   Oligarchy and Foreign Enterprise in Porfirian Chihuahua, Mexico, 1876-1911. Ph.D., University of Chicago.

White, Michael Charles
1976   The Continuum of Communication: Coalitions and Networks Among the Small Boat Tuna Fishermen of San Diego. M.A., San Diego State University.

Wiest, Raymond E.
1970   Wage-Labor Migration and Household Maintenance in a Central Mexican Town. Ph.D., University of Oregon.

Zeguidi, Khaled
1978   An Analysis of Industrial Composition and Growth in the Upper Rio Grande State Planning Region. M.S., Texas A&M University.

Demography

Bell, Mattie
1935   The Growth and Distribution of the Texas Population. M.A., Baylor University.

Blacke, John Herman
1973   Social Change and Population Trends in Mexico. Ph.D., University of California, Berkeley.

Bradshaw, Benjamin S.
1960   Some Demographic Aspects of Marriage: A Comparative Study of Three Ethnic Groups. M.A., University of Texas, Austin.

Bridges, Julian C.
1973   The Population of Mexico: Its Composition and Changes. Ph.D., University of Florida, Gainesville.

Clifford, Roy A.
1970   Sociological Study of the Growth and Decline of Mexican Population Centers, 1940-1960. Ph.D., University of Florida, Gainesville.

Grimes, Jeanne Johnston
1953   One Hundred Years of Population Expansion in Texas, 1850-1950. M.A., Southern Methodist University.

Hamby, James E., Jr.
1975   The People of Chihuahua: A Demographic Analysis. Ph.D., University of Florida.

Harmer, Dennis Dale
1979   The Nature and Determinants of In-Migration to Nonmetropolitan Texas, 1970-1976. Ph.D., University of Texas, Austin.

Hinojosa, Gilberto Miguel
1979   Settlers and Sojourners in the "Chaparral": A Demographic Study of a Borderlands Town in Transition, Laredo, 1755-1870. Ph.D., University of Texas, Austin.

McConville, J. Lawrence
1966   A History of Population in the El Paso-Ciudad Juárez Area. M.A., University of New Mexico.

Maxwell, Lawrence E.
1966   Residential Distribution of Occupations in Los Angeles. M.A., University of California, Los Angeles.

Phelps, Lynn Alan
1973   EDP and the 1970 U.S. Census as Used by the City of San Diego. M.P.A., San Diego State University.

Quinto, Bustaquio Visperas
1973   Analysis of the Variations Between Census Unemployment Data and Administrative Estimates for California. M.A., San Diego State University.

Rhoades, Cecilia C.
1981   A Comparative Analysis of Mexican Migration to the Mexican Border and into the U.S.: A Reappraisal of Ravenstein's Laws. M.A., University of Texas, El Paso.

Spaulding, Leslie E.
1954   Population Distribution in Arizona and New Mexico, 1950. M.A., University of Chicago.

Wilson, Foster W.
1966   Demographic Characteristics of Texas White Persons of Spanish Surname. M.A., Texas A&M University.

Society and Politics

Addison, Thomas
1971   Out of Home Care in the County of San Diego: A Description of a Fragmented System. M.S.W., San Diego State University.

Alexander, Gladys Martha
1942   The Position of Texas in the Relations Between the United States and Mexico. M.A., North Texas State University.

Andrade, Welton Edward
1975   San Diego Metropolitan Waste Water Management: Its Past, Present, and Future. M.P.A., San Diego State University.

Andress, Monte Richard
1975   World View and Millenarian Missionization in a Mexican Village. M.A., San Diego State University.

Arack, James Nicholas
1973   A Study of the Off-Campus Student in the San Diego Community Colleges. M.P.A., San Diego State University.

Armour, Brenda
1969   Can Racial Attitudes be Changed? An Evaluation of the Effectiveness of Two Programs Designed by the Citizens' Interracial Committee of San Diego. M.S.W., San Diego State University.

Bailey, Rusian
1979   The Implementation of Federal Air Pollution Control in the State of Texas. Graduate Nonthesis Paper, University of Texas, El Paso.

Becerra, Alejandro
1968   Report: Economic Welfare of Mexicans: In Mexico, the United States, and the United States-Mexico Border Area. M.A., University of Texas, Austin.

Benson, Elisabeth S.
1969   A Comparative Study of the Non-resident Applicants for AFDC and a Sample of AFDC Resident Applicants Approved from July Through October, 1968, in the Central District Office, San Diego County Department of Public Welfare, California. M.S.W. San Diego State University.

Bibb, Leland Eugene
1973   The LaMesa Town Center Project. M.P.A., San Diego State University.

Bierl, Raymond Manfred
1972   Poverty and Mental Retardation: A Study in Labeling. M.A., San Diego State University.

Blake, Robert
1948   A History of the Catholic Church in El Paso. M.A., University of Texas, El Paso.

Blew, Robert Willis
1973   Californios and American Institutions: A Study of Reactions to Social and Political Institutions. Ph.D., University of Southern California.

Boostrom, Roger Layton
1973   A Case Study of the Organizational Development of the San Diego County Air Pollution Central District. M.B.A., San Diego State University.

Boysen, Bernadine B.
1970   La Mesa Pentario: An Ethnography of Baja California's State Prison. M.A., San Diego State College.

Bridges, Julian C.
1961   An Examination of Some Aspects of Family Morality in Latin America. D.D., Southwestern Baptist Theological Seminary.

1969   A Study of the Number, Distribution, and Growth of the Protestant Population in Mexico. M.A., University of Florida, Gainesville.

Broaddus, Morgan
1955   The History of the Bench and Bar in El Paso County. M.A., University of Texas, El Paso.

Brook, Paula
1978   The Need for Affirmative Action in Public Education in El Paso, Texas. M.A., University of Texas, El Paso.

Browning, Elizabeth Ann
1978   A Critical Study of the Rhetorical Theories of Tom Hayden: Agitative Rhetoric in Divergent Contexts. M.A., Texas Tech University.

Bryson, Conrey
1959   El Paso Water Supply: Problems and Solutions, 1921-1959. M.A., University of Texas, El Paso.

Buckner, Dellos
1929   Study of the Lower Rio Grande Valley as a Culture Area. M.A., University of Texas, Austin.

Busey, James Lynn
1952   Domination and the Vote in a Southwestern Border Community: The 1950 Primary Campaign in El Paso, Texas. Ph.D., Ohio State University.

Bustamante, Jorge Agustin
1974   Mexican Immigration and the Social Relations of Capitalism. Ph.D., University of Notre Dame.

Cardenas, Gilbert
1977   A Theoretical Approach to the Sociology of Mexican Labor Migration. Ph.D., University of Notre Dame.

Cardoso, Lawrence A.
1974   Mexican Emigration to the United States, 1900-1930; An Analysis of Socio-Economic Causes. Ph.D., University of Connecticut.

Carney, John P.
1954   Leading Factors in the Recent Reversal of U.S. Policy Regarding Alien Contract Labor Agreements. M.A., University of Southern California.

1957   Postwar Mexican Migration: 1954-1955, with Particular Reference to the Policies and Practices of the United States Concerning Its Control. Ph.D., University of Southern California.

Casteñeda Alatorre, Fernando
1944   El tratado de 1906 celebrado entre México y los Estados Unidos de Norte-America sobre la distribución de las aguas del Río Bravo en el Valle de Juárez, Chihuahua. Masters, Universidad Nacional Autonoma de México.

Chacon, Ralph
1953   The Falcon Dam. M.A., University of Texas, El Paso.

Chan, Doris Yun-Yun
1975   Nutritional Intake of Children in Four Head Start Centers in Lubbock. M.S., Texas Tech University.

Chandler, Charles
1968   The Mexican-American Protest Movement in Texas. Ph.D., Tulane University.

Chaney, Homer Campbell, Jr.
1959   The Mexican-United States War as Seen by Mexican Intellectuals, 1846-1956. Ph.D., Stanford University.

Chatham, William Karl
1973   A Spatial Analysis of Social Visiting Patterns in San Diego. M.A., San Diego State University.

Christian, Chester C., Jr.
1961   Some Sociological Implications of Government VD Control. M.A., University of Texas, Austin.

Christian, Garna Loy
1978   Sword and Plowshare: The Symbiotic Development of Fort Bliss and El Paso, Texas, 1849-1918. Ph.D., Texas Tech University.

Clarke, Robert L.
1973   Regional Government in San Diego County. M.P.A., San Diego State University.

Clash, Thomas Wood
1972   United States-Mexican Relations, 1940-1946: A Study

of United States Interests and Policies. Ph.D., State University of New York, Buffalo.

Clay, James William
1969   Water-related Problems and Their Effects on the Spatial Arrangement of Agricultural Production in the Mexicali-San Luis Valley of Northwest Mexico. Ph.D., University of North Carolina, Chapel Hill.

Cline, Donald L.
1967   Farm Labor in Arizona since Termination of Public Law 78. M.A., Arizona State University.

Coalson, George O.
1955   The Development of the Migratory Farm Labor System in Texas, 1900-1954. Ph.D., University of Oklahoma.

Coker, William Sidney
1965   United States-British Diplomacy over Mexico, 1913. Ph.D., University of Oklahoma.

Coleman, Eugene Victor
1973   The Urbanization of the Sweetwater Valley, San Diego County. M.A., San Diego State University.

Cooney, John P.
1973   Definition of the Sociologic Vector in Comprehensive Land and Water Resource Planning. M.A., University of Texas, El Paso.

Cooper, Kenneth
1959   Leadership Role Expectations in Mexican Rural and Urban Environment. Ph.D., Stanford University.

Copp, Nelson G.
1963   Wetbacks and Braceros: Mexican Migrant Laborers and American Immigration Policy, 1930-1960. Ph.D., Boston University.

Cravens, Mattie Ella
1923   The Diplomacy Between the United States and Mexico Concerning the Mixed Claims Commission, 1868-1892. M.A., University of Texas, Austin.

Crocker, Eileen R.
1970   A Descriptive Study of AFDC Youth Ages Sixteen to Twenty-one Living in Own-Home Settings in San Diego, California. M.S.W., San Diego State University.

Crowley, Donald Wayne
1979   The Impact of Serano v. Priest: The Quest for Equal Opportunity. Ph.D., University of California, Riverside.

Crowley, Florence Joseph
1963   The Conservative Thought of José Vasconcelos. Ph.D., University of Florida.

Cruz, Gilbert Ralph
1974   Spanish Town Patterns in the Borderlands: Municipal Origins in Texas and the Southwest, 1610-1810. Ph.D., St. Louis University.

Cuellar, Robert
1969   A Social and Political History of the Mexican-American Population of Texas, 1929-1963. M.A., North Texas State University.

D'Antonio, William
1958   National Images of Business and Political Elites in Two Border Cities. Ph.D., Michigan State University.

Day, John C.
1971   Managing the Lower Rio Grande. Ph.D., University of Chicago.

Denny, John
1954   One Hundred Years of Free Masonry in El Paso, 1854-1954. M.A., University of Texas, El Paso.

Deveney, Bernard J.
1971   The San Diego County Board of Supervisors as a Political System. M.A., San Diego State University.

DeVille, Robert A.
1971   The Study of Political Socialization in Northern Mexico: A Methodological Critique. M.A., University of Texas, El Paso.

DeVore, Joyce McBride
1970   A Descriptive-Evaluative Study of the Youth Service Bureau, San Diego, California. M.S.W., San Diego State University.

Diaz, Arthur Joseph
1972   Diplomatic Relations Between the United States and Mexico, 1925-1928. M.A., San Diego State University.

Dobkins, Betty
1958   The Spanish Element in Texas Water Law. Ph.D., University of Texas, Austin.

Doleshal, David Jon
1973   An Analysis of Specific Content in Three Large Metropolitan Dailies. M.S., San Diego State University.

Dougherty, Daniel T.
1979   Electric Utility Regulation in Texas: The Case of El Paso Electric Company. M.A., University of Texas, El Paso.

Dougherty, John Edson
1969   Mexico and Guatemala, 1856-1872: A Case Study in Extra-legal International Relations. Ph.D., University of California, Los Angeles.

Driver, Walter W.
1973   A Study of El Paso Housing. M.A., University of Texas, El Paso.

Dunn, Sharon Ann
1977   The Effect of Court-appointed Versus Privately Retained Attorneys on The Disposition of Cases in a Federal District. M.A., University of Texas, El Paso.

Edington, Scot H.
1979   A Comparison of Seven Models for the Equalization of Educational Expenditures for Capital Outlay and Debt Service in the Texas Public Schools. Ed.D., Texas Tech University.

Edwards, Warrick Ridgely, III
1971   United States-Mexican Relations, 1913-1916: Revolution, Oil, and Intervention. Ph.D., Louisiana State University.

Elliot, Robert S.
1939   The Health and Relief Problems of a Group of Non-family Mexican Men in Imperial Valley, California. M.A., University of Southern California.

Fantini, Albino Edward, Jr.
1962   Illness and Curing Among the Mexican-Americans of Mission, Texas. M.A., University of Texas, Austin.

Foley, Edna
1950   A History of the William Eleveus Robertson Water Treatment Plant, El Paso, Texas. M.A., University of Texas, El Paso.

Fullerton, Frank P.
1968   The Implementation of the Chamizal Convention. 2 vols. M.A., University of Texas, El Paso.

Galzerano, Ethel Ann
1974   A Survey of the Attitude Political Cynicism in El Paso During the 1972 Presidential Campaign. M.A., University of Texas, El Paso.

García, Juan Ramon
1977   Operation Wetback, 1954. Ph.D., University of Notre Dame.

García, Mario Trinidad
1975   *Obreros:* The Mexican Workers of El Paso, 1900-1920. Ph.D., University of California, San Diego.

Garr, Daniel J.
1971   Hispanic Colonial Settlement in California: Planning and Urban Development on the Frontier, 1769-1850. Ph.D., Cornell University.

Gerome, Frank A.
1968   United States-Mexican Relations During the Initial Years of the Mexican Revolution. Ph.D., Kent State University.

Getty, Harry T.
1950   Interethnic Relationships in the Community of Tucson. Ph.D., University of Chicago.

Gibb, Charles Edward
1973   Regional Government and the San Diego County. M.P.A.,

Gibbs, William E.
1973   Spadework Diplomacy: United States-Mexican Relations During the Hayes Administration, 1877-1881. Ph.D., Kent State University.

Gibson, Delbert L.
1959   Protestantism in Latin American Acculturation. Ph.D., University of Texas, Austin.

Gilderhus, Mark Theodore
1968   The United States and the Mexican Revolution, 1915-1920: A Study of Policy and Interest. Ph.D., University of Nebraska, Lincoln.

Gildersleeve, Charles R.
1978   The International Border City: Urban Spatial Organization in a Context of Two Cultures Along the United States-Mexico Boundary. Ph.D., University of Nebraska, Lincoln.

Gorder, Bonnie Brunner
1974   Medical Requirements for Employment in Public Agencies in San Diego County. M.P.A., San Diego State University.

Gotshall, Elwood Rufus, Jr.
1970   Catholicism and Catholic Action in Mexico, 1929-1941: A Church's Response to a Revolutionary Society and the Politics of the Modern Age. Ph.D., University of Pittsburgh.

Graves, Ersilee Ruth Parker
1960   A History of the Interrelationships Between Imported Mexican Labor, Domestic Migrants and the Texas Agricultural Economy. M.A., University of Texas, Austin.

Greenleaf, Floyd Lincoln
1976   Diplomacy of the Mexican Revolution: Mexican Policy and American Response, 1910-1913. Ph.D., University of Tennessee.

Gregory, Gladys Grace
1937   El Chamizal: A Boundary Problem Between the United States and Mexico. Ph.D., University of Texas, Austin.

Guthrie, Charles N.
1975   A Descriptive Study of the Training, Organization and Cases of the Family Crisis Intervention Unit, San Diego, California. M.S., San Diego State University.

Gutiérrez, Emeterio, Jr.
1952   A Study of School Attendance of Migrant Students in Grullo, Texas. M.A., University of Texas, Austin.

Gutiérrez, Hector José
1975   Analysis and Redesign of Information System for Tijuana's Institute of Technology. M.S., San Diego State University.

Halla, Frank Louis, Jr.
1978   El Paso, Texas, and Juarez, Mexico: A Study of a Biethnic Community, 1846-1881. Ph.D., University of Texas, Austin.

Haney, P. L.
1948   The International Controversy over the Waters of the Upper Rio Grande. M.A., University of Texas, El Paso.

Hardy, Blaine Carmon
1963   The Mormon Colonies of Northern Mexico: A History, 1885-1912. Ph.D., Wayne State University.

Harrington, Marilyn H.
1977   A Study of Mass Media Use, Preferences and Needs of an Elderly Population in the San Diego Area. M.S., San Diego State University.

Harris, Charles Houston, III
1968   A Mexican Latifundio: The Economic Empire of the Sanchez Navarro Family, 1765-1821. Ph.D., University of Texas, Austin.

Harrison, Donald Fisher
1976   United States-Mexican Military Collaboration During World War II. Ph.D., Georgetown University.

Harshman, Carolyn Jean
1977   Flood Plain Management in San Diego County. M.P.A., San Diego State University.

Hellerman, Leon
1972   An Analysis of President Polk's Mexican Policy in Selected American History Textbooks for Secondary School. Ed.D., New York University.

Henn, Jacob B.
1971   Human Resource Development in the World Industrialization Process: The Case of Mexico. M.A., San Diego State University.

Hennessey, Gregg Robert
1977   City Planning, Progressivism, and the Development of San Diego, 1908-1926. M.A., San Diego State University.

Hill, Larry D.
1971   Woodrow Wilson's Executive Agents in Mexico: From the Beginning of His Administration to the Recognition of Venustiano Carranza. 2 vols. Ph.D., Louisiana State University.

Hinojosa, José
1979   Discretionary Authority over Immigration: An Analysis of Immigration Policy and Administration. Ph.D., University of Notre Dame.

Hobbs, Lola J.
1969   Participation, Influence and Self-Selection: A Study of Community Action Council Boards in San Diego County. M.S.W., San Diego State University.

Hoffman, Abraham
1970   The Repatriation of Mexican Nationals from the United States During the Great Depression. Ph.D., University of California, Los Angeles.

Hoffman, Nancy J.
1974   Mexican Emigration to the United States, 1900-1910. M.A., San Diego State University.

Holcombe, Harold Eugene
1968   United States Arms Control and the Mexican Revolution, 1910-1924. Ph.D., University of Alabama.

Horn, James John
1969   Diplomacy by Ultimatum: Ambassador Sheffield and Mexican-American Relations, 1921-1927. Ph.D., State University of New York, Buffalo.

Hudgens, Alice Gayle
1979   Hemisphericity and Its Implications for the Re-Design of Developmental Studies Programs. Ph.D., University of Texas, Austin.

Hufford, Charles H.
1929   The Social and Economic Effects of the Mexican Migration into Texas. M.A., University of Colorado.

Hull, Frank Leroy, Jr.
1973   The Effects of Braceros on the Agriculture Labor Market in California, 1950-1970. Ph.D., University of Illinois, Urbana-Champaign.

Hundley, Norris Cecil, Jr.
1963   Dividing the Waters: Mexican-American Controversies over the Waters of the Colorado River and the Rio Grande, 1880-1960. Ph.D., University of California, Los Angeles.

Hunter, James Lithgow
1974   Functions of Reclaimed Wastewater in San Diego County. M.A., San Deigo State University.

Ignasias, Charles Dennis
1967   Reluctant Recognition: The United States and the Recognition of Alvaro Obregon of Mexico, 1920-1924. Ph.D., Michigan State University.

Isaacs, Harold
1968   United States-Mexican Relations During the Gonzales Administration, 1880-1884. Ph.D., University of Alabama.

Jackson, Robena Estelle
1979   East Austin: A Socio-historical View of a Segregated Community. M.A., University of Texas, Austin.

Johnson, Robert Bruce
1964   The Punitive Expedition: A Military, Diplomatic, and Political History of Pershing's Chase After Pancho Villa, 1916-1917. Ph.D., University of Southern California.

Johnson, Tye Craig
1974   A Study of Forcible Rape in San Diego County, 1968-1972. M.A., San Diego State University.

Keefe, Edgar S.
1933   Denial of Justice as Interpreted and Applied by the United States-Mexican General Claims Commission Under the Convention of September 8, 1923. M.A., University of Texas, Austin.

Kelly, Duncan Peter
1975   An Investigation of Diversion in the San Diego Police Department's Youth Resources Program. M.S., San Diego State University.

Kemp, Roger Lark
1974   Survey and Analysis of Regional Planning Agencies Affecting Urban Growth in San Diego County. M.P.A., San Diego State University.

Kennedy, James David
1975   Factors Determining the Economic Feasibility of Wastewater Reclamation in San Diego. M.A., San Diego State University.

Kenney, Mabel
1950   Civilian Activities During World War II in El Paso, Texas. M.A., University of Texas, El Paso.

Kentner, Janet R.
1975   The Socio-political Role of Women in the Mexican Wars of Independence, 1810-1821. Ph.D., Loyola University of Chicago.

Kestenbaum, Justin Louis
1963   The Question of Intervention in Mexico, 1913-1917. Ph.D., Northwestern University.

Kimball, Dave Anthony
1973   A Fiscal Analysis: How Fare San Diego County's Suburban Cities. M.A., San Diego State University.

Kiser, George C.
1974   The Bracero Program: A Case Study of Its Development, Termination and Aftermath. Ph.D., University of Massachusetts, Amherst.

Knopp, Anthony Keith
1973   "The Will of the People": The International Public Opinion and the American Intervention in Mexico, 1914. Ph.D., Texas Tech University.

Kohl, Clayton Charles
1910   Claims as a Cause of the Mexican War. Ph.D., New York University.

Krassowski, Witold
1963   Naturalization and Assimilation-Proneness of California Immigrant Populations. Ph.D., University of California, Los Angeles.

Kroosz, Charles E.
1972   Food Price Differences in Two San Diego Neighborhoods. M.S., San Diego State University.

LaNasa, Marion Anthony, Jr.
1979   Decision-making by the Business Elites in the Post-Industrial Sunbelt City. M.A., University of Texas, Austin.

Lane, Janet A.
1972   United States-Mexican Diplomatic Relations, 1917-1942. Ph.D., Georgetown University.

Langford, Margaret H.
1969   The Public Image of El Paso. M.A., University of Texas, El Paso.

Langston, Edward Lonnie
1974   The Impact of Prohibition on the Mexican-United States Border: The El Paso-Ciudad Juárez Case. Ph.D., Texas Tech University.

Li, Ming dju
1949   An Introduction to the Study of the History of Methodist Churches in El Paso. M.A., University of Texas, El Paso.

Lipshultz, Robert J.
1962   American Attitudes Toward Mexican Immigration, 1924-1952. Ph.D., University of Chicago.

Liss, Sheldon Barnett
1965   The Chamizal Conflict, 1864-1964. Ph.D., American University.

Lopez, Pedro
1977   A Study of Unapprehended and Apprehended Aliens in El Paso: Characteristics and Reported Reasons for Coming to the U.S. M.A., University of Texas, El Paso.

Lou, Dennis Wingsou
1963   Fall Committee: An Investigation of Mexican Affairs. Ph.D., Indiana University.

Lyon, Jessie C.
1975   Diplomatic Relations Between the United States, Mexico and Japan: 1913-1917. Ph.D., Claremont Graduate School.

Lyon, Richard M.
1954   The Legal Status of American and Mexican Migratory Farm Labor: An Analysis of U.S. Farm Labor Legislation, Policy and Administration. Ph.D., Cornell University.

McAdams, Diana Claire
1979   Powerful Actors in Public Land Use Decision-making Processes: A Case Study in Austin, Texas. Ph.D., University of Texas, Austin.

McAlister, Robert T., Jr.
1968   The Relationship of Education and Income to Partisan Vote: The Case of El Paso, Texas. M.A., University of Texas, El Paso.

McCain, Johnny Mac
1970   Contract Labor as a Factor in United States-Mexican Relations, 1942-1947. Ph.D., University of Texas, Austin.

McCleneghan, Jack Sean
1979   The Effects of Media Interaction and other Campaign Variables in Mayoral Elections in Twenty-three Texas Metro Areas. Ph.D., University of Texas, Austin.

McConville, James Lawrence
1975   A Phenomenological Approach to Curriculum Metatheory: An Ethnomethodological Analysis of Affective Classroom Situations in a Borderlands Community. Ed. D., New Mexico State University.

McEuen, William
1914   A Survey of the Mexican in Los Angeles. M.A., University of Southern California.

Machado, Manuel Anthony, Jr.
1964   An Industry in Crisis: Mexican-United States Cooperation in the Control of Foot-and-Mouth Disease. Ph.D., University of California, Santa Barbara.

McReynolds, James Michael
1978   Family Life in a Borderland Community: Nacogdoches, Texas, 1779-1861. Ph.D., Texas Tech University.

MacWhorter, Carol Ann
1979   Health Region Three Elderly Needs Assessment. M.A., University of Texas, El Paso.

Maddox, Maude
1951   A Brief Survey of William Beaumont Army Hospital. M.A., University of Texas, El Paso.

Madero, Lydia
1979   The Ejido: A Survey of Views. M.S., Texas A&M University.

Markus de Kennedy, Anneliese
1974   The Office of Special Studies: A Study of the Joint Mexican Secretariat of Agriculture-Rockefeller Foundation Program in Agriculture, 1943-1963. Ph.D., University of North Carolina, Chapel Hill.

Martinez, John
1957   Mexican Emigration to the United States, 1910-1930. Ph.D., University of California, Berkeley.

Martinez, Oscar J.
1975   Border Boom Town: Ciudad Juárez Since 1880. Ph.D.,

University of California, Los Angeles.

Masingill, Eugene Frank
1957   The Diplomatic Career of Henry Lane Wilson in Latin America. Ph.D., Louisiana State University.

Maupin, Dorothy Carney
1968   El Chamizal: Settlement of a Boundary Dispute. M.A., Hardin-Simmons University.

Meador, Bruce Staffel
1951   Wetback Labor in the Lower Rio Grande Valley. M.A., University of Texas, Austin.

Mekuchonis, Sandra Bea
1975   Survey and Evaluation of Adapted Physical Education in San Diego City Schools. M.A., San Diego State University.

Meredith, Robert Addison
1968   The Treatment of United States-Mexican Relations in Secondary United States History Textbooks Published Since 1956. Ed.D., New York University.

Middagh, John
1952   Frontier Journalism in El Paso, 1872-1900. M.A., University of Texas, El Paso.

Miller, Eddie Lou
1968   The History of Private Welfare Agencies in El Paso, 1886-1930. M.A., University of Texas, El Paso.

Minge, Ward Alan
1965   Frontier Problems in New Mexico Preceding the Mexican War, 1840-1846. Ph.D., University of New Mexico.

Miranda, José Pablo
1964   An Exploratory Study of Mexican Foreign Students in Laredo, Texas, in Fall Semester, 1962-1963. M.A., University of Texas, Austin.

Moberly, Alan Lee
1964   Fences and Neighbors: El Chamizal and the Colorado River Salinity Disputes in United States-Mexican Relations. Ph.D., University of California, Santa Barbara.

Montgomery, Louise Falls
1979   Mexican Newspaper Elites' View of the Masses: Maintaining the Status Quo. M.A., University of Texas, Austin.

Montoya, Juan Alfredo
1979   An Analysis of the Disposition of Criminal Cases in the El Paso District Courts. M.A., University of Texas, El Paso.

Morrison, Ethel M.
1929   A History of Recent Legislative Proposals Concerning Mexican Immigration. M.A., University of Southern California.

Mueller, Clark Dean
1976   Decision-making in Mexico: The Politics of Population Policy Formation. Ph.D., University of Utah.

Mueller, Gerald E.
1973   Conflict Between Channel Morphology and Law Along the International Rio Grande. Ph.D., Johns Hopkins University.

Mullen, Colleen Mary
1979   Agrarian Reform and Political Violence: The Case of Sonora, Mexico. M.A., University of Texas, Austin.

Murray, Douglas Joseph
1979   The Relation Between International Politics and Domestic Politics: The Politics of North American Defense. Ph.D., University of Texas, Austin.

Neal, Joe West
1941   The Policy of the United States Toward Immigration from Mexico. M.A., University of Texas, Austin.

Nelson, Anna Louise Kasten
1972   The Secret Diplomacy of James K. Polk During the Mexican War, 1846-1847. Ph.D., George Washington University.

Nicoll, Marion
1951   Brief History of the El Paso Water System, 1881-1921. M.A., University of Texas, El Paso.

Nuñez, Theron R.
1963   Cultural Discontinuity and Conflict in a Mexican Village. Ph.D., University of California, Berkeley.

O'Connell, Mary-Margaret
1977   The 1920 Anti-alien Land Initiative: Perspectives in the San Diego Press. M.A., San Diego State University.

Oden, William
1959   Mud, Sticks, and Stones: The Use of Native Building Materials in the El Paso Area. M.A., University of Texas, El Paso.

Olinger, Calleen E.
1970   Domestic Water Use in the Española Valley, New Mexico: A Study in Resource Decision-making. M.A., University of Chicago.

Olinghouse, Elton Joe
1974   Planning for Governmental Spatial Organization in San Diego County. M.A., San Diego State University.

Osborne, Marie A. S.
1954   The Educational Status of Intrastate Migrations in Texas, 1935-40. M.A., University of Texas, Austin.

Parker, Janey Kathleen
1975   Historic Resource Planning for the Lower Rio Grande Valley State Planning Region. M.S., Texas Tech University.

Paulson, Ranene Carol
1978   Expectancy of Classroom Performance: The Effects of Students' Dialect, Students' Ethnicity and an Introduction to Sociolinguistics on Teacher Candidates' Perceptions. Ph.D., Texas A&M University.

Penton, Marvin James
1965   Mexico's Reformation: A History of Mexican Protestantism from Its Inception to the Present. Ph.D., University of Iowa.

Perez, Roberto
1978   Folk Medicine and Medical Change in Guerrero, Mexico. Ph.D., University of California, Riverside.

Poland, Wilma Don
1973   Study to Determine the Dental Care Needs of Preschool and Kindergarten Students in National City Schools. M.A., San Diego State University

Polizzi, Johnnie B. H.
1977   Language Attitudes in El Paso, Texas, Newspapers. M.A., University of Texas, El Paso.

Portman, Robert
1979   A Study of Undocumented Mexican Workers on a Texas Ranch. Undergraduate honors thesis, Dartmouth College.

Prestwood, Nadine
1949   The Social Life and Custom of the People of El Paso, 1848-1910. M.A., University of Texas, El Paso

Price, Glenn Warren
1968   The Origin of the War with Mexico: The Polk-Stockton Intrigue. Ph.D., University of Southern California.

Pridgen, William McKinley
1939   A Survey and Proposed Plan of Reorganization of the Public Schools in Zavala County. M.A., University of Texas, Austin.

Pyron, Darden Asbury
1975   Mexico as an Issue in American Politics, 1911-1916. Ph.D., University of Virginia.

Quigley, Robert Edward
1965   American Catholic Opinions of Mexican Anticlericalism, 1910-1936. Ph.D., University of Pennsylvania.

Rabe, William
1962   On to White Oaks: The Story of the El Paso and Northeast Railroad. M.A., University of Texas, El Paso.

Rainey, Helen
1949   A History of Organized Welfare in El Paso, 1892-1948. M.A., University of Texas, El Paso.

Ramirez, Armando Hipolito
1976   The Socioeconomic Impact of the Illegal Aliens on the

County of San Diego. M.P.A., San Diego State University.

Ramirez, Emilia Schunior
1951   "Wetback" Children in South Texas. M.A., University of Texas, Austin.

Reames, Edith Leslie
1973   A Study of the Present Status of Health Instruction of Selected Schools in San Diego Area. M.A., San Diego State University.

Renner, Richard R.
1957   Some Characteristics of Spanish-Name Texans and Foreign Latin-Americans in Texas Higher Education. Ph.D., University of Texas, Austin.

Riddell, Adaljiza Sosa
1974   Who Cares Who Governs? An Historical Analysis of Local Governing Elites in Mexicali, Mexico. Ph.D., University of California, Riverside.

Ring, Jeremiah J.
1974   American Diplomacy and the Mexican Oil Controversy, 1938-1943. Ph.D., University of New Mexico.

Rivera, Julius
1957   Contacts and Attitudes Toward the United States in a Mexican Border Community. Ph.D., Michigan State University.

Rivera-Worley, Maria del Carmen
1977   Class, Alienation, Familism and Utilization of Health-Care Facilities: A Mexican Sample. M.A., Texas Tech University.

Roberts, Donald Frank
1974   Mining and Modernization: The Mexican Border States During the Porfiriato, 1876-1911. Ph.D., University of Pittsburgh.

Robertstad, Janice L.
1975   Infant Mortality in El Paso County: Ethnic and Socioeconomic Correlates. M.A., University of Texas, El Paso.

Romney, Joseph Barnard
1969   American Interests in Mexico: Development and Impact During the Rule of Porfirio Díaz, 1876-1911. Ph.D., University of Utah.

Rowley, Ralph Alcorn
1975   United States Acquisition of the Spanish Borderlands: Problems and Legacy. Ph.D., University of New Mexico.

Rungeling, Brian Scott
1969   Impact of Mexican Alien Commuters on the Apparel Industry of El Paso: A Case Study. Ph.D., University of Kentucky, Lexington.

Rush, Thomas
1951   El Paso YMCA, 1886-1918. M.A., University of Texas, El Paso.

Sanchez, Billie Sue
1974   Marriage Deferment and Achievement: Antecedents and Consequences Among Rural Youth. M.S., Texas A&M University.

Sandoval, Salvador
1971   Political Socialization in Northern Mexico. M.A., University of Texas, El Paso.

Sanint, Zaida Castellanos
1979   Squatter Settlements in Latin America: The Basis of Social Integration. M.S., Texas A&M University.

Santoro, Carmela Elvira
1967   United States and Mexican Relations During World War II. Ph.D., Syracuse University.

Schatzman, Christopher G.
1977   The Regulation of Stationary Air Pollution in El Paso, Texas, 1951-1975. M.A., University of Texas, El Paso.

Schoonover, Thomas David
1970   Mexican-United States Relations, 1861-1867. Ph.D., University of Minnesota.

Schroder, John Herman
1971   To Give "Aid and Comfort": American Opposition to the Mexican War, 1846-1848. Ph.D., University of Virginia.

Schroeder, Edward James Michael, II
1973   Sacred Heart and the Catholic Church in Abilene. M.A., Hardin-Simmons University.

Scragg, Anne B.
1981   Problems in Professionalization of a Marginal Occupation: Midwifery in El Paso, Texas. M.A., University of Texas, El Paso.

Scruggs, Otey M.
1958   A History of Mexican Agricultural Labor in the United States, 1942-1954. Ph.D., Harvard University.

Sebesta, Charles Joseph, Jr.
1979   A Rural Multi-County Judicial District in Texas: A Sociolegal Analysis. M.S., Texas A&M University.

Self, Steven Lynn
1979   An Historical Analysis of the Role of Geography in the Secondary Schools of the United States: Texas a Case Study. M.A., University of Texas, Austin.

Sessions, Tommie Gene
1974   American Reformers and the Mexican Revolution: Progressives and Woodrow Wilson's Policy in Mexico, 1913-1917. Ph.D., American University.

Shearer, Ernest Charles
1940   Border Diplomatic Relations Between the United States and Mexico, 1848-1860. Ph.D., University of Texas, Austin.

Simonowitz, Haskell
1979   Political Opposition in a Mexican State: The *Partido Acción Nacional* in Baja California. Ph.D., University of California, Riverside.

Smith, Albion
1949   State Government in Texas. M.A., University of Texas, El Paso.

Smith, Cecil Bernard
1928   Diplomatic Relations Between the United States and Mexico Concerning Border Disturbances During the Díaz Regime, 1876-1910. M.A., University of Texas, Austin.

Smith, David Randolph Alexander
1973   San Diego's Cost of Aircraft Noise. M.B.A., San Diego State University.

Smith, F. M.
1969   Factors Influencing the Administrative Process in Mexico. Ph.D., University of North Carolina.

Solorzano, Rosalia
1979   Attitudes and Migration Patterns: A Comparative Study of the "Marias" from Ciudad Juarez, Chihuahua, and Tijuana, Baja California, Mexico. M.A., University of Texas, El Paso.

Sonnenberg, Timothy Clark
1979   Value Orientations of Educational Administrators and Teacher Union and Professional Association Officers in Texas. Ph.D., Texas A&M University.

Southerland, James Edward
1970   Mexican-United States Relations, 1857-1860: The Failure of Manifest Destiny. Ph.D., University of Georgia.

Steakley, Dan Lewis
1936   The Border Patrol of the San Antonio Collection Distict. M.A.,University of Texas, Austin.

Stegmaier, Harry Ignatius, Jr.
1970   From Confrontation to Cooperation: The United States and Mexico, 1938-1945. Ph.D., University of Michigan.

Stewart, Robert Edwin
1969   *Colonia San Martín de Porres:* A Study of Squatters' Housing in Tijuana, Baja California. M.S.W. (Project), San Diego State University.

Stoddard, Ellwyn R.
1961   Catastrophe and Crisis in a Flooded Border Community: An Analytical Approach to Disaster Emergence. Ph.D., Michigan State University.

Stokes, Rita Judd
1973   Health Care Services in the San Diego County Jail. M.S.W., San Diego State University.

Strauss, Julian
1956   The Bracero. M.A., University of Texas, El Paso.

Sybesma, Benjamin Cornelius
1977   Due Process in Prison Disciplinary Hearings. M.S., San Diego State University.

Taylor, Margery
1963   A Study of the Attitudes of Anglo-American Immigrants to Texas, 1820-1835. M.A., Hardin-Simmons University.

Tiltti, John Thomas
1978   Non-Border Search and Seizure: Authority of United States Border Patrol Agents Under Section 287-A of the Immigration and Nationality Act. M.A., University of Texas, El Paso.

Toney, W. T., Jr.
1973   A Descriptive Study of the Control of Illegal Mexican Migration in the Southwestern United States. M.A., Sam Houston State University.

Trow, Clifford Wayne
1966   Senator Albert B. Fall and Mexican Affairs, 1912-1921. Ph.D., University of Colorado, Boulder.

Tubbs, Lowell L.
1952   A Survey of the Problems of Migratory Mexicans. M.A., University of Texas, Austin.

Turchen, Lesta Van der Wert
1972   The Oil Expropriation Controversy, 1917-1942, in United States-Mexican Relations. Ph.D., Purdue University.

Tyler, Jerry Edwin
1974   The Cardenas Doctrine and Twentieth-Century Mexican Foreign Policy. Ph.D., Louisiana State University.

Urbina, Manuel, II
1976   The Impact of the Texas Revolution on the Government, Politics, and Society of Mexico, 1836-1846. Ph.D., University of Texas, Austin.

Valencia, Nestor A.
1969   Twentieth Century Urbanization in Latin America and a Case Study of Ciudad Juárez. M.A., University of Texas, El Paso.

Vetterli, Richard R.
1972   The Impact of the Multi-national Corporation on the Power Structure of Mexico and a Mexican Border Community. Ph.D., University of California, Riverside.

Viera, Michael Joseph
1978   Citizen Participation and the Housing and Community Development Act of 1974: A Study of Three California Cities. Ph.D., University of California, Riverside.

Villaseñor Martinez, Irene
1964   La Familia Mexicana. Dissertation, ITESCO, Guadalajara (México).

Vowell, Jack
1952   Politics of El Paso, 1850-1920. M.A., University of Texas, El Paso.

Wagner, Marion Kathryn
1969   The Community Welfare Council of San Diego County: Its Role in the Future Planning: An Exploratory Study. M.S.W. (Project), San Diego State University.

Walter, Paul
1938   A Study of Isolation and Social Change in Three Spanish-speaking Villages of New Mexico. Ph.D., Stanford University.

Webster, Michael Gordon
1972   Texas Manifest Destiny and the Mexican Border Conflict, 1865-1880. Ph.D., Indiana University.

Whalen, Norman
1964   The Catholic Church in Arizona, 1820-1870. M.A., University of Arizona.

White, Alice
1950   History of the Development of Irrigation in El Paso County. M.A., University of Texas, El Paso.

Williams, Christine S.
1977   An Evaluation of the Southeast San Diego Development Committee. M.P.A., San Diego State University.

Williams, Dean L.
1950   Some Political and Economic Aspects of Mexican Immigration into the United States Since 1941, with Particular Reference to this Immigration into the State of California. M.A., University of California, Los Angeles.

Wilson, Brenda Richardson
1976   Benefit-Cost Analysis of Water Importation to the Texas High Plains. M.S., Texas A&M University.

Woolever, Charles Edmund
1974   Campaign Contributions and Power in San Diego. M.A., San Diego State University.

Yielding, Kenneth Duane
1973   The Chamizal Dispute: An Exercise in Arbitration, 1845-1945. Ph.D., Texas Tech University.

Young, James Clay
1978   Health Care in Pichataro: Medical Decision Making in a Tarascan Town of Michoacan, Mexico. Ph.D., University of California, Riverside.

Yurtinus, John Frank George
1975   A Ram in the Thicket: The Mormon Battalion in the Mexican War. 2 vols. Ph.D., Brigham Young University.

Zelman, Donald Lewis
1969   American Intellectual Attitudes Toward Mexico, 1908-1940. Ph.D., Ohio State University.

Culture and Minority Groups (Excluding Mexican Americans)

Ablon, Joan
1963   Relocated American Indians in the San Francisco Bay Area: Concepts of Acculturation, Success and Identity in the City. Ph.D., University of Chicago.

Akita, Sakiko
1976   Japanese American Associations in San Diego: An Examination of Their Persistence. M.A., San Diego State University.

Albright, Linda
1973   A Survey of Marriage and Cultural Adjustments of Oriental Wives of American Citizens in Southern California. M.S.W., San Diego State University.

Alt, Arthur Lee
1973   Warfare Patterns Among Pre-Columbian American Indians. M.A., San Diego State University.

Anders, Gary Carson
1979   Dependence and Underdevelopment: The Political Economy of Cherokee Native Americans. Ph.D., Notre Dame University.

Anderson, E. Frederick
1967   An Investigation of Discrimination Against Negroes in Housing in the City of San Diego. M.S.W., San Diego State University.

Baker, Thomas Lindsay
1978   Silesians in Texas: A History of the Oldest Polish Colonies in America. Ph.D., Texas Tech University.

Baldwin, Mary Alice
1971   Culture Continuity from Chumash to Salinan Indians in California. M.A., San Diego State University.

Bauman, Marjorie Beth
1975   Organizational Preferences Among Ethnic Groups. M.S., San Diego State University.

Brady, Robert L.
1965   The Emergence of a Negro Class in Mexico, 1524-1640. Ph.D., University of Iowa.

Briscoe, Edward Eugene
1947   Pershing's Chinese Refugees: An Odyssey of the Southwest. M.A., St. Mary's University, (San Antonio).

Bryant, Jill Marie
1975   Patterns of Conflict Between Government and Minority Groups: A Cross-National Study. M.A., San Diego State University.

Burgess, Donald Harris
1963   Missionary Efforts Among the Tarahumara Indians. M.A., University of Texas, El Paso.

Busselen, H. J., Jr.
1962   A Study of the Federal Termination of a California Rancheria and Its Effects upon the Social and Economic Integration of the Indian Population Involved. M.A., California State University, Sacramento.

Cardoso, Geraldo da Silva
1975   Negro Slavery in the Sugar Plantations of Veracruz and Pernambuco, 1550-1680: A Comparative Study. Ph.D., University of Nebraska, Lincoln.

Carlton, Robert Lloyd
1977   Blacks in San Diego County, 1850-1900. M.A., San Diego State University.

Carroll, Patrick James
1975   Mexican Society in Transition: The Blacks in Veracruz, 1750-1830. Ph.D., University of Texas, Austin.

Christian, Jane
1963   Fourth Beginning: The Modern Revolution of the Navaho. M.A., University of Texas, El Paso.

Christiansen, Paige Walrath
1960   Hugo Oconor: Spanish-Apache Relations on the Frontiers of New Spain, 1771-1776. Ph.D., University of California, Berkeley.

Cloer, Carol
1974   Navajo Education: The "Long Walk" to Acculturation. M.A., University of Texas, El Paso.

Coates, Lawrence G.
1969   A History of Indian Education by the Mormons, 1830-1900. Ed.D., Ball State University.

Cullinane, Daniel
1955   Buffalo Soldiers. M.A., University of Texas, El Paso.

Dambourges Jacques, Leo Michael
1974   The Anti-Chinese Campaigns in Sonora, Mexico, 1900-1931. Ph.D., University of Arizona.

DeHart, Evelyn Hu
1976   Resistance and Survival: A History of the Yaqui People's Struggle for Autonomy, 1533-1910. Ph.D., University of Texas, Austin.

Delmez, Albert Jaures
1949   The History of the Cultural Missions in Mexican Education. Ph.D., University of Missouri, Columbia.

DeSomber, Myrna Ann
1975   Changing Play Patterns Among the Kumeyaay Diegueno Indians. M.A., San Diego State University.

Farrar, Nancy
1970   The History of the Chinese in El Paso, Texas: A Case Study of an Urban Immigrant Group in the American West. M.A., University of Texas, El Paso.

Foster, Robert Lyle
1974   Black Lubbock: A History of Negroes in Lubbock, Texas, to 1940. M.A., Texas Tech University.

Grantonz, Jelett L.
1971   A Survey into the Problems of Minority Employment in Governmental Agencies. M.P.A., San Diego State University.

Hamilton, J. A.
1948   A History of the Presbyterian Work Among the Pima and Papago Indians of Arizona. M.A., University of Arizona.

Hansen, Klaus J.
1963   The Kingdom of God in Mormon Thought and Practice, 1830-1896. Ph.D., Wayne State University.

Hester, Elbert Thomas
1975   Interethnic Conflict: Two Communities on American Frontiers. M.A., Texas Tech University.

Holt, Lottie Adele
1967   A Study of Placement Experiences and Length of Care of Negro Children Relinquished to Adoption Agencies in San Diego County, 1950-1964. M.S.W. (Project), San Diego State University.

Housewright, George M.
1972   The Changing Economic Status in Texas of the Latin-American and the Negro, 1915-1960. Ph.D., University of Arkansas.

Iverson, Peter
1975   The Evolving Navajo Nation: *Dine* Continuity Within Change. Ph.D., University of Wisconsin, Madison.

Jackson, Larry Joe
1979   The Development of Black Business in Texas, 1919-1969: From a Houston Perspective. M.A., Texas Tech University.

Jones, John R.
1977   White with Black: An Assessment of the Recollections of Aged Ex-Slaves Concerning Biracial Sexual Activity During Bondage. Graduate Seminar Paper, University of Texas, El Paso.

Kenner, Charles Leroy
1966   A History of New Mexican-Plains Indian Relations. Ph.D., Texas Tech University.

Kim, Chong-Soon
1974   Assimilation into the Host Society of Four Asiatic Groups, El Paso, Texas. M.A., University of Texas, El Paso.

Krause, Corinne Azen
1970   The Jews in Mexico: A History with Special Emphasis on the Period from 1857 to 1930. Ph.D., University of Pittsburgh.

Landon, Johnnie A.
1973   The N.A.A.C.P. in El Paso: An Instrument for Political Involvement. M.A., University of Texas, El Paso.

Lesser, Harriet Sara
1972   A History of the Jewish Community of Mexico City, 1912-1970. Ph.D., New York University.

Levinson, Robert Edward
1969   The Jews in the California Gold Rush. Ph.D., University of Oregon.

Lewis, Larry E.
1975   Ethnic Politics: The Minority of Minorities; The Native Americans. M.A., San Diego State University.

Liu, Judith
1977   Celestials in the Golden Mountain: The Chinese in One California City, San Diego. M.A., San Diego State University.

Lloyd, Stanley
1974   The Teton Sioux and the Indian Claims Commission. Graduate Seminar Paper, University of Texas, El Paso.

Luke, Donnie Leon
1977   The Non-white as Noble Savage: An Enduring Characteristic of American Literature. M.A., San Diego State University.

McNeley, James K.
1975   The Navajo Theory of Life and Behavior. Ph.D., University of Hawaii.

Martin, Kenneth E.
1975   A Profile of Successful Black Entrepreneurs in San Diego. M.B.A., San Diego State University.

Mayer, Vincent Villanueva, Jr.
1975   The Black Slave on New Spain's Northern Frontier: San José de Parral, 1632-1676. Ph.D., University of Utah.

Melody, Michael E.
1976   The Sacred Hoop: The Way of the Chiricahua Apache and Teton Lakota. Ph.D., University of Notre Dame.

Moore, Helen Anne
1979   Female Minority Students: Patterns of Social Conformity and School Commitments. Ph.D., University of California, Riverside.

Morgan, Elizabeth Nichols
1971   Oscar Lewis and the Culture of Poverty. M.A., San Diego State University.

Nagai, Nelson
1977   Japanese in California Agriculture. Unpublished paper. Department of Agricultural Economics, University of California, Davis.

Ng, Wing-Cheung
1979   The Labor Role of Asian Americans: Toward a Theory of Labor Market Segmentation. Ph.D., University of California, Riverside.

Nims, Amy Elizabeth
1941   Chinese Life in San Antonio. M.S., Southwest Texas State University.

Nissley, Maria
1973   In Search of Themes and Stylistic Traits in Tarascan Antiquity. M.A., San Diego State University.

Owen, Roger C.
1962   The Indians of Santa Catarina, Baja California, Mexico: Concepts of Disease and Curing. Ph.D., University of California, Los Angeles.

Palmer, Colin Alphonsous
1970   Negro Slavery in Mexico, 1570-1650. Ph.D., University of Wisconsin, Madison.

Pauchnick, Catherine J.
1971   The Cultural and Artistic Role of the Pre-Columbian Rain God. M.A., San Diego State University.

Peabody, Etta B.
1967   Efforts of the South to Import Chinese Coolies, 1865-1870. M.A., Baylor University.

Richardson, Robert Steven
1975   A Comparison of Black and White Consumption Patterns in San Diego. M.B.A., San Diego State University.

Robbins, Fred
1972   The Origins and Development of the African Slave Trade into Texas, 1816-1860. M.A., University of Houston.

Ruecking, Frederick Henry
1955   The Coahuiltecan Indians of Southern Texas and Northeastern Mexico. M.A., University of Texas, Austin.

Salmon, Robert Mario
1975   Seventeenth Century Tarahumara: A History of Cultural Resistance. M.A., University of New Mexico.

Sayler, Galen H.
1976   A Legacy of Hate: Western Apache-Anglo-American Relations on the Arizona Frontier, 1826-1873. M.A., San Diego State University.

Schwartz, Rosalie
1974   Runaway Negroes: Mexico as an Alternative for United States Blacks, 1825-1860. M.A., San Diego State University.

Simons, Suzanne L.
1970   Sandía Pueblo: Persistence and Change in a New Mexican Indian Community. Ph.D., University of New Mexico.

Smallwood, James M.
1974   Black Texans During Reconstruction, 1865-1874. Ph.D., Texas Tech University.

Stern, Jean
1971   A Thematic and Stylistic Comparison of the Mortuary Offerings of Ancient Western Mexico. M.S., San Diego State University.

Sutton, Imre
1964   Land Tenure and Changing Occupance on Indian Reservations in Southern California. Ph.D., University of California, Los Angeles.

Taylor, Richard Mangrem
1979   The Acquisition of Some Aspects of Standard Written English by Some Speakers of Black English. M.A., Texas A&M University.

Tiller, Veronica
1976   The History of the Jicarilla Apache Tribe, 1541-1970.

Ph.D., University of New Mexico.

Tweed, William Carleton
1975   The Seri Indians of Sonora, Mexico, 1760-1790. Ph.D., Texas Christian University.

Uhlmann, Julie M.
1973   The Impact of Urbanization on the Fertility Behavior of Pápago Indian Women. Ph.D., University of Colorado.

Valasco, Alfred Frank
1973   The Collapse of the Classic Lowland Maya: A Possible Solution. M.A., San Diego State University.

Wamble, Sharon Lynn
1977   Advertising Potential Within the Black Consumer Market. M.S., San Diego State University.

Ward, Carol Jan
1978   The Navajos of Chilchinbeto: The Dilemma of the Young Adult Generation. M.A., Texas Tech University.

Weideman, Margaret Pauline
1973   The Attitude Toward the Maintenance of Serbo-Croation Among Yugoslavs in San Pedro. M.A., San Diego State University.

Wilson, Charles
1972   Attitudes Toward the American Indians as Expressed in Selected American Magazines, 1865-1900. M.A., University of Texas, El Paso.

Woodward, Dorothy
1940   The Penitentes of New Mexico. Ph.D., Yale University.

Mexican Americans, Bilingualism

Acevedo, Baltazar A., Jr.
1979   Socialization: The Mexican American Mid-Level Administrator in Texas Institutions of Higher Education. Ph.D., University of Texas, Austin.

Acevedo, Roberto
1967   A Study of Decision Making by Caucasian-Mexican Unmarried Mothers Using San Diego County Adoption Service, Fiscal Year 1964-1965. M.S.W., San Diego State University.

Achor, Shirley Coolidge
1974   Of Thorns and Roses: Variations in Cultural Adaptations Among Mexican Americans in an Urban Texas Barrio. Ph.D., Southern Methodist University.

Adorno, William
1973   The Attitudes of Selected Mexican and Mexican-American Parents in Regard to Bilingual/Bicultural Education. Ph.D., United States International University.

Akery, Nichols
1955   An Exploratory Study of the Education of Spanish-speaking Children in the Primary Grades in Edinburg, Texas, M.A., University of Texas, Austin.

Allsup, Vernon Carl
1976   The American GI Forum: A History of a Mexican-American Organization. Ph.D., University of Texas, Austin.

Alvarado, Marie Therese
1979   A Two Year Comparison. Contrast Study of One Family's Code Switching in Three Languages. M.A., University of Texas, Austin.

Ambrecht, Biliana Maria Cicin-Sain
1973   Politicization as a Legacy of the War of Poverty: A Study of Advisory Council Members in a Mexican-American Community. Ph.D., University of California, Los Angeles.

Anderson, Martha Davis
1966   Latin-American Teenagers and the News in Ten Rio Grande Valley Districts. M.A., University of Texas, Austin.

Andrade, Sally Virginia Jones
1979   Family Planning Attitudes and Practices as a Function of the Degree of Cultural Identification of Female Mexican-

American College Students. Ph.D., University of Texas, Austin.

Armstrong, Roy A.
1972   Test Bias from the Non-Anglo Viewpoint: A Critical Evaluation of Intelligence Test Items by Members of Three Cultural Minorities. Ph.D., University of Arizona.

Baird, Janet Rae
1973   An Analysis of Mexican-American Culture in Kansas Migrant Programs. Ph.D., University of Kansas.

Barrera, Maria M.
1978   A Survey on the Status of Reading in Spanish in the First Grades of Texas Schools Involved in Bilingual Education Programs, with Emphasis on Scheduling, Language Usage, Materials and the Methodology for Initial Reading. Ed.D., Texas A&I University, Kingsville.

Barton, May
1950   Methodism at Work Among the Spanish-speaking People of El Paso, Texas. M.A., University of Texas, El Paso.

Berlanga, David, Jr.
1978   The English and Spanish of Mexican-American Bilingual Teachers. Ed.D., Texas A&I University, Kingsville.

Blayeck, Leda F.
1938   Food Habits and Living Conditions of Mexican Families on Farm Income Levels in the Upper Rio Grande Valley. M.A., University of Texas, Austin.

Blevins, Audie Lee, Jr.
1970   Rural to Urban Migration of Poor Anglos, Mexican-Americans, and Negroes. Ph.D., University of Texas, Austin.

Booker, Margaret
1937   A Study of the Dietary Habits of Mexican Families in Tucson, Arizona. M.A., University of Arizona.

Briegel, Kaye
1967   The History of Political Organizations Among Mexican Americans in Los Angeles Since the Second World War. M.A., University of Southern California.

Brittin, Dorothy Helen Clark
1974   Meat Buying Practices of Caucasians, Mexican-Americans and Negroes. Ph.D., Texas Tech University.

Bronson, Louise Fisher
1966   Changes in Personality Needs and Values following Conversion to Protestantism in a Traditionally Roman Catholic Ethnic Group. Ph.D., University of Arizona.

Brookshire, Marjorie
1954   The Industrial Pattern of Mexican-American Employment in Nueces County, Texas. Ph.D., University of Texas.

Brunton, Ann Marjorie
1971   The Decision to Settle: A Study of Mexican American Migrants. Ph.D., Washington State University.

Buriel, John Raymond
1977   Home and School Antecedents of Chicano and Anglo Children's Locus of Control. Ph.D., University of California, Riverside.

Cabaza, Berta
1950   The Spanish Language in Texas: Cameron and Willacy Counties, District 10A. M.A., University of Texas, Austin.

Calderon, Carlos I.
1950   The Education of Spanish-speaking Children in Edcouch-Elsa, Texas. M.A., University of Texas, Austin.

Camarillo, Albert Michael
1975   The Making of a Chicano Community: A History of the Chicanos in Santa Barbara, California, 1850-1930. Ph.D., University of California, Los Angeles.

Cameron, James William
1976   The History of Mexican Public Education in Los Angeles, 1910-1930. Ph.D., University of Southern California.

Campbell, Sherry Christine
1972   Meaningfulness Strength in Primary and Secondary Languages: Chicano Bilinguals. M.A., San Diego State University.

Cantu, Ethel Argetsinger
1977   The Effects of Bilingualism and Language Dominance on School Achievement. M.A., Texas A&I University, Kingsville.

Cantú, Ismael Sierra
1975   The Effects of Family Characteristics, Parental Influence, Language Spoken, School Experience, and Self-Motivation on the Level of Educational Attainment of Mexican Americans. Ph.D., University of Michigan, Ann Arbor.

Caples, Minerva
1979   A Content Analysis of the Mexican-American in the Elementary Basal Readers, Grades 1-6, Adopted by the State of Texas. Ed.D., Texas A&I University, Kingsville.

Caples-Osorio, Ronald W.
1979   Educational Aspirations of Selected Mexican American Elementary School Children Enrolled in Bilingual Education. Ed.D., Texas A&I University, Kingsville.

Cardenas, Blandina
1974   Defining Equal Access to Educational Opportunity for Mexican-American Children: A Study of Three Civil Rights Actions Affecting Mexican-American Students and the Development of a Conceptual Framework for Affecting Institutional Responsiveness to the Educational Needs of Mexican-American Children. Ed.D., University of Massachusetts.

Cardenas, Isaac
1974   Equality of Education Opportunity: A Descriptive Study on Mexican-American Access to Higher Education. Ed.D., University of Massachusetts.

Carmona, Roel G.
1978   A Study of the Knowledge of One Hundred Common English Idiomatic Expressions Exhibited by Bilingual Mexican-American and Monolingual Anglo-American Community College Students. Ed.D., Texas A&I University, Kingsville.

Carranza, Michael
1974   Evaluative Reactions of Bilingual Anglo and Mexican-American Adolescents Toward Speakers of English and Spanish. Ph.D., Notre Dame University.

Carrillo, Stella Leal
1965   Importancia economica y social de la poblacion mexicana en Estados Unidos de Norteamerica. Masters, Universidad Nacional Autonoma de Mexico.

Carroll, John Martin
1974   The Utility of Internal Colonialism as an Explanation for the Political and Social Marginality of Mexican-Americans. M.A., University of Texas, El Paso.

Castillo, Pedro
1979   The Making of a Mexican Barrio: Los Angeles, 1890-1920. Ph.D., University of California, Santa Barbara.

Clegg, J. Halvor
1969   Fonética y fonología del español de Texas. Ph.D., University of Texas, Austin.

Clements, Harold M.
1963   An Analysis of Levels of Living of Spanish-American Rural and Urban Families in Two South Texas Counties. M.A., Texas A&M University.

Clincy, Everett R.
1954   Equality of Opportunity for Latin-Americans in Texas: A Study of the Economic, Social and Educational Discrimination Against Latin-Americans in Texas and of the Efforts of the State Government on Their Behalf. Ph.D., Columbia University.

Coan, Barlett E.
1936   A Comparative Study of the American and Mexican Children in the "Big Bend" Area for 1935-36. M.A., University of Texas, Austin.

Collado-Herrell, Leida Ileana
1976   An Exploration of Affective and Cognitive Components

of Bilingualism. Ph.D., University of Maryland.

Corona, Bert C.
1955 Study of Adjustment and Interpersonal Relations of Adolescents of Mexican Descent. Ph.D., University of California, Berkeley.

Coronado, Leopoldo Angel
1979 The Effects of Differing Degrees of Bilingualism on the Cognitive Performance and Scholastic Achievement of Spanish/English Bilinguals. Ph.D., University of Texas, Austin.

Crasilneck, Harold B.
1948 A Study of One Hundred Latin-American Juvenile Delinquents in San Antonio, Texas. M.A., University of Texas, Austin.

Crawford, Jean Keith
1978 Aged Chicanos: Utilization of Health Services. Ph.D., University of California, Riverside.

Crisp, James Ernest
1976 Anglo-Texas Attitudes Toward the Mexican, 1821–1845. Ph.D., Yale University.

Darling, Henry B.
1975 The Costs and Benefits of a Modern Educational Industry for the Laredo, Texas, SMSA. Ph.D., University of Arkansas.

Dearman, Cecil J.
1947 A Socio-economic Study of Latin-American Farm Migrants in Texas. M.A., Texas A&M University.

DeHoyos, Arturo
1961 Occupational and Educational Levels of Aspiration of Mexican-American Youth. Ph.D., Michigan State University.

Díaz, Berta Ceballos
1958 A Descriptive Analysis of the Visiting Teacher Program in Selected Rio Grande Valley School Districts. M.A., University of Texas, Austin.

Dodd, Elmer C.
1930 A Comparison of Spanish-speaking and English Children in Brownsville, Texas. M.A., University of Texas, Austin.

Douglas, Helen W.
1928 The Conflict of Cultures in First Generation Mexicans in Santa Ana, California. M.A., University of Southern California.

Downs, Fane
1970 The History of Mexicans in Texas, 1820-1845. Ph.D., Texas Tech University.

Dunigan, Joseph L., Jr.
1970 The Religious Socialization of Mexican-Americans: A Functional Analysis of Catholic Education. M.A., University of Texas, El Paso.

Durkin, Hollis A.
1978 A Comparison of Female Attitudes Toward Physical Activity in Four Primary Culture Groups. M.S., University of Texas, El Paso.

Eaton, Arlinda Jane
1979 A Psycholinguistic Analysis of the Oral Reading Miscues of Selected Field-dependent and Field-independent Native Spanish-speaking Mexican American First-Grade Children. Ph.D., University of Texas, Austin.

Edmonson, Munro S.
1952 *Los Manitos:* Patterns of Humor in Relation to Cultural Values. Ph.D., Harvard University.

Elías-Olivares, Lucía E.
1976 Ways of Speaking in a Chicano Community: A Sociolinguistic Approach. Ph.D., University of Texas, Austin.

Emerson, Ralph W.
1929 Education for the Mexican in Texas. M.A., Southern Methodist University.

Eriksson, Magnus A.
1976 Rural Living and Chicano Political Attitude. M.A., University of Texas, El Paso.

Ermey, Jacqueline Marie
1974 The Acquisition of English Consonant Sounds by Spanish-speaking Mexican-American Children Four to Eight Years of Age. M.S., Texas Tech University.

Farmer, William A.
1937 The Influence of Segregation of Mexican and American Children upon the Development of Social Attitudes. M.A., University of Southern California.

Fellows, Lloyd W.
1929 Economic Aspects of the Mexican Rural Population in California with Special Emphasis on the Need for Mexican Labor in Agriculture. M.A., University of Southern California.

Fiebiger, Leo Joseph
1973 El Paso Manpower Needs Assessment for Educational Planning. Ed.D., New Mexico State University.

Flores, Noe E.
1979 Survey on Status of Chicano Literature in Selected Texas High Schools. Ed.D., Texas A&I University, Kingsville.

Foppe, Regina Elizabeth
1976 The Response of the Roman Catholic Church to the Mexican-Americans in West Texas, 1839, into Post-Vatican II. M.A., Texas Tech University.

Fretz, Barbara Beers
1974 An Exploratory Study of Foreign Language Acquisition and Evaluative Reactions to Spanish and English Speakers. Ph.D., University of Maryland.

García, Richard A.
1970 Political Ideology: A Comparative Study of Three Chicano Youth Organizations. M.A., University of Texas, El Paso.

Garza, Edward D.
1951 LULAC: League of United Latin-American Citizens. M.A., Southwest Texas State Teachers College.

Garza, Maria Luisa
1978 A Study of the Use of the Inter-American Tests of General Ability in Various South Texas Title VII Bilingual/Bicultural Programs. Ed.D., Texas A&I University, Kingsville.

Garza, Mary Jane
1979 The Effects of Training in Test-taking Skills on the Reading and Math Scores of Fifth Grade Mexican American Children. Ed.D., Texas A&I University, Kingsville.

Garza, Sherryl Ana
1979 Linguistic Acceptability of the Laidlaw Reading Series, Grades 1-3, to the Spanish-speaking Chicano Child in Texas. Ed.D., Texas A&I University, Kingsville.

Geilhufe, Nancy Lanelle
1972 Ethnic Relations in San Jose: A Study of Police-Chicano Interaction. Ph.D., Stanford University.

Gibson, Delbert L.
1959 Protestantism in Land-American Acculturation. Ph.D., University of Texas, Austin.

Goldkind, Victor
1963 Factors in the Differential Acculturation of Mexicans in a Michigan City. Ph.D., Michigan State University.

Goldsmith, Ross Paul
1979 The Effect of Training in Test-taking Skills and Test Anxiety Management on Mexican American Students' Aptitude Test Performance. Ph.D., University of Texas, Austin.

Gonzales, Jovita
1932 Social Life in Cameron, Starr and Zapata Counties. M.A., University of Texas, Austin.

Gonzalez, José Roel
1974 An Analysis of the English Segmental Phonological Problems of Mexican-Americans. M.A., San Diego State University.

Graf, Victoria L.
1979 Social System Variables Which Influence the Referral of

Ethnic Minorities for Placement in EMR Classes. Ph.D., University of California, Riverside.

Graham, Leon R.
1938   A Comparison of the English-speaking and Latin-American Students in the Mercedes, Texas, Schools. M.A., Southern Methodist University.

Graves, Theodore D.
1962   Time Perspective and the Deferred Gratification Patterns in a Tri-ethnic Community. Ph.D., University of Pennsylvania.

Green, Jamie Ruth Morgan
1979   The Acquisition of Distinctive Features by Spanish-speaking Mexican-American Children, Four to Eight Years of Age. M.S., Texas Tech University.

Griswold del Castillo, Richard A.
1974   *La Raza Hispano Americana:* The Emergence of an Urban Culture Among the Spanish-Speaking of Los Angeles, 1850–80. Ph.D., University of California, Los Angeles.

Guerra, Irene J.
1959   The Social Aspirations of a Selected Group of Spanish-Name People in Laredo, Texas. M.A., University of Texas, Austin.

Gunter, Dell Campbell
1958   Mass Media Use and Academic Achievement of Mexican-American High School Students. M.A., Texas Tech University.

Gurrola, José Domingo
1974   Historical Development and Economic Implications of the Mexican Labor Law. Nonthesis Graduate Paper, University of Texas, El Paso.
1974   Ciudad Juarez In-Bond Industry Wage and Salary Changes Between 1971 and 1974. Nonthesis Graduate Paper, University of Texas, El Paso.

Gutiérrez, Armando George
1974   The Socialization of Militancy: Chicanos in a South Texas Town. Ph.D., University of Texas, Austin.

Gutiérrez, Emeterio, Jr.
1952   A Study of School Attendance of Migrant Students in Grulla, Texas. M.A., University of Texas, Austin.

Gutiérrez, José Angel
1968   La Raza and Revolution: The Empirical Conditions of Revolution in Four South Texas Counties. M.A., St. Mary's University.
1976   Toward a Theory of Community Organization in a Mexican-American Community in South Texas. Ph.D., University of Texas, Austin.

Guzman, Ralph Cortez
1970   The Political Socialization of the Mexican-American People. Ph.D., University of California, Los Angeles.

Gynan, Shaw Nicholas
1978   Incipient Bilingualism in Anglo Preschoolers: A Case Study of Language and Social Context. M.A., University of Texas, El Paso.

Hall, Gilbert E.
1947   Some Legal Aspects of the Education of Spanish-speaking Children in Texas. M.A., University of Texas, Austin.

Harrison, David C.
1952   A Survey of the Administrative and Educational Policies of the Baptist, Methodist, and Presbyterian Churches Among Mexican-American People of Texas. M.A., University of Texas, Austin.

Harvey, Louise F.
1947   The Delinquent Mexican Boy in an Urban Area, 1945. M.A., University of California, Los Angeles.

Hayes, James Virgil
1952   An Analysis of Latin-American Partial Attendance and Dropouts in the Elementary Schools of Eagle Pass, Texas, in Recent Years. M.A., University of Texas, Austin.

Heller, Celia Stopnika
1964   Ambitions of Mexican-American Youth: Goals and Means of Mobility of High School Seniors. Ph.D., Columbia University.

Hernandez, José Amaro
1979   The Political Development of Mutual Aid Societies in the Mexican American Community: Ideals and Principles. Ph.D., University of California, Riverside.

Hicks, Elizabeth Estill
1979   Nahuatl-Spanish Bilingualism and Ethnic Attitudes in Different Communities: A Comparison. M.A., University of Texas, Austin.

Hocker, Phillip Norton
1973   Two-Stimulus Transposition as Demonstrated by Spanish/English Speaking Children from Bilingual (Spanish/English) and Monolingual (English) Instruction Classrooms. Ph.D., New Mexico State University.

Hogan, Milo A. V.
1934   A Study of the School Progress of Mexican Children in Imperial County. M.A., University of Southern California.

Holliday, Eileen Fiebig
1973   Classroom Testing Practices of Fifth Grade Elementary School Teachers in San Diego County Schools. M.A., San Diego State University.

Holliday, Jay N.
1935   A Study of Nonattendance in Miguel Hidalgo School of Brawley, California. M.A., University of Southern California.

Horton, Frances
1936   Food Habits and Living Conditions of Mexicans Dwelling in the Rio Grande Valley Between Roma and Mercedes. M.A., University of Texas, Austin.

Hough, John E.
1972   Post-High School Vocational and Educational Level of Male Mexican-Americans as Related to Scholastic Athletics. M.A., San Diego State University.

House, Novella Madden
1975   Effects of a Culturally Oriented Art Education Program on Rural "Disadvantaged" Chicanos. M.A., Texas Tech University.

Howe, Anna Lynn
1952   Proposals for the Organization and Administration of a Special Education to Improve the English Speech of Certain Spanish-speaking Pupils, Eagle Pass, Texas. M.A., University of Texas, Austin.

Irizarry, Richard
1979   The Relationship Between Creativity and Bilingualism. Ph.D., University of Texas, Austin.

Jackson, Lucile Prim
1939   An Analysis of the Language Difficulties of the Spanish-speaking Children of the Bowie High School, El Paso, Texas. M.A., University of Texas, Austin.

Jerden, Cecil M.
1939   A Study in Racial Differences in the El Paso Public Schools. M.A., Southern Methodist University.

Johnson, Henry Sioux
1964   Ethnic Group Differences in Certain Persons: Intellectual, Achievement and Motivational Characteristics. Ph.D., University of Southern California.

Johnson, Roberta M.
1932   History of the Education of Spanish-speaking Children in Texas. M.A., University of Texas, Austin.

Johnson, Wayman H. L.
1971   A Study of Students in the Education Opportunity Program at San Diego State College. M.B.A., San Diego State University.

Jones, Dixie Lee Franklin
1969   The Plight of the Migrant Child in the Lower Rio Grande Valley. M.A., University of Texas, Austin.

Jones, Lamar B.
1965   Mexican-American Labor Problems in Texas. Ph.D., University of Texas, Austin.

Jurado, Pete
1976   The Chicano Aggregation: A Barrio Gang. Nonthesis Graduate Project, University of Texas, El Paso.

Kellogg, Claudia Beatrice
1973   A Study of the Priorities of Educational Goals in the South Bay Union School District. M.A., San Diego State University.

Kelsey, Ruth M.
1932   The Comparison of Scholastic Standing Among Children of Native Born Parents with Children of Foreign Parents. M.A., University of Denver.

Kerr, Louise Año Nuevo
1976   The Chicano Experience in Chicago, 1920-1970. Ph.D., University of Illinois, Chicago Circle.

Kienle, John E.
1912   Housing Conditions Among the Mexican Population of Los Angeles. M.A., University of Southern California.

King, Francis Xavier
1976   Bilingualism and Academic Achievement: A Comparative Study of Spanish Surnamed Bilingual, Spanish Surnamed Monolingual, and Non-Spanish Surnamed Students. Ph.D., United States International University.

Kirstein, Peter Neil
1973   Anglo over Bracero: A History of the Mexican Worker in the United States from Roosevelt to Nixon. Ph.D., St. Louis University.

Kluckhohn, Florence
1941   *Los Atarquenos:* A Study of Patterns and Configurations in a New Mexico Village. Ph.D., Radcliffe College.

Knudson, Kathryn Helen Malloy
1978   The Relationships Among Affective Role-Taking, Empathy and Prosocial Behavior in a Sample of Mexican-American and Anglo-American Children of Two Ages. Ph.D., University of California, Riverside.

Kresselman, Harold B.
1948   A Study of 100 Male Latin-American Juvenile Delinquents in San Antonio. M.A., University of Texas, Austin.

Kurtz, Donald V.
1970   Politics, Ethnicity, Integration: Mexican Americans in the War on Poverty. Ph.D., University of California, Davis.

Landman, Ruth
1953   Some Aspects of the Acculturation of Mexican Immigrants and Their Descendants to American Culture. Ph.D., Yale University.

Lane, John Hart, Jr.
1968   Voluntary Associations Among Mexican-Americans in San Antonio, Texas: Organizational and Leadership Characteristics. Ph.D., University of Texas, Austin.

Lawrence, Penelope Demos
1977   Citizen Participation: A Study of Ten Mexican-American Groups in the City of San Diego. M.P.A., San Diego State University.

Leininger Pycior, Julie
1978   La Raza Organizes: Mexican-American Life in San Antonio, 1915-1930, as Reflected in Mutualista Activities. Ph.D., Notre Dame University.

Leis, Ward William
1932   The Status of Education for Mexican Children in Four Border States. M.A., University of Southern California.

Levenstein, Harvey A.
1966   The United States Labor Movement and Mexico, 1910-1951. Ph.D., University of Wisconsin, Madison.

Light, Jere Cook
1974   A Critical Analysis of Anglo and Mexican-American Cultural Patterns in Two Texas Border City Junior Colleges. Ph.D., University of Texas, Austin.

Linn, Charles Wesley
1979   A Comparison of the Cost-Effectiveness of a Stipend Versus a Non-Stipend Program for Adult Education in Hidalgo County, Texas. Ph.D., Texas A&M University.

Lopez, Joe Raymond
1975   Religion in Selected Works of Chicano Literature. M.A., Texas Tech University.

Loyola, José Gabriel
1974   Political Socialization: A Comparative Study of Different Ethnic School Children in Newark, New Jersey, and El Paso, Texas. M.A., University of Texas, El Paso.

Luhman, Reid A.
1974   The Social Bases of Thinking and Speaking: A Study of Bilingual Chicano Children. Ph.D., University of Kansas.

MacCarthy, Carrie B. H.
1939   A Survey of the Mexican Hardship Cases Active in the Los Angeles County Department of Charities, Los Angeles, California. M.A., University of Southern California.

McCary, Mallie M.
1953   These Minorities in our Midst: With Emphasis on Latin-Americans in Texas. M.A., University of Texas, Austin.

McDowell, John H.
1975   The Speech Play and Verbal Art of Chicano Children: An Ethnographic and Sociolinguistic Study. Ph.D., University of Texas, Austin.

McGarry, Sister Francesca
1957   A Study of Cultural Patterns Among Three Generations of Mexicans of San Antonio, Texas, M.A., University of Texas, Austin.

MacKay, Maryann
1975   Spoken Spanish of Mexican-American Children: A Monolingual and Bilingual School Program. Ph.D., Stanford University.

McLaughlin, Michael J.
1980   Chicano Paraprofessional Acculturation and Community Mental Health Ideology: Measuring the Bridging Function. Ph.D., University of Arizona.

McLeod, Joseph A., Jr.
1972   Baptists and Racial and Ethnic Minorities (Including Mexican-Americans) in Texas. Ph.D., North Texas State University.

Marin, Eugene Acosta
1973   The Mexican-American Community and the Leadership of the Dominant Society in Arizona: A Study of their Mutual Attitudes and Perceptions. Ph.D., United States International University.

Marston, Miriam
1950   The History of Alianza Patriota Revolucionaria Americana. M.A., University of Texas, El Paso.

Martinez Guerra, Manuel
1977   A Comparison in Time Orientation Between Mexican and American Business Students. M.B.A., San Diego State University.

Massey, Leonard Ellis
1953   Migration of the Spanish-speaking People of Hidalgo County, Texas. M.A., University of Texas, Austin.

Matthiasson, Carolyn W.
1968   Acculturation of Mexican-Americans in a Midwestern City. Ph.D., Cornell University.

Maybry, L.
1968   The Educational and Occupational Aspirations of Anglo, Spanish, and Negro High School Students. Ph.D., University of New Mexico.

Meador, Bruce S.
1959   Minority Groups and Their Education in Hay County, Texas. Ph.D., University of Texas, Austin.

Meierhoffer-Longoria, Lynn Vaulx
1978   Bilingualism and Domains of Language Behavior. Ed.D., Texas A&I University, Kingsville.

Morton, John Gilbert
1976   Spanish Language Immersion Camps: The San Diego Model with Emphasis on Administrative and Major Language Aspects. M.A., San Diego State University.

Muñoz, Carlos
1973   The Politics of Chicano Urban Protest: A Model of Political Analysis. Ph.D., Claremont Graduate School.

Myers, Deborah Anne
1977   Life Change Events, Psychophysiological Symptoms and their Relation to Drinking Patterns: A Multicultural Analysis. M.A., University of Texas, El Paso.

Nall, Frank C., II
1959   Levels of Aspiration of Mexican-Americans in El Paso Schools. Ph.D., Michigan State University.

Nelson, Kaye
1978   Difference in Self-predicted and Achieved Grade Point Average of Mexican-American and Anglo-American College Freshman Females. M.A., Texas A&I, Kingsville.

Officer, James E.
1964   Sodalities and Systemic Linkage: The Joining Habits of Urban Mexican-Americans. Ph.D., University of Arizona.

Ortegon, Samuel M.
1932   The Religious Status of the Mexican Population of Los Angeles. M.A., University of Southern California.
1950   Religious Thought and Practice Among Mexican Baptists of the U.S., 1900-1947. Ph.D., University of Southern California.

Ortiz, Leroy I.
1975   A Sociolinguistic Study of Language Maintenance in the Northern New Mexico Community of Arroyo Seco. Ph.D. University of New Mexico.

Pacheco, Henry Joe
1977   Chicano Political Behavior. Ph.D., Claremont Graduate School.

Paez, Leticia
1976   Ten Years in a Fishbowl: Surveys and Investigations in South El Paso. Graduate Nonthesis Project, University of Texas, El Paso.

Parsons, Theodore W.
1965   Ethnic Cleavage in California Schools. Ph.D., Stanford University.

Peñalosa, Fernando
1963   Class Consciousness and Social Mobility in a Mexican-American Community. Ph.D., University of Southern California.

Perales, Alonso M.
1979   The Effects of Teacher-oriented and Student-oriented Strategies on Self-Concept, English Language Development, and Social Studies Achievement of Fifth Grade Mexican American Students. Ph.D., University of Texas, Austin.

Peregrino, Santiago
1970   The Political Ideology of the Mexican-American in Southwest City: El Paso. M.A., University of Texas, El Paso.

Perez, Ernest
1979   Effects of Bilingual Education on Language Use and Language Preference of Fourth-Grade Mexican American Children in Four Bilingual Education Projects in Texas. Ph.D., University of Texas, Austin.

Perez, Soledad
1949   Mexican Folklore in Austin. M.A., University of Texas, Austin.

Phillips, Robert N.
1967   Los Angeles Spanish: A Descriptive Analysis. Ph.D., University of Wisconsin, Madison.

Pitt, Leonard M.
1958   Submergence of the Mexican in California, 1846-1890: A History of Culture Conflict and Acculturation. Ph.D., University of California, Los Angeles.

Porras, Normaina W. de
1971   Anamolias linguisticas en el español de un grupo de estudiantes bilingues. M.A., University of Texas, El Paso.

Porter, Charles Jesse
1940   Recreational Interests and Activities of High School Boys of the Lower Rio Grande Valley of Texas. M.A., University of Texas, Austin.

Post, Donald Eugene
1974   Ethnic Competition for Control of Schools in Two South Texas Towns. Ph.D., University of Texas, Austin.

Poulsen, Roger Lee
1977   Variables Discriminant of Problem Drinking Behaviors Among a Select Sample of Two-Year Multicultural College Students in New Mexico and El Paso, Texas. Ph.D., New Mexico State University.

Poulter, Virgil L.
1973   A Phonological Study of the (Spanish) Speech of Mexican-American College Students Native to Fort Worth-Dallas. Ph.D., Louisiana State University.

Provinzano, James
1971   Chicano Migrant Farm Workers in a Rural Wisconsin County. Ph.D., University of Minnesota.

Ramirez, Arnulfo G.
1974   The Spoken English of Spanish-speaking Pupils in a Bilingual and Monolingual School Setting: An Analysis of Syntactic Development. Ph.D., Stanford University.

Randle, Janice Ann Whitehead
1975   A Bilingual Oral Language Test for Mexican-American Children. Ph.D., University of Texas, Austin.

Remy, Martha C.
1970   Protestant Churches and Mexican Americans in South Texas. Ph.D., University of Texas, Austin.

Reyes, Ignacio
1957   A Survey of the Problems Involved in the Americanization of the Mexican-American. M.A., University of Southern California.

Riegelhaupt-Barkin, Florence
1976   The Influence of English on the Spanish of Bilingual Mexican-American Migrants in Florida. Ph.D., State University of New York, Buffalo.

Rinaldi, John Raymond
1975   An Evaluation of Two Counselor Preparation Models and Their Impact upon the Activities and Perceptions of Chicano Counselors. Ed.D., Texas Tech University.

Rincon, Edward Trillo
1979   Test Speed, Test Anxiety, and Test Performance: A Comparison of Mexican-American and Anglo-American High School Students. Ph.D., University of Texas, Austin.

Rios, Susan G.
1977   Internal-External Locus of Control and Perception of the Change Required by Life Events in a Multicultural Setting. M.A., University of Texas, El Paso.

Rivera, George Fred, Jr.
1971   *El Barrio:* A Sociological Study of Acculturation in a Mexican American Community. Ph.D., New York University, Buffalo.

Robertson, Clyde R.
1935   A Comparative Study of the Progress of American and Mexican Pupils in Certain Elementary Schools in Texas. M.A., University of Texas, Austin.

Robinson, Ellen Joyce Phillips
1977   A Study of English Language Development in Spanish-Dominant Five-Year-Old Children in the Sweetwater Public Schools. M.A., Hardin-Simmons University.

Rodriguez, Eugene, Jr.
1965   Henry B. Gonzalez, a Political Profile. M.A., St. Mary's University.

Rodriguez, Roy C.
1972   A Measurement of Political Attitudes in Mexican-American Civic Organizations. M.A., University of Texas, El Paso.

Rogers, Thomas G.
1927   The Housing Situation of the Mexicans in San Antonio, Texas. M.A., University of Texas, Austin.

Ross, William T.
1953   Social Function of the Godparent System in Tucson. M.A., University of Arizona.

Roth, Janine T.
1978   A Multicultural Analysis of Internal-External Locus of Control, Life Change Events and Anxiety. M.A., University of Texas, El Paso.

Ruby, Carrie L.
1953   Attitudes Toward Latin-Americans as Revealed in Southwestern Literature. M.A., University of Texas, Austin.

Saenz, Erasmo A.
1978   A Comparative Study of Language, Reading and Mathematics in a Bilingual Early Childhood Program. Ed.D., Texas A&I University, Kingsville.

Salinas, Medardo, Jr.
1976   A Comparison of the Levels of Personal and Social Adjustment Between Anglo-American and Mexican-American Adolescents in 6 AAAA Schools of the Rio Grande Valley of Texas. M.A., Pan American University.

Samora, Julian
1947   The Acculturation of the Spanish-speaking People of Fort Collins, Colorado, in Selected Culture Areas. M.A., Colorado A&M College.
1953   Minority Leadership in a Bicultural Community. Ph.D., Washington University.

Santos, Richard
1977   An Analysis of Earnings Among Persons of Spanish Origin in the Midwest. Ph.D., Michigan State University.

Savage, Fred
1955   Baptist Missions Among Foreign Language Groups in El Paso. M.A., University of Texas, El Paso.

Schoepfle, Gordon Mark
1977   Nogales High School: Peer Group and Institution in a Mexican-American Border Town. Ph.D., Northwestern University.

Scott, R. F.
1969   The Urban Mexican-American in the Southwest, 1932-1955. Ph.D., University of Southern California.

Scott, Wilbur Joseph
1972   The Effect of Industrialization on Anglo and Spanish Surname Populations in Sixteen Southwestern SMSAs. M.A., University of Texas, El Paso.

Sepulveda, Ciro
1976   *La Colonia del Harbor:* History of Mexicanos in East Chicago, Indiana, 1919-1932. Ph.D., Notre Dame University.

Shelton, Cynthia Jane
1975   The Neighborhood House of San Diego: Settlement Work in the Mexican Community, 1914-1940. M.A., San Diego State University.

Shelton, Edgar Greer, Jr.
1946   Political Conditions Among Texas Mexicans Along the Rio Grande. M.A., University of Texas, Austin.

Sherrill, Daniel Edward
1975   Migration to Colonia Buena Vista. M.A., San Diego State University.

Shockley, John S.
1972   Crystal City, Texas: Mexican-Americans and Political Change. Ph.D., University of Wisconsin, Madison.

Simmons, Ozzie G.
1952   Anglo-Americans and Mexican-Americans in South Texas: A Study in Dominant-Subordinate Group Relations. Ph.D., Harvard University.

Simmons, Thomas Edward
1976   The Citizen Factories: The Americanization of Mexican Students in Texas Public Schools, 1920-1945. Ph.D., Texas A&M University.

Smith, Clara G.
1936   The Development of the Mexican People in the Community of Watts, California. M.A., University of Southern California.

Smith, Margaret Jeanel Russell
1979   Correlates of Locus of Control in Mexican-American Eighth Graders. Ed.D., Texas Tech University.

Smith, William D.
1974   The Relative Growth of Savings and Loan Association Savings Deposits and Commercial Bank Time and Savings Deposits in El Paso, Texas. M.A., University of Texas, El Paso.

Snow, Ellen Genevieve Munson
1979   Self-Esteem and Peer Group Nomination of Anglo and Mexican-American Sixth Graders. Ph.D., University of Texas, Austin.

Sorley, Horace Eugene
1974   Marital Satisfaction in Interethnic Marriages Between Mexican-Americans and Anglo-Americans. M.S., Texas Tech University.

Sosa-Bonilla, Rosalinda
1979   The Education of the Mexican American: An Annotated Bibliography. Ed.D., Texas A&I University, Kingsville.

Spielberg, Joseph
1959   Social and Cultural Configurations and Medical Care: A Study of Mexican-Americans' Responses to Proposed Hospitalization for the Treatment of Tuberculosis. M.A., University of Texas, Austin.

Springer, Robert Lester
1961   A Curriculum Planning Guide for the Secondary Schools of El Paso, Texas. Ed.D., New York University.

Stewart, Arleen
1973   *Las Mujeres de Aztlan:* A Consultation with Elderly Mexican-American Women in a Socio-Historical Perspective. Ph.D., California School of Professional Psychology, San Francisco.

Stewart, Marlene M.
1971   Perceived Impact of Social Influences on the Retention of Armed Services Y.M.C.A. Volunteers: A Study of Mexican-American and Anglo-American Members of the Girls Service Organization. M.A., University of Texas, El Paso.

Taylor, Jacqueline Joann
1973   Ethnic Identity and Upward Mobility of Mexican-Americans in Tucson. M.A.,* University of Arizona.

Teschner, Richard V.
1972   Anglicisms in Spanish: A Cross-referenced Guide to Previous Findings, Together with English Lexical Influence on Chicago Mexican Spanish. Ph.D., University of Wisconsin, Madison.

Thomforde, Duane W.
1969   Political Socialization in South El Paso. M.A., University of Texas, El Paso.

Thompson, Roger M.
1971   Language Loyalty in Austin, Texas: A Study of a Bilingual Neighborhood. Ph.D., University of Texas, Austin.

Thurston, Richard G.
1962   Urbanization and Socio-cultural Change in a Mexican-American Enclave. Ph.D., University of California, Los Angeles.

Tipton, Lola Sue
1979   A Comparison of Academic Achievement and Attendance to Determine the Effectiveness of the Seven and Ten Month Programs for Selected Elementary School Migrant Children. Ed.D., Texas A&I University, Kingsville.

Torres, Salvador Roberto
1973   Creative Aspects of La Raza Inspired by Chicano Experience. M.A. (Project), San Diego State University.

Trejo, Arnulfo D.
1951   Vocablos y modismos del español de Arizona. M.A., Universidad de las Américas (Mexico City College).

Trevino, Robert Edward
1979   Bilingual-Bicultural Education in the Corpus Christi In-

dependent School District: A Process Evaluation. M.A., University of Texas, Austin.

Ulibarri, Horacio
1959   Teacher Awareness of Socio-cultural Differences in Multi-cultural Classrooms. Ph.D., University of New Mexico.

Vadi, José Miguel
1977   Mobilization Problems of Chicanos in a Southern California City. Ph.D., University of Wisconsin, Madison.

Vanderpool, Wayne Allan
1978   Development and Evaluation of a Modified Curriculum Design for Bilingual Vocational Education in the CVAE General Mechanical Repair Programs of the Lower Rio Grande Valley of Texas. Ed.D., Texas A&M University.

Vassberg, David Erland
1966   The Use of Mexicans and Mexican-Americans as an Agricultural Work Force in the Lower Rio Grande Valley in Texas. M.A., University of Texas, Austin.

Venegas, Moises T.
1973   Educational and Occupational Aspirations and Expectations of El Paso High School Students. Ed.D., New Mexico State University.

Villarreal, Jesus
1979   Chicano Earnings in Texas. M.A., University of Texas, Austin.

Villarreal, Maria Elena
1978   A Study of the Corrective Measures Used by Parents and the Self-Concept of Their Children. Ed.D., Texas A&I University, Kingsville.

Vogler, James D.
1968   The Influence of Ethnicity and Socioeconomic Status on the Pictorial Test of Intelligence. Ph.D., University of Arizona.

Waddell, Jack
1962   Value Orientations of Young Mexican-American Males as Reflected in Their Work Patterns and Employment Preferences. M.A., University of Texas, Austin.

Walker, Helen W.
1928   The Conflict of Cultures in First Generation Mexicans in Santa Ana, California. M.A., University of Southern California.

Walsh, Albeus
1952   The Work of the Catholic Bishops' Committee for the Spanish-speaking People in the United States. M.A., University of Texas, Austin.

Walter, Paul A.
1938   A Study of Isolation and Social Change in Three Spanish-speaking Villages of New Mexico. Ph.D., Stanford University.

Welch, Carol J.
1978   Income Inequality Among Mexican-Americans and Blacks in an El Paso Low Income Area: A Structural Analysis. M.A., University of Texas, El Paso.

Wells, Gladys
1941   Factors Influencing the Assimilation of the Mexican in Texas. M.A., Southern Methodist University.

White, Jean Dempewolf
1955   Time Orientation as Factor in the Acculturation of Southwestern Spanish-speaking Groups. M.A., University of Texas, Austin.

Williams, Brett
1975   The Trip Takes Us: Chicano Migrants on the Prairie. Ph.D., University of Illinois, Urbana-Champaign.

Winn, Charles C.
1972   Mexican-Americans in the Texas Labor Movement. Ph.D., Texas Christian University.

Zabala, José Maria
1979   Formas verbales en la produccion escrita de estudiantes Mexico-Americanos de la Universidad de Texas en El Paso. M.A., University of Texas, El Paso.

Zeleny, Carolyn
1944   Relations Between the Spanish-Americans and the Anglo-Americans in New Mexico: A Study of Conflict and Accommodation in a Dual Ethnic Relationship. Ph.D., Yale University.

History

Akers, Stephen
1976   The Arizona Struggle for Territorial Status, 1856-1868. Graduate Nonthesis Paper, University of Texas, El Paso.
1976   The U.S. and the Madero-Diaz Struggle. Graduate Nonthesis paper, University of Texas, El Paso.

Algier, Keith Wayne
1966   Feudalism on New Spain's Northern Frontier: Valle de San Bartolomé, a Case Study. Ph.D., University of New Mexico.

Allan, Robert A.
1971   Migratory Mexican Labor in the United States, 1917-1924. M.A., California State University, Hayward.

Ammons, Nancy C.
1931   The Spanish Conquest of New Mexico in the Sixteenth and Seventeenth Centuries. M.A., University of Oklahoma.

Anderson, Hugh Allen, Jr.
1975   Fort Phantom Hill: Outpost on the Clear Fork of the Brazos. M.A., Texas Tech University.

Archibald, Robert Reid
1975   The Economic Development of the Hispanic California Missions, Ph.D., University of New Mexico.

Bailey, David Thomas
1975   Stratification and Ethnic Differentiation in Santa Fe. Ph.D., University of Texas, Austin.

Baker, George Towne, III
1966   An Exposition Addressed to the Supreme Government by the Commissioners Who Signed the Treaty of Peace with the U.S. M.A.,* California State College, Fullerton.

Baquera, Richard V.
1978   Paso del Norte and Chihuahua, 1810-1821: Revolution and Constitutionalism. M.A., University of Texas, El Paso.

Barker, Bernice
1929   The Texas Expedition to the Rio Grande in 1842. M.A., University of Texas, Austin.

Barton, John
1963   El Paso, 1890. M.A., University of Texas, El Paso.

Beach, Frank L.
1963   The Transformation of California, 1900-1920: The Effects of the Western Movements in California's Growth and Development in the Progressive Period. Ph.D., University of California, Berkeley.

Bennett, Catherine
1939   The History of Education in Sauedo, Texas, to 1870. M.A., University of Texas, Austin.

Bents, Doris W.
1949   The History of Tubac, 1752-1948. M.A., University of Arizona.

Bradfute, Richard W.
1973   The Court of Private Land Claims and the Adjudication of Spanish and Mexican Land Grant Titles. Ph.D., University of Colorado.

Briegel, Kaye Linn
1974   Alianza Hispano-American, 1894-1965: A Mexican American Fraternal Insurance Society. Ph.D., University of Southern California.

Briggs, A. K.
1974   The Archeology of 1882 Labor Camps on the Southern Pacific Railroad, Val Verde County, Texas. M.A., University of Texas, Austin.

Brockman, Edward Burt
1977   The Military Activities and Operations of the Citizen Soldiers of the First New York Volunteer Regiment in California, 1846-1848. M.A., San Diego State University.

Brown, Lee Francis
1972   The Explorer, the United States Government and the Approaches to Santa Fe: A Study of American Policy Relative to the Spanish Southwest, 1800-1819. Ph.D., Loyola University of Chicago.

Brown, Maury Bright
1924   The Military Defenses of Texas and the Rio Grande Region, About 1766. M.A., University of Texas, Austin.

Brown, Robert Benaway
1951   Guns over the Border: American Aid to the Juarez Government During the French Intervention. Ph.D., University of Michigan.

Brown, Thomas Andrew
1974   An Episode in U.S. Foreign Trade: Silver and Gold, Santa Fe and St. Louis, 1820-1840. Ph.D., Ball State University.

Campbell, Elsie
1950   Spanish Records of the Civil Government of Ysleta, 1835. M.A., University of Texas, El Paso.

Carman, Michael Dennis
1974   United States Customs and the Madero Revolution. M.A., San Diego State University.

Carnes, Mary Loyola
1925   The American Occupation of New Mexico, 1821-1852. Ph.D., University of California, Berkeley.

Carter, Constance Ann Crowder
1971   Law and Society in Colonial Mexico: Audiencia Judges in Mexican Society from the Tello de Sandoval Visita General, 1543-1547. Ph.D., Columbia University.

Castanien, Donald Garner
1951   A Seventeenth Century Mexican Library and the Inquisition. Ph.D., University of Michigan.

Chandler, Robert Joseph
1978   The Press and Civil Liberties in California During the Civil War, 1861-1865. Ph.D., University of California, Riverside.

Chapman, Charles Edward
1915   The Founding of Spanish California: The Northwestward Expansion of New Spain, 1687-1783. Ph.D., University of California, Berkeley.

Chinn, Barbara
1967   The History of Lands Within the Pecos Division of the Texas Pacific Reservation. M.A., University of Texas, El Paso.

Christian, Garna Loy
1977   Sword and Plowshare: The Symbiotic Development of Fort Bliss and El Paso, Texas, 1849-1918. Ph.D., Texas Tech University.

Clark, Robert Carlton
1906   The Beginnings of Texas, 1684-1718. Ph.D., University of Wisconsin.

Clendenen, Clarence Clemens
1959   The United States and Pancho Villa. Ph.D., Stanford University.

Colton, Ray Charles
1954   The American Civil War in the Western Territories of New Mexico, Arizona, Colorado, and Utah. Ph.D., Maryland University.

Connor, Daniel
1949   Military Operations in the Southwest, 1861-1865. M.A., University of Texas, El Paso.

Cowling, Annie
1926   The Civil War Trade of the Lower Rio Grande Valley. M.A., University of Texas, Austin.

Crawford, Polly Pearl
1925   The Beginnings of Spanish Settlement in the Lower Rio Grande Valley. M.A., University of Texas, Austin.

Crudup, Robert E.
1933   The Gadsden Purchase. M.A., Oklahoma A&M University.

Cummings, Lewis
1967   Zack White, Pioneer Capitalist. M.A., University of Texas, El Paso.

Curry, Mary Basil
1965   Spanish Indian Policy in Louisiana, 1766-1785. M.A., University of Santa Clara.

Daddysman, James William
1976   The Matamoros Trade, 1861-1865. Ph.D., West Virginia University.

Daniel, J. M.
1948   La Junta de los Rios and the Despoblado, 1680-1760. M.A., University of Texas, Austin.
1955   The Advance of the Spanish Frontier and the Despoblado. Ph.D., University of Texas, Austin.

Davila, Adela B.
1975   El habla popular de Ciudad Juarez. M.A., University of Texas, El Paso.

Dewetter, Mardee
1946   Revolutionary El Paso, 1910-1917. M.A., University of Texas, El Paso.

Dominguez, Azucena (Susy) M.
1977   Phonological Variability in the English of a Mexican-American Bilingual. M.A., University of Texas, El Paso.

Dooley, Francis Patrick
1972   The Cristeros, Calles and Mexican Catholicism. Ph.D., University of Maryland.

Edwards, Warrick Ridgely, III
1971   United States-Mexican Relations, 1913-1916: Revolution, Oil and Intervention. Ph.D., Louisiana State University.

Estep, Raymond
1942   The Life of Lorenzo de Zavala. Ph.D., University of Texas, Austin.

Estrada, Richard
1975   Border Revolution: The Mexican Revolution in the Ciudad Juarez, El Paso Area, 1906-1915. M.A., University of Texas, El Paso.

Faulk, Odie B.
1962   The Last Years of Spanish Texas, 1778-1821. Ph.D., Texas Tech University.

Finch, Gail H.
1936   The Anglo-American Regime in New Mexico, 1846-1861. M.A., University of Oklahoma.

Fireman, Janet Ruth
1972   Spain's Royal Corps of Engineers in the Western Borderlands, 1764-1815. Ph.D., University of New Mexico.

Ganaway, Loomis Morton
1941   New Mexico and the Sectional Controversy, 1846-1871. Ph.D., Vanderbilt University.

Garner, Richard Lyle
1970   Zacatecas, 1750-1821: The Study of a Late Colonial Mexican City. Ph.D., University of Michigan.

Garrett, Kathryn
1935   The War of Independence in Texas, 1811-1813. Ph.D., University of California.

Gettys, James Wylie, Jr.
1974   "To Conquer a Peace": South Carolina and the Mexican War. Ph.D., University of South Carolina.

Giese, Anna Mae
1975   The Sonoran Triumvirate: Preview in Sonora, 1910-1920. Ph.D., University of Florida.

Gilson, William J.
1970   Socio-linguistic Study of Students Involved in the International Science Program. Graduate Nonthesis Paper, University of Texas, El Paso.

Glascock, Melvin Bruce
1969   New Spain and the War for America, 1779-1783. Ph.D.,

Louisiana State University.

Goldstein, Marcy Gail
1977   Americanization and Mexicanization: The Mexican Elite and Anglo-Americans in the Gadsden Purchase Lands, 1853-1880. Ph.D., Case Western Reserve University.

Gómez-Quiñones, Juan
1972   Social Change and Intellectual Discontent: The Growth of Mexican Nationalism, 1890-1911. Ph.D., University of California, Los Angeles.

Gooden, John
1965   Life and Experiences of the Forty-Niners on the Southwest Roads to California. M.A., University of Texas, El Paso.

Graebner, Norman A.
1949   The Treaty of Guadalupe-Hidalgo: Its Background and Formation. M.A., University of Chicago.

Graf, Leroy Phillip
1942   The Economic History of the Lower Rio Grande Valley, 1820-1875. Ph.D., Harvard University.

Graves, Donald
1962   Fence Cutting in Texas, 1883-1885. M.A., University of Texas, El Paso.

Guyler, Sam Lerert
1969   A Literary and Historiographic Analysis of Bernal Diaz del Castillo's "Historia verdadera de la conquista de la Nueva Espana." Ph.D., Cornell University.

Gwin, Adeline
1950   A History of San Elizareo, Texas. M.A., University of Texas, El Paso.

Hadley, Phillip Lance
1975   Mining and Society in the Santa Eulalia Mining Complex, Chihuahua, Mexico: 1709-1750. Ph.D., University of Texas, Austin.

Haller, Judith L.
1971   Unknown Compromise: Lincoln and New Mexico, 1860-1861. M.A., San Diego State University.

Hannon, Ralph L.
1966   The Gadsden Purchase, 1854-1884: An Historical Geographic Justification. M.A., Arizona State University.

Harman, Rhonda L.
1975   Linguistic and Language-Attitude Differences Among Latin American Students. M.A., University of Texas, El Paso.

Harris, Marilyn
1961   Arizona Land Grants: Cases Which Appeared Before the Court of Private Land Claims, 1891-1904. M.A., San Diego State University.

Hefferan, Violle Clark
1940   Thomas Benton Catron. M.A., University of New Mexico.

Hendricks, William Oral
1967   Guillermo Andrade and Land Development on the Mexican Colorado River Delta, 1874-1905. Ph.D., University of Southern California.

Hewitt, Harry Paxton
1963   The Opening of the Mines and the Defense of Nueva Vizcaya, 1600-1776. M.A., University of Utah.
1971   The Historical Development of Nueva Vizcaya's Defenses to 1646. Ph.D., University of Utah.

Hill, James
1951   A Diplomatic History of the Punitive Expedition into Mexico, 1916-1917. M.A., University of Texas, El Paso.

Hoffmann, Fritz L.
1935   Diary of the Alarcon Expedition into Texas, 1718-1719. Ph.D., University of Texas, Austin.

Hoskins, Lewis Maloney
1946   Class and Clash in Seventeenth Century Mexico. Ph.D., University of Michigan.

Hovious, JoAnn
1972   Social Change in Western Towns: El Paso, Texas, 1881-1889. M.A., University of Texas, El Paso.

Hruneni, George A., Jr.
1967   The Diplomatic Mission of Joel Roberts Poinsett to Mexico. M.A., University of Santa Clara.
1972   Palmetto Yankee: The Public Life and Times of Joel Roberts Poinsett, 1824-1851. Ph.D., University of California, Santa Barbara.

Hughes, Charles William
1974   The Decline of the Californios? The Case of San Diego, 1846-1856. M.A., San Diego State University.

Irby, James Arthur
1969   Line of the Rio Grande: War and Trade on the Confederate Frontier: 1861-1865. Ph.D., University of Georgia.

Jackson, Dorothy Jean
1940   Pershing's Expedition into Mexico. M.A., University of Texas, Austin.

Jacobs, Ken R.
1970   The Confederate Diplomatic Missions of John T. Pickett and Juan A. Quintero to Mexico, 1861-1865. M.A., Hardin-Simmons University.

John, Elizabeth Ann Harper
1957   Spanish Relations with the Indios Barbaros on the Northernmost Frontier of New Spain in the Eighteenth Century. Ph.D., University of Oklahoma.

Joseph, Harriett Denise
1976   Church and State in Mexico from Calles to Cardenas, 1924-1938. Ph.D., North Texas State Univeristy.

Kane, Nathaniel Stephen
1970   Charles Evans Hughes and Mexican-American Relations, 1921-1924. Ph.D., University of Colorado, Boulder.

Kantes, Stephen John
1976   Japanese-Mexican Relations and the Magdalena Bay Affair. M.A., San Deigo State University.

Kelly, Maria Ann
1975   A Chapter in Mexican Church-State Relations: Socialist Education, 1934-1940. Ph.D., Georgetown University.

Kerig, Dorothy Pierson
1974   A United States Consul on the Border During the Mexican Revolution: The Case of Luther T. Ellsworth. M.A., San Diego State University.

Kerr, Homer L.
1953   Migration into Texas, 1865-1880. Ph.D., University of Texas, Austin.

Kingrea, Nellie W.
1953   History of the Good Neighbor Commission in Texas. M.A., Texas Christian University.

Kirstein, Peter Neil
1973   Anglo over Bracero: A History of the Mexican Worker in the United States from Roosevelt to Nixon. Ph.D., St. Louis University.

Knowlton, Robert James
1963   The Disamortization and Nationalization of Ecclesiastical Property in Mexico, 1856-1910. Ph.D., University of Iowa.

Ladd, Doris Maxine
1972   The Mexican Nobility at Independence, 1780-1826. Ph.D., Stanford University.

Lamar, Quinton Curtis
1971   The Role of Lucas Alaman in Mexican-United States Relations, 1824-1853. Ph.D., Louisiana State University.

Landau, Saul
1954   The Bisbee Deportations: Class Conflict and Patriotism During World War I. M.A., University of Wisconsin, Madison.

Larrey, Martin Fermin
1962   The Yuma Colorado Settlements, 1775-1781. M.A., University of California, Santa Clara.
1965   A Viceroy and His Challengers: Supremacy Struggles During the Viceregency of Martin Enriquez, 1568-1580. Ph.D., University of California, Santa Barbara.

Leary, David Thomas
1970   The Attitudes of Certain United States Citizens Toward Mexico, 1821-1846. Ph.D., University of Southern California.

Lee, James Herbert
1974   Nationalism and Education in Mexico, 1821-1861. Ph.D., Ohio State University.

Lee, Raymond Lawrence
1946   Hapsburg Rule in New Spain in the Late Middle Sixteenth Century. Ph.D., University of Michigan.

Leef, Gladys Ruth
1976   George I. Sanchez: Don Quixote of the Southwest. M.A.,* North Texas State University.

LeMay, Donald Austin
1973   Joel R. Poinsett in Mexico, 1825-1829. M.A., San Diego State University.

Leonard, Glen Milton
1970   Western Boundary Making: Texas and the Mexican Cession, 1844-1850. Ph.D., University of Utah.

Lewis, James Allen
1975   New Spain During the American Revolution, 1779-1783: A Viceroyalty at War. Ph.D., Duke University.

Long, Stanton C.
1953   Early Nineteenth Century El Paso. M.A., University of Texas, Austin.

Long, William
1964   A History of Mining in New Mexico During the Spanish and Mexican Periods. M.A., University of New Mexico.

Lynch, Margaret A.
1935   Colonial Texas as a Frontier Problem. Ph.D., Boston College.

Mabric, Jacqueline Gertrude Barnett
1979   The *Frontier Times* Magazine, 1923-1954: An Index and Brief History. M.A., Texas A&M University.

Mabry, Donald Joseph
1970   *Accion Nacional:* The Institutionalization of an Opposition Party. Ph.D., Syracuse University.

McCarty, Jeanne
1978   Protestants and Prohibition in Texas, 1919-1935. M.A., University of Texas, El Paso.

McCarty, Kieran Robert
1973   Franciscan Beginnings on the Arizona-Sonora Desert, 1767-1770. Ph.D., Catholic University of America.

McClure, Wayne Hammer, II
1973   The Marques de Gelves: Viceroy of New Spain. Ph.D., Texas Christian University.

McCollum, Dudley Foster
1931   Spanish Texas. Ph.D., New York University.

McGranahan, Elizabeth Nadler
1974   The Crisis of the Believers: Anticlericalism in Mexican Government, 1855-1857. Ph.D., Catholic University of America.

McGrath, Sister Paul of the Cross
1930   Political Nativism in Texas, 1825-1860. Ph.D., Catholic University of America.

Macias, Anna
1965   The Genesis of Constitutional Government in Mexico, 1808-1820. Ph.D., Columbia University.

McKechnie, Marian Elizabeth
1970   The Mexican Revolution and the National Presbyterian Church of Mexico, 1910-1940. Ph.D., American University.

McKee, Okla Markham
1955   Five-Hundred Nondictionary Words Found in the El Paso-Juarez Press. M.A., University of Texas, El Paso.

McNeely, John Hamilton
1958   The Politics and Development of the Mexican Land Program. Ph.D., University of Texas, Austin.

Maughan, Scott Jarvis
1968   Francisco Garces and New Spain's Northwestern Frontier, 1768-1781. Ph.D., University of Utah.

Mazzaferri, Anthony J.
1968   Public Health and Social Revolution in Mexico, 1877-1930. Ph.D., Kent Sate University.

Michaels, Albert Louis
1966   Mexican Politics and Nationalism from Calles to Cardenas. Ph.D., University of Pennsylvania.

Miles, Robert
1972   An Examination of Article II of the Treaty of Guadalupe Hidalgo. M.A., University of Texas, El Paso.

Milligan, James Clark
1975   José Bernardo Gutierrez de Lara, Mexican Frontiersman, 1811-1841. Ph.D., Texas Tech University.

Morgan, William Abraham
1969   Sea Power in the Gulf of Mexico and the Caribbean During the Mexican and Colombian Wars of Independence, 1815-1830. Ph.D., University of Southern California.

Morton, Ohland
1939   The Life of General Don Manuel de Mier y Teran as it Affected Texas-Mexican Relations, 1821-1832. Ph.D., University of Texas, Austin.

Multerer, Raymond T.
1974   The Socialist Education Movement and Its Impact on Mexican Education, 1930-48. Ph.D., State University of New York, Buffalo.

Mulvihill, Daniel Joseph
1954   Juan de Zumarraga, First Bishop of Mexico. Ph.D., University of Michigan.

Murphy, Henrietta
1938   Spanish Presidial Administration as Exemplified by the Inspection of Pedro de Rivera, 1724-1728. Ph.D., University of Texas.

Murrah, David Joe
1979   C. C. Slaughter: The Cattle King of Texas. Ph.D., Texas Tech University.

Nathan, Deborah Ruth
1978   The Influence of African Slave Speech on the Phonology of Caribbean and Coastal Latin-American Spanish. M.A., University of Texas, El Paso.

Nelson, Al B.
1937   Juan de Ugalde and the Rio Grande Frontier, 1777-1790. Ph.D., University of California.

Nicholas, Cora S.
1947   The History of the Yuma Valley and Mesa, with Special Emphasis on the City of Yuma, Arizona. M.A., University of Southern California.

Nuttall, Donald Andrew
1964   Pedro Fages and the Advance of the Northern Frontier of New Spain, 1767-1782. Ph.D., University of Southern California.

Nwasike, Dominic Azikiwe
1972   Mexico City Town Government, 1590-1650: Study in Aldermanic Background and Performance. Ph.D., University of Wisconsin, Madison.

Overfelt, Robert Chellis, Jr.
1973   Benito Juarez: Government by Carriage, 1863-1867. Ph.D., Texas Christian University.

Parraga, Charlotte Marie Nelson
1976   Santa Fe de Nuevo Mexico: A Study of a Frontier City based on an Annotated Translation of Selected Documents (1825-1832) from the Mexican Archives of New Mexico. Ph.D., Ball State University.

Patterson, Jean Scarborough
1979   The Influence of English on the Spanish Syntax of El Paso-Juarez. M.A., University of Texas, El Paso.

Patton, Raymon
1953   A History of the Housing Authority of El Paso, Texas, and Low Rent Housing. M.A., University of Texas, El Paso.

Pearson, Jim B.
1955   A New Mexico Gold Story: The Elizabethtown-Red River Area. Ph.D., University of Texas, Austin.

Phillips, Richard Baker
1953   José Vasconcelos and the Mexican Revolution of 1910. Ph.D., Stanford University.

Pilant, James
1971   The Treaty of Guadalupe Hidalgo: Article X and the Protocol. M.A., University of Santa Clara.

Pineda, Hugo
1971   José Vasconcelos, politico mexicano, 1928-1929 (Spanish Text). Ph.D., George Washington University.

Pitchford, Louis Cleveland, Jr.
1965   The Diplomatic Representatives from the United States to Mexico from 1836 to 1848. Ph.D., University of Colorado, Boulder.

Pitt, Leonard M.
1955   The Foreign Miners' Tax of 1850: A Study of Nativism and Antinativism in Gold Rush California. M.A., University of California, Los Angeles.

Polich, John Leo
1968   Foreign Maritime Intrusion on Spain's Pacific Coast, 1786-1810. Ph.D., University of New Mexico.

Polzer, Charles William
1972   The Evolution of the Jesuit Mission System in Northwestern New Spain, 1600-1767. Ph.D., University of Arizona.

Poole, Richard Stafford
1961   The Indian Problem in the Third Provincial Council of Mexico, 1585. Ph.D., St. Louis, University.

Ports, Uldis Allen
1976   George White Marston and the San Diego Progressives, 1913-1917. M.A., San Diego State University.

Pratt, Francis E.
1965   The Obraje in New Spain: A Case Study in the Failure of Royal Authority to Impose Its Will. M.A., University of the Americas, Mexico City.

Ramirez, Karen
1971   Bilingualism and Bilingual Programs in El Paso: Kindergarten and First Grade. M.A., University of Texas, El Paso.

Rangel, Rudolph Stone
1975   Henry Lane Wilson and the Fall of Francisco I. Madero. Ph.D., American University.

Reisler, Mark
1973   Passing Through Our Egypt: Mexican Labor in the United States, 1900-1940. Ph.D., Cornell University.

Reynolds, Clarence Lynn
1974   Decision Making and Cultural Change: The Status of Spanish American Small Farms in Northern New Mexico. Ph.D., Southern Methodist University.

Riley, G. Michael
1965   The Estate of Fernando Cortes in the Cuernavaca Area of Mexico, 1522-1547. Ph.D., University of New Mexico.

Riley, John Denny
1976   Santos Benavides: His Influence on the Lower Rio Grande, 1823-1891. Ph.D., Texas Christian University.

Rosbach, Edith Virginia Hunter
1953   The History of the Mission Period of Pimeria Alta to 1828. M.A., University of Texas, Austin.

Rosenbaum, Robert J.
1972   *Mexicano* versus *Americano:* A Study of Hispanic-American Resistance to Anglo-American Control in New Mexico Territory, 1870-1900. Ph.D., University of Texas, Austin.

Ross, Oliver Dell
1953   Studies of Selected Mexican Communal Institutions: Colonial Period. Ph.D., Ohio State University.

Ross, Stanley Robert
1951   Mexican Apostle: The Life of Francisco I. Madero. Ph.D., Columbia University.

Rowley, Ralph Alcorn
1975   United States Acquisition of the Spanish Borderlands: Problems and Legacy. Ph.D., University of New Mexico.

Rubright, Lynnell
1967   A Sequent Occupance of the Espanola Valley, New Mexico. M.A., University of Colorado.

Ruecking, F. A., Jr.
1955   The Coahuilitecan Indians of Southern Texas and Northeastern Mexico. M.A., University of Texas at Austin.

Sanchez, Joseph Patrick
1974   The Catalonian Volunteers and the Defense of Northern New Spain, 1767-1803. Ph.D., University of New Mexico.

Sandels, Robert Lynn
1967   Silvestre Terrazas, the Press, and the Origins of the Mexican Revolution in Chihuahua. Ph.D., University of Oregon.

Sandos, James A.
1978   The United States and the Mexican Revolution, 1915-1917: The Impact of Culture Conflict in the Tamaulipas-Texas Frontier upon the Emergence of Revolutionary Government in Mexico. Ph.D., University of California, Berkeley.

Sandstrum, Allan
1962   Fort Bliss: The Frontier Years. M.A., University of Texas, El Paso.

Schmidt, Henry Contrad
1972   The Search for National Identity in Mexico, 1900-1924. Ph.D., University of Texas, Austin.

Schmitt, Karl Michael
1954   Evolution of Mexican Thought on Church-State Relations, 1876-1911. Ph.D., University of Pennsylvania.

Scott, Florence Johnson
1935   Spanish Land Grants in the Lower Rio Grande Valley. M.A., University of Texas, Austin.

Sensing, Welton Jerry
1954   The Policies of Hernan Cortes, as Described in his Letters. Ph.D., University of Illinois, Urbana-Champaign.

Shearer, Ernest C.
1939   Border Diplomatic Relations Between the United States and Mexico, 1848-1860. Ph.D., University of Texas, Austin.

Sherman, Ed
1962   A Decade of Exploration in the Southwest, 1846-1855. M.A., University of Texas, El Paso.

Sholly, Robert
1971   Alamogordo, New Mexico: A Case Study in the Dynamics of Western Town Growth. M.A., University of Texas, El Paso.

Simmons, Marc Steven
1965   Spanish Government in New Mexico at the End of the Colonial Period. Ph.D., University of New Mexico.

Sinkin, Richard Nathan
1972   Modernization and Reform in Mexico, 1855-1876. Ph.D., University of Michigan.

Smith, David Ryan
1979   Reconstruction and Republicanism in Grayson, Fannin, and Lamar Counties. Texas, 1865-1873. M.A., University of Texas, Austin.

Sotomayor, Elsie
1977   Historical Aspects Related to the Assimilation and Acculturation of the Mexican American People, 1848-1920. M.A., California State University, Fullerton.

Spears, Louis
1973   Galveston Island, 1816-1821: Focal Point for the Contest for Texas. M.A., University of Texas, El Paso.

Standart, Sister M. Collett
1974   The Sonoran Migration to California, 1848-1856. M.A., Dominican College (San Raphael).

Starnes, Gary Bertram
1971   Juan de Ugalde (1729-1816) and the Provincias Internas of Coahuila and Texas. Ph.D., Texas Christian University.

Stevens, Robert Conway
1963   Mexico's Forgotten Frontier: A History of Sonora, 1821-1846. Ph.D., University of California, Berkeley.

Stout, Joseph A., Jr.
1971   The Last Years of Manifest Destiny: Filibustering in Northwestern Mexico, 1848-1862. Ph.D., Oklahoma State University.

Sunseri, Alvin R.
1973   New Mexico in the Aftermath of the Anglo-American Conquest, 1846-1861. Ph.D., Louisiana State University.

Super, John Clay
1973   Queretaro: Society and Economy in Early Provincial Mexico, 1590-1630. Ph.D., University of California, Los Angeles.

Tate, R. C.
1942   History of Zavala County, Texas. M.A., Southwest Texas State University.

Taylor, James William
1976   Socioeconomic Instability and the Revolution for Mexican Independence in the Province of Guanajuato. Ph.D., University of New Mexico.

Tutino, John Mark
1976   Creole Mexico: Spanish Elites, Haciendas, and Indian Towns, 1750-1810. Ph.D., University of Texas, Austin.

Tymitz, John Paul
1973   British Influence in Mexico, 1840-1848. Ph.D., Oklahoma State University.

Valenzuela, Francisco
1975   Huerta, Villa and the German Connection, 1914-1917. Graduate Nonthesis Paper, University of Texas, El Paso.

Valenzuela, René
1975   Chihuahua, Calles and the Escobar Revolt of 1929. M.A., University of Texas, El Paso.

Valerio, Francisco Morales
1971   Antecedentes sociales de los franciscanos en Mexico: siglo XVII (Spanish Text). Ph.D., Catholic University of America.

Vaughan, Mary Kathryn
1973   Schools for Social Control: Mexican Educational Policy and Programs, 1880-1928. Ph.D., University of Wisconsin, Madison.

Vigness, David Martell
1948   The Lower Rio Grande Valley, 1836-1846. M.A., University of Texas, Austin.
1951   The Republic of the Rio Grande: An Example of Separatism in Northern Mexico. Ph.D., University of Texas, Austin.

Vincent, Gwendolyn Maxine
1976   The Runaway Scrape of the Texas Revolution with Special Emphasis on Its Enduring Effects: The Return and Effect on the Participants. M.A., Hardin-Simmons University.

Walz, Vina E.
1951   A History of the El Paso Area, 1680-1692. Ph.D., University of New Mexico.

Ward, C. F.
1932   The Salt War of San Elizario. M.A., University of Texas, Austin.

Ward, Forrest Elmer
1962   The Lower Brazos Region of Texas, 1820-1845. Ph.D., University of Texas, Austin.

Warner, Ted J.
1964   The Career of Don Felix Martinez de Rorrelaguna: Soldier, Presidio Commander, and Governor of New Mexico, 1693-1726. Ph.D., University of New Mexico.

Watkins, Lucy R.
1912   Mexican Colonization in the United States Border, 1848-1858. M.A., University of California, Berkeley.

Watson, Thomas Davis
1972   Merchant Adventurer in the Old Southwest: William Panton, The Spanish Years, 1782-1801. Ph.D., Texas Tech University.

Webb, Bert
1960   Controversies over Slavery and Secession in American Protestant Pulpits, 1844-1865. M.A., University of Texas, El Paso.

Webster, Michael G.
1972   Texas Manifest Destiny and the Mexican Border Conflict, 1865-1880. Ph.D., Indiana University.

Weeks, Charles Allen
1973   The Juarez Myth in Mexico. Ph.D., Indiana University.

Werne, Joseph Richard
1972   Guadalupe Hidalgo and the Mesilla Controversy. Ph.D., Kent State University.

West, Robert C.
1938   A Geographical Analysis of the Western Interior Path of Spanish Northward Expansion in New Spain. M.A., University of California, Los Angeles.

Westphall, Victor
1956   The Public Domain in New Mexico, 1854-1891. Ph.D., University of New Mexico.

White, Katherine H.
1961   The Pueblo de Socorro Grant. M.A., University of Texas, El Paso.

White, Theodore L.
1953   The Marquis de Rubis: Inspection of the Eastern Presidios on the Northern Frontier of New Spain. Ph.D., University of Texas.

Williams, Lyle Wayne
1970   Struggle for Survival: The Hostile Frontier of New Spain, 1750-1800. Ph.D., Texas Christian University.

Williman, John Baker
1971   Church and State in Veracruz, 1840-1940: The Concord and Conflicts of a Century. Ph.D., St. Louis University.

Wilson, Iris Higbie
1962   Scientific Aspects of Spanish Exploration in New Spain During the Late Eighteenth Century. Ph.D., University of Southern California.

Wilson, Thomas Ray
1944   William Walker and the Filibustering Expedition to Lower California and Sonora. M.A., University of Texas, Austin.

Yielding, Kenneth
1962   The Juan de Oñate New Mexico Entrada, 1596-1598. M.A., University of Texas, El Paso.

Zeitlin, Richard Henry
1973   Brass Buttons and Iron Rails: The United States Army and American Involvement in Mexico, 1868-1881. Ph.D., University of Wisconsin, Madison.

Zillich, Emily
1958   History of the National Guard in El Paso. M.A., University of Texas, El Paso.

Archaeology and Prehistory

Aten, Lawrence Edward
1979   Indians of the Upper Texas Coast: Ethnohistoric and Archeological Frameworks. Ph.D., University of Texas, Austin.

Bull, Charles Stuart
1977   Archaeology and Linguistics: Coastal Southern California. M.A., San Diego State University.

Ewing, Morgan Robert
1972   A History of the Archaeological Activity at Chichen-Itza, Yucatan, Mexico. Ph.D., Kent State University.

Foster, Michael S.
1978   Loma San Gabriel: A Prehistoric Culture of Northwest Mexico. Ph.D., University of Colorado, Boulder.

Herrington, Selma LaVerne Cloudt
1979   Settlement Patterns and Water Control Systems of the Mimbres Classic Phase, Grant County, New Mexico.

Ph.D., University of Texas, Austin.

Holt, Homer Barry
1979   Mexica-Aztec Warfare: A Developmental and Cultural Analysis. Ph.D., University of Texas, Austin.

McCluney, Eugene B.
1973   Bobcat Cave: A Contribution to the Ethnohistory of the Spanish Borderlands. Ph.D., Texas Christian University.

Noble, Rose Adele
1973   Physical Anthropology of Baja California. M.A., San Diego State University.

Nunley, J. P.
1971   Sociocultural Units of the Southwestern Texas Archaic: An Analytical Approach. Ph.D., Southern Methodist University.

Richardson, Sherrill E.
1972   Aztec Medicine: The Role of the Supernatural. M.A., San Diego State University.

Wooldridge, Harold Gene
1979   The Bald Eagle Cache: Implications for an Early Exchange System in the Jornada Region of South Central New Mexico. M.A., University of Texas, Austin.

Geology and Geography

Carlson, Alvar W.
1971   The Rio Arriba: A Geographic Appraisal of the Spanish-American Homeland: Upper Rio Grande Valley, New Mexico. Ph.D., University of Minnesota.

Carpenter, Nevin Shirley
1975   Images of the Spatial Impact of the Railroad: San Diego, 1851-1873. M.A., San Diego State University.

Cassell, Raymond Kelly
1947   The Land Use Systems of the Baja Rio Bravo in the State of Tamaulipas, Mexico. Ph.D., University of Michigan.

Darnell, William I.
1959   The Imperial Valley: Its Physical and Cultural Geography. M.A., San Diego State College.

Downs, Keith David
1977   The Preservation of Agricultural Lands Within Riverside County. M.A., San Diego State University.

Falter, Dale H.
1971   Tidal Currents in San Diego Harbor. M.S., San Diego State University.

Frazer, William J.
1959   Changing Patterns of Land Utilization with the Salt River Valley of Arizona. Ph.D., University of Michigan.

Gildersleeve, Charles Richard
1978   The International Border City: Urban Spatial Organization in a Context of Two Cultures Along the United States-Mexico Boundary. Ph.D., University of Nebraska, Lincoln.

Gritzner, Charles F.
1969   Spanish Log Construction in New Mexico. Ph.D., Louisiana State University.

Hornbeck, David, Jr.
1974   Spatial Manifestations of Acculturative Processes in the Upper Pecos Valley, New Mexico. Ph.D., University of Nebraska, Lincoln.

Hubert, Jacqueline Shields
1979   Ambient Air Levels of Particulates, Lead, Zinc, Cadmium, and Arsenic in El Paso, Texas. M.S., University of Texas, El Paso.

Kniffin, Fred Bowerman
1930   The Delta Country of the Colorado. Ph.D., University of California.

London, Ova Lee
1951   Geographic Aspects of the Tomato Industry of Texas. M.A., University of Missouri.

McLeod, Ronald Gordon
1977   Land Use Analysis of San Diego's Mission Bay Area Utilizing LANDSAT-1 Digital Data. M.A., San Diego State University.

Manera, Paul A.
1970   Physical Factors Limiting the Agricultural Development of Butler Valley, Yuma County, Arizona. M.A., Arizona State University.

Newkirk, William W.
1966   Historical Geography of Bisbee, Arizona. M.A., University of Arizona.

Quevedo, Hector Adolf
1977   Concentration and Distribution of Suspended Particulate Lead in the City of Juarez, Mexico. Ph.D., University of Oklahoma.

Uphoff, Thomas L.
1978   Subsurface Stratigraphy and Structure of the Mesilla and Hueco Bolsons, El Paso Region, Texas and New Mexico. M.S., University of Texas, El Paso.

White, Russell A.
1968   El Paso del Norte, the Geography of a Pass and Border Area Through 1906. Ph.D., Columbia University.

Widdison, Jerold G.
1958   Historical Geography of the Middle Rio Puerco Valley, New Mexico. M.A., University of Colorado.

Winsor, Robert A.
1966   The Geography of Poverty in Maricopa County, Arizona. M.A., Arizona State University.

Biology

Adams, Edward Blair, Jr.
1973   Characterization and Identification of Two Virus Diseases of Spinach in South Texas. M.S., Texas A&M University.

Beauchamp, Ruble Mitchel
1972   Floral Diversity of San Diego County, California. M.S., San Diego State University.

Brown, Charles E.
1967   Viticulture in Northwestern Baja California, Mexico. M.A., San Diego State College.

Condra, Gary Doyle
1978   An Economic Feasibility Study of Irrigated Crop Production in the Pecos Valley of Texas. Ph.D., Texas A&M University.

Conner, Molly Dea
1979   The Endangered Plants of Texas. M.S., University of Texas, Austin.

Cook, Thomas Carlson
1959   The Distribution of Certain Species of Exotic Eucalyptuses, Palms and Bougainvillas in Western Central and Southern Texas. M.A., University of Texas, Austin.

Flynn, Russell Leonard
1971   San Diego Bay's Commercial Sportfishery. M.A., San Diego State University.

Frank, Michael Dean
1979   The Economic Value of Irrigation Water in the Western United States: An Application of Ridge Regression. M.S., Texas A&M University.

Harris, Jeffrey Todd
1974   The Abalones of San Diego: A Problem in Resource Management. M.A., San Diego State University.

LeSueur, Hardeman David
1939   A Contribution to the Knowledge of the Flora of the State of Chihuahua, Mexico: A List. M.S., University of Texas, Austin.

Lincoln, Steven W.
1971   Vegetation Success on Cut Slopes Within the City of San Diego. M.S., San Diego State University.

Sye, Wen Fa
1978   Pesticide Residues in Wells and Canals of El Paso Area. M.S., University of Texas, El Paso.

Takht-Abnoussi, Gholamreza
1978 Some Physical and Chemical Properties Influencing the Permeability of Three South Texas Soils. M.S., Texas A&I University, Kingsville.

Fine Arts and Literature

Brady, Donald Vincent
1965 History of El Paso Theatre: 1881 to 1905. Ph.D., Tulane University.

Brown, Richard Lee
1978 Functions of Ambiguity in Three Hispanic-American Novels: *La Casa Verde, Rayuela, El obsceno parajo de la noche.* Ph.D., Texas Tech University.

Estes, David
1977 Community Influence in San Diego Performing Arts Organizations: An Institution Building Approach. M.P.A., San Diego State University.

Golden, Donna L.
1971 History of Theatre at San Diego State College from 1926-1970. M.A., San Diego State University.

Gourd, Robert D.
1975 Nondualism in the Teachings of Don Juan and the Bhagavad Gita. M.A., San Diego State University.

Green, Gwendolyn Davis
1979 *Brujeria* in New Mexico Folklore and Fiction. M.A., University of Texas, El Paso.

Hendricks, Patricia Ellen Dannelley
1979 Women and the Visual Arts in Twentieth Century Texas. M.A., University of Texas, Austin.

Hiester, Miriam Webb
1954 Los Paisanos, Folklore of the Texas-Mexicans of the Lower Rio Grande Valley. M.A., University of Texas, Austin.

Hillebrand, Terrell Lynn
1974 The Jaina Figurines: A Manifestation of Mayan Art and Life. M.A., San Diego State University.

Loya, Eugenio
1979 Seminario de literatura hispanoamericana. M.A., Texas A&I University, Kingsville.

Monteverde, Mildred
1972 Sixteenth-Century Mexican "Atrio" Crosses. Ph.D., University of California, Los Angeles.

Paredes, Americo
1953 Ballads of the Lower Border. M.A., University of Texas, Austin.

Quezada-Hori, Maria del Socorro
1977 Art and Revolutionary Ideology: The Role of the Mexican Muralist in the Legitimization Process of 1920. M.A., University of Texas, El Paso.

Razo, Margaret Rose
1977 Mexican Dances for the Secondary Physical Education Program. M.A., San Diego State University.

Repp, Carmel Ann
1976 Urban Renaissance in San Diego. M.A., San Diego State University.

Stewart, Donald Ray
1979 Three Modes of Realism in the Spanish American Novel: A Study of *El loco estero, Fruto vedado* and *Sin rumbo.* Ph.D., University of Texas, Austin.

Stewart, Janet Louise Beckwith
1979 The Concept of "lyrical novel" as Seen in Three Spanish American Novels. Ph.D., University of Texas, Austin.

Stuyt, Godfried Alexander
1979 Ethnic Festivals: Cultural Preservation and Tourism: A Comparative Study. Ph.D., Texas A&M University.

Trujillo, Luis M.
1961 Diccionario del espanol del Valle de San Luis de Colorado y del norte de Nuevo Mexico. M.A., Adams State College.

Williams, Gladys
1960 Orchestras and Bands: El Paso Music, 1880-1960. M.A., University of Texas, El Paso.

A

S

T

Borderlands Sourcebook,

designed by Edward Shaw and Bill Cason, was set by the University of Oklahoma Press in 10-point Garamond and printed offset on 55-pound Glatfelter B-31, with presswork by Cushing-Malloy, Inc., and binding by John H. Dekker & Sons.

Stoddard et al ed.

Borderlands Sourcebook: A
Guide to the Lit. on Northern Mexico & American Southwest

DEMCO